Praise for *Home Comforts*

"An extraordinary achievement that has no peer in this century and may well have none in the next."

—*Newsweek*

"What's appealing about Cheryl Mendelson is that she makes no assumptions about what high-thread-count linens, antiques, silver, and Miele vacuum cleaners people have. She is concerned instead that they have a well-run household. And she is full of revelations."

—Amanda Hesser, *The New York Times*

"Not only illuminating but also, most surprisingly, crisply entertaining."

—*Wall Street Journal*

"This is a practical book about how you make the bed and make a comfortable home. . . . It gives the reader all the information needed for the hands-on running of a home."

—*The Boston Globe*

"*Home Comforts* has a lot of answers to questions I've had, questions I never thought to ask, and answers to questions that have been asked of me."

—Laura Shapiro, *Time*

"[The] bible of good housekeeping."

—*People*

"This generation's most important book on the subject."

—Caitlin Flanagan, *The Atlantic*

"This extraordinary book is to be read for its wise counsel, its authoritative advice, and its illuminating insights into the management of the domestic realm. As if that were not enough, it is beautifully written."

—Witold Rybczynski, author of *A Clearing in the Distance, Home,* and *City Life*

"Writing with a warm over-the-fence intimacy and humor, Ms. Mendelson makes housekeeping into an art, most successful when it appears effortless. . . . It's hard to think of a better housewarming gift. Practiced homemakers who don't need their skills explained simply will enjoy a friendly chat."

—Stanley Trachtenberg, *Dallas Morning News*

"I loved *Home Comforts!* There's a mountain of information in these pages—everything from how to sort laundry to keeping fabrics from fading and from choosing the right lightbulb to create a special mood to making your own environmentally safe cleaning solutions. Here's a book that makes you want to go home again."

—Letitia Baldrige, author of *Letitia Baldrige's Complete Guide to the New Manners for the '90s*

"I've decided to let someone else besides Martha Stewart advise me on how to run my house. . . . Cheryl Mendelson has written a handy resource that answers all my housekeeping questions . . . giv[ing] dignity to the day-to-day job of keeping a house running."

—Jann Malone, *The Richmond Times Dispatch*

"Mendelson opens our eyes to the homes we inhabit yet know so little, to the fascinations of food and fabric, dirt and bugs, air and light. *Home Comforts* is a unique and absorbing book."

—Harold McGee, author of *On Food and Cooking*

"In this entrancing book, Cheryl Mendelson restores keeping house to its rightful place as the custodian of the peace, order, comfort, and sanity of our lives. . . . And in so doing, she helps to restore dignity, value, and craft to the work that creates and sustains the private space that nourishes our humanity."

—Elizabeth Fox-Genovese, author of *Feminism Is Not the Story of My Life* and *Feminism Without Illusions*

"Mesmerizing—and, in its own way, revolutionary."

—*Chicago Sun-Times*

HOME COMFORTS

The Art and Science of Keeping House

CHERYL MENDELSON

ILLUSTRATIONS BY
HARRY BATES

SCRIBNER
New York London Toronto Sydney

For Edward,

who made a home with me

SCRIBNER
1230 Avenue of the Americas
New York, NY 10020

First Scribner trade paperback edition 2005

SCRIBNER and design are trademarks of Macmillan Library Reference USA, Inc.,
used under license by Simon & Schuster, the publisher of this work.

For information about special discounts for bulk purchases,
please contact Simon & Schuster Special Sales:
1-800-456-6798 or business@simonandschuster.com

Designed by Carla Bolte, based on a design by Empire Design
Set in FFScala and Meta Plus

Manufactured in the United States of America

7 9 10 8

Library of Congress Cataloging-in-Publication Data
Mendelson, Cheryl (date).
Home comforts : the art and science of keeping house / Cheryl Mendelson.
p. cm.
Includes bibliographical references and index.
1. Home economics. I. Title.
TX145. M38 1999
640—dc21 99-37555
CIP

ISBN 0-684-81465-X
0-7432-7286-2 (Pbk)

CONTENTS

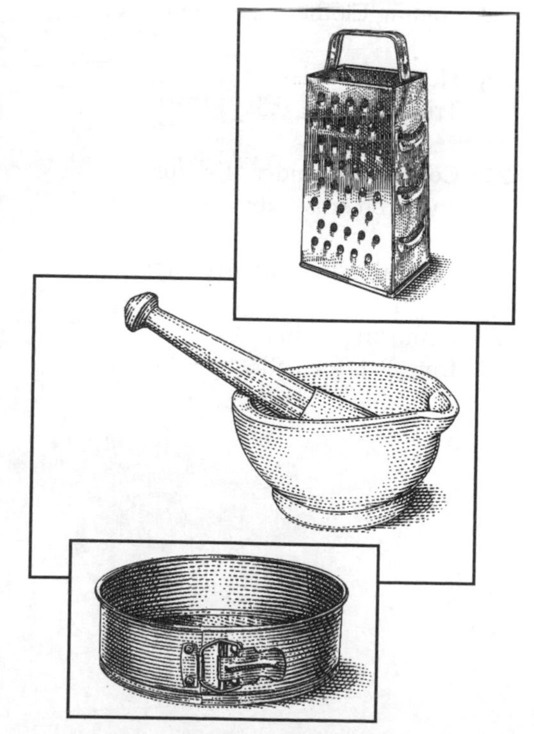

CLOTH

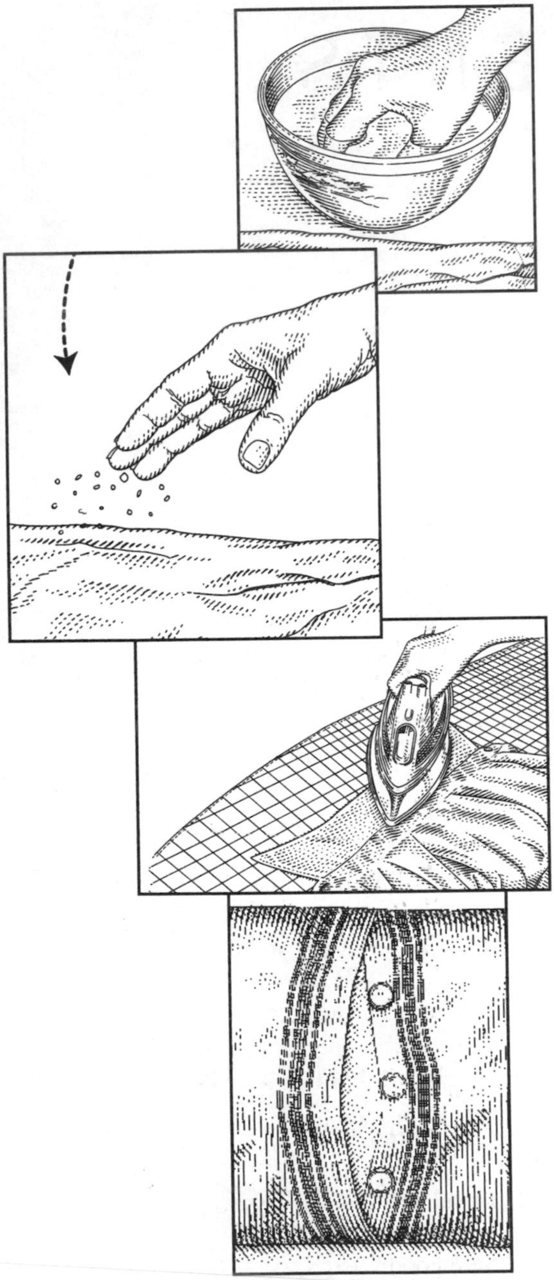

CLEANLINESS

DAILY LIFE

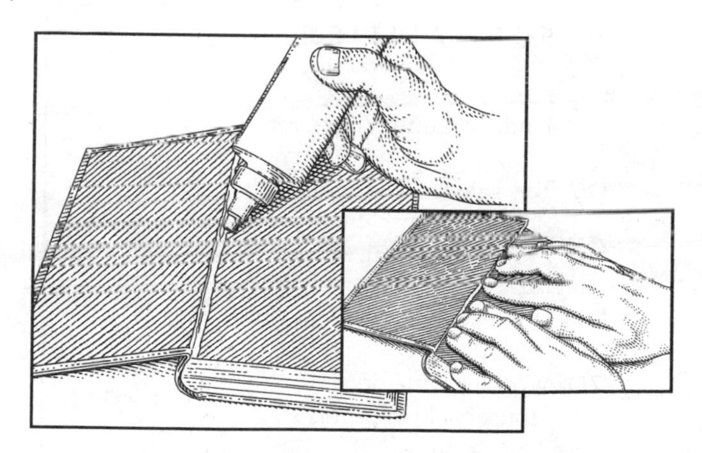

SLEEP

SAFE SHELTER

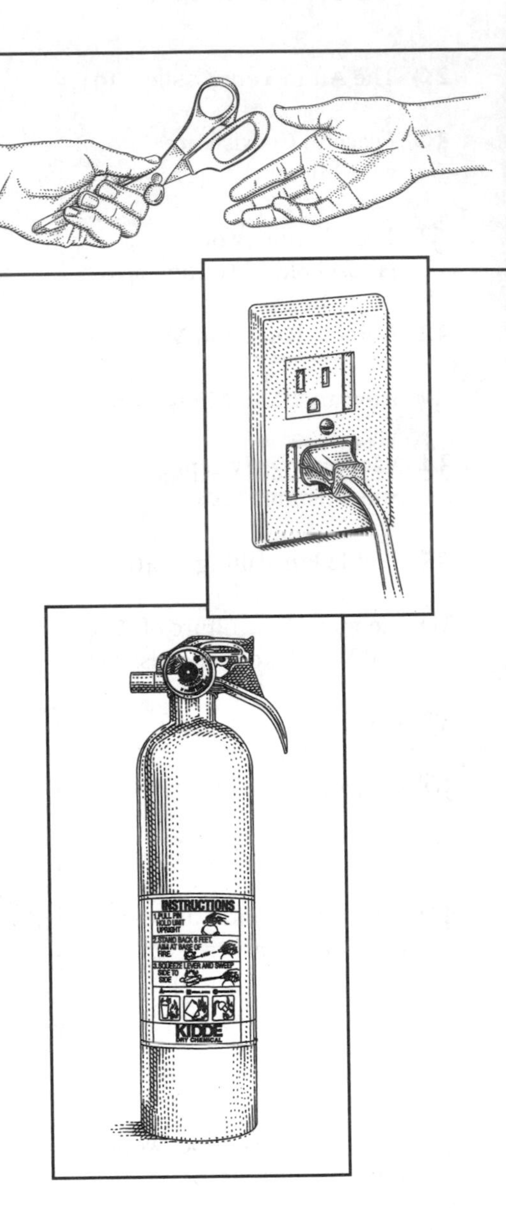

FORMALITIES

PREFACE

When you keep house, you use your head, your heart, and your hands together to create a home—the place where you live the most important parts of your private life. Housekeeping is an art: it combines intuition and physical skill to create comfort, health, beauty, order, and safety. It is also a science, a body of knowledge that helps us seek those goals and values wisely, efficiently, humanely. Such knowledge is drawn from practical experience, family traditions, the natural and social sciences, and many other stores of understanding and information.

Some of this skill and knowledge is directed toward keeping the home clean, but cleaning is only a part of keeping house, and in modern homes an ever-smaller part. Keeping house has always encompassed knowing and doing whatever is needed to make the home a small, living society with the capacities to meet the needs of people in their private life: everything from meals, shelter, clothing, warmth, and other physical necessities to books and magazines, music, play, facilities for entertaining oneself and others, a place to work, and much more. This book contains practical how-to-do-it material on many of these subjects, for both novices and those experienced in keeping house, and, because keeping house is a labor of love, it devotes space to its meanings as well as to its methods.

BEGINNINGS

1

My Secret Life

I am a working woman with a secret life: I keep house. An off-and-on lawyer and professor in public, in private I launder and clean, cook from the hip, and devote serious time and energy to a domestic routine not so different from the one that defined my grandmothers as "housewives." When I want a good read, I reach for my collection of old housekeeping manuals. The part of me that enjoys housekeeping and the comforts it provides is central to my character.

Until now, I have almost entirely concealed this passion for domesticity. No one meeting me for the first time would suspect that I squander my time knitting or my mental reserves remembering household facts such as the date when the carpets and mattresses were last rotated. Without thinking much about it, I knew I would not want this information about me to get around. After all, I belong to the first generation of women who worked more than they stayed home. We knew that no judge would credit the legal briefs of a housewife, no university would give tenure to one, no corporation would promote one, and no one who mattered would talk to one at a party.

Being perceived as excessively domestic can get you socially ostracized. When I made hand-rolled pasta for a dinner, I learned the hard way that some guests will find this annoying, as they do not feel comfortable eating a meal that they regard as the product of too much trouble. When my son was in nursery school, I made the mistake of spending a few hours sewing for him a Halloween astronaut costume of metallic cloth, earning the disgust, suspicion, and hard stares of many a fellow parent who had bought a Batman or Esmeralda costume. When I finally had to begin disclosing to friends and acquaintances just what the long book was about that I had been working on for so many years, I got a lot of those stares. Many times my courage failed me when painful silences followed my confession, "No, not a *history* of housework, an *explanation* of it—a practical book on how you make the bed and make a comfortable home," or "No, nothing about recipes, bouquets, gardening, monogramming, decorating, or crafts. It's about how a home works, not how it looks—what different fabrics are for, pantry and refrigeration storage, laundering and ironing, tuning the piano, cleaning and dusting, household records, books, laws, germs, allergies, and safety." I managed to persevere partly because not everyone responded with that stare; there was enthusiasm as well. And I was struck that no one responded with bored indifference. The topic was clearly hot—too hot for some people to handle, heartwarming to others.

Born Too Late

For me, too, the subject was actually something of a hot potato. I was raised to be a rural wife and mother, but I was born too late to find many openings for farm wives. Until I was thirteen, I lived in the Appalachian southwest corner of Pennsylvania, for most of the time on a working farm where I received an old-fashioned domestic education quite unlike the experience of the average girl in the 1950s. Early on, I learned baby care, housecleaning, laundering, gardening, cooking, embroidering, knitting, and sewing. I slopped the pigs, herded the cows, and helped out with the milking. I was proud to be able to pin a cloth diaper around a baby when I was six, and cook breakfasts of eggs, bacon, toast, and coffee for a large family and the hired help when I was nine.

Because housekeeping skills got respect in my world, I looked forward to keeping a house of my own one day. It was what I wanted, and part of me was confident that I could do it well. Another part doubted practically everything I had been taught. That was because my domestic education was a battlefield in a subtle war between my two grandmothers. These ladies, both expert in needlecraft, cookery, canning, and all the other arts of the home, each held an absolute conviction that there was a right way to keep house (the one she had been brought up with) and a wrong way (all others).

My maternal grandmother was a fervent housekeeper in her ancestral Italian style, while my paternal grandmother was an equally fervent housekeeper in a style she inherited from England, Scotland, and Ireland. In one home I heard Puccini, slept on linen sheets with finely crocheted edging rolled up with lavender from the garden, and enjoyed airy, light rooms with flowers sprouting in porcelain pots on windowsills and the foreign scents of garlic and dark, strong coffee. The atmosphere was open and warmly hospitable. The other home felt like a fortress—secure against intruders and fitted with stores and tools for all emergencies. There were Gay Nineties tunes on the player piano and English hymns, rooms shaded almost to darkness against real and fancied harmful effects of air and light, hand-braided rag rugs, brightly colored patchwork quilts, and creamed lima beans from the garden. My Anglo-American grandmother taught me to knit American-style, looping the yarn around the needle with a whole-arm motion. My Italian grandmother winced at the sight of this tiring and inefficient method and insisted I do it the way she did, with a barely visible, lightning flick of the last joint on her index finger. My Anglo-American grandmother sniffed at the other's idea of a gored skirt. The Italian thought it unwise to make beds, which should, she said, be *aired*. In one home, brows were raised and lips curled at the very idea of redeye gravy; in the other, at the idea of garlic. The Italian scarcely knew how to iron and sent out anything that needed it. The Anglo-American thought ironing the queenliest of the household arts, had every ironing aid known to humankind, and beamed at me when I had ironed-in creases in the sleeves of my cotton blouses.

Convinced that her own ways were best, each scolded me for doing things the way the other one did it, and each shook her head over the poor food and meager comforts of the other's household. Seeing my future as a housekeeper and a mother—yearning for the far-off joys of womanhood—I was faced with the dilemma of figuring out which of them knew the right way of doing things. Love of my mother and my own aesthetic nature inclined me toward things Italian, but love of my father and the society I lived in inclined me toward things American.

By the time I reached young adulthood, these questions no longer seemed to matter. Modern suburbia, where I found myself, had little interest in housekeeping and even less respect for it. Gamely I concluded that if the world no longer admired girls who sewed and cooked, in either the Italian or the American style, I would be up to date. I threw myself into studying, writing, and an academic career, and, not one to do things by halves (and determined to give myself much to regret in middle age), I made a youthful marriage to a man who ardently disliked domestic life. But my upbringing was not so easily overthrown. After an enjoyable year or two of antidomestic posturing, my true nature began to reemerge. One day when I arrived home in a rainstorm to find three wet, muddy dogs (ours and two of his friends) curled up in our unmade bed, I cried. That was a turning point. There followed a stage of rational discussion of our differences. At one point, I remember, I desperately constructed a philosophical defense of dusting under the furniture; and things got considerably less rational before the all-too-predictable end arrived.

But there is nothing like law school to take your mind off a divorce. My grandmothers, who had lived long enough to be mystified by the idea of a graduate degree in philosophy, never witnessed the further anomaly of a granddaughter who would become a lawyer. Despite the strenuous studies, as a newly single law student I reverted to domestic type. I immediately made a cozy, orderly little nest for myself in which I could study, make dinner for friends, listen to music, nurse my wounds, and live, unapologetically, the way I had wanted to for a long time. My father, amazed at the transformation, relaxed in my ample second-hand wing chair and said with a sigh, "At last you have a comfortable place to sit."

My Golden Age of domestic singledom was inevitably short-lived because I was graduated and began working excruciatingly long hours. At first I succumbed. My apartment was like a hotel room; I slept, showered, changed, and left. I did not cook, listen to music, or knit. I hired someone to clean, put up with dust on the books and grime in the corners, and entertained by meeting friends at restaurants. I felt like a cog in a machine.

Then one weekend I had a second domestic reawakening when I found myself with weekend guests who needed to be fed. Not only was I amazed to rediscover how gratifying it is to have people enjoy your cooking, but I was precipitated into some serious thought about cleanliness, sheets, the state of my pantry, and kitchen equipment. I was still making do with my half of the graduate student gear from my former life. After this, I began to try to control my hours at the office and to get at least a little time at home. Even a few hours, I found, were comforting. I got a good reading lamp to go with the wing chair, and I started on a novel. I put up a Christmas tree and invited friends with a child to help decorate it. Before long, I had a home once more, and living in it made me feel like a new person. I thought about housekeeping and how strange my life would appear to my grandmothers, and I began to collect housekeeping manuals, both old and new but mostly old, like the one my great-grandmother had used. I pored over them at bedtime, looking for my grandmothers' and mother's habits in them or finding to my astonishment that my grandmothers, both of them so right and so sure about everything, had not always done things by the book.

But most of this was socially invisible, so much so that it took me a long time to convince my new husband-to-be, when I finally met him, that I could actually cook. My former boyfriend, too, had set me down for a total housekeeping incompetent, and I had not bothered to enlighten him. He cooked and cleaned. I helped with the dishes, sometimes. When I took it upon myself to do marketing one day and came back with a reasonable collection of foods and supplies, he was floored. But my husband had to know the truth; this time I was going to start things out on the right footing. I told him straight out that the three-hole paper punch, a complete run of *PC Magazine,* and several collections of literary reviews did not belong in the kitchen cabinets over the sink and that I could not live with this. He shrugged, and so I married him.

Dousing the Home Fires

"Each day I long for home,
long for the sight of home."
—*The Odyssey*

The idea of writing a book about housekeeping first flashed into my mind in the laundry room a couple of years later, when I found myself hopelessly frustrated by the obscurities of garment care labels and wondering whether my laundering methods would lead to disaster. I thought about my great-grandmother's housekeeping book, and wished I had a modern book that would tell me the real story about fabrics and laundering in this day and age. With nowhere else to turn, I did what any lawyer would do: I went to read the "regs," the FTC regulations governing care labels. After painful study I learned, among other things, that an instruction to "dry clean" does not necessarily mean that you should only dry clean and not launder a garment. But overall I ended up with more questions than I started with. Besides, I reflected darkly, you shouldn't have to be a lawyer to figure out how to do the laundry.

Around this time I found myself facing many more household puzzles. I inherited my beloved uncle's grand piano, which had meant to him something like what my husband, son, home, computer, and CD player, all rolled into one, meant to me. I wanted to play it and care for it well, but had no idea whether I should vacuum out the dust in its depths, how often I should have it tuned, or what other care it might require. My husband and I had just renovated our apartment and found ourselves relying on our contractor for housekeeping advice. How, for example, should we clean and care for our newly polyurethaned wood floors? The contractor was confident and adamant: clean only with a mop *slightly* dampened with plain water. He insisted that we do the same in the kitchen, where he had painted a sealant over our Mexican tiles. Not only was nothing else necessary, he said sternly, but the wood floor would be damaged and the sealant dulled by anything else. This advice, which I found hard to believe, was wrong in both cases; but, intimidated by any word beginning with "poly" and by the very idea of a sealant, whatever that was, I followed it until the consequences (really dirty floors) were unmistakable. We had no notion of whether we would be better off using fluorescent or halogen or incandescent bulbs, and were unable to find someone who could lay out the pros and cons for us. And now we had a toddler and had become more conscious of cleanliness and germs. Could it be true, as the newspapers said, that soft-cooked eggs were no longer a safe food? (Yes.) Could it be true that I should start buying all those new disinfectant cleaners and soaps? (No.)

There were also reasons outside my own home that gave impetus to the idea of a housekeeping book. Over and over I found myself visiting homes where the predominant feeling was sepulchral, dusty, and deserted, or even hotel-like, as my own had once become. Perhaps a book that tried to explain not only the hows but the whys and the *meanings* of housekeeping was something the world could use.

I first learned that housework has meaning by observing my grandmothers. The reason they made a fuss when they saw a granddaughter doing things in a "foreign" way is that they knew—in their bones if not in words—that the way you experience life in your home is determined by how you do your housekeeping. Just as you can read a culture in the way its people fold a shirt (or do not), little domestic habits are what give everybody's home the special qualities that make it their own and let them feel at home there. Understandably, each of my grandmothers wanted me to make a home in which she could feel at home.

This sense of being at home is important to everyone's well-being. If you do not get enough of it, your happiness, resilience, energy, humor, and courage will decrease. It is a complex thing, an amalgam. In part, it is a sense of having special rights, dignities, and entitlements—and these are legal realities, not just emotional states. It includes familiarity, warmth, affection, and a conviction of security. Being at home feels safe, you have a sense of relief whenever you come home and close the door behind you, reduced fear of social and emotional dangers as well as of physical ones. When you are home, you can let down your guard and take off your mask. Home is the one place in the world where you are safe from feeling put down or out, unentitled, or unwanted. It's where you belong, or, as the poet said, the place where, when you go there, they have to take you in. Coming home is your major restorative in life.

These are formidably good things, which you cannot get merely by finding true love or getting married or having children or landing the best job in the world—or even by moving into the house of your dreams. Nor is there much that interior decorating can do to provide them. Making a home attractive helps you feel at home, but not nearly so much as most of us seem to think, if you gauge by the amounts of money we spend on home furnishings. In fact, too much attention to the looks of a home can backfire if it creates a stage-set feeling instead of the authenticity of a genuinely homey place. And going in for nostalgic pastimes—canning, potting, sewing, making Christmas wreaths, painting china, decorating cookies—will not work either. I count myself among those who find these things fun to do, but I know from experience that you cannot make a home by imitating the household chores and crafts of a past era. Ironically, people are led into the error of playing house instead of keeping house by a genuine desire for a home and its comforts. *Nostalgia* means, literally, "homesickness."

What really does work to increase the feeling of having a home and its comforts is housekeeping. Housekeeping creates cleanliness, order, regularity, beauty, the conditions for health and safety, and a good place to do and feel all the things you wish and need to do and feel in your home. Whether you live alone or with a spouse, parents, and ten children, it is your housekeeping that makes your home alive, that turns it into a small society in its own right, a vital place with its own ways and rhythms, the place where you can be more yourself than you can be anywhere else.

Despite these rewards, American housekeeping and home life are in a state of decline. Comfort and engagement at home have diminished to the point that even simple cleanliness and decent meals—let alone any deeper satisfactions—are no longer taken for granted in many middle-class homes. Homes today often seem to operate on an ad hoc basis. Washday is any time anyone throws a load into the machine, and laundering skills are in precipitous decline. Dishes are washed when the dishwasher is full. Meals occur any time or all the time or, what amounts to the same thing, never, as people serve more and more prepared and semi-prepared foods. And although a large, enthusiastic minority of home cooks grow more and more sophisticated, the majority become ever more de-skilled. Dirt, dust, and disorder are more common in middle-class homes than they used to be. Cleaning and neatening are done mostly when the house seems out of control. Bedding decreases in refinement, freshness, and comfort even as sales of linens, pillows, and comforters increase. It is not in goods that the contemporary household is poor, but in comfort and care.

These deficiencies of housekeeping can have serious effects on health. The decline of home cooking and regular home meals, along with the prevalence of the couch potato and television culture, coincide with skyrocketing rates of obesity and its related health problems. Allergy and asthma rates, climbing steeply in recent decades, are exacerbated by modern housekeeping practices. Those who live in disorderly and untended homes suffer higher accident rates. Inadequate cleanliness in the kitchen poses the danger of foodborne illness. Germs and mold anywhere in the home can cause infections and allergies.

Household activities of all kinds are becoming haphazard, not only cleaning, cooking, and laundering. Television often absorbs everyone's attention because other activities (such as music-making, letter-writing, socializing, reading, or cooking) require at least a minimum of foresight, continuity, order, and planning that the contemporary household cannot accommodate. Home life as a whole has contracted. Less happens at home; less time is spent there. Like the industrial poor of 1910, many people now, in order to work long hours with rare days off, must farm out their children for indifferent institutional care. People are tired, sleeping an estimated two hours less per night than people did a hundred years ago. There are fewer parties, dinners, or card games with friends in homes. Divorces break up countless households, and even in intact families frequent moves break ties to friends and neighbors. The homes that reemerge are thinner, more brittle, more superficial, more disorganized, and more vulnerable than those they replace. These plagues rain on the lives of both rich and poor. Many people lead deprived lives in houses filled with material luxury.

Inadequate housekeeping is part of an unfortunate cycle. As people turn more and more to outside institutions to have their needs met (for food, comfort, clean laundry, relaxation, entertainment, society, rest), domestic skills and expectations further diminish, in turn decreasing the chance that people's homes can satisfy their needs. The result is far too many people who long for home even though they seem to have one.

Obstacles to Housekeeping: Attitude!

Housekeeping is a subject that brings out attitudes. Generational issues are prominent, naturally enough, because we all associate housekeeping with our parents or children. Old fogies have always accused the young of declining competence. "You kids!" my grandmother's grandmother scolded her. "You don't even know how to make smoke go up the chimney." In times of great social or technological change, the young turn around and scorn the old. "Imagine saving string," my mother snickered, "or stretching the curtains on a stretching frame!"

And every generation makes the mistake of thinking that the next one will repeat its own experience. Many people in my parents' generation tried to avoid this mistake. They knew their parents were out of date, and they expected to be out of date too. They thought that they had nothing to teach us, their children, about housekeeping because our homes were going to be completely different from theirs. It is ironic, then, that in trying to be so very modern as to overthrow themselves before we even had a chance to, they made that same old mistake. They had experienced huge changes in housekeeping styles and technologies, but then, unexpectedly, we didn't. Although homes in 1955 were startlingly different from those of 1915, they would turn out to be remarkably similar to homes in 1995. This continuity matters. My feelings about my home are deepened by my perception that it is like my mother's; my hopes for our son are warmed by my expectation that someday he will find that his home is like ours.

By the 1950s most homes had long had electricity, modern plumbing, and heating, and the average home had a vacuum cleaner, a modern refrigerator, and an automatic washing machine and dryer. Automatic dishwashers were familiar to everyone, although not many people had one. Synthetic fibers, prepared soaps and detergents, and polishes were not new. Sewing and needlework of all sorts were already fixed in their new status as enjoyable leisure-time crafts, instead of the urgent necessities they had once been. Supermarkets sold packaged, sliced bread and chickens plucked and cut up. Compared with these changes, the innovations that came later, such as hand-held vacuum cleaners, microwave ovens, and a few computerized gadgets, do not save much labor or change the tenor of the home and its routines.

Other generational issues in housekeeping are harder to detect but can be emotional dynamite. Many middle-aged women of today had mothers who were dissatisfied housewives. These mothers taught their daughters not to get trapped but to get their degree and go out into the world and fulfill the mothers' frustrated ambitions. In droves, the daughters did just this—overall, a good thing. But there was in some cases a troubling subtext to this story. Some mothers actually gave their daughters another, whispered message as well: "Housekeeping is my consolation prize; it won't be fair if you get this and the career too." This was simply an extension of the housewife's message to her husband: "If you get the job and the public world, I insist all the more on my prerogatives in the home." Many young women have confided to me, sadly, that they felt sometimes as though they were being driven from things feminine and domestic by mothers who would not let them help cook or teach them anything of the mothers' own domestic crafts, no matter how much the daughters wanted to learn them. All too often, such women, supercompetent on the job, feel inept and lack confidence when they find themselves wanting to make a home of their own.

Thus it came about that for a couple of generations there were more and more children who were taught little about housekeeping except indifference. Those who lacked grandmothers or mothers who wanted them to learn about housekeeping usually never did learn anything about it and continue to regard it as alien territory. As adults who want good, well-run homes, they may succeed in mastering some practical skills, although a surprising number do not. Far more, however, find themselves quite conflicted about attempting domesticity. Their thinking is: I may do this dusting or laundry, but this is not really me.

Unfortunately, what a traditional woman did that made her home warm and alive was not dusting and laundry. Someone can be hired to do those things (to some extent, anyway). Her real secret was that she identified herself with her home. Of course, this did not always turn out well. A controlling woman might make her home suffocating. A perfectionist's home might be chilly and forbidding. But it is more illuminating to think about what happened when things went right. Then her affection was in the soft sofa cushions, clean linens, and good meals; her memory in well-stocked storeroom cabinets and the pantry; her intelligence in the order and healthfulness of her home; her good humor in its light and air. She lived her life not only through her own body but through the house as an extension of her body; part of her relation to those she loved was embodied in the physical medium of the home she made.

My own experience convinces me that there is still no other way to make a good home than to have attitudes toward home and domesticity modeled on those of that traditional woman. But most men and many women do not want to identify themselves with homes that they create through their housekeeping and through which they offer of themselves to others.

Their attitudes may have been learned originally at home, but they are constantly reinforced by the media. Advertisements and television programs offer degraded images of household work and workers. Discussions of the subject in magazines and newspapers follow a standard formula. The author confesses either to hating housework or to incompetence at it, jokes about the childish and mischievous aspects of poor housekeeping, then produces a list of "timesaving hints." It is scarcely surprising, then, that so many people imagine housekeeping to be boring, frustrating, repetitive, unintelligent drudgery. I cannot agree. (In fact, having kept house, practiced law, taught, and done many other sorts of work, low- and high-paid, I can assure you that it is actually lawyers who are most familiar with the experience of unintelligent drudgery.) And I am convinced that such attitudes toward housekeeping are needlessly self-defeating. You can be male and domestic. You can have a career and be domestic. You can enjoy keeping house. No one is too superior or intelligent to care for hearth and home.

Domesticity does not take time or effort but helps save both. It is just an orientation that gives you a sixth sense about the place you live in, and helps you keep it running with the same kind of unconscious and effortless actions that keep you from falling when you walk down stairs. This sixth sense lets you do things fast and cut the right corners, and helps you foresee and forestall the minor domestic disasters—spills, shortages, and conflicts—that can make life miserable when they accumulate. When it is absent, you are like an infant negotiating a flight of stairs for the first time. It feels hard and complicated. You have to focus your whole mind on it, and it wears you out.

Modern housekeeping, despite its bad press, is among the most thoroughly pleasant, significant, and least alienated forms of work that many of us will encounter even if we are blessed with work outside the home that we like. Once, it was so physically onerous and arduous that it not infrequently contributed to a woman's total physical breakdown. Today, laundry, cleaning, and other household chores are by and large physically light or moderate work that doctors often recommend to people for their health, as evidence shows that housework is good for weight control and healthy hearts.

Seen from the outside, housework can look like a Sisyphean task that gives you no sense of reward or completion. Yet housekeeping actually offers more opportunities for savoring achievement than almost any other work I can think of. Each of its regular routines brings satisfaction when it is completed. These routines echo the rhythm of life, and the housekeeping rhythm is the rhythm of the body. You get satisfaction not only from the sense of order, cleanliness, freshness, peace and plenty restored, but from the knowledge that you yourself and those you care about are going to enjoy these benefits.

Housekeeping requires knowledge and intelligence as well, the kind that is complex, not simple, and combines intellect, intuition, and feelings. You need a memory good enough to remember how things are done, where things are, what the daily routine requires, what everyone in the home is up to as it affects housekeeping, the state of supplies, budgets, and bills. You have to be able to decipher insurance policies, contracts, and warranties, manage a budget, and master the technical language of instruction manuals for appliances and computers. The ability to split your attention in several ways and stay calm is essential. You need to exercise creative intelligence to solve problems and devise solutions: efficiency measures that save money or time; psychological or social measures to improve cooperation; steps to improve physical comfort; analyses of why and how some routines break down. Housekeeping comprises the ability to find, evaluate, and use information about nutrition, cooking, chemistry and biology, health, comfort, laundry, cleaning, and safety. Above all, housekeeping must be intelligent so that it can be empathetic, for empathy is the form of intelligence that creates the feeling of home. Good housekeepers know intuitively what needs to be done in their homes because they know how their homes make people feel.

We should not overlook the relation of personal style and character to the character of a home. These are complicated subjects, but we can at least remind ourselves here how deeply they are involved in the subject of housekeeping. We can all observe for ourselves that warmhearted, reasonably well-organized people, not surprisingly, tend to keep well-functioning, cheerful, and welcoming homes, while people who live from one crisis to the next have homes filled with crises and chaos. Inconsistent people do housekeeping by fits and starts. People who think badly of themselves take these feelings out on their homes. Just as they have spots on their ties or runs in their pantyhose, their homes have stopped-up drains and a general air of disorganization. Alternatively, just as they may put excess stress on personal appearance in an effort to overcome self-doubt, so they may make their homes look forbiddingly perfect in an attempt to impress themselves and others.

Everyone knows chic, cool people whose homes are filled with striking furnishings but offer no place to be comfortable. At dinner the portions are fashionably small. Once you've admired the dish, its purpose is served whether or not you are still hungry. Some people are control artists or smotherers: five minutes in their homes and you need oxygen. You are asked if you are comfortable, and before you can answer you are offered pillows, told to try a new chair, and generally harassed to the point where you can't relax or think or talk. If you live with them, they are always doing more for you than you want, piling your bed high with blankets, cooking five-course breakfasts, and creating an uncomfortable sense of indebtedness.

Then there are those who are personally slatternly but keep immaculate houses, and the reverse. The pattern of a disheveled home and pristine person can reflect different sets of mind. Sometimes it is the way of the merely spoiled, who think everything should be done for them. But it may also be a single person's way of saying that he or she wants a mate: "I need someone to take care of me," or, perhaps, "It's not worth doing it just for me." In other cases it reflects a sense of being secretly contemptible.

But the housekeepers who have done the most to give housekeeping a bad name are those who are compulsive about it. Compulsive housekeepers clean houses that are already spotless. They arrange their shoes along the color spectrum in a straight line and suffer anxiety if the towels on the shelf do not all face the same way. They expend enormous effort on what they think of as housekeeping, but their homes often are not welcoming. Who can feel at home in a place where the demand for order is so exaggerated? In housekeeping, more is not always better. Order and cleanliness should not cost more than the value they bring in health, efficiency, and convenience.

Guilty housekeeping is another common style, almost as prevalent as compulsiveness. The guilt-ridden housekeeper always thinks that more should be done or that everything that has been done has not been done well enough. The floors were just swept? They look better, but I did not do a really good job on the corners and, besides, I neglected the closets. Moreover, I should also have spent time with my family and paid the bills. The guilt-ridden may eventually rebel against their own perception of endless duties in housekeeping and angrily let things go to hell.

In the modern world, it is easier to slide into neuroticism in housekeeping than it used to be. Thirty or forty years ago, compulsive housekeepers were easier to spot because there were generally accepted standards of what constituted adequate or good or excellent housekeeping, which they obviously exceeded. You did your wash on Monday, with sufficient skill to produce a certain range of results, and followed up quickly with ironing. Beds were changed on a certain day and made up by a certain hour of the morning. Vacuuming and dusting were done twice a week, serious baking once. Dishes were washed immediately after meals, and meals were made and served at home twice or thrice a day at regular hours. The Sabbath was marked with a more elaborate dinner.

Today, the disappearance of these social standards means that every household must invent for itself an ideal of a well-kept home and must choose its own standards of cleanliness and comfort. On the whole, this is a gain. No one wants to go back to the days of blushing over gray laundry and dirty dishes in the sink. On the other hand, the standards that operated in the past were grounded in practical reality. They balanced mental and physical comfort with the amount of effort required to achieve it, and they existed in a social world that assumed that life would include leisure and domestic enjoyment. They provided something crucial that the contemporary household lacks, which is a sense of *entitlement to a recognizable standard of everyday living*. Where standards are viewed as merely arbitrary and subjective, people come to feel that such comforts as fresh beds or good meals are not their right or are not worth working for.

Those of us who can gain some sense of the psychology of our own housekeeping will be freer to decide intelligently that some tasks are crucial enough to call for strenuous efforts while others are not. This book explores many kinds of pleasant possibilities in housekeeping without implying that anyone could, should, or must undertake them all. "Standards" are described, but they are offered as rights, entitlements, or suggestions for the sake of the reader's health, happiness, and enjoyment. The goal is always to pick and choose, to find the patterns and habits that work best for our own homes and that create the goods at home that we most value and need.

Setting Standards: When Is Good Enough Good Enough?

To the contemporary mind, the idea that happiness depends on good housekeeping might seem quaint or odd. A century or two ago, and in fact until the past few decades, it was taken for granted, and the quality of housekeeping was not beneath the attention of such great novelists as Jane Austen and Leo Tolstoy. Several of Charles Dickens's novels present an interesting variation on the whore/virgin theme when they contrast good housekeepers, who are lavished with praise, and bad housekeepers, who are described with appalled fascination. David Copperfield's first wife, Dora, who ties a basket of housekeeping keys to her waist in a childish imitation of real housekeeping, all but wrecks their marriage through her infantile incompetence. And though David realizes that he must forgive and love her anyway, Dickens helpfully kills her off and remarries David to Agnes, a genius of a housekeeper who even in childhood brought order and cheer wherever she went with her own little basket of housekeeping keys.

In *Bleak House*, the horrible Mrs. Jellyby serenely abandons her family to domestic squalor and confusion while she attends instead to charitable enterprises serving people a continent away. In contrast, Esther Summerson trips about creating comfort and order to the merry jingle of *her* little basket of housekeeping keys, and her guardian proves his good sense by appointing her his housekeeper within hours of meeting her.

Now, if you are a twenty- or thirty-something working person, you probably do not see yourself in Dickens's portraits of young ladies carrying baskets of keys (especially if you are a young man). But anyone can still respond to his portrayals of the chaos and unhappiness caused by defective housekeeping. Ruined and inedible meals, tools lost and broken, accidents, dirt, poor health, frustration, quarrelsomeness, shame—all these, which Dickens paints with vivid colors, are still the outcome of household neglect.

But what constitutes neglect? What is the point beyond which housekeeping becomes inadequate housekeeping today? Common sense says that it is the lowest level at which health and safety can be preserved and enough comfort and order maintained to ensure that people want to spend time at home, feel restored there, and do not have that haggard feeling of homelessness that travelers sometimes have even when they are perfectly well housed. Much housekeeping is justified merely on such rational, functional grounds as these. But in every age, people also do things to care for their homes that have no justification in concrete benefits for safety and health. Our forebears were fanatics about ironing, for example. Around 1900, they insisted on ironing everything from sheets to underwear even though this cost horrendous labor from women (and most did it themselves without maids, or did it alongside a maid) who were already devoting enormous amounts of labor simply to ensure survival. They were quite as capable as we are of appreciating that this was a lot of trouble for the sake of something they could have lived without. Feminist historians, in fact, have complained that the 1950s woman foolishly wasted on superfluous "work" the time she saved by using technological innovations. In calling the work superfluous, they devalue the goals of that era's housewives, and I am not convinced that they are being fair. But a brief glance at the history of dusting shows you why they might grumble.

In 1842, Catharine Beecher (Harriet Beecher Stowe's sister) thought that sweeping the parlor carpet and dusting all furniture, books, and knickknacks once a week was good enough. She mentions walls only with reference to spring cleaning (with the exception of kitchen walls, which need cleaning "often"). In 1908, Marion Harland called for daily dusting, weekly attacks on floors and carpets, and rubbing the dining room table with a drop of oil once a week. Walls and ceilings were to be attended to during "house cleaning," as both spring and fall cleaning were called. Around 1950, the authors of housekeeping books commonly recommended a dusting regimen of astonishing rigor for middle-class homes. You were supposed to dust all woodwork and furniture, including window frames, screens, and blinds, every day; dust the floors with a dust mop daily, vacuum carpets daily; brush all exposed surfaces on upholstery every day (or, if you had clean air in your area, two to three times a week), and do a complete brushing with an upholstery brush or vacuum, getting under pillows and in crevices, once or twice a month; vacuum wood floors once a week; dust walls and ceilings daily or weekly (as required by the air quality); and rub all furniture long and hard, with the grain, once a week. Whether people actually did *all* of this is open to question, but if they did, can this much labor be justified in terms of health benefits? Comfort? No doubt the dusting provided some of these benefits (and maybe partly explains the lower rates of asthma and allergy back then), but, equally doubtless, the amount of dusting outstripped such benefits. The point is that our mothers or grandmothers knew this as well as we do and thought it worthwhile anyway.

By midcentury my paternal grandparents, like most of their contemporaries, had acquired all the modern conveniences and gloried in them: vacuum cleaner, automatic washer and dryer, hot running water indoors, tiled bathroom and flush toilet, clean, modern heating system, enameled sinks and tubs, floors and walls that were not filled with dips and gouges. They enjoyed all these things in a house that sat yards away from the one in which my grandfather grew up, where my great-grandmother still lived without them. Modern supercleanliness represented to them and their peers deliverance from the dreary problems that had plagued their mothers' houses: chamberpots, smoke, grease, soot, grime, smells, ashes, bedbugs, fleas, mold and mildew, mud, stained porcelain and fabrics—all were fresh in their memories. Their excessive cleaning was rarely what it has sometimes been called: the neurotic behavior of bored women who could not think of anything more useful to do. It was a celebration of their release from centuries of a losing struggle with dirt, a celebration of new possibilities for comfort, beauty, and peace of mind that had so recently not existed even for the rich (who had always had their furniture dusted every day). For women who were domestic to the core, winning this war was comforting in a way we can hardly imagine.

It is difficult for us, who never experienced what my grandparents had so recently left behind, to realize the oppression of dirt, with its associations of death, discomfort, shame, and danger, and the free, light feeling that the modern home gave to those who remembered the labor its cleanliness had once cost. Cleanliness of this kind was the chief luxury that ordinary people gained through the new household technologies. So although all their cleaning and dusting was not entirely justified by its concrete benefits, it offered meanings and satisfactions that people wanted urgently. It gave their homes dignity and their lives an extra measure of contentment. Half a century later, few of us who grew up in the light, modern, clean homes of the 1950s and '60s have any such feelings and associations to motivate us. So we do not iron sheets, most of us do an unambitious dusting and vacuuming once a week, and in many other respects, too, we are willing to live with housekeeping that is merely "good enough." We understand better than people used to that it should be a matter of discretion whether we do anything more than that.

We should also understand, however, that we can permit ourselves to seek better than just "good enough" when it comes to our homes. It is just as important for us now as it was for people in 1800, 1900, and 1950. Dusting standards may have changed since the 1950s, but our homes still have to be to us what our grandfathers' homes were to them. Our homes are the center of our lives, and we should allow time and resources to make the most of them that we can, and to care for them in a way that consolidates and elaborates their meaning for each of us. At a minimum, we should avoid thinking that time spent on our homes is wasted time, or that our goal should always be to reduce the time and effort we spend on them.

Much housework is discretionary, but not *all* housework is. Minimum standards of cleanliness and order are inescapable necessities for health and happiness. It is up to each of us how to choose the dimensions of "necessary" in our own case. If this means that we can jettison without guilt a mother's or grandmother's idea of adequate dusting, it also means, on the other hand, that we still have to figure out just how much dusting represents the rational compromise between health and comfort and available time and resources. It is as true as ever that a dusty home is unpleasant and unhealthy to live in.

The ideological and economic fashions of each age provide masks to hide behind. When the message was "Stay at home and keep house," a woman who gave in to fears that kept her from doing something else could rationalize that she was doing her duty. Today, when the message is the opposite, "Go out and work," both men and women may rationalize the deficiencies of their home lives as necessary and unavoidable, saying that they do not have the time. Some people really *are* extraordinarily pushed and pressured. They need all the help they can get, and I hope this book will offer some. Other people are simply not cut out for domestic life, cannot avoid hating housework, and would perhaps be happier living in a hotel, barracks, ship, or monastery. But because it is true that whoever loves the end also loves the means, all of us who really do enjoy living in a well-kept home can come to enjoy the rituals of its care. The act of taking care of our homes brings comfort and consolation both in the enjoyment of the fruits of our labor and in the increasingly rare freedom to engage in worthwhile, unalienated, honorable work.

Using This Book

In writing this book I have constantly held two different audiences in mind. The primary one consists of beginners in housekeeping, especially young adults first setting up house or thinking of marrying or raising children. Also in this group are mature readers who for one reason or another have come to housekeeping late, as well as those who might be expert in one area but not others—skilled housecleaners, for example, who want to know more about food storage or fabrics. For the sake of this audience, I have included many basic details that will be obvious to experienced hands.

The other audience I have had in mind consists of those experienced hands. The members of this group will already have their own systems and methods in place (and I hope will excuse the didactic tone found here and there) but will be interested in learning more and keeping their knowledge up to date—perhaps on such subjects as lighting, safety, or newer materials and fabrics. Or, like me, they may simply enjoy reading about what someone else thinks and does about housekeeping. For their sakes, I have gone into more detail than beginners will need on some topics, such as the care of wood, fabrics, and laundering.

The brief summary of contents at the opening of each chapter, the table of contents at the beginning, and the ample index at the end of the book will help both groups navigate their way through the materials and find what they want. Readers should notice that many topics—bleach, disinfectants, and textile fibers, for example—are taken up in more than one chapter.

The parts of this book, listed in the table of contents, correspond to basic kinds of work that go into keeping up a home. Each kind of housework answers to some need that is satisfied in our homes: for order, neatness, food, clothing, cleanliness, activity, sleep, safety and an understanding of laws and business matters affecting our homes. The chapters contained in each part generally stand alone and can be read in any order. In some cases, however, you are better off reading two or more related chapters together. If you want details on laundering, for example, it will be helpful to read not only the chapter on laundering itself (chapter 21) but also those on fabrics, fibers, and care labels. If you are concerned about holiday safety, you will find relevant materials in the chapters on fire safety and electrical safety (chapters 60 and 61), and in other chapters as well, as indicated in the index and chapter summaries. If you have elderly houseguests, look at chapter 62, "Slips and Falls"; if there are or will be children in your home, look at all the safety chapters and pay special attention to chapter 65, "Additional Safety Measures for Children." Often, the text in one chapter refers you to other sections of the book that deal with related matters.

I hope all readers will keep in mind that what I have included here is one way of doing things, and, as I long ago learned so well from my grandmothers, in almost every aspect of housekeeping there are at least two good ways of doing things—and surely, if your grandmothers' ways were also considered, it would be many more than that. Wherever I thought it not self-evident, I tried to give the reasons why I use my own methods and systems. I hope this will help readers decide whether they wish to give them a whirl or whether they prefer something different.

2

Easing into a Routine

The organization of housework explained for beginners . . . Setting up schedules, standards, and goals . . . Saving time . . . Suggestions for shortening housekeeping . . . Learning the whys of housekeeping . . . Keeping lists . . . What systems and schedules do for you . . . Schedules for daily, weekly, monthly, semiannual, and annual housekeeping . . . List of weekly housecleaning chores . . . List of weekly laundering chores . . . Spring and fall cleaning . . . Order in which housecleaning is done, from room to room and within each room . . . Making things homey

Because most human needs are cyclic and recurrent, so is housework. Over and over, you need to sleep, eat, shower, change, laugh, relax, learn, and entertain. Over and over, your home must provide the means for you to do so in comfort and safety. The most important thing for any beginner to learn about housework, therefore, is that it goes by overlapping rhythms, schedules, and routines. These can be annual, seasonal, monthly, weekly, or daily. Each separate area of housework proceeds according to its own habitual order.

This chapter supplies an outline of these schedules and routines, with explanations of what they do for you and how you carry them out. But keep in mind three important points. First, *they are only summary suggestions intended to help beginners get the big picture.* Every family and every household develops its own methods and systems. The ones suggested here, quite typical and traditional, are easily modified to accommodate lighter or heavier housekeeping regimes and all varieties of personal taste. Second, here, as in many other parts of this book, *I have deliberately offered more detail than you may really need.* My spring cleaning list, for example, is so inclusive that my mother (a most thorough spring cleaner) objected to it. But let me assure you, as I tried to assure her, that I am not recommending that you do every task on the list or else move into a hotel. The list is intended to be inspirational and suggestive, so as to help beginners survey what would be useful in their own homes and avoid overlooking anything potentially important to them. Third, *beginners in housekeeping are not beginners for long*. What seems like a lot to digest when you read about it all at once begins to seem quite manageable in a short time, if you take it one step at a time.

Preliminaries

Setting Up Schedules, Standards, and Goals. People used to be fond of the old saying that a housewife's work is never done, but you do not hear it much anymore, perhaps because today, so often, the housewife's work is never started. In any event, this maxim, like most, is only half true. Yes, you can always think of something else that could be done, and yes, you will do more tomorrow, but in fact there really is an end to what your routine calls for this day or week or year. You, however, are the one who sets limits. Beginners should recognize the importance of setting plausible and explicit goals in housekeeping so that they know when they are done. In my experience, the most common cause of dislike of housework is the feeling that the work is never done, that it never gives a sense of satisfaction, completion, and repose.

To avoid this, you have to decide what ordinary, daily level of functioning you want in your home. There ought to be a word for this level, but there isn't. When I was a girl, my mother used to say, when everything was on schedule and as she wanted it, "The house is done." Whatever words you use, you need to create end points that will let you, too, say to yourself, "Finished!" Otherwise you will feel trapped and resentful, in danger of becoming one of the many unfortunates who hate taking care of their own homes.

Another trap to avoid is that of inflexible standards and unrealistic expectations. You need different goals for ordinary times and times of illness, stress, company, new babies, long working hours, or other interruptions of your home routine. People with large houses, many children or guests, active households, or invalid parents will have to spread themselves more thinly and should not expect to be able to keep house like the Joneses. Also, the fewer your resources of all kinds—money, help, appliances, skills, time—the more modest will be the level of housekeeping you can realistically hope for.

When you cannot have everything, establish priorities. Health, safety, and comfort matter more than appearances, clutter, organization, and entertainment. A jumbled closet may distract you, but it is much less urgent than clean sheets, laundry, or meals. Excessive dustiness can be unhealthy as well as uncomfortable; smeary mirrors (usually) aren't. Clean the rooms you spend the most time in and those where cleanliness is urgent (bedroom, kitchen, bathroom); let everything else go. Polishing gems and organizing your photographs can be put off indefinitely.

When you fall below your ordinary standards of housekeeping, a backup plan can help prevent the fall from turning into a free fall. Planning how you will engage in a *housekeeping retraction* at such times and return to ordinary standards when the crisis is past keeps you in control. The goal during these hard times is to adhere, more or less, to some workable minimal routine. If you can still cook simple meals and food preparation areas are safe and sanitary, if everyone has clean clothes, if the bedrooms are dusted, vacuumed, and aired and the bedding is fresh, you are doing well.

Saving Time. The stores are full of "timesaving" widgets and machines and the newspapers full of "timesaving" hints and tips. The widgets rarely live up to the promises, you probably have all the important machines already, and trying to keep house using hints and tips will drive you crazy. You will develop your own individual shortcuts as you develop skills and knowledge. It is often difficult to make good use of anyone else's shortcuts, for they tend to rely on habits and materials that may not be part of your housekeeping. I never use meat tenderizer or hairspray, for example, which are frequently relied on in housekeeping tips columns. Beginners need to work first on learning the basics. When they have their sea legs, they will be able to pick out tips that will work for them.

Aside from the basic modern conveniences such as vacuum cleaners, automatic washers, dryers, dishwashers, and microwave ovens, the most important source of significant savings in housekeeping time is knowing what you are doing. When you are practiced and knowledgeable, you can fly through chores in half the time. Skill and knowledge also let you use hired help and volunteered help much more effectively.

Learning Why. Whenever you can, learn why you do things one way rather than another. This is what enables you to be flexible, take shortcuts, use substitutes, and make changes that are improvements.

Keeping Lists. Good housekeepers are list-makers. Keep weekly lists of things to buy and jobs to do, such as calling service people or the piano tuner, performing special cleaning tasks, returning library books, or sewing on buttons. When you notice that any supplies are running low or you think of something it would be useful to get, write it down on that week's list. Before you go marketing, survey your pantry and refrigerator to see what's running low. Sit down and rough out menus for the week to come. Check cookbooks, if need be, to be sure you have all the ingredients on hand that you will need. Survey your laundry and cleaning supplies to be sure you have what you need to do the week's laundry and cleaning. Check the bathrooms and bedrooms for toilet paper, tissues, soap, and toiletries. Check your desk for paper, pencils, pens, and other items you use. Then remember to bring your shopping list when you go marketing.

SUGGESTIONS FOR SHORTENING HOUSEKEEPING

When time is short:

1. Pare your routines. Do only the essentials. Keep the kitchen clean, the dishes washed, food and other essentials stocked. Dust and vacuum only the bedroom or other areas where anyone sleeps or spends large amounts of time. Keep the beds in fresh linens. Take a few minutes to wipe down the bathroom and its fixtures with a good disinfectant cleaner.
2. Stay as neat as possible! Put things away as you go so that a sense of chaos does not develop.
3. Rely on foods that take little or no cooking. Use dishes you have frozen.
4. If you can afford to, hire help. If you do not usually hire cleaning help, have a bonded maid service come in for a day or half a day to do your weekly cleaning. If you can manage to keep up with the weekly chores but not with the less frequent ones, periodically hire help for them. Hiring someone to help with the heavy work of spring or fall cleaning is a particularly good idea and generally affordable. Find a neighborhood teenager whom you can pay to go to the grocery store or shopping center for you.
5. Send out the laundry or hire someone to come in and do it. Try to create less laundry.
6. If the situation is serious (illness, a new baby, a death), call on relatives and close friends for help.

Scheduling

What Systems and Schedules Do for You. Living in your home constantly uses up its good things—food, clean clothes, linens, shiny floors. Housekeeping routines provide for their continual renewal. The best way to begin keeping house is by setting up your routines and schedules. This can be done piece by piece and little by little; housekeeping is never all or nothing. At first, concentrate on a minimal daily and weekly routine. It may help to get a notebook or datebook devoted entirely to housekeeping matters. There are those who continue to keep a little housekeeping book their whole lives. I know an elderly man who writes down in his the contents of each closet and cabinet. This is how large, complicated households with many servants used to do things, with records of the number of sheets and jars of jam. Such detailed recordkeeping is not really necessary in the average house or apartment today, but some people will find it helps keep them on a system.

An increasing number of households do housework without any system, schedule, or routine, more or less reacting to each situation as it arises. This makes things harder, not easier. With systematic housekeeping, *most of the time you live comfortably:* supplies are not exhausted; dirt and laundry do not overaccumulate; plans and resources for at-home occupations and entertainments are in place. In nonsystematic housekeeping, chores are tended to only when the resources of one of the household's systems are exhausted: when there are no clean clothes or linens and there is school in the morning and stale beds tonight; when it is the dinner hour and the cabinet is bare; when dirt and disorder are beyond tolerating. When you keep house like this, domestic frustrations and discomfort begin to be felt long before you reach the point where you decide to do something about them. But when this point is reached, often the troubles cannot immediately be remedied because, without rational schedules, nothing ensures that time or resources will then be available to tend to the house. Moreover, the amount of work is more than it would have been had there been daily tending to chores; everything has become worse than it would have been. And worst of all, the only time you get to experience anything like a well-kept house is immediately after the emergency response measures are taken. The rest of the time—most of the time—you live badly.

A housekeeping routine not only prevents your home from growing seedy and sour between cleanings but also helps assure that you are willing to do the work, for, as experienced people all know, housework motivation can be a psychologically delicate matter. Cleaning, laundry, and other chores are far harder after you have let them go for two weeks; the energy you must summon to tackle them becomes greater the longer you have procrastinated. Not doing *some* housework leads to not doing even more housework.

If you have no system, you have to reinvent your housekeeping or debate what to do first every time you do it, and the required mental effort is a major obstacle, especially when you are tired. But a tired working person is often able to do things that are routine and habitual. No thinking is required; minimal inertia must be overcome. A chore that fits into a reassuring overall plan of housekeeping feels effective and worthwhile. But if you feel you are just tackling the worst problem in a home that is starting to go to pieces, it may hardly seem worth the effort.

To develop a set of routines for yourself, consider all the household work you have and divide it into portions that must be done daily, weekly, monthly or seasonally, and yearly or less often. The lists below summarize *typical* daily, weekly, monthly, and less frequently scheduled kinds of work.

Daily

Put soiled clothes in hamper and hang up other clothes

Clean sinks and tubs after use (including drains and traps)

Check soap, toilet paper, other supplies in bathroom; change towels if necessary

Prepare meals and clean up afterward

Put out fresh kitchen towels and cleaning utensils

Clean floors in high-use areas (kitchen, entryway) by sweeping, damp-mopping, or vacuuming

Make beds

Refill vaporizers and humidifiers (and clean if necessary)

Neaten; put away newspapers, magazines, and similar items

Do interim marketing, when necessary

Empty trash and garbage containers (evening)

Weekly

Housecleaning (see "A List of Weekly Housecleaning Chores," page 24)

Laundering

Minicleaning and minilaundering (see discussion below)

Marketing for food and non-food items

Odd jobs

Monthly, Seasonally, or Intermittently

Launder underbedding (mattress covers, pillow covers) and washable spreads and covers (monthly)

Turn mattresses (quarterly)

Wash or air pillows (quarterly)

Clean lampshades, light shades, or globes; dust lightbulbs (quarterly)

Wash mirrors

Clean the oven (as needed)

Wax floors (as needed)

Wash or wax woodwork (as needed)

Organize frequently used drawers, cabinets, closets (as needed)

Dust miniblinds and other blinds and shades (monthly), door tops, and other hard-to-reach areas where dust may collect

Wash windows, storm windows, and screens (as seasonally appropriate)

Clean blades of ceiling fans

Semiannually or Annually

Wash (or if necessary dry-clean) blankets, comforters, quilts

Remove out-of-season clothing from closet, clean and store it, replace with seasonal clothing (spring and fall)

Give away or throw away unused or worn-out articles

Clean and polish gems, jewelry, silver, brass, copper

Clean chandeliers and light fixtures

Have the piano tuned (twice a year)

Clean all walls, ceilings, and floors

Clean the basement and garage

Clean the attic (every two years generally suffices)

Wax the furniture

Vacuum books

Move and clean underneath heavy appliances and furniture such as stove, refrigerator, piano

Shampoo rugs and upholstery

Clean lampshades

Empty and clean all closets, drawers, and cabinets. Dust or wash china, crystal, knickknacks

Wash blinds, miniblinds, and shades

Dry-clean or wash curtains and draperies

Organize and/or store photographs, videos, CDs

Pay taxes and make official filings

Organize household business records, throw away superseded ones

Review insurance

Update household inventory

About the Daily Routine. A daily routine restores the household to a level of basic order twice each day: once before work or after breakfast, and once before bed. In the morning, you clean up the breakfast preparations, straighten up or neaten, air and make the beds, and hang clothes. In the evening, you clean up after dinner, neaten once more, take out the garbage, lock up, and before you go to sleep put dirty clothes in the hamper and hang other clothes. If you work away from home at a job, you want to come home to a neat, clean, fresh-smelling home. When you go to turn in, you do not want to be demoralized by an unmade, stale bed. If you stick to your daily routine, your average experience of your home will be of a comfortable degree of order and cleanliness. You'll wake to a fresh home, return to a fresh home after work, and never have to endure a stale bed, crumbs underfoot, sticky tables and counters, sour smells, fetid air, or grubby sinks, tubs, or showers.

Crumbs, stickiness, and any kind of dirt that contains food or is found in food areas should get high priority in your daily routine; clean it or sweep it up *promptly*. Take trash out at least once a day to discourage odor and vermin. To keep disorder from spreading, straighten—put things back in their proper places. (See chapter 3, "Neatening.") But some of the chores listed above as "daily" need not be done every day. Perhaps only once, twice, or three times a week, depending upon your habits and the level of traffic in your home, will you need to do the partial vacuuming in the living room or family room that my Anglo-American grandmother called "doing the middle of the floor." (But she did this, and more, each day.) You aim only at visible soil and ignore areas under cushions and furniture that you will attend to when you do your weekly housecleaning. Eat-in kitchens and dining areas, however, often need sweeping several times per day.

About the Weekly Routine. For at least a hundred years and probably much longer, the heart of housework was a weekly routine that assigned each of the major housekeeping chores to one day of the week. You see variants of the routine, but in my childhood people did washing (laundering) on Monday, ironing on Tuesday, sewing on Wednesday, marketing on Thursday, cleaning on Friday, and baking on Saturday. Sunday was the day of rest. For those of us who can remember the universality with which this system was followed through the mid-1960s, or even later in some areas, the speed and totality of its disappearance are breathtaking.

And in many respects, the old routine no longer makes much sense. Sewing and baking are anachronisms. Those of us who still bake and sew do it for fun and count it as leisure activity. Many people do little or no ironing. The number of major household chores has been reduced to three, perhaps three and a half, and some of these, especially laundering, do not take anywhere near the time or effort they used to.

But there is still room in the home for a weekly housekeeping routine, and I strongly recommend you devise one for yourself. This is the main thing you can do to make your home work well. Your list of weekly chores will still include marketing, housecleaning, laundering, and, sometimes, ironing. However, in place of a sewing day, you might have a day for doing odd jobs, such as mending, sewing on buttons or hemming, cooking ahead food for freezing, paying bills, or balancing your checkbook. You may also want a "minicleaning day," or a day on which you do an abbreviated version of your regular housecleaning. This is a particularly good idea for households that are very active or in which there are children, pets, allergies, or other situations that might make extra cleaning desirable.

Your weekly routine can assign the chores to different days of the week, as it did traditionally, or assign two or more weekly chores to the same day. For example, a possible weekly routine for a pair of working adults with no children, one cat, and a small house might be this:

Washing and ironing, if any, on Monday
Marketing on Tuesday
Minicleaning on Wednesday
Odd jobs on Thursday
Housecleaning on Saturday morning

When I was single, living in a studio apartment, and working, I usually did something like this:

Odd jobs on Tuesday
Marketing on Thursday
Housecleaning and washing and ironing on Saturday morning

You can do odd jobs or a minicleaning one week and not the next, depending on your needs.

Give some thought to how you assign your chores to the days of the week. Consider your housecleaning, for example. Although cleaning is now physically light work compared to what it used to be, it has replaced laundering, which is now almost entirely automatic, as the heaviest physical chore. If you do the housecleaning yourself, you want a regular day for it when you are likely to have plenty of time and energy. Working people with fair-sized homes who do their own housework usually prefer Saturday as cleaning day because they are too tired to do the biggest and most physically demanding part of housework after a day on the job. Saturday was the traditional cleaning day in many households in earlier times too. But in a studio apartment, or a small, lightly-lived-in home, not only can all the cleaning be accomplished after work, but all the laundry can often be done at the same time. Monday evening, at the start of the workweek when you are not tired and when housework is least likely to interfere with your social life, is a good evening to designate as combined cleaning and laundry day in households of this kind. A minicleaning day is most useful three or four days after your major housecleaning day.

In the old days, laundering was done on Monday, after the Sabbath rest, because it involved such backbreaking labor that you needed to be fresh and rested to get through it. If you are a stay-at-home housekeeper or have one working for you, you have little reason to hold to the traditional Monday washday. But the traditional rationale for a Monday wash often applies in the many households where all adults work and do their laundry in the evening after work (even if they hire someone to do their weekly cleaning). They may well find that Monday still works best because they are less tired at the beginning of the workweek. Even if you have no outside job, it pays to set aside a special day for laundering. Households in which there is a lot of laundry may prefer to have two laundry days, a major one and a minor one. But the common system of doing a load or two every day is inefficient in all but highly organized households and is easily vulnerable to disruption. (See chapter 20, pages 290–91 for a discussion of the reasons.)

If you are going to have two laundering days, you can help yourself stay organized by doing a different kind of laundry on each day—for example, towels and linens on one and clothing on the other. Cleaning day, when you are stripping the beds and putting out fresh towels, is also a good day to wash towels, sheets, tea towels, tablecloths, and other household linens. Clothes are better done on a separate laundering day because they are usually more complicated to sort and tend to, and they can best be washed on an

A LIST OF WEEKLY HOUSECLEANING CHORES	
Change the bed linens (once or twice weekly) and bathroom towels (twice weekly or as necessary)	Wash down entire bathroom: toilet, sink, tub, wall tiles, toothbrush holders and all fixtures, cabinets (exterior), mirror, floor
Vacuum rugs, floors, upholstered furniture, and lampshades	Wash all combs and brushes
Wash all washable floors	Clean entire kitchen: clean refrigerator; wipe down stove and other appliances inside and out; clean sinks, counters, and tabletops; extra-thoroughly wash backsplashes; scrub floors
Dust all dustable surfaces and objects, including pictures, mirrors, light fixtures, and light bulbs	Clean air-conditioner filters and humidifiers according to manufacturers' recommendations
Wipe all fingerprints or smears from doorknobs, woodwork, telephones, computer keyboards	Wash out and sanitize garbage cans

evening after work when you are doing nothing else. You can begin ironing while other clothes are washing or iron the next day. See chapter 23.

Thursday, the traditional day for marketing, still makes sense as a marketing day for many of us. This leaves Friday evening free for socializing, entertainments, relaxing, or collapsing, while ensuring that your home is stocked for the weekend. However, if you want to cook for freezing on Wednesday, Tuesday might be a better marketing day. Although many households market on Saturday afternoon, there are better ways to spend prime leisure time. Moreover, marketing can all too often conflict with other Saturday activities, creating a temptation to postpone it or leave it undone. Sunday afternoon is another possibility, but supermarkets on Sundays tend to be less well stocked and to offer goods that are less fresh. (Besides, you need one of your weekend days to be a day of rest.) Those who do their major marketing after work must be sure to prepare a thorough list to make the task go faster and leave a good part of the evening free.

Whatever day you choose, a weekly major marketing day is worth establishing. While most of us visit a local market several times a week for quick purchases of fresh produce, milk, or fish, it still makes sense to set aside one marketing trip each week to restock nonperishables and storable items such as cleaning or laundering materials, paper goods, canned goods, frozen goods, and other packaged goods. The satisfaction you get from having your shelves filled and ready for the unexpected is immense, and so is the frustration and annoyance that you suffer when basic stocks have not been replenished. A once-weekly major marketing also saves you from having constantly to run to the market during the week, which is a major source of wasted time in many households. You'll save money as well as time if you can cut back on these trips, because you'll find you have fewer opportunities for impulsive and wasteful buying. If you keep careful shopping lists and remember to check them, you can avoid extra trips for lightbulbs or milk.

Some people find that cooking dishes ahead and freezing them helps appreciably, even if it is done only once or twice a month. Try doing it either on the day you put aside for odd jobs or on Saturday afternoon, the traditional baking time, whenever it does not interfere with family and social activities. Children love to cook and like having their parents at home cooking, and homework and playdates can be supervised while you cook.

Designating one day in the week when you spend an hour (or two or three) doing accumulated miscellaneous chores helps every household keep itself together and organized. This is when you can clean a low-tech oven, go over the insurance policies to see if they are adequate, update your household inventory, make photograph albums, plan for your next month's housekeeping, and much more. You can use an odd-jobs day for monthly, seasonal, or intermittent chores—such as washing windows or walls—that cannot be fitted into your regular weekly housecleaning or laundering. You can also use an odd-jobs day for doing your annual and semiannual chores one by one, on an ongoing basis, and thus avoid the need for a massive spring or fall cleaning. Working people often prefer this arrangement because otherwise they are forced to use vacation and personal days for spring cleaning. But if your schedule can accommodate it, there is much to be said for the custom of special cleanings once or twice a year.

About Semiannual and Annual Routines: Spring and Fall Cleaning. "Spring cleaning" or "fall cleaning" is the name given to a massive, whole-house deep cleaning. The custom of a seasonal "housecleaning" in the spring arose because after two seasons of heating and lighting with wood, oil, gas, kerosene, and candles, the condition of the house made it essential. By winter's end, everything in the house was coated with a malodorous layer of black grease and grime, the ugliness of which would become ever more apparent as the days became longer and sunnier. So people cleaned everything—literally everything—as soon as the heating season was over and as soon as it was warm enough to do chores that cold weather made too inconvenient, such as beating rugs, taking mattresses and pillows outside for airing, or going into frigid areas of the home (the cellar or attic). They emptied every drawer, shelf, cabinet, closet, and room; cleaned them; and cleaned, washed, polished, or shined all their contents (drapes, mattresses, pillows, rugs, carpets, upholstery, crystal and china, silver, brass and copper, and so on); and then put everything back. Walls were washed or painted and cellars whitewashed. Because people often used separate furnishings for the warm and cold seasons, during spring cleaning they would also remove the winter furnishings and put out the warm-weather rugs, draperies, and bedclothes. During fall cleaning, preparations were made for another onslaught of cold and dirt, and the winter things were put back, bed curtains hung, wool carpets laid, and so on.

Most of the rationale for doing spring cleaning has now gone by the wayside. Modern heating and cooling systems prevent a clearly seasonal buildup of grime and enable us to do housework in all kinds of weather. I know no one who still uses different furnishings seasonally, with the exception that in most parts of the country people change the bedding and switch their seasonal clothing twice a year. And many people despise as heartily as our ancestors did the disruption of home life that spring cleaning causes. These are all reasons why some of us give up spring or fall cleaning and assign its various chores to odd-jobs days, getting them done one at a time.

But spring cleaning still has a place for anyone who can find the time for it or who rather likes the feeling of renewal that follows the major upheaval of turning your home inside out. Try it once before you rule it out. It is delightful to begin the new season with a home that has been scoured top to bottom, every drawer emptied, every piece of china washed, every bit of metal polished, every fabric washed, every square inch of all surfaces washed, polished, scoured, waxed, or otherwise brought to its finest state. This helps you feel motivated to keep things as pleasant as they are after the spring cleaning. It also means that you do not have a dozen big jobs constantly hanging over your head, getting in the way of your free time. Keeping up with the chores can feel onerous when you go at it piecemeal.

Fall cleaning is an excellent way to usher in the holiday season with its extra entertaining. You can do a fall cleaning instead of or in addition to a spring cleaning. Or you can do an additional fall cleaning in some years and not in others.

True spring cleaning should occur around the time when you stop using heat, typically sometime between the first day of spring and mid-April. Fall cleaning should be done six months later, typically in September and, at least in the cooler climates, no later than mid-October. Many people with children choose to do a fall cleaning that coincides with the beginning of the school year in late August, so as to clear closets, drawers, trunks, and other places where they store children's outgrown and worn-out clothes and toys. Then they can start the school year fresh with room for new school clothes and playthings. Spring and fall cleaning both involve closet clearing, so they are natural times for tag sales.

If you choose to have an annual or semiannual cleaning, you can make it as simple or elaborate as you wish. Remember that the chores listed on pages 21–22 are suggestions. Any chores you choose to omit can be done instead as miscellaneous odd jobs any time in the year or, if appropriate, put off until the next year. A full spring cleaning for an average suburban house and family might take up two or three days, rarely more. During this period you should plan on having no guests and doing only light cooking.

The Order of Work in Housecleaning: What Comes First?

Many beginners, struggling to define a rational sequence in which to do the household's cleaning, wonder if it even makes any difference. To some extent it does. A carefully planned sequence will let you avoid turning the entire house topsy-turvy at once and will keep you from disturbing clean areas while doing uncleaned ones. The order followed in traditional housekeeping is still efficient and is what I believe most people will like best. However, individuals will find that they wish to do things in a different order for reasons as objective as that their tub is in their kitchen, as in a London flat where my husband once lived, or as subjective as that the kitchen's disorder so offends them that they can think of nothing else until it is cleaned. The important thing is to have *some* sequence that you like and to follow it regularly.

The guidelines I learned at my mother's knee are these:

1. *Proceed from higher to lower.* Start upstairs and work your way downstairs; in general, clean higher places in each room before the lower (except, perhaps, when washing painted walls—see chapter 43, "Walls, Ceilings, Woodwork, and Windows.")
2. *Proceed from dry to wet.* Begin with dry rooms and areas without sinks, tubs, or toilets, then go on to wet rooms and areas.
3. *Proceed from inside the house to outside.*
4. *Begin with the chores that require waiting periods.* Start time-consuming automatic processes first—bed airing, laundry soaking, soup simmering—so that they can proceed while you do other things.

In practice, these guidelines will lead you to follow an order of work something like this:

Order of work from room to room. Begin with chores that include waiting periods. If you are going to do laundry while you clean, you should first gather and sort the clothes. When the first load is washing, begin on the bedrooms; keep the loads moving through the washer and dryer while you proceed with cleaning. This requires pausing to remove clothes from the dryer promptly and smooth them so that wrinkles do not set. (See chapter 22.)

Begin cleaning upstairs. Do bedrooms, offices, or sewing rooms, then hallways; do bathrooms last. If you have more than two floors, begin at the top of the house. As you descend, do the stairs between the floor you have just finished and the next floor down.

Do the ground floor last: first the living room; next the family room, den, or library; next the dining room; next the powder room or bathroom; the kitchen last.

After you have finished the inside cleaning, it is usual for those who have houses rather than apartments to do porches, patios, decks, and walks.

Order of work within each room. When you are cleaning a room, the basic idea is to avoid disturbing or soiling clean areas as you proceed to new areas. Usually you can do this by proceeding from insides (of closets, cabinets, refrigerators) to outsides, higher to lower areas, and dry to wet. Clean air conditioners and filters when you do the dusting in each room. Wash the floors last, and be sure to finish at the doorway so that you are not forced to walk over the wet floor.

Bedrooms: Strip the beds first and let them air. Next, tidy the room (if necessary, tidy closets or drawers first). Then dust. Wash picture glass and mirrors; wipe lightswitch plates, doorknobs, and doors as necessary. Then vacuum. Make the beds last. Remove and clean any vaporizers and humidifiers that require cleaning. Replace and refill them when you are ready to turn them on again.

Bathrooms: Tidy. If you use a soaking solution in the toilet, put it in immediately. Then clean the tiles or walls around the sink, shower, and tub, including shower curtains and doors. Next, clean the tub or shower stall, followed by the mirror, cabinet doors, doors, lightswitch plates, doorknobs. Then do the countertops, then the sinks. Finish cleaning the toilet (or clean it with a cleaner that does not require soaking). Sweep the floor. Wash the floor last. (You can wash lower walls and baseboards as you do the floor.)

Office, den, library, sewing room, family room, living room, dining room: Tidy, then dust. Wash picture glass and mirrors, lightswitch plates, and doors and doorknobs as necessary. Vacuum.

Kitchen: First tidy up. Then clean the stove and refrigerator. Empty any cabinets or drawers that have become dirty or disordered, wipe them out, and neatly replace the objects in them. Do backsplashes and cabinets, doors and doorknobs, lightswitch plates. Next, clean table- and countertops, then the sink. Then sweep or vacuum the floor. Wash the floor last. See chapter 9.

Utility rooms, attics, garages, basements: If you have a utility room or laundry room, it is usually best done after the kitchen, but that will partly depend upon where it is and whether you treat it more as part of your indoors or as part of your outdoors. Tidy. Clean appliances. Wipe cabinets, doors, doorknobs. Do countertops, then sinks. Sweep or vacuum the floor, then wash it.

VACUUM LAST!

There is a small but fierce debate about whether you should dust before vacuuming or vacuum before dusting. The answer is that you should dust first. The "floors first" rule is simply outmoded. Before there were vacuum cleaners, floors and carpets and rugs were often swept with brooms or carpet sweepers that raised a terrific dust. Housewives therefore did their floors first (laying cloths over everything else in the meantime), for if they had dusted first, they would have had to do it again after the dust from sweeping settled. Today you do not raise dust when you vacuum. (If you do, perhaps you should look into a new vacuum.) And if you spill dust on upholstery and floors while dusting, you can remove it when you vacuum.

Garages that do nothing more than hold the car overnight and little-used basements generally are cleaned only once or twice a year, although they may be swept out every week. When they are in daily use, they will require more frequent cleaning and perhaps weekly tidying, depending upon what activities they are used for. Attics that are used solely for storage generally need attention only every couple of years.

Outside: Sweep porches, patios, decks. Wash or hose them down as appropriate. Sweep walks.

But Is It Homey?

Those new to housekeeping may find themselves wondering if doing all this will really make their homes homey. The answer is that it will take you, in my personal estimation, about three-quarters of the way there. Housework in the seven basic areas outlined in this book is the source of most of the good things that make a place homelike—fresh sheets, good meals, airy, clean, orderly rooms, and so forth. But other things also affect the tone of the home.

Decor usually gets too much attention at the expense of other influences, but it certainly matters. If you are furnishing a home for the first time, be assured that you can suit your taste and still make a homelike home. I know people who have an avant-garde city apartment and a country home with rustic furnishings who seem to feel that only a countrified look is homey. This is surely wrong as a matter of principle, but it may be true that the signals they need to relax get sent only by Stickley furniture and wicker baskets.

It is best to know and follow your own real taste confidently instead of worrying about impressions and image. Artificiality and stiffness of decor are the most common enemies of a homey feeling. Sometimes when decor seems to subvert homeyness by its excessive grandeur or drop-dead coolness, this is really because it seems put on. As a general rule, anything you really like works—old, new, traditional, avant-garde.

That said, homeyness is easier to create in small, intimate rooms than in larger and grander ones, and many people think that if you really want your home to be *heimlich*, you should be sure to have a small one. I tend to agree, but I have seen people with enormous homes or open loft apartments create islands of intimacy in them by arranging furniture, partitions, or draperies so as to enclose small spaces.

There are ways of living in your home that make it homey as well, and you can get artful about it if you wish, consciously introducing habits and touches that make your place seem cozy and inviting when the occasion warrants. Usually what works best is an individual matter, which depends on your particular home, history, and tastes. There are some things that most people respond to as comfortable—sheets turned down and warmed, a newspaper left where someone will want to read it, a habitual cup of tea. You can always add to homeyness by remembering people's favorite dishes and how they like things prepared, particularly on their rough days or when there is a celebration to mark. It is also created by knowing the habits of the members of the household—a hook where this person wants to hang his cap, a basket where that one tends to leave keys and odds and ends from her pockets, a special drawer for a child's rock collection.

Fresh flowers, a bowl of good fruit, and homemade baked goods are, as always, easy, pleasant touches in your home. You want to provide pretty and good things like these and do something with them, no matter how simple, beyond merely buying. If you like arranging flowers, you can spend hours on it. If you don't, fortunately they look pretty if you just drop them in a glass with water. Three or four pieces of a fruit in season that you set out to ripen on your table are often more appealing (and sensible) than an elaborate selection of exotic fruits. The admixture of your own work, the element of foresight (you did this ahead of time so that this sight, smell, or taste would be available now), the respect granted to small pleasures and the home as their source—this gets right to the heart of the matter.

Many of us feel at home in places where there are good books, not only on shelves but on tabletops or other places where we might want to pause to read in moments of leisure. Guests appreciate a thoughtful assortment of books left at their bedside stand.

It is a cliché, but true, that a room that looks lived in looks more homey. This implies not that you should be less neat but that you should actually live in your rooms. When you talk, read and write, play music or games, or sew, you leave traces of this in the room. These traces then invite people not simply to look but also to be engaged. It makes them feel as though the room exists for people, to live in and do things in. Faked signs of life make the room feel desolate and lonely. Signs of real life make the room feel comforting and warm.

3

Neatening

Why some things out of place cause more things to get out of place . . . New habits to increase neatness . . . A place for everything and a time for things to be in them . . . Ongoing activities need not be put away . . . Temporary holding stations . . . Hiding things in closets makes the situation worse . . . Resentment about picking up after others

A friend from India once told me that in her country you would never find a stray piece of string or a rubber band on the street because material goods were so scarce there and people so poor that these would immediately be picked up and used. A modern American home throws away in the garbage every day food and goods that half the world would regard as riches to store and treasure. In this country a century ago, however, people both rich and poor lacked the plethora of movable objects that presently clog our homes: toys, games, magazines, papers, and gadgets of all sorts. The design of ordinary homes and furnishings has only recently begun to provide anything like proper storage for all these goods, enabling people to attempt to abide by the venerable household maxim, "A place for everything, and everything in its place."

Mess is such a dilemma for so many households that bookstores offer an amazing number of books on closet design and how to reduce clutter, and magazines offer articles on the emotional difficulties of throwing things away. Closet-renovation services are doing a tremendous business; they build all sorts of contrivances into your closets that enable them to hold far more of your goods. Big closets, using space efficiently with a variety of shelves, drawers, and hanging rods; underbed storage boxes; shelves and drawers lining the walls—all these and other storage ideas are worth pursuing. The how-to books and professionals will offer you ingenious suggestions that are genuinely helpful.[1]

But beyond creating a place for everything and learning not to purchase or retain useless things, achieving basic orderliness depends on learning a new set of habits, habits geared toward living with material plenty, for the likelihood is that your present ideas about how to stay neat were invented in a world that knew only material scarcity. True success involves changing your mind as well as your closets.

Broken Windows

In the hallway between our son's bedroom and our own, there stands a chair that serves various minor functions. One rushed morning I made the mistake of throwing my bathrobe and newspaper on it as I passed by. That evening, the chair held not only the bathrobe and newspaper but also my husband's dry cleaning, a plastic replica of the *Millennium Falcon* along with Luke Skywalker, a tube of antiseptic ointment, one copy of *PC Magazine*, and five Tinkertoys. (I remember because I recited the entire list to my smirking husband.) Yet this chair had stood entirely empty for the preceding six months.

Modern police successes are allegedly built on a sociological principle called the "broken-window theory." This theory says that any sign of social or physical neglect in a neighborhood causes people who are predisposed to antisocial conduct to feel more inclined to commit various crimes and misdemeanors. If there is one broken window and it isn't fixed, this suggests to malefactors that no one cares or that no one is in charge—that therefore it is safe to write graffiti on the walls, litter, and break other windows. This in turn suggests to more determined wrongdoers that they could get away with mugging and burglary. The first broken window, if not tended to, leads eventually to total social deterioration. Thus, by making sure that graffiti, broken windows, and "quality-of-life" crimes *are* immediately stopped or tended to, police have drastically reduced the serious-crime rates in many big cities. At least this is the claim, and there is good evidence that it is true. It sounds like common sense to most people.

The broken-window theory certainly applies to every individual home, and the reason why it does is clear. When people are cooperating in maintaining a household, the domestic equivalent of an unrepaired broken window can result in a chain reaction that eventually sees the home in complete chaos. It happens like this. Someone is reading in his favorite chair while sipping a cup of tea, after slipping off his shoes to get comfortable. His wife hands him an important piece of mail, and after reading it he walks off to make a telephone call, leaving behind the mail and the torn envelope, his novel spread to mark his place, his shoes, his half-empty cup, and the chair looking nicely sat in. He does not return to this chair for the rest of the day, forgetting his tea and novel after the telephone call and getting involved in something else. Now the "window" has been broken in this room. Anyone who walks in will feel entitled to add more disorder because the room is already slightly, even if pleasantly, disorderly. The next person therefore leaves her stack of papers at her chair and throws her sweater on it. After something like this happens four or five times, the room is littered, and the disorder soon spreads to the next room. Or say one person does a lackluster job cleaning up after a meal. Some dishes or pots or countertops are left unwashed. Everyone who walks into the kitchen afterward feels entitled to add to the mess, leaving a glass and plate on the counter or more crumbs on the table. (After all, there are already a dirty cup and bowl; two more won't matter.) The same chain of events can happen with chores. He did not market, so I will not (or cannot) cook or do the laundry or vacuum. It can also happen when you live alone, and you can find yourself responding to your own breaches of order or routine with still more disorder and disruption. In each case, the household is soon entirely out of control.

New Habits

Simply staying absolutely neat and doing the chores come hell or high water prevents a downward spiral, of course, and this is how things were done until the middle of the twentieth century. But in those days of few goods and simple lives, it was possible to stay absolutely neat without rigidity. Nowadays it is unrealistic, and excessively compulsive, to try to live in a way that avoids *any* breach of orderliness. Today, basic order is much looser but in its own way equally reliable. What this "relaxation" of the modern household amounts to is a set of habitual ways of containing the damage of the broken window, short of insisting that no windows ever be broken. If there is a secret to neatness in the contemporary home, learning these habits is it.

The new habits sound obvious to experienced people but not to novices in housekeeping, particularly if they came from a home that was old-fashioned. First, as to neatness, your inner standards must be adjusted to permit a certain number of things to be "out of place" without triggering the feeling that a rule has been broken or that the perfection of the room is thereby flawed. Thus newcomers to an area of the house do not feel entitled to escalate, or that "anything goes." There is still a place for everything, but things are only expected to be in them *at certain times*. Pickups come at the end of every activity insofar as possible. Otherwise, they happen before bed. You get up in the morning to a home to which order has been restored.

Second, as to what may be out of place: some things but not others. You leave uncompleted activities set up so as to be able to return to them conveniently later on. You leave your newspaper on your reading chair, your mending on the endtable, your mail or half-completed crossword puzzle and pencil on the kitchen table, your income tax calculations spread over the dining room table, a stack of CDs you are listening your way through on the carpet. Children may leave their setup for an elaborate pretend game or construction but *not* toys and games that they are finished with. Adults, too, put things away when they are finished. Neither children nor adults should leave out materials for more than one activity at a time.

You do not leave food or dirty dishes or glasses or remnants of snacks or meals out, as this is unsanitary. You do not leave wet towels in a heap on the bathroom floor, as they will not dry and then turn sour and get dirty. Nor do you leave the bed unmade or dirty clothes lying around. This makes more work for you, as the bed does not stay clean, and dirty clothes on the floor, which look ugly and are inconvenient, are not an activity but mere thoughtlessness. It is just as easy to put them in the hamper.

Third, you have to establish temporary holding stations for miscellaneous designated goods. These are places where it is permissible to leave things *before* they are put away. In our foyer we have a closet, a hat-and-coat rack, and a little chest with drawers that is there to hold letters ready for mailing as well as mail newly delivered, mittens, scarves, fliers from school, toys playmates have left that need to be returned, dry-cleaning receipts, and many other things that matter as you are coming in and going out. Before we had this chest of drawers, mail, letters to be posted, and receipts were constantly mislaid. Thus we not only made sure that there was a place for everything by putting the chest there, we also established a temporary holding station for things. The mail is not out of place there pending the time when it will be filed, answered, or thrown away. The toys and the receipts, while they are not in their places, are in the right place to be dealt with. If they accumulate there for a couple of days, still they do not get lost and they do not create a disorderly home. We know where to look for them.

Neat, well-organized homes tend to have a variety of these temporary holding stations. Consider establishing one whenever you see an annoying pattern of mess developing. Clothes hampers are an example of one that you already have: a place for holding dirty laundry temporarily until it is time to do something about it. But although homes have long had the need for clothes hampers, only recently have children brought home so much paper from school that it can take over the house. Many families benefit from establishing a holding station for children's letters from school, artwork, graded homework, announcements, and so forth. Make a drawer for them in your own hallway chest or in the kitchen, or establish a corner on the kitchen counter or in your desk, or put an attractive lidless storage box in a convenient spot. Periodically go through the box and throw away what is old and not worth keeping; put in a permanent place the artwork or compositions that you would like to save. (You might want to have a permanent large envelope for each grade for each child.) We have a book-shelving station in our home, just as libraries do. Without it, we found that there were books everywhere, growing dog-eared and in constant danger of mistreatment, while we could never find the ones we wanted. Many homes have magazine racks that work the same way. A junk drawer in the kitchen or elsewhere is both a temporary and permanent home for all the strange little plastic gadgets, rubber bands, and pieces of string that you cannot use or identify and think you might want someday. We have a shelf for holding old newspapers, and we empty it only once or twice a week. This keeps the papers around for a few days, which we find is useful: we often want to share an article or clip something but haven't time on the morning it comes.

Every temporary holding station has to go along with a day of reckoning, a time when you actually do sort the mail or the school papers, shelve the books, wash the laundry, and recycle the old newspapers. Otherwise the messes will begin again. Perhaps you will need to sort the school papers weekly, the mail daily. Even the junk drawer has to be sorted once or twice a year or you will not be able to open it.

The sad story of my friend K—— may bring this lesson home. She read in a magazine a rather extreme suggestion about how to produce quick order in your home, one that bears a misleading cousinly resemblance to the idea of temporary holding stations. The author suggested that when company is coming and your home is untidy you grab a shopping bag and run around throwing everything that is out of place into the bag; then store the bag in a closet for later unloading. When K—— found herself with eight shopping bags full of litter bulging out of her closets, she realized that this was really no solution for her. There were many problems with the plan. It came with no habit or plan for unpacking and sorting. It placed the litter out of sight so that she was never reminded to do something about it. It did not provide for keeping things in places where they could be found (in the way that you know your dirty laundry is in the hamper and I know the newspapers are on the shelf), and the problems it created were more painful than the messy apartment. For weeks she couldn't find things in the bags, and when she finally unloaded them it was an exhausting all-day chore.

Finally, it helps to develop a habit of neatening. When you go upstairs, carry up with you something that belongs there. You also promote neatness in your home, indirectly, when you keep to your household routines. When you neglect them, the sense of disorder and the out-of-control feeling that develop quickly lead to deterioration in basic orderliness and neatness. When you must disrupt your routines, keep chaos from developing by maintaining a reserve of whatever each routine provides—food, clean laundry, fundamental cleanliness—enough to keep things together until you can get back on schedule.

These are habits that will enable you to keep a neat and orderly household even though your home is filled with too many things and even though your schedule is unpredictable. When these habits are adopted, the place looks lived in—as though real human beings spend their time there doing serious, pleasant, and curious things. They do not live *for* the home but in it. It is not there for display but for comfort, rest, and the various activities of private life.

Picking Up After Others

Most of us resent having to pick up anyone else's litter, and as a general principle each member of a household should be responsible for picking up after himself or herself. Children can begin picking up toys and putting their clothes in the hamper as two-year-olds, and each year they can learn to do a bit more. (See the advice books on how to teach a child to put things away. When my son was a preschooler, I found *Dr. Spock's Baby and Child Care* and Penelope Leach's *Your Baby and Child from Birth to Age Five* helpful.) I myself, however, always permit an ongoing imaginative or constructive play activity to stay out, since I notice that putting it away destroys it, and I like encouraging elaborate games and constructions that last for days or even weeks. If you live with someone who is careless with her belongings, you might try establishing someplace where you put her things pending her putting them away herself. My husband and I both have home offices. When either of us is neatening and finds something belonging to the other, we put it inside the door of the other's office. This does not require us to put the other's things away, but order and harmony are preserved.

FOOD

4

The Whys and Wherefores of Home Cooking

Benefits of home cooking . . . Ease of modern home cooking . . . Finding time . . . Oven meals and other meals requiring little preparation time . . . Rethinking leftovers . . . Learning not to use cookbooks . . . Practicing skills . . . Meals off the shelf . . . Basic stores you need in refrigerator or pantry . . . Using convenience foods wisely . . . Real and spurious convenience . . . Convenience foods to avoid

Food is so pleasurable and powerful that it plays an essential role in creating a home that works. For your home to feel solid, meaningful, dignified, and warm, you must have the means and skills to produce good, nutritious food, to dream up pleasant menus, and to set the table and serve the food in an attractive manner that is familiar and comfortable to guests.

If you respect the importance of meals in your home, you gain a cornucopia of advantages that are acknowledged so rarely as to count among the best-kept secrets of our day. In addition to saving you money, cooking at home can help you be healthier, happier, and more secure, and it provides a wonderful way for you to be with your family. It takes less time than going out to a nice restaurant; you will enjoy better-tasting food and know much more about its history and preparation. Cooking at home also increases your control over the cleanliness and quality of ingredients and care that go into your food and establishes one more area in life in which you can be independent and knowledgeable.

Good meals at home satisfy emotional hungers as real as hunger in the belly, and nothing else does so in the same way. They promote affection and intimacy among those who share them. Characteristic, familial styles of cooking and dining, foods that "taste like home," are central to each home's feelings of security and comfort and to its sense of itself as a unique and valuable place. Cooking at home links your past and future and solidifies your sense of identity and place. When a home gives up its hearth, which in the modern world is its kitchen, it gives up its focus.

(The word "focus" is Latin for "hearth.") And the people who live there lose theirs too.

Home cooking can offer appropriate portion sizes, sophisticated attention to individual nutrition and diet needs, freedom from repetition (because people in their homes know what they have eaten today, yesterday, and last week), menus that reflect likes and dislikes in fat and salt levels as well as flavors, ingredients, and preparation styles. You can make almost anything in the world that you want, and you can make family or ethnic dishes just the way you like them. But commercially prepared foods have to appeal to the lowest common denominator of taste. (Without that, sales would not be high enough to turn a profit.) If you have satisfying, well-designed meals at home, you are going to be less prone to overeating and nibbling, not only because of the kinds of foods you are likely to prepare but because the very emotional satisfactions offered by home-cooked meals help assuage the empty feelings that make some of us eat when we are not really hungry.

These considerations are especially significant when it comes to home meals for children. The emotional comfort of home cooking for children is something every parent discovers. Sharing meals with the children in the privacy of your home, meals that you have prepared, reinforces your authority and beneficence in their eyes and helps increase their trust and pride in you and your abilities. You have the skill and knowledge to offer them good things; you take time and trouble for them. Moreover, if children do not become accustomed to the taste of healthy foods at home, they are an easy target for marketers who want them to buy unhealthy foods away from home—foods with high levels of fat, far too much salt and sugar, hidden ingredients, and, perhaps most harmful of all, textures and tastes that cannot be imitated at home. Once children's arch-conservative palates have become accustomed to the tastes and styles of fast food and other commercial foods, meals prepared at home that are healthier and better may nonetheless come to taste wrong to them.

Of course there are also times when a meal out is the most fun, most delicious, and easiest thing to do, and times when it would be absurd not to order a pizza. Home and health are at risk only when home cooking and eating are not routine and ordinary pleasures in life.

Then and Now: The Ease of Modern Home Cooking

Despite the clear benefits of living in a home capable of providing good meals, the institution of private cooking has long had its enemies who have insisted that we would be better off if we never bothered to market or cook. More than a century ago, various social critics and feminists, seeking to ease the burdens on women, denounced private cookery and sometimes contended that private homes should not even have kitchens. Because cooking was at the time among the most onerous of the housewife's many staggering domestic burdens, they believed such reforms essential to her liberation.

Some of these opponents of home cooking proposed that communities be designed with central kitchens that would provide all meals for resident families. Some thought a central dining room would be best. Others suggested that meals be delivered in warming devices to kitchenless homes, or that someone stop by the central kitchen to pick up the day's dinner. One scheme contemplated the use of vacuum tubes that would whoosh steaming-hot dinners to your dining room in seconds flat. A few dining communities on these models were in fact created, but they were short-lived.

The point of the old criticisms of home cooking is blunted by the fantastic ease of home cooking today compared with the nineteenth century. The labor of cooking has contracted until it now comprises only the last stages of assembly and heating—the creative and pleasurable parts. Refrigeration, commercial canning, and other excellent means of safe storage, superior stoves and ovens, microwaves, automatic cooking appliances, and the other accoutrements of the modern kitchen are only part of the story. You buy your chicken plucked, clean, cut up, and ready for the oven; meat is aged, cut, and trimmed; fruits and vegetables are sorted and washed free of mud; fish are cleaned, scaled, filleted. Important foods and foodstuffs that are often of high quality can be bought and do not have to be made at all. These include bread, breakfast cereals, dried pasta, ice cream, butter, cream cheese, cottage cheese, and all other cheeses, yogurt, sausages, hams, bacon, canned ready-to-eat fish such as tuna, salmon, mackerel, and clams, yeast, nut butters, jams, jellies, preserves, roasted coffee beans, pickles, relishes, and condiments of all sorts—mayonnaise, mustards, ketchup, vinegars, and dozens more.

The supermarket's rich offerings make possible an unprecedented degree of flexibility in home cooking. How much time you take to make a meal is largely up to you. You can make everything entirely from scratch or you can buy some foods partly or wholly prepared for you. Typical good home cooks today enjoy making long-cooking, all-from-scratch meals on days when they have extra time, but on weeknights after work usually choose meals that are quick to prepare. Often they rely on a combination of fresh, canned, and frozen foodstuffs to produce lovely, quick meals whose success is as much a matter of imagination and insight as of advanced cooking skills or time spent slaving over a hot stove.

Finding Time for Cooking

Some people have a genius for getting something tempting on the table in no time. But before we consider how they do this, it is worth deciding whether your goal, generally speaking, is really to get in and out of the kitchen as fast as possible. If you start out begrudging the time you give to cookery, you are going to create a false contest between cooking and enjoying yourself. Cooking in our day is pleasure, almost unalloyed pleasure, not an unpleasant means to an end. When you get home from work, you can use your time in the kitchen to slow down, regroup, and enjoy being physical—doing things with your hands, letting them get floury or wet, smelling good smells. Whether you cook alone or with others, this becomes a special time of the day that you soon find you cherish and do not want to miss.

Those who are most successful at accommodating the time pressure on the modern home are those who put effort into becoming good intuitive cooks. Many people go out to eat not because they really lack time to cook but because they simply do not know how to cook well enough to make good quick meals. Good cooks have physical skills that let them work quickly, and they have a good repertoire of thought-out, easy-to-prepare meals and dishes that they can turn to when time is short. They can add and subtract from this repertoire over time for the sake of variety, but they do not forget that most of us like a balance of the familiar and the new in our diets.

A few basic tricks can help you become the kind of intuitive cook who throws appealing things together confidently.

Make Oven Meals and Other Low-Preparation-Time Meals. New cooks soon learn the difference between cooking time and preparation time. The former is how long you have to expose foods to heat. The latter is how long you have to be engaged in preparing the food. Often, these two time periods are totally unrelated. I and many people I know often rely on what I call oven meals when we are short on time. This means a meal that cooks for a long time in the oven (usually one and a half to two hours) but takes only ten to twenty minutes to prepare before being put in the oven. A chicken or an appropriate cut of pork, veal, or beef can be roasted with fresh seasonal vegetables; you can bake potatoes in the oven at the same time. Add a salad and good bread, and you have a good, simple meal (along with the delight of a home filled with exquisite aromas while the cooking goes on). As you become more experienced, you can add little touches to oven meals that dress them up and make for variety—putting a mustard sauce on the chicken, or baking the vegetables in an easy casserole. Such simple oven meals are a godsend on evenings when you have to go out after dinner or have so many chores or so much other work to attend to that you do not want to do much in the way of cooking. While your dinner is roasting in the oven, you can do housework, supervise homework, or pay bills.

Some stovetop meals work in much the same way. There are many hearty soups and stews that can form the core of an excellent meal that take little time to prepare and will simmer along for hours with little attention while you busy yourself with other things. Many good cookbooks have recipes for these and will alert you that they are quick to prepare.

Then there are meals that take both short preparation time and short cooking time. Fish broils or poaches in minutes. You need to do nothing to it but place it under the heat or in the broth, and you end up with the healthiest of meals. Such vegetables as carrots, broccoli, or cauliflower steam in minutes. There are a thousand pasta or rice dishes and delicious sauces that are quick and effortless. My family likes various bean-and-rice dishes and bean soups. (There is nothing wrong with using canned beans when you are in a hurry.)

Rethink Leftovers. You can provide for days when you are rushed, and increase the versatility of your kitchen, by cooking extra quantities whenever you have time to do any serious cooking. As you plan your leftovers, the most important thing to keep in mind is your own tastes. People usually eat favorite foods as leftovers more easily than less-well-loved foods. But sometimes even well-loved foods can overstay their welcome. My family does not take to any fish dish the second day, or any leftover dish with cabbage or broccoli, although we otherwise like these foods.

Do not succumb to the widespread prejudice that you are deprived if you are eating leftovers. Leftovers do not really deserve their poor reputation, which is derived from a certain kind of leftovers that used to be common in American households. Until recently, mainstream American cooking was very old-style English, a largely defunct type of domestic cookery that was long subject to scorn for overemphasizing utilitarian factors at the expense of taste and pleasure. It was heavy, bland, greasy, and soggy, said its critics, designed to create lots of leftovers and to be consumed to the last stale crumb. Lest I be accused of anti-English prejudices here, I hasten to point out that my paternal grandmother was of part English ancestry and cooked in this very style.

My father venerated his mother's cooking, especially her way with leftovers. Any substantial meal she made wielded its influence for many days to come. Out of leftover mashed potatoes she made fried potato cakes, so she never failed to make at least twice the needed quantity at the first meal. Out of leftover meats she made stews, creamed meats, mock chicken, and meat ground up with pickles for sandwich spreads, so she made enormous roasts and birds. (My husband's mother, who also was very much a cook in this style, especially enjoyed creating disguised foods, such as meatloaf that was "really" something else. "You'd never know, would you?" she would insist triumphantly.) My father's admiration for his mother's abilities to stretch any dish out for a week was motivated more by principle than by taste. He had been brought up in the Depression, when a woman who could "make a meal out of nothing" was truly a miracle worker, the salvation of her family. He and others like him ate leftovers with apparent enthusiasm only because they believed this was right and good, not because they liked the tired food.

In Italian cooking there is no tremendous effort expended toward recooking with new ingredients, and in a different style, a food that was served in another style the day before. In my Italian relatives' homes, not only was the word "leftovers" never used, the whole idea was unknown. If there was soup or pasta, it was expected to last for two or three days. One simply had *more* soup or ravioli on subsequent days, not leftover soup or ravioli, and no one particularly minded having something again, assuming it was a well-liked food to begin with.

Comparing the two styles early on taught me this rule (which, like all rules, has important exceptions): if I wanted to serve leftovers, I should make Italian food; and if I wanted to cook like my Anglo-American grandmother, I should make no more than we needed for a meal. One reason Anglo-American leftovers were seldom desirable was the emphasis on roasted, broiled, and fried meat and fish. None of these is ever quite the same on reheating; they toughen and get dry, and their taste changes. Thus the cook is inspired to "make something else" of them, creating a dreary culinary netherworld of patties and cakes and croquettes, fish or meat mixed up with crumbs and eggs and onions, mournful shadows of their living selves. On the other hand, soups, stews, chili, tomato-based dishes and tomato sauces, and braised meats—all the long-cooking dishes so popular in many kinds of Italian cookery—usually improve on the second day, and almost all freeze well. If you are making roast chicken or meatloaf, make large ones or make two or three and freeze the extra ones. Make stock out of leftover bones and meat and keep it in the freezer. Freeze half a cake, cookie dough, and other favorites.

Consider the appearance and texture, as well as the taste, of the foods to be served more than once. Yellow vegetables such as squash and sweet potatoes tend to store and recook successfully. But spinach, sugar snap peas, and green beans suffer from deteriorating color and texture. Green beans that could not stand alone, however, might be fine in a soup or stew on the second day, or you might consider adding a vinaigrette and serving them cold as a salad. If the point of a dish is the crunchiness of its vegetables, you are unlikely to have luck serving it again tomorrow. Tossed greens will be too far gone the next day.

Root vegetables such as turnips, parsnips, potatoes, and carrots can often be re-served, but how successfully depends upon how they were first prepared. Purees and soups of these forward well. Mashed potatoes will have to be made into something else—for example, shepherd's pie or patties. Baked potatoes' taste and texture survive reheating passably well, yet there is much feeling against reheated baked potatoes, which are considered to be on a par with frozen commercial dinners. This attitude is a bit snobbish, but it has a point. Because there is nothing in the world easier to make than a baked potato for anyone with a potato, an oven, and the ability to think ahead for an hour, why not just make a new baked potato? There is occasionally a good answer to this rhetorical question—for example, because you have three of them unexpectedly left over and it is already lunchtime. However, I vote with those who think that it makes little sense to create extra leftover baked potatoes on purpose.

Learn How to Make a Meal Without Looking at a Cookbook. Good cooks know how to cook without looking at recipes. Of course they often use recipes too—for example, when they want to learn how to make new dishes, to be reminded of how to make old ones, to figure out why something never works well, to learn how to alter a dish, and to get inspiration. But they do not usually first think of dishes, consult recipes, and then collect ingredients to cook them. That is a laborious and time-consuming way to cook. If you are a cook who cooks only from recipes, you probably think it is hard to find enough time for cooking.

Intuitive cooks have learned basic cooking facts and techniques. For day-to-day cooking, far more important than memorizing a complicated recipe is knowing without thinking how much heat cooks a soft-boiled, hard-boiled, scrambled, or fried egg; the approximate cooking times of fruits and vegetables, whether chopped, whole, roasted, sautéed, or steamed; the effects of poaching, broiling, braising, roasting, sautéing, and frying on meat, poultry, and fish; when you can substitute parsley or celery leaves for basil, or cook a dish on top of the stove rather than in the oven; what combinations enhance the taste of ingredients; what garlic or cumin or rosemary is good with—all this an average competent cook knows without cracking a book. It may take a while to get to this point, but before long everyone who loves food and regularly spends time in the kitchen learning from his or her own mistakes will end up with these skills and many more.

Practice Skills. My Italian grandmother taught me that speed and physical dexterity in cooking techniques (and in all housework) are important; her hands moved faster than the eye could follow when they chopped and peeled. If you chop the celery in slow motion, you won't want to chop it very often. True skill involves not only producing the right result but being able to do so in a reasonable time, and the only way to learn speed is to practice, practice, practice. (But be safe! Do not go faster than you can without cutting yourself.)

The best way to learn all the skills of good cooking is to watch those who know how and imitate them. Adults are not too old to learn from their parents or grandparents. The learning aids available are superb, ranging from excellent classes in schools and on television and wonderful books that teach the fundamentals in ways that few cookbooks attempted before to videos that you can rewind and replay over and over. When you choose your sources, remember that different techniques are used in different cuisines and choose those that will help you acquire the skills needed for the type of cooking you prefer.

Be Prepared to Make Meals off the Shelf. It is always best to cook with fresh ingredients in season. But there are days when you cannot get to the market, or when at the last minute you find yourself missing something fresh that you need for the menu you planned. My husband once went to dinner at the home of a friend—a remarkable cook—whose plans for the evening were wrecked when she discovered that the package her butcher had given her contained venison liver, not venison steaks. In half an hour or so, after some hand-wringing, she produced instead one of the best plates of pasta he had ever tasted.

To be like my husband's friend and all other good home cooks, store a variety of foods that keep well and can quickly be turned into a meal without needing anything from the market, and develop a repertoire of meals or dishes that can be made from them. Restock these basic foods as soon as supplies are low. If you are a beginner, in time you will dream up your own off-the-shelf meals—"cabinet meals," a friend calls them. Meals I make this way include several pasta and rice dishes, bean dishes, egg dishes, and several canned tuna and salmon concoctions. The following foods are standbys that many people rely on when they cannot get to the market:

Relatively long-lasting fresh foods

Potatoes

Onions

Garlic
Ginger
Carrots
Celery
Apples
Oranges
Lemons
Eggs
Miscellaneous cheeses

Frozen foods

Selected fruits and vegetables
Stock
Meats or sausages that thaw well in the microwave
Ice cream

Canned or bottled goods

Tomatoes, whole or chopped
Tomato paste
Beans of all sorts: kidney, garbanzo, pinto, northern, etc.
Tuna fish or other canned fish (clams, salmon, etc.)
Selected fruits and vegetables
Olive oil
Vinegar
UHT* milk or condensed milk
Pickles, olives, salsa, and other relishes
Miscellaneous condiments: mustard, soy sauce, etc.
Jams and jellies
Syrups
Canned broth

Packaged and dried foods

Favorite types of pasta
Rice
Cornmeal
Breakfast cereals
Flour
Salt
Pepper or peppercorns
Dried herbs and spices: cinnamon, basil, cumin, mint, red pepper, rosemary, thyme, etc.
Sugar: white granulated, brown, powdered
Cornstarch
Baking soda
Baking powder
Coffee
Tea
Dried fruits: raisins, dates, figs, prunes, apricots, etc.

Add to or subtract from these lists in accordance with your own tastes. I know that I must always keep olives for various foods we enjoy, but a friend who detests olives always keeps anchovies, and another relies on a jar of capers.

Using these stocks, without marketing or spending much time cooking, you can quickly serve, for example, a light soup, followed by polenta with sausages; an omelette with vegetable filling and a baked potato; pasta e fagioli, or pasta and peas with ricotta or other cheeses. If you have some greens or green beans, you can make a hearty salad with the canned tuna. Italian and French cookbooks will suggest many tasty ideas for various "tuna and" dishes—pasta, tomatoes, white beans, garlic, fresh greens all go well. You can follow up any of these meals with fresh fruit, or, if you like a warm, sweet dessert, you could make apple tarts or stewed apples with brown sugar, cinnamon, and a little lemon juice. Dried fruits can be used for quick breads, cakes, or cookies, on

*"UHT" means "ultra-high temperature" pasteurization. UHT milk, if unopened, stays fresh for many months on the pantry shelf, but refrigerate it after opening. Check freshness dates on packages.

ice cream, in puddings, or as they are with some cheese.

Use Convenience Foods Wisely. Practically all foodstuffs used in the modern home would have been regarded as miraculous conveniences by our great-grandmothers. This truth has generally been forgotten, to the point that people commonly use the term "raw ingredients" to refer to foods that have undergone elaborate processing and preparation prior to sale: butter, pasteurized and homogenized milk, cottage cheese, ricotta cheese, a package of skinned and boned chicken breasts, a bag of roasted coffee beans, a bottle of olive oil, or a jar of mayonnaise. To keep things in perspective, it may help to consider the recipe for roast beef in one of my great-grandmother's cookbooks, which called for, among other things, a cow.

It is pointless to spurn convenience foods, and few people—the Amish, for example—really do. Many people enjoy making homemade yogurt, jam, or sausages. Many bake bread; this is fun and the bread is a heavenly delight. There is even a mini-fad of milling grains in a tiny home-milling machine. Some of us like to roll out our own pasta on special occasions. But most of us are glad to rely on convenience foods to increase variety and reduce drudgery in home cooking.

Real Convenience. Be alert, however, to whether a "convenience" is really there for your benefit or the store's. Sometimes it seems easier to buy a preselected bag of apples or package of green beans, but you are usually better off picking out your own so you can get exactly the amount you need and make sure none are bruised or broken. Grocers seem to pack one or two bad apples or strawberries into every package, which means that they have much less waste and you have much more. But if you know and trust your grocer, there is nothing wrong with buying a five-pound bag of onions or potatoes. It saves you a few minutes selecting and weighing at the market. Sometimes there is no choice, but, if you can, it is best to patronize a market that offers you the choice.

Canned and frozen fruits and vegetables are a real convenience. They take no washing, chopping, or cooking beyond heating. Of course, good fresh fruits and vegetables, in season, have much better taste and texture and offer better nutrition. But you are better off buying canned or frozen produce than produce that has traveled so far or been stored so long that it is nutritionally inferior to its canned or frozen counterparts. Discriminate among the brands and types, for not all taste the same, and buy unsalted and unsauced versions so that you can control flavor and healthfulness.

There are foods most people enjoy in their canned state, for this, after all, is a mode of preparation that can produce a tasty product. When I was a little girl, people in the country canned the products of their gardens. Canning was done with prized recipes, and often you could not wait for winter to sample the delicacies—relishes, vegetable salads, fruit preserves and jams. Supermarket canned goods contain some favorites, too, including canned tuna, tomatoes, some salsas, pumpkin and squash, all sorts of beans, and pickles. Others are a matter of taste, and what you like depends very much on what you are used to. For example, it is possible to develop a taste for canned evaporated milk. Where I grew up, people put it in their tea (but not, for some reason, coffee), and that combination tastes good to me to this day, although I could never bring myself to drink the stuff straight. Canned or bottled artichoke hearts are not at all like fresh artichokes but can be loved for their own sakes. The kind packed in water instead of oil leaves you more options for preparation.

Although it does not taste particularly like the fresh, canned corn tastes good and offers fairly good crunch. You would not use it in

WHAT PANCAKES ARE MADE OF

Ingredients for homemade pancakes from scratch:	Ingredients for pancakes using one famous pancake mix:
flour	mix
salt	
baking powder	
milk	milk
egg	egg
oil	oil

So the great convenience of the mix is that it saves you the trouble of measuring salt and baking powder.

dishes that you prepare to show off fresh flavor—corn chowders, for example—but you can put some in a vegetable soup when fresh corn is out of season. Canned green beans, peas, and asparagus are inferior to frozen, but neither canned nor frozen are particularly good. Bottled garlic is not a good substitute for raw, which is always available. Not everyone agrees with me, but I would rather have no broccoli than frozen broccoli, and I can think of nothing that could induce me to use canned potatoes.

My young son would not eat bottled applesauce and loved our homemade applesauce. (Check your cookbook; this is quick and easy to make.) One day he came home from nursery school to report that they had yellow peaches with "good juice" and asked why *we* couldn't have that. I tried him on my own stewed peaches with syrup, but these were voted inferior—not at all what he wanted. So I sighed and bought some canned peaches packed in light syrup, which made him happy, and I admit that the grownups, too, thought they were pleasant, even if inferior to homemade and tasting of can. I suspect that the pretty color of the canned ones and the texture were factors in his preference. I decided not to oppose him on this because, nutritionally speaking, canned peaches are a reasonable dessert. The lesson here is not "Buy canned peaches" but "Don't be irrational out of food snobbery." When health considerations cut the other way, of course, you have to stand your ground.

For health reasons, many people now eat fewer processed meats, especially ones with nitrates and nitrites, such as luncheon meats, bacon, ham, salami, and some sausages. Quite apart from questions about the healthfulness of such chemicals, these foods tend to be extremely high in sodium and often high in saturated fat. Still, sliced into a sauce or a dish of pasta with vegetables, sausages and cured meats can be an easy and flavorful means of filling out a quick meal. If you do not eat too much of these or serve them too often, they can be a real boon to the home on rushed days. Soy-based or other vegetarian sausages are also useful.

Mixes are sometimes a reasonable alternative and sometimes not. Often it is just as simple to cook from scratch. Cookbooks are full of simple recipes for cakes that will taste better than a mix and have a more interesting texture. (Of course, there are also some spectacularly difficult cakes in those books.) Those who are not accustomed to what homemade cakes taste or feel like in the mouth may not be pleased at first, for the mixes produce results that are invariably light, moist, and airy. Pancake mixes often offer no advantages at all.

Nonetheless, there are times when you would be foolish not to use a mix. Perhaps a domestic emergency occurs. Perhaps cupcakes must be brought to school tomorrow morning, but when you stop at the market on your way home from work, you cannot remember whether you have baking powder, cream of tartar, baking soda, nutmeg, cake flour, chocolate, or vanilla on your shelf, or you want to go through the "five items or fewer" line. So you buy the mix. Only a glutton for punishment would do otherwise. I have a hard time imagining emergency pancakes, but stranger things have happened.

Bread, yogurt and pasta are time-saving convenience foods. But if you enjoy cooking and have time, go ahead and try making some such things now and then. It is fun and gives your palate an education. Even people who know how to roll out their own pasta do so infrequently because it takes considerable time and muscle power. Premade pastas and pasta-making machines are a major convenience for pasta lovers. By and large, fresh pasta is better than frozen, and frozen is better than dried. But there is huge variation among brands, and dried pasta can be good. There is no reason to pay the high premium on fresh pasta if it strains your budget. When buying dried pasta, imported Italian brands are most reliably good. If you are buying fresh, try to get the recommendation of someone you trust or buy from a maker who specializes in Italian foods, for fresh pasta is costly and sometimes can be disappointing. Delicious filled pasta, such as ravioli and tortellini, can be bought fresh or frozen at fancy delicatessens, food specialty shops, and good supermarkets. You can make your own sauce for these easily and create a good meal in little time.

Spurious Convenience. Many foods that are marketed as convenience foods are not really convenient, do not taste particularly good, are not good for you, and are ridiculously expensive. When choosing convenience foods, consider flavor, read ingredient lists, check labels for fat, salt, sugar, and nutrient levels, and consider whether making it yourself would really take so much time. Everyone will have his or her own opinions as to which food should stay on the supermarket shelf, and these opinions will be as complicated as their lives. Rarely have I heard open discussion of the byzantine calculations that people today make routinely when they decide to buy, say, bottled tomato sauce rather than make it, but they would tax the brain of a mathematician. Who likes this and who does not; is there any basil at the market; can I work at home for an hour while something roasts or will I not get home until twenty minutes before dinner should be ready; did I remember to take something out of the freezer; is the brand with low-sodium on the shelf today; have we had this too often lately; if I make a big effort to try to buy and chop fresh tomatoes will that be the bit of extra pressure that wrecks my cheerfulness and makes me irritable with children or mate; is there a reason to serve something that the children especially love today? Given our complicated motivations, tastes, and goals, everyone is likely to have a list of foods not to buy that is different from other people's.

But most of us will be better off to resist buying, most of the time, some foods or

"CONVENIENCE" FOODS?

"Convenience" foods sometimes offer spurious inconvenience. The first cake mixes offered on the market were formulated so that the cook needed to do nothing more than add water and bake—and many buyers refused to use them because doing so made them feel useless. The manufacturers then reformulated the mixes to require the addition of an egg and milk just so that the cook could feel useful and creative.

types of food for reasons of health or taste—for example, highly sweetened and colored breakfast cereals, toaster pastries, frozen vegetable dishes with sauces, frozen dinners and entrees, canned spaghetti, or instant mashed potatoes. Some foods offer so little time savings that most of us usually have no reason to get them except in special circumstances, such as for office lunches or as a superior type of fast food. Precut and preselected salad greens and fruits are a case in point. It takes only a minute or two to pull a few leaves off a head of lettuce or cut the roots off some leaves of arugula. If you buy greens prepackaged, you deprive yourself of the choice of which greens you will use as well as any choice about their condition (which is hard to observe anyway in the closed package), and you actually pay a premium in price for this loss. (And, by the way, sometimes it is probably best to wash even prepackaged salad greens. See chapter 13, "Safe Food," pages 187–89.) It takes seconds to cut a melon and scoop out the seeds. Precut fruit is necessarily going to be less fresh, more prone to bruising, and more easily infected with pathogens.

If you buy cottage cheese without added fruits and vegetables, you can add your own when you serve it. This tastes better and leaves you the option of eating something different with it the next time: apple butter today; scallions, sweet red peppers, and cucumbers with fresh black pepper tomorrow. Sometimes you cannot find plain yogurt at the market, but it is worth looking for because flavored yogurts and milks are oversweetened and, unless sweetened artificially, have too many calories. You can add accompaniments to plain yogurt at home, if you wish, using only moments of your time to make your own low-calorie yogurt desserts: a spoonful of jam, apple butter, slices of banana, applesauce and cinnamon, sweetener plus a drop of vanilla or a little lime juice. Noodles and rice can be dressed up at home in seconds. Get suggestions from friends and cookbooks.

Canned chicken, stew, spaghetti, hash, chili, and similar canned dishes simply taste dreary to people accustomed to good cooking. Canned versions tend to be too soft or mushy, and are much less good for you than what you can easily and quickly make for yourself, as they are usually oversalted and contain too much saturated fat. Canned refried beans offer no particular advantage. You can make refried beans out of canned beans or cooked dried beans and enjoy better flavor, in about the same time it takes to open and warm a can of refried beans.

It is almost always a mistake to buy "flavored" foods. It takes only a few minutes with a cookbook to learn how to add your own spices, herbs, marinade, or breading. Bottled salad dressings are expensive, and few taste good. They are a prime example of how people are too often led to pay premium prices for spurious convenience. Homemade dressings not only taste better and cost less; the best of them are "instant" too. Many of us think that good olive oil and vinegar make the best-tasting salad dressing possible, and probably the healthiest. The substances added to flavored olive oils render the oil inappropriate for general use, and thus these oils, which are often costly, tend to go bad long before they are used up. See the discussion of the danger of botulism in flavored oils in the Guide to Common Food Pathogens, page 181. Flavored vinegars, too, are far less versatile. It is easy to add your own herbs or garlic to *small* amounts of oil or vinegar when you want herb flavors. Flavored creamy "gourmet" coffees contain partially hydrogenated vegetable fats and thus "trans fats," which are unhealthy. You can make a flavored coffee by adding cinnamon, cardamom (grind up one seed with your coffee beans), chocolate, or vanilla to an ordinary cup, and cookbooks offer more suggestions. Instant coffee simply doesn't taste as good as coffee made from freshly ground beans.

You might argue that if you want to eat such a silly food as flavored, sweetened, food-colored gelatin, as I occasionally do, you might as well buy it in individually packaged four-ounce premade servings as buy a box of Jell-O and mix it with hot water at home. But the premade stuff costs a great deal more. Moreover, many people are offended at the wastefulness of the elaborate, expensive packaging used for this playful, inexpensive food. The same goes for prepackaged puddings. Homemade pudding, custards, and "creme," made without mixes, are fast, easy, and good too, and you can make them as sweet, flavorful, and thick as you wish.

5

Breakfast, Lunch, and Dinner

What a real meal is . . . What protein and starch foods are . . . Three real meals are better than numerous minimeals or a life of snacking . . . Meals of the day . . . What breakfast is for and what to make . . . What lunch (or supper) is for and what to make . . . What dinner is for and what to make . . . Guidelines on how to put dinner together

This chapter and the next describe some of the traditions and conventions that define what we think a meal should be like, what breakfast, lunch, and dinner are all about, and the basics of serving appealing meals in the home—familiar customs that we take entirely for granted. Given that these customs are being challenged by strong social trends, however, it is worth pausing to reflect on what they are and how they serve us.

What Is a Real Meal?

The most basic convention governing food is the one that calls for us to eat meals, and having a meal is not the same thing as simply eating something. Meals have contents loosely prescribed by our customs, they occur at customary times of day, and they are served in customary ways. Whether or not people choose to eat real meals, they know one when they see one. Walk into almost any home or restaurant in this or any other Western country and you will observe that, with surprisingly few exceptions, what people consider a real meal is a triad comprising—at a minimum—one "meat" or other protein food, one starchy food, and one or more fruits or vegetables, depending on which meal it is. Cereal with skim milk and fruit or juice is a real breakfast; coffee and toast is borderline. A cheese sandwich and an apple is lunch; crackers and cheese is just a snack. Duck confit with polenta, greens, and olives is a delicious dinner; spaghetti with tomato sauce is just a course. There are gray and overlapping areas that menu planners puzzle over, but the basic idea, which my mother taught me and hers taught her, is that you need these three different kinds of food—at least—to make a satisfying, appetizing, healthy meal.

Of course, this pattern is to be used flexibly, adjusted to health, necessity, whim, fashion, and whatever else the particular moment or meal dictates. The triad is primarily a social or traditional idea, secondarily a nutritional one. What is experienced as a "real meal," and thus satisfies, has as much to do with expectation and experience as with appetite and nutrition, and may or may not be nutritionally sound.[1] But the triad is quite consistent with the USDA's Food Guide Pyramid or any other sensible nutritional guidelines you may follow, including vegetarian ones, and should be used along with these. It even incorporates some basic nutritional sense regarding "macronutrients"—substances necessary for health in relatively large quantities, such as protein, carbohydrates, and fats or oils—and fiber. (Vitamins, minerals, and other substances necessary in tiny quantities for health are called "micronutrients.") Although each member of the triad usually supplies more than one macronutrient and many micronutrients as well, a foodstuff is categorized as a protein or starch for meal-planning purposes only if it contains large quantities of the substance.

Besides its many crucial biochemical functions, the meat or other protein sustains satiety and prevents you from "crashing" from hunger too soon after a meal. The "starchy" food contains carbohydrates, which are necessary to satisfy your appetite quickly (so that you do not continue to feel hungry and overeat) and to give you energy. If you eat meals that are too high in protein or too low in carbohydrates, you may begin to feel tired, irritable, and hungry. The fruits and vegetables supply fiber and micronutrients, along with some protein and carbohydrates. Fats and oils, which serve a large variety of functions in your body (as, indeed, do all the necessary nutrients), are likely to come from any members of the triad, depending upon manner of preparation.

Proteins, Starches, and Fruits and Vegetables

Protein foods, those that include large amounts of protein, consist of flesh and other foods obtained from animals: beef, pork, lamb, mutton, sausage, game, poultry, fish, shellfish; eggs; milk and many milk products such as yogurt, cottage cheese, and other cheeses. (See also the listing for beans, below.)

Starchy foods, those that contain large amounts of carbohydrates, are usually made either of grains or of root vegetables and their products: wheat, barley, oats, corn, rye, millet, buckwheat, quinoa, triticale, pasta, rice, potatoes, sweet potatoes and yams, breakfast cereals, polenta and mush, grits, breads, pancakes and waffles, kasha, couscous. (Potatoes are vegetables but are always considered a starch dish when planning menus.)

Fruits include: apples, pears, cherries, peaches, plums, nectarines, berries of all sorts, melons of all sorts, oranges, lemons, limes, grapefruit, all other types of citrus fruit, kiwifruit, starfruit, bananas, coconuts, pineapples.

Vegetables include: green beans, peas, corn, celery, carrots, turnips, parsnips, asparagus, red peppers, green peppers, beets, lettuces of all types, cabbage, brussels sprouts, kale, mustard greens, collard greens, all similar greens, broccoli, cauliflower, squashes, pumpkin, cucumbers, onions, scallions, shallots, garlic, leeks, black-eyed peas, beans (kidney, black, northern, garbanzo, pinto, all other beans), tomatoes.

Beans, legumes, seeds, and nuts and their products (such as nut butters, tofu, and soy milk) are often used as meat substitutes because they contain substantial amounts of protein—much more than most other vegetables.[a]

Should Real Meals Be Abolished?

The organization of life around a pattern of three meals is, among Western nations, universal and long-standing. The Celts, the Renaissance Florentines, and the Pilgrims in colonial America all ate three meals a day, if they could get them. But for some years now, the idea has grown among some diet enthusiasts and nutritionists that it would be better for our health to eat five or more small, equal meals each day—to "graze"—and to throw out as outdated the idea of a main meal, especially one eaten in the evening. Others take a more moderate position, asserting merely that "grazing" can be done healthily if you find that your harried lifestyle leaves you too busy to sit down for regular meals. Both views offer comfort to the growing number of people who eat out more than they eat in or who for a variety of reasons find themselves missing meals and nibbling throughout the day. But most experts advise us to continue with our sensible traditional pattern of three meals—plus a snack, if needed.

Our meal patterns are significant customs that serve social and psychological purposes almost as important as their biological ones. To abolish meals would amount to rewriting the whole blueprint of private life in favor of something uprooted and isolating. What kind of expert is qualified to tell us to do this? Nutritionists and dietitians understand digestion and food chemistry, but when they turn from narrowly defined nutritional and health issues and address our social habits, they seem unaware that they are talking about historical artifacts with complicated psychological and cultural underpinnings—matters in which they have no expertise.

For a variety of compelling reasons, we continue to need real meals, especially a main meal. Frequent minimeals do not afford the heightened pleasures that food must provide to create a sufficiently important occasion for people to gather for the restorative conviviality of a meal. Practically speaking, in fact, you can accommodate such an experience only once a day, which is why you need a main meal. Because grazing is functional, solitary *eating*, rather than allowing for the relaxation and dignified enjoyments of dining, it offers little pleasure and does not restore you, physically or emotionally, the way real meals do. It is hard to think of five interesting minimeals seven days a week, yet such frequent eating keeps your mind on food all the time: what to have for the next meal, how to get it, how to store it, how to prepare it. The result, in my observation, is that people begin to overeat or undereat. America, the land of nibblers and grazers, of eating on the run on street corners, in cars, and at desks, is also the land of anorexia nervosa, bulimia, and obesity. In countries such as France, Italy, and Greece, where mealtimes are respected, there are fewer weight problems, heart problems, and other health problems associated with poor diet than we have.

Mealtime conventions both restrain and encourage eating by prescribing courses and portion sizes and by limiting the occasions during the day when you are called on to eat or think of food. Thus they make it more unlikely that people will eat either too little or too much. Conventional meals embody traditions designed to make you feel like a person, not a machine that needs fueling. The protection and perpetuation of these important and useful conventions is a major responsibility—and right—of the home.

If a lifestyle has been imposed on you that leaves you without enough time to eat real meals, I think you have a right to resent it and should insist on changing it. Everyone is entitled to the time and resources for a good dinner—and breakfast and lunch—every day, and that includes time to cook in one's own home and enjoy the food and the companionship of family and friends. These things are not luxuries but necessities.

The Meals of the Day

Each of the three daily meals—breakfast, lunch, and dinner, along with tea or a snack—has a definite function and is associated with characteristic or traditional dishes. Part of housekeeping is understanding what purpose each meal serves and how to meet it.

There is a present-day trend toward defying old-fashioned ideas of which dishes are appropriate for each of the meals of the day. Some nutritionists urge people to try soup or pizza or spaghetti for breakfast in hopes that this will get breakfast skippers to have a morning meal. Others serve traditional breakfast foods for dinner. There is nothing wrong with eating any foods that please you at any time of the day; the most important thing is to enjoy your meals and eat well. But you might weigh in the balance that traditional ideas of the appropriate dishes for breakfast, lunch, or dinner can serve to increase our feeling of variety in the menu overall. If you eat the same kinds of foods at all three meals, you cannot readily use the associations of a dish with one meal or another to set the character of a meal. Likewise, the use of certain foods and modes of preparation at different times of day often reflects practical matters of time, difficulty, appetite, and mood. So in principle anything goes, but if you are alert to all the factors that affect good menu choices you may find that in one respect or another you prefer traditional thinking about menus. This does not mean that you cannot be innovative or creative about menus. It only sets the parameters within which you will strive for something new and different.

About Eating Breakfast

What Breakfast Is For. Breakfast supplies food energy and nutrients to your body after its long overnight fast. Strong evidence shows that those who skip breakfast—especially children—perform poorly at school and work compared with those who eat breakfast. Breakfasting also serves important emotional functions. In an age when the home sends its residents out early in the morning for most of the productive day, eating breakfast is more important than it ever was. If you are going to spend nine or ten or more hours without intimacy, with your private and personal goals and interests suspended for the benefit of your work, you need to ensure that you first gather yourself emotionally and refuel yourself physically. Eating a meal, even a small one, helps you do both things.

Breakfast also helps get you oriented in the morning; it pulls you back from dreamland and into reality. Sleeping is a psychological regression, a withdrawal from the world back to a primitive part of your own mind. When you first wake up you have not entirely returned from that archaic place within you. Just as the concerns of your job recede when you get home at night, so the current concerns even of home and private life recede when you sleep and only gradually reassert themselves with full force upon your awakening. If the reconnecting process does not happen before you leave home, you tend to feel raw and off-balance for half the day.

This is why breakfast time is planning time in every household. The food helps sharpen your mind, and you begin thinking through your day, learning everyone's plans and setting your own. Children, who when they wake up in the morning have not interacted with their parents for eight to twelve hours, need to share breakfast with them to help keep alive the children's sense of parental affection and protection when they are apart during the day. This is as true for teenagers who would never admit it as for babies who are incapable of expressing the thought.

What to Make. The breakfast triad customarily consists of a grain food (starch), protein food, and fruit: toast, eggs, and juice; cereal with skim milk or yogurt and fruit; a bagel with lox or cream cheese and a slice of tomato; waffles with blueberries and sausages—plus, of course, a warm, stimulating, and comforting beverage such as coffee, tea, or hot chocolate.

Most people prefer a light breakfast. Not only do they want to face minimal cooking when they first awaken, but they have a modest appetite at that time of day. The rural tradition of a hearty breakfast persists in some places, particularly among farmers; more often such meals are not consumed except at "brunch" or on weekends, holidays, and vacations, when mornings are more leisurely. But a light breakfast still requires some protein; the milk, egg, yogurt, meat, or fish is what gives breakfast its staying power. The "continental" breakfast of rolls or toast and coffee is hard to defend, as it is short on practically everything. (It is greatly improved by a piece of fruit or juice and some skim milk or cottage cheese. The protein allowance for breakfast can be quite small.)

The breakfast appetite is not only modest but conservative. Many people skip breakfast entirely because their morning appetite is so fussy, or they want to eat the same thing every morning and complain about changes. This is the opposite of our attitudes at other meals, when we insist on novelty and lose our appetites if we are given the same thing two or three times in a row. This explains why nutritionists' efforts to persuade people to eat breakfast by assuring them that pizza and soup are fine breakfast foods are almost certainly doomed to failure. Someone who insists on a particular brand of raisin bran or a corn muffin for breakfast every day has not been hoodwinked into thinking that pizza is improper; he simply shudders at the thought of pizza first thing in the morning.

The conservatism of the morning appetite is a psychological phenomenon. When we are still making the slow journey back to full-fledged rationality (after our mental retreat during sleep and dreams), most people tend to want sweet, bland, gentle, easy-to-eat, comforting foods—in other words, childish ones. Throughout the Western world, we find that spicy-hot, acidic, or strong-textured foods that take vigorous chewing or cutting with a knife are usually avoided for breakfast at home, as are all the vegetables that children everywhere resist eating. Most of us prefer cereals and eggs, sausages (a bit spicy, but, unlike roasts, already ground up before we eat them), lox, whitefish, or other fish (more tender than a chop), breads, stewed fruits or fruit juices (no chewing or crunching), sweet jams, syrups, preserves, and so forth. However, if you have been up for a while and have gone out into the world—as is usually the case when you eat breakfast at a restaurant or have brunch instead of breakfast—you are ready to be a bit more adventurous: let them bring on the huevos rancheros with hot chili peppers. Of course, there are lucky people who wake up with fully matured appetites. They need no help figuring out something good for breakfast, but they may need to be more tolerant of others who are less fortunate.

For such reasons as these, habitual foods are useful to the home breakfast. Familiar foods at breakfast help people conquer tricky appetites and attitudes so that their inner children can be wheedled into eating something rather than nothing for breakfast. If you want to expand your breakfast menu, try including new or unusual fruits, grains, and cereals, especially whole-grain and higher-protein varieties. You might also try to include more lean proteins, such as vegetarian or soy-based sausages, tofu, and especially fish, which has always belonged on the breakfast table and has the further advantage of being quick to cook.

About Lunch (or Supper)

What Lunch Is For. Lunch has been called a "respite" from the day's toils, a break of sorts. But besides providing a short rest period, lunch exists to help you make the stretch to dinner. Employers and schools in this country are unwilling to give us time to let it be more, and its very origins work against its assuming any more meaningful character.

A couple of centuries ago everyone followed the custom of eating dinner at midday and supper in the evening. But just as dinner had already migrated from late morning to midday, so it continued to migrate—to three, then four, then five P.M., until, during the late nineteenth century in cities and suburbs, the dinner hour settled itself at about seven or eight P.M., and there it has remained in most Western countries. In rural areas, the custom of midday dinner survived much longer and still exists here and there on farms, and in our lingering habit of serving holiday feasts as early as one or two P.M. In Italy and Spain, and to some extent France, where people's domestic habits are still powerful enough to force businesses to accommodate them, the most important meal for many people may still come at midday.

When dinner got to be as late as two or three P.M., people began to need a snack in the late morning or at noon. And when dinner moved on to four or five P.M., they began to need a small meal at midday, and "lunch" was invented. Lunch was, therefore, makeshift from the start. It borrowed foods from breakfast and dinner, relying on remade and leftover foods, and it had no quarrel with cold or room-temperature foods. Lunch was supposed to be light and not demanding, either to cook or to eat. The lunchers want to save their time and their stomachs, and the cooks their energies, for the "real meal," dinner. Moreover, when lunch first came into vogue, it tended to be a ladies' meal (the gentlemen being tough enough to make it to dinner) and tended to stress light, delicate, and "feminine" foods. Lunch today bears marks of all these aspects of its history.

Most people eat lunch away from home, in which case lunch eating on weekdays affects home cooking only insofar as we try to offer different foods or to adjust the nutritional makeup of our other meals accordingly. But on weekends and vacations most people serve lunch in the home. People who work at home or rear children at home, or are retired, all routinely prepare lunches. Those who can unite the entire family at midday for a sufficient time may decide to aim for a midday dinner.

Usually at lunch you want light food, a minimum of cooking, and a meal that will not steal dinner's thunder. Lunch, therefore, is still light, quicker, less often hot, less often newly cooked, more often consisting of recooked or remade foods. But if you actually have a midday dinner, your evening supper will be the light meal of quick, cold recooked or remade foods.

What to Make. A satisfying lunch includes at least one protein food, one starchy food, such as a grain or root vegetable, and one vegetable. (Fruit is an excellent lunchtime dessert.) Sometimes it borrows the protein idea from breakfast. Omelettes, frittatas, and quiches with vegetables added are popular lunch dishes, for example, but fried, scrambled, or soft-boiled eggs are not usually served for lunch, except as complements to a hash or in some similar role. We often borrow the actual food for lunch from last night's dinner, too. We sometimes make the meal into lunch (or supper) rather than dinner by omitting any course before the main one and by serving the three components in one dish. Hearty soups, stews, chili, and "salads" of meats, fish, and other substantial ingredients have thus become lunchtime staples. Ordinary lunch menus include soup and salad with bread, a substantial egg dish with a salad of fresh vegetables, and one-dish meals such as shepherd's pie, beans and rice, or any of the many dishes of pasta plus a protein and vegetable. But the most important item on the American lunch menu continues to be the sandwich, a versatile, healthful invention for enjoying any protein food whatever—cold meat, poultry, egg, fish, cheese, nuts, beans—with a minimum of fuss, usually no cooking, and no need for utensils. A sandwich is protein plus grain, and if you add enough lettuce and tomatoes or other vegetables it turns into a meal. Even a burger-and-fries lunch is finger food in most homes and restaurants, although etiquette books may insist you use a fork for the fries.

About Dinner

What Dinner Is For. Breakfast prepares; dinner restores. Just as the purpose of breakfast is to send you out to your school or work fortified in mind and body, the purpose of dinner is to reclaim you for private life, pleasure, intimacy. Dinner is the most substantial meal of the day and the central daily event in the life of the home. It is the longest, largest, most elaborate meal, and it serves a variety of functions. Nutritionally, emotionally, and socially, dinner carries more of the burden than other meals of providing the benefits that derive from eating meals cooked at home.

We eat dinner in the evening—at least on weekdays—so that we can share the meal with others at a time when the day's work is behind us. This gives us peace of mind and the freedom to turn our attention to one another and to enjoy ourselves. A properly set table is desirable at all meals but is most important at dinner, the most formal meal. Dinner is usually composed almost entirely of freshly cooked warm dishes, unlike lunch and breakfast, which often feature uncooked or precooked foods that are eaten without utensils.

What to Make. Relatively informal dinners at home are typically served in two or three courses, a main course and a course preceding and/or following it. The courses that might precede the main course include appetizers, soup, pasta, or salad. Those that might follow are salad and dessert, and salad might also be served at the same time as the main meal. The main course includes the principal protein in the meal—the fish, fowl, meat, cheese, eggs, or beans—plus one or more vegetables. An important source of variety in home meals is the option of serving different sets of courses at different dinners: soup, main course, dessert on Monday; main course, salad, dessert on Tuesday; hors d'oeuvres, main course, salad on Wednesday, and so forth. More formal dinners, of course, would include all the courses in their traditional order—hors d'oeuvres, soup, main course, salad, dessert. Very formal dinners include even more.

All three elements of a good dinner can be supplied either in the main course or among the courses. For example, you could serve a small plate of pasta for an appetizer and follow with fish and vegetables (grain/starch, protein, and vegetable), or you might begin with a salad and follow with a dish that contains chicken and potatoes (vegetable, protein, and root vegetable/starch); or you could serve a one-dish meal that includes all three elements, such as beans and rice with salsa. I am not a fan of the one-dish dinner, however, even though magazines for nearly a hundred years have portrayed it as the solution to the busy woman's problems. It is often not much quicker to make or clean up after, and almost always gets eaten too quickly. Although some people enjoy main-dish salads for dinner, I generally tend to feel about them as I do about most one-dish meals, or to think of them as more like lunch—except in a heat wave, when they may taste refreshing.

Meals more slowly paced than one-dish meals tend to be, in my experience, better for your mood, your digestion, and your weight. When you begin your meal with foods such as soup or salad or light appetizers made of vegetables or fruits, which include plenty of water or fiber, your body gets more time to respond to your intake; you take the edge off your appetite with less calorically dense foods. When the meal is over, you feel satisfied and contented, and the diners have had a real chance to respond to one another.

Sandwiches are generally not considered dinner food because they are eaten with the fingers, are usually not cooked or warm, and are "casual." Of course, this is a convention, but it is a convention worth respecting often. The preference for more formality at dinner serves important purposes, and it is not in anyone's interest to do away with it. But it *is* in everyone's interest to do away entirely with feeling ashamed of how or what one cooks. If you cannot avoid having only sandwiches one day, the rational response is to feel slightly sorry for yourself, not to blame yourself.

GUIDELINES ON CHOOSING A DINNER MENU

Make sure that appetizers are light and small. If weight control is an issue, choose those that include plenty of fiber and water: soups, especially clear soups, vegetables, fruits, stuffed celery, and cut vegetables with low-fat dips.

If you are having guests, an appetizer that repeats the basic triad with miniature portions is a good way to keep the balance of the meal—for example, one or two meat or cheese-filled ravioli with a slice of grilled tomato or other vegetables.

Consider the additive effect of all the courses when deciding whether the meal is too heavy or too light for the people, the weather, or the season. If you are beginning with pasta, for example, do not serve polenta with the fish course. The two grain/starch dishes would be experienced as too heavy.

Do not serve in the same course two substantial starchy foods, such as rice and pasta, or potatoes and couscous or kasha. You may have two in one meal, if one is small enough to be merely a grace note. For example, if rice makes a modest appearance in your soup, that needn't stop you from serving a grain or potato in another course.

Consider the ingredients of each course in deciding whether the meal has a good nutritional (and aesthetic) balance. If you are beginning with a hearty vegetable soup, go light on vegetables with the main course. If you are beginning with a clear soup with a little parsley floating in it, you need to reinforce the vegetables by means of the salad or whatever you serve with the protein.

Cold or room-temperature pasta dishes are generally more appropriate for lunch than for dinner, but they may be used as appetizers at dinner.

You can treat beans as either a vegetable or a protein, but if you are using them as a vegetable try not to make them too prominent in quantity or spiciness.

If you are going to serve two proteins, one should have a minor presence and the other a major presence. Thus, if you are going to serve both fish and meat, serve them in different courses; you might begin with a fish appetizer or a fish soup, and follow with meat in the main course. Truly formal dinners have separate substantial fish courses, but for the modern stomach this constitutes a mighty feast indeed. The most common exceptions to the rule against two proteins for ordinary family dinners are the hunter's dishes that combine meat and poultry and fish soups or stews that contain two or more types of fish or shellfish—mussels, shrimp, lobster. Such dishes are considered hearty by most people nowadays, so if you serve one, choose lighter components for your other courses.

Do not serve the same ingredient in more than one course; avoid, for example, a soup with green beans and green beans again as a side dish.

Do not serve too many foods of the same taste character together. If you have a tomato-based soup in a first course, do not follow with a marinara sauce.

Opposites often go nicely together: acid/sweet, spicy/bland, hot/cold, crunchy/soft. If you are serving one spicy dish, say a curry, balance it with a cool and mild one such as yogurt.

Avoid serving two very strong-tasting dishes at the same meal.

Do not serve more than one highly salted food per meal.

Do not serve different foods of the same color together; for example, don't serve green vegetables with green noodles and pesto sauce.

In hot weather, lighter fare is more appetizing: more fruits and vegetables, fewer roasts, hearty soups, and meat stews. In cool weather, the reverse is true.

6

Serving Meals

Effect of an attractively set table . . . Offering food graciously . . . Tablecloths . . . Placemats and runners . . . Centerpieces and candles . . . Tables set for ordinary family meals . . . How to set the table . . . Serving the meal . . . Order of courses . . . Filling and removing dishes and glasses . . . Silver, china, and glassware . . . A beginner's set of china, flatware, and glassware . . . Dining rooms

Meals at home, however informal, should be treated as events that matter. All members of the household, including working parents and busy teenagers, will be happier if they take whatever trouble is needed to be home for meals regularly. Being on time is necessary if meals are to be a success. Otherwise, why should the cook take the trouble to get food ready for dinner? No one, children or adults, should leave the table except for the most important reasons until the meal is over. Turn on the answering machine and let the telephone ring. Turn the television and radio off, and put away books, papers, games, and toys. This puts the focus of the household on the meal and helps people to be emotionally present for it.

The Importance of an Attractive Table

The attractiveness of the table helps people give a meal the respect it deserves. Even everyday, informal meals merit an appealing presentation. Although on special occasions most people want to try for an especially beautiful and more formal table, it is the way you do things every day that sets the tone of the home. A table nicely set draws people to a meal and evokes the right attitudes for enjoying it.

Adults sometimes linger at the table over coffee or drinks to enjoy long discussions. Children should not be required to stay for this, of course, but they should certainly be encouraged to stay and listen quietly. Listening to the grownups talk around a table is one of the major ways children learn about being an adult—how you argue yet stay friends, how to tell a story or a joke, what you laugh at, what is worth talking about, and what ideas and values you respect. This is only one of those ordinary but important things that happen best in the context of a meal.

Offering Food

In offering food, the right touch is light. No one should feel pressured into eating. No one should fear that your happiness depends on their approval of your food. On the other hand, the right touch is not indifferent. Food offered with warmth and pleasure makes the meal feel nurturing. Accept compliments gracefully.

Announce the menu in advance so people can pace themselves for the greatest possible enjoyment of the meal. As with most announcements, brevity is best. Cooks or hosts who discuss every dish at length can make guests feel as if they are expected to be worshippers at a shrine.

Setting the Table

In the age of the automatic dishwasher it is just as easy to have an attractive table as a spartan one. The extra dishes take no longer to wash afterward when the machine does it for you.

Tablecloths. A tablecloth is always pleasing, especially at dinner. The cloth protects the table, protects the dishes, reduces noise and breakage, and looks beautiful. The reason to use real cloth, instead of functional plastic, is that it indicates to you, your family, and your guests the importance of the occasion. Cloth napkins are preferable to paper ones, and you might decide to use these even when you do not use a tablecloth. Whatever you may do in the family, cloth napkins are preferable when you have guests.

White damask is used only for dinner, and nothing but white damask or something equally elegant will do for a really formal dinner. (See chapter 16, "The Natural Fibers," page 235, for a discussion of damask.) Colored damask is not too elegant for any other meal, including informal family dinners. Other elegant cloths, such as those of lace and fancy cutwork, should be reserved for dinner or more formal luncheons. Prints and colored cloths of all sorts are good for any ordinary home meals.

Laying and laundering tablecloths and napkins creates no extra work for you, beyond larger washloads. Ironing them, alas, takes time. If you have no time for this and cannot either persuade an older child to try this pleasant work or pay someone else to do it, you have two alternatives. One is to buy wrinkle-resistant tablecloths, even though these are less desirable in other ways. See the discussion of resin treatments on pages 229–30 in chapter 15, "Transformations," and chapter 18, "Fabrics That Work," pages 271–73. The other is to use them wrinkled and to do what you can to reduce wrinkles without ironing. See suggestions on page 349. But most of us balk at the idea of using wrinkled cloths for guests. The old-fashioned electric rotary irons (or "mangles") that are now making a modest comeback let you iron many tablecloths almost without effort but produce less good results on cloths with extensive cutwork or embroidery.

A century ago, proper Victorian households did not hesitate to use tablecloths and napkins more than once, but this has come to seem unacceptable in the day of automatic washing machines. My own rule would be never to *count* on using a cloth for more than one meal, but often you will find that it is clean enough—when there are no guests—to use a second or even a third time, with careful brushing and spot-cleaning. If you put on a clean, everyday cloth for dinner, it may well make it through the next day's breakfast and lunch. But if you have used an

SPREADING THE CLOTH

Before spreading the cloth, lay a padding, liner, or "silence cloth" of felt, blanketing, or some similar cloth to help protect the table from warm serving dishes (truly hot ones will require trivets or other more effective protection) and reduce noise and the chance of breakage. The padding also helps the tablecloth look and hang better. You can buy one made for the purpose that will fasten around the table legs and not slip, or make one by cutting or folding an old flannel sheet or thin blanket to the proper size. At informal family meals, you can use a silence cloth or not, as you like.

Choose a tablecloth that will extend six to eight inches past the edge of the table for breakfast and lunch. The dinner cloth should extend eight to twelve inches past the edge. At more formal dinners, the cloth hangs twelve to eighteen inches. The traditional rule is that at most one fold or crease line, running the *length* of the table, may be visible on the cloth. But crisp checkerboard creases on less formal tables look very appealing.

When you will be serving dinner on a lace cloth, either place it directly on the table or place not only a pad or silence cloth but another plain tablecloth under the lace one so that the silence cloth does not show. Although a lace cloth looks beautiful when wood gleams through, it slips easily; and the other advantages of the silence cloth are lost as well.

The sideboard, too, should be covered with a cloth.

elegant cloth for dinner, it will be best to remove it and use a more appropriate one for breakfast. Napkins, too, can be reused if they are still clean. If you reuse napkins, everyone should have his or her own unique, identifiable napkin ring; replace the napkin in the ring after meals.

The cloth should be brushed, if necessary, between courses. You can brush the crumbs into a tray used for that purpose or into a plate. You can also use a napkin to do the brushing.

Some people have rustic wood tables or tables with other types of surfaces that will not be damaged by placing tableware directly upon them. Those who despise taking care of tablecloths should definitely acquire such a table, but even then it is worthwhile to lay a cloth sometimes, perhaps on one or two weekend dinners and always on feast days such as Thanksgiving.

You can buy commercial table pads that have a foam back and a vinyl front. Lay the foam next to the wood and the vinyl facing up. Do not leave the pad on overnight, and certainly do not leave it on a table indefinitely. Moisture may be trapped between the pad and the table, causing damage to the appearance of the wood. Although the foam-backed type is nonslip, I prefer a felt or flannel-backed padding. You can buy the nonslip type in a size that fits the table exactly. The softer felt or flannel-backed ones should overhang the table by a few inches.

Placemats and Runners. The idea of placemats is that they show the glory of your table while providing protection where it is needed. They feel informal and casual even when they are quite elegant. Some placemats require no ironing and are easy to launder, but others are quite as much trouble as any tablecloth. Runners, narrow lengths of plain or fancy-worked cloth that lie in the center of the table and extend its entire length (used over a tablecloth or a bare table), are less common today than they used to be, but they dress up a table and can be used to protect the center of the table when you use placemats.

Centerpieces and Candles. There was a time when a table without some decoration at its center looked as bare as hands without

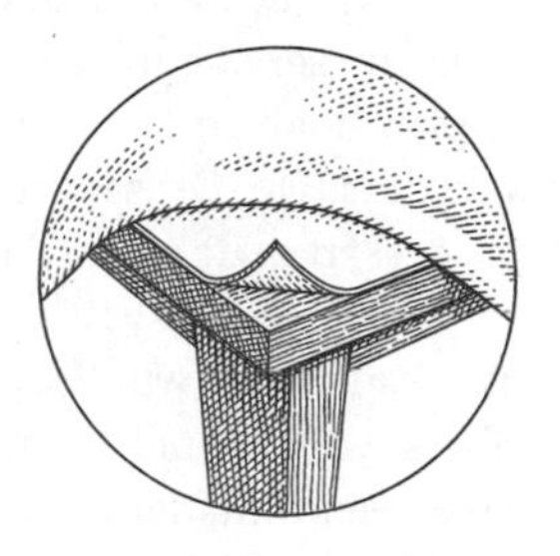

At more formal dinners, the tablecloth should show only one crease line that runs the length of the cloth. *Inset (in circle)*: A nonslip pad cut to the dimensions of the table may be used.

gloves and heads without hats. People still put centerpieces on holiday tables and tables set for guests, but many have ceased bothering for family meals. It is an easy and pleasant custom, however, and when you have one just for the family, it underlines the significance of even everyday meals.

A centerpiece at a family meal can be just a grace note: a few seasonal flowers or fruits or colored leaves in fall are all that is necessary. You can use anything: pretty vegetables, squashes, decorative china, dried leaves and flowers, your child's latest Lego or Tinkertoy construction. (Parents of young children: setting your child to work making a centerpiece for the dinner table makes the child feel useful and contented while you concentrate on cooking.) For formal and semiformal occasions, flowers are traditional, but you need not be traditional. Whatever you pick, it must be easy to see over and proportional to the size of the table. Avoid crowding plates and dishes with it.

Candles are only for dinner and only for after dark. They should flame above eye level (about eighteen inches high) so that people do not feel blinded. For safety's sake, do not set them too near the edge of the table or near anybody's elbow. Two or three candles at each end of the table are sufficient for a table set for six or eight. One candle at each end of the table does not give enough light and looks bare even when supplemented with other light. Or you can make candles part of a centerpiece and ignore their small contribution to the light, relying mostly on artificial lighting. (See chapter 47, "Kindly Light.") People used to say that it was an insult to guests to have unlit candles on the table, perhaps because it looked as though you did not think the guests important enough to waste candles for them or as though you were ignoring their preferences. I think you needn't worry about this today.

Setting Out Dishes and Flatware at Ordinary Family Meals. The rules for table setting are very bendable nowadays, so much so that it is hard to believe that anyone ever mourned for lack of ice cream forks or four different kinds of spoons for soup. ("Ice cream forks?" murmur today's readers.) Still, many conventions linger, because they are useful and pleasant. Even if you choose to flout them, it helps to know what they are so that you can cue your guests, to help them feel as comfortable as possible.

What goes on the table depends on which courses you are serving and what you are eating. At formal dinners, you begin by setting out very large service plates, upon which you set the appetizer or soup. For informal dinners at home, however, most people forgo these and either set the appetizer or the soup on the dinner plate or serve these courses with their own smaller service plates or saucers. The salad plate and dessert plates can be set directly on the table. Dessert cups and bowls go on the dessert plate or on their own smaller service plates. When you have guests, you set out bread plates with butter spreaders. Some think you should do this when there are no guests, no matter how informal the meal, but I let this be determined by the size of my table and what I am serving. If the table is crowded but the dinner plates have room and are not flowing with sauces or juices, I do not see why you should not put bread at the side of the plate—particularly if you are using the oversized dinner plates that have become popular.

At an informal home table, people sometimes lay out a fork, knife, and teaspoon when by formal principles only the fork would be required. The table knife may be used in place of a butter spreader for buttering the bread; the teaspoon will be used for dessert or coffee. You should suit yourself on all such matters. These gracious and efficient informalities for simple home meals are so common now that they have achieved the status of conventions.

HOW TO SET THE TABLE

All tableware should be spotless and gleaming. Place settings are twelve inches apart. Plates and flatware are set one inch from the edge of the table so that nothing gets knocked off. If possible, place settings should be directly opposite one another, to make conversation easiest.

The knives and spoons are placed to the right of the plate and the forks to the left, with two exceptions: the fork goes on the right when there is no knife, and an oyster fork goes either to the right or on the plate under the oysters. (If there is no knife at an informal family dinner, the fork may be placed at the left, simply to balance the spoon.) All implements face upward (the tines of forks and the bowls of spoons turn up), and the edges of knives are turned toward the plate. Spoons go to the right of the knives. The pieces that are to be used first are laid in the outermost positions, and no flatware is laid that will not have a definite function during the meal. Thus, if your menu calls for an appetizer of fruit, followed by soup, a main course, a salad, and a dessert, your table setting looks like the Illustration at the bottom right-hand corner of page 63.

The napkins are placed at the left of the forks (or in the center of the service plate when you use one) or, at lunch or breakfast, if you wish, on the plate. The napkin for dinner is folded in the manner described on page 355 at chapter 24, "Folding Clothes and Linens." Place it so that the hem is parallel to the edge of the table, the monogram or corner decoration is in the lower left, and the lower left-hand corner is open. (You can also fold the napkin so that it opens to the right, with the monogram or decoration in the bottom right-hand corner. Just be consistent.) The napkin for lunch may be folded into a triangle or pentagon. A plain rectangle fold is also suitable for any ordinary family meal.

Water glasses and children's milk glasses are set at the upper right edge of the dinner plate, at the tip of the knife. If wine will be served, the wineglass stands at the right of the water glass. If two wines will be served, the three glasses are set in a triangle, with the white wine foremost. A bread plate is set at the upper left edge of the plate. The butter spreader is parallel to the table edge, handle to the right for easy grasping. See the illustration at the bottom left-hand corner of page 63. When salad is served at the same time as the main course, you place it to the upper left of the dinner plate, as shown in the illustration at the bottom right-hand corner on page 63, or below the bread plate, if there is one.

Dessert utensils may be placed above the plate at the outset of the meal, as shown in the illustration at the bottom right-hand corner of page 63 or may be brought in upon the dessert plate, after clearing the table at the end of the meal, as shown in illustration E of the place settings for a formal dinner at the top of page 64.

The teaspoon for coffee or tea is placed on the saucer.

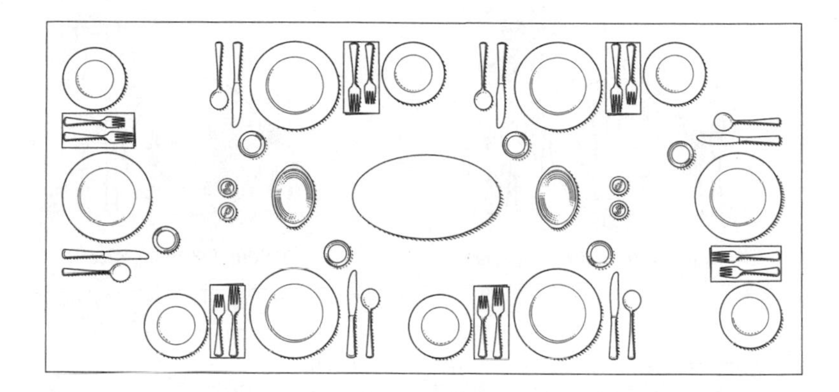

Informal Family Meal: The table is set for service by passing dishes around the table. No wine will be served; there are glasses for water, milk, or whatever other cold drinks are to be served. The first course will be soup, followed by salad, and then the main course. The salad plates are set out for ease in serving.

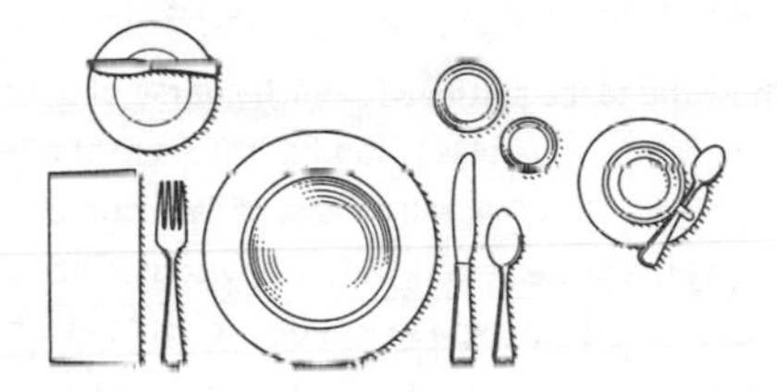

Place Setting for Breakfast: The breakfast will include first juice, then cereal, followed by ham and eggs and toast. Coffee or tea will be served with the food, not after it.

Place Setting for Meatless Lunch: The place is set for a lunch that begins with a fruit appetizer, followed by an omelette or quiche, and ending with a salad. No meat is being served, so there is no knife, and the forks are placed on the right in the order in which they will be used following the fruit.

Place Setting for an Informal Dinner: The positions of the fruit and soup spoons and salad forks indicate that the menu will include a fruit appetizer, soup, main course, and salad, one after the other. Water and wine will be served. A bread plate is placed above the forks.

Place Setting for an Informal Dinner: The positions of the soup spoon and salad fork indicate that soup will be served before, and salad after, the main course. To make serving the meal easy, the salad plates are set above the forks and napkins and the dessert implements are set above the dinner plates.

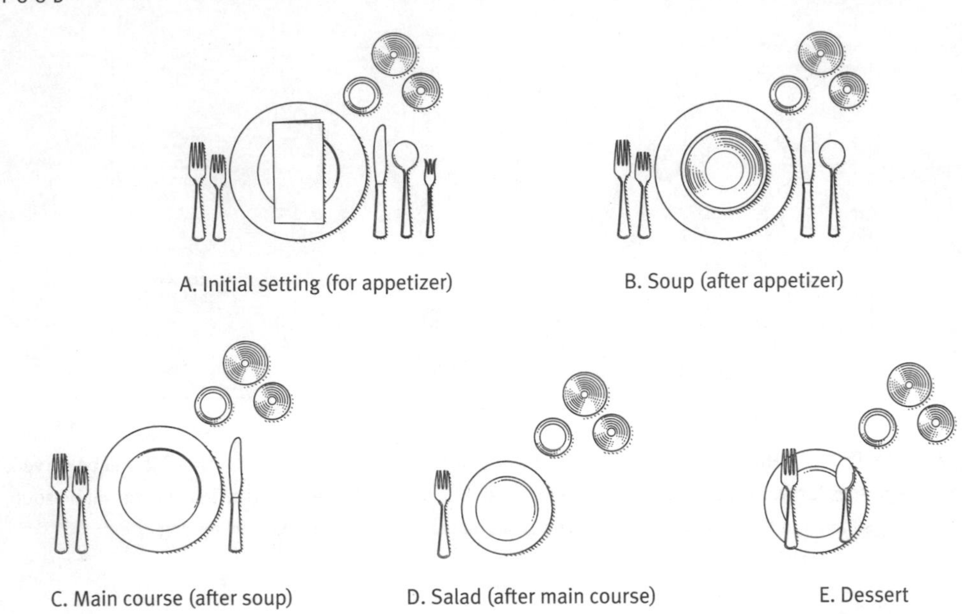

Place Settings for a Formal Dinner: Diagrams A through E show the place settings for each course of a formal dinner. Red and white wine will be served. The water glass and white wine glass stand at the base of a triangle, closest to the utensils. The red wine glass stands slightly behind. The meal will consist of five courses: oysters, soup, roast, salad, and, finally, dessert. Diagram A, showing the place setting before any course has been eaten, includes implements for the first four courses. (The dessert fork and spoon will be brought in with the dessert plate.) In diagram B, the oysters have been eaten and the place is ready for soup to be served. In diagram C, the soup has been eaten and the place is ready for the main course of roast. In Diagram D, the dinner plate has been removed and the salad plate has been laid. In diagram E, dessert is being served.

No matter how inconvenient it may seem, try to avoid commercial packages, boxes, bottles, and jars on the table: milk cartons, jam jars, ketchup and mustard, and bags and boxes of crackers or breads. This includes the butter and margarine tubs from the supermarket that are carefully designed to show no labels; they are still recognizable as a commercial product and look out of place. Put foods intended for the table into bowls and pitchers or on serving dishes.

Other Items on the Table or Sideboard. Place salt and pepper—shakers, grinders, cellars, or bowls—at convenient intervals, at least one set for every two people at more formal dinners. You can serve a basket of bread or place a roll on each bread plate. Set out butter for passing, if you plan to use it, or put pats of butter on each bread plate. Any relishes or condiments are also set out on the table. Plates, cups and saucers, and flatware that will be used later in the meal may be neatly stacked on the sideboard until needed. A water pitcher can go on the sideboard too, as can cream and sugar to be served later.

Serving the Meal

At ordinary home dinners, with or without guests, your goal is to present the meal gracefully, with some element of ritual but without the rigidity of formal meals or the coolness of meals in restaurants. The ritual has to feel like your own, not an arbitrary one imposed on you by some outside authority, which means that at every point you should try to think through why you are following it—whether for reasons of convenience, efficiency, beauty, comfort, or familiarity.

Order of Courses. Part of planning a meal is thinking about the logistics of cooking and serving, and this requires you to consider, first, the order of your courses. The traditional order of courses at dinner is: hors d'oeuvres or appetizers, soup, fish, meat or main course, salad, dessert. Service in the Italian style, now followed in many American homes when pasta is served, begins with the pasta course and continues through the main course, salad, and dessert. (An antipasto, of course, precedes the pasta.) The order of courses at breakfast is this: fruit or fruit juice; cereal; protein course (eggs with bacon, ham, or sausages) with accompanying potatoes or grits and breads (toast, bagels, Danish, and the like).

These courses are options, not requirements for a complete meal; hardly anyone still serves all of them at home meals. Informal home meals usually consist of two or three—for example, salad, main course, and dessert. But each course you choose is best served in relation to the rest of the meal using the traditional order or some variant that your household prefers. Some people prefer to serve all the courses at the same time, leaving each person to decide the order in which they will be consumed. My own feeling is that courses are best eaten sequentially, both because so many foods are best when they are freshly made and because it makes for a more leisurely, graceful meal and is more healthful.

The main exception to the rule about the order of courses at dinner is the salad. Salad after the main course is the European style, which was almost universally imitated in this country until the 1930s, when you begin to find references to the "California style" or "modern style" of serving the salad as a first course. The predominant habit at American informal home meals is now salad before main course, and it is a good custom for several reasons. Salad tastes especially good at the beginning of a meal when your appetite still has an edge. Children are more likely to eat it then, when they are really hungry. From the point of view of nutrition and weight control, it makes sense to eat a salad of tossed greens first, so that you temper your appetite with a serving of healthy, light greens. The traditional order, with salad following the main course, is more hedonistic, for the aim is to clear the palate and help you continue eating with gusto. You needn't make a permanent choice between the two styles, of course. You might choose to serve salad before (or with) the main course on weekdays, for example, and serve it after on special occasions or at more elaborate meals on weekends. It makes little sense, however, to follow the older order unless you are serving a fairly traditional salad. Any sufficiently acidic and light, simple concoction of greens or other vegetables, sometimes with a bit of fruit, will do. Creamy, protein-filled "salads" should precede, or be, the main course.

Filling and Removing Dishes and Glasses. Water glasses are filled about three-quarters full. Wineglasses are filled half full, or a bit more. Warmed dishes for hot food and chilled ones for cold food keep the food at its best longest. At informal meals people usually do not bother to warm or chill the plates, but this is hardly any trouble and sometimes really adds to the enjoyment.

There are two dominant styles of serving at informal family meals, and these may be combined if it seems convenient. In one style, a server has a stack of dishes and the food to be served, either at his place at the table or at the sideboard. The server fills the plates and they are passed hand to hand to each person. In the other, the serving dishes are placed at convenient places around the table, and the diners serve themselves, from serving dishes set (or held) slightly to their left, and pass the serving dishes on to the right until they have gone the full round of the table. Then the serving dishes rest again in the spot from which they started. Less often, the server will walk around the table carrying the dish and serving each person from the left. You may fill soup bowls at the table from a tureen, if you wish, or bring them to the table filled. Do whatever seems less likely to cause spills. Cold appetizers are usually placed on plates before the diners are seated, and hot ones are served after everyone is seated. Dinner plates, however, are always filled at the table.

The general rule is to serve people from their left and remove dishes from their right, except that glasses are filled and removed from the right so that you need not reach across anyone's plate to do so. Wait until the entire company has finished before removing any dishes because you do not want to rush those still eating. When you begin removing the dishes from one course, take first the left-over food in the serving dishes, then the used plates or bowls and flatware, then any unused dishes and flatware pertaining to that course. When dirty dishes are removed, they are never stacked at the table or in sight of the table, and are never, never scraped at the table. One or two persons are usually designated, or volunteer, to remove the plates, taking them two at a time. You can collect them at the sideboard and then carry them back to the kitchen in piles; however, if the walk back to the kitchen is long, you might find a cart useful so that you need not make too many trips.

When you are preparing the table to receive the dessert, take away all foods, serving dishes, salt and pepper, and so forth, and brush away any crumbs. Then proceed to serve the dessert. Most Americans like coffee with the dessert, but some prefer it afterward, often in the living room.

Silver, China, and Glassware

There was a time not long ago when it was nearly impossible to set a pretty table without having a lot of money. Young brides got advice on how to tough things out—how with imagination, "taste," and "spunk," they could give proper dinners with centerpieces of fall leaves, china from Woolworth's, and no oyster or ice cream forks, while they collected their fine china and real silver. In those days feelings of embarrassment and inferiority were the lot of many young people who had both a rigid idea of how things were "supposed to be done" and too little money to do them that way.

When young people started out in those days, they strove to acquire two sets of silver and two of china, one for "good" and one for "everyday." If you had lots of money, both sets were of fine china and real silver, but the good sets had more intricate, more elegant designs. If you had less money, you got the best fine china and real silver you could afford for good, and real but less expensive china and silver plate for everyday. Those who could not afford fine china or any kind of silver had to make do with whatever earthenware Woolworth's and other inexpensive stores sold, and this was likely to be either a gaudy imitation of the real thing or coarse, heavy, utilitarian stuff. There was nothing in between.

Today, you may be told that the system of keeping two sets of china and silver is dead, but that is not quite accurate. It has only changed to reflect some extraordinarily improved realities. Those who can afford to will still have two—or more—sets of china, at least one of which is costly and elegant. But at the lower price ranges, vastly improved quality and design are now available. Fine china of good design and strength and durability indistinguishable from the best is available at low prices from both new manufacturers and the old manufacturers of fine china. Stainless steel flatware is of high quality and such attractive design that many people prefer it for everyday use on the grounds that it is less trouble and, as compared with silver plate, more durable. Although many of us would not call good stainless steel inexpensive, it is

Flatware

Top row, left to right: Teaspoon, demitasse spoon, dessert spoon, fruit spoon, tablespoon, cream-soup spoon, soup spoon, iced tea spoon, sugar spoon

Bottom row, left to right: Dinner knife, fish knife, butter spreader, butter knife, pie or cake server, ladle, salad serving set, dinner fork, salad fork, oyster fork, lemon fork.

not nearly so costly as silver. These changes have swept away a lot of social suffering.

If you can afford only one set of china, you can find one that is versatile enough for both formal and informal occasions. But two sets are still more versatile than one and worth having if you can afford the purchase price and the shelf space. And if neither price nor space is a barrier, you can have two or more basic sets plus whatever pieces and partial sets you like—breakfast sets, tea sets, mixed sets, or collections of attractive individual pieces. If you are economizing, it is wise to begin with an attractive everyday set and collect another, finer set (or mixed pieces) as you can. The old rule against mixing patterns in one course is defunct, along with the rule against mixing cheap with expensive pieces. You can do anything that looks good. This includes having no sets at all but, instead, a collection of individual pieces, place settings, and whatever mixtures you like. I have seen this done most beautifully on a small scale—in studios and tiny apartments with tiny tables by people with little money and exquisite taste.

When you buy china, the minimum number of place settings that makes sense for most people is eight, and few people need more than twelve, at least at the outset. The most successful dinner parties are of six to eight people. At larger events—family reunions, for instance—people usually bring out both sets of dishes and perhaps borrow or rent more. Suggested minimum starter settings of china, flatware, and glass are listed below. Keep in mind, however, that each household has its special habits and tastes that should be consulted when decisions are made about what is absolutely necessary to begin with and what should be acquired as soon as there are the means. Champagne enthusiasts, for example, should get champagne glasses at the start.

Beginner's Set of China

Eight place settings each consisting of:
- dinner plate
- salad plate
- soup plate (or cup and saucer or service plate)
- dessert plate
- cereal bowl
- cup and saucer
- bread plate

Serving dishes, hollow ware:
- large platter
- small platter
- 2–3 serving bowls of different sizes
- sauce or gravy boat
- large pitcher
- cream pitcher
- sugar bowl
- teapot
- a few small serving dishes of varied sizes and shapes

Beginner's Set of Flatware

Eight place settings each consisting of:
- dinner knife
- butter spreader
- dinner fork
- salad fork
- teaspoon
- soup spoon

Serving pieces:
- large ladle
- small ladle
- sugar spoon
- salad-serving spoon and fork
- large meat-serving fork
- several serving spoons

Beginner's Set of Glassware
- 8 water tumblers (8 oz.)
- 8 juice glasses (5–6 oz.)
- 8 tall glasses (iced tea or highball) (12 oz.)

For wine and other alcoholic beverages:
- 8 all-purpose wineglasses, or 8 larger wineglasses and 8 smaller ones.

Dining Rooms

Architecturally speaking, the dining room is a fairly recent innovation. Even after dining rooms became common in the eighteenth century, Americans might or might not have had a room devoted solely to eating until well into the nineteenth. The modern trends have been to "relax" the dining room, to tear down walls, and to mix functions in rooms. But a real dining room devoted solely or primarily to one purpose is still worth having. Those who have none or have had to transform it into a home office or baby's bedroom, however, often create a dining corner or area in the kitchen or living or common room masterfully designed to do the trick.

The dining room—or whatever room you eat in—should be set up as much as possible to permit ready adjustment of heat, air, and light. Eating in a sweltering room, under a glare, or surrounded by stale smells is not pleasant. Sun and air are essential for freshening any room in which food is served.

Only three types of furniture are essential in a dining room. You need a generous table, chairs, and either a sideboard or a buffet upon which you can rest dishes and food for serving at table. It does not matter whether your table is round or cornered. Leaves for expanding are desirable. Choose a sideboard rather than a buffet only if it has built-in drawers or you have some other means of storing linens and silver close at hand in the dining room. You can put a china cabinet in the dining room, if you wish. Some people will bring in a tea cart or a serving table for serving dinner.

If you have a choice, it is pleasant to exclude from the dining room all furniture dedicated to functions other than dining, such as reading chairs and lamps, desks, stereo systems, and the like. But people who live in small apartments or houses do not have the choice. Sometimes the best way to preserve the dining room atmosphere is to use the dining room table itself, rather than some other piece of furniture, for reading, games, writing letters, or talking. You will need a protective mat or cloth if it is vulnerable to scratches. The size of the table invites the family to join together there. Some of the best times many of us have at home are those we spend gathered around a big table strewn with books, cards, letters and papers, cups, homework, and all the other paraphernalia of casual evenings together, pursuing our various chores and interests in the comfort of the common space.

Some houses have "breakfast nooks" in addition to the dining room, usually in or adjoining the kitchen, or a table large enough for meals set squarely in the kitchen. In older homes, breakfast and possibly lunch or supper were likely to be eaten in the breakfast nook, if there was one, but dinners were served in the dining room. Today, kitchens grow more and more popular not just for the family's informal meals but even for serving meals to guests, and kitchens grow ever larger and more luxurious. Serving dinner or a casual meal to guests in the kitchen can be fun. The cook gets company while he works, and family members and guests can be pressed into service. But I favor frequent use of the dining room if you have one.

Eating in the kitchen is most fun when novel, and the novelty doesn't last. You find yourself increasingly annoyed by heat, smoke, and lingering odors from cabbage or sausage during dessert. Cooking creates air pollution—combustion by-products, if you have a gas stove, and smoke and other cooking by-products no matter what type of stove you have. Sometimes the fan is noisy or you wish you could run the dishwasher, which may be hot and noisy both, or the cooking process itself may be hot and noisy—or the dishwasher may create strong smells of detergent. The mess that even the neatest cook at times creates while at work can destroy one's sense of peace and order. Simple meals, as breakfasts, lunches, and suppers usually are, can often be quite conveniently prepared and consumed in the same room. The sort of pleasure that belongs to dinner, however, ordinarily requires your most civilized setting, and this is doubly true when you have guests.

If you do not have a dining room, then you must do your best to control heat, light, air, odors, noise, humidity, and clutter in the kitchen so as to make meals there as appealing as you can. It is extremely helpful to have a kitchen fan over the stove that exhausts to the outside, a quiet, cool dishwasher, and effective air-conditioning, and to concentrate on neat habits. People used to be advised to hang a curtain or put up folding screens to shield the eye from the untidy sights of the kitchen. I once had a "kitchenette" with built-in folding doors that could be pulled shut to hide the last-minute disorder of cooking. But today, if you have a combination kitchen–dining room you most definitely should not try to hide the reality with screens or curtains. Simply make the kitchen as comfortable, neat, and clean as you can. If you can do this and provide good food, good company, and good cheer, your dinners are going to work far better than many served in fancier surroundings.

7

Stimulating Beverages

Caffeinated beverages: coffee, tea, and chocolate . . . Hospitality with coffee and tea: Should you be a purist? . . . Making coffee: freshness, roasts, storing and grinding coffee . . . How to use a vacuum maker, manual drip, electric drip, plunger or press method, percolator, espresso maker . . . Making steamed milk . . . Measuring coffee and water . . . Guidelines for making good coffee by any method . . . Making tea: Black, oolong, and green teas . . . Teabags . . . How to make tea . . . Using sugar, milk, spice, or lemon . . . Hot chocolate . . . Herbal teas . . . Alcoholic beverages . . . Aperitifs, digestifs, cocktails . . . Learning about wine . . . Temperature, uncorking, breathing, decanting, and serving . . . Glassware for wine and drinks . . . Storing wine . . . Wine with food

When you have visitors in your home for more than a few minutes, hospitality calls for you to offer them refreshment. Depending on time of day and whether or not the guests will be staying for a meal, you typically offer them coffee or tea, both of which contain caffeine, or some drink containing alcohol. Some sort of stimulating beverage is perhaps the most effective way to be hospitable, because it provides an extra measure of enjoyment beyond merely filling the belly or slaking thirst.

We use such drinks not only to make our guests welcome but also for ourselves, to round off meals, accompany snacks, or set off times of the day that are dedicated to restoration, enjoyment, or relaxation. Using them well is an important part of housekeeping. If you cannot boil an egg or make a bed, but you can and do make a nice cup of tea or coffee on the right occasion and serve it appealingly, you have gone farther toward making a good home than many a gourmet cook or compulsive housecleaner. You are getting right to the heart of the matter.

These drinks play such an important role that even those who avoid them, whether for medical, religious, or moral reasons, find substitutes in order to carry out all the important rituals of comfort and enjoyment that they sustain. Herb, grain-based, and decaffeinated coffees and teas can be used to replace regular coffees and teas; soft drinks, sparkling waters, ciders, or alcohol-free wines can be used instead of real wine.

Hundreds of years of tradition shape the ways in which we make and offer such drinks. This chapter contains only a primer on storing, preparing, and serving them successfully, but so vast is the lore associated with each of them that long tomes can be and have been devoted to them.*

Coffee, Tea, and Chocolate

Inexpensive, easy, and delicious, coffee or tea is called for when people in their homes take a break or gather to relax. Although Americans have never institutionalized afternoon tea, as the English have, in my own home I find that if we are at home between three and five o'clock, snack time for children and teatime across the ocean, we invariably have tea (or coffee); and if we have guests, they never refuse to share it with us.

Caffeine. Not everyone thinks caffeinated beverages are a good idea. We live in a world increasingly divided between those who have become fanatic drinkers of brown brews and those who avoid them entirely. As usual, the moderate course is probably best. Countless medical studies have failed to come up with much against coffee,[1] and some even suggest that tea offers health benefits.[2] On the other hand, their caffeine can make you jittery and sleepless if you drink too much of them or drink them too late in the day, and who knows what unpleasant statistics medical researchers might one day be spouting about those who drink too many cups per day.

Brewed coffee typically has about 100 mg of caffeine per 6-ounce cup (but may range anywhere from 60 to 180 mg); tea has about 40 mg per cup (but amounts may range from 20 to 90 mg). Some people who cannot drink coffee after dinner can drink tea without a problem; I know English people who cannot sleep without their bedtime cup of tea. Other people, however, especially older folks, are so sensitive to caffeine that even the tiny amount left in decaffeinated beverages bothers them, and there is evidence that as people get older their bodies retain caffeine longer. But no rule applies to everyone, and you must simply know your own reactions. If you cannot tolerate after-dinner caffeine, you might try herb teas. See page 82 below.

Decaffeinated versions of both tea and coffee are suitable when you wish to avoid caffeine. They do not taste as good as regular but are often quite drinkable. I like to add flavoring to decaffeinated coffee, such as a very small amount of cinnamon or a cardamom seed ground up with the beans.

There is a wide difference of opinion as to what is the proper age to give caffeinated beverages to children. French, Italian, and Hispanic families give a little coffee in a lot of warm milk to young children, and Irish and English tots are given tea. My family gave us both tea and coffee, diluted with lots of milk and sweetened with sugar, when we were preschoolers. My own view is that tea with milk is mild enough for a four-year-old to enjoy occasionally as a special treat. A little coffee, say 2 ounces, in a lot of warm low-fat milk with a teaspoon of sugar would contain about the same amount of caffeine as 8 ounces of Coca-Cola and much less sugar, and would provide significant amounts of many impor-

*Three of my favorites are *Jancis Robinson's Wine Course* (Abbeville Press, 1996); Corby Kummer, *The Joy of Coffee* (Houghton Mifflin, 1995); and Joel, David, and Karl Schapira, *The Book of Coffee and Tea* (St. Martin's, 1975, 1996).

AN ALTERNATIVE TO DECAFFEINATED TEA

Although some types of decaffeinated tea are acceptable, none come close to the flavor of regular tea. Thus the following suggestion, from James Norwood Pratt in his *Tea Lover's Companion* (Birch Lane, 1996), is particularly welcome. Mr. Pratt writes that 80 percent of the caffeine, being highly soluble, is extracted from the tea leaf within the first thirty seconds of steeping. So you can enjoy tea that is quite low in caffeine simply by discarding the water after thirty seconds (retaining the leaves) and then adding fresh boiling water to the leaves. I tried this and find that you still get a pretty good cup of tea—better, as promised, than decaffeinated.

tant nutrients (calcium, vitamin D, vitamin A, protein, and others) while Coke contains no nutrients whatsoever. Coffee-milk is nutritionally vastly superior to apple juice, too, which is essentially sweetened, flavored water, with very small amounts of a few minerals; its calories come entirely from fruit sugars (the equivalent of 6 to 7 teaspoons of table sugar in one cup of juice!). For these reasons I see no need to be shocked by the idea of occasionally—not regularly—giving children tea- or coffee-milk with a teaspoon or two of sugar, and my pediatrician agrees that this is probably healthier than giving them Cokes or endless glasses of apple juice.

Serving Coffee and Tea: Should You Be a Purist? Being delicate, tea seems to require pretty china—thin-lipped cups with saucers—but coffee may be served either in good china coffee cups or in hearty mugs. A distinction between porcelain coffee cups and teacups is sometimes drawn, and teacups are made slightly smaller; but few people pay much attention to this now.

Milk in coffee or tea renders the drink less bitter; sugar makes it sweet. Always be prepared to offer milk or cream and sugar to guests. (See suggestions as to lemon, sweeteners, and milk with espresso and tea, however, below, at pages 78 and 81.) So many people prefer honey to granulated white sugar that it is hospitable to keep it on hand even if you do not use it yourself. Milk adds calcium and other nutrients to an otherwise nutrient-free drink. Warm or cool milk will cool the drink a little too, a good thing as consuming things that are near boiling hot is not good for you. Once, most people agreed that cream or half-and-half (half milk, half cream) tasted even better than milk, and that whole milk tasted better than skim or reduced-fat milk. But cream, half-and-half, and whole milk contain unwanted saturated fats, so many people now use only skim or low-fat milk for coffee or tea. Many who have become accustomed to using skim say that they much prefer skim and find fattier milks and cream unpleasant. (I am still waiting for this to happen to me.) Whatever you prefer, it is hospitable to try to offer guests what they like. There are an increasing number of people who are what I call tea and coffee purists, who think that good tea and coffee should never be diminished with milk or sugar and therefore offer none. But this is a matter in which your guests' taste should be respected, because not everyone has a palate equipped for the rigors of black coffee.

Purists also think that you must make tea and coffee with spring water and tend to know the peculiarities of every bean and leaf from every region and nation and how to brew or steep each, measure down to the gram, and use timers and thermometers. But what I mean by serving a nice cup of tea or coffee is considerably less demanding. By all means, become as knowledgeable as you wish about the secrets of making good tea and coffee, but keep in mind that as a host you wish to make your guest happy with your coffee and happy with himself or herself. When you decide to become steeped in tea lore or coffee lore, you are taking tea and coffee out of the realm of the easy and quotidian into the realm of the arcane, rigidly disciplined, and spiritually high. This might be superior, desirable, maybe even noble, but *heimlich* it is not. The comfortable middle ground between instant decaffeinated beverages, on the one hand, and taking the pH of your water, on the other, is broad enough to accommodate a variety of temperaments, tastes, competencies, and expertise. The recipes set forth below are neither high nor low but middle of the road.

Making Coffee. I strongly recommend that you brew coffee and avoid instant coffee whenever you can. Non-instant, brewed coffee tastes far better—less bitter and more mellow—and is really not much more trouble to make than instant. In both cases you just need hot water and the ground roasted bean. Some people get in the habit of drinking instant coffee in the office, where there is no way to make real coffee, and get so used to its taste that they continue to use instant at home. But it would be better to stretch your palate a little for the sake of guests and make real coffee after office hours.

To make fresh brewed coffee, however, you do have to know a few things. First, you must choose your coffee. Coffee is produced in many different parts of the world, and there are characteristic taste qualities of coffee from specific regions. Good and not-so-good kinds of coffee may come from the same country, depending upon what part of the country it was grown in and who processed it. You must simply ask, try, and, sometimes, read. Price is a much less reliable sign of quality in coffee than it is in the more highly rationalized wine industry, so do not pay high prices unless a reliable person tells you the product is superior. (Besides, taste is more variable when it comes to coffee than it is with wine. The very rare and fine bean that some connoisseurs swoon over is not necessarily what others are going to find good.) Excellent coffee is available at very reasonable prices, but you do pay a premium for freshness and high-quality processing.

Freshness is a prime desideratum. If you know of a market that offers the roast dates of its coffees, patronize it by all means. Pay attention to how your market stores the coffees, too. They should not be standing open to the air. If they are selling flavored coffees, they should not be next door to unflavored ones, as beans invariably spill from one barrel to the next. Supermarket coffees, canned preground types, are almost always considered inferior by connoisseurs, and I agree with them. Not only is the type of coffee typically used undistinguished, but what you end up drinking is inevitably stale because coffee stales very quickly after being ground.

You must then select the roast you want. This you can often determine largely by

WHEN ARE WE GOING TOO FAR?

Back in the 1960s and '70s, good food, good coffee, and good tea were waiting to be discovered in this country. People were interested in taking trouble and learning more about these things, often because they had traveled or become friends with people from abroad and had experienced foods and drinks that they loved. Their instincts for improving food and drink were fairly trustworthy because they proceeded out of love—love of pleasure, of home, of friends, and of knowledge.

Nowadays, people have to cope with clouds of confusion raised by big business as it tries to make a profit off such impulses. You want better coffee? You like to cook? Someone out there is going to try to sell you a lot of expensive equipment, coffee beans, foods, books, and habits or, worst of all, a false sense of achieving quality and superiority when you become an "expert" about something that does not really fit into your life or your home or offer much real pleasure.

sight, choosing beans that are almost black, dark, medium, or light brown. But decaffeinated coffee may look fairly dark, even though it has not been dark-roasted, and different kinds of beans turn different shades of dark when roasted, so you must sometimes inquire. Other things being equal, dark roasts have the strongest taste, light the lightest. The darkest roast is called "espresso" or "Italian." Other dark roasts are called "French," which is sometimes medium dark and sometimes very dark, and "Viennese," which is usually a medium dark but in some places (my neighborhood) is the lightest of the darks. The experts tend to look down on the dark roasts, which the person in the street discovered only in the latter part of the twentieth century, because the roast flavor drowns out the coffee flavor. With very dark roasts, they say, the best coffee is indistinguishable from poor coffee, which offers unscrupulous marketers an opportunity to charge high prices for poor quality. I suppose this boils down to there being wisdom in buying only those very dark roasts that are less expensive—if you really can't tell the difference. But I am convinced that some dark roasts taste better than others. Although certainly the lighter dark roasts and the medium roasts retain more of the character of the underlying bean, the fact is that a good dark roast with hot milk is just indescribably delicious; it is absurd to imply that there is any degradation of taste or gullibility in enjoying it. Sometimes you can have one type of roast and sometimes another.

Blends of different roasts, for example, dark and medium, of beans from different regions are often very good. Although some experts will tell you not to try to blend coffees yourself, as it is a fine art and very complicated, I always do it, simply being careful never to offer any to coffee experts.

Storing and Grinding Coffee. It is far better to buy coffee as whole beans and grind it yourself at home. When you get the beans home, store them in an airtight container in a dark, cool, dry place. If you have bought a lot, store it in several different containers so that you need not continually expose the whole batch to air and humidity when you open it to get some. Experts used to advise us to freeze or refrigerate coffee beans, but now they point out that coffee beans readily absorb refrigerator odors, react badly to the moisture that condenses on them when removed from the cool, and are also harmed by extreme fluctuations in temperature when they are repeatedly taken in and out of the refrigerator. I certainly agree that coffee takes on refrigerator odors; it does this so effectively that you can actually use it as a refrigerator deodorant. But you needn't worry about ruining the flavor of your coffee from freezer or refrigerator odors if you simply use an airtight glass container. Moreover, freezing (and cooling) really do slow down the aging process; if you are going to keep your coffee beans more than a couple of weeks, it still makes sense to freeze them. I also suspect that in summer, when temperatures in my kitchen are sweltering and the humidity is at 90 percent, my coffee beans do better in the freezer than on the shelf even for a week or two.

Do not grind your beans until you are ready to make coffee, because ground coffee stales very quickly. (Keep ground coffee at room temperature in an airtight container, in a cool, dark place; use it up promptly.) If you have frozen the beans, you need not let them thaw before grinding; but the experts say that you'll get more flavor if you let the coffee warm up before brewing. If you have no grinder and you like coffee, put this inexpensive, long-lasting little machine at the top of your wish list. (There are expensive grinders, but very few people have any real need for them.) In the meantime, ask the store to grind your coffee according to your style of coffeemaker, store the ground coffee properly, and do not buy it long in advance.

The longer the hot water is going to be in contact with the ground beans, the coarser the grind you want. To get the finest grind, grind the beans long—for up to half a minute. To get a coarse grind, grind for only a few seconds. Have a store grind you some samples of each so you can familiarize yourself with the appearance of different grinds, and be sure to touch them as well as look at them. Very finely ground coffee is rather like superfine ground white sugar or table salt. Coarsely ground coffee has a grain something like that of granulated brown sugar, and medium is like granulated white sugar. As you read the list below of the appropriate grind for each common style of coffeemaker, keep in mind that there is inconsistent usage on this subject, probably because of different ideas about what "fine," "medium," and "coarse" mean. Whatever the words, the first type of maker in the following list needs the finest and the last the coarsest grind.

Espresso: very fine

Vacuum pot: fine

Drip coffeemaker: medium fine to medium

Percolator: medium to medium coarse

Melior or French press or plunger coffeemaker: coarse

In the plunger or press type, the water actually stands on the ground beans for about five minutes and thus needs the coarsest grind of all, whereas the espresso maker, which forces the water through in seconds, needs the finest.

How to Use Coffeemakers. The best coffeemaker is the one that makes coffee the way you like it most. I have tried all the different coffeemakers at one time or another, and my preferences have varied. Right now we use an electric drip machine (a Krups) most days, and for special occasions we haul out our vacuum maker. Some experts prefer coffee made in the vacuum pot, and I can vouch for its delicious taste. At times in my life I am in love with the special full flavor that you get with the Melior or plunger-type maker, at least until I become fed up with it because it is hard to wash. A drip coffeemaker is easiest, however, and the results are almost as good as the vacuum and plunger types. Electric drip machines, in general, are said to fall short of the ideal: they do not get the water quite warm enough (which causes weak flavor), they do not hold enough coffee (so it either overflows or, again, you make weak coffee), and they leave the water on the coffee too long (making the coffee more bitter). These criticisms do not apply to all makers; mine gets hot enough and holds enough coffee, but it does tend to be a bit too slow for best results. Like other good automatic drip machines, it produces fairly good coffee with great reliability. But leaving the coffee on the heated burner of the machine makes it taste terrible—bitter and acrid—very quickly.

The coffee that people in my generation grew up with—percolated—is booed by every critic. Yet when I visit my aunt, who to this day makes the strong percolated coffee that I remember from childhood, I think nothing could taste more delicious. (Not all percolated coffee is alike. See page 77 below.) And my husband and I, who follow all the conventional coffee ideas, have a secret love (at least it was secret until now) for what we call diner coffee, which you get from diners and cheap restaurants. It is near boiling hot and has a characteristic thin, strong, acid taste that you have to cut with milk and sugar. There is nothing like it to pick you up when you are out on a wintry day walking the city streets.

Vacuum Method. This method is not simple and carefree, but it is fun. The vacuum maker has two glass globes. The lower globe is a glass pot where the coffee is destined to end up. The other is a glass globe with a tube at its bottom; it is going to sit on top of the lower one for most of the brief process. It will

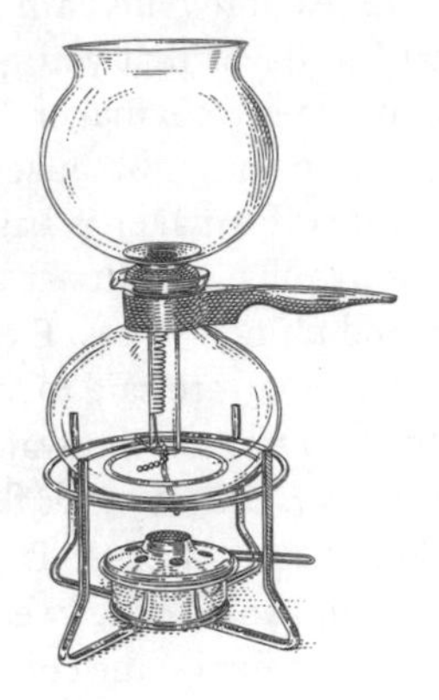

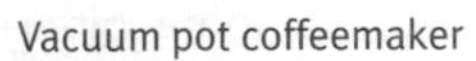

Vacuum pot coffeemaker

Manual drip coffeemaker

Electric drip coffeemaker

probably come with a stand that holds a small stove, a little fondue-type heating device that makes a flame. There is also a filter that goes in the tube—which all sounds obscure but becomes easy to understand when you have the machine in your hands.

To make your coffee, first bring a kettle of water to boil on your stove. (Some manufacturers' instructions permit you to put your lower glass globe, where the coffee eventually ends up, right on your stovetop, protecting it with a diffuser.) While this is heating, grind and measure your coffee, and place the filter in the upper globe (the one with the tube in it). Then put your measured coffee, ground fine, into the upper globe. Set the lower globe on the stand, pour in the boiled water, and light the flame under the globe.

You now put the upper globe on top of the lower one (both are unlidded), making sure that it latches on, creating an airtight seal. As pressure develops in the lower globe, the water is forced through the tube into the upper globe. Let it steep for two minutes, then turn off the flame.

The last step—a dramatic one—happens by itself after you turn off the flame: the cooling creates a vacuum in the lower globe that sucks the brewed coffee through the filter back down into the lower globe. When this is done, you remove the upper globe and set it in its stand. The coffee is ready to be served.

Manual Drip Coffeemaker. Gold filters are supposed to make better coffee than paper ones because they trap less of the coffee's essential oils. However, you can get good coffee with paper too. First bring a kettle of measured fresh cold water to boil. While this is heating, grind and measure your coffee. Then put the filter into the cone, and put the coffee into the filter. When the water has boiled, wait a moment. Then pour enough of the water on the coffee to dampen all of it, and wait a half a minute or a bit less. (This begins to dissolve the flavors so that they are readily released into the water.) Then pour the rest of the water into the cone. You may have to wait for some of the water to drip through before all of the rest can fit in the cone. It is best if you let the coffee drip into a thermal carafe of some sort, or pour it into a thermal container as soon as it is done dripping.

Electric Drip Coffeemaker. Follow the manufacturer's instructions. You merely insert a filter, put coffee in it, pour water in the appropriate place, and flick a switch to turn the coffeemaker on. Gold filters are supposed to be better than paper, as they do not

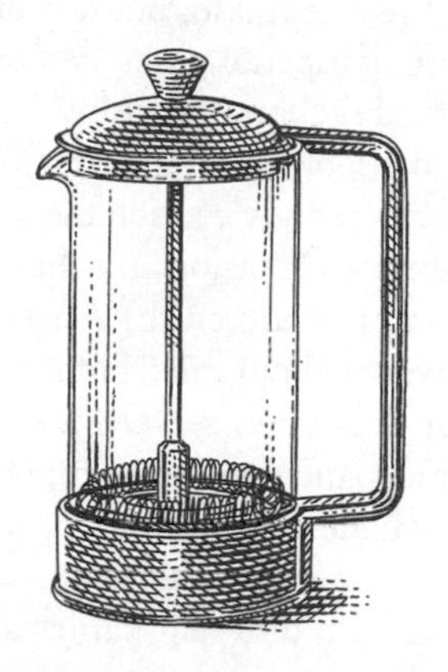

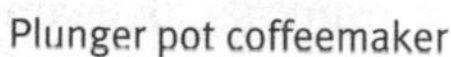
Plunger pot coffeemaker

Percolator

Moka pot espresso maker

hold any of the beans' essential oils. Be sure to measure and grind your coffee fresh, and use measured fresh cold water. To avoid bitterness, thermal carafes are best for receiving and holding the brew. Or you might turn off the electric burner under the glass pot, or pour the coffee into a thermal container after it is made to keep it both hot and good longer.

Plunger or Press Method. Set the kettle on to boil. In the meantime, measure and grind your coffee and place it in the bottom of the pot. When the water has boiled, turn it off and wait a moment, then fill the pot with hot water and put the plunger in place at the top. Wait about five minutes, or a minute more or less if you like your coffee more or less full-bodied. Then push down the plunger. You will need to push hard. If you want to keep the coffee warm, pour it into a thermal carafe.

Percolator Method. Fill the pot with water to the desired level, then measure coffee into the metal or plastic filter basket. The trick with percolated coffee, as with plunger coffee, is to use more coffee than with other methods, so that you get flavor without percolating it to death. Bring the pot to perk over moderately high heat. As soon as the first quiet perks appear, turn the heat as low as it will go to sustain the quiet perk. Never let it percolate furiously. Turn the heat down as far as possible and stand the pot at the edge of the burner, slightly ajar, or use a diffuser, so that the coffee does not get too strong. When the color in the glass dome at the top indicates that the coffee is finished, remove it from the heat.

Another point about percolated coffee to keep in mind is that you want a stainless steel or glass pot. Other metals may taint the flavor. Even with a stainless pot, you need to use it several times to "season" it; any new metal pot produces bad percolated coffee at the beginning. And you need to be as careful to wash the pot with hot, soapy water between uses as with any other type of pot.

Espresso. We think of espresso as a particular kind of coffee, but the word actually refers to a method of brewing. Coffee made in this style is exceptionally strong, thick, and full-bodied. Espresso is made by forcing hot water through finely ground coffee beans at a very high pressure, yielding a small amount of a highly concentrated brew. You can use any kind of coffee beans, but many people like a dark roast—the Italian or espresso roast. A serving of espresso is only about 1.5 to 2 ounces and is served in small "demitasse" cups. (A regular cup of coffee is about 6 ounces.)

There are several types of espresso makers. The most common kind in the home, the moka pot, is easy to use and inexpensive. Unfortunately, it does not produce a coffee drink as thick as espresso is supposed to be, but I would not decide not to have one for that reason. The brew it makes is still espresso-like, thicker and stronger than regular coffee—and delicious. The moka pot has three parts: a base or lower chamber, a metal filter that sits on the base, and an upper chamber that screws on above the filter. The upper chamber is where the espresso ends up. The moka pot sits directly on one of your stove burners. Put cold water in the lower half of the pot and fill the coffee filter chamber with very finely ground beans. It is important not to let the coffee grounds sit in the water, so be careful not to overfill the base of the moka pot. Set the metal coffee filter over the water in the lower chamber and screw on the upper chamber. Place the apparatus directly on top of one of the stove's burners and set on medium-low heat. The heated water is forced up into the coffee filter, and bubbles up through the grounds into the upper chamber of the moka pot. Wait to pour the espresso until the sound of bubbling subsides. You can open the lid at the top to look in to see whether you have collected a dark liquid in the upper chamber.

You can also use an electric pump espresso maker, which does make something that deserves to be called real espresso, but it is expensive and more temperamental. Follow the manufacturer's directions carefully. And if you are in the store looking for an espresso maker, be sure to ask for advice as to the different kinds of pump and "piston" machines for espresso making that are on the market.

Espresso is served without milk, but it can be sugared. Americans often serve espresso with a piece of lemon rind that can be rubbed around the edge of the cup, adding a little zest. There are several popular espresso-based milky drinks with different names according to the ratio of espresso to steamed milk that you use. For cappuccino, add approximately $^{1}/_{4}$ cup steamed milk to a shot of espresso, and top the mixture with $^{1}/_{4}$ cup milk foam. Caffè latte is a more diluted drink, mixing one part espresso with four parts steamed milk. It does not require foam on top. You can sprinkle ground cinnamon or chocolate on cappuccino. This, again, is an American custom, not an Italian one, but that's no reason not to do it if you like it.

Electric espresso makers often have a feature that allows you to make steamed or foamed milk to use with the espresso—this is a nozzle on the side that releases steam when you turn it on. To *steam* milk, put it into a heat-tolerant container, which should be no more than two-thirds full because the steamed milk will bubble up a bit; dip the nozzle *deep* into the milk, and turn it on. To *foam* the milk, the container should be no more than one-third full; let the nozzle bub-

Demitasse cup and saucer

Coffee cup and saucer

ble *close to the surface* of the milk. If you do not have an electric machine that makes steamed milk, just heat milk in a pot on your stove, but do not let it boil.

Measuring Coffee and Water. The standard coffee measure is supposed to hold two level tablespoons of ground coffee, but in fact, if you test them, you find that many hold more or less than this. Standard advice calls for using 1 coffee measure and 6 ounces of cold water for each cup of brewed coffee you wish to make. This will give you a medium-bodied cup of brewed coffee. Use a bit more or less than one measure per 6 ounces if you like a stronger or weaker brew, or use a measure that is a bit larger or smaller than the standard two tablespoons. Do not try to increase the strength of your coffee by using a finer grind than is proper for your coffeemaker; that will make bitter coffee or clog some machines. Instead, try using a bit more coffee.

Good Coffee by Any Method. There are a variety of practices that apply to making good coffee by any method:

- Use fresh, cold, good-tasting water. New York City tap water suits me, but some think it makes inferior coffee. There are no general rules, but if you do not like your coffee, try bottled spring water. Do not use distilled water; it is so soft that it over-extracts from the beans and produces a more bitter cup.
- Use a coffeemaker that will not taint the flavor of the brew. Glass, ceramics, and certain plastics are inert and are used for the best coffeemakers. If you use metal, make it stainless steel.
- Wash your coffeemaker and all its parts thoroughly after each use with hot, soapy water, and rinse it thoroughly. Traces of the last brew left inside the pot can ruin the flavor of the next. Clean out your coffee grinder thoroughly after each use too, or stale grinds will go into your next batch.
- The goal of every type of coffeemaking is to put on the beans water that is just under the boiling temperature, and to avoid touching the coffee with boiling water. In the scorned percolator method, try to minimize the temperature and duration of percolation.
- If you let the coffee sit on a heated burner on your stove or electric coffeemaker to keep warm, it quickly develops a bad flavor. A glass carafe should not be set directly over a flame, but there are contraptions—diffusers—that you can set between the carafe and the flame that help to protect the carafe.[3] Best of all, however, is to drip the coffee directly into a thermal carafe or to pour your brewed coffee into one.
- Coffee is always ruined by reheating.
- Heat your coffee pot and cone and/or metal filter before pouring in the boiled water. You may do this by boiling extra water and pouring some of it over the cone and into the pot. Then, of course, empty this water from the pot before proceeding to brew the coffee. It is also good to heat the cups with boiling water.
- Never reuse coffee grounds.

Making Tea. Just like coffee, tea is grown all over the world and subjected to different kinds of processing. The taste of tea depends on where it comes from as well as what has been done to it. Three basic methods of processing produce the three basic kinds of tea: black, oolong, and green. Black tea is oxidized or "fermented" for up to three hours, oolong tea is fermented for a shorter period, and green tea is not fermented at all. Oxidation makes for a stronger, "tea-colored" brew. Thus black tea is strongest and darkest; oolong second strongest and darkest; and green tea weakest and lightest.

Older supermarket teas were on a par in quality with supermarket coffees, but many—perhaps most—supermarkets now carry a wide variety of teas, including fine teas. Fine teas cost more, but not more than most people can afford to enjoy. If you go to your local coffee or tea specialty store, you will find a range of choices that is either exhilarating or dismaying, depending on your point of view. Those who are new to tea-drinking may find the list of teas below helpful in deciding what they might like to try. Or ask the clerk for suggestions.

Black Teas
Assam—full-bodied malt taste

Ceylon Breakfast—rich golden blend

Darjeeling—delicate muscatel flavor

English Breakfast—full-bodied blend

Irish Breakfast—robust and full-bodied

Keemun—fine black tea, with a "sappy" liquor

Lapsang Souchong—black tea with a distinctive smoky flavor

Orange Pekoe—name refers to type of tea; has no orange flavor

Russian Caravan—blend of black teas

Oolong Teas
Black Dragon—delicate, fruity tea

China Oolong—a pleasant blend

Formosa Oolong—known for "peach" flavor and aroma

Green Teas
Gunpowder—clear, yellow-green color and slightly bittersweet taste

Hyson—fragrant, bitter taste

Jasmine—blend of green teas and jasmine flowers, mild sweet flavor

Sencha—a Japanese green tea

Flavored Teas
Earl Grey—black tea flavored with oil of bergamot

Are Teabags Inferior? As to the taste of the tea, what matters is how good the tea is, not whether it is in bags or loose. But as a matter of fact, a lot of the tea that is put into tea bags is not good, and tea in bags may not be stored in airtight containers and in any event stales more readily. So while teabags need not offer an inferior tea, they often do. Certainly a nice pot of tea is more attractive than teabags on the edge of the saucer and a much more sensible way to make tea for more than one person. You can use bags to make a pot, of course. But they seem to make most sense when you are making just a cup for yourself. If you do not use bags, you use a small infuser to make a cup, and you use a larger infuser, or an infuser basket, to make a pot.

How to Make Tea. In coffee-making you always try to get the water cooled to slightly below the boiling point. In tea-making, however, you always try to keep the water as close to the boiling point as you can, but without applying direct heat, as this ruins the tea.

You begin by putting a kettle of fresh, cold water on the stove to boil. Set over high heat a separate small quantity of water for warming the teapot. (But put no tea into the pot until you have warmed it.) Shortly before the kettle boils, warm the teapot with water from the second pot. Then pour it out and put in the tea—1 teaspoon of black tea or one teabag for each 5½ ounce cup of tea you plan to make. (Use ½ teaspoon per cup for oolong, and 2 teaspoons per cup for green tea.) You can put loose tea right into the bottom of the teapot, into one or more infusers or tea balls, or into the infusion basket that some teapots contain. Do not pack an infuser full of tea, or the tea will not have room to expand when it becomes wet. It should be no more than half full.

Immediately when the kettle boils, bring it to the pot and pour, holding it close to the mouth of the teapot so that the stream of water does not get cooled by the air during pouring. Put the lid on the teapot; cover it with a tea cozy, if you like, to insulate the pot and keep in the warmth. Brew black tea for three to five minutes; oolong for about five min-

Teapot with infuser

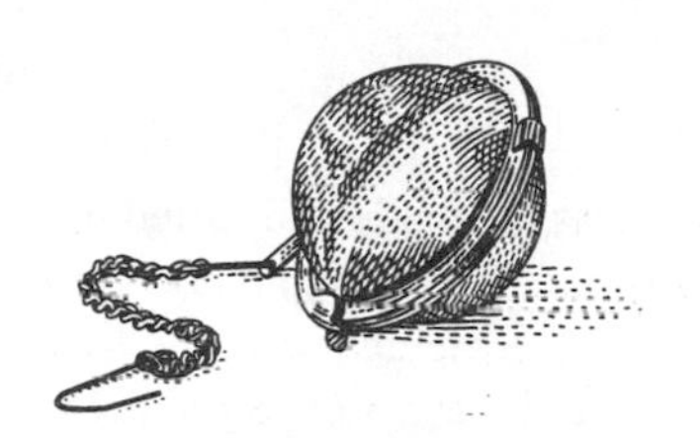
Tea infuser

utes; and green teas for only a minute or two. Do not be misled by the fact that the tea's color ripens long before that. You need the full brewing period to get all the flavors. Near the end of the steeping period, gently rock the pot so as to mix the brew and water evenly, and then let the leaves settle again.

Once the tea has steeped, you need to remove the leaves from the tea so that the brewing stops or the tea will begin to become bitter. You do this in one of two ways. You can simply pull out the infuser, infusion basket, tea balls, or teabags; or, using a strainer so that leaves and sediment do not come with the brew, you can pour the tea into a new teapot that has also been preheated.

Reusing Tea? Tea made from previously used leaves is not as good as tea made from fresh leaves. On the other hand, it tastes tolerable, and is economical.

Lemon, Milk, Sugar, and Spice? Milk and sugar are good in most black teas, and so is lemon. You never use lemon and milk together; lemon curdles milk. But, generally speaking, the more delicate the tea, the less desirable is anything that will dilute it or overpower its taste. Thus Darjeeling and oolong are usually served without milk or lemon. Lapsang Souchong and green tea are not served with milk or sweetener. Honey is often good in tea, but it has a more intrusive flavor than sugar. Strong-flavored honey drowns out much of the flavor of delicate teas. Spices often drown out the tea, too, but spiced tea is a pleasant change now and then.

Making Hot Chocolate. Hot chocolate, another mildly caffeinated beverage, deserves a mention here. Every good all-purpose cookbook has a recipe. I use this one:

To make hot chocolate, measure two heaping teaspoons of sugar, one heaping teaspoon of powdered unsweetened chocolate, a tiny pinch of salt, and one cup of milk for each cup of chocolate. (Many cookbooks omit the salt, but it brings out the chocolate flavor nicely.) First mix together the dry ingredients; then add milk one teaspoon at a time, stirring constantly to prevent lumps from forming, until you have a creamy smooth mixture. Stir in the rest of the milk and place over medium heat. Stirring constantly, heat the mixture just to the boiling point. Remove from heat and add one small drop of vanilla per cup (a scant teaspoon for four cups). To make a rich dessert, add whipped cream. Children like hot chocolate with marshmallows floating on it.

The better the chocolate you use, the better the drink. Low-fat and skim milk taste very good, even if whole milk tastes better. Hot chocolate is not so good made with plain water, but hot chocolate mixes usually have dried milk in them. Hot chocolate mixes and syrups cost more and offer spurious convenience. Presweetened chocolates and mixes give you less choice about how sweet and chocolatey you want your drink.

Herbal Teas

Herbal teas are made with dried parts of certain aromatic or fragrant plants. In common parlance, "herbal" teas are any that have no caffeine and have not been decaffeinated. Many of these taste delicious, with or without sugar, honey, or a sweetener. Some of them are reputed to be nutritious or to contain substances that increase resistance to various kinds of illnesses, and many of the plants commonly used for herbal teas in fact have medicinally active ingredients. Some can be dangerous if overused or used by vulnerable people.[4] It is not likely, however, that any dangerous teas will be on your grocery store shelves. In my supermarket I can buy herbal teas of rosehips, blackberry, raspberry, and strawberry leaves, chicory, mints of various sorts, chamomile, jasmine, lemon verbena, and lemongrass, and of cinnamon, cloves, cardamom, coriander, and other spices. Various fruit-flavored drinks are sometimes sold as herbal teas, including peach, cherry, cranberry, orange, and lemon.

Just as with regular tea, you make herbal tea by pouring boiling hot water over a bag or infuser containing the tea and then letting it steep. Store herbal tea in a dark, dry, cool place in an airtight container.

WHAT IS AN HERBAL TEA?

According to the Schapiras' *Book of Coffee and Tea,* if the aromatic or fragrant plant originates in the tropics it is called a spice, and if it comes from a temperate climate it is called an herb. But, they point out, this is a rule with many exceptions, such as cinnamon, a spice that makes an excellent "herbal" tea.

Alcoholic Beverages

Wines are enjoyed, as foods are, for their taste. Mild warmth and relaxation is sought with a glass of spirits; but becoming "high" is undesirable. Although the drink after work has not disappeared, it is not nearly as common as it once was as a way to make the transition between work and home or to get over a bad day.

If you do not drink, you may still wish to be able to accommodate guests who do. This is a gracious and moderate course, which is not hard to follow. Simply keep on hand some good scotch, sherry, vodka, soda water, gin, tonic, a couple of unopened bottles of red wine and a few of white, and some sort of brandy or cognac or liqueurs. You can say pleasantly, "We do not drink, but perhaps you would like . . ." and then offer whatever component of your bar is proper for the occasion. But if you are not interested in keeping wine or drinks and their makings at home, don't. You need never apologize for this. Simply explain the situation matter-of-factly, and express dignified regret in consideration of the feelings of any guests who might feel a little disappointed.

Aperitifs and Digestifs: The Cocktail Hour. During the cocktail hour, the period before dinner when alcoholic drinks are served with appetizers, the drinks best served are known as "aperitifs," and typically they are grape- or wine-based drinks with a higher alcohol content than wine but lower than hard liquor. They help enliven your appetite by virtue of their alcoholic content, which releases inhibitions. Cocktails are mixed drinks that contain hard liquor—scotch, whiskey, gin, vodka, or rum. Throughout the twentieth century until the 1970s, cocktails were so popular as predinner drinks that this period of the day is still called the cocktail hour. Since then there has been an extended decline in their popularity, interrupted by the occasional vogue, but they have never regained their preeminence as predinner drinks, partly because people wish to drink less hard liquor and partly because these drinks never made much sense before dinner anyway. Cocktails are so strong that they often spoil your appreciation of the wines and foods to follow. Aperitifs made of grapes, such as dry sherry, Dubonnet, Campari, vermouth, Madeira, or champagne, or mixed drinks based on such drinks, are more rational choices.

At casual dinners, white wine and beer often work well as the predinner drink. Full-bodied red wine is a trickier choice because it will drown out many flavors to follow. But a lighter red, to be followed at dinner by a heavier one, would work. A white wine before dinner, even a glass of the white that you will have at dinner (or during the first course), always makes sense. (In the 1980s the wine spritzer, a half-and-half mixture of soda water and white wine, was popular among those who wanted to drink less alcohol but join in the predinner drink ritual.) Beer enthusiasts, especially young ones, insist that the right beer is excellent before, during, and after meals. There are those, however, who experience beer as overly filling, perhaps because it is usually consumed in larger volume than wine or other drinks, or perhaps because it is fizzy.

"Digestifs" are drinks served after dinner, in theory as an aid to digestion. But whereas there is some scientific support for the idea that you eat more, and with more enjoyment, if you drink a small amount of some aperitif beforehand, there is none that I have ever heard of for the idea that you will digest your meal better if you sip a little port or cognac. Many traditional digestifs are grape-based, but some people enjoy whiskeys, beers, and other types of drinks after dinner. What all digestifs tend to have in common is strength of some sort: very high alcohol content, very great sweetness, or very powerful taste. Such drinks are best enjoyed after the meal, for obvious reasons.

Aperitifs, digestifs, and cocktails are remarkably fashion-sensitive and have the same ups and downs in popularity as hemlines.

Cocktails. If you wish to serve cocktails in your home, you have to stock a bar with what you need in the way of liquors, soda, tonic, various flavorings, garnishes of olives or onions, juices, etc., and all the implements, ice buckets, jiggers, shakers, and glassware you will need for making and serving them. You can aim for a less elaborate bar, one that can handle a few standard drinks (plus the latest fad or two), or a more elaborate one that can produce just about anything. Besides the fashionable drinks of the moment, there are certain more standard cocktails—martinis, Manhattans, old-fashioneds, margaritas, Rob Roys, gin and tonics, or sidecars—that never go completely out of fashion. Beginners can find out what is what in any of many enjoyable and reliable books on the subject that are perennially available.

A cocktail party is one that serves only hors d'oeuvres or appetizers—no dinner or supper—along with cocktails. Cocktail parties are less popular than they used to be, partly because people work so much more than they used to that there is no one to prepare or attend them. Cocktails can also be served at any evening party, and you can hold a party at the cocktail hour without cocktails, instead offering wine, champagne, aperitifs, beer, or soft drinks.

Wine

Learning About Wine. There are excellent books, classes, and teachers to help you learn what kinds of wines are best suited to your tastes and meals. You can begin by buying what a friend or restaurant served that you liked. Then get one of the many excellent introductory books about wines and learn the meaning of all the things that the labels say so that you can choose to acquire for yourself the same wine, winemaker, grape, year, or wine region, knowing what you are doing. (My own favorite, *Jancis Robinson's Wine Course*, is both astonishingly fact-filled and a delight to read.) Experiment broadly: reds, whites, rosés, dry and sweet wines, light and heavy, aperitifs, dessert wines, Madeira, and port. Whenever you try something you like, turn to your books and learn as much as you can about what pleased you. Good wine stores and knowledgeable clerks can sometimes offer invaluable assistance also.

Wines go in and out of fashion just as cocktails do—Australian reds enjoyed a vogue in the 1970s, Chardonnays were hugely popular in the 1980s, Beaujolais Nouveau in the 1990s. But this is a fact that beginners should rejoice over. Although not every wine fashion appeals to connoisseurs, a beginner who serves the latest fad can be more confident that his or her choice will be acceptable. It is fun, too, to be au courant, and a little grouchy to insist on ignoring popular taste entirely. There is time enough to buck the trends, or set them, when you are no longer a beginner.

If you plan to serve wines, you must learn to store, chill, and serve them properly.

Temperature. White wine, rosé, Beaujolais (a red wine that is fruity and light like a white), and Beaujolais-type California wines should all be chilled before serving. Lighter whites are best when served at 40–50°F, so you might pop these in the refrigerator in the morning of the day they are to be served and then take them out to warm slightly close to serving time. (Your refrigerator, if it is properly cool, chills them to just below 40°F.)

Full-bodied whites and light reds are best served at 50–60°F; put these in the refrigerator for one or two hours. Or chill them in an ice bucket. To do this, first remove the cork and place the bottle in the bucket. Then fill the bucket with ice cubes. Lastly, fill it with cold water. The cold water will chill the wine much more rapidly than the cold air of the refrigerator will. If you have no ice bucket and you have forgotten to chill your wine, put it in the freezer. But do not forget to remove it before the wine freezes, the cork pushes out, or the bottle cracks.

Full-bodied reds are best served between 60° and 66°F—a fairly cool room temperature by American standards. I do not worry much about cooling reds so long as my room is below 70°. When it is over 70°, I put a red in the refrigerator for a little while. Connoisseurs often have small cooled storage areas or coolers for their wines.

Uncorking. Pierce the cork with your corkscrew right down its center, and make sure that it goes all the way. You may break the cork if you do not. If you should mangle the cork hopelessly, you have no choice but to push it into the bottle. Then decant the wine through a strainer or a *clean* coffee filter or cheesecloth to catch the bits of cork. Good wines, by the way, tend to have good long corks.

Uncork sparkling wines such as champagne very carefully in order to preserve the bubbles (you don't want it to go flat) and to prevent the wine from fizzing out and being wasted. You first peel off the foil wrapping around the bottle opening. Then you loosen the metal wires that hold the cork down, while keeping your hand on top of the cork—otherwise, if pressure has built up inside, the cork might pop off when the restraining wires are gone. Now you want to loosen the cork enough to let some gas escape without removing it from the bottle yet. To do this, tightly grip the cork so that it will not get away from you and gently turn the bottle, not the cork, while you gently push up on the cork with the thumbs. Gas should slowly bubble out around the cork, with a soft hissing. There may or may not be a gentle pop. When the hissing subsides, push the cork out and pour. But in case things do not work out as planned, keep a glass at hand to catch any champagne that fizzes out suddenly.

Breathing. To taste its best, wine, especially red wine, must be uncorked and exposed to the air for a period of time before it is drunk. This is called letting the wine "breathe," and it gives the wine a mellower, less sharp flavor. Those new to wine-drinking may be surprised at how profound the difference is in taste before and after breathing. White wines, rosés, and very light Beaujolais need very little breathing time, perhaps five or ten minutes. Most reds will need much more, how much depending upon a number of factors.

One rule of thumb with reds is that the younger the wine, the longer it needs to breathe, since airing the wine is a way of aging it by exposing it to oxygen. If the wine is already very aged, you can send it over the hill by letting it breathe too long. The type of grape the wine is made of also affects breathing time. Red Bordeaux and various Chiantis need a great deal. A Bordeaux under five years may need as much as two hours, while one between five and ten years may need only one hour. Burgundies and pinot noirs tend to need between a half hour and an hour. The heavier Beaujolais should be treated like burgundies. Some very old wines may need very little breathing time, but others may need fairly substantial breathing periods. If you are uncertain, be sure to consult your wine book or ask a knowledgeable clerk when you buy your wine—especially if your wine is a fine one.

Decanting. Decanting—pouring the wine out of its bottle into a decanter or pitcher—hastens the breathing process by exposing a larger surface area to the air. It is really necessary only when sediment has collected or when you wish to hasten breathing; otherwise it is perfectly all right to pour wine from its bottle.

Because white wines do not collect sediment, you never need to decant them, although you may if you wish. Wines are stored on their side, which means that the sediment is stirred up when you pick up the bottle for drinking; and every time you tip the bottle to pour a glass the sediment is disturbed anew. With reds, you should first stand the bottle for an hour or so before decanting so that the sediment has a chance to settle on the bottom of the bottle. Then pour the wine out slowly with light shining behind the bottle so that you can see when the sediment first appears in the neck of the bottle. When it does, stop pouring. Later on, when there has been more settling of the sediment, you can salvage still more of the small amount of wine that you left in the bottle.

Beautiful crystal decanters have long been favored for wine, but these (if they are real crystal) contain lead, which can be leached out by the wine. Letting wine stand for any period of time in crystal decanters, to breathe or for refilling glasses, is therefore not a good idea, unfortunately. See chapter 44, "China and Crystal," pages 548–50.

Serving and Glassware. Ordinarily, one bottle of wine or half a bottle of a dessert wine serves four people. Do not fill the glass more than half full; this means that to serve an ordinary four-ounce serving of wine you need an eight-ounce glass, and you may use an even larger one if you wish. If you are serving two wines with dinner, provide different glasses for the two wines and set them in a triangle with the water glass. See chapter 6, "Serving Meals," page 64. Serve the lighter wine first and the heavier second. At a formal meal, when cheese is served after the salad, keep the red wine for the cheese course, and serve the dessert wine when the sweet is served. You can serve cognac or a digestif with coffee or after it.

Wineglasses are stemmed so that you can hold the stem and not warm the wine with the warmth of your hand. They are large, relative to their contents, to permit swirling the wine, which releases its bouquet, and the sides curve in at the top to prevent the wine from sloshing over the top when it is swirled. The two main shapes in wineglasses are the tulip, which curves in slightly at the top, and the burgundy glass, a sphere with its top sliced off. Occasional wine drinkers and beginners may prefer to use an all-purpose wineglass, a medium-sized tulip-shaped glass that can be used for whites, reds, cham-

Glassware: Top row, left to right: Red wine glass, brandy snifter, white wine glass, all-purpose wine glass, champagne glass (tulip)
Bottom row, left to right: liqueur glass, martini or cocktail glass, short tumbler, tall tumbler, sherry glass

pagne, or dessert wines. Wineglasses are highly variable in size.

Champagne does not need swirling because its bubbles carry up its bouquet. Champagne glasses come in three shapes. The tulip is taller and narrower than the wine tulip. The flute is like the tulip except that the top does not curve in. The coupe is a very shallow, broad bowl. Champagne lovers disfavor the coupe because it lets the champagne go flat sooner by exposing a wide surface area to the air; and it does not show a pretty stream of bubbles ascending from the bottom of the glass to the top, as do the flute and tulip.

Storage. Many experts say that wine ages best if stored at 55°F, although a few hold out for slightly colder storage. Jancis Robinson says that 40–59°F is ideal, but 59–68°F is not likely to do any great harm.[5] What is most important is that the wine experience no rapid change in temperature, as wine will be harmed more by an abrupt shift than it would be by a gradual seasonal warming over a period of many weeks. The experts disagree about the effect of light on wine during storage. At one extreme, surely you should not expose it to direct sunlight, and at the other it is clear that perfect and constant darkness is not required. But you probably do not need to get fanatical about exposure to light, particularly when you remember that wine bottles are colored and filter out a great deal of light anyway.

You can get a wine-storage refrigeration unit installed in your home that will keep the wine at an ideal temperature, but you must weigh the pros and cons. Some connoisseurs point out that if a power outage would subject your wine to a violent shift of temperature, you might be better off using your cellar and exposing the wine to gradual, subtle warmings and coolings. But if you live in an overheated city apartment and intend to get serious about fine wines, artificially cooled wine storage is your only sensible option. Those who wish to be a bit less serious yet still enjoy their wine should keep it in the coolest closet they have. Make sure that there are no hot-water pipes passing through any of its walls, and place the bottles where they will not be bumped. If you use your cellar, watch out for areas near your furnace, hot-water heater, or washer and dryer that may grow too warm or show great fluctuations in temperature.

Some who store very fine wines worry about vibrations, which can keep sediment stirred up and cause corks to loosen. Subways, trains, and big trucks that frequently pass by can cause problems, although vibrations pose less of a threat to wines than heat and temperature swings. I cannot imagine any threat from vibrations to ordinary good wines in ordinary homes if wine is stored in an out-of-the-way place not subject to bumpings and bangings.

Store wine on its side so that the cork stays wet. If the cork dries out, it may shrink and admit air, which would ruin the wine. You should not turn or move the bottles, so position them in such a way that you can read their labels without moving them or picking them up.

Which Wine? There are customs governing which wines complement which foods, but none rise to the level of rules. In the long run, your own tastes are your best guide. Beginners, whose tastes are in the process of being formed, can get much good advice from books, friends, and professionals. Beginners used to be told, "Whites with fish and white-meat poultry; reds with red meats." This is not really wrong; it is just not always right. What you really want is not to overpower the wine with the food or the food with the wine. A strong-tasting wine will leave you unable to taste a delicate dish properly, and strong-tasting food will overcome a gentle wine. In fact, fish and poultry are often delicate and go well with light whites, but not always. Red meats often do really go well with full-bodied red wines. You definitely want the latter for spicy sausages. But there are full-bodied whites that will stand up to almost any meal, light reds that are good with milder foods, and so forth. With vegetarian meals, go by the strength and nature of the tastes. Strongly spiced dishes and tomato-based dishes will demand stronger wines. With desserts, drink sweet dessert wines, or, more generally, make sure the wine is sweeter than the food.

You need not drink French wine with French foods or Italian wines with Italian food. When you are in doubt, it is sometimes a good bet to go with a wine of the same national or regional origin as the food you are choosing. But you can always find a French wine to grace an Italian meal or a California wine to serve with a curry.

8

The Center of a Dwelling

Setting up the kitchen . . . Is the kitchen just for cooking? . . . Storing kitchenware . . . Convenient storage for glasses, flatware, pots and pans, canned goods, detergents . . . Basic equipment for the kitchen, including linens, utensils, small appliances, knives . . . Knives and knife sharpeners: choosing, sharpening, caring for, and storing knives . . . Pots and pans and bakeware . . . Materials used in cookware and their properties . . . Glass, enameled cast iron, cast iron, stainless steel, copper, aluminum and anodized aluminum, nonstick cookware, tin

. . . this all-electric room
where ghosts would feel uneasy,
a witch at a loss, is numinous and again
the centre of a dwelling
not, as lately it was, an abhorrent dungeon . . .

—W. H. Auden, "Thanksgiving for a Habitat"

Democracy made kitchens come to life again. In other times, kitchens may have been little more than dungeons where servants toiled. But in today's servantless homes, where shining, sweet-smelling kitchens are equipped with the latest labor-saving devices, cooking has been transformed into an art that everyone can be proud to master. Even though the hum of electricity has replaced the magic of a live fire, the modern kitchen is once more the warm center of the home.

Setting Up the Kitchen

Is the Kitchen Just for Cooking? As the one room in the house that can give you a full dinner or a hot cup of tea, the kitchen has a special drawing power that tends to transform it into a general working and lounging area. If someone is in the kitchen cooking, other members of the household or neighbors wander in to help or chat, and while we are there talking, chopping, and stirring, we begin to do almost anything else—fold the laundry, make business and social telephone calls, balance the checkbook, glue a broken toy, put photos into albums. And whereas eating and socializing in the kitchen used to be done only by poor people and servants, it is now quite likely to happen in the homes of the super-rich. For better or worse, many people entertain and serve guests in their kitchens rather than in their dining rooms.

In some homes, the kitchen becomes the household's command center. Even people who have desks or offices devoted to household affairs tend to use them primarily for storage or for doing their income taxes. It is the kitchen table or countertop that they actually use to make daily business and medical calls, deal with service and repair personnel, and plan their week, even though it offers none of the conveniences of a desk.

The multifunctional kitchen system cannot avoid some inefficiencies. It gets crowded. Cooking does not always combine well with clothes-folding, check-writing, or photo-sorting. Reading at countertops takes up space needed for chopping. A kitchen table used as a desktop produces a paper trail between the kitchen and the real office or desk, and you may be left wondering where the electricity bill is.

Some people build large kitchens and establish a desk and computer in one corner to resolve at least some of these problems. My own vote, if apartment living gave me a free choice, would be for a middle course: a large kitchen and some limits on its use for extraculinary functions. Rather than move the household desk or office into the kitchen, I would have these adjoining the kitchen so that there is easy traffic between them. An office, if it were the right size, could also conveniently offer some work space—especially tabletop surfaces—to homes that children (and adults) often complain have "no place to *do* anything."

And I would make sure that the kitchen provides well for all its central cooking functions. Your stove, for example, should have an outdoor exhaust, and the kitchen itself should have excellent ventilation. If you often cook for several people, you are likely to want far more cabinet space than builders and architects want to give you; and you may find you can make good use of more refrigerated space than your mother had—an extra freezer or small refrigerator. You can install a wine cooler that will keep your wines at the desirable temperature. A pantry, generous in size, with controllable temperature and humidity, ought to be thought of as a kitchen necessity, but it is still an unusual feature in today's homes.

Every kitchen needs—and rarely has—enough shelves for cookbooks, reference books on nutrition and foods, and other housekeeping books. My great-grandmother had one cookbook and one housekeeping book, but many homes today rely on a small kitchen library. Its books should be shelved far enough away from cooking areas to stay free of oily residues, or perhaps kept behind glass doors. (A friend whose two passions are cooking and books thinks cookbooks should not be stored in the kitchen at all.) If you want to do much lounging in the kitchen, while cooking or otherwise, it is important to have a table in the kitchen with some chairs. A table with some shallow drawers is most useful. It can be used as a food preparation area, a desk (if you keep paper, pencils, and a calculator in one of the drawers), or a place for snacks or informal meals. Or you can keep flatware or napkins in the drawers. I find a table more comfortable and inviting than a bar with stools, but this is purely a matter of taste.

Function over Fashion: Store Most Dishes, Pots, Pans, Utensils, and Foodstuffs in Closed Cabinets or Drawers. Before letting the potential looks of a kitchen sway you, it is important to ask yourself how the kitchen will really work. One design trend that goes in and out of fashion is a preference for open shelves and racks for wall-hanging utensils (instead of storage in drawers, cabinets, or other covered places). It is a nostalgic style intended to evoke thoughts of a colonial kitchen, but for the average kitchen it works poorly. Professional chefs hang out lots of pots and utensils because they use most of them constantly. Although you might think it is more convenient for you too to have things visible than to have to dig for them in cabinets and drawers, it probably isn't, as I learned from unpleasant experience. Exposed surfaces in kitchens (including walls, ceilings, light fixtures, lightbulbs, and ceiling fans) get dirty faster than anything else in your home. I once had a small, charming, "architect-designed" kitchen that had open shelving for everything—even for foodstuffs in cans, bottles, boxes, and bags. These quickly became coated with a particularly unpleasant and hard-to-remove mix of dust and oil. I was glad to leave this kitchen behind, and, ever since, I have stared skeptically at pictures in magazines of shining knives and pots hanging behind a stovetop, where they will soon be spattered with food and grease. Pots and pans that have been hanging out for a week without washing should be thoroughly cleaned before use. Unless placed near the cooking and food preparation area, where they grow dirtiest most quickly, there is no point in hanging them out instead of storing them in cabinets, where they will stay usably clean much longer. Of course, kitchen utensils may be stored in the open if you have plenty of time or can hire someone to wash everything every couple of weeks. But it is hardly the best course for the time-pressed household. New homes now often feature "appliance garages" that enable you to keep blenders, food processors, mixing machines, and other appliances out of sight.

It is convenient to keep out a few things that you use very often. Potholders must be kept at the side of the stove, where you can reach them immediately. Some people like to keep out their favorite paring or chopping knives, along with an assortment of spoons of different sizes and a saucepan or sauté pan or anything else that is used every day or two. Many of us keep a half dozen wooden spoons of different sizes at the side of the stove in an open container ready to be grabbed when needed. The spoons are used and washed constantly, and the container needs a weekly wash. All other frequently used items should be easily reachable in drawers or cabinets close to the stove and counter area where you chop and prepare foods for cooking.

How to Store Things Conveniently. There is no rule about which things go in which cabinet except that you should balance four factors: keeping like things together; putting heavy things lower and lighter things higher; keeping all foods away from heat (even canned foods; see chapter 12, "Bread and Honey"); and keeping things near the places where they will normally be used. The point of keeping like with like is to make things easier to find, to retrieve, and to replace: put all canned goods together; do the same with dry staples such as sugar, flour, and salt. Experienced people often store things in the following ways, but you may have reasons not to:

Glasses and china usually go in overhead cabinets near the sink and dishwasher. This is to make them easy to reshelve after washing up. Glasses are often placed directly over the sink so that you can reach for one to get a drink of tap water. Some people set cups, glasses, and other pieces upside down so that they do not collect dust. See also chapter 44, "China and Crystal," pages 546, 548, on how to store fine china.

Flatware usually goes in a drawer either near the dishwasher, for easy replacing after washing, or near the table, for easy table-setting.

Serving and cooking dishes and bowls are usually placed together in a cabinet of their own or on two or three shelves of their own.

Some people have both kitchen china and kitchen glassware, for less formal meals and snacks, which is stored in the kitchen as described above, and fine china and glassware or crystal that gets stored in a china cabinet, which is usually in the dining room or may be built in, as with a butler's pantry. A china cabinet is placed to be convenient for display and for setting the table in the dining room. Good silver or other tableware is kept in a chest of drawers or the sideboard in the dining room, for ease in setting the table there. The sideboard, if it has drawers, may also contain table linens, cloths, napkins, underliners, occasional dishes, silver serving dishes. Silver is properly displayed in glass-doored cabinets, but it will tarnish faster this way than if wrapped in tarnish-retarding cloths and kept out of sight. So display it only if you have either the time to polish or help with the polishing.

Most kitchens have one or more utensil drawers near the stove so that you can reach for what you need quickly while you are cooking. Every kitchen needs one or more drawers for linens. Kitchen linens include dish-drying towels, dish-washing cloths, potholders, cheesecloth (used for cooking and miscellaneous purposes), and, where used in the kitchen, tablecloths, cloth napkins, and placemats. You can also hang some or all of your potholders for handy use, but be sure to keep them washed.

The best way I know of to store knives (those that you do not keep out on magnetic or other holders) is in shallow, wooden knife trays that are kept in drawers. Large, upright wooden block-style stands with holes in which different-sized knives can be inserted are difficult to clean. Crumbs and spatters get inside the deep holes and are all but impossible to get out.

Canned, bottled, and packaged foods can be stored in high or low cabinets, as suits you, with two qualifications. It is easier to store heavier things low and lighter things high; and heat rises. All foodstuffs, even canned and bottled ones, must be kept at cool to moderate temperatures. Try to keep these out of cabinets that adjoin the stove, refrigerator, or dishwasher, as these appliances generate heat. Experienced cooks will usually store in one cabinet, or together on one or more shelves, all baking goods (flours, sugars, salt, baking powder), all spices and herbs, all condiments (nonrefrigerated oils, vinegars, Worcestershire sauce, molasses, soy sauce), all canned vegetables, fruits, fish or meats, and so forth.

Pots and pans can conveniently be placed near the stove, both because they can take the heat and because that is where you will want to use them. Generally, because they are heavy, you will want to place them in lower rather than overhead cabinets.

Every working kitchen has an assortment of cooking aids and utensils of awkward sizes and shapes: colanders, strainers, peelers, sifters, cooking thermometers, salad spinners, rolling pins and pastry boards, measuring cups and spoons, and, in my own case, a few old plates and bowls that I keep specially for cooking purposes (for getting tastes, mixing up cornstarch and water, or stacking chopped things on until it is time to put them in the soup) and never use for food service. It works well to keep all such things together, putting some in a cabinet and some in a drawer, depending upon their size. These should be near your most important food preparation surfaces—where you will be mixing, cutting, and so forth—or near the stove, where they also get much use.

Many households establish a small miscellany drawer in the kitchen—everyone calls it the junk drawer—which holds all the little things that you do not know what to do with: rubber bands, corks, stray paper clips, popsicle sticks, string, package-carrying handles, unidentified widgets that you think you had better hang on to. These are messy drawers full of fascination to children, who can spend hours making strange machines out of their contents.

Customarily, cleaning materials, soaps, and detergents are stored under the sink. This is good practice with two exceptions. When there are infants or young children in the house, nothing potentially harmful or toxic should be stored in an accessible low cabinet, and all cleaning materials, toxic and not, should be stored in childproof cabinets. Second, no detergents in granular form, especially dishwashing detergents, should be stored where they may be exposed to humidity or wetness, as they will cake and harden. If it is quite dry under your sink, however, they may be stored there.

Basic Kitchen Equipment

I know of someone whose entire adulthood, from age twenty-one on, seems to have been spent in moving from one place to another. When she gets to a new home, she immediately opens her packed box of kitchen utensils and pulls out her favorite large stirring spoon, which her mother gave her when she set up her first kitchen; the spoon helps reconcile her to having to start all over and makes her feel at home. So pick your kitchen equipment well, and when your children leave home to set up their own kitchens, you will have a sufficiently evocative spoon to give them to help create the spirit of home wherever they go.

Almost everyone needs the same basic ensemble of kitchen gear. Beyond the basics, you should add to your kitchen equipment as your tastes and habits suggest. You don't need tablecloths if you have no kitchen table. If you make Chinese food, you will want a wok; if you diet, a food scale; pizza makers need a pizza stone. If you like to make soups, fresh juice, or fresh pasta, an extra-large and fine stockpot, an electric juicer, or a pasta machine might be high on your list. Beginners do best to choose multifunction tools and buy specialized things only when they feel sure they will need them often. It is all too easy to end up with drawers or cabinets full of expensive, fancy gadgets that are never used.

Choose plastic or wooden utensils for nonstick cookware that requires them. Manufacturers of some new types of nonstick ware advertise that they can be used with metal utensils. Ask carefully, and read labels, when you purchase anything of this kind. Choose all your equipment with thought about how well it functions, how hard it is to care for, and how long it will last. Your cooking character develops in tandem with your tools: you learn to do it in the way your equipment allows, and you do not learn anything that you cannot try for lack of necessary tools.

Kitchen Linens

Basic Kitchen Linens

Tablecloths and napkins for a kitchen table, if any (for as many days per week as you use them)

1 dozen drying or tea towels (3–4 of these should be linen for glass, crystal, and good china)

1 dozen dishcloths or "dishrags"

6 potholders

2–3 pieces of cheesecloth for cooking, straining (keep separate from cheesecloth used for cleaning)

2–3 aprons that cover at least from midchest to midthigh

Assorted kitchen rags (see pages 105–6, "Different Kinds of Rags, Cloths, and Towels"): 6 large old towels or pieces of terrycloth for big spills; 6 smaller rags, for dirty jobs and smaller spills and a rag bag, box, or drawer to keep them in

See chapter 18, "Fabrics That Work," on selecting good kitchen linens.

The Kitchen Desk

Even if your kitchen desk, like mine, is a drawer and a tabletop, you still need a few basic desk materials in it for jotting down lists, recipes, and notes and for doing minor arithmetic.

Basic Desk Equipment

Writing paper

Pens and pencils

Pencil sharpener

Handheld calculator (optional)

Kitchen Utensils, Equipment, and Knives

With most tools, you get what you pay for; the best things are the costly ones. Kitchenware has recently begun to include exceptions to this rule, as there seem to be more and more eye-catching, highly designed kitchenware items that work poorly even though they are ridiculously costly. Choose sturdy materials: high-quality plastics, stainless steel, and wood. Knives present a special case; see pages 94–98.

Replace can openers when they are dull. Replace chopping boards when they chip, splinter, or develop grooves. Replace anything wooden when it becomes warped or rough or begins to split. Use everything until it simply doesn't work.

Basic Utensils

1 or 2 manual can openers (even if you also have an electric one)

"church key"–style bottle opener

corkscrew

2 large stirring spoons

slotted spoon

6 wooden spoons of assorted sizes and shapes (a couple with very long handles)

large fork

soup ladle

rubber spatula or scraper

1 or 2 pancake turners

mechanical eggbeater

large strainer

small strainer

colander

vegetable steamer

potato or vegetable peeler

wire whisk

potato masher

mortar and pestle

kitchen shears (sharpen when dull)

grater

citrus-fruit juicer

pepper mill

4–6 storage jars, light-proof and airtight

6 or more tight-lidded plastic refrigerator/freezer storage tubs (in all sizes)

funnel

tongs

1–2 scoops

skewers

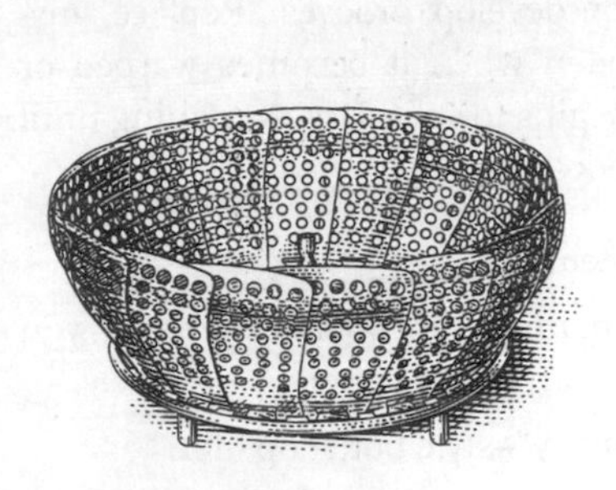

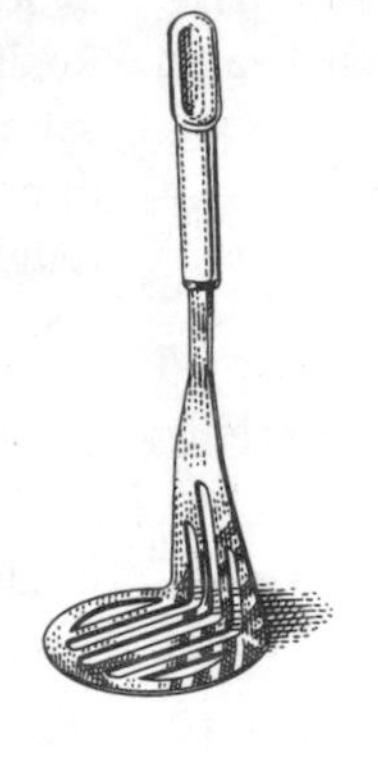

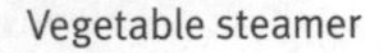

Vegetable steamer

Potato masher

Mortar and pestle

tea infuser

2 or 3 plastic chopping boards

grinder or food mill (optional)

vegetable brush (optional)

fat separator (optional)

Basic Measuring Equipment

2 sets of measuring spoons

quart-sized or pint-sized glass measuring cup

cup-sized glass measuring cup

set of nesting cups (for dry measuring)

coffee measure

meat thermometer

candy thermometer

all-purpose quick-read cooking thermometer

refrigerator/freezer thermometers

timer

Basic Small Appliances

portable electric mixer and/or full-size electric mixer

toaster or toaster oven (especially useful if you have no microwave oven)

blender and/or food processor

coffee grinder (optional)

coffeemaker (optional)

Basic Dishwashing Equipment

dishwashing tub or plastic sink liner

draining mats

dish-drying rack

nylon mesh scrapers for nonstick and enameled cookware

metal scratchers for pots, pans, utensils

bottle brushes

dishcloths or sponges and dishtowels

Basic Kitchen Cutlery

5" all-purpose utility knife

3" paring knife

8–9" chef's knife

long slicing (carving) knife and/or boning knife

long serrated knife (optional)

sharpening steel and knife-honing stone or electric honer

Note on Knives and Knife Sharpeners. If you are going to cook, you need a couple of really sharp knives. Good knives are expensive. When shopping for a good knife, heft

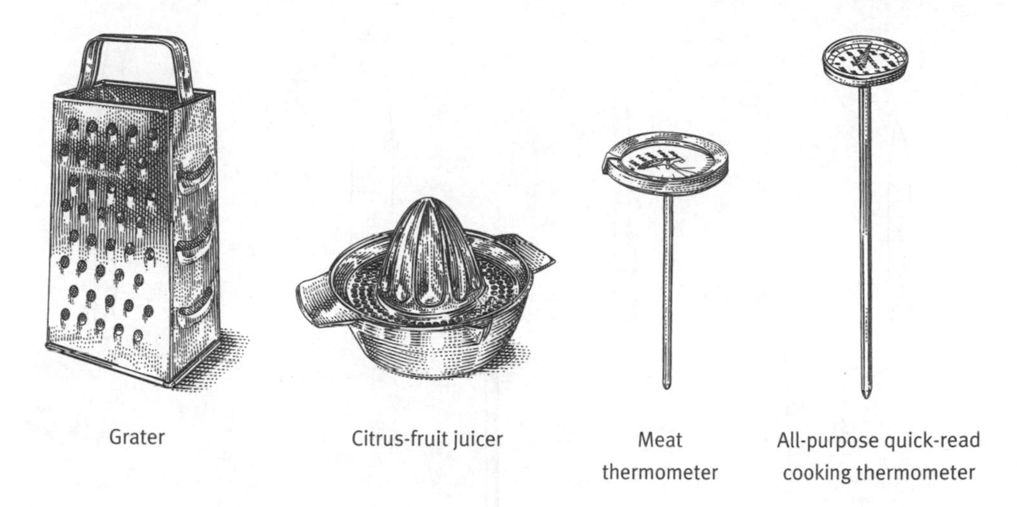

Grater

Citrus-fruit juicer

Meat thermometer

All-purpose quick-read cooking thermometer

the knife in your hand to see if you like the feel of it, because what one person finds comfortable the next might not. Rather than buying a set, it is more practical first to buy one knife made by a particular manufacturer and see how you like it over a period of use. If you are delighted with it, then, and only then, should you think about buying other pieces from the same maker. You might try a friend's knives, too, to see how you like knives made by other manufacturers. If you are on a budget, use inexpensive stainless steel knives until you can invest in good ones. Good knives will last for what is always said to be "a lifetime." That may be a bit exaggerated in some cases. But you really should get twenty or thirty years' good use out of a knife, if you take care of it. Keep all good knives out of the dishwasher.

Stainless Steel vs. Carbon Steel. The best kind of knife—at least what most reliable experts consider the best kind of knife and what all good stores nowadays will offer you as their best—is a good high-carbon stainless steel knife, one that you have to sharpen but that does not rust. These knives will always look bright and shiny. Because they contain less carbon than the old rust-prone carbon steel knives (discussed below), they are harder and hold their edges better. Although in theory they can be rendered just as sharp as carbon steel knives, ordinary people in their homes are probably not going to be skilled enough to get them as sharp as they might be. These high-carbon stainless knives do not hold flavors the way carbon steel knives do.

My favorite knives, however, are carbon steel, the kind that rust and spot. Carbon steel (.01 tool steel) is softer than stainless steel, which means that these knives are easier to sharpen. The average person in his or her home can make these very sharp, and this is why I like them best. But carbon steel, being soft, also requires sharpening and steeling more often; it does not hold its edge. Carbon steel knives rust readily and soon stop looking new and shiny. They also seem to hold food flavors much more than harder metals and to pass them on to the next food; I have more than once gotten garlic- or onion-flavored potato or fruit slices as a result of using my carbon steel paring knife. (Rub a lemon slice over it to get rid of the lingering flavors and rinse and dry thoroughly.) They can leave rusty marks not only on towels but on apples and other light-colored foods. If you have these knives, be sure to wash them by hand and dry them carefully.

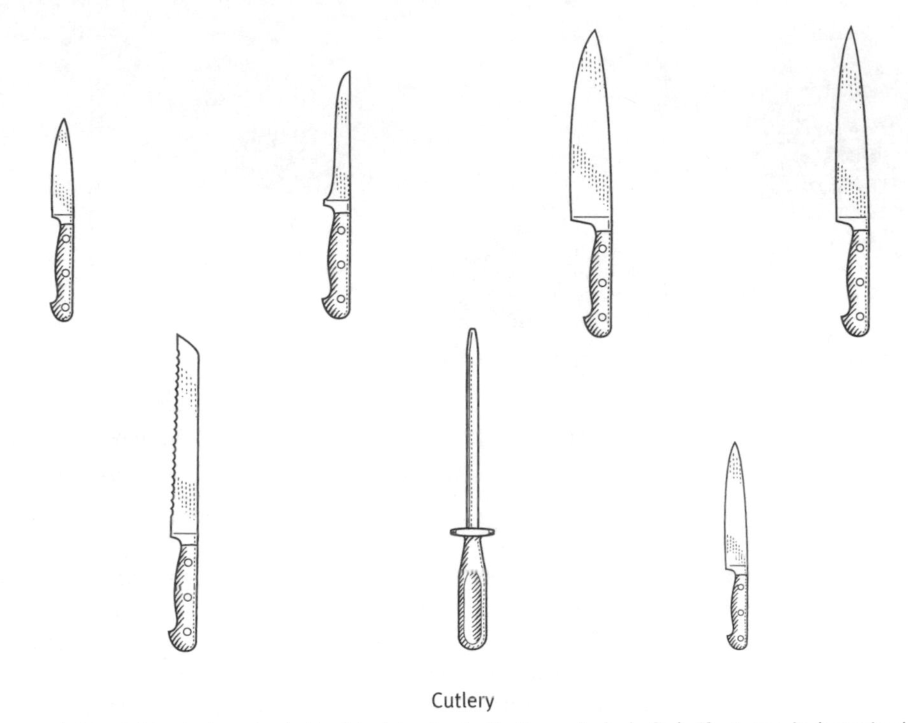

Cutlery

Top row, left to right: 3-inch paring knife, 6-inch boning knife, 8- or 9-inch chef's knife, 8- or 9-inch carving knife
Bottom row, left to right: Serrated knife, sharpening steel, 5-inch utility knife

Some people put oil on them after drying to protect against rust. I do not care for this idea, but if you do, use some flavorless oil (other than olive oil, which is too acidic). Like all good knives, carbon steel knives must *never* be put in the dishwasher and never left to soak. Besides growing dull more easily than other knives, they almost always have wooden handles that can be ruined, and they rust horribly in the dishwasher. I expect you are now dissuaded from using my favorite kind of knives, which in any event can be hard to find, although knife specialty stores sometimes carry them.

The least desirable knives are those that claim never to need sharpening. These are very hard, low-carbon stainless steel knives, which dull slowly because they are so hard. But they do grow dull; and when that happens you have to throw them away because they are too hard to sharpen. I do not find that they are terribly sharp to begin with. (Serrated knives, too, cannot be sharpened.)

Good knives are hand-forged and made of one piece. The bolster (the slightly thickened part between the functioning blade and the handle) is continuous with the rest of the blade; there is not one material inside and another out. Forged blades are better than stamped ones because the forging process arranges the molecules of the metal in such a way as to render it stronger. The tang of a good knife goes all the way back to the end of the handle, where you can see it at the seam. (This is called a "full tang," as opposed to a "partial tang.") The handle is riveted on, not glued. The handle on a good knife may be of wood or high-quality molded plastic. Wood feels best and is not so slippery but also does not last so long as high-quality plastics. (The dishwasher is ruinous to wooden and glued-on handles.)

Some people fear that wood knife handles develop cracks and crevices over time in which bacteria can hide and grow.

What Knives Are For. A "chef's knife" is used for chopping, dicing, mincing, and cutting. It has a point so you can pivot it and do assembly-line chopping jobs with a rocking motion. You cut food with this kind of knife on a chopping board.

Carving knives are used for getting thin, even slices of cooked meats and poultry.

Paring knives are for peeling, cutting, and trimming small items that you hold in your hand while you work, such as a potato or an apple.

Utility knives are for paring, cutting, and odd jobs.

Serrated knives, which require a sawing motion, work well for breads, cakes, fruits, and tomatoes. I prefer a sharp paring knife for fruits and vegetables, but if you have no really sharp one you will find the serrated edge helpful for breaking the skin of fruits.

A boning knife has a heavy blade that can conquer tough joints of meat and poultry, raw as well as cooked. It will also be used on fish. (A longer, narrower version, usually, is specifically recommended for fish.)

Which Knives? People have gotten more and more fetishistic about knives as they actually use them less and less. People who buy their skinless, boneless chicken already cut up for stir-frying still want a full complement of expensive kitchen knives displayed on their magnetic knife holders on the kitchen wall. Actually, you do not need many to start. Skilled and dedicated cooks with money for luxuries will find uses for a variety of special-function knives, but they can do a fine job without them too. Good stores typically suggest the set of four to six knives listed on page 94. You could actually get along with the first three or just the second and third, but then you would often not have tools for two people to work side by side.

This "beginner's set" is precisely what my family had for its advanced set all through my childhood. We had two "paring" knives—a bigger one (a utility knife) and a smaller one—and two "butcher knives" (a chef's knife and a carving knife). When I got older, we finally acquired one serrated "bread knife," which we had done perfectly well without until we actually stopped making the crusty homemade bread on which it might have been used. If a farm family could get by with these, most families today could get by with half of them. (My father always had a large penknife for jobs outside the kitchen that required a knife.)

Using and Storing Knives. The ascendancy of stainless steel knives in American kitchens means that some people forget how dangerous sharp knives can be. They casually test the knife edge with a finger and store knives, blade up, in jumbled all-purpose drawers—or even jam them into the utensil holder in dishwashers where unsuspecting hands may blindly grope. In kitchens where people are serious about knives, that would cause frequently bloody fingers, because a properly sharp knife will cut at the barest touch. This is the secret of paper-thin, even slicing, well-carved birds and roasts, and lightning-quick chopping.

To keep knives from growing dull too quickly, keep them out of dishwashers. To keep the edge on your good kitchen knives keen, do not use them for odd jobs such as cutting tape or string or cardboard. Rather, keep a sturdy pocketknife, penknife, or "jobs" knife in a handy place for such chores. The USDA tells us that, for sanitary reasons, plastic chopping boards (in good condition, without grooves) are better than wood, but they make your knives dull faster than wood will. (See page 175.) Stone and stonelike surfaces are to be avoided. Try to use as little force as you can when you press down with your knives. Unnecessary force will dull and bend the sharp edge. If you keep your knives reasonably sharp, you will not be tempted to use too much force and bend or break the edge—or accidentally cut yourself by sawing away with all your might.

Knife-Sharpening. A dull knife does not necessarily have a blunt edge. Typically the real problem is that the thin, sharp edge is bent over from pressure applied during use. Sometimes the edge breaks off. There are two things you do about this, and both require a bit of skill and knowledge. You can unfold or straighten the edge out again, or, especially if the edge can't be unfolded or is broken, you can create a new edge.

The first type of sharpening, unfolding the edge, should be done every time you use a knife, and, on a long, hard job, occasionally in the course of it. This is called "steeling," and you do this with a sharpening steel, the long, rounded metal stick, perhaps covered with vertical grooves, that you see sold with knife sets. If you have seen butchers or your grandfather rubbing two knife blades against each other before beginning a job, you have seen essentially the same procedure.

In the second type of sharpening, called "honing," you actually grind away part of the metal of your knife to sculpt a new edge, using a whetstone or sharpening or grinding stone or a knife-sharpening machine. This you do infrequently, only when steeling begins to fail to give you a keen edge. Not all knife edges are alike, however, even if they are initially equally sharp. Depending upon their shape, they may be more or less vulnerable to breaking and folding in the future. Thus sharpening a knife can sometimes make matters worse, not better.

Taking your knives to a professional sharpener is best, but there are not many of these around. Stores that specialize in selling knives will usually offer this service. Home knife sharpeners can eat up your knives or produce edges that are not shaped properly for strength and endurance; and they can be expensive. Only a reputable retailer specializing in cutlery will be able to tell you what is best and instruct you in its careful use. (Some stones must be wet with water when you use them, to prevent heat damage, or lubricated with an oil. Ask when you buy, or go to a knife store and ask.) The technology of home sharpeners is changing and improving, so find an up-to-date dealer. Your other choice, still best for those with the option, is to take your knives to a professional knife sharpener now and then.

You cannot actually make a new edge on serrated knives, but you can straighten their edges by steeling. When this no longer works, you have to discard them and get new ones.

Pots, Pans, and Bakeware

The basic set of pots and pans described below enables you to roast, simmer, fry, stir-fry, steam, braise, and stew, to make almost any pasta or rice dish, to make soups, and to cook vegetables of all sorts in most common styles. If you wish to make cakes, pies, breads and quick breads, cookies, muffins, or other oven-baked pastries, you will also need a set of basic baking utensils.

Basic Set of Pots and Pans

4–5" skillet

8–10" skillet (cast iron or with nonstick coating, or one of each)

large 8–12 quart stockpot (also for cooking pasta) (stainless steel with aluminum core)

2–3 saucepans of assorted sizes (stainless steel with aluminum core, or 1 or 2 with nonstick coating): 1/2, 2 1/2, and 4 1/2 quart

large lidded enameled cast-iron casserole or dutch oven

large roasting pan with rack

anodized aluminum sautéing pan

coffeepot/coffeemaker (see chapter 7, "Stimulating Beverages")

teakettle (whistling type)

teapot (ceramic, glass, silver, or silver plate)

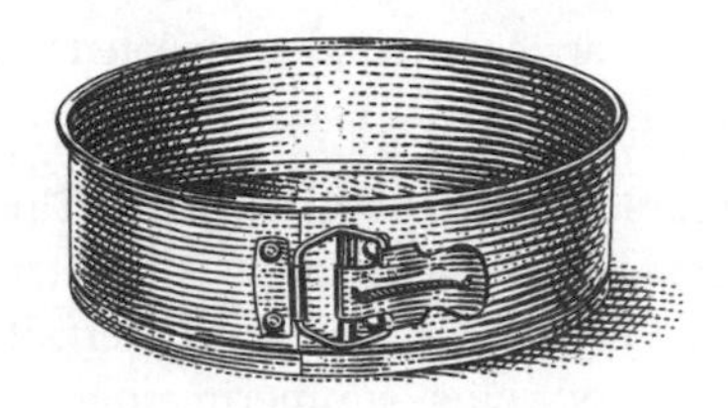

Springform pan

Basic Bakeware

2 round 8" or 9" cake pans

2 9" or 10" pie pans

1 or 2 loaf pans (9×5 or 10×4)

1 or 2 square cake pans (8×8 or 9×9)

rectangular cake pan (13×9)

set of 3 graduated-size mixing bowls (glass or stainless steel)

1–2 muffin pans

2 cookie sheets

rolling pin

flour sifter (large)

8×2 or 8×3 springform cake pan (optional)

pastry board (marble is best; wood is cheaper and works fine)

Know Your Materials

Before choosing cookware, learn what materials are available and what their characteristics are. Each material presents tradeoffs; you will have to determine which type is best for you. A brief summary of materials commonly used for cookware may be found on pages 100–102. Refer to chapter 9, "Kitchen Culture," for general instructions on cleaning cookware.

If a material is a good *heat conductor,* it heats or cools rapidly, and it will be responsive. You need a good conductor, for example, when you want to bring something rapidly to a boil and then cool it suddenly. Some materials are heat-retentive; they hold the heat rather than cooling off quickly. Different materials also conduct heat more evenly or less evenly. If a material conducts heat unevenly, hot spots may form that could burn a sauce. Flimsy, lightweight pots and pans will not distribute heat so evenly as heavier ones.

Your cookware should perform whatever function you intend it for and at the same time be as *inert* or *nonreactive* as possible; it should not change the taste, odor, color, or chemical composition of your food, and it should certainly not contaminate it with any dangerous substance. We have all heard how the Romans poisoned themselves by storing and cooking food in pottery that contained lead, and you have surely experienced food that has picked up a metallic taste from a can, pot, or container. No cookware is absolutely inert, but some types are nearly so. Choose the most inert cooking materials—such as enameled or nonstick surfaces or stainless steel—for acidic foods or for foods such as soups, stews, and stocks, which you will simmer or cook for a long time. For storing foods in the refrigerator or freezer, plastic or glass containers are best.

Do not forget the importance of handles. Metal handles can go in the oven and the dishwasher (if the pot can). If they are not the stay-cool type, can you live with them? Some good pots lack stay-cool handles. Cheap plastic handles can melt, but more costly good ones won't. Wood handles will not get so hot as many metal ones, but they can scorch or wear out, and are destroyed in the dishwasher. Carefully examine how handles are attached to make sure that the construction is strong. Screw-on handles break or come off more often than do one-piece metal handles or riveted-on handles.

Some people think you shouldn't put any good pots in the dishwasher. They are right that the dishwasher is hard on everything. Even "dishwasher-safe" metals are stressed, dulled, and worn by the contrasts of heat and cold, friction, and strong detergent in the average dishwasher. Others advise you to go ahead and put in your aluminum and stainless steel pots and pans—if they have metal handles. They are right that such cookware will probably survive the abuse for a long, long time, even if it does not look so pretty as it would have otherwise. The decision is yours. Remember that plastic and wood handles are the most likely to be harmed.

Consider the requirements of your stove also. Electric stoves and flat-top stoves require heavier, flat-bottomed pans that will cover the heating element evenly and will not dent or warp. If you have an induction cooking unit, which operates by using a magnetic field to transfer heat, you must use iron. Cast iron and enameled cast iron will work. Steel or stainless steel pots and pans are suitable for induction cooking units only if they are magnetic, but sometimes they are not. (Check their labels or call the retailer or manufacturer.) You cannot use glass or ceramic cookware, copper, or aluminum on induction cooking units. In microwaves, you cannot use metals (or china with gold and silver decorations) or materials that might melt or contaminate the foods, as some plastics will. Glass, plastics labeled microwave-safe, most food-safe ceramics, and china with no metallic decorations or metal-laced glazes are all acceptable.

Glass. All glass cookware is highly inert. Most glass cookware (*not* ordinary glass tableware and *not* crystal) is suitable for microwaving and freezing as well as baking. Most glass cookware is not suitable for stovetop cooking or any type of cooking that puts it in direct contact with a flame or heat source, but some is. Follow your manufacturer's instructions on safe use and care, and keep them for future reference. Glass cookware retains heat well but conducts it poorly and thus may cook foods unevenly. Its breakability is another potential problem. Its transparency, however, can be fun and useful too. It is ideal for coffeepots and good for pie pans and other bakeware. It is generally dishwasher safe, but always develops a dull, scratched appearance after repeated washing in the dishwasher.

Enameled Cast-Iron Cookware. This type of cookware is naturally stick-resistant and its enameled surface is highly inert. It is excellent for stewing, simmering long-cooking dishes, and braising; it is poor for browning. It conducts heat slowly and holds heat. However, it tends to nick or chip and wear away. Some manufacturers say you can put it in the dishwasher unless it has wooden handles or some other destructible part. My opinion is that this wears it out much faster.

Cast Iron. Cast iron is exceedingly heavy, which means it never dents, bends, or warps, and it lasts a long time. The usual phrase "a lifetime" is, for once, no exaggeration; cast iron lasts for several lifetimes and gets passed from grandparent to parent to child. It is quite cheap. It heats and cools slowly but evenly. (In fact, it cools so slowly that I have occasionally burned myself on the handle of a cast-iron skillet long after it was removed from the heat.) It is excellent for browning and, as it ages, it turns dark brown or black and becomes more and more naturally resistant to sticking. Cast iron rusts if you are not careful, and rust can discolor foods. (Cast iron cannot go in the dishwasher and should not be soaked, but it can go into the oven.) It tends to leach iron into foods, particularly acidic foods (i.e., it is somewhat reactive), and can give them a metallic taste. This sometimes matters aesthetically, but it is not a health problem except for those who must avoid iron. It can even help people with iron-deficiency anemia. It should not be used for deep-fat frying because the iron accelerates the chemical processes that cause rancidity in cooking fats.

Stainless Steel. Stainless steel is the least reactive of the metals used for pots and pans. High-grade cookingware of stainless steel is made of iron, 18 percent chromium, and 10 percent nickel. (This is what 18/10 means.) Unlike iron, stainless steel does not rust or tarnish, but acid or salt left on it long enough will begin to corrode it. For this reason, it can be discolored by mustard, mayonnaise, vinegar, and lemon juice that are left standing on it for long periods. Like iron, stainless steel does not warp or dent, and retains a good flat bottom. It is fairly heat-retentive, but not so much as cast iron.

Stainless steel heats slowly and unevenly and gets hot spots. Therefore, stainless steel pots are often made with an aluminum inner core or copper bottom for better, more even heating. What some people (myself among them) regard as the very best pots now available are made of stainless steel with an aluminum core. This combination gets you the good conductivity and even heating of aluminum (see "Unanodized Aluminum," below) plus the nonreactivity and the resistance to warping and denting of steel.

Stainless steel is fairly easy to clean and is generally regarded as dishwasher-safe so long as it has metal handles. But some manufacturers advise you to keep their stainless steel products out of the dishwasher; check the care instructions for yours.

Copper. Copper has the highest heat conductivity of all the metals used for pots and pans, which means it both heats and cools quickly and is highly responsive. Thus it has been favored for making delicate sauces and other cooking that calls for great precision. It is expensive.

Copper tarnishes, is readily reactive with many foods, especially acidic ones, and can make you quite sick if you take in too much. So copper is not used alone for cookware; copper pots and pans are lined with tin or stainless steel. When they are lined with tin, they may have to be relined when the tin begins to wear down, which is a somewhat expensive proposition. To have this done, go to any good kitchenware store. It will either do the work or refer you to someone who will.

Copper bowls are desirable for beating egg whites stiff because the copper ions they put out help prevent the foam from deflating and help make it creamy. (You won't get sick from the small amount of copper that you take in from the bowl.)

Copper kitchenware is definitely not for you if you are short on time. It requires polishing, and you will not be able to put it in the dishwasher.

Unanodized Aluminum. Aluminum conducts heat almost as rapidly as copper but not evenly, which means you can burn foods in it. But it is highly responsive. It can dent or warp because it is not so strong and hard as iron or steel. Its light weight, however, is often highly convenient. Unanodized aluminum is somewhat reactive with foods, especially acidic ones such as tomato-based dishes or those that contain wine or fruit, sauerkraut, vinegar. It is also reactive with salty foods. Aluminum can heighten the sulfur flavor and cooking odor of cruciferous vegetables such as cabbage, broccoli, and brussels sprouts. It can discolor acidic foods or egg-based foods. If you store salty or acidic foods in aluminum pots (or touching aluminum foil), aluminum will leach out into the food and surface pitting may even occur on the pots.

According to the Food and Drug Administration, there is no evidence that ingesting aluminum is harmful. Aluminum pots and pans came under suspicion some years back as a result of the hypothesis that Alzheimer's disease was caused by the ingestion of excess amounts of aluminum. This theory is no longer taken seriously, and aluminum cookware is back in favor. However, it is true that aluminum cookware releases aluminum into food and that in some cases this tends to result in off-flavors and colors. And even if it does not cause Alzheimer's and even if we get far more aluminum naturally in our foods and in over-the-counter medicines such as antacids, this is no good reason to feed yourself still more aluminum derived from your cookpots. Thus you might consider not using aluminum pots for stock, soups, stews, and other long-cooking dishes, for acid foods (such as those containing citrus juices, tomatoes, vinegar, or wine) or salty foods, or for food storage. For the latter purposes, stainless steel, glass, enameled cookware, and plastic or glass storage containers are better choices.

You can usually put this type of metal pot in the dishwasher, unless its handles cannot take it, but always check the manufacturer's instructions. Alkaline substances such as strong detergents or ammonia can darken or mar it. See page 113.

Anodized Aluminum. This is a stick-resistant surface, but it is so extremely hard that it is genuinely long-lasting. Some manufacturers even say that you can use metal utensils on it and that if you find marks that look like scratches after doing so, they are actually just metal deposits from the metal utensils. They'll come off if you use a special cleaner designed for anodized aluminum pots, such as Dormónd. My anodized aluminum pot, however, most definitely is scratched by metal utensils and should only be used with wooden or plastic utensils. Be sure to check the manufacturer's instructions for your own. Anodizing is a process that thickens the oxide film that naturally forms on the surface of aluminum, hardening it and making it more scratch-resistant. Some anodized aluminum pots are also treated with a nonstick coating, which is said to be quite durable. Anodized aluminum is highly inert and reacts less with food than does regular aluminum. But even anodized aluminum will react if food is stored in it for long periods. Using it for food storage is not recommended. Keep it out of the dishwasher or it will discolor.

Nonstick Substances. Nonstick substances are highly inert, but they wear and scratch, exposing the next layer of the pot, which is usually aluminum or steel. (The general cooking properties of the pots are those of the underlying metal.) Newer nonstick coatings are much more durable than those of the first generation, but most still require you to use plastic or wooden utensils, which suggests that they should still be regarded as vulnerable. Some are made with the same material as Teflon pans, except with more coatings, which results in greater durability. Some of them release fumes when heated to extremely high temperatures, so observe the manufacturer's instructions on use and care. Nonstick pots and pans are considered healthy both from the standpoint of their nonreactivity and because they permit you to reduce your use of fats and oils. To many people, these are far more important characteristics than the convenience of easy cleaning, which is not always all it is cracked up to be. Manufacturers generally recommend against putting nonstick cookware in the dishwasher.

Tin. Some copperware is lined with tin, but otherwise it is rarely used in cookware; it is soft, wears away, and has a low melting point. See "Copper," above. Tin is less reactive than copper, but it reacts with some foods. It can cause gastrointestinal illness if too much is taken in. This used to occur when certain foods were stored in their tin cans after opening.

9

Kitchen Culture

Good kitchen habits . . . Cleaning up as you go . . . Restoring the kitchen after each use . . . Kitchen manners . . . Different sets of rags, cloths, and towels for different purposes . . . Hand-washing the dishes . . . Scraping and stacking . . . Disposing of oily and wet food remnants . . . Order in which dishes are washed . . . Removing burned-on material . . . Rinsing, draining . . . Hand-drying vs. air-drying . . . Odors adherent to dishes and pots . . . Using an automatic dishwasher . . . What cannot go in the machine . . . Cleaning kitchen appliances

The kitchen is the most complicated room in the house, with its powerful machines for cooling, heating, washing, grinding, and beating; its water supply and faucets, sinks and drains; its foodstuffs—hot, cold, wet, dry, sour, and sweet. These capacities make the kitchen feel alive and make it attractive to living things, not only ourselves but also various undesirable creatures, including furry, six-legged, odorous, and microscopic ones. To keep its systems operating at their best and to avoid sharing your kitchen with other forms of life, you have to tend it several times a day. If you don't, it lets you know you have neglected it by malfunctioning in unpleasant ways. If you do, it hums, looks and smells inviting, and fulfills your contradictory wishes for things that are wet and dry, hot and cold, clean and messy. When you finally achieve a modus vivendi with your kitchen, you have been acculturated. You have learned a way of life.

Kitchen Habits

Some people may be strangers to the cultu of the kitchen, unfamiliar with the rhythr of giving a kitchen daily care because t have had nothing to do with one until t find themselves in charge of one. For t sakes, I include the following basic info tion on living with and in a kitchen in that results in a center for the home that is fresh and sweet, orderly, safe, and functional.

Clean Up the Kitchen as You Cook. A good cook usually cleans and neatens while cooking, finding time to clean while food is stewing or simmering. He or she tries to wipe the counter down frequently and sanitize the chopping board between uses; clean up the peels or crumbs or spills; when possible, he or she washes, dries, and puts away (or puts in the dishwasher) dishes, pots, pans, and utensils that are finished with or puts them to soak so they will be easy to clean when the time comes. Not only does this make the final cleanup easier, the cooking itself is more pleasant. When you are cooking something complicated, there is nothing like being surrounded by towering heaps of food-encrusted bowls and pots to give you a panicky feeling. But, of course, a kitchen in use looks used. It is strewn with dishes that are out of place, sticky pots, heaps of chopped foods, piles of peels, dripping utensils, and other signs of healthy life.

Clean up kitchen spills, wherever they are, immediately—in the refrigerator or on the floor, stove, or countertop. Otherwise hey are harder to clean up, can cause acci- nts, and can cause cross-contamination of ds. As part of this clean-as-you-go process, r leave foods out of the refrigerator for a te longer than necessary. This will help the chances both of spoilage and of tal cross-contamination. See chapter Food." Before you sit down to a meal, put away all foods used in n so that nothing spoils. Then st of the last-minute mess until ished eating. You may wish to vers from dinner before enjoy- coffee or tea so that you feel long as you want.

Restore the Kitchen to Its Order and Cleanliness. nup consists of returning the kitchen to order. Your goal is to prevent spoilage and the growth of dangerous or unpleasant microorganisms, to prevent stale or rotten odors, to create clean-feeling and clean-looking surfaces throughout the kitchen, and to preserve neatness and orderliness. This means getting rid of all traces of cooking and eating. Do this soon after every meal or chaos will arrive with amazing speed. It is especially important that this be done before you go to sleep.

First, safely store away all foods.

Second, wash, dry, and put away all dishes, pots, pans, flatware, and utensils. See "Washing the Dishes," below.

Third, do a general wipe-down. Sinks, drains, counters, table, and stovetops should be washed clear of any food or greasy film and debris, and should be wiped dry. Pot scratchers and similar cleaning materials should be thoroughly washed with hot, sudsy water until clear of food debris, then left to drain dry. Depending upon what you have been cooking, you may wish to soak these cleaning materials in a bleach solution for sanitizing. Be sure to sanitize chopping boards as necessary. (Chapter 13 explains how to sanitize in the kitchen.) Wipe fingerprints off doors and handles, and wipe chairs or stools clean, if necessary.

In the evening, take out the trash and clean up the trash can. Wash the trash can during weekly cleaning. Each night wipe it free of any spills or crumbs, dry it out, and line it with a fresh lining bag. Keeping trash as dry as possible is most important. Drain foods before putting them into the trash. If you are discarding spoiled or moldy food, secure it tightly in an opaque plastic bag and make sure that the trash can is tightly lidded. (This helps ensure that children and animals are not tempted to get into it.) Be aware of the recycling laws in your area. (See chapter 64, "Poisons, Hazardous Substances, and Proper Disposal of Hazardous Household Wastes.") Cans and bottles should be rinsed out before recycling. Flatten cardboard cartons and crush boxes to compact them. Many districts require that you tie up old newspapers with string or twine for recycling.

Run hot water down the drain or pour baking soda or a bleach-and-water solution down the drain to freshen it up and forestall odors developing in the night. If cooking liquid from fish or cabbage or the liquid from a can of tuna or something else that produces strong odors has been poured down the drain, you must be sure to flush the drain out thoroughly or the kitchen will be malodorous in the morning. Put wiping cloths in the laundry (but first hang wet ones to dry), and hang out fresh towels and wiping materials. If you use a tablecloth, change it for the morning. The last step of the cleanup is sweeping the floor.

Finally, update your list of food or supplies that are low or exhausted, based on what you may just have used or noticed.

Good Kitchen Manners. Do not place food directly on any surface that you would not eat from. Generally speaking, foods should not be prepared directly on countertops or tabletops, as this creates hazardous opportunities for cross-contaminating foods with microorganisms. It is far safer to place food only on serving or cooking plates, dishes, pots, or pans, on chopping or preparing boards, or in drainers, colanders, and the like. Purses, briefcases, toys, and other objects that are often set on the floor or the ground should be kept off kitchen tables and counters. Pets, too, must be kept off tables and countertops.

The kitchen sink should be almost entirely reserved for chores connected with foods and things that touch food. This is because germs in the sink can easily contaminate foods. For the most part, the kitchen sink is not for washing your face or hands. So many homes lack a laundry tub these days that it is tempting to hand-wash laundry in the kitchen sink, but this is not a good idea either. If you have no laundry tub or sink, use a portable plastic tub and empty it into the toilet. My Italian grandmother was extremely rigid about this. You were permitted to do nothing in the kitchen sink but wash foods and dishes. No matter how many extra steps it cost you, you had to go up to the bathroom or down to the cellar to wash your hands. The dog's dish had to be washed in the cellar, his water dish filled there. You could not empty a flower vase in the kitchen sink or even cut and arrange flowers there. My own procedure on washing my hands is to wash them outside the kitchen before I begin cooking. However, if my hands get floury, sticky, or wet with meat juices during the cooking, I wash them in the kitchen sink. Otherwise, I could hardly cook; I would be constantly running in and out of the kitchen. (I often wonder whether my grandmother managed to keep her hands cleaner when she cooked than I do.)

Different Kinds of Rags, Cloths, and Towels. Use separate cloths, rags, and towels for different kitchen purposes. Dishcloths are used for dishes, sinks, counters, and tabletops. Rags are used to wash the floors and clean up spills. Hand towels are used for drying people's hands. Dish towels are used for drying dishes. In addition, it is convenient to set aside some cloths, towels, or rags within each category to be used for very dirty jobs of that sort. For example, you can have some dishcloths that you use for very dirty pot-washing jobs or for mopping up nasty countertop spills; you can permit these to acquire stains. Give them vigorous laundering, but take no special measures if stains do not come out. Save other cloths or rags for lighter, cleaner jobs. Fine linen towels are reserved for chores that will not stain them—drying and polishing glasses, crystal, china, and silver.

Keep *plenty* of cloths and rags on hand for all your purposes. This is a most important point. If you have plenty of cloths, towels, and rags, you need never hesitate when you are working, washing down the counter or doing the dishes, to replace one if it becomes soiled or comes into contact with something that should not be spread around.

You can hang your kitchen rags, cloths, and towels to dry on a rack kept for that purpose, or you can hang them to dry on the side of a laundry basket. Launder your dish towels separately from rags you use for dirty jobs, such as floor-washing.

After any kitchen cleanup, remove the soiled linens and cloths and replace them with fresh ones.

For drying your hands in the kitchen, when you are cutting up raw chicken or meat or doing other chores that might leave pathogens on your hands, use paper towels rather than run the risk of leaving dangerous microorganisms on a hand towel that someone else will use before preparing the salad greens.

Dishwashing

Having grown up washing dishes, I am surprised to find that so many people have not been initiated into the mysteries of this ancient and ritual-laden art. My husband, an orderly, logical person who actually enjoys washing dishes, hadn't a clue about ordinary dishwashing procedures when I married him. He stacked dirty dishes and pots on both sides of the sink; he put washed ones down among the unwashed, rinsed ones among the unrinsed. He did not set dishes to drain; to this day he tends to let water pool in them. He still follows no particular order of washing; a glass might be washed after a skillet and before a plate, then another glass, then the paring knives, then a cup. He is not bothered by food particles that are hard to see or those that are on the outside of a bowl or pot. He tends to walk away from the job midway and return a couple of hours later, seeing no reason not to break it up. To me, this all seems something like heresy or insanity or the end of civilization. Traditional dishwashing rules are so ingrained in me that I could far more easily walk off and leave all the dishes unwashed than bring myself to wash glasses after skillets or mix washed and unwashed items on one side of the sink.

About Hand-Washing Dishes. No matter how high-tech and efficient your dishwasher may be, you need to know how to wash dishes by hand. When you're cooking and have soiled bowls, pots, or utensils that you need to use again immediately, you can't wait to run the machine; you must also know how to hand-wash all the things that cannot go into the machine. When the dishwasher is broken or too full, you have to hand-wash everything. And sometimes you want to hand-wash things because they seem too few to run the machine for and you do not want them to sit in the machine until it fills. If you do it properly, hand-washing produces safe and bright dishes.

Instructions appear below for washing by hand *all* the soiled dishes, glasses, flatware, serving dishes, pots, pans, and utensils created by an entire dinner. Most of the time, however, you have only a few things to wash by hand and the rest go in the dishwasher. Follow the same basic routine in either case.

However you wash the dishes, there are many good reasons for you to get them washed quickly. First, it's just easier and more pleasant. The sooner you do them, the easier they are to get clean and the sooner your kitchen looks inviting again. Food-laden dishes attract pests, get smelly, and grow bacteria, sometimes dangerous ones. Moreover, accidents happen more easily when the dishes are left half done; leftover food particles spill or drip where they shouldn't; dishes are left where they can be knocked over and broken; things that are needed are not ready for use. Use good hot water and detergent for washing, rinse thoroughly, and promptly put away clean, dry dishes. This is orderly, efficient, attractive, and the most effective way to keep your dishes free of microbial contamination.

Keeping Organized During and After the Meal: Avoid Delaying or Interrupting Eating. Although you try to wash as many things as you can while you are cooking, there are usually last-minute items that cannot be washed because dinner awaits you. If these look hard to clean, quickly scrape them off or pour off liquids or oils. Then fill them with plain hot water or, if they are greasy, hot sudsy water, and put them in the sink or on the stove over very low heat (the liquid should not boil) so they can soak while you are eating. Otherwise, food remnants will harden on them and make your washing job much harder. Be careful not to burn yourself on a hot pot; remember that if you put water into a hot cooking pan it may sizzle and splatter on you.

Sometimes you can begin the dinner cleanup and dishwasher loading in the interval between the main meal and coffee or dessert. Put the dinner plates, salad plates, and glasses in the dishwasher while the coffee drips or while people are chatting as they wait for dessert. But do only as much as you can without sacrificing a comfortable meal schedule.

Clearing, Collecting, and Preparing. When the meal is completely finished, your first priority is to put away foodstuffs *quickly*. After that is done, clear the table, stove, and counters completely, then carefully wash down and dry their top surfaces. When you are finished, none of your cooking, food-preparing, or eating surfaces should be damp, tacky, oily, or crumb-ridden (except, perhaps, the area where you have dirty dishes stacked for washing).

Scraping and Stacking. To ready things for washing, scrape food off all dishes, pots, pans, and utensils and rinse them, loading into the dishwasher everything that belongs there and stacking the rest on the counter to one side of the sink. (Some people like to set a draining mat under the dirty dishes.) Use a wooden or rubber spatula for scraping; for hard-to-remove food, use pot scratchers appropriate to the material you are cleaning—nylon for nonstick pans and china, and metal for cast iron—and work under running water. Pour fats and oils (and food waste if you have no garbage disposal) into a food-waste receptacle, not into the sink. Some people like to wipe oils out of pots and pans with paper towels.

Stack the dirty dishes, *like with like,* near the sink in the order in which they will be washed: glasses; silver or flatware; plates, bowls, cups and saucers; serving dishes; mixing dishes and bowls; and pots, pans, skillets, casseroles, and cooking utensils. Tradition calls for stacking on the right side of your sink (which is usually the dishwasher side), but left-handers, iconoclasts, and those with dishwashers placed elsewhere may choose the left.

Now do some preliminary muscle work on heavily soiled items and those you left soaking during the meal because they were covered with hard-to-remove or burned-on food. Get the major soil off using pot scratchers, brushes, abrasives, or whatever is effective and safe for the material. Then stack these, too, still damp and probably still oily or imperfectly clean, in their proper washing order beside your sink.

Setup: Rack, Mat, and Dishpan. On a clean countertop to the left of the sink, or opposite the side where you have set the dirty dishes, set a clean dish-draining rack on a draining mat, with the edge of the latter placed so that it drains into the sink. If you do not have a rack and mat, or you have only a few dishes, you can lay a clean, thick dish towel to catch drips. Or, if you have an empty and clean dishwasher, set the dishes to drain in there. But remember that if you use both racks, the top one will drip onto the bottom, so use just one rack or plan on less air-drying and more towel-drying.

Set up a place to rinse the dishes. Usually the other section of your double sink is best. If you do not have a double sink, place a rubber or plastic dishpan on one side of the sink and rinse on the other. (And by all means

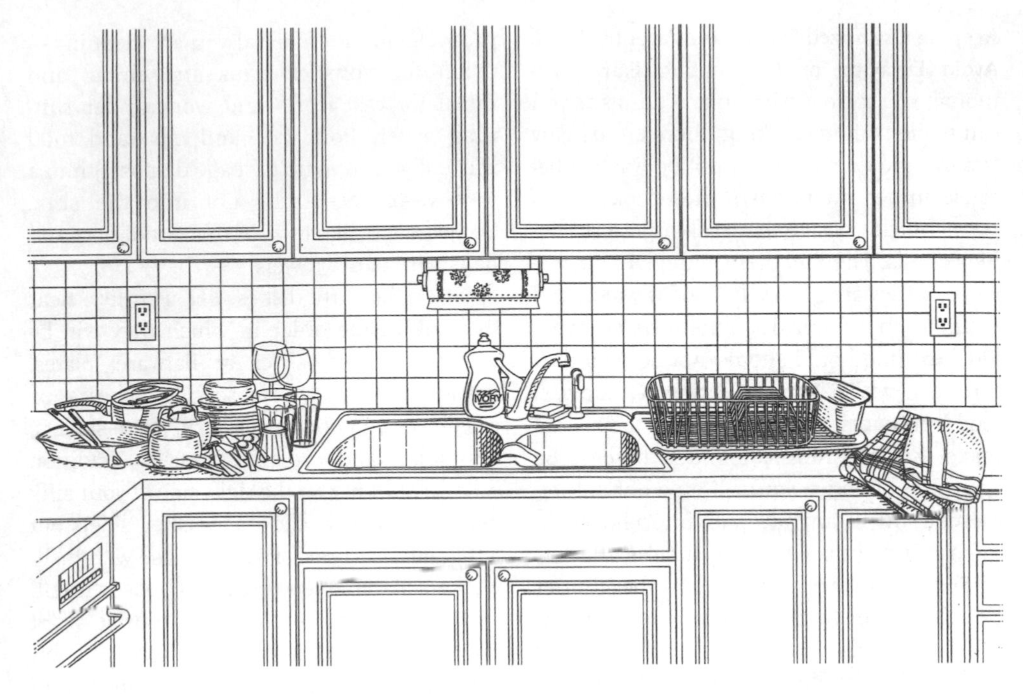

Dishes ready for washing by hand

DISPOSING OF OILY AND WET FOOD REMNANTS

Do not pour oils, fats, or liquids containing food remnants directly down the drain, and do not let crumbs or food particles wash down. (Small amounts of fats and oils can usually be sent through the garbage disposal with plenty of cold water. But check the manufacturer's instructions.) If you are emptying food liquids into the sink, be sure to use a drain filter or strainer basket or pour them into your garbage disposal. Otherwise you will eventually get clogged drains. Do not expect to see blockage tomorrow. It may take a year or even several for a block to develop, but it is a memorable and expensive event when it finally happens. Moreover, you may develop odorous and germ-filled drains in the short term, and this can make a kitchen really unpleasant, not to mention less safe. To deodorize drains, see chapter 42, "Pipes and Drains."

Those with garbage disposals, of course, will use the disposals for all their grindable wastes. People without garbage disposals can keep an old lidded can or container to receive food waste. Like most people in New York City, I do not have a garbage disposal (disposals were not legal here until recently), so I keep a small waste container lined with a leakproof plastic bag on the countertop beside the sink for fats, oils, scrapings, leftovers past their prime, dripping plastic from meat wrappings, paper towels used in food preparation and cleanup, and the contents of my sink drain basket. You'll find that the paper part of the waste absorbs liquids. Those with disposals can use a container of this kind for the portion of their food waste that cannot go into the disposal. When your mini–waste collector is filled, fasten the bag tightly and put it in your garbage can. When you are at home, you might fill it and change the liner two or more times each day, depending on what sort of day it is. The receptacle must be washed, relined, and left clean, dry, and empty each evening as part of your final cleanup.

CLEANING OFF BURNED OR BAKED-ON MATERIAL

To get off hard-to-remove, burned, or baked-on food debris, first remove all that you can with a wooden spoon or rubber spatula. Then try scrubbing with an abrasive pad, pot scratcher, or brush that is safe for your pot or pan. Do not use a harsh abrasive material on any surfaces that would be scratched or damaged. On nonstick enameled ware, anodized aluminum, ceramic, and glassware, nylon or plastic scrubbing pads are required. Other pots and pans can usually take metal scouring pads and steel-wool soaped scouring pads or other soaped scouring pads. Coarse metal scouring pads, when you can use them, are what work best for hard crusts. When you use an abrasive scrubbing pad, you can sprinkle some scouring powder on materials that will not be harmed. (There are specially formulated ones for stainless steel, copper, and other metals.) Check whether the scouring powder contains bleach and whether the bleach is safe for the material. On anything not made of aluminum, a little baking soda may help; on aluminum, try cream of tartar.

When these methods fail, try soaking (or more soaking). After scraping off all the soil that you can, soak the article in plain hot water or a detergent-and-hot-water solution; you can leave really hard problems soaking overnight. Alternatively, fill the pot or pan with a solution of detergent and water, and let the pot simmer on the stove until the material loosens. For especially hard jobs, try soaking in a solution of automatic dishwashing detergent and water according to the directions on page 114 below.

Caution: Do not soak good knives or any utensils that are made, wholly or in part, of wood, bone, ivory, or cast iron.

have a double or triple sink if you possibly can. It is among the most important of all kitchen conveniences.) If you do not use a dishpan, put in a protective rubber mat or line the sink with a towel to wash delicate glass and china.

Collect your dishcloths, sponges, pot scratchers, bottle brushes, and other preferred utensils. These should all be absolutely fresh and clean.

Fill your dishpan or sink no more than two-thirds full with water as hot as your hands can bear. This will be hotter than your bath water. It should be a bit uncomfortable to leave your hands in it for a sustained period. Wearing lined plastic gloves is better for your skin and enables you to use even hotter water. If the water begins to cool, run in a little more hot water.

Add dishwashing liquid at any time before you begin washing, enough to make the water feel slightly slippery and look moderately sudsy. You have enough if your dishes do not feel oily after washing and readily come clean. You have too much if they take forever to rinse. Pay attention to whether you have a "regular" or a concentrated "ultra" formula, or you can end up with gallons of suds.

Washing the Dishes. Begin with perfectly clean, hot, sudsy water. Wash the dishes that are least soiled first and progress to those that are most soiled, as this entails the fewest changes of water. As noted above, you usually begin with glass and silver or flatware, which need very hot water so that they dry quickly without streaks or spots. Real silver tarnishes, too, especially if you let salt or salty food stand on it, so you want to do it promptly.

Do not put oily or dirty items in with relatively clean ones such as water glasses. You will simply make the cleaner items dirtier and have to change the water sooner. Drain the dishpan or sink and get fresh water and detergent if the water becomes oily, if it is not sudsy enough, if it is too dirty with food waste, or if it is too cool.

To reduce the chances of breakage, wash like with like: glasses and plates are more likely to be broken by a heavy pot than by other glasses and plates. Do not overcrowd the dishpan or sink. When you are washing delicate or valuable pieces, do *one at a time.* (On washing fine china and crystal, see chapter 44, "China and Crystal.") If two glasses get stuck one inside the other, do not try to force them apart or they may break and cut you. Fill the inside glass with cold water (to make it contract), and stand the outer one in warm water for a couple of moments (to make it expand). Then gently part them.

Scrub the immersed items with a clean brush, dishcloth, dishmop or whatever other utensil is suitable for the item, removing all food remnants and oils, until it is absolutely clean. Bottle brushes are indispensable for bottles and vases that you cannot easily get your hand or a dishcloth into. Use a circular motion and gentle pressure on easy-to-remove dirt. Hard-to-remove soil often responds to a brisk back-and-forth motion, applied with much force. When your cleaning tool or cloth is dirty, get a fresh one. I prefer a cotton dishcloth with a waffle weave or some similar thick-and-thin weave. Its bumpy surface provides gentle rubbing power; you can scrunch it up to fit in tight places; you can rinse it clean easily; and you can feel food bumps through its thin places with your fingers and use your fingers and nails through it to rub bumps off. You can't do any of that with a brush or sponge. And a waffle weave is highly absorbent; it holds plenty of water. In the end, you have to use your hands to tell you if the dishes are clean; your eyes will not always find the residues or oiliness that your fingertips can.

As soon as your water feels oily or unclean or lacks suds, pour it out and run another tub or sinkful. Proceed in this fashion until all the items are washed.

Wash the dishes promptly; don't let them sit for long periods in dishwater that is growing tepid. Don't wash dishes in their soaking liquids. Pour this off and wash them in fresh hot, sudsy water.

To remove coffee and tea stains on china, plastic, and glassware, soak the items for five to ten minutes in a solution of one tablespoon regular chlorine bleach to a gallon of water (or slightly less than one teaspoon per quart). Then rinse and dry.

Note that those who insist that hand dishwashing is unsanitary would be right if it were done with lukewarm water filled with oils and debris and if dishes were left to sit for long periods, allowing microorganisms to breed in the wet, food-rich environment. But good hand dishwashers in fact always use only fresh hot, sudsy water for washing and rinse the dishes thoroughly with very hot water.

Rinsing. As you wash each item, set it in the other sink, or at the other side of the dishpan, or on a clean mat or towel if it is delicate, until you have a half dozen or so pieces collected. Now (and before the suds dry on the dishes) rinse them *very thoroughly* with running tap water as hot as you can safely use. This prevents dullness, streaks, spots, and a soapy taste in your food when you use the dishes later. If your tap water is not very hot, you might even first rinse them under the tap, then pour heated water (170–180°F would be good) over them. If you make it hotter, you have to start worrying about things cracking from the heat.

Hot rinse water works best not only to rinse off suds but to kill microorganisms, prevent spotting, and speed drying. A hot glass or plate will air-dry, if you drain it properly, almost immediately. A hot, dry dish will quickly show a drastically reduced bacterial count.

If water is not plentiful, you can rinse by repeated dipping in a tub of hot water. But you'll have to change the water when it collects a little soap.

Draining. Set items properly in the draining rack so that water does not pool in them. If you are draining on a towel laid on the counter, set bowls, cups, and glasses so that they tilt slightly. You can do this by making a slight fold in the towel or by setting something relatively flat at its edge, such as a clean plastic cutting board. If you set them down flat, moisture is trapped under them; they do not dry, and they provide an environment in which bacteria can grow. If cups or bowls hold water in their bases while draining, be sure that you empty them out or pat the water out with a towel.

If your draining rack fills up, you might stop and empty out all the pieces that are dry before continuing with your washing.

Is Hand-Drying or Air-Drying More Sanitary? Some kitchen safety experts nowadays discourage the hand-drying of dishes, pointing out that air-drying is far more sanitary. In principle, this advice is good; in practice, more needs to be said. The main reason for the safety experts' advice to let dishes air-dry is the widespread habit of drying them with towels that are not fresh. Studies have shown that used and damp towels become home to many bacteria—from hands, dishes, countertops, and so on. Using a bacteria-laden towel to wipe dry your dishes spreads bacteria all over them. You can towel-dry perfectly safely if you use clean towels. When you want to towel-dry, *begin with a perfectly clean, fresh towel—not one that you used and hung to dry this morning or one that you dried your hands on—and change to a new towel when the one you are using becomes damp or soiled.* If you are drying an enormous load of dishes, you might go through half a dozen or more, so stock plenty in your drawer. They are cheap, easy to launder, and long lasting. Use paper towels for cast iron if you are worried about rust marks on your towels. Use different towels for drying dishes, hands, and countertops and other surfaces. A towel should never be used on the floor.

How to Dry the Dishes by Hand. If you have drained dishes properly, you will need to do nothing more than pat out drops collected in bases—so the water does not fall on dry dishes—before turning them over and putting them away. Usually you'll need to towel-polish spots off the glasses and silverware, just as your grandmother did, even if you do let them air-dry. Stainless steel and aluminum pots and pans may also look streaked or spotted unless you give them a brisk rubbing with a towel. You must be sure to hand-dry cast-iron pots and pans so that they do not rust. After I hand-dry my cast-iron pots, I set them over a hot burner for a few seconds to drive off the last drops of moisture. Be careful not to burn your hand when you remove them from the heat!

It is best to dry glass, crystal, and fine china with linen towels, which are lint-free and highly absorbent. Those called "glass towels" are especially good, but high-quality good cotton towels are also nonlinting.

Rub with a circular motion to remove excess moisture until things feel dry to the touch and show no streaks, spots, or lint. To dry the inside of a glass, wrap two or three fingers in a dish towel, insert them in the glass and rub all around. Or you can stuff some of the towel in and turn it all around. But beware of putting in your whole fist or cramming in the towel tightly; the glass might break. There is a characteristic curved-line scar that results from this mistake.

Putting the Dishes Away. Air-drying is definitely not easier and more sanitary if it means you are tempted to leave your dishes standing in the drying rack day in and day out, as if it were a convenient storage spot for fresh cups and glasses. Not only is this unsightly, but it exposes the washed things to splashes, dust, sneezes, breaks, and the unforeseen conduct of children and others. Put the dishes away as soon as they are dry. If you have used good hot rinse water, that will take only a couple of minutes. You need to be particularly careful to put dishes away promptly if your drying area is adjacent the stove and work areas of your kitchen, where splatters and spills can easily happen.

Air-drying will also fail to accomplish its purposes if you set dishes so they cannot drain properly or if they are designed in such a way that they cannot. Standing water is ideal for bacteria to grow in.

Finally. When you are finished washing the dishes, clean the dishpan with dishwashing liquid or a scouring powder. Then rinse it thoroughly, dry it, and put it away. Empty, wash, dry, and reline your food-waste receptacle, if you keep one. Next, wash or scour the sink and adjacent countertops with an appropriate cleaner; then rinse and wipe them dry. Be sure to empty the sink's drain basket of any food particles that have gathered there, and clean it and the drain carefully. This is a prime site for germs to grow. You may, now and then, wish to sanitize the drain at this point or when you close up your house for the evening before bed. (See page 175.)Last, either wash out your sponges or dishcloths thoroughly, ending with a soak in a sanitizing solution as described in chapter 13, "Safe Food," or put them, along with used towels, in the laundry when they are dry. (Let them dry somewhere in your laundry area. If you dry them in the kitchen, someone will be tempted to use them.) In my grandmothers' day, people would have boiled, bleached, or sunned them to be sure they had been rendered sanitary.

Washing the Dishes in an Automatic Dishwasher. Follow the instructions in the instruction booklet. Learn the characteristics and functions of each cycle of your machine, and use the appropriate cycle to get good results and save energy when possible.

A few basic rules apply to most automatic dishwashers:

Let the water spray do its work. Look inside to learn where the water spray comes out. Turn the soiled sides of items toward the water, and do not set tall items where they will block the spray. Never let spoons and forks nest, as this prevents water from getting in between. Instead, insert them alternately turned up and turned down. Overloading will prevent the spray from reaching many of the dishes.

Do not load glasses or dishes so that they touch; be especially careful with thin glass and china and stemmed glasses. They might jostle one another and break or get scratched. Aluminum pieces can leave black or gray marks on dishes. (Use Bon Ami or another mild scouring powder to remove them.) Load articles in such a way that they drain and dry, with bottoms up.

Silver should not go in the dishwasher, but if you do put it in, place it so that it does not

ADHERENT ODORS AND FLAVORS

Some odors and flavors will cling to dishes and cutlery despite washing in hot, sudsy water and thorough rinsing, and, sometimes, even despite a rugged washing in the automatic dishwasher. Wooden utensils and bowls, nonstainless knives, cast-iron pots and skillets, aluminum pots and pans, and old or porous ceramics are especially vulnerable to such problems. But even ordinary china and flatware will take an odor sometimes. Chopped garlic and onion, fish of all types, and curries are among the foods most likely to cause the problem. Some helpful preventive and curative measures are as follows:

- Rinse dishes and utensils completely free of all food that may leave odors as quickly after using as possible. Be especially careful to rinse them thoroughly before putting them in the dishwasher or into a dishpan with other dishes.
- Rub lemon slices over cast-iron or rust-prone pieces that have taken an odor or flavor. Then immediately rinse, wash in hot, sudsy water, and dry thoroughly.
- Soak them (briefly, if they are rust-prone or wooden) in a solution of hot, sudsy water plus a little baking soda. Then rinse thoroughly.
- Soak them (briefly, if they are rust-prone or wooden) in a solution of hot, sudsy water plus a little chlorine bleach. Then rinse thoroughly.

KEEP APPLIANCE MANUALS

Be sure to read thoroughly and retain the instruction and use and care booklets for your automatic dishwasher and all other home appliances. Browse through them now and then to refresh your memory about the correct use of your appliances. Note cleaning, maintenance, and safety instructions, too.

touch other metals, particularly stainless steel, as this may result in permanent marking or pitting of the silver. Load sharp things with their points down for safety. Don't crowd the silver; water flow to each piece will be impeded, and it won't come clean.

Ordinarily, china, glass, stainless steel, plastic kitchenware, and—depending on how you feel about it—aluminum (see discussion below) are dishwasher-safe. But check manufacturer's instructions.

Do *not* put in the dishwasher:

Delicate china, especially antiques, hand-painted items, and pieces with gold or silver trim. Dulling and cracking are dangers; decorations and paint can chip, fade, or come right off. The heat, force of the water spray, strength of the detergent, and friction are all potential causes of damage.

Crystal. It scratches, dulls, and breaks.

Decorated glasses. The decorations wear off.

Milk glass. It may yellow.

Cast iron and tin. They rust.

Pewter. It may pit, tarnish, or discolor.

Silver. It will scratch, tarnish, or be marked or discolored; some pieces may undergo structural damage. Patinas or finishes may be ruined.

Gold. It discolors.

Sharp knives. Keen edges will dull (or can cut someone emptying the dishwasher). Glued-on handles (hollow ones) will loosen. Wooden handles will eventually crack, warp, roughen, and be ruined.

Bone or ivory. Handles on utensils or flatware made of such materials will be harmed by the wetness, heat, and detergent inside the dishwasher.

Wood. It roughens, warps, and eventually cracks.

Certain plastics. Check manufacturer's instructions for each kind. Disposable types melt.

Aluminum, unanodized, depending on your wishes. On the subject of aluminum the Soap and Detergent Association says: "Plain aluminum will darken when exposed to water, some foods, detergents, and alkaline cleaners such as ammonia or a heated solution of baking soda and water. The degree of discoloration depends partly on the length of contact and metal (some alloys are more resistant). Aluminum can be washed in the dishwasher if the discoloration or the necessity of additional cleaning with steel wool or an acid cleaner is not objectionable."

Some anodized aluminum pots and pans. Check manufacturer's instructions. Anodized aluminum tends to discolor in the dishwasher. According to the Soap and Detergent Association, aluminum "with a colored or metallic copper or gold look, usually on the lids of pans and molds," also has an anodized coating that is not dishwasher-safe.

Many other nonstick pots and pans. Check manufacturer's instructions.

The upper level of the dishwasher is generally designed to receive glassware and other delicate items, and you are supposed to keep these out of the lower rack, but this isn't always the case. When you see advice or instructions on the labels of dishes or plasticware about what should go in the upper rack, you are usually being told whether or not something should be kept farther from the heating element in your machine; in many (but not all) machines, placing heat-vulnerable items in the lower rack would put them too close to the heating element.

The modern rule is that you do not rinse your dishes before placing them in the dishwasher; you just scrape off bones and food and let the dishwasher do the rest. But you must remove baked-on debris or hardened foods before placing dishes in the dishwasher. Nonetheless, I still rinse most of my dishes before I put them in. One reason is to ensure that they will come out of the dishwasher completely clean and free of food odors. Another is that rinsing helps to reduce the premature aging that automatic dishwashers inflict on dishes, glassware, and eating utensils. The extra friction caused by food particles flying around in the dishwasher causes quicker dulling and scratching. Rinsing also results in fewer instances of soil getting baked on by the machine in its drying cycle.

Hard-to-remove soil should be scrubbed with a brush or appropriate scratcher, or softened by soaking and then scrubbed, before automatic dishwashing. Try soaking the item in hot water or, with really hard-to-clean pots and pans, fill them with water and let simmer on the stove; if the pans are greasy, use dishwashing soap and hot water. (Never, however, put dishes in the machine coated with regular hand-dishwashing soap. This can cause too many suds.) For very hard-to-remove soil, such as baked-on foods, manufacturers of automatic dishwasher detergent recommend soaking in a solution of one tablespoon of dishwasher detergent per quart of hot water. Do not do this with silver or other materials that might be injured. Make sure the dishwasher detergent is dissolved before putting things in, or you may get marking or pitting.

Use automatic dishwasher detergent and no other kind. It is specially formulated to make low suds, and it's strong. It does not matter whether you use gel or granules or liquid—just so long as you use one designed for a dishwasher. The wrong kind of detergent can cause serious inconvenience. My neighbor, having just had a baby, hired someone inexperienced to come in to help with housecleaning. This helper put hand-dishwashing liquid in the machine and then had to spend more than an hour clearing out the enormous volume of suds that was produced. When my neighbor called the manufacturer for help, she was told that there was nothing that could be done but to keep bailing suds until they were gone.

Put the detergent into the dishwasher's detergent dispenser, not on the dishes or flatware, where it may cause marks or pitting. Make sure the dispenser is dry or the detergent will cake.

If you are getting spots on your glassware, try using a rinse agent (solid or liquid). You are especially likely to benefit from one if you are using an energy-saving cycle or not using your drying cycle.

To remove coffee or tea stains on china, plastic, and glassware, mix one-eighth cup regular chlorine bleach with one cup water and pour the mixture into the bottom of the dishwasher before starting the wash cycle. *But do not use bleach if you have loaded anything made of aluminum, nonstainless steel, or silver in the machine, as they may be discolored.*

Use hot water. Even if your dishwasher heats its water, as many modern models do, it heats it hotter if water enters your machine already somewhat hot. Mine, for example, should be given water no cooler than 120°F in order for it to give its best performance. (Remember this if you rely on your dishwasher for sanitizing. See chapter 13, "Safe Food," pages 176–77.) Hot water cleans better, rinses better, kills more germs, and aids drying without spots. The Soap and Detergent Association recommends that your dishwasher water reach at least 130°F for effective washing, and advises that if your dishwasher does not heat water, your water heater should be set at 140°F to ensure the correct washing temperature. (But see chapter 65, "Additional Safety Measures for Children," page 753, on safe and desirable tap-water temperatures.)

While the dishwasher is running, complete all the steps listed under "Finally," above, in the discussion of hand-washing dishes.

When the dishwasher has finished running, your dishes will stay safe and clean until you use or unload them. But it is best to unload them as soon as they are dry, so that no one accidentally starts mixing dirty dishes with the clean ones. Also, once you begin unloading, finish. A half-empty dishwasher is far more likely to be mistaken for one containing dirty dishes.

Sanitizing Dishes. Ordinary dishwashing, especially in the dishwasher, kills many germs. But you might want to take extra steps to kill any pathogens on dishes, pots, pans, or utensils if someone in the household is seriously ill or is immunocompromised either by disease or by medical treatment. See chapter 13, "Safe Food," pages 172–74.

Cleaning Kitchen Appliances

Clean all your kitchen appliances in the manner prescribed in the instruction booklet supplied by the manufacturer. *Unplug all electric appliances before cleaning them. Never immerse electrical appliances in water even when they are unplugged.* Your care booklet will inform you of other safety concerns and of any potentially damaging cleaning materials and methods that you should avoid.

Refrigerators. Cleaning your refrigerator often and carefully is one of the most important jobs in your home. Because fresh foods are stored there, there is always the possibility that germs from spills, molds, old foods, or soil will contaminate the new ones. Moreover, refrigerator odors can easily develop. These are unpleasant in themselves, and they can taint the flavor of milk and other susceptible foods so much as to make them inedible. Refrigerator odors can also make your entire kitchen smell bad.

Every other day or so, check the contents of the refrigerator to be sure that everything is fresh. Throw away immediately anything that is growing spotty, moldy, smelly, slimy, or soft. Pick through bags of fruit or vegetables and make sure each piece is sound; one rotten piece will cause the rest to rot. Even if leftovers look and smell all right, throw them out if you know that they are more than two or three days old, or sooner if you are sure that no one will eat them. Check milk for freshness dates and cheeses for molds. Rotate foods so that the oldest are kept in front, to be used first.

Washing out the refrigerator is part of your weekly cleaning routine. As part of this cleaning, make a survey of your freezer and throw out anything that is past its prime. Note which items are coming to the end of their storage lives so that you can plan to use them in the near future. Try to time your weekly marketing to fall after your weekly cleaning so that you have a fresh, spacious place to receive the new food. This will save much waste. It will also help you shop better because you will be more aware of what you need and what you do not need.

How to Wash the Refrigerator. Try to wash the refrigerator before you market so that it is relatively empty and you do not have to cause fresh meats or other highly perishable foods to get warm.

First, remove as many drawers and shelves as possible, setting foods such as fruits and vegetables that are not highly perishable temporarily on the countertop. Crowd highly perishable foods together as best you can on one or two shelves that you leave in the refrigerator. Wash the drawers and shelves you have removed, using hot, sudsy water, rinse them well, and let them drain. Wipe one shelf dry and replace it in the refrigerator. Move the highly perishable items to this shelf, and now remove and wash the shelf they had been standing on.

Now, unplug the refrigerator. Do not alter the temperature control dial when cleaning. *Manufacturers warn that you must unplug the refrigerator for washing. Alternatively, you can flip the circuit breaker that controls the refrigerator. In any event, you must be careful to avoid washing or splashing lights, switches, and control dials.*

Before replacing the rest of the shelves and drawers, wash the interior walls and all other surfaces of the refrigerator. Work quickly. Use a pot or bucket of warm, sudsy water. (Beware of using hot water on cold glass shelves; they might crack.) Baking soda in the water softens it and adds some deodorizing power; use about four tablespoons per quart. Any mild detergent will do, including hand-dishwashing liquid, so long as it has no strong odor. You might use one of the perfume-free ones if you find that detergent odors cling in the refrigerator. Some manufacturers recommend that you use a baking-soda-and-water solution only, with no detergent, but I find that this does not work as well.

If you have mold in your refrigerator, add chlorine bleach to your detergent-and-water solution. Chlorine bleach will kill the mold and also act as an effective deodorizer. It helps clean too, but don't use too much bleach or you will get bleach smells in your refrigerator. (On how much chlorine bleach to use, see chapter 30, "Peaceful Coexistence with Microbes," page 433.)

Start from the top and go to the bottom to avoid dripping on cleaned areas. If food is stuck on, first try wetting the spot and letting it stand for a few minutes. Or try soaking a clean cloth in soapy water and setting the cloth to stand on the area. If the food will not come off after soaking, try a nylon-mesh pad such as those that are recommended for use with nonstick cookware. Be sure to get into cracks, corners, and seams. Mold and bits of rotting food that stick in these out-of-the-way places are often the cause of refrigerator odors. If necessary, dig at them with something that poses no danger of scratches or punctures (a chopstick or toothpick, for example) to remove hardened gunk; it either is mold or will provide a home for molds and other contaminants. Above all, your job is to keep mold out of the refrigerator.

Wash the gaskets too. If mold has grown on the gaskets, wash them with a bleach-and-detergent solution. (See directions on page 433 for making the solution.) Scrub stubborn spots with a nylon-mesh pad. When you have finished washing, wipe all surfaces thoroughly with fresh warm water to rinse them. Then wipe them dry.

Be sure to plug the refrigerator back in or turn the electricity back on when you are done.

How to Wash the Freezer. You need not wash the freezer every week, but clean it as soon as you notice that crumbs or spills are present. The technique is the same. Unplug the refrigerator or flip the circuit breaker. Work very quickly. Remove all the items and place them in the refrigerator or a large ice chest while you clean. Or, if you can, move them to one side of the freezer while you clean the other. Remove shelves for washing, and wash the sides and the bottom as you did when cleaning the refrigerator.

During your weekly cleaning, make a survey of your freezer's contents. Throw out anything that is too old to eat. Ice cubes, too, get old and pick up freezer odors; discard them when they are no longer fresh.

How to Defrost a Manual-Defrost Refrigerator. Do not wait to defrost until you have glaciers in your freezer compartment. Waiting too long makes this job much harder and more time-consuming when you get to it and causes the refrigerator to run less efficiently in the meantime. When a modest amount of ice accumulates in the freezer, choose a day when both the freezer and your refrigerator are as close to empty as you can get them. To begin, either switch off the electricity to the refrigerator or unplug it. Remove everything from the freezer. (Set food in an ice chest, if you have one, or on the back porch if it is below freezing outdoors. Otherwise, consider waiting a couple of days until you use things up.) Set a pan of hot water in the freezer. When the water has cooled, check to see if the ice has softened enough to pull out with your hands. Repeat as necessary. Wear gloves to remove the ice if the cold bothers you too much, or use a rubber spatula to dislodge it. *Use no sharp implements or ice picks!* These can puncture the lining of the freezer, causing it to malfunction. Empty the drip tray under the freezer as soon as it has filled with water from the melted ice. When the freezer is ice-free, wash the freezer and the drip tray, rinse them, and dry them, exactly as you do the rest of the refrigerator. Replace the drip tray. Plug the refrigerator back in, or turn the electricity back on.

Other Important Refrigerator-Cleaning Jobs. Some refrigerators have drip pans at their bases or under their freezer compartments. If your refrigerator has a drip pan anywhere, it is *most important* that it be emptied and sanitized frequently—especially the drip pans at the bottom of the refrigerator. Molds and other microorganisms grow in drip pans. Every week, as part of your weekly cleaning routine, pull it out, empty it, wash it thoroughly with a hot, soapy solution, and rinse it. Then sanitize it with a bleach solution, letting it stand for a few minutes. (See page 175.) Drain it and let it air-dry briefly before putting it back in its place.

Your refrigerator's condenser may need vacuuming every three to six months, or more often if there has been some dust-producing condition in your home, such as renovations or the presence of pets. See your manual on where to find the condenser and how to vacuum it. Twice my refrigerator has stopped cooling in the middle of a heat wave as a result of dust accumulating on the condenser.

Wash down the refrigerator's exterior with a solution of mild detergent and water or baking soda and water. Vacuum the grille; occasionally remove it, vacuum off dust, and scrub it with a brush and soapy water. Wipe it dry and replace it.

Modern refrigerators often have special features such as icemakers and drink dispensers. These may require special care. For safe and sanitary use of these and other special features, consult your manual.

Garbage Disposals. Follow the manufacturer's recommended procedures. Garbage-disposal units are self-cleaning for the most part. There are commercially prepared aids for degreasing, deodorizing, and cleaning the disposal—for example, a disk in paper that you drop in with running water while operating the disposal. Or grind small bones or fruit pits, using plenty of water, or ice in the disposal. Hard materials such as these help scour the mechanism. (But avoid putting in fibrous materials such as cornhusks, artichokes, and rhubarb; they can block or damage the disposal.) Or you can

DEODORIZING THE REFRIGERATOR

You can prevent refrigerator odors by regularly throwing out rotten and moldy foods; washing the refrigerator thoroughly every week with sudsy wash water to which you add some baking soda or a little chlorine bleach; putting odorous foods into airtight containers or wrapping them carefully with plastic wrap. If, despite your careful wrapping and tight containers, refrigerator odors from fresh stored foods arise, you can counter them by setting an open box of baking soda in the refrigerator. Or you can spread baking soda or activated charcoal on a shallow pan or tray to get more surface exposed to the air.

run lemon peels, or a solution of baking soda and water, through the disposal to clear odors. Always use plenty of running water.

Stoves and Ovens. Consult your manufacturer's instruction manual for care and cleaning instructions. *Some stoves have metal trim that will be ruined by ammonia, cleaning substances that contain ammonia, and other strongly alkaline cleaning substances.* (After thoroughly ruining the shiny trim on a brand-new stove, I learned this lesson well.) Most modern stove manufacturers also recommend against the use of any strong abrasives, gritty powdered cleansers, steel wool, or—in the case of self-cleaning ovens—commercial oven cleaners. Oven cleaners will harm many external stove surfaces as well as self-cleaning ovens, so *beware.*

Keep stoves clean while cooking by using moderate temperatures when frying or boiling. Hard boiling and frying cause splatters. Lay a splatter guard over skillets. Put a cookie sheet under pies and other dishes in the oven to catch drips that bubble over. Do not overfill oven dishes; use generous roasting pans. Once spills and splatters happen, clean them up as soon as possible, preferably while you are still cooking if you can do so safely; the heat of the stove will bake them on and make them harder to remove.

During your weekly cleaning, take the burner pans and burner grates off gas stoves. On electric stoves with removable heating elements, remove the heating elements; then remove the reflector bowls beneath them. Soak burner pans, grates, and reflector bowls *(not the heating elements from electric stoves)* in a solution of dishwashing liquid and hot water. Simply wipe off the electric stove heating elements, *when they are cool,* with a well-wrung cloth dampened with hot, soapy water. (These are usually not heavily soiled because their heat burns off spills while you are cooking.) Then wipe them dry.

While the burners and grates are soaking, wash the stovetop with a solution of mild detergent and hot water. To remove stubborn food particles from the stove exterior, first dampen them and let them stand until they soften, or leave a cloth soaked in hot, soapy water sitting on the stubborn soil. If they still will not come off and if your manual does not recommend against doing so, try using a nylon-mesh cleaning pad of the sort recommended for nonstick pans. You can try to do the same, or try a mild abrasive cleanser, with your burners and grates if soaking does not soften the food enough to allow removal. But even a mild cleanser may scratch them, in which case you must decide whether you most abhor scratches or stuck-on food.

Wash the oven door and accessible sides of the stove in the same fashion. However, if your stove has an electronic control panel, you should not use plastic scratching pads or abrasives of any sort on this, for it may scratch. If food gets stuck there that you cannot wipe off, dampen a cloth with hot, sudsy water and hold it against the hardened food until it softens.

During daily cleanups, it is usually sufficient to wipe the burners and baskets in place when you clean the stovetop. Be careful not to try to clean a hot burner.

Be sure to wipe the walls and countertops near the stove with hot, sudsy water, for food often splatters in these areas.

Some people still have old-fashioned or antique stoves with porcelain enamel finishes. When I was a child, we had one that my Italian grandmother had acquired new, which had long since been relegated to the cellar. There was a fine crazing (a network of fine cracks) over its surface, caused by a well-meaning guest who had tried to wipe the then-new stove, while it was still hot, with a cloth dipped in cold water. This was a tragedy that my grandmother mourned for thirty years or so. Be careful to avoid putting *anything* cold on the porcelain surface when it is hot or you, too, will get crazing. Let the porcelain cool first. In fact, avoid touching the porcelain with anything that is of a very different temperature. The other major caution to observe with these stoves is to clean up food spills, especially acidic ones, as soon as possible, or they will cause permanent stains. Avoid cleaning them with abrasives. Even gentle abrasives will scratch and wear away the surface.

How to Clean the Oven. Clean self-cleaning ovens in accordance with the instructions in your manual *and in no other way*. If you use regular oven cleaners inside such ovens, you may destroy their self-cleaning surfaces. It can take two to four hours for the self-cleaning process to finish, and it may produce a lot of heat in the meantime, so plan ahead. You will probably wish to be out of the kitchen. You must not try to clean grates, burners, or broiling pans in the self-cleaning oven. They, and it, are not made for this.

To clean non-self-cleaning ovens, buy a commercial oven cleaner and read the instructions and cautions carefully. These usually contain lye, although you can get noncaustic ones. Be careful to avoid breathing the fumes of lye-based oven cleaners. Consumer Reports' *How to Clean Practically Anything* recommends that you wear goggles and a paper dust mask for this procedure. Use rubber gloves, wear long sleeves, and exercise every caution to avoid letting the cleaner touch your skin. Ventilate well! Do not try to do this on a day when you must keep the windows shut. You may breathe in fewer fumes if you do not use the aerosol type of cleaner.

Before you begin, spread newspaper on the floor under the oven door to collect drips. (The cleaner may ooze out the cracks around the door.) Wearing rubber gloves, apply the cleaner all over the oven in the manner directed on the label, including the inside of the door, and close the door tightly. Wait for the recommended period—usually two or three hours or overnight. Then, again wearing the rubber gloves, wipe off the cleaner with paper towels or disposable rags; dispose of these in a container you have at hand. Rinse the oven carefully, using a cloth dipped in plain warm water, until the cleaner is entirely removed. If there are any remaining spots of soil, they will probably come off now if you rub them with a nylon-mesh pad.

You can usually clean the broiling pan as you would any other soiled pan, and it is usually dishwasher-safe—if you can fit it in the dishwasher. I once moved into a new home and found in the non-self-cleaning stove a broiling pan that was black with years of neglect. In this situation, I coated the broiling pan with oven cleaner when I cleaned the oven, and it came brightly clean. Make sure to rinse the broiling pan extremely thoroughly afterward if you do the same.

How to Clean Cooktop Griddles. Follow the manufacturer's instructions. A cooktop griddle is usually removable. You simply take it off when cool, wash it in hot, sudsy water, and rinse it. If there is burned-on dirt, soak the griddle or work on it with a nylon-mesh pad. Check the manufacturer's instructions as to stronger abrasives.

Radiant-Element Stoves and Cooktops. Manufacturers prescribe specialized cleaning routines for these, and you must follow the manuals carefully. Manufacturers may also provide cleaning liquids.

Microwaves. Wash after each use that creates steam or food spatters or spills, and during each weekly kitchen cleaning. Use warm, sudsy water (any mild detergent will do); then rinse and dry. Never use commercial oven cleaners in a microwave oven! Be sure to wash top, bottom, and sides, window and door, inside and outside, because food can splatter. Also be sure to clean the door seals and seams. This ensures that food sticking there does not prevent the door from sealing properly when you close it. Wipe the oven dry. To get off food that is sticking, wet the area with your detergent solution and let it stand for a moment. If it still will not come off, use a nylon-mesh pad designed for nonstick cookware. Ordinarily, the exterior will wipe clean with a soft cloth dipped in a solution of water and mild detergent. Treat the control panel with great care; use no abrasives or strong cleaners.

Many microwaves and convection ovens come with accessory racks, pans, and other inserts made of a variety of materials. Some may be metals that can take the strongest types of abrasives; others may be more delicate. Your manual will give you advice on care.

Some models have a removable grease filter on the ceiling. To clean this, remove it according to instructions, soak and agitate it in hot, soapy water (no ammonia if it is aluminum), rinse it, and shake out the excess moisture. Then replace the filter.

Can Openers. Remember not to immerse the electrical element of an electric can opener! Unplug it before cleaning. Some models have a detachable cutting element. You can take it off and immerse it or put it in the dishwasher. Others you must wipe, in place, with a cloth soaked in warm, soapy water, after unplugging the machine. All can openers, electric and manual, should be washed with soap and water after each use, by the way, as they can be a source of cross-contamination of foods. Food from inside cans gets on the cutting edge. If left there, microorganisms may grow and contaminate the food from the next can you open. If you are having trouble getting food debris out of the crevices, try a clean toothbrush.

Toaster Ovens. Check your instruction manual before proceeding. Unplug your toaster and wipe it inside and out with a solution of mild detergent and hot water. Rinse with a cloth dipped in plain warm water, and wipe dry. Take out the shelves and, if the manufacturing instructions permit, soak them and scrub them with abrasives or scouring pads, or whatever else is necessary, to get off any burned-on food. During your weekly cleaning, do not forget the crumb tray. Take out the crumb tray, empty it of crumbs, and thoroughly wash it, rinse it, and wipe it dry. The instructions on cleaning my crumb tray would permit the use of any sort of abrasive to remove burned-on food.

Waffle Irons. Practically all waffle irons on the market are nonstick. But most waffle irons today come without a detachable grid. Unfortunately, waffle irons without detachable grids are so hard to clean that it is enough to make you give up making waffles.

Detachable grid type. To wash a waffle iron with a detachable nonstick grid, first unplug it and detach the grid. Put it to soak while you clean the base. Wipe the base inside and out with a cloth dipped in sudsy, warm water and wrung out. Then rinse it by wiping it with a cloth dipped in plain warm water and wrung out. Finally wipe it dry. By this time any baked-on batter on the grid, which you have left soaking, will have softened, and you can clean it as you would any nonstick surface. Use a nylon-mesh pad or a brush that is not too scratchy.

Nondetachable grid type. To wash a waffle iron that lacks a detachable grid, first unplug it. Clean the exterior and other areas in the same manner as described above for irons with removable grids. Scrub the grid with a brush dipped in sudsy, warm water and shaken free of excess water, making sure that you clean each tunnel of the grid. Be sure that your brush is not so stiff that it will scratch a nonstick surface.

If you have let the adherent waffle batter grow hard, take a cloth, soak it in hot, sudsy water, then wring it out just enough to stop it from dripping and lay it on the grid until the crumbs soften. Don't let drips go in seams where they might get to the wiring. Once you have gotten off all the food particles, using a soft brush or well-wrung cloth—a thin old dishcloth is best—and a solution of water with not too much detergent (or you will have a miserable time rinsing it off), scrub the grids. The trick is to do this without dripping water into the electrical elements. When you finish this, rinse them thoroughly with a cloth dipped in warm, clear water (again being careful about dripping), or your next batch of waffles may taste soapy. Then wipe them dry. Run your finger down the grids and make sure you feel no trace of oiliness. If you do, again apply slightly soapy water, rinse, and dry.

Baked-Enamel Exteriors of Major Appliances. Some major appliances have baked-enamel exteriors; these scratch easily. This surface is commonly used on washers and dryers. Avoid all abrasives. A cloth dampened with a mild detergent-and-water solution is all you will need.

Miscellaneous Appliance Advice. Wash food processors, blenders, choppers, juicers, and similar machines immediately after using them. (A friend's pasta-machine instructions, however, recommend you wait until the pasta dries so that it can easily be brushed off.) Read instruction books carefully for safety advice. *Always be sure all appliances are unplugged first. Never immerse any portions that contain electrical wiring.* Usually you can hand-wash or put in the dishwasher all the nonelectrical parts. As for the electrical parts—bases and so forth—you simply wipe the exterior with a cloth that has been dipped in warm, sudsy water, then well wrung. If these appliances stand on your countertop, put covers over them so they do not get dirty and dusty standing out. Or store them in cabinets or "appliance garages." Usually such small appliances require little or no maintenance.

10

To Market, to Market

Marketing to ensure food safety . . . The best way to fill your basket . . . Observing freshness dates . . . What different types of dates on packages mean . . . How to select fresh fruits and vegetables . . . How and when you can ripen fruits at home . . . Seasonal availability of common fruits and vegetables . . . How to choose canned, bottled, and packaged goods . . . How to choose fresh meats, poultry, and fish

"Blessed shall be thy basket and thy store."

—Deuteronomy 28:5

I decided to include a marketing chapter in this book as a result of scenes I often observe in my local food market. This market is located across the street from a large university, in the middle of a lively and diverse city neighborhood. Its cramped aisles, filled with young and old from both communities, often see as much teaching as goes on across the street on campus. The students, puzzling over artichokes and avocados, do not hesitate to buttonhole anyone passing by who looks serene and knowledgeable and beg for assistance. "Do you think this is ripe?" they ask, and when they see that such a person has chosen flounder or halibut at the fish counter, they buy the same thing. The frequency with which this sort of thing happens convinced me that many who are learning how to stock a kitchen of their own for the first time might find information about how you make good choices of fresh foods especially useful.

Safe Marketing: In General

It will do little good to store and cook foods safely at home if they are maltreated by your market, or on the way to the market and to your home. Bacteria and other microorganisms, some of which can cause food poisoning, grow extremely rapidly at room temperature. (See chapter 13, "Safe Food.")

Check for Temperature Safety in the Store. If you are buying hot foods, such as roasted chicken, meatballs, or other cooked foods from the deli department, make sure they are kept *very* hot; make sure foods that should be chilled—fresh meats and poultry, eggs, milk, salads, precut fruits or vegetables—feel *very* cold to the touch. Try to patronize the same market frequently and observe habits there: do you see milk and eggs (and other foods that should be chilled) left standing outdoors or in aisles for long periods?

Shop first for inedibles, such as paper towels and soap. Next, pick out nonperishables: canned and bottled things and anything else that you will store outside the refrigerator or freezer, such as sugar, salt, dry cereal, flour, canned and room-temperature bottled foods. Next, buy refrigerated things, such as milk, cheese, fresh meat and poultry, and fruits and vegetables. Last, buy hot cooked foods and frozen foods. Do not buy frozen foods stored above the freezer line or protruding above the top of a freezer display case.

Put hot things with other hot things in your basket and keep them separate from chilled or frozen foods; they will help each other stay hot. And put cold and frozen things together in your basket, separated from the hot ones, so that they can keep each other cold.

Watch to see how your groceries are bagged. See to it that hot and cold things are bagged or boxed separately. Meats and other foods that might drip liquids or raw juices (especially meat, fish, and poultry) should be placed in additional plastic bags to ensure that they do not drip onto other foods during transit.

Get home with your food as fast as you can; don't make stops on the way home. In hot weather, put groceries in the passenger area of your car, not in the trunk, and turn on the air conditioning. If there will be an unavoidably long trip home, bring an ice chest in your car to keep your cold and frozen foods chilled during the trip. If your groceries are going to be delivered and you will get home long before they do, try to carry just the hot and cold items with you, in two different bags. When you get home, unbag and properly dispose of hot and cold foods first, chilling, freezing, or heating them as necessary. If hot foods have not been kept at 140°F or if cold foods have been allowed to reach temperatures exceeding 40°F for two hours (or as little as one hour in hot weather—over 90°F), throw them away; they are no longer safe. Check the labels of unfamiliar foods to see if they require refrigeration.

Avoid Cross-Contamination. Do not buy packages of meat, poultry, or fish that are dripping liquids, for this might contaminate other food. This would be particularly dangerous if drips got on foods that will be eaten without cooking, such as apples or lettuce or cheese.

If you are buying cooked fish or shellfish, notice how it is displayed. Does it lie next to raw fish that might touch it or exude liquids that touch it? Is raw fish being lifted over it? If so, do not buy it.

Observe Dates on Food Packages. If food is undated, write the date of purchase on the label when you put it away at home. This will save you racking your brain later on trying to remember when you bought it. When dates are printed on packaged, wrapped, or canned foods, be sure you know what the dates mean. Unfortunately, the meaning varies from item to item. Food dating is not federally mandated for anything except baby food and formula. State laws are variable, and many states require little in the way of dating. Even when dates are given, some products may be sold after their dates have passed, so long as they are "wholesome." In

FOOD DATING

Pull-By or Sell-By Date. The sell-by date states the last date on which the product should be sold. Foods with sell-by dates may include meats, eggs, milk, cottage cheese and other cheeses, orange juice in cartons, and yogurt. These foods are safe for use after that date, provided they have been transported and stored in a proper manner for a safe period of time thereafter (including the time they are stored at home). Milk, for example, if it has been kept chilled before and during its stay in your home, is good for two or three days after the sell-by date; yogurt for two days, eggs for three to five weeks, cheeses a few weeks. The Food Keeper, on pages 131–41, tells you how long, usually, foods are good after the sell-by date when properly stored.

Freshness or Best-If-Used-By Date. UHT milk, bakery goods, packaged cereals, and some packaged precut vegetables are included among the foods that have best-if-used-by dating. After the specified date, the product becomes stale or no longer has peak quality, but it may still be safe and edible. Such goods are often sold at discount prices after the date has passed. Sometimes you also see foods such as mayonnaise and jam with a best-if-purchased-by date. This is the last date on which the manufacturer guarantees peak quality, but since commercially prepared mayonnaise and jam are the kinds of foods that, stored unopened in a cool, dry pantry, will last months or years, they are good to use for a period after the date, assuming proper home storage. See the Food Keeper for recommended home-storage periods for such foods.

Expiration or Use-By Date. Federal law mandates use-by dating on baby food and baby formula. This refers to the last date recommended by the manufacturer for use of the product; after this there may be a decline in taste or performance. Never buy baby food or formula past its use-by date. Do not buy any foods if you are not sure you will use them by the use-by dates or if the use-by date has passed. Yeasts and doughs may not perform properly after these dates, and you'll get flat breads or rolls.

Pack Dates and Coded Dates. Most canned goods are stamped with codes that in some cases indicate dates. "Closed" dates are there for the use of the manufacturer and are not intended for use by consumers. "Open" dates are dates you can read. If you need to know anything about coded dating, you can usually call the manufacturer to find out.

many states it is legal, in fact, for the retailer to change the date on meat that has been cut up and wrapped in the retailer's own meat department if it is still wholesome.

Do not overshop! Crowded refrigerators and freezers do not work so well as uncrowded ones. Overstocked pantries become laden with items past their peak that will have to be thrown away, and you will be tempted to use foods that are no longer fresh.

Selecting Fresh Fruits and Vegetables

Freshness is not everything when it comes to picking unprocessed fruits and vegetables, but it's close. Flavor and nutritional qualities have other determinants too, but here our concern is with food storage. Usually there is no date-labeling to help you select fresh produce (except with some precut fruits and vegetables or those in life-extending modified-atmosphere packaging—see chapter 13, "Reduced-Oxygen or Modified-Atmosphere Packaged Foods," pages 187–89). You need to develop some horse sense about picking fruits and vegetables that are not going to expire immediately upon unpacking. But don't hope for perfection in yourself or your grocer. The occasional rotten apple is something we have to live with.

In general, avoid buying fruits and vegetables that have bruises, soft brown spots, browning, wilting, mold (any mold whatsoever!), slimy spots, holes, punctures, cuts, shriveling, wrinkling, or yellowing or other improper coloring. With experience, you will learn a great deal about desirable traits in fruits and vegetables. In addition, beginners can start by avoiding produce that shows the negative signs described in the following two lists, based on information from the USDA.

Vegetables. Avoid buying:

Asparagus with spread-out tips or vertical ribs or ridges, and very thick asparagus. This means that it is old and likely to be tough. Also avoid limp, flat stalks.

Beets that are elongated with scaly areas at the top; get small or medium-sized smooth beets.

Broccoli with a yellowish-green color (purplish tops are all right), or open or large buds. You want tender, firm stalks that are not splitting, and compact buds.

Cauliflower whose flowerets are separating or are speckled with black or brown spots.

Celery that is limp, splitting, or woody.

Cucumbers that are mushy, bruised, or have soft spots. Cucumbers that are very large may have too many seeds and too little flesh, so buying the biggest may not be best. Old cucumbers get woody and dry.

Eggplants that are shriveled, or those with rust spots or bruises.

Mushrooms with caps that are not closed to the stem or, if they are open, that show dark, discolored gills instead of pink or light-tan gills. Avoid shriveled and bruised mushrooms. Get plump, firm, cream-colored ones.

Onions that have thick, woody centers at their tops or are sprouting green shoots.

Peppers with very thin walls (which may be evidenced by cuts or punctures or light weight for their size).

Potatoes that are sprouted or shriveled or green, or have a great many eyes.

Tomatoes with cracks, deep brown cracks around the stem, bruises, or shriveled skin. Green or yellow areas indicate that the tomatoes are not fully ripe.

Turnips with lots of leaf scars around the top. An old turnip will be woody and fibrous instead of firm and moist inside. If turnips seem light in weight for their size, this is a sign that they are woody.

Winter squash and pumpkins without at least an inch of stem. If they are picked without the stem, they will rapidly decay around the area where the stem was broken off. They should be heavy for their size, without cracks.

Fruits. Avoid buying:

Avocados with dark, sunken spots in irregular patches or cracked or broken surfaces. Most ripe avocados are green, but some varieties turn purplish-black, maroon, or brown as they ripen. The color will be all over if it indicates ripening.

Bananas with more than a speckling of brown—unless you are contemplating banana bread, which requires overripe bananas (not rotten ones). A light speckling usually means that they are perfect for eating. They can become overripe in less than a day when the temperature is very warm.

Cherries that are shriveled, have dried stems, or look dull.

Cantaloupes that combine very yellow base skin on the rind with softness or large bruises. A ripe cantaloupe will have a firm rind and a yellow base skin. (I have read that a cantaloupe with a stem is underripe; the stem indicates that it was hard to break the melon off the vine. But, outside a garden, I have never actually seen a cantaloupe with a stem.) Avoid cantaloupes with mold near the stem scar.

Grapes with brown, brittle stems.

Honeydew melons that are dead white or green-white are immature or underripe.

They are ripe when they are yellow-white to creamy in color.

Lemons, limes, oranges, and grapefruits that are very lightweight for their size or that have rough, hardened, or shriveled skin, soft spots, or dull skin. Juicy citrus fruit feels hefty in your hand. Note that a greenish cast does not necessarily mean that an orange is unripe.

Nectarines that are hard or dull or shriveled.

Pears whose flesh near the stem is weak.

Pineapples with watery eyes or an unpleasant odor—signs of overripeness. Underripe pineapples have a dull yellow-green color, little aroma, and dull, tight pips. A mature pineapple has a good pineapple aroma and is heavy and firm. On the color of mature and ripe pineapple, see the discussion below of ripening fruit at home.

With some fruits, it helps to be aware of things that do not matter, as well as the signs listed above that do. For example, on apples you need not worry about scald (those tan or brown rough patches of skin that are not associated with bruises). On grapefruits, you need not avoid scars or discolored patches other than bruises. Florida or Texas oranges that show tan, brown, or blackish speckling or mottling are fine. These are *not* signs that the fruit inside is not good. In fact, some of the best-tasting, thin-skinned varieties commonly have these marks.

Ripening at Home. One way to ensure that fruits are ripe when you want to eat them, and not before, is to buy them before they are ripe and ripen them at home. You cannot do this with all fruits. Fruits that will not ripen at room temperature include berries of all types, citrus fruits of all types, grapes, dates, currants, figs, pomegranates, rhubarb, and watermelon. Common types of fruit that ripen at home are listed below. In general, fruits that have not fully ripened will be harder and greener (or paler or show some other unripened color) than fruit that is ready to eat. Once fruit is ripe, most kinds should go in the refrigerator. Bananas should not go in the refrigerator, and tomatoes should only as a last resort. See the discussion immediately below.

Apricots: Ripen at room temperature.

Avocados: Leave firm avocados at room temperature on the countertop for three to five days.

Bananas: These ripen best between 60° and 70°F, out of direct sunlight, which may cause uneven ripening. At higher temperatures they will ripen extremely quickly. If you keep unripe bananas below 56°F for more than two hours, they will never ripen tastily, so unripe bananas should never be refrigerated. Ripe bananas can be prevented from overripening in the refrigerator, however. Their skins may turn dark brown, but they'll still be good to eat. Note, though, that bananas cause strong refrigerator

RIPENING IN A BAG

You can ripen fruit faster at home on the counter by putting it into a bag or in an enclosing bowl. The explanation is that many fruits release ethylene gas, which causes them to ripen. The bag (or, to a lesser extent, the bowl) traps the ethylene gas near the fruit and thus hastens the ripening. Paper bags are recommended over plastic bags, as the plastic ones trap more moisture, which can lead to molding. (Perforated plastic bags help with the molding problem but may let out too much of the ethylene.) Fruits that ripen nicely in a paper bag include kiwis, peaches, nectarines, apricots, bananas, tomatoes, plums, pears, avocados, and apples. If you add a banana or an apple to the bag in which you are ripening another fruit, it will further hasten the process.

odors and readily impart strong flavors to other foods.

Cantaloupe and other melon: Firm, underripe melon will ripen in two to four days at room temperature.

Kiwi fruit: Firm kiwis will ripen in a few days at room temperature. When ripe, they will feel soft but not mushy.

Nectarines: Firm fruit with bright color will usually ripen within two or three days at room temperature.

Peaches: Hard peaches with bright color will ripen in one to three days at room temperature. Sometimes they will ripen overnight.

Pears: Hard pears will ripen in a couple of days at room temperature.

Persimmons: Unripe ones will ripen if kept at room temperature for a week. I have read that you can ripen a persimmon by wrapping it in foil and leaving it in the freezer overnight, but I haven't tried this.

Pineapples: An unripe mature pineapple (dark green, plump, firm, heavy) will turn orange or yellow or reddish-brown within a few days at room temperature. It will also get softer and less acidic, but it won't get sweeter.

Tomatoes: Put them in a warm place out of direct sunlight—on your countertop or on a shaded tabletop on the deck or back porch in the summer. If you refrigerate your tomatoes, they won't ripen. Even when they have fully ripened, refrigeration causes a mealy texture, and it's best to keep them unrefrigerated unless otherwise they are going to overripen and rot. You have to choose the lesser of evils. One possible solution to this dilemma is to put fully ripened tomatoes on the shelves in the door of your refrigerator where it is less cool. You can even get a couple into the butter compartment in the door, where it tends to be warmer (often 50°F or more).

Seasonal Availability of Fresh U.S. Produce

Another way to be sure of long-lasting fresh produce is to be aware of what items are seasonal, whether you are buying early or late in the season, and whether the produce you are buying has been stored for some time or has just come from the farm this morning. Now that the market for produce in the United States is largely nationwide and often international, you can get almost anything fresh at almost any time of the year. Winter crops in Florida, California, and the Southwest keep all parts of the United States in fresh produce year-round.

Imported produce also supplies local markets out of the local season, but it may be more expensive. Although there are notorious cases of outbreaks of foodborne illness caused by imported produce, it is so far unclear whether imported produce is more likely, overall, than domestic to carry pathogens. Domestic produce has also caused illness. Likewise, with respect to pesticide residues, the existing evidence, though incomplete, indicates that imported produce does not necessarily carry more residues and sometimes has less. Imported produce that is frozen or canned must be identified as such on the labels. But no federal laws and few state laws (Florida and Maine, for example, are among the exceptions) require that unprocessed produce be labeled "imported" or show its place of origin.[1] Fortunately, fresh produce grown in this country is often labeled as such, and you can sometimes guess from the season and the lack of a label that fresh produce is imported.

Even types of produce that are available from domestic sources year-round have their peak seasons when supplies are especially plentiful, choice, and well-priced. For the items listed below, these seasons may occur roughly as given in "Seasonal Availability of Vegetables," below. Long seasons of availability reflect cultivation of the fruit or vegetable in different parts of the country with different growing seasons. To make the best choices, find a grocery that tries to offer a good selection of local and other fresh produce. It helps to learn about the farms in your area—what they grow and when the crops are harvested—and to get to know a grocer or green marketer who is both informed and informative.

Seasonal Availability of Vegetables. Most vegetables show fairly uniform quality and availability year-round: lettuce, carrots, radishes, cabbage, celery, green beans, a wide variety of greens, depending on the season (kale, mustard greens, chicory, endive, turnip greens, chard, collard greens, spinach, watercress), mushrooms, broccoli, summer squash, potatoes, sweet potatoes, turnips, and onions. The vegetables listed below are available as shown (based largely on information from the USDA).

Vegetables (U.S.)

Asparagus: April–August. In the Northeast, local asparagus is available in spring. (Imported asparagus in the markets September–March, the U.S. off-season, comes mostly from Mexico; other suppliers are Peru, Chile, Guatemala, Argentina, and Ecuador.)

Artichokes (California): April–May

Brussels sprouts: peak in October–December, but some availability in much of the rest of the year

Cauliflower: most abundant September–June, but available all year

Chicory, endive, escarole: primarily winter and spring

Corn: most plentiful from late spring through early fall, but some availability year-round

Cucumber: best and most plentiful in summer

Eggplant: most plentiful in late summer

Parsnips: best in late winter

Peas: late spring or early summer

Peppers: most plentiful in late summer, but available all year

Pumpkins: fall

Potatoes: new potatoes are ready in late winter and early spring, February–April. (Red-skinned potatoes at other times of the year are probably old potatoes.)

Rhubarb: January–June

Rutabagas: mostly available in fall and winter

Tomatoes: year-round, but best and most plentiful from midsummer through early fall in north and central regions

Winter squash (acorn, butternut, Hubbard): most plentiful in early fall through late winter

Seasonal Availability of Fruits. Some fruits are available from domestic sources year-round; these include avocados, lemons, and limes. Bananas are not commercially grown in this country; they come from Central and South America. The only state that grows pineapples is Hawaii. (Other pineapples come from Puerto Rico and Mexico.) The fruits listed below are seasonally available as shown (based largely on information from the USDA).

Fruits (U.S.)

Apples: late summer through fall. Stored apples are available throughout the year in widely varying quality. U.S. grades for apples, in descending order of quality: U.S. Extra Fancy, U.S. Fancy, U.S. No. 1, U.S. Utility. (Apples from West Coast states are usually marketed under state grades similar to the U.S. grades.)

Apricots: June–July

Berries (raspberries, blackberries): most plentiful and best in July–August, but some may be available in spring. (Berries sold in other seasons are imported, usually from Latin America.)

Blueberries: May–September

Cherries: May–August

Cranberries: September–January

Grapes: most plentiful late summer and fall

Kiwi fruit: California kiwis are harvested October–November and marketed through May

Grapefruit: all year, but most abundant January–May

Melon:
- Cantaloupe: May–September
- Casaba melon: July–November
- Crenshaw melon: July–October, peak August–September
- Honeydew melon: most abundant July-October. (Imports are available in winter and spring.)
- Persian melon: August–September
- Watermelon: May–September, peak June–August

Nectarines: June–September

Oranges:
- Navel: November–early May
- Valencia, western: late April–October
- Valencia, Florida and Texas: late March–June
- Parson Brown: October–February
- Hamlin: October–February
- Murcott: late February–April
- Pineapple orange: late November–March
- Florida Temple: early December–early March

Peaches: May–November, peak July–August

Pears:
- Bartlett: early August–November
- Anjou, Bosc, Winter Nellis, Comice: November–May

Persimmons: fall and early winter (California)

Pineapples: most abundant March–June, but available all year

Plums: June–September

Prune plums: August–October

Strawberries: from Florida beginning in January. Best supply is spring, May–June

Tangerines: late November–early March, with peak supplies in December–January. For Murcott, see "Oranges."

Eggs

Choose only grade AA or A eggs with uncracked, clean shells that are stored in a refrigeration unit. Make sure they are quite cold to the touch. Check the package for a date if one is required in your area.

Canned, Bottled, and Packaged Goods

When buying anything canned or bottled, make sure the exterior of the container is in good shape. Avoid rusty, leaking, heavily dented cans, bulging or swollen cans, or lids that bulge. A bulging can or lid indicates gas building up inside as a result of bacterial activity. Avoid cans with a dent on a seam or rim, because this may damage the seam; but small dents that do not loosen a seam or pierce or weaken the can are probably nothing to worry about. On bottles, make sure the lid is untampered with and tight and that the bottle is unchipped and uncracked. Packaged goods—in boxes, cartons, bags, and so forth—should be tightly sealed (the outside as well as the inside liners) and without holes or gouges. Never buy canned, bottled, or packaged goods whose labels are missing, stained, or torn.

When buying canned fruits and vegetables, you can make some determinations of quality by discriminating among manufacturers and by observing the U.S. Department of Agriculture (USDA) grades:

Grade A fruits and vegetables are superior in appearance as well as flavor and texture, and they are the most expensive.

Grade B fruits and vegetables are of very good quality—only slightly less than grade A. You'll lose little (or sometimes nothing) in flavor but will get produce of slightly less perfect appearance, vegetables that are slightly older, or fruit that is a bit less sweet or less well colored.

Grade C is entirely wholesome and safe but is definitely less lovely and may contain some broken and uneven pieces. Vegetables will usually be older; fruits will be less sweet. They are the least expensive.

The best canned tomatoes tend to be Italian, and those from the San Marzano region tend to be the best of all.

Fresh Meats and Poultry

Fresh meats and poultry have sell-by dates. Buy none whose sell-by dates have expired, and try to select packages with the most distant selling dates (but remember that in many states the retailer can redate "wholesome" meats that it has packed itself). Learn to judge when meats and poultry look and smell fresh. But your greatest protection is a reliable and honest retailer or butcher.

Buy no meats or poultry that are not kept thoroughly chilled. Put your finger on the package to make sure it feels very cold. Buy none that are in leaking, broken, or damaged packages. They should be tightly wrapped.

If you are learning to judge meats and poultry, take every opportunity to examine cuts that you know are fresh with your eyes and *nose*. Fresh raw meats and poultry have odors that are quite unlike the good smells of cooked meats and poultry, but are not strong, tainted, or rotten-smelling. If you ever let meat stay a bit too long in the refrigerator, waft some air from the meat toward your nose before you throw it out, so you become familiar with the scent of meat that is just beginning to go bad. You want to reach the point where you can detect the faintest scent of spoilage.

Discoloration can be a sign that meats and poultry are not fresh, but they may be going off even though their color looks normal to you, and an unattractive dark, purplish color in beef may *not* mean that it is not good.

When buying poultry, avoid dry, hard, purple, or broken skin or skin with hairs. Look for moist, smooth, unbroken skin. Do not buy frozen poultry if you see brownish areas of freezer burn; this may mean long or improper storage. Cut-up poultry goes bad faster than whole birds; turkey goes bad faster than chicken. Fresh sausages and cut-up or ground meats or poultry go bad faster than those that are not ground.

Fresh Fish and Shellfish

The traditional rule about buying fish is "not on Monday," and in this age of weekend marketing you could probably add "and not on Sunday either." This is because markets may not have fresh shipments on these days.

Fresh fish does not smell fishy, unpleasant, or strong. It is moist, without dry or discolored edges. The eyes are not cloudy or sunken; they are bright and they bulge. The gills are pink or red. The flesh should be elastic and firm to the touch. Scales are shiny and firmly adherent to the skin; they should not feel slimy. A fresh fish will float in cold water.

Anything with a hard shell—lobsters, crabs, clams, mussels, oysters—should be alive when you buy it. Live clams, mussels, and oysters, if open, close tightly when tapped. Crabs and lobsters should be moving.

If fish is packaged with a sell-by date, make sure that the date has not expired.

As with meats and poultry, buying from a reliable and honest retailer is your best protection. A good fish market will pack your fish in ice for you to ensure that you get it home safely on a hot day. Do not put the package in the trunk of your car on a hot day. Keep it in the passenger area, preferably with the air conditioning on, and preferably on ice. If your market does not pack fish in ice, remember to bring an ice chest with you when you shop.

THE FOOD KEEPER

Excerpted, with permission, from *The Food Keeper: A Consumer Guide to Food Quality and Safe Handling*[2]

(Developed by the Food Marketing Institute, Washington, D.C., with the Cornell University Institute of Food Science, Cornell Cooperative Extension)

Food Storage Guidelines. The storage times listed in the food storage chart below are intended as useful guidelines; they are not hard-and-fast rules. Some foods may deteriorate more quickly and some foods may last longer than the times suggested. The times will vary depending on the growing conditions, harvesting techniques, manufacturing processes, transportation and distribution conditions, nature of the food, and storage temperatures. Remember to buy foods in reasonable quantities and rotate the products in your pantry, refrigerator, and freezer.

Shelf Stable Foods	*Unopened in Pantry*	*In Refrigerator After Opened*	*In Pantry After Opened*
Baby Food, Jars or Cans			
Fruits & vegetables	2 mos. after date	2–3 days	
Meats & eggs	2 mos. after date	1 day	
Cereal, dry mixes	Use-by date		2 months
Formula	Use-by date	1–2 days	
Bacon Bits, Imitation	4 months		4 months
BAKING INGREDIENTS			
Baking Powder	6 months		3 months
Baking Soda	18 months		6 months
Biscuit or Pancake Mix	15 months		Pkg. use-by date
Cake, Brownie, and Bread Mixes	12–18 months		Pkg. use-by date
Cornmeal, regular degerminated	6–12 months	12 months	
stone ground or blue	1 month	2–3 months	
Cornstarch	18 months		18 months
Flour, White	6–12 months		6–8 months

Shelf Stable Foods	*Unopened in Pantry*	*In Refrigerator After Opened*	*In Pantry After Opened*
Flour, Whole Wheat	1 month	6–8 months	
Frosting, canned	10 months	1 week	
Frosting Mixes	12 months		3 months
Beans, dried	12 months		12 months
Canned Goods, Low Acid (such as meat, poultry, fish, gravy, stew, soups, beans, carrots, corn, pasta, peas, potatoes, spinach)	2–5 years	3–4 days	
Canned Goods, High Acid (such as juices, fruit, pickles, sauerkraut, tomato soup, and foods in vinegar-based sauce)	12–18 months	5–7 days	
Cereal, Ready-to-Eat	6–12 months		3 months
cook before eating (oatmeal, etc.)	12 months		6–12 months
Chocolate, unsweetened and semi-sweet, solid	18–24 months		1 year
Chocolate Syrup	2 years	6 months	
Cocoa and Cocoa Mixes	Indefinitely		1 year
Coffee			
Whole Beans, non-vacuum bag	1–3 weeks	3–4 months frozen	
Ground, in cans	2 years	2 weeks	
Instant, jars and tins	12 months		2–3 months
CONDIMENTS			
Barbecue sauce, bottled	12 months	4 months	1 month
Catsup, tomato; cocktail sauce or chili sauce	12 months	6 months	1 month
Chutney	12 months	1–2 months	
Horseradish, in jar	12 months	3–4 months	
Mayonnaise, commercial	2–3 months	2 months	
Mustard	12 months	12 months	1–2 months
Olives, black and green	12–18 months	2 weeks	

Shelf Stable Foods	*Unopened in Pantry*	*In Refrigerator After Opened*	*In Pantry After Opened*
Pickles	12 months	1–2 months	
Salad Dressings, commercial bottled	10–12 months	3 months	
Salsa, picante and taco sauces	12 months	1 month	
Cookies, packaged	2 months	8–12 mos. frozen	4 weeks
Crackers	8 months	freeze or refrig. 3–4 months	1 month
Diet Powder Mixes	6 months		3 months
Extracts: vanilla, lemon, etc.	3 years		1 year
Fruits, dried	6 months	6 months	
Garlic, chopped, commercial jars	18 months	Refrigerate; use by date on jar	
Gelatin, flavored	18 months		Use all or reseal for 3–4 months
unflavored	3 years		
Gravy, jars and cans	2–5 years	1–2 days	
dry gravy mixes	2 years		Mix entire packet
Herbs, dried	1–2 years		Store in cool, dark place, 1 yr.
Honey	12 months		12 months
Jams, Jellies, Preserves	12 months	6 months	
Juice, boxes	4–6 months	8–12 days	
Lentils, dried	12 months		12 months
Maple Syrup, pure genuine	12 months	12 months	
Marshmallows, Marshmallow Creme	2–4 months		1 month
Milk, canned evaporated	12 months	4–5 days	
Molasses	12 months		6 months
Mushrooms, dried	6 months		3 months
Nuts, jars or cans	12 months	4–6 mos., freeze 9–12 mos.	
Oils, olive or vegetable	6 months		4–6 months
walnut, macadamia, other nut oils	6 months	4 months	
vegetable oil sprays	2 years		1 year

Shelf Stable Foods	*Unopened in Pantry*	*In Refrigerator After Opened*	*In Pantry After Opened*
Pasta, dry, made without eggs	2 years		1 year
dry egg noodles	2 years		1–2 months
Peanut Butter, commercial	6–9 months		2–3 months
Peas, dried split	12 months		12 months
Pectin	Use by pkg. date		1 month
Popcorn, dry kernels in jar	2 years		1 year
Commercially popped in bags	2–3 months		1–2 weeks
Microwave packets	12 months		1–2 days popped
Potato Chips	2 months		1–2 weeks
Potatoes, instant	6–12 months		6–12 months
Pudding Mixes	12 months		3–4 months
Rice, white or wild	2 years		1 year
brown	1 year	6 months	
flavored or herb mixes	6 months		Use entire amt.
Sauces and Mixes, nondairy (spaghetti, taco, etc.)	2 years		Use entire amt.
cream sauces with milk solids	1 year		
Shortening, solid	8 months		3 months
Soda such as carbonated cola drinks, mixers:			
Diet sodas, bottles or cans	3 mos. after date	2–3 days	
Regular sodas, bottles	3 mos. after date	2–3 days	
Regular sodas, cans	9 mos. after date	not applicable	
Soup Mixes	12 months		Use entire amt.
Spices, whole	2–4 years		Included in total
ground	2–3 years		Included in total
Paprika, Red Pepper, Chili Powder	2 years	Store in refrig.	
Sugar, Brown	4 months		Sugar never spoils
Granulated	2 years		
Confectioner's	18 months		
Sugar Substitutes	2 years		

Shelf Stable Foods	*Unopened in Pantry*	*In Refrigerator After Opened*	*In Pantry After Opened*
Syrup, Pancake, maple & other flavors	12 months		12 months
Tapioca	12 months		12 months
Tea, Bags	18 months		12 months
Loose	2 years		6–12 months
Instant	3 years		6–12 months
Toaster Pastries, fruit filled	6 months		Keep foil packets sealed
nonfruit fillings	9 months		
Tomatoes, sun dried, packed in oil	12 months	6–12 months	
packed in cellophane	9 months		3–6 months
Vinegar	2 years		12 months
Yeast, dry, packets and jars	Pkg. use-by date	Refrigerate open jars	
Water, bottled	1–2 years		3 months
Worcestershire Sauce	1 year		1 year

*Foods Purchased Refrigerated**	*Refrigerated*	*Frozen*
BEVERAGES, FRUIT		
Juice in cartons, fruit drinks, punch	3 wks. unopened; 7–10 days open	8–12 months
CONDIMENTS		
Refrigerated pesto, salsa	Date on carton; 3 days after opening	1–2 months
Sour cream-based dip	2 weeks	Doesn't freeze well
DAIRY PRODUCTS		
Butter	1–3 months	6–9 months
Buttermilk	7–14 days	3 months
Cheese, Hard (such as Cheddar, Swiss)	6 mos. unopened; 3–4 wks. opened	6 months
Cheese, Soft (such as Brie, Bel Paese)	1 week	6 months
Cottage Cheese, Ricotta	1 week	Doesn't freeze well
Cream Cheese	2 weeks	Doesn't freeze well
Cream, Whipping, ultrapasteurized	1 month	Do not freeze
Whipped, sweetened	1 day	1–2 months
Aerosol can, real whipped cream	3–4 weeks	Do not freeze
Aerosol can, nondairy topping	3 months	Do not freeze

*Foods Purchased Refrigerated**	*Refrigerated*	*Frozen*
Cream, Half and Half	3–4 days	4 months
Egg substitutes, liquid		
unopened	10 days	Do not freeze
opened	3 days	Do not freeze
Eggnog, Commercial	3–5 days	6 months
Eggs, in shell	3–5 weeks	Do not freeze
Raw whites	2–4 days	12 months
Raw yolks	2–4 days	Do not freeze well
Hard Cooked	1 week	Do not freeze well
Margarine	4–5 months	12 months
Milk	7 days	3 months
Pudding	Package date; 2 days after opening	Do not freeze
Sour Cream	7–21 days	Doesn't freeze well
Yogurt	7–14 days	1–2 months
DELI FOODS		
Entrees, cold or hot	3–4 days	2–3 months
Store-sliced lunch meats	3–5 days	1–2 months
Salads	3–5 days	Do not freeze
DOUGH		
Tube cans of biscuits, rolls, pizza dough, etc.	Pkg. use-by date	Do not freeze
Ready-to-bake pie crust	Pkg. use-by date	2 months
Cookie dough	Pkg. use-by date, unopened or opened	2 months
FISH		
Lean fish (cod, flounder, haddock, sole, etc.)	1–2 days	6 months
Fatty fish (bluefish, mackerel, salmon, etc.)	1–2 days	2–3 months
Caviar, nonpasteurized (fresh)	6 months unopened; 2 days after opening	Do not freeze
Caviar, pasteurized, vacuum packaged	1 year unopened; 2 days after opening	Do not freeze
Cooked fish	3–4 days	4–6 months
Smoked fish	14 days or date on vacuum pkg.	2 months in vacuum pkg.

*Foods Purchased Refrigerated**	*Refrigerated*	*Frozen*
SHELLFISH		
Shrimp, scallops, crayfish, squid, shucked clams, mussels and oysters	1–2 days	3–6 months
Live clams, mussels, crab, lobster and oysters	2–3 days	2–3 months
Cooked shellfish	3–4 days	3 months
MEAT, FRESH		
Beef, Lamb, Pork or Veal chops, steaks, roasts	3–5 days	4–12 months
Ground meat	1–2 days	3–4 months
Variety meats (liver, tongue, chitterlings, etc.)	1–2 days	3–4 months
Cooked meats (after home cooking)	3–4 days	2–3 months
MEAT, SMOKED OR PROCESSED		
Bacon	7 days	1 month
Corned beef, in pouch with pickling juices	5–7 days	1 month
Ham, canned ("keep refrigerated" label)	6–9 months	Not in can
Ham, fully cooked, whole	7 days	1–2 months
Ham, fully cooked, slices or half	3–4 days	1–2 months
Ham, cook before eating	7 days	1–2 months
Hot dogs, sealed in package	2 weeks	1–2 months
Hot dogs, after opening	1 week	1–2 months
Lunch meats, sealed in package	2 weeks	1–2 months
Lunch meats, after opening	3–5 days	1–2 months
Sausage, raw bulk type	1–2 days	1–2 months
Sausage, smoked links, patties	7 days	1–2 months
Sausage, hard, dry (pepperoni), sliced	2–3 weeks	1–2 months
PASTA, FRESH	1–2 days or use-by date on package	2 months
POULTRY, FRESH		
Chicken or Turkey, whole	1–2 days	12 months
Chicken or Turkey, parts	1–2 days	9 months
Duckling or Goose, whole	1–2 days	6 months
Giblets	1–2 days	3–4 months

*Foods Purchased Refrigerated**	*Refrigerated*	*Frozen*
POULTRY, COOKED OR PROCESSED		
Chicken nuggets, patties	1–2 days	1–3 months
Cooked poultry dishes	3–4 days	4–6 months
Fried chicken	3–4 days	4 months
Ground turkey or chicken	1–2 days	3–4 months
Lunch meats, sealed in package	2 weeks	1–2 months
Lunch meats, after opening	3–5 days	1–2 months
Pieces covered with broth or gravy	1–2 days	6 months
Rotisserie chicken	3–4 days	4 months

*Note: Storage times are from date of purchase unless specified on chart. It is not important if a date expires after food is frozen.

*Bakery Items**	*Shelf*	*Refrigerator*	*Freezer*
Bread, commercial	2–4 days	7–14 days	3 months
Bread, flat (tortillas, pita)	2–4 days	4–7 days	4 months
Cakes, Angel Food**	1–2 days	7 days	2 months
Chiffon, Sponge	1–2 days	7 days	2 months
Chocolate	1–2 days	7 days	4 months
Fruit Cake	1 month	6 months	12 months
Made from Mix	3–4 days	7 days	4 months
Pound Cake	3–4 days	7 days	6 months
Cheesecake	No	7 days	2–3 months
Cookies, bakery or homemade	2–3 weeks	2 months	8–12 months
Croissants, butter	1 day	7 days	2 months
Doughnuts, glazed or cake	1–2 days	7 days	1 month
dairy cream-filled	No	3–4 days	No
Eclairs, dairy cream-filled	No	3–4 days	No
Muffins	1–2 days	7 days	2 months
Pastries, Danish	1–2 days	7 days	2 months
Pies, Cream	No	3–4 days	No
Chiffon	No	1–2 days	No
Fruit	1–2 days	7 days	8 months

*Bakery Items**	*Shelf*	*Refrigerator*	*Freezer*
Mincemeat	1–2 days	7 days	8 months
Pecan	2 hours	3–4 days	1–2 months
Pumpkin	2 hours	3–4 days	1–2 months
Quiche	2 hours	3–4 days	2 months
Rolls, yeast, baked	3–4 days	7 days	2 months
yeast, partially baked	Pkg. date	7 days	
filled, meat or vegetables	2 hours	3–4 days	

*Bakery items containing custards, meat or vegetables, and frostings made of cream cheese, whipped cream or eggs must be kept refrigerated. Bread products not containing these ingredients are safe kept at room temperature, but eventually they will mold and become unsafe to eat.

**Refrigerate any cake with frosting made of cream cheese, butter cream, whipped cream or eggs.

Foods Purchased Frozen	*Freezer*	*In Refrigerator After Thawing*
Bagels	2 months	1–2 weeks
Bread Dough, commercial	Use-by date	After baking, 4–7 days
Burritos, sandwiches	2 months	3–4 days
Egg Substitutes	12 months	Date on carton
Fish, Breaded	3 months	Do not defrost. Cook frozen.
Fish, Raw	6 months	1–2 days
Fruit such as berries, melons	4–6 months	4–5 days
Guacamole	3–4 months	3–4 days
Ice Cream	2–4 months	Not applicable
Juice Concentrates	6–12 months	7–10 days
Lobster Tails	3 months	2 days
Pancakes, Waffles	2 months	3–4 days
Sausages, uncooked	1–2 months	1–2 days
precooked	1–2 months	7 days
Sherbet, sorbet	2–4 months	Not applicable
Shrimp, shellfish	12 months	1–2 days
Topping, Whipped	6 months	2 weeks
TV Dinners, Entrees, Breakfast	3 months	Do not defrost. Cook frozen.
Vegetables	8 months	3–4 days

Fresh Produce	*Shelf*	*Refrigerator*	*Freezer*
FRUITS*			
Apples	1–2 days	3 weeks	Cooked, 8 mos.
Apricots	Until ripe	2–3 days	No
Avocados	Until ripe	3–4 days	No
Bananas	Until ripe	2 days, skin will blacken	Whole peeled, 1 month
Berries, Cherries	No	1–2 days	4 months
Citrus Fruit	10 days	1–2 weeks	No
Coconuts, fresh	1 week	2–3 weeks	Shredded, 6 months
Grapes	1 day	1 week	Whole, 1 month
Kiwi Fruit	Until ripe	3–4 days	No
Melons	1–2 days	3–4 days	Balls, 1 month
Papaya, Mango	3–5 days	1 week	No
Peaches, Nectarines	Until ripe	3–4 days	Sliced, lemon juice & sugar, 2 months
Pears, Plums	3–5 days	3–4 days	No
	Shelf	*Raw, Refrigerated*	*Blanched or Cooked, Frozen*
VEGETABLES**			
Artichokes, whole	1–2 days	1–2 weeks	No
Asparagus	No	3–4 days	8 months
Beans, Green or Wax	No	3–4 days	8 months
Beets	1 day	7–10 days	6–8 months
Cabbage	No	1–2 weeks	10–12 months
Carrots, Parsnips	No	2 weeks	10–12 months
Celery	No	1–2 weeks	10–12 months
Cucumbers	No	4–5 days	No
Eggplant	1 day	3–4 days	6–8 months
Garlic, Ginger Root	2 weeks	2–3 weeks	1 month
Greens	No	1–2 days	10–12 months
Herbs, Fresh	No	7–10 days	1–2 months
Leeks	No	1–2 weeks	10–12 months
Lettuce, Iceberg	No	1–2 weeks	No
Lettuce, Leaf	No	3–7 days	No

VEGETABLES**	*Shelf*	*Raw, Refrigerated*	*Blanched or Cooked, Frozen*
Mushrooms	No	2–3 days	10–12 months
Okra	No	2–3 days	10–12 months
Onions, dry	2–3 weeks	2 months	10–12 months
Spring or Green	No	1–2 weeks	
Peppers, Bell or Chili	No	4–5 days	6–8 months
Potatoes	1–2 months	1–2 weeks	Cooked and mashed, 10–12 months
Rutabagas	1 week	2 weeks	8–10 months
Spinach	No	1–2 days	10–12 months
Squash, Summer	No	4–5 days	10–12 months
Winter	1 week	2 weeks	
Turnips	No	2 weeks	8–10 months
Tomatoes	Until ripe	2–3 days	2 months

*Raw fruits are safe at room temperature, but after ripening, will mold and rot quickly. For best quality, store ripe fruit in the refrigerator or prepare and freeze.

**Some dense raw vegetables such as potatoes and onions can be stored at cool room temperatures. Refrigerate other raw vegetables for optimum quality and to prevent rotting. After cooking, all vegetables must be refrigerated or frozen within two hours.

11

Cold Comfort

Desirable refrigerator and freezer temperatures; relative humidity . . . What foods should be stored in the refrigerator . . . Guidelines for refrigerator storage: how to store butter, coffee, spices, oils . . . Should you leave supermarket wrappings on? . . . Avoiding refrigerator odors; which foods cause and take odors . . . How to refrigerate produce; which fruits and vegetables should be placed in bags . . . When a cool storeroom would be better than a refrigerator . . . Refrigerating eggs, leftovers, fresh herbs, ROP or MAP foods . . . How long leftovers will keep . . . Freezer storage; which foods should not be frozen . . . Power outages

The refrigerator—the reason we get to eat fresh foods all year long—has taken the place of the hearth as a symbol of the comfort of food. The image of a woman's face lit by the fire as she stirs a cheerfully bubbling pot has been replaced by the image of someone's face lit by the refrigerator light as he or she peers in, looking for something to munch on. Fires and hearths were beautiful and inspired hundreds of poetic images, but few poets have composed verses about refrigerators, which are ungainly and ungraceful. In fact, to compare someone or something to the homely refrigerator is a common form of humorous derogation. The associative power of food, however, is such that, despite the refrigerator's aesthetic deficiencies, we are comforted by its hum much as people were once comforted by the crackling of the fire, and when we open a malfunctioning refrigerator to find darkness and warmth we feel an emptiness that is something like what people used to feel when the fire was dead and cold.

Despite how important our refrigerators are to us, practically and emotionally, most people probably underuse or misuse these splendid machines. Experts on home food storage would like us to rely on them even more than we have been accustomed to, and to be a bit more careful in doing so.

Refrigerator and Freezer Temperatures

Generally Speaking. To keep your food safe and ensure its long life, you must keep your refrigerator cold. The USDA says to keep your refrigerator at 40° and your freezer at 0°F. Other food-storage experts say that your refrigerator compartment is best maintained at temperatures above 32° and below 40°F, say 34–38°F. The ideal storage temperature for many refrigerated foods, in fact, is as close as you can get to 32°F without freezing. But according to the 1999 *Food Code* (a U.S. Public Health Service set of model regulations for food services without the force of law), studies show that home refrigerators are far too warm, with typical homes showing refrigerator temperatures between 41° and 50°F, one in four with temperatures over 45°F, and one in ten showing temperatures of 50°F or higher![1]

Because it is so important, and so difficult, to gauge whether your refrigerator is actually in the safe temperature range, get a thermometer for your refrigerator and another one for the freezer compartment. "Refrigerator-freezer thermometers," which register temperatures from 70°F down to –30°F, can be bought at a hardware store or home center. The thermometers will tell you quickly when something is going wrong and will help you select the desirable control setting. If you do not have a thermometer, you can tell that your refrigerator is too cold if milk or leftovers get ice in them. It is too warm if you notice that milk turns sour too quickly or that things do not feel quite cold to the touch.

Frequently opening the refrigerator raises its temperature, so you should avoid doing so unnecessarily. The refrigerator may also tend to warm up in hot, humid weather. The more foods you crowd into your refrigerator, too,

Thermometer for refrigerator or freezer

the warmer the foods may be; crowding interferes with the free circulation of air. Aside from these factors, your refrigerator may also have warmer and colder regions inside, depending on its type and design.

Frostless and self-defrosting refrigerators tend to have uniform temperatures throughout. But the coldest place in many refrigerators is likely to be the bottom, because heat rises. The meat drawer is often thought of as the coldest spot, but it may or may not be so. In manually defrosted refrigerators, in which the meat tray is right under the freezer, this may be the case. (If you are in doubt, use your thermometer to find out.) The bottom of your refrigerator, too, may not be much colder than the top nowadays because fans in many refrigerators circulate the air and keep the temperature much more uniform. The difference between the bottom and the top of my own refrigerator is only one degree. Wherever your refrigerator is coolest, and at the back of the shelf, is where you should keep fish, fresh meats, poultry, and milk and other fresh dairy products, as well as any other foods that need cold temperatures. (Remember that fish spoils even more readily than meat; it should always be kept very cool.) Ideally, all these would be stored just above freezing, at 33° or 34°F. (Don't let them freeze.) But if your refrigerator will not keep things this cold, do not worry; they keep well as long as temperatures are at 40°F or below. Most leftovers should also be kept at 40°F or below.

The refrigerator's door shelves are likely to have a more variable temperature because the door gets the most exposure to the room air and its shelves are shallow; the butter compartment, which is in the door, is likely to be the warmest place on the door. Even if the door gets as cool as the rest of the refrigerator overnight, when no one is opening it, it will probably have a more widely fluctuating temperature during the course of the day as people open it. The fronts of all the shelves, like the door shelves, are likely to be warmer and have a more widely fluctuating temperature during periods of high use than the backs of the shelves. For this reason, do not store eggs, refrigerated biscuits, rolls, pastries, or cookie dough in the refrigerator door; place them at the back of the shelf. Butter, too, should be placed neither on the refrigerator door nor in the butter compartment, as it should have chillier storage. (See pages 146 and 153, below.) You may safely keep on the refrigerator door (within proper storage time limits, as shown in the Food Keeper, pages 131–41) opened bottles of pickles and vinegary relishes, maple syrup, jams, preserves, ketchup, mustard, and horseradish; ground coffee in an airtight glass container (but see page 74); soft drinks; beer; wine; and oils.

Keep your freezer at 0°F or even a bit colder, but remember that this will make for slower thawing. If your freezer does not reach this temperature, you cannot rely on your frozen foods to stay fresh and safe for the periods ordinarily recommended for frozen foods (see the suggested storage periods in the Food Keeper, pages 135–41); store foods in such a freezer for only a few days. If your freezer holds steady at 0°F or colder, you can assume your food will be safe for the recommended periods. Be sure to date foods when you freeze them so that you know how long they have been stored.

Use a thermometer to test the temperature in various parts of your freezer. If you find that some areas are colder, place new additions to the freezer in those areas so that they freeze as quickly as possible. Move them later, after they are frozen.

Humidity in the Refrigerator. The most humid places in your refrigerator are likely to be the fruit and vegetable drawers; being closed, they retain moisture that evaporates from the produce they contain. If your model has a lever for controlling the humidity, it probably works by closing or opening air holes. The highest humidity is produced by closing them altogether. The bad news, however, is that these drawers often do not really make much of a difference. Using a "hygrometer" (see chapter 29, "The Air in Your Castle," page 401), I found throughout my refrigerator a relative humidity considerably lower than ideal. Depending upon the day and what was stored, the relative humidity of my refrigerator shelves ranged from about 55 percent to 40 percent, and in the produce drawers from 85 percent to 40 percent. When I called the manufacturer to inquire about this, I was told that low refrigerator humidity, even in produce drawers, is typical. And many refrigerators provide even less humidity than mine because they recirculate air from the freezer into the refrigeration compartment, and the frigid freezer air is exceedingly dry.

Thus your refrigerator air is likely to be quite dry, unless you accidentally (and temporarily) steam it up by putting in, say, a bowl of hot soup without a tight cover. Cover hot or warm liquids; you don't want odors or steam condensing in your refrigerator. Circulating dry refrigerator air helps discourage mold, but it can also dry and shrivel, harden, or impart odors to foods and fresh produce that are left uncovered.

Which Foods Should Be Stored in the Refrigerator?

In some instances the choice of refrigeration storage is simply a matter of how long the food will look or taste best. In others, it is a matter of life and death. Read labels! If a product label says to refrigerate, refrigerate! If it says to refrigerate after opening, it is *extremely* important that you do so. As the lists below show, nowadays it is considered best to refrigerate many items—such as whole-grain flours, sauces and condiments, maple syrup, some spices, and certain oils—that most people used to keep on a pantry shelf. Read through the lists and make a mental comparison with your own practices to see if you wish to make any changes in your habits. Some of the foods listed below are discussed at greater length in the paragraphs following the lists.

The following foods must be stored in the refrigerator:

Fresh milk and cream of all types; whipped cream, sour cream, and whipped and sour cream substitutes

Butter

All cheeses: cottage cheese, farmer's cheese, ricotta cheese, grated cheese, cream cheese, processed cheese, soft and hard cheeses. (Exception: processed cheese in aerosol cans should be stored at room temperature or the spray will not work.)

Eggs and any food containing eggs (even one yolk or white) such as custard, pudding, and egg-containing or chiffon pie fillings or toppings, including pumpkin pie and pecan pie

Fresh meats, poultry, and fish, processed and cured hams, sausages, luncheon meats, and frankfurters. (Exception: canned hams or meats with labels specifying refrigeration only after opening.) *Note that some canned hams must be refrigerated even before opening; check labels.*

Leftovers of all sorts: meats, fish, poultry, casseroles, vegetables, fruit salads, pasta, rice

Tofu (and change the water daily after you have opened a sealed package)

Most fresh produce (exceptions are listed on pages 149–50)

Whole-grain flours and meals, wheat germ—store in airtight, moisture-tight containers. (Whole-grain products contain oils that will turn rancid quickly unless refrigerated. In very hot weather, refrigerate all flours.)

Bacon bits and similar products of textured protein

Dry yeast

The following foods must be refrigerated after opening:

UHT milk

Canned milk

Baby food and formula

Canned food of all sorts (remove from can for refrigerator storage; place contents in glass or plastic container with tightly fitting lid or plastic wrap)

Maple syrup, genuine (but you probably need not refrigerate molasses, honey, corn syrup, imitation maple syrup, or other pancake syrups)

Chocolate syrup

Jams and jellies

Marshmallow cream

Peanut butter, natural

Dried fruits

Nuts and seeds, in or out of the shell, and any canned or packaged nutmeats (including pine nuts)

Nut and seed oils, such as peanut, walnut, macadamia, or sesame oil

Mayonnaise

Canned shredded coconut

Icing or frosting

Grated cheese

Olives

Pickles

Salsa

Relishes

Paprika, red pepper, chili powder

Worcestershire sauce, soy sauce, barbecue sauce, and other sauces

Butter turns rancid if not kept quite cool. If you regularly keep it cool enough, in fact, you may find that you become more sensitive to rancid undertones in your butter. To ensure that it stays fresh, the best policy is to freeze most of your butter, keeping on a cool refrigerator shelf only as much as you will use in the next few days. Be sure to wrap or cover butter well; this also keeps it from becoming rancid by preventing oxidation. Never leave butter standing at room temperature to keep it soft. If you need soft butter in a hurry, microwave it for a few seconds.

Peanut butter that contains hydrogenated oils may be stored outside the refrigerator in the pantry. Peanut butter that does not contain hydrogenated oils will separate—oil will rise to the top—and will not stay fresh unless you refrigerate it. Hydrogenation is the process that transforms vegetable oils that are liquid at room temperature into oils that are solid at room temperature; this is done by artificially "saturating" unsaturated fats. Health authorities usually recommend you avoid hydrogenated and partially hydrogenated oils. Thus it is probably better to buy unhydrogenated—and unsweetened—peanut butter and store it in the refrigerator.

I feel it is probably best to refrigerate after opening all cooking and salad oils that you are going to keep for more than a few weeks—including corn oil, canola oil, and olive oil. Most food-storage experts (including the authors of the Food Keeper) believe this unnecessary, but there are a few experts who recommend it on the ground that all oils will become rancid faster when exposed to higher temperatures. I side with what seems to be the minority because at times I used to pick up rancid flavors in my shelf-stored oils, which never happened again after I moved all the oils into the refrigerator. Note that olive oil thickens when refrigerated but quickly liquefies again when it warms to room temperature. You can keep some in a small bottle that can be set out ahead of time to warm quickly when you need it. Or running warm water over the tightly closed bottle will liquefy the oil very quickly.

Store ground paprika, red pepper, and chili powder in the refrigerator after opening; they mold rapidly. Other spices may be stored in the pantry, but refrigeration will extend the life of all spices, as their oils are vulnerable to heat, air, and light just as other oils are. Refrigeration makes good sense when you have no cool, dry place outside the refrigerator to store spices. Fresh and freshly ground spices are far superior to dried and ground ones.

Low-sodium soy sauce must be refrigerated immediately after opening. Regular soy sauce kept at room temperature after opening will retain its best taste for about a month. After that, you can cook with it for another two months, but the flavor will not be good enough for uncooked dishes. Unopened soy sauce will keep in a cool, dark pantry for two years.

Coffee stays freshest longest if it is kept cool, dry, and in the dark, but many experts think it should not be refrigerated. However, coffee beans can be frozen for long-term storage—more than a couple of weeks. Use an airtight glass container in the freezer so as to prevent the beans from absorbing freezer odors. (See page 74 on refrigerator and freezer storage of coffee.)

Vinegar is said not to need refrigeration. If it turns cloudy, it is still good. However, once or twice I have found mold on wine vinegar, so I now refrigerate it. If you find mold on vinegar, throw it *all* away.

General Guidelines for Safe and Effective Refrigerator Storage

Do not overload your refrigerator. A crowded refrigerator cannot keep foods cool enough. Leave room for air to circulate, for that is what is doing the cooling.

Keep your refrigerator stocked in an orderly fashion. Not only is this attractive and soothing, it is more efficient and safer. Rotate foods so that you use the old ones first. When you buy new things, place them behind the old ones. Become familiar with the refrigerator and freezer lives of the foods you ordinarily eat. Throw away items that have been stored for longer than their recommended storage periods. Signs of spoilage or age include decay, browning, sliminess, softness, curdling, and off odors or tastes. (If you suspect that food has begun to spoil, *do not taste it* to find out; even a taste can sometimes be deadly.) Decay and mold spread from food to food, so go through bags and pick out and discard pieces that are molding or going bad. It is true that one rotten apple, or potato, can spoil the whole bag.

As to supermarket food wrappings and packages, see the discussion below about worries over DEHA in plastic cling wrap. If the plastic wraps on your food are of a safe type:

- Keep cheese in the supermarket wrap until you open it. Then rewrap it tightly in a plastic bag or waxed paper to prevent mold.
- Leave ricotta cheese, cottage cheese, and yogurt in the supermarket cartons or plastic tubs they come in, even after you open and use them. (However, once you have removed some for serving, never return it to the tubs or containers.)
- Leave all meat, poultry, and fish that you intend to use soon on a refrigerator shelf in the store wrapping. Wrapping and rewrapping just multiplies the opportunities for bacteria to get in and out of the packages.[3] Put a plate beneath them to catch any drips, or put them in drip-proof plastic bags, or place them on the very bottom of the refrigerator if it is cold enough there. You do not want bacteria-laden drips to contaminate other food, especially food that will be eaten without being cooked.

After pouring milk or cream from the carton into a bowl or pitcher, never pour it back. Put the pitcher in the refrigerator, covered, or pour the contents into a clean, tightly covered plastic container. Always keep milk and dairy products in tightly closed, lidded, or covered containers.

Recent newspaper reports have raised questions about the safety of some brands of plastic cling wrap used by supermarkets and people in their homes for wrapping food. Some of these, it appears, contain a plasticizer known as di-(2-ethylhexyl) adipate, or DEHA, which can leach into food, particularly food with a high fat content, such as cheese and cold cuts, and is feared by some researchers to be an "endocrine disrupter" and a health hazard. It is still unknown whether DEHA is safe or unsafe at the levels at which it leaches from plastic wraps into foods, and respectable experts offer opinions on both sides of the issue. Pending resolution of the safety debate, or until reliable authorities inform us that manufacturers are no longer making DEHA-containing plastic wraps, some experts think it may be wise to remove all plastic cling wrap from supermarket-wrapped meats, cheese, and cold cuts. Before rewrapping them, use a cheese slicer to remove the outside layer of cheese and try to slice or scrape off a fine layer of meat. Then rewrap such foods in safe plastic bags or cling wraps. Those labeled "polyethylene" on the box are among the types that definitely do not contain DEHA. Or, if it is appropriate for the type of food you are storing, place it in a Tupperware or similar container and close the lid tightly. You can also try to buy meat from a butcher and have him wrap it in paper; and have your cheese sliced from a wheel and wrapped in paper or placed in a plastic bag. When you put plastic wrap over food in bowls, do not let it touch the food. Avoid microwaving foods covered with plastic wrap.

Whenever possible, store foods in smaller, flatter containers rather than larger, taller ones, and use two or more containers or packages rather than one for faster chilling. Buy two smaller packages of meat instead of one large one. This is safer because the smaller containers chill faster. Glass and plastic containers designed for food storage are good for refrigerator storage; they will not taint the flavor of the leftovers or leach metals or other chemicals into the food.

To avoid refrigerator odors, clear the refrigerator of old, rotting, spoiled, or molding foods, and follow the cleaning instructions set forth on pages 115–17. Carefully wrap the following foods, which commonly cause refrigerator odors, or store them in airtight plastic containers:

- Strong cheeses
- Cooked cabbage, broccoli, brussels sprouts, cauliflower, and other cooked vegetables of the cabbage family
- Cooked or cut raw onions and garlic, chives, and other members of the onion family and foods containing them
- Fresh basil
- Bananas and foods containing them
- Cut melon
- Cooked poultry, such as roasted or stewed turkey or chicken
- Hard-boiled eggs

The odor of chopped raw onions and garlic always seems to get out no matter how tightly lidded their storage containers. Unpeeled garlic and onions, in their papery skins, cause no refrigerator odors so long as they are fresh and hard. (Use mesh bags or no bags at all to help prevent rotting by allowing air circulation.) When onions and garlic get old and soft, the problem starts; mushy onions cause a bad refrigerator odor.

Some foods, including the following, are especially likely to absorb refrigerator odors, and they too should be carefully wrapped or stored in closed containers:

- Milk
- Eggs
- Butter and margarine
- Dairy foods

I have read that grapes and celery absorb odors, but I myself have never experienced problems with these.

About Refrigerating Produce

By and large, it is a bad idea to wash fruits and vegetables before putting them away in the refrigerator. It is especially bad for soft things such as berries and mushrooms, for you will inevitably bruise them while washing and you will not be able to dry them, and then they will rot and mold quickly. The same is true, to a lesser degree, of most fresh produce. Besides, you will have to wash it again before cooking or eating it, so you do not gain much.

Most fruits and vegetables keep best when they are stored at quite cool temperatures of just over 32°F. (Exceptions are discussed below.) Typically, higher temperatures do not ruin them but shorten their lives. Beware of freezing them, for they generally have a spoiled taste or texture or rot quickly once they have been frozen. Although they usually do not freeze except when the temperature is at least slightly below 32°F (the freezing point of plain water), do not take chances.

If you find that your fruits and vegetables wither fast—if they quickly get wrinkly skins or go limp—they are probably too dry. Most fruits prefer a high relative humidity of 85 to 90 percent, or even higher for pears and apples. Most vegetables like anywhere from 85 to 95 percent relative humidity. A few like a humidity level that is a bit lower than this, say between 65 and 75 percent; these include garlic, onions, winter squash, and pumpkins. Refrigerator air is usually much drier than this. Produce will keep best in the fruit and vegetable drawers, where it is protected from the drying, circulating air in the refrigerator.

But even though you put your fruits and vegetables in the produce drawers (separate drawers for fruits and vegetables), you still need to put most of them in bags or other containers to make sure they do not shrivel and dry out. Perforated plastic bags are usually best. Perforated bags hold moisture from the produce but permit air to circulate so that moisture does not condense in the bag; this delays rot and mold. Or you can use plastic containers with loose lids or regular plastic bags, leaving them open or poking a few holes in them. Just be sure that you get air circulation somehow.

You need not bag oranges, lemons, grapefruits, and other citrus fruits; winter squashes; cucumbers, eggplants, and other items with thick skins; or onions, shallots, or garlic in their papery skins. (You can keep those with papery skins in a mesh bag for convenience. Leeks and green onions or scallions should be stored in perforated plastic bags.) Remove the leafy tops of carrots, beets, radishes, and turnips before bagging and refrigerating, and they will last longer. (The tops may draw moisture out, causing these vegetables to shrivel. Leave an inch or so of stem so as to avoid breaking the flesh.) One expert on food storage recommends that you store mushrooms in an open carton or box (the cardboard box they come in) with a damp paper towel on top to prevent withering. Figs should be stored in unperforated plastic bags.

Whatever you store your fresh fruits and vegetables in, keep each different type of fruit or vegetable in a container separate from the others—only apples go in the apple bag, only carrots go in the carrot bag. This is necessary because different sorts of fruits and vegetables give off different gases that can cause others to deteriorate. For example, the following types of produce do not get along well with each other in storage and should be kept apart:

Store carrots away from apples, as the gas emitted by the apples may give the carrots a bitter taste.

Store potatoes away from apples. Gas from the apples may make the potatoes sprout, and the potatoes may make the apples mold or rot.

Store onions and potatoes separately. Each emits a gas that will shorten the storage life of the other.

Store leafy greens separate from eggplants and tomatoes, which will cause the greens to go bad faster.

When a Cool Storeroom Would Be Ideal for Produce, But You Do Not Have One

Most, but not all, of your fresh produce will last longest if stored in the refrigerator. In other cases, there is a judgment call: the food would be better off in a cool storeroom than in a refrigerator, but it is better off in a refrigerator than at room temperature. Those who have a subsidiary cooling unit that could be kept slightly warmer than their refrigerator could use that for several of the foods discussed in this section. A wine cooler, too, can serve this purpose. A cellar, pantry, attic, window well, porch, or garage might provide good storage conditions in the winter months, if you can ensure adequate humidity and you are sure the foods will not freeze.

Here is a list of foods that, at least ideally, would not be refrigerated:

Fruit that you wish to ripen should not be refrigerated.

Bananas should not be refrigerated. They blacken in the refrigerator after a couple of days. Their odor can also easily taint the taste of other foods in the refrigerator. You can freeze peeled bananas.

Grapefruit may be stored in a cool, dry place outside the refrigerator or in the warmest place in the refrigerator. Storage temperatures of about 50°F would be best. Other citrus will be better off in the refrigerator.

If your refrigerator is quite cool—below 38°F—ideally you would not store your potatoes in it. Below this temperature range, their starches turn to sugar and they begin to sprout. The best place to store potatoes is in a cool, dark, humid place—at 40°F and 90 percent relative humidity. If they are stored in a light place they become green and bitter. (If this happens, you can cut off the green part and use the rest.) If you have no cool storage space outside the refrigerator, you are probably better off putting potatoes in a perforated plastic bag in the warmest place in your refrigerator. You can usually get quite a few into the door shelves.

Sweet potatoes would find 55–60°F, 80–90 percent relative humidity ideal. If you have a cool spot outside the refrigerator for these, that would be best. If you do not, you are probably better off putting them in the refrigerator. As with regular potatoes, you might find they do better on a shelf in the door. Throw them away as soon as they show mold. (Study them closely at the market, too, to see if they are already moldy, as I find they frequently are in my neighborhood.)

Once tomatoes are ripe, they also keep best at 55–60°F in a very moist environment. (This temperature will also keep unripe tomatoes from ripening.) At lower temperatures they tend to become mealy. If you cannot provide relatively cool temperatures outside your refrigerator and you cannot yet use fully ripened tomatoes, you are better off putting them on the refrigerator door, or in the butter compartment, rather than letting them rot.

Dried peppers should be hung in a cool, dry, airy place, where they will keep for about a year.

Sweet peppers, which do best at 40–55°F and 90–95 percent relative humidity, will last far better on the refrigerator door in a perforated plastic bag than on a warm, overdry shelf.

Pumpkins and winter squashes will not keep very long in the average city apartment. They are ideally stored at 50–55°F and 70–75 percent relative humidity. Pumpkins go bad fairly fast at room temperature, so when they are small enough to fit, keep them in the refrigerator. (Remember to avoid any with a bruise, cut, or puncture, for pumpkins go bad even faster after any break in the skin.) Winter squashes can also be stored in the refrigerator.

Some people recommend storing onions and garlic outside the refrigerator in a cool area, with humidity at about 68–75 percent. I find that refrigeration, however, is superior to storage at warm room temperatures. Onions and garlic will sprout, soften, and rot fairly quickly when stored at warm temperatures.

About Refrigerating and Freezing Eggs

Count on keeping eggs no longer than three to five weeks from your date of purchase.

At home, do not wash the eggs. Doing so removes a natural protective coating from the shell. Keep eggs in the store carton and put them at the back of your coldest refrigerator shelf, not on the refrigerator door. Keep the egg cartons closed to protect the eggs from odors and from the drying effects of the air circulating in the refrigerator.

If you crack any eggs transporting them home, you can salvage them. Break them into a clean container, cover it tightly, and refrigerate. But use them within two days. This is also what you should do with leftover whites or yolks when your recipe calls for yolks or whites only. You can cover the yolks with cold water so that they do not dry out.

You can freeze eggs if you first beat the yolk and white together. You can also freeze whites alone. But, one cooperative extension service recommends, to freeze yolks alone, mix four yolks with a pinch of salt and one and a half teaspoons sugar or corn syrup. They will be good for up to six months. If eggs are accidentally frozen in their shells, keep them frozen until needed; then defrost them in the refrigerator. But discard any eggs that crack when frozen.

About Refrigerating Leftovers

Do not refrigerate any leftover canned food in its can. Remove the food from the can and place it in a clean plastic or glass container, either lidded or tightly covered with plastic wrap, and place it on a refrigerator shelf. The cans would leave a metallic taste, and although it is against the law to use lead in the cans, the seams of a few cans—imported ones—are still soldered with a material containing lead. Once such a can is opened, lead may leach into the food.

For safety reasons, all leftovers should be *immediately* stored in the refrigerator in airtight, leakproof containers or wraps. If there are large quantities, divide the food into smaller batches and place it in separate shallow containers so that it cools as fast as possible. Remove the stuffing from poultry and meats and refrigerate it in a separate container. If left in, it might take longer to cool than is safe.

The table below lists safe cold-storage time periods for various prepared and leftover foods.

COLD-STORAGE TIME FOR PREPARED AND LEFTOVER FOODS

	Refrigerator	*Freezer**
Egg, chicken, tuna, ham, or macaroni salad (store-prepared or homemade)	3–5 days	Don't freeze well
Hard-boiled eggs	1 week	Don't freeze well
Soups and stews Vegetable or meat-added	3–4 days	2–3 months
Prestuffed pork and lamb chops, stuffed chicken breasts	1 day	2–3 months
Cooked meat, meat dishes	3–4 days	2–3 months
Gravy, meat broth	1–2 days	2–3 months
Fried chicken	3–4 days	4 months
Cooked poultry dishes	3–4 days	4–6 months
Chicken pieces, plain	3–4 days	4 months
Chicken pieces, covered with broth, gravy	1–2 days	6 months
Chicken nuggets, patties	1–2 days	1–3 months

*The recommended freezer times indicate how long quality is preserved.

Source: Excerpted from Cold Storage Chart, in "A Quick Consumer Guide to Safe Food Handling," Home and Garden Bulletin No. 248, August 1995, U.S. Department of Agriculture Food Safety and Inspection Service.

About Storing Fresh Herbs

Fresh herbs such as dill, parsley, cilantro, mint, tarragon, and basil generally preserve their flavor better in the freezer than in the refrigerator. Wash, drain, and pat them dry with paper towels. Wrap small quantities in freezer wrap, or place them in separate freezer bags and seal tightly. Freeze. These will be good for cooking but not attractive enough to use as garnishes.

For short-term refrigerator storage, most herbs can be placed in plastic bags or tightly lidded plastic containers and washed just before using. Basil, however, is hard to store outside the freezer and will not last long anywhere. It tends to turn black quickly both in a very cool refrigerator (and makes strong refrigerator odors) and in a very warm room. If you buy it with roots, it will last a little longer. Try making a basil bouquet: put the roots in a glass of water and loosely cover the leaves with plastic wrap or damp paper towels. Experiment to see if it lasts longer in your refrigerator or on your countertop. Or, try wrapping it in damp paper towels and placing it in an open plastic bag in the refrigerator. (You can make bouquets of other herbs as well; but always store other herbs in the refrigerator.)

Ginger root, which is a spice, not an herb, can be stored in the refrigerator in a perforated plastic bag. Periodically slice off what you need. It molds readily, so examine it before using. Be sure to cut off the moldy parts plus at least one and one-half inches more.

A Note on Refrigerating Reduced-Oxygen or Modified-Atmosphere Packaged Foods

Many foods in the market are offered in "reduced-oxygen packaging" (known as ROP) or "modified-atmosphere packaging" (known as MAP). Such foods often require continued refrigeration, at the store and in your home, and always must be used by the dates stamped on the packages to be safe. In addition, some ROP foods are precooked and some are not. You must always follow package directions as to refrigeration, dates, and cooking. See chapter 13, "Reduced-Oxygen or Modified-Atmosphere Packaged Foods," pages 187–89, for more information.

Freezer Storage

Freeze all fresh meats, poultry, and fish that you are not going to use in a few days. Freeze all leftovers that can be frozen if you are not going to use them within the time periods specified in the Food Keeper, pages 131–34, or the Cold Storage chart, page 151. The colder your freezer, the faster foods freeze, and the faster foods freeze, the better the quality and safety of the food. Slower freezing causes bigger ice crystals to form in the food. These puncture cell walls and cause more damage. The foods' texture and taste decline. (Slow thawing of meat is preferable, however, as it keeps in more juices—another reason to prefer thawing in the refrigerator. You might remember the maxim: Freeze fast, thaw slow.)

The guidelines below set out some basics of safe and effective freezing. For more detailed information on blanching and otherwise preparing fresh foods for freezer storage and on foods that freeze well, consult a basic all-purpose cookbook such as *The New Good Housekeeping Cookbook,* or call your local cooperative extension service. Many cooperative extension services have posted excellent and detailed information about freezing foods on the Internet. (See "Acknowledgments and Sources" for information on the cooperative extension system and how to contact your local branch.)

General Freezing Guidelines:

- Do not overload the freezer. Make sure air has room to circulate.
- Wrap foods in safe material designed for frozen-food storage, and seal it to be air- and moisture-proof.

- Put dates and content labels on packages before you freeze them. Otherwise you will not know what is in each package or when you must use something because it is near the end of its storage life.
- Food that comes in great volume or quantity should be broken into smaller packages for faster freezing. Use shallow containers, and when you are freezing more than one, spread them around the freezer so that air can circulate, causing them to freeze faster. Once they are frozen, you can stack them together for convenience and saved space. Stacking them together after they are frozen will in some instances help to prevent freezer burn too.
- Freeze no more than three pounds of food per cubic foot of freezer space within a twenty-four-hour period. Your freezer cannot freeze more than this efficiently. Too much food added at one time may cause the temperature to rise temporarily, shortening the life and quality of the foods already in the freezer and causing the freezer to take too long to freeze the new food.
- *Do not refreeze thawed meats.*
- Twice-frozen foods are of poor quality because the ice crystals increase.
- If foods begin to thaw but still contain plenty of ice crystals, it is probably safe to refreeze them.
- When you buy fresh or frozen meats, fish, or poultry, freeze them in their original store wrappings. But if you want to store them for longer than two months, overwrap them with freezer wrap or a plastic bag to make the wrapping air- and moisture-proof. Fresh meats, and sometimes frozen ones, are packed in a permeable plastic that is inadequate for longer-term freezing. Freezer wrap is designed to be more moisture-vapor-proof and keeps meats, poultry, and fish better than ordinary plastic wrap.
- You must be especially careful to wrap meats well because fats, especially the unsaturated fats that occur in fish, pork, lamb, poultry, and veal, oxidize (become rancid) readily when exposed to air. Fat that oxidizes tastes bad and is unhealthy. Beef freezes best because its saturated fats oxidize less easily. Cut off fat from all meats, and wrap the meat tightly in air- and moisture-proof freezer wrapping. Try to squeeze out all air from under the wrapping. Or overwrap the store wrap carefully. Oxidizing occurs even more rapidly in the presence of salt, and that is why bacon and ham can be stored only for a relatively short period in the freezer.
- Fried and broiled meats can be frozen, but they tend to become tough and dry.
- Fish freezes less well than meat. It tends to be dry or stringy after freezing.
- Bread should be frozen in tight wrapping. (I have read that when thawing bread you should wait until the moisture inside the package is reabsorbed by the bread; otherwise the bread will be too dry. This sounds right to me, but if I'm in a hurry I never do wait, and the bread always seems to be of fine quality.)
- Keep butter (but not whipped butter) in the freezer unless you are going to use it within a few days, in which case it may be refrigerated instead.
- When you can, season foods after freezing and thawing, when they are to be eaten, rather than before freezing. Various seasonings may grow stronger during

FREEZER BURN

Whitish or discolored areas on the surface of solidly frozen foods is probably freezer burn. This is simply a dried-out area caused by air, usually owing to a hole in the package. Food that has freezer burn is safe to eat. Just cut off the portion that is freezer-burned because it probably will not taste good.

freezer storage—black pepper, cloves, onions, and garlic, for example. But do not worry unduly about freezing foods that contain these ingredients. In my experience, it usually turns out well.

- The following items should not be frozen:

  Salad greens
  Garlic
  Raw cabbage
  Raw celery
  Raw tomatoes
  Corn on the cob (it loses flavor)
  Whipped butter (it separates)
  Buttermilk
  Sour cream
  Yogurt
  Cream cheese
  Neufchâtel cheese
  Eggs in shell
  Creamed cottage cheese (dry curd is all right to freeze)
  Ricotta cheese
  Whipping cream (ultrapasteurized)
  Hard-boiled eggs (the whites get hard, rubbery)
  Luncheon meats (they weep)
  Cured meats for longer than one month (they are salty and thus become rancid quickly)
  Milk sauces and gravies (they may curdle)
  Watermelon
  Cake batter
  Cream pie filling or custards
  Mayonnaise
  Salad dressing

Power Outages

In case of a power outage affecting either a separate freezer or your refrigerator, keep the room in which the appliance is located as cool as possible.

The refrigerator compartment can keep the food cool for about four to six hours, depending on whether the room in which the refrigerator stands is warm or cool. Leave the door of the refrigerator closed so that the cold air is retained. You can also try to keep it cold inside by putting in block ice. If you have a refrigerator thermometer, take readings as best you can (but do not open the door only for that purpose) to try to determine just how warm the food got and for how long.

If fresh meats, fish, poultry, milk, leftovers, and other foods that must be kept chilled reach the danger zone—over 40° and under 140°F—for two hours, throw them away. See chapter 13, "Safe Food."

The freezer may keep food frozen for two days if it is full. If it is half full, it will keep food frozen for about one day. You can add dry ice—not regular block ice—to keep it cool. (Dry ice is colder and will not melt and leave your freezer full of water.) But be careful not to touch the dry ice with your bare hands or to breathe its fumes. Follow the directions that your supplier gives you for the use of dry ice.

12

Bread and Honey

Advantages of a cool, dry, dark pantry . . . Crisping crackers and softening brown sugar after it hardens . . . Salt, sugar, acids, and other natural preservatives . . . What foods belong in the pantry . . . Guidelines for good pantry storage . . . Shelf life of certain foods . . . Storing bread in pantry or freezer, not refrigerator . . . What to do if you find insects in dry food

If you are like most Americans, you have no pantry. The typical middle-class American kitchen, and in many cases even the highly luxurious one, does not provide this amenity. We put canned, dried, bottled, and packaged foods in our kitchen cabinets or cupboards instead. The problem with this is that kitchen cabinets tend to be warmer and more humid than is ideal for longer-term storage. If you are buying a house or renovating your kitchen, you might consider whether a cool, dry food-storage place might be created. In the meantime, those who, like me, lack one will need to avoid stocking more than they can use before it passes peak quality or goes bad. A house typically has many possibilities for food storage that apartments lack. Cellars, attics, sheds, garages, window wells, back porches, and many other places might offer cool storage for part or all of the year. If you have a large refrigerator, you can store some foods there that would be better refrigerated than left at room temperature.

About the Pantry

Temperature. Keep the pantry or the cabinets where you store canned and packaged goods cool. This means keeping these areas as distant as possible from stoves, ovens, refrigerator motors, and other heat-producing machines.

Even canned and packaged dry foods retain their quality longer and better, and their nutrients are better preserved, if they are stored at temperatures lower than 85°F; 75°F is better; and, in fact, the cooler the better, down to 50°F or so, which is ideal. Canned goods will quickly deteriorate in quality at temperatures over 100°F and in excessively cold temperatures as well.[1] In summer, I have found my own food cabinets baking at higher than 90°F. Yes, air conditioning will keep the room cooler, but sometimes you go away and turn off the air conditioning for hours, days, or weeks at a time.

Humidity. Your pantry or storeroom for packaged and dried foods—such as cereals, crackers, cookies, flour, sugar, salt, cornmeal, rice and other grains, and dried spices—should be dry. Humidity promotes the growth of molds, which ruin the taste and appearance of foods and are unhealthy. Bread, baked goods, and many other foods, by the way, will begin to mold much more slowly if they contain preservatives such as calcium propionate or sorbates. These preservatives are harmless; the mycotoxins produced by molds are carcinogenic. (See the Guide to Common Food Pathogens, pages 178–79, in chapter 13 for more on molds.) Humidity can also cause crackers, cookies, chips, and cereals to lose crispness. Although sugar, salt, baking powder, and baking soda will not mold, humidity will cause caking, especially of brown sugar.

Darkness. Your pantry or food-storage shelves should be dark except when you are in the pantry or looking in. Light causes deterioration of many foods, from bottled vegetables to oils to flours. Open shelving for bottled and packaged goods, therefore, is not a good idea, no matter how colonial it looks, unless you carefully place foods in opaque containers. In colonial times, people knew enough to keep fresh foods in root cellars, down well shafts, and in other cool, dark places.

What Goes in the Pantry and What Doesn't

For a list of basic foodstuffs that many experienced people like to stock in their pantries, see pages 42–43.

Most canned, bottled, and packaged goods, before they are opened, should be stored in the pantry or food cabinet, not in the refrigerator or freezer. But practically all canned and bottled foods must be refrigerated after opening. Read labels. Never store any food that is labeled "Keep Refrigerated" in the pantry or food cabinets.

The following foods are all appropriately stored in the pantry:

TO CRISP CRACKERS

To crisp crackers, chips, cereals, and similar foods after they have absorbed too much moisture, spread them out on a cookie sheet and bake in a hot oven (425°F) for five minutes.

TO REVIVE STALE BREAD

To revive stale bread, wrap it well in aluminum foil and heat it to 140°F. Remove it from the oven as soon as it has reached the desired temperature. You may find that the crust has gotten tougher, but the rest of the bread will be improved.

TO SOFTEN BROWN SUGAR

You can try storing brown sugar in a tightly lidded jar to prevent its hardening after you open the box it has come in, but often this does not work as a tiny amount of moisture in the air is enough to cause the problem. To soften brown sugar, spread it on a cookie sheet as best you can. Then heat it in a low to moderate oven (250–300°F) until it softens; this will take ten minutes or so. Or microwave it on high in a microwave-safe container for a couple of minutes. If you put a slice or two of apple in the container with the sugar, the moisture helps soften the sugar (and the cooked, sugary apple—when it cools—is delicious). The sugar will start to harden again when cool, so measure it fairly soon.

SALT, SUGAR, ACID, AND DRYNESS: NATURAL PRESERVATIVES

When foods are very salty or sugary, they draw water out of bacteria, which either kills the bacteria or keeps their numbers down. Thus sugar and salt keep in the pantry indefinitely. Many sweet or salty foods will also keep for long periods. Many types of candy, stored in a tightly closed container, last for a long time on the shelf. Honey and pancake syrups keep without refrigeration for about a year; molasses will last for six months. Genuine maple syrup, however, tends to mold and eventually ferment in the pantry (after it is opened), as it is less concentratedly sweet than these others.

Acidity and dryness also discourage bacteria. Vinegar, with a pH ranging from 2.4 to 3.4, is too acidic to be friendly to bacterial growth, so you ordinarily need not refrigerate it, and it will last safely on your pantry shelf for as long as a year. (But see page 146.) Pickling and brining use a potent combination of salt and vinegar or other acid to preserve and flavor foods at the same time. Nowadays we refrigerate our pickled foods after opening them so as to keep them crisper and better-tasting. But pickles always used to be stored in the pantry—in the pickle barrel or jar—and some stores still sell pickles from the barrel, at room temperature.

Meats such as bacon and ham are still sometimes salt-cured (and sometimes are both salt-cured and smoke-cured, smoke being another "natural" preservative). Cured meats last longer than fresh meats, but *all* meats are such desirable homes to bacteria that they must be refrigerated even after curing to keep them safe.

Because dryness is antimicrobial, flours, mixes, pasta, rice, and dried beans may all be stored in the pantry. Molds, however, may afflict dried foods if your pantry gets too humid.

Foods containing enough alcohol, a general disinfectant, can also live long on your pantry shelves. It is the presence of alcohol that keeps your vanilla, almond extract, and other flavoring extracts, as well as alcoholic beverages, safe for long periods on your shelves without refrigeration.

Unopened canned and bottled foods (which should usually be refrigerated after opening): Canned meats (but see exceptions below), milk (UHT as well as canned), vegetables, fruits, soups, milk, broths, and prepared foods of all types; pickles, olives, relishes, salsa, jams and jellies, condiments such as mustard, ketchup, mayonnaise, and soy sauce. Wheat germ that is vacuum-sealed in a bottle should be refrigerated or frozen after opening.

Honey, molasses, imitation maple syrup, pancake syrups (but see exceptions below)

Cooking and salad oils (but see exceptions below; and also note my own practice, page 146). Close lids tightly.

Dried spices and herbs

Vanilla, lemon extract, almond extract

Pasta and noodles of all sorts

Prepared dry cereals

Coffee and tea

Chips, crackers, cookies

Rice

White and refined flours (but see exceptions below)

Dry mixes for cakes, muffins, brownies, puddings

Chocolate powder, baker's chocolate, chocolate chips

Most candies

Dry soup mixes

Worcestershire sauce

Dried beans, peas, and lentils

There are, however, exceptions, so *read package labels carefully*. Among the exceptions are these:

- Some canned hams must be refrigerated even before opening. Read labels!
- Coffee beans to be stored more than a couple of weeks will remain fresher if you freeze them.
- Chocolate syrup and real maple syrup should be refrigerated after opening.
- Nut oils should be refrigerated after opening.
- Paprika, red pepper, and chili powder should be refrigerated after opening.
- Whole-grain foods such as flours, cereals, cornmeal, brown rice, and other grains should be frozen or refrigerated; they contain natural fats and oils that can become rancid at room temperature very quickly. Rancid flours and meals have a bitter, acrid taste, and they are bad for you. In very hot weather, consider refrigerating all grains and meals in airtight containers.

General Guidelines for Good Pantry Storage

A collection of pantry lore, old and new, follows. These are good habits that will keep the pantry orderly and pantry foods fresh and safe.

Guidelines for the Pantry

- Keep your pantry and pantry shelves clean! Dust and crumbs contain molds and microorganisms, which can spread to foods kept in the pantry, and they cause stale and sour odors. They also attract pests.
- You do not need shelf paper if you have washable shelves that are neither painted nor varnished. The purpose of shelf paper was to prevent things from sticking to paint or varnish. But well-chosen shelf paper looks fresh and cheery, and if you like it and have the time to replace it periodically, by all means use it. There is also a mesh shelf liner that helps prevent chips and breakage.
- Arrange your pantry in an orderly fashion. This is attractive, efficient, and safer. When you store like things with like, you know what you have on the shelf and you do not overbuy or drive yourself wild looking for things. Moreover, unless you have an orderly pantry, you cannot properly rotate your foods in the manner described in the next paragraph. Date foods that lack label dates when you purchase them, so that months later you know how old they are. Just scribble the date with a marker as you unpack after marketing.
- Rotate foods in the pantry; when you buy new canned or packaged goods, store them behind older cans or packages of that type of food so that you use the old ones first.
- Keep foods tightly wrapped in air-proof and moisture-proof wraps and containers. Make sure your canisters are air- and moisture-proof and also opaque.
- Make sure packages are sealed and unbroken. If holes or tears appear, check to see that the contents are in good shape and pest-free; then rewrap or repackage.
- Once you have opened cookie, cereal, or other packages or boxes, fold over the inner bag tightly and reclose the outer package tightly. You can resort to rubber bands or tape if nothing else works.
- If you find on your shelves any cans that have rust or serious dents, throw them away. (A slight dent that is not on a rim or a seam is probably all right.)
- Throw away any bulging cans, and don't use food that spurts from the can or looks or smells funny. The bulging and spurting is caused by gas building up inside, and it means that the food is dangerously spoiled. *Do not taste the contents of such cans* (not even a tiny touch on your tongue), and throw them away. (See chapter 13, "Safe Food.")

Guidelines for Storing Various Types of Foods On the shelf life of foods, refer to the Food Keeper, pages 131–41.

- Bread that you are going to use soon should be wrapped and stored in the pantry, on the counter or shelf, or in a bread bin, at room temperature. Wrapping prevents the bread from drying out. However, if you leave the wrapping a little loose around the bread, this may help prevent moisture from condensing inside and thus help prevent molding. To keep Italian or French bread crusty, use a paper wrap or bag, and be sure to use the bread quickly. Do not store bread near bananas, onions, or other odorous foods; it readily takes on flavors.

- Remove some of the bread from the package and freeze it if you think you will not be able to use it before it goes stale. Commercial breads with preservatives keep fresh at room temperature for three or four days or even longer; bread that lacks preservatives may go stale in as few as one or two days. If bread is sliced before it is frozen, you can generally remove as many slices of frozen bread as you need and thaw them on the counter or in the microwave or toast them if you are in a hurry. Bread preserves its quality through the thawing and microwaving and toasting well.

FREEZE BREAD OR STORE AT ROOM TEMPERATURE

In his book *On Food and Cooking* (Scribner, 1984), the great kitchen rationalist Harold McGee explains something I had always noticed but refused to accept because it made no sense to me: that refrigerated bread goes stale faster than bread kept on the counter. This happens, says Mr. McGee, because bread becomes stale quickly at temperatures just above freezing, and extremely slowly at temperatures just below freezing. So while freezing is a good way to keep bread fresh, refrigerating isn't. One investigation showed that at a refrigerated temperature of 46°F bread stales as much in one day as it would in six days at 86°F. Moreover, the faster the bread is frozen, the less time it spends in the temperature near and above 32°F and the less readily it goes stale. So you should either store your bread at room temperature or freeze it as quickly as you can.

- You should not refrigerate bread, even though you can freeze it, as it goes stale rapidly in the refrigerator. But there are no absolutes. Bread that does not contain preservatives (and, in hot, humid weather, even bread that does contain preservatives) will mold quickly at room temperature. Once a little mold forms on bread, you must throw it all out. Thus refrigeration might be better than pantry storage at very warm temperatures. But freezing bread is always a better alternative than refrigerating it.
- High-acid canned foods, such as tomatoes and foods made with tomatoes, fruits, sauerkraut, and any foods containing vinegar, should be kept on your shelf no longer than twelve to eighteen months. Keep low-acid foods (which include most canned meats and poultry, stews, soups that are not tomato-based, and vegetables such as corn, potatoes, green beans, spinach, peas, pumpkin, and beets) no longer than two to five years. If you tend to keep canned goods for long periods, write the purchase date on the label of each can so you can keep track of its age. After the desirable storage period has passed, throw the can away.
- Canned beets and asparagus do not store as well as other vegetables. They retain top quality for only six months or so.
- Produce in glass bottles usually has a better flavor than that in cans but is subject to light deterioration. Keep glass jars in the dark.
- Dried mushrooms can be stored in the pantry for about six months before opening and three months after opening.
- Turn cans of evaporated milk top to bottom every month or two so that the solids do not collect in a hard-to-remove mass at the bottom of the can.
- Keep spices and dried herbs (other than paprika, red pepper, and chili powder, which should be refrigerated) tightly sealed in light-proof containers, and store them in a cool, dark place. Fresh spices

that you grind yourself are best. Air, heat, and light cause deterioration, especially the loss of the essential oils in spices, which largely carry their flavor.

- Store tea in an airtight container once the package is open. A real tea can of some sort is a good thing to have.
- Store flour and meal in airtight containers. You can put the whole package of flour or meal into a jar or canister, or you can pour out the contents into the canister. (Remember to store whole-grain meals and flours in the refrigerator.)
- *Follow instructions on the labels of ROP and vacuum-packed foods.* Many of them require refrigeration, or refrigeration after opening, and are not safe stored on a cabinet shelf.

Pests in the Pantry

Your local extension service may give you advice on this subject that I have never been able to bring myself to follow. If you open your flour or cornmeal and find an association of beetles, weevils, meal worms, or other small creatures enjoying life there, you are not to panic and throw it out, unless the insects are *numerous;* these types are not harmful. Instead you are to get out a fine-mesh strainer or sifter and sift them out. Next put the flour, meal, or whatever had been infested into an air- and moisture-tight container and freeze it. (This gives you insurance that no progeny are left alive.) Then use the flour or meal with confidence.

I have experienced three such infestations in my housekeeping life, two limited to a single box or package and one that affected several packages. What had happened was that I had bought items that were already inhabited at the market, and, in the third case, the infestation had spread from there at home. I could never manage even the straining or sifting, let alone eating food made of the flour or meal afterward, and so I simply threw all the infested foods out. Perhaps you will be more rational. The advice, in any event, does not apply to cockroaches, which can carry harmful or dangerous microorganisms.

Whatever you choose to do about the infested package, take steps to protect your other foods against infestation. Remove everything from the cabinet and wash it thoroughly. One cooperative extension service I spoke to says you can use a pesticide approved for food areas in cracks and crevices that are difficult to clean. Without using pesticides, I successfully cured all three of my infestations with no recurrence. But your situation may be different, and you may find that you need pesticides.

After you have washed the cabinet, examine all the boxes and packages that were stored in the vicinity of the infested one to be sure there are no insects in any of them. I found insects in a few packages that had never been opened; the insects either had bored through the paper side of the package or had managed to squeeze through a seam somewhere. If the packages are free of insects, replace them on the shelves when the shelves dry. Otherwise, throw out or sift, then freeze, as before.

Remember that cross-infestation can be avoided if you keep vulnerable packages in plastic containers with tight lids. Most important, remember that bugs in the flour or meal have *nothing* to do with cleanliness, only with your luck. They are in no way due to your housekeeping.

13

Safe Food

Causes of foodborne illness . . . Recommended safe cooking temperatures . . . How to use thermometers for food effectively . . . Cooking red meats and hamburgers, poultry, eggs, and fish safely . . . Buying pasteurized foods . . . Two rules for serving foods safely . . . Cooling and thawing safely . . . Guidelines for avoiding cross-contamination . . . Washing fruits and vegetables . . . Sanitizing food-contact surfaces . . . Chopping boards . . . Sanitizing drains and disposals, dishcloths, brushes, pot scratchers, sponges . . . Effects of washing in the dishwasher . . . Guide to Common Food Pathogens . . . What to do about contaminated foods . . . Reduced-oxygen or modified-atmosphere packaged foods . . . Cooking by-products: safe cooking with meats, fats, and oils

All of us who want to eat good home-cooked food owe it to ourselves, and to our friends and families, to educate or reeducate ourselves on the subject of food safety. For some years now, several circumstances of modern life have combined to create new risks of foodborne illness. First, there are a number of new, emerging pathogens, as well as virulent new strains of old ones, that can live in food and make us sick. Our parents and grandparents did not have to deal with *E. coli* O157:H7, *Cyclospora, Cryptosporidium, Campylobacter, Listeria,* and *Yersinia,* but we do. Second, the food industry has changed. Food comes to us not only from all over the country but from all over the world, and meats, poultry, and eggs are produced at huge, centralized, factory-like places. In some instances, such changes have meant that food is more likely to be contaminated with pathogens. At the same time, never were children so likely as they are today to grow up and leave their parents' homes, remaining entirely uneducated in how to run a kitchen so as to keep food safe.

This chapter, therefore, offers a primer on food safety in the home kitchen, explaining how foodborne illness arises and what our chief means of preventing it are. Extremely effective and simple means of prevention are available to all of us. Yet it is so easy to succumb to irrational fears of food that newcomers to the art of running a kitchen should keep the following reminders in mind as they read. This chapter is full of information on dangers that you cannot see, taste, or smell, and you should learn about these and the simple steps you can take to reduce the risks from such hidden dangers. But it is as true as it ever was that most dangers of foodborne illness coincide with conditions that are not at all mysterious. Bad-tasting, moldy, discolored, or rotten food is far more likely to be unhealthy and unsafe than food that is not. Kitchens in which surfaces, dishes, pots and pans, and chopping boards are soiled with crumbs, grease, spills, and smears are more likely to cause illness than sparkling clean ones. Yes, there are cases in which people follow all the rules and still get sick. But it is overwhelmingly true that foodborne illness is the result of simple and obvious mishandling of food: we fail to wash our hands or our foods, to cook foods well, to refrigerate them promptly and effectively, and to avoid cross-contamination. Once you have adopted good basic kitchen and cooking habits, it is time to stop worrying. The food in our country is generally of high quality, and your careful handling of it gives you a comfortably wide margin of safety.

Foodborne Illness: In General

Every year, tens of millions of us suffer from foodborne illness. This is serious business: it can result in severe complications or death. As always, the very young, the very old, sick and immunosuppressed people, and pregnant women are more vulnerable to harm than others. Usually, however, illness caused by contaminated foods is more uncomfortable and humiliating than life-threatening.

When it happened to me, within hours of ingesting contaminated food I began to vomit and developed diarrhea. Within a couple of days I felt fine again. But many foodborne illnesses do not follow this pattern. For one thing, they may not appear until days after you ate the bad food. *Staphylococcus aureus* usually appears in two to three hours, salmonellosis in twelve to twenty-four hours, and botulism most commonly in twelve to thirty-six hours. But *E. coli* has an incubation period of about three to eight days; *Campylobacter* infection comes on in two to five days; *Cyclospora* may take a week to make you sick. Listeriosis can develop anywhere from one to ninety days after consumption, but a few weeks is typical. Diarrhea, cramps, and vomiting, which may be mild or severe, are common symptoms but are not universal. Some kinds of food poisoning cause weakness, chills or fever, headaches, blurred or double vision, difficulty in breathing, the symptoms of meningitis, or flulike illness.

All food contains microorganisms. Some are harmless or even beneficial. But others, called pathogens, can cause illness in one of two ways. First, they themselves can invade your body and make you ill when you eat food containing them. This is called infection by the microorganisms. Second, microorganisms can produce toxins—harmful chemicals—in food, which will make you ill when you eat the food even if the microorganisms that produced the toxins are destroyed. For example, the bacterium *Staphylococcus aureus* will be destroyed by cooking, but its toxin will withstand heat, refrigeration, and freezing. The toxin that causes deadly botulism, however, would be destroyed if boiled for ten or fifteen minutes. Illness caused by ingesting toxins is called intoxication (but this type of intoxication, of course, has nothing to do with drunkenness).

To make your food safe, you must protect against infection with microorganisms that grow in foods *and* against poisoning, or intoxication, by toxins that microorganisms may have produced.

Like all living things, microorganisms need a favorable environment to survive and grow in, not too acidic or too alkaline,[1] not too hot or too cold, free of chemicals that might poison them (such as disinfectants or acids), and providing adequate food and water. Some bacteria are hardy—like some plants and animals—and survive under extremely unfavorable conditions. Others are impervious to one set of hardships but vulnerable to another; perhaps they will survive freezing but not heat, or perhaps they can tolerate a salty medium but not an acidic one. Just like other living things, some microbes are tougher than others of the same type. And just like most plants and animals, they can often live for a while in bad conditions, say without food or water, and start to thrive when some comes along; during the bad times they may simply survive, dormant, without growing or multiplying. (The Guide to Common Food Pathogens, pages 178–86, gives a summary of basic facts pertaining to some common food pathogens.)

Much of our food potentially provides both nutrients and water along with other favorable conditions for luxuriant microbial growth. So do wet chopping boards, knives and utensils, food-soiled or wet countertops, sink basins, dishes, drains, sponges, pot scratchers, damp dish towels and dishcloths, and our own hands. A minuscule crumb of food is a mountain range of sustenance for millions of bacteria. Spills and sticky or oily surfaces provide ample supplies for veritable armies of microbes. By the same token, where things are clean and dry, bacteria and other microbes are going to be vastly reduced in number. Even a "clean" but wet countertop can be home to millions of bacteria, but you can create a staggeringly reduced bacterial count simply by drying it off and keeping it dry for a couple of hours. The simplest and most important rule of food safety is: keep your kitchen clean and dry.

The presence of pathogens in foods that you have consumed does not guarantee that you will become sick. That depends on many factors, including the state of your health and resistance and just how many microbes or how much toxin you consumed. To some extent, it even depends on what you are used to, as we all tend to become accustomed to the microbes we commonly encounter in our own homes. Infectious sickness follows only when you ingest an "infectious dose" of pathogens. (See chapter 30, "Peaceful Coexistence with Microbes," pages 423–24.) Although it may take shockingly few microbes to give you certain kinds of food poisoning, for example by *E. coli*, there are many kinds, such as certain strains of salmonella, to which healthy adults may succumb only if they consume tens or even hundreds of thousands of the causative pathogen. More microbes also produce more toxin; and although the tiniest taste of some toxins, such as the one that causes botulism, can be deadly, generally you are worse off the more you take in. Thus the real goal of many kitchen safety rules is to create conditions in and around your food that are unfavorable to the *growth and multiplication* of dangerous microbes. That way, even if some bad ones do survive, there may be so few that they cannot make you sick, or you may get a mild illness rather than a severe one.

Temperature

Safe Temperatures and the Importance of Using Thermometers. Our most important means of killing and reducing the numbers of pathogens in our foods is temperature control: refrigerated storage and adequate cooking. People knew this and made food safe long before they knew there were such things as bacteria. Today, most of our kitchen behavior continues to be intuitive and customary, not science-based. We make things safe by doing things the way our parents did. Food-safety experts, however, urge you to make a change and introduce to your kitchen and cooking customs safeguards that our parents and grandparents often did not have: *use thermometers*—to test food temperatures, refrigerator temperatures, and freezer temperatures. They mean going beyond the occasional use of a candy thermometer or meat thermometer for the turkey.

Most bacteria grow in the temperature range between 40° and 140°F and are destroyed at higher temperatures. Bacteria that cause foodborne illness usually multiply most rapidly at between 60° and 125°F. Molds, like bacteria, can grow over a broad temperature range. They usually grow best between 64° and 86°F and are destroyed at temperatures over 140°F.

We refrigerate foods at 40°F or below so as to create an environment unfavorable to the multiplication of microorganisms. Refrigeration slows down the growth of most microorganisms without killing them and without stopping their growth entirely. It keeps food from spoiling for a few days. But as all of us know from unpleasant experience, sooner or later even food stored in the refrigerator spoils or grows moldy; and some bacteria can grow better in cold temperatures than others. Your freezer, which should be kept at 0°F, keeps food much longer because temperatures this low generally stop microbial growth altogether. However, most bacteria are not killed by freezing either. They will again begin multiplying as soon as they are thawed and returned to the favorable temperature range. The foods may become inedible from other causes in the meantime: rancidity, loss of texture, drying out.

Temperatures above 160°F do not merely prevent growth but actually kill most microorganisms. This is why cooking is our most important defense against food poisoning. Some bacteria, however, form "spores," hard shells that protect them from environmental dangers such as extreme heat. Such spores do not die but "rest" until conditions are favorable once again. Some bacterial spores are practically indomitable, surviving even boiling. Spores are one reason why food may become unsafe again even after cooking unless the food is kept in the proper temperature zone: when the food after cooking cools down to within the zone of temperatures favorable to bacteria, the spores that survived will start to grow again. (This is one of the key dangers to be guarded against in home canning. See the information about *Clostridium botulinum* in the Guide to Common Food Pathogens, pages 180–81.) Commercial canning processes use a combination of very high temperatures plus pressure, which can destroy spores, to achieve the impressive safety record of commercial canned goods. If you serve home-canned foods, especially those that are low in acid, such as stew or corn, the USDA recommends that you boil them for at least ten minutes before serving. (Add one minute of boiling for every one thousand feet you are above sea level.)

Once you have brought food to a safe temperature by cooking, keep it hot (over 140°F) until it is eaten. This helps prevent any bacteria or spores that chanced to survive the cooking (or were newly introduced into the food by some accident after cooking) from having a chance to multiply in it. For the same reason, you should cool foods to below 40°F quickly. Otherwise, the food spends a dangerously long time passing through the risky temperature zones in which microbes multiply (between 40° and 140°F). And you should keep foods cold (40°F or less) that are supposed to be cold. Be sure to reheat leftovers thoroughly before serving them. Liquids or wet foods should be brought to a rolling boil. Bring other foods, including leftover meats and poultry, to at least 165°F.

The USDA recommends that you always use a meat thermometer to be sure that your food has actually reached and been maintained at the recommended safe temperatures. (A meat thermometer will sometimes work for other kinds of foods.) The cooking temperatures to which you should heat foods in the table below are recommended by the USDA.

Using Thermometers for Food Effectively. Insert the thermometer in the places that are likely to get hot last. The leg of your turkey may register a high temperature even when the meat deep in the breast is still uncooked or when the stuffing is not nearly cooked enough for safety.

> In poultry, insert the meat thermometer into the inner thigh area near the breast, not touching bone.
>
> Test the stuffing separately, and test it twice—once just before the stand time and once at its end. The stand time is the time that you leave your bird to stand at room temperature immediately after cooking and just before serving. The temperature of the stuffing will probably continue to rise throughout the stand time.
>
> In meats, make sure the thermometer is in the thickest part and away from bone, fat, and gristle.
>
> Insert the thermometer in the thickest part of casseroles and egg dishes, but make sure it does not touch the bottom.
>
> In thin items such as chops or ground-beef patties, put the thermometer in sideways.[2]

You may use either of two main types of meat thermometers, but be sure that you use a meat thermometer and not a candy thermometer or some other kind. One type of meat thermometer is ovenproof. You insert this type in the food before you put it in the

COOKING TEMPERATURES

Eggs—Cook until yolks and whites are firm

Egg dishes—160°F

Ground meats and meat mixtures
- Turkey and chicken—165°F
- Veal, beef, lamb, pork—160°F

Fresh beef
- Medium rare—145°F
- Medium—160°F
- Well done—170°F

Fresh veal
- Medium rare—145°F
- Medium—160°F
- Well done—170°F

Fresh lamb
- Medium rare—145°F
- Medium—160°F
- Well done—170°F

Fresh pork
- Medium—160°F
- Well done—170°F

Poultry
- Chicken, whole—180°F
- Turkey, whole—180°F
- Poultry breasts, roasts—170°F
- Poultry thighs, wings—180°F
- Stuffing (cooked alone or in bird)—165°F
- Duck and goose—180°F

Ham
- Fresh (raw)—160°F
- Precooked (to reheat)—140°F

Miscellaneous
- When holding foods for serving, or at buffets, keep hot foods over 140°F; keep cold foods under 40°F.

Source: Cooking temperatures table in "A Quick Consumer Guide to Safe Food Handling," House and Garden Bulletin No. 248, August 1995, USDA, Food Safety and Inspection Service.

oven and leave it there during cooking until it shows that a safe temperature has been reached and the food is done. The other is a quick-read type. You cannot leave it in the food. If your food is in the oven, pull out the oven shelf and insert the quick-read meat thermometer in the proper place in the food for a good test reading: about two inches into the thickest part of the food *not touching the bone.* It registers in about fifteen seconds. *Be sure to wash any thermometer with hot, sudsy water after use and before reinserting to test temperature again.* Washing ensures that any harmful bacteria present in the food before it achieves a safe temperature are not reintroduced later by the thermometer itself.

Some poultry comes with pop-up thermometers already inserted. They are accurate if properly placed, but it is wise to use another thermometer to test the bird in a few other places just to be sure. You can also buy your own pop-up thermometers.

Test microwaved food for safe temperatures with a thermometer too; be sure to test in several places. (There are thermometers specially designed for use in microwaves.) Microwave cooking presents special risks because it leaves cold spots in the food in which microorganisms can survive. To ensure that all parts of the food have warmed to safe temperatures, cover the food with a lid or vented plastic wrap. This makes steam build up underneath and helps get all parts of the food warm. Remove the dish and stir thoroughly a couple of times during cooking, and turn the dish in the microwave, or move it now and then, so that different parts of it warm. If a microwaving recipe calls for standing time, obey the recipe! Cooking goes on during this period from heat already absorbed by the food.

Some Guidelines for Food Safety

Cooking Red Meats and Hamburgers Safely. Use your eyes when you cook. Red meats should be cooked at least until they turn grayish or brown, without any pink or red flesh or juices, inside or out. Pork is usually well cooked when the juices run clear. Because of deadly outbreaks of illness caused by *E. coli* O157:H7 in undercooked hamburgers, the USDA recommends that *no one*—especially children, the elderly, and immunosuppressed or otherwise vulnerable people—eat rare or medium-rare hamburger or any other dishes that include raw, rare, or pink beef. Moreover, because of some evidence indicating that ground beef can be unsafe even when it is not pink, the USDA strongly urges everyone to *use a meat thermometer to test the doneness of hamburgers.* The desirable temperature is 160°F inside the thickest part of the patty.

Ground meats, such as hamburger, are more dangerous than others because grinding spreads any dangerous microbes throughout the meat. Thus a hamburger patty is more likely to have *E. coli* in its pink middle than a steak, which is likely to harbor bacteria on its outside where they are more readily reached and killed by the heat of cooking. But rare meat of any kind poses risks. It takes very few *E. coli* O157:H7 to cause illness, and the illness can be deadly. Children, immunocompromised people, the elderly, pregnant women, and sick people of any description are particularly vulnerable to serious harm from rare and undercooked meats.

Cooking Poultry Safely. Pathogens such as *Salmonella enteriditis, Campylobacter jejuni, Staphylococcus aureus,* and *Listeria monocytogenes* are estimated to be present in a substantial percentage of all poultry sold for food in this country. The Centers for Disease Control documented 39,027 cases of salmonellosis in 1996 and estimates that the number of unreported cases each year runs to the hundreds of thousands or higher.

Cook poultry at least to the USDA-recommended temperatures. Poultry is generally cooked safely when the juices run clear, but you cannot be sure unless you test with a meat thermometer. The USDA recommends that you cook stuffing separately because of the frequency with which people fail to get it hot enough inside the bird and suffer illness as a result. If you really want to cook stuffing in the bird, however, do not place the stuffing inside until immediately before cooking, and do *not* buy prestuffed turkeys. When you have tested both the bird and the stuffing with a meat thermometer to make sure each has reached a safe temperature (in the manner recommended on page 165), remove the stuffing immediately and place it in a separate serving bowl. Never cook a stuffed bird in the microwave. Because the microwave heats foods unevenly, you cannot be sure that all parts will reach a safe temperature. You can address questions about safe cooking techniques for poultry and stuffing to the USDA Meat and Poultry Hotline at 1-800-535-4555 (or 447-3333 if you're calling from Washington, D.C.). Or write to your local cooperative extension service.

Cooking Eggs Safely. Given many people's taste for lightly cooked egg dishes, perhaps even more important than the increase in contamination of poultry is the contamination of eggs with salmonella. Strains of this bacterium infect hens' ovaries and get into the egg in its shell. The USDA urges us to exercise greater caution in our use of eggs. Everyone can eat hard-cooked eggs, as hard-cooking them, by boiling or frying, kills salmonella bacteria. All of us, but especially all vulnerable people (the very young and old, sick people, immunosuppressed people) should avoid eating any eggs with soft or runny yolks—soft-boiled, over light, sunny-side up, or prepared in similar styles. The USDA recommends that healthy adults who are determined to eat eggs that are not completely firm follow the cooking time guidelines below to reduce risk. Doing so is intended to partly hard-cook the yolk all around its outside and get the middle hot and thickened but not hard.

Fried eggs: cook 2 to 3 minutes on each side; 4 minutes in a covered pan.

Scrambled eggs: cook until firm throughout.

Poached eggs: cook 5 minutes over boiling water.

Soft-cooked eggs: Cook 7 minutes in the shell in boiling water.[3]

All foods made with raw eggs, and recipes for foods containing raw eggs, should be avoided: meringue, eggnog, homemade mayonnaise, homemade ice cream, Caesar salad, chilled chocolate mousse, or béarnaise or hollandaise sauce. (Many of these foods can be made using pasteurized egg products or substitutes. To find revised recipes, contact your local cooperative extension service or find an up-to-date cookbook that offers recipes that rely on pasteurized eggs or other substitutes for fresh eggs.) Do not taste egg-containing foods before they are cooked—cookie dough, raw egg noodles, cake batter, various pie fillings, or pudding. It is especially hard to deny tastes to your children when you remember happily licking the spoon or bowl in your own childhood and suffering no harm from it, but it is necessary to do so. Refrigerate cooked eggs and foods containing them promptly when meals are over. Even hard-cooked Easter eggs should not be left out of the refrigerator. If they have been unrefrigerated for more than two hours, throw them away. Hard-boiling an egg in the shell destroys much of the natural protection given by the shell. Thus, even though cooking kills bacteria in the egg at the time of cooking, it also renders the hard-boiled egg less resistant to future contamination than an uncooked one. Refrigerate hard-boiled eggs and use within a week.

Cooking Fish Safely. Fish is generally cooked when it flakes with a fork and no longer looks wet or rubbery inside. Eating raw fish or shellfish is playing Russian roulette. All fish and shellfish must be thoroughly cooked. Cooking shellfish just enough to open the shells is definitely insufficient to destroy many dangerous types of microorganisms, and eating such shellfish is a common cause of food poisoning. Raw or undercooked oysters and clams—even when fresh and when taken from "clean" water—may harbor any of several dangerous microorganisms, such as *Vibrio vulnificus,* an emerging pathogen that is extremely dangerous to people with liver and immune disorders and other illnesses.

Buy Pasteurized Milk, Dairy Products, and Juices. Pasteurization is an indispensable heat treatment for many foods. *Always* buy pasteurized dairy products; never consume raw milk or cheese or other products made from raw milk. Always buy pasteurized juices and cider, too; especially avoid serving unpasteurized juices or cider to children or other vulnerable people. Serious outbreaks of illness have occurred from *E. coli* in unpasteurized apple juice and cider.

Two Basic Rules for Safely Serving Foods. The first rule of thumb recommended by food-safety experts is this: keep hot foods hot and cold foods cold. This means to keep hot foods at 140°F or higher and cold foods at 40°F or below. At a buffet, use heating devices to keep the hot dishes at temperatures of at least 140°F. Use ice to keep cold foods at temperatures of 40°F or lower. Put foods in the refrigerator or keep them heated on the stove until you are ready to serve them. Marinate foods in the refrigerator, not on the countertop.

The second rule for keeping food safe is the "two-hour rule." Hot foods and cold foods that are left at temperatures lower than 140°F and higher than 40°F for more than two hours should be thrown away, no matter how heartbreaking this seems or how it hurts your budget. If the air temperature exceeds 90°F, throw away any food that stands out for one hour. Don't taste foods to see if they still taste good. Much dangerous food tastes and looks good, and is still dangerous even if you recook it. Heat may not destroy toxins in food even though it destroys the bacteria that produced the toxins.

Cooling and Thawing Safely. As cooked food cools, say from 150° down to 35°F, it necessarily passes through temperatures between 40° and 140°F, the range most favorable to the growth of bacteria. Therefore, when you are ready to store food, you must try to cool it as quickly as possible, so that it spends a minimum of time in that dangerous zone. To achieve this, you are advised by the USDA to put foods *in the refrigerator or freezer for cooling.* Do not first let the stock or soup or roast cool on the stove or countertop. You are also advised to break food down into smaller portions for cooling and freezing, because even in the refrigerator or freezer large batches take too long to cool or freeze. Put leftovers in shallow, small containers. (Be sure that they do not leak or drip.) If you are refrigerating stuffing, take it out of the bird or roast and put it in a separate container to speed the cooling process.

You may object that putting things in the refrigerator or freezer when they are still hot temporarily warms the refrigerator or freezer and makes it run more. You are right, but this does not last long. The benefits of doing so definitely outweigh the costs. (To avoid heating up the refrigerator or freezer, however, I sometimes cool soups or stocks by cooking them down, then adding ice cubes until they again reach the proper volume.)

The USDA urges you *not* to thaw foods at room temperature, on the counter. If you thaw a frozen chicken on the countertop, the outside of the chicken reaches room temperature while the inside remains frozen. Salmonella and other microorganisms can begin multiplying in those outer portions even while the inside is too cold. Your safest bet is to *thaw foods in the refrigerator.* This ensures that no part of the food ever exceeds 40°F. When thawing foods in the refrigerator, put a plate under them so that juices do not drip onto other foods or onto shelves where they might contaminate other foods.

Refrigerator thawing takes foresight. It can take days to thaw a large chicken or turkey in the refrigerator, depending upon how deeply the bird was frozen and how large it is. Allow twenty-four hours for each five pounds of weight; for example, for a fifteen-pound bird, allow seventy-two hours, or three days. If you need to thaw something faster, the USDA recommends the cold-water method. Fully immerse the frozen bird, wrapped in leakproof plastic, in cold water. Allow thirty minutes per pound, and change the water every thirty minutes. This would produce thawing in the following time periods:

8–12 pounds .... 4–6 hours
12–16 pounds .... 6–8 hours
16–20 pounds .... 8–10 hours
20–24 pounds .... 10–12 hours

The fastest of all thawing methods is the microwave. When you do this, however, you must cook the bird *immediately* after thawing it. The time required varies not only with the size and nature of your food but with the power and make of your microwave. Refer to your manufacturer's instruction booklet. My microwave will thaw a three-pound whole chicken in a little over twenty minutes; yours may be different. Of course microwave thawing may be impossible for large items such as turkeys. Moreover, you may find that microwave thawing negatively affects the texture, tenderness, or moistness of certain foods. In some cases, however, it is ideal—for example, when you want fast thawing of stocks and soups.

Avoiding Cross-Contamination

You would never lick a fork after you had speared raw chicken with it. But many people unthinkingly engage in kitchen practices just as dangerous as this. Cross-contamination is what happens when food pathogens in one food are transferred to another food. Although the food-safety experts tirelessly warn us against it, the classic route to illness from cross-contamination is still traveled hundreds of times each year: someone cuts up raw chicken, meat, or fish on a chopping board or plate or other surface, and then, without first washing and sanitizing the chopping surface, chops salad vegetables on it. The raw flesh leaves a pathogen on the chopping board, which is picked up on the lettuce or cucumbers and then eaten in a raw salad. No one gets sick from eating the flesh, since it is first cooked to a safe temperature, but the whole family becomes deathly ill from eating the apparently harmless salad. To avoid cross-contamination, you must be sure not to accidentally introduce pathogens into foods, especially foods that are to be prepared and stored in ways that will not kill bacteria or prevent them from multiplying.

Cross-contamination can happen in a hundred different ways. One food can drip contaminated drops onto another. One unsafe ingredient can contaminate an entire dish. A transfer can be effected through a spoon, a pot, or a chopping board. Your own hands all too often supply the route whereby bacteria travel from one food to another. Even the most experienced cook can benefit from reading through the rules set forth below.

Guidelines for Avoiding Cross-Contamination

Wash your hands for fifteen to twenty seconds in comfortably hot, sudsy water. Much foodborne illness is caused by a failure to exercise this basic rule of hygiene. If you wear plastic gloves, you still have to wash, in the same way, with the gloves on, because they pick up microorganisms too. Wash your hands especially carefully after using the toilet, changing a baby's diaper, blowing your nose, or touching a pet, a cage, or the cat-litter box. Wash your hands before you cook anything. Not only that, continue to wash your hands throughout the cooking process, especially after you have handled anything raw or likely to harbor pathogens. This means washing your hands before and after you cut up raw poultry, fish, meat, or any other animal food. (Then wash and sanitize your chopping boards and implements too.) Wash your hands before and after handling raw fruits or vegetables. Wash your hands when you have finished handling one foodstuff and are going to work on another. Cover cuts, sores, or boils on your hands or face with a waterproof dressing or wear disposable plastic gloves.

Always touch food with your hands as little as possible. Use utensils instead. Be especially careful to avoid touching food if you have had a foodborne illness or any type of diarrheic illness.

Be careful about what you dry your hands on. Use either paper towels or a clean cloth towel, that is, one that has not previously been used.

Don't sneeze or cough over or near food.

Never place other foods on a chopping board, plate, or other surface on which you have previously placed raw meat, poultry, fish, or eggs unless you first wash it thoroughly in hot sudsy water. For additional protection, sanitize the chopping board. (Instructions for sanitizing are given on page 173.) In fact, the experts recommend that you keep at least two chopping boards. Use one chopping board for fruits, vegetables, and bread, and keep one or more other chopping board *only* for meats, fish, and poultry. In any event, wash and, if you wish, sanitize any chopping board immediately after using it in the preparation of raw meat, poultry, or fish.

Wash any chopping board, plate, or other food-contact surface with hot, sudsy water after chopping fruits and vegetables on it, too, for these can also harbor pathogens, even though illness from such sources is less common. (Wash the produce too.) Always keep in mind that whatever touched the board will touch the next food on the board—unless you first wash or wash and sanitize.

After using knives or other utensils on food—especially raw meat, poultry, fish, or eggs—thoroughly wash them in hot sudsy water before using them on other foods. For additional protection, sanitize knives according to the instructions on page 173

Put plates or platters under foods that might drip in the refrigerator. Be extremely careful not to let raw fish, meat, or poultry liquids drip onto foods that will be eaten without cooking. Wrap foods in plastic wrap or put them in plastic bags to protect them.

Watch out for drips, splashes, and accidental mixings. Move things out of the way when you have to carry packages of raw meat, poultry, or fish, and try to carry them in leakproof packages or on plates. Keep raw meats, fish, poultry, and eggs well separated from cooked foods and from foods that are to be eaten raw, such as fruits and vegetables.

When liquid from meat, poultry, or fish spills onto your counter or into your sink, immediately wipe it up and wash the counter or sink with hot, sudsy water.

Immediately wash with hot, sudsy water or place in the dishwasher any utensil, plate, or pot that has come into contact with raw meat, fish, eggs, or poultry. And *never* pull a utensil out of the dishwasher, rinse it under the tap, and use it. The utensil may have touched something dangerous. Rinsing under the tap will not get it clean enough for safety.

Keep the refrigerator and pantry shelves, drawers, and walls clean so that stored food does not become contaminated from food stored there earlier or from molds growing there.

Use different spoons to stir different bowls and pots. If you used a spoon to stir a dish when it was raw or not adequately cooked, thoroughly wash it before you use it to stir the same dish later. Otherwise, microbes left on the spoon by the food in its raw state will reinfect it.

Every time you taste food you are preparing, use a clean spoon or fork. Do not put a utensil that has gone into your mouth into food that will be eaten by others. Germs in your mouth may be deposited into the food by means of the spoon or fork. Likewise, never use your own eating utensils to serve or taste food in a serving bowl at the table.

Serve foods only with perfectly clean plates, bowls, pots, and utensils. *Never serve food on a plate that has been touched by raw meat, poultry, eggs, or fish.*

If a recipe calls for you to baste food with its marinade, reserve some for this purpose *before* you put the food in the marinade. Make sure that the marinade cooked with the food comes to a rolling boil. Marinades that will not immediately be cooked with the food that was marinated should be discarded. If there were any dangerous bacteria on your raw chicken or meat or fish, they will have contaminated the marinade too.

Never put leftover foods or condiments back into the jars or cartons out of which they originally came. That is, do not pour milk or cream from the table pitcher back into the carton in the refrigerator; do not put mayonnaise back into the mayonnaise jar; do not put leftover chicken or tuna salad back in the plastic container in the refrigerator from which you served it. This way you avoid contaminating the original source if the part that was taken out has somehow become contaminated.

Do not mix leftovers with fresh foods unless you are going to eat the mixture immediately, and make sure the leftovers are fresh enough to eat. (And preheat cooled leftovers to at least 165°F before eating them.) Remember that you shorten the storage life of any food when you mix it with food that is about to expire.

Store fruits and vegetables in their own bags and places. Store newly bought ones separate from old ones; do not put the old head of lettuce into the bag with the new one.

Keep pets out of food preparation areas, and off tables and countertops.

Washing Your Foods

Thoroughly Wash Fruits and Vegetables. Do this just before using them, not before putting them in the refrigerator. Even if you are going to peel the produce, *wash it thoroughly before you peel it* because otherwise your knife or peeler or fingers could pick up microorganisms and carry them through to contaminate the underlying flesh of the produce. Washing helps remove not only dirt, but microorganisms and any traces of pesticides. Food scientists say that washing probably decreases the risk of getting sick but does not eliminate it, particularly because bacteria may adhere tightly. Still, the experts agree: *wash produce thoroughly,* even if you plan to peel it.

Before washing, remove all outer leaves. Wash hard-skinned produce such as cucumbers, apples, or eggplant by scrubbing hard and thoroughly, under a hard stream of running cold water, with no soap, until all visible soil is removed. The force of the running water, like the scrubbing, helps carry off microorganisms as well as dirt. If there is no visible soil, wash or scrub hard under running water anyway. Use a clean vegetable brush for scrubbing, especially on root vegetables such as carrots and potatoes. Bacteria are especially likely to be numerous in bits of soil that adhere to vegetables. Even if you see no soil on them, root vegetables are still more likely to harbor bacteria from the soil. Vegetables fertilized with manure are particularly suspect.

Of course, you cannot scrub or rub soft-skinned produce such as berries, mushrooms, lettuce, or greens without macerating them. The best technique for washing these is to wash them in a stream of water as hard-running as it can be without ripping or bruising the produce. Gently rub off the dirt or soil under the stream. You can put berries and similar items into a sieve or colander, running the water over them as you gently bounce or turn them. Wash all vegetables for a *long* time. A few seconds won't do.

You may have seen newspaper or magazine articles telling you to wash produce with soap, but the FDA and the USDA do not recommend using soap; its residues might remain on or get absorbed into the food. (Some authorities say soap may also break down the skin of the produce, rendering it more susceptible to bacterial invasion.)

Washing helps reduce any pesticide residues on foods, as does peeling away skins and rinds and tearing off outer leaves.[4] In peeling, of course, you sacrifice the nutrients and fiber in these portions of the foods.

Wash Lids of Cans. Use a little hot, sudsy water and dry with a clean towel or paper towel. Be sure to wash and dry thoroughly the crack at the circumference of the lid where dirt tends to resist washing out. Don't forget that the can has been handled by strangers and perhaps has sat in warehouses, in storerooms, and on shelves for days, weeks, or months. It has collected dust and, perhaps, insect or rodent droppings, hairs, pesticides, cleaning substances, or heaven knows what. If you do not wash it, the liquid inside the can will wash the dirt on the lid into the contents when you press down while opening.

Sanitizing

The USDA believes that using your dishwasher or washing your dishes with hot, sudsy water ordinarily gives you all the protection you need against pathogens. Sanitizing offers added protection in certain circumstances. Effective sanitizing requires a germicidal agent that kills a broad spectrum of microorganisms; for surfaces and objects that are going to touch food, you need one that will be safe around food, even without being rinsed off. For home use on utensils and surfaces that will touch food, the USDA and the FDA recommend regular household chlorine bleach (a 5.25 percent solution, ap-

SAFETY SUMMARY

Wash your hands!

Cook foods hot enough and long enough.

Keep hot foods hot (140°F or higher) and cold foods cold (40°F or lower) while waiting to serve them or storing them. Do not eat foods that have been kept at improper holding temperatures for two hours or more (or for one hour in temperatures of 90°F or higher).

Refrigerate leftovers quickly.

Chill or freeze food rapidly in small quantities.

Reheat leftovers to 165°F.

Thaw foods in the refrigerator, in ice water, or in the microwave, not on a countertop or at room temperature.

Avoid cross-contamination.

Wash vegetables and fruits carefully.

Keep fingers out of food. As much as possible, avoid handling food; use utensils.

proximately, of sodium hypochlorite). It kills a broad spectrum of bacteria, viruses, and molds; it is fast, highly effective, and cheap; and it quickly breaks down into harmless components. When you are sanitizing *non-food-contact* surfaces, such as ordinary countertops or tabletops on which you do not place food directly, you can use any commercial sanitizing product you like. Look for an EPA registration number.

In addition to the details given below, further information on sanitizing and disinfecting can be found in chapter 30, "Peaceful Coexistence with Microbes." Keep in mind that the sanitizing and disinfecting methods ordinarily recommended for the kitchen are backup measures, intended to reinforce other sound habits, not replace them. They do not produce germfree surfaces and objects, but, properly used in conjunction with those habits, help reduce the numbers of bacteria, including potentially harmful ones, so that you have an increased margin of safety. Those who wish to target specific pathogens or who are dealing with situations that pose serious health threats should seek medical advice or the advice of public health authorities in their own communities.

How to Sanitize Food-Contact Surfaces. A basic sanitizing method for all hard food-contact surfaces and objects in your kitchen, wooden and others, is this:*

First, wash the surface carefully with hot, soapy water, making sure that no soil or food particles remain; then rinse thoroughly with plain, clean water.

Second, if possible, immerse it in a sanitizing solution made up of one teaspoon of household chlorine bleach and one quart of water.† Leave it in the solution for a few minutes. If it is something that cannot be immersed—for example, a countertop—then flood it with the sanitizing solution, keeping it wet for a few minutes.

Third, take it out of the sanitizing solution and let it air dry, or pat it dry with clean paper towels. *Do not rinse!*

In this way you can sanitize chopping boards, plates, utensils, sinks, countertops, and any other hard objects or surfaces that have come in contact with raw meat, poultry, fish, eggs, or other foods likely to harbor hazardous microorganisms. It is not a bad idea to sanitize all chopping boards now and then, even if you have not used them for especially hazardous raw foods, even those labeled antimicrobial (see page 175).

Why We Do It This Way. When you are sanitizing, *cleaning comes first.* Before sanitizing food-contact surfaces or objects, you must always first thoroughly wash them with sudsy, hot water. Otherwise, the sanitizing may be ineffective. Remarkably more bacteria can live on a tiny crumb of meat or in a drop of sauce than on any wet or unsanitized countertop; the more food is present, the more bacteria. Even more important, *organic matter*—food particles, the remnants of spills, crumbs of any sort—*can inactivate some antimicrobial products and solutions,* including chlorine bleach, preventing them from doing their germ-killing job. See chapter 30, pages 420 and 431–35. This is why the first and most important line of defense against pathogens in the kitchen is ordinary cleaning—getting rid of crumbs, bits of food,

*But do not use chlorine bleach on nonstainless steel, copper, aluminum, or silver. It may be used on stainless steel but not for extended periods of time.

†You may read recommendations to use stronger recipes. The USDA, however, says this recipe is effective. Stronger solutions might leave residues or cause unpleasant bleach smells. In other places in this book, such as chapter 30, different recipes are recommended for other purposes.

spills, and sticky or oily surfaces. Use some muscle power when you clean; scrub hard, and spray with a strong stream of water.* Notice also that *you should not rinse after sanitizing food-contact surfaces;* anything that touches the surface after sanitizing has the potential to recontaminate it. Thus any products to be used for sanitizing food-contact surfaces should not leave toxic residues behind.

Alternative methods are feasible. For example, the 1999 *Food Code* (a set of model regulations for food services, without the force of law)[5] permits sanitizing food-contact surfaces and utensils by immersion in water that is maintained at 171°F or higher for thirty seconds.[6] (If you want to do this, you should first thoroughly wash the items in hot, sudsy water and rinse them; after immersion in the hot water, the items should be allowed to air-dry.)

Some people just put their chopping boards in the dishwasher after using them, and this is probably effective. (See "Sanitizing in the Dishwasher?" below.) However, it is often impractical—for example, when you want to use a chopping board again right away, when it is not dishwasher-safe, or if you do not know how hot your dishwasher gets.

Microwave sanitizing, too, is theoretically possible, and you may see recommendations in newspapers and magazines to use this method. To me it seems unwise. There are no reliable guidelines for the home use of this technique, and there are grave uncertainties involved. For one, microwaves differ from one another and do not all produce the same results. For another, various studies have shown that microwaving works with some objects but not others. Plastic chopping boards, for example, will not get hot enough to be sanitized. Microwaves' spotty heating can be a problem too. Until the food-safety experts announce that they think either of these methods is a good idea for the home, and explain just how dishwasher or microwave sanitizing might effectively be done in the home for different sorts of objects and surfaces, the bleach method for sanitizing food-contact surfaces continues to be a choice that is simple and highly effective.

Which Surfaces Should Your Food Touch? Food belongs on properly maintained and sanitized chopping boards, pastry boards, properly washed and dried pots, pans, dishes, and utensils. Some countertops are designed to be used for food preparation. However, if you want to chop and prepare foods on your countertop, your home should follow rules designed to keep it scrupulously clean and safe. If you cut up chicken on your countertop, you should sanitize the countertop and follow the same rules regarding cross-contamination, with scrupulous care, as you do for chopping boards. You must also ensure that none of the following items are ever put on your countertop: unwashed hands, newspapers and magazines, bags of groceries, toys, bookbags, knapsacks, purses, or briefcases. These objects may have touched the floor, the ground, the sidewalk, or the grocery store checkout counter. If you do not set foods on countertops, this rigor is not necessary and you need to do much less sanitizing. In my home, I find that it is much less trouble to use a clean plate or chopping

*Bacteria have been found to create an invisible, strongly adhering, slimy layer or film of cells, called a biofilm, on even hard and smooth surfaces such as stainless steel. Some research indicates that a biofilm is not easily removed with chemical means alone—for example, detergent or sanitizer—because the film prevents penetration by the chemical. Mechanical force, such as a stream of hard-running water or scrubbing, was found to be important in getting the film off. ("Microbial Attachment Similar for Wooden, Plastic Cutting Boards," *Food Chemical News*, September 30, 1996.)

board than to have to sanitize the counter before using it and worry about who did what on the countertop while I was out of the room. Do not forget that if the kitchen rules are to work, everyone in the household must follow them.

A Note on Chopping Boards. Food-safety experts recommend that you keep two chopping boards: one for raw fish, meat, and poultry, the other for produce and everything else. This in itself goes far to prevent cross-contamination, especially contamination of foods to be eaten raw, by dangerous bacteria from raw fish, meat, or poultry. The debate on whether plastic or wooden chopping boards are better is now regarded as settled in favor of plastic ones. Glass cutting surfaces, too, are recommended over wood for raw meat, fish, and poultry. This is the USDA's latest and best word, although it regards wood cutting boards that are used *exclusively* for raw meat and poultry as acceptable. Wood chopping boards can conceal bacteria in their grooves and pores.[7] Throw away any chopping board—no matter what it is made of—as soon as it shows grooves or nicks, because these can hold bacteria and food particles and render the board difficult to clean. To keep all cutting boards clean, the USDA recommends washing them with hot, sudsy water after each use; then rinse and air-dry or pat dry with fresh paper towels. Nonporous acrylic, plastic, or glass boards and *solid* wood boards can be washed in an automatic dishwasher (laminated boards may crack and split). (To sanitize chopping boards, follow the instructions on page 173.) By the way, although hard, nonporous surfaces of plastic make the most sanitary chopping boards, they are harder on your knives. They will dull them more rapidly than wood, so be prepared to sharpen as necessary.

If you have chopping boards that are labelled "antibacterial" or "antimicrobial," always wash and sanitize them in the same way and on the same occasions as you would any others. They are not intended to be used to replace or substitute for ordinary safe food practices. (The real nature and life span of their antimicrobial efficacies is currently unclear, but you can be sure that if you have gotten raw chicken juices contaminated with pathogens on your chopping board, its antimicrobial action will *not* render them harmless.)

Sanitizing Non-Food-Contact Surfaces and Objects

Hard Surfaces and Objects. Hard surfaces and objects that do not come into contact with food—sinks, countertops, refrigerator drip trays—can be sanitized in the same way as hard food contact surfaces. See page 173.

The Drain and Disposal. Sanitize your kitchen sink drain, connecting pipe, and garbage disposal once or twice a week following your final kitchen cleanup in the evening. This will help control odors as well as keep your kitchen safe. Food particles trapped in this moist environment provide a felicitous habitat for microorganisms, which may grow there in astonishingly high numbers. Contaminated drains are associated with increased risks of acquiring a foodborne illness. To sanitize your drain, connecting pipe, and garbage disposal, the FDA recommends that you make a sanitizing solution of one teaspoon of regular chlorine bleach in one quart of water and pour it down the drain. Or you can use any commercial sanitizing agent according to the directions.

Cloth. Use towels, cloths, and rags prodigally in your kitchen. Keep plenty around, and when they get even a little damp or soiled, get fresh ones. When they are damp and soiled, they grow microbial armies. If you wipe down a countertop with a bacteria-laden towel or cloth, you spread bacteria everywhere. If you go through several of each every day, that's good. They are easy to launder. Ordinary laundering of dish towels, hand towels, dishcloths, aprons, potholders, cheesecloths, pastry cloths, dishrags, and other kitchen cloths will generally make them safe. Washing them with chlorine bleach sanitizes them, and like my mother and grandmothers before me, I do this automatically with all kitchen linens. Some people do not like to use chlorine bleach so often, but they might wish to do so on occasion—say when they have some particular reason to be concerned (or when the linens are beginning to look dingy). To give yourself this valuable option, never buy cloth for the kitchen that you cannot bleach. (To sanitize kitchen towels, rags, and cloths of all sorts, see chapter 27, "Sanitizing the Laundry.")

Brushes, Pot Scratchers. Cleaning implements such as brushes and various types of abrasive scratchers should be washed entirely free of food particles with hot, sudsy water every time you use them. Squeeze out the excess water until they are as dry as possible. If necessary, you can sanitize them as follows: Immerse brushes and pot scratchers in a solution of one tablespoon regular chlorine bleach per gallon of water, and let soak for five to ten minutes. Drain and let air-dry.

Odors indicate that bacteria are growing. *The absence of odors, however, is no guarantee of safety, not even in so-called anti-bacterial cleaning implements.* Wash all implements frequently in hot, soapy water, being careful to remove food particles that adhere to them, and do not keep them too long.

Sponges and Dishcloths. I am no fan of sponges for cleaning in the home. Sponges are havens for bacteria; tiny food particles get deep inside, and sponges stay wet for long periods of time. The bacteria that survive deep inside sponges are smeared around your kitchen every time you use them. Do not use sponges to clean up after raw meat, poultry, eggs, or fish. If you choose to use them for such a task, you *must* discard or sanitize them afterward or they will simply spread contamination to everything they touch.[8] Even when you are not aware of wiping up any particularly hazardous material with your sponges, you should occasionally sanitize them anyway. Studies show that typically they hold large numbers of potentially hazardous microorganisms.

When sanitizing sponges, first get the sponges quite clean of food and other soil. (Remember that sanitizing agents do not work so well in the presence of organic matter.) Wash the sponges thoroughly by hand with hot, soapy water, repeatedly squeezing them so as to get out food particles and all organic matter, rinse them thoroughly. Then mix a gallon of water with 3/4 cup regular chlorine bleach in the sink. Soak sponges in the bleach solution for five minutes. Rinse and air-dry. You can sanitize dishcloths this way, too. Dry them in the sun or in the dryer.

What was said about odors in brushes and pot scratchers, above, also goes for dishcloths and sponges. It means bacteria are growing, *but if a cloth or sponge lacks odors, this is no guarantee of safety.*[9] Launder your dishcloths frequently; use one or more fresh ones each time you do a kitchen cleanup or wash the dishes. Wash sponges often with hot, soapy water, and do not keep them long.

Sanitizing in the Dishwasher? If you were running a food-serving establishment and wanted to sanitize dishes and utensils in the dishwasher, the 1999 *Food Code* would require that your machine first wash them with proper detergents or other cleaning chemicals, using a wash-water temperature of 150° to 165°F, depending upon the type of machine. Then it would require that the machine do a sanitizing hot-water rinse, either by immersion for thirty seconds in water 171°F or hotter, or mechanically, usually at a temperature of not less than 180°F. By comparison, my dishwasher is designed to wash at 140°F and "sani-rinse" at 160°F.

Many of us would not be able to comply with these regulations at home because our machines don't get hot enough. Some dishwashers get only as hot as the tap water, which is usually around 140°F or even much lower in many homes. Self-heating dishwashers may or may not get hotter than that; how hot even they get may depend upon the temperature of the tap water they receive. Few of us know how hot our machines are supposed to get, let alone whether they actually get that hot. Still, even if your dishwasher, like mine, does not heat its water as hot as 180°F, it probably gets pretty hot, and once your dishes have been washed and dried inside it they are likely to be quite safe for use, given the potent combination of heat, strong detergent, and drying they have been subjected to. Moreover, hard, nonporous objects such as utensils and dishes, when freed of soil, subjected to a bath of strong detergent in good hot water, and thoroughly dried, are terribly uncongenial homes for bacteria. We do not really need to worry much about our dishes and utensils when they have been washed and dried in an ordinary dishwasher.

I would worry, however, about relying on a dishwasher to clean or sanitize things that a dishwasher is not designed for. I was surprised to learn that several of my friends had begun to follow recommendations, given on television and published in newspapers and magazines, to "sanitize" kitchen cloths and wiping rags, sponges, and similar soft and porous materials in the dishwasher. In my opinion, this is a dubious proposition. Dishwashers are not designed to clean soft, spongy objects. The objects they are designed for are hard and do not hold water or food particles. Sponges and cloths are left sopping by a dishwasher, for unlike clothes washers, dishwashers have no spin cycle. Moreover, unless you wash these soft things thoroughly before you put them in the dishwasher, they may remain full of food particles, for a dishwasher does nothing that will remove them. Even if you got all the food off them before putting them in the machine, why wouldn't food flying around inside become reimbedded? If a germ or two manages to live through the dishwashing cycle (maybe it did not get hot enough long enough or maybe it was a heroic bacterium), it will find itself in microbe heaven—a warm, protected environment with plenty of food and drink and not much competition. And if you then leave everything in the dishwasher overnight, the microbes will have plenty of time to multiply themselves a few million times. Or suppose that all the germs are actually killed but your sponges and rags still contain food debris. The minute you take them out of the dishwasher, they are going to come into contact with whatever microorganisms are hanging around in the vicinity and provide them with a lot of sopping wet food.

Pot scratchers, vegetable brushes, and various other cleaning utensils also tend to trap food particles. Because of such doubts, I prefer washing by hand and then sanitizing pot scratchers, abrasive pads, and sponges in a bleach solution.

Guide to Common Food Pathogens

Food Molds and Mycotoxins

Molds that grow on food sometimes produce toxic substances called mycotoxins. These are dangerous in varying degrees, depending on their type. *Aspergillus flavus,* a food mold that commonly attacks corn and peanuts and to a lesser extent barley, wheat, and other foods, produces a group of mycotoxins, called aflatoxins, that are extremely dangerous. Acute symptoms of aflatoxicosis can arise about three weeks after eating moldy grains. But it is believed that long-term, low-level ingestion is dangerous too. Aflatoxins are thought to be carcinogenic. Indeed, they are among the most carcinogenic substances known to exist for rats, but it is still not clear whether or to what extent they may be human carcinogens. A link with liver cancer is suspected. Their other effects in humans, aside from acute toxicity, are also unclear. Among other things, it is believed that they may worsen cirrhosis of the liver and Reye's syndrome and may weaken the immune system. Other mycotoxins can also cause acute poisoning and have been implicated in the development of various types of cancer (of the esophagus, stomach, kidney, liver), infertility, liver and kidney disease, and other ailments.

Disease attributable to consumption of mycotoxins is believed to be quite low in the United States as compared with other countries, particularly those with warm, humid climates where people are more likely to consume moldy grains and other moldy foods than they are here. Although much remains to be learned about mycotoxins, no one doubts that they pose health dangers, that the dangers increase in proportion to their quantities in the diet, and that their presence in food should be reduced or eliminated.

IF A SOFT FOOD IS MOLDY—THROW IT ALL AWAY!	IF A HARD FOOD IS MOLDY—SOMETIMES YOU CAN SAVE SOME
A soft or liquid food that shows any sign of mold—even the tiniest speck—must be discarded *entirely.* Molds can put out tendrils that you will not see, tendrils that can penetrate far into soft or liquid foods, and the toxins disperse throughout. Foods counting as soft include jams and jellies, syrups, apple juice, bread, pies, cakes and other baked goods, soft cheese such as Brie or American cheese or other soft yellow kinds, sour cream, yogurt, cottage cheese, flour, cake, peanut butter, hot dogs, bacon, meat pies, opened canned ham, sliced deli and luncheon meats, cucumbers, tomatoes, spinach, lettuce, kale and other leafy vegetables, corn (including corn on the cob) bananas, peaches, melon, all softer fruits, nuts, whole grains, and rice.	With a hard food, such as a block of cheese or a hard salami, you can sometimes cut the mold off, but you must cut away at least one inch extra as a safety margin. (Some authorities say one and one-half inches.) This often means, practically speaking, that you must throw away the whole chunk—for example, if a block of cheese is only an inch thick to begin with, or if it is two inches thick and has molded on both top and bottom. Foods that are hard enough to consider trimming in this fashion include: hard cheeses (Swiss, cheddar), hard fruits (apples, pears), and hard vegetables (potatoes, turnips, parsnips, carrots, heads of cabbage, cauliflower, brussels sprouts, broccoli, bell peppers).

Molds can grow on just about any food: grain, flour, bread, cereal, jam, fruit juice, meat, nuts, leftovers. When moldy foods look or taste or smell bad, as they often do, people will throw them away. But sometimes there are no off-putting sights or tastes or smells connected with the contaminated food. Apple juice is often found to contain low levels of mycotoxins that no one can taste. A piece of slightly moldy peanut ground up in the peanut butter will never be noticed. And mycotoxins may be present in foods that have never been moldy. For example, if cows are fed moldy food, their milk and the dairy products made from it may contain aflatoxins. Government regulation is necessary to protect us from dangers like these. At home we must protect ourselves.

To protect against ingestion of mycotoxins at home, it is important to throw out food that has become moldy and to examine all stored foods carefully to be sure that mold has not begun to grow. Even a *spot* of mold is a call for action. Do not *sniff* moldy foods. Their spores can induce respiratory illnesses. If you find any mold at all in a box of cereal, cake mix, flour, or other grain food, *throw out the entire box.* Never eat a moldy or shriveled peanut. You will have less waste if you avoid buying more food than you can use before it goes moldy. Sometimes you can save part of a food that has gone moldy. Very often you cannot.

Mycotoxins are not readily destroyed by freezing or heating. Thus cooking will not make contaminated foods safe. (From 20 to 80 percent may survive cooking.) Preservatives, therefore, are relied on. The growth of food molds is inhibited by a number of food additives, including sodium bisulfite, sorbates, propionate, and nitrates, as well as by a number of natural substances in foods such as peppers of all types, mustard, cinnamon, and cloves. Bread that has not been treated with preservatives molds readily and becomes tainted with mycotoxins, especially in warm weather. (The condition called ergotism or St. Anthony's fire, common in medieval Europe, was caused by a mycotoxin produced by a mold that grew in rye bread. Aflatoxins may also be produced by bread molds.) If you buy bread without preservatives, it is best to freeze it and thaw it in the microwave as you need it.

Molds are considerably less inhibited by salt and sugar than are bacteria and, unlike most bacteria, grow well in acid media. Acids may be consumed by molds. Thus moldy foods sometimes also become less acidic and then also become bacterially contaminated.

Bacteria

Bacillus cereus. *Bacillus cereus,* which occurs widely in nature, can be the cause of a short illness lasting up to a day. There are two strains. In one strain, which causes a diarrheal illness that lasts for about a day (with onset about eight to sixteen hours after consumption), the bacterium produces a heat-labile toxin; in the other, which causes an emetic illness also lasting about a day (onset in one to six hours), it produces a heat-stable toxin. (It is unclear whether the heat-labile toxin is produced in the food or the gut, however.) *B. cereus,* a problem in food services that hold food for long periods before serving, tends to contaminate plant foods such as cereals, corn or cornstarch, flour, rice, fried rice (so commonly the case that some sources refer to illness caused by *B. cereus* as the "Chinese restaurant syndrome"), baking products, potatoes, and cold soups. But sometimes animal foods, cooked vegetables, ice cream and milk, and tapioca and other puddings are the source. The cause is usually food left in the danger-zone temperatures too long—for example, by cooling too slowly. This bacterium forms spores—hard, protective shells. (See page 164.)

Campylobacter jejuni. This bacterium is a potential contaminant of many foods of animal origin, including unpasteurized milk and cheeses and chicken. It is readily killed by heat, acid, salt, and dryness, so ordinary food-safety practices should be sufficient to guard against it. Yet it has in recent years emerged as a major cause of diarrhea in the United States and the rest of the world as well, causing more cases of illness than salmonella. This is because it is so widely present in food, and ingestion of a very small number of the bacteria can result in infection. Onset is usually in three to five days, but this varies. Symptoms range from mild to severe, and, as always, it is more dangerous to more vulnerable people—the very old, the young, the immunosuppressed, and the sick. In moderately severe cases, symptoms may include malaise, fever, vomiting, or grossly bloody stools. In some cases, bacteremia, Reiter's syndrome, Guillain-Barré syndrome, or urinary tract infection may result. It usually resolves in a few days to a week, but some cases are prolonged. Serious complications can result. It does not form spores. It causes illness through infection.

Clostridium botulinum. Botulism occurs rarely, but it is so dangerous that every household should understand it. The toxin produced by *Clostridium botulinum* is one of the most deadly substances known. It is a neurotoxin; it attacks the peripheral nervous system. There is an antitoxin, but it must be administered quickly. *C. botulinum* is widespread in nature, being found in the soil, water, on plants, and in animals and fish. It produces spores that are harmless unless they get into foods that supply the proper growing conditions, at which point they will germinate and produce the deadly toxin. These growing conditions include: a low-acid environment (*C. botulinum* grows only at a pH of 4.6 or higher), a temperature between 40° and 120°F, and the absence of oxygen.

Symptoms of botulism come on twelve to thirty-six hours after consumption of the toxin; they include weakness, dizziness, and sleepiness, followed by blurry or double vision, reduced salivation, hoarseness, and great thirst. Death is caused when the diaphragm is paralyzed, preventing breathing. The merest taste of the toxin can be deadly, so *never* taste food—especially anything canned at home—to see if it is spoiled. You can destroy the toxin (but not the spores!) by boiling the food for ten to fifteen minutes.

Low-acid canned goods that have been improperly processed, then stored and eaten without boiling are a typical source of botulism. Foods that have been associated with botulism are low-acid canned vegetables such as green beans, corn, and spinach; fish; fruits; condiments such as chili peppers or chili sauces; tomato relishes; and other foods that are not necessarily cooked before being eaten, such as cold soups, tuna fish, or mushrooms. The most common cause is improper home canning: either the heat and pressure applied are insufficient to kill the spores, or they are not applied for long enough. Having survived the canning process, the spores germinate in the airless environment of the stored cans or jars and produce toxins. Later someone eats the contents of the jar without boiling them for the requisite period. Because home canning is still a common cause of botulism in our day, experts recommend that you boil *anything* canned at home before eating it. Most outbreaks are caused by canned goods that contain food that is eaten without having been cooked.

Commercially canned foods are extremely safe and are the source of botulism extremely rarely. Still, now and then someone runs across a can of food that has gone bad. I once found an impressively bulging can of green chili peppers (imported) on my pantry shelf. I have a friend who once opened a can that had become so gassified inside that it shot liquid in the air. When you are buying canned goods or intending to eat home-canned foods, be alert for the following dangers:

Cans, containers, or lids that leak, bulge, or are damaged or cracked

Containers whose contents spurt or foam when opened

Food that smells or looks abnormal

In recent decades there have been several instances of botulism not attributable to canned goods. This was surprising, since the anaerobic conditions favorable to *C. botulinum* occur uncommonly. Each instance involved relatively new foods or methods of preparation combined with an abuse of temperatures. In one instance, baked potatoes were cooked in foil and then left at room temperature for several days. The foil apparently created an anaerobic environment around the potato. In another, a vacuum-packed salad served on an airplane flight in Europe was the cause. Here the oxygen was intentionally removed from the container so as to extend the life of the salad; then the salad was held at temperatures over 40°F. There have been outbreaks of botulism, including one in this country in which seven people died, from vacuum-packed smoked fish as well. The smoking and salting of the fish had been insufficient to destroy all *C. botulinum*, and it was left at dangerously warm temperatures. Still another case involved food oils to which flavorings such as garlic were added; the oil created an anaerobic environment around the garlic that, in turn, supplied bacteria. The oil was then stored at room temperature. (It is best not to make any flavored oils that are not intended for immediate use. But if you do, store them in the refrigerator.)

To learn the latest in safe home-canning practices, consult your local cooperative extension service.

Clostridium perfringens. This bacterium, like *C. botulinum*, is widespread in nature (in soil, dust, air, sewage, human and animal feces, and raw foods) and also produces spores. Meat and meat products (but not usually cured meats), gravies, and casseroles are common causes of food poisoning from *C. perfringens*. Also, like *B. cereus*, it tends to be a problem in food services that cook food and then hold it for long periods before it gets consumed. The cause is generally slow cooling, long storage at improper temperatures, or a failure to reheat to a proper temperature. Although it does not produce much toxin in foods, it does so in the intestines after being consumed. The diarrheal illness it causes develops in eight to twenty-four hours, after large numbers of the bacteria have been consumed, and lasts for about a day. It is relatively mild, except in vulnerable people, and does not last long (and probably often goes unreported).

Escherichia coli. This bacterium has received great attention in the press in recent years, and for good reason. Various strains of *Escherichia coli* commonly inhabit the intestinal tracts of people and animals where they usually do no harm. But it is now believed that pathogenic strains of *E. coli* are a common cause of the diarrhea travelers often acquire. Some types of *E. coli* cause a mild diarrhea; others produce severe diarrhea, possibly with blood or mucus in the stool, stomach pains, and vomiting. One strain of this ubiquitous bacterium, *E. coli* O157:H7, has been responsible for several outbreaks of virulent, often deadly illness. It may cause attacks of bloody diarrhea with cramps, mainly in adults. In children, it can produce hemolytic uremic syndrome, which is characterized by acute renal failure, hemolytic anemia (reduction in red blood cells), and thrombocytopaenia (reduction in blood platelets). This syndrome can result in kidney damage or even death. Children, the elderly, and sick and immunosuppressed people are especially vulnerable. *E. coli* O157:H7 has been contracted through ground meat that is undercooked, raw milk, soft cheeses (imported Brie in one outbreak), lettuce, unpasteurized apple juice and cider, and possibly chicken. *E. coli* survives freezing but is readily killed by heat. Hygienic practices are important, especially adequate washing of hands. Ordinary safe food practices—especially cooking ground meats to recommended safe temperatures and avoiding cross-contamination through cutting boards—provide good protection against it.

Listeria monocytogenes. This bacterium began to be regarded as a serious problem only in the 1980s. Water, soil, sewage, humans, and animals, including domestic pets, may carry it. Vegetables fertilized with manure may carry it; in one outbreak in Canada, coleslaw made from cabbage fertilized with manure was the source. An outbreak involving several hospitals in Boston in 1979 was traced to a raw-vegetable garnish made of celery, tomatoes, and lettuce. Chocolate milk, raw milk, soft cheeses, fish, meat (especially sausages and deli meats), and chicken have been contaminated with it. It is resistant to processing; it survives freezing, direct sunlight, and long-wave ultraviolet light. It is alleged to have survived pasteurization in one instance, but the literature is conflicting on this point. Like *Yersinia enterocolitica* (discussed below), it grows at refrigerated temperatures, but slowly. It shows growth in the range of 32° to 107.6°F, with greatest growth at 86° to 95°F; at temperatures of 41°F or below it grows extremely slowly. It does not grow in moderately acidic media.

Although this bacterium is widespread in nature, infection is not correspondingly common, because people become ill only after ingesting high numbers of highly pathogenic strains. But it is of great concern because, depending on the type, it is so often fatal. The vulnerable groups—the very young, the very old, sick people, pregnant women, and the immunocompromised—are the most likely victims. The infection is especially dangerous during pregnancy, sometimes resulting in premature delivery of stillborn or ill infants. *Listeria* can cause a mild flulike illness, meningitis, septicemia, and other symptoms. In vulnerable people, it can also result in serious complications. The incubation period varies widely, from one to ninety days, with a few weeks being typical. The Centers for Disease Control estimates that in this country in one year there are 1,700 cases, that about 450 adults die of it, and that 100 fetal and newborn deaths are attributable to it. Protection is provided by keeping foods *very* cool in storage, and by following all ordinary safe food practices, including keeping foods out of the danger zone of temperatures and reheating adequately after cooling. It cannot hurt to wash vegetables thoroughly.

Salmonella. There are a couple of thousand types of salmonella that can cause food poisoning, and they are one of the most common causes of food poisoning in this country. Typhoid fever is one of the salmonella infections (caused by *S. typhi*). These bacteria grow in the intestinal tracts of people and animals and in raw meat. Likely carriers are food handlers, pets (dogs, cats, birds, turtles, fish, iguanas), rodents, and insects such as flies and cockroaches. Foods that have been most commonly involved in outbreaks include eggs and poultry and foods containing them (chicken and turkey and their stuffings or salads made of them, custards, cream cakes, eggnog, mayonnaise, and homemade ice cream) but also meat and meat-containing foods (pies, hash, sausages, chili) as well as milk and milk products—usually raw milk or cheese made from it.

Salmonella bacteria do not produce toxins; they cause an illness called salmonellosis by infecting the body. Symptoms arise within a day or less and usually last for one or two days; diarrhea, cramps, nausea, or vomiting are likely. Sometimes there are chills and fever, or mucus or blood in the stools. The very young and old, the sick, and immunosuppressed people are more vulnerable to this as to other infections. Some strains cause more serious infection than others, and some are resistant to antibiotics. Deaths from salmonella are uncommon except among the vulnerable groups, but symptoms can be severe, with a possibility of serious complications.

Food infected with salmonella does not look, taste, or smell different. The bacteria are readily killed by heat. To prevent infection, follow the general rules on food safety and safe cooking temperatures.

Shigella. Shigella, the bacterium that causes dysentery, comes from human beings. Associated with poor hygiene, it passes from person to person and through contaminated water, food, and flies. Food-service workers with poor hygiene can spread it to food, especially those foods that are much handled, such as potato salad, tuna salad, macaroni salad, chicken salad, and shrimp salad, and foods that are not kept at safe temperatures. Ordinary safe cooking and storage practices protect against it, and personal hygiene is important in preventing its spread. Although shigellosis is generally a more severe condition than salmonellosis, it is less common. There are between fifteen thousand and twenty thousand cases a year in the United States, most of them in children under the age of two. Symptoms include diarrhea (often bloody), abdominal pain, fever, and vomiting. Onset is from seven hours to seven days, and in most cases the illness lasts for a few days.

Staphylococcus aureus. This bacterium is a common cause of foodborne illness. It comes from people and animals. Introduced into food, it produces a dangerous toxin that is heat-stable, colorless, odorless, and tasteless. It grows well in protein foods and foods with high levels of salt or sugar: milk and milk products, custards, cream-filled bakery goods, puddings, meat, meat products such as sliced roast beef and ham, salads, and pies. Sliced ham and similar foods served at buffets and kept too long at room temperature are often the source of foodborne illness caused by this bacterium. Foods that have received a lot of handling and touching are much more likely to harbor the bacteria and thus its toxin. Illness caused by the toxin comes on quite rapidly after the contaminated food is eaten—within two or three hours—and is usually brief (one to two days). Few people die of it. The symptoms include nausea, vomiting, cramps, diarrhea, headache, weakness, chills, and fever. Personal hygiene is an important preventive measure—bathing and washing hands. Keep your hands away from your nose, mouth, hair, and skin infections. Don't cough or sneeze on your food. Use utensils, not hands, when making food. Don't dip your finger in food to taste it. If you have a cut or wound on your finger, wear plastic gloves. Follow all the general rules for food safety.

Vibrio cholerae. This bacterium is the cause of cholera, a disease characterized by diarrhea or bloody diarrhea, nausea, and vomiting. Dangerous dehydration can result, and cholera often causes death. Water that has been contaminated by human waste is the main source of cholera infections. Thus fish and shellfish, although not the only food sources, are the most common ones. There are still periodic epidemics of cholera, a dangerous infection, around the world, but it is uncommon in this country. Cooking destroys *V. cholerae,* but food must be cooked long enough. Cholera is one of the many dangers associated with eating undercooked or raw seafood.

Vibrio parahaemolyticus. This bacterium generally contaminates crabs, oysters, shrimp, lobsters, and other seafood, and causes infection when seafoods are eaten raw or undercooked or when raw or undercooked seafoods cross-contaminate cooked seafoods. (When you buy cooked shrimp or other fish at your market, pay attention to whether it is lying too close to uncooked fish or whether it is placed in such a way as to be dripped on when uncooked fish is removed from the case.) It is easily killed by ordinary cooking. Proper cooking—steaming just to open the shell is *not sufficient*—and *careful refrigeration* of seafood, in accordance with ordinary safe food practices, will help protect against it. The incubation period is usually between nine and twenty-five hours but can vary from two hours to four days. The symptoms include severe abdominal pain, nausea, headache, chills, and fever. Infection generally resolves within about three days but can last up to eight days.

Vibrio vulnificus. This bacterium, another emerging pathogen, is extremely dangerous to the vulnerable groups, particularly those with liver disease. It grows in water and causes human illness in undercooked and raw seafood, particularly oysters and clams. Adequate cooking kills it. Steaming shellfish just enough to open the shells is *not sufficient;* you need to boil oysters for three to five minutes after the shells open. Although *V. vulnificus* tends to infect only those with underlying illness or weakness of some sort, among this vulnerable group the death rate is frighteningly high, 40 to 60 percent. There is initially malaise, then chills and fever and great weakness. Sometimes, but not usually, there is vomiting and diarrhea. People with liver disease have a risk of death from this bacterium almost two hundred times greater than others. To protect against it, *never* eat raw oysters or other raw seafood, and cook them well. Carefully avoid cross-contamination; follow all other safe cooking rules.

Yersinia enterocolitica. *Y. enterocolitica* is found in animals and in water. Concern about infection by certain strains of this bacterium first arose in the 1970s, and its worldwide incidence has increased greatly from the late 1960s through the present. Pathogenic strains have contaminated chocolate milk, raw milk (goat's and cow's), powdered milk, and even pasteurized milk from one processing plant; tofu packed in contaminated water; and pork and other meat. Poultry, fish, game, vegetables (bean sprouts packed in contaminated water), and drinking water have also been sources. It will grow in refrigerated foods, but slowly. It is destroyed at temperatures over 140°F. Although it is only rarely fatal, it puts vulnerable people (the very young, old, and sick) at risk, and can result in serious complications. Illness from this bacterium is most commonly found in children under the age of seven. It has an incubation period of one to eleven days (usually two to five), and the illness can take five to fourteen days to run its course. It causes diarrhea and great abdominal pain. In severe cases, septicemia, meningitis, arthritis, or other serious illnesses may arise. Ordinary safe cooking practices and good personal hygiene are important protections.

Protozoa

Toxoplasma gondii, Sarcocystis, Giardia lamblia, Entamoeba histolytica, Cryptosporidium, and *Cyclospora cayetanensis* are all protozoa—one-celled animals—that can cause foodborne illness. *Entamoeba* is the cause of amoebic dysentery. Cryptosporidiosis amounts to a self-limited case of diarrhea in most healthy adults, causing serious problems only in immunosuppressed people and other vulnerable or weak people. *Giardia lamblia* causes diarrhea, cramps, and nausea. The incidence of foodborne illness caused by protozoa is quite low compared with that caused by bacteria. Nonetheless, *Cryptosporidium* appears to be on the increase. There was a massive outbreak in Milwaukee in 1993 when this microorganism got into the city water supply. And *Cyclospora,* a newly emerging pathogen that repeatedly made the news in the 1990s, was all but unheard of before this. In 1996, at least one thousand people in twenty states got sick from *Cyclospora* infections. Its incubation period is about a week, after which it causes a severe diarrheic illness, with cramps. Serious weight loss is a common effect. Unlike many types of foodborne illness, however, it can last for weeks or even months. Both of these (like all foodborne illnesses) are dangerous diseases for vulnerable people.

Toxoplasmosis is typically acquired from eating raw or very rare meat, especially pork or mutton, or from contact with a cat's litter box or feces, which is why pregnant women are advised to stay away from the litter box. Although in healthy adults it produces a mild flulike illness, all vulnerable people (the elderly, young children, the sick, immunosuppressed people) can be made very ill by it, and all should follow safe food practices and avoid cat litter and feces, just as pregnant women do. Freezing does not kill it; cooking does.

All these protozoa are killed by cooking. Raw and undercooked foods cause the trouble: drinking water and raw sausages (*Cryptosporidium*); strawberries and salad vegetables (*Giardia*); raw or undercooked beef and pork (*Sarcocystis*); raspberries, basil (or pesto made from it), and lettuce (*Cyclospora*). Worldwide, contaminated water and other foods are also sources.

Because raw fruits and vegetables are so often the carriers of these organisms, washing such foods carefully is important.

Viruses

Many viruses are spread through foods. Among the most significant of these are the Hepatitis A virus, Norwalk-type viruses, and rotaviruses. These viral illnesses usually cause vomiting and sometimes, but not always, diarrhea or fever. Contaminated water is a common source. Fish, especially from cold northern waters, can be infected with viruses, and raw seafood is a major source of human infection. Insects and rodents can carry them. There are cases involving unheated foods such as salads and frosting. Vegetables can be contaminated with the hepatitis virus if they are watered with contaminated water or fertilized with human excrement. Strawberries from Mexico recently caused an outbreak. Milk can carry hepatitis. (Viruses can survive pasteurization.) Any food handled by infected persons that is not thoroughly cooked afterward is potentially contaminated.

Viruses may not be killed unless food is thoroughly heated. Some viruses are killed at temperatures exceeding 149°F; others must be heated to the boiling point. Steaming shellfish just to the point of opening is always inadequate. Acidity tends to deactivate viruses, and additives such as sulfite and ascorbate do too. Freezing kills some viruses; others can actually be transmitted by ice. According to one authority, "The process of depuration, in which shellfish are placed in sterile water for 48-72 hours to allow them to cleanse themselves, is effective against bacteria but not viruses."[10]

Poor hygiene is often a cause of viral contamination of food. Washing hands and taking effective measures against cross-contamination are all the more important given the heat resistance of some types of viruses.

Parasites

Trichinella spiralis is the most common parasite to cause foodborne illness. It causes trichinosis, and is acquired when someone eats meat, usually pork, that contains the larvae of the *T. spiralis* worm. The larvae then mature in the victim's stomach and go on to form new cysts in the muscle tissues of the new host. Early symptoms include abdominal pain, nausea, fever, and diarrhea; later there is muscle pain, tenderness, and fatigue. Untreated, the disease is extremely dangerous. Hogs are much less commonly infected with *T. spiralis* than they used to be, but there are still about fifty cases of trichinosis per year in the United States. *T. spiralis* is killed by heating or by freezing for twenty days at -10°F or lower. (The National Pork Producers Council recommends a temperature of 170°F for cooked pork, although the USDA calls for a slightly lower temperature, 160°.)

Tapeworms and flukes can be acquired from raw or undercooked meat or fish. Nematodes and anisakis, a roundworm, may be acquired from raw fish. Proper cooking offers protection from all of these.

What to Do About Contaminated Foods*

Here is what the U.S. Department of Agriculture (USDA) recommends if you encounter suspect food in your kitchen or elsewhere:

Call the local health department if:

- The suspect food was served at a large gathering.
- The suspect food is from a restaurant, delicatessen, sidewalk vendor, or other commercial or institutional kitchen.
- The suspect food was prepared and packaged in a retail grocery store.
- The suspect food is a commercial product.

Other authorities to call:

Foodborne illness involving a USDA-inspected meat or poultry product may also be reported to the toll-free Meat and Poultry Hotline at 1-800-535-4555. (Callers in the 202 area code should call 447-3333.)

Foodborne illness involving other products that cross state lines may be reported to the nearest Food and Drug Administration (FDA) office, listed in the local phone book.

Foodborne illness involving products that are sold only within the state may be reported to the state health department or the state department of agriculture.

Try to have the following information available when calling:

Your name, address, and daytime phone number.

The name and address of the event, party, or establishment where the suspect food was consumed or purchased.

The date that the food was consumed and the date of purchase.

If the suspect food is a commercial product, have the container or wrapping in hand for reference while on the phone. Most meat and poultry products have a USDA or state inspection stamp and a number that identifies the plant where the product was manufactured. Many products also have a code indicating when the item was produced. This information can be vital in tracing a problem to its source.

Dispose of suspect foods safely:

To dispose of suspect home-canned products, it is best to enclose the food, in its original container, in a heavy garbage bag marked POISON and place the bag in a trash container that is not accessible to homeless people, children, or animals.

*The material in this section is excerpted from the USDA Food Safety Inspection Service booklet "Preventing Foodborne Illness," Home and Garden Bulletin No. 247, September 1990, pages 20–21. It has been partly reordered.

If a suspect canned food is opened in your kitchen, thoroughly scrub the can opener or other utensils, containers, counters, etc., that might have contacted the food or its container. Discard any sponges or cloths used in the cleanup. Wash your hands thoroughly.

Promptly launder any clothing that might have been spattered.

Preserve the evidence:

If a portion of the suspect food is available, wrap it securely in a heavy plastic bag and place it on ice in a secure container marked DANGER. Write down the name of the food, when it was consumed, and the date of the illness. Store the container away from children, pets, and other foods, in a location where it will not be mistaken for edible food. The sample may be useful to medical personnel treating the illness and to health authorities tracking the problem.

If they are available, also save the container, wrapping, and any metal clips used on the original package. This is where you can find the number that indicates the plant that a meat or poultry product is from.

Reduced-Oxygen or Modified-Atmosphere Packaged Foods

Many foods in the market are offered in "reduced-oxygen packaging" (known as ROP) or "modified-atmosphere packaging" (known as MAP). *ROP foods often require continued refrigeration, at the store and at your home, and must be used by the date stamped on the package. In addition, some ROP foods are precooked and some are not, and some require refrigeration after opening but may look just like foods that do not. You always must follow package directions as to refrigeration, dates, and cooking.*

ROP actually refers to a variety of packaging techniques, all of which reduce or remove the oxygen in the air inside the package, which may be replaced partly or wholly with another gas, such as nitrogen or carbon dioxide. The effect of reducing oxygen is to create a less favorable environment for the growth of many bacteria and thus to extend the life and storage quality of foods. It does *not* result in a product that you can put on your pantry shelf and expect to stay edible the way canned food does.

ROP techniques include all of these:

- Cook-chill (uses a plastic bag from which air has been expelled and which is filled with hot cooked food);
- Controlled atmosphere packing, or CAP (the reduced-oxygen atmosphere in a package is maintained throughout the shelf life of the product by agents placed inside the package that bind oxygen or sachets that emit gases);
- Modified-atmosphere packaging, or MAP (packing a product in an atmosphere that contains a different proportion of gases, with reduced oxygen, from air, which normally contains 78.08 percent nitrogen, 20.96 percent oxygen, and 0.03 percent carbon dioxide);
- *Sous vide* (a sort of pasteurization that does not make food shelf-stable, involving partially cooked ingredients, vacuum-sealed packages, rapid cooling and reheating to specified temperatures before

opening—many restaurants, even expensive ones you'd assume were making everything, use *sous vide* foods for appetizers or other components of meals);
- Vacuum packaging (reduces air and hermetically seals package to create a near-perfect vacuum).

In my local supermarket, I have found precut salad greens, packaged carrots, precooked polenta, meats, and many precooked foods in ROP packaging. Such products are not identified as ROP on their labels. *Always read labels carefully to determine whether foods require refrigeration.*

ROP foods pose complex safety problems to the food industry. Low acid foods that are stored in no-oxygen, nonbreathable packaging face the predictable problem: *Clostridium botulinum* grows in anaerobic environments, and some ROP foods are not processed in ways that would kill the spores of this bacterium. Keeping temperatures low helps to discourage its growth, but improper refrigeration would permit it to grow and create its deadly toxin. ROP also inhibits the growth of spoilage bacteria that could alert you to a problem by producing odors, rot, or slime; in other words, the food may continue to look perfectly fresh even though it is deadly. Other bacteria are also worrisome in some ROP products. Bacteria that continue to grow slowly in relatively low temperatures, such as *Listeria,* have an extra-long time to grow with extended-life products. If ROP foods were to be held at improper temperatures, these and other pathogens might reach dangerous levels. The food industry's answer to these sorts of problems is often to provide other barriers to the growth of bacteria besides low temperature—such as salt or acid. But some ROP foods lack fall-back barriers. "Use-by" dates thus offer important back-up protection in some cases.

In the meantime, studies show that "temperature abuse" routinely happens both in retail establishments and homes. According to *Supermarket News* (October 13, 1997): "Checks on temperatures of modified-atmosphere packages of fresh-cut salads [in retail establishments] over the past three years have showed a high level of abuse . . . Of 300 packages tested, 78% had a temperature greater than 45°F . . . What's more, 17.5% of the 300 packages had a temperature greater than 55 degrees." The 1999 *Food Code* complains that many people in their homes, too, do not maintain cold enough refrigerators for safety of ROP foods.

ROP packaging is considered safe by the 1999 *Food Code* when properly carried out by trained people, when there is no recontamination of food during processing, and when proper refrigeration is used at every step of processing, packing, distribution, and storing—including home storage. Although incidents of food poisoning involving ROP foods seem to be rare in recent years—outbreaks involving vacuum-packed fish occurred some years ago, causing several deaths—some experts fear we could see more of them unless we become more aware of the refrigeration requirements for ROP foods.

If you purchase ROP foods, here are some safety guidelines that the facts seem to warrant:

- Buy ROP foods only if they bear a "use-by" date which has not expired, and scrupulously observe such dates at home.
- Look for and follow label instructions as to storage (in the refrigerator or freezer) carefully!
- Carefully observe the refrigeration of ROP foods in supermarket cases. Make sure they feel cold to the touch. Buy only from highly reputable markets. Observe the habits at your market.
- Keep ROP foods that require refrigeration carefully refrigerated at home.
- If an ROP package contains precut fruits, salad greens, or vegetables, use it quickly after opening. Cut produce no longer has

natural resistance to invasion by microbes. It is going to go bad quickly.

- If salad greens in a sealed package say "washed" *and* "ready to eat," some reliable authorities say you need not wash them before eating them, especially if they are products of large, reputable food companies. (I would wash even these, however, if they were to be served to any vulnerable people, such as the very young, the elderly, or the sick or immunosuppressed.) Always wash prepackaged salads that do not explicitly say "washed" and "ready to eat." And wash any greens sold in bulk or in open displays or that are not in a sealed package, even if they are said to be "washed."
- Carefully follow the instructions on the label regarding cooking.
- If you are going to freeze an ROP product, do so quickly after buying it.

Cooking By-Products: Safe Cooking with Meats, Fats, and Oils

If you have a gas stove, keep the flame well adjusted so as to prevent carbon monoxide emissions. Some research suggests that combustion by-products from gas stoves (and other stoves that produce flames), such as nitrogen dioxide, can aggravate asthma, increase rates of respiratory problems, and reduce lung function. Some kitchen air pollution is also produced by the cooking itself—smoke or tiny droplets of oils and other foods, for example. Keeping the windows open whenever possible and making sure the stove has an exhaust to the outside helps significantly to reduce the concentrations of all these and other possible irritants in the air.

Research suggests that certain cooking techniques are associated with the creation of carcinogens in meats. High-temperature methods of cooking can produce "heterocyclic amines," or HCAs, in cooked muscle meats. HCAs are suspected carcinogens. Although no one knows whether or to what extent they really pose a cancer risk, it is known that the higher the temperature and the longer the cooking time, the more HCAs are formed. The cooking techniques most associated with their production in meats are frying, broiling, barbecuing, and grilling—particularly charcoal grilling. Microwaving, stewing, boiling, and poaching cause little or no formation of these substances, presumably because all these techniques cook foods at temperatures of 212°F or lower. Oven roasting and baking fall in the middle, producing more than the latter and less than the former methods. Partially cooking meats in the microwave, and finishing cooking by other methods, is recommended as a means of reducing HCAs. The liquid that forms when meats are cooled contains the precursors of HCAs. If you pour it off, the amount of HCAs in the cooked food is reduced. In addition, those who wish to reduce their consumption of HCAs can eat meats cooked medium instead of well done and avoid gravy made from meat drippings.

Higher-temperature cooking of fats and oils, too, is thought to produce carcinogenic and unhealthy substances in the air as well as in foods. (This is yet another reason why you should choose lean cuts of meat and trim away all visible fat, aside from the benefits in weight control and heart-healthiness.) The production of toxic (and bad-tasting) compounds from the breakdown of fats and oils tends to occur at a temperature called the "smoke point," when smoky fumes are produced from the overheated oils—a sight every cook is familiar with. You can choose cooking oils with higher smoke points. Vegetable oils, generally speaking, have higher smoke points than animal fats and oils. But among vegetable oils, sesame oil, extra-virgin olive oil, and Crisco—a hydrogenated vegetable oil—have low smoke points, in the range of 350° to 400°F, comparable to that of lard and butter; clarified butter, or ghee, and non-virgin olive oil have higher smoke points than regular butter and extra-virgin olive oil. Peanut oil, safflower oil, grape seed oil, canola (rape seed) oil, and corn oil all have high smoke points of around 440°F to 450°F.

Fats and oils get rancid—oxidize—just sitting on the shelf and aging; cooking oxidizes fats rapidly. Do not reuse cooking fats and oils. The old-fashioned habit of keeping a jar of cooking fat on the stovetop and pouring fats in and out of it for weeks on end was extremely unhealthy, but, fortunately, it has all but disappeared.

CLOTH

14

The Fabric of Your Home

Modern fabrics . . . Fiber content labels, care labels, low labeling . . . Warp and filling yarns . . . Thread (fabric) count and its effect on durability . . . Plain weave, twill weave, satin weave, and other common weaves . . . Weft and warp knits . . . Jersey, garter, rib, cable, tricot, and other knits . . . Carded and combed yarns, staple and filament yarns . . . Twist . . . Natural vs. synthetic fibers and the environment . . . Effect of fiber content and other factors on fabric comfort . . . Absorbency and permeability of fibers . . . Hydrophilic natural fibers and hydrophobic man-made fibers . . . Effect of fiber content and other factors on look, feel, resilience, durability, cleanliness, and launderability . . . Glossary of fabric terms

Most parents have had the experience of observing their child's intense attachment to a beloved rag of a blanket or a disintegrating bit of cloth diaper. As many of them know, professional psychologists give the child's lovey the cold-sounding name "transitional object" and explain it as an attempt to evoke maternal comfort by creating a symbol of Mother. Cloth, or something similarly soft and fuzzy, is the all but inevitable infantile symbol of a mother whose touch comes through blankets and diapers from within moments of birth. In fact, the child's first work of art, motivated by the longing for security and affection, is this transformation of a grubby bit of cloth into something invested with the power to satisfy that longing.

In our adult lives, cloth continues to play intertwined aesthetic and functional roles. Textiles—from Oriental rugs to gleaming damasks—are the single most powerful source of domestic beauty. At the same time, they provide protection and comfort of a kind nothing else in the home can offer, shielding us and objects around us from cold, heat, dirt, damp, air, and light and from hard and rough surfaces that might bruise or scratch. The emotional warmth and security of a home, in our world, depends to a remarkable extent on the resonance of the sensations aroused by cool sheets, soft carpets, fabric-filtered light, nubby upholstery, thick towels, and so forth. By intricate chains of memory and association, these link up eventually to the primordial feelings of comfort, safety, love, and warmth that were first experienced through the medium of cloth in infancy.

All of us inevitably become textile connoisseurs. Nowadays, however, our taste is usually unconscious and inarticulate because, for a variety of historical reasons, most of us know far less about textiles than ordinary people once did. We may know what we like when we see or touch it, but we do not know what to look or ask for or how to use and care for fabrics. This diminished understanding of what so intimately concerns all of us is partly due to our increasing distance from the manufacturing, production, and care processes. But there is also far more to know than there used to be.

Until the late nineteenth century, Western peoples were familiar with the domestic use of four or five of the so-called natural fibers. Even in 1940, a housekeeper had to understand, by and large, the use and care of fabrics made of only six fibers: silk, linen (flax), cotton, wool, rayon (a generic name for a group of cellulosic fibers drawn from natural sources such as wood pulp), and acetate (a generic name for a group of fibers composed of cellulose acetate). By 1960 this number had more than doubled, swelled by the addition of several completely synthetic fibers. These included nylons, acrylic and modacrylic, olefin (polypropylene), and polyester. In the past few decades there has been an explosive increase in the number of processes and treatments, mechanical and chemical, to which fibers and fabrics are subjected, as manufacturers have sought not only to develop new "miracle" fabrics but to improve the appearance and function of the old ones. Endless modifications, combinations, and blends of each of the fibers are possible—for whiter whites, enhanced flame resistance, water repellency, resistance to shrinking or pilling or static electricity buildup, and a hundred other purposes. The result is fabrics and fabric care and cleaning requirements the identity and nature of which not even professionals can always discern by mere visual or tactile examination.

The government mandates labels that identify fiber content and provide care instructions as the solution to the problem of figuring out safe and effective care procedures. It also requires fiber content labels that specify which different fibers are contained in a garment and their percentages by weight—for example, "100% cotton" or "50% cotton, 40% polyester, 10% nylon." (Explanations of care labels, and lists of terms and symbols commonly employed on them, are provided in the Glossary of Care Label Terms and Symbols, pages 286–87.) Valuable as they are, care labels are not a perfect solution. First, the information given on them is exceedingly limited, even when correct, which it sometimes is not as a result of mistakes, negligence, or, occasionally, intention. "Low labeling" (when manufacturers recommend a more conservative treatment than is necessary) is common. But even when the instructions are valid, they do not tell you what rationale lies behind them, so you do not know what consequences, great or small, you risk if you use procedures different from those recommended. And many people do not really know how to read and interpret care labels. For these reasons, relying on care labels is often a frustrating business. But it is not nearly as frustrating as not having any care labels at all—a situation you will sometimes encounter with household furnishings such as tablecloths, sheets, blankets, or draperies, for which the law does not currently require care labels.

The fiber content label fills in some of the blanks that the care label leaves open. Once you learn the fiber content of the article, you in theory learn much about the nature of the fabric—whether it is durable, wrinkle-prone, stain resistant, hot or cool, absorbent, and so forth. In practice, however, people today are so little familiar with the properties of different fibers that to learn that a piece of upholstery or a garment is made of a cotton/synthetic blend or of acrylic in fact tells them little. And even if you understand the properties of the fiber or fibers used in the fabric, you also need to know something about the way the fabric is made and the quality of its manufacture to be sure you know how it will feel and function, how durable it will be, and how best to care for it. This chapter (together with the next, which describes the characteristics of the fibers most commonly used for clothing and household furnishings) explains the basics of choosing and evaluating fabrics. A basic knowledge of these things is a foundation that enables you to continue to build your understanding of fibers and fabrics from each casual encounter.

The appearance, potential uses, and safe care of fabrics are determined by five factors: fiber content, yarn construction, weave or knit, dyes, and finishing and other treatments. In this chapter, I take up the first three factors in the reverse manufacturing order, first considering the weave, then unraveling the weave to consider the yarns it is composed of, and finally examining the fibers used to make the yarns. Dyes and finishing treatments, which may be applied at practically any step in the manufacturing process—on raw fiber, yarn, fabric, or even finished garments—are taken up in chapter 15.

Weaves and Knits

In woven fabrics, the yarns interlace; in knits, the yarns interloop. Woven fabrics are made on looms. The lengthwise threads on a loom are called the "warp" yarns, and the crosswise yarns are called "filling"—or "weft" or "woof"—yarns. (See the illustration below.) When weaving is done well with good-quality yarns, a pleasing smooth, regular pattern is formed from the interlacing of the warp yarns and the filling yarns. The pattern of the weaving largely determines what type of cloth is being made—batiste, damask, oxford cloth, or corduroy. (These and many other useful terms relating to fabrics are explained in the Glossary of Fabric Terms, pages 212–20.)

To determine the quality of the weave, hold the fabric up to the light. It should have no knots, weak spots, protruding yarns, crooked or broken yarns, or overthick yarns (slubs). The weave should be firm, close, uniform, and even.

Thread Count (Fabric Count). A fabric's thread count, now called the fabric count by textile professionals, tells you just how closely woven it is. (I will use the old term because it is still widely used on packages of sheets and other household goods.) The stated thread count on packages or in catalogues helps you evaluate the nature and quality of the goods offered for sale.

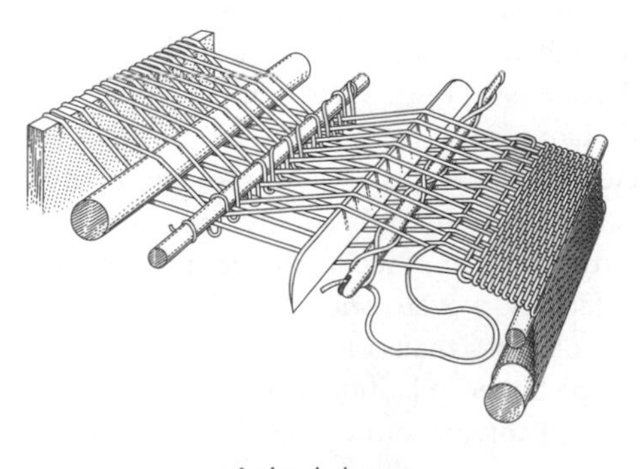

A simple loom

THREAD COUNT AND DURABILITY

The durability of cloth is a function of many factors besides thread count, including the weight of the cloth, the type and quality of the fibers comprising the fabric, the overall construction of the cloth and its yarns, the nature and quality of the weave, and the types of finishes used. Do not assume, therefore, that you are getting the most durable sheets or shirts when you pick those with the highest thread count. Higher thread count means greater durability only when the comparison is between *similar* fabrics woven with *the same type of yarn*. If the yarn used to produce the higher thread count is thinner and weaker, the fabric is not necessarily stronger. A satin weave is less durable than a twill, and heavier cloth wears better than lighter. Thus coarse, heavy-duty cotton fabrics used for work clothes wear longer than sateen fabric of combed Egyptian cotton and a thread count of 310.

A fabric may be manufactured with a tight or a loose weave. In a tight or compact weave, the yarns lie more closely together than in a loose weave. The thread count tells you just how many warp and filling yarns per square inch there are in the fabric. A thread count of 64 x 60 means that the fabric has 64 warp yarns and 60 filling yarns per square inch. The finer the yarns, the more of them can be compressed into the space of an inch; the coarser the yarns, the fewer of them go into an inch. Thus muslin sheeting made of a coarser yarn may be quite closely woven even though its thread count is less than that of percale sheeting made with a finer yarn. ("Coarse" and "fine" here refer to yarn diameter, not yarn quality.) All else being equal, closely woven cloth is stronger and more durable, because it contains more yarns than a loosely woven one. A tight weave also shrinks less than a looser one and holds its shape better in laundering.

The thread count may also be expressed in one number; that is usually how it is done for sheets, pillowcases, and other household linens. The number given on the package labels is obtained by adding together the number of warp yarns and the number of filling yarns per square inch. This style of expressing the thread count is chosen because most such household items have a "balanced construction"—that is, they have roughly equal numbers of warp and filling yarns. A thread count of 220 in a balanced construction, for example, indicates that there are about 110 warp yarns and 110 filling yarns per square inch. When fabrics have an unbalanced construction (unequal numbers of warp and filling yarns)—say 100 x 60—it is more informative to see the numbers separately because the properties of balanced and unbalanced constructions are different. The yarns in a balanced construction take wear evenly, so, other things being equal, the fabric tends to wear more evenly and thus to be more durable than fabric with an unbalanced construction. But other things are not always equal. One authority gives this rule of thumb: a fabric with a high thread count but poor balance will wear better than one with a low thread count but good balance.[1]

If you want to determine the thread count of a fabric, you can try to count the yarns yourself, but this can be difficult with high thread-count cloth. Using a ruler and a pin (and a magnifying glass if you need to), count off the number of either filling or warp yarns in a quarter-inch square of fabric and—if it is a sheet or other fabric with a balanced construction—multiply the number by eight; you'll end up with a figure that roughly repre-

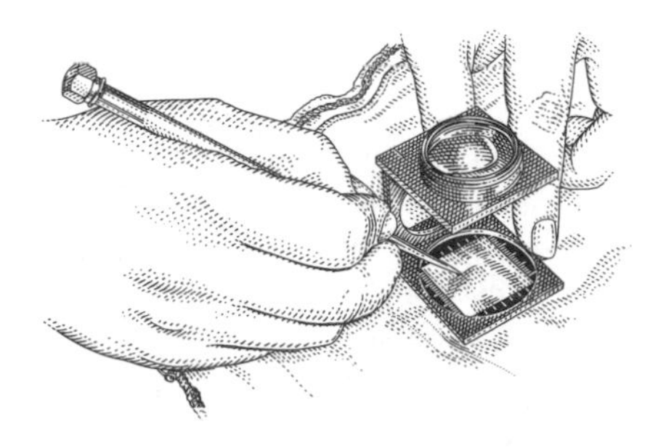

Taking a thread count (or fabric count) with a professional's pick and magnifying glass.

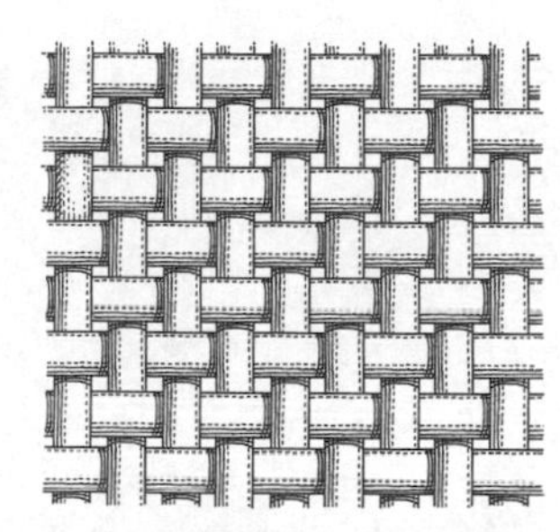

Plain weave: Each filling yarn goes over and under each warp yarn, making a pattern of squares.

Plain-weave handkerchief with lace trim

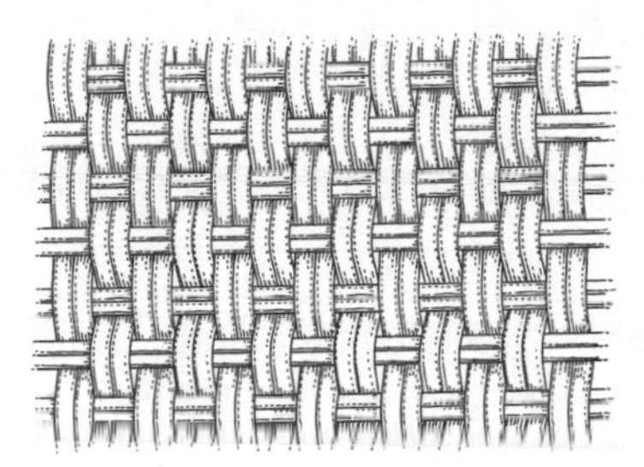

Basket weave: Two warp yarns pass over and under two filling yarns.

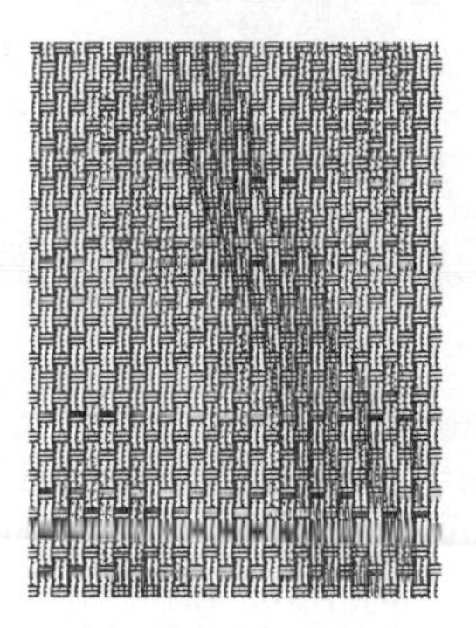

Fabric woven in basket weave

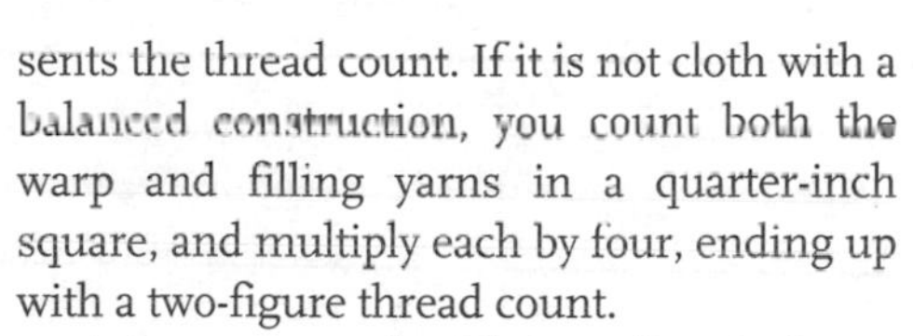

sents the thread count. If it is not cloth with a balanced construction, you count both the warp and filling yarns in a quarter-inch square, and multiply each by four, ending up with a two-figure thread count.

A fine weave of a fabric ordinarily has a better "hand"—feels better on the hand—and is more expensive than a coarser one.

Plain Weave, Twill Weave, and Satin Weave. There are only three basic weaves, of which most other weaves are variations: plain weave, twill weave, and satin weave. They vary in the way the lengthwise (warp) yarns are crossed by the filling (weft) yarns. Each of them can be found in looser and tighter and in coarser and finer versions, made of virtually any type of fiber or blend of fibers.

In plain weave, each filling yarn alternates over and under successive warp yarns all across the fabric, and on its return across the fabric the filling yarn goes under and over alternate warp yarns. Plain weave appears identical on both sides and has no right side or wrong side unless it is napped or printed or otherwise finished differently on one side. Plain weave is used in dozens of fabric types, including broadcloth, calico, cambric, challis, percale, seersucker, blanket cloth, and tweed. Most sheets are plain weave. (But there are also sateen and twill-weave sheets as well as knitted-fabric sheets.) Plain-weave fabrics will generally be quite durable when the thread count is high. They may wrinkle more than twills.

There are several variations on the plain weave, of which the most common are the basket weave and ribbed or corded weaves. The basket weave creates fabrics that are usually loosely woven. It is often used for draperies and other furnishings because it hangs well. It is also somewhat wrinkle resistant and flexible. It is not particularly durable, however, because it is of loose construction and contains yarns with little twist. Thus it is less suitable for many kinds of clothing than

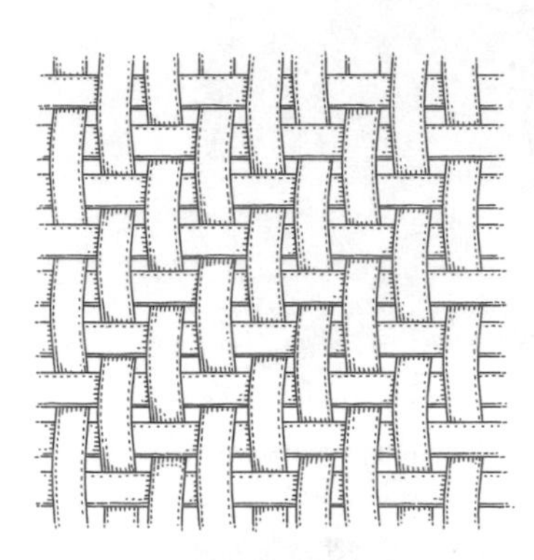

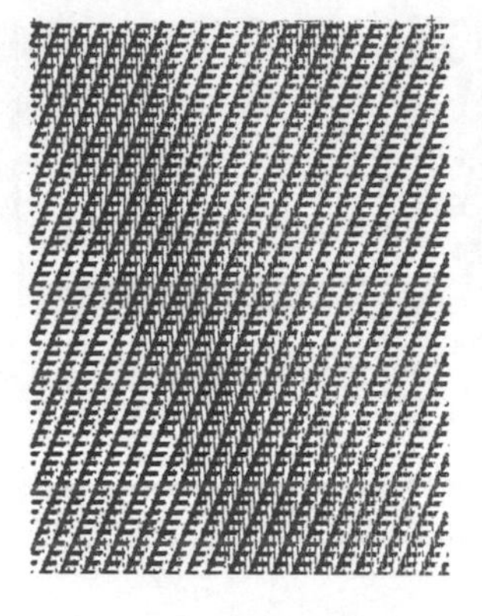

Twill weave: One or more warp (or filling) yarns go over at least two filling (or warp) yarns. The next warp (or filling) yarn(s) do not go over the same yarns as their neighbors. Instead the point of intersection is moved up or down by one or more yarns, creating the characteristic diagonal in the twill weave.

Herringbone twill

a balanced plain weave. Ribbed or corded fabrics (such as poplin, taffeta, faille, or ottoman) are created by using double the number of warp yarns as filling yarns, with larger filling than warp yarns; they are less durable than balanced plain woven fabrics because of the increased abrasion to which the raised cords or ribs are exposed.

The second basic weave, the twill weave, has a characteristic diagonal pattern that can be varied to form attractive patterns by changing the direction of the diagonal, as in the herringbone weave. When the diagonal is more prominent on one side than the other, this side will be the face of the twill. A twill weave is more durable than a comparable plain woven fabric, and usually the steeper the diagonal of the twill line, the greater its strength and durability. Suits and coats are often made of fabrics in a twill weave. The long-favored denim, famous for its hardiness, is also a twill weave, as are gabardine, foulard, many tweeds, and serge. While twill fabrics are not perfectly wrinkle resistant, they are more resistant to wrinkling than are plain-woven fabrics.

A satin weave tends to be less durable than plain and twill weaves, because the yarns are given less twist—in order to make the fabric smoother and more lustrous—and because the long floating yarns on the fabric surface are more subject to snag and wear. (Floats are the length of the warp between the filling yarns.) Satin weave, however, is valued for this smooth, lustrous surface, which is desirable for elegant clothes. The shiny side of the satin weave is its face. Satin weaves also drape well. They are warmer and more absorbent because they are compact weaves: a great amount of fine yarn is woven into a small space. This gives satin weaves high thread counts despite their lower durability.

Other Common Weaves. Besides the three basic weaves, there are a few others with which it is useful to be familiar.

Double-woven cloth is usually chosen for its greater warmth and body. Double-cloth weave is made on a loom capable of simultaneously weaving two layers of fabric and joining the layers so as to create a single fabric. Double-woven fabrics may have different weaves on their two sides—for example, plain weave on one side and twill on the other. Many double-woven fabrics are reversible.

Leno weave is done on a loom capable of crossing two adjacent warp yarns. It is used to make lightweight, open-mesh fabrics,

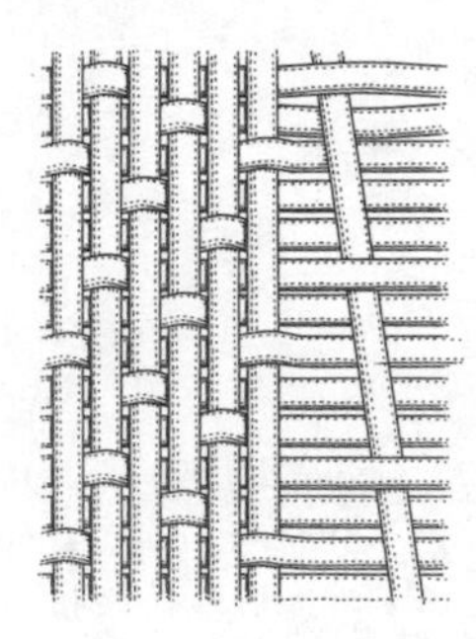

Satin weave: The warp yarns float over two or more filling yarns, creating a smooth, lustrous surface.

Satin weave fabric

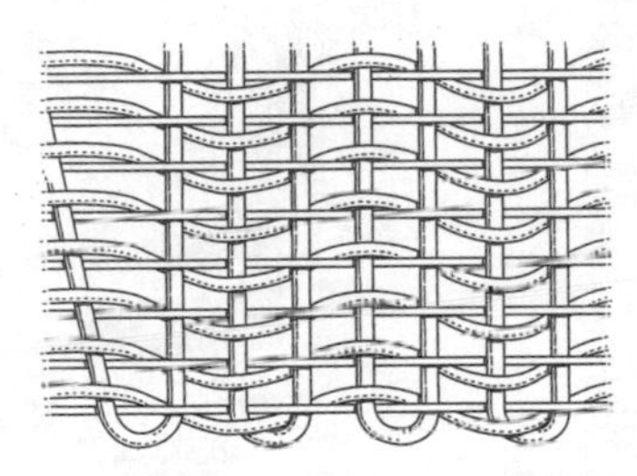

Gauze weave used in marquisette

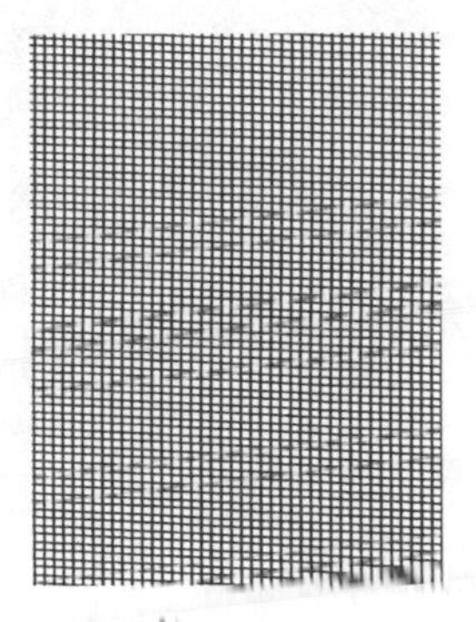

Marquisette

such as marquisette. This weave is also called gauze weave.

Dotted swiss cloth is a familiar example of a fabric created by swivel weaving, in which decorations such as circles or dots are woven into the surface of the cloth. Swivel weaves create the same design on both sides of the cloth. These fabrics typically are delicate enough that rough treatment in the laundry or elsewhere can pull the decorations out. Similar decorations are produced by lappet weaving, a method in which additional warp yarns are used to create small designs that are not the same on both sides of the cloth. Lappet-woven fabrics tend to be more durable than swivel-woven fabrics because the ends of the decoration threads are more securely fastened.

The dobby weave creates simple designs by means of a mechanical attachment to a plain loom. Bird's-eye is the name of a typical fabric having dobby weave. The jacquard weave creates fabrics with highly intricate designs. Jacquard weaving is done on a jacquard loom, which uses punched cards that control the movements of the warp yarns. This intricate type of weaving is used to make fine linen damasks, upholstery fabrics, silk brocades, and tapestries.

Many weaves that were associated entirely with one sort of fiber a hundred years ago are now often available in virtually any sort of fiber one might wish. Serge, for example, once meant a very strong worsted (that is, a fabric of combed wool fibers) in a twill weave. Now serge may be made of wool, rayon, silk, or other fibers, and "worsted" refers to any type of yarn spun of longer, smoother, stronger yarns. Velvet originally meant a fabric made of silk, but now the word refers to any pile fabric with a plain or twill back and warp yarns forming the pile—

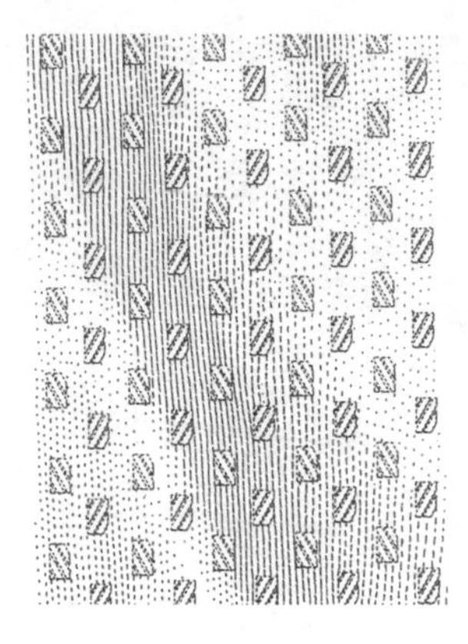

Two dobby-weave fabrics: The right-hand sample shows a dobby-weave fabric with a moiré.

Two jacquard-weave fabrics

silk, rayon, nylon, cotton, or synthetic. Flannel was once a wool fabric, but it may now be any napped, soft, loosely woven cloth of either plain or twill weave.

Knits. Knitted fabrics have characteristics unlike those of woven ones. Although woven ones, in general, hold their shape better, knitted ones tend to drape better and be less susceptible to wrinkling. By and large, knits deserve their reputation for being good travel choices. Knitted fabrics are usually more stretchy or elastic than woven fabrics and thus are famous for fit and comfort. But, because they are stretchy, they may bag, sag, or lose their shape if not well constructed. Knits are particularly prone to pilling and snagging because of their loose construction and the low twist of their yarns. Unless treated, knits, especially those made from cotton, have a strong propensity to shrink. Synthetic fibers are often used in knits, exclusively or in blends with natural fibers, to resolve such problems. When made of absorbent fibers, knits are exceptionally absorbent. They are highly air-permeable, and for that reason they are not good wind breakers. They are ideal for cool weather when they are thick and made from fuzzy, crimped fibers such as wool. Such knitted fabrics trap warm air near the skin very effectively. On the other hand, thin knits such as cotton T-shirts are especially comfortable for warm-weather wear.

Commercial knitwear is made by one of two processes: weft knitting or warp knitting. Weft knitting, like hand knitting, creates fabric by moving yarns horizontally back and forth across the fabric. Weft knitting permits rapid changes of design, but weft knits will run and unravel if a loop gets broken. Warp knitting creates fabrics in which the yarns run vertically in the fabric. Warp knits have less stretch than weft but will not run or unravel.

Weft Knits. Plain knit, also called jersey, is the basic knit stitch. (This is called stockinet when you do it at home by hand, knitting alternating rows of knit and purl stitches.) Jersey fabrics stretch both lengthwise and widthwise, but considerably more in the width. They are smooth on the right side (unless made with nubby yarns), showing vertical rows of Vs, and slightly nubby on the wrong side. They are commonly used for T-shirts, men's underwear, sweaters, socks, gloves, and other apparel. Jersey knits will unravel at the ends and form runs, too. Unless steps are taken to prevent it, they tend to curl up (crosswise, or across the width, toward the face of the fabric and lengthwise toward the back side of the fabric). The more stitches per inch, the better a jersey knit holds its shape.

Links-links, or purl knit, looks like the fabric a home knitter creates doing garter stitch (knitting entirely in knit stitch or purl stitch), or plain knitting. It looks the same on front and back. Raised rows alternate with indented rows, which are only clearly visible if you stretch the material lengthwise. It is often used for babies' and children's clothes because it stretches both lengthwise and widthwise, but more in the length. Purl fabric is also commonly used for sweaters and other apparel. Like jersey knits, it unravels at both ends and can develop runs.

A rib knit produces alternating raised and indented rows ("ribs"), each consisting entirely of knit or purl stitches. In rib knits, the ribs run vertically and the stretch comes from their crosswise extension. (In hand knitting you make ribs by alternating a fixed

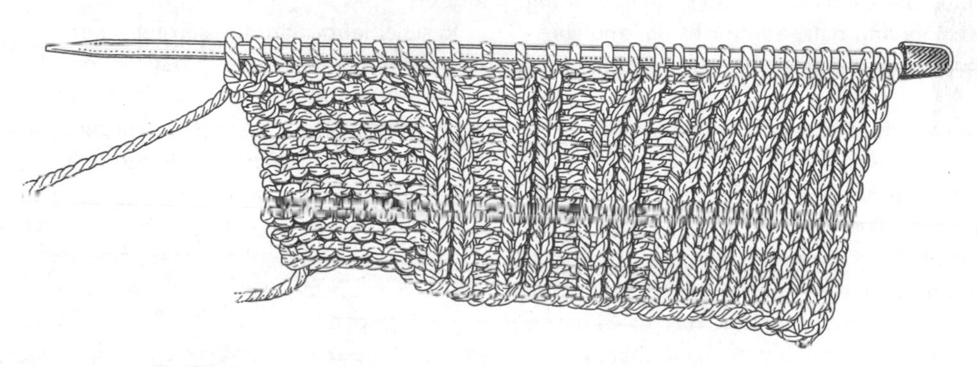

Front side of hand-knitted sampler: From left to right, plain knitting (or garter stitch), rib knit, and stockinet.

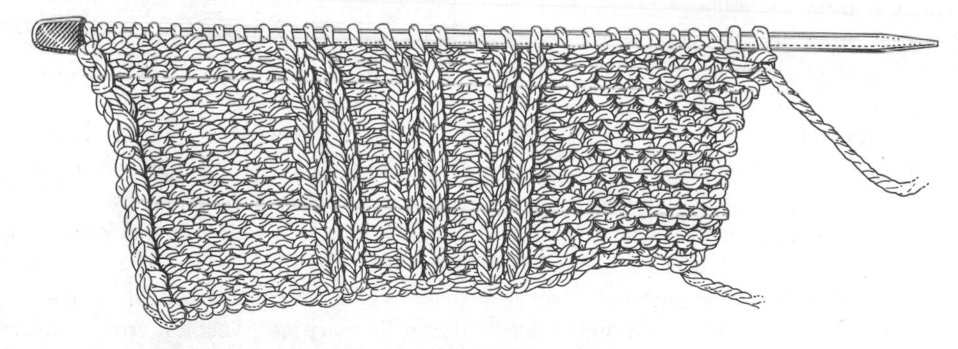

Reverse side of knitted sampler: From left to right, stockinet, rib knit, and plain knitting.

Cable stitch

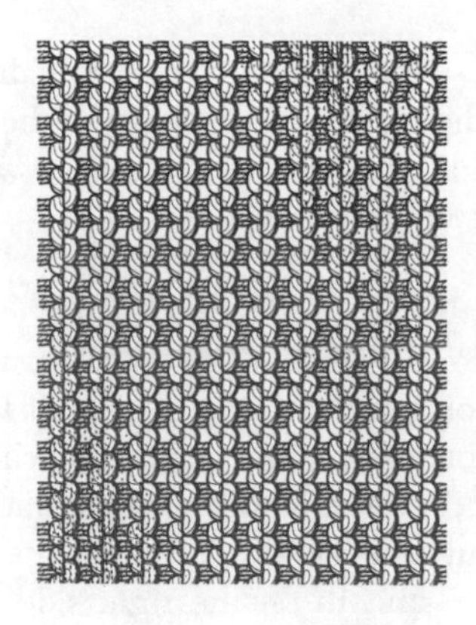
Raschel knit fabric

number of knit and purl stitches, creating alternating columns of stockinet and garter stitch.) Because rib knit stretches more in the width than in the length, it is good for waists and wristbands in sweaters: it will stretch to allow you to put on the garment and then contract to fit your wrist or waist snugly. Rib knit is also used for the bodies of close-fitting sweaters and hats. Some ribs do, and some do not, look the same front and back.

Cable stitch is used to make the plaited, interweaving decorative columns that appear on many sweaters and afghans.

Double knits are rib knits with two layers of loops. They are similar to double-woven fabrics. They are produced on knitting machines that have two sets of needles working simultaneously. The fabrics produced have a firmness and stability of shape that is comparable to that of woven fabrics. At the same time, double knits, like all knits, are naturally wrinkle resistant. Double knits are used for women's suits and dresses, some men's wear, and much sportswear.

Warp Knits. Tricot knits are the most common type of warp knit. They are produced on the tricot knitting machine, which can use very fine yarns, such as those used to make lingerie fabrics. It can also produce a wide range of designs but does not easily permit changes of design or complex designs. Tricot knits look like rows of chains on the right side and rows of Vs or zigzags on the back (reverse) side. (You might need a magnifying glass to see this.)

Tricot fabrics drape well, are soft, have good wrinkle resistance, and are elastic and strong. They are also open enough that air and moisture can pass through, promoting comfort.

Raschel fabrics are the second main type of warp knit. They are produced on the raschel knitting machine, which permits more versatility and complexity in design patterns and quicker change in design than tricot machines. The raschel knitting machine, for example, can produce heavy blankets, bedspreads, carpets, pile fabrics, fine laces, and veils, using any type of fiber whatsoever.

Both tricot and raschel knitting machines are used to make elasticized fabrics and waistbands, swimsuits, stretch foundation garments, and the like.

Lace. Lace is an openwork fabric of yarns that are twisted, looped, braided, stitched, or knotted together to form patterns. Although handmade lace is still produced for sale, almost all lace today is machine made (usually on warp knitting machines). Machine-made lace is usually much less expensive and much more durable than handmade lace. Any lace pattern that can be produced by hand can also be produced by machine. Most patterns produced by machine today can be found in design an-

ton are. Flax and cotton, moreover, are subjected to repeated mechanical and chemical treatments that alter their appearance, shape, color, and other qualities. When we refer to the products of these enormously complicated manufacturing chains as "natural" and regard nylon as "synthetic," we are saying more about our own preferences for the familiar and the traditional than about the characteristics of the cloth.

This is not to say that preferences for natural fibers are necessarily arbitrary. Natural fibers have characteristics that really make them, in many instances, the best choice for furnishings and clothing, especially clothing to be worn next to the skin. For one, they are all hydrophilic (water-loving or -attracting), whereas most manufactured fibers (except for rayon, a cellulose-based fiber) are hydrophobic (water-hating or -repelling). This is what makes the natural fibers more absorbent, which is, as we shall see, a prime factor in their superior comfort under many circumstances. But by and large, the best choice of fiber for a particular function cannot be based on the thin distinction between natural and synthetic. A synthetic carpet backing that is rot-proof is preferable to a jute one that is not. A drape made of light-resistant synthetic fibers will last much longer and cost less than a silk one that will all too soon fall to pieces from the effects of ultraviolet radiation (and the synthetic might even look as good). But the prejudice against synthetics is not easily removed because it has been infected with status perceptions. Wrongly but persistently, synthetics are associated with bright, unfading colors, smoothness, neat creases, durability, and cheapness, and are disdained. Meanwhile clothes that wrinkle, fade, shrink, bleed, and develop holes become signs of superior taste and class, and deeper pockets, as these characteristics, equally mistakenly, are identified as the attributes of "natural" fibers such as cotton.

Sometimes the prejudice goes the other way, too, in favor of synthetics when they make little sense. People may sometimes choose synthetics for certain types of exercise and sportswear only because they feel that shiny, stretchy, "high-tech" fabrics are the right fashion statement for the exercise club, or because the symbolic value of synthetics rises in the sports world. Predictably, too, when natural fibers are chosen out of a sense of moral superiority, a backlash in favor of fun and self-indulgence cannot be long in coming, and this, as well, partly explains certain trends in favor of synthetic fibers where they are not necessarily better. The production of newer, high-priced, luxury versions of older synthetics is another development that has probably done more than anything else to erode prejudice against synthetics.

Environmental concerns have tended to push people toward buying natural fibers, but the facts do not present us with a clear-cut choice for one or the other on environmental grounds. Environmental issues in the textile industry are exceedingly complex. You must weigh not only the effects of elaborate agricultural, production, and manufacturing processes, but also the finishes and dyes that are likely to be used on both sides; the number of years the two kinds of fabrics are likely to survive; whether they are likely to be dry-cleaned or laundered, how they will be laundered, and the relative advantages and disadvantages of those processes environmentally; any waste or disposal problems created by a particular fiber; whether the fabric will be recyclable; and what reforms are ultimately possible in each case. There are studies that suggest that cloth makes its biggest impact on the environment not during the manufacturing process but while we own it, as a result of dry cleaning and laundering.

Most synthetics are made of petroleum products, a nonrenewable resource. Natural fibers are made of renewable resources. But the agricultural and manufacturing processes that produce cotton, for example, create staggering amounts of pollution in the form of pesticides (common estimates are that from 25 to 50 percent of the world's pesticides are devoted to cotton crops), defoliants, other herbicides, fungicides, chemical fertilizers such as nitrates, enormous poundages of bleach, softeners and fading agents, sizing agents such as polyvinyl acetate, resins, including polyurethane resin, acrylic, and formaldehyde resins, dyes (because the excess goes down the drain and, unless biodegradable, passes into the soil and surface water), and the large quantities of energy and water needed to carry out these processes. Pollution from these substances affects the earth, water, and air. Similar concerns have been raised about other natural fibers, although the problems associated with silk, wool, and linen appear to be smaller because smaller quantities of such fibers are produced. Sheep for wool require millions of acres of land for grazing and sheep dips containing phosphorus or chlorine. Chromium mordant dyes used on wool in underdeveloped countries can create toxic sludge.*

Industry and government have not been indifferent to these environmental problems. Reforms have been instituted, and more are likely to come, both formally, through environmental regulations, and informally, through manufacturers' attempts to clean up their production processes and through the production of "transitional," "green," and organic cottons. "Transitional" cottons are those grown without pesticides but on soil that has not been clear of pesticides and chemicals long enough to qualify as organic. "Green" cottons are not organic—that is, they have been grown with pesticides and chemicals—but they are "minimally processed": they may have used low-impact or nontoxic dyes or closed-system dyeing; they may be unbleached or undyed; they may be stone-washed (which is considered environmentally better than using chemical softeners) or enzyme-softened (which may be better than both). Preshrinking may be done by washing, with no chemicals; starch may be used rather than polyvinyl acetate. There are even naturally colored cotton fibers—mostly in green and brown—that require no dyeing.

Some environmentalists favor the increased use of hemp for fabrics because it can be grown without pesticides, fertilizers, and other chemicals required for cotton growing. Laws in this country make it difficult to be a legal hemp grower because of hemp's great similarity to the marijuana plant, which is illegal to grow. The type of hemp plant used in textiles is a different strain, however, and cannot be used for drugs. In many states, laws to make it easier to grow this type of hemp have been proposed in recent years. The push to grow more hemp has also coincided with a push toward developing better and more attractive types of hemp fabrics, and these have been given some attention by clothes designers in recent years.

Because the manufacture of viscose rayon (which constitutes 95 percent of the rayon currently marketed) has always been a highly polluting process, the pressure of environmentalism has led to the introduction of a new rayon fiber, under the brand name Tencel and the generic name lyocell, that is now being promoted as environmentally favorable or low-impact. Like all rayon, lyocell is made of cellulosic polymers derived from wood pulp, which is a renewable resource that uses little fertilizer or pesticides. But lyocell is said to be taken from sustainably harvested tree farms; and, unlike conventional rayon, it is made in a solvent spinning process that is "close-looped," meaning that the dissolving agent is used over and over rather than being discarded as waste with each new batch. The Achilles' heel of this product, as with all rayon, is the pulp-making process, which releases mas-

*Only about 50 percent of raw wool by weight is in fact fibrous material. The rest is oils or fats, excrement, dirt, and other matter, which all goes into the sludge. From this unsavory potpourri lanolin is extracted and subsequently used in the manufacture of such items as peppermint cremes and lipsticks.

sive amounts of natural and unnatural chemicals into the environment.

Other attempts to make natural fibers available without harmful pollution include various kinds of recycling. Wool has always been recycled. (See chapter 16.) Cottons, however, have not been; only recently have some companies begun shredding and respinning cotton fabrics into yarns by relatively clean processes.

It is difficult to find any objective evaluation of the effects of all this. The environmental regulations are said to have brought about real improvements. But none of the organic or low-impact fibers so far constitutes a significant share of the market. (Of about 13 million acres of cotton production in the United States in 1997, 100,000—less than 1 percent—were dedicated to organic and transitional cottons.) They cost considerably more than conventional cottons and rayon. Unless a product is labeled to show that it is both organically grown and processed, moreover, the buyer often does not know which improved procedures were actually used. All of these products and procedures offer real benefits, or at least could make a real difference if they amounted to somewhat more than a small drop in a large bucket. Alas, the sacrifice required on the part of a buyer determined to purchase only environmentally virtuous natural-fiber products, in terms of variety, cost, and quality, is still immense.

Spokespeople for synthetic fiber manufacturers argue, with some justice, that the production of low-impact cotton and even expensive organic cotton has a greater negative environmental impact than polyester production, both because of the enormous amounts of water and energy that cotton growing consumes and because the manufacture of even these virtuous products typically creates chemical pollutants as by-products. They point out that the manufacture of synthetics involves no growing or raising process to complicate matters, and synthetic fiber manufacturing continually reuses solvents rather than discarding them as waste. Dyeing synthetic fibers (other than acrylics) does not require prior bleaching, which uses massive amounts of water to prepare the fibers; synthetic fibers are already white. Although there are as yet no efforts toward recycling synthetic textiles (and these are unlikely anytime soon because of the complications presented by textiles made of blended fibers), plastic beverage bottles have been recycled and used to manufacture synthetic fabrics that are made into outerwear.

Those who wish to fight pollution with their textile-buying habits might sensibly try buying only goods manufactured in countries with expensive pollution-control regulations—our own, many Western European countries, Canada, Australia, and Japan. Many Asian, African, and Central and South American countries do not have such laws. Avoiding overfrequent laundering and dry cleaning of clothes and furnishings is environmentally prudent too. But perhaps the surest bet of all, at least for the time being, may simply be not to buy so much. (An academic specialist in textiles told me that the annual rate of consumption of textiles is about 40 kilograms per person in the United States, 20 kilograms per person in Europe, and 2 to 3 kilograms per person in Asia.) This would mean buying things that last longer and learning how to clean, preserve, and mend them so as to extend their lives. So far there has been no call for the really revolutionary solution: an end to fashion, the pleasant habit that keeps most of us buying new clothes and furnishings when old ones are quite serviceable.

Effect of Fiber Content on Fabric Performance; Interplay with Other Determinants.

Comfort Is Partly Subjective. Fiber content strongly affects how comfortable a fabric feels. Some types of polyester now have a pleasing silky or cottony hand, but older types had a slight harshness, and many types still do. Wool can be scratchy. Coarse weaves of many fibers are literally painful when worn against the skin. Medieval penitents who donned coarse sackcloth undershirts chose an effective means of self-torment.

Some scientific bases for the comfort factor of various kinds of fabrics are discussed below, but the reader should remember that the final test is in the wearing. If you find a fabric comfortable (or not), that is all that counts. Comfort depends not only on the characteristics of the fabric but on those of the wearer—how much he or she perspires, skin sensitivity, bodily responses to environmental factors, and so forth. In addition, some places on the body are more sensitive, warmer, or cooler than others; and some people's bodies are more sensitive, warmer, and cooler overall than others'. Dressing for comfort means juggling a lot of subjective factors with the objective ones.

Comfort Effects of Absorbency and Permeability of Fibers; Dressing for the Weather. A fabric's comfort in different kinds of weather depends largely on the extent to which it is permeable to air and water vapor. In fact, the interactions of skin, perspiration, air, fabrics, and environmental heat and moisture are so complicated that scientists only now feel they are beginning to unravel their mysteries, which would require whole books to explain thoroughly.

At temperatures around 85°F, so textile scientists tell us, the amount of heat produced by the human body and the amount lost to the environment are in equilibrium, and you will feel warm enough without clothes. Although the naked body can accommodate cooler temperatures to some extent by contracting its blood capillaries or shivering, it will start feeling chilly and uncomfortable at temperatures only a little lower; you will begin to want something on. At slightly higher temperatures, the body dilates the capillaries and sweats to cool itself; you may find yourself wanting to remove layers of clothing. But although wet skin is less comfortable than dry, it does not follow that in very warm weather no clothing is more comfortable than light clothing. Clothing can cool you down and protect you from the heat of the sun.

Whether a fabric holds heat well or poorly is a profound determinant of the comfort it affords. Relatively recently, people thought that the comparative warmth or coolness of different fabrics was mostly a function of how well, comparatively, their fibers conducted heat. I was taught as a girl that it was because linen was a good heat conductor (it conducted heat away from the body) that it was cool and because wool was a poor heat conductor (it did not conduct heat away from the body) that it was warm. This was not accurate.

In fact, all textile fibers are rather poor heat conductors, and fabrics can be excellent insulators. Metals will conduct heat a thousand times better. But the air warmed by your body is trapped by the textile material. Woven textiles, being nothing more than a latticework of air and textile fibers, thus create an extremely effective and lightweight insulation, holding heat near your body and preventing it from being lost to the wind or the surrounding cooler air. The thicker a fabric and the more air pockets it has, the better it holds heat. (Note that a thick fabric may or may not also be heavy.) The coolest fabrics, therefore, are the thinnest, smoothest, most loosely constructed ones, for these are least effective in holding a layer of warmed air around you. Napped, pile, and fuzzy fabrics, of whatever fiber, tend to be warmer than smooth ones, because they hold air in the interstices between the fibers that make up the fuzz. Linen (flax), whose fibers are extremely smooth and are readily woven into very fine and air-permeable fabrics that are nonetheless strong, is thus highly valued as summer wear. Flannel sheets, which have a fuzzy surface that traps air, feel warmer than regular sheets. Wool fibers, which are even fuzzier and are scaly and quite crimped, trap a great deal of air and thus make an extremely warm fabric. Yet because wool worsteds that are smooth and fine can be woven, there are summer-weight wools too (although they could never compete with linen for coolness). Silk is often warm, but it is usually considered summery because it can be woven into lightweight and highly breathable fabrics—fabrics that permit air to pass in and out. Even linen yarns can be knitted into a rather spongy, dense material fit for cooler weather. Thus, although fiber content is quite important to how cool or warm a fabric is, it is by no means the whole story.

The way a fabric reacts to moisture is almost as important as the way it holds heat in determining whether people feel that it is comfortable. A complicated interplay occurs among the effects of moisture, air and other factors, and fabrics. The comfort goal in moisture management is to keep your skin neither too wet nor too dry. Dry skin feels scratchy, and it itches. Wet skin is uncomfortable too. Fabric acts on it more abrasively; it is more vulnerable to infections from funguses or other microorganisms; if your feet are sweating you are more likely to get blisters. Your skin naturally and constantly loses moisture—through perspiration—even when it feels perfectly dry. In a hot environment, you will notice when you begin to sweat. You feel cooler when the perspiration evaporates from your skin. Usually what you want your clothing to do is let your perspiration move away from your body; usually, therefore, absorbent fabrics are far more comfortable against the skin than unabsorbent ones.

The so-called natural fibers (cotton, linen, silk, wool, ramie, hemp) and the cellulosic man-made fibers (rayon and lyocell) are all absorbent and hydrophilic or water-attracting. Synthetic fibers such as polyester, nylon, acrylic, and polypropylene are all unabsorbent and hydrophobic or water-repelling. When an absorbent fabric is placed on your skin, water evaporating from your skin surface will be taken right into its fibers. Highly absorbent fabrics can often hold great quantities of moisture before they become saturated; thus they can keep you quite comfortable unless you perspire a great deal. When the fibers and the air trapped in and near their interstices all begin to fill with moisture, the insulating ability of the fabric will be decreased, and you may also start to feel cooler. As the saturation point of the fabric is reached, for example, on a very hot day when you are exercising actively, your skin may begin to feel wet again. If a fabric releases absorbed water readily through evaporation, it is less likely to become or stay saturated and it is likely to remain more comfortable. How readily the moisture evaporates from the fabric depends only partly on fiber content; fabric and yarn construction and garment construction are also extremely important, as are the environmental temperature and humidity. Wool, by the way, has extraordinary advantages in cold, damp weather. Not only does it take in enormous quantities of moisture before becoming saturated, it actually releases enough heat as it becomes wet to help you feel warm.

Fabrics remove moisture from the skin by mechanisms other than absorbency. Synthetic fibers as well as natural ones, for example, may *adsorb* or *wick*. (The latter term, not yet in many dictionaries, gradually worked its way from textile-industry jargon into advertisements for the public.) "Adsorbency" refers to a fabric's capacity to attract water to its surface. The more surface area a cloth has, the more water it can hold on its surface, which partly explains the longer drying time for cotton towels with looped-fiber surfaces compared to those with cut pile (or "velour")—the former simply have a greater surface area to adhere to. When fabrics "wick" moisture, they draw it off the skin surface and pass it along their interstices (without absorbing it), where it evaporates into the air at a rate determined by fiber type, the atmospheric relative humidity, and other factors. If you put the edge of a cotton towel in water, you can watch the water wick up the cloth.

Such hydrophilic fibers as cotton, linen, and rayon tend to hold moisture longer than the hydrophobic ones such as nylon, polyester, and polypropylene, which dry more readily; this slight dampness contributes to their keeping you feeling cool in warm weather. On a hot summer day, you will love the coolness—hence the ever-popular cotton T-shirt for a summer's jog. It's better than bare. But if you are cross-country skiing on a frigid day and sweat to the point of soaking your cotton undershirt, you put yourself at risk for dangerous hypothermia. That is why sports experts often recommend that for cold-weather sports you wear a wicking type of fiber next to the skin so as to get perspiration off the skin and let it evaporate rather than saturate the fabric. Not all synthetic fabrics wick, however, or wick sufficiently to make you comfortable in the extremes of cold weather or warm, humid weather, particularly when you are exercising heavily. (And not all forms of exercise produce enough perspiration to make high wickability the chief desideratum of next-to-skin clothing.) Wearing ordinary polyester, nylon, or other synthetics in the summer can make you feel hot and clammy. Among synthetics, polypropylene naturally wicks well. Some synthetics are constructed so as to wick well; the fibers in one type are actually hollow tubes through which perspiration can pass. There are also finishes applied to synthetic fabrics that promote wicking.

A fabric's "breathability," as the retailers call it, really refers to its permeability to water vapor; this is another factor that strongly affects comfort. Various coatings applied for waterproofing, for example, render fabrics impermeable to water vapor in the way that vinyl upholstery or rubber and plastic are impermeable. As your perspiration evaporates, it cannot pass through such fabrics into the surrounding air; you feel wet and uncomfortable. The hotter it is, the more water-vapor permeability you will want in your clothes and the less you will enjoy sitting on a vinyl car seat or upholstery that is completely impermeable. The most comfortable rain gear is impermeable to moisture from the outside but permits water vapor from the inside to pass through, so you do not become wet from your own perspiration. There are new fabrics, such as Gore-Tex, that do this.

Garment construction also matters greatly to your comfort. Never underestimate the simple effect of unbuttoning your coat or of loose or vented clothing that lets air in. Unzipping can be far more effective than wicking. Close-fitting garments are warmer than loose ones, just because they do not let the air inside them move around much. Tight cuffs and collars and waists also keep the air in and restrict its flow. Double-breasted garments insulate better than single-breasted ones. Unbuttoning your collar, loosening your tie, removing your scarf, taking off one insulating layer—all are actions that can overpower the effects of fiber content and construction. On the other hand, no amount of loosening and unbuttoning is going to make your Norwegian wool sweater endurable in August on the beach.

Aesthetics: Look and Feel. In the world of textiles, a fabric's "hand" refers only to its feel on the hand, not to its feel on other parts of the body and not to its feel, in general, on the skin. In fact, your hands and other parts of you can respond quite differently to the same fabric, which explains why the sheet or shirt that feels so lovely when you handle it in the store can give quite an ugly sensation when pressed against your back. To say that a fabric has a good hand is a purely aesthetic evaluation. Yet the fabric's hand contributes significantly to its comfort.

Fiber content strongly affects how smooth, rough, silky, soft, hard, or luxurious a fabric feels. The satiny feel of some silks can never be matched by wools, no matter how finely woven. Many 100% polyesters lack the pleasant sensations of linen and cotton on the skin. The softness of good wool cannot be achieved with cotton or linen. Each of the major fibers, as rendered in an ordinary plain-weave construction, has a unique, all but indescribable hand that is so familiar to us that we tend to use the fiber names archetypally and to speak of cottony, woolly, silky, and linenlike sensations. Still, remarkable things can be done in the process of constructing the fabric. Cottons can feel flannelly. Synthetic yarns can look and feel woolly or cottony.

The look of a fiber can be as variable as its hand. Some fabrics are lustrous; some have a dull surface. Luster is produced by a number of factors. Very smooth fibers, such as silk, are highly lustrous. Linen, which is also smooth, has a pleasing subtle luster, but cotton, a rougher fiber, generally has little unless it has received a treatment to give it luster. Synthetics can often be produced in both lustrous and dull versions. (There are various chemical treatments and weaves that will produce a luster too.) Drapability—how well a fabric falls into pleasant folds—is strongly influenced by fiber content. Wool, silk, and nylon drape softly and gracefully, but for crispness you need cotton or linen. How successfully a fabric dyes is also mostly a matter of fiber content. Linen is hard to dye, and silk is famous for dyeing with gorgeous colors. (Unfortunately, for the same reason, linen resists staining and silk stains outrageously easily.) Acetate takes no ordinary dyes; special ones had to be developed for it. Many synthetics not only dye well but resist fading—an important factor in determining how long upholstery or a garment or curtain will be serviceable.

Resilience. Fiber content strongly affects a fabric's resilience, or how readily it wrinkles. Manufactured fibers other than rayon tend to have excellent resilience. Nylon is the most popular material for carpets because, among other things, it is highly resilient, over and over springing back after being crushed underfoot. Wool, another traditional fiber for carpets, is also highly resilient but costs much more than nylon. Everyone knows that cotton wrinkles and linen wrinkles horribly unless they have received a treatment that controls wrinkling. A simple test for resilience is to crush a bit of the fabric in your hand for a few seconds and see whether it emerges wrinkled.

Durability. The durability of fabrics depends on many factors, including yarn and fabric construction and finishing treatments. Fiber content is a major determinant of tear strength, that is, resistance to ripping when the fabric is pulled in opposite directions. But a fabric's abrasion resistance (how well it resists rubbing or friction) is another strong determinant of durability, and fabrics with excellent tear strength may have little abrasion resistance. Silk is considered a durable fiber because it is strong, in fact stronger than cotton, but it has less abrasion resistance than cotton. Durability is to some extent relative to use; a weaker fiber with good abrasion resistance might outlast a stronger fiber with poor abrasion resistance if it is used in such a way that it is subjected to little pulling but much rubbing (say, as a handbag lining or a polishing cloth). Spandex, the weakest of all fibers, has good durability not only because of its high resistance to abrasion but also because it is elastic. If a fabric is somewhat weak but elastic, such as spandex or to a much lesser degree nylon or wool, the danger of tearing is reduced because the fabric will give before the pull produces a tear. Generally speaking, thicker fabrics are more durable than thinner ones of the same type. Even the degree of smoothness of the fabric can affect its durability; a smooth fabric, all else being equal, may last longer because it will not pull and snag on surfaces it comes in contact with.

Some fabrics deteriorate readily with exposure to sunlight, and others will fade. Light-fast fibers, obviously, are more durable choices for draperies. See "Choosing Ultraviolet-Light-Resistant Fibers" in chapter 18, page 268. Susceptibility to moths and mildew strongly affects the durability of fabrics. A rough rule of thumb is that natural fibers may be damaged by insects and mildew, and synthetics usually are not. (The susceptibility of various natural fibers to silverfish, moths, and mold is discussed in chapter 16.)

Cleanliness. Some fibers have an inherent tendency to stay clean. Fabrics that tend to soil less may have a longer life because washing and cleaning gradually wear out cloth.

Smooth fabrics such as linen tend to be cleaner than other fabrics because rough surfaces trap and hold dirt more readily; cotton's rougher surface means that it soils more than linen. Unabsorbent fabrics do not readily attract dirt, and resist staining simply because matter that would otherwise stain remains on the surface of the fabric, where it is more easily removed. That is why upholstery fabrics often benefit from some synthetic fiber content—most synthetics are unabsorbent—or stain-repelling treatment. However, several synthetic fibers have a tendency to build up static electricity, which tends to attract lint and dirt. Many synthetics also tend to be oleophilic and hydrophobic—they attract oil and repel water—which means that they tend to oil-stain and to resist getting thoroughly wet and clean in the laundry. Napped and pile fabrics also tend to resist stains because their construction prevents the soil from easily penetrating the cloth; it stays on the surface where it can more readily be removed. Of course, napped and pile fabrics are by no means stain-proof.

Launderability. Launderability is determined greatly, although not solely, by fiber content. Because most soaps, detergents, and laundry solutions are alkaline, fabrics that tolerate alkalinity well are typically highly launderable, and those that do not tolerate alkalinity usually require dry cleaning or special handling. This is why fabrics composed of plant fibers, such as cotton, linen, and ramie, are often launderable while those derived from animal matter, such as wool and silk, are more problematic. Plant fibers are made of cellulose polymers, which are sensitive to acids but can tolerate a fair degree of alkalinity. Silk, wool, and other hair fibers are composed of protein polymers, which are more resistant to acids but less resistant to alkalies than cellulosic fibers. Although many silk and wool articles can be washed with mild or nonalkaline soaps or detergents if special care is taken, more often than not they should be dry cleaned—for this and other reasons. (For laundering instructions for each type of fiber, see chapters 16 and 17. See also the discussion of laundering "Superwash" wool in chapter 16.)

The vulnerability of particular fibers to acids and alkalis may be increased with heat or may not be present at all except at high temperatures; that is one reason why laundry instructions sometimes recommend using cold or lukewarm water. There are other substances besides soaps and detergents, such as foods, household cleaning products, household chemicals, and medicines, some of which are strongly alkaline or acidic, that may damage fabrics they come into contact with. (See chapter 31, "The Chemistry of Household Cleaning.)

Synthetics may have chemical vulnerabilities to alkaline solutions or dry-cleaning fluids; thus some are either not launderable or not dry-cleanable, although many are both.

Glossary of Fabric Terms

Abrasion resistance. The ability of a fabric to withstand rubbing without suffering damage to its appearance or function.

Art linen. Closely woven, round-thread (not calendered or beetled; see chapter 15) linen, used mainly for embroidery, in plain weave. It is also used for dresses and table linens.

Bark crêpe *(krape)*. Fabric with rough, bark-like surface, used for coats and dresses. Of wool, rayon, or manufactured fibers.

Batiste *(buh-TEEST)*. Sheer, fine, combed cotton or cotton blend in plain weave, used for soft dresses, shirts, infants' wear, nightgowns, lingerie.

Bedford cord. Heavy, corded fabric with cords running along the warp. Used for coats, suits, uniforms, upholstery.

Bengaline *(BEN-guh-leen).* Lustrous corded fabric with ribs running in the direction of the filling, like grosgrain but heavier. Used for dresses, coats, ribbons.

Bisso. A fine, crisp, sheer linen made of wiry yarns, which is sometimes called altar cloth and is used for that purpose.

Boiled wool. Very densely felted wool fabric; used for coats, jackets, slippers.

Bouclé *(boo-KLAY).* Cloth knitted or woven with a novelty yarn that has protruding loops or curls.

Broadcloth. Originally meant a high-quality, closely woven woolen worsted fabric wider than 27 inches, in a twill or plain weave. Now refers to cotton and cotton/polyester plain-weave fabrics in solid color or print.

Brocade *(bro-KADE).* Heavy jacquard-woven fabric with raised floral or figured designs. Often has a satin-weave figure on plain or twill-weave ground. Originally was a heavy silk with gold or silver thread, and often still has that appearance.

Brocatelle *(brock-uh-TELL).* A stiff upholstery fabric, similar to brocade, with raised or puffed figures, usually in silk, rayon, or cotton.

Buckram *(BUCK-ruhm).* A plain-weave, coarse cotton fabric given a stiff starched or sized finish.

Burlap. A coarse plain-weave fabric usually of jute.

Calico *(KAL-ee-ko or KAL-i-ko).* A plain weave printed with small designs, of cotton or cotton blend.

Cambric *(KAME-brik).* A soft, plain-weave linen or cotton fabric, calendered to give it luster, often used for dainty and delicate things such as handkerchiefs, underwear, aprons, and blouses, but it comes in heavier weights as well. It is also called handkerchief linen, linen lawn, or linen batiste.

Camel hair. Lightweight, warm, soft-napped fabric, made from the natural-colored hair of a camel. Frequently mixed with wool. Used for coats, sweaters, blankets.

Canvas. Any strong, firm, heavy plain-weave fabric. Usually of cotton, sometimes of linen or hemp.

Cashmere. Soft, fine fabric made entirely from the soft undercoat of cashmere goats or from fine wool mixed with the soft hair. Widely used in coats, suits, sweaters, shawls.

Cavalry twill. A twill weave fabric with a steep, double twill line. Used for uniforms, sportswear, riding habits.

Challis *(SHAL-ee).* A lightweight, soft wool, cotton, rayon, or combination of fibers in a plain weave, usually printed with a small design. Used for dresses, blouses, pajamas. Originally wool or silk.

Chambray *(SHAM-bray or SHAM-bree).* Usually cotton, but may be made with a combination of fibers. Yarn-dyed fabric, plain weave, with colored warp and white filling thread (or contrasting color in filling thread, which produces an iridescent effect). Depending upon weight and quality, used for shirts, dresses, and work or play clothes.

Chamois cloth *(SHAM-ee).* Cloth of cotton or synthetic fiber that has been napped so as to resemble chamois leather.

Charmeuse *(shar-MOOZE).* Lightweight, soft fabric that has a semi-lustrous satin front and a dull back, with hard-twisted warp yarns and crêpe filling yarns. Made of silk, cotton, or synthetics. Sometimes refers to cloth that is given a somewhat lustrous finish, for example, by mercerizing.

Cheesecloth. Very open, plain-weave, lightweight fabric of carded cotton yarns.

Chenille *(shen-EEL).* The term refers to two types of fabric. One is made by tufting, a process in which yarn is "punched" through a backing fabric. Chenille robes and bedspreads are made this way. This type of chenille fabric can show a pattern or may have a "velvet" pile surface. The other type of chenille fabric is made of chenille yarn, which has pile protruding all around it, so as to show patterns in pile.

Cheviot *(SHEV-ee-uht).* Twill weave, in wool or worsted yarns, with a rough, hairy surface, good for sportswear.

Chiffon *(shiff-ON).* Very lightweight, sheer silk or silky synthetic, made in a plain weave with a very fine, hard-twisted yarn. Its surface is dull; it is used for dressy blouses, scarves, dresses, veils.

China silk. A soft, lightweight, plain-weave silk, used for blouses, linings. Rayon imitations of china silk are common.

Chino *(CHEE-no).* Sturdy plain- or twill-weave cotton used for sportswear, dyed a khaki color.

Chintz. A glazed, crisp cotton in close plain weave, usually in bright prints, often big florals. It is used for draperies, slipcovers, and, in light weights, summer dresses.

Clear finished. Worsted whose yarns and weave are clearly visible because the fuzz and nap are singed or sheared.

Covert *(KUHV-ert or KOH-vert).* Twill-weave fabric woven with yarns of two shades of the same color, usually tan and brown, so that the fabric looks speckled or mottled. Of wool, cotton, or other fiber.

Corduroy. A strong, durable pile fabric with lengthwise ridges of cut pile called wales. Usually of cotton. Used for casual clothes and sportswear.

Crash. Relatively coarse plain weave, medium weight, made of uneven, slack-twisted yarns in various qualities. In cotton or linen, often with colored borders. Used for toweling, table linens, draperies.

Crêpe *(krape).* Any fabric with a grained, crinkled, or textured surface.

Crêpe de chine *(krape-d'SHEEN).* Very light, fine, plain-weave silk with a fine-textured crêpe. It is woven with filament silk yarn in the warp and hard-twisted filament silk yarn in the filling. It is also made with spun yarns in warp and filament yarn in the filling.

Cretonne *(KREE-tahn or kri-TAHN).* Like chintz, but with an unglazed, dull surface. Usually in big florals and used for interior decorating purposes such as upholstery, draperies, slipcovers.

Crinoline *(KRIN-uh-lin).* Any of a variety of stiff, plain-weave fabrics used for support, for example, to hold out full skirts. Lighter weight than buckram.

Crocking. The transfer of color from a fabric to other surfaces as a result of rubbing.

Damask *(DAM-uhsk).* Cloth with jacquard-woven floral or geometric designs, used for tablecloths, towels, bedspreads, and other household linens, as well as upholstery and drapes. Usually in white or one or two colors.

Denim. A sturdy, twill-weave cotton used for work and play clothes, blue jeans. Often has

Damask

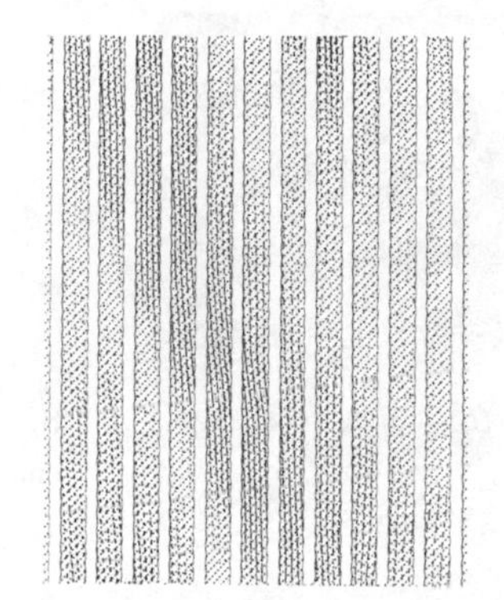
Dimity

blue (indigo-dyed) warp and white filling threads.

Diaper. A woven pattern that shows repeated units of design that are all connected to one another or cover the whole surface of the cloth.

Dimity (DIM-*i-tee*). A thin, sheer, plain-weave cotton, with cords in the warp, often in stripe or check. Used for dresses, aprons, bedspreads.

Dobby. Any fabric woven on a dobby loom. These fabrics have small woven-in geometric figures such as bird's-eyes, diamonds, and so forth. See illustrations on page 200.

Doeskin. Fine quality, smooth finish, satin-weave wool fabric with a slight nap, or similar napped fabric of other fibers. Used for coats, pants, uniforms.

Donegal tweed (DON-*i-gall*). Woolen tweed of medium- to heavy-weight, originally handwoven in the county of Donegal, Ireland, but now any Irish tweed. In a plain or twill weave with a single color in the warp and a mix of colors in the filling yarns. Used for suits and coats.

Dotted swiss. Any fabric with dots created by swivel weave or lappet weave or by flocking. It is usually crisp, with a lawnlike background. Used for summer clothes, children's wear, curtains.

Double cloth. Fabric with two layers joined in weaving. Used for overcoats, sweaters, blankets, upholstery.

Drill. A durable, closely woven, medium-weight cotton twill used for khaki and ticking.

Duck. A closely woven, durable, heavy cotton plain-weave fabric. Used for belts, bags, tents, awnings, sails. Also called canvas, but usually lighter than canvas.

Duvetyn (DYU-*vuh-teen or duv*-TEEN). A very softly napped, drapable fabric that looks suede like or like a compact velvet.

Faille (*file*). Somewhat shiny, closely woven silk, cotton, rayon, or synthetic fiber fabric with a flat, crosswise, fine ribbed surface, similar to grosgrain. Used for dresses, suits, coats.

Filament. A fiber of indefinite length or of very great length. Filament yarn is made of one or more filament fibers gathered together.

Flannel. Napped plain-weave or twill cloth originally of wool, now usually of cotton.

Flannelette. A lightweight cotton flannel, often used for nightwear or baby clothes.

Fleece. A heavyweight, bulky woolen fabric with a long, fleecy nap, used for coats.

Fleur-de-lis (*flure-d'*LEE *or flurr-d'*LEE). Floral design resembling an iris.

Foulard (*foo*-LARD). Lightweight, plain-woven or twill silk or rayon fabric, soft, usually printed in small figures. Popular for neckwear, soft dresses, blouses, robes.

Frosting. Change in, especially lightening of, fabric color as a result of abrasion or rubbing.

Full-fashioned knit. A garment made from pieces that have each been knitted to a given shape. Such garments usually have a better fit.

Gabardine (GAB*'r-deen*). Sturdy, firm, clear-finished fabric in twill weave, with steep diagonal lines on the face of the cloth. Made of worsted, cotton, and other fibers. Used in suits, coats, sportswear.

Georgette. Thin, lightweight, crinkly silk fabric with a pebbly crêpe surface as a result

Gingham

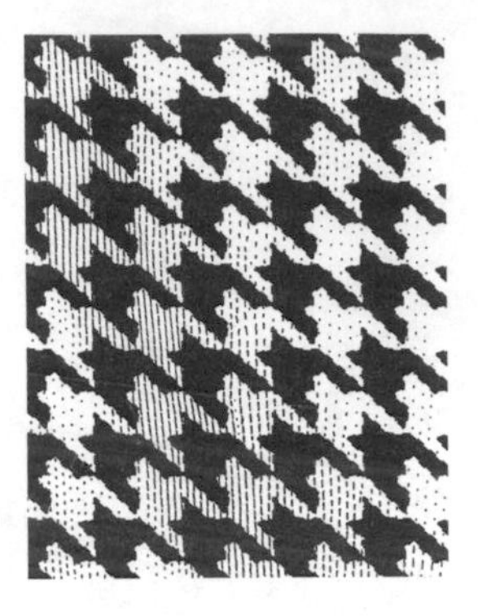

Houndstooth check

of its hard-twisted yarns. The fabric has stiffness and body despite its light weight. Sometimes made of synthetics. Used for dresses, blouses, gowns, hats.

Gingham (GING'*m*). A plain-weave, medium-weight cotton fabric with a check (sometimes plaid or striped) design. Varies from coarse to fine, light fabrics. Commonly used in summer dresses and play clothes.

Greige (*grazhe*—rhymes with beige) **or gray goods.** Undyed, unfinished fabrics.

Grenadine. Open-weave dress fabric made of silk or synthetic fibers.

Grosgrain (GRO-*grane*). Closely woven, ribbed fabric with heavier crosswise ribs than poplin. Familiar in ribbons. Made in silk, cotton, rayon, polyester.

Hand. The tactile qualities of fabrics, or those perceived by touching, squeezing, or rubbing them with one's fingers.

Herringbone. A twill with rows of alternating left- and right-hand twill lines. Usually seen in coats, jackets, wool dresses. (See illustration on page 198.)

Holland. Plain-weave linen or cotton, heavily sized and sometimes glazed. Used for window shades. (Formerly referred to a fine, plain-weave linen shirting fabric, especially from Holland.)

Homespun. Cloth woven at home rather than a factory. Or any loosely woven, fairly heavy plain weave, with coarse, uneven yarns, which looks handloomed.

Honeycomb. A dobby-woven fabric with a textured pattern of raised squares or diamonds that look like a honeycomb. Also called waffle cloth. Used for clothes and furnishings.

Hopsacking. Actually burlap, but the term also refers to any coarse, rough cloth in a basket weave or other weave with a similar look. Used primarily for sportswear, suits and coats, draperies.

Houndstooth check. A variant of the twill weave in which yarns of two different colors produce a jagged check effect.

Huck towel. A towel in a dobby weave, usually woven with borders or names, in color, such as the sort of towel you see at hotels or clubs.

Huckaback. Cotton or linen toweling in bird's eye or honeycomb dobby weave, or with a rough, pebbly surface, and with loosely twisted filling yarns or long floats to increase absorbency. See Huck towel.

Hydrophilic. Tending to attract water; absorbent (of water).

Hydrophobic. Tending to repel water; unabsorbent (of water).

Irish tweed. Tweed made in Ireland, usually with white warp and colored filling yarns.

Jacquard (JACK-*ard*). Any fabric woven on a jacquard loom. The jacquard loom creates intricate designs woven into the cloth by means of punched cards that enable it to handle far more threads than other looms. Brocades, damasks, and tapestries are all types of jacquard fabrics.

Jersey. A smooth, plain-knit fabric of wool, cotton, rayon, or synthetic blends. Used for dresses, shirts, sportswear, underwear. Called stockinet in handknitting. See illustration on page 201.

Lace. An open-network fabric of twisted, looped, or knotted threads, usually forming intricate patterns.

Lamé *(la-MAY)*. Any fabric with metallic threads woven in for decorative purposes.

Lawn. Fine, sheer, crisp-finished cotton or linen of plain weave. Less crisp than organdy or voile. Used for children's clothes, summer dresses, sleepwear. See "Cambric."

Madras. Cotton from the Madras region in India, either in natural color or vegetable dyed, often in colored plaids, stripes, or checks. Its tendency to fade and bleed as a result of the dyes used is periodically the object of faddish admiration.

Marquisette *(mar-ki-ZETT)*. Leno-weave open-mesh fabric, very light in weight, of cotton, silk, or synthetics. Used for curtains, dressy evening fashion. See illustration on page 199.

Matelasse *(mat-el-lass-AY or mat-luh-SAY)*. Double-cloth woven on a jacquard loom to create a quilted or stitched surface. Used for bedspreads and draperies. Originally made of padded silk.

Melton. A dull, smooth, heavy, very short napped, quite durable wool fabric used for coatings and outerwear. Looks somewhat like felt. Also comes in fibers other than wool.

Mohair. Fibers from the hair of the angora goat, or a soft, woolen fabric made from mohair, in plain or twill weaves.

Moiré *(mwah-RAY or mah-RAY)*. Any fabric with a wavy, water-marked design. Taffeta fabrics often receive a moiré finish, and some plain-weave fabrics are printed with the design.

Moleskin. A napped cotton fabric with a suedelike hand. It is made in a strong, heavy weave of coarse, carded yarn. Used for sportswear and work clothes.

Monk's cloth. Loosely woven, heavy basket-weave cotton, usually in brownish or oatmeal colors. Often used for upholstery, drapes, or other furnishings.

Mousseline *(moose-uh-LEEN)*. The French term for muslin; refers to a finer fabric than our own cotton muslin. Used in the United States, it denotes any of several lightweight, sheer, crisp fabrics of a variety of fibers. "Mousseline de soie"—literally, "silk muslin"—is a lightweight, plain-weave, sheer, crisp silk or rayon that resembles chiffon. It is used primarily for evening wear.

Muslin. Originally a substantial plain-weave cotton, fairly strong and heavy. Now also refers to similar fabrics made from blends of cotton and other fibers. It exists in various weights and qualities and has highly varied uses, from heavy sacking to light dresses.

Nainsook *(NANE-sook—rhymes with "look")*. Plain-weave, soft, lightweight cotton fabric of varying grades, usually dyed in pastels. Made from the same gray goods that are turned into batiste and cambric. Used for ladies' blouses and babies' clothes.

Net or netting. Any fabric made of threads, string, or twine worked into open mesh. Of any fiber.

Organdy. A sheer, stiff, transparent plain-weave cotton, treated to make it permanently stiff.

Organza. Thin, transparent, stiff fabric of rayon or silk, used for evening wear.

Ottoman *(OTT-uh-muhn)*. A crosswise-ribbed fabric similar to faille or bengaline but with heavier ribs. Wool, cotton, silk, or synthetic fibers may be used.

Oxford cloth. A plain- or basket-weave cotton, used for shirting. Usually has a double-yarn warp and a single filling thread. Oxford

Fabric with moiré finish

Paisley design

chambray is oxford cloth with colored warp and white filling yarns.

Paisley. Any fabric printed with a traditional paisley design. The paisley design, which originated in Paisley, Scotland, has a teardrop shape with a curving point.

Peau de soie *(po-d'*SWAH*)*. Literally "skin of silk," denotes a soft, good-quality silk (or silky synthetic) satin cloth with a dull surface. Used for dresses.

Percale *(purr-*KAL*—rhymes with "Al")*. A closely woven, plain-weave cotton, used for dresses, blouses, sheets. Percale has a thread count (fabric count) of 180 or higher.

Pile fabric. Any fabric in which one set of yarns (pile yarns) stand vertical to the base fabric. May be made by weaving, knitting, and tufting. May have a looped or velvety surface. Examples are terry cloth, velvet, velveteen, and corduroy.

Piqué *(peek-*AY *or pik-*AY*)*. Any woven or knitted fabric with a raised pattern or quilted-looking surface. Usually of cotton; sometimes of synthetics. Woven piqués are usually medium- or heavyweight, rather stiff fabrics with raised crosswise cords, often used for collars, cuffs, dresses.

Plissé *(pliss-*AY*)*. Has a puckered or blistered surface appearance in stripes created by a chemical treatment. In cheap goods, it may wash out. Looks like seersucker.

Pointelle. Any ribbed knit with tiny holes or openings in a pattern

Polished cotton. A plain-weave cotton with a glazed finish.

Pongee *(pahn-*GEE*)*. Raw silk fabric often in a natural tan color, with a rather uneven, crude texture. The term is also used to refer to cotton or rayon cloth of a similar weight and texture.

Poplin. Plain-weave dress goods in which the filling is heavier than the warp, producing a fine, crosswise rib surface appearance. Most commonly a medium- or heavyweight cotton fabric, but also in wool, silk, synthetics.

Ragg. Formerly a fabric made from waste clippings of wool or used wool. Now may refer to new wool fabrics or garments made with multicolored yarns or made to resemble rough fabrics or garments of waste, used, or recycled wool.

Rep. Fabric with narrow, lengthwise ribs made with unbalanced plain weave.

Resilience. Ability of a fabric to spring back to its original state after being crushed or wrinkled.

Rib or ribbed fabric. Any woven fabric with a cord or ridge either lengthwise or crosswise, such as poplin, grosgrain, and rep. Any knit fabrics with lengthwise ribs on both sides.

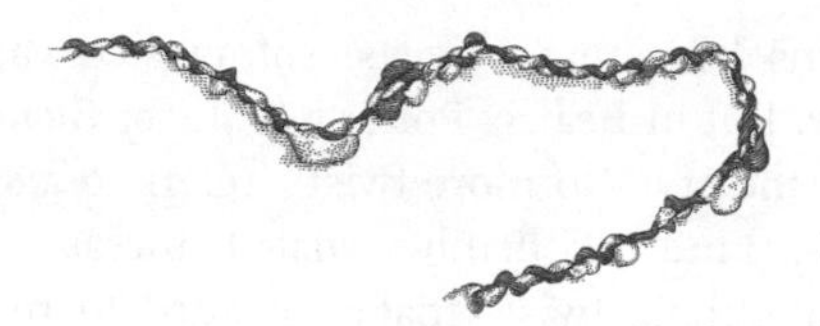
Novelty yarn with slubs

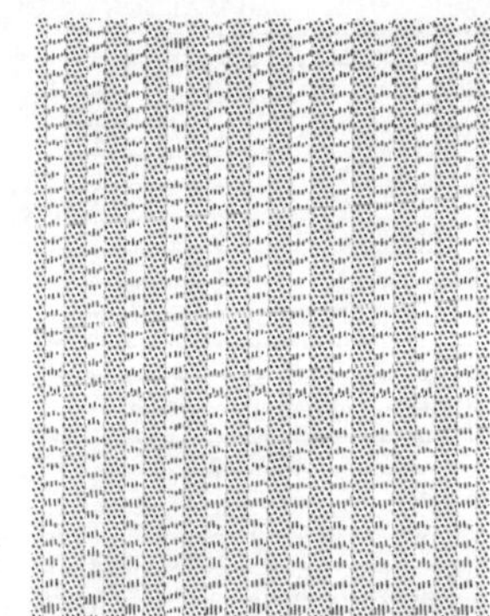
Seersucker

Sailcloth. Strong, durable fabric of linen, cotton, jute, or nylon or other synthetics. Used for sails, play clothes, upholstery.

Sateen. A cotton fabric in a lustrous satin weave with filling yarn floats.

Satin. Originally referred to silk fiber in a satin weave, but now may refer to man-made fibers in a satin weave too. Highly lustrous, slippery. Used for evening wear, lingerie, linings. Any fabric made in a satin weave.

Seersucker. A dull-surfaced, medium-weight fabric with crinkly rows woven in. A variation of a plain weave. It is used for summer clothes. Classically of cotton fiber, but now made from synthetic fibers too.

Selvage. The edges of cloth that are finished in a tighter weave, and sometimes with a different weave or heavier threads, to prevent their raveling. (Note, however, that some modern-weave selvages do not look this way anymore.) Sheets usually have selvages along the sides, with hems at the foot and head of the sheet.

Serge *(surj)*. Smooth twill made from heavy worsted yarns, clear finished.

Shantung *(shan-*TUHNG*)*. Rough silk in plain weave with irregular filling yarns that give it a slubbed or textured effect; originally of wild silk. Sometimes refers to similar-looking fabrics in fibers other than silk.

Sharkskin. Medium- to heavyweight sleek fabric with slightly lustrous surface. Usually in a basket weave, of wool, rayon, silk, or synthetic fibers. Used for tailored suits, slacks, and sportswear.

Sheeting. Fabric of size, construction, and weight suitable for bed sheets.

Slub. A thick place in yarn, caused by uneven twisting or irregularities in the fibers. Sometimes slubs are intentionally created for a fashion effect. Otherwise they constitute a flaw.

Staple. Fibers of medium or short length. Used to make spun yarns.

Suede cloth. A plain-weave fabric napped on one side. Made of cotton or other fibers.

Suiting. Any fabric suitable for coats or suits.

Surah *(*SORE*-uh)*. Lustrous twill weave of silk, rayon, or synthetic fibers suitable for soft-tailored garments and neckwear. Available in solids, prints, plaids.

Taffeta *(*TAFF*-et-uh)*. Any of a group of fabrics, all plain-weave, fine, smooth, and crisp, usually with a fine crosswise rib. Originally of silk, now of almost any fiber.

Tattersall. A style of English plaid; usually has crossing lines in two colors forming squares on the background of a third color.

Tear strength. Ability of fabric to resist tearing.

Terry cloth. Cotton-pile woven or knitted fabric with uncut loops on one or both sides.

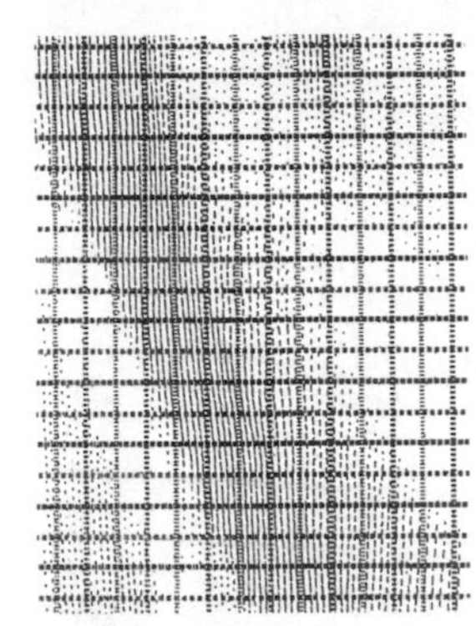

Tattersall plaid

Ticking. A type of drill cloth with alternate stripes of white and colored yarn. Used mainly for mattress, upholstery, and pillow covers. Term may be used to refer to any strong, durable, closely woven fabric used for such purposes.

Toile *(twahl)*. The term means, simply, cloth or fabric, or more particularly a linen cloth. It has come to be associated with "toile de Jouy," printed linens made in Jouy, France.

Tricot *(TREE-koh)*. A fine-waled warp-knit fabric, often used for underwear, sleepwear, and gloves. Of cotton or synthetic fibers.

Tulle *(tool)*. Fine, soft, sheer silk (or silky synthetic) net fabric, usually with tiny hexagonal mesh. Used for veils, gowns, bridal gowns, dance costumes.

Tussah *(TUHSS-uh)*. A sturdy, rough or coarse, loosely woven silk fabric, especially fabric made from Tussah silkworm (wild silk) fibers.

Tweed. Any rough-surfaced woolly fabric, usually woven in two or more colors, either plain or patterned. Originally a rough homespun fabric of heavy woolen yarns, today almost any fabric that is nubby and rough, with mixed colors. Now of wool or almost any other fiber.

Twist. The number of twists or turns per inch given a thread or yarn. Hard-twisted yarns have many twists, soft-twisted yarns few. But in Beatrix Potter's *Tailor of Gloucester*, the cry "No more twist!" refers to a specific kind of firmly twisted thread, the "buttonhole twist" that is needed to make the last of the twenty-one buttonholes in the mayor's new waistcoat.

Union cloth. A fabric with cotton warp and filling of reused wool, usually heavily napped. Used for heavy overcoating.

Union linen. A fabric with cotton warp and linen filling. Sometimes this is called union cloth.

Velour. Thick, soft woven or knitted fabric with a deep pile (deeper than velvet). Mainly used as a suit or coat fabric.

Velvet. Fabric with short, thick, smooth pile. Originally of silk, now of many types of fiber.

Velveteen. A cotton velvet. It has a short, thick pile and a dull surface.

Voile *(voil, rhyming with "oil," or vwahl)*. Plain-weave, lightweight, sheer, crisp fabric made of hard-twisted spun yarns, loosely woven. Used for dresses, blouses, and curtains. Of cotton, silk, rayon, worsted.

Waffle cloth. Any fabric woven on a dobby loom loom in a wafflelike pattern, such as honeycomb or waffle weave.

Waffle knit. Knit fabric with a pattern of wafflelike squares.

Waffle weave. See "Waffle cloth."

Whipcord. A fabric made from worsted. Similar to gabardine but with a steeper twill. Has a hard, wiry hand. Used for riding clothes and other highly tailored garments. Now may be seen in many fibers other than wool.

Zibeline *(ZIB-uh-leen)*. A woolen coating fabric with a long, lustrous, hairy nap of straight fibers laid in one direction.

15

Transformations

Synthetic vs. natural dyes . . . Colorfastness . . . Vat dyes . . . Fiber or stock dyeing, piece dyeing, garment dyeing . . . Crocking and frosting . . . Pigments and prints . . . Finishing treatments for absorbency, antisepsis, antistatic, antiwrinkling . . . Beetling, bleaching, calendering, crêpeing and similar procedures, flame resistance, glazing, mercerizing, mothproofing, napping and sueding, preshrinking, resin treatments, soil resistance, ultraviolet protection, stiffening treatments, and water resistance

What happens to cloth after it is woven may substantially transform its look and behavior and, more often than not, is what matters most to us when we go looking for clothes or furnishings. We tend to take the structure and fiber quality of the cloth for granted. What we want to know is what color it is and whether we have to iron it or wash it separately. The answers often depend on what dyes and finishes have been used.

Inferior dyeing can wreck the appearance of the finest cloth and greatly reduce its usable life, or cause expense in dry cleaning or the inconvenience of separate or hand-washing. Modern finishing treatments, from resins that prevent wrinkling to napping that creates a warm, fuzzy surface, significantly affect how you care for the cloth, what you can use it for, and how it looks.

Dyes

Almost all dyes used on textiles today are synthetics, derived from coal-tar distillates or petrochemicals rather than from plants, minerals, or animals. Functionally, synthetic dyes are available that are considered superior in almost every respect to natural ones. Environmental and health issues have occasionally been raised concerning synthetic dyes, however, and some synthetic dyes have been found to be potentially carcinogenic and banned from use.[1] Natural dyes, on the other hand, are hard to find and expensive, and they may present environmental problems of their own as a result of the use of toxic metals, such as chrome, copper, tin, and zinc, to improve colorfastness and light resistance. Aluminum and iron may be relied upon as substitutes for these metals, but they are less effective. The production of natural dyes also requires the use of much agricultural land.

Colorfastness, the resistance of color to removal or extraction, is a complex set of behaviors. Fastness may be tested against different substances used in laundering, such as soap or detergent, bleach, and water (cool, warm, and hot), or in dry cleaning (a variety of solvents); light; acidic and alkaline solutions; heat; and perspiration. Some colors withstand laundering of any sort but fade in the light; these, obviously, should not be used for drapery or upholstery. Some fade or bleed in laundering but not in dry cleaning. Vat dyes, so called because they are applied in a vat, are widely used on cellulosic fibers such as cotton, linen, or viscose rayon. They result in color with excellent fastness to washing and to light. But such colorfastness is not always considered desirable. Among dyes commonly in use today, indigo, used for blue jeans and other blue denim cloth, inevitably fades, and is valued for this property. I know of someone who refused to wear a pair of inexpensive blue jeans that had a herculean resistance to fading: they looked like new even after half a dozen launderings with chlorine bleach.

A dye's performance is determined not only by the type of dye but also by what fabric and fiber it is used on and the method used to apply it. Dye (or pigment) can be applied at almost any point in the manufacturing process. It may be added to the solution out of which man-made fibers are produced (referred to as "solution dyed" or "producer dyed") or to the fibers out of which yarn will be spun ("fiber dyed," "stock dyed," or "top dyed," tops being the long fibers out of which wool worsted is spun). Or it may be applied to the yarn out of which fabric is woven ("yarn dyed"); or the woven fabric may be dyed in the piece or after the garment is made ("piece dyed" and "garment dyed"). Tweeds are stock dyed; the fibers are dyed before they are woven into yarn. Gingham, chambray, and denim are yarn dyed, as are most fabrics containing two or more colors of yarn, such as plaids or checks. The dyeing of already made-up articles is fraught with dangers. Poor penetration by the dye at seams, discoloration of trim, uneven color, and similar problems all become more likely. As a rule of thumb, the earlier in the production process the color is added, the more likely the product is to have uniform coloring, good penetration, and good colorfastness, but these are likelihoods, not guarantees.

Colorfastness and uniform color are not the only important characteristics of a good dye or dyeing process. Good dyes will not readily yellow or otherwise discolor. Good color will neither crock (transfer color to other surfaces when rubbed against them) nor frost (show areas where color has been rubbed off by abrasion). When jeans are stone-washed, they are subjected to abrasion to create frosting intentionally, but ordinarily this effect is unwelcome. Frosting can result unintentionally when the dye has not penetrated the fabric thoroughly. As the outside of the fabric wears off from abrasion, so does the dye, and light areas begin to show.[2] Bleeding of dyes is also a headache for home launderers. Manufacturers are required to warn you on care labels to wash items likely to bleed separately from others, which might otherwise pick up the color left in the wash water by the bleeding articles. But this can be exceedingly inconvenient. (Remember that towels sometimes bear no care labels. If they have bright or deep colors, wash them separately a few times—after which, if they are the product of a good manufacturer, they will cease giving up color.)

Pigments, which do not actually unite with the fibers, as dyes do, but are attached to their surface by means of resins, can be used on any type of fiber. They tend to be fast to light and bleach. When deep colors are achieved with pigments, however, the colors sometimes have a tendency to crock. Pigments have fair fastness to washing. Pigments are also used in a dyeing process for manufactured fibers called "mass pigmentation," in which the pigment is added to the spinning solution. This is as yet not a versatile method, and certain technical problems stand in the way of its widespread use. However, it is desirable for dyeing polypropylene satisfactorily. It provides lightfastness not available by other means in nylon and polyester.

Prints are fabrics with colored designs (usually created with pigments) that are applied to their surfaces. The design can be screened, heat-transferred, rolled, or stamped onto the cloth or applied to it in still other ways. In poor-quality prints, you may see bits of pattern askew or off their proper place, areas that have not received color, a lack of fine detail, fuzzy edges, and similar imperfections.

As the case of the unfading blue jeans illustrates, we should not assume that fading in fabrics after a few launderings is natural and unavoidable. Care and skill in the use of dyes can produce products that resist bleeding, crocking, frosting, and discoloration. Unfortunately, once the ordinary buyer has examined a fabric for good appearance, he or she has no way of judging further how the dyeing will perform with use and with laundering or dry cleaning. Catalogues sometimes announce that a garment is yarn dyed; or occasionally a tag boasts of "only pure natural dyes"—a probable contradiction in terms, according to one expert in textile dyes. But aside from what you can learn by performing some simple home tests for colorfastness (see page 300 in chapter 20, "Gathering, Storing, and Sorting Laundry"), you are usually forced to glean bits of information from the fabric's appearance and care label. It is truly a case of caveat emptor, for not even the principle that you get what you pay for holds at the retail level; many expensive items fade. Your best bet, which is by no means infallible, is to get what information you can from your retailer and to buy from reputable manufacturers and those whose products have proved colorfast in your home laundry. (In a store recently I saw a stack of knit tops displayed with the sign "Garment dyed!" As garment dyeing is typically a sign of lower rather than higher dyeing quality, the management of this store either labored in ignorance of its stock-in-trade or believed that its customers did.)

Finishing Treatments

When you purchase nonwrinkling shirts or blouses, mercerized thread for your sewing box, flame-resistant potholders, jeans with a suedelike hand, chintz upholstery fabric, or soil-resistant tablecloths, you bring home fabric that has been subjected to a certain finishing treatment through chemical or mechanical means. These and other finishing treatments can profoundly affect how well the fabric will function, how durably it will do so, and how you will have to care for it during its useful lifetime. Thus when you understand finishing treatments you can choose fabrics more wisely and take better care of them. Immediately below, descriptions are set forth of finishing treatments commonly applied to fabrics used in clothing and furnishings in the home. (Chapter 16 takes up in detail proper care for fabrics subjected to wrinkle resistance and other resin finishes.)

Finishing Treatments Commonly Applied to Fabrics

Absorbent Finishes. The natural absorbency of cottons, rayon, and linen may be increased by the use of absorbency treatments. Underwear and towels are sometimes treated for absorbency. Some treatments, applied to sanitary napkins, tampons, towels, and other materials used for drying and absorbing moisture, may increase absorbency dramatically. A variety of chemicals and resins is employed, depending on the fiber being treated and the use intended. Nylon and polyester may also be subjected to treatments to increase their absorbency. Sometimes they may be specially manufactured to increase their wicking capacity. Synthetics so treated are said to feel more comfortable against the skin, especially in warm and humid weather. But such claims are regarded skeptically by some, and I have been told that they have not stood up to double-blind trials. Mercerization (see "Mercerizing" on page 228) increases the absorbency of cotton (but is employed for other reasons). The absorbency of natural fibers is decreased by resin treatments, fabric softener, and constructions using extremely tightly twisted yarns or weaves.

Antiseptics; Mildew Control. Antiseptic finishes may be used to help prevent athlete's foot, or to control odors in shoe linings, bedclothes, diapers, underwear, and socks. There are also finishes that can help prevent damage to fabric by mildew and rotting on shower curtains, carpets and rugs, and elsewhere. The presence of various antimicrobial substances is indicated by the use of words such as these in labels: "antiseptic," "bacteriostatic," "antibacterial," or "mildew-resistant." (Linen, cotton, and rayon are particularly susceptible to mildew; silk and wool will also mildew, although somewhat less readily; most synthetics will not mildew, but some tend to retain body odors, and for this reason receive antiseptic finishes.)

Antistatic Treatments. Many synthetic fibers, especially polyester and nylon and their blends, are prone to building up static electricity when subjected to friction. (Olefin—polypropylene—an exception, tends to be low-static.) Garments made of these fibers gather static electricity when you wear them or tumble them in the dryer; carpets become charged when you walk over them. Among the natural fibers, wool and silk may develop static cling, too, particularly when the humidity is low, but not to the extent that synthetics do. Clinging, climbing, and minor electrical shocks and sparks that may be painful or even dangerous (for instance, in the presence of flammable gases) or destructive (to delicate electronic equipment) are some potential consequences of static electricity in clothing and furnishings. Static may also cause fabric to attract dirt. To prevent static buildup, manufacturers sometimes use antistatic finishes, but these are not durable. New forms of certain synthetic fibers have been developed with built-in resistance to static. If you are buying nylon carpeting, this is a feature to insist on.

At home one can use antistatic sprays or fabric softeners to reduce static effectively. Or one can choose naturally low-static or nonstatic fibers. Humidity reduces the amount of static electricity produced by friction.

Antiwrinkling Treatments. Antiwrinkling treatments rely on the use of resins that combine with two or more adjacent molecules of the fibers of cellulosic cloth in a chemical process called cross-linking. (See "Resin Treatments," pages 229–30.) Cross-linking is what diminishes wrinkling. If a fabric has been subjected to a wrinkle-resistance resin treatment, it may need some ironing after laundering but will tend to resist wrinkling during wear, and any wrinkles acquired during wear will tend to fall out when the article is hung up. Fabrics so treated are referred to by a variety of familiar names: "permanent press," "wash and wear," "durable press," "easy care," and "minimum care."

Because cross-linking weakens cotton fabric, most permanent-press fabrics are cotton/polyester blends. The polyester in the blend is not weakened by the treatment, and treated blends thus have more strength than all-cotton fabrics. (The polyester confers other advantages too. See chapter 17, "The Man-Made Fibers and Blends.") Some newer treatments, however, cause less deterioration in the strength of cottons, and more durable easy-care 100% cottons are becoming more common. These are not yet as strong or as resistant to wrinkling as the blends.

Antiwrinkling treatments are of two major types: precured and postcured. Precured treatments are applied to fabrics before they are sewn into garments, with the result that they may be hard to work with. Precisely their wrinkle-resistant properties make it difficult for them to contour properly to body shape or to be pressed into creases. Drip-dry clothes have been precured; you hang them to dry and they regain their shape and smoothness with little or no ironing. You see few drip-dry clothes nowadays, however, as most clothes are postcured.

The postcured wrinkle-resistance treatments are applied after the fabric is sewn into garments or other finished products. One problem with postcured treatments is that articles treated with them are difficult to alter: creases, pleats, curves, seams, and the like are built into the fabric's "memory" and cannot readily be moved around. A second problem is that the crease lines are even weaker than the rest of the fabric: they may lighten or abrade.

The durability of any wrinkle-resistant resin finish depends on a number of factors: the type of resin, the quality and type of application procedure, the degree of saturation, the care used in applying the treatment, and the care of the wearer in following the instructions on the garment label. Resin antiwrinkling treatments are not permanent, but they are fairly durable, lasting for up to fifty washes. Such treatments usually reduce wrinkling without preventing it entirely; the amount of wrinkling you actually get also depends on such factors as the type and amount of resin used, the skill and care with which it has been applied, and how the garment is laundered and dried.

Antiwrinkling treatments are not applied to synthetics except in blends because many of these fibers have built-in wrinkle resistance.

There are "durable-press" treatments that create permanent creases and pleats in wool and wool blends. These rely on resin or chemical treatments, and they are of varying durability.

A nonresin wrinkle treatment for cellulosic fibers, without the negative side effects of resin treatments, also exists. The liquid ammonia durable-press treatment, which is used only on cloth that is made of 100% cellulosic fiber, involves placing the fabric in an ammonium hydroxide bath in which temperature, fabric tension, time, ammonia concentration, and other factors are carefully controlled. It is a sensitive and expensive process and therefore not widely used. It is fairly durable, lasting for between forty and fifty launderings. The buyer, however, will find no indication on tags that it has been applied.

Wrinkle-treated garments should be machine-washed and tumbled dry on the permanent-press cycles. See chapter 21, "Laundering."

Beetling. Beetling is the process in which linen fabric is pounded with wooden mallets until the yarns are permanently flattened and the weave of the cloth is closed. Table linens are usually beetled. Because beetling makes the yarns smoother, it increases luster. Beetling will give linen cloth a uniform thickness and render it more flexible. Ironing with hard pressure renews the flattened look of the yarns after laundering.

Bleaching. Unless it is to be used in its natural color, cloth must be bleached to whiten it or to prepare it for dyeing. Substances used for this purpose include chlorine bleaches—sodium hypochlorite (also used as a household bleach, as in Clorox) or sodium chlorite—and hydrogen peroxide and sodium perborate (the household bleach Snowy or Clorox 2), but a number of other chemicals may be used at various points in the bleaching process. Some Irish linen is still whitened by bleaching in the sunlight, a process called "grass bleaching." Bleaching by any means generally weakens the cloth to some degree.

Sunlight, however, is considerably more gentle than chemical bleaching. Manufacturers sometimes also apply optical brighteners to fabrics, which simply alter the way the fabric reflects light, creating an appearance of brightness and masking yellowish hues. Most all-purpose detergents contain optical brighteners too.

Calendering. The term "calendering" refers to any of several processes in which fabric is subjected to great pressure and/or heat, in a type of ironing using large rollers. Calendering renders fabric smooth and lustrous. It is not a durable treatment when applied to cotton without resins. But when resins are used with calendering to create glazed, ciré, embossed, moiré, or Schreinerized fabrics (see the following paragraph), or when calendering is applied to thermoplastic fibers such as polyester, it is durable.

Crêpeing, Plissé, Embossing, Moiré, Schreinering. The use of heat, pressure, or acids, bases, and other chemicals on textiles can produce decorative effects. Crêpe can be produced either by weaving techniques and yarn construction or by passing fabric between specially engraved rollers. Crêpe produced by engraved rollers will eventually wash out, whereas the former methods render the crêpeing permanent. Embossing and moiré are also done with engraved heated rollers. Embossing produces a design by raising a pattern on the fabric or causing a depression in certain portions of it. It is permanent on thermoplastic fibers but not on cotton unless the cotton is treated with resins that are resistant to water and dry cleaning. Moiré is permanent only on thermoplastic fibers, such as acetate, polyester, and nylon, or on natural fibers treated with resins. Nylon can be chemically treated to crinkle it. The use of sulfuric acid on sheer cotton produces organdy; it stiffens the fabric and makes it translucent. But if the acid treatment is not properly done, it can seriously weaken the cloth.

Plissé (a crêpe effect) is the result of the application of caustic soda (sodium hydroxide). The chemical shrinks the area to which it is applied—mercerizing the area, in effect—and produces puckers. Chemically produced plissé is less permanent than real seersucker, which is produced by weaving. Plissé may come out under ironing, but seersucker will not. Seersucker can be distinguished from plissé by its clearly defined, alternating crinkled rows and smooth rows. By stretching the fabric and seeing how persistent the decorative effect is, you can gain some indication of how permanent it may be.

Embossing. See "Crêpeing."

Emerizing. See "Napping."

Flame-Resistance Treatments. There are only two flameproof fibers, both inorganic: glass and asbestos. Organic fibers are at best flame resistant; that is, after the fiber is ignited, flaming is prevented, terminated, or inhibited, whether or not the ignition source is removed. Flame retardants are substances that render fabrics flame resistant; they slow or stop the eruption and spread of flames but do not entirely prevent burning. Most treated fabrics will extinguish as soon as they are removed from the ignition source. The idea behind flame-resistant treatments is that they provide enough time to extinguish or to escape a fire before grave harm occurs. Wool and silk are naturally somewhat flame resistant, but various finishes may render either of them less so. Some modacrylic is also naturally flame resistant. Some synthetics can be rendered permanently flame resistant during the manufacturing process without the use of flame retardants.

Unless treated, cotton, linen, rayon, acetate, nylon, and polyester ignite and burn readily. In all cases, the construction of the fabric, as well as fiber content, affects flammability; napping, pile weaves, loose weaves, soft-twisted yarns, and light weight all increase flammability.

Prior to the passage of legislation in 1953, there had been tragic fires and injuries caused by highly flammable fabrics and wearing apparel. Some of these involved napped or pile fabrics of viscose rayon that would flash-burn and engulf a wearer in flames in an instant following contact with a spark. The 1953 law, as later amended, prohibits the sale of highly flammable fabrics as apparel but requires that fabrics be flame resistant only when used in children's sleepwear, rugs and carpets, mattresses, and mattress pads. Small rugs and carpets need not meet the standards if they bear a label stating, in part, "Flammable . . . Should Not Be Used Near Sources of Ignition." Upholstery is governed only by voluntary industry standards. The law on children's sleepwear requires it to be durably flame resistant, that is, able to undergo at least fifty launderings without losing its flame-resistant qualities.

Before you take too much comfort in the existence of this limited law, you should know that the test—known as the 45-degree-angle test—for whether a textile is "dangerously flammable" (as provided in the federal Flammability of Clothing Textiles Standard) is widely regarded as inadequate. This test requires, among other things, that you hold a piece of fabric at a 45 degree angle and apply to it a flame of a specified size for one second. If it burns at a certain rate within a certain time, then it is banned for use in apparel in this country. Unfortunately, as one text points out, dry newspaper would not fail this test. Cotton/polyester blends, untreated for flame resistance, are often more dangerous than either 100% cotton or 100% polyester. Yet such blends are not "dangerously flammable" under the 45-degree-angle test. (They are difficult to treat for flame resistance, as the treatments—heavy back-coatings—tend to yield materials with an unpleasant hand.) Moreover, some fabrics pass this test that might melt or emit toxic fumes or suffocating amounts of smoke when exposed to a flame. These characteristics can render them more dangerous than a textile that fails the test and thus legally counts as "dangerously flammable." Melting synthetic fabrics may adhere to the skin, causing worse burns than flaming fibers; heavy fumes and smoke can be lethal. Better regulations to remove these and other irrationalities, however, are resisted by interests in the textile industry. A proposed molten drop test, for example, that various types of synthetic cloth would have failed (even though they passed the 45-degree-angle test) was dropped.

Flame-resistance treatments have been problematic in other respects as well. One of the flame retardants widely used earlier was subsequently determined to be a carcinogen. A substitute developed for it was then found to be mutagenic. Some flame retardants, when they burned, were found to produce toxic fumes or large amounts of smoke, which were hazards in themselves. Some flame-resistant finishes tend to worsen the fabric's hand, producing harshness and stiffness, or weaken it. Bleaches, fabric softeners, soaps, and nonphosphate detergents tend to render them ineffective. To reduce the possibility of skin reactions, you should wash flame-retardant-treated fabrics before wearing them.

In 1996, the Consumer Products Safety Commission amended the rule requiring that all children's sleepwear be flame resistant, effective as of June 8, 1998. The amendment to the rule, which has aroused fierce opposition, contains two major provisions. First, it exempts from the flame-resistance requirements all sleepwear for infants under nine months of age. Second, it permits sleepwear for children of any age to be made of untreated (non-flame-resistant) cotton so long as it is snug fitting or contacts the skin at all points. (Snug-fitting clothes ignite less easily and burn less readily than loose-fitting or flowing ones.) Aside from these two categories, cotton sleepwear must still be treated to render it flame resistant. So far as I am aware, United States manufacturers no longer make children's sleepwear that is treated with flame retardants, but some imported cotton pajamas are. In addition, flame-resistant pajamas of synthetic fibers continue to be widely available. But if you find pajama-like cotton garments for children over nine months that are neither treated to render them flame-resistant nor snug fitting, they will continue to be labeled "Not intended for sleepwear."

When cotton sleepwear has been treated with flame retardants, this typically is done with tetrakis hydroxymethyl phosphonium (THP) salts, which are said to be both effective and safe from a general health standpoint. Such treatments last for fifty or more launderings. But clothes so treated cannot be washed with chlorine bleach or any product containing chlorine bleach or with ordinary nonphosphate detergents. This can be a problem in those areas that ban phosphate detergents, although there are nonphosphate detergents on the market that state that they will not harm flame-resistant finishes. Unfortunately, THP-treated cloth produces fumes and heavy smoke when it burns.

Nowadays, however, most children's sleepwear is made of synthetic fibers (such as polyester or modacrylic) that are intrinsically flame resistant—at least for legal purposes (that is, they pass certain tests)—and need no treatment with flame retardants. There are also flame-resistant variants of rayon, acrylic, and polypropylene. Modacrylic can be made with quite good flame resistance, and acrylics are flame resistant to a degree. Experts point out, however, that given the insufficiencies of the legal standard, no matter what you buy, all you can be sure of is that the fabric passed the test, not that the fabric is necessarily safer than another.

Glazing. Glazing creates a stiff, shiny appearance. Chintz and polished cotton are familiar glazed fabrics. Older-style glazes of starch or wax are not durable. Some modern glazes are created by baking or calendering resins onto the fabric, and these are more lasting.

Mercerizing. Mercerizing is used principally on cotton yarns and fabrics. They are treated with a solution of caustic soda, causing the fibers to swell up into a round shape and shorten. The effect is that the fabric or yarn becomes stronger, more lustrous, and easier to dye. The fabric also acquires an improved hand and drape. Cotton sewing thread purchased for use in the home should always be mercerized.

Mildew. See Antiseptics.

Mothproofing. Silk, wool, fur, and other hair fibers are susceptible to damage by insects that feed on the protein in such fibers. Moth larvae eat wool and fur; carpet beetles eat wool, fur, and silk. Wool blends are vulnerable in the same ways that wool is, and should receive the same treatment. Insectproofing that will not come out with laundering or dry cleaning is built into some wool fabrics, such as carpets and upholstery and, apparently, some clothes. Some of these treatments kill the larvae when they try to eat the fibers; others render it indigestible by the larvae. According to one authority, however, none of the substances presently being used for such purposes is completely effective.

Less durable mothproofing can also be applied during dry cleaning. If woolen articles have not been treated, preventive measures should be undertaken at home. See the discussion of mothproofing in chapter 16 on pages 251–52; see also chapter 58, "Closets for Clothes and Linens."

Napping; Sueding; Sanding; Emerizing. Napping gives fabrics a fuzzy surface. It is accomplished by giving the yarns from which the fabric is woven a slack twist when they are spun, then passing the woven fabric over a roller covered with wires ending in small hooks. The hooks pull up fiber ends out of the fabric and create the fuzziness or nap. (In brushing, brushes are used to raise the nap.) Napping creates air pockets in which warmth can be trapped; thus napped fabrics, such as flannels, are warmer. Napped fabrics are also more stain resistant because the nap prevents substances from penetrating deep into the fabric. Napping should not be confused with pile, in which additional threads have been woven into the cloth, creating raised loops (which are sometimes cut) on the surface.

Sueding, or sanding, is similar to napping except that the roller that the cloth moves over has a sandpaper surface that abrades the cloth, producing the familiar suede finish. Like napping, sueding can render cloth weaker. In sandwashing, sand is put in a wash bath to abrade and soften the fabric. Emerizing uses gentler, emery-covered rollers to produce the sort of suedelike surface you find on many garments of polyester microfiber.

Plissé. See Crêpeing.

Preshrinking. Whenever you can, buy preshrunk finished goods. You can usually buy preshrunk fabrics for home sewing as well, but when you cannot you should usually wash them before sewing so as to preshrink them yourself. Unfortunately, continued shrinking of any preshrunk goods may occur, and this shrinking may continue in small increments over many washings.

There are many antishrinking procedures, ranging from simple washing to mechanical, chemical, and resin treatments, and combinations of these. The familiar "Sanforized" trademark indicates that the cloth, woven cotton and rayon, was subjected to a standardized, highly effective method of compressive shrinkage, and that additional shrinkage will not exceed 2 percent. (Compressive shrinkage subjects fabrics to a controlled shrinking process that results in uniform shrinking and ensures that additional shrinkage will not exceed a given percentage.) There are other trademarks reflecting compressive shrinkage and other antishrinking treatments.

Wools are subjected to a similar variety of preshrinking methods using water, chemicals, or thermosetting resin treatments. Fulling is a laundering process to which wool may be subjected to clean it and to produce a controlled degree of felting, or drawing together of the wool fibers. Fulled fabric is smoother and fuller, denser and more compact, which makes it warmer. Thus fulled woolens such as melton (which is a heavily fulled, napped, closely woven fabric) are used to make overcoats. Worsteds are only lightly fulled, if at all. If an antishrinking effect in wool is derived from the use of chemicals, shrinking may develop after several launderings when these are finally washed away. The "Superwash" trademark indicates that wool has received chemical and resin treatments that render it durably shrink resistant and machine washable. See chapter 16, "The Natural Fibers," page 246.

Resin Treatments. Textile resins are "prepolymers" that are applied to cellulosic fibers (cotton, linen, rayon) or blends containing them to produce a variety of effects: permanent creases or wrinkle resistance, resistance to shrinkage, permanent stiffness or crispness, shine or luster, water repellency, and decorative effects such as ciré, moiré, embossing, and so on. The resins most commonly used for these purposes are urea, glyoxal, carbonate, and melamine formaldehyde compounds. Resins work not by coating the fibers but by linking adjacent cellulosic molecules so that the resins actually form part of the structure of the cloth.

When resins were first used, years ago, health questions were raised about them because they were found to emit formaldehyde fumes. The odor was often unpleasant; some people are allergic to formaldehyde or can become sensitized by it; there was fear that the formaldehyde might be carcinogenic. Newer, lighter application procedures and low- and non-formaldehyde-emitting resins, however, have by and large answered these concerns. (Newer resins still emit an extremely low amount of formaldehyde, but documented cases of sensitivity to resin-treated cloth in this country are rare.) Various experts seem to agree that resin-treated cloth is safe, recommending simply that you launder resin-treated articles once before using them to remove the tiny amount of free formaldehyde they may contain. There are also resins that contain no formaldehyde, which are often used on infants' and children's wear (because younger folk are more sensitive), but these tend to be more costly and less effective.

The application of resins, however, is not without other side effects, bad and good. On the negative side, they will render fabrics less absorbent, which means they are less comfortable, particularly in hot, humid weather. The cloth will also have a less pleasant hand and be weaker—up to 50 percent weaker—and less resistant to abrasion. Treated cloth will also develop a tendency to oil-stain, just as synthetic fibers do, and may develop static cling. Resin-treated fabrics may require different, milder laundry treatments. (See chapter 16, "The Natural Fibers," pages 249–50.) On the other hand, besides reducing shrinking and wrinkling, resins will cause the cloth to dry faster and will act as a stiffener, which renders many cotton garments more attractive. And both the positive and negative side effects of resin treatments are reduced by newer resins and by lighter applications.

See also "Antiwrinkling Treatments," above.

Sanding. See "Napping."

Schreinering. See "Crêpeing."

Soil-Resistance Treatments. Apparel, tablecloths, upholstery fabrics, and other textile goods used in the home can receive treatments or finishes that make them more accident-proof and soil resistant. Soil-resistant treatments are of two types: soil release and soil repellent.

Soil repellents. A soil-repellent fabric has received a treatment that renders it resistant to soil by causing water and/or oil to bead on its surface rather than penetrating immediately. This gives you a chance to wipe dirt and spills off before they can do damage. Such treatments are now available for both wool and synthetic carpets. There are many different kinds of soil repellents, and they do not all do the same thing. Some repel only water. Fluorocarbon polymers such as Scotchgard and Zepel repel both oil and water. Soil repellents generally will reduce the absorbency of fabrics but not their breathability. Soil-repellent treatments are applied to both natural and synthetic fibers as well as their blends.

Soil release. Soil-release fabrics have received a treatment that causes them to come cleaner during laundering. Soil-release treatments are applied only to synthetic fibers and their blends or to durable-press fabrics, that is, to oleophilic/hydrophobic fibers or to those that, as a result of resin treatments, resist thorough wetting, and thus thorough cleaning, during laundering. Without soil-release treatments, any of these fabrics may need some laundering pretreatment to ensure against "ring around the collar (or cuff)" or to help remove soil in areas of the garment that are particularly likely to pick up body oils or greasy food stains, such as collars, cuffs, and the midriff area.

Soil-release treatments are not all the same. Fluorocarbons work by making a film that prevents the oil from making direct contact with the fibers, so that a detergent-and-water solution can more easily wash it away. Others work by trying to make the surface of the fabric more hydrophilic through the application of chemicals. According to one textiles authority, those soil-release treatments that create a more hydrophilic fabric surface have various beneficial side effects: they can improve the garments' comfort level by increasing their moisture takeup, soften the hand, reduce static buildup, decrease soil redeposition during laundering, and reduce pilling. This expert points out, however, that soil-release treatments actually seem to cause fabrics to soil more heavily than nontreated ones.[3] Soil-release treatments have varying degrees of durability; some will last the life of the garment.

Combination soil-repellent and soil-release finishes. Note that the application of fluorocarbon copolymers (Scotchgard and Zepel) renders fabric both more soil repellent and more soil releasing.

Skin Protection from Ultraviolet Rays. More protection is naturally provided to your skin against the ultraviolet rays of ordinary sunlight by clothes that are made of thicker, tighter weaves. Darker clothes are more protective than lighter-colored ones (although they feel hotter) because they absorb more ultraviolet radiation. Dry clothes are more protective than wet ones, because the latter are more transparent. As far as cloth construction and color go, therefore, in warm weather you have something of a Hobson's choice between comfort and protection.

Some fabrics are manufactured to provide extra protection from the dangerous rays of the sun, through chemical treatments or cloth construction or a combination of these. Such cloth tends to be fairly light and cool yet offers at least as much protection as dark, tight weaves. See also chapter 18, "Fabrics That Work," page 275.

Stiffening. Cottons and linen may be given temporary stiffness or crispness by the use of starches or sizing. These terms are often used interchangeably, but "sizing" should properly refer to any substance used to stiffen a fabric, and "starch" only to starch solutions, that is, solutions containing $C_6H_{10}O_5$. A wide variety of substances may be used for temporary stiffening—from starch to resins. Starches tend to be crisper and sizings softer. Both will wash out and, if the original crisp look and feel are to be retained, must be replaced on laundering. Overstarching or oversizing may be used to conceal inferior goods. If goods after washing become hopelessly limp, they may have been overstarched. If you suspect overstarching, rub the fabric between your hands to see whether any starch will powder off. (For a discussion of starching or sizing at home, see pages 348–49 in chapter 23, "Ironing.")

Many more or less permanent stiffening treatments are also in use. These work by altering the structure of the fiber with resins. The application of resins has a variety of side effects, good and bad. See "Resin Treatments," above.

Sueding. See "Napping."

Water-Resistance Treatments. Fabrics that are absolutely impermeable to water are called waterproof. Those that are called water repellent have a coating of some hydrophobic chemical that causes water to bead up on their surface rather than soaking through immediately. These fabrics have varying degrees of resistance to water but sooner or later are penetrated. Waterproof articles are made of or coated with a continuous layer of some water-insoluble material such as plastic, rubber, vinyl resins, and the like; thus they are impermeable to air as well as water. Waterproofing is generally permanent. Water-repellent treatments, however, have varying degrees of durability. Some lose their effectiveness with washing or dry cleaning or both. Durable water-repellency treatments are possible using any of a number of chemicals and resins that will withstand both laundering and dry cleaning. Many of them confer other advantages such as wrinkle resistance and stain resistance. Silicone treatments, while economical and highly effective, do not launder as well as they dry clean. Fluorochemical water repellents, such as Scotchgard or Zepel, which function as soil repellents too, to some extent repel oil as well as water. When water-repellent garments become less effective as a result of cleaning or washing, they may be retreated by the dry cleaner. Labels and the occasional knowledgeable sales clerk are your only sources of information about water-resistance treatments.

16

The Natural Fibers

Advantages of understanding fibers . . . Linen fabric manufacture . . . Judging damask . . . Properties of linen . . . Why we are more careful with linen fabrics today . . . Laundering delicate vs. sturdy linen fabrics . . . About bleaching, avoiding shrinking, drying linen . . . Cotton fabric manufacture . . . Properties of cotton fibers and fabrics . . . Caring for cotton fabric . . . Manufacture of wool fabrics . . . Judging quality in wool . . . Worsted vs. woolen yarns . . . Properties of wool . . . Caring for wool fabrics . . . Hand-washing and machine-washing wool fabrics . . . Manufacturing silk fabrics . . . Raw, pure dye, duppioni, and wild silk . . . Properties of silk fiber and fabrics . . . Caring for silk fabrics . . . Bast fibers and their properties and uses . . . Permanent press and resin-treated cotton, rayon and finer fabrics and their blends . . . Washable antiques, heirlooms, and other fragile or valuable linen . . . Mothproofing wool

Imagine two shirts of identical bright color and cut, indistinguishable except that one is made of cotton and the other of polyester. One may fade, and the other almost surely will not. One may pill, the other won't. One will wrinkle, the other will hardly wrinkle at all. One will be cool and comfortable in hot, sticky weather, the other may not be. These examples by no means exhaust the list of differences, all of which are functions of the fiber content of the two garments.

When you buy clothes, linens, towels, drapes, or other cloth goods for the home, you unavoidably choose one kind of fiber, or blend of fibers, over another. That choice determines how well the cloth will function in the role you envision for it, how it will feel, how long it will wear, how attractive it will remain as it ages, and how you will have to clean and care for it. To choose on the basis of style or look alone can lead to repeated experiences of frustration and unnecessary expense. To help you choose wisely and increase your awareness of how different fibers behave, in this chapter and the next I summarize the nature of the major fibers used in clothing and furnishings and offer a summary of how fabrics made from each of them are best cared for.

The natural fibers have a long and distinguished history. Linen, cotton, silk, and wool have each been used in cloth making for millennia. They have been so important in our history that our language carries dozens of phrases and ideas borrowed from the manufacture and use of cloth of natural fiber from calico cats and gingham dogs to getting fleeced, wearing sackcloth, and buying shoddy work or goods. Sometimes a restaurant disappoints you with its run-of-the-mill food. You might prefer tweedy friends to homespun ones, but certainly you want no sleazy ones.* The same richness of connotation cannot be expected of the synthetics, which are so recent. A young woman might be glad that her hair is flaxen and her skin like satin, but she will not cotton to being compared to polyester.

We draw upon the rich meanings of the natural fibers in a different way when we choose to put one rather than another on our backs or in our homes. Linen is dignified, and often seems capable of heights of refinement and elegance that cotton cannot reach. Cotton is whatever you want it to be—plain or fancy, sensible, businesslike or whimsical, as you wish. Its very versatility works against its being a symbol of anything. Wool is comfortable, protective, warm, and prudent. Silk, as the fiber of true velvets, satins, and flowing chiffon scarves, retains an image of luxury and sensuousness. In each instance these associations are derived from something in the way the fiber actually works or feels. A better acquaintance with the cloth made of these fibers will enable you to do more with fabrics in your home and to care for clothes and furnishings more successfully.

Linen

About Linen. Linen is so highly venerated that people tend to think of it as precious and delicate. But linen is available in sturdy constructions as well as fine. While some linens are fit for royal boudoirs and fragile lace on christening gowns, others are suitable for hard work as towels, bandages, everyday sheets, and other ordinary items. Flax is a remarkably strong, durable, and functional fiber. Linen is chosen for the finest damasks and the most delicate laces partly because it is lustrous and smooth but also because it has superior strength, launders so well, and lasts so long. Linen towels, handkerchiefs, clothes, nightgowns and nightshirts, sheets and pillowcases, and upholstery are often both lovely and exceptionally serviceable.

Linen fabric is made from fibers of the flax plant's stem, which, like other plant fibers, are made of cellulose polymers. Good-quality linen is expensive, especially in the United States, which imports all of its fine linen and uses only small quantities of it each year. Linen is produced in many European countries. Traditionally, Belgian, Irish,

*Run-of-the-mill goods are goods before they have been inspected or sorted for defects or flaws. When sheets and pillowcases were sold as "run of the mill," therefore, you were not guaranteed first quality. Applied to cloth, "sleazy" means flimsy, limp, or loosely constructed when it should not be. A loosely woven sheet, for example, would be sleazy.

and Italian linen are the most prized. Courtrai flax, grown in Belgium, creates the strongest and finest yarns, but Irish workmanship has long been regarded as superior. Belgian linen has a faint yellow cast; Irish linen is often skillfully sun-bleached to a prized degree of whiteness. French linen, also of high quality, is characteristically woven of round yarns, that is, it has not been put through the beetling process that is used to flatten linen. See “Beetling” on page 225, chapter 15.

Not all linen produced in these countries is of the highest quality, however. The Confédération Européenne du Lin et du Chanvre, known as CELC, is an association of linen producers from Austria, Belgium, France, Germany, Italy, the Netherlands, Spain, Switzerland, and the United Kingdom (including Northern Ireland). CELC, through its promotional organization, Masters of Linen, authorizes the use of its international linen trademark by producers who agree to meet its standards. The logo's presence indicates that the linen meets the Masters of Linen quality standards of construction, strength, dimensional stability (resistance to shrinking), and colorfastness. The logo is also an indication that you will find reliable care information—often a boon on tablecloths and other household fabrics because no United States laws require care labels on articles other than apparel. Hang tags bearing the logo denote the fiber content of the linen fabric, that is, pure (100%) linen, minimum 50% linen, or linen union (cloth with cotton warp and linen weft). Although the Masters of Linen logo is helpful, you must still judge the quality of individual pieces for yourself.

Manufacture of Linen. A process called hackling separates flax into long fibers and short fibers, or staple. The fibers are then spun into yarn for weaving or knitting. Only long staple, called line, is used for fine linens—handkerchief linen, fine tablecloths, fine lingerie, and dresses. Thus the label “pure linen” is not necessarily a guarantee of high-quality fabric. For very fine linen, hackling is done by hand to produce longer fibers than can be obtained by machine hackling. Short fibers, called tow, however, might be used in a very thin, smooth, closely woven fabric. Dish towels that are 100% linen but have a bumpy, slightly rough texture are of tow, as are linen draperies and upholstery. If it were possible to untwist and examine the length of the fiber in linen fabric, you could determine for yourself whether the fiber is line or tow: line fibers are twelve to twenty inches long; tow fibers are shorter than twelve inches.

The characteristic smooth texture of line linen reflects the smoothness of flaxen yarn. Usually linen yarns used for table linens (but not those used for dress linens) are also subjected to beetling, which gives the fabric its characteristic flat, lustrous appearance. Beetling also renders linen more flexible and gives it a uniform thickness.

In its natural state, flax fiber ranges in color from pale yellow or cream to dark brown. To get white linen, the fibers or fabric must be bleached. The more the cloth is bleached, unfortunately, the weaker it becomes. The traditional Irish method of bleaching it by laying it out on the grass in sunlight is less damaging than the chemical bleaching that is more commonly done. Whatever method is chosen, linen may be bleached a little or a lot. (There are four grades of bleached linen: fully bleached or full white, three-quarters bleached, half or silver bleached, and quarter bleached.) Bleaching is used not only to produce lighter cream and white shades but to make it easier to dye the linen fibers to intense hues. Flax fibers' hard, nonporous surface resists taking color. Brightly colored linen will have been much bleached and therefore may be weaker and have a shorter wear life than linen that has been less bleached. Nonetheless, if it is vat dyed or if it bears the

Masters of Linen logo, it will have good colorfastness.

Fine linen is characterized by close and regular weaving and a smooth surface, free of bumps or knots. Fuzziness of any degree indicates either lower quality or the presence of another fiber blended in. Linen is available in many different weights, from very sheer to very heavy, and in very tight to very loose weaves. The heavier the weight of a linen fabric, the more durable it tends to be and the better it stands up to laundering. Fine flax cambric, for example, is delicate, while linen duck (a canvaslike fabric) is hardy.

Fine table linens are almost always jacquard-woven in single damask or double damask. Damask's woven patterns show on both sides. Double damask has twice as many filling yarns as warp yarns, which makes its pattern show more distinctly. The thread count of double damask ranges from 165 to 400. In single damask, which usually has a balanced construction (equal numbers of warp and filling threads), the thread count is from 100 to 200. The higher thread counts are more desirable in both kinds of damask.

JUDGING DAMASK

Double damask is not necessarily superior to single damask. If low-quality yarns are used for double damask and high-quality for single, the single may be better. To be of better quality than single damask, double damask should have a higher thread count, superior yarn, and careful design and weaving. In durable, high-quality damask, the yarns are very even and the weave very close; otherwise the yarns will slip and the floats will wear out sooner. In general, longer floats are more beautiful, shorter floats more durable. The most beautiful, high-quality damasks are made of linen rather than cotton because the long, smooth flax fibers, when woven into damask's long floats, do not pull out, fuzz up, and wear out as readily as cotton fibers do.

You can assure yourself that you are getting good quality by examining the cloth with eyes and hand, by relying on reputable manufacturers, and by obtaining knowledgeable sales assistance when it is available.

Properties of Linen. Flax fibers are strong and can be rendered into hardy, durable linen fabrics as well as delicate ones. The strength of the best linen is equaled only by fabrics made of nylon and polyester. Flax is considered a durable fiber both because of this strength and because of its good resistance to abrasion (rubbing) and to the deteriorating effects of sunlight. However, wrinkle-resistance treatments and bleaching, especially strong chemical bleaching, will weaken it. (Wrinkle-resistance treatments will also render it less absorbent and affect its hand; see pages 224–25 and 229–30.) As it ages, it softens in a way that many people particularly enjoy.

Flax fibers' smooth surface neither attracts nor holds dirt and stains as much as less smooth fibers, including cotton, do. Linen clothing feels cool and comfortable in hot weather—more so than fabrics made from any other fiber. This is both because flax fibers are so smooth and flat and because they are one of the most absorbent of all fibers. (Even a linen garment will not be cool, however, if it is lined with a hot or inabsorbent fabric, so be sure to check the fiber content of linings.) Linen also dries quickly—faster than cotton fabric—and does not lint. Thus it makes excellent towels, handkerchiefs, and bandages. Linen is naturally crisp. It has more body than cotton and drapes better. Linen fabrics may shrink a bit when washed (unless they have been treated or are labeled "nonshrink"), but they shrink less than untreated cotton. It is always best to buy linen fabric preshrunk if possible. The presence of the Masters of Linen logo indicates that linen fabric will resist shrinking.

Linen is not resilient—that is, it will wrinkle readily—unless treated to prevent wrinkling or blended with a less wrinkle-prone fiber. It is inelastic, too; linen clothes should be carefully fitted, for they will not "give" in wear. Because linen is stiff, a crease should not be routinely or repeatedly pressed in firmly or eventually the linen will actually crack there. Articles that are stored folded, such as sheets and tablecloths, may weaken along the fold line if they are always folded in the same way or if they are left folded for long periods, so periodically refold them or roll them on tubes. (See "Caring for Linen" below.)

Linen is vulnerable to mildew but not to moths. It has good light resistance, more than cotton, eventually deteriorating only with long exposure to light. Concentrated acids, or even dilute acids if they are hot, can damage cellulosic fibers like linen. Over time, acid perspiration will also weaken it. If linen is stored in a starched state, silverfish may attack the starch and harm the linen.

Despite its fine qualities and its various superiorities to cotton, linen is often so expensive that you are better off investing in cotton if your budget is limited. And although linen compares favorably with cotton in so many respects, it is considerably less versatile. There are fewer types of linen cloth, and it bears many fewer constructions. Linen is available in quite a few excellent blends with both natural and synthetic fibers. Look for the Masters of Linen trademark for assurances of quality with respect to colorfastness, shrinkage, strength, and cloth construction. Or, for colorfastness, look for a label that says "colorfast" or "vat dyed."

Is Linen Delicate? Those Times and These Times. Household linens, such as sheets, towels, and lingerie, are likely to have care labels that prescribe laundering. All other linens today tend to have care labels that call for dry cleaning.

When it comes to highly tailored garments such as linen suits and jackets, and furnishings such as draperies, upholstery, and the like, take the dry-cleaning prescription very seriously. By home-laundering a dazzling linen summer suit whose care label prescribed dry cleaning, I turned it into a limp, shrunken, crooked-threaded mess. There are times, however, when both manufacturers and home launderers are a bit too timid about laundering linen. It is, after all, in principle, a strong, durable fabric. Not so long ago people did not hesitate to bleach, boil, and scrub linen vigorously, using strong chemicals like washing soda, to ensure that it was white, germ-free, and gorgeously gleaming. But today, even a care label that instructs you to wash the linen article does so in a way that makes you nervous. When you stop to consider why this change has taken place, it may help you to decide how you wish to treat your own prized linen fabrics.

In part, today we need to use more caution because our linens are less sturdy than linens were in the old days, when they were much heavier in weight, resin-free (resin treatments weaken cloth), and often made of the finest-quality flax. However, the gentle treatments recommended for linen today are not always addressed to its fiber content. For example, linen can take a lot of heat—hot wash water and a very hot iron—without damage. (A strong fiber by nature, linen is even stronger when wet.) Yet you are usually told not to wash it in hot water, and certainly not to boil it! One reason for the change is that dyes in colored modern linens may bleed or fade, whereas in the old days linen wasn't dyed at all but came in shades of white, tan, and brown. Another reason is that the manufacturer thinks you will be angry if the article shrinks, whereas people expected and allowed for some shrinking in the old days. They did not use fitted sheets (there *were* no fitted sheets); rather, they got their sheets—and nightgowns, chemises, shirts, and tablecloths—big enough to shrink somewhat and still fit. And whereas today people tend to buy linen for its looks, in the old days people valued it as much for function as for its beauty. It was inconceivable to the sanitarily minded Victorian that you should not render your bed and body linens germ-free by boiling or that you should not do everything in your power to render them snowy white. It was precisely because linen resisted staining and soil and because sturdy linen *could* endure strenuous laundering that it was used for bedding, tablecloths, towels, underwear, and nightgowns.

A final difference that matters is that in the good old days people were expert ironers and used very hot irons. Today's manufacturer is worried about what the home launderer will do when faced with the job of restoring a flat rectangle of a tablecloth—let alone a garment of complicated construction—to its smooth, prelaundered appearance. Many modern irons do not even get quite hot enough to do linen well. Most people just don't expect to iron or even know how to do fine or complicated ironing of an article that has to be very damp, requires a very hot iron, and may need starch, so the manufacturer shrugs and writes on the care label, "Don't even try." (But you can certainly learn this simple and satisfying skill, and quickly too, if you are willing to practice and survive less than stellar results until you pass beyond the beginner's stage.)

It is, of course, always safest to follow the care labels. There are many reasons why care labels on linen articles might call for dry cleaning or very gentle laundering, even though linen is in principle a sturdy, highly washable fabric. To summarize and provide a few other examples:

Heirloom and antique linens always require special handling. (See pages 250–51.)

Linens may have water-soluble finishes that will dissolve in the wash, leaving you with a hopelessly limp, unsightly garment.

If linen is not preshrunk—and it often is not—it may shrink significantly when washed, especially if the fabric has a loose weave.

Linen articles may have trims or linings that are not washable.

Many colored linens are prone to fading and bleeding.

The manufacturer may fear that the skill required to iron some linen garments properly, especially heavyweight ones, will exceed the talents of the average person.

Ironing dark and bright-colored linens might cause seams and dart lines to turn white.

The fabric may be a blend that includes some fiber that requires a more conservative treatment than flax.

Loosely or delicately constructed linens might unravel, tear, snag, or shrink in the wash. Linen damasks that are not of the highest quality may be loosely woven with low-twist yarns and long floats.

Any construction or weaving factors that render other fabrics delicate may be present in linen fabrics. (See pages 294 and 306–7.)

Because of such contingencies, *it is risky to disregard care labels on linen.* And of course any risks are magnified by the premium in price that you pay for good linen. The high cost is enough to drive any of us to extreme caution.

Caring for Linen.

Choosing a Good Laundering Technique. Laundering linen differs from laundering cotton in several respects. First, bleaching will usually be unnecessary, and chlorine bleach should usually be avoided. Second, shorter or gentler agitation is called for. Third, linen is best dried out of the dryer. *In laundering any type of off-white linen, be cautious about the use of laundry detergents. Most contain optical brightening agents, which can change the color or create a dappled effect on some off-whites.* (One manufacturer of linen damasks also advises against using detergents or other products that contain optical brighteners on *white damask* because, the manufacturer says, this will detract from the appearance of the subtle pattern. See "Optical brighteners," pages 325–26, and "Detergents and soaps, mild," pages 322–24, in the Glossary of Laundry Products and Additives.

Cautious, conservative laundering is required for antique or heirloom linens; linens of very fine or delicate construction; less sturdy or lower-quality damasks; sheer fabrics; loose weaves, or weaves with long floats or low-twist yarns; lace; embroidered (especially hand-embroidered) fabrics; cutwork; and similar linens. If you do not want to tackle the laundering of such linens, there are businesses that specialize in laundering antique and fine linens of all sorts.

The experts disagree on the best ways to launder linen. To a large extent, the disagreements reflect different ideas about how long you should expect linen to last. If you really wish and expect washable sturdy linen to last a lifetime, you should give it the gentle treatment described below as suitable for *washable delicate* linens. But if vigorous cleaning is more important, consider whether you should choose the method directed for *washable sturdy* linens. (To clean antiques, heirlooms, and other fragile or valuable cottons and linens, see pages 250–51. The instructions immediately below are *not* appropriate for such items.)

Cautious Laundering Methods for Washable Delicate Linens

These instructions apply to *washable delicate* linens that have not become fragile through age and are not being preserved for posterity.

Washable delicate linens may be hand-laundered in mild detergent in the manner described in chapter 21, "Laundering," on pages 313–14. Or they will do fine on the gentle cycle of your washing machine, set for a short wash. If you have no gentle agitation setting, you might consider *very briefly* machine-washing delicate linens on regular agitation, but this requires you to exercise your judgment as to just how delicate the articles are. For protection while machine-washing, especially if the pieces have fringes, ties, or loose trim, place them in a mesh bag or an old pillowcase and fasten it closed. Use warm water for white linens and lukewarm for colored (or, if the colored linens bleed readily, cool). Use a mild detergent (preferably one without optical brightening agents if you are laundering off-whites or white damask). If you prefer a mild soap to a detergent, be sure that you have soft water. Rinse very thoroughly with plain cool water. (Those who are uncertain how to choose a mild detergent should read "Detergents and soaps, mild," in the Glossary of Laundry Products and Additives, pages 322–24.)

To remove spots or stains or general dinginess or yellowing, first try soaking the fabric overnight in warm water with mild detergent. (However, protein stains—blood or egg, for example—get a cool water soak; see the Guide to Stain Removal on pages 387–90.) Next, resort to sun bleaching and then to oxygen bleach, as described below. (I myself am willing to chance even chlorine bleach to cure stains or dinginess in delicate linen when I reach the point at which I feel I have nothing to lose.)

To dry linen, *do not wring;* roll it in a towel to remove excess moisture, then dry flat away from sources of heat. Hanging to dry can stress delicate fibers but will be fine for a sheer linen nightgown or blouse (one that you wear—not an antique). Use your judgment.

You can avoid ironing delicate lace if you gently pull it to its proper shape and then pin it to the towel or weight it down around the edges with something harmless to prevent its curling up or drying crooked. Watch out that you do no harm with the pinning; put the point of the pin through holes in the lace.

If ironing will be safe and is necessary, take the linen up while it is still fairly damp. Then iron sheer or delicate linens on the wrong side with a medium iron, and iron less sheer, less delicate linens on the wrong side with a hot iron. (See "Ironing Linen" in chapter 23, "Ironing," pages 346–47.)

Laundering Washable Sturdy, Nonshrink, Colorfast or White Linens

The following instructions apply to *washable sturdy* tablecloths, sheets, woven towels, clothes, and similar linens. Linen that has not been Sanforized or preshrunk may shrink moderately, and the hotter the water the more shrinking you may expect. (See "About Shrinking in Linen," below.)

Use hot water and regular laundry detergent unless you need to avoid optical brighteners (on certain off-whites or on white damask—see "Optical brighteners" in the glossary at the end of chapter 21).[1] If you use soap, make sure you have soft water. Set the machine for gentle or slow agitation or—if you have only one agitation speed—a short agitation period. (Although some experts think regular agitation is fine, my experience suggests that linen's brittle fibers last longer if they are not beaten about too much. A front-loading washing machine, however, would be fine on "regular.") Use a fast spin. Rinse thoroughly; using the extra-rinse option on your washer is a good idea. *Do not wring*. When you are having trouble getting linens clean with the foregoing procedures, add a long presoak, overnight if the problem is stubborn, with hot water initially.

Wovens linens can be hung to dry; knits should dry flat. (See "About Drying Linen," below.) Iron with a hot iron. (See pages 346–47 in chapter 23, "Ironing.")

About Bleaching Linen. If you launder linen well and rinse it well, it is not likely to need bleaching. But sometimes dinginess develops or stains or spots occur. If bleaching becomes necessary, sun-bleaching is gentlest. To whiten linen and help remove spots, sun-bleach by laying the freshly washed, damp article in the sun, putting a sheet or some other protection under it. Make sure it will not be injured or soiled by animals or children. (The habit of laying stained fabrics on a bush to bleach them gave rise to the expression, "If that doesn't take the rag off the bush.")

City dwellers may cautiously resort to chemical bleaches on whites. On colorfast colored and white linens, try oxygen bleaches if you feel the linens need bleaching. If you need to avoid the optical brighteners or bluing that oxygen bleaches typically contain, consider using plain hydrogen peroxide (see page 317). Chlorine bleach is generally unnecessary, but I have made occasional use of it, without mishap, on white, sturdy, washable linen that grew dingy. I use chlorine bleach on linen dish towels at each laundering; after several years, none has developed holes or any other apparent weaknesses.

About Shrinking of Linen. If you wish to use hot water, be sure to buy sturdy, well-made linens that are Sanforized or preshrunk or that are big enough to undergo some shrinkage and still fit. (The presence of the Masters of Linen logo indicates that the fabric should be dimensionally stable.) If you are deliberately shrinking non-preshrunk linens, however, be alert to size and to decorative patterns, such as those that are meant to track the edge of the table. If linen is not preshrunk and you cannot permit any shrinkage, you might consider dry cleaning it, because even washing it in cool water and drying it flat or on the line will produce a bit of shrinking on each laundering until it is finally completely shrunk. But sooner or later—usually sooner—dry cleaning produces grayness, dinginess, or limpness in white or light linen. So be sure to search for a reliable dry cleaner and make your standards known when you deliver your linens.

About Drying Linen. Tumbling in the dryer causes linen fabric to become terribly wrinkled; all the tumbling is hard on the fabric, and for many household linens it is quite unnecessary as they dry quickly and you must iron them very damp. Flax, keep in mind, is a rather brittle fiber. Thus good care for linen fabric includes not bending and jerking it too much, especially when it is dry. One manufacturer actually recommends removing linen from the washer after the spin cycle and ironing it right away. This manufacturer probably has in mind the front-loading type of washing machine common in Europe but not the United States, which spins laundry much dryer than ours do. However, the advice does make a point: you want linen to be quite damp when you iron it, so there is no reason to risk damage by tumbling it dry. If you feel you must put sturdy linen in the dryer, keep the drying time short and be sure to remove the linen when it is still very damp. If you are concerned about shrinkage, dry the linen on a low setting.

It is best, however, to hang an article made of linen to dry or to dry it flat. When it is the proper degree of dampness for ironing, roll it up tightly, place it in an airtight plastic wrap or bag, and put it in the refrigerator or freezer if you do not intend to iron it within a few hours. If you are going to iron it soon, wrap it so that the dampness does not evaporate in the meantime.

On ironing linen, see pages 346–47 in chapter 23.

Cotton

About Cotton. Cotton is the true "miracle fiber." It is the fiber of democracy: it can be anything it wants to be, ambitious or humble, and its qualities can be enjoyed by rich and poor alike. More cotton is used in the United States than any other fiber.

Cotton, like flax, is a cellulosic fiber. It is derived from the fuzzy fibers surrounding the seeds of the cotton plant. It has many of the virtues of flax. It is absorbent, cool, crisp, smooth, and strong, even if, in each case, less so than linen. The quality of cotton fabric, like that of linen, is determined by the closeness and regularity of the weave and the construction of the fabric as well as the kind of cotton plant that provided the fibers from which it was made. The cotton plant determines the fiber's color, strength, luster, fineness or coarseness, and the length of the staple—short, medium, long, or extralong. (Long-staple cotton is $1\frac{1}{8}$ inches or more in length; extralong is $1\frac{3}{8}$ inches or more.) In general, the longer the staple, the better and the more costly the cotton fabric made from it and the more strength, smoothness, softness, luster, and durability it has.

Measured by these criteria, the best kind of cotton fiber is said to be Sea Island cotton, first grown off the coast of Georgia and now grown in the West Indies. This is a lustrous fiber with the finest and longest staple of all cottons (from $1\frac{1}{2}$ to $2\frac{1}{2}$ inches), and therefore it is used to manufacture the very finest cotton fabrics. It is now available only in small quantities, and you are unlikely to find many fabrics made of it. I have encountered men's shirts of Sea Island cotton, and I have bought Sea Island cotton fabrics in a piece goods store.

Pima cotton, another superior type of cotton, is a crossbreed of American and Egyptian cottons that is grown in Texas, the Southwest, and southern California. Pima cotton, like Sea Island cotton, is extralong staple (its staple length ranges from $1\frac{3}{8}$ to $1\frac{5}{8}$ inches), uniform, very fine, lustrous, strong, and light in color, which means it needs less bleaching than darker cottons. The Supima Association is an organization of Pima cotton farmers that promotes Pima cotton and authorizes the use of the Supima trademark only on fabrics of 100% Pima cotton. (The Supima Blends trademark indicates that the fabric contains at least 60% Pima cotton. The other 40% may be composed of other types of cotton or other types of fibers.)

Egyptian cotton, grown largely in the Nile Valley, is a third extralong staple, better-quality cotton, with a staple length running from $1\frac{1}{2}$ to $1\frac{3}{4}$ inches. It comes in a number of varieties; although all are long or extralong staple, not all are of the highest quality, and you cannot rely on labels announcing "Egyptian cotton" as a guarantee that you are getting the best. Egyptian cotton fibers range from light cream to dark tan; they are said to be less uniform than Pima cotton fibers.

When purchasing goods bearing labels indicating that they are made of "Sea Island" or "Egyptian" cotton, look to see whether they are said to be of 100% of this type of cotton; otherwise they may be made of a mixture of fine and less fine cottons or other types of fiber. When purchasing Pima cotton goods, look for the Supima trademark or for a statement about the percentage of Pima cotton the article contains.

Most United States cotton, however, as well as most of the world's cotton, is Upland cotton; most cotton goods, including clothes, towels, sheets, and diapers, are made of Upland cotton. The Seal of Cotton, with its familiar cotton boll, is a registered trademark of Cotton Incorporated, an industry organization supported by growers of Upland cotton. This seal indicates fabric made 100% of Upland cotton; the Natural Blend trademark indicates that the fabric contains at least 60% Upland cotton. Upland cotton, too, comes in a number of varieties and staple lengths, and these are of different quality, but none are as long and strong as Sea Island, fine Egyptian, or Pima cotton; its staple length averages $^{13}/_{16}$ to $1\,^{1}/_{4}$ inches. Yet quality in cotton is to some extent relative to purpose. In towels, for example, my preference is for Upland cotton, which seems to me to be most absorbent and soft.

South American cottons are to be found on the market in a wide range of quality. Asiatic cotton imported into the United States is almost always of relatively short staple and is usually used only for lower-quality cotton goods.

Fine-quality cotton goods will often be labeled "combed cotton." Combed cotton fabric is made of combed yarns that contain the longest of the long-staple cotton fibers. Combed yarns are stronger, smoother, and more durable than carded yarns and make higher-quality fabrics.

Properties of Cotton. Cotton fibers are naturally very absorbent, and so are fabrics made of them. Cotton fabrics are often preshrunk. If they are not, they tend to shrink; the more loosely woven the fabric, the more it will shrink. Cotton cloth wrinkles, but not quite so much as linen. The cotton knits that have been so deservedly popular for so long wrinkle less than cotton wovens. In addition, much cotton fabric on the market, including cotton in blends, has been subjected to wrinkle-resistance treatments. (But these tend to alter the cloth's hand, weaken it, and render it less absorbent. See "Resin Treatments," pages 229–30, and "Antiwrinkling Treatments," pages 224–25.)

Cotton fabric is cool, but not quite as cool as linen because its fuzzier, less smooth surface holds warmed air. Although cotton fabric is highly absorbent, it dries more slowly than linen. It can be delightfully cool on a hot summer's day, therefore, as it grows damp from perspiration. Cotton is also strong and durable, although, once again, a bit less so than linen. Cotton fabrics are generally crisp and hold their shape well. Cotton fiber is inelastic but cotton fabrics may acquire "give" or "stretch" from their construction or that of their yarns, for instance, through crêpeing or knitting. And because cotton fibers have a relatively rough surface, cotton fabrics are not quite as dirt- and stain-resistant as linen. One of cotton's chief advantages over linen, however, is that it takes dyes very well, although colorfastness varies from poor to excellent, depending on the dye and the dyeing process. Cotton fabrics generally have low luster, but those made of long-staple cotton fibers have higher luster.

Like linen, cotton fabric is stronger wet than dry. It has fairly good resistance to degradation by light, but it will yellow and weaken with prolonged exposure to sunlight. It mildews readily if left damp but will not be attacked by moths. (In cotton/wool blends, however, moths might attack the wool.) Like all fabrics made of cellulosic fibers, cotton fabric is vulnerable to strong acids. Acidic perspiration has a slightly deteriorating effect on cotton over time. Certain other acids occasionally used in the home, such as hydrochloric, sulfuric, and oxalic acid, will quickly do damage; the hotter and stronger the acidic solution, the greater the damage.

Cotton fabrics are available in every conceivable quality, coarse and fine; in a huge variety of woven and knitted constructions; and in blends with both natural and synthetic fibers.

Caring for Cotton. Subject to the usual caveats regarding finishing treatments, dyes, loose or otherwise delicate weaves, trims, and linings, cotton garments are in principle machine washable, withstand vigorous and strong detergents, and are also dry-cleanable. Cotton clothes, bedsheets, and tablecloths can be laundered on the regular wash cycle, unless the care label indicates otherwise or unless the article in question is delicate in some respect. Unless treated or preshrunk to prevent it, woven cotton fabrics shrink modestly, and knitted cotton fabrics less modestly. Avoiding hot water and high dryer temperatures reduces shrinkage of cotton knits.

Cotton fabrics may safely be bleached with ordinary household bleaches as long as this is done properly and they are rinsed thoroughly. Chlorine bleach, used according to the manufacturer's directions, is usually safe on white and colorfast cottons. (But prolonged use weakens the fabric. See "Bleaches" pages 316–19, and "Optical brighteners," pages 325–26, in the Glossary of Laundry Products and Additives.) Cotton that has been resin-treated to make it wrinkle resistant is weaker, however, and may last longer if you avoid bleaching it with a chlorine bleach.

Cotton fabrics tend to yellow with age or long exposure to sunlight. For this reason, you often hear these days that if you line-dry cotton you should put it in the shade. Keep in mind, however, that this is the *long-term* effect of sunlight. The short-term effect is that sunlight bleaches cotton—whitens whites and fades colors. If I had a clothesline, I would put white cotton in the sun if I wanted to whiten it, but I would not leave it there for more than a few hours, and I would always put colored cottons (and other colored fabrics) in the shade. If your cotton has yellowed from sunlight, by the way, you can usually bleach the color out. (My mother tells me that boiling for forty-five minutes or an hour with detergent will do the trick, too, but no one today has facilities for boiling, so I do not recommend this for bulky items.) Another problem with line-drying cotton is that some cotton is treated with optical brightening agents that yellow in the sunlight. But this problem seems to be rare. Yellowing from either cause tends to show up only on white or light cottons, for instance, on a pastel blue that turns dull.

Cotton fabrics can take a hot iron, and woven cottons usually need ironing unless they have received a resin treatment to reduce wrinkling, in which case the warm or permanent-press setting is usually recommended. Use starch or sizing for added crispness.

On the care of permanent-press cotton and cotton blends, see pages 249–50. See also pages 264–65 in chapter 17, "The Man-Made Fibers and Blends."

Wool and Other Hair Fibers

About Wool. Nature designed wool for comfort. Wool fabric, woven from sheep's fleece, offers you a bit of what it gave the sheep: warmth, softness, cushioning, protection from dampness, and absorbency. Almost all wool fabrics that you can buy are made from sheep's wool, but the term "wool" on a garment's label can also refer to fibers obtained from the fleece of Angora or cashmere goats and to fibers drawn from the coats of the camel, alpaca, llama, and vicuña. Wool fibers are the warmest of all natural fibers. They can absorb a great amount of moisture without feeling damp and are naturally water repellent. Wool fabric will not keep you dry in a pouring rain, but it will easily keep a sprinkle or a chilly mist at bay. Moreover, as wool fibers absorb water they actually release heat. This means that in cold, damp weather wool fabric will feel remarkably warm and comfortable, a fact that has been well appreciated for millennia. Wool fibers can also be woven into fabrics that are so lightweight and porous that they are considered suitable for summer wear. Wool is also widely used for furnishings, especially upholstery, carpets, and rugs. Wool fabric can be smooth or rough, fine or coarse. Although raw wool fibers are the weakest of the natural fibers (and grow still weaker when wet), wool fabrics can be constructed to be extremely durable. Wool fabrics are generally more expensive than either cotton or linen because of wool's expensive production process, beginning with the breeding of sheep.

Wool fibers are classified in two main ways: according to the kind of sheep the fiber comes from and according to the kind of fleece. Merino sheep are the source of merino wool fibers, the finest, softest, strongest, and most elastic wool fibers; because of these qualities, merino wool is the warmest type and spins into yarns well. But merino is not the most durable. The names of the sheep whose wool is most durable are not likely to appear on labels. ("Shetland" and "Botany" refer to places the sheep are raised—the Shetland Islands in Scotland and Botany Bay in Australia.) There is a wide variety in the quality of wool fibers, but quality is relative to function; the coarse, durable wool that makes a good carpet would make a rough, uncomfortable sweater.

Classification by type of fleece reflects the age and condition of the sheep and its fleece. Lamb's wool is a fleece of very fine quality. Fabrics of lamb's wool are the softest of all, but less strong than those made of mature wool. Hogget wool, the first shearing off year-old sheep, is highly desirable because it is still quite soft yet stronger than lamb's wool. Later shearings, from older (and dirtier) sheep, are progressively less desirable for clothing fabrics. Other decidedly inferior classes of fleece are taken from slaughtered or badly nourished sheep. Taglocks are the inferior (torn or discolored) pieces of any fleece.

New Wool and Recycled Wool. Previously manufactured wool yarn and fabrics may be recycled and used in new products. When recycled wool, known also as "shoddy," "reclaimed," "reused," or "reprocessed" wool, is added to new wool, it can add durability, especially if it was of a good grade, but at the cost of some warmth, softness, and resilience. Although the term "recycled" may be relatively new, the practice of recycling wool is quite old. Products containing recycled wool may well be of good quality, and they are generally less expensive than 100% new wool fabrics. The Wool Products Labeling Act requires that labels state what percentage, by weight, of wool is contained in a fabric and how much of it is new (or virgin) and how much recycled. A label guaranteeing 100% new wool does not, however, and is not intended to, guarantee a wool fabric of superior quality, let alone one superior to all fabrics containing recycled wool. Even very inferior grades of wool, such as pulled wool (from slaughtered sheep), might properly be identified as 100% new wool. A fabric made of a high-grade recycled wool would be superior to one made of low-grade new wool.

American Wool

Pure New Wool Woolmark

Harris Tweed Certification Mark

Evaluating Wool. The Wool Products Labeling Act does not require any indication of the breed of sheep or the type of fleece used in a garment or other wool product. Thus it can be difficult to determine the quality of the wool fiber used. There are several trademarks you can look for that help in assessing the quality of wool fibers and fabrics. The Woolmark is the trademark of The Woolmark Company. It may be used only on fabrics of 100% new wool that meet The Woolmark Company's quality specifications. The Woolmark Company also has a Woolblendmark, a trademark to be used only on articles made of at least 60% wool fibers; it, too, may be used only by manufacturers who meet The Woolmark Company's quality specifications. The presence of the logo of the American Wool Council, a division of the American Sheep Industry Association, indicates that the article contains a significant percentage of wool that originated in the United States—at least 20% in all-natural-fiber articles or 30% when blended with synthetics. As a condition of receiving permission to use the logo, the manufacturer agrees to use it only on goods of highest quality, samples of which it agrees to supply to the American Wool Council. Genuine Harris tweeds, which are known for their quality of construction, durability, and exclusive designs, can be identified by the symbol of the Harris Tweed Authority.

Tags or labels indicating that the fabric is of merino wool are one means of determining good quality. The indication on the label of the proportions of new and recycled wool fiber tells something about the relative durability and resilience of the fabric, but, unless you know about the quality of both, this information is of limited use. A "Superwash" or "H_2O Wools" (J. P. Stevens Company) label indicates that the wool fabric has been resin-treated to render it machine-washable. (See page 246.) You should be sure to read the care label to see whether hand-washing or dry cleaning is going to be necessary. Labels may also indicate preshrinking treatments, treatments rendering wool washable, antiwrinkling treatments, permanent creasing, and so forth.

Much can be learned by sight and touch. If wool feels harsh and stiff, it is of an inferior grade for use in clothing. If it feels very soft and resilient (that is, it does not wrinkle when crushed in the hand), it is of a high grade for this purpose. But softness and resilience are not a guarantee of strength. The addition of some reprocessed or reused wool may indicate increased durability. Napping tends to weaken any fabric; if wool is highly napped it may not be strong. Tightly twisted yarns are stronger than loosely twisted yarns; and yarns in two or more ply are progressively stronger than single-ply yarns. Always observe the quality of the weave. You can usually rely on the representations of reputable retailers and manufacturers and knowledgeable sales clerks, but I find that many sales clerks are as much in the dark as I am.

Different grades of wool may be blended during the manufacturing process to make a hardier or less expensive fabric. Wool/synthetic blends (the percentage of each fiber will be noted on the label) often combine beauty with comfort, serviceability, and economy. Wool fiber contributes softness, warmth, absorbency, and drapability while synthetic fibers can add increased wrinkle resistance, crease retention, or strength to the fabric and help prevent sagging, bagging, or stretching. Wool/microfiber blends have been particularly praised as giving the appearance and hand of a fine-quality wool.

Worsted and Woolen Yarns. Wool yarns fall into one of two types: worsted and woolen. Long wool fibers are used for worsted yarns. They are separated out from short ones and laid parallel (by several processes, including carding and combing) before spinning. The long wool fibers spin into a smoother and firmer yarn. Short wool fibers are used for woolen yarns. They are not combed and are rendered nonparallel so they will spin into fuzzier yarns than worsted yarns.

Worsted fabrics have the flat, hard, smooth feel of tailored wool suits and dresses. Worsted fabrics are usually found in twill rather than plain weave. Worsteds are considerably stronger and more wrinkle resistant than woolens, and they resist dirt better because they are not fuzzy. However, they can develop unattractive worn, shiny spots.

Woolen fabrics feel soft and fuzzy. Their fuzziness renders them warmer than worsteds but less durable. They are often napped, which gives even more softness but means they hold dirt more readily. Woolens are familiar in sweaters, blankets, sportswear, and jackets.

Oiled wool has had more natural lanolin left on the fibers than usual, which creates extra water repellency, and thus might be used in heavy, water-shedding sweaters.

Properties of Wool. Wool is a soft—not crisp—fabric. Although technically wool is a weak fiber, fabrics made from it are exceedingly durable. Wool fabrics have good resistance to abrasion, and both woven and knit wool fabrics can be constructed so that they have excellent strength. Hard-twisted wool yarns, in two or more ply, make very durable fabrics. Wool has fairly good resistance to pilling, which increases its durability in uses such as carpeting. (Although wool fabrics pill, the pills break off and thus do not accumulate as they do on fabrics made of synthetic fibers.) Wool fabrics drape gracefully.

Wool fabrics tend to be warm because wool fibers have scales and crimps, which create air pockets that trap body warmth. It is also highly absorbent. It can hold great quantities of perspiration and atmospheric moisture while still feeling dry. Moreover, as wool absorbs water it liberates heat and makes the wearer feel even warmer; thus it well deserves its reputation as the fiber of choice for cold, damp climates. Wool fabric is resilient (resists wrinkling). Wrinkles will disappear when the garment or fabric is steamed. But because its resilience is reduced when it is wet, you should not walk on a wet wool carpet or wear a wool garment you have just steam-pressed.

Wool fabrics shrink in water unless treated. Woolens shrink more than worsteds, but both shrink. Look for the "Superwash" mark on tags or for some other trademark or label indication that the wool will resist shrinking in water. Wool/synthetic blends may be more resistant to shrinking in water than 100% wool that has received no nonshrinking treatment, but such blends are sometimes more prone to pilling. Wool ordinarily has low static buildup but in a very dry atmosphere can become quite static-charged. It is stain-resistant; liquids will run off wool or penetrate it slowly, giving you time to blot them up. Dust and dirt often brush off wool. But it can also absorb and hold odors.

Wool fabrics are highly vulnerable to damage by moths. Sometimes they are given a mothproof finish.

Although wool resists mildew, it may succumb if left damp for a long period. Wool has low resistance to ultraviolet radiation.

Caring for Wool. Wool tends to hold dirt. Because of wool's elasticity, wool garments should be allowed to "rest" for twenty-four hours in order to return them to shape before they are worn again. According to one authority, wool garments should also be left to rest for a few days after dry cleaning or washing. If wool fabrics are left to rest, their fibers age or "anneal." The wool molecules actually rearrange themselves into more energy-efficient configurations.[2] To prepare a garment for resting, empty the pockets, button or zip it up, and hang it straight. Brush wool garments after wearing and allow them to air, properly hung on a hanger, before replacing them in your closet. Brushing not only helps keep the cloth clean, it is also good protection against moths; airing will reduce odors.

Wool, however, does not hold body odors as synthetics sometimes do and actually gets rid of underarm odors by absorbing them. To freshen and unwrinkle wool garments, hang them in a steamy bathroom or use a steaming device. You will help wool garments stay clean longer if, after brushing and before airing, you simply wipe them down with a barely damp white, lint-free cloth. Make sure you let them air-dry afterward before replacing them in the closet or drawer.

Wool fabrics are usually dry-cleaned. Some are washable, but wool is softened by moisture and heat, and shrinking and felting may occur when the fabric is washed, especially in alkaline solutions. Because shrinking and felting are much less of a problem with dry cleaning, most care labels call for this.

WASHING WOOL

Hand-washing. Before washing a sweater or other garment, draw its outline on a piece of sturdy paper or cardboard. To control shrinking, use cool water (but not icy-cold water) with a mild, neutral soap or detergent suitable for wool and for cool-water laundering.* You might try lukewarm water if the item is heavily soiled. Soak for three to five minutes. Then lift from beneath the article and gently squeeze suds through the material. Leave the garment in the water for as short a period as possible; the longer it is in, the more its fibers swell and weaken. Since wool loses strength when wet, wool fabrics should never be pulled, twisted, or wrung while wet. Rinse the article thoroughly in clear, cool water. To dry, roll it in a towel and squeeze gently. Then, using your drawing as a guide, block the garment to its original shape. If you need to, pin it to the shape. Let it dry flat on a towel or other clean surface away from direct heat or sunlight.

Machine-washing. Most wool blankets require dry cleaning. Some wool blankets, afghans, and certain wool sweaters and other garments can be machine-washed. Be sure to check the care label before proceeding, however. And before machine-washing a sweater or other garment that might lose its shape, draw an outline of it on a piece of paper or cardboard. Test for colorfastness before laundering any colored wools, especially prints. On machine-washable wool blankets, see chapter 26, page 359.

"Superwash" indicates a 100% wool fabric that can be machine-washed and -dried because it has undergone chemical and resin treatments that eliminate felting and shrinkage. The Superwash treatment is permanent.

To reduce pilling from abrasion during laundering, use plenty of water. Set the machine on "gentle" or "delicate" for agitating, but use a fast spin; you want slow agitation, but you want to get the wool as dry as possible. Use cool wash water (lukewarm if the item is heavily soiled), and a mild detergent safe for wool and suitable for cool water and *machine washing.* Dissolve the detergent before adding the wool item. Fabric softeners are unnecessary. Wash each item briefly. Never leave wool to soak for more than a few minutes; keep the wash as brief as possible. Rinse with cool water.

Dry flat, blocking as for hand-washing, unless the care label instructions permit machine drying, in which case you will probably be instructed to use a low temperature. Superwash wools can be tumbled dry; be careful not to overdry. When you have air-dried blankets, sweaters, and other soft wools, you may then wish to put them in the dryer for a few minutes on the air-fluff cycle, which uses cool air, to fluff them up.

*One acquaintance recommends using shampoo on wool. This course is a bit risky, however, as some shampoos are quite alkaline and some contain medicines, colorants, conditioners, and extras that could harm or discolor your wools. However, it is true that a neutral or slightly acidic, gentle shampoo that contains no colorants or additives might clean wool nicely. Be sure to test first, and avoid products that look milky rather than clear, that contain conditioners or other additives, or that have bright or unusual colors.

Even wools that can be washed require extreme care in laundering. Because ordinary laundry detergents all create an alkaline wash-water solution, wool should be washed with special detergents. Use a gentle soap or detergent that is nonalkaline or near-neutral pH. (See "Detergents and soaps, mild" in the glossary at the end of chapter 21.) Make sure the soap or detergent is effective in cool water. Hot or warm water with detergent can cause astonishing shrinkage: your size 38 sweater can emerge toddler-sized. Washable white wool may be bleached, if you are careful about it, with hydrogen peroxide but not chlorine bleach. (See page 317.) Do not dry wool in the sunlight, especially white wool, as this can render it yellow or dull.

Store wool clothes, blankets, and carpets out of light and dampness, and make sure they are perfectly clean when they are put away; moths and other insects will be attracted to soils. On protecting wools from moths, see "Mothproofing Wool," pages 251–52.

Do not iron wool; press it, using a damp press cloth. (See chapter 23, "Ironing," page 343.) Ironing wool dry will make its fibers brittle and damage them.

Silk

Sumptuary laws in sixteenth-century England forbade the wives of poor men to wear silk gowns or French velvet bonnets. Such finery was considered suitable only for the wives of men who had at least a horse to ride in the king's service. For centuries, silk has been regarded as the most desirable, elegant, and luxurious of all fabrics, and it continues to hold that status despite keen competition from synthetics and blends.

Silk is made of the filament secreted by the silkworm, the larva of a moth, to form its cocoon—the only natural fiber that comes in filament form. It is smooth, soft, lightweight, lustrous, strong, and resilient, with excellent drapability. Because it has only moderate resistance to abrasion, it is not an ideal choice for upholstery fabrics that are to take hard wear, but it may be quite durable in other uses. Silk takes dye—and, alas, stains—more readily than any other natural fiber, and today, as in the past, much of the appeal of silks lies in the gorgeous colors and patterns applied to them.

Production; Types of Silk. After silk cocoons are sorted and softened, several silk filaments unwound from a cocoon are combined and wound onto a reel, forming a long, raw silk strand called reeled silk. Reeled silk is then "thrown." Throwing is a kind of twisting of the reeled-silk filaments into threads. Thrown silk is used to make fine and sheer fabrics, such as georgette, taffeta, voile, crêpe de chine, organza, and grenadine.

Spun silk is produced when short lengths of silk filament are carded, combed, and spun into threads just as wool, cotton, and linen are. Because of the short staple of spun-silk yarn, spun-silk fabric tends to become fuzzy with wear (the short fibers rub up). Spun-silk fabrics have less strength and elasticity than thrown-silk fabrics but otherwise have the same characteristics. Spun-silk fabrics are usually less expensive than filament (thrown) silk fabrics. Spun-silk fibers are used in blends and in pile fabrics such as velvet.

The gum that covers the natural silk fibers is boiled off, ultimately resulting in fabric that weighs less and has less body. Manufacturers may "weight" silk by adding metallic salts to make up for the lost weight and give the silk more body and better drape. But heavily weighted silk is less elastic and more vulnerable to damage by sunlight, perspiration, and dry cleaning. It may crack or split. Because heavily weighted silks were once a problem, federal regulations require that heavy weighting be disclosed on the label.

Raw silk is silk that has not been processed to remove the gum. Fabric woven of raw silk is bumpy and irregular, and is less expensive.

Pure dye silk is silk that contains no metallic weighting, although it may contain limited amounts of water-soluble substances such as starch or gelatin used in dyeing and finishing processes. Good pure dye silk is superior to and more durable than weighted silks; not only does it retain its natural elasticity, but it usually has a greater amount of silk yarn woven into it, rendering it stronger than weighted silk.

Duppioni silk fabric is made from fibers from the double or interlocking cocoons that can occur when two silk worms spin the same cocoon or spin cocoons side by side. Since these fibers are irregular, the fabric made from them has a thick-and-thin look.

Most silk fabric is made from cultivated silk fiber—silk fiber from the cocoons of silkworms raised especially for the production of silk filaments. Wild silk or tussah comes from a wild species of moth, usually the tussah silkworm. Wild silk is not the same as raw silk, and may or may not be raw. It is less lustrous and coarser than cultivated silk. Wild silk fabrics—such as pongee or shantung—are both durable and less expensive than pure dye silks.

Properties of Silk. Silk fabrics are generally considered summery. Filament silk can be woven into sheer cloth that air readily penetrates, which makes it comfortable on all but the hottest and most humid days. But spun silks can be made into fairly warm garments. Silk is also highly absorbent and, like wool, can take in much perspiration and atmospheric moisture and not feel damp. This makes it a more sensible choice for undergarments and lingerie than silklike but inabsorbent synthetics. Silk is naturally somewhat wrinkle resistant.

Because it is somewhat elastic, it has a comfortable give when worn and does not readily stretch out of shape. Silk does not pill and has moderate abrasion resistance. It has a very slight tendency to build up static, especially in a dry environment. Carpet beetles will attack silk. It has poor resistance to the effects of ultraviolet radiation. It does not readily mildew but may do so if left damp for a long time. Silk, like cotton and wool, is woven into a great variety of fabrics and blends.

Caring for Silk. Silk does not attract or hold particles of dirt readily because it is so smooth. But it is perhaps the most readily stainable of all fibers. Most care labels for silk recommend dry cleaning. Silk is significantly weaker when wet and, because it is a protein fiber like wool, is vulnerable to alkalies, even mild ones.

On the other hand, some silks have had chemical treatments to render them washable; these washable silks *cannot* be dry-cleaned. Read care labels carefully. Such silks do not appear lustrous and smooth in the manner of classic silk, and according to one text that I consulted, their proper laundering is a matter of debate. Some say that machine-washing will permanently alter them (presumably for the worse) and recommend only hand-washing in cool water with gentle soap or detergent. Others say you can machine-wash them. Both groups caution that these articles must be washed separately because their dyes bleed. As for drying, tumble them on a cool setting in the dryer, or hang the garments to dry. Iron them while still damp.[3]

Some silk fabric that has not been chemically treated to render it washable can nonetheless be laundered, but this must usually be done with special care. *Never* wash glossy, dressy silks; if you do, it is all too likely that they will never look that way again. Some of us at times successfully wash silk despite care labels saying not to, but we do this at our own (considerable) risk. If the silk is not a pure dye silk, the weighting may wash out, leaving you with an irremediably limp garment. And the colors may run. Always test for colorfastness in an inconspicuous area before attempting to launder silk. Silk crêpes must always be dry-cleaned, as they shrink disastrously when wet. Skill is required in both the washing and ironing of silks at home.

Washable silks that have not been chemically treated to render them washable should be washed gently by hand in lukewarm water and mild soap or detergent. (See pages 313–14.) Regular laundry detergents are alkaline; the hotter and more concentrated the alkaline solution, the more damage will be done to silk. Chlorine bleach will cause silk to disintegrate. Hydrogen peroxide or sodium perborate bleaches may be used on white silks with caution. Do not leave silk soaking for long periods. Because silk weakens a little when wet, it might be harmed by wringing or rough tumbling.

Water often leaves spots on silk (as a result of sizings and other finishes applied by manufacturers), but the spots generally come out upon laundering. Iron silk on the reverse side when it is still damp, or use steam and a press cloth on a medium setting. (See chapter 23, "Ironing," page 343.) Wrinkles that develop in wear will often come out as the garment hangs.

Perspiration weakens and discolors silk, and the aluminum chloride in some antiperspirants and deodorants also harms it. The use of dress shields is therefore advisable. Wash out perspiration as soon as possible, before it has a chance to do damage. If yellow areas develop in the underarm area of *white* silks, try an oxygen bleach. (See "Perspiration," pages 369–70, and "Yellowing," pages 372–73, in chapter 26, "Common Laundry Mishaps and Problems.")

Bast Fibers

Bast fibers are strong fibers obtained from the inner bark of a variety of plants. Linen is a bast fiber. There are three others that may show up at home in clothes, furnishings, or utilitarian objects of various sorts: jute, ramie, and hemp.

All the bast fibers are cellulosic, like cotton and linen, and thus have similar physical and chemical properties. For example, they are absorbent, they are vulnerable to acids but not to mild alkalies, and they can usually be bleached, if care is taken (but jute, being one of the weakest cellulosic fibers, can be damaged by bleaching). If washable, they can be laundered, usually, as linens and cotton are.

Jute. Jute is derived from the jute plant, grown in Bangladesh, India, Thailand, and China. It is the stiff, inelastic fiber from which burlap, bags, rope, and similar comparatively inexpensive, rough goods are made. It also finds some uses in carpentry, as a backing fabric, and as a binding thread. It must be kept dry—it rots if left damp.

Ramie. Ramie, also called China grass, is grown in the Philippines, China, Brazil, and many other places. Its fiber is white or cream-colored, very strong, and lustrous. Ramie fabric is similar to linen but more brittle, which limits its use for apparel and furnishings. Increasingly, however, it is being included in blends used for such products. Unlike linen and cotton, ramie resists mildew, although it will eventually mildew if left damp for a long time. In blends with cotton, rayon, nylon, and polyester, it contributes strength and benefits from the flexibility of the other fibers. It is used for clothing (especially in blends), for twine, and for upholstery fabrics.

Hemp. Italy has traditionally grown the best hemp, which is a stiff, rough, and durable fiber taken from the inner bark of the hemp plant. Hemp is used to make cords, twine, and ropes (especially for ships, because it is strongly resistant to rotting or weakening in water), canvases and tarpaulins, in carpet manufacture, and in some furnishings. Lately it has been used more and more for clothes too. (See page 206.)

Miscellaneous Issues in Caring for Natural Fibers

Permanent Press (Durable Press, Wash-and-Wear, or Wrinkle Resistant): Resin-Treated Cottons, Rayons, Linens, and Their Blends. For several reasons, laundering can be problematic for permanent-press or durable-press cottons, rayons, linens, and blends containing these and other natural or man-made fibers. First, cotton, rayon and linen fabrics, including cotton, rayon, or linen blends, that have been subjected to resin treatments to create wrinkle resistance or permanent creases or pleats are significantly weaker than those that have not; hence harsh washing procedures may significantly shorten the fabric's life. In addition, permanent-press fabrics tend to take up and hold soil that gets deposited in the wash water and emerge from the laundry gray or dingy. Third, such resin-treated fabrics are particularly prone to oil staining and, in some cases, to retaining body odors.

Despite such problems, home laundering is the cleaning procedure of choice for permanent-press clothes. Commercial laundering is usually too harsh. You should wash all new clothes and linens before using, but it is especially important with those that have been subjected to a resin treatment, so as to remove any remaining formaldehyde. (However, not all permanent-press garments have the problem today.) Permanent-press washing and drying cycles should always be used. Use plenty of water and make smaller loads, as overcrowding in the washer will also tend to cause wrinkling. The permanent-press cycle cools off the washed clothes with cool water so that when they spin they do not take a wrinkled imprint; it also spins them more slowly for the same reason. The permanent-press dryer setting includes a cool-down period at the cycle's end so that clothes do not wrinkle from sitting, heated, when the dryer stops tumbling.

Before washing, examine the usual wear areas: collars and cuffs, pleats and darts, creases, the seat of pants. If necessary, make repairs before washing. If wear is apparent, you may prolong the life of the garment by using the gentle washing cycle a with a warm or cool wash, cool rinse, and slow spin. Because the fold and crease lines on permanent-press articles tend to be even weaker than the rest of the fabric, it is often a good idea to wash and dry permanent-press articles turned inside out.

Frequent washing is the key to keeping permanent-press clothes clean and fresh-smelling. Use pretreatments on pillowcases and cuffs, collars, and other areas that take up body oils and odors; the use of pretreatment products that contain solvents is a good idea. Also use plenty of detergent and warm or even hot wash water (when it is safe for the fabric), not cold, to keep permanent-press clothes clean.

Tumbling dry, followed by prompt removal from the dryer, is necessary to get the full benefit of wrinkle-resistance treatments on permanent-press articles. But drip-dry clothes should usually have no spinning in the washing machine, no wringing, and no machine drying; their care labels will prescribe hanging to dry or drying flat. In some cases, mild soap should be used; check the care labels. Hang clothes carefully, "finger ironing" them—smoothing and straightening them with your hands—especially at seams. Sometimes a quick touch with an iron will be necessary to reduce a bit of puckering.

Chlorine bleach may not be recommended for permanent-press cloth because the cloth has been weakened. In addition, some permanent-press clothes will yellow if exposed to chlorine, although this problem appears to be unusual nowadays. In any event, use chlorine bleach with caution. In my experience, though, an occasional light bleaching does no harm.

Washable Antiques, Heirlooms, and Other Fragile or Valuable Linen. Extremely delicate and aged fabrics cannot be washed at all. You can at times vacuum these by using a protective screen and the low setting, with open vents, on your vacuum cleaner. (See page 472 in chapter 35, "Textile Furnishings.")

Sometimes washable antiques and heirlooms will be sufficiently cleaned by merely soaking for half an hour or so in plain, soft, lukewarm water. To avoid potentially damaging handling, you can lay the piece on a nylon screen or in a plastic colander and gently immerse it in the plain-water bath. This will dissolve dust and acids that may have collected on the fibers and thus extend the life of the fabric. After the soak, pour off the water and gently add another bath of pure, soft, cool water for rinsing. Then raise the screen or colander out of the water and let the piece drain and dry while still resting on it.

If more cleaning is necessary, add some very mild, neutral detergent to your water bath and let the article soak for a few minutes. Orvus WA Paste (manufactured by Procter and Gamble) is often recommended for this purpose by museums and conservators. (If you choose instead to use a mild soap, be sure that your water is soft and that you rinse thoroughly.) Then pat the piece gently to get water to pass through it. Or you may let it lie on a nylon screen or colander, as described above, and gently raise and lower the screen to get the water to run through the cloth. If the piece does not come clean, repeat. Pour off the wash water. Then rinse gently with plain, cool water in the same manner as you washed until absolutely all soap or detergent residues, along with any dirt that has been removed, are rinsed away.

Use no bleach of any sort, including sun bleaching, on very fragile pieces. If you are determined to get spots or stains out of a fragile piece, you can try additional soaking in a solution of lukewarm water and mild detergent. If the piece is neither valuable nor very important and if its appearance is marred, you might escalate to sun bleaching, then to the more risky expedient of stronger detergent (one without optical brighteners or bluing).

As for chemical bleaching to remove stains or to lighten a dingy piece, try it only if you have nothing to lose or if the piece is not too important or valuable. Avoid commercial oxygen bleaches, as these contain laundry boosters, optical brighteners, and bluing. If you wish to try an oxygen bleach, consider using plain hydrogen peroxide. (See page 317.)

To dry, blot or press with a towel and then let dry flat—all on the screen or colander if you are using one or, if you are not, on a clean white towel. Dry away from sunlight and heat.

Mothproofing Wool. The most important thing you can do to keep your clothes and carpets free of moth damage is to keep them clean. Moths will be attracted to grease and food stains on clothes. Frequent vacuuming and occasionally cleaning or shampooing will give carpets in use all the protection they need. Clothes that are frequently worn and laundered will also not be moth damaged. You should make sure that clothes and carpets in storage are perfectly clean, but they will also require additional protection.

Brushing wool articles frequently, and always after wearing, and cleaning them before they are stored will help remove any eggs that may have been deposited. Storage in an airtight compartment at or below 40°F will prevent eggs from developing and hatching. Ironing at temperatures greater than 130°F kills them.

Home chemical treatments work by either repelling or killing the insects. Repellents may prevent the deposit of eggs but will not destroy eggs already deposited, and they do not last long. The most popular repellent, cedar, is at best modestly effective, in my experience. It has been determined that cedar oil will kill young larvae (not older ones or eggs), but it is hard to see how cedar-lined closets or cedar chips, blocks, hangers, and chests are going to expose the young larvae to a lethal dose of cedar oil. The hope is that moths will not wish to lay their eggs in a cedar-scented environment, but I have had moths flutter happily out of my cedar-laden closets and found moth holes in cedar-surrounded garments. So far as I have been able to determine, there is no scientific evidence—at least not yet—for the theory that moths will avoid cedar-laden areas.

Some people tout dried orange peel and various spice mixtures and potpourris as repellents. These have scents that will appeal to many, but, again, I have found no scientific evidence that any of them really works as a moth repellent. (My Italian grandmother used both lavender and dried orange peel, but only for their scent, not to repel moths.) As for commercial moth repellents that may use secret or unnamed ingredients, their effectiveness is also a mystery. Of course, it does not hurt to try any nontoxic products that interest you.

Naphthalene and paradichlorobenzene, typical ingredients in mothballs and other antimoth devices today, will actually kill moths, larvae, and eggs, provided the storage is airtight and compact so that the atmosphere can be saturated; if it is not, the chemical released is not strong enough to do the job. The chemical-containing device should be hung above the clothes because the vapors, which are heavier than air, will flow downward. Unfortunately, both naphthalene and paradichlorobenzene are also toxic to humans, and paradichlorobenzene is a carcinogen. The U.S. Environmental Protection Agency (EPA) recommends that you use devices containing paradichlorobenzene only in areas sealed off from your living space, such as garages or attics. I would follow the same advice when using naphthalene mothballs, crystals, or flakes.

17

The Man-Made Fibers and Blends

Viscose rayon, cuprammonium rayon, high wet-modulus rayon, and lyocell and their care . . . Acetate and triacetate and their care . . . Nylon and its care . . . Polyester and its care . . . Acrylic and modacrylic and their care . . . Spandex and its care . . . Polypropylene and its care . . . Microfibers . . . Blends . . . Caring for hydrophobic synthetic fibers

Man-made or manufactured fibers have been used to make fabric for more than a century. Rayon, invented in the late nineteenth century, began being commercially produced in this country in 1910; acetate was commercially produced by the 1920s. Both of these are based on plant, or cellulosic, fibers. When nylon was introduced, with great fanfare, in 1939, it was the first fiber made entirely from synthesized or manufactured chemicals. Many other entirely synthetic fibers followed in short order. By 1960, acrylic and modacrylic, olefin, polyester, and spandex fibers were all well known, and fabrics composed of innumerable blends of two or more synthetics or of synthetics and natural fibers became popular. These new fibers constituted a revolution.

Man-made fibers other than rayon and acetate—the synthetics—are unabsorbent and hydrophobic. (Rayon and acetate fibers are based on cellulose and therefore are absorbent.) The synthetics are also thermoplastic—that is, they melt or soften when enough heat is applied and harden when they are cooled. As a result, creases or smoothness can be programmed into the cloth by a process called heat setting. If the cloth is smoothed when hot enough, it stays smooth unless it is rendered that hot once more. Thus such cloth needs little or no ironing. Similarly, if a fabric made of synthetic fibers is creased when at the right temperature, it will stay creased unless it is once more brought to that temperature. Care labels on clothes made of synthetic fibers often call for low to moderate temperatures in washing and drying and a cool-down period in the dryer; this is to avoid setting in wrinkles. Likewise, these fabrics should be ironed at low to medium settings. (See pages 264–65.)

Rayon

Rayon is made of regenerated cellulose derived from cotton fiber or wood pulp. The variety of rayons on the market makes it difficult to generalize about its properties. Not only are there different types of rayon, but each type can be produced in both thrown or filament yarn and spun yarn, and the characteristics of these spun and filament yarns may be markedly different. Rayon filament yarns produce silk-like fabrics. Spun rayon can be napped, finished, and constructed to resemble fabrics of cotton, linen, and wool. (Such rayon fabrics, however, will function quite differently from the fabrics of natural fibers that they resemble.) Rayon fibers can be effectively blended with many other fibers, natural and synthetic.

Viscose Rayon. Most rayon you buy is viscose rayon. Its name derives from a step in its processing in which a cellulose mixture is transformed into a viscous solution. This type of rayon is usually identified on the fiber content label merely as "rayon" or, often, "viscose."

Fabric made from viscose rayon is usually soft and drapable with a pleasant cottony hand. It is weaker than silk, linen, cotton, and wool. It is highly absorbent—even more than cotton or linen—and cool, characteristics that make it one of the most comfortable of fibers, especially in warm weather. Viscose rayon fabric may stretch when it gets wet and shrink as it dries, and may even stretch and shrink with changes in atmospheric humidity; thus it is usually a poor choice for draperies. Unlike cotton and linen, rayon fabrics lose much strength when wet, so laundering may not be recommended or may have to be done with gentle agitation. Unless given a shrink-resistant treatment, viscose rayon fabrics tend to shrink more than comparable cotton fabrics. Viscose rayon fiber is modestly more elastic than cotton or linen but less elastic than silk and wool. Rayon fabric tends to be rather limp or lacking in body.

Viscose rayon fabric tends to lack the resilience of silk and wool and therefore wrinkles readily. Its inherent tendency to wrinkle is one of its biggest disadvantages, but this may be reduced by wrinkle-resistance treatments and by careful engineering of the construction of the yarn and fabric. When buying an item made of rayon fabric, crumple it for a few seconds in your hand and then release it to determine how much it wrinkles.

Prolonged exposure to sunlight may cause weakening or yellowing of viscose rayon fibers and fabrics. Viscose rayon fabric mildews if left damp. It is vulnerable to silverfish but not to moths. Like all cellulosic fibers, viscose rayon fiber is vulnerable to acids but has good resistance to alkalies.

Cuprammonium Rayon. Cuprammonium rayon, also known as Bemberg or cupra rayon, is named after a step in its processing in which cellulose is dissolved in a cuprammonium hydroxide solution. The buyer may be told only that it is "rayon." Cuprammonium rayon is soft, lustrous, and silky, and usually is produced as filament rayon. Fabrics made from cuprammonium rayon tend to be more resilient than viscose rayon—that is, they do not wrinkle so easily. Cuprammonium rayon fabrics also tend to have greater abrasion resistance than viscose rayon. Thus they make excellent linings as well as women's dresses and blouses.

High Wet-Modulus Rayons. Rayon fibers have been developed which have greatly increased strength when wet, comparable to that of cotton; these can be mercerized and rendered shrink resistant with compressive shrinkage treatments. These fibers are known as high wet-modulus rayon or modified rayons or high-performance or Polynosic rayons. Fabrics made from high wet-modulus rayons often look and feel like high-quality cotton fabrics, and tend to have more body and stiffness than viscose rayon fabrics, but they can also be silky or woolly. Because they have better wet strength, these types of rayon are more readily launderable than viscose rayon and can usually be machine-washed (subject, of course, to the usual caveats). Acid perspiration will cause some types of high wet-modulus rayon to deteriorate.

Lyocell (Tencel). Lyocell is the generic name of a new rayonlike, cellulosic fiber that is more wrinkle resistant, shrink resistant, and stronger than viscose rayon. It is absorbent, with an appealing soft, luxurious hand. Like rayon, it is derived from wood pulp, but it is produced through an environmentally more favorable process. It tends to be more expensive than viscose rayon. Lyocell is used both alone and in blends with linen, cotton, rayon, and wool fibers.

Caring for Rayon Fabrics. The buyer of clothes or furnishings made of rayon fabrics should be sure to check care labels before purchasing. Many inexpensive pieces of rayon sportswear may require the inconvenience of hand-washing or the expense of dry cleaning. High wet-modulus rayons, however, are usually machine-washable.

Many, but not all, types of viscose rayon have a smooth surface that sheds dirt readily. Theoretically, viscose rayon may be both dry-cleaned and laundered. For many reasons, however, dry cleaning is more frequently recommended. Viscose rayon fabrics weaken greatly when wet and often shrink, bleed colors, go limp, and wrinkle badly after washing. Laundering more quickly wears them out. Viscose rayon fabrics are frequently given water-soluble finishes and sizings that may dissolve in laundering, resulting in changes for the worse in the fabrics' hand and drape.

Launderable viscose rayon should be handled very gently during laundering. It is more vulnerable to all sorts of chemicals than cotton, including alkaline laundry solutions. It should usually be hand-washed in mild detergent and warm water, then squeezed, not wrung or twisted, to remove excess water, unless the garment care label explicitly permits machine washing. When it does, it usually calls for using a shorter, delicate agitation cycle. Viscose rayon knits should be dried flat; woven viscose rayon fabrics should be hung to dry. White viscose rayon will ordinarily not turn gray or yellow with cleaning or laundering and therefore usually needs no bleaching, but household bleaches may be used, with care, on white viscose rayon, so long as it is not blended with another fiber that cannot be bleached. Some types of rayon are much sturdier than regular viscose rayon, so do not hesitate to take advantage of vigorous laundering methods when you find them prescribed on a rayon fabric care label.

Viscose rayon fabrics should usually be ironed damp on a low to medium iron or with a steam iron. Some rayon fabrics develop a shine from ironing, so use a press cloth or iron the fabric on the wrong side. (See chapter 23, "Ironing.")

Acetate and Triacetate

Properties of Acetate and Triacetate. Acetate, or cellulose acetate, is made in a process that begins by treating cellulose, derived from wood, with acetic acid. Acetate fabrics are often lovely. They are smooth, very lustrous, and silk-like in appearance and hand. Triacetate, acetate's chemical cousin, is more versatile and may be constructed into fabrics that resemble those made of rayon, cotton, wool, or silk fibers. Both acetate and triacetate fabrics drape attractively. They tend to be more expensive than those made of cotton, rayon, or polyester.

Acetate and triacetate, however, are both weak fibers, and fabrics made of them have poor abrasion resistance. Acetate fabrics become significantly weaker when wet, which means that they must usually be dry-cleaned; when launderable, acetate fabrics must be washed with great care. Triacetate is less weakened by wetness and can usually be machine-washed and -dried. Fabrics made from acetate and triacetate are more elastic, warmer, and more wrinkle resistant than rayon, and shrink less. Triacetate is quite wrinkle resistant—more so than acetate—and when wrinkles do form in a triacetate garment they tend to fall out when it is hung for a while.

Acetate and triacetate have a little absorbency, but much less than fibers classified as hydrophilic. Both are classified as hydrophobic, and fabrics made of them tend to feel uncomfortable in hot, humid weather. They are useful in items such as raincoats or shower curtains that need some water resistance. Both are used in dresses, blouses, and other clothes, as well as draperies and curtains, but not in articles that will receive hard wear. Although linings are often made of acetate, its weakness and poor abrasion resistance mean that otherwise durable coats with acetate linings will need new linings long before the rest of the coat wears out. Acetate's low absorbency can interfere with the comfort of summer garments lined with it.

Both acetate and triacetate are thermoplastic, triacetate more so than acetate. Triacetate can receive permanent heat-set pleats and creases; acetate cannot. Triacetate can take much more heat than acetate before melting. Acetate will melt and stick to a hot iron, but triacetate melts at a higher temperature than irons reach.

Both acetate and triacetate have good pill resistance. They do not mildew and will not be attacked by pests (except that silverfish might harm the cloth in the process of devouring any starch in it). Both fibers, but triacetate more than acetate, tend to build up static unless they have received antistatic treatments. Acetate and triacetate have moderate resistance to the ultraviolet radiation in sunlight. Concentrated solutions of alkalies or acids will harm them. Acetate and triacetate and their blends will be destroyed by nail polish remover, paint remover, and other solvents that contain acetone.

Special acetate dyes are used on acetate, and may bleed, fade in laundering or in contact with atmospheric gases (a phenomenon known as "fume fading"), or discolor with perspiration. Solution dyeing solves these problems; the color of solution-dyed acetate is fast to washing, atmospheric gases, perspiration, and light. Triacetate is less likely to be discolored or weakened by perspiration and is less prone to fume fading and fading during washing than acetate.

Caring for Acetate and Triacetate. Dry cleaning is usually recommended for acetate fabrics because acetate fibers are fragile, lose strength when wet, and are highly temperature-sensitive. Triacetate, however, is usually machine-washable. When acetate is launderable, either gentle machine-washing or hand-laundering will be recommended. Lukewarm water, not hot, is usually recommended—or acetate fabric will shrink and wrinkle—and mild soaps or detergents. Bleaches will not ordinarily be necessary on white acetate because it tends to stay white, but if there are stains, household bleaches may be used cautiously. Bleaches may also be useful on white fabrics that are blends of acetate with other fibers that do not stay white. Colored acetate fabrics should not be soaked because they will bleed. (Solution-dyed acetate, however, will have color that is fast to laundering.) If you hand-wash acetate or triacetate fabrics, do not wring, twist, or rub them. You may wish to use a fabric softener now and then.

Roll acetate items in a towel. Dry knits flat and hang wovens to dry, unless the care instructions permit machine-drying. Usually you can tumble-dry triacetate; use the permanent-press cycle (at medium to low temperatures) to take advantage of the cool-down period, and remove the items promptly. If either of these fabrics is left to sit warm in a dryer, it will wrinkle. Triacetate will need little to no ironing, but it can take a hot iron. (It may be billed as wash-and-wear.) Acetate fabric will need damp ironing on its wrong (back) side at low to medium temperatures, or on the right side using a press cloth.

Nylon

In a remarkable marketing event, nylon hose were offered for sale throughout the United States on May 15, 1940, following an extraordinary advertising campaign addressed to a public already disposed to admire rather than disdain man-made fibers. It is difficult for us today to imagine how a mere article of clothing could cause such a stir in the world, or how eager women were to get rid of silk hose that ran, sagged, and bagged.

The word "nylon" refers to any member of a group of similar compounds (polymers) called polyamides. These polymers are made from coal, petroleum, air, water, and sometimes cereal waste products such as oat hulls or corncobs.[1]

Properties of Nylon. Nylon fiber comes in many chemical forms that are sold under a variety of trade names and differ greatly in their properties. Spun and filament yarn nylons also differ significantly from one another. However, the various types of nylon fiber share some common characteristics. Nylon fibers are light and strong and highly resistant to abrasion. They are also extremely elastic—second only to spandex and rubber. Such qualities make nylon fibers exceptionally well suited for use in hosiery and sheer fabrics. Nylon fibers are also resilient, so nylon fabrics resist wrinkling, and wrinkles that develop during use or wear fall out easily. In looks and hand, fabrics made of nylon often have a silky luster, but nylon fabrics can easily resemble those made of cotton, wool, or other fibers in their appearance and hand.

Nylon can be made into warm fabrics. It is low in absorbency (although it is more absorbent than other hydrophobic fibers such as polyester, polypropylene, or acrylic), and nylon fabrics can feel hot and sticky in warm, humid weather. A tightly woven, light, filament nylon, which is impermeable to air, heat, or moisture, makes an excellent windbreaker or raincoat, but it may trap moisture inside and make you feel cold and clammy in winter or hot and sticky in summer. Spun nylon, used in sweaters and socks, is warmer than filament nylon because its fuzziness traps additional heat. And because nylon can be rendered into exceptionally fine, sheer, and light fabrics that air readily penetrates, it is also used for summer wear.

Newer types of nylon fabrics and new treatments applied to nylon (and other synthetics) have been developed to solve some of nylon's problems with moisture and comfort. There are now a few types of nylon that wick moisture quite effectively. Fabrics made from nylon microfibers may be waterproof yet breathable, with a pleasant hand. Such fabrics therefore have a different comfort profile from those made of older types of nylons.

Nylon is not damaged by mildew, moths, or other pests. It is much weakened by exposure to sunlight, but neither sunlight nor laundering causes dyes used on nylon fabrics to fade. Perspiration can discolor it. Many types of nylon tend to have annoying problems with pilling and static buildup. Modifications of nylon fiber that render it static resistant, however, are available.

Nylon's resilience, elasticity, and spectacular strength are relied on in a variety of highly desirable blends with both natural and synthetic fibers.

Caring for Nylon Fabrics. Care labels usually recommend laundering nylon, although in principle it is dry-cleanable. But nylon is somewhat difficult to launder well. As a hydrophobic fiber, it holds oily soils and stains rather tenaciously but at the same time needs gentle treatment. To avoid a buildup of oily soil or odor, follow the methods recommended at pages 264–65, "A Note on Caring for Hydrophobic Synthetic Fibers": frequent washing, pretreating, presoaking, plenty of detergent, warm water, and so on. Being static-prone, nylon attracts dirt and lint. It also tends to take up dirt from the wash water when it is laundered. You can use ordinary soap or detergent to launder nylon. Always wash white nylon separately from any colored fabrics, no matter how pale, because of the strong propensity of white nylon to pick up any hint of color and turn dingy. Once this happens, you will probably not be able to remove the dinginess. Bleaching is usually unnecessary. If you feel you need to use a bleach, you might try an oxygen bleach. Do not use chlorine bleach; it tends to yellow nylon.

When laundering, use gentle (slow) agitation and a slow spin (or a brief spin, if you have no choice of spin speed), with warm wash water and a cool-down rinse. Thorough rinsing is advisable. Set the dryer at low temperature, using the permanent-press cycle, which has a cool-down period, and remove promptly when dry to avoid setting in wrinkles. (Nylon is thermoplastic.) Iron at a low to medium setting.

Use a fabric softener to reduce static problems and wrinkling and to improve the hand.

To reduce pilling, turn articles inside out for washing and drying, use plenty of water, and keep the agitation and tumbling periods short.

Polyester

If nylon is the king of synthetics, polyester is the queen. Like nylon, it is produced from substances derived from coal, petroleum, air, and water. As with nylon, its introduction was heralded by an enormously successful advertising campaign whose most memorable moment was the exhibition at a press conference of a man's suit that had been worn for sixty-seven days, immersed twice in a swimming pool, machine-washed, and never pressed. The suit was still wearable.

Polyester fiber comes in many chemical and structural varieties, each with characteristics different from the others, some expensive and some inexpensive. Polyester filaments of different shapes may be created, and these will have distinct properties. The basic solution out of which the filaments are made may be modified by the addition of substances that produce various effects. Special finishes may be applied to the filaments. As with other synthetics and silk, the fibers can be rendered into filament yarns or spun yarns. Because of all the variations, only rough generalizations about polyester are possible.

Properties of Polyester. Many polyester fabrics are crisp and light, but they can be found in medium and heavy weights too. Polyester fabrics are made in both lustrous and nonlustrous versions, napped and not napped, with and without bulk, and in knits and wovens. They tend to drape fairly well. (Fabrics made from spun polyester yarns drape better than those made from filament yarns.) Their hand can be slightly harsh, but in some types, especially newer ones and in "microfiber" versions, the hand can be soft, silky, or satiny, and generally quite pleasant to the touch. An outstanding characteristic of polyester fabric is its great resilience (wrinkle resistance); it needs little or no ironing. A highly thermoplastic fiber, polyester readily heat-sets into permanent creases. Ordinary polyester is an inabsorbent, low-wicking, hydrophobic fiber; but modern variants and treatments have been developed to alter these characteristics.

As a group, polyester fabrics are quite strong and durable, but they range from relatively weak to exceptionally strong. None of them weakens when wet. Polyester fabric is highly abrasion resistant, but it tends to pill. There are pill-resistant variants. (These, however, are said to lose some abrasion resistance.) Polyester fabrics have some elasticity but much less than nylon; they do not stretch or bag or shrink.

Polyester fabrics can be warm or cool to wear, depending on their construction. New variants are vaunted as having state-of-the-art heat-insulating capacities. The inabsorbency and nonwicking character of most unmodified polyester, however, means that many find it uncomfortable worn next to the skin, as it traps moisture. There are new types of polyester designed to wick moisture well—some actually have tubes or channels in the fibers through which moisture can pass—and these are said to be more comfortable. There are also variants that are more absorbent. Polyester's inabsorbency, however, means that it dries quickly and does not stain easily, except by oil, which stains it readily. Most polyester accumulates static electricity, but there are static-resistant variants.

Polyester fabrics are resistant to damage from both alkalies and most acids. Polyesters have good resistance to damage by sunlight, are unaffected by mildew, moths, and other insects, have good colorfastness, and are usually quite impervious to damage by perspiration.

Like some other hydrophobic fabrics, polyester tends to retain body odors. Polyester athletic wear has sometimes received antimicrobial treatments that help to reduce the odor problem. Soil-resistance treatments are sometimes used to help achieve better laundering results.

Caring for Polyester Fabrics. Polyester fabrics may be dry-cleaned or laundered. Because polyester fiber often holds static electricity, it also tends to attract and hold dirt and lint. Any ordinary laundry detergent can be used to launder it, and any ordinary household bleach can be used. But white polyester very often stays white without bleaching. Fairly warm water is safe to use. To conquer the oil-stain and odor problems, wash frequently, pretreat the problem areas, use a presoaking period, use plenty of detergent, and use warm or hot rather than cold water. (See "A Note on Caring for Hydrophobic Synthetic Fibers," pages 264–65.) One text particularly recommends using pretreatment products that contain organic solvents and detergents that contain grease- or soil-release agents. (See "Pretreatments and prewash stain removers," in the Glossary of Laundry Products and Additives, pages 326–27.)

When polyester is properly dyed, it is highly colorfast in laundering. But if residual dye remains in the fabric, it can bleed into the laundry water and badly stain certain other fabrics, such as acetate and nylon. To test for this, touch some acetone (acetone nail polish remover will do) on an out-of-sight spot on a new polyester garment. If you get color removal, wash the garment separately at first.

Drying polyester in a dryer is recommended because the fluffing helps prevent wrinkling, but clothes should be removed promptly from the dryer or wrinkles may be set in. Use the permanent-press cycle, which has an automatic cool-down. Use fabric softener if necessary to soften or reduce static cling. It will probably not be necessary to use it at every laundering.

Polyester fabrics do not wrinkle much, but if any ironing becomes necessary, they should be ironed at a low to medium setting. They will melt with excessive heat.

To reduce pilling, wash and dry polyester garments turned inside out, reduce agitation and tumbling time as much as possible, and use plenty of water.

Acrylics

Acrylic (polyacrylonitrile) and modacrylic are made from petroleum derivatives. The modacrylics are modified acrylics with slightly different properties.

Acrylic tends to be used as a staple fiber in fabrics that are soft and woolly, fluffy, or fuzzy; most acrylic fabrics look and feel like wool. But there are some smooth acrylics and some that feel like cotton fabrics. Acrylic fabrics are made into a wide range of garments and furnishings, from sweaters and sportswear to rugs and draperies. Modacrylics, which can be soft and fleecy or furry, are often used in fake furs, wigs, carpets, and draperies; because they have good flame resistance, they are also used in children's sleepwear. Both acrylics and modacrylics are well suited to napped and pile constructions.

Properties of Acrylic and Modacrylic. The various types of acrylic and modacrylic fibers bear a family resemblance to one another, but the two fiber families also have some significant differences. Used often as a wool substitute, both have the virtue of being light and warm yet stronger and less expensive than wool. Their strength, however, is less than that of linen, cotton, or silk. Acrylics weaken when wet; modacrylics do not.

Fabrics made from these fibers have fair to good abrasion resistance and very good to excellent resilience (wrinkle resistance). They tend to pill, but not always. All have little elasticity and do not stretch (unless the yarn is crimped) or sag. They will not shrink unless exposed to high temperatures or steam. Acrylic and modacrylic fibers are thermoplastic and can be heat-set to retain pleats and creases.

Acrylic and modacrylic fabrics have low absorbency and can be uncomfortable in muggy weather. All will hold static electricity unless treated. All are oleophilic—oil-loving—and prone to being stained by oil. They have good to excellent resistance to ultraviolet radiation and usually have good resistance to perspiration. They are unaffected by mildew or by moths or other insects. They have good colorfastness. Modacrylics are flame resistant. Pilling is a problem with many acrylics. For those who find wool irritating, acrylics are an excellent alternative. Acetone and acetone-containing substances such as nail-polish removers will harm modacrylics.

Caring for Acrylic and Modacrylic Fabrics. The suggestions that follow are generally applicable, but particular finishes or constructions might require different treatment. Pay careful attention to care label instructions on acrylic and modacrylic fabrics. A "dry-clean only" instruction on a care label may mean that the fabric has been given a water-soluble finish that, if removed by laundering, will leave the fabric with a harsh hand.

Acrylics tend to hold oily soil and body odors. Because they develop static electricity, these fibers also tend to attract and hold dirt. Frequent cleaning, pretreating, presoaking, and using plenty of detergent will help resolve any such problems. Dry cleaning is not usually recommended, but in principle almost all types of acrylic and modacrylic may be dry-cleaned. They may also readily be laundered with mild soap or detergent in *cool* water—acrylics are highly heat-sensitive and will shrink—on the *gentle* cycle or by hand, without wringing, rubbing, or twisting. But modacrylic fabrics with a pile construction should usually be dry-cleaned only or treated with a fur-cleaning process. Household bleaches may be used. To avoid static problems, reduce wrinkling, and give a good hand, use a fabric softener.

For those acrylic or modacrylic fibers that are prone to pilling, the problem may yield to the usual precautions: turn such articles inside out for laundering and drying, use plenty of water, and keep the agitation and tumbling periods short. More delicate articles should be hand-washed. If the article is being hand-washed, avoid rubbing or wringing.

Woven and firmly knitted acrylic fabrics should usually be dripped dry. Heavy acrylic knits should be dried flat. Sometimes you can tumble them dry on a low heat, but you *must* include a cool-down period. Be careful to keep the dryer temperature low.

Ironing may not be necessary at all. If it is, use a low iron setting.

Spandex

Spandex, developed in the 1950s and early 1960s, is the generic name for a group of fibers made of different types of polyurethane. (In Europe, spandex fibers are called elastane. Lycra is a trade name for spandex) Spandex fibers are "elastomeric," that is, very stretchy. And, as everyone knows who has worn fabrics that contain spandex, it is stretchy in a different way from nylon or other stretch fabrics. The fibers of the latter do not really stretch much; their elasticity comes from the straightening out of crimps in the filaments. Spandex, by contrast, can pull out to five or more times its own length and promptly contract to its original size. Its stretchiness makes it ideal for athletic clothes, tights, knits, sportswear, foundation garments, support hose and swimsuits.

Properties of Spandex. Spandex fibers are rather weak. Nonetheless, they are durable because they have good abrasion resistance and such great elasticity that in ordinary wear they are never stretched far enough to reach their breaking point. They are extremely resilient and flexible, so fabrics of spandex appear smooth, unwrinkled, and neat. Spandex itself does not pill, but fabrics containing spandex often pill because they contain other fibers that do.

Spandex is highly inabsorbent, even more so than polyester. Spandex fabrics are virtually all blends that include only a small percentage of spandex. The other fibers usually comprise more than 90% of the fabric by weight. Exercise clothes, for example, might be made with a small amount of spandex and a large amount of cotton, producing a fabric that is at once cool, absorbent, and stretchy. It is because these blends have so little spandex that they are so comfortable. Foundation garment and swimsuit fabrics usually include a larger percentage of spandex—from 15 percent to 50 percent.

Spandex has good resistance to light. All types of spandex are unaffected by mildew or by moths or other insects. Colorfastness varies from poor to good. All types of spandex resist damage from sea water, perspiration, body oils, cosmetics, and suntan lotions, which is important in fabrics used for exercise, foundation garments, and swimwear.

Caring for Spandex Fabrics. Because spandex is almost always found in blended fabrics that include much more of the other fibers than of spandex, it is important to read the care and content labels carefully. A rule of thumb in laundering blends, aside from following care instructions, is to use the most conservative procedures required by any fibers present. The suggestions offered below are applicable to spandex alone, not to any fibers it might be blended with.

All spandex fibers can be both dry-cleaned and laundered. They are machine washable with ordinary soaps and detergents in warm, not hot, water; high heat will damage the elasticity. Wash whites separately. Some care labels on spandex-blend garments recommend drip drying; if you are careful, you can machine-dry on a low setting. Delicate articles, however, should be hand-washed and line-dried.

White spandex may be yellowed by body oils, perspiration, chlorine bleach, and smog.

To avoid yellowing, launder frequently and use a nonchlorine household bleach. Spandex fibers might be weakened or yellowed if exposed to a chlorine bleach. The spandex in swimsuits gradually deteriorates—and loses elasticity—after repeated exposures to the chlorine in swimming pools. (The spandex is usually hidden, however, so that if yellowing also occurs, it often cannot be seen.) Your spandex-blend swimsuits will last longer if you rinse them out after you wear them to swim in chlorinated water. Sodium perborate bleaches are safe for spandex. (See "Bleaches" in the glossary at the end of chapter 21.)

Spandex fibers do not shrink in water, but some will lose elasticity and weaken if exposed to hot water. Avoid high temperatures in the dryer and on the iron. If ironing is necessary, iron quickly on a low setting.

Olefins (Polypropylene)

Olefins are produced from ethylene and from propylene, petroleum by-products that are inexpensive and available in great quantities. The olefin fiber most used in the home is polypropylene. It is a fiber with many excellent traits, as well as a few negative ones that limit its uses. Currently it is used for, among other things, rugs, upholstery fabrics, rope, disposable diapers, and apparel, especially sportswear and activewear. Polyethylene, which is used for furnishings, car upholstery, blinds, and awnings, is omitted from the discussion that follows. It differs substantially in character from polypropylene and is much more limited in use.

Properties of Polypropylene. Polypropylene is extremely lightweight—the lightest of any fiber. It can be made into very lightweight, warm sweaters and blankets. Among its other merits are that it can be made into fabrics that are strong, abrasion resistant, and wrinkle resistant. Polypropylene fabrics can be heat-set into creases that are permanent, so long as they are not exposed to high temperatures. Polypropylene fibers are extremely inabsorbent (the least absorbent of all the synthetic fibers). Some assert that polypropylene wicks extremely well, and it has become a popular choice for active sportswear. Whether or not polypropylene fibers actually wick well, however, is a matter of debate. Unlike a fabric made from a hydrophilic, absorbent fiber such as cotton, polypropylene fabric will not become soaked with perspiration and lose its heat-insulating ability; thus it has been favored for cold-weather sportswear. And unlike many other synthetic fibers, it resists static buildup. Polypropylene is not harmed by mildew or by moths or other insects. Pilling is often a problem for polypropylene fabrics.

Other problems that afflict polypropylene fabrics are poor dyeability (which producers have made slow progress in improving), strong sensitivity to heat and light (it has the lowest resistance to ultraviolet radiation of all fibers), extremely low absorbency, and ready oil-staining and odor-holding. Its heat and light sensitivity can be substantially reduced with chemical additives, resulting in fibers with adequate resistance for most uses. Its laundering problems, especially those caused by polypropylene's oleophilic tendencies, are less tractable.

Caring for Polypropylene Fabrics. Like other hydrophobic, oleophilic fibers, polypropylene is prone to retaining oily soils from, for instance, food spills or the body. On the other hand, it is quite resistant to water-based stains, which can sometimes just be wiped off—a real virtue in carpeting. Dry cleaning is not usually recommended for polypropylene because it shrinks in perchlorethylene, the most commonly used dry-cleaning fluid; if dry cleaning is recommended, an alternative solvent will be specified on the care label. If dry cleaning is necessary, the cleaner should be made aware of the item's fiber content.

Unfortunately, polypropylene does not readily launder clean, as it can take neither hot water (it shrinks) nor vigorous agitation. Polypropylene may be washed only in warm or cool water, with gentle agitation. Most soaps, detergents, and bleaches may be used. Because it is prone to oil-staining and holding body odors, getting it really clean and fresh is difficult. Polypropylene tends to be low in static, but if you do have a static problem, use a fabric softener. Because it is quite heat sensitive, line-dry or tumble dry polypropylene with cool air or at the lowest dryer setting followed by a cool-down period. It dries very readily, so do not be tempted to turn up the heat out of fear that otherwise it will take forever to dry. Be most careful with irons! If an iron touches polypropylene fabric, it may melt; using a press cloth with a cool iron is wise.

Microfibers

Microdenier, or microfiber, fabrics are woven from superfine fibers. You will sometimes see the term "microfiber" used to refer solely to polyester microfibers, these being the most familiar in apparel, but there are also rayon, nylon, and acrylic microfibers.

Only in the past decade have manufacturers begun to produce superfine fibers or microfibers, generally defined as those of less than one denier. The sizes of silk and man-made fibers are specified in "deniers," or in terms of their linear density.[2] One denier of a given fiber is defined as the weight in grams of 9,000 meters of the fiber. For example, if 9,000 meters of polyester weighed 1 gram, this polyester would be 1-denier; if 9,000 meters of it weighed 3 grams, it would be 3-denier. (A "tex" is $^1/_9$ of a denier, or the weight in grams of 1000 meters of fiber.) Higher deniers (or tex numbers) imply bigger (greater diameter) fibers, but because different kinds of fibers have different weights, you cannot conclude that 1-denier nylon is the same diameter as 1-denier polyester. The first microfibers were one denier, or about the same denier as silk. Now manufacturers sometimes use even "ultrafine" microfibers, with a denier of 0.3 or less. Until these developments, man-made fibers were either fine (less than or equal to 2.2 denier, medium (2.2 to 6.3 denier) or coarse (greater than 6.3 up to 25 denier).

A yarn composed of microfibers contains more filaments and has more surface area than yarn with the same diameter that is composed of regular fibers. This produces a number of effects. All microfiber fabrics tend to have a very soft, silky hand and excellent drapability, strength, great abrasion resistance, more warmth (because they trap more air), and improved moisture wicking, which contributes to improved comfort. They resist pilling. They are well suited for outerwear, providing both excellent water repellency and good breathability. They can also show superb color contrasts in prints. Microfibers frequently contribute to excellent blends.

Despite the improvement in hand, some observers say that microfibers still look synthetic and lack the beauty of natural fibers. They tend to be expensive—often as expensive as silk—and they tend to retain the general characteristics of whatever synthetic they are made of. For example, polyester microfibers are inabsorbent, may oil-stain, and may develop static unless they receive modifications or treatments to control such problems. Microfibers may be more heat sensitive because their thin fibers are more readily penetrated by heat. One reliable source recommends that you use only a cool iron on polyester and nylon microfibers to avoid glazing or melting the fabric and that you avoid applying heavy pressure with an iron, which can cause shine and ridges on the fabric.[3]

Blends

Blends are fabrics that contain two or more fibers, which may be natural, synthetic, or both. The qualities of blends depend on the proportions of each fiber in the blend and on the finishes and treatments that are applied to it. In judging the characteristics of blends, a rule of thumb is that the resulting fabric will have the properties of each fiber in the degree to which that fiber is present in the blend. The most successful blends unite the best qualities of the blended fibers, but there are often trade-offs. Cotton/polyester blends are more wrinkle resistant than 100% cotton fabrics and more comfortable than 100% polyester fabrics. However, they can pill (like polyester) and overall may be more likely to stain than either polyester or 100% cotton because they may contain the vulnerabilities of both fibers. Blends improperly made or cared for may lose shape or pucker if one fiber shrinks and the other does not. Skillfully made blends, however, often unite superb looks, easy care, and excellent performance.

Examples of deservedly popular blends are far too numerous to list. Cotton/rayon blends often have better crispness, luster, sheen, and hand than a fine 100% cotton. With the proper treatments, cotton/rayon blends may also have better shape retention, washing properties, and strength than a 100% cotton given similar treatments. Rayons with good resistance to alkalies can be mercerized in cotton blends, and wrinkle-resistance treatments weaken them less than they weaken cotton or other types of rayon. Rayon or cotton will contribute good hand, looks, and absorbency when blended with polyester, acrylic, triacetate, or nylon.

A polyester/rayon or polyester/cotton blend is likely to look and feel better than 100% polyester but will often fall short of the comfort and good hand of a fabric containing all cotton or rayon or a fabric with a higher percentage of cotton or rayon. The more polyester the article contains, the more wash-and-wear properties it will have, but a higher percentage of cotton or rayon than polyester will give the fabric greater absorbency and a better hand. When cotton/polyester blends are given wrinkle-resistance treatments, polyester's strength is important because cotton is weakened by the finishing process.

Blended with wool, polyester and other synthetics enhance abrasion resistance and easy-care properties (wrinkle resistance, crease retention) and help to prevent sagging, bagging, and stretching. The wool adds beauty, warmth, and elasticity. The greater the percentage of wool, the warmer the blend will be and the less likely to pill (but not all such blends are prone to pilling). A garment of wool and triacetate is cooler than wool alone, is more wrinkle resistant, and holds its shape better.

A Note on Caring for Hydrophobic Synthetic Fibers

Hydrophilic fibers (all the natural fibers and rayon and lyocell) absorb both oily and water-soluble soils, but since they also absorb water and detergent very readily, they tend to give up both types of soil easily too. Man-made fibers such as polyester, nylon, triacetate and acetate, spandex, polypropylene (olefin), acrylic, and modacrylic are all, to one degree or another, hydrophobic. Polypropylene and polyester are exceedingly hydrophobic, and nylon is moderately so. Hydrophobic fibers do not readily absorb water; they may even repel it, and it takes them longer to get wet. They do, however, readily retain oil (they are oleophilic) and do not readily give it up. On the positive side, this means that they shrink less and tend to repel water-based stains, such as coffee and sugary stains, just as they tend to repel water. On the negative side, because it is so hard to get them good and wet, it can also be hard to get them good and clean—especially when it comes to oily dirt and stains, such as greasy tomato sauce. They may retain body odors and oils. Fabrics made from synthetic fibers tend to pill.

Synthetic fibers, for the foregoing reasons, in most ways require the same type of laundering as resin-treated cottons and cotton blends. Laundering frequently, pretreating (particularly with solvent-containing pretreatment products), using plenty of detergent, and using the warmest water the fiber will tolerate—all the procedures recommended for resin-treated cloth—help conquer the oily soil and odor problems that you sometimes experience with synthetics. Turning garments made of synthetic fibers or their blends inside out helps too, as this reduces pilling. Use the permanent-press cycle on your washer, with its cool-down rinse and slower spin, with plenty of water, and avoid overcrowding, so as to reduce or avoid wrinkling and excess abrasion in the washer; the dryer's permanent-press setting, too, includes a cool-down period so that hot clothes do not sit and wrinkle.

Because hydrophobic fibers resist wetting, the main trick in laundering them is to leave them in the water for a longer time than you ordinarily need with cottons and linens. The best way to do this is with a good long presoak with plenty of detergent or a presoak product in the hottest water safe for the fiber. You can also increase the wash/agitation period, but this increases the amount of abrasion the fabric is exposed to and hence may increase pilling too.

If oil stains will not respond to laundering, dry-cleaning solvents or stain removers containing dry-cleaning solvents, whether used professionally or at home, will often work. If you use them yourself, observe all cautions on labels. They are highly flammable.

Soil-release treatments are often applied to synthetic and wrinkle-treated fibers. These are chemical finishes that make the fibers more absorbent and hence more wettable. They work well at improving the washability of these fabrics for as long as they last, but such treatments tend to become less effective over time. Some last longer than others. If treated with soil-release finishes, permanent-press clothes will generally wash free of both oil- and water-based stains in ordinary home washing procedures. Some types of durable-press and wash-and-wear fabrics are treated with antimicrobials to reduce odor problems.

18

Fabrics That Work

General guidelines for choosing fabrics for clothes or furnishings . . . Choosing ultraviolet-light-resistant fabrics . . . Dish towels and dishcloths . . . Bath towels and hand towels . . . Bath rugs and mats . . . Table linens, sizes of tablecloths and napkins . . . Upholstery . . . Rugs and carpets . . . Carpet padding or underlay . . . Clothes that are cool, warm, low- or no-iron, UV protective

A beautiful cotton tablecloth I once bought turned out to be a madras print with bleeding dyes, a fact I discovered only when I brought it home and read all its labels. Such dyes are unsuitable for a tablecloth, which requires frequent, vigorous laundering. Because this madras cloth had to be washed in cold water, separately from the rest of the laundry, I could not get oily food spots out of it. Even with cold-water washing, its lovely colors turned muddy after only two or three trips through the washer, and it became downright ugly. If I had read labels before I bought it, instead of letting my eyes make the decision, I could have had an equally pretty cloth that would have stayed pretty.

The lesson here is that you cannot assume that an article sold for a particular function is well designed to perform that function. The store shelves all too often contain eye-catching textile goods that do not make sense when you try to use them. Suggestions for finding fabrics that work in household jobs, from towels to upholstery, and for avoiding the frustration, expense, and inconvenience of poor choices, are set forth in the material below. For guidance on how to choose bed linens and blankets, see chapter 57, "Beds and Bedding."

Choosing Fabrics for Clothes or Furnishings—In General

Read the care label, the fiber content label, and any other information on labels or pack-

Flat-felled seams on denims

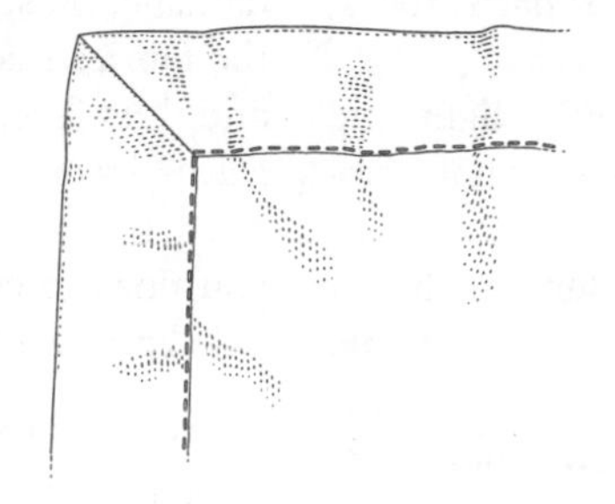

Mitered corner

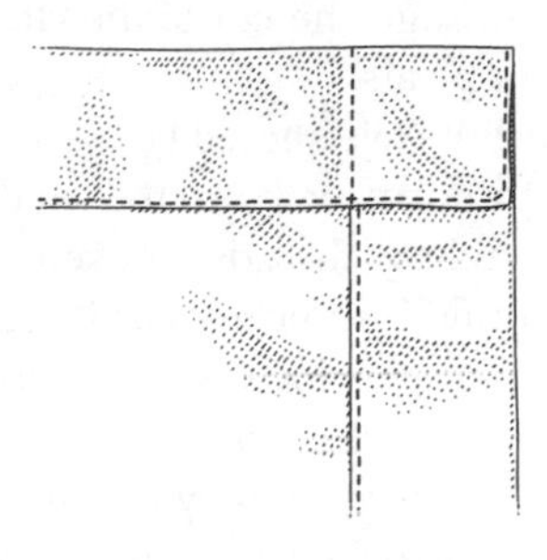

Nonmitered corner

ages before buying. Look for logos that convey information about the nature or origin of a fabric. Look for evidence of finishing treatments or types of dye used, for example, a tag that says that an article is vat-dyed or yarn-dyed, or is a madras print. If an article's care instructions are not appropriate for the use you intend, consider whether you should try to find one with more appropriate care instructions or whether it would be wise to risk ignoring the care label. Avoid inexpensive goods that are expensive or impossible to clean.

Carefully examine clothes and furnishings inside and out before buying. Evaluate them in terms of probable comfort, durability, and functioning: examine their construction, finishes, fiber content, and workmanship.

Buy preshrunk goods whenever possible.

Choose reputable retailers and manufacturers to reduce your risks from unknowable factors. A company whose major business for many years has been manufacturing towels is more likely to sell you a towel that performs well than a company whose major asset is a fashion logo. Of course, every rule has its exceptions, except perhaps the rule of caveat emptor.

Seams should hold together tightly and not pull apart. Look at the kinds of seams that are used. Although plain running stitch is the right type of seam on many articles, flat-felled or other reinforced seams have much more strength and are desirable in play or sports clothes. Better quality sweaters and other knits often provide a length of matching yarn attached to a hang tag for use in case you ever need to make repairs.

Stitching should be small, smooth, straight, even, and tight. Look at the hems on sheets and towels, and at the quilting stitches on mattress pads and comforters. Mitered corners are often a sign of quality in bed and table linens.

Buttons should be securely attached, with a shank or thread shank, so that they fit readily into the buttonholes. On a heavy winter coat or other heavy garments, buttons should be attached with heavy-duty thread or by some other extrastrong means. Extra buttons should be provided. Buttonholes should be neatly and closely stitched all around.

Look for linings in blazers, jackets, skirts, and other garments. These improve the wear, hang, comfort, and appearance of many kinds of clothes and are usually a sign of better quality.

Although we all sometimes like clothes of a rough cut for fashion reasons, better kinds of clothing are usually shaped to the body, sometimes so subtly you can barely detect how it is done. Look to see whether a dress or shirt is simply square or shows shaping through the cut of the cloth or darts, tucks, or pleats.

Weave should be even, close or tight, and uniform, with no crooked threads, knots, protruding threads, broken threads, or slubs (unless slubs are put there intentionally, for example, for fashion reasons). You should not see thick or thin spots except where this is done purposely for effect. You should not see crooked lines in the weave. The yarns should be of uniform size, and the individual yarns should show uniform diameter.

Goods should be cut straight. Unfold napkins and other flat goods (handkerchiefs, blankets, sheets) and hold them up to the light. You should be able to see that the threads are parallel and perpendicular to the edge of the cloth. The shape should be even and square at the corners.

Color should be even and uniform and penetrate well. Check for color penetration at the seams and darts especially.

Avoid overstarched goods—those whose appearance, body, or firmness is actually a function of starches that will launder out. If you rub the fabric between your hands, sometimes you can actually see excess starch powder out.

Choosing Ultraviolet-Light-Resistant Fibers

The chart below gives a rough ranking of the various textile fibers in accordance with their ability to resist the degradation—loss of strength, deterioration, yellowing, and other ill effects—caused by exposure to the ultraviolet radiation in sunlight and other types of light. Resistance to degradation as a result of exposure to light is obviously crucial in furnishings, especially draperies but also carpeting and upholstery. Treatments are sometimes available that increase a fiber's resistance to UV radiation, however, and other factors are also relevant. For example, southern light causes more damage than other light; higher humidity increases the rate of damage. Most importantly, the dyes used on the fabrics may have low resistance to light, and thus fade, even though the fibers themselves have good light resistance. Thus the chart gives only some of the relevant facts you need to consider when assessing probable light resistance.

Excellent Ultraviolet-Light Resistance

Acrylic

Modacrylic

Polyester

Good Resistance

Linen

Cotton

Rayon

Acetate and Triacetate

Poor Resistance

Nylon

Wool

Silk

Olefin/Polypropylene

Choosing Dish Towels and Dishcloths

Functional properties

Highly absorbent

Soft, flexible

Nonlinting, especially for drying china and glass

Durable

Care characteristics

Dish towels and dishcloths must be launderable and colorfast, and they should be able to take hot washing and drying temperatures, ordinary laundry detergents, and chlorine bleaches. When you launder kitchen toweling, you want to be able to remove food stains and sanitize. Avoid buying towels with care labels that say "Wash separately" or "Wash with like colors" or "No bleach."

Good choices

There are stalwart defenders of cotton dish towels, but in my opinion linen are best. For drying glass and china they are particularly desirable because they do not lint. Huckaback or huck toweling makes a fine towel. Crash towels are also good. They are cheaper and rougher than another, finer, type of plain-weave towel called a "glass towel" or "dish towel." ("Huck," "huckaback," "crash," and other fabric terms used in this chapter are defined in the "Glossary of Fabric Terms" at the end of chapter 14.) The words "glass towel" or "dish towel" may be woven into such towels. They are indeed good for drying glass and china because they have smooth, hard-twisted yarns to prevent linting. Glass towels often come in white with blue or red checks or stripes, but some are in prints as well. Damask dish towels look beautiful but may be less absorbent because of the tightness of their weave.

Cotton towels, too, come in crash or huckaback weaves and various plain weaves, especially basket weaves. They are a bit less absorbent and more likely than linen to yellow or gray with age and to lint. But cotton still makes an excellent towel and is less expensive than linen. Good-quality cotton towels do not lint. Cotton terry-cloth dish towels are widely available in a range of styles and quality.

Glass towel

Waffle or similar spongy weaves, terry cloth, and basket weaves will be naturally wrinkle resistant, so these are for you if you can bear neither to iron dish towels nor to look at wrinkles. Crash and glass towels work fine in their wrinkled state, but you might roll them tightly around a tube while they are warm from the dryer to smooth them out. Or fold them neatly and set a weight on the stack while they are still warm. (See chapter 23, "Ironing.")

Choose dishcloths for washing dishes in any spongy, bumpy, soft weave of cotton, such as a waffle weave. The raised portions of the weave provide good friction for rubbing dishes clean, and a good, spongy weave will hold plenty of water. Thickest is not necessarily best, however, as you will be unable to get into small places with very thick fabrics and you will be less able to feel bumps through such fabrics with your fingers.

Choosing Bath and Hand Towels

Functional properties

Soft

Highly absorbent

Durable

Thick or thin, according to preference

Care characteristics

Traditional housekeepers sought bath and hand towels and washcloths able to take hot water and dryer temperatures, ordinary detergents, and—if needed—chlorine bleach. This is because you want to be able to sanitize them if necessary and to be able to remove stains and soils wiped off the skin. You will search long and hard before you find any today that have care labels permitting such vigorous laundering. But I find that towels can quite often be laundered vigorously despite care label instructions to the contrary. (See chapter 19, "Carefully Disregarding Care Labels.") Towels should always be colorfast. Avoid buying towels with care labels that say "Wash separately" or "Wash with like colors." This is a care instruction that makes no sense for towels. But care instructions to wash separately for the first two or three launderings are not objectionable, as this indicates that the towels are really colorfast but may hold some excess dye that will readily and permanently wash out.

Although colored towels are lovely, it is not a bad idea to stock some plain white towels as well. White towels, usually, can take the most vigorous laundering with hot water, strong detergents, and chlorine bleach; thus they are not hard to keep looking good. Not only are they attractive in the bath, you will find many uses for them outside the bath, such as laying wet clothes on them to dry, rolling wet clothes in them, and for hot and cold compresses; everyone finds further uses special to their own homes.

As to thickness, half the members of my family hate thick towels, insisting that they make it hard to get behind the ears or between toes. They like old towels worn to thinness or inexpensive thin, new towels. The others insist on thick towels for their luxurious softness and ability to hold more moisture.

Most towels will shrink a little; towels of lower quality may shrink greatly, often becoming misshapen in the process.

Good choices

Turkish towels or cotton terry-cloth towels, which were introduced in the late nineteenth century, are wonderfully soft and absorbent for the bath. And nothing beats cotton terry-cloth washcloths, which mildly abrade the skin to remove soil, oil, and dead cells. Although cotton is less absorbent than linen and, when dry, initially resists moisture, the loops on the face of terry towels help them to pick up more moisture and to hold more of it than other towels, including linen ones. The most absorbent towels have the most pile loops, which should be long and not too tightly twisted. When the loops are cropped to form *velour* terry, the cloth feels velvety and shows prints well but is much less absorbent. Terry towels with cotton pile and a polyester back will still be fairly absorbent, since most of the drying that your towels do is with the pile. (Polyester in the back adds strength and durability.) A tight, balanced weave, preferably a twill, is desirable. But the thread count of the towel is less important in determining absorbency than the weight of the towel: heavier towels are more absorbent.

Look for dense, thick, firm towels with high pile, even selvage edges, and small, even hem stitches. Hold terry-cloth towels up to the light to check the quality of the underlying weave. Feel it for softness and resilience. Avoid towels that lack that cottony, dry, terry-cloth feeling and instead have a certain (seductively pleasant) silky or smooth feel. In my experience, the latter are not very absorbent until they have received years of wear and grown more cottony.

TOWEL SIZES

Towel sizes are not uniform from manufacturer to manufacturer. The sizes below are common, but do not be surprised to encounter different dimensions. Store six sets of towels per person plus one or more sets for guests.

Finger or guest: 12 × 18; 11 × 16; 14 × 22

Hand: 18 × 30; 16 × 30; 20 × 32

Bath: 24 × 46; 28 × 52

Bath sheet: 38 × 72; 36 × 70; 40 × 70

Bath mat: 19 × 27; 22 × 36

Washcloth: 12 × 12; 13 × 13

Although you see extralong-staple Egyptian and Pima cotton towels praised, I prefer terry-cloth towels made of Upland cotton, which seem to me more absorbent and softer. Towels of extralong-staple cotton, however, grow softer and more absorbent as they age.

Most people in this country would never exchange the great comfort, absorbency, and reasonable prices of terry-cloth towels for old-fashioned linen bath towels. These lacked a pile and were made in a variety of weaves, such as huck, honeycomb, or waffle weave. Linen bath towels vied with terry-cloth through the opening decades of the twentieth century and are still favored in some places in Europe. They are often quite large but quickly grow damp and soaked and can chill you in cold bathrooms; they wrinkle readily. They can be quite beautiful, especially those with long, silky fringes. But although people look more elegant wrapped in the folds of fine, fringed linen fabric after a bath, people wrapped in terry towels are warmer and more comfy. If you would like to try this type of linen bath towel, the most sensible, and the warmest, have thick, spongy weaves such as waffle weave and natural colors—creams, tans, and off-whites. The most beautiful are in jacquard or dobby weaves. You may be able to find such nonterry bath towels in cottons as well.

Some companies make linen terry-cloth towels, often marketing them especially to men. These towels are invigoratingly scratchy and quite absorbent, especially after a couple of washes, but the ones I have seen are not nearly so pretty as cotton terry cloth.

Hand towels of linen are traditional. They come in beautiful damask weaves or huck, crash, honeycomb, or waffle weaves. Linen towels are absorbent and durable, do not yellow or turn gray, and can take strong laundering. Cotton terry is more absorbent than other types of cotton hand towels, but all are good. Guest hand towels often are delicate and elegant, with fringe, embroidery, cutwork, or lace. These require careful ironing to look good.

Bath Rugs and Mats

Functional properties

Absorbent

Slip resistant

Care characteristics

Bath rugs and mats should be easily launderable and colorfast. Although bleaching is not so important for bath mats and rugs as for towels and sheets, it is always easier to get out potential stains using a chlorine bleach. Nonslip backings on bathroom rugs are indispensable. (Usually you can machine launder these; if the care label says not to, do not buy the rug.) Bath mats, which are often made simply of thick, absorbent woven cotton, have no nonslip backings. Be careful using them! Laying them on a bathroom rug that has a nonslip back sometimes solves the slippage problem and keeps the rug drier as well.

Table Linen

Functional properties

Absorbent

Smooth hand

Crisp, drapable

Durable

Care characteristics

Tablecloths and napkins, ideally, should be able to take hot-water laundering, ordinary commercial detergents, and chlorine bleach, for they will be exposed to food, drink, and lipstick stains, among others. In practice, few care labels prescribe vigorous laundering for table linens. Yet unless you can at least sometimes use your strongest laundry weapons, you may not be able to keep them looking good. Although you might take risks with everyday table linens to get out stains, you can face agonizing choices when it is your beloved damasks or lace, hand-embroidered, or cutwork cloths that have become spotted. Therefore consider whether you should choose table linens that minimize such risks: whites and colorfast table linens in heavier weights, for example, are better able to endure the occasional stain-removal trauma. Linen gives up stains and soil more readily than cotton but, on the other hand, is more readily damaged by bleach.

Table linens of untreated cotton or linen will require ironing. If natural fibers receive wrinkle-resistance treatments, you may find you are satisfied with their appearance with little or no ironing. When natural fibers are blended with synthetics, too, you can often get by with little or no ironing. But both resin-treated cloth and cloth containing hydrophobic synthetic fibers tend to oil-stain. If you buy these, therefore, look for labels that say the cloth has received soil repelling and soil-releasing treatments to make laundering them easier. (See chapter 15, "Transformations," on soil-resistance treatments, pages 230–31.)

Sizes

Breakfast or lunch cloths should hang over the edge of the table from 6 to 8 inches. The dinner cloth should hang over the edge 8 to 12 inches. The more formal the occasion, the longer the desirable overhang—from 12 to 18 inches for formal dinners. There are those, however, who object to the tablecloth hitting the chair seat. More than 12 inches of overhang will cause the cloth to begin folding up on the chair. The suggestions below, there-

Shape	*Table Size*	*Cloth*	*Persons Seated*
Square	28" × 28" to 40" × 40"	52" × 52"	4
Round	30" to 42" diameter	52" round	4
	42" to 44" diameter	60" to 68"	4 to 6
	42" to 46" diameter	68" with fringe	4 to 6
	42" to 54" diameter	68" with fringe	6
	42" to 60" diameter	72" round	6
	64" to 76" diameter	90" round	6 to 8
Oblong	28" × 46" to 36" × 64"	52" × 70"	4 to 6
	36" × 56" to 42" × 62"	60" × 80"	6 to 8
	42" × 60" to 48" × 72"	72" × 90"	6 to 8
	42" × 72" to 48" × 90"	72" × 108"	8 to 10
Oval	28" × 46" to 36" × 54"	52" × 70"	4 to 6
	36" × 56" to 42" × 62"	60" × 80"	6 to 8
	42" × 60" to 48" × 72"	72" × 90"	6 to 8
	42" × 72" to 48" × 90"	72" × 108"	8 to 10

fore, are rough and must be adapted to the occasion. Allow for shrinkage in laundering when you choose your table linens. As with sheets, expect most of the shrinkage to occur in the length—up to 10 percent.

Napkin sizes have grown smaller over time, and are not particularly standardized. Hundreds of years ago, they were truly blanketlike—in the eighteenth century, perhaps a square yard or even larger—but more petite napkins are now the rule, as the expectation is that you will not soil your hands, face, or clothes while eating, or at least not much. In general, the more formal the occasion, the more ample the napkin should be. Luncheon napkins may be from 12 × 12 to 18 × 18 inches. Cocktail napkins will be even smaller. Dinner napkins vary from 18 × 18 to 24 × 24 inches. Banquet napkins may be from 24 × 24 to 32 × 32 inches.

Good choices

Linen, cotton, rayon, and blends of these with synthetic fibers are all sensible choices for tablecloths and napkins, depending on your goals. To avoid or reduce ironing, choose tablecloths and napkins in permanent press fabrics or fabrics made of synthetic fibers and their blends. For best launderability, choose untreated white cotton and linen, but plan to iron. Less absorbent fabrics, such as synthetics, blends, and resin-treated cloth, do not make ideal napkins. For formal and elegant tables, choose damask in linen or cotton. Generally speaking, you get greater durability in linens with greater weight. Those of us with a budget usually aim to have one or two elegant tablecloths for special occasions and some relatively casual ones for ordinary uses.

Extra work in laundering and ironing will usually be required if you choose tablecloths that are embroidered, have cutwork, or are lace or trimmed with lace. Although handmade lace of natural fibers is expensive and requires thoughtful laundering and ironing, machine-made lace is often easy to care for—machine washable or no-iron—and affordable.

Choosing Upholstery

Functional properties

- Durable
  - Abrasion resistant
  - Strong
- Ultraviolet light–resistant—nonfading
- Nonshrinking or preshrunk
- Colorfast
- Nonpilling
- Nonshedding
- Nonstatic
- Good hand (not harsh, slick, or scratchy)
- Flame resistant

Care characteristics

The most important care consideration is to make sure that the fabric of your upholstery is cleanable by the method you prefer to use: home or professional wet cleaning (a new professional cleaning technique that can often replace dry cleaning) or shampooing, or professional dry cleaning. If you plan on wet cleaning, you must inquire carefully about colorfastness and shrinking. Soil-repellent and soil-release treatments are *always* a good idea for upholstery fabrics.

Good choices

Almost all fibers have been adapted for use in upholstering, and well-designed blends and synthetics are often good choices. When you choose a synthetic or blend, inquire about whether it is prone to the problems that synthetics often face, such as pilling and static. People most often go wrong when they buy a fabric for upholstering which is intended for draperies, apparel, or some other use, and thus lacks the strength and abrasion resistance that upholstery fabrics need for enduring the hard wear they will receive. Silk is elegant and beautiful, but it stains readily and cannot take much abrasion; thus it is not a practical choice for places that will get hard use or in places where children and pets will play.

Choosing Rugs and Carpets

Functional properties

Durable

Abrasion resistant

Resilient

Nonpilling

Nonshedding

Nonstatic

Ultraviolet light–resistant—nonfading

Colorfast

Flame resistant

Care characteristics

As with upholstery, the most important consideration is to make sure that a rug or carpet you are buying can be cleaned by the method you would plan to use on it: can it be cleaned by home shampooing using a machine or professional cleaning, or must it receive gentle hand cleaning? Soil-repellency or soil-release treatments are a good idea, and some carpets are more naturally stain resistant than others.

Good choices

See chapter 35, "Textile Furnishings."

Choosing Carpet Padding, Cushion, or Underlay

Functional properties

Level of cushioning
  Proportional to carpet
  Thickness proper for comfort
Insulating effect
  Noise
  Heat and cold
Nonmildewing

Care characteristics

This is not usually an issue. Carpet padding is generally cared for by vacuuming now and then.

Good choices

Other things being equal, choose thinner padding for thinner carpets and thicker padding for thicker carpets, but the Carpet and Rug Institute recommends a maximum thickness of 7/16 of an inch. For high-traffic areas, choose less cushiony, harder types. It is tiring to walk a great deal on a highly cushioned surface, and also difficult when you are wearing high-heeled shoes. For low traffic, softer types of padding will work. A thicker padding is good where you want noise insulation.

Have the pad cut to the correct size. If you have a carpet pad that does not extend to the edge of the carpet, over the years this can cause premature wear; an unattractive line can develop at the place in the carpet where the pad stops. The thicker the pad, the worse this problem can be. A carpet pad that is larger than the carpet is unsightly.

When evaluating durability, remember that jute will mildew if it gets damp and a synthetic will not. Fiberglass-based pads are recommended for high-traffic areas and for rugs on which office chairs or other rolling or frequently moved furniture are placed; they last longer and are less likely to disintegrate under such pressure than other types of padding. Sponge rubber is available in various thicknesses and degrees of firmness, but only thinner, firmer types will be sufficiently durable for high-traffic areas. Polyurethane foam is also available; the type I have experience with was best suited for lighter uses, as in a small child's room. Felted padding made of hair is sold in many thicknesses and degrees of firmness, but it is not very durable and should not be used in heavy traffic areas.

Clothing

To stay cool, look for:

Fabrics of linen, cotton, rayon

Absorbent fibers

Smooth fibers and fabrics (avoid spun fibers, or napped, pile, or fuzzy fabrics)

Open, smoother, looser weaves or knits such as mesh or seersucker

Lightweight fabrics

Light colors

To stay warm, choose:

Wool and acrylic

Fuzzy fibers, crimped fibers

Fabrics with pile or nap

Tight weaves, thick weaves, thick knits, satin weaves, especially in heavier weights

Heavyweight fabrics

Dark colors

To reduce ironing, choose:

Any woven synthetic other than rayon; wool; silk; permanent-press and wash-and-wear clothes

Seersucker

Waffle weaves and similar weaves

Napped or pile fabrics

Knits of all sorts

Corduroy

To gain protection from the sun's ultraviolet rays, choose:

Tightly woven fabrics (avoid loose or open weaves such as basket weaves or gauze)

Blue denim

Satin weaves and other smooth-surface weaves

Fabrics treated to render them UV resistant

Dark colors

Dry clothes—wet ones transmit more UV radiation

See also chapter 15, page 231.

19

Carefully Disregarding Care Labels

Inaccuracy of many care labels, low labeling . . . FTC regulations; how to interpret care labels . . . What the care label means when it is silent, when it gives warnings, when it does not mention ironing, and when it prescribes no bleach or non-chlorine bleach . . . What care labels do not have to tell you . . . When to disregard care labels and when not to . . . What to do when the care label procedure causes damage . . . Glossary of care label terms and symbols

Following Dr. Seuss's example, I feel obliged to warn the reader that this chapter is dangerous. It contains advice on when and why you might wish to disobey that fundamental law of the modern laundry: "Follow the instructions on the care label!" Those of you who are beginners *should* follow the care labels unless it is clear you have nothing to lose—for example, when the garment looks so awful that you are never going to wear it again in its present state and there is no way to remedy it if you limit yourself to care label instructions. Even then, you have to think of your chagrin when someday you find out that you could have saved it by trying another remedy that you had not known about. If this sounds too frustrating, follow that care label, or hand the problem over to a professional. Otherwise you risk the destruction of your fabrics, their colors, or their appearance. I have handed garments to my dry cleaner saying, "Try anything. It's ruined as it is, so I will not blame you if you make it even worse trying to fix it."

Those of you who are not beginners should also be prepared to accept the risks, because in this area no one can offer you certainty, least of all someone who has never even seen the fabric or problem you are dealing with. First survey the risks (including the possibility that you might render a wearable garment unwearable) in your mind and decide if you can accept failure. Remember, if it is a T-shirt, this means merely a little money and some inconvenience; if it is an expensive cashmere sweater, this could leave you with quite a hole in your pocket and nothing to wear this weekend.

The Uses and Limits of Care Labels

All wearing apparel (except footwear, gloves, hats, and other head and hand coverings) and piece goods used for home sewing of apparel sold in this country, including imported clothes and piece goods, are subject to the care labeling rules promulgated by the Federal Trade Commission. These rules require the manufacturer to attach a permanent label to each garment telling the buyer how to clean it. The regulations require that the label tell you at least one form of regular care, washing or dry cleaning, needed for the ordinary use and enjoyment of the product, and that it warn the buyer against procedures that the buyer might assume are safe if in fact they would result in damage to the product or others being laundered with it.* The instructions on the label must cover trim, lining, buttons, and any other permanent part of the garment.

Surveys show that most home launderers pay attention to instructions on care labels, and textile and laundering experts unanimously advise you to follow care labels. If you do not, you run the risk of ruining your garments and ruining your chances of a refund or replacement as well, for if you follow improper laundering procedures, any damage is considered your own fault. This seems fair enough until you look at some of the practicalities.

Every home launderer will have had plenty of experiences like my own with care labels. Among my son's new school clothes one year, for example, were two 100% cotton knit shirts, one in green and one in red, made by different manufacturers and bought at different stores. I would have bought neither of them if I had bothered to read the care labels, which specify treatment that is not the most practical for the clothes of the active son of busy parents: "Wash separately, cool water. Dry flat." One of the shirts bled dye at every washing, even in cool water; it faded quickly and accumulated some oily stains that were impossible to get out with cool water. The other shirt never bled dye at all, not even in hot water, never faded, and shrank just enough to fit perfectly, even after repeated tumble-drying on low heat. Its care label instructions were flat wrong, but there was no way to determine this without bringing it home and experimenting; it looked just like the other shirt, which really did require separate washing.

For another example, I have an oversized, white cotton T-shirt that I bought in 1986 whose care label says, "Machine wash warm. No bleach." I have machine-washed it in hot water hundreds of times, usually with chlorine bleach. It has hardly shrunk at all, and although it has become comfortably soft and thin after more than a decade of good wear, it still looks white and attractive. Overcautious labels when it comes to bleaching appear to me to be almost the rule rather than the exception, but the problem is the opposite

*In a few instances, the care instructions may appear on a hang tag or package rather than being permanently affixed to the garment. This is true of reversible clothes whose appearance might be ruined by a visible label. It is also true of garments that can be cleaned by any normal methods without harm. In the latter case, the hang tag must show the statement "Wash or dry-clean, any normal method." This means that you may wash and dry at hot temperatures, use all types of bleaches, including chlorine bleaches, and dry-clean with any ordinary solvents. If a product cannot be cleaned by any method, the manufacturer is required to attach a label saying so—for example, "Do not wash, do not dry-clean" or "Cannot be successfully cleaned."

when it comes to ironing. My family's closets are full of shirts that lack any care label instruction as to ironing but that nonetheless require regular ironing to look presentable.

As an experiment, I once sorted my laundry according to the exact instructions on the care labels. Although in quantity I had enough to make up three or four good-sized loads, if I had obeyed the labels I would have had to wash at least three times that many loads, as practically no two garments were labeled identically. No experienced home launderer actually washes twelve or more loads instead of four. Thus we all become care label skeptics, defying the labels without hesitation.

Inaccurate labeling and "low labeling" (labels that prescribe more conservative care than the garment really needs) are both quite common. Nonetheless, some of our skepticism about labels is in fact mistaken. We might fail to recognize that a label is accurate if (for example) a garment labeled "Dry-clean only" seems perfectly all right after being laundered. The effects of laundering may become apparent only after the third or fourth wash, and those effects may include shrinkage, fading, weakening, or the loss of beneficial treatments and finishes. By the time you discover that the label was right all along, it is too late to save the garment.

In other cases, a garment's care label simply cannot give the whole picture. Knowledgeable readers will appreciate, given how complicated a fabric's cleaning story can be, that manufacturers should not be faulted for not getting all the nuances on a square inch or two of care label. Moreover, what constitutes the "best" treatment will in some respects turn on the goals and skills of the person who will apply it: Is longer wear or whiter appearance more important? Is expense any object? Is the buyer a skilled and willing ironer?

A care label is intended to help you launder safely and effectively by giving you some simple guidelines. Care labels are not intended to do away with your need to know, more or less, what you are doing when you putter around in the laundry. I have often wondered whether we would be better off if we had regulations that required manufacturers to inform us about the characteristics of the products instead of the rather authoritarian care label system that asks us to obey simple-minded instructions blindly without giving us any hint of the reasons behind them. But because there is no likelihood that the system will change, you are going to find yourself wanting and needing to use laundry procedures other than the ones that are recommended on the labels.

There are three main reasons to ignore care labels sometimes. The first is that you want to do a better job than you believe is possible with the recommended treatment. The second is that you want to take less trouble or expense than you believe is necessary to get the garment clean safely and effectively. The third is that you want to wash in one load clothes whose care labels would require different treatment. Before you can decide to ignore a label you need to be able to make educated guesses about whether an alternative procedure is safe. This requires being able to spot potential problems and decide when the risk is worth it. *You must also be prepared to accept the loss when you guess wrong.* I repeat: If you are a novice, just follow the care labels. The less you know, the greater the risks of doing anything else. Sooner or later, however, every novice develops an instinct for fibers, fabrics, and laundering, and discovers for himself or herself when the risks are small enough to justify taking a chance.

The FTC Regulations: What Care Labels Tell You

The glossary at the end of this chapter sets forth definitions of certain standard terms and symbols that are permitted on permanent care labels. If you do not know the meaning of terms or symbols on your clothes' care labels, refer to this glossary. Better yet, photocopy it and tape it to the wall or put it on a bulletin board in your laundry.

When manufacturers write care labels, they are obliged to do so the way the FTC regulations tell them to. The heart of the rules they must obey is contained in the following provisions quoted from the regulations, which deal with washing and dry-cleaning instructions on care labels:

(1) Washing, drying, ironing, bleaching, and warning instructions must follow these requirements:

(i) Washing. The label must state whether the product should be washed by hand or machine. The label must also state a water temperature that may be used. However, if the regular use of hot water will not harm the product, the label need not mention any water temperature. [For example, "Machine wash" means hot, warm, or cold water can be used.]

(ii) Drying. The label must state whether the product should be dried by machine or by some other method. If machine drying is called for, the label must also state a drying temperature that may be used. However, if the regular use of a high temperature will not harm the product, the label need not mention any drying temperature. [For example, "Tumble dry" means that a high, medium, or low temperature can be used.]

(iii) Ironing. Ironing must be mentioned on a label only if it will be needed on a regular basis to preserve the appearance of the product, or if it is required under paragraph (b) (1) (v) of this section, Warnings. If ironing is mentioned, the label must also state an ironing temperature that may be used. However, if the regular use of a hot iron will not harm the product, the label need not mention any ironing temperature.

(iv) Bleaching.

(A) If all commercially available bleaches can safely be used on a regular basis, the label need not mention bleaching.

(B) If all commercially available bleaches would harm the product when used on a regular basis, the label must say "No bleach" or "Do not bleach."

(C) If regular use of chlorine bleach would harm the product, but regular use of a non-chlorine bleach would not, the label must say "Only non-chlorine bleach, when needed."

(v) Warnings.

(A) If there is any part of the prescribed washing procedure which consumers can reasonably be expected to use that would harm the product or others being washed with it in one or more washings, the label must contain a warning to this effect. The warning must use [the] words "Do not," "No," "Only," or some other clear wording. [For example, if a shirt is not colorfast, its label should state "Wash with like colors" or "Wash separately." If a pair of pants will be harmed by ironing, its label should state "Do not iron."]

(B) Warnings are not necessary for any procedure that is an alternative to the procedure prescribed on the label. [For example, if an instruction states "Dry flat," it is not necessary to give the warning "Do not tumble dry."]

ITCHY LABELS

Sometimes labels are made of stiff, scratchy material that irritates the skin—especially children's sensitive skin. If you cut the care label off and you think you need it as a reminder, pin it to a bulletin board in your laundry with a note saying, for example, "Manufacturer X's Striped T-shirt." Better, but more trouble, is to reattach it to the garment, with firm stitching, someplace where it is less irritating, say at a side seam within a couple of inches of the bottom hem.

(2) Dry-cleaning.

(i) General. If a dry-cleaning instruction is included on the label, it must also state at least one type of solvent that may be used. However, if all commercially available types of solvent can be used, the label need not mention any types of solvent. The terms "Drycleanable" or "Commercially Dry-clean" may not be used in an instruction. [For example, if dry cleaning in perchlorethylene would harm a coat, the label might say "Professionally dry-clean: Fluorocarbon or petroleum."]

(ii) Warnings.

(A) If there is any part of the dry-cleaning procedure which consumers or drycleaners can reasonably be expected to use that would harm the product or others being cleaned with it, the label must contain a warning to this effect. The warning must use the words "Do not," "No," "Only," or some other clear wording. [For example, the dry-cleaning process normally includes moisture addition to solvent up to 75 percent relative humidity, hot tumble-drying up to 160°F, and restoration by steam press or steam-air finish. If a product can be dry-cleaned in all solvents but steam should not be used, its label should state "Professionally dry-clean. No steam."]

(B) Warnings are not necessary to any procedure which is an alternative to the procedure prescribed on the label. [For example, if an instruction states "Professionally dry-clean, Fluorocarbon," it is not necessary to give the warning "Do not use perchlorethylene."]

What the Rules Do and Do Not Mean

Although the discussion that follows often talks about what care labels "say," starting in 1999 the labels may use symbols instead of words. The symbols are to be interpreted just as words are and must obey the same rules as the words. (For an eighteen-month period, manufacturers are required to use words along with the symbols, to allow people time to learn them. At the end of this period, manufacturers may, but are not required to, use the symbols alone. The symbols, which have long been used abroad, are already somewhat familiar to Americans through their use on imported goods.)

Most care label instructions you will encounter are straightforward. Some instructions have implications that are not so obvious, however.

The Meaning of Silence. Often, it is what the care labels do *not* say that creates confusion. For example, when *both* dry cleaning and washing are safe for regular use on a product, the rules do not presently require the manufacturer to say so on the care label. Rather, under the rule as it now stands, "the label need have only one of these instructions." Thus, a label that says "Dry-clean" tells you neither that you can nor that you cannot also wash the article without harming it.* And if the label says "Machine wash," you have been told nothing about whether it can also be dry-cleaned or whether dry cleaning would harm it.

Sometimes, however, silence on a care label means that, in some respect or other, any-

*The FTC is now considering an amendment to the rules that would require manufacturers to include a washing instruction for any article that can be washed. The amendment would also require manufacturers to be able to substantiate that washing would be inappropriate for any garment labeled only "Dry-clean." The FTC is also considering requiring that all garments that carry a dry-cleaning instruction also carry a "wet-cleaning" instruction, if that method, too, would be appropriate. Wet cleaning is a new environmentally favorable cleaning technology that uses water instead of dry-cleaning solvents and is safe for a wider variety of fabrics than normal laundering.

thing goes. For example, a label that says nothing about washing, drying, or ironing temperatures means that any temperatures are safe. A label that says nothing about bleach means that all household bleaches are safe and can be used regularly. "Machine wash, tumble dry" means that any temperatures for washing and drying and all types of household bleach may be used.

Warnings. The words "only," "do not," and "no" are always warning words on care labels. Warnings mean that harm is likely to ensue, in one or more washings, if the instructions are not followed. In addition, if the label says "Wash with like colors" or "Wash separately," despite the absence of obvious warning words, you are being warned that the article *is not colorfast* and may bleed dyes onto anything washed with it. For example, if a label says "Dry-clean only," the word "only" makes this a warning against machine washing; and the instruction means that machine washing will be harmful. (Since this is a warning, the manufacturer has to have evidence that the procedures warned against really would be harmful.) But note that there is also an implicit warning against a stronger alternative when a care label specifies a gentler one; for example, a label that prescribes warm water is implicitly warning you not to use hot, even though no warning words are used explicitly.

Ironing. If a label says nothing at all about ironing, that *is supposed* to mean that no ironing is needed to "preserve the appearance" of the garment. But this provision of the rules, so far as I can tell, is routinely ignored; many garments that require ironing have care labels that do not mention ironing. Presumably manufacturers think that telling people they have to iron would not be a big selling point.

Bleaching. If a label says "No bleach," this does not mean that the article will stay white or bright without bleach, or that bleach is unnecessary. Some garments that are marked "No bleach" do not stay white without bleach. You may infer only that the manufacturer is telling you that all types of household bleach can reasonably be expected to harm the product in one or more washings.

If regular use of chlorine bleach would harm the product but regular use of a non-chlorine bleach would not, the label *must* say "Only non-chlorine bleach, when needed." This instruction seems to tell you that you are to use a non-chlorine (or oxygen) bleach only when the product starts to look dingy, but—whatever the instruction is really intended to mean—in practice this would often be a mistake. In general, non-chlorine bleach is effective only when used regularly to *prevent* a dingy appearance from developing and can do little to remove it when it has already developed. Nonetheless, the manufacturer, it seems, has no lawful choice but to give you this exact wording, misleading as it may be, if it wants to warn you against using chlorine bleaches but not against other types of bleach. This required wording is misleading in another way, too: it does not allow for cases in which "irregular" or *occasional* use of chlorine bleach might do no harm.

What Care Labels Do Not Have to Tell You. You should not assume, when you read a care label, that the manufacturer is trying to give you *the least expensive* or *the best* or even *both of two equally good* sets of care instructions. The rules do not require this, and care labels very often do not do so.

When care labels give warnings, they are not required to explain what danger is being warned against, how big a danger it is, or how likely the danger is. Care labels never tell you *why* one procedure is recommended rather than another, whether it is because a garment might fade, shrink, pill, or go limp or shapeless, whether invisible finishes may dissolve, and so on. Care labels do not tell you whether the product has received wrinkle-resistance or other treatments or whether any instructions on the label are there to protect a finish. Manufacturers are not required to tell you on care labels how much shrinking you can expect, nor when instructions are geared toward preventing shrinkage.

Care labels are not required to tell you when starch or sizing is necessary to restore the crisp appearance of a garment, or when ironing should be done when the clothes are damp. Apparently, they are also not required to give instructions on the use of soaps or detergents, softeners, bluing agents, boosters, and the like, and they rarely do, except, occasionally, to advise the use of mild soap or detergent.

At the present time, care labels are not required on sheets, mattress pads, tablecloths, blankets, towels, rugs, upholstery, and many other textile products used in the home. (Care labels are also not required on shoes, gloves, hats, handkerchiefs, neckties, and similar items of attire.) Wisely, manufacturers often include care labels on towels, linens, and other textile goods for the home even though they are not required. When care labels are absent, as often happens on imported towels and linens especially, you have to rely entirely on labels describing fiber content—which are, fortunately, required by the Textile Fiber Products Identification Act for all domestic and imported textiles—and use care procedures appropriate to the fibers.

Disregarding Care Labels Carefully

Below are listed some ways in which it often pays to depart from care label instructions. By following these guidelines, I sometimes ruin something, but in the long run my laundering is more effective and more efficient.

If you, too, wish to defy care labels at times, your best protection is to *understand fabrics and fibers.* (See chapters 14, 15, 16, and 17 for general information about fabrics and the care procedures appropriate to fabrics made of different types of fibers. See also "Bleaches," pages 316–19, in the Glossary of Laundry Products and Additives, and chapters 21 and 22 on home laundering and drying.) If you wish to launder or clean in a way other than the one recommended on a care label, you should be sure you are aware of the general nature of the fiber and construction you are dealing with and what is *generally* safe and effective in laundering such a fiber and construction, even though particular articles may have to be treated differently. To try to figure out whether the garment is actually launderable or cleanable in the way you intend, you should look for hints on the care label, on hang tags, and on fiber content labels, and you should examine all parts of the garment—its trim, linings, interfacings, buttons, and so on. Consider the weave and the yarn construction. Before proceeding, test for colorfastness, yellowing, and the like. Ask sales personnel whether they have any experience with the type of garment in question. Manufacturers may recommend a given procedure for a variety of reasons that you can only guess at.

- By using chlorine bleach on white fibers that are bleachable in principle, such as cotton, linen, or polyester. (To learn about a fiber's bleachability see chapters 16 and 17.) *Always test first, watching for yellowing, fading, color change, bleeding, or other negative effects.*
- By occasionally using chlorine bleach on colored articles, *if home testing indicates that chlorine bleach is safe.*
- By sometimes laundering, by hand or machine as seems best, articles whose care labels say "Dry-clean," when they are of a type or construction that typically is launderable. This calls for judgment and is only for the experienced.
- By washing polyester and nylon in warm water, although labels recommend cold, so as to get better cleaning.
- By using lukewarm water on washable wool sweaters and silks when care labels call for cold or cool.

- By washing colors that fade in warm, not cool, water, choosing cleanliness over color preservation. (But be sure to wash clothes that bleed separately from others or with others of like color, as appropriate.)
- By washing colorfast and white woven cottons and linens in hot or warm water, although labels recommend warm or cold. (Watch out for shrinking in knits or loose weaves.)
- By washing sturdy cotton blends and synthetics (not those containing viscose rayon, acetate, or other delicate and heat-sensitive fibers) in the regular cycle or permanent-press cycle when the label says "Gentle" or "Delicate." (Make sure there is no likelihood of pilling or tearing.)

You can also depart from care label instructions in the direction of being *more cautious* rather than less so. The usual reason to do this is to combine a stray item or two with a larger load, by giving it a less rigorous treatment than it could safely take. For example, you can:

- Wash or dry clothes at cooler temperatures than care labels direct.
- Wash or dry clothes with shorter or gentler agitation and spin cycles than care labels direct.
- Wash clothes with milder laundry products than care labels direct.
- Wash clothes without bleach that could safely be bleached.
- Hand-wash clothes whose label says to machine-wash.
- Dry flat or hang dry clothes whose labels permit tumbling dry.

The potential cost of using milder or gentler or cooler treatments is that clothes may not come as clean. Over time, dirt retained in the fibers weakens them and makes clothes appear gray and dingy or even feel unpleasant. However, the effects of retained dirt are not going to show up if you *occasionally* or *infrequently* make this compromise, for the sake of fewer loads. You would probably never wish to wash heavily soiled children's play clothes in cold water with mild detergent, for they simply will not come clean. But play clothes with moderate soil that you usually give strong treatment to would probably do fine if they were occasionally washed in warm water with permanent-press clothes on the permanent-press cycle—especially if you have pretreated any stains or heavy soil marks.

When Not to Disregard Care Labels

If you are in the habit of ignoring care labels, you will minimize your risks if you know that *some care label instructions should never or rarely be disregarded:*

For General Reasons

- Obey care labels on garments made by manufacturers whose care labels you have found reliable or important in the past.
- Obey care labels that are carefully written or provide a lot of detail. In my experience, this unfailingly indicates a degree of attention to proper care that is a sign of the instructions' importance and reliability.
- Obey care labels on expensive garments that you cannot afford to damage or replace.

For Reasons Related to Construction of Garment, Fabric, or Yarn

- In laundering specialty items, of whose construction and materials you know virtually nothing, follow care labels carefully. For example, always follow care labels on materials that are flocked, glued, furry, or otherwise unusually constructed.
- Generally, obey care label instructions on upholstery, rugs, quilts, draperies, and down-filled or feather-filled articles such as pillows, comforters, and sleeping bags. Not only are these things expensive, but

they often have constructions or treatments that require special care. Remember that curtains and draperies are often not washable, particularly those made of very loose weaves or silk velvet.

- Obey care labels on highly tailored items, especially those made of delicate or expensive fibers such as linen, silk, or wool.
- Never ignore "Dry-clean" or "Dry-clean only" instructions on crêpe—especially silk or rayon crêpes, which may shrink dramatically—or on other high-twist yarn constructions or low-twist yarn constructions.[1] (Shrinkage of up to 50% will result if a fabric made of highly twisted yarns is immersed in water.)

For Reasons Relating to Fiber Content

- Never disobey care label instructions to dry-clean dressy, glossy silks.
- Beware of defying dry-cleaning instructions on any crisp, tailored, or heavily sized linen or cotton garments. Never launder tailored linen suits unless the care label permits it.
- Obey all care labels on fiberglass!
- Never ignore instructions to use gentle treatment on rayon, acetate, or fabrics of delicate or fragile construction (open weaves, netting, lace).
- Never ignore instructions to use mild soap or detergent or cool water with silk or wool.
- Never ignore instructions to dry-clean acrylic or modacrylic, as this may be prescribed because the garment has a water-soluble finish. Laundering might cause a hard hand.

For Reasons Relating to Dyes and Finishes

- Never ignore laundering instructions for any garments with special or unusual finishes.
- Never ignore laundering instructions on items treated with flame retardants to render them flame resistant; this may harm the flame-resistant finish.
- Never ignore care instructions on water-repellent articles; this may render the article non-water-repellent.
- Pay attention to temperature or permanent-press instructions for washing or drying wrinkle-resistant, easy-care, or permanent-press garments or you may get wrinkling.
- Never ignore instructions to wash separately or with like colors unless you have thoroughly tested and have proof that a garment will not bleed. (But *always* follow care labels of colored or printed silks.)

When Instructions Relate to Bleaching

- Obey care labels that forbid bleaching wool, silk, leather, mohair, spandex, and nylon; on fabrics with colors that run; and on any colored fabrics that you have not successfully tested for bleachability. Obey care labels about bleaching on any fabric or finish that is not generally bleachable.

When Instructions Relate to Ironing and Drying

- Never use a hotter iron than a label instructs without carefully testing it first in an inconspicuous area to be sure that the fabric will not scorch, glaze, or melt.
- Almost always follow drying instructions. Although knits whose care labels say to dry flat can often be tumbled dry on low, it is very likely to result in some shrinkage. This might be tolerable if you expect and allow for it.

What to Do When the Procedure Recommended by the Care Label Causes Damage

If an article is damaged when you launder or clean it in accordance with the care instructions, the FTC recommends that you return the article to the retailer who sold it to you. The FTC suggests that if the retailer refuses to "resolve the problem," ask for the name and address of the manufacturer. "In your letter, fully describe the garment and give all the information that is on the labels and tags," advises the FTC. "Estimate how many times the garment has been washed or dry-cleaned and give the full name and address of the store where you bought it." You can also get in touch with the FTC, and you should definitely do so if the manufacturer fails to give you satisfaction. Write to: Correspondence Branch, Federal Trade Commission, Washington, DC 20580, or call: 202-326-3693. The FTC will not attempt to resolve your grievance, but the information you provide it "may reveal a pattern or practice requiring action by the Commission. You may be contacted if the FTC decides to investigate."

In my experience, however, retailers and manufacturers are almost always happy to make an exchange or refund.

Glossary of Care Label Terms and Symbols

Machine wash. Use washing machine, hot, warm, or cold setting.

Machine wash, warm. Use washing machine, warm setting. (Hot water should not be used.)

Machine wash, cold. Use washing machine, cold setting. (Hot or warm water should not be used.)

(Note that the absence of any instruction concerning bleaches or ironing should be interpreted as meaning that all commercially available bleaches may be used on a regular basis without harm, and that no ironing is necessary to preserve the appearance of the garment.)

Hand wash, cold. Wash by hand in cold water. (Machine washing and warm or hot water should not be used.)

Only non-chlorine bleach. Non-chlorine bleach can safely be used when needed. (Regular use of chlorine bleach would harm the product.)

No bleach. [Do not bleach.] Use no bleach. (All commercially available bleaches would harm the product when used on a regular basis.)

Tumble dry. High, medium, or low dryer temperature setting can safely be used.

Tumble dry, medium. Medium or low dryer temperature settings can safely be used. (The hot setting should not be used.)

Tumble dry, low. Low dryer temperature settings can safely be used. (The hot and warm settings should not be used.)

Iron. High, medium, or low iron settings can safely be used.

Warm iron. Iron on a medium temperature setting. (The hot setting should not be used.)

Cool iron. Iron on the lowest temperature setting. (The hot and warm settings should not be used.)

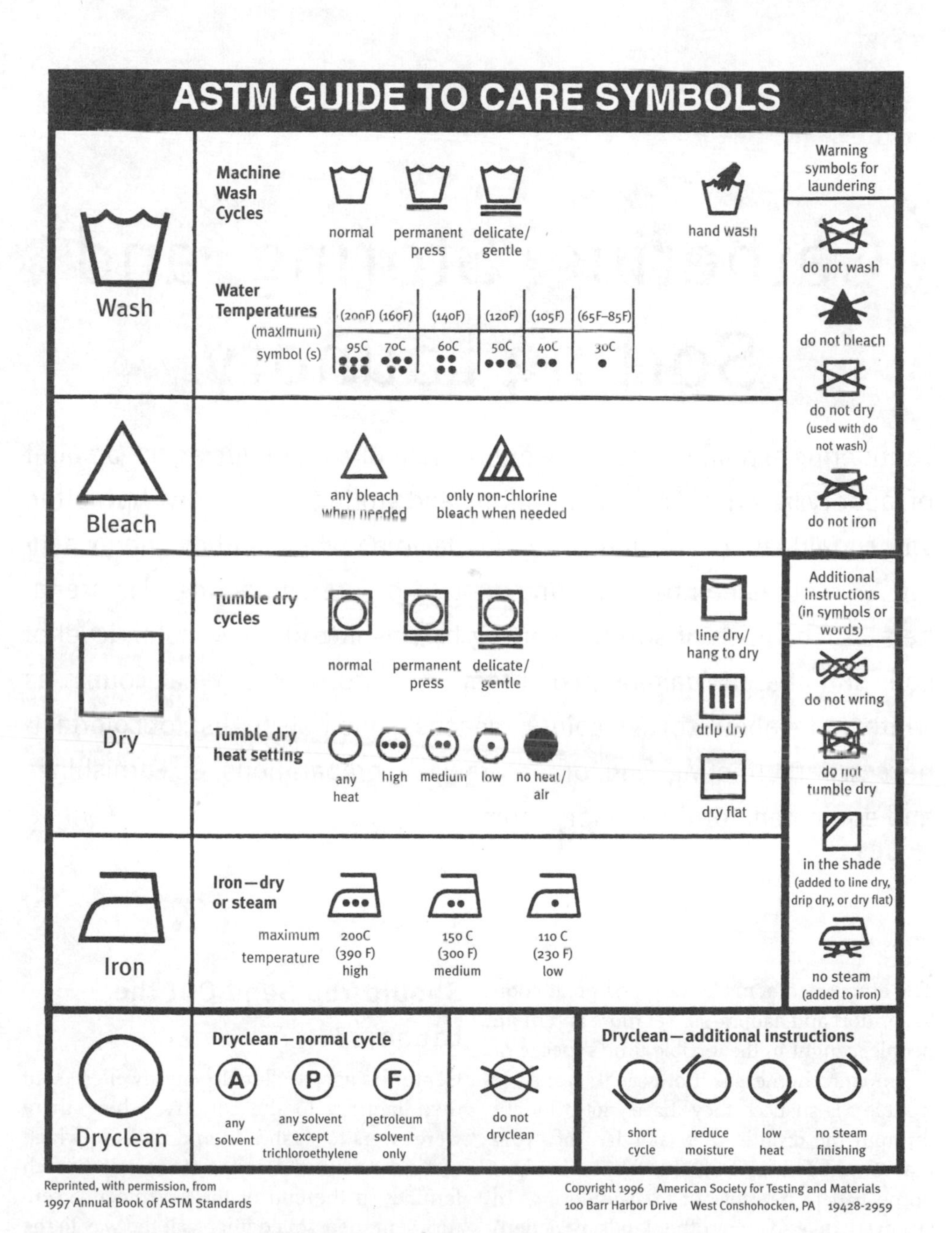

This figure illustrates the symbols used for laundering and drycleaning instructions. As a minimum, laundering instructions should include, in order, four symbols: washing, bleaching, drying, and ironing; and drycleaning instructions should include one symbol. Additional symbols or words may be used to clarify the instructions.

20

Gathering, Storing, and Sorting Laundry

Laundering at home vs. sending out the laundry . . . Reducing the amount of laundry in your home . . . Gathering and storing the laundry; how often you should launder; laundry day . . . Deciding when clothes need washing . . . Clothes hampers . . . Why we sort before laundering . . . Care labels . . . The rules of sorting; sorting by washing method, color, level of soil, potential for damage; compromises in sorting . . . What counts as white, more about sorting colors, bleaches, and how to test for colorfastness . . . Pretreating and other prewash preparations . . . Furnishings and equipment for the laundry room

The automated home laundry is a great boon to comfort and happiness. Yet more and more people, caught in the terrible time-squeeze of the modern home, see it only as the cause of trouble. I suspect they have not thought through the drop in their standard of living that would follow if all the fabrics in their home had to be sent out for laundering. In any event, like so many other kinds of modern housework, home laundering is much more a matter of knowing than of doing a lot. Once you know how, home laundering takes little trouble and provides great benefits.

Should You Send Out the Laundry?

Centuries ago, well-to-do city dwellers sent their laundry to the country, where there were rivers to wash it in and fields in which to spread it in the sun. Aristocratic French families at the end of the seventeenth century sent their soiled linens all the way to the Caribbean for laundering. By 1900, the custom of sending the laundry out (or sometimes of having a laundress come do it) had been adopted by other classes and was widespread. This system had some inconveniences—lost clothes, poorly laundered clothes, damage, stains, clothes and linens that could not be used because they were away being laundered—but these were overridden by its great benefits. One hundred years ago laundering was highly labor-intensive and required elaborate facilities for washing and drying, including boilers, wringers, and mangles, a whole collection of irons and ironing equipment, drying contraptions of various sorts, and ample space indoors and out. Few city families could supply all this muscle power, time, equipment, and space—or know-how—so out went the laundry, or, in some cases, in came the poor laundry women.

Then came automatic washing machines and other improvements for home laundries, and the private home again took on the sole responsibility for the job. Commercial laundries disappeared by the hundreds. That is why some feminists who wish to relieve women of the burdens of housekeeping have bitterly complained that home laundering is a case of a battle once won and then lost again. The calls for once more giving up home laundering, now that women have gone out to work in such numbers, have become louder and louder. In my view, home laundering is so easy, convenient, inexpensive, and successful that it is here to stay for most of us. There are those, however, for whom sending it out would be the best thing to do.

If you are single and working long hours or are part of a two-career family with children, you may sometimes find that this is the best choice for you. I know from experience that nothing cheers you up, when you are tired and stressed from work, like someone delivering bundles of crisp, clean laundry. I also know from experience, however, that commercial laundries do not do nearly as good a job as you can at home, cause much faster wearing and fading of clothes and linens, and will rarely give the individual attention to cherished garments or expensive linens that you will. You have to give up either having especially nice things or trying to keep them looking good. Laundries also impose on you the same inconveniences of sending the laundry out as they did at the turn of the century. The garment you desperately need for a trip cannot be retrieved from the bowels of the laundry establishment until the appointed day, and even then maybe not. Special sheets or extra towels unexpectedly needed for company may be gone. Damage (cracked buttons, discoloration, fading) and loss are still possibilities to be contended with, although they happen less often than you might expect.

The greatest problem for most people, however, is the large expense of sending the laundry out. It costs much, much more than doing the wash at home, even when the laundering services are mediocre. To have it done with anything approaching the delicate attention to individual garments and laundry problems that can be offered at home costs more than most people, even those who are relatively well off, can afford.

Many people can afford the occasional use of good commercial laundries, however, and taking advantage of this possibility when you must work extralong hours, or when you or your children are sick, or when there is a series of meetings you must attend at the time when you would ordinarily be laundering, can be such a boon that it is worth dipping into your emergency nest egg for this service now and then. Using commercial laundries only occasionally has the additional advantage that it causes less overall wear and tear on your clothes than habitual commercial laundering. Another option is to use commercial laundering services for some portion of your laundry; shirts are the classic choice here because they almost always require ironing. Just sending out the shirts saves a significant amount of time and causes a minimum of inconvenience. (But be sure to stock more shirts in the wardrobe than you would find necessary if you were doing them at home.)

You can also have someone come to your home to do your laundry, but you must take care to pick a conscientious person who knows how to do it, for the damage caused by sloppy or ignorant laundering can be immense. You might try asking the prospective employee to describe his or her laundering procedures. Questions about care labels, using bleach, permanent-press cycles, and drying temperatures tend to smoke out areas of ignorance. Even when you hire someone who understands laundry basics, however, you cannot expect the same kind of knowledge and attention you would give the task yourself; nor can you expect to pass along everything you know—about your clothes, linens, and fabrics as well as about laundering—if you have limited time to devote to training someone. And if you are going to sort, pretreat, and do a few handwashables yourself, you are not going to save much time by having someone else do the rest, which, after all, does not take much time. What it takes is your being at home for a few hours at a time, so that you can change loads and remove loads from the dryer. You can be doing many other things while the laundry proceeds.

There are times when you truly cannot manage to be at home for a few hours. More often, however, the hours are available, but doing the laundry is felt to be a strain and a bother in a busy life. When this is the case, the cause is often a lack of experience and know-how combined with the absence of a routine that includes laundering. Habitual conduct takes the least effort, and doing what is habitual soothes rather than stresses. Know-how reduces the amount of attention a task takes and the amount of annoyance you experience in carrying it out, and enables you to focus on other things. Know-how in laundering also enables you to make the things you care about look good and last long.

REDUCING LAUNDRY

You can reduce the amount of laundry you have to do each week by taking any or all of the following steps:

Hang towels to dry carefully after each use.

Instead of putting lightly worn outer garments in the clothes hamper, spot-clean them (if necessary), let them air, and hang or fold them neatly.

Wear T-shirts, dress shields, camisoles, or slips under shirts, blouses, and dresses.

Protect clothing with smocks or aprons when you clean, cook, or do other messy jobs.

Use good bed manners to save laundering of bed linens and blankets. Avoid lying or sitting on the bed wearing street clothes; and always wash at least your face and hands before getting into bed. Make up your bed in the traditional way described on pages 664–68 in chapter 56, "The Cave of Nakedness."

Gathering and Storing

Laundry Day: How Often Should You Launder? Once upon a time, Monday was laundry day, and this was such an onerous chore in the nineteenth century that it was called "blue Monday." Although there is no longer any compelling reason for most of us to launder on Monday, doing laundry only once or twice a week is still more effective and efficient than doing a load or two every day.

The first step in preparing to do laundry is to accumulate a stock of soiled clothes and linens to wash. This stock should be large enough to produce the best washing results. If you wait until a good stock is accumulated, you will have fewer temptations to give some items improper treatment by washing them with a load of dissimilar items. It is inefficient and ineffective to run washers and dryers with very small loads; clothes come cleaner if washed in medium or larger loads and if articles of different sizes, large and small, are mixed loosely together in a load. (See chapter 21, "Laundering," page 311.) This sort of mix will also help prevent the load from becoming unbalanced. (When the load becomes unbalanced, the washing machine may automatically shut down or dance wildly across the floor.) Clothes dry faster, too, if the dryer has at least a medium fill.

On the other hand, the accumulation of laundry should be small enough to be completed in a reasonable amount of time, and each laundry day should be fairly close in time to the last one—a week or less. The longer the dirt stays on fabrics, the harder it is to remove. In many instances, articles should receive interim treatment to prevent permanent staining or discoloration. Dirt, particularly perspiration and many food stains, also weakens fabrics, causing them to deteriorate, fade, or turn yellow. Mildew and odor are more likely to develop if laundry sits unwashed for a while; mildew can permanently discolor fabrics. And, of course, the sooner the laundry is washed, the sooner the clothes and linens are available for using again.

Choosing one day a week when most of the laundry is always done will go far toward making laundry easier to do while keeping life pleasant and orderly. One may choose to do a smaller wash of similar items on a second washing day—say, toddlers' clothes or towels and linens or other items requiring relatively uncomplicated treatment. Those working out of the home full-time may find it preferable to do roughly equal amounts of laundry two evenings per week so that weekends may be more leisurely.

It is possible to do small amounts of laundry several times a week or every day. This system actually tends to work best in large, highly organized households, particularly those in which someone stays home to keep house. But it tends to be adopted, as a kind of default system, in more disorganized households where no one stays home. Frequent laundering geared to the needs of the day makes it hard to get properly sorted and balanced loads. Besides, this method never gives one a sense of repose, freedom from an accomplished chore. Nor does it lead one to form expectations and habits in accordance with what clothes and linens will be available for use at a given time. And because it requires you to attend to the laundry so frequently, it is a system that tends to break down, creating disorder and crisis and more frustration. The system of doing laundry once or twice a week depends on having a stock of clothes and linens that will last a week and be adequate for occasional emergencies as well—but this is a condition easily met in the era of inexpensive fabrics and automatic laundering equipment. Some people manage to have even fewer, but longer, laundry days by stocking extralarge quantities of clothes and linens, a satisfactory procedure so long as proper stain-removal procedures and pretreatments are used on stored soiled clothes. Centuries ago, the difficulties of laundering meant that in some large, wealthy households linens were washed only annually or semiannually. These households held astonishing stores of linens, dozens of sheets and tablecloths, for this was necessary to get from one rare laundering day to the next. (See chapter 57, "Beds and Bedding" for a discussion of adequate stocks of linens in modern households.)

When Do Clothes Need Washing? All new clothes, sheets, and other household fabrics that are launderable should be washed once before they are used. After this, wash launderable clothes, linens, and household textiles when they look, feel, or smell dirty. Even if they look fine, you should launder them if you know that they have accumulated dirt and dust, because particulate dirt and dust will contribute to wearing them out. Particles of dust cut into cloth like tiny knives, weakening it and rendering it susceptible to holes and tears. Perspiration, food, and other substances that get on clothes during wear cause deterioration or discoloration in many fabrics.

On the other hand, because laundering and dry cleaning also age cloth, you should avoid resorting to them too frequently. Most of us today do tend to over-launder simply because laundering is so easy; children find it much easier to deposit a barely worn garment in a laundry hamper than to hang it nicely for airing or fold it nicely for the shelf. Of course, if you have perspired heavily in a garment, you must wash it before wearing it again, and what used to be called "body linen"—underwear and other intimate clothing—always needs washing after just one wear. But if you get a spot on a fresh garment, try washing or cleaning off just the spot, with plain water or a cleaning fluid (unless the garment is a silk that may water-spot or unless the spot cleaning may leave a ring or faded spot—test your procedure first in an inconspicuous area). And rather than throw the shirt you wore for an hour into the laundry hamper, put it on a hanger and let it air, then replace it in your closet for wearing again. Brush and air clothes and blankets, especially woolens, after use. Sometimes you can simply wipe down wools and synthetics with a barely damp, white, nonlinting cloth to keep them clean longer. (If you do this, be sure to air them until they are absolutely dry before replacing them in drawers or closets.) Wear T-shirts under dress shirts, and dress shields, camisoles, or slips under blouses and dresses. By these means, you can often keep launderable garments free of visible soil and heavy perspiration so that they remain fresh enough for two or more wearings before laundering. All this is even more important for clothes that must be dry-cleaned.

Clothes Hampers. As clothes and linens become soiled through regular use, collect them in a clothes hamper or other receptacle. Let towels and other damp articles dry before you put them into the hamper, and place the hamper in a dry room, not in the bathroom (unless you have a bath suite with a dry room separate from the shower and tub). Stored damp laundry may mildew or become malodorous, and the odor can taint the air in the room where they are stored. Gathering soiled laundry in an airy container, such as a wicker or woven basket or hamper, will help avoid this problem. (You can sprinkle baking soda in a hamper to deodorize it as well; the soda can go right into the washing machine, as it is a gentle detergent booster.) Lidded baskets of wicker or similar material with a polyurethane coating are a good choice for hampers; air can enter through the interstices, and the smooth coating protects clothes from being snagged and protects the container itself from being damaged by moisture.

Very greasy, muddy, or heavily soiled clothing should be stored separately if there is any danger of the soil getting on other articles in the hamper. Fine and delicate items should also be stored separately for laundering so as to avoid their coming into contact with soil, odors, snags, or anything else that might harm them. A smooth cloth sack that will breathe and can be hung in some convenient place (not your clothes closet) works best. Later on, these items are laundered separately to protect them from harsher cleaning methods that they will not easily withstand.

Sorting the Laundry

The laundry-maid should commence her labours on Monday morning by a careful examination of the articles committed to her care, and enter them in the washing-book; separating the white linen and collars, sheets and body-linen into one heap, fine muslins into another, coloured cotton and linen fabrics into a third, woollens into a fourth, and the coarser kitchen and other greasy cloth into a fifth. Every article should be examined for ink or grease spots, or for fruit or wine-stains.

—*Mrs. Beeton's Book of Household Management*, 1861

Why Sort? Sorting is the process of separating soiled clothes and linens into heaps or piles such that all the articles in a pile can safely receive similar laundry treatment—similar washing methods, washing products, water temperature, washing vigor and duration, and, usually, drying methods, times, and temperatures. Sorting the laundry has become more complicated than Mrs. Beeton (who wrote what became the bible of British housekeeping for more than half a century) ever dreamed of, because there are so many more fibers, finishes, and constructions to deal with. Even care labels may seem to complicate matters instead of simplifying them. I recently counted ten different sets of laundry directions included on the care labels of the clothes included in *one* medium-sized load (out of three loads washed that day in my home). Drying instructions add even more complications. If you tried to obey each care label to the letter, you might end up with thirty or forty laundry loads on every laundry day. As a result of these complications, a kind of minicrisis of sorting has developed in which the old rules no longer seem to work, and the standard consequence of a breakdown in rules and values has ensued: the youth have become skeptical and nihilistic. They do not believe it is possible to figure it all out. They do not sort their clothes for laundering, and they sneer that sorting makes no difference.

But they are wrong. You can still figure out how to sort, and if you don't sort, over time your clothes will suffer the subtle or not-so-subtle bleeding of dyes that turns all light-colored clothes dull pink or dingy gray, along with shrinking, pilling, tearing, and other problems. Damage can be mild or immense. The bad effects of undesirable laundering habits are often cumulative and long term. You will not necessarily see them at once; they appear over weeks and months. Some people know very well what is the cause of their pink undershorts, and towels and sheets of uniform dinginess, but they believe that their time is so short that bright, attractive colors, good fit, and unpilled knits are luxuries that they cannot afford. But doing laundry well takes little more time than doing it poorly, and endless shopping to replace goods that prematurely look bad or function badly takes far more time in the long run. Besides, when you find something you like, you want it to last. Most of us cannot afford to buy whatever we want whenever we want it, even assuming that another shirt just like the ruined one could be found.

Care Labels. Chapter 19, "Carefully Disregarding Care Labels," tells you how to interpret and follow care labels and provides explanations of terms and symbols used on care labels. Sorting clothes properly requires reading all their care labels. The care label warns you against procedures that will likely do damage and tells you a safe way to clean the garment. If reading a lot of care labels seems onerous and you are not accustomed to it, be assured that as you gain experience you come to know your own clothes and linens. Eventually, you will read care labels only when you first buy and launder things, as you get into the habit of keeping this kind of information in mind. *If you, like me, choose to second-guess care labels, it is virtually guaranteed that sooner or later you are going to wreck something.* Ignoring care labels has led me to turn a crisp linen suit into a limp rag and to shrink a chic rayon/acetate dress so severely that I was unable to pull it on over my shoulders. When this happens to you, be prepared to shed philosophical tears and blame no one but yourself.

Rules of Sorting. Once the laundry has been gathered, sort it into piles according to these five rules: (1) sort by washing method, (2) sort by color, (3) sort by level or kind of soil, (4) sort according to whether some clothes will cause other clothes to pick up lint, snag, tear, and so on, and then (5) make sorting compromises, as necessary and safe, to create a reasonable number of good-sized loads.

First, sort according to washing method. Separate washable clothes and linens, in accordance with their fiber and fabric type, into four piles corresponding to the four basic laundering procedures: regular, permanent-press, gentle machine-washing, and hand-washing. (In chapter 21 you will find a description of each of these laundering procedures and how to carry them out.) This is done *roughly* as set forth below. All laundering rules have their exceptions.

Regular Machine-Washing. Sturdy white and colorfast cottons and linens. Normal or regular washing treatment is appropriate for sturdy cottons that have not received antiwrinkling treatments or other finishes that need special protection. Close plain and twill weaves and sturdy knits, such as T-shirts and underwear, diapers, towels of all sorts, wrinkly sheets, work clothes, play clothes, and sportswear, ordinarily receive laundering on the regular cycle of the machine. (See "The Regular Cycle," pages 304–5, in chapter 21.)

Permanent-Press Machine-Washing. Permanent-press or other cloth treated for wrinkle resistance and most synthetics. Wrinkle-treated, durable-press, or "easy-care" cotton, linen, and rayon fabrics and blends get washed on the machine's permanent-press cycle, as do most garments made of synthetics, including polyester, nylon, some spandex, and polypropylene and blends containing such fibers. (See "The Permanent-Press Cycle," pages 305–6, in chapter 21.)

Gentle Machine-Washing. Fine cotton knits, machine-washable silk, wools, acrylics and modacrylic, some spandex, triacetate, some washable acetate, viscose rayons, and blends and items with linings containing them. Laces, netting, fringed items, embroidery, fine lingerie, loosely knitted or loosely woven articles, and other fine, sheer, or delicately made articles of any fiber need gentle washing. This cycle is also proper for sheer weaves such as cambric or lawn; satin weaves and other weaves with floats (these will snag and abrade easily), irregular surfaces, low yarn counts, or open or loose weaves of any sort in which there are spaces between yarns (because these are prone to snagging and shrinking); washable laces; articles with fragile or loosely attached trims, ties, or decorations that might get pulled off in vigorous washing; anything unusually susceptible to abrasion, pilling, or snagging; and many specialty items, including nonwoven materials or those bonded with various adhesives. (See "The Delicate or Gentle Cycle," pages 306–7, in chapter 21.)

Hand-Washing. Some washable acetate, washable delicate acrylics, silks, wools, rayons, some cotton knits, and especially fragile, old, or other delicate articles. The difference between this group and the previous one is only a matter of degree. Especially delicate fibers and constructions, and fabrics that have become fragile through age should be hand-washed. Panty hose and stockings are safest washed by hand, too, but you can try putting them in the machine on the gentle cycle in a mesh bag if you are willing to risk occasional snags or runs. (See "Hand-Washing," pages 313–15, in chapter 21.)

When sorting by fiber content and construction, do not forget that some washable garments are made of two or more fibers or constructions that might ordinarily get two or more different treatments. If so, always choose the more conservative. For example, if a dress has a delicate, sheer top but a sturdy cotton skirt, give it gentle treatment. If a shirt is a cotton/polyester blend, wash it as though it were polyester. Pay attention to linings, trim, buttons, and similar parts of a garment that might take treatment different from the rest.

Although there are four different laundry procedures, you may use only one, two, or three of them on any given day. I rarely use more than two—regular, and either gentle machine-washing or hand-washing.

Second, sort by color. Once you have sorted your laundry into piles according to the type of laundering that it will receive, divide each of those piles into color-compatible groupings. The basic color groupings are these: all white, mostly white (prints with a white background, towels with a colored stripe at the border), and light, medium or bright, and dark colors. As much as possible, wash things of the same hue together. Separate out bleeding colors for separate washing or for washing with like colors, as necessary. You should also divide the color piles into those that will and those that will not receive some sort of bleaching. Generally speaking, white and colorfast colored articles made of bleachable fibers are the components of the wash that can benefit from bleach of some sort.

Third, sort by type and degree of soil. Separate out of the foregoing piles any extra-heavily soiled articles or those with heavy grease, mud, or other soil. If you live in the city, as I do, you will have to do this very rarely—perhaps only when your child has a muddy day at the playground or if you have cloth diapers to wash. Articles with heavy or unusual soil and stains, particularly greasy or oily ones, must be washed separately from clothes without such soil (and sometimes from each other) for two reasons. First, there is a danger that the heavy soil or stains would be redeposited on more lightly soiled clothes and not come out. (Seriously stained items, for this reason, should always be washed separately or the stain may spread to other items in the wash.) White and light-colored clothes are particularly susceptible to turning dingy, gray, or yellow if washed with heavily soiled items. Second, heavy and unusual soils usually demand special, more vigorous treatment to which you may not wish to subject your ordinary wash. Stronger treatments cause faster wearing and fading and are inappropriate for many fibers and fabric constructions. Diapers should be laundered only with other diapers, using a presoak and sometimes a double wash as well.

If you have serious infectious illness in your home, you may also wish to wash the clothes, towels, and linens of the sick person separately. I know elderly women who tell me that in their day you would also have separated handkerchiefs, bed linens, and body linens from table linens for laundering; it would have been considered unsanitary to mix them up. No one does this anymore. Only diapers still are (and should be) washed separately as a routine matter. But keeping germ-laden material separate, especially when a household member is ill, is a good idea.

Get off as much of the soil as possible before inserting the clothes into the washing machine, scraping it off with an old table knife if necessary, or rinsing briefly by hand in a separate basin or laundry tub. Scrape or rub off mud from the garden.

Fourth, sort according to whether clothes will cause others to pick up lint, snag, tear, and so on. Separate out of each of the foregoing piles any clothes that might mechanically damage or spoil the appearance of other clothes in the load. Again, if your laundry is at all like mine, potentially damaging and linting articles are rarely a problem (at least since my son disdained overalls and I gave up my chenille bathrobe). This category includes items that produce lint or pick up lint easily and those with heavy buckles or clasps, zippers that might catch lace or ribbons, or other features that might cause damage. What is dangerous is relative to the other clothes in the load. A buckle or clasp might tear chiffon, lace, or net or other open weaves but not denims. Clothes and linens that produce lint include some towels and other terry-cloth items, especially when they are new; flannel; chenille bedspreads or bathrobes; and rags or fabrics that are fraying. Clothes and linens that will attract or hold lint include those that develop static electricity (polyester, acrylic, nylon, and other synthetics primarily) and pile fabrics like corduroy and velvet. Linting fabrics should be washed separately from any of these that would show the lint badly. For example, dark clothes will show white lint far more than white or light ones will. Note that household furnishings such as washable draperies, small rugs, and slipcovers often produce lint and should almost always be washed separately.

Fifth, make compromises! After you have completed sorting by these rules, make compromises to reduce the number of loads if you find yourself with a large number of single-item loads or loads that are very small. Compromises are *occasional* choices made in the interests of efficiency. Engaged in regularly, they will eventually spoil your clothes and linens. If you have time, the better way is simply to hand-wash the one or two items—the shirt that bleeds, the one unbleachable white item—that do not belong with a load according to the foregoing criteria. Here are some guidelines for making effective sorting compromises:

- Combine bleach-fast, nearly-all-white prints with pure whites, excluding orlons and nylons, and treat all as you would the pure whites. (But see the discussion of whites, colors, and bleach below.)
- Wash synthetic and natural-fiber whites together, giving them all permanent-press treatment. Synthetic whites that receive permanent-press washing can usually take bleach, even if they do not need it. So if you would have used bleach on the natural fibers and you can confirm (by checking labels or testing) that the synthetics can take it, use bleach.
- If color, colorfastness, and soil type do not preclude it, include items that can take more strenuous treatment in a load that is to receive less strenuous treatment. For instance, colored cotton T-shirts that are only lightly soiled could be given permanent-press or gentle treatment now and then, even though ordinarily they require stronger washing techniques. Or put nylons and polyesters that you would ideally give permanent-press treatment in the gentle cycle to wash, making sure you use a cold rinse (and adjust the drying treatment too).
- When an article is not heavily soiled, combine it with any color-compatible load that is to receive milder or less vigorous treatment.
- Wash light coloreds with bright coloreds, or bright coloreds with dark coloreds. Watch out for bleeding dyes.

More about Whites, Colors, and Bleach; Testing for Colorfastness

Whites and Nearly Whites. What, for sorting purposes, counts as white? "White" means only white. Off-whites and creams are not whites, and neither are mostly white prints. Whites are best washed only with other fabrics that are all white. For the sake of making up a load, however, you may occasionally compromise this principle according to the guidelines sketched below. *White or light nylons and orlons*—orlon has not been made since 1990, but some is still in use—will pick up any faint hint of color in the wash water, even the all-but-invisible taint of pastels, and may become dingy or gray. If this happens, it may be quite difficult or impossible to restore their original whiteness. With other fibers, however, such an accident is often reparable. (See also chapter 26, "Common Laundry Mishaps and Problems," page 368.)

If you have a number of whites with an occasional touch of color, it is best to wash them separately in a load made up of other such items. However, washable articles that are all white with some colorfast colored trim—for example, men's athletic shorts made in white cotton with colored piping, sheets or pillowcases with edges sturdily satin-stitched in colored or black thread or with colored embroidery, or white dish towels with a band of colorfast color at each hem—may sometimes be treated as whites for sorting purposes. Any color on such items is almost always fast to detergent and water; if it were not, there would be no way to launder it without tainting the white with the color of the trim. (Unfortunately, you may find occasionally that you have purchased just such a ridiculous item. I once bought a child's bathing suit, marked "Machine washable," whose red stripes, after being immersed in ordinary chilly lake water, proceeded to bleed enthusiastic-red on white beach wraps and continued to do so after any number of immersions. Such an article should be returned to the retailer or manufacturer.) Other items that may occasionally be treated as whites for sorting purposes are colorfast prints that are mostly white with a little color—a white shirt with fine pinstripes, a sheet with pastel flowers, or white pajamas strewn with colored balloons. *But test all of these for colorfastness to detergent and water before adding any to a white load. (Testing is explained on page 300.)*

Bleaching Whites and Mostly Whites. The appearance of whites and mostly whites can sometimes be dramatically improved with the use of bleaches. Almost all colors that are fast to detergent and water are also fast to oxygen bleach, which can practically always be used safely. On using bleaches, see "Bleaches" in the glossary at the end of chapter 21. When mostly white items (white with a colored border, piping or trim, or mostly white prints) are also fast to chlorine bleach, they usually benefit from an occasional bleaching with chlorine bleach. (Use the *tests for bleach-fastness* on page 300. Remember that the color in a white-background print might be fast to hot water and detergent but *not to bleach.*) In my own household, almost all such fabrics are chlorine-bleachable, including towels, children's print cotton knit undergarments, pajamas, and shirts. On quality goods, care labels often do not proscribe chlorine bleaches. But low labeling (care labeling that prescribes more conservative treatment than is necessary) is common on white and mostly white cottons and linens. On most washdays I use chlorine bleach on several articles whose labels proscribe it, without the slightest damage, and many of these have been receiving chlorine bleach now and then for years. *However, using any kind of bleach when the care label says not to is risky; some all-white fabrics should be bleached neither with chlorine bleach nor with all-fabric bleach. You must always test.* Even when your test shows no damage, you must think about the long-term effects and possible forms of damage that will not show up right away; there are many reasons (besides the possibility of causing the colors to run) why such an instruction might be included.

If you occasionally use a chlorine bleach on articles with bleach-fast colors, you may nonetheless notice over the long run that this makes the colors fade a bit more quickly than they otherwise would. This result may be acceptable in many instances or, at least, it may be preferable to the alternative of dingy, yellowed, or grayish-looking clothes. *If you are not prepared to accept any degree of increase in fading, do not use chlorine bleach on these articles.* Try an oxygen bleach instead.

Off-whites and pastels will lighten if you regularly subject them to chlorine bleach, and may eventually turn white. Do not wash pieces of matched sets separately, or they will fade at different rates and look unmatched. Never bleach one piece of a matched set and not the others. Nonetheless, you can occasionally wash *very* light bleach-fast pastel or cream-colored cotton sheets or an off-white cotton blouse that has become dingy or gray with whites that are being chlorine bleached. This treatment usually helps remove the dinginess. But, as it is risky, it should be done only infrequently and cautiously, only with very light colors and off-whites that have already been washed several times, and never in loads including nylon or orlon.

Light, Bright, and Dark Colors. When you sort clothes for laundering, divide the loads initially by color intensity, separating the laundry into light and pastel colors, medium or bright colors, and dark colors. Even clothes that are theoretically colorfast may lose a tiny bit of color each time they are washed. That tiny bit of color from, say, a navy blue shirt will be invisible if deposited on a forest green skirt but it could muddy a pastel yellow one. Hue matters too. You will keep colors most clear and true if to the greatest extent possible you wash like colors together—oranges with reds, bright blues with purples, navy with black, light tan with cream. This is a principle that must be compromised to some degree each time you wash.

Separating Out Clothes Whose Dyes Bleed Color. Care labels that say "Wash separately" or "Wash with like colors" should be taken *very seriously;* articles that lack care labels should be carefully tested for colorfastness before washing. Instructions of this kind indicate that the dyes in the articles are likely to bleed during laundering and give an ugly, unwanted coloration to all the clothes washed in the same load. The story behind the labels, however, is slightly complicated. Some dyes that bleed will do so to some extent—sometimes greatly—every time they are washed; others will bleed only very little, but visibly. Those that bleed greatly should always be washed separately. Those with dyes that visibly bleed very little should be washed only with like colors. Many other items, such as towels, have dyes that bleed the first two or three times they are exposed to water, or to water and detergent, and then stop. These items are actually colorfast; the fabrics are simply giving up excess dye on the first few washes. (A good manufacturer will make this clear on the label by instructing you to wash the article separately or with like colors for two or three washes only.) If your care labels simply say "Wash separately" or "Wash with like colors," be observant. Retest the garments after two or three washes to see if they are still bleeding color.

Denim, madras, and fabrics dyed with vegetable or "natural" dyes are among those that bleed color their entire lives. Fluorescent colors, too, tend to pose problems. (You should not treat fluorescent dyes with stain removers unless you have first tested them.) Blue denims, whose notorious fading is sometimes valued and sometimes deplored, depending on the current fashion, continue to bleed a little color even if they are "stonewashed" or "prewashed" when you buy them. New blue jeans that have not been prewashed or faded should be washed only with very dark blues and colors darker than the jeans—deep brown, charcoal, black. You may safely wash blue jeans that have faded to light blue with medium-color loads, always keeping in mind that the more closely you can match the colors of any colored load, the better—that is, it is best to wash the blue jeans with medium purples or grays or greens.

Madras garments are supposed to fade, and one is supposed to prize the changes in their looks as the different colors in them fade and merge over time. They must *always* be washed separately.

If you have a garment that will bleed or if a care label advises you to wash it "with like colors" and you lack any like colors, you are going to have to wash it alone; this may mean by hand if your washer cannot accommodate a very tiny load without coming unbalanced or wasting too much water and energy (something to think about when you are buying clothes and linens).

Remember that many dyes tend to fade more over the lifetime of the garment when you use hotter water, stronger detergents, and stronger bleaches. Preserving color and getting the cleanest wash are goals that have to be balanced.

If you have a washing disaster involving dyes that bleed, try the suggestions on page 368 in chapter 26.

Bleaching Colored Clothes. For dinginess or grayness in colored clothes, use an "all-fabric" or oxygen bleach. Many colored clothes, especially prints, are also fast to chlorine bleach. Test first to ensure that all articles in a load are fast to whatever bleach you are using.

Pretreating and Other Prewash Preparations

Once the laundry is sorted, final preparations for washing are done as follows:

Pretreating. Pretreat stains, spots, and heavily soiled areas either while you are sorting and making loads or, if the problem is likely to be hard to remove, as soon as possible after the garment becomes soiled or stained. Pretreatments are often especially useful on cuffs, collars, the undersides of sleeves that have rested on desks or papers all day, and the area at the waist that leans against a table or desk edge. Pretreatments are particularly important for oily stains and areas that take up body oils on synthetics, and the cooler the wash temperature to be used, the more important they are. (See "Pretreatments and prewash stain removers" in the glossary at the end of chapter 21.)

To pretreat, rub a little liquid detergent or spray or rub a pretreatment product or stick on the soiled area. You can also rub the area with a paste of detergent and water or pure bar soap (one that contains no moisturizers, medications, or dyes); dampen the area first when you use either of these treatments.

If there is *any* question as to the safety of a pretreatment substance, it should be tested on an inconspicuous area of the garment, on the wrong side of a hem or on a seam allowance. Simply apply the pretreatment product to the test area, wait ten minutes or so, and then check for ill effects: staining, fading, bleeding, or other problems. If you have done a good deal of pretreating, you may not need as much detergent in the wash water as you would otherwise have used.

Preparing the Clothes. Some commonsense precautions are necessary to prepare the clothes for the machine or washtub:

- Turn inside out blue jeans and other articles that may fade or whose color may abrade (if you wish to prevent that); also turn inside out articles made of synthetic fibers, knits, and other articles prone to pilling or that have poor abrasion resistance. The creases of cotton fabrics that have received resin treatment to prevent wrinkling are particularly vulnerable to abrasion. Turn corduroys inside out to avoid wearing down the pile and to reduce lint. Heat-transfer, pigment, or other prints that might rub off will also be safer turned inside out. But remember that turning a garment inside out can make it hard to get heavy soil or stains off the protected right side; sometimes you will want to omit this step for the sake of a cleaner outcome.
- Check pockets, cuffs, pleats, and folds for coins, keys, crayons, pens, tissues, papers, lint, and so on. Hard objects, such as coins and keys, can damage the washer and dryer tubs' smooth surfaces, leaving rough places that might snag, tear, or abrade clothes. Crayons and pens can mark much of the load. Tissues, paper, lint, and the like will adhere to the laundered clothes and prove troublesome to remove.

TESTING FOR COLORFASTNESS TO LAUNDRY PRODUCTS

You must test for the colorfastness of dyed clothes and linens to any substance with which you plan to launder them: detergent, bleach, boosters, pretreatments, and stain removers. Some dyes will run or fade in a solution of water and detergent but would not be affected by plain water; some will bleed when you use hot water but not warm. Some will bleed in a pretreatment solution or in bleach but would not run in a solution of mere detergent and water. Test with hot or warm water if you will be washing in hot or warm water; the action of the bleaches and other laundry additives is increased in hotter water.

Pretreatments and stain removers sometimes have special ingredients that can cause some dyes, especially fluorescent dyes, to run, so be particularly careful to test neon pinks, electric blues, and other fluorescent colors.

Choose an inconspicuous area for testing, such as the wrong side of a hem or on a seam allowance, so that if your test leaves a spot, it will not show. Be sure to lay the cloth in such a way that the solution does not penetrate through to visible areas.

Recipe for testing fastness to detergent Follow the directions on the product. If there are none, mix one teaspoon of dry or liquid detergent in a cup of warm or hot water (whichever you will be using). Apply enough solution to soak a small hidden area of the garment and wait for a few minutes. Then press the area with a clean white cloth, tissue, or paper towel to see if any color comes off. If color comes off or if you perceive a color change on the garment, it has failed the colorfast test. If you perceive nothing, rinse and let dry, and observe again (because it may look darker while it is wet). If you see no color change, it is colorfast to your detergent at the temperature of the water you will use.

The quick, easy, *less reliable* way to test is to make a cup of water of the proposed temperature, add a teaspoon of detergent, and dip a corner of the fabric in it. If the water turns color, the fabric is not fast to detergent in water of that temperature.

Recipe for testing fastness to chlorine (sodium hypochlorite) bleach Use the method recommended on the product. Or add one tablespoon of chlorine bleach to ¼ cup water. Apply the solution to a hidden area, such as a seam allowance, and wait one minute. Then blot the spot dry with a clean white cloth, tissue, or paper towel. If color comes off or if you perceive a color change on the garment, it has failed the colorfast test. Look for yellowing and other changes as well. If you want to be very sure there has been no color change, rinse the item and wait until it dries to draw conclusions, as sometimes it is hard to tell while fabrics are wet.

Recipe for testing fastness to other wash additives Follow instructions on the label for testing. If there are none and if the product is not a liquid, mix it with enough water to get a solution somewhat stronger than the one you will have in the washing machine, making sure that all of the product is dissolved. Apply enough solution to soak a small inconspicuous area of the garment. Or, if the product is a liquid, simply apply a little, undiluted, to an inconspicuous area of the garment. Wait ten minutes and then look for any changes of color, fading, bleeding (press a clean paper towel to the area), or other damage. Then rinse and let dry to be completely sure there is no change.

When testing an activated oxygen bleach, be sure to read and follow the manufacturer's instructions, which may specify a more concentrated testing solution and a longer exposure time than is usually called for.

- Place in a mesh bag hosiery, articles that tear and snag, such as lace, articles with fringe that might fray, tangle, or become detached, and small items that might otherwise get lost. A zippered pillow cover or a pillowcase with the opening secured can be used in place of a mesh bag. (Small items like baby socks, contrary to what you may have heard, are never actually sucked down the drain pipes, which have filters;

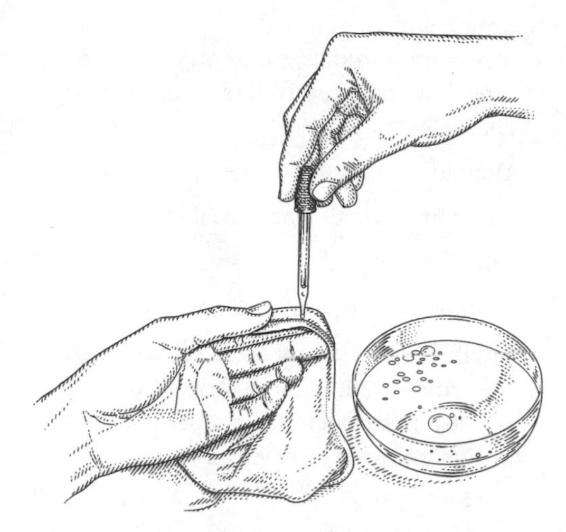

Test fabrics for colorfastness and bleachability on an out-of-sight area.

they disappear into sleeves, pant legs, and dresses and are folded, unnoticed, into towels and sheets.) Hosiery can get twisted or knotted or can snag on almost any rough surface. Heavily soiled pieces may not wash clean, however, in a mesh bag. You may have to hand-wash them.

- Pins should usually be removed before washing because of the possibility that they will rust or that the pinned fabric will tear. Cuff links, buckles, and other metal attachments pose the same dangers—and the additional danger, according to washing machine manufacturers, that they can damage the enamel inside the machine—and, if possible, should be removed. Buckles on sturdy fabrics that will not be harmed by pins could be fastened inside pant legs instead.
- Tie together sashes or other long pieces that might knot and tangle the wash. Button long sleeves to each other or to shirt fronts to prevent them from tangling. Pin things together only if you are certain that the pin will not rust and that the fabric around the pin will not tear during the wash. Some people like to pin little items to a bigger one, such as a towel, to be sure that they are not lost, but do this only if you are sure that it will do no harm.
- Mend tears and tighten loose buttons before laundering. Tears will grow larger and buttons may come off and be lost in the wash.
- Remove decorations, linings, buttons, or other trim or attachments on a garment that are not washable. Of course you can do this only if you know how to reattach them. If sewn-in linings are not washable, few of us are up to undertaking to remove them and sew them back in later; such garments should be dry-cleaned. (If you are astonished to learn that someone might go to the trouble of removing and then resewing a delicate button or piece of lace trim for the sake of laundering something safely, the perspective of the nineteenth century may help. Good washing practice then called at times for taking a dress apart entirely for washing or other cleaning and sewing it back together later!)
- Check each load for matching: does it contain any pieces that belong in sets? Does it contain any socks without mates? If so, consider adding the other parts of the set, even if they are clean, so that all parts will fade to the same degree. Always wash sock mates together or they may become different colors.

Useful Furnishings and Equipment for Laundry Rooms

The ideal laundry room would contain facilities that many of us have little room for. From the following list of useful features, you might select those that particularly fit your needs and your available space:

Indoor drying line

Drying racks, including a mesh one for drying knits flat

Hanging facilities, including a hanging rod, broad-shouldered hangers, and trouser and skirt hangers

Ample tabletop or countertop space for folding and stacking

Shelves for folded laundry

Shelves and cabinets for storing laundry products, stain-removal products and equipment, and mending equipment

Ironing board and iron, plus ironing aids such as a sleeveboard or press cloth

Windows providing good natural light for checking color compatibility of loads, colorfastness, success of pretreatment, color-matching sock mates, and so on

Small bulletin board with care label terms and symbols, notes on care for different articles, reminders, stain-removal charts, etc.

Double laundry tub

One or two small plastic basins

Small washboard

Clothes brushes and lint removers

Small sewing basket with scissors, needles, and several basic colors of thread for quick repairs such as reinforcing seams or tightening or removing buttons

21

Laundering

Knowing how your washing machine washes . . . The regular cycle, permanent-press cycle, gentle or delicate cycle, and adjustments and variations of these . . . Water level, temperature, hardness and softness, water softeners . . . Making balanced loads that are the right size, choosing order of loads, starting up the machine, adding detergent and other laundry products . . . Hand-washing delicate things . . . Hand-washing sturdy things . . . Cleaning the washer and dryer . . . Glossary of laundry products and additives

You can launder more efficiently and effectively if you understand what goes on under the lid of your automatic washing machine when you close it. Most people do not. Many laundry failures and frustrations can be chalked up to the illusion that it is not necessary to know what the different cycles on washing machines do, or why they are recommended for certain fabrics and fibers.

The type of automatic washing machine that most people in this country have in their homes is a top-loading machine that "agitates," or churns or jerks the clothes back and forth, by means of a post in the center of the tub, to wash and rinse them. As it drains the wash and rinse waters, it spins the clothes at ever-increasing speeds until the great "centrifugal" force of the spinning presses out so much water that the clothes do not drip—are "damp dried"—when they are finally removed. On such machines, you usually have a choice of three standard laundering cycles: "normal" or "regular," "permanent press," and "delicate." Normal or regular washing typically consists of a regular (fast or vigorous) agitation and fast spin for both washing and rinsing. Permanent-press washing uses a regular agitation and slow spin and automatically provides a "cool-down rinse" before spinning. Gentle or delicate washing uses gentle (slow) agitation and slow spinning. Top-loading machines probably also have settings allowing you to make at least the following separate adjustments:

- the size of the load (the amount of water that will flow into the tub)
- the temperature of the wash water
- the temperature of the rinse water
- how long the clothes will agitate in the wash portion of the cycle (a maximum of twelve to fifteen minutes is typical)
- whether the agitation will be regular (fast) or gentle (slow)
- whether the spin will be fast or slow
- whether there will be an extra "deep" rinse.

Thus you can vary each laundering cycle to fit the characteristics of the load. These three ways of washing, together with handwashing, are the four basic laundering procedures used in the home. The four basic procedures are explained and described in detail below.

The Regular Cycle

When you wash on the regular cycle, you usually choose the maximum length cycle or near it (say ten to fifteen minutes), with hot wash water and a cold rinse, and you use an all-purpose or heavy-duty detergent. If the clothes are very dirty or greasy, you would use extra amounts of detergent. The vigorous mechanical action of the regular cycle, plus the extra cleaning efficacy of the hot water and strong detergent, are suitable for sturdy cottons and linens and for highly soiled work, play, and athletic clothing.

Particularly heavily soiled clothes, including diapers (which are washed separately from other garments), may benefit from a presoak or even two washes. Presoaking (which used to be called just "soaking") and double washing are two different variations of the regular cycle. The presoaking cycle on an automatic washer lets clothes sit in water to which a detergent, a presoaking product, or both have been added. (Some machines alternate intervals of stillness and gentle agitating during the presoak.) Then, without draining or rinsing, the machine enters its wash/agitation cycle. Sometimes a presoak is all the extra help that is needed to get very dirty clothes clean. A presoak can be quite successful in brightening up white and light-colored fabrics that have grown dingy and in getting items that are wholly or partly made of synthetic fibers clean and fresh smelling. (Do not use chlorine bleach with an enzyme-containing presoak product, as the bleach will inactivate the enzymes. Add bleach, if you feel it will be needed, after the presoak product has had a chance to work.) Presoaking is a powerful laundering procedure that requires absolutely no labor—only foresight.

A double wash can be combined with the presoak cycle if you wish. To do a double wash, use *two separate* batches of wash water and add detergent *twice*. For the first wash, put in detergent and whatever boosters or other additives you like, and set the machine either for a six-minute regular wash or for a presoak plus a six-minute regular wash. Be sure you are present when this is finished, because the next step is to set the washer forward to the spin/drain part of the cycle manually, *skipping the rinse*. When the load has drained, manually reset the control back to the beginning of the wash cycle, add detergent, bleach, and so on, just as you would do normally (as though you were starting the load), and wash again. The first wash carries off the bulk of the dirt in the clothes, ensuring that the washing and rinsing in the second will be more effective. Because of the extra detergent you have used, you should use an extra rinse to be sure you have cleared it. Then feel the clothes; if they still feel soapy, do a third rinse.

Hot water gets clothes cleanest, and most detergents and other laundry products are more effective in hotter water. Hot water best removes heavy soil and grease and keeps whites white. But it will also tend to cause more fading and more bleeding of colors that

FRONT-LOADING WASHING MACHINES

Some manufacturers in the United States market what are known as "high-efficiency tumbling" or "horizontal-action" front-loading washing machines. The newer type of front-loading machine has a washing action and other characteristics sufficiently different from those of top-loading machines (and from older-style front-loading ones) to require some adjustments in your laundering style. Although they are said to be more effective at cleaning clothes, this is sometimes disputed. That they are considerably more energy efficient and use much less water than top-loading machines is not disputed. Where a European-made horizontal-action machine uses 15 to 17 gallons to do a medium load, a top-loading agitator might use 30 to 40 gallons (and more for larger loads). All washing machines of this type spin clothes much drier than a top-loading agitation machine. This results in a further saving in energy, as the clothes need much less time in the energy guzzling dryer. Many manufacturers of this type of washer vaunt their superior rinsing, which is said to get out more detergent and dirt residues and thus prevent dinginess from developing. The new front-loading machines are more expensive, sometimes greatly so.

European front-loading models tend to have smaller capacities and much longer wash cycles than American top-loading machines. Although you can set the European front loaders for shorter periods for lightly soiled clothes, they take as long as 1½ hours to clean, say, sturdy cotton clothes and linens that are moderately to heavily soiled. (But a friend tells me that in England everyone she knows uses a "quick" wash setting to avoid such long cycles.) European models add to their cleaning power by including a self-heating feature. Temperatures on European models may exceed 200°F, while European-made machines marketed in this country may go as high as 170°F. Insofar as your fabrics cannot be washed in very hot water or are made with dyes that fade too much in hot, you will have little reason to pay extra for a self-heating feature.

The larger American versions of the new type of front-loader have somewhat shorter wash cycles than European front loaders. They lack the self-heating feature but, like the European models, they use less energy, water, and detergent—65 percent less energy, 40 percent less water, and 30 percent less detergent—and spin clothes much drier than conventional top-loading machines. However, you may need low-sudsing detergents, which may be more expensive than regular detergents.

When you use these new machines, ordinary fabric care principles continue to apply. Like standard machines, they automatically give you a cold rinse and reduced water temperatures when you set them for permanent press or gentle cycles. You may still want to turn your permanent-press clothes inside out. You may still want to use a greater volume of water for clothes and linens that are low in abrasion resistance or that tend to pill, such as polyester and certain other synthetics. Although their manufacturers claim that the new front loaders are gentler on fabrics and cause less abrasion, this is disputed. If it turns out to be true of at least some models, however, you may be able to give clothes and linens that pill or are low in abrasion resistance a longer wash period.

are not colorfast and more shrinking in clothes that tend to shrink. Many knits have a propensity to shrink and thus are better washed in warm or cool water. Warm water is far more effective at cleaning than cool. See pages 308–10, below.

Bleach is often used for whites and colorfast colors on the regular cycle.

The Permanent-Press Cycle

The permanent-press cycle is usually best for synthetic fibers other than acrylic, modacrylic, rayon, and acetate (which usually require gentle treatment or hand-washing) and for wrinkle-resistant cottons and linens and blends of these. The permanent-press cycle uses regular (vigorous) agitation for a shorter time period (say eight minutes up to ten for heavily soiled clothes) than the regular cycle so as to reduce abrasion and wear and tear on synthetic fibers, some of which pill, and on resin-treated fibers, which are weaker than their untreated counterparts. It provides a cool-down rinse and a cold final rinse so that heat-sensitive fibers do not go into the spin cycle while warm or hot. It uses a slower spin speed so that wrinkles are not set into synthetic fabrics or permanent-press clothes by the spin pressure. (Wash-and-wear fabrics, however, should not be spun at all. Remove them from the washer after the rinse, press them dry with a towel, and carefully hang them to dry.) The wash water is usually warm, but occasionally hot or cold will be needed. Ordinary all-purpose detergents are usually fine for the clothes that receive this treatment; sometimes deodorizing detergents are advisable for odor-retaining synthetics.

To help reduce the pilling produced by abrasion during washing, turn any clothes that might pill inside out. You should also use more water than you would for a comparable load of cottons or linens, as this diminishes the amount of rubbing against one another that the articles undergo. For example, fill the machine with water to the "large" load level when you are washing a medium-sized load or to the "medium" load level when you are washing a small load. And be sure to add the correct amount of detergent for the *increased* water level.

The downside of reducing the abrasion, of course, is that you also reduce the cleaning power of the wash, as abrasion—rubbing together—is one of the things that gets out dirt during the agitation. To get synthetic fibers clean, you will usually need to *pretreat problem areas and give a long presoak in detergent and water as hot as the fiber can bear* (which is often hotter than the care label indicates). Deodorant detergents or laundry boosters are helpful because of the odor-retaining potential of many synthetic fibers such as polyester, acrylic, and polypropylene. When it is safe for the fabric, chlorine bleach deodorizes effectively. Warm water, rather than the cool that is often recommended on care labels, does a better job at getting odor out too. If you are having odor problems on synthetics whose label recommends cold-water wash, try lukewarm water rather than cold; and if that does not work, try warm or hot water—but *never on polypropylene or other especially heat-sensitive fibers*. Warm wash water, pretreating, presoaking, not skimping on detergent, and frequent washing all help to minimize problems getting synthetics and permanent-press clothes clean and fresh.

Fabric softener is appropriate for permanent-press clothes, but you need to use it only every two or three launderings. If you use it too often, you will get a greasy buildup. Softeners help diminish static and give a smooth hand. Liquid softener is used in the final rinse; machines with an automatic dispenser will hold it until then, so you need not remember to come and add it. Softener sheets that go in the dryer are also good. Detergents that include softeners are not recommended. Note that the old rule specifying regular-cycle laundering of whites does not usually apply to synthetic whites. Whites that are synthetic or wrinkle-treated probably will need the permanent-press cycle. Many white synthetics will stay white without bleach. If they do not, they often can take and will respond to ordinary household bleaches, but there are exceptions.

The Delicate or Gentle Cycle

Delicate or gentle laundering is the most variable of the washing machine treatments because the profile of "delicate" fabrics is so variable. The gentle cycle is needed sometimes because of a garment's fiber content (machine-washable silk and wool, viscose rayon, acrylic and modacrylic, and acetate) and sometimes because of its delicate construction (lace, very sheer fabrics, loosely woven or knitted ones). The slow, short agitation (six to eight minutes or even less) and spin typically used on the delicate cycle offer mechanical protection and reduced abrasion to delicate constructions, weak fibers, and fibers that weaken when wet. The cool to warm wash water, cold rinses, and mild detergents and soaps (preferably liquid ones when you are using cold water) protect fragile fibers and finishes from harsh chemical cleaning action.

It is helpful to be aware of why you are using gentle treatment so you can vary the delicate cycle effectively. For example, machine-washable acetate and viscose rayon need special treatment both physically and chemically. They need cooler temperatures, detergent that is gentle and works with cooler temperatures, and gentle agitation and slow spin. Knits of cotton, cotton/polyester, and rayon will shrink in hot water, but they may not need mild detergent. An untreated white cotton dress with a cotton lace collar trim that might detach from the collar may not be harmed by strong detergent or hot water, but it should receive brief, gentle agitation. Some linens might do best with gentle agitation, hot water, and all-purpose detergent. Strong bleaches, too, are sometimes safe for fabrics that need gentle agitation or spinning in order to minimize the risks of tearing or excessive wrinkling.

Agitation and spinning do not subject fabrics to the same kinds of stresses. Spinning or fast spinning should be avoided on some sturdy wrinkle-treated and thermoplastic fabrics only because it may set in wrinkles. Spinning exerts an enormous force on fabrics that presses the cloth against the walls of the machine, squeezing out the water. Quite often you will be able to use a fast spin in the gentle cycle; wool, for example, is so elastic that after hand-washing washable wool sweaters you can spin them dry in your machine using the fast spin setting without fear of harming them.

More central to true "gentle" treatment is gentle agitation. Agitation jerks and pulls fabrics. This forces water back and forth through the cloth, dissolving and lifting out dirt. It also abrades—causes a constant rubbing of one item against another—which is part of what gets them clean. Agitation does no harm to sturdy cloth, but it can cause pilling on fabrics prone to pilling, as many synthetics are; it can weaken cloth with low abrasion resistance; and it too can result in tearing of extremely delicate fabrics. You can reduce abrasion and wear and tear on very fragile items by placing them in a mesh bag for laundering. (This also prevents very small items such as baby socks from being lost.) Ample water further reduces abrasion. Vigorous spinning might not harm a garment that would be badly affected by long and vigorous agitation. Machine-washable wool, for example, should be gently agitated for a very short time, if at all, but can be spun fast to get it as dry as you can.

Besides these variations in why items need "gentle" treatment, there are all the ordinary differences between them in color, colorfastness, degree and type of soiling, and so forth. Because of this great variability, few people can wash all their delicates in one load. If your machine has a "mini-basket," that helps. If it does not, you may find it efficient to hand-wash some of your delicates.

Fabric softeners are advisable occasionally for synthetics that will receive gentle treatment. Liquid softeners are added to the final rinse water. Softener sheets are added to the dryer.

Water—How Much, How Hot, How Soft?

Quantity. Use the setting on your machine that is proper for the size of your load. Too much water results in poor cleaning because there is too little rubbing and abrasion. Too little water will also result in poor cleaning, along with poor rinsing, detergent

OPTIONS FOR ADJUSTING AND VARYING THE THREE BASIC AUTOMATIC WASHING MACHINE CYCLES

- *Water quantity according to size of load.* Larger, dirtier loads need more water. Permanent press, wool, and fabrics that pill should be washed with more water than other clothes. More water reduces wrinkling in permanent press, knits.
- *Water temperature.* Hot water is best for cleaning and sanitizing. Cool is best for reducing shrinking and fading. Use cool water for presoaking protein stains, for example, blood or egg. The cooler the water temperature, the longer you should wash/agitate the clothes and the more important is a presoak.
- *Water softeners.* Helpful where water is hard (has high dissolved mineral content). See "Water Softeners," below.
- *Detergent.* Larger loads, harder water, colder water, and heavier soil all require more detergent. If you do a presoak, you should use up to 50 percent more detergent than you would normally use for the load. Or add a presoaking product in addition to the regular amount of detergent proper for the load. (See the Glossary of Laundry Products and Additives at the end of this chapter.)
- *Detergent boosters.* Boosters can help in cold water, hard water, or with extra-dirty laundry. (See the glossary at the end of this chapter.)
- *Bleach.* Add to wash water for whitening, brightening, and cleaning. Chlorine bleach also sanitizes and deodorizes. (See the glossary at the end of this chapter.)
- *Bluing.* Can help yellowing whites look white again. See the glossary at the end of this chapter.)
- *Length of agitation/wash period.* Longer agitation gives greater cleaning; shorter agitation causes less wear and tear and abrasion.
- *Speed of agitation/wash period.* Fast cleans better. Slow cleans more gently, and causes less pilling. Delicates, permanent press, and machine-washable wools need slower or shorter agitation.
- *Speed of spin.* Slow is gentler for very delicate articles. Fast gets things drier.
- *Additional final rinse.* Useful to avoid dinginess and premature wearing caused by detergent and soil residues incompletely rinsed out of clothes. Also useful when doing diapers or other clothes that go next to infants' sensitive skin (or anyone else with sensitive skin) to be sure soap or detergent is completely washed out. Useful when using extra detergent or boosters or doing double washes, to be sure extra cleaning product is completely removed. Useful for whites to be sure bleach and any other residues that might affect the fabric are removed.
- *Liquid fabric softener in final rinse.* Reduces static, gives soft hand to synthetics, renders pile fabrics fluffier. Or use dryer softener sheet. (See the glossary at the end of this chapter.)
- *Use of liquid starch in final rinse.* Gives added crispness to cottons, linen, rayons. Or use spray product while ironing. (See the glossary at the end of this chapter.)

and laundry-product residues in your clothes, dinginess, and a harsh feeling. It also causes excessive abrasion and wears out your clothes prematurely. If you use too much detergent or other additives for the amount of water, you can get excessively high concentrations of chemicals on your clothes and damage them. The recommendations of the manufacturer of your machine as to the amount of water needed for a certain amount of laundry are highly reliable.

Water Temperature. For the best laundering results, but not necessarily the most energy-efficient results, choose the hottest wash temperature the fabrics will bear without shrinking, fading, or suffering other damage. The hotter the wash temperature, the better any laundry soap or detergent will work. Warm or cool water rather than hot, however, keeps many colors brighter. Some laundry products advertise that they work better than others in cold water. That may be true, but it does not mean that they would not work still better in warmer water. No matter what detergent you are using, warm or hot water is always better than cold for cleaning oil and grease stains.

Laundry experts agree that no detergents will work properly in water temperatures below 65°F. Washing your clothes in such cold water can cause lint, poor cleaning, and residues of undissolved detergent. Granular detergents may not readily dissolve or mix into cold water. Before you decide to use cold water, consider also that "cold" in one geographical location may be remarkably different from "cold" in another, and perhaps neither of those is what a detergent manufacturer means by "cold." If you live in Florida, your "cold" water in August will be lukewarm; in northern Michigan, your cold water in January will be frigid indeed- probably below 65°F. The Federal Trade Commission is considering changing care label rules to permit the use of such terms as "cool" and "lukewarm" to describe wash-water temperatures. In the meantime, these are the temperatures that manufacturers have in mind when they talk about cold, warm, and hot laundering (and dishwashing) water temperatures:

Cold water: 80°F (26.7°C) or colder

Warm water: 90° to 110°F (32.2 to 43.3°C)

Hot water: 130°F (54.4°C) or above

It is worthwhile to acquire an inexpensive thermometer for testing your home water temperatures. You may find that there is a significant difference between what your water heater is set for and what gets delivered at the faucet. The wash water cools once it is in the washer, too, so that you may begin a load with hot water but end with much cooler.

The hot-water setting on your washing machine, unless you have one of the models that heats its own water, is only as hot as your tap water. Most people's homes have tap water between 140° and 150°F. New hot-water heaters are preset in the factory at 120°F, but people sometimes raise the settings at home. Safety experts recommend tap water temperatures not higher than 120°F in households with children or very elderly people. On a day when your hot-water heater is set at 140°F and your cold tap water is 60°F, if you choose the "warm" setting on your washing machine you will probably get wash temperatures of about 100°F (which feels comfortably warm to the hand). This will provide good cleaning for much of your laundry, if less cleaning power than hot water. But if your hot water is 120°F and your cold is 40°F, your "warm" may be only about 80°F, which is considered cold under care label rules.

Water temperature affects more than cleaning power. Hotter water kills microorganisms and gives better sanitizing. Hot enough water kills dust mites too. Colder water minimizes shrinking and fading, and it is better for presoaking many protein stains, such as blood. When dyes, fiber content, and construction are suitable:

- Use hot water for sturdy whites, pastels and light prints, diapers and soiled baby bibs and clothes, heavily soiled work, garden, sport, and play clothes; clothes and linens of those sick with infectious diseases; on oily or greasy dirt; dish towels and dishcloths, bath towels and hand towels, face cloths, pillowcases and sheets and other household linens; and cleaning rags and cloths.
- Use warm water for permanent press, colorfast brights, and dark colors.
- Use cool for delicates, fabrics with dyes that run or bleed, fabrics that are lightly

soiled, soaking protein stains such as blood, and rinsing.

Cold water is generally recommended for rinsing your clothes after they have been washed. Most home washing machines let you set your automatic controls for any temperature wash and offer you, at the least, a choice of cold or warm rinsing. (With some coin-operated machines, you may have no choice as to rinse temperature.) Cold rinse water is perfectly adequate in all but exceptional circumstances. It is more energy efficient, even when you factor in the qualification that your dryer may take longer to dry clothes that have been chilled by the cold-water rinse. A warm rinse is a bit more effective at removing dirty, sudsy water from your clothes and linens. Try a warm rinse, or a couple of them, at times when you need especially effective rinsing—for instance, for the clothes or linens of someone with sensitive skin; for a delicate fabric from which you wish to remove all possible residues of detergents or other laundry additives; or if you are working on trying to remove dinginess or grayness or yellowness from whites.

Quality: Water Softeners. If you have hard water, you probably know it already—your shampoo struggles to foam, and you may get mineral deposits around your faucets. It might still be useful to have your water tested to see just how hard it is so that you can make appropriate adjustments when you launder. Manufacturers have the following levels of softness and hardness of water in mind when they make their recommendations as to how much detergent or bleach or other product you should use:

	Soft	*Moderately hard*	*Hard*	*Very hard*
Grains/gal	0.0–3.5	3.6–7.0	7.1–10.5	10.6+
Parts/million or mgs/liter	0.0–60	61–120	121–180	180+

Many people install mechanical water softeners in their homes. These use ion-exchange resins to remove the minerals; they "exchange" the calcium and magnesium ions for sodium ions provided by the resins.

If your water is very hard and you have no mechanical water-softening system, you can add a packaged water softener to your laundry. Remember to use the softener in the rinse water as well as in the wash water. There are two varieties of packaged softeners: nonprecipitating and precipitating. Nonprecipitating types (such as Calgon) "sequester" the offending minerals and hold them in solution; the water remains clear. These usually contain polyphosphates. Precipitating softeners combine with the minerals to form a precipitate or residue that turns the water cloudy. The precipitate can stick to clothes or your washer. Precipitating softeners usually contain sodium carbonate (washing soda) or sodium sesquicarbonate. TSP and borax are both precipitating softeners. You can buy water softeners at the supermarket or your local hardware store. Be sure to follow the product instructions.

If your water is only moderately hard, you will probably need to do nothing more than use enough of a good detergent that contains water softeners. But in this case it would be better to avoid detergents that contain carbonates. (Read labels carefully.) The unpleasant potential effects of using a carbonate detergent if you have hard water include stiff, harsh towels; fading, dullness, dinginess, or graying; a white powdery residue on dark clothes; reduced wrinkle resistance in permanent-press clothes; increased abrasion; and buildup of a crust in the washer.

To remove hard-water mineral residues from clothes, soak the clothes in a solution of 2 cups white vinegar to 1 gallon hot tap water for 15 minutes, in a *plastic* container. (Do not use a metal or other container that will be affected by the vinegar, which is a mild acid.)

There are other strategies besides adding water softeners that will help you cope successfully with hard water. Try using a phosphate detergent; using hotter wash water;

adding more detergent and making sure it is fully dissolved before adding clothes; using more bleach; and sorting with special care, particularly keeping greasy or more heavily soiled clothes entirely separate from lightly soiled or delicate things.

Washing in the Machine

Making Balanced, Properly Sized Loads. As though you had not already expended a Solomon's store of wisdom in sorting your clothes, when it comes to putting them in the machine there are still other factors to consider. The physical size and composition of the load also affects how clean your clothes become. Every load should be composed of a mixture of small and large items, because this mix produces the best action for cleaning and keeps the machine balanced. No load should be too small—you usually need at least what your machine designates as "small"—because the clothes should rub together to some degree to get clean. (Some washing machines have a water-saving "minibasket," a small tub that fits into the machine for doing miniloads.)

Overloading can cause a smorgasbord of problems. Overpacked loads will not come clean. Water cannot circulate adequately or carry off all the soil through the clothes during washing and rinsing agitation when clothes are jammed together. Clothes will retain soil and soap, each of which will make them look dingy and weaken the fibers. Overloading can cause excessive linting and increased pilling and wear because crowded wash articles rub against one another too much. Extra water is desirable for permanent press, many synthetics, delicates, and machine-washable wool, to reduce abrasion and, if the fabric is susceptible, pilling. About three dozen cloth diapers is as many as should be washed together in one load in a top-loading machine.

Overcrowding can also cause wrinkling. To get the most wrinkle-free wash possible, make sure the clothes have plenty of room to move in the water. Permanent-press clothes and machine-washable knits will need more room to move in the water than other clothes to reduce or avoid wrinkling. Never wash any load of permanent-press clothes that is larger than medium-sized, and always use the next larger water setting: use "large" for medium, "medium" for small. Very large items like bedspreads, blankets, and sheets need more room to move in the washer than smaller ones.

Gauge the size of your loads by seeing how full they make the machine before you add water, and carefully review your instruction manual on this subject. My machine uses the following scale for judging load size:

Small:	1/3 full, loosely loaded
Medium:	1/3 to 1/2 full, loosely loaded
Large:	1/2 to 3/4 full, loosely loaded
Extra-large:	3/4 to completely full, loosely loaded

Once you are used to your machine, you will no longer need to load in clothes to see how full it is; you will be able to estimate this automatically.

Order of Loads. People who have limited supplies of hot water for washing will first wash the loads that require the hottest water: whites, cottons, linens, and heavily soiled clothes. Then they will do the loads requiring warm water and finally those that take cold Those with plenty of hot water (which is most of us nowadays) can choose any order that is convenient. For my family, it is usually most efficient to wash first the clothes that take longest to dry—towels, thick bedspreads, and heavy denims.

Starting Up the Machine. Once the loads are ready, set the machine dials to the proper wash cycles, water levels (load size), temperatures, spin and agitation speeds, and running times, designating a presoak or extra rinse if you wish. The right load size, according to the instructions in your washing machine's instruction booklet, is crucial; you want enough water to get your clothes clean with the optimal amount of abrasion and without wasting water and energy. If your machine does not have an automatic lint cleaner, clean the lint filter before each use.

Adding Detergent, Bleaches, and Other Products. Fill the machine with water and add the detergent *before* you add the load of clothes. If you put in the clothes first and then fill the machine with water and add detergent, the detergent may not fully dissolve or be thoroughly mixed and you may get uneven cleaning or stains in spots where detergent sat on the clothes undiluted. At any time after an inch or more of water has accumulated, you can add the proper amount of detergent to the machine. There are directions on the boxes or bottles about how much to use. You need more detergent if you are using higher water levels, no matter how little laundry you actually put in, since you want to create the right concentration of detergent in the water. Similarly, if you have a large- or extra-large capacity machine, it uses more water than a regular-capacity machine to do small, medium, or large loads; thus you need proportionally more detergent. (See the detergent manufacturer's instructions.) You should also add more detergent if your water is extra-hard or less if your water is extra-soft. *If you are doing a presoak, you should add up to 50 percent more detergent than would otherwise be called for or add a separate presoaking product.* You can stir the water with a big wooden paddle or extralong wooden spoon or run the machine for a minute, making sure that the detergent and other laundry products are completely dissolved and mixed; only then add the clothes. Detergents may not dissolve readily in cold water. If you tend to have problems with undissolved detergent, try a liquid detergent. Or first dissolve the correct amount of powdered detergent in a quart of lukewarm to warm water (the warmer the water, the more easily the detergent dissolves) and then add this to the machine. For information on when and how to add fabric softeners, see page 324.

Bluing, water softeners, oxygen bleaches (which often contain bluing), and boosters should be added, and thoroughly stirred or mixed, when you add the detergent, before the clothes are loaded. Such products can be used in the presoak if you are doing one. Years ago, before automatic or fully automatic washers were used, bluing was added in the final rinse, but this is inadvisable in automatic washers because the clothes are already inside when you want to mix the bluing with the water. It is very important to make sure that oxygen bleach and bluing are thoroughly mixed into the wash water, or you can end up with light spots or blue streaks on your clothes. (These blue streaks can be cured. See "Bluing" in the glossary at the end of this chapter). Never pour oxygen bleach directly on clothes. Oxygen bleach needs time to work; it will be more effective if you use it in a presoak or in extended washing, and, especially, if you use it regularly and with water as hot as the fabrics can bear.

When the detergent, oxygen bleach, and other additives are thoroughly dissolved and mixed, add the clothes, dropping them in loosely, one piece at a time, separately around the post. Do not string long objects around the post because this leads to tangling.

Follow the manufacturer's instructions for using chlorine bleach. For best results, add chlorine bleach five minutes after the clothes have agitated in the water-and-detergent solution. This permits the additives contained in some detergents—optical brighteners, oxygen bleach, or enzymes—time to do their work; chlorine bleach can interfere with the action of such additives. (See "Chlorine Bleach" in "Bleaches," in the glossary at the end of this chapter.) Some newer-model machines have bleach dispensers that automatically delay adding the chlorine bleach for a few minutes. If yours does not, simply pour bleach into the bleach dispenser five or six minutes after the wash cycle begins. If you do not have a bleach dispenser, add *diluted* bleach to top-loading machines manually as follows. Mix the correct amount of chlorine bleach (see the manufacturer's instructions, paying careful attention to load size) with 1 to 1½ quarts of water; then stop the washing machine's agitation by opening the lid, pour in the bleach solution, and stir with a long wooden spoon or paddle. Close the machine to let it continue washing. (Front-loading machines that I have seen do not permit manually adding diluted bleach after the machine has begun washing; you must use the automatic dispenser.) You can add chlorine bleach, following these instructions, at any point during the wash cycle when you can count on having a few minutes for it to work before the wash water drains. *Be careful to ensure that chlorine bleach is not splashed or poured directly on fabrics, as this can cause holes, weakened fibers, or serious discoloration.* Such splashing can occur when you are pouring bleach into your machine's automatic bleach dispenser. When using chlorine bleach, your goal is to ensure that the bleach is thoroughly mixed into the wash water and never touches dry clothes. If the bleach will be used when the clothes are not agitating, stir *diluted* bleach in with a wooden paddle or big wooden spoon to mix it well.

If the washing machine becomes unbalanced during operation and rumbles or stops, open the lid and redistribute the clothes in a balanced manner and close it again. The machine should start up automatically.

When the machine has finished a load, remove it for drying promptly. This will reduce wrinkling. Moreover, wet clothes will support rapid microbial growth; odors and even mold will develop if you leave wet clothes long enough. In warm weather, wet clothes can develop a sour smell overnight. If that happens, you must wash them again, for the smell will not come out during drying.

Hand-Washing

Hand-Washing Delicates. The care label regulations define hand-washing as "gently squeezing action." This action is what is being prescribed when a label tells you to hand-wash; usually you hand-wash because the fabric is so delicate, so weak, or so weakened when wet that it could not take agitation or spinning without damage. Sometimes hand-washing is prescribed because a fabric loses dye so quickly that only the briefest immersion in water can be tolerated without serious fading.

To hand-wash delicate items, usually you should immerse them for a few minutes in a basin of cool to lukewarm water in which some mild detergent or a specialty cleaning product designed for delicate fabrics has been mixed. See "Detergents and soaps, mild," in the glossary at the end of this chapter. If the hand-washing instructions on labels do not specify any particular water temperature, this means that any temperature—hot, warm, or cold—is safe. Keep dye-bleeding articles immersed for the shortest possible time.

The gentlest hand-washing, which should be used for panty hose and stockings, loose knits, and other delicate items, consists of carefully patting the article until wetted with sudsy water, then squeezing it, forcing water through the fabric in the process, until the soil has been lifted. Silks, woolens, and rayons may be gently dipped up and down. Especially delicate items are simply immersed in sudsy water, soaked, and perhaps patted briefly. Delicates not vulnerable to abrasion may be gently rubbed against each other or against themselves. If delicates are heavily soiled, you might try a presoak or a pretreatment of just the heavily soiled spots with mild detergent when this is safe for the fabric.

Rinse with clear cold water, using the same technique as when washing, until all soap or detergent is removed. Several rinse baths may be necessary. The rinse is finished when the water no longer has a slippery feel. You may wish to use gloves when doing hand-washing to preserve your skin and the laundry too. If you don't wear gloves, be sure that you have no rough fingernails (and apply a moisturizer to your hands afterward).

Unless otherwise instructed, roll delicate hand-washed items in a towel to remove excess water. (Make sure that the towel will not bleed color to the garment and that the wet garment will not bleed color to the towel.) Never wring delicate fabrics, many of which are very weak when wet. Wringing out clothes is much harder on them than spinning or agitating in the washer. Never wring wash-and-wear or permanent-press clothes, as wringing will wrinkle them.

Delicates should usually be hung to dry or dried flat. (See chapter 22, "Drying the Laundry.") You can place them on a drying frame that provides a mesh for support beneath them while allowing air to circulate on all sides. Or you can lay them on a clean, dry towel that does not bleed and will not be harmed if the garment bleeds. Knits and stretchy items should be blocked to their proper shape and dried flat to prevent stretching. (See page 246 in chapter 16 on blocking.) To speed drying, turn an electric fan on the clothes. Dry them out of direct sunlight. For suggestions on washing old or other very fragile fabrics, see pages 250–51 in chapter 16.

Hand-Washing Sturdy Articles. Sometimes you want to hand-wash something that is not delicate. You are in a hotel, it is midnight, and you need a garment for the morning. Or you have a muddy pair of overalls whose soil you do not want to contaminate a load of other clothes, or perhaps you have one or two small things that are not worth running the machine for, or you feel that without individual attention a particular garment will not come clean.

Hand-washing can be vigorous as well as gentle. In fact, hand-washing can be more harsh than anything your washing machine can do. If you are dealing with especially dirty clothes, hand-scrubbing, when the clothes are sturdy enough to take it, can be far more effective than machine-washing and sometimes is your only hope. The combination of physical action and chemical action is more effective than either alone, and the addition of heat (in the water) makes it even more so.

Use protective rubber gloves, ordinary laundry detergent (if appropriate to the fiber), and the hottest water that is suitable to the fabric and the soil and that your gloved hands can bear. When it would be safe for the fabric, presoaking the item in extremely hot water before you scrub it is highly effective—using whatever detergents, boosters, bleaches, or pretreatment products are appropriate. Use only *cold* water, however, for articles that bleed, and never presoak these. Immerse them in water for the shortest possible time consistent with getting them clean.

To scrub a sturdy article, grasp the cloth in both hands and rub it against itself, concentrating on the areas with heaviest soil, perhaps the cuffs, knees, and collar. Alternate this rubbing with repeatedly immersing and swishing and squeezing the article in soapy water. This rinses away dirt that you have loosened by your scrubbing and gets you fresher soapy water to continue scrubbing with. If the water becomes too soiled, drain it and start over with fresh water and detergent.

If you find that you wash hard-to-clean sturdy items by hand more than occasionally, you might find it useful to have a small washboard (like the larger one your grandmother or great-grandmother had) to handle deeply ingrained soil in play clothes, gardening clothes, work clothes, or sportswear. Try this

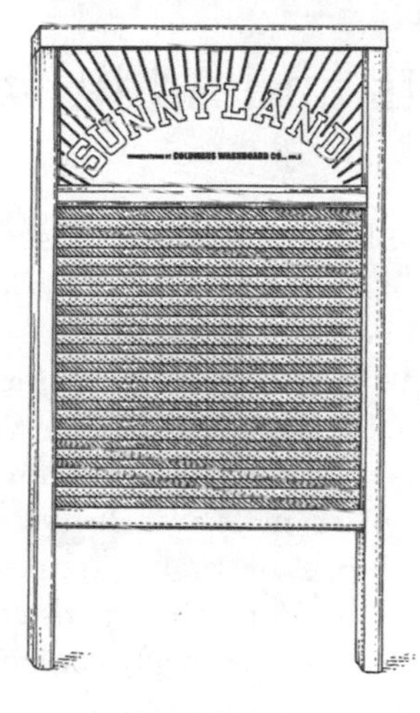

Washboard

especially on mud, oil or grease, food stains, collar rings, and any other soil that resists coming clean in the machine. Just scrub the fabric up and down against the bumps on the washboard.

If you do not have a washboard, you can scrub the fabric with a small soft brush or toothbrush or against another cloth, such as a clean white terry towel, or scrub it against itself as described above. *All such procedures, while often effective, can be very hard on the cloth*—harder than a washboard, whose surface is smoother.

When you can see that you have gotten the article clean, rinse thoroughly as many times as it takes to get out every last bit of suds. Wring the article out by first twisting the cloth, then grasping it at both ends with one hand rotated as far forward as it will go and the other as far back as it will go. Then reverse the rotation of your fists so as to tighten the twist, forcing out water. (Remember that these are techniques to be used only on *sturdy* hand-washables!) This takes muscles, and it's good exercise. After wringing, you may still want to roll the item in a towel, as you do with delicates, to get out even more water and decrease the drying time.

If the article can take it, put it in the dryer on the proper temperature or hang it on a line outdoors. Otherwise, hang or dry flat as described in "Hand-Washing Delicates," page 313.

Never use these harsh hand-washing methods on delicate items, unless, of course, the soil or stain is so serious that the article will be unusable if it is not removed. In this situation, you have nothing to lose by trying progressively harsher treatments.

Washers and Dryers

Check your instruction booklets for any maintenance chores. Some automatic washers have filters that need cleaning periodically. You should wash out the tub in your washer occasionally. First wipe out any dirt or lint particles with a damp cloth, then run the machine through a short wash cycle with laundry detergent and hot water, spin, and rinse with plain water. If you need to clean and sanitize the washing machine tub, make a solution of liquid chlorine bleach, detergent, and water in the proportions specified in chapter 30, page 433, and let it stand in the tub for a few minutes before draining it. Then refill with plain water to rinse, and drain again.

Dryer filters need constant cleaning; too large a collection of lint causes the dryer to operate inefficiently and is a fire hazard. In addition to emptying the filter frequently between loads, you should clean in and around the opening in which the filter sits, as lint tends to collect in this entire area. Vacuuming there with the crevice cleaner attachment is helpful. Now and then, wipe the inside of your dryer with a well-wrung cloth dampened with a mild detergent-and-water solution.

The exteriors of washers and dryers are usually made of baked enamel, which scratches easily but readily wipes clean with a cloth dampened in a solution of mild detergent and water or any mild, nonabrasive all-purpose household cleaner.

Glossary of Laundry Products and Additives

Acid. See "Vinegar."

Alkali. See "Ammonia," "Borax," "Detergents and soaps," "Detergents and soaps, mild," "Trisodium phosphate," and "Washing soda." Laundering solutions of water and detergent typically are alkaline (have a pH greater than 7).

Ammonia. Ammonia is an alkaline substance that can be used as a laundry booster. It will sometimes brighten a load of laundry and help detergent perform better. Add 1/2 cup of household ammonia to the laundry water before you add clothes. *Do not add ammonia to any laundry water that has been treated with chlorine bleach: the combination of ammonia and bleach releases toxic fumes.*

Average load. When a product label tells you to use a certain amount of detergent or soap for an average load, it is important to realize what it means by "average":

5–7 pounds of clothes

Moderate soil

Medium (moderately) hard water: 3.6–7.0 grains of minerals per gallon or 61–120 parts per million or milligrams/liter

Average water volume: 17 gallons (64 liters) for top-loading washing machines and 8 gallons (30 liters) for front-loading machines

My observation of my neighbors suggests to me that what detergent manufacturers consider "average," many people consider rather small. Thus detergent manufacturers are surely right when they say that one of the main causes of poor laundering is using insufficient detergent. If you use too little, the soil will redeposit itself and your laundry will be gray and dingy. If you use too much, however, your machine will not be able to rinse it out properly and your laundry will come out stiff and boardlike.

Bleaches. Bleaching is the process of applying oxidizing or reducing agents to fabrics so as to chemically transform dark or colored materials in textile fibers into colorless, soluble ones that can be washed away. (Oxidation is the removal of one or more electrons from an ion, atom, or molecule. Reduction is the addition of one or more electrons. Both processes result in making stains colorless.) Household bleaches usually contain oxidizing agents such as sodium hypochlorite (chlorine bleach), sodium perborate, potassium monopersulfate, sodium percarbonate, and hydrogen peroxide.

Bleaching makes fabrics whiter and cleaner, which causes them to look brighter; chlorine bleaching also deodorizes and sanitizes them. But if used improperly, bleaches can fade dyes and weaken cloth. Different household bleaches vary considerably in strength. Strong bleaches can eat holes in cloth if accidentally splashed on it at full-strength. Part of the art of laundering is learning to pick a bleach appropriate for the fabric, a process of weighing costs and benefits. One factor to be weighed in the balance is that bleach helps to remove dirt and detergent residues, which can also cause deterioration in cloth, and that a fabric that does not look good has also failed to "last."

When your eyes tell you that your clothes or linens are stained or heavily soiled or appear gray, dingy, dull, or yellow, you may wish to use bleach. Follow the instructions on the product's label. The process becomes intuitive as you gain experience with it. The product label tells you which of the commonly available chemical bleaches (discussed below) is included in the product. Advice on which bleach to use is included below.

Sunlight: natural bleaching In ordinary sunlight, nature has provided an effective bleaching agent that is gentler than chemical bleaches. Sunshine has a greater bleaching effect on damp fabrics than on dry ones, so if you want to bleach a cotton sheet, towel, or T-shirt, or a linen tablecloth, wash it and spread it out in the sun on a sheet or other clean white cloth, or hang it on a line. You can get slight results in one day, and slightly more results with two or three. Sunlight can fade dyes, so dry colored things in the shade. Prolonged exposure to sunlight, as with other bleaches, will cause fabrics to deteriorate. White cotton yellows with prolonged exposure to sunlight, but the effect of moderate sun exposure on cotton is to bleach it. (Yellowing is not likely to be visible on colored fabrics other than pastel blues.) Vigorous laundering, especially with chlorine bleach, will usually take out such yellowing in white cottons.

Hydrogen peroxide Dilute solutions of hydrogen peroxide can be used for household chemical bleaching. Hydrogen peroxide is an oxygen bleach. (The other oxygen bleaches convert to hydrogen peroxide in solution. See "Oxygen bleaches" below.) Hydrogen peroxide is recommended for bleaching delicate fabrics and washable white wool and silk and can be an important aid in stain removal. You can buy a 3% solution of hydrogen peroxide for various household uses at your drugstore; this is already dilute enough to be safe on fabrics, but add water if you wish. It comes in a brown bottle that is intended to keep it from deteriorating from exposure to light. Hydrogen peroxide loses its effectiveness over time. (To be sure yours is active, try the simple home test provided in chapter 30, "Peaceful Coexistence with Microbes," page 434.)

Be sure to test the hydrogen peroxide in an inconspicuous area for safety for the fabric before using it as a bleach. Soak fibers other than wool in the peroxide solution for thirty minutes, but wool can be harmed by soaking and should be removed after a few minutes. Rinse thoroughly.

Although you can, in theory, also use any good commercial oxygen or all-fabric bleach for delicates and washable white wools and silks, all-fabric bleaches usually contain bluing, optical brighteners, laundry boosters, or other additives. Plain hydrogen peroxide is desirable when such additives are not suitable for your fabric.

Oxygen bleaches The household oxygen bleaches, also known as "all-fabric" bleaches, include sodium perborate, potassium monopersulfate, hydrogen peroxide, and sodium percarbonate. All of these except hydrogen peroxide come in powdered form. When dissolved in water, the inorganic peroxide compounds they each contain convert to hydrogen peroxide (plus some residue, such as sodium borate or sodium calmite), and this hydrogen peroxide is the actual bleaching agent in each of them. The hydrogen peroxide reacts with soil and organic materials, either rendering them colorless or breaking them up. This chemical bleaching action, in the strengths in which we use such products in our homes, is gentler than chlorine bleaching.

Powdered oxygen bleaches usually contain a number of other substances: builders and surfactants such as sodium carbonate, optical brighteners, bluing agents, and perfumes. Enzymes are also used in some. Oxygen bleaches are safe for almost all whites, colorfast dyes, fibers, and fabrics. They should not be used on dyes that are not colorfast, on extremely delicate or old fabrics, and on some wools or silks. They are said to be good for maintaining whiteness and brightness but not very useful for restoring whiteness once it has been lost. Thus you must use them regularly to reap their benefits.

Their effectiveness depends on four factors: temperature, time, concentration of the active ingredient, and pH of the solution. Oxygen bleaches need an alkaline environment to be really effective. Sodium carbonate, which is often added to commercial bleaches, increases the alkalinity of the washwater solution. In addition, oxygen bleaches need hot water—140°F or higher. The typical load of laundry in this country, however, is washed at lower temperatures. Activated oxygen bleaches, such as Biz, contain a chemical catalyst that significantly improves their functioning at lower wash temperatures, but most oxygen bleaches sold in this country are not activated. With all oxygen bleaches, the longer the exposure, the greater the effectiveness of the bleach. And the lower the water temperature, the longer you need to expose fabrics to oxygen bleaches. (This is unlike chlorine bleach, which both works well in lower wash water temperatures and completes its work within a given period after which further exposure is not useful; see the discussion of chlorine bleach below.) Thus presoaking or using an extended washing period when you use an oxygen bleach can improve its effectiveness.

Despite their comparative mildness, oxygen bleaches can occasionally do damage when used on the wrong fabrics, so test them following the manufacturer's instructions, before using, on an inconspicuous area of the garment if there is any question as to their safety. Test detergents that contain oxygen bleaches too. Oxygen bleaches can be used safely on fabrics that have received wrinkle-resistance resin finishes.

Oxygen bleaches should be added to the presoak or wash water with the detergent, before the clothes, in the amounts recommended by the manufacturer for the load size. Make sure that the bleach is thoroughly mixed and dissolved before putting the clothes in.

Chlorine bleach Chlorine bleach, ordinarily sold for home use as a 5.25% solution of sodium hypochlorite, is the strongest household laundry bleach. Its aesthetic and hygienic contributions to laundering are both important. It will whiten whites, brighten colorfast colors, remove stains, and remove mildew. It also cleans, increases the effectiveness of laundering in cooler water, sanitizes, and deodorizes. It is inexpensive.

Chlorine bleach is usually safe on sturdy white and colorfast cottons and on most fabrics made of manufactured fibers (other than spandex and nylon). When used at proper concentrations, it is safe for the majority of washables. Improperly used, it can drastically weaken cloth, eat holes in it, and fade clothes and linens. Proper use means diluting the bleach according to the manufacturer's instructions, using the recommended quantities, adding it to the machine in the recommended manner, and not spilling bleach on clothes. You risk damage to your clothes and linens if you use chlorine bleach in defiance of care label instructions. *If you have any doubt, test the effect of diluted chlorine bleach in an inconspicuous area.* (See pages 300–301.) Be sure always to test all components of a garment before concluding that it is safe for chlorine bleaching; facings, interfacings, linings, and trim are sometimes vulnerable when the garment-in-chief is not. In addition, read the fiber content label, and for each fiber listed on the label, determine whether any household bleach may safely be used on it.

When using chlorine bleach in your laundry, always observe these cautions:

- Frequent chlorine bleaching will usually cause some fading in colored articles (essentially in all but a few vat-dyed ones), and overfrequent bleaching will harm fabrics made of some types of fibers, resulting in a weakening of the cloth and, possibly, frayed areas or holes. Using more bleach than the manufacturer recommends can also create these problems.
- Chlorine bleach should never be used on silk, wool, leather, mohair, nylon, spandex, and many fabrics treated with flame retardants. It may yellow or weaken spandex and permanently damage the fibers of silk, wool, and mohair. It may yellow nylon.
- Chlorine bleach is not recommended for sheer, fine, weak, or delicate fabrics, or

fabrics with trim or decoration that fit such a description.

- Too much bleach can cause yellowing.
- Spilled or splashed bleach can result in holes or discolored spots in clothes and linens, such as pale blotches on dark fabrics.
- Some permanent-press clothes and fabrics that have been given optical brightening finishes may yellow if exposed to chlorine bleach. If you are worried, test in an inconspicuous area.
- When exposed to chlorine bleach, some resin-treated fabrics may yellow or may retain a chlorine odor. If you are worried, test in an inconspicuous area.
- If your water contains a great deal of iron, chlorine bleach may cause rust stains to appear on fabrics.
- *Do not mix chlorine bleach with acids, ammonia, or acid- or ammonia-containing products. Doing so will produce a toxic gas or other deadly or dangerous reactions.* See page 432 in chapter 30, "Peaceful Coexistence with Microbes."

Use the quantity of chlorine bleach recommended on the bleach container for the load size (and choose the proper load size setting on your machine). Although you can damage your clothes if you use too much bleach, you can get poor results if you use too little.

Chlorine bleach should be added after the clothes have agitated with the detergent for five or six minutes. The reason for delaying is that contemporary detergents almost always contain optical or fluorescent brighteners and sometimes contain enzyme cleaners. Chlorine bleach may interfere with the action of optical brighteners and inactivate enzyme cleaners. Waiting five or six minutes before you add the chlorine bleach gives the brighteners and enzymes time to complete their work. You need not wait, of course, if your detergent does not contain these substances. (Some detergents also contain oxygen bleaches, which are inactivated by chlorine bleach and interfere with its working as well.)

Some newer-model washing machines have bleach dispensers that automatically delay adding the bleach for five minutes or so. If your machine has this feature, you can add bleach while the machine is filling and it will automatically delay adding the bleach to the wash water until the clothes have been agitating in the sudsy water for several minutes. If your machine lacks this feature, you can simply add bleach to your bleach dispenser at the proper time (five or six minutes after the clothes have been washing in the detergent-and-water solution). Bleach dispensers automatically dilute the bleach so that it is not too strong for your clothes, but watch out that you do not splash or spill undiluted bleach on your laundry in the process of adding it to the bleach dispenser.

If your machine has no liquid bleach dispenser, you add the bleach manually, *but you must always dilute chlorine bleach* before adding it to the wash water in which the clothes are agitating. (You *never* add chlorine bleach to dry clothes.) To do this, mix the bleach with at least one quart of water; then add it at the proper time, stirring the bleach mixture into the washer with a long wooden paddle or wooden spoon to be sure that it mixes well. The bleaching action of chlorine bleach is completed in about five minutes—a little less in hot water, a little more in cold water.

Chlorine bleach loses potency as it ages. When kept for emergency purposes as a disinfectant for water during floods or for other important functions, it should be replaced every six months. When kept for laundering or other ordinary household cleaning purposes, it should be replaced every nine to twelve months. Chlorine bleach should be stored out of the reach of children.

Bluing. Bluing is a colorant added to the water in which you wash white clothes. It neutralizes any yellowish tinge in the color of whites, thereby making them look whiter, although at the same time less bright or a bit duller. (Or at least we North Americans think whites look whiter and cleaner when they are more blue-white than yellow-white. I have read that to South Americans a red-white is what looks clean.)

You can usually buy bluing separately in the supermarket. It is also contained in some commercial oxygen or all-fabric bleaches and in some detergents and other laundry products. If you would like to try bluing, follow the label instructions carefully. You are generally told to add it when you add the detergent, before you put the clothes in the washer. You can add bluing in the rinse, but in automatic washers the clothes are already inside at this point, which increases the risk that you will cause blue spots or streaks as a result of insufficiently mixed bluing. It is important to make sure that bluing is thoroughly mixed in the wash water. But if you should end up with blue streaks on your clothes, this is a nuisance rather than a disaster; these wash out. See "Blue Spots or Streaks," page 370, in chapter 26, "Common Laundry Mishaps and Problems."

Boosters and laundry aids. See "Borax," "Builders," "Trisodium phosphate," and "Washing soda."

Borax. Borax is an excellent all-around laundry aid and booster. It is gentle. It cleans, deodorizes, and helps get rid of stains. It also is a water softener and acts as a buffer, maintaining alkalinity in wash water.

It makes an excellent diaper soak because it deodorizes and helps clean and whiten the diapers while rendering them more absorbent. Add 1/2 cup borax to the diaper pailful of warm water. It can be used together with chlorine bleach. You can also add 1/2 cup to the wash water for diapers.

Borax will boost the cleaning ability of mild detergents but at the cost of rendering them less mild. Add 1/4 cup borax and 1–2 tablespoons of mild soap or detergent in a sinkful of warm water and soak the garments for ten minutes. Rinse in clear, cool water and blot with a towel or roll in a towel. This preparation is not for use on silks or wools, or for any very delicate or fragile items.

Builders. Builders are substances added to detergents to improve their functioning. They soften the water, inactivate acids, buffer the washing solution in order to maintain alkalinity, and prevent the redeposit of soil.

Chlorine bleach. See "Bleach."

Color removers. Color removers, manufactured by dye manufacturers, contain sodium hydrosulfite ($Na_2S_2O_4$—also called "sodium hyposulfite"). A color remover is a reductive bleach (not an oxidizing bleach like ordinary household bleaches). It does not literally remove color. It destroys many dyes on fabrics to prepare them to receive another dye. It should be used only on white clothes or on clothes that you intend to strip of color; and it should be used with great caution.

If you have yellowing of a white garment caused by a chlorine-retentive finish, such as a resin used to render cloth wrinkle resistant, a color remover may be effective in rendering it white again. A color remover may also help when you have ruined a white or light article by washing it with another garment whose color ran. *Follow the instructions on the package carefully. Be sure that the color remover is safe for the fabric. Remember that color removers will indeed destroy the color in colored garments and linens.* Color removers are sold in drugstores, hardware stores, home centers, and large supermarkets. See also "Whitener/brighteners."

Detergents and soaps. Detergents contain surfactants to increase the wettability of the fabrics to be cleaned, builders and boosters of all sorts to increase cleaning power, antiredeposition agents that keep dirt suspended in the wash water and prevent it

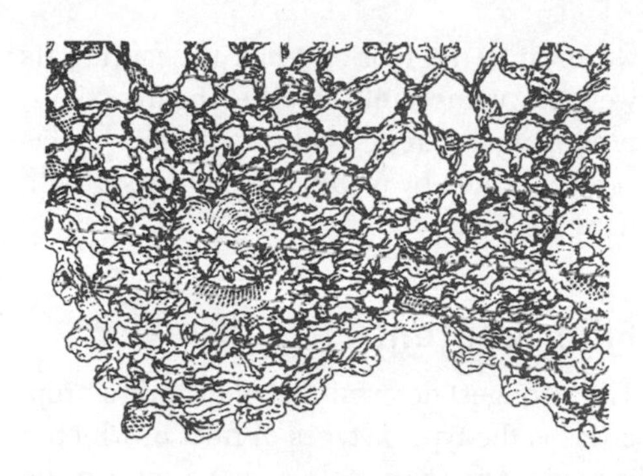
Handmade lace

Machine-made lace

thologies that feature lace patterns owned by kings and queens centuries ago.

By its nature, lace tends to be delicate and easy to tear. Handmade lace should generally receive exceedingly gentle care. Laces can sometimes be machine washed but often requires handwashing. The proper care of lace, like other fabrics, depends on the type of fiber of which it is made. Cotton, linen, silk, rayon, polyester, and other fibers are all commonly used for making lace today.

Yarn Construction

Carded and Combed; Staple and Filament Yarns. In the case of wool and cotton, the process of spinning raw natural fibers into yarns begins with carding or combing the fibers. Carded fibers have been arranged in parallel fashion by a carding machine. The ropelike structure formed is called sliver; it can be spun to form carded yarn. Combing is a process in which the sliver is carded again, rendering the fibers more parallel to each other and removing the shorter fibers. Yarn made from combed fibers is called combed yarn. Combed yarns, of whatever fiber, produce superior fabrics that are stronger and smoother than those made of carded yarns. Articles made of combed cotton yarns, therefore, are so identified on labels to enable the buyer to know that they are of higher quality. Fuzzier woolen yarns are made from carded yarns; wool worsted, a smoother type of wool fabric, is made from combed yarns. See chapter 16, "The Natural Fibers." Linen yarns, too, are spun out of both short-staple fibers, called tow, and long-staple fibers, called line. Fine linen articles are always of line.

Silk is the only natural fiber that comes in filament lengths—that is, very long strands of up to a couple of thousand feet—as well as short (staple) lengths produced as waste in the process of reeling the long silk from cocoons. Whereas the staple-length silk fibers are spun into yarns the same way that cotton is, reeled silk filaments are twisted together in a process called throwing.

Synthetic fibers may be manufactured as staple that will be spun into yarns like cotton or wool fibers or as filaments of indefinite length that will be thrown like silk filaments. Rayon exists in both staple and filament forms, but it is mostly used in staple form.

Filament (or thrown) yarn may have strikingly different properties from spun yarn of the same fiber. For example, spun nylon would be used for sweaters and blankets, but filament nylon is necessary for silky lingerie and undergarments. Spun silk is less lustrous, strong, and elastic than thrown silk and tends to become fuzzy in use because the staple fibers rub up. Generally speaking, fabrics of spun yarn usually have a better hand and are fuzzier and softer, less smooth or slick, less lustrous, more adsorbent (because of a greater surface area—see pages 209–10), more water-vapor permeable, warmer, and more insulating; they trap dirt more easily, produce more lint, pill more, slip less when you are sewing with them, and snag less than filament yarns of the same fiber and size.

Filament yarns, in turn, can be manufactured in different forms that result in fabrics of widely varying properties. Synthetic "textured" filament yarns (made of filament fibers that do not lie straight, close, and parallel) give greater comfort than older types of synthetic fabrics, which were made of flat multifilament yarns (made of straight filaments that pack close together and lie straight and parallel to one another). Newer textured yarn fabrics thus do not lie so flat on the skin and do not feel as hot and clammy as flat yarn fabrics. They let more water vapor and air pass through, have greater adsorbency, and, in general, feel more comfortable. They also have a better hand, one more similar to that of spun yarns. Today, most clothing fabric made of synthetic fibers uses textured yarns.

Twist. In all types of yarn, the tightness of the twist in the yarn has a major effect on the characteristics of the finished fabric. Fabrics of harder-twisted yarns, other things being equal, are stronger, smoother, more elastic, more resilient, more abrasion resistant, more absorbent and adsorbent, less prone to pilling or snagging, and even more comfortable on the skin. Up to a point, hard-twisted yarn also tends to shrink less, but both very low twist and very high twist yarns will shrink more—sometimes *much* more—than yarns with a moderate to high twist. Extremely hard-twisted yarns may also begin to weaken from the stress of the twist. Very fine, hard-twisted yarns are used for sheer fabrics, such as georgette, chiffon, and voile. Soft-twisted yarns are necessary for soft woolen fabrics. Crêpe fabrics are created when hard-twisted yarns with both right-hand and left-hand twists are woven into the fabric. When the fabric gets wet, the yarns kink in different directions, producing the crêpey look. Many other effects can be created by using different twists, both hard and soft.

Fiber Content

The strongest determinant of a fabric's properties is the type or types of fiber of which it is made. A fabric's coolness or warmth, durability, strength, washability, dry-cleanability, absorbency, cleanliness, softness, smoothness, resilience (proneness to wrinkling), hand, and many other properties, as well as its cost, are affected as much or more by the fibers it is made of than by construction, weave, finish, dye, or any other single factor. How you clean and care for garments and furnishings is affected more by fiber content than by any other factor. (Chapters 16 and 17 give details on the characteristics and care of each type of fiber commonly used in clothing and furnishings in the home.)

Natural Versus Synthetic Fibers. Some people insist on using only "natural" fibers, but "natural" is a term of doubtful meaning in this context as in so many others. Applied to fabrics, it denotes fibers of plant or animal origin, such as cotton, linen (flax), silk, or wool. These, the major natural fibers, are derived, respectively, from the downy coverings of the seeds of cotton plants, the stalks of flax plants, silkworms' cocoons, and sheep's wool. Other fairly common plant, or "cellulosic," fibers used to make clothes and household furnishings are jute, hemp, and ramie. All other fibers, such as rayon, nylon, polyester, acetate, acrylic, and spandex, are termed "synthetic," "man-made," or "manufactured." But the distinction between natural and synthetic fibers is somewhat strained. The plant and animal substances from which the "natural" fibers are derived are indeed naturally occurring, but wood pulp, coal, and petroleum products are provided by Mother Nature, just as flax and cot-

from resettling on the clothes, and a variety of other chemical agents. Laundry detergents usually contain optical brighteners. (See pages 325–26.)

Detergent names that include the word "ultra" are concentrated, so you can use less of them. This "new" type of product is in fact old. When detergents were first manufactured, people were used to using laundry soaps, which had much greater volume. It took less detergent than soap to get the laundry clean. But people resisted buying a small box of detergent, even though it would last just as long and produce clean clothes, for the same price as a bigger box of soap, out of a feeling that they were being cheated. So the detergent manufacturers included fillers in their products so that the boxes would be as big as soap boxes and you would need to use about the same amount of detergent as soap to do a load. This is how things stood from that day until the 1990s, when, finally, detergent manufacturers decided that they could sell little boxes and bottles to those of us who have little shelf space and, unlike our great-grandparents, tend to think new or different is better. This results in the problem, however, of making it more difficult to estimate how much you need. If you switch back and forth from "ultra" to "regular" detergents, you may lose your sixth sense for getting the right amount and you can forget which one you are using and accidentally add too much or too little. Follow the instructions on the package and use the measure in the box to help minimize the chances that this will happen.

Detergent names that include the word "free" contain no dyes or perfumes or fragrances. People who are prone to allergic responses to such substances prefer these. (I wish manufacturers could be convinced to offer products with just a *little* pleasant fragrance, but they usually seem to offer only the extremes of chemical-smelling products "free" of perfume and those that bowl you over with their heavy odor.)

The terms "heavy-duty" and "all-purpose" are often used interchangeably to refer to detergents formulated for use on the whole family laundry—all types of soil and washable fabrics (except those that must be washed with "mild" or "gentle" soaps or detergents). These detergents are too strong—that is, alkaline—for some fibers, such as silk, wool, and many delicates. "All-purpose" sometimes means a detergent that is suitable for general household cleaning purposes as well as for laundering. All-purpose or heavy-duty detergents come in both granular and liquid form. Liquids are preferable when cold water makes it difficult to dissolve granules and for convenience in pretreating spots and stains. They are sometimes superior for washing out oily soils and food stains. Granular (powdered) detergents are said to be especially effective on clay and ground-in dirt.

Both all-purpose and mild laundry detergents often contain bleaching agents (oxygen bleaches) that some fabrics cannot take. See "Detergents and soaps, mild." The presence of bleaches in laundry detergents is not altogether a blessing. Such bleaches are often ineffective under ordinary laundry conditions. They are inactivated by chlorine bleach. Their presence reduces your freedom to choose whether you will use bleach, how much you will use, and when. Detergents containing bleach may be used only on items that are safe in oxygen bleaches. You must be careful to dissolve or mix such detergents in the wash water thoroughly, too, before adding the clothes.

Some laundry detergents contain enzyme cleaners. These are more effective on organic and protein stains such as blood, eggs, grass, vomit, urine, excrement, and other body soils.

Detergents that contain *fabric softeners* are not recommended. The softener gets in the way of effective cleaning. If you want to use fabric softener, add it separately during the rinse or in the dryer.

Phosphate detergents clean better than nonphosphate detergents, because phosphates are better "builders" or laundry boosters. But in many places the amount of phosphates permitted in home laundry detergents is strictly limited, or phosphates are prohibited by law, to protect the environment.

Light-duty detergents contain no or low levels of builders or boosters, but they may contain optical brighteners, oxygen bleaches, or enzymes. This group includes hand dishwashing liquids and laundry detergents designed for baby clothes and fine fabrics. Some can be used in automatic washers and some cannot. You must read the labels.

Detergents and soaps, mild. When you are told on a care label to use a mild detergent, the manufacturer probably is telling you to use one that has a neutral or near-neutral (only slightly alkaline) pH. But since laundry detergents give you little information on their pH, it can often be difficult to determine whether a detergent is "mild." Most commercial laundry detergents are to one degree or another alkaline. The more alkaline they are, the more harsh, and—the other side of the coin—the better they tend to clean. Ordinarily, a mild detergent is going to be less effective at cleaning heavy soil or stains than products that advertise themselves as "strong," "stain-fighting," "heavy-duty," "powerful" and the like. However, some more mild detergents clean better than some less mild ones. Mildness and cleaning effectiveness are related but not identical.

If you are worried about whether a product is mild, call the toll-free number on the product label to confirm whether it is suitable for a given fiber or fabric. Sometimes you will be told the pH or whether the product is "slightly" or more alkaline if you ask. Also, remember that detergent and soap formulations change. If the box or bottle of a product that you are used to says "new" or "improved" or "with" some new ingredient, try to confirm that the change does not alter its mildness. But keep in mind what one textile expert told me: do not go overboard worrying about whether a detergent is mild enough. Practically all commercial laundry detergents in this country are fairly mild. One detergent manufacturer I spoke to pointed out that you can get a milder laundering effect with any detergent by simply using less of it. Even if a detergent is mild to begin with, you must follow label instructions for its use to be sure of gentle laundering, including directions as to water temperature.

Mild detergents for hand-washables To find a good mild detergent for hand-washables, look for those that describe themselves as "mild" or "gentle for your hands" or "good for fine washables." For very delicate fabrics and especially for antiques and heirlooms, textile conservators, museums, and my mother often recommend Orvus WA Paste, a mild, neutral detergent made by Procter and Gamble. Orvus WA *cannot* be used in the washing machine. You will also often find gentle but expensive detergents designed solely for hand-washing lingerie and hosiery or delicate fabrics in department store lingerie departments or linen or lingerie stores; but you need not buy an expensive product to get good results. Inexpensive dishwashing liquids, which also cannot be used in the washing machine, often have a neutral or near-neutral (only slightly alkaline) pH; otherwise they would hurt your skin when you washed the dishes. But look for those that advertise themselves as "gentle to your hands." It may be an excess of caution, but it is probably safer to pick only plain dishwashing products—those without special ingredients or additives—for use on fabrics.

Mild detergents for machine-washables As for products that *can* be used in the washing machine, some detergents spe-

cially formulated for wool or delicate fabrics are suitable for the washing machine as well as hand-washing; carefully read the labels to see whether a particular product can be used in the machine. Some commercial laundry detergents, especially those that are often recommended for baby clothes (such as Ivory Snow powder, Ivory Snow Liquid, or Liquid Dreft), are only slightly alkaline. But some "baby" detergents are alkaline, and some regular detergents (such as Liquid Cheer and Liquid CheerFree) are nearly neutral (very slightly alkaline).

Optical brightening agents and enzymes in mild detergents Some mild detergents contain optical brightening agents. These do not make the detergents less mild, nor do they harm any fibers. But they can change the hue or the appearance of a few types of fabrics, including some khakis, "natural" cottons, off-whites, and creams, especially imported linens and damasks. The following detergents, which are only very slightly alkaline (that is, they are mild), contain no optical brightening agents: Liquid Dreft, Ivory Snow Liquid, Liquid Cheer, Liquid CheerFree, and Delicare. (None of these contains bluing either, which makes them all well suited for natural and off-white shades of linen and cotton.) Dishwashing liquids, too, contain no optical brighteners, but of course they cannot be used in the washing machine. Powdered Dreft and powdered Ivory Snow contain low levels of brighteners. Optical brighteners may be present in some products even though they are not listed in the ingredients.

A detergent that contains enzymes may still be mild. Enzymes typically used in laundry products are themselves neutral and safe for any type of fiber or color. See "Enzyme laundry and presoak products." It is other agents in products that render them alkaline. An enzyme presoak, for example, may contain boosters that would not be good for a delicate fabric. Detergents that contain bleaches, too, should usually be avoided when you are trying to select a mild detergent. The label will always tell you if a product contains bleach.

Which is milder—soap or detergent? You will encounter many recommendations to use soap and not detergent in washing fabrics as well as other materials in the home because, it is claimed, soaps are milder and clean more gently. In fact, it all depends on which soap and which detergent you are talking about. (Soap is, technically and chemically, a detergent. Some writers refer to "synthetic detergents" to distinguish them from soap itself. But I will ignore the technical and chemical similarity and use the terms as most people do.) As one textiles expert explained to me, soaps are always alkaline in water, and many detergents are nonalkaline. There are harsh soaps; there are neutral and very mild detergents. Ivory Bath Soap is mild; Octagon, Fels Naphtha, and similar brown soaps are strong. (For an explanation of what soaps and detergents are, see chapter 31, "The Chemistry of Household Cleaning," pages 437–39.)

Not only are some detergents milder than soaps; soaps are harder to work with. They may leave residues in clothes and are difficult to rinse, which is especially problematic for delicate fabrics. The harder your water, the worse are such problems. You can buy laundry soap bars and liquid laundry soaps from some health food stores, mail-order suppliers, and Internet-based vendors, but the last of the laundry soap flake products, Ivory Soap Flakes, is no longer made. You can also use any bar soap that does not contain moisturizers or similar additives, such as Ivory bath soap, for small jobs. Either rub the bar on the garment, or with a knife or cheese slicer shave fine pieces off the bar and dissolve them to get sudsy water. If you resort to bath-soap bars, you must beware of the ingredients included in some that are good for or harmless to the skin but bad for fabrics, such as moisturizers or dyes. Many people, myself included, sometimes use Ivory bar soap for hand-washing delicates, either rubbing it right on the fabric or shaving pieces off the bar and letting them soften in the wash water. Not all bath and hand bars are soaps. Some are detergents.

Make sure your water is soft before using soaps. If it is not, soften it with a nonprecipitating water softener. Otherwise the soap will react with the minerals in the water to form curds that stick to clothes and are hard to get off. Soaps need warm or hot water to be really effective.

Enzyme laundry and presoak products. Enzyme cleaners are found in many pretreatment or presoak products, stain removers, detergents, and some oxygen bleaches. You should test these products on an inconspicuous area of a piece of laundry before using them just as you do other laundry additives; but by and large they are safe for all washable fabrics. They are valuable for helping to remove organic or protein-based stains, including bodily substances (such as blood, vomit, and urine), eggs, dairy products, grass stains, and chocolate.

Several enzymes are used in enzyme cleaners, and they work on different types of soil. Amylase works on starch soils. Lipase works on fatty and oily soils. Protease works on protein soils. A detergent may contain more than one. Cellulase helps to reduce the graying of cotton and pilling and aids in removing particulate soil. To remove fuzz from wrinkle-resistant cottons, the Fabricare Institute recommends laundering with a product that contains a cellulase enzyme.

The key to the effective use of products containing enzymes is to allow them time to work. Let garments soak in an enzyme presoak for half an hour or longer. Chlorine bleach will inactivate enzymes, so add it only when you have finished the enzyme treatment. If your laundry detergent contains enzymes, add chlorine bleach after the clothes have agitated for five minutes. See also "Detergents and soaps, mild."

Fabric softeners. Fabric softeners are supposed to make cloth fluffy, soft, and pliable, minimize wrinkles, make ironing easier, and help prevent the static electricity that commonly plagues fabrics made from synthetic fibers. They are also said to be helpful in fluffing up the pile in pile fabrics. I never use them, and I know at least two professors of textiles who also never use them. Marketers say that people use fabric softeners because they like their nice smell.

These products achieve their effect by leaving a waxy coating on fabrics. The main problems they cause, therefore, are reduced absorbency and the tendency of the waxy coating to find its way onto other fabrics and onto your skin. Avoid using fabric softeners on towels, T-shirts, underwear, sheets, and pillowcases; these and any other fabrics used on and near the skin are comfortable only when absorbent. You should also avoid using fabric softeners too often, because their wax builds up, leaving garments feeling greasy and exaggerating their inabsorbency. Fabric softeners may also reduce the effectiveness of flame retardants. Wash and dry items treated with flame retardants in loads that will not receive softening treatment.

Liquid fabric softeners, if you use them, are added to the final rinse water in your washing machine. If you have a softener dispenser, you can add liquid softener at the beginning of the wash cycle and it will be added at the proper time. If you do not, be sure to dilute, mix, and dissolve softeners thoroughly in at least a quart of water before adding them to the rinse water, for if they touch clothes directly they can cause spots. If this happens, rub with a bar of pure soap and rewash them. You may need to repeat the process.

Dryer softener sheets are saturated with a waxy substance that melts in the heat of the dryer and coats the clothes as they tumble. If you like, cut one into two or four pieces and just use one of the parts for a lighter dose of softener that will still have a good effect. This is especially helpful when your load is not large.

There is not much difference in quality between the two types of softener. Some people think that the liquid type is slightly better at softening while the dryer sheets are slightly better at stopping static buildup, but both do both things well.

Some detergents contain fabric softeners, but the fabric softeners impede their cleaning. It is better to use a separate fabric softener.

Clothes that are line-dried, especially towels, often have a rough, stiff, boardlike feeling. Tumbling towels and other things that would dry stiff on the line is softening in and of itself, without the addition of any fabric softener. But tumbling also exaggerates static problems for synthetics because of the friction it produces.

Heavy-duty detergent. See "Detergents and soaps."

Hydrogen peroxide. See "Bleach."

Laundry disks. You may have encountered advertisements for laundry disks, globes, balls, spheres, or doughnuts. Reliable authorities recommend you not waste your money on any such devices. These are "alternative" laundry products that purport to clean clothes without the use of laundry detergents or other ordinary laundry pretreatment and washing products. Typically, they allege that some part of the device—ceramic beads, magnets, or "activated water"—emits negative charges or far-infrared electromagnetic radiation, reducing the surface tension of water and permitting it to penetrate fabrics more readily. Studies of such products, however, indicate that water alone is just as effective at cleaning clothes as water to which laundry disks or similar devices have been added. (Indeed, it seems that reasonable people are sometimes deceived about the effectiveness of such devices because they are not aware of how effective plain water is.) Moreover, scientists say that the manufacturers' purported "scientific" explanations of how the disks function are baseless and illogical. Some states have taken legal action and levied heavy fines against companies for claims made in connection with the sale of such devices. Among the organizations that do not recommend their use are the Consumers Union, International Fabricare Institute, Maytag Corp., and the Soap and Detergent Association.

Light-duty detergent. See "Detergents and soaps."

Mild detergent. See "Detergents and soaps, mild."

Optical brighteners. Optical brighteners are now used in almost all laundry detergents, including most gentle or mild ones, and in oxygen or all-fabric bleaches. The list of ingredients on the package may include such terms as "optical whiteners," "fluorescent whitening agents," or "brighteners." These are colorless dyes that absorb the energy of invisible ultraviolet rays in light and re-emit it at a lower, visible spectrum wavelength. This makes white fabrics appear whiter and colors appear brighter in the presence of ultraviolet radiation, that is, in unshielded fluorescent light or daylight. Optical brighteners will be ineffective in incandescent light, which emits very little ultraviolet radiation, so you may find that your clothes are more brilliant by day in your office than by night at home, where indoor lighting is almost always incandescent.

United States manufacturers also apply optical brighteners to almost all white and pastel-colored fabrics during the manufacturing process. The brighteners in the fabrics will sometimes (infrequently, it appears) turn yellow when exposed to sunshine or to bleach. Yellowing of fabrics treated with optical brighteners may also result simply as a result of aging, for these colorless dyes, like all dyes, fade; in fact, they have a rather low fastness to light. When this happens, not only does your fabric lose the whiteness optical brighteners supplied, but the fading by-products are themselves yellowish, which may give the fabric a yellow cast. According to the International Fabricare Institute, decomposition of optical brightening agents can also be caused by dry cleaning and steam finishing, washing with alkaline detergents and bleach, or exposure of optical brightening agents on fabrics to chlorine bleach.

The optical brighteners in detergents are intended to maintain the white or bright look that fabrics have when they are new as a result of being treated with optical brighteners. But you can run into trouble when you use detergents (or other laundry products) that contain optical brighteners to wash fabrics that have *not* been treated with optical brighteners. If you use a product that contains brighteners as a pretreatment, this can lighten the color or even create an ugly dappling or spotting on untreated fabrics. I learned what optical brightening agents ("OBAs") were through the sad experience of buying some imported linen towels, in an off-white hue, that had a label bearing these words: "OBAs will affect shade." This meant that if you used a detergent with optical brighteners, you might change the hue of the towels. Not knowing what OBAs were, I had no idea that I was actually using them. Laundering did indeed alter the hue and produced mottling of the color. Generally speaking, imported fabrics, especially linens in tan or off-white shades, are more likely to be untreated than others. Some famous-brand American manufacturers use imported fabrics that are not treated, so you cannot avoid the problem just by buying American. Watch out for khakis and "natural cottons" in particular. A manufacturer of linen damask also recommends that you not use optical brighteners on white damasks.

As of the time of writing, the following national-brand laundry detergents contained no optical brighteners: Ivory Snow Liquid, regular powdered Cheer without bleach, CheerFree, Liquid Cheer, Liquid CheerFree, powdered Dreft and Liquid Dreft, and Delicare. Powdered Dreft and powdered Ivory Snow contain low levels of brightener. In addition, dishwashing liquids, which can often be used for hand-washing delicate fabrics, contain no optical brighteners. See also "Detergents and soaps, mild" and "Bleach: Chlorine bleach."

Oxygen bleaches. See "Bleach."

Potassium monopersulfate. See "Bleach: Oxygen bleaches."

Pretreatments and prewash stain removers. Pretreatments and prewash stain removers in liquid form are usually applied just before laundering. Pretreatment sticks, however, may be used as much as a week in advance of laundering without danger of mildew, so they are useful when you are concerned about a stain setting if you do not immediately launder an article. Rub the stick on the fresh stain; then put the soiled item in the laundry hamper until laundry day.

These products should be tested on an inconspicuous area of the fabric just as you test other laundry products. Optical brighteners or other ingredients they contain can cause light spots or color loss in certain fabrics. This is particularly important on neon or fluorescent dyes, which they may cause to run or fade. They may also contain enzymes. See "Enzyme laundry and presoak products," above.

Prewash treatments and stain removers work well on oily and greasy stains, including skin oils and perspiration, food stains, cooking oil, lotions, and cosmetics. They may be detergent-based or they may contain isopropyl alcohol, dry-cleaning fluids, or other petroleum-based solvents. Those containing solvents or grease- or soil-release agents are particularly likely to be effective at removing oily and greasy soil from polyester and other synthetic fibers. Sometimes you can tell by reading the ingredient list whether a pretreatment product contains solvents or grease- or soil-release agents, and sometimes you cannot. I know of one case where the manufacturer no longer lists its soil-release agent, yet still includes it in the product. Usually the pretreatment products with pump dispensers are detergent-based and those with aerosol sprays contain solvents; but this may not always be the case.

Sal soda. See "Washing soda."

Soap. See "Detergents and soaps" and "Detergents and soaps, mild."

Sodium carbonate. See "Washing soda."

Sodium perborate. See "Bleaches: Oxygen bleaches."

Sodium percarbonate. See "Bleaches: Oxygen bleaches."

Suds, soap and detergent. When you are laundering with soap rather than detergent, the amount of suds is an indication of the cleaning power. So when you use soap, make sure you have plenty of suds. Look for soapsuds as firm as beaten egg whites.

But the suds level does not correlate with the cleaning power of detergents. Low-sudsing detergents can be stronger cleaners, and high-sudsing detergents weaker cleaners.

Suds of both soaps and detergents are decreased by heavy soil and hard water and increased by light soil and soft water. If you develop excess detergent suds, sprinkle a little rubbing alcohol on them or drop a little piece of bar soap in the water. Chlorine bleach makes suds creamier.

Low-sudsing detergents are preferred for front-loading washing machines. They may also be preferred for certain jobs, such as washing pillows and comforters. They work fine in top-loading machines too.

Sunlight. See "Bleaches: Sunlight."

Surfactants. Surfactants are substances contained in detergents that lower the water's surface tension, making it "wetter." This enables the surface being cleaned to become wet more readily and thus enables soil to be loosened and removed more readily. Surfactants also keep soils emulsified and suspended in the water rather than resettling on the material being washed. See chapter 30 "The Chemistry of Household Cleaning," pages 437–39.

Trisodium phosphate. Trisodium phosphate, sometimes called TSP, is a laundry booster and a water softener. It is a strong alkali and therefore cannot be used on protein fibers such as silk or wool.

Vinegar, white. You can add white vinegar, an acid, to the final rinse water of your laundry as a "sour" to neutralize any residual chlorine bleach or alkalinity from the detergents and to help prevent lint. Add the white vinegar to the machine when the final rinse water has finished filling; use 1 cup per load, a bit more for extra-large loads. *Caution:* do not add vinegar to any laundry load or laundry water that contains chlorine bleach! This can produce hazardous fumes.

Washing soda. Washing soda (sodium carbonate or sal soda) is a very old laundry aid, and it is still a good, very strong detergent booster or "builder" and laundry deodorizer. It is marketed under different trade names, which often contain the word "soda." Read the ingredients on labels to find out if a product is mostly washing soda. Washing soda, an alkali, helps at cutting grease, and it is a water softener. Follow the manufacturer's instructions, or use 1/2 cup per regular (normal) load or 3/4 cup for an extralarge load. Observe proper cautions when using it.

Washing soda is also effective as a pretreatment for many stains, including food stains, grease, diaper stains, lipstick, and crayon. To use it as a stain pretreatment, work 4 tablespoons into a paste with about 1/4 cup water. Dampen the stain and, wearing rubber gloves, rub the paste into the stain. To use washing soda as a presoak, use 1 tablespoon per gallon of warm water or 1/2 cup per regular washing load. Drain the clothes before washing. (If you wish, you can then add another 1/2 cup to the wash water as a booster.)

You should exercise caution when using a strong caustic substance such as washing soda. It should *never* be used on wool, silk, or other protein or animal-origin fibers. Also avoid using washing soda on any delicate cellulosic fibers. Use rubber gloves to keep it off your skin.

Water softeners. See "Borax," "Builders," "Trisodium phosphate," and "Washing soda."

Whitener/brighteners. Whitener/brighteners, unlike color removers, are not bleaches of any sort and do not remove color. Rather, they are "optical brighteners," or colorless dyes that absorb invisible light (in the form of ultraviolet radiation) and re-emit it in the form of lower-energy visible light. See "Optical brighteners." Both color removers and whiteners/brighteners are sold in drugstores, hardware stores, home centers, and large supermarkets. See also "Color removers."

22

Drying the Laundry

Using the automatic dryer . . . What goes in the dryer . . . Load size, temperature, moisture sensing, cycle choices, avoiding overdrying, sorting for drying, operating the dryer . . . Using the dryer to unwrinkle . . . Line drying . . . How to hang things on the line . . . Hanging dry on hangers or hanging racks . . . Drying flat

Most people today have no choice but to dry laundry indoors in an automatic tumbling dryer or on a hanger, a rack, or an indoor line. These are all fine methods, and among them they provide the best choice for drying some kinds of fabric. For those who have the option, however, outdoor line drying gives the freshest result and would be my preference for all those clothes and linens for which it is suitable. This chapter canvasses how and when to use each of these options.

The Automatic Dryer

What Goes in the Dryer. Most clothes and linens can safely be dried in the automatic dryer. The exceptions are fiberglass, rubber, certain especially heat-sensitive fabrics, such as polypropylene, many acetate, acrylic, and spandex fabrics, plastic, certain knits, drip-dry clothes, and many delicate fibers and fabrics, including viscose rayon. Drip-dry clothes should be hung to dry. Towels, flannels, and other pile and napped fabrics, on the other hand, need tumbling in the dryer to fluff them up. Ordinarily, they should not be dried flat or hung to dry. Superwash, and similar treated wools, may be dried in the dryer on a low setting (unless the care label says not to), but other wools must be dried *outside the dryer.* Once wool articles have dried outside the dryer, however, they can then be fluffed up on a setting that uses no heat, often called "air fluff."

Load Size. A washing load is usually about the same size as a drying load. Drying loads, like washing loads, should be neither too small nor too large. A dryer with a full, wet load looks two-thirds empty. Remember that clothes will fluff up and take up more space when they are dry. Too small a load will dry more slowly, as the tumbling action requires a minimum fill level to work properly. If a load is too small, add a few clean, dry items—say, two or three nonlinting towels of compatible color—to bulk it up. Too large a load will wrinkle, lint excessively, and dry very slowly and unevenly because air will not be able to circulate freely around the clothes. An overlarge load can also block the vent and cause heat damage to clothes.

Temperature. Home dryers always give a choice of temperatures. Regular, the hottest temperature, is for sturdy cottons—T-shirts, towels, cotton underwear, sheets, preshrunk blue jeans, and so on. Care labels on articles that may be dried on regular should simply say "Tumble dry." In general, the hotter the drying temperature, the greater the likelihood of shrinking, so this setting is also reserved for preshrunk or low-shrink fabrics. The medium setting is for permanent-press, wrinkle-treated clothes, many synthetics and blends, lightweight cottons and linens, some knits, and those whose care labels direct "Tumble dry medium." The low or delicate settings are for more heat-sensitive garments, including some synthetics, fine lingerie, sheer fabrics, and most cotton knits, as well as for those whose care labels direct "Tumble dry low."

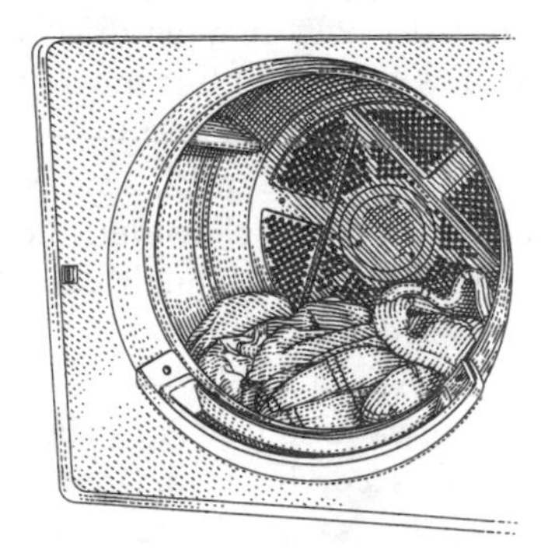

A properly loaded clothes dryer

Moisture Sensing. Many home dryers now also offer "electronic drying," in which the machine automatically senses the moisture level and turns off when it is reduced to the level you select, from "more" or "very" dry, to less dry. The very dry setting is for items you wish to get extra-dry as well as hard-to-dry items like rugs, very heavy clothes, and towels. The less dry setting should be used for cottons and linens that you are going to damp-iron, although I find that they still need steam ironing or sprinkling. (See "Avoiding Overdrying; Damp Drying," below.)

Cycle Choices. Home dryers let you set drying time with a timer. Most home dryers also offer a choice of cycles: regular, permanent press, permanent press with extended cool-down, and air-fluff. The regular cycle has a short cool-down period at the end, for less wrinkling and easier handling when you remove the clothes. The permanent-press cycle has a long cool-down during which, on many machines, a warning buzzer sounds to let you know that you will have to remove clothes soon. This is because permanent-press clothes, when warm, may wrinkle if left to sit in the dryer, and may even do so if they are only slightly warm after the cool-down. The extended cool-down feature adds a second long cool-down period, during which the warning buzzer sounds every five minutes. Its function is to keep the clothes moving and cooling when you cannot immediately remove them. Unless you are hovering near the machine, you should always use it, for it maximizes your options and minimizes the risks of wrinkling. These are useful features that many people fail to take advantage of.

"Air fluff" or "fluff dry" simply uses unheated air. It can be used to fluff pile fabrics or knits or to dry plastic shower curtains, diaper liners, and other items that should not be exposed to heat.

Avoiding Overdrying; Damp Drying. Success in using an automatic dryer consists in not overdoing it. Overdrying causes shrinking, wrinkling, a harsh, dry hand, and yellowing. Such yellowing is especially problematic for whites, lights, and pastels. On synthetics, the hand or texture may sometimes be permanently ruined by overheating.

To avoid overdrying, set the temperature and timer conservatively or, when you can, use electronic drying. The longest drying times are necessary for the largest loads and the bulkiest, thickest items, such as towels and blue jeans. Sheets and pillowcases might be dry in less than twenty minutes, but towels can take up to an hour. When you are estimating drying time, remember that a cool rinse extends the drying time. Drying in your automatic dryer also takes longer when the room in which the dryer sits is colder.

You should not aim for absolute dryness. Remove clothes while there is still a hint of dampness in thick seams or at elastic bands. Linen, especially, should never be dried bone dry; it needs a little moisture to stay supple (and usually requires damp ironing). Blue jeans and other play and work clothes have very thick seams that dry slowly. To get the seams completely dry in the dryer, you would have to overdry the fabric in the rest of the garment, shrinking it, imposing unnecessary wear and tear, tying up the dryer when you need it, and using up energy. So remove jeans and all similar articles when the flat portions are dry, and let them finish drying outside the dryer. Hang them over a clothes rack near the dryer or over a chair back that will not get used, or simply fold them loosely and set them on a table or shelf somewhere.

Sorting for Drying. When drying, you must read and follow care labels carefully. Shrinking, yellowing, linting, pilling, abrading, melting, and other problems can result from using an overhot dryer. Elastic fibers can become inelastic, and white fibers can yellow if machine dried at too high a temperature. Some elasticized garments should not be machine dried at all.

Just as you cannot wash together items that might bleed color on one another, you cannot dry them together either. *Beware of mixing together wet color-sorted clothes in the dryer.* Do not dry items that are not colorfast with whites or light-colored loads. All other sorting instructions for washing—instructions as to linting, avoiding damage from buckles and pins, preventing tangles with sleeves, sashes, and trims, removing decorations, keeping matched sets and pairs together, turning inside out, using mesh bags for delicate and small articles—also apply equally to dryer loads.

Separate slow-drying clothes and linens from quick-drying clothes and linens. Otherwise, the latter will overdry. Turkish (terrycloth) towels, blue jeans, heavy work clothes, thicker knits, rugs, and the like dry slowly. Sheets and pillowcases, medium and light weight woven cottons and linens, and synthetics dry more quickly. (Polyester and other synthetics tend to dry very quickly, much faster than, say, even lightweight cotton knits.)

Keep clothes and linens that are to be dried with a fabric softener sheet separate from those that are not. Softener sheets are most appropriate for synthetic fibers. Fabric softening sheets should not be used on diapers, towels, dish towels, rags, sheets, T-shirts, cotton underwear, and any other articles that must be absorbent to work well and feel good. Fabric softener gives clothes and linens a waxy coating that reduces their absorbency. You will not need fabric softener at every laundering. If you use it too often, it tends to build up and give a greasy feeling.

Usually clothes that need similar washing temperatures also take similar drying temperatures. But if (as a compromise load) you have washed synthetics and wrinkle-treated clothes together with untreated cottons or linens, you may wish to dry them separately so that you can give some and not others permanent-press treatment.

One care label instruction that I sometimes ignore is commonly included on cotton knits—to dry flat. You can buy cotton knit sportswear big enough to fit after some shrinkage; dry it only on low heat, and remove it when still slightly damp. Doing this entails a *risk* that the garment will shrink more than you predict or that there was some other reason for the instruction besides potential shrinkage, perhaps yellowing or pilling. In the long run, however, you will save a good deal of drying time and are likely to get satisfactory results.

Operating the Dryer. Each time you dry a load, check the lint filter and empty it if necessary. Sometimes it will be necessary to do so in the middle of a large load as well. (Make sure the dryer is off before you do this.)

Choose appropriate temperatures, times, and cycles. Place a fabric softener sheet in the dryer if you intend to use fabric softener. (Try using them only every two or three washes to avoid a softener buildup.) For a small load or for a light softening effect, you can cut a sheet of fabric softener into halves or quarters and use only a piece.

Shake out each wet item to be dried. Then throw it loosely in on the others, one by one. If you throw in clothes from the washer knotted together in an impenetrable mass, they are likely to take forever to dry, or some will overdry while others remain damp because air cannot circulate around them.

If clothes have emerged sopping from the washer, put them back in for another spin if you can or, if you can't, roll any heavy or thick items in a towel before placing them in the dryer. Otherwise they will take forever to dry.

Remove all clothes from the dryer promptly when they still have a mere hint of dampness. This is especially important for thermoplastic fibers, permanent-press and wrinkle-treated clothes, and cottons that are to be ironed, to prevent or reduce their wrinkling. Remove articles that are to be dampironed when they are still fairly damp, roll them up, and then cover them so that they stay damp until you are ready to iron. (Linen should usually be dried outside the dryer, but if you put it in, take it out when still quite damp, especially if you are going to iron it.) Many dryers have a "damp dry" setting. It gives a short drying time, perhaps twenty minutes, followed by a short cool-down.

Hang or fold clothes promptly upon removing them from the dryer or they will take on wrinkles sitting in the basket. As you do so, shake each one out and give it a snap, as though you were cracking a whip. This helps them to return to their proper shapes. You can greatly improve their appearance and reduce the need for ironing if you finger-press them: smooth the seams, pull shapes straight, unfold edges so that they lie flat, and so on.

When you have folded or hung clothes that are still slightly damp from the dryer, let them stand on a shelf or table for a while if necessary to air and complete drying. Often they dry from their own warmth while you are folding. If they don't, avoid putting them away until they dry more thoroughly or you will get musty smells in dressers and closets.

If clothes that have dried flat or on the line, such as knits, small rugs, pile fabrics, or sheets, feel stiff or harsh or look wrinkled or flat, put them in the dryer on "air fluff" (cool air) for a few minutes after they dry to soften and fluff them up.

Unwrinkling with Your Dryer. You can use your dryer to unwrinkle clean, dry clothes (from, say, a suitcase or drawer) by tumbling them on reduced heat for five to ten minutes. It sometimes helps to throw in a clean, slightly damp, *nonlinting* towel to make a little moisture.

Line Drying

Our language shows the effect of centuries of drying wet linens and clothes outdoors when we speak disapprovingly of "airing laundry in public" or "letting it all hang out."

Outdoor clothesline

Years ago, when everyone had to hang their laundry out on the line, it was common for some people to feel ashamed at the quasi-public display of their linens and underwear, especially if they showed stains and tears. Older friends say that worst of all was hanging out the rags that all women used before the days of disposable sanitary napkins and tampons. Today, it is hard to imagine anyone being embarrassed by their underwear, now that we see billboards of celebrities in theirs. But my suburban friends tell me that you still need a private backyard to line-dry your laundry unembarrassedly because many people think that their neighbors' laundry flapping in the breeze ruins the appearance of the neighborhood and will complain when they see it.

To my mind, whether laundry on the line is unattractive depends on what kind of laundry it is and how it is hung. When I was a girl, hanging out the clothes was an art widely understood in the countryside. Familial style was given some leeway, but there were nonetheless ways you did this and ways you didn't; the rules were so clear that I remember one elderly lady stifling unseemly giggles when she saw the work of a novice. If those days ever come back, the instructions below will save you from social humiliation.

Line drying outdoors produces appealingly fresh-smelling clothes and linens, and sunlight is a natural sanitizing and bleaching agent. (The dryer's heat also kills germs.) Line drying is good for almost all washables. It is not a good choice for fabrics that will stretch when wet, such as wool and loosely knitted articles, and for articles that need fluffing to look their best—terrycloth, chenille, flannels, and other napped and pile fabrics. Nor should you hang filled articles such as comforters or sleeping bags over the line; the fill drops to the ends, clumps, and will not dry. Items such as towels, which take very long to dry, you may find inconvenient to hang out. Many clothes feel stiff after drying on the line, particularly if there is little wind to blow them soft as they dry. Towels, especially, tend to get boardlike and stiff on the line and need some tumbling to make them soft. You might tumble towels until they are half dry, then move them to the line for finishing—or vice versa. Knits, too, often need some tumbling (usually on low or cool) to regain their softness, whether before or after drying flat. Delicate clothes and fabrics should be dried flat rather than line dried. Fabrics that should not be exposed to the sun can be line dried indoors.

If you hang things carefully, they will often look smooth when they are dry, and you can minimize or avoid ironing. The best weather for line drying, if you have a choice, is warm, dry, and sunny with a moderate breeze. You need some wind to billow wrinkles out of the fabric and hasten drying. Line drying can seem interminable on a humid, airless day. But avoid extremely windy days.

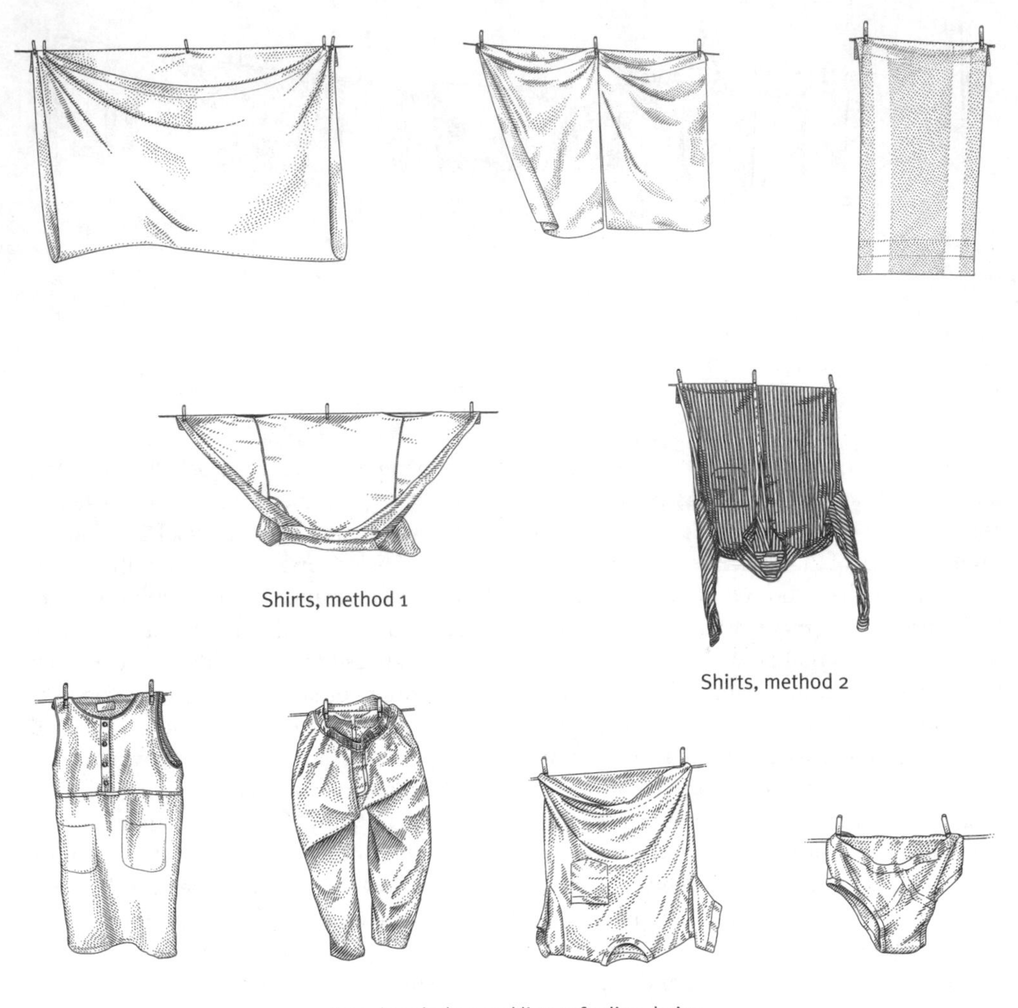

Shirts, method 1

Shirts, method 2

Hanging clothes and linens for line drying

The flapping is wearing on the clothes; the wind is hard to work in and sometimes blows clothes off the line. Avoid freezing weather also. It is painful to hang out wet things in such weather, and they will take forever to dry. Besides, water expands when it freezes; that can result in damage to fabric whose fibers have absorbed water. The idea that freezing outdoors is good for the wash is an old wives' tale, born, no doubt, out of the superstition that great suffering always produces great good.

Make sure that your line and clothespins are clean. Wash the line, if necessary, with some ordinary detergent in water or household cleaner. Make sure it is sufficiently taut, strong, and secure that there is no danger that the clothes will drag or drop.

Keep a plentiful store of clothespins and do not stint on using them. (Look for sturdy ones; some are shoddily made.) You can use old-fashioned wooden push-down pins (no spring) for sheets, towels, play clothes, and other articles that will not pull out of shape or

HOW TO PIN LAUNDRY ON THE LINE

Sheets: Fold the sheet hem to hem, then fold three to four inches of one hem over the line and pin at both ends. Pin the corners of the other hem a few inches inside the first two. The sheet should open toward the wind so it blows out like a sail. Run your hands down the selvage edges to smooth them and make sure that the sheet is hanging square and even.

Pillowcases: Fold one side of the opening over the line, pinning at both corners, allowing one side to sag open. You want the pillowcase to fill up like a sail in the wind.

Handkerchiefs: Fold in half over the line and pin at both ends.

Towels: Fold three to four inches of one end over the line and pin at both corners. Towels will line dry to be much softer and fluffier if you shake them energetically before you hang them on the line. Make them snap. This loosens up the pile very effectively. Shake and snap them when you take them off, too, to soften them.

Shirts and blouses: Method 1—hang by the tail, turning under three to four inches over the line, fronts opened out to the sides. Pin at placket ends and side seams, if necessary. Method 2—hang by the tail, turning under three to four inches, but fold the fronts in.

Dresses: If the dress is straight, pin it by the shoulders. If the dress has a full or gathered skirt, pin it by the hem, shoulders hanging down. But straight dresses, and the tops of many full dresses, dry with fewer wrinkles and a better shape if you hang them on hangers.

Skirts: Turn over the waistband of straight skirts and pin at both ends. Hang gathered or full skirts by the hem.

Pants and shorts: Turn the waist over and pin at both ends, or, for pants, use a trouser frame.

T-shirts and undershirts: Fold the hem a few inches over the line and pin at both ends.

Underwear or panties: Fold the waist over the line and pin at both sides.

Bras: Pin by the hook end.

Socks: Pin by the toe.

Hangers: If you want clothes on hangers to dry outside, make sure they will not blow off the hanger. Sometimes you can pin them on at the shoulder, but this may leave holes in fine and light fabrics, so be careful. If you hang a hanger outdoors, on the clothesline or elsewhere, watch out that it does not blow off. Try pinning the hanger to the clothesline with a clothespin, making sure that the garment is securely fastened to the hanger.

stretch. Plastic are less likely to leave marks on the clothes—but be sure they are clean. For knits and stretch wear, including underwear, panties, T-shirts, and knit dresses, use clip-on pins (with a spring).

Usually you will turn three or four inches of the fabric over the line, enough to be sure that the fold will not slip or come undone, especially important if there is a strong breeze. Heavy pieces will be more secure if you turn one-third to one-half of them over the line. On windy days, too, turn over more, for more security. Do not let clothes drag on the ground. Be sure that the pin gets a good grip. To the extent possible, hang sheets, tablecloths, and similar flatwork so that their hems are parallel to the line—widthwise. This takes less room along the clothesline and puts the stress of hanging on the warp yarns (they run lengthwise), which are stronger than the filling yarns. When hanging blankets or other large, heavy items, lay them over two lines so as to distribute their weight. (See the illustration on page 359.)

Hanging clothes properly reduces wrinkles and makes ironing more easy. The wind smooths wrinkles (and softens and dries clothes quickly, so try to hang garments so that sleeves, skirts, and legs billow out in the breeze. To accomplish this with sheets, pillowcases, skirts, and other pieces with double layers, hang them so that the fold (or the closed end of the pillow case) hangs down and the open, hemmed edged are pinned to the line; do not pin the fabric taut on the side from which the wind is blowing but let it sag down a bit, so that there is an opening for the wind to enter. (See the illustration on page 334.) Otherwise, however, it is best to pull the pinned edges of the clothes taut to reduce wrinkles. In addition, you should finger-iron and smooth the pinned-up clothes; pull seams, collars, and pockets straight and hang items so that the lines of their construction run neatly parallel and perpendicular to the clothesline. Otherwise the clothes will dry with funny bumps and shapes.

To prevent fading, dry colored clothes in the shade or turn them inside out, or both. White linens usually benefit from drying in direct sunlight, which gives them a gentle, natural bleaching. White and light cottons may eventually yellow with prolonged exposure to sunlight, so some experts recommend that they be hung in the shade for drying. My view is that the more typical effect of sun on white cotton—for, say, an afternoon on the clothesline after each laundering—is to bleach it, which I like.

Where it will not make a thick lump of cloth that will take too long to dry, it is labor-saving and space-saving to pin the ends of two garments together so that you use only half as many pins. For example, you pin a pillowcase to the end of a sheet and then pin a second pillowcase to the end of the first, creating a continuous line rather than one with breaks between the items. (See the illustration on page 333.) But you cannot let two items touch if one has bleeding dyes that would be visible on the other.

Remember that clothes dry at very different rates. If you are short on line space, run out to check on the clothes periodically to see whether some are dry. Sheets dry very quickly in the breeze and take up lots of line. You'll soon be able to take them down and hang up other things. Line-dried clothes are unlikely to get overdried on the line, since they are not exposed to artificial heat, but do not leave them out on the line overnight. Articles that are to be ironed should be taken down when they are still a bit damp, rolled up, and covered with a towel or placed in a plastic bag so that they do not dry out. Iron them promptly so that they do not rot or mold.

Fold immediately all clothes that will not be ironed. As you take down clothes for folding, shake each item and snap it—that is, hold it at one end and sharply crack it like a whip. This fluffs and shapes the article. Avoid putting laundry in a basket unfolded, and especially never leave it that way for a period of time, for this will cause much wrinkling and ruin the good effects of your careful hanging.

If you are line drying indoors, be sure to shake out the clothes vigorously before hanging them. This is necessary to reduce wrinkles and help them to dry less stiffly since you have no breezes to soften them.

Hanging Dry on Hangers or Hanging Racks

Dresses, blouses or shirts, jackets, permanent-press clothes, and pants that do not go in the dryer are usually best dried on hangers, for this preserves the shape of the garments and reduces wrinkles. Other items can be hung on drying racks or clotheshorses. Wash-and-wear or drip-dry clothes should always be carefully hung to dry and finger-pressed (smoothed and straight-

Jacket on hanger

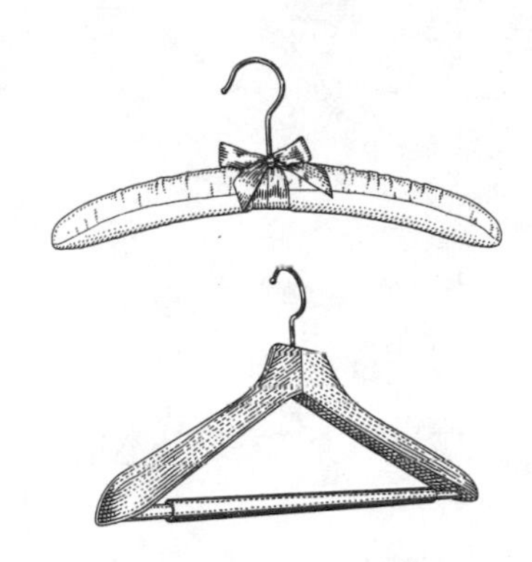
Nonrusting hangers with broad shoulders are best for hanging clothes to dry.

ened), particularly at seams. It is usually best to hang clothes to dry on wide hangers, for this distributes the weight of the garment better. A thin wire hanger produces strain on a very narrow band of cloth and creates unwelcome creases around the shoulder area. Jackets should be hung on hangers designed for jackets, which have wide rests for the shoulders. There are also thick padded or inflated plastic hangers that are good for drying.

When drying dresses, blouses, and shirts, hang the garments straight and smooth. Hang slips and dresses by their straps, if they have them. Button, zip, or snap them up so that the cloth is pulled properly to shape the garment. Press or smooth collars, facings, seams, trim, and pockets with your fingers, especially on wash-and-wear clothes. This little step can make ironing of many garments unnecessary and reduces it considerably on all. Use a trouser frame for "hanging" pants. This pulls them taut so they do not wrinkle and creates a crease in the right places. Or hang them over a wide hanger. (If you hang them from their cuffs on a trousers hanger, the cuffs may not dry.)

Dripping garments can be hung in the bathtub or shower stall, either on a drying frame or a line. The stores are full of good gadgets for these purposes.

Underwear, hosiery, and other articles that do not need to be hung on a hanger can be hung on racks.

Indoor drying on hangers and racks can be speeded by turning an electric fan on the clothes.

Drying Flat

Clothes that must be dried flat rather than hung include fabrics that stretch when wet, such as many knits and wools, and very delicate articles that should not be pinned or blown on the line or that should not be subjected to the stress of their own weight during hanging. In addition, smaller articles, particularly knits and items made of fast-drying synthetics, such as panties, bras, or hosiery, dry so quickly on a frame or rack that there is little reason to expose them to the high temperatures and static-producing friction of a dryer. They'll last longer and look better dried flat.

When drying clothes flat, keep them away from direct sources of heat, which may produce shrinking. Dry colored items out of direct sun. Pick a warm, dry room in which the air will readily take up moisture, or, if drying

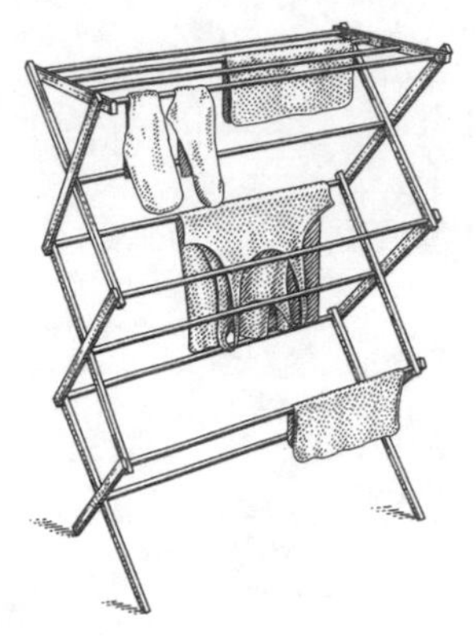
Drying rack

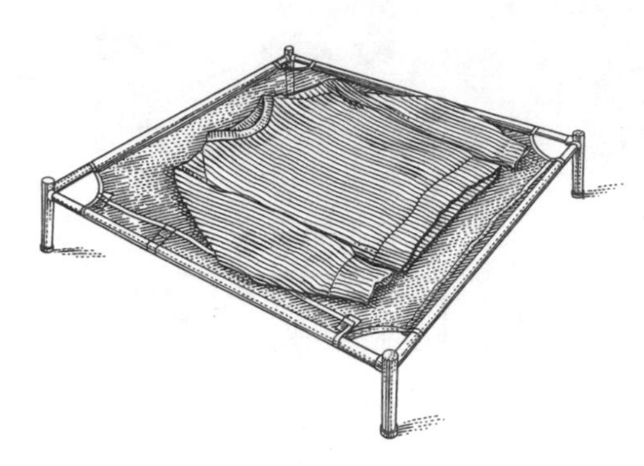
Flat drying rack

outdoors, a warm, dry day. Knits, especially sweaters, and other garments that hold lots of moisture, should be laid on a mesh rack, which speeds drying by permitting air penetration from below as well as above, or on a thick, absorbent towel. (If the article to be dried bleeds color, choose a towel that does not matter or that is of like color. And be sure that you do not lay the drying article on something that will bleed color into it.) Articles that do not hold a great deal of moisture, such as hose or panties, can be laid on a sheet. Whatever you are drying, be sure to protect wood or other surfaces that might be vulnerable to moisture if there is a chance that moisture will soak through.

If you turn over long-drying items, they will dry faster, but you should not disturb carefully blocked articles such as sweaters or other wool or knit clothes.

You can hasten drying of clothes laid flat by turning a fan on them.

23

Ironing

What should and should not be ironed . . . Sprinkling or dampening before ironing . . . Ironing temperatures . . . Techniques for pressing, ironing, and steam ironing . . . Airing the ironing, and avoiding under-ironing and over-ironing . . . Ironing clothes, flatwork, linen, table linens, sheets . . . How to avoid ironing . . . Starches and sizings . . . How to clean the iron

Ironing gratifies the senses. The transformation of wrinkled, shapeless cloth into the smooth and gleaming folds of a familiar garment pleases the eye. The good scent of ironing is the most comfortable smell in the world. And the fingertips enjoy the changes in the fabrics from cold to warm, wet to dry, and rough to silky. There is nothing like keeping the hands busy with some familiar work to free the mind. You can learn Italian while you iron, as a friend of mine did, or you can simply think.

What to Iron

Untreated cotton and linen woven fabrics almost always need ironing to look their best. Outer clothing made of such fabrics is a top ironing priority. Tablecloths, napkins, curtains and draperies, doilies, dresser scarves, and similar decorative pieces often do not look good without ironing, and since they exist at least half for appearance's sake, it is worthwhile to iron them.

Sheets, pillowcases, and flat-woven dish towels are a different matter. They need not be seen, and they do not function better if ironed. If you are short on time, you should eschew the luxury of ironed sheets and dish towels. But they are indeed luxuries to enjoy when you can. Crisp, smooth sheets dramatically change the aesthetic appeal of your bed and heighten your sense of repose. Pretty ironed dish towels make the kitchen look cared for when they are hung out; and, when you change them following a morning or evening cleanup, they provide a ready symbol of freshening and renewal. Such things enlarge the vocabulary of your housekeeping, give you more attractive things to say with it. On the practical side, a newcomer to the kitchen can be sure that an ironed towel is fresh.

You need not—and should not—iron terry-cloth towels and washcloths, small rugs and mats, diapers, mattress, crib, and bumper pads, comforters or other filled articles, sweatpants and sweatshirts, spandex stretch tights and other stretch athletic wear, seersucker, or pile fabrics such as velvet and chenille. Some people like to iron men's cotton knit underwear, woven cotton boxer shorts, and women's knit and synthetic-fiber bras and panties. This is fine for those who like both the work and the result, but unnecessary.

You may be satisfied with the way permanent-press and wrinkle-resistant clothes and linens look with no ironing at all, but these articles vary in just how wrinkle resistant they are. Wrinkle resistance may also decrease after many launderings. "Permanent-press" treatments are sometimes more accurately called "durable press" because they actually last through about fifty launderings, but many permanent-press clothes and linens look better after some touch-up ironing. You must consult your own priorities and tastes as well as the appearance of the garments, to determine whether and how much you wish to iron them.

Sprinkling Clothes and Linens

Permanent-press and synthetic fabrics sometimes iron well when dry, and, if they do not, a steam iron will supply all the moisture necessary. These fabrics usually need little or no ironing anyway. When some smoothing is desirable, their thermoplasticity makes them responsive to the warmth of the iron alone.

Untreated cottons, rayons, and silks must be slightly damp to iron out properly. They should feel as though you had left them outside overnight in summer and they became damp with dew. Linen should feel even more damp. The easiest way to get things this damp is to remove them from the dryer or line before they have gotten entirely dry. But this is not always convenient to do. When it is not, you can render them damp either by using a steam iron or by sprinkling them with water.

Sprinkling clothes is a little more trouble, but cottons and linens are far easier to iron and look far better after sprinkling than steam ironing alone. When fabrics are properly sprinkled, the moisture has a chance to penetrate the fibers and spread uniformly throughout the fabric. Steam from the iron does not penetrate so deeply or so uniformly.

The best procedure is to sprinkle clothes the night before they are to be ironed so that

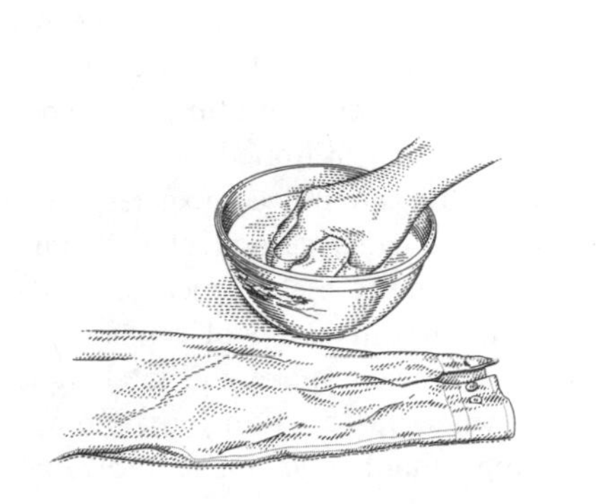

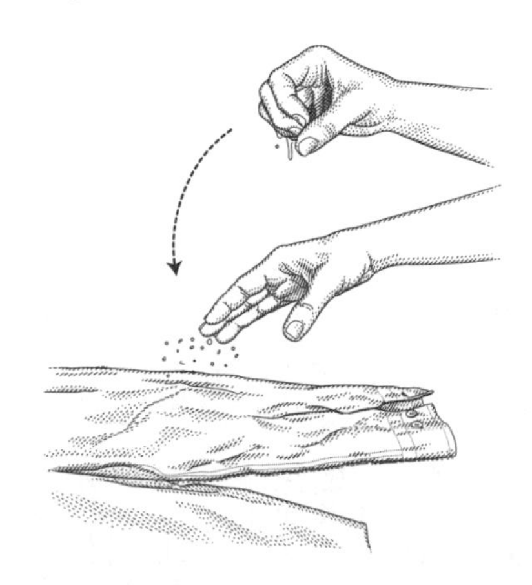

Sprinkling clothes by hand to dampen for ironing

the moisture permeates the cloth. If you cannot do this, allow at least an hour before you will iron. Clothes that will sit overnight before ironing should be placed in a tightly closed plastic bag and stored in the refrigerator or someplace else cool; otherwise there is danger of mildew. If they will not be ironed within twenty-four hours, put them in the freezer. Chilled, sprinkled fabrics make for smooth and pleasant ironing.

Use the hottest water that is comfortable to your hand for sprinkling because warmer water spreads more quickly. Some people like to spray fabrics with plain warm water from a spray bottle or to sprinkle with a sprinkle bottle. I find such bottles a nuisance as they tire your hand. But if you would like to try using one, you can make one by punching holes in the lid of a screw-top jar, testing it until it works to your satisfaction. If you prefer sprinkling by hand, as I do, fill a basin or sink with warm water and dip your fingers in. Then shake them with a snap over the fabric with your palm facing you (as though you were making the familiar hand-and-finger gesture that means something like "I'm impressed"). Whether you use bottles or sprinkle by hand, you very lightly scatter water drops all over the article until it is covered with droplets as evenly spaced as you can manage. Shirts, dresses, pants, pillowcases, and other articles with fronts and backs must be sprinkled front and back, but flatwork, such as sheets, tea towels, or tablecloths, need be sprinkled only on one side. Experience, and nothing else, will finally enable you to judge with great accuracy whether you have sprinkled enough or too much. Linen should be sprinkled damper than cotton.

When the garment has been sprinkled, fold it lengthwise until it is narrow enough to make a conveniently sized roll; then roll it tightly. If the roll is not tight, the moisture will not be able to spread evenly through osmosis and the garment will dry. Store the rolls in a clean plastic bag or cover them with something that will not permit the moisture to evaporate. If you have slightly damp clothes from the dryer or line that you intend to iron, you must roll and cover and store them the same way to avoid their drying prematurely or mildewing.

You can roll up a stack of sprinkled napkins or dish towels. Or if the fabric is thin, as with handkerchiefs, sprinkle only every other one and then roll up the stack. The water will spread from the sprinkled ones to the unsprinkled, and they will not be too damp.

In deciding how damp to make your cloth, allow for the dampening effect of spray starch or sizing, if you plan to use it. If an article is too damp, simply spread it out to the air and let the moisture evaporate a bit while you iron something else.

Rolling sprinkled pillowcases for ironing

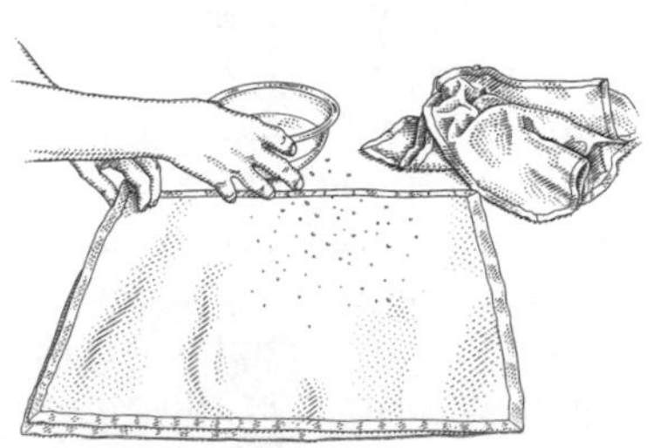

Stacking and sprinkling napkins

Rolling stacked and sprinkled napkins for ironing

Ironing Temperatures

The international symbols for ironing temperatures consist of one, two, and three dots.

One dot: cool (low temperature—248°F, 120°C), synthetics

Two dots: warm (medium temperature—320°F, 160°C), silk and wool

Three dots: hot (high temperature—370°F, 210°C), cotton and linen

These suggested temperatures are roughly applicable to the categories indicated. Consult chapters 16 and 17 with respect to particular textile fibers and "General Ironing Strategies," below, for more specific information on proper ironing temperatures.

My unscientific impression is that many irons today do not reach particularly high temperatures, even when set for maximum heat, and that it can be hard to get heavier cottons and linens to look good. Higher wattages indicate more heating power. If you can pick up an old iron (with an intact cord and plug) at a second-hand store or tag sale, you might find it useful on clothes or linens that need a really hot iron.

Before Beginning

Make sure that your ironing board is well padded and covered with a smooth, secure, clean, heat-resistant cover. Make sure that there are no mineral deposits inside the iron or in its steam holes and that the soleplate of your iron is clean. Mineral deposits or scorched material on the soleplate will come off on whatever you are ironing. If you have any doubts, heat and/or steam up the iron and test it on a rag. (See "Cleaning the Iron," below.)

Also test the iron's heat before beginning so as to avoid scorching or melting the fabric with an over-hot iron. Test on a rag of similar composition or on an inconspicuous place on the garment.

Ironing Techniques

Pressing. The terms "ironing" and "pressing" are often used interchangeably, but they are in fact different things. In ironing, you slide the iron back and forth over the cloth; in pressing, you simply press the iron in one spot and then lift it. Pressing is used on tailored and lined suits, especially men's, on wool, on silk and some rayon, on net, and on pile fabrics. Pressing is used to avoid crushing the cloth, giving it a shine, or stretching or scorching or otherwise harming it with the heat of the iron. This is done partly by not sliding the iron and partly (and usually) by using a "pressing cloth." This is simply a cloth that you lay over the fabric, pressing through it rather than touching the iron directly to the garment. Use unbleached muslin, white cheesecloth, or just a clean white dish towel for a pressing cloth. There are translucent pressing cloths that let you see what you are doing. A pressing cloth is sometimes used in ironing as well as in pressing.

Most pressing is best done professionally. At home, we usually wish to do only a little touching up by way of pressing. But it happens that one finds oneself with a wrinkled suit and an appointment when the dry cleaner is closed for the holiday, and home pressing has to be done. On these occasions, the best thing to do is to do as little as possible. First try steaming out the wrinkles, with a hand steamer if you have one or in the shower if you don't. Then try to press out intractable wrinkles. Using a dampened pressing cloth and working only on the wrinkled areas, apply the iron with a slight pressure and then lift quickly. Press on the wrong side as much as possible. Beware of creating shiny areas or seam marks on seams, lapels, and pockets by pressing too hard or too long. If you should happen to create a shine, try gently brushing with a clothes brush to remove it, or rub gently with a slightly moistened clean sponge or clean white face cloth or towel.

To press wool. Put a heavy, nonlinting, nonbleeding terry-cloth towel under the garment to prevent seams and folds from leaving imprints on the garment's surface. Press on the wrong side using steam or a damp pressing cloth and medium iron. Wool will develop an unpleasant shine if the iron directly touches the right side. Lift the iron after each pressing. Do not go back and forth, as this will stretch the fabric, and iron in the direction of the weave. Do not iron the garment until it is absolutely dry; stop when the fabric is smooth and almost undetectably damp.

To press silk ties. Press on the wrong (back) side. Lay thick silks or ties on a terry-cloth towel. Place a dry pressing cloth over the article. If wrinkles will not come out, place a damp pressing cloth over the dry one.

General Ironing Strategies. Whether you are pressing or ironing, you lay the article on the ironing board and smooth it out. Iron as large an area as you can, then put down the iron so that you can use both hands to rotate the article around the board in preparation for ironing a new area. When you are ironing, one hand works at smoothing the garment and pulling it taut while the other works the iron. When you put down the iron, either stand it on its heel or place it on a nonflammable stand.

In real ironing, as opposed to pressing, you use moderately paced, steady back-and-forth strokes of the iron, with slight downward pressure; you usually press down more heavily on the forward strokes than on the return motion. Today's irons are very lightweight. Some people, myself included, find that ironing is easier with a heavier iron with a very smooth stroke. The weight means that you have to apply less muscle power.

- Begin ironing with those items that are to be ironed at the lowest temperatures and end with those that will be ironed at the highest temperatures—for example, polypropylene first (using a pressing cloth) and linen last.
- Keep a sprinkle or spray bottle or damp sponge at hand for spot dampening in case you accidentally iron in an unwanted crease or in case the cloth dries before you have finished ironing. You will sometimes also wish to redampen a pressing cloth.
- Spray starch and spray sizing should be kept at hand, too, if you intend to use them. Spray lightly from a distance of six to ten inches with the bottle tipped at an angle. Follow instructions on the bottle. You can choose to starch only collars, cuffs, and plackets, or those areas plus fronts. The traditional way is to use more starch on these areas and less on others. Because it is easy to scorch spray starch, you may wish to turn down the heat on your iron. (For more on what to starch, see "Starches and Sizings" below.)
- To avoid unwanted creases on collars, iron from the points in, using short strokes. After ironing, the collar should be folded down and softly creased with your hand, not the iron. Iron the wrong side (the back) of the collar first, then the right side.
- French cuffs, too, should be softly creased after ironing with the hand, not with the iron.
- To avoid unwanted creases where the cloth has slack—for example, in a hem—use short strokes and stop short when you see that the slack is going to fold and crease. Try moving the iron toward the wrinkles from different directions.
- To avoid shine, iron fabric on the wrong side or use a pressing cloth. This is a particularly good idea on dark cottons, linens, rayons, and silks. (Silk should always be ironed on the wrong side with a pressing cloth; the same goes for any rayon that tends to develop a shine.) If shine develops on thick seams or elsewhere, wipe lightly with a barely damp cloth. When ironing double thicknesses, like collars,

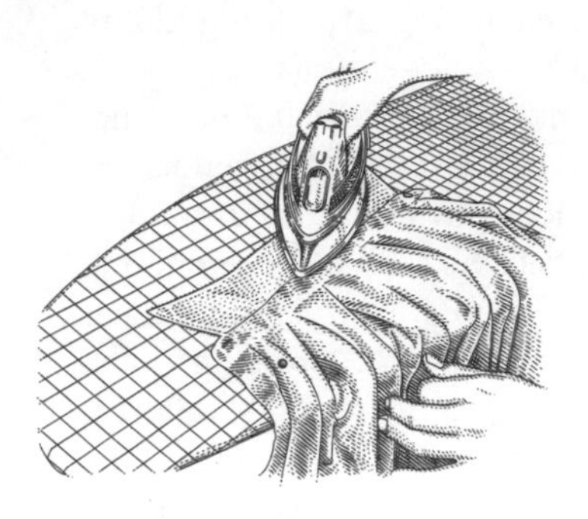

Ironing a shirt collar

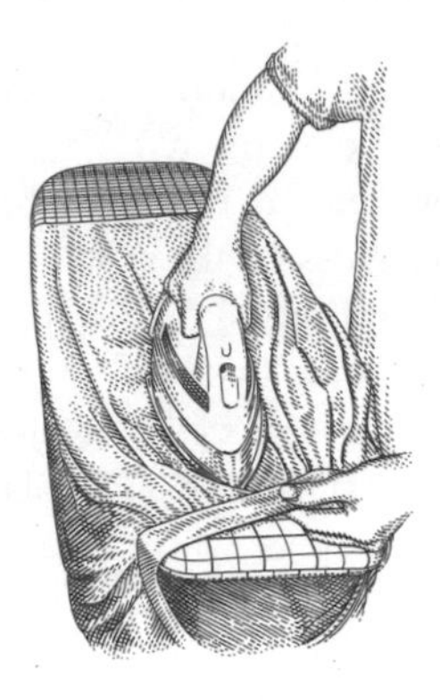
Ironing a gathered skirt

Ironing a pant leg

pockets, and cuffs, do the wrong side first and, if necessary to avoid shine, use a pressing cloth on the right side.

- Nose the iron gently around buttons, hooks, snaps, and zippers; never iron over them. Buttons will sometimes melt and will frequently crack if you iron over them.
- Close zippers, snaps, and hooks before ironing plackets. But leave button plackets unbuttoned.
- To iron gathers, begin at the edge of the cloth opposite the gathers, and wiggle the point of the iron into the gathers.
- To iron puffed sleeves or pockets, stuff them with tissue paper or a small terry towel or washcloth.
- Some people like to use a sleeve board for shirt sleeves. (Set the sleeveboard on the ironing board and pull the sleeve over it.)
- To iron pleats, first lay or pin them in place. (Some people like to pin them to the ironing board cover.) Then, holding the pleats taut against the pressure of the iron, iron them in long strokes going from waist to hem.
- Lay embroidered or sequined cloth on a Turkish towel, then iron it on the wrong side with a pressing cloth. This keeps the embroidered patterns raised and prevents cracking of the sequins or scratching of the soleplate.
- Use a pressing cloth when ironing lace and cutwork. This will ensure that you do not accidentally cause a tear with the point of the iron.
- Never iron pile fabrics. Velvet should be steamed, not ironed, unless the manufacturer otherwise directs. To steam corduroy, lay it on a Turkish towel. Then hold your steam iron just a fraction of an inch up from the surface of the wrong side and release steam. This will refresh the pile.
- Untangle fringe while it is still wet.
- Ironing can stretch certain garments or fabrics out of shape. Iron bias-cut clothes and other stretchy fabrics, including wools and knits, in the direction of the weave—that is, in the less stretchy or non-stretchy direction. In the case of bias-cut skirts, this means that you should not iron from hem to waist, as you usually do. Use a press cloth, if the fabric is especially stretchy, to reduce the iron's drag.

Steam Ironing. Wait until the iron is hot enough to steam the water. When you have not sprinkled the clothes damp, steam is helpful in ironing practically any fiber. Choose a proper steam level for the fiber—most for linen, down to practically none for 100% thermoplastic synthetics. Use the

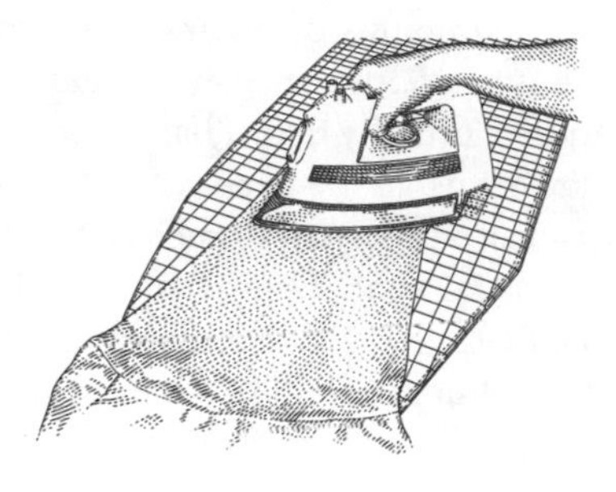

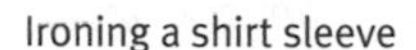
Ironing a shirt sleeve

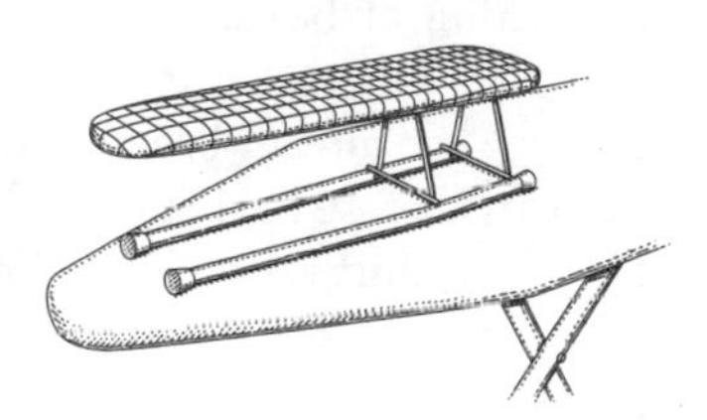
A sleeve board

steam button to eject a steam spray on cuffs, collars, and other thick places.

Airing the Ironing; Avoiding Under- and Over-Ironing. It is a basic rule of ironing that you iron things until they are dry. If you leave things too damp, they will feel rough and look rumply afterward. They may also develop a faint unpleasant odor or mildew if you put them away in that state.

But there is dry, and then there's *dry*. Some people over-iron in an effort to get the article bone dry, but this is a mistake. Scorching, yellowing, or melting of synthetics are some of the obvious effects of over ironing. Shininess, brittleness, and a harsh hand can also be produced. You should stop ironing just a fraction of a degree before the flat of the cloth is perfect for use and wear, letting the last tiny increment of moisture evaporate from the heat of ironing. At this point, when the flat has a bare suggestion of dampness in it, the seams will be slightly more damp than this, but that is all right, for now you are going to *air* the ironing. Airing carries off the excess moisture without the dangers of over-ironing. One hundred years ago the ironing was aired religiously, usually overnight, often in front of the fire.

To air laundry in this day and age, fold or hang each ironed article carefully, but *do not put it away* until both flat and seams feel perfectly dry to the touch. Folded articles may be aired on a table or shelf, but do not stack them on top of one another until the airing is completed. Shirts and dresses can be hung on hangers on a rack in the laundry room or in some other convenient area for airing. If you do not air them this way before replacing them in your closets, they are likely to carry dampness into your closets and create a musty smell that is very hard to get rid of.

Ironing Clothes. When ironing clothes, follow an order in which there will be minimal rewrinkling of the already ironed sections as you proceed. This means following three basic rules.

1. Iron all parts that have a double thickness—ties, bows, collars, cuffs, sleeves, pockets, and the like—because they will wrinkle less readily than larger, thinner areas like shirt backs. Collars, cuffs, plackets and facings, hems, and other parts of the garment that have two right sides should be ironed inside first. When ironing pockets, hems, or facings on the right side, use a pressing cloth to avoid ironing marks at raised places. If an article is lined, turn it inside out and iron the lining first. Iron set-in pockets from the wrong side with garments turned inside out.

2. Iron the nonflat portions, like ruffles, shoulders, and puffed sleeves, before the flat portions. Ironing these requires more turning and twisting of the garment, which could cause flat, unstructured areas to rewrinkle if they had already been ironed.
3. Iron the top parts before the bottom parts (the shirt part of a shirtwaist dress before the skirt, the top of pants before the legs) so that you do not have to scrunch up the ironed lower section, rewrinkling it, to get at the top.

Some say you should also iron small parts before large parts. But I find that these three rules cover the ground thoroughly.

Ironing Flatwork. Much flatwork can be done extremely well and quickly on an electric rotary iron or "mangle." These machines have a heated roller that presses the cloth. They take out wrinkles but do not produce quite as fine a result as hand ironing. They are now all but unknown in the United States, but they were common equipment in middle-class homes here until the early 1960s, and they remain popular in some European countries. I am told that Americans are once again beginning to ask for them; you see them now and then in appliance stores. I acquired one several years ago because our household habits produce a great deal of flatwork to iron—sheets and pillowcases, tablecloths and napkins—since we prefer untreated cottons and linens. The rotary iron saves great amounts of ironing time and effort, but it is a fairly expensive machine and uses more electricity than a hand iron.

Rotary iron or mangle

Rotary irons, in the hands of skilled operators, can also be used for much clothing, especially casual wear, T-shirts, and children's play clothes that benefit from a quick smoothing but do not need fine, close ironing. Skilled users do shirts and dresses too, perhaps with some hand finishing, but this takes practice. Cutwork and embroidery or other designs that create raised patterns will definitely need hand ironing, although on flatwork with decorated hems and edges you can often do the flat on the rotary iron and then finish the embroidery and lace with a hand iron. These areas need the point of the iron to get close to raised areas in the fabric.

When ironing or mangling sheets or tablecloths or other large items, lay an old sheet or tablecloth on the floor so that items that reach the floor will not be soiled.

Ironing Linen. Some experts now sometimes recommend a warm, not hot, iron for linen. If linen or a blend containing linen has received resin treatments for wrinkle resistance, it is true that you should avoid a hot iron and follow the care label instructions. (The permanent-press setting may be recommended.) In addition, very sheer and lightweight linens may iron well with a warm iron. Subject to this and other caveats about blends, resins and finishes, and the like, however, linen is not harmed by the temperatures of a hot iron. Not only that, it is quite hard to iron most linen free of wrinkles on a medium iron. Even cambric or lawn, which may not need a hot iron, will not be harmed by it unless you let it rest upon them until they dry and burn. It is not difficult to avoid doing this. Almost any fabric would be injured if you left a hot iron standing on it.

To iron well, linen should be quite damp—damper than cotton needs to be for good results. Steam from a steam iron is adequate for sheer linens, but I find it easier to sprinkle medium-to-heavy-weight linen fabric. When you dampen, allow for the additional dampening effect of spray starch, if you are using it. Stretch and smooth damp linens into their proper shape before ironing. Ironing on the wrong side, or with a pressing cloth, will prevent a sheen from developing. But on damask and other light-colored linens a sheen is desirable; these you iron first on the wrong and then on the right side. Darker linens should be ironed only on the wrong side.

Linen is rather brittle when completely dry—and the drier it is, the more brittle—so it should not be ironed bone dry; stop while there is still a suggestion, barely detectable, of dampness. Be particularly careful not to iron creases too dry or too sharp or the cloth might be weakened along the creases and eventually crack. (This is particularly a danger with ironed linen that is stored flat. It is best to store it unironed unless you plan to use it soon.) Hang ironed linen clothes while they still retain a hint of dampness at the seams or hems, and leave them out to air dry. Replace them in closets or drawers only when such dampness has evaporated; this will happen quickly.

Good linen tablecloths and napkins stay crisp without starch. But if your table linens or linen clothes have gone limp (even if they shouldn't have), starch will often restore the look you want. Fancy napkin-folding requires starch.

Table Linens. Ironing instructions are provided here; for folding instructions, see chapter 24.

To iron round tablecloths, begin at the center and work out, turning the cloth as you go.

Iron table napkins flat; do not iron in the creases.

Damasks, especially of linen, are supposed to look glossy or shiny after ironing, and they are ironed on both sides, wrong side first. Fold square and rectangular tablecloths in half lengthwise and iron first on the wrong side, until half dry, and then refold and iron until near dry on the right side. Linen is brittle, especially when dry, so take special care to be sure that crease lines are not ironed dry and that you iron along the crease line gently. Remember to move any creases an inch or two at each ironing so that the cloth does not wear out along the crease.

Etiquette forbids creases on the cloth for formal dining or, at best, tolerates one middle crease line *lengthwise.* A crease across the middle offends the eye. If you are one of those who want no creases whatever on your cloth—not even down the length—after ironing on both sides and avoiding the center, softly fold the cloth into thirds and iron the small unironed strip down the center of the cloth. For informal dining, ordinary checkerboard squares caused by folding will be tolerated by everyone, and some, myself included, think they are pretty and fresh-looking. The rule against any but a lengthwise center crease is of relatively recent vintage; through the eighteenth century, tablecloths were purposely ironed in accordion pleats and checkerboard creases that were valued for their contribution to the table's beauty as much as the china or silver set upon it.

It is best to store tablecloths unstarched and unironed, if it will be some time before they are used, and to iron them just before they are needed. Doing this gives you very wrinkle-free cloths on the table but also creates more work and details to keep in mind at the last minute.

Sheets. The highest traditions, which are by and large extinct, should survive at least in memory. Perhaps some people will wish to adopt them on their wedding night or similarly rare and grand occasions. These dictate that sheets, especially top sheets and more especially linen sheets, be ironed. Some actually like sheets ironed on both sides.

Ironing flat sheets.

Long method. Fold the sheet in half crosswise (hem to hem), wrong sides together, and iron on both (right) sides. (If you wished to iron the sheet on both sides, you would first fold it in half crosswise (hem to hem), *right* sides together, and iron both sides—the wrong sides. You would then go on to refold, wrong sides together, and iron the right sides.) Fold again crosswise (fold to hem), creating quarter folds, and iron both sides. Fold again crosswise (fold to hem), creating eighth folds; iron both sides. Then fold lengthwise, or selvage to selvage. Fold lengthwise again, fold to selvage, twice. The completely folded and ironed sheet is divided into thirty-two sections.

Short method. Iron only once, after the initial folding in half. Then fold as above.

Abbreviated method. Fold in half crosswise (hem to hem). Iron the bottom hem, selvage edges, and eighteen inches of the top hem (the foldover portion). Then fold as above.

Ironing fitted sheets. Ironing fitted sheets is usually not necessary since they are pulled taut by the mattress and are further smoothed by the pressure, moisture, and warmth of bodies upon them. Moreover, they do not show. But some people like the more finished smoothness of ironed fitted sheets. If you are going to iron yours, you can do the fitted corners by stuffing them with a small terry towel. Or you can leave the fitted corners unironed and iron only the flat portions. Otherwise, iron as for a flat sheet.

Caution for those who never iron sheets. When I got married and joined my linen stores with my husband's, I was initially mystified by the dozens of small but growing holes along the selvages and hems of my husband's good-quality cotton sheets. I soon determined that the holes were caused by the creases of permanent, natural wrinkles in those places, wrinkles that did not unwrinkle even in laundering. (Cloth weakens along any permanent crease lines.) Even if you do not wish to iron your sheets, you might try ironing out just their selvages and hems now and then, to avoid getting such holes.

Starches and Sizings

Starches are plant starches, usually corn starch nowadays, but formerly wheat or potato starch and other substances were commonly used. Starches are used to stiffen; add crispness, body, and glossiness; promote soil resistance (dirt particles adhere less easily to smooth, starched surfaces); and make ironing easier.

If you like cottons, cotton blends, and linens that have not been resin-treated for wrinkle resistance, you may also enjoy them ironed with a bit of starch. I like a little starch on cotton shirts, dresses, and skirts. Sometimes I starch just the collars, cuffs, plackets, and perhaps the shirt fronts. When you want to fold napkins into elegant or unusual shapes, starching is usually necessary; starched napkins are not soft to the lips, but they look more formal. Starch is a good idea whenever or wherever you want extra body or stiffness, or when you want a garment to continue to look ironed after you've been wearing it for hours. Starch should not be used on sheets, underwear, diapers, towels, or filled or stuffed articles. (Back in the 1940s and 1950s, starched pillowcases were de rigueur, and I know one lady who says she still cannot sleep on an unstarched pillowcase. I like the appearance of starched pillowcases and even enjoy their crisp feel. Most people do not.) Fancy hand towels for guests—lacy, embroidered, damask, etc. (not terrycloth towels)—are usually starched crisply.

Spray starch is applied as you iron. You can put liquid starch in the final rinse of the

TO REDUCE OR AVOID IRONING

- Choose low-wrinkling clothes and linens. (See page 275, chapter 18.)
- Use a mangle (rotary iron), on all flatwork, casual clothes and play clothes, and sportswear.
- If you like non-wrinkle-treated sheets but do not wish to iron them, dry them on the line, being sure to hang them neatly, smoothing hems and selvages, in such a way as to ensure that the wind will billow them out. They will come very smooth. If they feel at all stiff—as can happen, particularly when there is no breeze—tumble them on cool for a few minutes in the dryer to soften them up. (But they will soften almost immediately when you sleep on them.) Yet another way to dry things smooth without ironing is to tumble them in the dryer; promptly remove them and fold them tautly while they are still warm and before they are bone dry. If you let them sit in the dryer, they will wrinkle. After removing them—from the line as well as the dryer—shake them out well, pull them sharply into shape, and snap them, that is, give them a crack as one might crack a whip. Stack them neatly, place them at the bottom of the stack in your linen closet, and place something quite heavy on top of the stack. Or, rather than folding them, fold them while they are still hot into halves or quarters and then roll them tautly around a cardboard roll.
- Dry synthetics and wrinkle-treated clothes on the permanent-press cycle. Remove them from the dryer and fold them promptly.
- Use a trouser frame when drying pants. It stretches them taut so they do not wrinkle and creates creases in the right places.
- Never leave laundry sitting in the laundry basket unfolded; this causes much wrinkling. Hang and fold clothes carefully, and keep drawers and closets uncrowded.
- If you plan to wear items again, hang or fold them neatly after you take them off.

wash, using the amounts recommended on the label. If you wish to use liquid starch on some but not all of the contents of a load, do the starching separately in a clean basin.

On synthetic fibers and blends with a high percentage of synthetics, what are called "sizings" are usually preferable. Sizings are also stiffeners. (Technically, starches are sizings too, but in supermarket products the terms are used as I describe them here.) Sizings usually contain sodium carboxymethylcellulose, a derivative of cotton that dries and stiffens when exposed to heat. You spray store-bought sizing on when you iron. Sizing is softer than starch and irons at lower temperatures. That is why it is usually recommended for synthetics, which cannot be ironed at higher temperatures. You can use it on cottons and linens, too, when they do not need much stiffness. You can make an old-fashioned sizing at home using unflavored, uncolored gelatin, available at your grocery store—use one packet to two quarts of hot water. This is good for small, delicate items that need gentle stiffening. Just dip them in, and be sure to get all the parts equally wet. Let them dry, then iron with a steam iron or sprinkle to dampen.

Cleaning the Iron

If spray starch sticks to the soleplate of your iron, make a paste of baking soda and water and brush the soleplate with an old, clean toothbrush dipped in the paste. If you do not have immediate success, let the paste stand for a few minutes and then scrub vigorously. Or simply buy a commercial cleaner for the soleplate at your home center or hardware store. I have also seen recommendations to use white vinegar for this purpose, but in my experience vinegar is not effective. Whatever you use, it's best to work on the problem as soon as possible. The longer you wait, the harder it becomes to remove a stuck-on substance, and scorched-on spray starch tends to come off on garments when you are ironing.

When your steam iron becomes clogged as a result of mineral deposits in your water, you can dissolve them—unless the manufacturer's instruction booklet says not to—by pouring some white vinegar into the water tank, turning on the iron, and letting it steam for a few minutes. (White vinegar *is* effective for this.) After cleaning with vinegar, iron a clean rag of some sort so that any residues are deposited on the rag. Then cool the iron and rinse with cold, plain water. Some irons require that distilled water be used in the tank. If you frequently have trouble with clogged steam holes, perhaps yours requires this; check the instruction booklet.

24

Folding Clothes and Linens

Why clothes and linens should be folded properly . . . How to fold suit jackets, shirts, blouses, jackets, and sweaters, T-shirts, dresses, pants and shorts, skirts, underpants, socks, napkins, tablecloths, blankets, sheets, pillowcases, towels, handkerchiefs . . . How to put a duvet (comforter) into a cover . . . Using tissue paper in folding

When I was a girl, every week my mother and I folded sheets together in a brisk dance, moving quickly and always turning the folds in the same direction. Periodically she would give the sheet a good sharp snap, which would jerk my end out of my hand if I didn't hang on tight. Tablecloths, sheets, and other large, unwieldy items really are folded most easily by two congenial people of roughly the same height. But when I first kept house as a single woman, I learned to lay the part that would otherwise drag on the floor on a bed or sofa. I rather liked not having to worry about the other person's suddenly giving a violent snap to her end.

Folding smaller pieces after laundering was always done by a daughter, sitting at a table. Each article was to be folded in just the right manner. Neat, separate stacks of napkins, handkerchiefs, T-shirts, towels according to their size, and piles of rolled-up sock balls, arranged according to owner, were first set on the table and left to air, if necessary, then set carefully in a basket and carried around the house to their proper storage places: linen closet, dresser drawers, or kitchen drawers.

The folding and hanging styles described in this chapter are those used in my family. Other styles might be just as good or better. But it is useful to have some habitual way of folding so as to keep things neat and wrinkle-free and to use drawer and shelf space most efficiently.

Suit Jackets. Suit jackets are hung in a closet or carried in a garment bag for traveling whenever possible. When they must be folded into a suitcase or stored flat, the following folding method works well. Put your hands into the shoulders of the unbuttoned jacket,

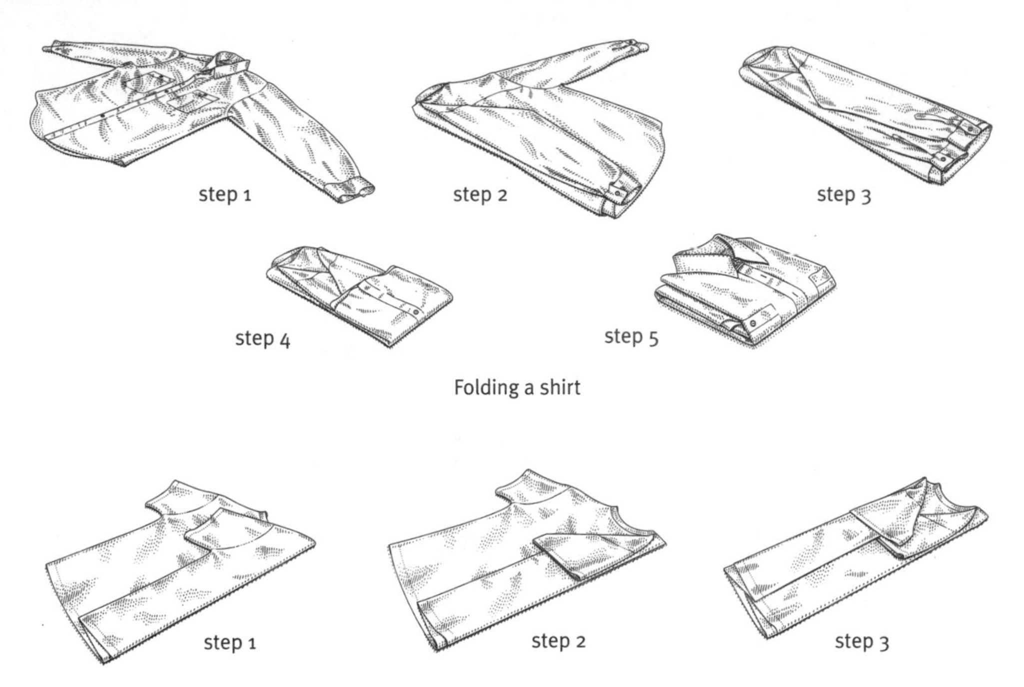

Folding a shirt

Folding a T-shirt (see "Folding a shirt," above, for steps 4 and 5)

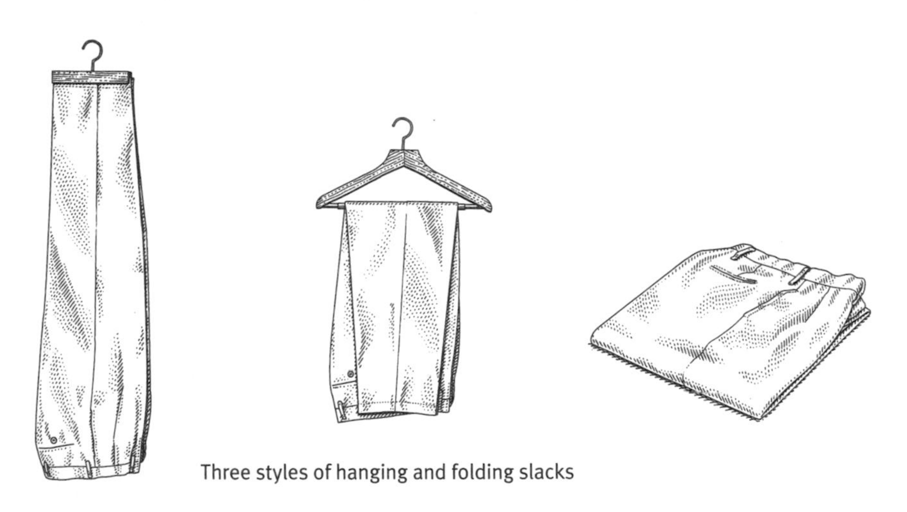

Three styles of hanging and folding slacks

grab the ends of the shoulder pads, and turn the shoulders inside out. Without letting go, pull the shoulders together, in the process folding the jacket inside out along the side seams. The back and sleeves now lie between the left and right front. Straighten up and align the side seams, make sure that sleeves and hems are aligned, and open the lapels. If your suitcase or drawer is large enough, you can instead simply fold the unbuttoned jacket in half lengthwise, with the lapel edges together and the side seams together.

Shirts, Blouses, Casual Jackets and Sweaters, and T-Shirts. If the shirt has buttons, button it at top, middle, and bottom. Then lay it facedown. Fold both sides of a shirt or blouse so that they meet in the back, with the sleeves aligned with the side folds. Fold the tail up to the cuffs, making a straight

Folding a skirt

Folding boxers

Folding panties

Folding a dress

line at the bottom. Then fold in thirds crosswise. Casual jackets, long-sleeved sweaters, pullovers, and cardigans are folded the same way, except that there is no tail to be folded up. Do T-shirts as you do other shirts. A child's T-shirt may need only one crosswise fold, in half; but an adult's you may wish to fold into thirds, depending upon the size of the T-shirt and what fits comfortably in your drawer or on your shelf.

Dresses. Dresses should almost always be hung rather than folded, unless they are to go in a suitcase or other type of flat storage. To fold a dress for a suitcase, lay it front down. Fold the top as though it were a shirt or blouse. Fold the bottom hem to the knees. Then fold at the waist.

Pants and Shorts. Pants are usually hung by their cuffs on trouser hangers. Or fold them over a hanger with a thick bar or a paper guard so that a cross-wise crease does not form. Shorts may be folded and placed in a drawer. Whether hung or put in a suitcase or drawer, pants and shorts are folded as follows: align the inseams and outer seams of the legs and fold so that a crease forms properly at the front center of the legs. In well-made garments, the crease should run all the way to the top of the pants, joining the front waist pleats. Fold in the front placket along the pleats.

Skirts. Lay the skirt front down, with zippers and plackets closed. Fold the sides in toward the center. Then, if it is not a short skirt, fold crosswise in thirds. The idea is to avoid a vertical crease line down the front center or a horizontal crease line halfway down the front.

Underpants. The folding is the same for men's and women's. Fold in half crosswise, so that the crotch meets the waistband. Then fold into thirds. Underpants can also be laid flat, unfolded, in stacks, if they are not too large, or they can be rolled.

Socks. There are three ways to fold socks. Method 1, in which they are folded into balls, looks good and is space-efficient but tends to stretch out the top of the socks, especially all-cotton socks. In this method, you lay one sock on top of the other. Starting at the toe, roll them up together to the ribbing. Open the top of the outside sock and pull it over the roll. In method 2, the socks are simply rolled up together. This is neat and space-efficient, but the rolls can come undone and socks separated. It's the best method for careful adults but not for children and those of us who sometimes rummage wildly through our drawers. In method 3, you place one sock on top of the other, then fold one top over the other. This keeps pairs together in all but the wildest rumpuses.

Napkins. When folding napkins, always fold loosely by hand. Do not iron creases in. A large dinner napkin is folded in a triple screen fold lengthwise, then in another triple screen fold crosswise, producing a square. You can then fold again in half, if you prefer a smaller rectangular shape to a larger square shape or just to save some room on the table. However you fold it, if there is a monogram or corner decoration, it should end up in the lower left-hand corner when the napkin is placed at the left of the forks. (The lower right-hand corner is also fine; just be consistent.)

A smaller dinner napkin is simply folded into a rectangle: in half twice, ending with the monogram or decoration in the lower left corner.

The luncheon napkin and napkins for informal occasions may be folded any way you like—for example, like a dinner napkin, in a triangle, or in a wedge formed from the triangle. To make a wedge, the two points of the triangle are folded to the back in thirds, forming a pentagon with two long sides. The monogram or decoration is in the point, which points downward.

Tablecloths. Tablecloths should be either rolled around a cardboard tube or *loosely* folded, so as to avoid creases as much as possible. (One lengthwise crease is acceptable.) You can also hang tablecloths if they are not

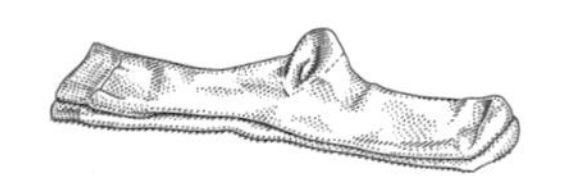
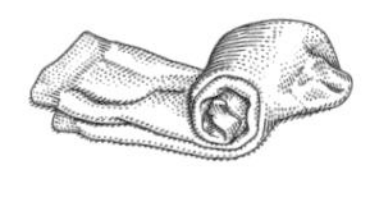
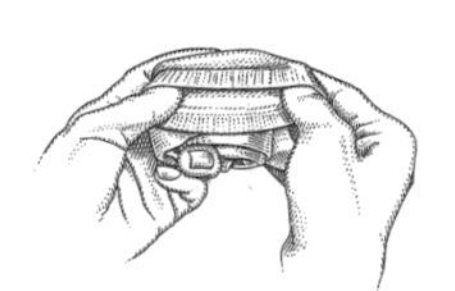

Folding socks, method one

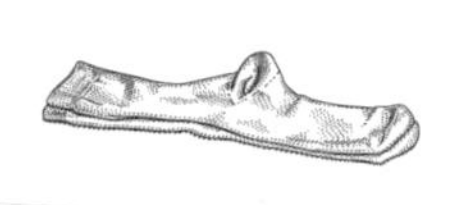

Folding socks, method two

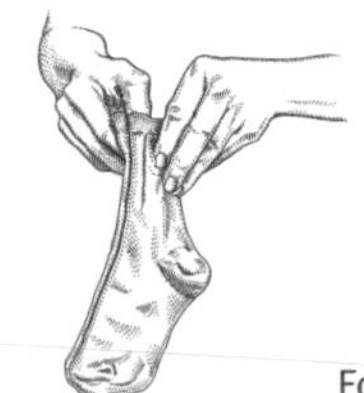
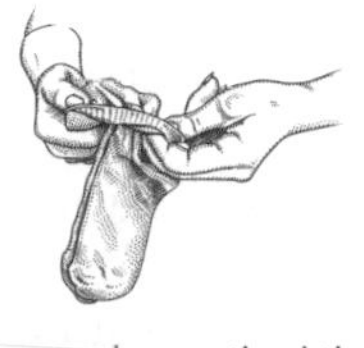
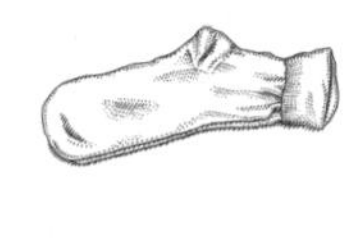

Folding socks, method three

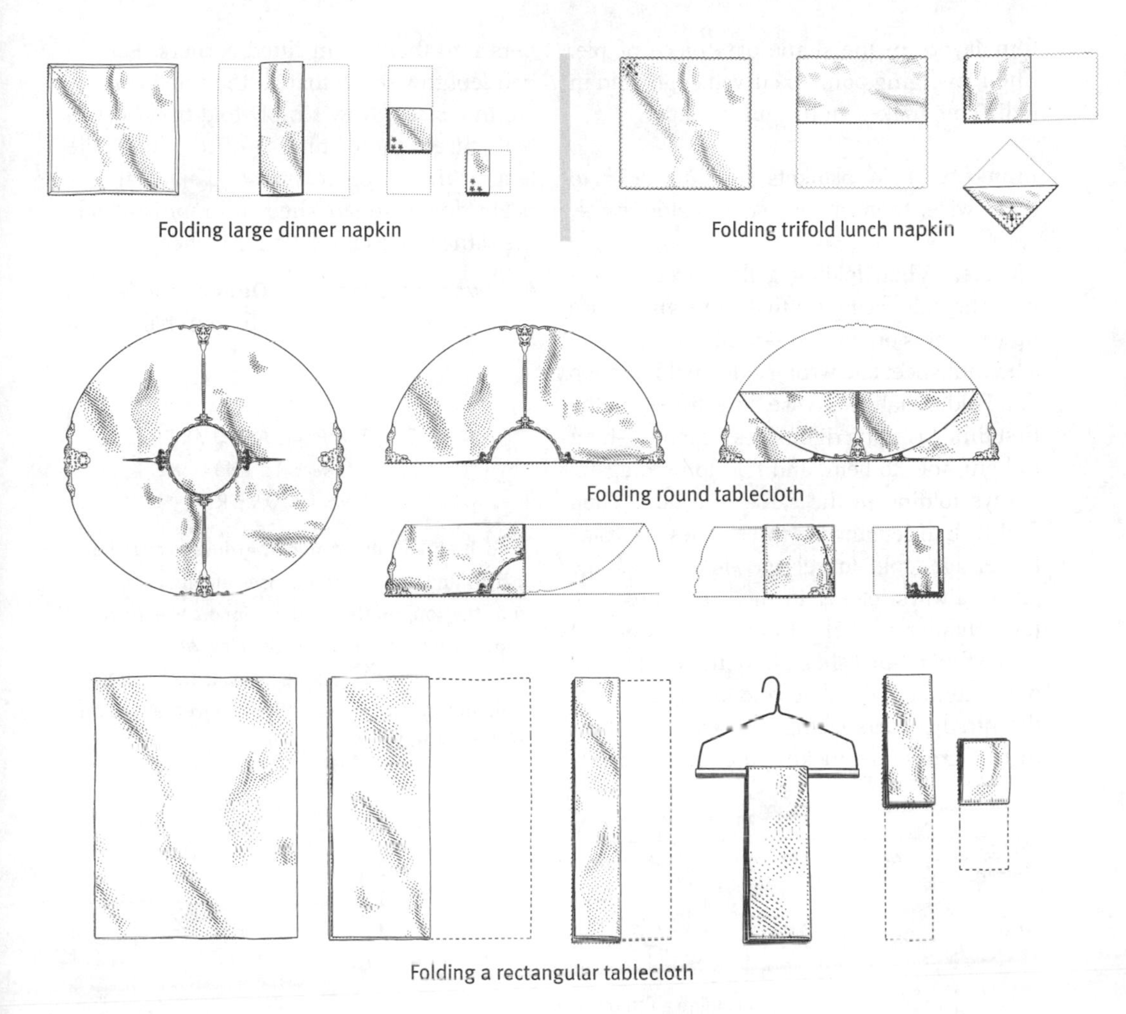
Folding large dinner napkin

Folding trifold lunch napkin

Folding round tablecloth

Folding a rectangular tablecloth

too wide. Simply fold loosely in half twice, lengthwise, and fold over a hanger with a thick, round bar to avoid causing a crease.

If you wish to fold your tablecloths, large square and rectangular tablecloths may be folded in half three times lengthwise, forming eight layers (the first fold brings wrong sides together), then two or three times crosswise. The number of crosswise and lengthwise folds may be increased or decreased depending on the size of the tablecloth and your drawer space. If you wish the fold lines all to point upward to the right side of the cloth, fold the tablecloth in fourths as follows. Bring each side edge to the middle of the cloth, creating two folds along the sides of the cloth. Then fold again lengthwise along the middle line where the two side edges meet, so that the two edges are inside. Do the same with the crosswise folds.

Fold round tablecloths in half, to form a half-moon shape, with wrong sides together. Then fold in half lengthwise, bringing the arc of the half-moon to the fold. The center of the arc should be even with the center of the fold. Fold lengthwise again if necessary—as for a large cloth. Then fold in half crosswise twice, or three times if the cloth is large. You will have a rectangle. Small round tablecloths are sometimes folded this way: Fold in half twice, forming four layers in the shape of a piece of pie. Then, bringing point to curved edge, fold in half. This makes an irregular shape.

Blankets. Fold blankets in half, head to foot, twice, then in half, side to side, twice.

Sheets. When folding a flat sheet, hold it with the side facing up that you want to face up when it is on the bed—right side up if it is a bottom sheet and wrong side up if it is a top flat. Fold in half crosswise three times, on the first time bringing right sides together—hem to hem, fold to hem, and fold to hem again, always folding in the same direction. Then fold in half lengthwise three times—selvage to selvage, fold to selvage, fold to selvage again, always folding in the same direction. (See chapter 56, "The Cave of Nakedness.")

To fold a fitted sheet, have the wrong side of the center of the sheet and the right side of the fitted corners facing you. Fold the sheet in half crosswise, tucking the top fitted corners into the bottom fitted corners. Fold in half lengthwise, so that all the fitted corners are in a stack. Now simply fold the sheet in half three more times—once along the length and twice crosswise. This makes a neatly folded fitted sheet of approximately the same size as the folded flat sheet.

Pillowcases (Standard, Queen, and King). Fold in thirds lengthwise, then in half cross-

HOW TO PUT A DUVET (COMFORTER) INTO A DUVET COVER

Fold both the duvet and the duvet cover into halves and then quarters. Insert the folded duvet into the top quarter of the folded cover so that the duvet's end and the opening of the duvet cover are aligned. Pick up both at the opening, hold tightly, and shake until the duvet falls to fill the entire cover.

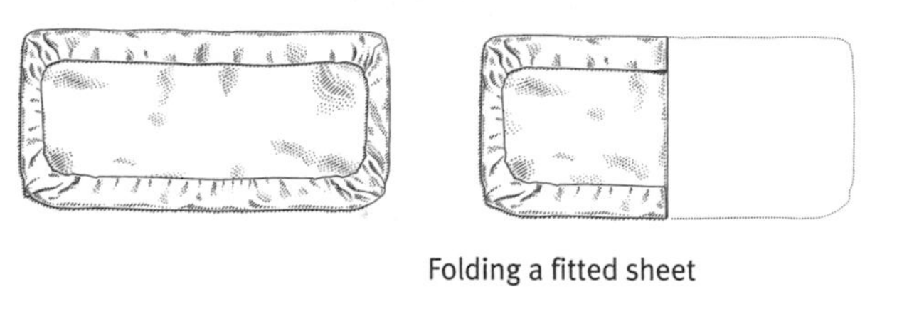

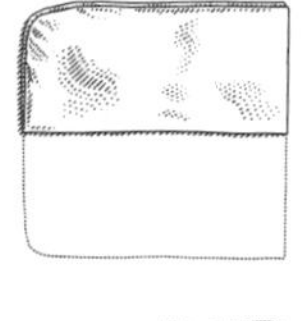

Folding a fitted sheet

Fold two times crosswise

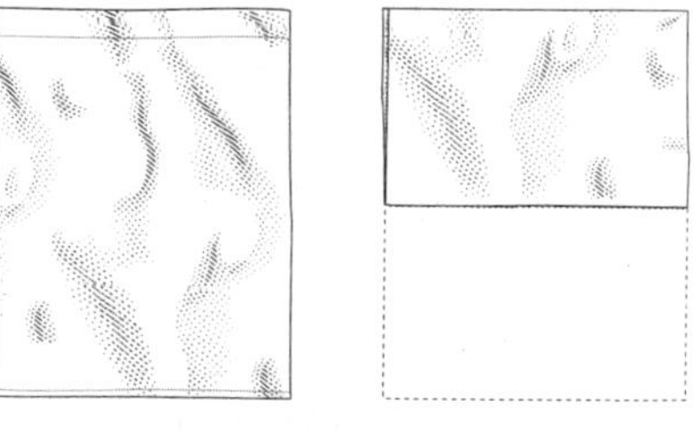

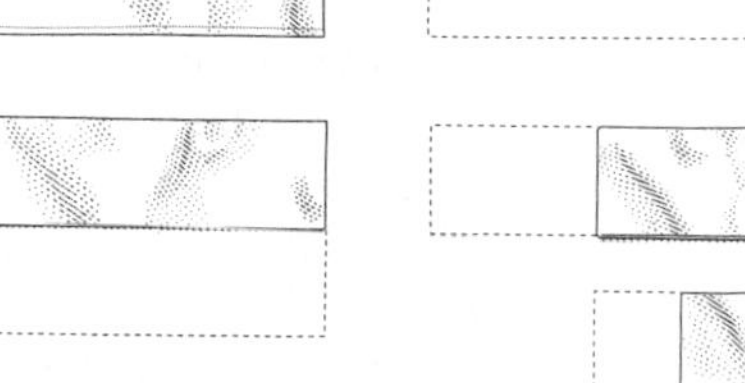

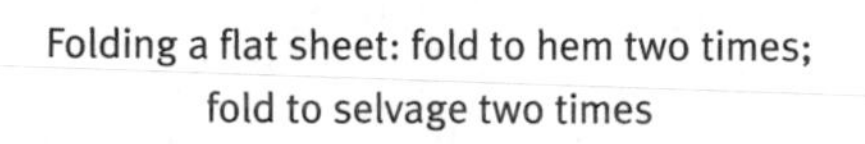

Folding a flat sheet: fold to hem two times; fold to selvage two times

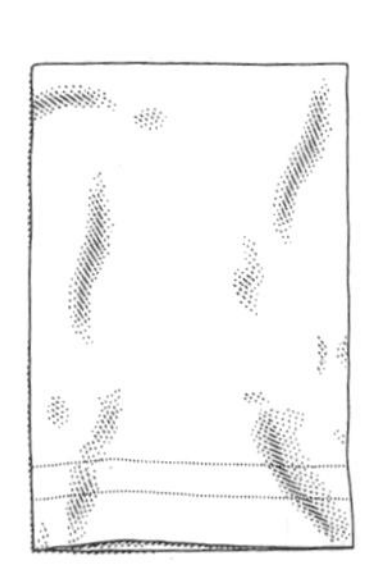

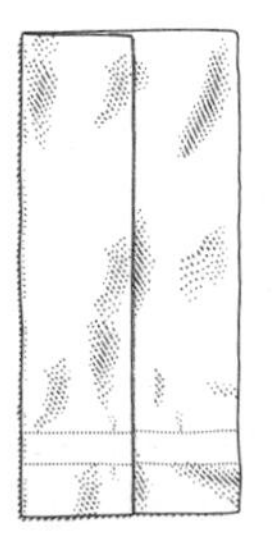

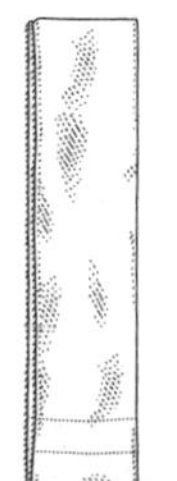

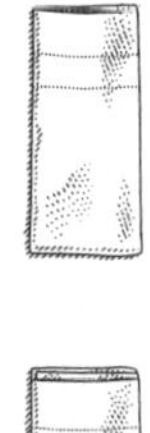

Folding a standard pillowcase

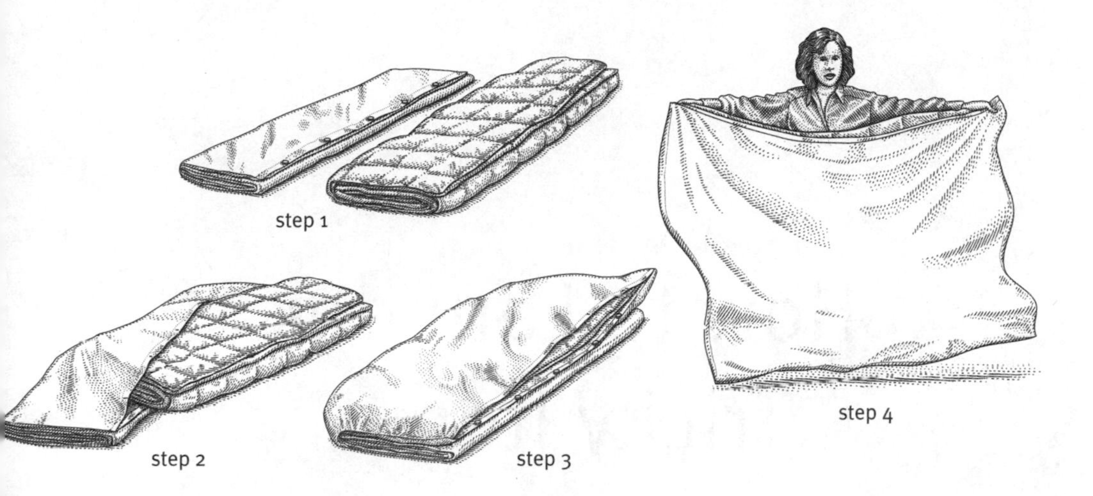

Filling a duvet cover

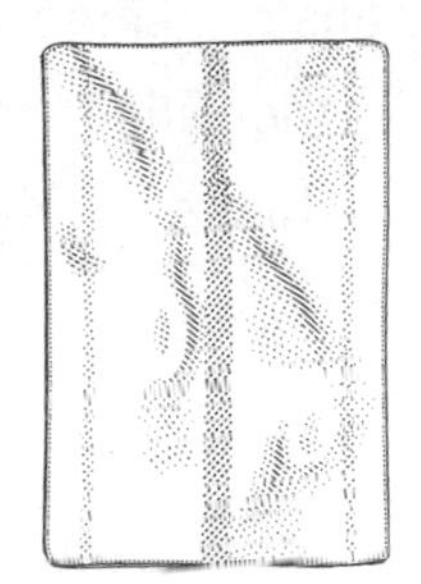
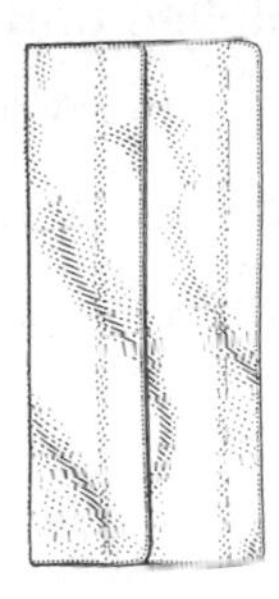
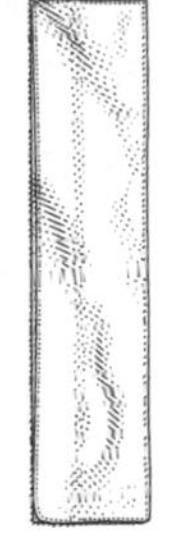
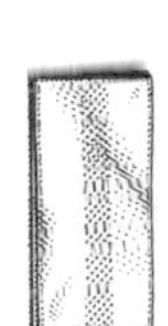

Folding a dish towel

wise once or twice depending upon your shelf or drawer space. Or reverse this, folding in half crosswise twice, then three times lengthwise. Either way will prettily display trim or lace at the opening of the pillowcase.

Pillowcases (European). Try folding these in thirds along both dimensions.

Towels. Dish towels, tea towels, bath towels, and hand or guest towels can be folded in thirds lengthwise, then folded in half or thirds crosswise, depending upon the size of the towel and its thickness. Thinner towels are more easily folded many times. This method shows trim nicely and lets you hang the towels with their vertical folds in place; you need not refold for hanging.

Handkerchiefs. Fold men's handkerchiefs in half three times, forming rectangles. Fold women's handkerchiefs twice, forming squares.

USING TISSUE PAPER IN FOLDING

Folded articles in suitcases, on shelves, or in drawers resist wrinkling better if you lay tissue paper over them so that it is folded up with the garments. You can also stuff puffy sleeves and hats with tissue paper. When you are putting things into long-term storage, especially antiques, heirlooms, or other precious fabrics, use acid-free tissue paper.

25

How to Launder Tricky Items

How to launder blankets, nonwool and wool . . . Curtains and draperies . . . Shower curtains . . . Diapers . . . Gloves and mittens . . . Lingerie, undergarments, foundation garments . . . Down- and feather-filled clothes and furnishings . . . Polyester-filled clothes and furnishings . . . Kapok and foam fillings . . . Knits . . . Cotton knits . . . Quilts

Every home contains some clothes and furnishings that are launderable but cannot be washed in the standard ways or present unusual laundering difficulties. Suggestions are included below for the successful laundering of a number of such items: blankets; curtains and drapes; diapers; gloves and mittens; delicate lingerie, undergarments, and foundation garments; pillows, comforters, and garments filled with down, feathers, polyester, or other materials; and quilts. When the methods suggested are incompatible with care labels on any such articles, however, you should follow the care label.

Blankets, Nonwool. Be sure to look for a care label; blankets do not always have one, but, when they do, *follow it*. Before you decide on laundering, test for colorfastness. Nonwool blankets are almost always machine-washable and machine-dryable, assuming that your washer and dryer are large enough for them. Blankets should be washed singly, one by one. To be sure a blanket will fit, try it out in both your washer and your dryer before proceeding. If it is too large, send it to a professional laundry or take it to a laundromat that has extra-large machines. If you prefer or if your dryer is too small, blankets can be line-dried or dried flat.

To launder washable nonwool blankets, fill the washer with water. Use the warmest temperature safe for the fiber and construction. Warm is usually best because nonwool blankets will generally be made of a synthetic or a cotton knit or loose weave and will have a soil type that is readily removed with warm water. (But only hot water would kill germs and dust mites.) Put in sufficient detergent and thoroughly dissolve it before adding the blanket. Arrange the blanket loosely and evenly around the post. Let it soak for twenty minutes, then wash on the gentle cycle. Rinse with cold water. Spin dry on the fast (or high) setting.

Tumble dry at the temperature proper for the fiber and construction—usually low to medium. If you are line drying, spread the blanket over two lines to distribute its weight, preventing strain and stretching. If you are drying flat, try spreading it on the lawn on an old sheet. Sometimes even though the dryer is too small for drying a blanket, it is large enough to hold it for a few minutes of air-fluffing after it has dried. You can also shake, snap, or brush the blanket to fluff it.

If you are forced to dry a blanket indoors on a line or rack, you can turn an electric fan on it to hasten drying.

Blankets, Wool. If there is a care label that says "dry-clean only," obey it. If the blanket is of Superwash wool, follow the instructions on the care label (and see chapter 16, "The Natural Fibers," pages 245–47.) If there is no care label, you must use your judgment. Dry cleaning will be safe, but home laundering using proper procedures will probably be safe too— and some people feel that they can give gentler care at home. But be sure to test for colorfastness with whatever detergent you plan on using.

Measure the blanket first so that you can restore it to its original dimensions after it is washed. As with other blankets, wash each wool blanket separately and alone.

Use a *neutral*, mild detergent suitable for wool (see "Detergents and soaps, mild," pages 322–24), for use in cool water, and for machine laundering. Use cool water, making sure that the detergent is thoroughly mixed and dissolved before you put in the blanket. (Cool, by the way, does not mean icy cold. See "Water Temperature," pages 308–10, in chapter 21.) And if the blanket is heavily soiled, risk-takers like myself might try lukewarm water. Years ago, if there was heavy soil, people might even have tried a regular detergent as well—but, you may

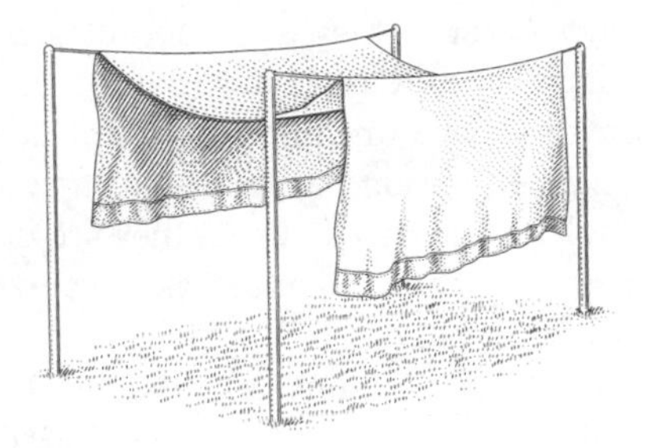

Blanket spread over two clotheslines to dry

wish to try an extra amount of your mild detergent instead. (We risk-takers are also probably more tolerant of less-than-ideal results than others may be.) Be sure to use plenty of water. Soak the blanket for a few minutes, say five or fewer, *and no longer*. Agitate on *gentle* very briefly—for a minute or two. Or, to be more cautious, do not agitate at all; just stir the blanket gently with a long wooden paddle or spoon. Then manually set the machine forward to spin dry, using the fast spin speed. Then fill again with cold water to rinse, agitate briefly, for a minute or two (or stir gently), and spin dry on the fast setting again. Repeat the rinse if necessary.

Dry the blanket by laying it flat on a rack or laying it outside on an old clean sheet, stretching the blanket gently into its proper dimensions; refer to your original measurements to be sure. Or hang the blanket over two or three clotheslines to distribute its weight, pulling it gently into good shape. If you are drying a blanket indoors, you can hasten the process by turning an electric fan on it. If your dryer is large enough, air-fluff the blanket after it is dry, without heat. If you cannot do this, shake the blanket and brush it gently with a clothes brush to soften and fluff it up after it is dry.

Curtains and Draperies. Read care labels on curtains and draperies carefully, or consult your retailer at the time you buy as to their washability or dry-cleanability. Many curtains and draperies are not washable, whether because they are made of a nonlaunderable fabric such as silk velvet or because they have unlaunderable trim or for some other reason. In this case, they are probably dry-cleanable. But if they are quite delicate or worn, you must alert your dry cleaner to the situation.

Even when curtains and draperies are washable, they may not be machine-washable. And even when they are machine-washable, they should almost always be washed on the gentle cycle. This is so for several reasons. First, the type of soil they are likely to collect is usually easy to get out with gentle washing. Second—probably the most important consideration—they are constantly exposed to light while they are hanging, which causes deterioration of the fabric. Laundering can tear or fray them when they have been weakened by light. Third, they are often made in constructions, such as lace or extremely loose weaves, that demand gentle treatment. To choose between machine-washing on a gentle or delicate cycle and hand-washing, and to choose water temperature and detergents, use the same criteria that govern in other cases. (See chapter 21.) Choose lukewarm or cool water to avoid shrinkage with fibers that may shrink. Tumble dry on low if shrinkage is a problem, or line dry if you wish to avoid any heat or abrasion.

Fiberglass curtains and draperies, which are not sold very often anymore, should be hand-laundered, not dry-cleaned, unless there is a care label stating otherwise. They should *not* go into your washing machine or dryer. Not only do they need a very gentle wash, but glass fibers will break off in the machines and be picked up by the next load you do. When glass fibers become embedded in fabrics they can cause severe skin irritation. (Fiberglass drapes must by law bear tags or labels saying they can cause skin irritation.) To launder fiberglass drapes and curtains, place them in a large laundry tub with water and detergent. Wearing rubber gloves, swish them around, then soak until the dirt has loosened. Swish again; then rinse thoroughly. Press water out of the curtains or drapes with your hands (still wearing rubber gloves)—do not wring—and then line dry. Afterward, rinse the tub very thoroughly to ensure that all fiberglass fibers have been removed.

Curtains, Plastic Shower. Washing machine manufacturers may recommend that you not wash plastic shower curtains in the machine because they can become brittle with age and crack. I have washed them in the machine many times without encountering this or any other problem. But if you cannot afford to have your shower curtain crack or if you are very attached to it, perhaps you had better not try to machine-wash it. Scrub it by hand with a medium-soft brush or cloth wetted with detergent and water as hot as the hand can bear. Test for safety first in an inconspicuous area; then, if you wish, add a little bleach (perhaps 3/4 cup per gallon) to help with mildew. Rinse thoroughly when clean. You can also clean shower curtains by spraying them with any nonabrasive bathroom cleaner, letting the cleaner stand, and then wiping and rinsing.

Diapers. If you use cloth diapers, try to wash diapers at least every other day; every day is best. In the meantime, collect dirty diapers in a pail to soak. Before putting a soiled diaper in the pail, scrape off excess matter into the toilet with a tool dedicated to this function, say an old table knife or spatula. Or dip the dirty diaper in the toilet, holding one end tightly, and flush to rinse. Then place diapers in the pail with warm water and 1/2 cup borax per gallon of water to help remove stains and deodorize. Adding chlorine bleach to the pail also helps remove stains, deodorizes, and kills bacteria. One leading bleach manufacturer recommends using 1/4 cup chlorine bleach per gallon of water and soaking for five minutes; rinse before laundering. (You may also add chlorine bleach to the wash water, as described below.) Or buy a special diaper-soaking product and use according to directions.

When you are ready to launder the diapers, which should be done separately from all other laundry, first let the machine begin filling. Add detergent; when it is fully mixed and dissolved, dump the contents of the diaper pail into the machine. Do a regular wash cycle with hot water and a mild detergent or one formulated for sensitive skin or for baby's skin; adding chlorine bleach in the quantities recommended by the manufacturer sanitizes and deodorizes. Give at least two rinses. Dr. Spock recommends that you rinse three times if your baby has sensitive skin. Do not overcrowd the machine. About three dozen diapers are the maximum that should go in a top-loading large-capacity machine with the water level set to its maximum level.

Drying diapers in the sunshine kills germs, but they will probably not feel as soft after line drying as after tumbling dry; and the dryer heat, too, kills germs. Do not use fabric softener, as this makes diapers less absorbent.

Diaper services will bring you clean, sterilized diapers (and sometimes training pants too) and take away the dirty ones. If you use a diaper service, you just scrape off loose matter from the diapers and place them in the pail the service provides. Do not rinse them. Do not add any chemicals or additives to the pail unless the service provides them.

Gloves and Mittens, Leather. Do not wash suede or lined leather gloves. Other leather gloves you may be able to launder; consult any care instructions supplied by the manufacturer. (Usually there are none, unfortunately.)

To wash launderable leather gloves, begin by emptying the fingers of any dust or debris or lint that has accumulated inside. Then wash them in warm water made sudsy with a mild soap or detergent. Squeeze water through the leather gently. Rub a little extra detergent directly on especially soiled areas. Then turn them inside out and wash the inside in the same manner. Rinse the inside thoroughly, then turn the gloves right side out and rinse the outside thoroughly. Dry flat. Work them with your hands two or three times as they dry to prevent their drying stiff. If you wait until they are dry to do this, you may cause them to crack. When they are half dry, put them on to shape them. If they do dry stiff, wet them a little before working them to soften them up. When they are completely dry, rub them with a little leather conditioner.

I have read that you can sometimes remove light dirt and spots from leather gloves by rubbing with a clean gum eraser. This sounds plausible but potentially injurious if you are not gentle, and I have never tried it. Before you do, I recommend that you test the procedure out first by trying it on an inconspicuous area of the glove.

Gloves and Mittens, Wool. First be sure to remove any lint or dirt from the inside of the gloves. Then machine-wash on gentle or hand-wash washable wool gloves exactly as you wash wool sweaters, not forgetting to test first for colorfastness and to trace them first for blocking. See chapter 16, page 246. Roll in a towel to remove excess water, then dry flat. Brush with a fabric brush when the gloves are dry to restore fluffiness to the nap. Do not try to turn them inside out or shape them when they are wet.

Gloves, Nonwool Woven Fabric. These will usually require washing by hand separately from other clothing, as they are particularly likely to bleed or to pull apart. Use warm, sudsy water made with mild soap or detergent, and squeeze it gently through the gloves. If there are especially soiled spots, work a little soap into them and let them soak for a few minutes. These gloves are usually too delicate to turn inside out for washing the inside. Rinse very thoroughly. Roll in a towel, then dry flat.

Lace. Machine-made lace is often machine-washable. Snagging, tearing, and tangling when machine-washing lace can be reduced or prevented by placing lace in a mesh bag for laundering. Use the gentle cycle and mild detergents, moderate temperatures (lukewarm for cotton and linen laces, as they may shrink), and cool-downs and gentle spins for synthetics. All-lace items are usually very lightly soiled, so you can keep the wash cycle short. They dry quickly, too. If they keep their shape well, you can just put them on a drying rack. If they need shaping or if shrinking is a danger, follow the instructions for delicate laces in the following paragraph. Cotton or linen lace may shrink if you dry it in the dryer, but this is not a problem for polyester. You might even let polyester lace curtains or draperies finish drying on the curtain rod, but, of course, if they need some touching up with an iron this is not feasible.

Very delicate laces, especially handmade ones, should be hand-washed. Place in a basin, let soak for a few minutes in a solution of lukewarm to warm water with mild soap or detergent, then gently pat—this presses water through the fibers—until clean. Rinse very thoroughly. Press with a towel to remove excess water, then dry flat on a flat mesh rack or on a dry towel, arranging the lace in its proper shape. You can use a gentle tug to do this. You will sometimes read that you should pin lace down to dry it. If you are careful (and use nonrusting pins), this will do no harm and may obviate the need for ironing by keeping the lace from rolling or getting out of shape.

Lingerie, Undergarments, and Foundation Garments. A clerk at one of New York City's fine department stores once told me that the expected life span of a good bra is six months. After that you can expect limpness, discoloration or dinginess, and loss of elasticity. What she said is true unless you follow my mother's advice, in which case you can do considerably better than this.

How Good Girls Wash Their Underclothes. My mother taught me that you were supposed to hand-wash panty hose, bras, panties, slips, camisoles, girdles (which are making a comeback), and all other fine lingerie immediately after use. Many women still follow this policy, and their bathrooms are moist with dripping silks and hosiery almost every night. To wash fine lingerie, use plain, mild detergent in lukewarm water. Ivory bath soap was what Mother used, and it is still a good choice; but mild detergents are easier to rinse out and work better in hard water than soaps. The specialty cleaners made for lingerie are always good, too, in my experience, and they have nice perfumes. But they are almost always terribly overpriced. Plain, mild dishwashing detergent works just as well. Never rub and scrub; simply soak for a couple of minutes, then press and squeeze suds through the fabric. Rinse thoroughly in lukewarm water and roll in a clean, colorfast towel to remove excess water. Dry small items flat or on a drying rack. You can hang slips by their straps. Do not use clothespins on stretchy parts—it will harm their elasticity. Do not put fine lingerie in the dryer, except on a no-heat setting. (See the discussion below in "How Most Women Wash Their Underclothes.")

The reason for washing intimate garments immediately after wear is that they are worn next to the skin, where they absorb perspiration, skin oils, antiperspirants, perfumes and their oils, and lotions and moisturizers, as well as ordinary dust and dirt from the environment. Perspiration will cause natural fibers to deteriorate. Dust and dirt affect all fibers negatively. Many chemicals contained in antiperspirants, perfumes, and other substances used on the body will also discolor, stain, or cause deterioration in fine fabrics. In each case, the longer the substance stays on the fiber, the greater the damage or the more permanent the stain or discoloration. These causes can also produce loss of elasticity over time. If you wash the garments immediately, thoroughly, and very gently, they may stay fine and fresh-looking for years, not months.

How Most Women Wash Their Underclothes. Since few of us have time to care so nicely for nice things, what many of us do is buy less delicate, machine-washable fabrics and fibers for everyday use and take out the elegant, delicate ones only on weekends and special occasions. Check care labels to be certain that what you buy for everyday use is indeed machine-washable. Practically all less delicate foundation garments and lingerie are machine-washable nowadays, including most stretch undergarments. If for hygienic reasons you wish to be able to use hot water and bleach on panties or other undergarments, avoid silk and buy white or colorfast cottons or polyester with cotton crotches. The cottons are likely to shrink, so get them large enough to fit after shrinking.

Wash soon after wear. Turn panties inside out for laundering. Panty hose, articles with delicate lace, or articles that tangle up (such as bras) can be placed in mesh bags for laundering (and drying items that go in the dryer) when you want to avoid hand-washing. Fasten the bras so that they cannot catch in other garments; this also reduces tangling.

Use the gentle cycle and wash for five minutes or so, using warm water, cool rinse, and mild detergent on those garments that require it—otherwise use a regular detergent. Or you might use regular detergent every now and then to do a very thorough cleaning, and mild detergent in the meantime. Be particularly careful not to overheat stretch fabrics, which will lose elasticity, and avoid using chlorine bleach on spandex, nylon, and silk.

Dry underclothes on a drying rack or simply lay them on a towel or sheet on the floor. Much women's lingerie and underwear dries so quickly that the dryer is really unnecessary. (Cotton underpants can take longer.) The heat of the dryer ages such garments greatly, often discolors them, causes their elasticity to decline far more rapidly, and offers no real convenience. If you let them air-dry, moreover, you avoid static cling. Of course, fabric softener would remedy this problem too, but it also reduces the absorbency of the fabrics, and when fabrics go next to the skin you want them to be absorbent.

On removing yellow perspiration stains from lingerie, see chapter 26, "Common Laundry Mishaps and Problems—Yellowing."

Down- and Feather-Filled Articles. Down-filled and feather-filled pillows, comforters, jackets, sleeping bags, and other filled articles can be difficult to clean: they are unwieldy to launder at home and expensive to send out. This makes it important to keep them clean as long as you can so that they need laundering or dry cleaning less frequently.

According to contemporary manufacturers, the trick in cleaning these filled articles is to avoid stripping the down and feathers of their natural oils in the process. These oils sustain the loft and resilience of down and feather, which in turn are the source of the articles' warmth and soft comfort. Although both dry cleaning and laundering will to some extent remove oils, most manufacturers today seem to regard *laundering* as the cleaning method of choice for down- and feather-filled clothes and furnishings. You occasionally run into a care label that prescribes dry cleaning, however, and when this happens you should obey it. Only the manufacturer knows what finishes (for example, water repellency) or other features of the article might be vulnerable to damage from a given cleaning method. You also occasionally run into a care label that says hand-wash or have dry-cleaned only by an *experienced* dry cleaner (using only certain solvents, and *clean* solvents)—a clear indication that some people have not had the best luck when sending these sorts of things out for dry cleaning.

Instructions for laundering down- and feather-filled articles today are much more cautious than they were fifteen or twenty years ago. Then (and in many instances now) the standard advice was to wash washable pillows on the machine's regular cycle for eight to ten minutes, with ordinary detergents, and to dry them at "regular"—that is, hot—temperatures. This certainly would produce cleaner, faster-drying pillows than the more conservative instructions you find now, but manufacturers of such articles say they now understand better than they once did the harm that rough laundering can cause.

Many manufacturers—perhaps a majority—now recommend that you use only a soap to launder their filled products, on the grounds that soap will be more neutral and milder than a detergent and less likely to strip oils. When pressed, one told me that a really mild, neutral, *powdered* detergent would be acceptable, although not as good as soap. However, the idea that soaps necessarily are milder than detergents is mistaken, and until someone informs me of any other reason for choosing soap for laundering down- and feather-filled objects, I will continue to use a mild detergent. (See "Mild soaps and detergents," pages 322–24.) Whatever you choose, rinse thoroughly; the residues of soap or detergent left in the filled items can eventually cause deterioration.

Although some manufacturers still provide instructions for washing their filled products in a regular top-loading machine, many now recommend that you either *hand-launder* their filled products or machine-wash them only in a *front-loading tumbling machine*. The idea here is that the rough, jerking agitation in a regular top-loading machine can pack the down or push it out of its proper place (so that it becomes poorly distributed throughout the article) or can rip out delicate seams or baffling. Whatever type of machine you have, first make sure that it is really large enough to wash, thoroughly rinse, and spin dry bulky filled articles. (I know someone whose machine's spin mechanism was ruined when she washed a heavy comforter in it.) When you think about drying your comforter in your home dryer, remember that the dryer has to accommodate its much larger dry size as well as its wet size.

The risks of not following care labels are extremely hard to calculate with filled articles, and the potential damage is great. There is not only the launderability of the down filling and ticking to consider, but also that of linings, outer fabrics, trims, zippers, and finishes. So follow care labels. If you have none or have to fill in for care labels that leave too much to your imagination, you might use one of the following laundering recipes. (Test for colorfastness or other qualities as necessary.)

Three Methods of Washing Down- and Feather-Filled Clothes and Furnishings

Hand-washing. Hand-washing a large filled object takes some physical vigor. It also takes a large laundry tub. Make sure yours is large enough before proceeding. If not, use the bathtub. Fill the tub with warm or lukewarm water and add a mild powdered detergent (preferably a low-sudsing one) or soap. Make sure the soap or detergent is thoroughly dissolved and mixed before adding the article to be washed. Place the article in the sudsy water and let it soak for a few minutes, pressing out air bubbles with your hands. Then wash by gently pressing the sudsy water through it (and pressing out air bubbles); continue this for a few minutes to be sure you are getting the article clean. Drain the wash water. Fill with fresh cool water and rinse by the same pressing technique. Repeat until all traces of suds are gone. *Do not wring.* Squeeze out excess water. As the squeezing part of the hand-laundering tends to be onerous and as drying takes so very long, you might wish to *spin* the article in your washing machine to get out some excess moisture. Spinning it does not jerk or beat or twist the article as do agitating or wringing—front-loading tumbling machines spin too—and it can help you get the filled article dry much more quickly. Just set your washing machine control forward to the spin, skipping the fill and the agitation cycle.

Machine-washing, front-loading. If you have a tumbling front-loading machine that is large enough, simply wash with warm or lukewarm water and a mild powdered detergent or soap. Rinse thoroughly with cool water. If need be, do an extra rinse.

Machine-washing, top-loading. Make sure that your machine is large enough. When washing in an agitating top-loading machine, use *gentle* agitation and fast spin with warm or lukewarm water and mild powdered detergent (preferably a low-sudsing one) or soap. First partially fill the machine and dissolve the detergent and then add two pillows or other filled items for balance, pressing them down to expel the air. Let the machine continue to fill and wash. As the objects wash, open the lid now and then to press out air. (Because air pockets often form inside filled articles, it sometimes helps to wet down the article thoroughly and spin it in the machine first; then wash it as prescribed.) Rinse thoroughly with cold water. Do an extra rinse if necessary.

Be *careful* when you lift the wet filled object. Do not pick it up by one end or all the wet filling will fall to the other and be packed down. For similar reasons, never hang filled articles to dry; the filling will fall to the ends, clump, and fail to dry quickly enough, and the article can be ruined.

Whatever washing method you use, you can tumble dry on low. This takes a very long time—several hours, perhaps, for a comforter or other large or thick object. You can speed drying by putting a couple of clean, dry, colorfast towels in the dryer to take up moisture. It also helps to put in two or three tennis balls or clean tennis shoes to knock any clumps apart. Or you can half dry the article in the dryer, then continue the drying in the air. Whatever you do, it is important to get down- and feather-filled articles completely dry. If you leave them damp, they will smell and mildew. Note, however, that feathers and down always have a strong, rather unpleasant smell when they are wet. Do not be alarmed; this will go away after you dry them.

Polyester-Filled Clothes and Bedding. Polyester-filled pillows, comforters, jackets, and other articles are highly washable. You can wash polyester-filled articles by hand or machine. Use lukewarm or warm water with the regular cycle. Dry on regular (hot), making sure that thick items are thoroughly dry. Use low-sudsing detergents.

Kapok and Foam Rubber. *Do not wash kapok pillows. Do not dry foam rubber pillows in the dryer.* Foam rubber poses a fire hazard in the dryer.

Knits. Knits vary greatly according to fiber content. Cotton and linen knits that are not preshrunk will shrink less if they are washed in cold or warm rather than hot water and if they are dried on the low to medium setting. (In general, the hotter the water, the greater the danger of shrinking.) Some knits will require blocking (see page 246) and should not be machine-dried. Wool knits often should be dry-cleaned because of their propensity for shrinking and felting. Knits of Superwash wools can readily be machine-washed and machine-dried. Polyester, acrylic, and other synthetic knits are far more resistant to shrinking and can almost always be successfully machine-washed. See the recommendations in chapter 17.

Knits, cotton. Fine cotton knits, especially all-cotton lingerie, nightgowns, and fine sportswear, will lose their silky hand or lustrous appearance if subjected to hot washing or drying temperatures. Hot temperatures will make them shrink and grow rough, less soft, and thick or felt-like. To preserve their fine look and feel, use the gentle cycle, cool to lukewarm wash water, and dry on a rack. When they are dry, tumble them in a cold dryer to soften them up. Such gentle laundering will usually get these articles clean and fresh.

But children's cotton knit play clothes that are covered with ketchup or chocolate milk are another matter. Gentle laundering with cool water will not remove these stains. Ordinary T-shirts and cotton underwear, which are subjected to heavy wear and perspiration and body oils, also need more vigorous laundering. First treat stains, remembering that hot water sets protein stains. Then give these a regular wash with warm to hot water and tumble them in a low to warm dryer (but buy them large enough to shrink). If you keep them long enough, they will grow thin and supple with repeated laundering and wearing; some people like them best this way.

Quilts. You should carefully read care label instructions to see what cycle, water temperature, and detergent are recommended for washing quilts. Very often, however, you end up with a quilt that has no care label. In that case there are three main potential difficulties that you must be alert to if you wish to wash it.

First, the quilt must be neither too old nor too delicate to endure laundering. Fragile, faded, worn cloth is all too likely to break, tear, and pull apart even in the gentlest laundering procedures. If you own heirloom, aged, or antique quilts that are very valuable, you had better consult a conservator about cleaning. Very old and delicate quilts should probably not be laundered or dry-cleaned at all but would ordinarily benefit from careful vacuuming through a screen. (See chapter 35, "Textile Furnishings," page 472.) Quilts that are not excessively delicate, old, or valuable, however, can ordinarily be cleaned either by dry-cleaning or laundering.

But—and this is the second problem to be alert for—many quilts are either not made entirely of launderable materials or contain at least some materials that are not colorfast. The two main types of filling used in quilts are cotton and polyester batting. In principle, both are washable, but you also have the shell and lining to keep in mind. You must make sure that *all* the fibers in the shell of a crazy-patch quilt are launderable and that *all* the different patches are colorfast to at least lukewarm water and mild detergent. Test as best you can in inconspicuous areas, and try not to let the test water run through to another piece or part of the quilt. (You can stop as soon as you find the first patch that bleeds.) Remember to test all types of cloth or thread used, including the lining, trims and embroidery threads. A patchwork quilt of silk velvet squares, lined with silk, will clearly not be washable at all, but other quilts may mislead you. I have seen a quilt of cotton patchwork in which just a few of the squares were made of fabric whose dyes ran. This quilt had to be dry-cleaned, as the silk velvet one would.

The third problem can arise even with quilts whose fibers and dyes are fit for laundering. To survive laundering well, quilts must be firmly stitched, and the filling, in particular, must be firmly stitched down. Otherwise, it moves around during laundering and forms lumps inside—a state of affairs that generally cannot be cured without taking the quilt apart.

Once you have determined that it is safe to proceed with washing, you must choose between hand-washing and machine-washing (choosing a cycle appropriate to the fiber and delicacy of the quilt). If you choose to hand-wash, you may in certain cases still wish to spin dry in the machine.

New, store-bought quilts can usually be washed and dried in the machine; these tend to have a highly launderable polyester shell and polyester filling. Such quilts can be laundered in the same way as ordinary washable blankets. Water temperature, type of detergent, and choice of regular, permanent-press, or delicate cycle depend on the same criteria as in other cases—fibers, finishes, type of filling, type and quality of construction, trim, and likelihood of shrinkage. When in doubt, the safest choices are always lukewarm or cool water, mild detergent, and the gentle cycle.

Tumble dry, dry flat, or line dry, then air-fluff, based on the same type of determinations. More delicate quilts should be dried flat. If you line dry, spread the quilt over two lines so that its weight is distributed more broadly. Or lay it on a sheet on the grass, turning the quilt over when it is half dry. If you are an apartment dweller, lay your quilt gently over a drying rack, and turn a fan on it.

26

Common Laundry Mishaps and Problems

Fading and bleeding dyes . . . What to do if a colored garment's bleeding dye tints a load of wash . . . Fading of acid, indigo, and fluorescent dyes . . . Fading caused by light . . . Loss of color from abrasion . . . What to do about fading . . . Grayness or dinginess . . . Holes and tears . . . Lint . . . Perspiration . . . Pilling . . . Spots or streaks: blue, brown, or light spots . . . Spots from uneven cleaning or soiling . . . Miscellaneous causes of spots . . . Streaks, residue, stiffness due to hard water . . . Yellowing due to perspiration, skin oils, or antiperspirants, hard water, chlorine bleach, inadequate rinsing, sunlight, or heat and age

Laundering problems have solutions in most but not all instances. The material in this chapter can help in diagnosing a variety of common laundering difficulties and, where possible, suggests remedies when things have gone wrong. In laundering, however, as in so many things, prevention is always better than cure. Good basic laundering techniques can usually prevent the misfortunes catalogued below.

Fading and Bleeding

Some dyes bleed slightly every time you wash a garment, even though the color of the garment does not seem to change. Other dyes, such as indigo, "wash down," or fade, a little every time you wash them; these dyes are more likely to be used on natural fibers. Dyes may also fade as a result of exposure to water, hot water, prolonged soaking, detergents, and bleaches of all types. Abrasion, exposure to dry-cleaning fluids, light, ozone, and many other factors can cause fading.

Clothes and linens whose colors run should be washed separately from others or, if the loss of color is slight, washed with articles of like color. If a print has dyes that run, unless it is a madras print in which the effect is desired, it cannot be laundered and must be dry-cleaned.

People used to add salt or vinegar to the wash water in an effort to "set" dyes that run, and you still see this suggested in various "tips and hints" books and columns. Doing so might help reduce dye loss by reducing the alkalinity—and the cleaning power—of the wash water. It does not actually cause any color to "set," however. The amount of salt or vinegar needed to do that would be very large (10 percent of the weight of cotton goods in salt, or 3 to 5 percent of the weight of wool or silk goods in vinegar). Moreover, salt or vinegar will not, in any event, set many classes of textile dyes.

What to Do If a Dye Runs and Tints Other Clothes. If a garment bleeds color that ruins the appearance of other articles in your laundry, do not dry them. Remove the offending piece and rewash the entire load using the strongest detergent, the hottest water, and the strongest type of bleach safe for the fabric. If this does not work, on *white* articles you might try a color remover. (See "Color removers," page 320.) Follow instructions and cautions on the package to the letter.

Fading of Acid Dyes. Silk, wool, cashmere, and nylon may be colored with acid dyes that discolor when exposed to underarm perspiration or prolonged exposure to soap or detergent and water. I know of no remedies for this problem in colored garments. For whites that have yellowed, see "Yellowing" below.

Fading of Indigo Dyes. Indigo dyes produce various shades of blue which bleed and fade, particularly when exposed to bleach. Most people like their blue denims faded. Still, such garments should be washed with like colors or with darker colors that will not be tinted. However, if something is tinted by an accidental washing with blue denim, simply rewash it; the color will come out.

Fading of Fluorescent Dyes. Many fluorescent dyes are much less colorfast than other dyes, so wash fluorescent-dyed articles separately unless they pass a colorfastness test. Do not use stain removers or pretreatments on them without first testing in an inconspicuous area.

Fading Caused by Light. Light fading has no cure. But see chapter 47, "Kindly Light," on prevention.

Loss of Color from Abrasion. Some types of dyes will rub right off fabrics. This is a phenomenon everyone is familiar with in blue jeans. The white areas at the knees and the seat of the pants develop because these are the points of highest abrasion. To forestall some of this—assuming that you want to—wash garments inside out.

The color on fiberglass curtains can also rub off against contact points, for example, the windowsill or furniture that touches the curtain.

What to Do About Fading. Usually there is no good solution to faded fabrics. Sometimes redyeing is possible, but my only notable successes with redyeing have been with blacks, which can really look like new. Before attempting redyeing, carefully study the home dye instructions. Some fibers, such as acrylics and polyesters, will not take home dyes. If the fading is irregular, redyeing may not produce uniform color and you may find you preferred the faded look.

Grayness or Dinginess

If your laundry or some piece of it appears gray or dingy, rewash. Begin with a presoak, using the strongest detergent (and plenty of it), the hottest water, and the strongest type of bleach that are safe for the fabric. Do an extra rinse. You might also try a double wash or the addition of a laundry booster such as borax. Be sure to rinse thoroughly after any such effort; detergent residues themselves will cause a dingy appearance. On whites, if all else fails, including bleach and strenuous laundering, you might try a whitener/brightener. (See "Whitener/brighteners," page 328.)

Holes and Tears

The common causes of holes and tears in fabrics, when these are not caused by long wear and use, are excessive bleaching, failure to rinse out bleach and detergent thoroughly, bleach spills, failure to dilute bleach properly before adding it to wash water, prolonged exposure to sunlight, or exposure to any of a wide variety of destructive household chemicals, such as acid toilet bowl cleaners and depilatories. Occasionally tears result if a fabric is washed with a pin in it, or when one garment gets caught on the open zipper, buckle, or hook of another.

Overloading the washer produces faster wear, which eventually results in fraying, holes, or tearing. Sometimes clothes catch on a rough, broken place inside the dryer or washer. It is imperative to locate such damage and have it repaired before you use the machine again.

Mice, insects, moths, or other pests can eat holes in fabric.

Lint

Lint consists of fuzz or bits of thread and fiber that rub off fabrics during laundering, drying, and wearing. Lint rubbed off one article in a load can cling stubbornly to all the others in the load, making them look unattractive. When the lint is of a different color from the article it clings to, it looks especially unpleasant. Fabrics with a pile and those made with fuzzy fibers—such as terry-cloth towels or chenille bathrobes—usually lint more than others because it is easier to rub fibers off them. But almost all fabrics will produce at least a little lint. Tissues left in the pockets of articles thrown into the wash load, however, are the most common cause of lint problems.

If your clothes frequently come out of the laundry covered with lint, be sure that you are sorting properly and preparing garments adequately for the wash. Separate the lint-giving articles (such as chenille) from the lint-taking ones (such as polyester) in the washer and the dryer; avoid washing or drying polyester or other synthetics with towels. Empty pockets of all contents, especially tissues and other debris. (See chapter 20, "Gathering, Storing, and Sorting Laundry.")

Besides improper sorting, lint may be caused by overloading of the washer or dryer, which causes increased abrasion. Another possible cause is overdrying; by creating excess static electricity, it can cause lint to stick to clothes more stubbornly instead of being deposited in the lint filter. Or you may simply need to empty the lint filter more often in either washer or dryer or both. Most washing machines nowadays have automatic lint removal.

Rather surprisingly to us lay launderers, using too little detergent can cause excess lint. Just like dirt, lint is held in suspension in the water by chemicals in detergents that prevent soil redeposition. When you use too little detergent, not only dirt but lint gets redeposited on the clothes.

Mildew

Fabrics made of natural fibers will mildew if they are left damp or even if they are stored in a place with high atmospheric humidity and little air circulation. For recommendations on removing mildew, see "Mildew," page 389.

Perspiration

Perspiration is usually mildly acidic as it emerges from your pores, but tends to turn alkaline when exposed to the environment. The pH of individuals' perspiration, however, does not always fit the rule and may be acidic or alkaline, depending upon variations in metabolism. Dyes and some textile fibers are affected by perspiration, and different effects are likely depending upon whether the pH of the perspiration is acidic or alkaline.

Fading, yellowing, discoloring, or weakening of cloth after prolonged exposure is quite common.

The most important thing to do to protect fabrics from such damage is simply to clean or wash frequently clothes and other fabrics that have skin contact. In the case of silk, it is advisable to wash or clean the garment as soon after wearing as possible. For other preventive measures and cures for problems caused by perspiration in clothes, see "Yellowing—Perspiration," page 372.

Pilling

If pilling—the rubbing up of little balls of fiber on the surface of the cloth—is or may be a problem, try turning garments inside out for laundering and drying. Or you can put them in a mesh bag, making certain that it is securely closed. A shorter or slower agitation or tumbling period is also helpful. When the type of soil and kind of article permit, hand-wash without rubbing or scrubbing and either line-dry or dry flat. It is said that using fabric softeners helps too. Note that strong fibers may actually pill worse than weaker ones because the fibers that are rubbed into little balls do not break off but cling tenaciously to the surface.

The foregoing techniques are designed simply to reduce the amount of rubbing on the fibers. But because the fabric unavoidably gets rubbed in use and wear, there is not much that can be done to prevent entirely the pilling that develops on fabrics like sheeting or shirt material that are made of polyester blends or polyester and some other synthetic fibers.

There is a downside to turning garments inside out to prevent pilling: sometimes pills then develop on the inside of the garment rather than the outside. If the garment is worn next to the skin, this can feel rather uncomfortable. Turning a garment inside out also makes it more difficult to get the outside clean.

You can buy pill-removing gadgets at houseware stores. These are safer than shaving them with a razor.

Spots or Streaks

Blue Spots or Streaks. Blue spots or streaks usually consist of undiluted or undissolved detergent or fabric softener. They might once have been due to unmixed bluing, too. Few people use straight bluing anymore, but it is an ingredient in many detergents and all-fabric bleaches. To prevent detergent spots, dissolve and mix detergent in the water before adding clothes. To prevent softener spots, add softener to the dispenser at the start of the load or, if you add it during the final rinse, first mix it with water to dilute it before adding it to the rinse water. To prevent bluing spots, see "Bluing," pages 319–20.

To remove undissolved detergent that is adhering to clothes, one detergent manufacturer suggests that you soak the article for an hour in a vinegar/water solution—1 cup of white vinegar to 1 quart of water—and then rinse thoroughly. My own method (so far 100 percent successful) is to soak the article in water as hot as it will bear until the detergent dissolves and then to rewash.

To remove fabric softener spots, rub with bar soap and rewash. You may need to repeat the process.

To remove bluing streaks, rewash.

Brown Spots. Brown or yellow spots on fabrics can be caused by iron in the water or iron that is deposited on fabrics by a steam iron. If your water contains too much iron, chlorine bleach may result in further discoloration. (The water on our family farm, for example, is so iron-rich that if we use chlorine bleach the clothes all turn tan.) To cure iron spots, see "Yellowing: Hard Water," page 373. Do not use chlorine bleach to cure rust or iron-caused spots; this will only make the problem worse.

Brown spots may also be caused by a failure to rinse chlorine bleach out completely; by soil or soap or detergent or other residues left in the cloth that oxidize over time; by fabric softeners, when liquid softener is not fully mixed with the water or is not completely dissolved or when softener sheets in the dryer do not move around freely. (The softener spots may also be blue. See "Blue Spots or Streaks," above.)

To prevent brown spots, always rinse laundry thoroughly. Brown spots caused by oxidized residues often may be cured by soaking and laundering with the strongest detergent, the strongest bleach, and the hottest water that the type, age, and condition of the fabric warrant. Follow by normal laundering with one or two extra-thorough rinses. On more delicate fabrics of cotton or linen that cannot take strong detergents or bleaches, the spots may remain. If they persist, try pouring on a solution of lemon juice or white vinegar mixed in equal parts with water. If you get partial results, repeat until the mark is gone. Or try a paste of salt and vinegar. This treatment is not for old or very delicate fibers, however. On such items, if you very much want to get rid of the spots, you had better consult a specialist.

Storing linens and clothes in acid-free paper will prevent those brown spots that are caused by chemicals in woods and other materials they may rest against in storage.

Light Spots. Pretreatments—the direct application of liquid detergent or a detergent paste to some areas of a fabric and not others—can cause light spots on some fabrics. Such light spots on unbleached, off-white, tan, or natural cottons and pastel cottons are sometimes due to optical brighteners in the products. (See "Optical brighteners," pages 325–26.) Over time, the rest of the garment may become similarly lightened and the spots may disappear. If this doesn't happen or you do not wish to wait, one detergent manufacturer advises that you can usually at least accelerate the process of evening out the color in the following way. Make a solution of 1 cup of a heavy-duty detergent to 2 cups of warm water in a total amount sufficient to submerge the article. When you are sure that the detergent is thoroughly mixed or dissolved, soak the article for two hours. If you have to, weigh it down (with something that will not bleed colors or do any other harm) to keep it entirely submerged, or the part that sticks out of the solution will be a different color from the rest. Wring the article out. Then rewash without adding more detergent, and rinse very thoroughly. Repeat the entire process if necessary until uniform coloring is achieved. If you are dealing with one piece of a set, remember that it will be a different color from the others unless you subject the entire set to this procedure.

Spills of bleach or other chemicals can sometimes produce light spots too. Undiluted chlorine bleach splashed on dry cloth can completely strip most dyes. Some colored cottons will spot as a result of direct contact with non-chlorine bleaches. This will not occur if the bleach or bleach-containing detergent is first dissolved in water before you add the clothes. There is generally no remedy when color has been stripped or spotted by a bleach accident. Even redyeing will not remedy the problem because the cloth will not dye evenly.

From Uneven Cleaning or Soiling. Polyester and polyester blends have an affinity for oily soil and a tendency to hold oily soil even when laundered. Particularly troublesome areas of clothes are any that contact skin and hair, around the chest and shoulders, and where the face and hair rub on pillowcases made of blends or polyester. Soak the problematic article in a solution of 1 cup of heavy-duty liquid laundry detergent to 2 cups of warm water for a couple of hours, then rewash in warm water without additional detergent. Rinse thoroughly. An extra rinse or two may be necessary to remove all the detergent. To keep this problem from arising, do not treat polyester and other synthetics more gently than is necessary. Launder frequently, pretreat (especially with solvent-containing pretreatment products) and presoak, and use plenty of detergent and the hottest water that the fabric can bear.

Miscellaneous. Household chemicals often contain strong acids, bases, alcohol, or other strong chemicals that can affect the dyes on clothes or eat right through fabrics. Be careful to keep all of these away from fabrics: hair permanents, hair dyes, toilet bowl cleaners, scouring powders, pool chemicals, acids (including battery acids), bleaches, antiseptics, astringents, and any other strong household chemicals.

Benzoyl peroxide, which is used in acne medications and cosmetics, selectively removes many dyes, especially blue ones. If a susceptible color, say a blue, is mixed with other dyes, benzoyl peroxide might remove the blue and leave the rest, making a red spot on a purple dress, for example, or a leaving a yellow spot on a green carpet. Problems resulting from this chemical may appear in places that contact the face or neck, such as collars, sheets or pillowcases, and towels.

Fiberglass curtains and drapes may be colored by pigments held in acrylic binder resins that can dissolve in solvent cleaners. Thus they cannot be dry-cleaned. They should be washed by hand unless care instructions specify some other method.

Streaks, Residue, Stiffness, Harshness, or Premature Wear from Abrasion Caused by Hard Water

Some nonphosphate detergents used in hard water can cause a buildup of residues that can make fabric appear streaky, render it stiff or harsh to the touch, and even contribute to its premature wearing out as a result of increased abrasion. Clean out such residues by soaking the article in a solution of a cup of white vinegar per gallon of plain water in a plastic container. (Do not use a container that will rust or react with the acid vinegar.) Rinse thoroughly. To prevent the problem, use a nonprecipitating water softener with the detergent, or change to a liquid detergent.

Yellowing

There are many reasons why fabrics develop yellowed areas or become yellow overall. The chief ones are covered in this section.

Perspiration, Skin Oils, and Antiperspirant Stains. Any buildup of perspiration, skin oils, or antiperspirants on fabrics can result in yellowing. Everybody's shirts tend to turn yellow under the arms, men's shirts to a greater degree than women's because men perspire more than women. Polyester fabrics in particular may turn yellowish in areas with the greatest skin contact as they age, because they tend to hold any oil, including skin oil. There are both preventive and curative measures for this problem that are very effective.

To prevent perspiration yellowing on the underarm area of garments, men might wear undershirts and women might wear dress shields, especially when they are wearing silk. For your information, if you have never used them, dress shields are little padded wedges of cloth that attach to your blouse, slip, or bra or come sewn on a bralike garment. There are also disposable ones. (You can sometimes buy them where lingerie is sold. I have also found them in the kind of variety store that also carries sewing materials and in sewing and piece goods stores.) Undershirts or dress shields will absorb perspiration, oil, and antiperspirants, and you can wash them with brutal effectiveness. Unfortunately, many men feel as enthusiastic about undershirts as most women feel about dress shields. A second preventive measure, effective on any area of a garment, is to wash it (or dry-clean it) frequently and as soon after wearing as you can, because the longer perspiration stands on the cloth, especially silk, the more damage it does.

Once the problem has developed, the solution for hardier fibers (not silk or wool) is to do one or two exceedingly vigorous launderings. Try pretreating the affected areas, and then presoak for up to thirty minutes using an enzyme-containing presoak. Launder with the hottest water the fiber will bear, using plenty of detergent—more than normal or with a detergent booster added. Use the strongest bleach the fabric will bear as well. Rinse *very* thoroughly (synthetics in cool water).

Even when silks can be washed, they cannot take prolonged soaking, strong bleaches and detergents, or high water temperatures. Thus you must wash washable silk promptly and frequently. Try sodium perborate bleach on washable white silks, but only after testing.

If yellow perspiration stains have appeared in the underarm areas of hand washable lingerie such as bras, slips, or camisoles, try pretreating by rubbing the affected area with a pure bar soap or a mild detergent formulated for fine and delicate washables. Let it soak in sudsy water for up to thirty minutes. Then wash the article normally, rubbing together the wrong sides of the fabric in the stain area if you can.

Hard Water. Certain types of minerals (iron and manganese salts) in the water will cause clothes to yellow or to acquire yellow or brownish spots. Use a nonprecipitating water softener to keep this from happening. (See pages 310–11 in chapter 21.) Iron spots may also be deposited on fabric by a steam iron. To remove yellow or brown streaks or overall discoloring caused by minerals in the water, use a rust remover advertised as safe for fabrics. These are available in hardware stores, in houseware stores, and from washing machine dealers. Or you can work on spots by spreading the fabric over a pan of boiling water and squeezing lemon juice on it, or by immersing in a solution of equal parts lemon juice or white vinegar and water. (Lemon juice is more effective in my experience.) *Do not use chlorine bleach on clothes suffering from this problem.* It will only make the stain worse.

Chlorine Bleach. Chlorine bleach will produce yellow discoloration of silk, wool, nylon, and spandex. This discoloration is permanent.

Chlorine bleach may also produce a yellow discoloration on some white or light-colored, resin-treated cotton, linen, or resin-treated blends containing these fibers. I have never experienced this, and it seems to be quite unusual today. Chlorine bleach can cause yellowing of fabrics that have been treated with optical brighteners. This problem, too, appears to be quite uncommon. Sometimes interfacings have been resin-treated, even when the fabric of the garment has not. When bleached, the interfacing yellows and shows through the shirt, making it look unattractively two-toned. This possibility illustrates the risks of ignoring care label instructions and of *failing to test bleach on all components* of a garment. You can use a color remover on whites to try to remove the yellow coloration.

If you fail to rinse chlorine bleach out of clothes and then put them in the dryer, the heat can turn the chlorine left in the clothes yellow. Wash the clothes again and rinse them very well.

Overheating in the dryer can also cause yellowing of white or light fabrics.

Inadequate Rinsing. Alkaline salts from laundry products may remain in the fabric after washing and rinsing are completed. These residues can cause yellowing, discolor dyes, and irritate skin. The solution is to use less detergent, use more rinse water, or do one or more additional deep rinses. Institutional laundries add a "sour"—that is, an acidic compound—to neutralize alkalies. You can make your own sour by adding a cup (more for extra-large loads) of white vinegar to your rinse water.

Sunlight. Sunlight can produce yellowing in two circumstances. First, prolonged exposure to sunlight will turn white or very light cotton yellow. (This will not happen with rayon or linen.) The short-term consequence of putting cotton in the sun, however, is that it bleaches. If you line-dry white cottons, you can try to take care not to leave them out too long or else hang them in the shade. Yellowing caused by sunshine can be diminished by chemical bleaching.

You may read that sunlight can also produce yellowing in some fabrics that have been treated with optical brighteners. (See "Optical brighteners," pages 325–26.) It is true that when some optical brighteners are exposed to sunlight, they break down, causing clothes to appear yellowish and duller or to have a gray cast. They are particularly vulnerable to breaking down when they are wet, so that this problem might happen as a result of line drying. I am told, however, that laundering removes these degradation by-products, and because we generally launder frequently, they are gone before we start to see them.

Heat and Age. Aging is in large part a slow oxidation of the cloth, a process that naturally produces yellowing in many types of fabric. Heat speeds up the natural aging process. If you store clothes in hot places, such as in unventilated attics or near radiators, or overdry clothes in the dryer, yellowing is likely to result. Always store clothes in cool, dry places, and be careful to use proper dryer settings and to remove clothes from the dryer when they are just one degree less dry than you want them.

Sometimes laundering with bleach, where possible, will cure this type of yellowing. The optical brighteners in laundry detergents can sometimes help too. Or try using a whitener/brightener. (See "Whitener/brighteners," page 328.)

White wools that yellow can sometimes be brightened by bleaching with hydrogen peroxide. Or you can try a whitener/brightener, although this will produce a bluish-white that makes wool look like something else, such as an acrylic, an effect that many people dislike.

An overhot iron can scorch or yellow fabrics.

Polyethylene Bags. Plasticizers in the plastic bags used by dry cleaners may migrate to clothes and cause yellow places. I know of no cure, but this is easy to prevent by removing the bags when you bring the garments home. This is better for them in any case. (See chapter 58, "Closets for Clothes and Linens.")

27

Sanitizing the Laundry

Getting rid of germs on cloth . . . Germicidal effects of ordinary laundering and dry cleaning . . . Chlorine bleach and other disinfectants for the laundry . . . Laundering away dust mites and mite allergens . . . Importance of hot water . . . Lice and nits, fleas . . . Textile dermatitis . . . Poison ivy and other plant allergens

The home laundry sometimes has to deal with clothing or bedding that has been contaminated by more than ordinary soil. When microorganisms, dust mites, vermin, or allergic substances adhere to fabrics, the best solution is almost always a trip to the washing machine. Home laundering is usually your most effective means of sanitizing textile goods.

This chapter describes the ways in which ordinary laundering has sanitizing effects and the ordinary means by which we can heighten these effects in our home laundries. None of the methods discussed guarantees germ-free fabrics. They are merely ways of reducing the numbers of pathogens that may adhere to fabrics as part of ordinary good housekeeping. Those who wish to target specific pathogens and those who are dealing with situations that pose serious health threats should seek medical advice or the advice of public health authorities in their own communities.

Infectious Microorganisms

Germs and Cloth. Long before anyone had ever heard of bacteria, it was discovered that cloth could transmit infection from the sick to the well, a fact that was used for both good and ill. The plague and the pox were sent to enemies on infected fabrics. The spread of infectious disease was restrained by avoiding contact with contaminated cloth and burning the clothes and linens of victims. The eponymous bunny of *The Velveteen Rabbit* has to be saved by magic because it is to be burned, along with all the other fabrics that touched the skin of the child who has just survived scarlet fever.

Scientific research confirms that microorganisms—bacteria, viruses, yeasts—survive on fabrics for significant periods of time and survive transfer from one cloth to another. One study, in fact, has found that some fibers are more hospitable than others to certain viruses. In the age of antibiotics, advanced indoor plumbing, and vaccinations, however, sickroom routines that were familiar in every household through the early twentieth century are now forgotten. No smelly disinfectants are used to wipe down every surface and utensil near the sick one. No linens are burned or boiled, and handkerchiefs, "body linen," and bed linens of the sick are not laundered separately. By and large, this is as it should be.

In every household, however, there are times when it is valuable to exercise a degree of special caution—for example, in the case of infectious illness, dirty diapers, or flood-contaminated textiles. It is helpful for all of us to understand how ordinary laundering procedures include physical, thermal, and chemical elements, each of which has profound sanitizing effects. Of course, in the event of a natural disaster or serious illness, you must seek expert advice on what safety measures you need to take. Your local extension service will have valuable information on disinfecting after a flood or other disaster. Your medical advisors will have guidance on household disinfection when there is infection in the home. You may also wish to contact your local public health agency.

Germicidal Aspects of Ordinary Laundering and Dry Cleaning. If you did nothing more than agitating cloth goods in plain water in your washing machine, this would to some degree be sanitizing. Plain water physically removes vast numbers of microorganisms and sends them down the drain—alive and well, perhaps, but gone from your clothes and linens. When the water is hot, the sanitizing effect of agitating in plain water is greatly increased, for water that is hot enough kills germs. More water, hotter water, and longer exposure to heat increase the sanitizing effects of laundering. Ordinary detergents inactivate great numbers of microorganisms. Many studies have shown that sodium hypochlorite (household chlorine bleach) is a highly effective germicide in the laundry, and adding chlorine bleach to your wash also increases the sanitizing effect of cooler water washes. The heat of the dryer kills off still more microorganisms, and so does dryness per se. If you hang your clothes to dry in the sun, the ultraviolet radiation from the sun kills many microorganisms. Hot irons are also highly germicidal. Thus germs are killed very effectively by the procedures of ordinary laundering in hot water with detergent and bleach, tumbling in heat or sunning, and ironing.

But plain laundering, while sufficiently germ-killing for normal household purposes, should not be overestimated. It does not permit you to be confident that you have killed any particular microorganism that you may be targeting, or that the fabrics have been completely disinfected. Home laundries are not set up to permit you to monitor or maintain the water temperature; few home washing machines even deliver water initially hot enough to kill many microorganisms. The amount of bleach used may not be sufficient. The duration of the germicidal action may not be long enough to be effective. For example, the polio virus would be inactivated within ten minutes if exposed to temperatures exceeding 122°F (50°C), but hepatitis B would require higher temperatures. *Candida albicans,* a yeastlike pathogen that causes one type of vaginal infection and is thought to be transmittable on underwear, survives in ordinary laundering with a water temperature of 120°F. You would have to launder articles at 158°F or higher to kill it, or iron them with a hot iron.

If clothes or furnishings are not washable but must be dry-cleaned, the solvents and heat of the steam used in professional dry cleaning, too, will have a germ-killing effect. But the sort of dry cleaning you do yourself at coin-operated machines does not use steam and is not recommended, for example, as a way of cleaning flood-soiled clothes.

Disinfecting in the Laundry with Chlorine Bleach. Chlorine bleach kills a broad spectrum of microorganisms and serves as an excellent general household disinfectant for fabrics that are not harmed by chlorine bleaches. (Oxygen or all-fabric laundry bleaches are *not* effective disinfectants. Refer to the discussion of chlorine bleach, pages 318–19, for information on which fabrics chlorine bleach is safe for. See also chapters 15 and 16.) To disinfect laundry, one bleach manufacturer recommends the following procedure: Thoroughly mix 1 cup of chlorine bleach for each 16 gallons of water in your washing machine. Add bleach-safe clothes. Soak ten minutes, then add detergent and start the wash/rinse cycle. Rinse well. If clothes are already in the machine, dilute the bleach with 1 quart of water before adding it. (See also "Diapers," on pages 360–61.)

Other Disinfectants. To disinfect clothes and linens that cannot tolerate chlorine bleach, the use of quaternary compounds or pine oil or other phenolic disinfectants is sometimes suggested. These disinfectants can be found in various household cleaning products such as pine oil cleaning disinfectants (Fyne Pine or Texize-O-Pine) or in sanitizers used by janitorial, dairy, or poultry supply companies ("quats" such as Roccal, Zephrin, or End-Bac). Such disinfectants will say "disinfectant" on the label and will bear an EPA registration number, but they are not laundry products, are not especially formulated for use as laundry disinfectants, and usually bear no instructions, or very limited instructions, on how to use them on fabrics. Look for them in drugstores or in dairy or janitorial supply stores.

Quaternaries would have to be added at the beginning of the rinse cycle, as they are inactivated by detergents. Pine oil and phenolic disinfectants would have to be diluted before adding or mixed well in the water before clothes are put in, but could be used in the wash, at the beginning of the cycle, or the rinse water.

As with laundry products, you would have to test such disinfectants for their safety for different fabrics. Phenolics and pine oil disinfectants, for example, cannot be used on wool or silk. The odor of pine oil can cling strongly to fabrics afterward. Quaternaries are said to be safe for all fibers but not for all dyes; they can cause color change in some.

Use the highest water setting, the hottest water, and the longest wash cycle your machine permits. The Lee County, Florida, Public Safety Division publishes on its Web site the following information on how much of these types of disinfectants should be used:

> In top-loading washing machines, use 4 tablespoons of Roccal or 2 tablespoons of Zephrin. In front-loading machines, use 2 tablespoons of Roccal or 1 tablespoon of Zephrin.
>
> When using pine oil disinfectants, such as Fyne Pyne, King Pine, Pin-O-Pine, or Texize-O Pine, add 1 cup to top loading machines and 1 cup to front-loading machines. (Read labels to be sure products contain at least 80% pine oil.)
>
> When using phenolic disinfectants, such as Pine-sol, Al-Pine, or Sea-Air, add 1 cup to top-loading machines and 1/2 cup plus 2 tablespoons to front-loading machines.

For further information on how to use these or other disinfectants effectively in situations where this is important for health or safety, contact your local public health authority, your local extension service, or your doctor.

Dust Mites

Dust mites are actually arachnids—bugs, not germs—which are so tiny that you cannot see them without magnification. They do not cause infection, but they cause allergies in some people. (See "Dust and Dust Mites," chapter 33.) Dust mites are killed by laundering at high enough temperatures. One study finds that wash water temperatures of 131°F kill dust mites after ten minutes and notes that at cooler temperatures the acaricidal (mite-killing) effect is not increased by detergents or other chemicals tested. Some authorities, however, recommend higher wash temperatures, 140°F or 150°F. One study determined that water below 113°F killed no mites at all and that water at 122°F killed 49.7 percent of them. Thus there is speculation that the increase in cold-water home laundering in recent decades is among the many factors that may have caused an increase in the incidence of allergic asthma, as the cold-water washing has inadvertently rendered bedding more mite-ridden than it was in the good old days of boiled bedding.[1] Since the water cools during agitation in home washers, you might begin with 140°F or higher just to be sure the water stays in the proper range for ten minutes. (See "Water Temperature," pages 308–10, in chapter 21.)

Laundering is perhaps most important, however, in removing the allergens produced by dust mites. Wash water of any temperature removes over 90 percent of dust mite allergens, even when it leaves the mites alive and well (and clean, presumably). Dry cleaning, by comparison, kills all the mites but does not remove the allergens, which may cling for very long periods of time. This is a strong reason to buy only launderable bedding and blankets. Weekly launderings at 140°F or higher of all bedding—sheets, pillowcases, blankets, and mattress pads—is best to keep dust mites and dust mite allergens at low levels. As stored clothing can also harbor large numbers of mites, you might wash it before wearing, especially if you notice any allergic symptoms when you put such an article on.

Lice and Nits; Fleas

Water temperatures of 150°F will kill lice and nits (leave laundry in the water for ten minutes to be sure), so laundering is effective to rid fabrics of these miserable pests. (Some say you need only a temperature of 140°F or even 130°F, but since the water in your machine cools during the wash, the hotter you begin the wash the better.) You should wash all sheets, pillowcases, blankets, comforters (duvets), and clothes, including hats and coats, that the afflicted person has been in contact with. (And if it is not head lice but body lice of some sort, you must be sure to do a good job washing underwear.) Then dry all items in a hot dryer for twenty minutes too, just for good measure. If you cannot wash certain items, dry cleaning is also effective. Or place things in airtight plastic bags, tightly sealed, and leave them for thirty days, which is longer than nits can survive at room temperature. Away from the human body, the lice themselves die much sooner—within three days. The plastic-bag option is an especially good idea for headsets, helmets, and similar items.

Fleas and their eggs will also be killed by hot-water laundering.

Textile Dermatitis

Many people are allergic to residue left on cloth by detergents and other laundry products. The solution to such problems is careful rinsing, the use of products that contain as few inessential additives, such as perfumes, as possible, and changing products until you find one that does not irritate. If these measures do not work, consult your doctor. But there are also allergic reactions to certain textile fabrics. Allergic reactions have been associated with cloth made of nylon, fiberglass, rubber, and wool fibers. When nylon fabric first appeared, many people reported that it made them itch. It turned out that nylon fabric required more rinsing than people were used to doing and that soap was the cause of the itching, which ended with adequate rinsing. In the past, spandex, too, was sometimes associated with allergic problems, but it is apparently no longer made with the problematic substance. And it is not clear that all discomfort described as "allergic" by sufferers is really that. Dermatologists find that many people report "allergies" to polyester or nylon fabric that may reflect experiences of ordinary skin irritation, perhaps the result of these fabrics' being unabsorbent.

Whatever the nature of the difficulties, the solution is to stop wearing what itches you, to stop wearing it next to the skin, or, in the case of fiberglass, to stay away from it. If it is synthetics that bother you, switch to natural fibers. If it is wool, substitute acrylics. Acrylic functions and looks like wool and is nonirritating and nonallergenic. Wearing a thin cotton or silk liner or T-shirt under a wool sweater may be enough for many people.

Poison Ivy, Oak, or Sumac

Poison ivy, poison oak, and poison sumac are forms of allergic dermatitis caused by substances contained in these plants. The allergenic substances can be transferred from the plants to clothing or other fabric, or from someone's skin to fabric. Either way, the next person to touch the fabric can come down with a case of poison ivy, oak, or sumac. Both ordinary good laundering and dry cleaning will remove the offending substance and render fabric safe.

28

Removing Stains from Fabrics

Tolerating stains . . . Recognizing a potential stain . . . Common staining substances . . . What removes what . . . Stain-removing substances to stock in your home . . . Chemical vulnerabilities of certain fibers . . . Uses of detergent and water, bleaches, acids, alkalies or ammonia, solvents . . . Common stains that respond to solvent-based removers . . . Common household solvents . . . Commercial stain removers and pretreatment products . . . Removing printer toner powder . . . Stain-removing techniques . . . Stain removal mistakes to avoid . . . Removing unknown stains . . . Guide to stain removal

If a beautiful object has a tiny flaw, some people do not notice it and others notice nothing else. In dealing with stains, the most important skill you can acquire is the ability not to be bothered by small imperfections that you cannot fix. Many fabrics are ruined by overzealous and unrealistic attempts to make them perfect. If you find that your pleasure in a favorite textile object is spoiled by a minor flaw, consider whether this is because you equate stains with dirt. Stains are not dirt; they are inadvertent dyeings. While dirt should continue to arouse your fighting spirit, it is perfectly all right to surrender to insignificant stains. But when stains threaten to pass your tolerance threshold, you should be prepared to act quickly.

Sometimes acting quickly means running for help. When a stain afflicts a very valuable or obscure material, the wisest course, usually, is not to tackle it yourself but to seek the help of an appropriate expert. Where clothing and household fabrics are at stake, that is usually a dry cleaner; if the care label on the article advises dry cleaning, in fact, going to the dry cleaner is usually the only thing you can do other than apply dry-cleaning fluids or solvent spot removers yourself. Take the article to the dry cleaner as fast as you possibly can. Point out the area of the stain and explain what caused it. Do not leave it to the dry cleaner to notice the stain and guess what it is. If the object is an antique, an heirloom, or a work of art, consult a conservator. Check the yellow pages of your telephone directory or the directory of the nearest city, or call a local reputable antique dealer. Dealers often know of a good conservator who can deal with your problem.

For times when you decide to deal with stains yourself, you will want a compact chart, like the Guide to Stain Removal, pages 387–90, that tells you what substances and techniques are likely to be effective for removing common types of stains. Tape a copy of it to the wall in your laundry room. This chapter describes the basic materials you should keep in the house for fabric stain removal purposes and explains the basic ideas and techniques that will help you deal with most household stains successfully.

Recognize a Potential Stain When You See One

Whether a substance will actually stain depends on the fiber and the fabric and what sorts of stains they are particularly vulnerable to. It also depends on what cleaning procedures the fabric in question can tolerate. Delicate antique lace that will not take bleaching or rubbing is a far more difficult case for stain removal than sturdy cloth, carpets, or upholstery that you can subject to vigorous cleaning measures.

What Removes What

There is more than one way to skin a cat and to remove a stain. You will read widely different remedies for the same kind of problem, all of which may work. But there are also cats that won't be skinned and some stains that you have to give up on. Some stains will respond gradually, so that you will have to apply your remedy half a dozen times before you are completely successful. You may need all your patience. Test the effect of any substance you choose to use on an inconspicuous area of the fabric. Many substances that will remove stains sometimes cause fabrics to deteriorate or affect dyes or finishes.

The following collection of home stain-removing agents will serve for most purposes. The majority of the items included are also used in other ways in the home.

COMMON STAINING SUBSTANCES	
Red wine	Ink, including felt marker ink
Purple grape juice	Rust
Berries, cranberries, and their juices	Wax, candle or other
Chocolate	Dyes
Grease or oil, from food, cars, machines, tools, cosmetics	Nail polish
Blood	Shoe polish
Tar	Lipstick and other makeup
Crayon	Perspiration (sometimes)
Paint, latex or enamel	Mud (sometimes)
	Grass

All-purpose detergent
White vinegar
Lemons
Bleaches
  Hydrogen peroxide (3 percent solution)
  Commercial oxygen (all-fabric) bleach
  Household chlorine bleach
Ammonia
Rubbing alcohol
Fingernail polish remover (acetone type)
Solvent-type cleaning fluids, dry-cleaning fluids, or spot removers (for use on items that require dry cleaning)
Nonsolvent stain or spot remover (these contain detergents and water and cannot be used on items that require dry cleaning)
Enzyme pretreatment product or detergent
Laundry stain pretreatment product (some contain solvents)

1. Detergents. The best stain remover for practically all types of textile "stains" is plain detergent and water as hot as the fabric will bear. I follow common usage in referring to just about any soil as a "stain," but in my family we used that word to refer only to marks that would not come out at all after ordinary efforts. When you read ads for substances that remove food and grease "stains," don't be deceived. Rarely will extraordinary efforts be necessary to remove spaghetti sauce or butter smears from your child's clothes. Usually, if you simply scrape off the excess and throw the article into the washer with hot water and detergent, the "stain" disappears. Detergents remove food stains and oils and grease very effectively. Using a solvent-containing prewash stain remover is particularly helpful, especially on synthetic fibers. See chapter 17, pages 264–65. In general, when fabrics are prone to staining or just to be sure, you should pretreat spots. Presoaking laundry is also highly effective. Enzyme presoak products help with food soils.

If, after washing, you find a spot, do not dry the article and certainly do not iron it. Heat sets many stains. Instead, try to treat the stain again while the article is still wet.

2. Bleaches. Bleaches are used in stain removal to render the staining material colorless and invisible, as well as to help actually remove it. A mild bleach such as hydrogen peroxide will be safe for almost every white fabric. It will remove most fruit stains. Test it before using on any colored fabrics. Chlorine bleaches can be tried on chlorine bleach–safe fabrics (most whites, some colorfast colors) to lighten or remove a wide variety of stains, among them those caused by coffee, tea, soft drinks, Popsicles and fruit ices, children's medications, grass, mustard, fruits or fruit juices, ink, or blood. But chlorine bleaches will not work on rust. (See the Guide to Stain Removal, pages 387–90, on removing various stains with bleach.)

3. Acids. Acids are used on rust, oxides, and mineral deposits. If a clothes hanger leaves rusty marks on a shirt, you might apply a solution of lemon juice with water or

CHEMICAL VULNERABILITIES OF CERTAIN FIBERS

Even when diluted, chlorine bleach damages wool, silk, mohair, leather, and other protein-based fibers. It also harms nylon and spandex.

Acetone (contained in nail polish remover and paint thinner) harms acetate, triacetate, and modacrylic.

Cellulosic fabrics are more vulnerable to acids, and protein fibers are more vulnerable to alkalies.

Polypropylene (olefin) is damaged by perchloroethylene, the dry-cleaning solvent most commonly used by dry cleaners. (Polypropylene can be dry-cleaned with other solvents.)

white vinegar mixed with water, then rinse thoroughly and launder (or see "Rust," page 390, in the Guide to Stain Removal). You could try the same solution on brown or yellow spots in stored linens, as these tend to be caused by oxidized residues of soil or detergent. (In each case, half-and-half proportions are usually good enough, but you might sometimes try full strength for more effect. Some people add salt to the lemon juice solution. You must test a vinegar or lemon juice solution on an out-of-sight area of the article, just as you test detergents and spot removers, as such a solution can adversely affect some fibers and some dyes.) Refer to chapter 31 for a discussion of common household acids and bases and related subjects. There are also commercial rust-removing preparations, such as RoVer or Whink, which you can buy at home centers, houseware and hardware stores, or stores where washing machines are sold. These commercial preparations contain acids (hydrofluoric acid or oxalic acid); read their labels and follow all cautions carefully.

Warning! Do not mix acids or acid-containing substances with chlorine bleach or substances containing chlorine bleach. This will produce hazardous fumes.

4. Ammonia. Ammonia, which is alkaline, is sometimes used to neutralize acid substances. For example, you are sometimes advised to apply ammonia to fresh perspiration stains or stains from antiperspirants, which tend to be acidic. With old perspiration stains, you are advised to apply white vinegar because they will have oxidized. You are also advised to try ammonia on fresh urine stains and white vinegar on old, for the same reasons. Then rinse and wash the garment.

Warning! Do not mix ammonia or preparations containing ammonia with chlorine bleach or substances containing chlorine bleach. This will produce hazardous fumes.

5. Solvents. Use appropriate solvent-based cleaners to remove non-water-soluble substances. You can remove enamel paint or varnish with turpentine but not with plain soap and water. (See the guide at the end of this chapter.) Although some stains, such as oily or greasy soils, can be removed both by solvents and by water-and-detergent solutions, others can be removed only with some sort of solvent. Solvents, which are nonpolar liquids, remove stains caused by substances that are not water soluble. (See chapter 31 for an explanation of polarity.) Water is very highly polar. Polar substances remove stains caused by water-soluble substances. The more nonpolar a substance is, the more nonpolar a solvent you need to dissolve it. Drycleaning fluids are nonpolar solvents. Below is a list of substances that may require or respond to solvent-based removers. Note, however, that stains from these substances—especially ink—may be permanent no matter what you do. (They may also respond to other methods of removal than the application of some solvent. Check the Guide to Stain Removal, pages 387–90.)

Chewing gum
Lipstick
Eye makeup and other makeup
Shoe polish
Fingernail polish
Tar/asphalt
Enamel paints
Grease
Ballpoint pen ink
Felt-tip marker ink (unless labeled "washable")
Wax
Crayon
Glue (some types)

When you are dealing with an unknown stain, begin working on it with water, which is highly polar, or a water-and-detergent solution. If this does not work, try solvents in order of decreasing polarity—rubbing alcohol, then a commercial solvent-containing spot cleaner, and so forth. The following list of common household solvents gives them in order of *decreasing polarity*.

Rubbing alcohol (30 percent water and 70 percent isopropyl alcohol) (polar)

Fingernail polish remover (ethyl acetate) (slightly polar)

Commercial stain removers containing ethylene dichloride (very slightly polar) or other solvents

Hydrocarbons (nonpolar)—*extremely flammable and volatile*

- Dry-cleaning fluids (perchloroethylene, trichloroethylene petroleum distillates, Varsol)
- Turpentine

Hydrocarbons are dangerous. Keep tightly sealed. Use only with plenty of ventilation and always far from potential sparks or flames. (See chapter 60, "Fire," and chapter 64, "Poisons, Hazardous Substances, and Proper Disposal of Hazardous Household Wastes.") *Fabrics treated with hydrocarbons should always be rinsed before washing.* Less volatile solvents may also pose risks. Always read label cautions carefully and follow them to the letter.

6. Enzymes. Enzymes help to remove organic and protein-based stains. Such stains include bodily substances (blood, mucus, feces, urine, vomit), most food stains (egg, catsup, gravy and meat, grease, milk and milk products), grass, mud, and some glue. As not all enzymes work on all such stains, enzyme-containing products for the laundry usually contain more than one enzyme. Heat may set some protein-containing stains. Thus you are advised to soak many of them in cold water. This is standard advice for stains of blood, egg, meat or gravy, milk or ice cream, urine, or feces. As food stains are likely to contain more than one staining substance—say, both catsup and grease—you usually work on the protein part first so as to avoid setting it.

7. Color removers may be used on certain white fabrics. (See "Color removers," page 320.) These contain sodium hydrosulfite, a strong bleaching agent. Make sure it is safe for the fabric you intend to use it on.

TONER POWDER

Heat will set spots on fabrics caused by toner powder from your computer's printer. If you should soil your clothes with toner powder, wipe it off with a clean dry cloth and wash it out with cold water.

COMMERCIAL SPOT REMOVERS AND PRETREATMENT STAIN REMOVAL PRODUCTS

Commercial spot removers may contain solvents or surfactants or both. Among the solvents that may be present in spot removers are ethylene dichloride and isopropyl alcohol. Some laundry pretreatment soil and stain removal products contain dry-cleaning fluids.

Stain-Removing Techniques

1. Act quickly before stains have a chance to penetrate too deeply or to set. On the other hand, do not use any new substance, including laundry pretreatment products and "safe" stain removers, on any fabric without first testing it on an out-of-sight place to see if it damages the fabric or color. Always follow instructions on labels and packages. If a fabric's care label prescribes dry cleaning, spot and stain removal too must be done with dry-cleaning fluids. Practice triage when you mop up spills. To save the heirloom tablecloth from what promises to be permanent damage, sacrifice your cotton shirttail, if that happens to be the only absorbent material you

have at hand. (Rational triage presupposes that you know which spills are likely to be highly staining and which are likely to be easy to remove.)

When you have more than one potential remedy, always begin with the gentlest and end with the strongest.

In order for your efforts to be successful, a stain remover must penetrate as deeply into the material as the stain. It must be of a type able to dissolve the particular kind of stain. It must be applied in sufficient quantity to dissolve *all* of it.

2. Gently blot up liquids with a clean, absorbent white cloth or paper towels or sponges. In theory, you could use colorfast cloth, but it is best not to take a chance that the wiping cloth would compound the problem. Do not let your blotting material get so wet that you cannot carry it off without causing new drips to fall in new places. Scrape off solid material with a knife or spatula. Do nothing to spread the stain. Wipe, pat, blot, or scrape from the outer edge to the center of the spot. (If you are using a solvent-based cleaner, be sure to provide plenty of ventilation. If your cleaner is flammable, keep it far from sources of sparks or flames.)

3. When removing stains from clothes and linens, work from the wrong side of the cloth to the right side to ensure that you do not simply force the stain in deeper when you apply a cleaning agent. One way to do this is by draping the article wrong side up over a basin and pouring the stain-removing substance through it. Another is to make an absorbent pad under the fabric of clean white paper towels or other absorbent material, and lay the fabric, wrong side up, upon it. In the latter case, you then apply a small amount of your cleaning solvent or agent on a clean white cloth and begin to pat the stain (from the wrong side), working from the outside toward its center so as not to spread it. When the absorbent material underneath begins to absorb the staining material, change it for fresh. Continue in this fashion until the entire stain is removed.

4. When there is no danger of spreading the stain further, and only on sturdy fabrics—such as denim, muslin, or gabardine—that can stand the abrasion without pilling or tearing, you might try rubbing or scrubbing with your cleaning agent. Mechanical action helps the cleaner to penetrate and act effectively.

5. Once you have removed the stain, you must rinse thoroughly and then launder the fabric to remove entirely any last traces of your cleaning agent or soil. *You must wash out dry-cleaning fluids (and spot removers containing dry-cleaning fluids) before placing an article that has been cleaned with them in the dryer.* (Otherwise you create a fire hazard.)

6. *Do not mix different stain removal products together.* Not only is there no guarantee that the mixture will be effective, but you may inadvertently mix a chlorine bleach with ammonia or some other substance that will react and produce dangerous reactions or hazardous fumes.

7. In stain removing, there are a number of common mistakes to take care to avoid:

- Avoid soaking protein stains in hot water. The heat will cook the stain into the fabric.
- Avoid ironing any kind of stain or using heat to tumble dry the article, as this may make the stain more resistant to removal.
- Use detergents, not soap, when removing stains, as stains that contain tannins may become permanent when exposed to soap. There are tannins in alcoholic beverages, beer, berries (cranberries, raspberries, and strawberries), coffee, cologne, felt-tip pen or washable ink, fruit juice (apple, grape, and orange), soft drinks, tea, and tomato juice (this list is from the Ohio State Cooperative Extension Service). Detergents will not have this effect.
- Do not try to remove rust with a chlorine bleach; it will worsen the stain.

- Do not use automatic dishwasher detergents, which are very alkaline and may irritate your skin or harm wool, silk, nylon, or other fabrics.
- Shampoos, which are sometimes recommended, are no more effective than detergents and cost more. Those that are colored, opaque, or milky may contain staining ingredients or prove difficult to rinse out because they foam so much.
- Do not iron candle wax. This drives the wax deeper into the fabric, making it hard for a solvent or detergent to reach it, and more permanently sets any color in the wax too. But see page 387.
- Do not use hair spray as a remover of, for instance, ballpoint pen ink. It is the alcohol in hair spray that seems to help. But the gums and lacquers in hair spray get in the way of the solvent's action and must then be removed themselves.

Removing Unknown Stains

The following procedures for attempting to remove stains of unknown origins are provided by the University Extension, University of Missouri.* Follow each step until the stain is removed. Then wash the garment according to instructions on the care label.

- Soak the stain in cold water for twenty minutes. Work liquid laundry detergent into the area and allow to stand for thirty minutes. Rinse. If you suspect that it might be rust, treat with rust remover before using bleach. This gets the rust out before you use bleach. Bleach will make rust stains worse. Launder in the washer using the regular cycle with hot or warm water. Silk and wool cannot take chlorine bleach and should be soaked in warm water and agitated very briefly, if at all. Air dry.
- Soak the stain overnight in an enzyme presoak. Launder.
- Sponge the stain with dry-cleaning fluid. Let stand for twenty minutes. Rub with detergent. Rinse thoroughly.
- If the fabric can be bleached, mix equal parts liquid chlorine bleach and water and apply with an eye dropper. Do not use on wool, silk, spandex, or noncolorfast items. For these fabrics, sprinkle oxygen bleach on the stain and dip briefly in very hot or boiling water. Launder immediately.

If the stain remains after all these steps have been completed, nothing can be done to remove it.

*Reprinted with minor alterations from "Stain Removal from Washable Fabrics," by Sharon Stevens, Department of Textile and Apparel Management, University of Missouri—Columbia (1993).

Guide to Stain Removal from Clothes, Linens, and Other Household Fabrics*†

General Rules

- Read care labels to see if the article is dry-clean only or wash only.
- Treat stains promptly. Fresh stains are easier to remove than old ones. If the stain is on a nonwashable fabric, take it to the dry cleaner as soon as possible. Tell the stain and the fiber content of the garment.
- Read and follow package directions when using any stain removal product.
- Always test stain removers on an inside seam or other hidden part of garment for color fastness. To test, apply product and let stand 2–5 minutes, then rinse. If color changes, do not use product on garment.
- When using a bleach, do not try to bleach just one area of garment; bleach the entire garment to prevent uneven color removal.
- When treating, place stained area face down on a clean paper towel or white cloth. Apply stain remover to the under side of the stain, forcing stain off the fabric surface instead of through it.
- Never put chemical dry-cleaning solvents directly into washer.
- Thoroughly rinse and air dry areas treated with dry-cleaning solvents before placing in washer, to avoid a fire.
- Do not mix stain removal products together. Some mixtures, such as ammonia and chlorine bleach, produce hazardous fumes.
- Always launder washable items after treating to remove residues of the stain and the stain remover.
- Have patience; it takes a little extra time and effort to remove some stains.
- Remember, some stains cannot be removed.

Adhesive Tape, Chewing Gum, Rubber Cement. Harden surface with ice; scrape with a dull knife. Saturate with a prewash stain remover or cleaning fluid. Rinse, then launder.

Baby Formula. Pretreat or soak stain using a product containing enzymes; soak for at least 30 minutes or several hours for aged stains. Launder.

Beverages (coffee, tea, soft drinks, wine, alcoholic drinks). Soak stain in cool water. Pretreat with prewash stain remover, liquid laundry detergent, or a paste of powder detergent and water. Launder with the bleach safe for that fabric. *Note:* Older stains might respond to treatment with an enzyme product, then laundering.

Blood. Soak *freshly stained* garment in cold water for 30 minutes. Rub detergent into any remaining stain. Rinse, then launder. *Dried stains* should be pretreated or soaked in tepid water with a product containing enzymes, then laundered. *Note:* If stain remains, rewash, using a bleach that is safe for that fabric.

Candle Wax. Harden with ice, then remove surface wax with a dull knife. Place wax stain between clean paper towels and press with a warm iron. Replace paper towels regularly to absorb more wax and to prevent transferring the stain. Place stain face down on clean paper towels. Sponge remaining stain with a

*Excerpted from "Stain Removal Guide," prepared by Dr. Everlyn S. Johnson, Extension Apparel and Textiles Specialist, Mississippi State University Extension Service, and published on the Service's Web site.

†See also "Guide to Carpet and Upholstery Stain Removal," pages 481–87.

prewash stain remover or dry-cleaning fluid; blot with paper towels. Let dry, then launder. *Note:* If any color remains, relaunder with a bleach that is safe for that fabric.

Catsup/Tomato Sauce. Rinse in cold water, then soak in cool water with 1/4 cup detergent per gallon of water. Spray with a prewash product; launder with a bleach that is safe for that fabric.

Chocolate. Treat the stain with a prewash spray or pretreat with a product containing enzymes. If stain remains, relaunder with bleach that is safe for that fabric.

Coffee, Tea (plain or with sugar/sweetener). Flush stain immediately with cool water if possible; or soak for 30 minutes in cool water. Rub the stain with detergent and launder with bleach that is safe for that fabric.

Coffee, Tea (with cream only). Sponge stain with a dry-cleaning solvent. Air dry. Rub with detergent, then launder in hottest water safe for that fabric (with bleach that is safe for that fabric). Pretreat or soak older stains with an enzyme product, then launder.

Collar/Cuff Soils. Rub area with a stain stick product and let remain for 30 minutes, or longer for heavy stains; launder.

Cosmetics. Pretreat with stain stick, prewash stain remover, liquid detergent, or a paste of granular detergent or laundry additive and water, or rub with bar soap. Work into dampened stain until outline of stain is gone; rinse. If greasy stain remains, soak in an enzyme product. Rinse and launder.

Crayon (few spots). Treat the same as for candle wax, or rub dampened stain with bar soap. Launder with hottest water safe for that fabric. *Washer load of clothes* can be washed in hot water, using a laundry soap (not detergent) plus 1 cup baking soda. If colored stain remains, launder again, using chlorine bleach, if safe for the fabrics. Otherwise, pretreat or soak in a product containing enzyme or an oxygen bleach using hottest water safe for fabric, then launder.

Dairy Products (milk, cream, ice cream, yogurt, sour cream, cheese, cream soup). Pretreat with stain stick or soak in an enzyme presoak product for 30 minutes if stain is new, or several hours for aged stains; launder.

Deodorants, Antiperspirants. Treat *light stains* with a liquid detergent and then launder. Pretreat *heavy stains* with a prewash stain remover. Allow to stand 5 to 10 minutes. Launder, using an all-fabric bleach.

Dye Transfer (white garment that has picked up bleeding dye from other garment). Remove stains with a commercial color remover; launder. If stain remains, launder again with chlorine bleach, if safe for that fabric. For colored fabrics and whites that cannot be chlorine bleached, soak in oxygen bleach or an enzyme presoak product, then launder. *Note:* Proper sorting before laundering and not allowing wet clothing to stay in washer after cycle is completed helps prevent this type of stain.

Egg. Pretreat with an enzyme product for 30 minutes for new stain, or several hours for aged stains; launder.

Fabric Softener. Moisten stain and rub with bar soap. Rinse, then launder. If stain remains, sponge area with rubbing alcohol or dry-cleaning solvent. Rinse thoroughly and relaunder.

Fingernail Polish. Try nail polish remover, but do not use on acetate or triacetate fabrics. Place stain face down on paper towels and flush with remover. Replace paper towels regularly. Repeat until stain disappears; rinse and launder. Some polishes may be impossible to remove.

Fruit Juices. Soak garment in cool water. Wash with bleach that is safe for that fabric.

Grass Stains. Pretreat with stain stick or soak with an enzyme product. If stain remains, and if safe for dye, sponge stain with alcohol (dilute alcohol with 2 parts water for use on acetate). If stain still remains, launder in hottest water safe for fabrics, with bleach that is safe for that fabric.

Grease (motor oil, animal fat, mayonnaise, salad dressing, butter, cooking oil and car grease). *Light stains* can be pretreated with a spray stain remover, liquid laundry detergent, or a detergent booster. Launder in hottest water safe for fabric. Place *heavy stains* face down on clean paper towels. Apply cleaning fluid to the back of stain. Replace towels frequently. Let air dry; rinse. Launder in hottest water safe for that fabric.

Ink. Test stain with water or dry-cleaning solvent by placing a drop of each on stain. Use method that removes more of the ink. *Ballpoint ink* stains can be placed stain face down on white paper towels. Sponge with rubbing or denatured alcohol or dry-cleaning solvent, or rub detergent into stained area. Repeat if some stain remains. Rinse; launder. *Drawing ink* usually cannot be removed. Try flushing with cold water until pigments are removed; rub liquid detergent into stain; rinse. Repeat process. Soak in warm sudsy water to which 1 to 4 tablespoons of household ammonia per quart of water have been added. Rinse thoroughly. Launder in hottest water safe for that fabric, with bleach safe for the fabric. *Felt tip or India ink*—Usually cannot be removed. Try pouring water through the stain before it dries, until pigments are removed. Allow to dry. If you notice some reduction in stain, sponge with dry-cleaning solvent. Allow to dry. Rub liquid household cleaner into stain. Rinse. Soak stain (possible overnight) in warm water to which 1 to 4 tablespoons of household ammonia have been added. Rinse and repeat treatment if necessary; launder.

Iodine. Rinse from back side of stain under cool, running water. Soak in solution of color remover, or sponge with a solution of sodium thiosulfate crystals (available at drug store). Rinse and launder.

Lipstick. Place face down on paper towels. Sponge area with dry-cleaning solvent, or use a prewash soil and stain remover. Replace towels frequently; rinse. Rub light-duty liquid detergent into stain until outline is removed; launder. Repeat treatment if needed.

Liquid Paper. Sponge the stain with amyl acetate (banana oil). Air dry. Repeat treatment if necessary. Rub gently with detergent, then launder.

Mercurochrome or Merthiolate. Rinse out as much of the stain as possible under cool, running water. Soak for 30 minutes in a solution of 1/2 teaspoon ammonia per quart of water. Rinse; if stain remains, soak in a solution of 1 quart warm water and 1 tablespoon vinegar for one hour. Rinse thoroughly and allow to dry. Launder with detergent and bleach. For delicate fabrics, apply alcohol and cover with pad moistened with alcohol. Change pads frequently until stain is removed. Rinse; launder.

Mildew. Launder stained items using chlorine bleach, if safe for that fabric. Otherwise, soak in an all-fabric bleach and hot water, then launder. If some stain remains, sponge with hydrogen peroxide. Rinse and relaunder. Dry in sunlight. Badly mildewed fabrics may be damaged beyond repair.

Mud. Let dry, then brush off as much mud as possible; or rinse under running water and let soak overnight. For *light stains*, pretreat with a paste of dry detergent and water, liquid detergent, or a liquid detergent booster; launder. Pretreat *heavy stains* by presoaking with a laundry detergent, a product containing enzymes, or a container of water with 1/4 cup each of ammonia and liquid detergent; launder. *Red clay* can be rubbed with a paste of vinegar and table salt. Leave for 30 minutes. Launder with hottest water safe for that fabric and bleach. Repeat if needed.

Mustard. Treat with a prewash stain remover, or dampen with water and rub with bar soap. Launder with chlorine bleach, if safe for that fabric, or use an all-fabric bleach.

Paint. *Water-based paint,* such as latex acrylic stains, should be rinsed in warm water while stain is still wet; launder. This stain usually cannot be removed after it dries. For *oil-based paints,* including varnish, use the solvent listed on the label as a thinner. If label information is unavailable, use turpentine. Rinse. Pretreat with prewash stain remover, bar soap, or detergent. Rinse and launder.

Perfume. Treat with prewash stain remover or liquid laundry detergent; rinse and launder.

Perspiration. Treat with prewash stain remover, or dampen stain and rub with bar soap. If the color of the fabric has changed slightly, apply ammonia to fresh stain or white vinegar to old stain; rinse. Launder in hottest water safe for that fabric. Stubborn stains may respond to pretreating with a product containing enzymes, then launder using an all-fabric bleach.

Pine Resin. Sponge the stain with cleaning fluid; let air dry. Rub with detergent and launder as usual. If stains persist, apply a few drops of household ammonia. Air dry. Launder, using liquid laundry detergent.

Pollen (tree or flower). Sponge, then flush with dry-cleaning solvent. Let air dry. Rub gently with detergent. Launder as usual, using bleach that is safe for that fabric.

Rust. Apply a commercial rust remover. Follow manufacturer's instructions. **Do not use chlorine bleach on rust.**

Scorch. Launder with chlorine bleach, if safe for that fabric. Otherwise, soak in an all-fabric bleach and hot water, then launder. *Note:* Badly scorched stains cannot be removed.

Shoe Polish. Pretreat *liquid shoe polish* with a paste of dry detergent and water; launder. Use a dull knife to scrape residue of *paste shoe polish* from the fabric. Pretreat with a prewash stain remover or cleaning fluid; rinse. Rub detergent into dampened area. Launder with chlorine bleach, if safe for fabric, or an all-fabric bleach.

Tar. Act quickly before stain dries. Use a dull knife to scrape excess tar from the fabric. Place stain face down on paper towels. Sponge with cleaning fluid. Replace towels frequently for better absorption. Launder, using hottest water safe for that fabric.

Tobacco. Moisten stain and rub with bar soap; rinse. Pretreat with stain stick or soak in an enzyme solution; launder. *Note:* If stain remains, launder again using chlorine bleach, if safe for fabric, or use oxygen bleach.

Urine, Vomit, Mucus, or Feces. Treat with prewash spray or pretreat with a product containing enzymes. Launder with chlorine bleach that is safe for fabric, or use an all-fabric bleach.

Yellowing of White Cottons or Linens. Fill washer with hot water. Add twice the detergent as normal. Place items in washer and agitate four minutes on regular cycle. Stop washer and soak clothes for 15 minutes. Restart washer and agitate 15 minutes. Complete the wash cycle. Repeat process if needed.

Yellowing of White Nylon. Soak garment overnight in an enzyme presoak or oxygen bleach. Launder, using hot water and twice as much detergent as usual with an oxygen bleach.

CLEANLINESS

29

The Air in Your Castle

Effects of inadequate ventilation, signs of inadequate ventilation, desirable levels of ventilation . . . Desirable indoor temperatures, indoor and outdoor methods of cooling using air conditioners, shade trees, awnings, window shades, blinds, solar shades and screens, and other means . . . Desirable indoor humidity levels, effects of excess and insufficient humidity . . . How to measure and control indoor humidity . . . Indoor air pollution caused by household chemicals used for cleaning and other purposes, chemicals used in hobbies and work, pesticides, ozone, formaldehyde, asbestos, radon, lead, off-gassing and fumes produced by fabrics and carpets, microorganisms, house dust . . . Indoor pollution caused by furnaces, stoves, heaters, and fireplaces; combustion byproducts, carbon monoxide; unvented heaters, wood stoves, gas stoves . . . Tobacco smoke . . . Air-cleaning devices such as filters and air-cleaning machines; effect of houseplants

Dr. J. H. Kellogg—of Battle Creek, Michigan, Corn Flakes, and a 1994 movie, *The Road to Wellville* (based on T. Coraghessen Boyle's novel), which exploited his eccentric theories about health—wrote a *Household Manual* (1877), which was fierce on the subject of ventilation. Open the windows and let in the sun, he insisted. Airtight houses are unhealthy, and cold air will not make you catch a cold. He scolded about unvented stoves and molds and their spores, and preached that houseplants make the air wholesome. He loathed cigarette smoking, which he said illustrates "the readiness of human nature to seize upon anything which promises gratification of the senses, no matter how filthy, how disgusting, how pernicious, or how fatal in its ultimate consequences." In 1869, Kellogg's less-fanatical contemporaries, Harriet Beecher Stowe and her sister Catharine Beecher, had also published a book on household management. It too contained long, technical discussions of good and bad air—listed in their table of contents under "Household Murder," a title that nicely sums up their views on unvented stoves and sleeping with the windows closed.

The post-Victorian world denigrated such sermonizing on fresh air as outmoded asceticism based in part on an antagonism to anything physical, including natural body odors. More sympathetic souls pointed out that the Victorians had more odors to worry about than we do; after all, they still usually lacked running water for bathing, and used chamber pots. All agreed in dismissing as unscientific the belief that foul-smelling air carries pestilence. But the winds of change are blowing in the other direction.

Today, the scientific recommendation is again: *ventilate*. Although many airborne dangers are imperceptible, sometimes foul-smelling air really can make us ill. Overheated houses waste energy, make us drowsy, and become too dry for optimal health and comfort. Unvented stoves once more pose public-health problems. We may not find the florid vocabulary of Kellogg and the Beechers to our taste; "putrefaction," "pestilence," "fetid exhalations," and "disagreeable effluvia" do not exactly capture the negative qualities of our modern dirty air. But these writers' recommendations for household health and safety where ventilation is concerned are often sound. The worldwide increase in allergic diseases in the past thirty years appears to be attributable more to poor air indoors than outdoors. We spend more time indoors than people used to—typically, twenty-three of the twenty-four hours; the air indoors is more polluted than it used to be and is many times more polluted than the outdoor air, even in industrialized areas.

Despite this, and despite the cautions on air quality in the home that are set out below, readers will do themselves a favor if, on the subject of indoor air quality, they recognize that the unexciting middle ground is also the solid ground. In the vast majority of cases, any problems that exist are mild ones that should raise mild, rational concern and prompt modest and simple remedial efforts. Unfortunately, almost anything said about the subject tends to arouse excessive alarm and, in some of us (including me), purely psychological symptoms. When I wrote the section below about chemical fumes from common household products, I developed an eerie heaviness in my chest and a heightened sensitivity to chemical smells, even though to the best of my knowledge I was not exposed to any hazardous fumes and was enjoying healthy air blowing in from outdoors. All symptoms disappeared as soon as I did not have to think about volatile organic compounds.

Although some substances, such as carbon monoxide, radon, lead, asbestos, and various hazardous household chemicals, may occur in the home under circumstances that pose either immediate or long-term threats to life and health, for most of us improved indoor air is not a life-and-death matter. Nonetheless it promises real advantages in comfort and health that are well worth striving for. The advantages are greatest for those who spend most of their time in the home—infants and children, sick people (especially those with heart and lung ailments), the elderly, and pregnant women—all of whom tend to be more vulnerable than others to poor air quality.

The Indoor Climate

Ventilation. The energy crisis of the 1970s was an occasion for renewed concern about ventilation. When fuel prices rose sky-high, the message went out: build tight and weatherize. As a result, ventilation in many homes and offices decreased, often dramatically, and people began to talk of "sick-building syndrome"—a condition in which occupants of a poorly ventilated office building with windows that don't open develop respiratory and eye complaints and other illnesses. Homes can also suffer from this syndrome. In any tightly sealed structure, pollutants build up in the air when they are not diluted or discharged by outdoor air. These pollutants include volatile organic compounds[1] which are contained in cleaning products, polishes, cosmetics, paints and varnishes, thinners and strippers, glues, and many other household substances, in addition to gases, humidity, dust, smoke, fungi, bacteria, and viruses.

In houses that are not tight, fresh air seeps in at door and window frames, vents, cracks, attics, basements, and many other places. As a result, nontight, uninsulated homes in years past had one or more—some say as many as three or four—complete changes of air each hour. Because all that fresh air requires heating in winter, those who have high air-exchange rates (the rates at which outside air replaces indoor air) have heating bills to match. By having your house weatherized and tightened, you can significantly decrease both. (You can never render a home completely airtight.) But indoor air pollution increases—and available oxygen decreases—as the air-exchange rate goes down. Thus, although weatherizing usually allows enough fresh air to enter for adequate ventilation, and weatherizing your home is almost always safe and beneficial, authorities recommend against tightening homes with inadequate ventilation or specific pollution problems such as unvented gas cooking stoves, unvented heating stoves, potential radon accumulations, or urea-formaldehyde foam insulation or other significant formaldehyde-emitting sources.

The popularity of weatherizing has focused attention on desirable rates of ventilation. For certain living areas in homes—but not high-humidity or high-pollution areas such as kitchens, bathrooms, or workshops—the American Society of Heating, Refrigerating, and Air-Conditioning Engineers (ASHRAE) Standard 62-1989, followed in many building codes, recommends at least 0.35 air changes per hour, or at least fifteen to twenty cubic feet of fresh air per person per minute (cfm). Many in the industry regard the ASHRAE standard as inadequate even as a minimum; the ideal would be higher. Consider that 0.35 air changes per hour would amount to eight and a half complete air changes in a day. In your grandparents' drafty old house, there were probably twenty-four to seventy-two air changes per day or more. In homes in Britain, it is estimated that "the rate at which indoor air is exchanged for fresh air is now ten times lower than it was thirty years ago, with a considerable increase both in humidity and in concentrations of indoor pollutants and airborne allergens."[2]

When it comes to good ventilation, not all rooms of your home are equal. Some, such as kitchens, bathrooms, and laundries, are more humid or generate more pollution and thus need more ventilation. The Home Ventilating Institute, a nonprofit, independent industry organization, recommends fifteen air changes per hour for kitchens with fans exhausted to the outdoors. (Kitchens with range hood fans exhausted to the outdoors, however, will need considerably less ventilation because this type of fan is far more effective in the kitchen.) For bathrooms, the Institute regards eight air changes per hour as optimal for controlling moisture build-up and keeping down mold and mildew; more air changes in the bathroom would make people feel chilly, and fewer would not be enough to achieve adequate moisture control. Moreover, it makes sense to be particularly careful about ventilation in rooms in which you spend more time. Harriet Beecher Stowe and her sister were right about bedroom ventilation: you spend so much time sleeping that the quality of air in this room matters more to your health than does the air in your living room.

Signs that ventilation is inadequate in your home include odors, stuffiness, mold or

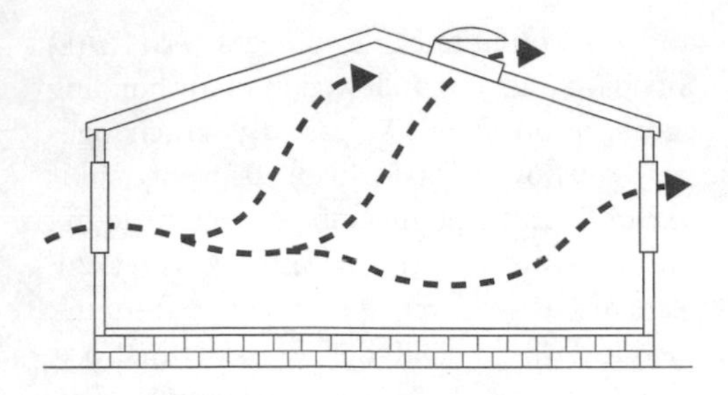

Using windows effectively for ventilation

mildew, and moisture condensation on walls, windows, or other cool places. Windows and doors are our primary means of controlling ventilation. Air from outside, unfortunately, not only raises the heating bill but often does not enter the parts of the house that most need fresh air. To move air through your house, open the windows, if possible, both on the side of the house from which the breeze is coming and on the opposite side. Keep interior doors between these sites open so the breeze can get through. If there is no consistent breeze from a given direction, you can create a draft by opening windows at the highest and lowest points possible in your home, creating what is called a "chimney effect." (See the illustration above from a Department of Energy booklet.) The higher your high window—for example, a skylight that opens—the better this system works. Reinforce this effect with window fans that draw in the proper direction: in on the side the breeze enters and out on the side you wish the breeze to exit. Control the amount of breeze by raising or lowering the windows. Ceiling fans do not bring in fresh air, but make you feel cool and are effective at mixing new air with old.

Some new homes are built so tightly that when the windows are closed they have as few as one to three air changes per day. In Sweden, where new, tight homes may have only 0.1 air changes per hour, home builders install mechanical ventilation systems; they usually employ "heat exchangers" or "energy recovery ventilators" for this purpose. These are mechanisms that transfer the heat of the indoor air that is being expelled to the cold air coming in. This is energy efficient because much of the heat in the outgoing air is preserved, not lost. At the same time these machines provide all the benefits of ventilation: overly humid indoor air goes out, and indoor pollutants are vented outdoors and diluted indoors with fresh, warmed air. Energy recovery ventilators will also retain humidity to prevent overly dry air. Heat exchangers are sometimes designed to work in summer to cool incoming air, too, but they are said to be most cost-effective in cool climates. Mechanical ventilators are being employed more and more often in the United States. They can be used with air filters, including HEPA filters, but they are not primarily designed to function as air cleaners. (HEPA—High Efficiency Particulate Air—filters are defined as those that remove 99.97% of particles greater than 0.3 microns in diameter.)

Temperature

Desirable Indoor Temperatures. Americans do not need to be advised to keep warm. They keep warmer than any other people whose climate requires them to rely on artificial heat in winter. In the 1970s, they had to be persuaded to lower their thermostats to 65–68°F—the desirable temperature range in the average home that houses healthy adults and children. As always, you must exercise special care for the very old and the very young. Dr. Spock says that babies of eight pounds or more are fine during waking hours at 65° to 68°F, the same temperatures recommended for older children and adults. The World Health Organization recommends 61°F (16°C) as a minimum indoor temperature for healthy adults and older children. It, too, recommends a warmer minimum indoor temperature of 64.4°F for young children, the handicapped, and the sedentary elderly.[3] In my experience, this is still too low for comfort among the elderly. (At 64°F, even young people want a warm sweater when they are reading or enjoying other quiet activities, but perhaps not when they are physically active.) As low as 60°F is a comfortable sleeping temperature for healthy adults, older children, and, according to Dr. Spock, babies who weigh more than eight pounds. But the very young, the elderly, and vulnerable persons should sleep in rooms warmer than this. (Babies under eight pounds do not yet have effective bodily heat regulators, so consult your pediatrician.) Your doctor should be consulted with respect to desirable sleeping temperatures for these members of the household. Those who sleep too lightly may be surprised to discover the comforts of a cool bedroom. But be careful not to get too cold, however, as this can also cause you to sleep too lightly.

When choosing safe and comfortable room temperatures for your household, do not overlook the interplay between temperature and relative humidity, particularly in winter. In winter, if you bring frigid, dry air indoors and heat it, its relative humidity drops drastically, particularly at temperatures of 70°F and higher. (See the explanation for this at pages 399–400, below.) This is both uncomfortable and less healthy—another reason to keep the thermostat at 68°F or lower in winter. In summer, when homes in most parts of the United States are uncomfortably hot for one or more months, an air conditioner effectively dehumidifies as it cools, and its filter helps clean the air. The dehumidifying effect also helps control mold and mites. However, with air conditioners and central air conditioning, proper service, cleaning, and maintenance are essential to prevent the growth of fungi and bacteria in moisture collected in the condensate pan, on coils, in ducts, and at other sites in the system. You can remove the front of your unit and clean the coils, the area behind them, and the blades on the blower, which can become thickly coated with dirt and mold that may then blow into your room. ("Humidifier fever" and hypersensitivity pneumonitis can be caused by microorganisms that grow in air conditioners and humidifiers.) Filters should be changed or cleaned at intervals recommended by the manufacturer.

Room or "evaporative" coolers consume one-fourth of the energy used by conventional air conditioners, and are effective. They are not placed in windows, so they are often recommended for windowless rooms. They, too, require cleaning and maintenance to prevent the growth of molds and microorganisms.

If you dislike or cannot afford air conditioning, you can still have a livably cool home in most climates. Although nothing but these machines will cool a house in the hottest climates, you can make your home appreciably cooler by other means.

External and Structural Means of Cooling. Some of the most important steps to improve cooling can be taken outside your house.

Shade trees, those miraculously refreshing coolers, can lower temperatures in the surrounding area by as much as 9°F, and deciduous trees do you the favor of dropping their leaves in winter, allowing the sun to penetrate to light and warm your home. Elm, oak, maple, sycamore, and ash, which are deciduous trees that form good umbrellas, are popular choices for shade trees. My grandparents' home was kept pleasantly cool in summer by the shade of catalpa trees. Bushes and vines on trellises near the house are also effective. The dramatic cooling effect of trees and bushes is not entirely due to sun blockage. The process of photosynthesis itself produces water that cools the surrounding air as it escapes the leaves, and trees' leafage also absorbs solar heat.[4]

Shade trees should be planted on the northeast-southeast and the northwest-southwest sides of your home. Avoid planting them on the south side (unless where you live is hot all year), because you will want southern sunlight in winter, and even bare branches block it considerably. Be careful not to block cooling breezes with your trees by putting them too close to the house. Place trees where their roots will not damage pipes, septic tanks, underground wires, or the foundation of your home.

Artificial shade works too. Awnings, louvers, and shutters are available in great variety. Properly installed awnings, according to the U.S. Department of Energy, can reduce heat gain on southern windows up to 65 percent and up to 77 percent on eastern windows. Like leaves, awnings come down in winter so you can get light and warmth when you need it. Before air conditioning took over American cities, lovely awnings were everywhere. In New York, you could walk for block after block and never leave the shade of the awnings on apartment houses and office buildings except to cross the street. Light-colored awnings reflect more heat and light than darker ones. You can buy slatted awnings that do not block so much of the view.

Shutters, although permanent, can be opened or closed, so you need not worry about losing sun on cold or cloudy days. However, they keep out breezes along with the sun, and when closed block all light. On the plus side, they provide a bit of security and help insulate when it is cold. Rolling shutters and shades can often be controlled from the inside, but will still keep out all light when fully extended.

Insulation, weatherstripping, and caulking are as effective at keeping heat out as they are at keeping it in. Insulating an attic cools a house significantly because that is where much of the heat would otherwise enter. Insulating walls is considerably less important, and insulating floors does virtually nothing. Venting an attic is another excellent means of cooling; according to the Department of Energy, ventilated attics may be up to 30°F cooler than nonventilated ones.[5] Place intake vents low and exhaust vents high. You may need professional help to do this properly.

Heat can be reflected from your home by several means. White-painted exterior walls reflect most solar heat away from your home while dark ones absorb most of it. You can buy reflective roof coatings, and tinted window coatings (which will darken your rooms). Avoid any tinting or cooling coatings on your southern windows if you want light and heat from the sun in winter.

Interior Means of Cooling Without Air Conditioners. Window shades inside your home will help cool it, but—with the possible exception of solar shades—not so much as external shades will. If you cannot have outside shade, you should put up sun- or heat-blocking window coverings: indoor solar shades, window shades, venetian blinds, miniblinds, pleated or accordion shades, shutters, draperies, curtains, or whatever else suits you. In choosing, remember that a tightly woven, opaque fabric admits less heat and light than a loosely woven, transparent one, and that light colors reflect more heat. Two layers of draperies provide more insulation than one, and like all insulation will protect against both cold and heat. The closer the draperies hang to the wall, the more insulation they provide.

Venetian blinds are less good as insulators, but they have the advantage of being adjustable to permit different levels of light and air to enter. If you put up two layers of draperies, each with its own drawstring, and venetian blinds, you will have the best of all worlds: insulation, light, and air as and when you want them. Your home will look like a grandmother's—my grandmother's, in fact. But her home was pleasantly cool all summer and warm and draft-free all winter. Pleated and accordion shades are attractive, and you can order them in a range of light-admitting levels, from translucent to opaque. They can be raised and lowered easily. However, unlike venetian blinds, they block a fixed degree of light, they block some air, and when the wind blows, they clack against the window frames. Plain, old-fashioned window shades, although sometimes less pretty in the lower price brackets, do nearly as well for less money and provide somewhat less clacking, although they, too, will flap noisily when the wind is strong.

Proper ventilation can also help cool your home, but only when the air is cooler outside than inside. The Department of Energy recommends that you ventilate in the cool of the morning and evening, and shut windows and employ shade devices in the heat of the afternoon. If you have cool nights where you live, let in the night air; according to the Department of Energy, if, the next day, outside temperatures rise to 85° or 90°F, a well-insulated house will warm up by only 1°F per hour.

In addition to shading and ventilating, you might also attempt to reduce heat from indoor sources, such as appliances and lights. Do not use a conventional oven at all in hot weather. Try to use dishwashers, clothes dryers, and stoves as little as possible, and close the doors to the rooms in which they are operated. Fluorescent lights produce much less heat than incandescent lights do. Window and room fans are also effective at making you feel cool, and they can be used to increase ventilation. Ceiling fans can make you feel four degrees cooler.

Humidity. The humidity levels that feel most comfortable are also, usually, the most healthful. Most homes will do well if they maintain a relative humidity of between 40 and 50 percent. According to the Environmental Protection Agency (EPA), 30 to 50 percent is best for controlling many biological contaminants in the home.

The best measure of moisture in the air is relative humidity, the percentage of moisture actually present in the air compared to the maximum amount the air could hold at a given temperature. Hot air can hold more moisture than cold air can. Thus if the outside air is 30°F and has a relative humidity of 90 percent, and that same air is sent in-

SOLAR SCREENS AND SHADES

You can buy solar screens, solar shades, solar films, and various types of treated glass to block the sun's heat, light, or UV rays, or all three. When considering window treatments, take into account the climate where you live, and consult a window professional before making any big purchases or changes. Think carefully before buying any type of window or window shade that will permanently reduce the level of natural light in your home.

The most expensive choice is to buy window glass that has already been tinted to block solar radiation. Products that have a low shading coefficient block the sun's UV rays. The lower the shading coefficient, the better the product is at blocking heat and UV rays. If the glass also has a low "coefficient of heat transmission" or "U" value, it will block heat; double-paned and insulated glass has this property. Other solar-protection products can be applied directly to the surface of windows. Usually they are difficult to apply. Have a professional do it or the coating may bubble. Even when the coating is properly applied, bubbling or peeling can develop if the coating is exposed to excessive heat. The benefits of any type of treated, tinted, or coated glass vanish when the windows are open.

Solar screens and solar shades are practical choices. Sun screens placed outside the windows typically are made of a vinyl-covered woven synthetic material. Interior sun shades, which may be pulled down, are often made of Mylar. Both are effective, the exterior screens somewhat more so. Exterior screens will also keep out insects and let breezes and light in. They can block 70 to 80 percent of the sun's heat, or more, and they work even if the windows are open. Both types come in different sizes and colors, and in materials of different thickness.

side and warmed to 72°F, it now has a relative humidity of 19 percent. If the air outside is 15°F with a relative humidity of 70 percent, inside at 72°F its relative humidity will be 8 percent. The natural humidity level in my home in winter is a too-low 25 percent. (As heating and cooling experts have been fond of pointing out for at least seventy years, the relative humidity in the Sahara Desert is 25 percent.)

The humidity level in any house or room is determined partly by indoor factors, partly by outdoor ones. For example, kitchens and bathrooms in most homes generate a lot of moisture. Tight construction can trap this moisture in a house just as it traps smoke and dust. In buildings that are not particularly tight, or in any ordinary house when the windows are open, the humidity level indoors is largely determined by the level outdoors.

Very high and very low relative humidities can affect your comfort and your home adversely. At high relative humidities, the body has a reduced capacity to cool itself by perspiring when the weather is warm and a harder time feeling warm when the weather is cool. Low relative humidities may cause eye and nose irritation and itchy, dry skin. Low relative humidities increase static electricity in carpets and woolen and synthetic fabrics used for clothes and upholstery, and they also increase the production of ozone, an eye and lung irritant. Furniture, pianos, violins, other musical instruments, and almost anything made of wood, leather, or other organically derived material will fare ill at both high and low humidities. Wood can shrink and crack when dry, and swell when damp.

High relative humidities promote rust, water condensation (which in turn promotes dry rot and the deterioration of wood), stains on walls and ceilings, the growth of fungi (mildew and mold) and the proliferation of their spores, dust mites, the off-gassing of pressed woods, carpets, furnishings, and other materials, and increased numbers of some airborne viruses and bacteria. Several studies have confirmed a connection between damp homes and increased occurrences of respiratory symptoms such as coughing, phlegm, wheezing, and asthma. Dampness may produce such symptoms by promoting increased levels of allergens, irritants, and infectious agents, or by reacting with substances in the air. Higher levels of airborne dust particles (which may contain allergens) were found, in one study, in homes with relative humidities exceeding 45 percent.[6] It is hypothesized that moisture in the air may combine with nitrogen dioxide and sulfur dioxide (combustion by-products commonly present in the air of the home) to produce acids that help cause respiratory problems.

Fungi, which are a major source of allergens in the home, flourish at relative humidities of 75 percent or more; they will grow, but more slowly, when the humidity is lower. Several studies have found a significant connection between the presence of mold and respiratory and allergic complaints. Dust mites, which are widely recognized as one of the key causes of asthma, thrive in moderate to high relative humidities (over 50 percent) but decrease markedly in number at relative humidities of 45 percent or lower. Mites may disappear entirely at the low winter humidities experienced in many homes. (But their allergens may linger. See chapter 33, "Dust and Dust Mites.") The quantities of animal and cockroach allergens in the air may also increase with the humidity.

Low humidity, on the other hand, is generally associated with an increased incidence of colds and flu, and studies indicate that humidifying dry buildings reduces the number of respiratory illnesses. Some studies suggest that many airborne bacteria and viruses that cause flu and colds (for example, when a sneeze produces aerosols laden with the infectious agent that are breathed in) tend to be inactivated quickly at room temperature when the humidity is in the middle range (between 40 and 60 percent). (Such infectious microorganisms are also transmitted by direct contact. See chapter 30, "Peaceful Coexistence with Microbes.") Thus rates of colds and flu infections are believed to increase both when the humidity is below 40 percent and when it is above 70 percent. Although there have been few studies of the effects of relative humidity on pathogenic bacteria, what evidence there is suggests that the same rule of thumb may hold for many pathogenic bacteria as for viruses: the midrange of relative humidity appears to be less favorable for their survival than extremes of dryness or moisture.[7]

Indoor relative humidities can thus affect how frequently people acquire infectious diseases, but the frequency will be greatly influenced by a number of other factors. Many infectious diseases are transmitted by routes that are not affected in the same way by relative humidity, so far as we know. The incidence of airborne infection will tend to be greater when more than one person in the household has the infection (because more of the infectious agents will be cast into the air). The incidence of airborne transmission—but not transmission by other routes, such as direct contact—will tend to decrease or be nonexistent where there is a high ventilation rate with fresh air.

For comfort, for avoiding damage to home, furnishings, and possessions, for reducing dust, irritants, and air pollutants, and for reducing the incidence of many allergies and infections, a relative humidity of between 40 and 50 percent is probably best for the home. If you want to minimize allergies from dust mites, aim at the bottom of this range. (See chapter 33, "Dust and Dust Mites.") Even lower relative humidities are sometimes recommended for allergic children, but you should consult your doctor about this. If you are more concerned about dry skin, you will prefer the upper end of this humidity range.

Hygrometer

How to Measure and Control Humidity in the Home. To create the proper relative humidity in your home, in summer you may wish to try a dehumidifier in your basement or other damp areas, and in dry seasons a humidifier in dry areas. You should also buy a hygrometer—an inexpensive device that measures humidity—if your humidifier does not have one built in. (Hygrometers are sold in hardware stores and home centers.) Because relative humidity can vary greatly from room to room, you may want more than one hygrometer in order to monitor each room where you are concerned about the humidity level. Without a hygrometer, you must rely on the weather report, your own sensations of dryness or dampness, or obvious signs of excess moisture such as condensation on windows and other cold surfaces, or mold growth.

If your home lacks a vapor barrier—waterproof material inserted in a wall behind the plaster that prevents moisture from penetrating and condensing inside the wall—a humidifier can overhumidify your home, damaging your walls and causing fungi to grow inside them. Excess humidity can also wreck your plaster. I know of two families who caused the plaster to crack and fall off the ceiling by humidifying or steaming for a croupy child pursuant to a doctor's orders. Some experts recommend that whenever you use an artificial means of humidifying your home, you aim at the bottom of the recommended range (40 to 60 percent relative humidity) so as to avoid pockets of over-humidity and the consequent danger of mites, molds, or structural damage.[8] But if someone in the home has allergies it would be wise to consult your doctor before using a humidifier.

Air conditioners automatically dehumidify air as they cool it. Because cool air holds less moisture, when steamy outside air is cooled, some of the moisture it contains condenses speedily. Thus air conditioners can help reduce molds and mites by depriving them of needed moisture to grow and, in the case of molds, by enabling you to keep the windows shut against spores. You can dehumidify closets, cupboards, cabinets, and other small, enclosed areas with silica gel crystals or other moisture-absorbent materials or desiccants. See chapter 58, "Closets for Clothes and Linens." Home centers and hardware stores sell bags of absorbent crystals you can hang in closets or other problem areas. A lightbulb left burning in a damp closet will help dry it out. But don't create a fire hazard; be sure nothing is left touching or near the bulb. Exhaust fans vented to the outdoors effectively remove excess humidity and indoor air pollutants in bathrooms and kitchens. Every home should have these, but many do not. Ventilating or placing moisture barriers in crawl spaces, basements, and attics can prevent excessive humidity buildup. Dehumidifiers are said to help significantly anywhere in the home, including the basement. Like most other air-treating machines, dehumidifiers have trays that must be emptied and cleaned at recommended intervals to prevent molds and microorganisms from growing.

When excess dampness in your home cannot be remedied by these or other means, call in expert help for diagnosis and treatment. You may need better drainage in the vicinity of your basement, or a mechanical ventilating system. In any event, persistent dampness is not a problem you can safely ignore.

In the Air

You can ensure that the air in your home is wholesome only if you know what substances tend to take up residence there, their effects, and whether and how they should be removed.

Housekeeping and Other Household Chemicals. Housekeeping has always made use of strong chemicals. One main difference between the households of today and those of a hundred years ago is that today's housekeeper need not mix and prepare polishes and soaps. Here, for example, are recipes for polishes given in the housekeeping manual my great-grandmother used:

> *Furniture Polish.* One and a half ounces each alcohol and butter of antimony, one-half ounce muriatic acid, eight ounces of linseed oil, one-half pint vinegar. Mix cold.
>
> *Stove Polish.* Add to one pint benzine, one ounce pulverized resin; when dissolved, mix any good and finely ground black lead, using the above just the same as you would water for mixing stove polish. Apply with a small paint brush, and rub it smooth, as it dries rapidly; when dry, polish with a soft stove brush; very little rubbing is required. For sheet-iron use the benzine and resin alone, apply with soft rags, and rub rapidly until dry and shining.

My grandmother's stove polish was a stew of poisons. Yet my great-grandparents and grandparents, most of whom lived to ripe old ages, really did keep muriatic acid (hydrochloric acid) and powdered lead in their sheds and cabinets, along with lye, mercury, paris green (used as a pesticide), spanish fly (used against flies in the barn), and benzene, as well as substances commonly seen in many homes today—kerosene, turpentine, paint thinner, ammonia, sodium hypochlorite (ordinary chlorine bleach), and others. In their drafty houses, fumes probably dissipated quickly. Chilblains were the problem.

The sensible attitude, according to most authorities, is to be careful and restrained in the use of chemicals of all sorts in the home, to follow manufacturers' instructions precisely, and to ventilate the home thoroughly, especially when you are using chemical products in a workshop or when cleaning. When used in improperly ventilated rooms and contrary to manufacturers' instructions, some household chemicals can induce symptoms ranging from mild headaches, nausea, and eye irritation to dizziness, faintness, and heart attacks and other potentially fatal effects. In our far tighter houses, the fumes and vapors of housekeeping chemicals—polishes, solvents, waxes, cleaners, and sprays of all sorts—tend to lead to higher concentrations of chemical pollutants, and more kinds of them, than before. (On the potential dangers of fire and explosions from some household chemicals, see chapter 60, "Fire," and chapter 64, "Poisons, Hazardous Substances, and Proper Disposal of Hazardous Household Wastes.")

Oven, drain, and toilet cleaners are among the most powerful chemicals used in the home. Powdered oven cleaners, when mixed with water, release ammonia vapors, which can be dangerous to inhale. Many oven cleaners contain lye, a dangerous caustic that can injure the skin, eyes, and internal organs. Household drain cleaners, too, are often composed mostly of lye. These can be extremely hazardous if by accident they should be ingested, or spilled on skin or clothing. When lye is sprayed (for example, in a spray oven cleaner), some of it gets into the air, and may be inhaled. *If alkaline or acidic cleaners are mixed with chlorine bleach (sodium hypochlorite), they create toxic or deadly by-products. Never mix chlorine with any other cleaning substance.* (See chapter 30, page 432.) Avoid using them in the same area (so as to prevent their fumes from mixing in the air). In a recent study of causes of hospitalization for chemical-related respiratory diseases, it was found that exposure to the fumes of a household cleaning product, or to fumes created by the improper mixing of household cleaning products, accounted for 24 percent of all those hospitalized who were not exposed at work.

Other household products such as some cleaning products, moth balls, spot removers, fabric or rug and upholstery cleaners, dry-cleaning fluids, air fresheners, wood and floor cleaners, paints, spray paints, varnishes, strippers, thinners, glue, and adhesives leave vaporous traces in your home's air—of paradichlorobenzene, naphthalene, benzene, methylene chloride, trichloroethylene, tetrachloroethylene, perchloroethylene, toluene, and other volatile organic compounds and petroleum distillates. Such substances are potentially harmful and must be used carefully; some may damage the brain, central nervous system, liver, kidney, or lungs. All are extremely dangerous or fatal if ingested. Exposure to high levels of their fumes can be irritating, painful, or harmful to eyes, mucous membranes, lungs, and other organs. (Their labels suggest other dangers, including flammability and explosiveness.) Some, such as toluene (found in glue, among other products), are neurotoxins; that is, they cause various ill effects in the brain and central nervous system. In addition, some, such as benzene and trichlororethylene, are known to be carcinogens; methylene chloride, paradichlorobenzene, and perchloroethylene cause cancer in animals. The sources of benzene in indoor air include tobacco smoke, fuels, solvents, detergents, ink, and paints. The most effective moth treatments use paradichlorobenzene. Trichloroethylene, tetrachloroethylene, and perchloroethylene are dry-cleaning fluids. They are used in spot removers, and enter the air in your home from dry-cleaned clothes. Trichloroethylene is also used in other household products, as well as in copying and printing machines. At exposure levels too low to cause acute poisoning and death—say, the levels one might experience using paint stripper in an unventilated area—methylene chloride, found in such products as paint strippers, aerosol propellants, spray paints, and air fresheners can cause depression of the central nervous system, confusion, memory loss, and lethargy, as well as complications for people with preexisting heart disease or coronary artery disease.

Aerosol products offer insignificant added convenience, and they cost more and pollute the air in your home far more powerfully than spray pump and plain bottle or can dispensers. Aerosols often contain such propellants as propane and nitrous oxide, which are themselves air pollutants. Propane is a flammable gas used in fuels. Nitrous oxide is laughing gas, used by dentists because of its effect on the central nervous system. The amounts of these substances that enter the air when you use an aerosol spray according to manufacturers' instructions are not going to kill you, or even make you feel sick in a well-ventilated room. But you cannot avoid breathing them in; it is natural to wonder whether they have adverse long-term health effects. It is prudent, therefore, to do without aerosols in favor of liquid dispensers and spray pumps.

Some people resort to aerosols to solve odor problems. Air fresheners, however, aerosol or nonaerosol, are not a good solution. Some air fresheners contain chemicals that are toxic in varying degrees. In the past, some air fresheners contained chemicals that did nothing to remove odors but instead reduced your ability to smell by affecting receptors in your nose. (It is dangerous to be unable to smell; you should be able to detect smoke, rot, and other odors that indicate a threat to health or safety.) Other air fresheners contained paradichlorobenzene.

According to the Chemical Specialties Manufacturers Association (CSMA), at present air fresheners for the home contain fragrance as their main ingredient, and no home air fresheners contain paradichlorobenzene, xylene, naphthalene, benzene, or ingredients such as formaldehyde that deaden the capacity to smell. Paradichlorobenzene is sometimes used as a crystalline deodorizing block in urinals in public restrooms or toilet bowls, however, and paradichlorobenzene and naphthalene are still used in moth repellents. When they are present in a product, the label will say so, according to the CSMA, and will prescribe appropriate cautions.[9] Some investigators say that air fresheners for the home still may contain toxic substances. Whatever the truth, you cannot effectively mask an undesirable odor with another odor, so you should not buy air fresheners to solve odor problems. It would probably also be wise to use no air perfumes, fragrances, or scents unless you feel sure you know what they contain. The most pleasant way to scent the air is with fragrant plants or flowers. There are also potpourris of herbs, flowers, and spices; just read labels carefully to see that these are the sole ingredients. Use all air fragrances sparingly; you can inadvertently use too much because your nose may become so accustomed to the scent that you do not notice it even when it is so strong that your guests are overwhelmed.

The Centers for Disease Control (CDC) does not recommend the use of disinfectants sprayed in the air to kill germs or odors in hospitals.

New homes and those that have undergone renovations have elevated emissions from paints and other building and installation materials for the first few months. If you are moving into a new home, ventilate well during this period, or, if any member of the household is sensitive, try to arrange for a waiting period before you move in.

Working and Playing. Hobbies and arts and crafts can contribute serious pollutants to the air. Welding, soldering, and sanding can burden the air with dust or fumes and should be done only outdoors or in extremely well-ventilated areas. Glue, epoxy, paint, varnish, shellac, polyurethane, and paint strippers and removers can emit fumes containing such dangerous substances as benzene, methylene chloride, and toluene. Methylene chloride, used in spray paints, solvents, and paint and adhesive removers, vaporizes when used, and can be inhaled. Paint strippers should not be used indoors at all, and persons with heart and lung problems should avoid them altogether.

Excellent ventilation is crucial when using any of these substances. Follow all manufacturers' cautions and safety instructions to the letter. *Never* use paint, varnish, polyurethane, or paint stripper in a closed space. Allow ample time for rooms that have been painted or varnished to air—several days at a minimum. If you paint or varnish furniture (with any type of varnish), let it air in a garage or some other place separate from your living quarters before using the furniture in your home.

Avoid storing containers of fuel, unused paints, and other organic supplies in your home. They can leak fumes or cause dangerous accidents. But do not throw them out with the garbage. Follow proper procedures for hazardous-waste disposal in your area. (See chapters 60 and 64)

Pesticides. Commercial pesticides are almost always composed of substances that can be dangerous to people as well as insects. Try to keep your exposure to any pesticide to a minimum. Pesticide poisonings and exposures are extremely common, and the typical victim is a child. If you must have your home treated for insects, carefully air it afterward until no trace of fumes remains before you reenter. Chlordane, which is carcinogenic in animals, was applied until 1987 to the soil below and around the foundations of buildings to protect them against termites. Its vapors can sometimes rise into the air of the home, even years after treatment. Another pesticide, pentachlorophenol (PCP), which is used to preserve wood, has been found to continue to vaporize for years after application. People have become sick in PCP-treated houses. Mothballs contain paradichlorobenzene or naphthalene. The EPA suggests that you store clothes with moth repellents containing this substance only in separately ventilated areas such as attics or garages.

Dispose of pesticides on a toxic-waste pickup date, at a special toxic-waste disposal site, or in the manner directed by your local sanitation department. Do not throw them out with the garbage. (See chapter 64.)

Ozone. Ozone is good when it is up in the stratosphere protecting us from dangerous ultraviolet radiation. It is unwelcome here on the ground, where it harms trees and crops, or inside buildings, where it harms our lungs, eyes, and mucous membranes. You may have smelled it around some electrical appliances and after lightning storms. It is also produced by some types of air ionizers and air cleaners that, for this reason, are not recommended. Electrical discharges from these sources in effect oxidize oxygen, producing ozone (O_3) out of oxygen gas molecules (O_2) and oxygen atoms (O). Ozone problems appeared in the home in the 1980s when many people set up home offices with copiers and laser printers whose operation produced small amounts of ozone. More recent models, however, are usually designed to be low-ozone or ozone-free.

Ozone production is increased as relative humidity decreases, and the combination of ozone and low relative humidity is particularly unhealthy. The solutions to ozone problems include investing in the latest low-ozone-producing equipment, turning off equipment that is not in use, humidifying, and, as always, ventilating.

Formaldehyde. Formaldehyde is a gas with an easily recognizable smell that enables most people to detect its presence at low concentrations. It is used as a disinfectant and as a preservative, and is found in a wide variety of resins, wood products, furniture, and paper products such as grocery bags, waxed paper, paper towels, and facial tissues. Formaldehyde is also emitted from fabrics that have been treated for wrinkle resistance, and occurs in various other household products and furnishings. It was the subject of scandal some years ago when many people were made sick by the off-gassing of formaldehyde from building materials used in their homes. Formaldehyde is found in urea-formaldehyde foam insulation and in adhesive resins used in plywood, particleboard, furniture, and carpeting.

Urea-formaldehyde foam insulation was the first formaldehyde culprit to be publicized. This substance is an effective and relatively inexpensive insulator when blown into walls and then sealed. But formaldehyde gas can be released from these walls into the air of the home. The quantity released depends on a variety of factors, including the care with which the foam was made and the injection and sealing were performed. Even when properly used, however, this type of insulation will leak some formaldehyde; high temperatures and humidity seem to increase this effect. Urea-formaldehyde foam insulation was banned for a while by the Consumer Product Safety Commission, but this ban was overturned in the courts. Although legally it may now be used again, except where banned by local laws, adverse publicity and a flood of lawsuits by homeowners have effectively precluded its use in the United States since the early 1980s. Emissions of formaldehyde from foam insulation decline over the years, eventually reaching negligible levels.

Formaldehyde is a carcinogen in animals and produces illness in people. Exposure to formaldehyde can cause eye, nose, and throat irritation, coughing, respiratory distress, headaches, and dizziness, and some people will become allergically sensitized to it. Anyone who experiences illness that may be attributable to formaldehyde should seek medical advice.

A variety of steps may be taken to reduce formaldehyde emissions in the home: remove whatever product is emitting the formaldehyde; increase ventilation; wash permanent-press clothes immediately after purchase; thoroughly air out permanent-press draperies in a ventilated basement or unused room or outdoors until a day or two after you detect no odor; apply varnish, paint, or polyurethane to unfinished furniture or pressed-wood products. Over time, formaldehyde off-gassing will subside, but this usually takes a number of years. Some state and local health departments will test homes for the presence of formaldehyde.

Asbestos. Asbestos is a powerfully carcinogenic mineral that causes such deadly diseases as lung cancer, mesothelioma (cancer of the lining of the chest and abdominal cavity), and asbestosis when tiny, invisible fibers of it become airborne and are inhaled. Such diseases have long been recognized: insurance companies stopped issuing policies for asbestos workers in 1918. The process is insidious; disease may not appear for twenty or more years after exposure. Smokers are at much greater risk for developing disease from asbestos exposure than are nonsmokers.

Asbestos in the home is not likely to become airborne unless it is damaged, crumbling, or deteriorating, or it has been tampered with. Even when it does become airborne, its levels in the home are usually quite low. But because the risk of disease increases with the quantity of asbestos inhaled, all authorities recommend extreme caution when dealing with asbestos, and urge you to call in professionals to handle asbestos hazards. Your job is simply and solely to recognize a potential asbestos problem and take it immediately to the right helpers. Reliable identification of asbestos requires laboratory testing, and should be done before you attempt expensive repairs that you may not need. Before you begin any repairs or remodeling in your home, evaluate the possibility that doing so will pose an asbestos problem.

If you think you have found asbestos, *stay away, seek professional advice, and in the meantime do nothing to disturb it. Only professionals can safely sand, drill, cut, saw, hammer, scrape, sweep, dust, vacuum, or remove materials containing asbestos.* Vacuuming, sweeping, and dusting always cause an increase of airborne particles, and you don't want to increase the number of airborne asbestos particles. If the asbestos is in good condition, you will usually be advised that the best course of action is simply to leave it alone. If remediation is required, however, it generally takes the form of removal or repair by encapsulating, sealing, or covering the asbestos.

Stringent regulations now control products that use asbestos, but this was not true in the past. Asbestos was often used for insulation, fire protection, and soundproofing until 1973, when the EPA prohibited its use for these purposes. In 1975, the EPA also prohibited its use in pipe covering if the material would easily crumble after drying. The Consumer Product Safety Commission (CPSC) forbade the use of respirable asbestos in patching compounds and artificial fireplace ash and embers in 1977. In 1986 the CPSC promulgated a labeling requirement for all products that contain asbestos: asbestos paper and millboard; asbestos cement sheet; dry-mix asbestos furnace or boiler cement; asbestos wood or coal stove-door gaskets; asbestos stove mats and iron rests; central hot-air furnace duct connectors. Finally, in 1989, the EPA instituted a phased-in ban on almost all asbestos products by 1996. The following advice on where and when asbestos in the home is likely to be a problem comes from "Asbestos in Your Home," a pamphlet prepared by the American Lung Association in conjunction with the EPA and the CPSC:

> Common products that might have contained asbestos in the past, and conditions which may release fibers, include:
>
> *Steam pipes, boilers,* and *furnace ducts* insulated with an asbestos blanket or asbestos paper tape. These materials may release asbestos fibers if damaged, repaired, or removed improperly.
>
> *Resilient floor tiles* (vinyl asbestos, asphalt, and rubber), the backing on *vinyl sheet flooring,* and *adhesives* used for installing floor tile. Sanding tiles can release fibers. So may scraping or sanding the back of flooring during removal.
>
> *Cement sheet, millboard,* and *paper* used as insulation around furnaces and wood-burning stoves. Repairing or removing appliances may release asbestos fibers. So may cutting, tearing, sanding, drilling, or sawing insulation.
>
> *Door gaskets* in furnaces, wood stoves, and coal stoves. Worn seals can release asbestos fibers during use.
>
> *Soundproofing* or *decorative material* sprayed on walls and ceilings. Loose, crumbly, or water-damaged material may release fibers. So will sanding, drilling, or scraping the material.
>
> *Patching* and *joint compounds* for walls and ceilings, and *textured paints.* Sanding, scraping, or drilling these surfaces may release asbestos.
>
> *Asbestos cement roofing, shingles,* and *siding.* These products are not likely to release asbestos fibers unless sawed, drilled, or cut.
>
> *Artificial ashes and embers* sold for use in gas-fired fireplaces. Also, other older household products such as *Fireproof gloves, stove-top pads, ironing board covers,* and certain *hairdryers.*
>
> *Automobile brake pads* and *linings, clutch facings,* and *gaskets.*

This pamphlet and other materials on asbestos and indoor air pollution are available from your local chapter of the American Lung Association (check the telephone directory in the nearest large town or city) and from the United States Consumer Product Safety Commission, Washington, DC 20207. For further information, call your state environmental protection department or contact the regional office of the EPA in your area. There is a CPSC hotline that can give you information on certain appliances and products that contain asbestos, including brands and models: (800) 638-CPSC. Or call your state or local health department. When hiring a contractor, choose only a certified asbestos-removal professional.

Radon. Radon is a dangerous radioactive gas naturally produced by the breakdown of uranium in the ground. It is a potent cause of lung cancer, as the tragic experience of uranium miners exposed to elevated levels of this gas proves. Radon risks, like asbestos risks, are greatly increased in smokers.

In many homes radon is found in concentrations many times higher than those found outdoors. When radon develops in the soil, it sometimes seeps into cracks in foundations and other openings, and thus enters the air in houses and buildings. More infrequently, radon present in well water is drunk, is released into the air during showers and other household activities, or is emitted by building materials derived from the earth. But radon is believed to be less dangerous when swallowed than when breathed in.

The EPA hypothesizes that low-level radon exposure in the home produces as many as fourteen thousand lung cancer deaths per year. One recent study estimated that 11 percent of lung cancer deaths in smokers and 30 percent of lung cancer deaths in those who have never smoked are attributable to radon. Critics of such claims argue that there is no evidence that at low levels radon has any measurable ill effects. Nonetheless, at present the EPA recommends testing all homes below the third floor for radon. (Apartment dwellers above the third floor need not worry.)

Never decide that your home is safe because your neighbor's is. Two adjacent houses may have different radon test results. You may also have heard that radon problems tend to be specific to particular neighborhoods or geographical regions. That is true, but individual homes may have radon problems in areas

ASBESTOS DOS AND DON'TS FOR THE HOMEOWNER

- Do keep activities to a minimum in any areas having damaged material that may contain asbestos.
- Do take every precaution to avoid damaging asbestos material.
- Do have removal and major repairs done by people trained and qualified in handling asbestos. It is highly recommended that sampling and minor repairs also be done by asbestos professionals.
- Don't dust, sweep, or vacuum debris that may contain asbestos.
- Don't saw, sand, scrape, or drill holes in asbestos materials.
- Don't use abrasive pads or brushes on power strippers to strip wax from asbestos flooring. Never use a power stripper on a dry floor.
- Don't sand or try to level asbestos flooring or its backing. When asbestos flooring needs replacing, install new floor covering over it, if possible.
- Don't track material that could contain asbestos through the house. If you cannot avoid walking through the area, have it cleaned with a wet mop. If the material is from a damaged area, or if a large area must be cleaned, call an asbestos professional.

—American Lung Association, with the U.S. Consumer Product Safety Commission and the U.S. Environmental Protection Agency where other homes do not. Nor should you decide against testing because you believe that your house is too well sealed or too well ventilated or too new. The only basis for feeling confident about the absence of radon problems is a proper radon test.

You can have your home tested by a professional or a state-licensed tester, or you can test it yourself with a radon-testing kit. Use only a kit whose package states that it meets EPA requirements. In order to achieve an accurate result, follow the guidelines and instructions for radon testing established by the EPA and your state or local health department. Because radon levels in a home can vary from day to day and season to season, some of these guidelines aim at making your test results reflect average radon levels, and because radon levels tend to be higher in the lowest parts of the home and to be affected by breezes and other factors, the tests contain instructions intended to preclude results that will either exaggerate or understate the typical radon levels in your home. Both long-term and short-term testing kits are available, as are many different passive and active testing devices. (The latter require power to function.) When you have completed the test at home, you send the testing device to a laboratory for analysis. A written report of the results will be returned to you.

Once testing is completed, you must decide whether to take action. The EPA currently recommends that you act if the results of one long-term test or the average of two short-term tests show radon levels of four picocuries per liter (4 pCi/l) or greater. The EPA advises that remedial steps can generally reduce the levels to below 2 pCi/l. The average home in the United States has 1.3 pCi/l, and the average outdoor level is 0.4 pCi/l. The Indoor Radon Abatement Act of 1988 specified that in the long term we should aim to achieve indoor levels that are no higher than those outdoors.

Radon gas detector

Given that the risks increase with the level of radon, you may wish to take action to reduce the radon in your home even if its concentration is below the EPA's action level. Modest and inexpensive steps to improve your home's ventilation rate seem prudent, and can be as simple as opening the windows or installing fans or ventilation systems. When you are tightening your house for energy-conservation purposes, moreover, keep in mind that if you cut the ventilation rate in half, you will double the radon concentration.

Once you have determined that you must take action to reduce radon, the EPA advises that you seek the assistance of a professional who is state certified, or listed in EPA's Radon Contractor Proficiency (RCP) Program, or both. Remedial steps that a qualified contractor might take include using fans, vents, pipes, and soil suction (in which radon is routed away from your house by pipes in the ground that vent the gas to the air above your house), repairing cracks in your basement floor and walls, and performing subslab depressurization (in which suction pipes are inserted in the slab under the house), sealing, natural ventilation, and mechanical ventilation.

Lead. Most people know that lead poisoning is serious business, especially where children are concerned. Most are also aware that lead can occur in paint, water, food, china and crystal. But some people are surprised to learn that lead can contaminate the air in their homes. Sometimes the source of indoor lead dust is outdoors. This happened in 1990 in Lynn, Massachusetts, when a sandblasting operation on a railroad bridge spread lead-contaminated dust throughout the neighborhood where the bridge was located; the lead was carried indoors in the air and on shoes and clothes. Sometimes the source of the problem is indoors. Leaded paint may have been used in any home built before the 1970s and may still exist hidden under newer layers of paint. When this paint peels, crumbles, or deteriorates, or is sanded, rubbed, scraped, or disturbed in any way, it can be ground up into lead-containing dust that becomes airborne. Breathing in such dust is one of the most common sources of lead poisoning in children.

Inexpensive kits are available for lead testing of hard surfaces in your home. There are also kits for testing tap water in your home for lead; or you can send samples of your water to your public health department (or other local authority) or to a private laboratory for testing. In the meantime, if you are not sure whether you have lead in your pipes, run the water for a minute—until it runs cold—when you get up in the morning and any other time the tap has been unused for a long period. This ensures that you do not drink water that has had many hours to leach lead from the pipes. Do not drink or cook with water from the hot tap; hot water dissolves lead more readily.

Finding out whether you have lead in the air of your home is less simple, unfortunately. You can hire a trained professional to come to your home for a thorough inspection and analysis. Your doctor can test you and your children. If elevated levels of lead are found in the blood, you will probably be visited by your local department of health. If lead paint is discovered, you may or may not have to do something about it, depending on its condition and location, whether you have young children, and whether they have elevated lead levels in their blood. Remedial steps include removal, encapsulation or effective covering, and simple cleaning techniques. Some authorities claim that simply cleaning up any lead dust that forms is as good as or better than engaging in an expensive and possibly dangerous lead-abatement program. You cannot choose the proper response without expert advice, and neither can you carry out the remedial work safely on your own. Note that some studies show that vacuuming carpets with HEPA vacuums does not help reduce the lead-dust levels because these vacuums suck as much new dust up from the lower reaches of the carpet as they remove.

Encapsulation techniques, such as wallpapering or painting over the problem areas, are intended to prevent lead-containing dust from forming. Encapsulation techniques must take into account potential danger spots, such as doors and windows, which may stick and rub against floors or door or window frames and cause the formation of lead dust at the sticking points. They also require attentive maintenance; sometimes lead dust forms anyway and must be removed.

When lead paint must be removed, or when you intend to renovate, remodel, or remove walls or plaster containing lead paint, hire professionals trained in lead abatement. They are hard to find and charge high fees, but the work is dangerous. Such projects—or any repairing, sanding, scraping, or sawing of any areas or objects containing leaded paint—can create airborne dust contaminated with lead. Dust produced from renovations will have to be kept from seeping into the rest of the house by sealing off work areas with thick plastic sheets and duct tape. I know from sad experience, however—fortunately with lead-free dust—that despite such efforts you can end up with dust coating your entire house. Children and pregnant women may be advised to stay out of the home entirely until any lead dust unavoidably created has been removed. When the work has been completed, you may face a major cleanup operation throughout your home, not just in the painted or renovated area.

For information on how to find qualified lead-abatement contractors in your area, call your local or state health department. Some locales keep lists of qualified contractors. The EPA has designed training courses in lead abatement that are administered by many states, and some contractors will be able to show you a certificate stating that they have completed this course. Postings of people offering to do lead abatement are also available on the Internet.

Off-Gassing and Fumes Produced by Fabrics and Carpets. Draperies, upholstery, rugs and carpets, and clothes can put out irritating gases, such as formaldehyde or dry-cleaning chemicals. Some synthetics and plastics may let off gas if heated by the sun or otherwise. Newly installed synthetic fiber carpeting, and carpeting adhesives in particular, may sometimes produce shockingly strong odors for periods lasting from a few days to weeks, rendering a room unlivable in the interim. Be sure to inquire about such problems before you purchase and install carpeting. Low-emission alternatives are available. Look for the green and white label of the Carpet and Rug Institute, indicating low-emission levels; and see the discussion and suggestions on pages 468–69 in chapter 35, "Textile Furnishings."

Microorganisms. When there is inadequate ventilation in the home, the concentrations of all microorganisms in the air, including pathogenic ones, increase proportionately. This can increase the incidence of infections and allergic reactions such as flu, colds, chicken pox, allergic rhinitis, and asthma in members of the household. Increasing your ventilation is an obvious first step. But you can also reduce the number of microorganisms polluting the air by controlling indoor humidity and keeping clean all machines that affect your air: air conditioners, humidifiers, vaporizers, dehumidifiers, heating and cooling systems, ventilators, and refrigerators. Pay special attention to their drip trays. If you have water-damaged or soaked carpets, upholstery, or building or other materials from leaks, floods, or accidents, you may have to consider getting rid of them or replacing them if you cannot dry them within a day or so. After that, molds and bacteria will have begun to grow, and they are difficult to eradicate. After a flood or other natural disaster or water damage from other causes, seek and follow the advice of your local public health department.

House Dust. House dust, which can contaminate the air and surfaces in the home, presents a number of housekeeping issues that are addressed separately in chapter 33, "Dust and Dust Mites."

Furnaces, Stoves, Heaters, and Fireplaces

Any fire that burns in your home is in competition with you for the oxygen in the air, and produces by-products that become harmful above certain concentration levels. The basic principles governing the use of fire in the home are these: first, supply an adequate source of oxygen for the fire, and second, supply a method of venting combustion by-products.

All effective and well-maintained furnace systems are set up to do just this. Intake vents supply air for oxygen, and exhaust pipes and vents carry off the smoke and gases produced when fuel of any kind burns. Fireplaces draw air from the room and, if all goes well, send the by-products up the chimney. Vented heating stoves, whether they burn wood, pellets, oil, kerosene, or any other fuel, have vents that permit them to draw air from the room; the air exits through pipes to the outdoors. Almost all clothes dryers have outdoor exhausts too. But some people use space heaters and room heaters that have flames but lack vents; gas and wood-burning cooking stoves and ovens often lack outdoor exhausts. Inadequate air supply and malfunctioning or nonexistent exhaust systems can produce extremely serious air problems.

Carbon Monoxide. The by-products given off by stoves and heaters depend on the type of fuel, how hot the fire is, how much air is supplied, and other factors. All fires, however, produce carbon dioxide (CO_2), a colorless, odorless gas normally present in the atmosphere and usually harmless. (At high concentrations, carbon dioxide can cause headaches, loss of judgment, and suffocation; at lower but still elevated levels it is also considered unhealthy.) Carbon monoxide (CO) is produced only when there is inadequate oxygen, a situation that results in incomplete combustion of the carbon present in fuel so that carbon monoxide rather than carbon dioxide forms. Carbon monoxide is a deadly, odorless, colorless gas. It can produce grogginess or confusion, fatigue, headache, nausea or vomiting, dizziness, blurred vision, rapid breathing, and, in great enough quantities, unconsciousness and death. In many instances, its symptoms are confused with those of the flu or food poisoning.

If flues and dampers on furnaces and heating stoves are not properly set or are blocked, if there are cracks in pipes, loose gaskets, or other entry points for combustion by-products, or if chimneys are blocked, carbon monoxide may be produced and build up inside the home. Every year, more than two hundred fifty people in the United States die from carbon monoxide poisoning in incidents involving combustion appliances. The EPA recommends that you have all fuel-burning appliances inspected by a trained professional at the beginning of every heating season: oil and gas furnaces, gas waterheaters, gas ranges and ovens, gas dryers, gas or kerosene space heaters, fireplaces, and wood stoves. All should be installed, maintained, and operated in accordance with all manufacturer's instructions, especially the warnings, cautions, and safety tips. Have flues, vents (including the dryer's outside vent opening), and chimneys inspected and cleaned. If they are blocked or malfunctioning, this can cause carbon monoxide build-up. Avoid having any unvented fuel-burning stove, heater, or appliance in your home. But if you do have one, never operate it unless you open a window a couple of inches—at least; keep the doors to the room open too.

Carbon monoxide is also present in car and lawn mower exhaust fumes, and each year some people die when cars or mowers are left running in an attached garage and their fumes penetrate the home. When starting your car, first open the garage door, then turn on the motor and immediately drive out; likewise, turn the motor off immediately upon entering the garage. Do not warm up the car in the garage, even with the garage door open. Do not turn on the motor while you are doing maintenance or repairs on your car in the garage. Do not turn on or store lawn mowers in the garage. Remember that weed trimmers, snow blowers, chain saws, generators, and small motors can also create carbon monoxide problems. In all cases, be alert to the possibility of a carbon monoxide problem, particularly if you notice headaches, grogginess, fatigue, dizziness, nausea, vomiting, confusion, or flulike symptoms.

WHAT TO DO IF YOU SUSPECT CARBON MONOXIDE POISONING

If you or anyone in your family experiences symptoms that you think could be caused by carbon monoxide, get fresh air immediately; open doors and windows, turn off combustion appliances, and leave the house. Call the fire department. Seek medical attention. Tell the doctor that you suspect carbon monoxide poisoning. If your carbon monoxide detector goes off, you should immediately ventilate: open your doors and windows. Check everyone for symptoms of carbon monoxide poisoning, especially infants and others who have trouble communicating.[10]

WARNING SIGNALS OF CARBON MONOXIDE PROBLEMS WITH FURNACES, HEATING SYSTEMS, OR FUEL-BURNING APPLIANCES*
The following situations are possible signs of carbon monoxide danger:
streaks of carbon or soot around the service door of your fuel-burning appliances;
absence of a draft in your chimney (indicating blockage);
excessive rusting on fuel pipes or appliance jackets;
moisture collecting on the windows and walls of furnace rooms;
fallen soot from fireplace;
small amounts of water leaking from the base of the chimney, vent or flue pipe;
damaged or discolored bricks at the top of your chimney;
rust on the portion of the vent pipe visible from outside your home.
*Excerpted from "Questions and Answers About Carbon Monoxide and CO Detectors," Underwriters Laboratories.

Carbon monoxide poisoning frequently occurs when charcoal is used indoors for cooking or heating. In the past, sentries in the British Army, who warmed themselves outdoors with charcoal burners, would sometimes place the burners in the open doorways of their sentry boxes, only to die of carbon monoxide poisoning. Never burn charcoal or operate a barbecue grill indoors—not even in a fireplace or basement—or near doors or windows.

Carbon monoxide detectors are recommended by all safety experts. But, as the EPA cautions, they are no substitute for proper use and maintenance of your fuel-burning appliances and should not lull you into a false sense of security. Carbon monoxide detectors show a wide range of reliability in tests, with some failing to alarm even when carbon monoxide levels reached high levels. Others alarmed even at very low levels that pose no health risk. This can be particularly frustrating in that, unlike the situation with smoke alarms, you cannot easily confirm that there is no danger from an odorless, colorless gas such as carbon monoxide. Be sure to read consumer publications for advice and look for the Underwriters Laboratories certification on any detector you buy.

Like smoke alarms, carbon monoxide detectors make a shrieking noise when set off. Be sure that you get one that sounds an alarm, not one that just measures the level of carbon monoxide; otherwise you will not be alerted to danger while you sleep or at any other time unless you go and read the indicator. Remember that a carbon monoxide detector does not detect smoke or fire!

Read your manufacturer's brochure carefully and install and place carbon monoxide detectors in accordance with the manufacturer's instructions. Generally, you will be advised to put at least one on every level of your home. Be sure to put one in your bedroom or just outside your bedroom where you are sure to hear it while you are sleeping. Various household chemicals and cleaning substances can damage the carbon monoxide detector's sensing device, so you will be advised to install it at a distance from these. You may get false alarms if you install one in your kitchen, garage, or furnace room. Your man-

Carbon monoxide detector

KNOW YOUR ALARMS

A safe home probably contains smoke alarms, a carbon monoxide detector, and perhaps a burglar alarm. Thus it behooves you to become familiar with the alarm sound that each makes, and to make sure that each member of the household is familiar with the sounds too. If you wake up to a shrill alarm in the middle of the night, you do not want to be guessing at whether the danger is fire, carbon monoxide, or intruders.

ufacturer's instruction booklet will contain additional important cautions about placement and use of your carbon monoxide detector.[11]

If your carbon monoxide detector is wired into your electrical system, test it monthly; if it is battery-operated, test it weekly and replace the battery once a year or more frequently if your manufacturer recommends this. Leave the battery in the detector; don't use it in your Walkman or your child's toy. You can make the yearly change of batteries at the same time as you change your smoke detector batteries—in the fall when you set your clock forward at the end of daylight savings time.

Unvented Space Heaters. Unvented kerosene and gas space heaters, which increased in popularity when fuel prices rose dramatically in the 1970s, should not be used in the home. Kerosene heaters are banned in some states. California requires unvented kerosene heaters to bear a label stating "not for residential use." Nonetheless, the vast majority of the fifteen to sixteen million of them now in use are in people's homes. *They pose serious fire and burn hazards in addition to creating potentially dangerous gases.* See chapter 60, "Fire." Newer, improved models, which are safer in several respects, are considerably less likely to produce carbon monoxide than are the older ones, but the older ones are still in use in many homes. Moreover, studies show that kerosene and gas heaters produce excess amounts of carbon dioxide, nitrogen oxides (nitrogen dioxide and nitric oxide), formaldehyde, and carbon monoxide. One study showed that sulfur dioxide (SO_2) was also produced by kerosene heaters.

Nitrogen dioxide (NO_2) is a colorless, odorless gas that irritates mucous membranes in the eyes, nose, and throat. Exposure to high concentrations can cause shortness of breath; low levels can increase the risk of respiratory infections. Nitrogen dioxide may affect lung function in young children, and some animal studies suggest that it contributes to the development of emphysema. Sulfur dioxide is a pungent, toxic gas that forms one of the destructive ingredients in smog. The Consumer Products Safety Commission warns that unvented kerosene heaters, particularly in closed rooms, can cause health problems in asthmatics and people with lung disease and heart disease. Others are not likely to suffer harm from these heaters' combustion byproducts, however, so long as the heaters are used in well-ventilated rooms and are not used for long periods of time. *It is extremely dangerous to sleep in a room in which an unvented heater or stove is burning.*

Burning Wood. Carbon monoxide poisoning can be caused by wood fires too. Wood-burning stoves and fireplaces, like kerosene heaters, produce carbon monoxide, carbon dioxide, and nitrogen oxides, in addition to benzopyrene, a carcinogen, and respirable suspended particulates. Because wood stoves and fireplaces are vented, their combustion by-products enter the home only when the venting system malfunctions through improper installation, downdrafts in the chimney, cracks in the stovepipe, or other problems. Nonetheless, studies have shown that such by-products almost always do enter to some degree, producing elevated levels of breathable particles and benzopyrene. Your total exposure from wood burned in the fireplace for pleasure will likely be too low to cause harm. But some studies raise questions about the health effects of fireplaces and wood-burning stoves used as major sources of heat, or for cooking. Several studies suggest that children in households that use wood-burning stoves for indoor heat have significantly higher rates of respiratory illness.

Wood stoves should be checked for proper installation, inspected frequently for leaks in stovepipes, and adjusted at regular intervals. Fireplace users should employ proper techniques for causing the chimney to draw, and for reducing smoke. Do not use green wood, chemically treated wood, or damp wood in stoves or fireplaces. Open the flue before lighting the fire and do not close it until the ashes are cold. Tight-fitting fireplace doors are also recommended. Good ventilation is necessary in rooms with wood stoves or fireplaces so that the fire can draw enough oxygen. See chapter 48, "Fireplaces."

Gas Stoves. Gas stoves are used in 60 percent of the homes in the United States. They do not really boil water faster than electric stoves do, as is commonly believed, but they permit you to change cooking temperatures far more rapidly. Unfortunately, when gas cooking stoves are not vented to the outside, they cause elevated levels of carbon monoxide, nitrogen oxides, formaldehyde, and respirable particulates in the home. According to one study, the levels of carbon monoxide produced after two burners and the oven are lit for two hours are more than two and a half times greater than the EPA's maximum allowable eight-hour average concentration for outdoor air. (There are no comparable standards for indoor air.) People who unwisely use their cooking stoves for heating purposes create increased levels of indoor air pollution. Pilot lights also cause pollution. Use a range or dryer with an electric spark-lighting system. Make sure any area in which a pilot light is burning is well ventilated.

There is controversy about the health effects of cooking on gas stoves. Several studies have found increases in respiratory illnesses in children, and decreased lung functions in children and adults, in homes with gas cooking stoves, but other studies do not agree. The weight of the evidence at present seems to lean toward the existence of at least some negative health effects.

Until more is known, the commonsense response to these worries is simply to install a range exhaust to the outdoors over your gas stove (if you do not already have one). This is an easy way to prevent most of the combustion by-products of your stove from building up indoors. A second response is to improve the overall ventilation in your kitchen and the rest of your home. Opening the window always helps, but an exhaust fan over the stove or range hood that simply recirculates the air in the room does not help. It can even make things worse; unless it is cleaned and its filter replaced frequently, it can support the growth of molds and microorganisms and cause offensive odors. Finally, some cooks settle for a gas stove cooktop (with an exhaust to the outdoors) and an electric oven, a readily available combination that can significantly reduce the level of air pollution from combustion in your home air. You should have your gas range and all other gas appliances (dryer, furnace) inspected and, if necessary, adjusted at regular intervals. If the flame on your gas range or any pilot light burns yellow or orange (instead of blue), you need to call for service. Finally, never use a gas range for heat. (See also chapter 60, "Fire.")

Tobacco Smoke

Smoke from cigarettes, cigars, and pipes is probably the most serious of all indoor air problems. Publicity about the lethal effects of smoking and of breathing secondhand tobacco smoke is so widespread that there is little point in repeating the sad statistics here. Secondhand smoke is particularly dangerous for children and for those with heart or lung disease. Tobacco smoking adds to indoor air not only the usual products of combustion, but other carcinogens, including nicotine, that are drawn from the tobacco itself—about forty carcinogens in all. The more smoke, the greater the levels of these substances. Smoking sometimes aggravates the effects on health of other air pollutants, such as asbestos and radon. The best solution is for the smokers to stop. Smoking outdoors helps, as does smoking next to a window. No one should ever smoke indoors when children are present. Increasing ventilation in the home is essential; good air-cleaning machines also help quite a lot.

Air-Cleaning Devices

Air Filters and Cleaners. Heating and air-conditioning systems help clean the air in your home by filtering it as it passes through. Filters should be cleaned regularly at intervals recommended by the manufacturer to ensure that you reap their benefits. They can block only large particles, however.

Air-cleaning machines are also available, and a good one is highly desirable in homes with smokers or other air problems. Some are more effective than others. Technology in this area changes, so check consumer product research publications before buying. Choosing a machine of the right size and maintaining it carefully are essential if you are not to waste your money. Those with HEPA filters are most effective. These are said to remove just about everything that gets into the air: mold spores, pollen, animal dander, dust, tobacco smoke, and some bacteria. A HEPA filter cannot trap gases. Most air cleaners are not designed to remove gases, but some have absorbent materials that can trap some gases. Air cleaners are also said to be fairly ineffective with dust-mite allergens because these remain in the air for only a short time before they resettle on surfaces. At present the EPA does not recommend using air cleaners to remove radon. In general, according to the EPA, source control is the most effective solution to indoor air pollutants. Air cleaners should be used only as a backup measure.

Houseplants. You have probably read that plants clean the air. Plants really can remove gases and vapors such as carbon monoxide, formaldehyde, benzene, and trichloroethylene from the air of your home. But, says the EPA, a reasonable number of houseplants cannot remove enough pollutants to make a difference. It is pleasant to think that a philodendron might make my air clean, but I believe the EPA. Those who believe in the plants recommend that you set out two to three plants in eight- or ten-inch pots for every one hundred square feet of floor space. The larger and more numerous the plants, they say, the cleaner your air, and the longer you keep them, the more effectively they clean. Note that the EPA, however, also cautions that watering too many plants in your home can increase humidity and lead to mold and other problems. It is probably best to choose the variety and number of your houseplants according to your tastes and what will thrive in your home without creating an over-humid indoor environment.

30

Peaceful Coexistence with Microbes

Overuse of antibacterial agents in the home? . . . Microorganisms in the domestic environment, where they are and how they got there; chief types: bacteria, viruses, and fungi . . . Recipe for infection . . . Cleaning and disinfection, how to wash your hands, antimicrobial hand soaps ordinarily not necessary; first clean, then sometimes disinfect; sanitizers and disinfectants, when and where used; special cautions for homes with infants; clean tools and materials; keeping things dry . . . Glossary of sanitizers and disinfectants, including instructions for sanitizing with chlorine bleach

All of us learn in school that billions of microorganisms live on our skin, in our bodies, and in our homes at all times, but unless we are doctors, nurses, microbiologists, or neurotics, we never think about this again. My eighth-grade science teacher tried to dissuade us from kissing each other by having us kiss petri dishes and then culture them so we could see how the germs on youthful cherry lips produced repulsive growths. The fuzzy petri dishes convinced no one to give up kissing, and our misguided teacher succeeded only in publicly humiliating one poor boy whose dish sprouted a surprisingly florid and varied crop.

When science discovered the role of microorganisms in spreading dangerous infections, neurotics gained a whole new arena in which to be irrational and doctors began to encounter patients who went to bizarre lengths to avoid infection, not only forgoing kissing but also refusing to touch door handles or engage in ordinary social handshaking. Many people have mild tendencies this way. If you are one of them, it may help to keep in mind that nothing that lives in your kitchen sink or on your toilet handle can compare to what thrives in any healthy person's nose—an ecosystem that no one can or should do anything about. Nor have there been any epidemics arising from poor housekeeping practices. Nonetheless, good housecleaning should aim, within reason, to minimize the dangers posed by pathogenic microorganisms. Most households can probably afford to undertake a few reforms in this area of housekeeping without danger of going to extremes.

The advent of antibiotics made people much less fearful of germs than they were in the first half of the twentieth century, when sick-nursing for serious infections was often done at home rather than in hospitals and when disinfection could mean the difference between life and death. Now, however, the rise of AIDS and antibiotic-resistant forms of tuberculosis, the increased incidence of certain kinds of foodborne illness, and the advent of frightening new diseases, beginning with Legionnaires' disease in the 1970s, have caused people to fear infections once more. In response, the supermarket and store shelves are blossoming with hundreds of new antiseptic and antimicrobial products. The ready availability of these easy-to-use, pleasant-smelling disinfectant cleaners leads people with more money than time to substitute the use of germ-killing chemicals for cleaning. These habits are worrisome.

Cleaning (removing dirt with ordinary detergents or soaps), not disinfecting or sanitizing (killing germs with germicidal agents), is the best frontline defense against infectious sickness in the home. The discriminating, informed use of household disinfectants and sanitizers can be a prudent reinforcement for cleaning, but can never substitute for it; such reinforcement is discussed below.* (Killing germs in food and on surfaces that might touch food, however, is taken up separately in chapter 13, "Safe Food.")

Overuse of Antibacterial Agents in the Home?

So many dishwashing liquids, household cleaners, hand lotions, hand sanitizers, soaps, and sponges are now formulated to contain disinfectant and sanitizing substances that it can be hard to buy products that lack them. This phenomenon has begun to alarm some scientists and doctors for at least two reasons.

Their first concern is that the public will be misled about the potential efficacy of the products, or believe that ordinary cleaning and hygienic practices will be rendered unnecessary by reliance on disinfectants. Some of this is due to misleading labeling and advertising: For example, some dishwashing liquids labeled "antibacterial," the smaller print shows, are actually claimed to be antibacterial for washing hands, not dishes. By making no claim about killing germs on dishes, the manufacturer avoids going through the EPA registration process for antimicrobials—the FDA, not the EPA, regulates products that are for killing germs on hands—and avoids having to prove that the product works to kill germs on dishes. Yet many people will conclude, as I initially did, that this is what the product is for, given that its label prominently states that it is antibacterial and is to be used for dishwashing. The remarkable proliferation in the mid 1990s of products impregnated with antimicrobials (usually triclosan), such as toys, kitchen utensils, and chopping boards, raised similar concerns. This use of antimicrobials was originally permitted under an exemption from EPA registration for antimicrobials added to products to prevent them from rotting or otherwise deteriorating as a result of microbial action. Yet before 1998, when the EPA finally put a stop to it, such products were advertised as being effective against a

*The EPA draws a distinction between sanitizers and disinfectants, which is explained below. This book follows common usage, however, in using the terms interchangeably.

WHAT IS AN EPA-REGISTERED ANTIMICROBIAL?

The FDA regulates antimicrobial hand soaps and substances that will be used either on your body or on processed food, or that can reasonably be expected to migrate into processed food. The EPA regulates all other antimicrobials. EPA-registered antimicrobials are not for use on or in the body. They include ordinary household disinfectant cleaners intended for use on hard or inanimate surfaces such as floors, walls, tiles, bathroom surfaces, and so on.

The EPA registers several types of antimicrobials, and products must pass various tests to be registered in one or another of these categories. An antimicrobial that controls disease-causing organisms, such as Escherichia coli, Salmonella, or rotavirus, is called a "public health antimicrobial." The EPA will register a public health antimicrobial only if its manufacturer submits adequate data to support its claims of efficacy against specific pathogens; and unless manufacturers register their products they may make no public health claims for them. Even when public health antimicrobials are registered, their manufacturers are not permitted to claim in any way that they are effective against diseases rather than disease-producing microorganisms.

Depending upon whether a product can meet certain performance guidelines, a public health antimicrobial is classified as a bacteriostat, a sanitizer, a disinfectant (which is more strongly antimicrobial than a sanitizer), or a sterilizer (strongest of all). In addition, the EPA registers certain antimicrobials as fungicides or virucides. Once products are registered in one or the other of these categories, their manufacturers are limited in what claims they may make for the product.

A bacteriostat is a substance that inhibits the growth of bacteria in inanimate environments, preventing, say, rotting or odor of textiles or deterioration of paint. A bacteriostat must be registered if public health claims are made on its behalf. Thus, if a manufacturer claimed that a chopping board treated with a bacteriostat killed common food pathogens, it would have to be registered and efficacy data submitted to prove its claims.

A sanitizer is a chemical that kills a certain percentage of specific test bacteria within a specific short time span. A sanitizer approved for use on food-contact surfaces (such as chopping boards) would have to kill 99.999 percent of the test organisms; a sanitizer approved for use only on non-food contact surfaces (such as walls, floors, or tubs and sinks) would have to kill 99.9 percent of them. Sanitizers reduce the number of microorganisms to a safe level according to public health codes or regulations; but they do not necessarily eliminate all the microorganisms on a surface. A sanitizer's label may state that it sanitizes, significantly reduces, or reduces the number of bacteria by the appropriate percentage. Disinfectants destroy or irreversibly inactivate all test microorganisms but not necessarily their spores. Disinfectants can be classified as "limited" or as "broad spectrum" (meaning they destroy both gram-negative and gram-positive bacteria). (There are also "hospital" disinfectants, which must meet more stringent performance guidelines.) A disinfectant that is classified "limited" must state clearly what its limits are, for example, by explaining which microorganisms it works against. Labels on broad-spectrum disinfectants may state that they are effective against common household germs. A sterilizer destroys or eliminates all forms of bacteria, fungi, and viruses, including their spores—the most difficult form of microorganism to destroy. Fungicides' and virucides' labels must state accurately which fungi or viruses they are effective against.

The labels on EPA registered sanitizers or disinfectants also provide instructions for use as well as warnings about possible dangers. When you are using disinfectants or sanitizers, you must *follow the instructions precisely,* particularly as to waiting periods following application of the product, or you will fail to get the disinfectant or sanitizing effect the label promises.

variety of human pathogens. Such public health claims are not permissible under the law on behalf of products whose efficacy has not been proven in the registration process.

Does the public understand that many ordinary household disinfectants are inactivated by organic matter—food spills or excrement or other plant- or animal-derived substances? If you fail to clean a surface before attempting to sanitize it with certain kinds of products, you may not sanitize it at all. Further, antimicrobials must be used exactly as manufacturers or other experts advise, and usually you must apply them for a specified period of time in order to produce the desired effect. Different kinds of antimicrobials are effective in different degrees against different types of microorganisms, and usually, while they greatly reduce the number of certain microorganisms (including benign ones), they do not entirely get rid of them. Perhaps most important, there is no evidence at all that in the home they make any difference in whether or not people get sick. These aspects of the problem have been addressed by the Association for Professionals in Infection Control and Epidemiology (APIC),[1] which in 1997 issued a position statement, "The Use of Antimicrobial Household Products." As the statement is brief and illuminating, I quote it in full:

> *Background*
>
> Recently, manufacturers have begun introducing agents with antimicrobial activity into household products such as toys, food preparation items, hand care products, etc. According to a *Wall Street Journal* article of January 7, 1997, "Since the start of 1996, nearly 150 products making antibacterial claims have come out, nearly double the number launched in 1995. These products are marketed to the consumer with the implication that their use will lower the risk of infection."
>
> *Description of Issue*
>
> We are concerned that the public may develop a false sense of security and may not be aware of the continued need for valid hygienic practices (e.g., handwashing). In addition, most of the products make an "antibacterial" claim, but many childhood and adult communicable diseases of concern are viral in nature.
>
> Despite inquiries to 11 different companies, APIC has received no information related to the efficacy of these products with consumer use.
>
> *Conclusion*
>
> There is no proven infection prevention benefit in the use of these products. APIC does not advocate the use of antimicrobial household products which are marketed with the implication of preventing infections.

Not only is there no evidence that such products help reduce the incidence of infection in the home, but some scientists fear that they will have the opposite effect. They anticipate that indiscriminate use of these products may lead to the development of resistant bacteria—bacteria that can no longer be killed by the disinfection agents or even bacteria that are resistant to antibiotics. Professor Stuart B. Levy warns:[2]

> If we go overboard and try to establish a sterile environment, we will find ourselves cohabiting with bacteria that are highly resistant to antibacterials and, possibly, to antibiotics. Then, when we really need to disinfect our homes and hands—as when a family member comes home from a hospital and is still vulnerable to infection—we will encounter mainly resistant bacteria. It is not inconceivable that with our excessive use of antibacterials and antibiotics, we will make our homes, like our hospitals, havens of ineradicable disease-producing bacteria.

Professor Levy hypothesizes that using antimicrobials indiscriminately might unfavorably affect the balance of microbial life in the home. Antimicrobials kill some microbes, benign as well as pathogenic, and leave behind those that are harder to kill, or resistant ones. These survivors might then multiply excessively in the absence of competition from the ordinary microbial inhabitants of the household. If pathogens should be among these, we might inadvertently be exposing ourselves to greater danger, not lesser, of infection. In addition, the common household use of antimicrobials that leave long-lasting, active residues, he theorizes, increases the likelihood that the surviving bacteria will become resistant. Among the types of antimicrobials that leave active residues are quaternary ammonium compounds, phenolics, iodophors, and triclosan (a type of phenolic). (See the Glossary of Sanitizers and Disinfectants, pages 431–35, for more information on these and other types of antimicrobials.) Such products are unnecessary for ordinary good and sanitary housekeeping. According to Professor Levy, when ordinary cleaning with soaps and detergents is not sufficient (see pages 427–29 on when you may need to do more), you are best off using the old household standbys for disinfection. Chlorine bleach, isopropyl alcohol, and hydrogen peroxide all quickly dissipate (they evaporate or break down), leaving no long-lasting residues that might continue to kill benign bacteria and increase the growth of resistant strains even after target pathogens have been removed. All are effective against a broad spectrum of microorganisms found in the home. Washing hands with ordinary soap, too, rather than with products containing antibacterials, is for all ordinary purposes perfectly adequate in the home.

Professor Levy's research gives initial support to his hypothesis that the indiscriminate use of antimicrobials in the home might lead to the development of bacteria that are resistant either to disinfectants or to antibiotics. Nonetheless, many respectable scientists are skeptical, and much further research is required to establish who is right. In the meantime, even those who doubt that any real danger will be found believe it is crucial to continue to investigate the situation carefully. Moreover, experts on both sides of the issue agree that except in households with especially vulnerable people—such as newborns, the elderly, people with suppressed immune systems from diseases or cancer or organ-transplant treatments, or any other very sick people—antimicrobials have limited usefulness in the home. Experts on both sides of this issue also agree that in the limited situations in which antimicrobials are useful, the best choice for a general disinfectant in the home is a properly diluted chlorine bleach and water solution. Get your doctor's advice if any members of your household are especially vulnerable.

Microorganisms in the Domestic Environment

Where Are They and How Did They Get There? Microorganisms take up residence in three major domestic locales. First, they live on surfaces, materials, and objects in the home, ranging from bathroom sinks and kitchen counters to food, fabrics, and books. Second, they live in the air of the home. Third, microorganisms may live in the water, but the responsibility for rendering tap water safe usually belongs to the municipality, not homeowners. (If you have a well or if you have no safe public water source, ask your local cooperative extension service or public health department for advice and assistance.) Safe food storage and preparation is taken up in chapter 13. On clean air, see chapter 29.

One source of the microorganisms in the home is our own bodies. Microorganisms are spread by coughs, sneezes, and saliva that land on used tissues, magazines, dishes, cups, and telephones; some that live in the intestines get deposited in the environment or on hands at the toilet or diaper-changing table, and are carried off from there; hands pick them up in a thousand places—from clothes, furniture, books, other hands—and redeposit them alive and well in a thousand more. Foodstuffs introduce a great variety of microorganisms into the kitchen; meats, poultry, vegetables, fruits, and cheese deposit molds, bacteria, and viruses on our drain boards, countertops, dishes, sinks, and utensils. We carry them from one part of the house to another on our persons, on objects, and on cleaning materials and utensils. Flies, cockroaches, fleas, mice, and other pests can also carry them from one place in a house to another, or from outside to inside. They blow in on the wind and float in the water. Whatever anyone tracks into the house on shoes gets deposited on the floor. Most of these creatures basking in the warmth of your home are harmless, or even beneficial. But in most homes at most times some pathogens, too, are thriving even though they do not usually make us sick.

Chief Types of Pathogens in the Home: Bacteria, Viruses, and Fungi

Bacteria. The bacteria that sometimes turn up in people's homes include Escherichia, Pseudomonas, Staphylococcus, Streptococcus, Salmonella, and Legionella. Pathogenic strains of such bacteria under the right circumstances can cause illnesses ranging from gastroenteritis or "food poisoning" to boils and other skin infections, sore throats, and pneumonia. Wet places in the home, such as kitchens, bathrooms, laundries, hot tubs, whirlpool baths, and basements harbor the most bacterial growth because bacteria need moisture to thrive. Somewhat less obvious contamination sites, perhaps, are bath mats, buckets, mops, kitchen and cleaning sponges, cleaning cloths and rags of all sorts, used or damp dishcloths and dish towels, chopping boards, kitchen counters, stove tops, and tabletops. Any standing or pooled water is a potential home for dangerous bacterial growth. Humidifiers, dehumidifiers, vaporizers, and air conditioners can provide moisture that supports the growth of bacteria as well as fungi, amoebae, and protozoa. Merely keeping things dry goes far toward keeping bacterial counts low. Dry sponges, towels, sinks, counters, and basements—all are likely to have low bacterial counts.

Contaminated foods spread harmless as well as harmful bacteria on kitchen surfaces and utensils. Hands contaminated with pathogenic bacteria can spread them to food that, in turn, spreads them to chopping boards, to different hands, and to other foods. Bacteria may also survive in the air after a sneeze or when a flushing toilet spews minute amounts of liquid in the air, or in the vapor emitted by some types of humidifiers.

Some species of a group of bacteria called enterobacteriaceae, after the Greek word *enteron*, which means "intestine," are capable of making us a little sick or very sick depending on the circumstances. They are likely to be present in areas of potential fecal contamination in the home, such as diaper pails and changing tables, toilets and toilet brushes, sinks and tubs (because we wash there), and any places that fecally contaminated hands are likely to touch. Studies regularly find them thriving in the kitchen in sinks, drains, and sponges.

Viruses. Pathogenic viruses are spread in the air by sneezes and coughs. Some viruses also survive on surfaces, often for prolonged periods, where they can be picked up and transferred, and cause new infections. The rhinovirus, the cause of many colds, survives the transfer from hands to hard surfaces, and even survives drying out, well enough to be able to return to other hands and cause other colds. You can also catch colds by breathing in virus-laden droplets of moisture in the air. Influenza A and B viruses can probably be transmitted from contaminated environmental surfaces, although it is believed that their primary transmission route is through the air. Influenza A could probably be contracted from heavily contaminated paper tissues for as long as a few minutes and from heavily contaminated hard, nonporous surfaces for as long as two to eight hours. Enteroviruses, like enterobacteriaceae, enter the home through fecal contamination. Rotavirus, a major cause of diarrhea and hospitalization, especially among children, is readily spread by surface contamination. So is respiratory syncytial virus (RSV), a common cause of infections of the lower respiratory tract in children. RSV survives for up to thirty hours on environmental surfaces, and contamination from such surfaces is one important means by which this virus is transmitted.

Fungi. Fungi are probably the most abundant and diverse group of species on earth. They include yeasts, molds, and mildew. Many fungi are highly beneficial, playing important roles in the production of cheese, bread, antibiotics, vitamins, and enzymes, as well as in biodegradation.

Fungi especially like damp areas. They grow best at relative humidities of 75 percent or higher and grow more slowly or not at all at lower relative humidities. They prefer slightly cool temperatures—from 50 to 60°F—but will accommodate themselves to a broader range. Thus they adorn shower curtains, tile grouting, and food, whether refrigerated or not; flourish in cellars, crawl spaces, and laundries, and on damp linens and other fabrics; and thrive in the refrigerator drip pan and in air conditioners, humidifiers, dehumidifiers, and vaporizers that are improperly operated or cleaned. They live naturally outdoors in soil and on vegetation, where they help to rot or break down organic matter. The same kind of organic matter can also be their target inside your home. They can rot any damp wood, from furniture to fireplace logs, and can rot your walls from the inside out. Their spores float in the air everywhere. They cannot be entirely prevented from contaminating the air in the home, where they contribute greatly to the suffering of allergic people. Hypersensitivity pneumonitis (or "humidifier lung") is an inflammation of the lungs caused by exposure to mold in the home.

Fungi also cause infections such as ringworm (tinea) and athlete's foot. Fungal infections tend to be mild and local, but they are hard to get rid of at times. In unusually vulnerable individuals, such as immunosuppressed people, they can be life threatening and exceedingly difficult to treat. Aspergillus, for example, a ubiquitous fungus that lives in the soil and is commonly present in the home, is usually harmless, but it can cause allergic pneumonitis in some people and, in immunosuppressed people such as transplant patients or people with AIDS, can cause a dangerous systemic infection.

In addition to their ability to cause allergies and infections, molds can spoil the taste and appearance of food and render it dangerous to eat. See the Guide to Common Food Pathogens, pages 178–79.

Recipe for Infection

The presence in the house of a pathogenic microorganism, of whatever kind, does not automatically mean someone will get sick. For a specific sickness to result from the presence of a pathogen, several other conditions must be met. First, this microorganism must get inside a human being, usually through a wound, the mouth, the nose, or the conjunctiva of the eyes. Microorganisms usually cannot penetrate the skin itself. (The exceptions to this rule, such as schistosomiasis and ringworm, are rare.) Second, the microorganism must gain entry in sufficient numbers to constitute an infectious dose. Third, the human being who is inoculated with the infectious dose must be vulnerable to the infection at that dose level. A microbiological definition of "clean," therefore, would refer to the absence of *sufficiently high numbers* of *harmful microorganisms* in places where they might find *entry* into a *vulnerable person's* body.

People are vulnerable to microorganisms in different degrees. The very young and the elderly tend to have less resistance to infection than others do; in general, less-healthy people will tend to be sicker, and will be infected by smaller doses, than the healthy. The vulnerable include those who already have serious infections or illnesses such as tuberculosis, those undergoing chemotherapy for cancer, transplant patients, people with AIDS, and other immunosuppressed people. If any people who fit these descriptions live in your home, you will at times want to take more stringent precautions than usual for their protection—or for your own. Ask your doctor and other medical professionals for advice.

Bacteria generally measure between one and two microns, and viruses are even smaller. (A micron is one-millionth of a meter, which is approximately forty inches long.) Because microorganisms are so small, it is possible to take in an infectious dose in a tiny crumb of food or an invisible droplet of moisture in the air. Many microorganisms can survive on surfaces in your home—countertops, sinks, magazines, toilet handles, light switches, sheets—for periods of time ranging from a few minutes to days, depending on the type of organism and the atmospheric conditions of temperature and humidity. When you touch these surfaces, you can pick up infectious material on your hands; when you touch your hands to your eyes, nose, or lips, you inoculate yourself, perhaps with an infectious dose. But what constitutes an infectious dose varies not only from victim to victim but also from microorganism to microorganism and strain to strain. Among foodborne pathogens, shigella has a rather low infectious dose; as few as one hundred organisms can make a healthy adult sick.[3] Whether you become infected with Salmonella depends greatly on your age, health, and even the kind of food that carried the bacteria. Very young or elderly people might become ill from consuming ten to one hundred Salmonella bacteria, but healthy adults might be sickened only if they ingest as many as a million of them. Of some strains of E. coli, you would need to ingest about one million to become sick, but fifty or fewer of the deadly E. coli O157:H7, some scientists say, may make you sick.[4] (See chapter 13.)

Although you may need quite a dose of influenza virus to come down with the flu, you can get that dose from surfaces or tissues that someone sick with flu has touched. Cold and flu viruses tend to spread rapidly around the home because they inevitably get into the air where you cannot avoid inhaling them, and they readily contaminate hands that in turn contaminate a hundred household objects. Such diseases are probably contracted both by inhaling the viruses and by self-inoculation after they are picked up when hands touch some contaminated surface. Opening the windows and ventilating the home reduce the number of airborne pathogens and thus can help reduce the chances that you will take in enough of them to get sick by that route.

Cleaning and Disinfection

Some infections caught at home are unavoidable. Your goal must be not total freedom from infection, but the reduction of the risk of infection and protection against dangerous infection. This is accomplished in four ways: frequent washing of hands; frequent and thorough surface cleaning followed, *in appropriate circumstances,* by a judicious use

WASHING HANDS IS CRUCIAL

Aseptic techniques were introduced in medicine in the nineteenth century, when Dr. Ignaz Semmelweis, a Hungarian obstetrician, noticed that the washing of hands in obstetrical units greatly reduced the incidence of puerperal fever (postpartum infection of the uterus). Even today, contaminated hands continue to be a major source of hospital infections, and the washing of hands continues to be the major defense against the spread of infection in hospitals. The same is true in your home.

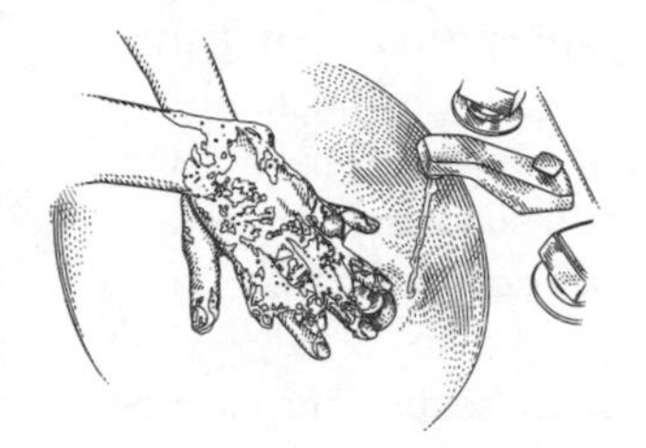

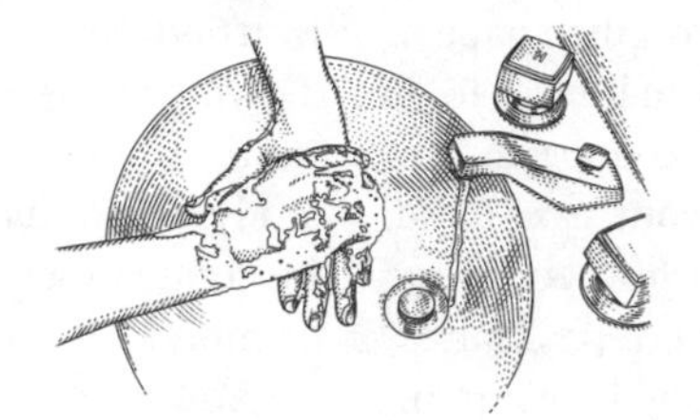

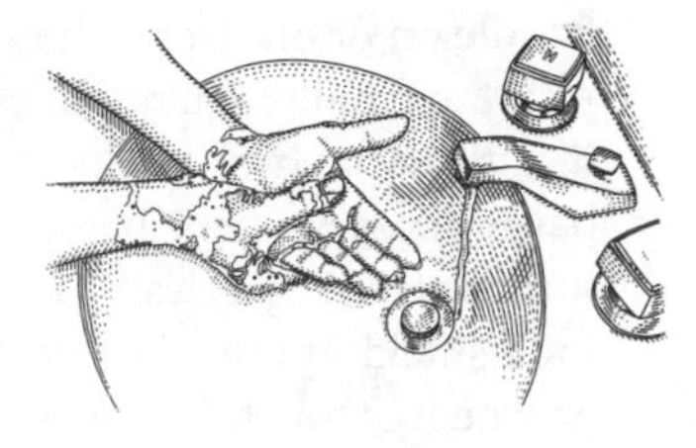

of disinfectants; the use of noncontaminated and noncontaminating tools and materials in cleaning; and keeping things dry.

Washing Hands

The Importance of Washing Your Hands. Our hands are probably the most important means by which nonairborne and nonwaterborne pathogens in our homes are spread to surfaces and other people. Frequent hand washing is one of the most important means we have of defending against pathogens in the home. Remember to wash your hands after using the toilet, changing a diaper, emptying a diaper pail, cleaning the toilet, or accidentally touching the toilet-bowl brush or changing table; after handling raw meat or poultry or touching any material with which they were in contact; after touching or cleaning pets, litter boxes, or cages; or after scrubbing floors or doing any dirty job around the house or yard. My husband and I noticed that when we had a baby in diapers, we both got occasional, mysterious, short-lived attacks of "intestinal flu," despite our efforts at good hygiene. These attacks disappeared with the diapers. I think this must happen to many people with infants because of the unavoidable diaper change on a park bench or lawn where your options for washing your hands effectively are somewhat reduced. (I also wonder about diaper-changing tables in public restrooms, where you can wash your hands but not everything that touches the changing table. Laying clean paper towels under your changing mat or the baby, if possible, is a good idea.) Thoroughly drying your hands after washing further reduces the number of microorganisms. Moisture is favorable to the survival of microorganisms, and it makes their transfer from your hands easier.

In hospitals and day-care centers, where fighting infection is an urgent necessity, taps are often turned on with paper towels or foot pedals to avoid cross-contamination from tap handles. Homes cannot be run like hospitals. But if your hands are potentially dangerously contaminated (for example, if you've just handled raw chicken), you might use a paper towel or piece of toilet paper to turn the tap

HOW TO WASH YOUR HANDS

First, moisten your hands with water; then add soap or disinfectant cleanser. Soaps, especially those that contain antimicrobials, are potentially harsh on the skin, and they will be more harsh on dry than on moist skin. Use 1 ml of plain liquid soap or 3–5 ml of antimicrobial liquid soap—usually one squirt, if the dispenser is functioning properly. (A teaspoon is approximately 5 ml.) Produce a fair lather with cake soaps.

Vigorously rub all areas of the hands—palms, backs, fingertips, the spaces between your fingers, wrists, thumbs, and under the fingernails and rings. Continue washing in this manner, after applying the soap, for about fifteen seconds, or longer if necessary. (Experts variously recommend from ten to twenty seconds.) One nurse specialist in infection control advises that you can gauge your washing time by the time it takes to sing "Yankee Doodle."

Rinse thoroughly under running water.

Dry with a clean, dry towel or paper towel. Rub vigorously, both to increase dryness and because the friction itself removes some microorganisms.

handle on or off. Depending on the shape of your tap handle, you might even be able to do it with your arm or elbow. Whenever you have turned on the tap with your bare hand, turn it off using a clean paper towel or tissue for a shield. It must in any event be cleaned, or whoever touches it next may be contaminated with whatever was on your hand.

Rinse cake soap before and after use and store it in a draining dish so that it dries. Do not keep adding more soap to a liquid-soap dispenser that has been used, because doing so will increase the risk that the soap becomes contaminated. Instead, use it all up and replace it, or thoroughly clean the container and then refill it with fresh soap. This way, if it has become contaminated you are at least sure to decontaminate it when it is empty.

Hands should not be washed in the kitchen sink, which is close to food and food preparation. This is an instance of a more general principle of household organization: Keep food and everything that is near or touches food strictly separate from anything that is near or touches human waste, such as the diaper pail, which should never come near the kitchen. Never wash out even your finest silk underwear in the kitchen sink. See chapter 9, "Kitchen Culture," page 105.

Hand lotions or creams help keep your hands unchafed and comfortable, and chafed, raw skin holds more bacteria, and is more easily infected. Hand lotions and creams may in time become infected with bacteria, so choose a small container that will quickly be used up. Use a pump or other dispenser jar rather than a dip-style jar.

Antimicrobial Hand Soap: Unnecessary in Ordinary Circumstances. Both plain soap and water and antimicrobial soap help substantially to reduce the numbers of microorganisms on hands. Plain soap and water kill many microorganisms. Just as important, they mechanically lift them and wash them down the drain. Washing in plain soap and water thus greatly reduces the number of transient microorganisms on your hands. The more effectively you rub and scrub, the more microorganisms you remove. One study found that plain soap-and-water washing reduced the test bacteria by 90 percent or more.

Antimicrobial hand soaps and cleaners kill or inactivate more transient microorganisms than plain soap does. The Centers for Disease Control recommend, nonetheless, that even hospital personnel use *plain* soap for hand washing in routine patient care, and that antimicrobial products be reserved for use before caring for newborns, persons in high-risk units, and severely immunocompromised patients (to protect especially vulnerable patients from being infected by something on the caretaker's hands). If most of us follow the same rules in our own homes, we will probably use no antimicrobial hand cleansers at all, unless, perhaps, we have a new baby, an immunocompromised person, or another very sick or vulnerable person resident in the household. Except in such special circumstances, antimicrobial hand cleansers probably will make no difference. They are also more expensive, and some of them are more harsh on the skin. This last fact can actually make their use counterproductive. If the skin cracks or chafes, it is far more susceptible to invasion by microorganisms; raw skin has higher bacterial counts than healthy skin. If you use one of these products, therefore, try to pick one that does not dry or chap your skin. If you are using it for general purposes, do not pick one designed to be used (for example) only as a fungicide. See what the label says about its efficacies. Remember that products that kill bacteria may be no better than plain soap when it comes to viruses or funguses.

First Clean; Then Sometimes Disinfect

About Disinfecting and Cleaning. By keeping your home clean you greatly reduce its level of microbial contamination. Cleaning—removing dirt, grime, and grease with a solution of water and detergent or other all-purpose cleaning substance—washes away many microorganisms and their sources of food and moisture. The sanitizing and disinfecting methods ordinarily recommended for the home are backup measures, intended to reinforce sound cleaning habits, not replace them They do not produce germfree surfaces and objects, but, properly used in conjunction with those habits, help reduce the numbers of bacteria, including potentially harmful ones. Those who wish to target specific pathogens or who are dealing with situations that pose serious health threats should seek medical advice or the advice of public health authorities in their own communities. (For information on sanitizing food-contact surfaces and other surfaces in the kitchen, see chapter 13, "Safe Food," pages 173–77.)

Using sanitizers or disinfectants effectively means recognizing when their extra measure of protection might be helpful (see the suggestions below) and understanding which ones best suit your purposes. The glossary on pages 431–35 gives a brief description of sanitizers and disinfectants that might be used in the ordinary household. One among them is a particularly good choice, on surfaces for which it is safe, for a wide variety of household purposes: household chlorine bleach—sodium hypochlorite in a 5.25 percent solution—mixed with water, is inexpensive, chemically simple, environmentally harmless, effective as a general disinfectant, long familiar to medical science, and generally considered safe.

On surfaces that are not used for food, chlorine bleach can sometimes be used simultaneously with detergent in a one-step cleaning and disinfection process. See instructions on pages 433–34. Or you can first clean the surface and then disinfect it with a bleach solution, as you would do with food-contact surfaces. (On sanitizing food-contact surfaces, see chapter 13, page 173.) The reason for cleaning first when you wish to disinfect is to remove organic matter—blood, feces, or food, for example—that might inactivate bleach and certain other household disinfectants. (See the glossary on pages 431–35 for more information on this subject.) You can also buy commercial one-step disinfectant cleaners. When the product instructions tell you to, you will have to clean first and then disinfect if you wish to get the sanitizing or disinfection benefits of the product. When you have questions, call the toll-free information numbers that almost all such products supply.

Usually, instructions for using sanitizers and disinfectants include provisions for an appropriate *contact time*. For adequate sanitizing and disinfecting, *you must leave the sanitizing or disinfecting agent on the surface for whatever period of time the instructions prescribe.* Waiting periods of thirty seconds, or one, five, ten, thirty, or more minutes are common. If you were to rinse the disinfectant off too soon or (in the case of those that are not to be rinsed) use the surface too soon, the product would not yet have done its work. The necessary contact time varies from disinfectant to disinfectant, some work faster than others.

Whether or not you are going to clean and disinfect in one step or clean first and then disinfect, use some elbow grease when you clean. Microbes can fairly quickly—in as little as twenty minutes—attach themselves to kitchen and other household surfaces; other microbes can then attach themselves to these, forming layers twenty to thirty microbes thick. Embedded in these layers of microorganisms may be bacteria, yeasts, molds, algae, and food particles. The biofilm sticks tenaciously to even the slickest, hardest, least-porous surfaces, including glass and stainless steel. Worse, microorganisms embedded in biofilms are more resistant to sanitizers, and the longer they remain, the harder it is to kill them. *Scrubbing*—muscle power—helps remove a biofilm.

When and Where. Sanitizers and disinfectants are useful outside the kitchen in the following ordinary household circumstances:

- Regularly, on the toilet, inside and out, and on surfaces and floors near the toilet
- Occasionally, in the tub and shower stall to prevent mildew as well as bacterial growth
- In whirlpool baths and hot tubs, in accordance with manufacturers' instructions
- Frequently, in sink drains and connecting pipes
- Wherever a musty odor appears (an indication of mold)
- Regularly, in diaper pails or when washing diapers
- Regularly, on changing tables (but see "Special Cautions for Homes with Infants," below)
- In damp basements
- When children or pets have accidents
- When cleaning pets' cages and litter boxes (But be sure what you use is safe for the pet. Phenolic disinfectants should not be used around cats; see page 435.)

Sanitizers and disinfectants may be useful around people who are especially vulnerable to infection (infants, the elderly, the immunosuppressed, and other very sick people) or simply when there is infectious illness in the home and you want to minimize the chances that others will catch it. To protect these vulnerable persons, you should follow your doctor's advice and observe all food-safety practices. To control the spread of infections (a cold, the flu, diarrhea, gastroenteritis), in addition to washing your hands frequently and vigorously, use scrupulous care in disposing of diapers and human or pet waste and used tissues. Soiled handkerchiefs should be promptly washed, using chlorine bleach, detergent, and hot water. In case of serious infections, give that same laundry treatment to the sick person's clothes and bedding; until these items are washed, store them separately where they will not be touched accidentally. Disinfectants for cleaning the toilet and bathroom always make sense when a member of the household has a gastrointestinal infection. Avoid sharing cups, glasses, plates, and flatware at all times, but especially when there is infectious illness in the home. A casual rinse of dishes, glasses, and cups used by the infected person will not decontaminate them. Use the "normal" cycle (or the longest, hottest cycle available) on the dishwasher, if you have a dishwasher. If not, wash them by hand with sudsy, hot water, scrubbing vigorously, rinse them thoroughly in hot, fast-running water, and air-dry them, or dry them with a fresh, clean towel, as described on page 111. Use a broad-spectrum disinfectant cleaner on all surfaces that the infected or vulnerable persons may touch—places where fingerprints tend to accumulate: telephone receivers and touch-tone pads, doorknobs, handles, cabinet pulls, on/off switches (on radios, stereos, televisions, and other appliances), light switches, computer keyboards, refrigerator handles, faucets, and toilet handles. Children's toys, in households with children, are often the means by which one child passes infections to others.

Choose a disinfectant targeted to your problem—for example, something that kills fungi in areas where mold or mildew is a problem, or something that kills viruses if you are trying to prevent the spread of colds by wiping contact sites.

Floors generally pose lower risks of spreading infection, at least for adults, because they are dry, are infrequently skin-contact sites, and are not involved in food preparation or other processes tending to introduce pathogens into the body, unless they become the scene of some child's or pet's accident. In this case—or wherever such accidents occur—disinfection is advisable. Some people choose to use disinfectant cleaners on their floors when they have a crawling infant or toddler. Whatever type of cleaner you use on the floor, let it dry thoroughly and air out any fumes before you let the child play on it. See "Special Cautions for Homes with Infants." These circumstances aside, frequent washing of floors without disinfectants seems to me to be good enough.

Many people follow the custom of removing their outdoor shoes when they return home. This is a particularly good practice when there are crawling and toddling babies in the home or children who play on the floor. Most people in this country, however, will not want to ask business or social visitors to take their shoes off unless they are as intimate as family, but the Japanese and old Dutch custom of removing shoes indoors makes good sense. Shoes track in mud, fecal matter, decayed food, and, in cities, where spitting on streets is common, human sputum; the imagination can supply many more unpleasant possibilities.

Special Cautions for Homes with Infants. Infants and young children are far more sensitive to the ingredients in sanitizers and disinfectants than others are. Many people will remember the tragedies in the 1960s that resulted when infants were accidentally exposed to heavy doses of hexachlorophene. Cleansers containing hexachlorophene can cause brain damage in newborns. In another case, newborns in a hospital developed hyperbilirubinemia when their cribs were scrubbed with a phenolic disinfectant cleaner. Hospital personnel failed to ventilate properly before placing the babies in the cribs; the illness was produced by the infants' inhaling the vapors. In light of such possibilities, it would be prudent to rinse thoroughly and dry and air completely all disinfected surfaces before putting an infant on or near them, and to avoid using phenolics around infants. Air out rooms, cribs, bedding, and any other object or place that might otherwise expose a young child to fumes or vapors. It is not necessary, by the way, to use disinfectants on children's crib mattresses or frames unless they have become soiled with urine or feces. The use of disinfectants (a solution of chlorine bleach and water is safe and effective) is always a good idea on the changing table and in the diaper pail. You will often need to sanitize bedclothes, sleepwear, and other infants' and toddlers' clothes as well. Hot water, detergent, and, sometimes, chlorine bleach are all that is needed. See chapter 27, "Sanitizing the Laundry."

CLEANING UP MICROBE-LADEN MESSES

Paper towels are particularly useful for small spills or messes of anything likely to be germ-laden, such as juice from raw chicken or a pet's or child's accident. For bigger spills, you may find it more convenient to use old cloth towels or rags kept for this purpose. Wear plastic disposable gloves for cleaning serious or very messy spills. If you use paper towels, when you have finished, put the soiled towels into a plastic bag, seal it, and put it in the garbage. If you use cloth towels or rags, you must clean the cloth when you are finished. If you wiped up flushable matter, get it off as you would empty a diaper: hold the end of the cloth, still wearing your plastic gloves, and dip it in the toilet until it washes free of matter. Wring excess water into the toilet. If necessary, scrape the cloth with a plastic knife and then throw away the knife. If you wiped up nonflushable matter, hold the rag or towel in a large plastic bag and try to shake off the matter into the bag. Then rinse the rag or towel in the toilet; launder in hot water with detergent and chlorine bleach. Now wash up the area where the spill was with hot sudsy water. Use a disinfectant cleaner or follow the directions for disinfecting with chlorine bleach on pages 433–34. When you have finished, wash your hands.

Clean Tools and Materials. Use fresh, clean materials and utensils. Damp cleaning cloths, sponges, mops, and other damp or dirty cleaning tools become reservoirs for enormous numbers of bacteria. If you sanitize surfaces and then wipe them with a contaminated towel or sponge, you will recontaminate them. Cloths, sponges, and other cleaning utensils should be used only once and then laundered in hot water with detergent and chlorine bleach or, if not launderable, washed by hand in hot, sudsy water, rinsed, and then soaked in a solution of bleach and water. (Sanitizing sponges, pot scratchers, and other kitchen cleaning devices in a bleach solution is described in chapter 13, page 176.) If you change washing and scrubbing cloths and towels frequently, you will need a large stock to get you from one laundry day to another. Paper towels or other disposables have the advantage of being free of microbial contamination, but they are less effective and more expensive. See chapter 32, "Aprons, Rags, and Mops," pages 447–48.

Keeping Things Dry. Because enterobacteria, Pseudomonades, molds, and other microorganisms usually thrive in dampness, keeping surfaces and objects dry helps tremendously to keep microbial counts low. A kitchen counter left dry over a period of a few hours will show a substantial decrease in bacteria. The same is true of a dry bathroom, which also will not mildew. (When you wipe down countertops, sinks, tiles, tabletops, and other surfaces to dry them, you also help preserve them from gradual damage over the years from chemicals in the water.) If your carpets get wet, dry them thoroughly as quickly as you can, so mildew and bacteria do not have a chance to take hold. Once they do, they are difficult or impossible to eradicate. Do not allow water to stand anywhere in your house—not in basements, in refrigerator drip trays, around leaking pipes, or anywhere else.

Wipe surfaces dry only with clean materials, always from an area of probable absence of contamination toward areas of probable heavy contamination, and use a separate drying cloth on the latter. Ventilation that speeds drying times is important in humid rooms or rooms with wet surfaces and much moisture.

In the bathroom, towels and washcloths should be permitted to dry thoroughly before reuse, or a fresh supply of towels and washcloths should be provided. The sharing of bathroom towels should be discouraged. I dislike using sponges for cleaning the bathroom. If you prefer sponges, use them only once before disinfecting them. The dark, wet insides of sponges provide an ideal breeding ground for microorganisms. Do not leave sponges on the side of the tub or sink where they will repeatedly be rewet. All sponges (including loofah sponges), pumice stones, and other exfoliant bath aids should be treated with disinfectant between uses because of their ability to support the growth of pathogenic bacteria that, according to medical reports, have caused unpleasant skin diseases. People tend to leave loofah sponges in the shower, where they stay more or less continuously wet, providing an ideal growth medium. If you cannot manage to disinfect loofah sponges between uses, drying alone will reduce the bacterial count somewhat, but only after periods of as long as two weeks. When loofah sponges are rewetted, bacteria return in huge numbers overnight. Children's bath toys, too, should not be left holding water. They should be washed, rinsed, and left to dry in the sunshine. Soak them now and then in a solution of chlorine bleach and water. (Then rinse and dry.) I would particularly avoid any toys that are difficult to drain or that drain incompletely. (This is the voice of sad experience speaking, as I have found pockets of black mold in a couple of my own child's bath toys, in crevices and concealed areas where moisture was retained.)

Whirlpool baths and hot tubs have frequently been the cause of skin infections. Clean and sanitize or disinfect them in accordance with manufacturers' instructions.

Sunshine. The ultraviolet radiation in sunlight kills germs. Much of the sun's ultraviolet radiation, however, is filtered out of sunshine that comes in through ordinary window glass. Lay furnishings, toys, and fabrics out in the sun to get the best effect. See chapter 47, "Kindly Light."

Glossary of Sanitizers and Disinfectants

If you buy a household disinfectant or sanitizer in the supermarket, be sure you have selected a product that has significant antimicrobial properties. Look for an EPA registration number on the label, and read the label carefully to see what sort of effectiveness it has and to make sure that the product you select will do the job you want done—kill mold or mildew, funguses, viruses, or bacteria, or act as a broad-spectrum general household disinfectant.

Any commercial disinfectant or sanitizing product will have explicit instructions for its use on the label. *You must follow the instructions precisely in order to get the benefit of the product.* You may be instructed to clean a surface before using the product on it. *A waiting or contact time may be prescribed.* Because different products are formulated differently, instructions will vary greatly from product to product as well. *Never assume that one product should be used like another or will do the same job as another.* Many disinfectants are toxic. *Read and observe all cautions on labels.*

Alcohol. Alcohol is a useful household disinfectant that is effective against a wide range of microorganisms and has been used for that purpose for centuries. A solution of 70 percent isopropyl alcohol and 30 percent water is a better sanitizer than 100 percent alcohol. (This is because proteins are denatured more readily in the presence of water.) Organic matter can readily inactivate the sanitizing effect of alcohol.

Alcohol is less versatile as an all-purpose sanitizer for the household than chlorine bleach for a couple of reasons. First, even in a 70 percent solution, it is *highly flammable* and requires considerable caution in its use. Because of its flammability it should not be used on large surface areas, for example. Isopropyl alcohol (rubbing alcohol) and methyl alcohol (wood alcohol) are toxic and bad-tasting. Ethyl alcohol, the type of alcohol in alcoholic beverages, is more expensive. For areas or objects where there will be no food contact, isopropyl alcohol is effective and less expensive than ethyl alcohol. Isopropyl alcohol can be bought at the drugstore in a 70 percent solution. Ethyl alcohol, also called "ethanol," is used in some commercial disinfection products sold at the supermarket.

Chlorine bleach. Household chlorine bleach (sodium hypochlorite, usually in a 5.25% solution) is an excellent all-purpose tool for cleaning, sanitizing or disinfecting, and deodorizing. It is effective against a wide range of bacteria, viruses, and molds. But if you are targeting any *particular* microorganism, rather than trying for a *general* disinfect-

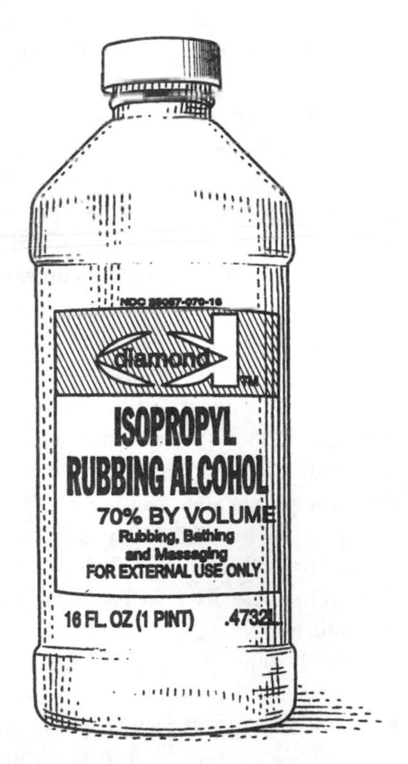

Rubbing (isopropyl) alcohol

DANGER! WHAT HAPPENS IF YOU MIX CHLORINE BLEACH WITH CERTAIN KINDS OF HOUSEHOLD PRODUCTS

If you mix chlorine bleach with *acids or preparations containing acids*, you will cause chlorine gas (Cl_2) to be produced. It is toxic and extremely dangerous. This can happen if you mix chlorine bleach with drain cleaner, toilet-bowl cleaner, or other acidic preparations used in the home. If you mix chlorine bleach with *ammonia or preparations containing ammonia*, you will cause the production of chloramine gas, which is noxious and irritating to the lungs and can be deadly. This would happen if you mixed chlorine bleach with window cleaners or all-purpose liquid cleaners that contain ammonia. Other hazardous or noxious by-products of improperly mixing chlorine bleach with these and other chemicals are also possible.

Beware of inadvertently mixing chlorine bleach with acids or alkalies. For example, automatic dishwasher detergent, which is far stronger than regular dishwashing liquids, contains chlorine bleach and therefore should not be mixed with ammonia. Some powdered bathroom cleaners contain chlorine bleach. Drain cleaners may be either strongly acidic or strongly alkaline. Some tile cleaners are acidic.

Aside from water and ordinary laundry detergent, you should never mix chlorine bleach with anything unless you are specifically instructed to do so by a reliable authority. If you have questions, call a local public health authority, the poison control number in your area, or the manufacturer's toll-free number printed on the label of whatever product you are using.

ing effect, get expert advice. The suggestions given below are not suitable for such specific purposes. Household chlorine bleach does not kill every microorganism, and it works at different speeds against different types. Used properly for ordinary household purposes, however, it is not only effective, it is also inexpensive, versatile, and safe for food-contact surfaces, most objects in the home, and the environment. You can buy it at supermarkets, hardware stores, home centers, and some drugstores and sundry stores.

Like many other disinfectants, chlorine bleach solutions that contain more than 200 parts per million (ppm) of available chlorine (about one tablespoon per gallon) are toxic. Chlorine-bleach solutions are corrosive, and irritating to the skin. Carefully follow instructions for the use of chlorine bleach. Store it in a safe place, locked out of the reach of children. Never store chlorine bleach in any bottle other than the one it comes in from the store, and never store any other substance in an old bleach bottle. Doing so may mislead someone into thinking that a bottle does not contain bleach when it does. Familiarize yourself with the safety instructions on the product label, including instructions about what to do in case of accidental ingestion. Always observe this caution: *do not mix chlorine bleach with acids, ammonia, or acid- or ammonia-containing products. Doing so will produce a toxic gas or other dangerous reaction.*

Most commercial preparations of sodium hypochlorite, such as Clorox, are 5.25 percent solutions, but some are lower and some are as high as 6 percent. All the instructions for sanitizing given below presuppose a 5.25 percent sodium hypochlorite solution. Do not fall into the error of thinking that undiluted bleach is a stronger and better sanitizer than diluted bleach. Rely on the directions provided by the manufacturers.

A chlorine-bleach solution acts quickly but, like all disinfectants, it acts against different microorganisms at different speeds. The presence of organic matter—blood, food, or other plant or animal matter—will inactivate it.

If you wish to sanitize food-contact surfaces in your home, chlorine bleach is recommended by the USDA and the FDA because it does not accumulate and leaves behind no active or toxic residue. It quickly breaks down, leaving ordinary salt and water behind. (This is one reason why those who are concerned with the overuse of disinfectants in the home recommend using chlorine bleach to disinfect.) Used according to instructions, chlorine bleach is a good choice for disinfecting your baby's bleach-safe equipment, toys, bottles, and utensils on those occasions when you think this advisable. If, after sanitizing with bleach and then allowing surfaces to dry, you detect chlorine odors, the most likely explanation is that the solution was too strong. But we have a remarkable ability to smell chlorine. According to the USDA, we can detect 0.01 ppm of chlorine; our ability to smell chlorine is more than five thousand times greater than our ability to smell ammonia. The bleach smell does not mean that the object or surface is not safe to use.

After six months or so, undiluted household bleach may no longer be fresh and should not be used for sanitizing or disinfection. After nine to twelve months, bleach kept for laundering purposes should also be replaced.

Note: For sanitizing and disinfection, use only "regular" or "plain" bleach. Wear plastic gloves when cleaning with bleach solutions to protect sensitive skin. When in doubt, test materials before using bleach solutions on them. Do not splash bleach on clothes, furniture, wood floors, rugs, or other surfaces.

Instructions for Disinfecting Non-Food-Contact Surfaces with Bleach

When you are cleaning *hard non-food-contact surfaces,* you can clean and disinfect in one step by adding bleach to detergent and water. (Do not clean and sanitize food-contact surfaces in one step. *Follow the instructions on sanitizing food-contact surfaces* on page 173.) This type of solution is highly effective for a variety of chores. A leading manufacturer of household bleach gives the following suggestions for making a solution that will clean, disinfect, and deodorize:

$^3/_4$ cup of bleach

1 gallon of warm water

1 tablespoon of powdered laundry detergent

Using solution, wash surface or object clean. Then keep it wet with the solution for at least five minutes. Rinse and let dry.

You may use the foregoing cleaning and disinfecting solution in your bathroom, kitchen, and nursery, on all the hard surfaces, substances, and objects listed below. (But avoid letting bleach solution contact metal fixtures.)

Bathtubs

Showers

Sinks

Porcelain

Ceramic tile (be careful with dark or colored grout)

Marble

Plastic

Fiberglass

Enamel-painted woodwork and walls

Latex-enamel-painted woodwork and walls

Baby furniture such as cribs, changing tables, high chairs; washable toys

Plastic mattress covers and plastic crib bumpers

Stoves

Diaper pails (deodorizes too)

Refrigerators, both interior and exterior (deodorizes too)

Indoor garbage cans (deodorizes too)

The manufacturer also gives the following suggestions for cleaning, deodorizing, and disinfecting a variety of surfaces and in the home:

- Disinfecting and cleaning floors of vinyl, linoleum, no-wax, ceramic tile: Mop with a solution of 3/4 cup of bleach per gallon of water. Keep wet for at least five minutes. Rinse with clear water and air-dry.

- Cleaning hairbrushes and combs: Immerse in a solution of 3/4 cup bleach and one gallon of warm water for at least five minutes. Rinse. Let air-dry; stand brushes on bristles.
- Sanitizing and deodorizing cat litter boxes: First, empty and wash with sudsy water; rinse. Then wash with a solution of 3/4 cup of bleach per gallon of water. Keep the surface wet for at least five minutes. Then rinse.
- Pet food and water bowls: Wash with sudsy water and rinse. Then fill with a solution of 1 tablespoon of bleach per gallon of water. Let stand for two minutes. Drain and air-dry.
- Sanitizing and deodorizing outdoor garbage cans: First, empty and wash with sudsy water; rinse. Then wash out with a solution of 3/4 cup of bleach in a gallon of water. Keep the surface wet for at least five minutes. Then rinse again.
- Bleaching and sanitizing the laundry: See chapter 27.
- Deodorizing and whitening diapers: See chapter 27.
- Disinfecting and deodorizing kitchen cloths (bleachable dishcloths and synthetic sponges) and the sink at the same time: See chapter 13, pages 175–76.
- Flowerpots and planters: Wash thoroughly with soapy water and rinse. Then soak for five minutes in a solution of 3/4 cup of bleach and 1 gallon of water. Rinse again.
- Freshening cut flowers: Add 1/4 teaspoon of bleach to each quart of cold water in the flower vase. This will help your cut flowers stay fresh longer by killing bacteria that would otherwise begin to rot them.
- Cleaning and deodorizing vases: To remove stains and odors from a flower vase, wash it with warm, sudsy water, rinse, then fill with a solution of 3/4 cup of bleach per 1 gallon of water and let stand five minutes. Rinse.

Heat. With heat, you can sterilize, but if you have any need for sterile objects or surfaces, you should consult a doctor or other appropriate expert to learn how to do it properly for your purposes. Boiling, baking, steaming in a pressure cooker, and burning are all means often available at home, but you must know what temperature the item must reach, what means of heating will reach it, and how long the item must be kept at that temperature. It is not necessarily easy to do. High temperatures can be required for long time periods, how long depending on your goals, what you are disinfecting, and whether you are using wet or dry heat. Heat sterilization is suitable only for objects that will not be damaged by heat.

Hydrogen peroxide. Hydrogen peroxide (H_2O_2) works against many bacteria, viruses, and molds. It is usually sold in a 3 to 5 percent solution. It is generally used as a household bleach and antiseptic. See page 317.

Hydrogen peroxide is usually purchased at a drugstore. It should be stored in a dark bottle to preserve it. In nine months to a year, it may have become inactive. Test it by taking a small sample and adding to it, with an eyedropper, one drop of chlorine bleach. If it is active, it will bubble vigorously. (The reaction that will occur is this: $NaClO + H_2O_2 \rightarrow Na+ + Cl- + H_2O + O_2$.)

Iodophors. Iodophors are iodine-containing compounds that are used for disinfection and sanitizing. (They are also used to make antiseptics.) They leave an active residue and dissipate slowly. Look for "iod- or "iodo-" in the list of ingredients. Because these compounds contain iodine, they may cause stains. They are only slightly corrosive, and they are only slightly affected by the presence of organic matter. They are an effective antibacterial.

Phenolic compounds. These include phenol (C_6H_5OH) and analogous compounds used as disinfectants. Pine oil is a phenol. You can buy phenols, such as Pine-Sol, in grocery stores. You can sometimes, but not always,

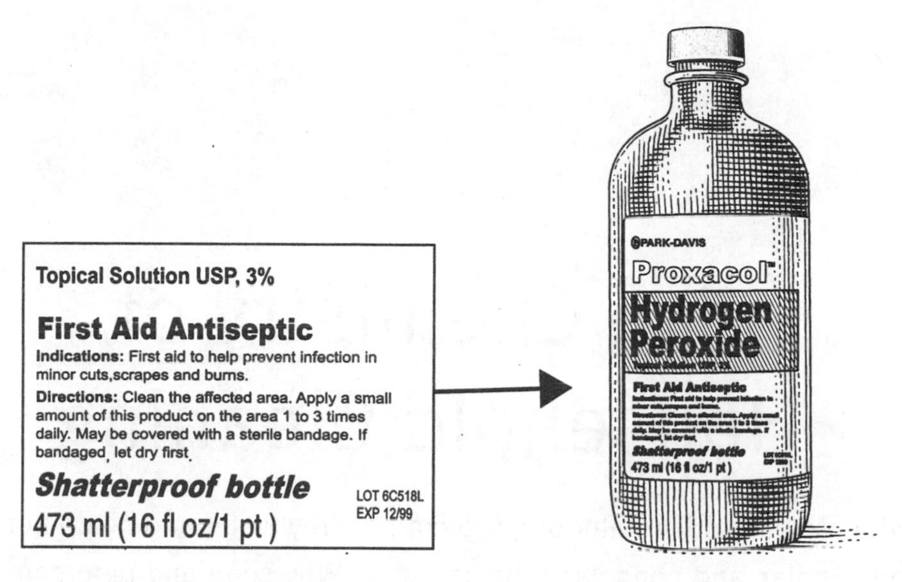

Household-strength (3%) hydrogen peroxide

tell that a product contains phenols or phenolic derivatives by looking on the label for chemical names that include the term "phenol"—for example, ortho-phenylphenol. Phenolic compounds leave a bacteriostatic (bacterial-growth-inhibiting) residue. They should not be used in a baby's room or on a baby's things, especially beds and bedding, or near a baby. Phenolics are also toxic to cats.

Quaternary ammonium compounds. Quaternary ammonium compounds (called "quats") are used in some laundry products, in some household and bathroom disinfectant cleaners, and in some mouthwashes and skin cleaners. They are low-level disinfectants that hospitals might use for sanitizing noncritical areas such as floors or walls. You can often tell whether a product contains quats by looking in the ingredient list for the names of chemicals ending in "-ium chloride" or "-ium bromide"—for example, cetyldimethylbenzyl-ammon*ium chloride* or cetylpyridin*ium chloride*. But there are exceptions. For example, alkyl dimethyl benzyl ammonium saccharinate is a type of quat.

Quats can be inactivated by soaps or detergents, but quats themselves are often used in cleaning products. They are not corrosive and are less affected by organic matter than are bleaches or certain other household sanitizers. Quats tend to leave an active residue. You can buy quats at drugstores or janitorial supply stores or in the supermarket in some disinfectant cleaning products.

Triclosan. Triclosan (trichlorohydroxy diphenyl ether), a phenolic derivative, is used in deodorant toilet cleaners and antibacterial soaps and hand soaps to kill bacteria on the skin and to control body odor. It is also used as the antimicrobial agent in many new antibacterial products, ranging from toys to chopping boards to bedding.

31

The Chemistry of Household Cleaning

When to use sudsy water or a solvent . . . Why water and oil do not mix: ionic, polar, and nonpolar substances . . . Why soap and detergent also work on oil and grease . . . Acids and alkalies, what pH means, list of pHs of common household substances . . . Homemade cleaners and recipes for making and using them . . . Abrasives

Readers who dislike anything technical may skip this chapter. But for those who can tolerate a short excursion into high school science, it contains much traditional household lore. If you are the sort of housekeeping beginner who has always wondered why you are supposed to be unable to keep house without white vinegar and baking soda, you can find here brief explanations of these and other highly useful snippets of household chemistry.

To clean your home confidently and successfully, it helps to understand why every household makes use of the same four basic types of chemical cleaning agents: soaps or detergents in water, solvents (such as dry-cleaning fluids), acids, and alkalies. (These categories can overlap.) A few simple chemical concepts explain why these are used for certain standard household purposes, and show why many of us continue to make occasional use of the recipes for homemade cleaners set forth in this chapter. Aside from the four basic types of chemical cleaning, household cleaning is also accomplished through scrubbing or abrasion (discussed briefly in this chapter), suction, and other means of physically removing dirt. See, for example, chapter 34, "Vacuuming, Sweeping, and Dusting."

Some household chemicals are hazardous. See the cautions in chapter 64, "Poisons, Hazardous Substances, and Proper Disposal of Hazardous Household Wastes."

When to Use Sudsy Water and When a Solvent

You cannot clean anything greasy or oily with plain water. Grease and oil are not soluble in water. Most dirt on our bodies and clothes and much dirt in our homes—especially in kitchens—is combined with grease or oil. To clean grease and oil, you can use either soaps and detergents, mixed in water to make a sudsy solution, or a solvent-based cleaner. Because solvents are usually more toxic, more expensive, more odorous, less versatile, and flammable, soaps and detergents are what we try to use whenever possible on clothes, dishes, and other materials and surfaces in the home. We turn to solvents for cleaning things that cannot withstand water, hot water, or soaps or detergents.

Why Water and Oil Do Not Mix: Ionic, Polar, and Nonpolar Substances. Dirt, foods, cleaners, and other substances in the home can be divided into three chemical categories: ionic, polar, and nonpolar. Ionic compounds are those whose smallest units are charged particles called "ions," such as ordinary salt and hydrogen peroxide (H_2O_2). When salt (sodium chloride, NaCl) dissolves in water, its chemical units dissociate into one positively charged sodium ion (Na+) and one negatively charged chloride ion (Cl−). Polar substances are composed of molecules that have different charges at each end. For example, water molecules, which are polar, have different charges, negative and positive, at their sides or ends. Nonpolar molecules, such as those that make up olive oil, do not. Because they are polar, water molecules bond tightly to one another: the positively charged hydrogen atoms of one molecule are attracted to the negatively charged oxygen atoms of another. This is why water, unlike olive oil, beads on flat surfaces and has a high surface tension (as though a skin on its surface holds the drop of water together). Some other examples of familiar substances made of ionic, polar, and nonpolar molecules include:

Ionic: salt, baking soda ($NaHCO_3$), hydrogen peroxide

Polar: water, alcohol (wine, spirits, rubbing alcohol), lemon juice, vinegar, chlorine bleach

Nonpolar: grease, oils such as cooking oils, fat from meats, furniture oils, dry-cleaning fluids, mineral spirits (paint thinners), floor waxes

As a rule, substances made of polar molecules do not mix with substances made of nonpolar molecules. And generally speaking, the more polar a substance is, the more soluble it is in water, and the more nonpolar it is, the less soluble in water. When grease or oil is mixed with water (for example, when olive oil is mixed with vinegar, which is mostly water), the water bonds so tightly to itself that it forces the grease or oil molecules to form separate globules; they don't mix. Nonpolar substances are also considerably less effective at dissolving ionic compounds such as salt, because they do not attract the charged Na+ and Cl- ions away from one another. Salt, for example, will not dissolve in olive oil—one more reason to put a little vinegar on the salad

But nonpolar substances are effective solvents for one another; to put it in other words, nonpolar substances dissolve in other nonpolar substances. So dry-cleaning fluids are good for removing body oils and grease splatters from clothes, and you can remove wax with mineral spirits.

Why Soap and Detergent Also Work on Oil and Grease. Soap and detergents are surfactants. Surfactants reduce the surface tension of water. This causes the water to spread and to wet objects rather than bead up on them; when surfactants are mixed with water, oil and grease in the water are emulsified—they stay mixed or spread throughout the water in tiny droplets. The explanation for this is that surfactants' molecules have long, complicated hydrocarbon chains, one end of which is polar and the other end of which is nonpolar. The polar end is attracted to water: it is water-loving or hydrophilic. The nonpolar end is soluble in oil and grease and repelled by water: it is water-hating or hydrophobic. The nonpolar ends of these sur-

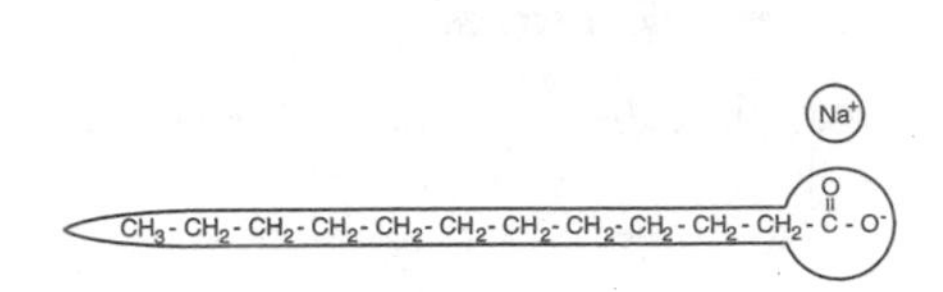

Surfactant molecule

Surfactant molecules clustered around a piece of oily dirt, their polar heads in the water and nonpolar tails in the oily dirt.

factant molecules form a kind of circle-barrier around a droplet of oil in water, with their water-insoluble ends next to the oil and the water-soluble ends away from it. When the oil is emulsified, the polar ends of the surfactant molecules keep the droplet suspended in the water and keep it from joining other oil droplets and separating into large globules. Thus it can be rinsed out of fabrics or off countertops with water.

Both soaps and detergents are, or contain, surfactants. Chemically, soaps and detergents are similar, but detergents—also called "synthetic detergents"—are made from petrochemicals. Soaps are produced by mixing animal or vegetable fats and oils with some strong alkali such as sodium hydroxide (caustic soda—NaOH) or potassium hydroxide (caustic potash—KOH). Hard soaps, such as bar soaps, are generally made with sodium hydroxide, and liquid soaps are usually made with potassium hydroxide. Soaps often contain many other ingredients—from moisturizers, abrasives, deodorants, and bactericides to perfumes. Soaps are now rarely used for laundry, although cleaning soaps such as Murphy Oil Soap remain in use.

Soap has been supplanted as queen of the laundry by synthetic detergents because soap causes a scum to form when used in hard water. Hard water contains calcium or magnesium ions that combine with the soap to form insoluble salts, or scum, which then is deposited on clothes in the washing machine or on bathroom tiles and bathtubs. It looks ugly, and it can be hard to dislodge. Soap also is problematic when it is used in the presence of acids, for they will render the soap inactive and create a different kind of scum. Skin and clothing often contain acids from the decomposition of perspiration or from food spills. Thus, the average load of laundry contains some acids, and these cause problems for laundry soap.

There are four types of detergents: anionic, nonionic, cationic, and amphoteric. Anionic detergents are the ordinary high-sudsing types generally used in laundry and all-purpose detergent products. Anionic detergents do essentially the same chemical job that soaps do, without causing hard-water scum to form. They are more powerful and less expensive than cationic or nonionic detergents. Unlike cationic and nonionic detergents, however, they can be partly deactivated by too-hard water. For this reason, alkaline substances are often added to anionic detergents (and to soaps, which are also anionic). The alkalies react with acids in the hard water and help the anionic detergents clean better, and, in the case of soap, also reduce scum formation. (Borax, which is an alkali often added for this reason, deodorizes and leaves a clean smell because it removes odor-causing acids.)

Nonionic detergents are used for low-sudsing laundry detergents and dishwasher detergents. They are effective in hard water and work well on most types of dirt, especially oily dirt. Some cationic surfactants are used in fabric softeners and fabric-softening detergents. All soaps and detergents are antibacterial to some extent. But certain cationic detergents—quaternary ammonium compounds, or "quats"—have a stronger antibacterial effect and, therefore, are used as sanitizers or disinfectants. Amphoteric detergents are mild and are widely used in shampoos and personal-care products, and in some household detergents.

Both soaps and detergents work better in warmer water and with the aid of mechanical action, whether muscle power applied in scrubbing or rubbing on a washboard or the agitation of a washing machine. Despite the advantages of detergents, some people prefer soaps because detergents are made from petroleum products, a nonrenewable resource, unlike the fats and alkalies from which soaps are made. It is not true that soaps are necessarily "milder" than detergents. Some soaps are harsh, and some detergents quite mild. See "Detergents and soaps, mild," on pages 322–24.

Laundry detergents marked "heavy-duty" or "all-purpose" are perfectly good all-purpose cleaners for the household. These are detergents that contain various "builders"—substances that enhance the detergent solution's alkalinity and ability to emulsify grease and oil or inactivate water hardness. Phosphates are the builders that have most commonly been used, but they are now banned in many states—a decision the soap and detergent industry is still protesting.* See "Phosphates," below. Light-duty detergents, such as dishwashing liquids, are those that contain no builders. They are milder. Mild, generally, means neutral or near-neutral in pH. Strongly alkaline solutions burn the eyes and are harsh on the skin and on many household materials as well. Shampoos that do not burn the eyes have a pH between 6.0 and 7.0.

Acids and Alkalies

The efficacy of a household cleaner for any given purpose is in great part a function of its pH, the number that expresses how acidic or alkaline it is. Which substances clean which kinds of dirt, and what cleaners are safe for what materials, are strongly affected by pH. The pH scale runs from 0 to 14, with 7 as neutral. The higher the number over 7, the more alkaline the solution is. The lower the number under 7, the more acidic the solution is. Pure water is neutral, with a pH of about 7, but rainwater is slightly acidic, with a pH of about 6. (Pure water, by the way, should not be confused with potable water or plain tap water. Drinkable tap water and bottled water—unless the bottled water is distilled—contain many minerals and other substances in addition to H_2O.)

A water soluble substance is alkaline if a solution of the substance in water contains a greater concentration of hydroxyl ions (OH^-) than of hydrogen ions (H^+). It is acidic if, when mixed with water, the resulting solution contains more hydrogen ions than hydroxyl ions. Because most dirt and body soils are slightly acidic, most good cleaners are at least slightly alkaline. The term "base" is a synonym for "alkali," and "basic" is a synonym for "alkaline." (I use "alkali" and "alkaline," however, to avoid confusion.)

*Automatic dishwashing detergents are exempted from the ban on phosphates because of the difficulty the industry has had in attempting to formulate an effective nonphosphate product. However, some "ultra" versions of automatic dishwashing detergents do not contain phosphates.

Alkalies make it possible to clean without too much rubbing. Soap and soap-containing products and detergents are alkaline and perform well only in an alkaline solution. Automatic dishwashing detergents, all-purpose laundry soaps and detergents and hard surface cleaners (liquid or granules) are usually alkaline to one degree or another, but hand dishwashing detergents and "mild" detergents are neutral or close to neutral because more alkaline solutions are too harsh on the skin. (Some hand dishwashing liquids advertised as good for "sensitive skin" are actually slightly acidic.) These milder alkalies nonetheless work well sometimes because you add a little muscle power to the chemical power they provide. Because soaps and detergents form alkaline solutions, acids are sometimes added to shampoos to lower the pH to prevent them from burning your eyes. You sometimes see such products advertised as "pH balanced."

Alkalies, such as ammonia, are good at cleaning acidic, fatty, and oily dirt, which is why laundry products and kitchen cleaners tend to be alkaline. Because alkalies readily remove oily dirt, they are not good for cleaning surfaces painted with oil-based paints. They can remove the oil from the paint, causing it to dry, crack, or peel. They can also darken or otherwise damage aluminum.

Acids can remove soap scum and hard-water deposits (calcium carbonate). Many bathroom cleaners, therefore, are mildly acidic. Acids—such as lemon juice or white vinegar—will also remove discoloration on aluminum, brass, bronze, and copper; rust on iron; and rust stains. Strong acids can damage clothing, leather, some metals, ceramic tiles, and other materials in the home. We enjoy eating many foods that are weakly acidic, such as tomato sauces and salad dressings containing vinegar. *But strong acids are extremely toxic if ingested.*

Both alkalies and acids are found in the household in different degrees of weakness and strength. *Strong alkalies and acids can cause serious injury to skin and eyes, and if swallowed can cause serious injury or death. Do not induce vomiting after accidental ingestion of such substances, as they can cause grave damage in the process of being ejected from the body. Instead, immediately call your local poison control center and follow the instructions you are given.*

Here is a list of various foods and substances commonly found in the home, arranged according to pH, beginning with the strongest alkalies and ending with the strongest acids:

Very Strong Alkalies:

13 Lye, caustic soda, (NaOH—sodium hydroxide) (found in some oven cleaners and drain cleaners, e.g., Drano)

Caustic potash (KOH)

11.8 Washing soda, sal soda, or sodium carbonate (Na_2CO_3) (added to detergents as a builder and to cleaners and presoaks to increase alkalinity; used in some drain cleaners)

Moderate Alkalies:

11 Household ammonia (ammonia gas [NH_3] in a 5 to 10 percent water solution) (a grease cutter, wax stripper, and general soil remover)

9–11 Detergents, soaps, window cleaners, mildew cleaners, most bathroom scouring powders, liquid cleaners, builders

9.28 Borax (a white crystalline powder)

Mild Alkalies:

8.35 1 percent solution of baking soda, or sodium bicarbonate ($NaHCO_3$), and water

8.3 Seawater

8.1 Soap

9 percent solution of baking soda and water

7.8 Eggs

7.5 Blood

Neutrals

7 pure water, milk, sugar water, salt-water

Fabuloso All-Purpose Liquid Cleaner

Orvus WA Paste

Ultra Palmolive Pots and Pans

Ultra Palmolive Antibacterial

Dawn and Ultra Dawn

Very Mild Acids:

6+ Some dishwashing liquids for "sensitive skin"

5–6 Rain in unpolluted environments

5.1 Seltzer water or carbonated water (contains carbonic acid [H_2CO_3], which breaks down and gives off carbon dioxide as fizz)

Cream of tartar in water

5 Boric acid solution (H_3BO_3) (used in eyewash)

4.2 Tomatoes

4 Rain in polluted environments (can be as low as 2)

4 Orange juice

Moderately Strong Acids:

3.1 White vinegar (5 percent acetic acid)

3 Carbonated beverages, apples

2.3 Lemon juice, lime juice (contain citric acid)

2.1 Citric acid

Very Strong Acids:

1.1 Sulfuric acid (NaHSO4) (found in many dry toilet-bowl cleaners)

0.8 Hydrochloric acid, or muriatic acid (HCl) (found in many liquid toilet-bowl cleaners)

Oxalic acid ($H_2C_2O_2$) (effective as a rust remover, but toxic; contained in some scouring powders recommended for rust removal, such as Zud and Barkeeper's Friend)

Homemade Cleaners

Homemade cleaning solutions have become a subject of widespread interest, and they can in many cases be convenient, effective, and economical. They are also, usually, "green"—in other words, environmentally favorable or nontoxic. Unfortunately, they are often less effective than commercial products. To replace the cleaning power of the stronger chemical you choose not to use, you must often provide additional muscle power or waiting time or both.

Homemade-cleaner recipes found in newspapers and magazines are sometimes unreliable. For example, if you contemplate using ammonia and water to clean windows because ammonia, an alkali, will cut grease and dirt, does it make sense that you should add vinegar too? Vinegar is acidic and will tend to neutralize the ammonia. Yet recipes for window-cleaning liquids that recommend doing just that often appear in prominent publications. I have seen one recipe that calls for mixing ammonia, baking soda, and vinegar—as though the three great home-cleaning agents must be triply powerful when combined. But this is not how cleaners work. A mixture of baking soda and vinegar works as a gentle drain cleaner, however, because the mechanical action of the fizzing (caused by the release of carbon dioxide gas—see the recipe given below) in the drain helps remove clogs.

Several cautions should be kept in mind when you mix your own cleaners:

Do not mix chlorine bleach with acids, alkalies, ammonia, or substances that contain them. Such mixtures produce a toxic and hazardous gas or other dangerous reaction. (See page 432.) In fact, avoid mixing toxic ingredients with anything else unless you have consulted a reliable authority. (Manufacturers will be glad to share safety information about their products with you.)

Do not mix more than you are going to use in the near future, for a solution may lose efficacy over time. When using chlorine bleach as a sanitizer, mix it fresh on the day you are going to use it.

Store toxic and flammable materials in carefully, clearly, and accurately labeled containers, and store them in safe places out of the reach of children. People in your home might otherwise be misled as to their contents, and you yourself might forget what is in an old bottle at the back of a shelf. *Never use food containers for this purpose.* Not only may chemicals in your solution react with residue in the containers, but someone might mistake it for food.

Follow all safety instructions on labels.

Always ensure adequate ventilation when mixing toxic, flammable, or strong-smelling substances.

All-Purpose Disinfectant Cleaner

Recipes for all-purpose disinfectant cleaners are given on pages 433–34.

Mild All-Purpose Cleaner

Mix 4 tablespoons of baking soda with a quart of warm water. Wipe with a soft cloth or sponge dipped in the solution. Rinse with clear water. This is good for wiping out the refrigerator and the oven (when the latter is not heavily soiled with baked-on food), as it both cleans light soil and deodorizes. It will not remove heavier dirt.

Strong All-Purpose Cleaner

1. Add 1 tablespoon each of ammonia and liquid laundry detergent to a pint of water.
2. Add 1/2 cup of washing soda (see page 440) to 1 gallon of warm water.

Either of these cleaners can be used in kitchens and bathrooms and on wrought iron, appliances, ovens, etc. Neither should be used on fiberglass or aluminum.

Mild, Gently Abrasive Cleaner

Add enough drops of water to baking soda to form a paste. This can be used to remove crayon from painted walls and easily scratched plastic surfaces.

Window Cleaner

Most commercial window cleaners contain a combination of water, ethyl or isopropyl alcohol, and ammonia. They contain no abrasives, because they might scratch glass. They contain no soap or detergent that might leave a film or residue. The ammonia cuts dirt and oil. The alcohol cleans polar soils and helps the water evaporate quickly so that the windows are not streaked. You can make a good window cleaner yourself with this recipe: 45 percent water, 45 percent rubbing alcohol, and 10 percent household ammonia.[1] Exact measurements are not important. Put it in a clearly marked spray bottle. This is quite as good as any product you can buy.

Cleaner for Regular Drain Maintenance Solution

Do not use these recipes for clogged drains.

1. To clean and deodorize, pour 1/2 to 1 cup of baking soda down the drain. Then slowly drip warm water into it. If you add the water too quickly, the baking soda will be washed away before it has a chance to do any cleaning. Do this every week or two to help prevent clogs from forming.
2. This cleaning recipe is stronger. Add 1/2 cup of washing soda to a gallon of warm water. Pour hot water down the drain. Then pour down the washing-soda solution; then pour hot water down again.
3. This recipe deodorizes, sanitizes, and cleans. Mix 3/4 cup regular chlorine bleach, 1 gallon warm water, 1 tablespoon powdered laundry detergent. Fill your sink with the solution; then drain. Rinse with plain water.

Drain-Clog Cleaner

Do not use these recipes if there is standing water in the sink or tub. See chapter 42, "Pipes and Drains."

1. Pour 1/2 to 1 cup of baking soda down the drain; then slowly pour 1/2 to 1 cup of white vinegar after it. (The fizzing reflects this reaction: $NaHCO_3 + HC_2H_3O_2 \rightarrow CO_2 + NaC_2H_3O_2 + H_2O$.) Cover the drain if possible, and let sit for five minutes. Follow with a gallon of boiling water. The source of this recipe, the Extension Service of Mississippi State University, in cooperation with the United States Department of Agriculture, explains that the vinegar and baking soda break down fatty acids from grease and other food wastes into soap and glycerine, so that the clog can wash down the drain. (I would add that if the clog persists, you should try using your plunger after pouring down the liquids, and if this does not work, repeat the whole process.)
2. The Plumbing-Heating-Cooling Information Bureau recommends for moderate clogs that you pour boiling water with a few teaspoons of ammonia down the drain. The water-and-ammonia solution will break up grease, and you can then use your plunger to loosen it.

Lime and Mineral Deposit Remover.

Because lime and mineral deposits are made of calcium and other salts that dissolve in acid, they will soften with a white-vinegar poultice. Soak a rag or paper towel in white vinegar and leave it around the faucet or other trouble spot for about an hour. The deposits should then be soft enough to remove.

Aluminum Pot Cleaner.

Fill pot with water and add 2 tablespoons of cream of tartar or one-half cup of white vinegar per quart of water. Bring the solution to a boil; then let it simmer for ten minutes. Wash and dry as usual.

> **DRAIN CLEANERS**
>
> Most commercial drain cleaners are made of a concentrated solution of NaOH—lye—and a little aluminum. The aluminum produces bubbling, and when the NaOH dissolves, it produces heat; heat melts the grease that blocks drains and the bubbles agitate it. The NaOH reacts with the grease to form a soap and eats away hair. These products are highly toxic and corrosive and must be used with great caution. They can damage drainpipes. Follow the instructions on the labels.

Stainless Steel Pot Cleaner

Fill pot with water and add 1/2 cup of white vinegar. Bring to a boil; then simmer for an hour. This will remove mineral deposits.

Chrome and Stainless-Steel Cleaner

You can clean mineral deposits off chrome and stainless steel by wiping them with a soft cloth dipped in undiluted white vinegar.

See also chapter 45, "Metals."

Oven Cleaner

This procedure is *not* for self-cleaning or non-stick ovens. Ordinary ovens, however, can be cleaned of most debris with it. First wet the oven surface; then sprinkle it with baking soda. Rub it with fine steel wool. Wipe off the scum with a damp cloth or sponge. Repeat if necessary. Rinse well and dry. (To rinse, wipe repeatedly—until the surface is squeaky clean—with a cloth rinsed in clear, warm water.) A thick, well-burned-on mass is not likely to respond to this method, but you can often get most of the oven clean this way and save the commercial oven cleaner made of strong chemicals for the part that remains.

Borax

Borax is a mild alkali that will deodorize carpets, litter boxes, and laundry. It is used as a detergent booster. It cuts grease. It deodorizes by reacting with odor-causing acids. This substance can be toxic if ingested, and should be stored and handled carefully.

Trisodium Phosphate (TSP)

This phosphate is an effective cleaner and is often used as a builder. It can be used for general household purposes. Painters like to use it to wash surfaces in preparation for painting because it rinses away completely, leaving no residue. See also "Trisodium Phosphate" in the glossary at the end of chapter 21.

Abrasives

Abrasion cleans by physically grinding off the unwanted dirt. Abrasives usually consist of small particles of hard minerals, such as calcite, feldspar, quartz, pumice, talc, and sand or silicates. They are used in soaps, cleansers, and cleaning tools to add mechanical cleaning and polishing power to chemical power. Abrasives are also used by themselves—rottenstone, whiting, and pumice, for example. Abrasives used in most households include sandpaper, steel wool, and abrasive mesh cleaners made of plastic, nylon, and metal. In general, the larger and harder the particle or material, the harsher the abrasion, and the greater the possibility of scratching or dulling softer surfaces to which abrasion is applied. Mesh cleaners made of nylon or plastic are mildly abrasive. Fine steel-wool is moderately abrasive. Metal brushes and mesh cleaners and coarse steel wool are strongly abrasive.

Always choose the most gentle abrasive that will do the job. Harsh abrasives will harm glass, ceramics, porcelain, plastics, vitreous enamel, nonstick and other cookware, painted surfaces, plated and highly polished metals, and many other household surfaces.

Scouring powders unite chemical cleaners with abrasives, and sometimes both are harsh. In strong powders, such as Zud for example, oxalic acid may be an ingredient.

PHOSPHATES

Phosphates, such as trisodium phosphate and sodium triphosphate, are salts that form alkaline solutions in water. They are added to detergents as builders because, like borax, they inactivate acids. This prevents the formation of one kind of scum and helps soaps and detergents clean more effectively.

The first effective detergents for the laundry contained phosphates, and it is still true that phosphate detergents clean better. Environmental concerns, however, have resulted in restrictions on their use. Phosphates that get into the waterways cause eutrophication. That is, they cause water plants to grow so excessively that they clog the waterways. Then plants on the bottom die for lack of sunlight, rot, and in rotting use up all the oxygen in the water. Without oxygen, the water cannot support life and becomes useless. Eventually the pond, lake, or stream itself succumbs. (Fertilizer runoff is a major source of continuing phosphate pollution.)

TOILET-BOWL CLEANERS

Most toilet-bowl cleaners contain strong acids because the discolorations and scale buildup in toilets usually consist of hard-water deposits composed mostly of calcium carbonate ($CaCO_3$), which is dissolved in acids. Solid bowl cleaners tend to contain sodium hydrogen sulfate ($NaHSO_4$). The liquid types usually contain hydrochloric acid (HCl). *Never mix these cleaners with chlorine bleach.* These cleaners will also remove rust stains from the toilet bowl.

In addition to acid, some toilet-bowl cleaners contain bubbling agents, such as $NaHCO_3$, to help break up the scale, but also to make them look like powerful cleaners in the eyes of those who do not know that acid, not bubbling, is doing the real work. The blue color that some manufacturers add is also just there for appearance's sake. Blue looks clean to many people.

BAKING SODA

Sodium bicarbonate ($NaHCO_3$), or baking soda, is a white crystalline powder with chemical and physical properties that give it capabilities for cleaning, deodorizing, leavening, buffering, fire extinguishing—even toothbrushing.

It cuts dirt and grease because it is mildly alkaline, reacting with fatty acids to form compounds that are mild detergents (as stronger alkalies do less gently). It effervesces in water and fizzes in vinegar, enabling it to lift soil. A gentle abrasive, when worked into a paste with a little water, it makes a mild scouring powder. Some of it dissolves to make an alkaline cleaning solution and some gently abrades the surface being cleaned.

As a deodorizer, it works neither by perfuming or masking odors nor by absorbing them. It chemically neutralizes odors. Pleasant odors are neutral in pH. Most unpleasant odors are caused by strong acids (e.g., sour milk) or strong alkalies (e.g., rotten fish). Baking soda reacts with the odor molecules to bring them to a more neutral pH. Baking soda works best as a deodorizer in a confined space—for example, a closet or a refrigerator. The deodorant effect is also present when baking soda is dissolved in water, so you can use it as a laundry or cleaning deodorizer too. It works in shoes (sprinkle in dry), on your body, and even in your mouth as a mouthwash (gargle with soda and water). Baking soda can be used for these and many other cleaning and deodorizing jobs:

Chrome

Drains and garbage disposals

Porcelain enamel

Tiles

Walls and woodwork

Coffee pots

Refrigerators

Diaper soaks

Baking soda is a buffering agent, which means that it tends to cause acids to become more alkaline and alkalies more acidic, balancing out at 8.1 (or slightly alkaline). It also causes the buffered solution to resist changing from this pH.

Baking soda is highly effective against class B fires (for example, grease fires) and also effective against class C fires (electrical fires), but should never be used on class A fires (wood, paper, and cloth) because the powder will only scatter the burning material. It is a good fire extinguisher for class B and C fires because, when heated, it breaks down to give off carbon dioxide, water, and sodium carbonate:

$$2\,NaHCO_3 \rightarrow Na_2CO_3 + H_2O + CO_2$$

CO_2 is more dense than air, so it crowds out the fire's source of oxygen and smothers it. The water cools and smothers the fire, and the sodium carbonate residue aids in smothering it.

Most powdered cleansers are milder now than they were years ago, and several have come out in different formulae—nonabrasive, gently abrasive, and strongly abrasive—so look carefully at the label so you can be sure to buy the kind of formula that suits your purpose. If you have trouble determining whether or not a powdered abrasive is gentle or harsh, you can sometimes tell by reading its recommended uses. If it is recommended for use on fiberglass, for example, it is likely to be gentle; fiberglass will readily scratch. Dry baking soda is an abrasive gentle enough for fiberglass.

Among scouring powders, a paste of baking soda and water is the gentlest. Bon Ami and Soft Scrub are considered gentle abrasives. Regular Comet and Ajax are moderately abrasive. Zud and Barkeeper's Friend are quite abrasive.

32

Aprons, Rags, and Mops

Dressing for the occasion, clothes for cleaning . . . Rags, cloth rags vs. paper towels . . . The art of rag making, ragbags . . . Tools for cleaning . . . Cleaning liquids and powders, polishes and waxes

Every home can use a cleaning closet, a place that can be closed up and rendered childproof, in which to keep cleaning paraphernalia: detergents, scouring powders, bathroom cleansers, polishes, and waxes; rags, mops, brushes, and brooms; a plunger; cleaning clothes; and other tools, cleaning substances, and conveniences used for regular or emergency cleaning. When you open a well-stocked, tidy closet containing exactly what you need, housecleaning feels doable and it is easier to get started. It is also easier to stay well stocked when everything you have is kept in one place; you can scan the shelves and readily see what is in short supply or lacking. You can tape a list of basic supplies inside the door and check it against the closet's contents. If you cannot keep all such things in one closet, you might have two separate storage spots—one for tools and one for cleaning substances.

Materials for washing dishes and cleaning the food-preparation areas of the kitchen are dealt with separately in chapter 9.

Dressing for the Occasion: Cleaning Garb

When you clean the house, remove rings, bracelets, and any watches but the most utilitarian. Wear comfortable shoes, with support and cushioning and nonslip soles. If you have a special pair devoted to this purpose, you can keep them in your cleaning closet.

Although many of us wear aprons when we cook, I know hardly anyone who puts one on to do housework, even though this is a useful, clothes-friendly, and laundry-reducing habit. Instead we wear old clothes to perform potentially dirty chores. A friend keeps an assortment of oversized T-shirts in her cleaning closet, and uses them as smocks over her clothes when she cleans. But nothing beats a real apron or smock with several pockets for carrying coins, paper clips, pins, screws, and other small objects back and forth, for wiping your hands on without remorse, for keeping your midriff free of oily stains and grime, for sticking pins in, and the like. When you take it off, you can sit down to lunch or tea in a clean shirt without changing.

Pictures of 1950s housewives vacuuming in pearls, high heels, and an apron seem funny now, but probably only because we have forgotten the context. My grandmothers always insisted on doing housework nicely dressed (although not in pearls and high heels). Whatever their differences, they each donned and doffed the same kinds of aprons according to the same housekeeping and social patterns. They wore plain white muslin ones for everyday. The apron went on first thing in the morning and came off when they ate and when the day's housework was done. These work aprons, however, were for the eyes of the family only. They were removed before the door was opened to admit anyone else. Fancy, frilled, and embroidered aprons came out when there was cooking to be done in the presence of company, but even these would be removed for answering the door. Thus the aprons were used to protect a distinction between the private and public part of home life.

You may wish to tie a scarf around your hair or wear a cap, as everyone would have done in the days before showers and detangling hair conditioners, when women's hair might be a couple of feet long and washing it was a once-weekly ordeal.

Besides a covering for your clothing, you will need rubber or plastic gloves for any job that requires you to immerse your hands in liquids, for any potentially dirty job, and for any job involving strong chemicals. You might find it useful to keep a box of disposable plastic gloves in your cleaning cabinet.

A dust mask is one part of a cleaning ensemble that no one used until recently. For dusty jobs—cleaning a long-neglected attic, getting all the ashes out of the fireplace, raking leaves in the yard—wear a dust mask to keep airborne debris out of your mouth and nose. A well-fitting face mask is doubly important for asthmatics and others who are allergic. Have some goggles in the cleaning closet, too, for keeping dust or fumes out of your eyes when you are doing especially rough chores, such as cleaning the fireplace or manually cleaning an oven.

When doing your weekly cleaning, it is a good idea to keep the windows open as much as you can, so you will need to dress to accommodate the weather. (Ventilating the rooms is as important to the cleaning as anything else you do.) A loose, launderable sweater or sweatshirt that lets you move but can go under your smock is another useful item to have in your cleaning closet.

Rags

Cloth vs. Paper. For most purposes, rags are better than sponges or paper towels. Cloth cleans better than disposable materials and is far easier to work with. It is hard to know whether cloth or disposables offer the more environmentally correct solution, but I vote in favor of cloth. Worn-out bath towels are better than anything else for big spills, and small towels of thin terry, cotton knit, or other soft, absorbent cloth are good for small spills. Paper towels are inconvenient (and expensive) for big spills, which might absorb entire rolls. A sponge or mop will have you wiping and squeezing a few dozen times and will be harder to clean or launder than old towels or rags. But you can just cover a spill with an old towel or two that you have reserved for dirty jobs, and the spill is soaked up. Then launder the towels. Usually you can launder a lot of rags and cleaning materials together.

Rags are much preferable to paper towels for hard jobs because they do not disintegrate when you scrub with them and they hold much more liquid. They are also superior to sponges for difficult jobs. You cannot feel through sponges with your fingers well enough to know whether a surface is free of bumps of hardened food or other matter. You cannot apply finger and nail pressure through a sponge so easily. And you would poke holes through paper towels if you applied pressure when using them. Rags are more sanitary than sponges.

The Art of Rag Making; Ragbags. Make distinctions among your towels, cloths, and rags. A fundamental rule of housecleaning is that separate things are used for cleaning or wiping dishes, kitchen sinks, counters and tabletops, floors, bathroom tubs and sinks, and people. Except for those to be used on the kitchen floor, moreover, cloths and rags to be used in the kitchen should generally be stored in the kitchen, not in the ragbag in the general cleaning closet. Keep different sets of rags for doing dirty jobs and for lighter, cleaner jobs—for example, old, thin terry cloth for washing floors and soft, white flannel for dusting wood and china. Old bath and kitchen towels, T-shirts, flannel sheets and pajamas, and soft knits of sorts all make good rags. Any nonlinting, absorbent, soft, white or *absolutely* colorfast cloth will do.

Cut rags to convenient sizes for your hand and purposes. Keep some big towels for big spills, and some soft white squares for dusting. If you cut the rags with pinking shears, they are less likely to fray at the edges.

Store your different types of rags in different ragbags or boxes, and keep plentiful supplies for all purposes. When you dirty one while cleaning or dusting, you want to be able to reach for the next without hesitation. When choosing materials to make rags, avoid or remove buttons, studs, zippers, and even thick and lumpy seams, such as the flat-felled seams on denims. These can harm surfaces and are hard to work with. After housecleaning, throw all your dirty rags into the washing machine—separately, not with your regular laundry—and launder them with hot water, detergent, and chlorine bleach; tumble them dry in a hot dryer. They are now sanitized and ready to be returned to the ragbag for the next cleaning day. (If you cannot launder them immediately, hang them on a rack or line until you can—but do not use them.)

Tools

You do not need many tools for housecleaning. With experience, however, most people develop strong tastes for certain types—for example, a yarn mop instead of a sponge mop—and special habits that require more tools than are included in the basic list that follows.

- Rags
- Broom
- Dustpan with brush
- Mop (sponge or other)
- Handheld vacuum
- Vacuum cleaner (with disposable bags, if your machine requires them), and attachments
- Dust mop
- Plunger
- Brushes
- Bucket(s)
- Box (or basket or bag), for carrying a kit of cleaning materials

Cleaning Liquids and Powders; Polishes and Waxes

The supermarket shelves beckon, but it is best to keep things simple. Choose one strong all-purpose cleaner and one mild one. Find a disinfectant cleaner for the bathroom and the toilet. Stock any waxes, polishes, or finishes appropriate for your floors or furniture. You need not stock cleaning materials that you use rarely. Instead, go get them at spring cleaning time or whenever the occasion arises and try to buy no more than you will use. (Recipes for homemade cleaning concoctions are set forth in chapter 31.)

All-purpose detergent cleaning powder or liquid (Spic-and-Span, Fantastic, Mr. Clean, or any other you like)

Mild detergent (Orvus WA Paste or Fabuloso, for example)

Bathroom sink, tub, and tile cleaner, disinfectant

Powdered or liquid abrasive cleaners

Toilet-bowl cleaner, disinfectant

Window cleaner (such as Windex, or make your own)

Household ammonia, or ammonia plus detergent

White vinegar

Baking soda

Chlorine bleach

Floor polishes or waxes, if necessary, according to the types of floor in your home—wood, tile, resilient flooring, stone, marble, and so forth

Silver polish and other metal polishes

Furniture waxes or polishes

33

Dust and Dust Mites

Why we cannot live with dust . . . Dust as a contributor to rising allergy rates . . . Temperature and humidity levels favorable to dust mites; sites where dust mites are likely to be numerous . . . Controlling dust mites and their allergens by placing allergen-proof covers on beds and bedding, by dusting and vacuuming, by HEPA filter vacuuming . . . Pet hair and dander, insects and insect allergens, pollen, fungi, microorganisms, tobacco smoke, and other components of house dust

The humblest and most inevitable contaminant of the air and surfaces of the home is

dust that rises up,
And is lightly laid again.[1]

Two contrasting attitudes toward dust have emerged in the late twentieth century. On the one hand, many harried working people have decided that so long as dust remains under the couch they are not going to worry about it. To these people are addressed the anticleaning stories that appear in most newspapers each spring, filled with wit about dust bunnies, just how rarely the authors vacuum, what their ancestors would think about that, and how they have found peace of mind nonetheless. On the other hand, many people have begun to recognize the health dangers of a laissez-faire policy toward dust accumulation. Sooner or later, house dust always rises up from its hiding places. Dust under the sofa becomes dust in the nose, the eye, or the soup. Particles become airborne when a breeze swoops them up from floors, furniture, and other surfaces. Dust is disturbed by walking, dancing, or the dropping of shoes on the floor; fixing the bed, and pillow fights. Tight houses without ventilation have higher levels of airborne dust because the indoor dust is not diluted with enough outside air. And the tight-house effect is exacerbated in homes that are seldom vacuumed and cleaned.

Dust is uncomfortable underfoot or at hand and unendurable in a bed. It causes problems in computers and CD players, always looks unpleasant, and carries hard-to-break connotations of death, decay, sin, carelessness, abandonment, and loneliness. As for its effect on your health, the Victorians were right to believe that dust is an irritant to the eyes, nose, and lungs; it attracts pests, promotes unpleasant odors, and can transmit infections. Modern medicine adds the accusation that it causes allergies.

All house dust contains a variety of allergens, and house dust is implicated in the alarming rise in the rates of asthma and other allergic diseases in recent years. The statistics on this precipitous rise are staggering. It is estimated that forty to fifty million people in this country are currently affected by one allergic disease or another. Thirty-five million have chronic sinusitis, and twenty million, excluding asthma sufferers, have hay fever (allergic rhinitis). Fifteen million have asthma (5.4 percent of the population), and five million of those asthma sufferers are children. The rate of incidence increased about 75 percent from 1980 to 1994. In children age eighteen and under the incidence of asthma increased 72 percent from 1980 to 1994. Deaths from asthma in 1994 alone numbered 5,787; death rates from asthma more than doubled from 1975 to 1995. Rates of hospital admission for asthmatic attacks are also increasing. Costs from these trends in suffering and fear, medical treatment, and lost work and school time are enormous.

There is substantial reason to believe that tight houses and increased levels of dust are significant factors in producing these disturbing statistics by causing increased exposure among the susceptible population to dust-mite, pet, and other indoor allergens. (Cats, dust, and grass pollen are thought to be the three main triggers of asthmatic attacks.) Many allergic people, especially asthmatics, are sensitive to allergens contained in house dust. Whether or not any individual develops allergies depends on a combination of inherited vulnerability and exposure to allergens. If a child has an inherited susceptibility—a strong possibility if the father or mother is allergic, and a very strong possibility if both are—there is good evidence that the risk that the child will develop certain allergies can be decreased by avoiding *early* exposure to allergens. The level of exposure to allergens in the first year of life appears to have an effect on whether or not a child will eventually develop asthma or other allergic conditions, as well as on how serious the allergies become. (Some scientists suspect that exposure even in utero has an effect, which makes me wonder whether women who may pass on genetic susceptibility to allergies might possibly reduce their children's later risks of allergies by avoiding unnecessary exposure to allergens during pregnancy. At any rate, it couldn't hurt to try.) Low levels of exposure early in life appear to reduce both the incidence and the severity of later allergic conditions,[a] but one can also become sensitized as an adult.

Dust Mites

The Habits and Natural Habitat of Dust Mites. House dust has many components, few of them less savory than dust mites. These are ugly arachnids—bugs—whose only merit is that they are too small to be seen except under a microscope. They are present in many homes in numbers ranging from few to appallingly many. They feed on the scales of our skin, on our pets' skin, and on other organic material.

Dust mites' excreta and pulverized bits of their tiny corpses are small enough to become airborne and find their way into the lungs. To most people they are harmless, but although they spread no diseases, they are strongly associated with allergic rhinitis and dermatitis, and are thought to be one of the most common triggers of asthma attacks. Vulnerable people, those with a genetic predisposition, who are exposed to sufficiently high levels of the allergens of dust mites develop these ailments in great numbers.

Dust mites prefer darkness, warmth, and humidity, conditions that the average household supplies for at least part of every year. They are far more common and populous in warm and humid climates, and their numbers increase explosively when the relative humidity exceeds 50 percent and the temperature reaches 70°F or more—77°F is said to be optimal for mites. They die when the relative humidity goes below 45–50 percent. Because of their love of humidity, dust mites tend to be absent or few in number at high altitudes, which are dry. (Dust mite allergens may actually increase during periods of low humidity, however, because the mites die and their corpses break down and create allergenic debris.) Studies in Boston and Chicago showed that mites are much more likely to be found in houses than in apartment buildings. And the higher the apartment, the fewer the mites. In both cases, this is probably because the farther a dwelling is from the ground, the less damp it is likely to be. (Houses sit on the ground and may have damp basements. But I know children with dust allergies who live in tall apartment buildings.) In the southeastern United States, favorable conditions for mites exist year-round. In large parts of the mid-Atlantic and central Midwest, favorable conditions exist in the summer; mite growth is also favored in centrally heated houses in the Pacific Northwest. In areas in which conditions are unfavorable for as long as four months in a row each year, dust mites are unlikely to be able to establish themselves in a home.

Dust mites are usually found in greater numbers in bedrooms than in other areas of the house, because sleeping bodies and bedding create an environment with plenty of food and moisture. Our skin, when it rubs against bedclothes, produces great quantities of scales. Each of us perspires approximately a pint of water into our beds and bedroom air each night. Skin scales fall onto carpets and floors and rub off on beds, pillows, sheets, blankets, mattress pads, comforters, and mattresses. Mites can take up residence in any of these and, unless you prevent it, they find sustenance sufficient to stay and raise many generations of new mites. A study in England reported that one-tenth of the weight of a six-year-old pillow was composed of dust mites, dust-mite excreta, dead dust mites, and skin. Mattresses similarly become laden with them, and the floor and carpeting around and under the bed are favorite haunts. Pets' sleeping spots are other preferred habitats, as are upholstered furniture, rugs, carpets, quilts, woolen blankets and clothes, and the spaces under sofas, dressers, and other furniture, where skin scales tend to drift. Stuffed toys in children's rooms are known as "mite farms" in the allergy literature. The soft little balls affectionately called "dust bunnies" that accumulate under the furniture also contain mites, mite excreta, and skin scales—along with bacteria, insect parts, mold spores, and other debris.

Mite allergens do not float in the air unless they are somehow disturbed. Thus, even though a home has dust mites and a large reservoir of mite allergens, just walking into the home may not cause an allergic reaction in someone with an allergy to mites. The allergens also settle fairly rapidly after being strewn into the air by careless dusting, vacuuming with a vacuum cleaner with inadequate exhaust filtration (which will blow dust back out into the air), making beds, punching pillows or having pillow fights, beating carpets, moving furniture, and similar activities. But when you sleep in your bed or sit on an upholstered sofa, you are placing yourself close to allergens and in a position to breathe them in. Thus if you wake sniffly in the morning or sneeze after housecleaning, you may have been given a clue that dust-mite allergens are present.

Controlling Dust Mites. The presence of dust mites does not imply dirtiness, and they are a normal part of environments that offer favorable physical conditions for their survival. However, they can be controlled by effective housekeeping. To some extent, you may choose your level of caution. If you are allergic, you already know that you must go to great lengths to preserve your health and comfort and that you must follow the cleaning advice of your allergist, which may be more rigorous than that given here. Likewise, anyone who has an infant or child in the home may wish to be careful about dust-mite allergens so as to avoid sensitizing him or her, or aggravating the symptoms of any child already sensitized.

Keep Bedding Mite- and Allergen-Free. The most important precaution you can take in the battle against mites is to use mite- and allergen-proof covers for pillows, mattresses, box springs, and comforters. These can be ordered from companies that specialize in allergy-control products, and can be found in some stores that sell household linens. Vinyl and plastic were once used for this purpose, but they are uncomfortable. Newer materials prevent mites and allergens from passing through yet are water-vapor permeable, soft, and comfortable, with a luxurious hand; they are available in a range of prices. It seems wise to use them on all beds, whether or not anyone in your family is now mite-sensitive. See chapter 56, "The Cave of Nakedness."

In addition, it is advisable to wash sheets, pillowcases, blankets, and mattress covers with *hot* water—over 130°F. See chapter 27, "Sanitizing the Laundry." Wash bedroom curtains the same way. Even cool wash temperatures will remove dust-mite allergens, but only hot water will kill the mites. Dry cleaning will also kill the mites, but it will not remove the allergens.

If you use allergen-impermeable pillow covers, it probably does not matter whether you use synthetic or feather or down pillows, but we all should follow our doctors' advice. And it is worth noting, because allergic people are often advised to use polyester pillows rather than feather or down ones, that two studies raise questions about the superiority of polyester pillows when it comes to allergens and allergic reactions. One found that there was a substantially lower risk of serious asthmatic attacks among children using feather pillows than among children using polyester ones.[3] The other found that after six months of use, new polyester pillows contained about eight times as many dust-mite allergens as new feather pillows—a significant difference.[4] Do not use foam rubber pillows, which can support the growth of mold, further aggravating allergies.

Controlling Temperature and Humidity. You can also do your best to keep heat and humidity below levels that support mites. Reduce the relative humidity in your home to 45 percent or less—especially in the bedroom—and keep temperatures below 70°F; otherwise you need even lower humidity. See chapter 29, pages 401–2, on reducing humidity with air conditioners in the summer, exhaust fans, dehumidifiers, and mechanical ventilation systems that remove humid air and add dryer air. You cannot kill mites by turning up an electric blanket to high and leaving it on the bed, but you can kill them by freezing them. Some people whose children are asthmatic tuck their comforters and stuffed toys into a deep freezer every month for six hours. This kills the mites, but the items must be washed, too, to remove allergens.

Dusting, Vacuuming, Airing, and Sunning. Removing dust in your home by regular dusting and vacuuming is important, but in households that are fighting allergies those chores must be done properly or they are counterproductive. Even when dust mites die, their allergens, preserved in their feces and corpses, stay in your home for a long time. The allergens are impelled into the air by bed making, walking, running, and any other activity that produces air currents, including, most discouragingly, sweeping, vacuuming, and dusting. Dusting furniture, books, and knickknacks can raise quite a lot of dust. But the amount of dust made airborne by dusting can be somewhat minimized by using slightly dampened cloths, getting rid of feather dusters, and learning proper dusting techniques. See chapter 34, "Vacuuming, Sweeping, and Dusting."

Vacuuming with a good vacuum cleaner is much better than sweeping with brooms or mops. But ordinary vacuum cleaners spew out small particles (such as dust-mite allergens and other allergens) through their filter bags, exhausts, and joints at which the hoses and nozzles connect. For people who are allergic, and particularly those who are asthmatic, this creates a situation worse than leaving the allergens resting peaceably under the sofa. In fact, one authority complains, such vacuums provide one of the few ways that could be devised to get large amounts of mite allergens airborne. The familiar smell of vacuuming is, in part, the smell of dust reentering the air.

Those with allergies should, if they can possibly afford to, purchase a vacuum cleaner that uses a HEPA filter—a high-efficiency particulate air filter—and has especially tight engineering to control dust emissions. (A HEPA filter removes 99.97 percent of particles greater than 0.3 microns in diameter.) A central vacuuming system that vents to the outdoors also solves the problem. These options are more expensive than ordinary vacuum cleaners. A less-expensive alternative is to use a vacuum that a consumer research organization recommends as low in dust emissions, and use specially designed high-filtration vacuum bags with it. These will increase the ability of your vacuum to retain small dust particles, although not to the extent of a true allergy-control vacuum with a HEPA filter. With all vacuum cleaners, remember to change the bag before it is completely filled. A full bag causes worse dust emissions. Once you have a tolerably clean-running vacuum, you can substantially reduce mite allergens by frequent vacuuming, being sure to vacuum mattresses, pillows, box springs, comforters, carpets, furniture, and draperies, and under furniture, especially beds, sofas, and other places favored by pets. Vacuuming, however, neither kills nor removes mites, which effectively cling to fibers deep within carpeting and other materials.

Among other steps doctors often recommend for the homes of asthmatics and other allergy sufferers: either wash children's stuffed toys frequently or remove them from their bedrooms, and remove from bedrooms other dust catchers, such as pennants, books, and wall hangings. Check with your doctor before taking such measures, which can distress children greatly. For serious cases of asthma, doctors may recommend removal of all carpets from a home in favor of bare hardwood or tile. Or they may recommend removing carpeting from the bedroom, where it is particularly undesirable. If you choose hard, bare floors instead of carpeted floors, you will remove an enormous breeding ground for mites, as carpets typically hold a hundred times more allergens than bare, hard floors. If you feel you must have carpeting, use short-napped rather than long-napped rugs, and use area rugs instead of large carpets or wall-to-wall carpeting. Substituting synthetic for wool-fiber carpets may reduce the amount of airborne mite allergens, perhaps because the synthetics develop a static charge that holds particles rather than releasing them into the air when disturbed.

Good ventilation and light in the bedroom and other rooms, and thorough airing of the bed and bedclothes probably help diminish dust mites and allergens. One prominent researcher and allergist told me that thorough sunning will kill dust mites, vindicating yet another bygone spring-cleaning custom.

Air filters and cleaners probably do not help much to get rid of dust-mite allergens, although they can be quite effective for other purposes, because dust-mite allergens remain airborne for only a short time before they resettle on surfaces, beyond any filter's reach.

Clothing. Dust mites can live in clothes. A wool sweater or pair of slacks that is put away without having been cleaned retains perspiration and skin scales sufficient to support armies of mites. Research has found that during a month of storage, mites and allergens greatly increase. The best solution for clothes that can take it is laundering in hot water often, and always before putting them away for any long period of time. Wool garments and others that must be dry-cleaned or laundered at temperatures too low to kill mites should be thoroughly aired and sunned before replacing them in closets or drawers; try to wash or dry-clean them frequently, especially before storing them.

Acaricides (Mite Killers). A method for killing mites and reducing allergens that is often recommended consists of the application of a tannic acid solution, in combination with an acaricide, to carpets and furniture at regular intervals. The tannic acid denatures mite excreta and particles (and cat dander as well) so that they are no longer allergenic; the acaricides kill the mites. (Test tannic acid in an inconspicuous area before using it, to see if it stains. Some products are said to be quite unlikely to stain if used properly.) Some experts are unenthusiastic about this method, as it requires a lot of effort and may not do much good. The acaricide most commonly recommended at present, benzyl benzoate, is not safe for homes with crawling infants and toddlers. Moreover, because the effects are short-lived and treatments must be repeated, the whole process can become expensive.[4]

Pets

Pet hair and dander are major components of house dust in all homes with furry pets, and are one of the major causes of allergies. Dogs and cats are the typical sources of animal allergens, but almost any furry or feathered creatures—gerbils, guinea pigs, hamsters, rabbits, birds—can trigger allergies. Anyone allergic to one species, moreover, is likely to develop allergies to others. Information on pets, allergies, and housekeeping in homes with pets is presented in chapter 55, "Pets."

Other Components of House Dust

Insects. Parts of spiders and dead insects of all sorts and their egg cases, saliva, and excreta form another irritating and allergenic component of house dust. Crickets, flies, beetles, fleas, moths, and roaches can cause allergic problems, but the most troublesome in this respect, and most common, is the cockroach. A study of homes with cockroaches found cockroach allergens in all samples of house dust tested. And with cockroaches, as with dust mites, there seem in recent years to be increasing levels of infestation and increasing numbers of sensitized people. (A heavy infestation of cockroaches will produce a characteristic unpleasant smell that is in itself a form of air pollution.)

Mere household dirtiness does not in itself cause cockroach infestations. Once they are in your apartment or house, roaches may survive on materials that you cannot get rid of, such as soap and the glue in book bindings. However, you can certainly aggravate the problem by providing crumbs and ready moisture. Effective means exist for getting rid of cockroaches. Ask your local cooperative extension service, check out supermarket products, or call an exterminator. There are progressive, enlightened exterminators these days with some new tricks, but they are still hard to find. (People living in apartment buildings must be prepared for renewed infestations when their neighbors call an exterminator, for it is well documented that when one apartment is treated the roaches will flee to another one that is not.)

It is unclear to what extent roach allergens, like mite allergens, continue to be airborne in the home after the roaches themselves have been killed. Careful cleaning and vacuuming in all areas where they had flourished—in kitchen cabinets, on kitchen floors, and in bathrooms and basements—seems advisable. Roach infestations are usually found in kitchens. But when children eat or snack in their bedrooms, cockroach allergens may be high there, as they may be in dens or family rooms if food is eaten in these rooms. Bathrooms are also favorite haunts.

PREVENTIVE MEASURES AGAINST COCKROACHES

Preventive measures against cockroaches include putting all food away, washing dishes immediately after eating, and taking the trash out each evening. Do not leave damp sponges lying in the sink, and be sure to wipe your sink and countertop dry, as moisture attracts roaches. Do not keep cardboard boxes or paper grocery bags in your home; cockroaches often live and lay eggs in them. After the infestation (in your home and neighboring apartments) is conquered, undertake cleaning measures to get rid of allergens that have accumulated. Vacuum, scrub, and dust surfaces in and near infested areas. The kitchen floor, especially, and all baseboards should be thoroughly washed with hot, sudsy water and rinsed, and holes and crevices near floorboards caulked. Empty out all kitchen cabinets and drawers, thoroughly wash them with hot, sudsy water, and rinse and dry them before replacing dishes and foods. First vacuum, then seal joints and cracks where roaches hide. A silicone sealant often will do the job. Caulk all holes and crevices around countertops, sinks, stoves, refrigerators, and cabinets.

Pollen, Fungi, and Microorganisms. Hayfever sufferers are probably aware that pollen blows into their homes and mixes with the house dust. Fungi (which include yeasts and molds)—Penicillium, Aspergillus, Cladosporium, and many others—can grow inside the home on any surface, in drip pans, inside walls, in the refrigerator, in rotting wood, or in any damp place, and their spores can blow in on the wind. They and their spores are common components of house dust, and when the dust becomes airborne they are breathed in. Fungi can cause both allergies and infections. Bacteria and viruses survive well in dust, but I have not encountered any modern scientific apprehensions about dust as the source of infectious disease. In 1901, a doctor named T. Mitchell Prudden wrote a book called *Dust and Its Dangers* in which he insisted that dust carried, along with many other bacteria, the live bacillus that caused tuberculosis, and called for intelligent housekeeping to prevent dust from spreading this dreaded disease. Contemporary scientists would no doubt scoff at the idea that dust was ever a significant means by which tuberculosis was transmitted, but they would confirm that all sorts of microorganisms thrive in house dust.

Mice and rats, when they are present, contribute most unpleasantly to dust. Besides leaving hair and dander, as all other furry creatures do, mice dribble urine as they explore in order to mark where they have been. They also drop feces dozens of times a day, and these droppings carry allergens and sometimes diseases. The deadly hantavirus can be contracted simply by breathing the air near the excreta of rodents that carry it. (Not all types of rodents are carriers. Deer mice, which live primarily in the West and Southwest, appear to be the primary but not the sole reservoir of hantavirus in the United States.)

Nicotine from tobacco smoke attaches itself to house dust and can be inhaled long after the smoker has crushed out the cigarette or cigar butt or emptied the pipe.

Finally, dust harbors a motley collection of crumbs, hairs, fluff from cloth, flecks of playdough, mold, and other debris of our home lives, as well as traces of the miscellaneous kinds of dirt that we track in or that blows in. Be sure to use doormats; wipe your shoes before entering your home. Clean your floors regularly.

34

Vacuuming, Sweeping, and Dusting

Vacuuming, sweeping, and dusting to preserve surfaces from dust abrasion . . . Floors, sweeping with brooms, dusting with mops, dusting by hand, vacuuming bare and carpeted floors . . . Choosing an effective suction setting . . . About vacuum cleaners . . . Vacuuming upholstery . . . Dusting furniture and other household objects, aids to dusting, treated cloths, dusting marquetry, gilding, gesso, and similar surfaces

Vacuuming, sweeping, and dusting are our major ways of removing dirt and dust without water or solvents. We suck them up, sweep them up, and wipe them up. Regular vacuuming, sweeping, and dusting are the most important actions you can take to prolong the lives of floors of all sorts, carpets, and most kinds of furniture. Dust, especially when it contains an admixture of sand, is abrasive. When you walk on dusty floors—whether they are of wood, stone, marble, ceramic or nonceramic tile, or some other hard surface—you grind dust into them and dull them. Dust and dirt are even more harmful to carpets and upholstery, settling deep into their fibers and making tiny cuts that hasten their deterioration.

Beginners should not fear that the work of sweeping, vacuuming, and dusting is time-consuming. These are quick, light chores. Those who are pressed for time can make them still quicker by avoiding the accumulation of objects that will need dusting and vacuuming. Dusting floors on hands and knees is an option that only serious housecleaners will consider; everyone else will vacuum or use a dust mop, which rarely takes long and is comfortable, satisfying work. Once you know the basic techniques, and the reasons for them, you can fly through these chores.

Floors

Vacuuming every day is best for your floors. I feel obliged to say this even though most people, myself included, are unable to do this. But if you vacuum or dust all the floors thoroughly on cleaning day and partially one or two days a week between cleaning days, you can still keep your floors in good condition. By a partial cleaning of the floors, I mean vacuuming or dusting in high-use areas, traffic corridors, and areas that you notice tend to accumulate dust and dirt, even if it is not visible on casual inspection. (Such accumulations of dust will be circulated in the room by air currents.)

Carpets should be cleaned by vacuuming. Bare floors can be vacuumed, hand-dusted, or dusted with a dust mop. Vacuuming does an excellent job on bare floors, but hand-dusting is best. (Yes, this means on your hands and knees. I once read about a health spa that had its clients do this because the exercise is so beneficial. But kneel on something soft or you may develop a painful condition known as housemaid's knee.) Dust-mopping is the least effective, but the mop and the dust cloth both offer one advantage over the vacuum: when used with pressure, they are better at removing a fine layer of grime that adheres slightly to the floor and cannot be picked up by suction. A handheld vacuum for occasional spot work is useful. When you are cleaning the entire floor, begin on the side of the room opposite your intended exit, and end at the door. On wood floors, rub, wipe, or vacuum in the direction of the grain of the wood. Never use furniture dusting sprays or dusting aids on floors. These make the floors too slippery, and some contain substances that would cause problems if you wanted to refinish your floors.

How to Sweep Floors with a Broom. If you have children or you cook a great deal, your kitchen is likely to need sweeping more than once each day. Garages, workshops, playrooms, utility rooms, porches, and other areas that see hard action are also sites for sweeping. You can use a vacuum for the kitchen if you like—crumbs do no harm inside the vacuum bag—but I find it easier to use a broom for the sort of quick, frequent removal of large particles that the kitchen and other heavily used floors require. Get a good, sturdy broom. I prefer nylon or synthetic bristles for smooth, level indoor surfaces, such as the kitchen floor, but some people prefer corn brooms, which are made of straw. Be sure to rest such brooms with the bristles unbent, because once they are bent they tend to stay that way. Very stiff, tough corn brooms are good for uneven surfaces such as sidewalks and some cellar floors, porches, and decks because their bristles are uneven.

Begin at the walls and aim to collect the dirt in the center of the room—which means

Sweeping dirt

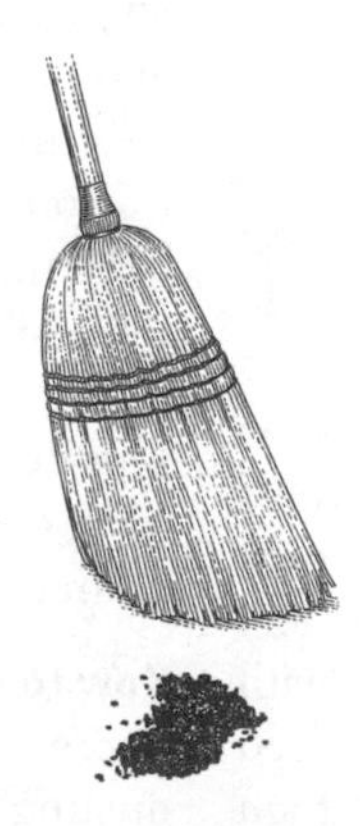
Dirt swept into a little pile

Sweeping pile of dirt into dust pan

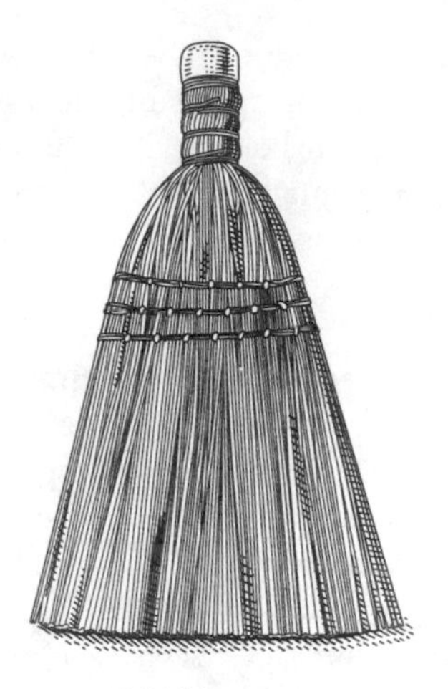

Whisk broom

it will be swept the shortest distance. Sweep the dirt toward you, brushing it with repeated, light strokes from all corners of the room, until you have a tidy little heap that can be brushed into a dustpan. Do not lift the broom up off the floor at the end of a stroke or you will fling dust and dirt into the air. Sweep the little heap of dirt into the dustpan and pour it into the trash. If you can manage this with the broom, well and good, but it is probably easier to use a brush or little whisk broom for sweeping into the dustpan. You should brush all the dirt in that you can, then move the dustpan back a couple of inches and sweep up the line of dust that was left; repeat this last step until all the dirt is in. (If you have trouble kneeling down to do this, there are long-handled brushes you can use more comfortably.)

The kind of dust that wood floors collect in your living room, office, study, den, library, family room, or bedroom is less amenable to sweeping with a broom. It is too light and fine, and a broom is too scratchy for these floors. Use a vacuum, mop, or dust cloth in these areas. Before vacuum cleaners were invented, carpets were swept with brooms or carpet sweepers, but this released tremendous dust into the air; the dust then settled down over carpeting, furniture, and anything else in the room that was not covered with dusting sheets. If you do not have a handheld vacuum, use a whisk broom or brush to sweep up crumbs or other dry messes on the surface of carpets or upholstery. Sometimes the brush works a little better than the handheld vacuum.

How to Use a Dust Mop. Dust mops work better if you dampen them *slightly* with plain water. Make strokes of the mop (on wood floors, along the grain of the wood) in one direction, or you will simply push the dirt back and forth. Lift the mop slightly to move it back for the beginning of a stroke. You must do this carefully or you will raise dust that will soon settle comfortably back on the floor. Watch out that you don't catch the mop in a sliver of wood and pull it up. If you can, shake the mop out a window or door periodically to clear it of dust. (This presents a quandary if you are a city dweller. Sometimes you have no window out of which to shake the dust because your windows are barred or screened. In my city, it is illegal to shake a mop out the window, and I am sure the same is true in many other cities. You are forced to resort to shaking the dust into a trash can or plastic bag, picking the dust off the mop by hand, or vacuuming it.) When the mop gets dirty, wash it. Choose a dust mop with a removable all-cotton head so you can simply shake it out or vacuum it and put it in the washing machine with your cleaning rags.

Some people go over their floors with a dust mop after vacuuming to remove that fine, adherent layer of soil that sometimes remains. Use a different technique for this: press down with the mop and go back and forth (on wood floors, in the direction of the grain of the wood).

How to Dust Floors by Hand. Hand-dusting floors is done in the same manner as the dusting of furniture. Choose a cloth and use the technique described in "Dusting Furniture and Other Household Objects," below. You can go back and forth in straight lines, or make elongated ovals, in either event going in the direction of the grain and wiping with a slight downward pressure. Turn or fold the cloth as soon as it has picked up a coat of dust, and switch to a clean cloth when it is soiled all over. Dust the baseboards at the perimeter of the room as you go. Be careful not to let the cloth catch in a loose sliver and pull it up. When the loose dust and dirt have been picked up from the area you are working on, give it a final pass using firm downward pressure to pick up the fine layer of adherent dust that is the last to go.

How to Vacuum Hard-Surface Floors and Carpets. On bare floors and delicate, antique, and Oriental carpets, use the bare-floor vacuum attachment, or what some manufacturers call the "universal" floor attachment. This will have a row of brushes at the rear to catch any dust that might otherwise escape the suction. The attachment's little rubber wheels prevent it from scratching the floor.

Although beater bars and power brushes should not be used on bare floors, valuable and vulnerable carpets, or Oriental rugs, they are helpful on many other carpets and rugs. The power brush is designed to separate the fibers of the carpet's pile as it rotates so that the airflow can reach in and pull out dust and dirt. The beater bar beats the pile so that the dirt is loosened and can be sucked up. The higher the pile, the more power you need to move the carpet fibers apart and beat loose the dirt. The power brush is also excellent for removing pet hair. If you have a lot of carpeting in your home, you should have a vacuum with a beater bar or power-brush attachment. If you have no beater bar or power brush, use the ordinary brush on your machine. The general opinion is that an upright vacuum with a beater bar is the most effective, but that a canister with a power brush does an excellent job too. The mechanical action of these tools, however, can be too harsh for Oriental or other valuable or irreplaceable carpets. These tools can break the pile fibers and cause them to wear out prematurely. Oriental and certain other rugs also may have looped fringes, and the bristles of the brush can catch in the loops and pull them out. Be cautious about using a beater bar on shag rugs or other long-pile rugs. Set the beater bar high and lower the suction to reduce the risk of pulling out strands of the pile. It is safest to vacuum these without the beater bar or power brush, but, unfortunately, less effective.

Vacuum wood floors with the grain of the wood. Repeated strokes, back and forth, will ensure that you have removed all the dust. (This is unlike dust-mopping, in which the strokes go in one direction. When you vacuum, each repeated swipe picks up more dirt, but when mopping you would merely push the dirt back and forth if you did this.) On carpets, use slow, deliberate, overlapping strokes. You need not press down. Pressing is counterproductive because it impedes the airflow. (It is hard to convince yourself that the extra muscular exertion is not helping, but you will be able to see that the floor still gets clean without it.) Fringe on a carpet should be approached from the middle of the carpet out; reduce the vacuum suction to avoid damaging it.

Other things being equal, the harder or denser the material you are vacuuming, the stronger the suction you need. If your machine permits you a choice, use the highest suction setting to clean hard, bare floors, the second-highest on Oriental carpets—they are dense carpets with rather stiff backings—and the third on wall-to-wall carpeting. But if you are vacuuming an heirloom rug, use only gentle suction. (See "About Rugs and Carpets" in chapter 35.)

Go a little more slowly on carpets to give the suction time to work. You can go a little less slowly on bare floors.

You need not worry about occasionally picking up greasy or slightly damp crumbs when vacuuming in the kitchen. A wet mess that got sucked up might ruin the vacuum bag, but crumbs will dry in the vacuum bag. You should never vacuum up water or spills. Empty or change vacuum bags outdoors if possible, or in a well-ventilated area if not.

About Vacuum Cleaners. Your vacuum cleaner does more than any other appliance you own to keep your home clean and healthful. Money spent to procure a vacuum that is clean-running and effective is well spent. If you are buying a new one, try to choose a model that does not spew a great deal of dust into the air. Vacuum cleaners that are not well designed will leak dust out of gaskets, joints, and bags. Moreover, all vacuum motors create their own dust when running, which, unless properly filtered, will also be spewed into the air of your home. This dust, which is composed of particles large enough to cause lung damage, is a kind of indoor air pollution that it is worth trying to combat. If you detect a familiar strong odor when you turn on your vacuum cleaner, it is time to put a new vacuum cleaner on your "to buy" list, for this is the smell of the dust being created and recirculated by your vacuum. Allergy sufferers should have a model that uses a HEPA filter, but everyone should aim to have a machine that produces as little dust as possible.

A second factor to consider when you buy a vacuum is how much airflow or suction it really has, for this is what determines how well it cleans. You cannot judge airflow by amperage alone. Horsepower is a better indication of suction strength. Two machines with the same amperage do not necessarily have the same airflow. One could be of superior design and hence have better airflow. Switches and lights, too, require additional amperage; a machine that has them

VACUUM ATTACHMENTS AND THEIR FUNCTIONS

The *all-purpose* or *universal brush* works well on shelves and books (not to be confused with the floor attachment some manufacturers call "universal").

The *smooth floor brush* (with two rows of bristles) is for high-shine smooth floors such as parquet, stone, or vinyl.

The *radiator brush* is for radiators and narrow shelves and crevices.

The *crevice nozzle* is for getting into narrow spots, cracks, and corners.

The *dusting brush* is for floorboards, curved surfaces, and carved surfaces.

The *upholstery nozzle* is for vacuuming sofas, cushions, curtains, fabric furniture covers, mattresses, and similar furnishings.

WHAT SUCTION SETTING?

Carpets will not come clean if the vacuum's suction is too high. For successful cleaning you will need a slight gap between the tool and the surface to be cleaned, or the surface will block the tool and no dust will be sucked up. High suction can bury the tool in the carpeting. This produces an effect similar to what happens when you vacuum draperies and the cloth is pulled into the tool, cutting off the airflow. Not only does it result in failure to clean, it also puts undue stress on the machine's motor and belts. On hard, bare surfaces—for example, wood or tile—this blockage cannot happen. Therefore on these surfaces you can and should use the highest setting, which will pull dust from the natural grooves, indentations, and seams. Use the lowest setting on draperies, upholstery, and throw rugs.

These are guidelines, not rules. Experiment when vacuuming; you may find that the recommended setting does not work so well on your particular carpet or floor as another would.

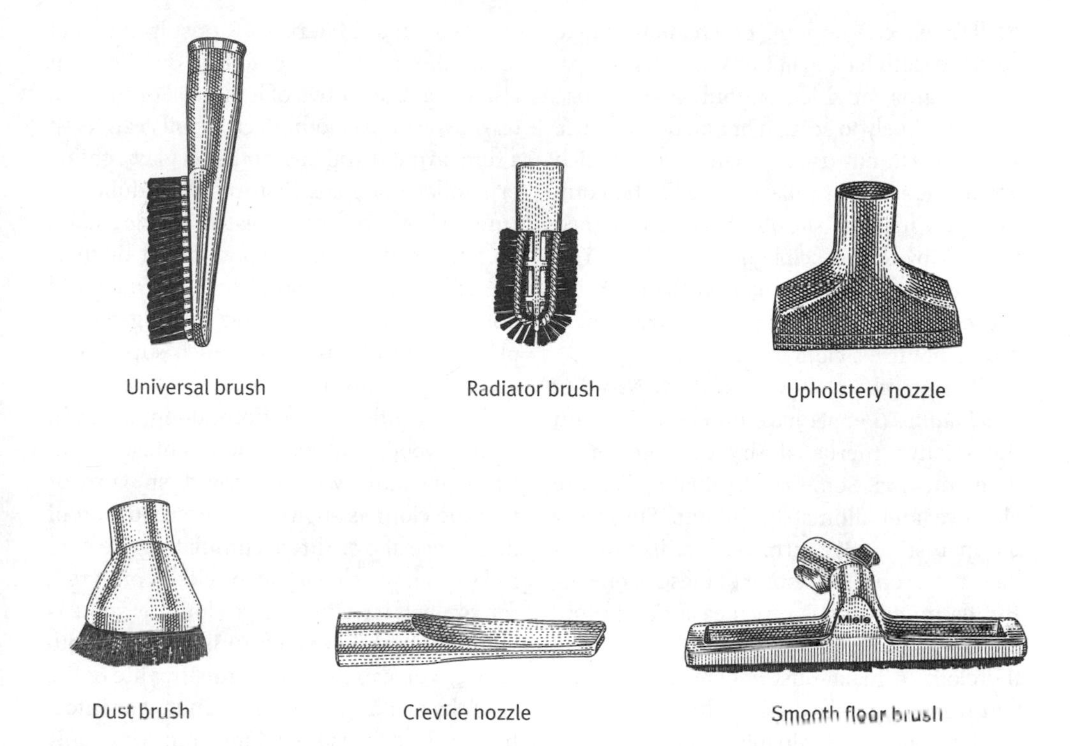

Universal brush
Radiator brush
Upholstery nozzle
Dust brush
Crevice nozzle
Smooth floor brush

might post a higher amperage but have less cleaning power than a machine with lower amperage.

Central vacuuming systems offer many advantages. Because the motor and filter mechanisms are not in the room where you are vacuuming, you avoid the dust problems. This advantage is lost, however, if the motor is placed in an area from which air will be recirculated into the house. This is often the case when the basement or a garage is chosen. A second difficulty to watch out for is the distance of the hose from the motor: the further away, the weaker the suction. Be sure that you are getting vigorous cleaning power in all areas where you need it.

Vacuuming Upholstery

Vacuum upholstery thoroughly once a week. Vacuuming will prevent dust from settling into the cloth and render far less frequent the need to clean the upholstery—a worthy goal. Vacuum all sides of cushions, under cushions, in cracks and crevices, and on backs. Use the appropriate attachments for vacuuming smooth upholstery fabrics and those that have a nap. If you have time, vacuum the visible surfaces a second time during the week.

When vacuuming delicate upholstery and antiques, set the suction level of the vacuum on low. If necessary, further protect them by covering them with a nylon or plastic screen and vacuum through the screen with the upholstery nozzle. Or cover the head or nozzle of the vacuum with netting secured with a rubber band. This reduces the force of the suction and prevents any loose fabric, threads, or fringe from being sucked into the tube. Do not use downward pressure on the fabric.

Dusting Furniture and Other Household Objects

Use a clean, washable cloth of soft cotton, such as a well-worn dish towel or a piece of flannel, cheesecloth, or chamois. Make sure the cloth has no buttons, zippers, snaps, thick seams, or thick buttonholes, because these are likely to scratch or abrade furniture surfaces. Do not use synthetic fibers, which are nonabsorbent, unless you like the commercially made dust cloths that are designed to work by the principle of static cling. You want a hint of fuzz or nap on the cloth because dust adheres better to the fuzz or nap, but do not use a cloth that lints.

Dampen the cloth very slightly. *Never get wood damp.* (People have different views on the relative merits of dry dusting versus damp dusting. Some say dry dusting is more abrasive and ultimately dulling. Some say damp dusting may harm wood or its finish. I have never observed either of these ill effects. But damp dusting is much easier and more effective.) You want just enough moisture in the cloth to make dust adhere to the cloth; you are not trying to dissolve dirt on surfaces. For heirlooms and valuable antiques, conservators recommend using distilled water. On wood, ceramics, pottery, and glass, do not use a cloth that has unraveling edges or hanging threads; these might catch on slivers of wood, lacquer, moldings, knobs, or other protrusions or loose pieces. If the wood you are dusting has rough sections or splinters, try brushing with a soft brush or vacuuming with a soft-brush attachment to avoid any danger that the cloth will snag. You may find it easier to dust intricately made pieces or sections of decorative china, ceramics, chandeliers, vases, or woodwork with a soft, small artist's brush, such as a natural-hair or hogshair brush. Never use stiff-bristled brushes for this purpose.

On wood, you may wish to use a spray-type dusting aid or an impregnated cloth. Not all commercially treated or impregnated cloths contain silicone oil, but if yours does, consider whether you mind using it on your wood possessions. See pages 492–93 in chapter 36, "Floors and Furniture of Wood and Woodlike Materials." Consult the label or call the manufacturer to find out. You can also put a drop or two of lemon oil or mineral oil on your dust cloth. Because oils can leave a film, avoid using oily cloths on glass, china, or similar materials that might be dulled or smeared. Never use a treated or oiled cloth on paintings or other works of art or their frames. Oily films can also attract dust and hold it on surfaces. I find dusting with a plain, slightly damp cloth much superior to dusting with oils or sprays.

With gentle oval motions along the grain of the wood, and with the slightest downward pressure, wipe off the dust. Turn or fold the cloth as soon as the used portion of its surface shows dirt accumulating. Be sure to keep an ample supply of cloths on hand, for you will have to change cloths as soon as you no longer have a clean part of the cloth to use. You can extend the dusting life of the cloth by shaking it out the window or into a bag, but because shaking removes only some of the dust you'll need a new cloth sooner or later when you are doing lots of dusting. Use only a fresh cloth to dust especially valuable, cherished, or antique items. Lift, do not slide, objects such as lamps and knickknacks to dust under and around them. Avoid soiling upholstered surfaces adjoining wood. Use a soft brush, if necessary, to get dust off clawed furniture and out of grooves, curlicues, scrolling, carving, and cracks. Wash soiled dust cloths or other washable dusting tools after each use.

Do not use feather dusters. They remove dust poorly and fling it into the air. Unless they are synthetic, they are not washable. If a feather should break while you are swishing, the sharp edge of a quill might scratch wood surfaces.

When dusting antiques, marquetry, gilding, gesso, gold leaf, crumbling or flaking lacquers, or any furniture with loose pieces, cracks, or splinters, take special care. Do not use a cloth. Instead use a soft, dry brush, as gently as you possibly can. A cloth duster might catch and pull pieces loose. Never use a damp cloth on gilding, painted gesso, or old paint. (Never let water in any form touch these areas.) If pieces of veneer or splinters come off antiques or good furniture, carefully save them—no matter how small they are—for future repair by a professional. Never rub gilding or gold leaf. Gold leaf and gilding on valuable antiques (picture frames as well as furniture) should be cleaned only by a trained professional.

35

Textile Furnishings

About rugs and carpets . . . Fiber qualities . . . Effect of structure: tufted and woven carpets . . . Pests . . . Chemical emissions . . . Preserving carpets and rugs with good household habits . . . Shampooing carpets . . . Stains and spills . . . Cleaning valuable antiques, Oriental rugs, and delicate carpets . . . Safeguards for delicate carpets . . . Shampooing delicate carpets . . . Spills and stains on delicate carpets . . . Caring for rugs made of rushes, grasses, sisal, and similar materials . . . Upholstery . . . Preventing soiling of and damage to upholstery . . . Shampooing upholstery . . . Leather upholstery . . . Draperies . . . Lampshades, dusting lampshades, cleaning fabric shades by immersion and parchment and plastic shades by nonimmersion methods . . . Glossary of rugs and carpets

All furnishings made of textiles require the same basic care. They must be vacuumed at frequent intervals and washed or dry-cleaned at less frequent ones. The frequency with which you vacuum and clean them will vary according to the type of fabric and the level of use they receive. By vacuuming regularly you not only extend the life of your furnishings, but also increase the intervals between the times when you will need to subject them to the laborious, and sometimes expensive, ordeal of shampooing or dry cleaning.

About Rugs and Carpets

The purpose of fabric floor coverings is to provide a softer, more beautiful, more comfortable surface for walking, standing, and, sometimes, sitting, and to act as an insulator for noise and warmth. They are also used to protect a hard surface such as wood or marble from wear. How a carpet looks, feels, and wears, and how easy or hard it is to maintain, are determined both by the fiber from which it is made and the construction of the fabric. (The terms "rugs" and "carpets" are for the most part used interchangeably, but there is some tendency to use "rugs" to refer to smaller floor coverings.)

Fiber Qualities. Ninety-nine percent of all carpets today are made of synthetic materials. Silk and cotton are rarely used for floor coverings because they lack resilience and, for this purpose, sufficient durability. Wool, which is the most expensive carpet fiber commonly in use, accounts for only 0.6 percent of domestic carpet manufacture—a dramatic change from 1950, when wool accounted for 97 percent. Nonetheless, the finest rugs are still made of wool, and all carpeting still strives to match the appearance and qualities of wool carpeting. Wool is durable and does not attract static, dyes beautifully and subtly, feels soft and pleasant, has a natural luster, and is wonderfully resilient—it springs back when stepped on. In appearance, none of the synthetics can match wool. Wool's appearance and its good functional qualities are a combination that has so far proved unbeatable, despite the many excellences of synthetics and the many flaws of wool. Wool weakens and bleaches with prolonged exposure to light. Although it is not particularly prone to mildew, it will mildew if left damp. It can be attacked by the larvae of moths and carpet beetles. Wool holds dirt, is less stain-resistant than synthetics, retains odors, and is not easy to clean.

All of the major synthetic fibers used for carpets—nylon, polyester, polypropylene, and acrylic—are more stain-resistant than wool because they are relatively unabsorbent. A water-based spill can often be wiped off carpets made of synthetic fibers, but they are prone to being stained by oils. None of them will be attacked by moths or beetles. They also resist abrasion better. Nylon is extremely durable and can take a great deal of bending and twisting without breaking. Polyester is less durable than nylon. Some types of polyester, nylon, and acrylic tend to pill when abraded. Unless they receive an antistatic treatment, many types of nylon, acrylic, and polyester will develop a static-electricity charge; this is annoying and uncomfortable and attracts lint and dirt. Polypropylene has good resistance to pilling and static, but it is less resilient than nylon.

The ability of carpets to withstand exposure to light is an important factor in their durability. Synthetics that have been solution dyed will have excellent colorfastness to light. Natural fibers have varying degrees of colorfastness. As for the fibers themselves, polyester and acrylic are most resistant to ultraviolet rays. Nylon and wool fibers—the one the most common and the other the most beautiful and expensive of carpet fibers—both have poor resistance to light. Silk and polypropylene fibers have the lowest resistance of all. See page 268 in chapter 18, "Fabrics That Work."

Effect of Structure. Both tufted and woven carpets can give good wear, but, other things being equal, woven rugs are generally considered more desirable than nonwoven or tufted carpets, and they are more expensive. (See "Tufted carpets" and "Woven carpets" in the Glossary of Rugs and Carpets, pages 480 and 481.) The design of woven carpets is often preferred. In high-traffic areas, with a woven rug you needn't worry about yarns getting pulled out, as you must with tufted carpets. And woven rugs, unlike tufted carpets, do not need a secondary backing, which can present wear problems of its own. (The layers can separate, for example. See the illustration on page 479.) But other things may *not* be equal: a well-made tufted carpet of good design and material will be superior to a poorly made woven one.

The denser the carpet, the better it wears—that is, the more closely the tufts occur to one another or the more yarn in the pile weave, the more durable the carpet. Carpets with a thicker pile wear better than those with a thinner pile. Carpets whose surface yarns have a harder twist are more durable than those with a softer twist. Carpets made of thicker yarn are more durable than those made of thinner yarn.

With tufted carpets, the more securely the tufts are fastened to the backing, the better the carpet will hold up and the better resistance the carpet will have to runs. The material most commonly used for backings for tufted carpets is polypropylene, which does not mold, mildew, rot, or shrink. But woven rugs with jute as a backing are subject to all those ills and must be protected from dampness. Polypropylene is now more commonly used than jute as a backing for woven carpets.

Level types of pile wear better than multilevel pile because pressures get distributed more widely on the former. With a multilevel carpet, the yarns that stick up highest take a disproportionate amount of wear and give out faster. Carpets with deeper pile are harder to vacuum; shag carpets are particularly hard to keep clean. But a thick, deep pile feels softer and more luxurious than a thin, hard pile, and a carpet with soft-twisted surface yarns feels softer than one with hard-twisted yarns. A thicker, softer pile insulates against noise and holds in heat better.

See the Glossary of Rugs and Carpets, pages 478–81, for more information on structures and types of rugs and carpets.

Pests. Unfortunately, rugs and carpets, whether of natural or synthetic fibers, can host various pests. Such floor coverings offer favorable environments to dust mites, which cling deep in the pile and thrive on the skin scales and other edibles that collect there. Moths and carpet beetles in their larval phase eat wool.

Carpets in use will not be damaged by carpet beetles and moths so long as the carpets are frequently vacuumed; and vacuuming with a low-emission vacuum will substantially reduce the level of dust-mite allergens. (See chapter 33, "Dust and Dust Mites.") Because mites, beetles, and moths all like damp, dark conditions, keeping the humidity down, supplying good ventilation, and letting in some sunshine, along with frequent, thorough vacuuming, will usually suffice to keep pest problems at bay. Carpets in storage, however, are highly vulnerable to damage from beetles and moths.

If you must store carpets and you can store them in an area apart from your living space, use mothballs or other moth repellents, as described on pages 251–52 in chapter 16, "The Natural Fibers." Some carpets are treated to resist moths and beetles. According to manufacturers, these treatments pose no danger to children or pets.

Chemical Emissions from Carpets. New carpeting made of synthetic fiber often emits volatile organic compounds into the air. The emissions may be from the backing or the adhesive used to lay wall-to-wall carpet. The odor of such emissions is often surprisingly strong and unpleasant. There are disputes about how harmful such fumes are. Some people seem to get headaches, allergic reactions, or flulike symptoms from the fumes. There is no hard evidence that worse harm results. However, there is little reason to think that breathing such compounds does you any good.

Usually, emissions from new carpets subside greatly within a few days, but they can continue at a lower level for a much longer period. The remedy is to open doors and windows and use fans to bring fresh air in. The Carpet and Rug Institute (CRI), an industry organization, recommends you do this for forty-eight to seventy-two hours and that you call your retailer if the problem persists. (And if the problem persists, so should your ventilation efforts.) The Carpet and Rug Institute suggests that you might consider scheduling installation of new carpeting at a time when most family members will be out of the house. Having had a taste of this problem, I strongly endorse that suggestion, especially for families with infants, young children, or members with allergic tendencies, and further suggest that you try to find a way to be absent for a few days, leaving your home to ventilate, if possible, particularly after installation of a large amount of carpeting. If you are allergic or sensitive to dust, you should also try to avoid being around when your old carpet is lifted and new carpet is laid. This process can create a great deal of temporary air pollution. Vacuum and clean carefully after the removal.

When buying new carpets and carpet cushioning or mats, look for the green-and-white label of the Carpet and Rug Institute. This indicates that the item has met CRI low-emission standards as part of a voluntary testing program carried out by the CRI; insist that the installer use adhesives with the CRI label too. Although some observers express doubt about whether the CRI standards are stringent enough, this is clearly a step in the right direction and will probably be the only way you have of assessing the potential emissions of any new American manufactured carpeting you buy. It is also a good idea to ask your retailer to roll out and air your new carpeting before delivering it to you.

Preserving Carpets and Rugs. Regular, proper vacuuming is the most important action you can take to preserve the good looks and quality of your carpets and rugs. (See pages 461–63 in chapter 34, "Vacuuming, Sweeping, and Dusting," for advice on how to vacuum.) Dirt and dust not only ruin the appearance of carpeting; they are ground deep into the carpet where they cut and destroy the fibers of the pile and the carpet's backing. This will eventually cause worn areas to appear. A thorough vacuuming on cleaning day and a partial vacuuming once or twice a week between cleaning days will keep your carpets in good condition and the dust and allergen levels down.

The second most important part of carpet care is having good cushioning or matting. Carpet cushioning adds to comfort by increasing softness and providing insulation. Functionally, the extra cushion prevents dirt from being ground into the carpet and saves wear by absorbing some of the impact of footsteps as well. It also creates a suction layer, or air pocket, between the floor and the carpet, which improves the effectiveness of vacuuming. (See pages 274–75 and 462.)

A third major means of preservation is to use doormats at each entrance to your home, preferably one immediately inside and one immediately outside each door that opens to the outdoors. (You may need just one of these if you live in an apartment building with carpeted hallways that are frequently vacuumed.) The mats will absorb great quantities of dust and dirt that would otherwise be tracked onto your carpets and floors. You can also do wonders for your carpets by carefully wiping shoes and boots at the door or, even better, taking them off at the door. These steps will save much labor in vacuuming and shampooing. They will also save the additional wear on the carpet that these cleaning measures extract. Unfortunately, cleaning the carpet also contributes to its aging in direct proportion to the vigor of the cleaning procedure. The goal, therefore, is not only to clean the carpet but insofar as possible to keep it from getting dirty in the first place.

You can help preserve your carpets through some simple habits and practices. Use casters and protectors under furniture legs to prevent the pile from being crushed or broken. You can get these with pointed legs or prongs so that they themselves do not crush or mat the pile. (If your synthetic carpets develop impressions, place an ice cube on them and the fibers will regain their loft. Do not do this with natural-fiber carpets or rugs.) Never walk on any carpets when they are wet, but be especially careful not to walk on wet wool carpets. Wool is less resilient when wet, and you may damage the fibers. Turn the carpet periodically so that light and traffic wear and age it uniformly. Move the furniture now and then so that the pile is not permanently crushed or matted. Clip stray pile yarns that are too long. Whenever you move furniture, always lift it; never push it across the carpet. Pushing and sliding are hard on both rugs and furniture. Do not use delicate and valuable rugs in high-traffic spots, such as entries and hallways, or in high-abrasion spots, such as stairs and turns or corners. If a carpet develops an edge that rolls or turns up, iron it flat on both sides using a damp pressing cloth. This condition usually is a result of walkers' pushing the edge up with their feet as they pass. It is not only unsightly but will damage the fibers of the carpet over time.

Improper storage can result in damage to carpets. Wool carpets are far more likely to be attacked by pests in storage than when they are left on the floor, because pests like dark, damp, undisturbed areas. If you must store a carpet, never fold but roll it, right side out (so as not to crush the pile), fringe to fringe, if it has any. Antiques or delicate heirlooms should be lined with acid-free paper and placed in acid-free boxes. (This protects them from contact with environmental hazards without creating any new ones.) Roll larger carpets on a roller. Do not roll them so loosely that wrinkles will form or so tightly that the carpets cannot breathe and the pile is crushed. Stored wool carpets should be aired periodically to reduce any moisture that may have accumulated, and to allow you to check for insect infestation.

Carpets, like people, flourish in temperatures of about 70°F and relative humidity of about 50 percent.

Shampooing. Old-fashioned housewives shampooed the carpets at every spring cleaning, and this is still the most hygienic schedule. If no one in the household is troubled by allergies, you can preserve appearances with less-frequent shampooing. The schedule depends on the amount of traffic and dirt and the number of children to which your carpets are exposed. If you give your carpets thorough, regular vacuuming and traffic is light to moderate, shampooing every two or three years can suffice to keep them looking good. Whether sooner or later, there inevitably comes a day when dirt and spots have accumulated and vacuuming no longer restores a good appearance. Then you must shampoo.*

There are four methods of carpet shampooing: with commercial rug-cleaning products and a vacuum cleaner; with a rented or purchased cleaning machine; by professional cleaners in the home; or by professional cleaners out of the home at a cleaning

*There is some evidence that some episodes of Kawasaki syndrome, a dangerous illness of children, were associated with exposure to rug shampooing. Kawasaki syndrome, which is the main cause of acquired heart disease in children in this country, predominantly affects children under five. Although the connection between Kawasaki syndrome and rug shampooing is not regarded as proved, you may wish, if there are crawling babies, toddlers, or preschoolers in the home, either to avoid shampooing or spot-cleaning rugs or to have the carpets sent out for cleaning and thorough drying before they are returned. Whenever you shampoo carpets, you should ventilate the room well, so do not attempt to shampoo carpets or upholstery in cold, damp weather. Choose a time when drying is likely to be quickest and when you can leave doors and windows open.

company. Each of these methods has strengths and weaknesses, and it is wise to choose on a case-by-case basis. None of them, however, should be used on valuable antique rugs, which should be cleaned only by professionals who specialize in such work. Send any silk rug to an expert.

Thoroughly vacuum the carpet before using any method of shampooing.

The first shampooing method, using commercial rug shampoos and cleaning products and a vacuum, may not be the most pleasant, but it is the cheapest. Effective foam sprays, liquid shampoos, and powders are available in supermarkets, hardware stores, and home centers. Dry shampooing, however, should probably be reserved for small areas. Follow the directions on the product. Never overwet the carpet. Mildew can result unless both pile and backing are of synthetic fiber. Even when mildew is not a worry, an overwet carpet of any fiber takes a long time to dry and cannot be walked on because it is more vulnerable to soil and stain. (Also, in some instances its fibers are weaker and more easily damaged when it is wet.) Always vacuum or rinse out all chemical cleaners thoroughly; their residue can damage the carpet and hasten resoiling, and may be toxic. When scrubbing these products into carpets, a brush is recommended because it does not flatten the pile so much as a sponge does. A sponge is good for blotting; a natural sponge is more absorbent and creates no risk of transferring color onto the carpet.

Steam- or dry-cleaning equipment can be either rented or bought. Dry cleaning compounds need a much shorter drying time (approximately one hour), and are good for spot cleaning and for high-traffic areas. Do not overwet the carpet with them. Dry-cleaning fluids pose a fire hazard. Use them only with plenty of ventilation. (See cautions in chapter 60, "Fire.") It can be difficult to remove all of the cleaning chemicals in the carpet, and it may take a second procedure. A steam-cleaned carpet can take many hours to dry. Steam cleaning does a more thorough job, but the quality of the work depends on the skill of the operator. In general, rented equipment is cumbersome, the cleaning chemicals are expensive, and the results vary. Often the increased cost of hiring a professional carpet-cleaning service to come into your home is worth it. Many services pick up, clean, and return your carpets to you in a thoroughly dried state, and also do competent repairs. (This is not feasible, of course, for wall-to-wall carpeting.) With all professional services in the home, you should research the best companies in your area.

Stains and Spills. With spills, time is of the essence; once set, many carpet stains are nearly impossible to remove completely. Act swiftly, and remove as much of the spill as you can. Blot, do not rub, spills with an absorbent white towel or paper towel. Sometimes you can spoon them up too. The main consideration is not to make matters worse by spreading the spill more widely. For a liquid spill, sparingly pour soda water or seltzer over the area; the bubbles will cause more of the spilled substance to rise to the surface, which should then be blotted quickly.

Once the spill is contained, try to remove any remaining stain with carpet shampoo or commercial stain removers, following product instructions. Most spills, once contained, can also be dealt with effectively using the *foam* from the suds of a solution of water and a mild detergent. Brush lightly, then wipe off the excess foam with a clean cloth. Rinse with a half-and-half solution of white vinegar and water to remove any alkalinity left by the cleaner. Finally, rinse with plain warm water, taking care to blot thoroughly. Carry out both rinses either by spraying the liquid onto the carpet, taking care not to get it too wet, or by patting it on with a clean white cloth or paper towel. Then blot it with a dry white cloth or paper towel.

Consult the Guide to Carpet and Upholstery, pages 481–86, for stains that do not respond to this treatment.

Cleaning Valuable Antiques, Oriental Rugs, and Delicate Carpets. Your goal with rugs that are old, delicate, or valuable should be to lift dirt while avoiding the damage to the delicate fibers of the pile that can be caused by bending, pulling, and crushing them during cleaning. There is a troublesome trade-off here, because dirt will harm carpets too. For less-delicate but valuable rugs, the trade-off between damage caused by dirt and damage caused by the vacuuming itself tilts toward removing the dirt more effectively: the best guarantee of long life for such a carpet is a high level of cleanliness. For a very delicate, very old carpet, the balance tilts the other way: use every possible caution. There are many in-between cases for which you must simply consult your own wishes and intentions. If you have irresolvable doubts, ask a specialist.

Safeguards. A number of safety measures should be taken when caring for old, delicate, and valuable carpets. First, and most important, never use a power brush. Vacuum only with reduced suction. If you cannot turn down the power of the vacuum, reduce its suction by placing a screen of nylon or plastic over the nozzle of the vacuum or by laying a screen over the carpet. This is especially desirable on carpets with fringe, particularly if it is hand-knotted. The screen reduces suction and prevents the vacuum from sucking fringe or fiber into the hose. Vacuum old and delicate carpets and rugs in the following way: using the "universal" floor attachment, vacuum in the direction of the pile slowly, getting off as much dirt as possible; then go over the carpet one more time (with a hand brush, gently, if you have vacuumed through a screen) against the direction of the pile to stand the fibers up and restore their natural sheen. Once a year or so, give it a deeper vacuuming by hanging it vertically, for example, on the back of a chair or two chairs, and going over it slowly with a handheld vacuum of no more than one horsepower.

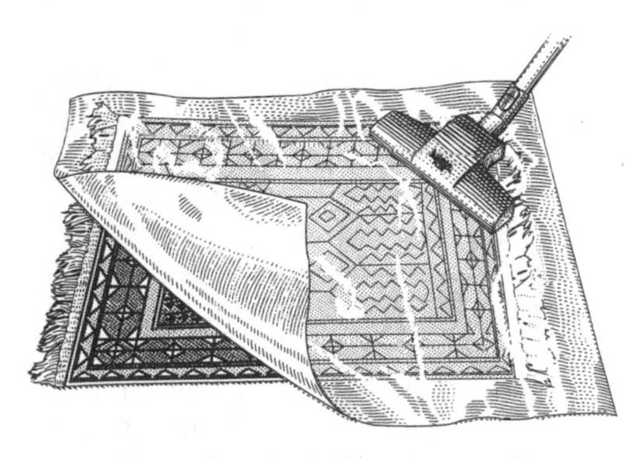

Vacuuming carpet with screen over it

Cleaning an older or delicate carpet with any sort of liquid will result in a loss of fiber (in a disastrous case, a large loss of fiber), and therefore is inadvisable. Wet cleaning or shampooing and dry cleaning should be done only by specialists and on the recommendation of specialists.

With old and delicate carpets, observe somewhat more rigorously the cautions you observe for ordinary carpeting. For example, place carpets needing special protection out of high-traffic areas, such as entryways and hallways, and high-abrasion areas, such as stairs, turns, and corners. Extremely delicate and valuable rugs do not belong on the floor at all; hang these on walls or lay them on tables. Others may go on the floor in places where no one will be tempted to walk on them. If a valuable, somewhat vulnerable carpet has been placed where it generally needs vacuuming more than once a week, it should be moved. Frequent cleaning as well as frequent soiling will cause it to wear more quickly. Keep antique and other valuable rugs out of all light, natural and artificial, as much as possible, especially direct sunlight; make sure that any light striking them strikes uniformly. Keep the humidity moderate. Do not let furniture stand where it will crush the pile.

For the most valuable and most delicate carpets, you should take all of the foregoing safety measures. For others, choose the level of caution that makes a comfortable compromise between the importance of the rug and your time and willingness to take trouble.

Shampooing Delicate Carpets. Generally speaking, do not attempt to shampoo valuable carpets yourself. Too much can go wrong. However, with those troublesome carpets that fall in the gray area of "somewhat old but not really a valuable antique" or "delicate but not really irreplaceable," you might trust yourself to give them a gentle moist cleaning in the manner described below. Be certain that you believe the benefits of doing so outweigh the possible costs.

The mildest wet cleaning you can perform is simply to sponge the rug gently with a natural sponge or clean white cloth dipped in spring water and wrung dry. (Tap water is too heavy with chemicals, and distilled water will remove too many natural oils.) First, however, carefully test a few fibers at an edge for colorfastness by wetting them with your cloth or sponge, then wiping them with a clean, dry white cloth and observing whether dye comes off. If not, then proceed with your sponging. Afterward, dry the carpet quickly and thoroughly. Wipe it with a clean white towel to take up as much moisture as possible. Then air the carpet. Open the windows and use fans, if necessary, to increase the ventilation. Carry out such an operation only in warm, dry weather.

For a slightly less mild cleaning, brush the carpet gently with the *foam* of a solution of mild detergent and water. Orvus WA Paste, manufactured by Procter & Gamble, is an excellent choice. See "Detergents and soaps, mild," pages 322–24. Do not use commercial rug shampoos or strong cleaners. You will need a bucket of mild detergent and water, a second bucket of plain water, a soft brush, and a clean white cloth. First, in a small, inconspicuous area at the edge, test to be sure the colors in the carpet will not run. Make a good foam in your solution of detergent and water. Then dip the soft brush in the foam only—not in the water—and gently brush the carpet with the foam. Start on the reverse side of the carpet and work from the middle out in a circular motion, cleaning a small section at a time. Rinse by wiping off the foam with a well-wrung cloth that has been dipped in plain water, being careful not to soak the carpet. Once finished with the reverse side, flip the carpet and proceed in the same manner on the right side. Dry the carpet thoroughly, as described above, by first wiping it with a clean white towel and then airing it. Finally, brush the top side of the carpet gently with a soft, dry brush to raise the pile.

Spills and Stains on Delicate Carpets. Accidents involving valuable and delicate rugs require fast action. But do not attempt to deal with such stains yourself.

Immediately try to isolate the substance, blotting or gently scraping up what you can. Then wrap the carpet tightly in plastic so as to avoid the drying of the stain—if this happens it is likely to set forever—and make haste to the nearest professional cleaner or conservator.

Caring for Rugs Made of Rushes, Grasses, Sisal, and Similar Natural Materials. Use rugs of rushes and grasses only in dry areas of your home. They will rot or mold if they are left damp. Stronger, more coarsely woven types can be used on the floor like any other rug. Fine and delicate ones will quickly break down and tear if you walk on them.

Vacuum such rugs front and back. Then lift them and vacuum the floor under them. I have never attempted to wash such a rug, but I have read that it can be done. I would be wary, however. Especially if the rug has colors or is painted or decorated, I would attempt to wash it only if the manufacturer or retailer assured me that washing would do no harm. Test the effect of water and mild detergent in an inconspicuous area before beginning.

The trick is to try to avoid soaking the rug and to dry it quickly so that it does not mildew or deteriorate. Use a solution of mild detergent and water and a soft brush or cloth. A stiff brush, or even a not-so-stiff brush, may damage the fibers or designs or decorations on some weaves. Wash the rug quickly. Rinse it thoroughly. Then dry it fast. Hang it on a clothesline in the sun, or over a drying frame or in any other fashion that lets air go through. Do this outside if you can. (You may see suggestions to hose the rug down, if you are outside, but I would hesitate to soak such a rug.) Apartment dwellers can resort to a terrace, bathroom, or kitchen.

Upholstery

Vacuum upholstery once a week according to the instructions in chapter 34.

Shampoo upholstery as needed. Once every year or two is usually enough unless you have a large family or an unusually active household. You can hire professionals to come into your home to do this modestly onerous task. You can also purchase or rent equipment and do the job yourself. Or you can do the job without machines, using hand brushes. (It takes a bit of muscle, and can raise a little anxiety or frustration because you may fail to remove the soil.) If you have antique upholstery that you wish to preserve, however, you should have the job done by a trained professional.

Preventing Soiling and Damage to Upholstery. Because upholstery cleaning is often only moderately successful, it is important to concentrate on preventive measures: vacuuming, using soil repellents and cloth protectors of various sorts, and using care and caution. When preventives fail, you must keep in mind that upholstery is generally not intended to last for anywhere near a lifetime.

Soil-resistance treatments and guards work well. Soil repellents help by causing spills to bead up rather than to soak in and by creating a barrier against dirt. You can apply these yourself with spray or have the job done by professionals. If you apply a soil repellent yourself, be sure the product you choose is recommended for the fiber you have and apply it as evenly as possible. Note that some soil repellents work on both oil- and water-based soil, but others do not. Read labels, or if you hire professionals to do this job, be sure to ask what you are getting before you commit yourself.

Crocheted antimacassars—the small lace and cloth circles, rectangles, and squares that used to adorn the backs and arms of chairs and sofas—are quite out of fashion, but if hair oil ever becomes popular again, pull them out of the attic immediately. The young will deduce that these are launderable materials used as soil guards on the high-soil areas of upholstery. They will not remember how, in the days before daily shampoos, oil spots on walls and furniture from people's heads were a major cleaning problem. (There is a mild, morose character in Dickens' *Bleak House*—Mr. Jellyby—whose custom of sitting in a certain spot to indulge in despair is indicated by a greasy spot on the wall where his head habitually lolls.) Hair and skin, even with our frenzied bathing and shampooing, continue to have natural oil and a bit of soil on them that is transferred to upholstery. Some people still preserve the backs and arms of upholstered furniture by acquiring arm guards and back guards made out of the upholstery material, hoping that these will not be noticed. Others take advantage of a bit of a vogue in slipcovers. These are all good ideas. You could also design up-to-date antimacassars in some washable fiber.

Light will cause most fabrics and wood to fade and deteriorate, but there is a vast difference in the susceptibility of different fibers and dyes to light. Choose the more light-resistant types for your upholstery. Place antiques where direct light will not strike them. Place all furniture in such a way that light strikes it uniformly. It is remarkable how quickly bleaching can occur.

Shampooing Upholstery. Begin with a thorough vacuuming. If you have slipcovers, simply remove them and launder or dry-clean as appropriate. Follow the care label instructions. If you plan to wash them, you must ensure that they are preshrunk when you buy them or that the initial fit is loose enough to tolerate whatever degree of shrinkage you are told you can expect. When you are worried that launderable slipcovers may shrink, wash them in cold water and either line dry or tumble on low/gentle until they are three-quarters dry, then replace them on the furniture while they are still slightly damp.

The best way to shampoo upholstery yourself is almost always to use a home steam extraction machine. (This is also the method professional cleaners use.) If you do not own one, you can rent one. This machine shoots cleaning solution into the upholstery, then sucks the dirty water back out with tremendous force, so you are not left with soggy cushions that will mold before they dry. At the same time, your cleaning solution is able to penetrate the fabric, which is the only way to get it really clean. Proceed according to manufacturers' instructions. Use any commercial upholstery shampoo that works in the machine. Always test a patch first in a hidden area. Do not use the furniture until it has dried thoroughly, and do everything in your power to ensure that it dries quickly. Good ventilation and low relative humidity will help. (Dirt adheres more readily to damp surfaces, and dampness can leach colors from clothing, paper, and other materials.)

It is best to shampoo upholstery by hand when the soiled upholstery is too delicate to tolerate machine cleaning and not worth the expense of professional cleaning. Hand-shampooing works well on light, even soil and on fabrics without nap, and is the method to use on occasional small pieces of furniture. Most of us, however, would find the job of cleaning several large pieces in this manner quite tiring, and, considering the labor expended, the results obtained can be disappointing when this gentle method of cleaning is applied to heavy soil or stubborn stains.

There are many methods of hand-shampooing. One popular method is to spray a commercial upholstery cleaner onto the fabric; rub it as vigorously as the cloth will tolerate with a brush or sponge; then vacuum. Some methods are wet; some use solvents. Just be sure to follow whatever specific instructions are on the product you buy. To shampoo upholstery in the traditional way, you will need a clean cloth, a soft brush, a bucket of clean water, and a bucket of a very sudsy solution of upholstery shampoo and water. Make sure the upholstery shampoo is safe for your upholstery fabric. (Orvus WA Paste is excellent for this.) Dip the brush into the *foam or suds only*. Do not actually get the brush wet. Using *only the suds*, brush a small section of the upholstery as vigorously as the fabric will tolerate. Rinse by wiping the foam off with a well-wrung cloth dipped in the clean water. Continue in this manner until the entire piece is finished. The main object is to avoid soaking the upholstery. If it gets soaked, it may rot inside or smell unpleasant forever after. Do not remove covers from pillows; clean them in place. Let the upholstery dry thoroughly; then vacuum it. Never use upholstery when it is damp.

Leather. You need not clean leather-upholstered furniture or desktops more than once a year under ordinary circumstances. First dust; then use saddle soap or another leather cleaner according to the product directions. (Waxes and polishes formulated for woods and other surfaces contain solvents that may harm leather; don't use them.) After cleaning leather, let it dry before using it again. If the leather seems too dry or is beginning to crack, use a conditioner after cleaning. Be sure to select products that will not darken light leathers. If you are in doubt, test in an inconspicuous place.

You can wipe leather with water to clean off an occasional spot so long as you do not let it get damp through. Never let water stand on leather. Sun will bleach and cause deterioration of leather, and heat will make it crack and dry.

Draperies

Launder or dry-clean draperies as necessary—that is, when vacuuming does not make the draperies look good or when you know that they are quite dirty even if they look all right. For suggestions on laundering draperies, refer to chapter 25, "How to Launder Tricky Items." Obey the care labels, particularly when they forbid either laundering or dry cleaning.

To vacuum, use the upholstery nozzle, and set the suction level on low. Begin at the top and go to the bottom, using short, repeated strokes. In bedrooms, vacuum draperies weekly. In other areas, if weekly vacuuming is not feasible, try for a once-monthly vacuuming, or simply do it as often as you can get to it. It is a quick job.

Lampshades

Nothing much has changed for fifty or more years when it comes to taking care of lampshades. The newer synthetic fibers of which some lampshades are made are perhaps less expensive than silk or linen, but not much easier to clean once they are fastened to the frame.

Dusting Lampshades. Because most lampshades are either difficult or impossible to wash or dry-clean, dusting them frequently and carefully is all the more important. By doing so you can put off the vile necessity of cleaning them for a long time. You can also preserve the life of the shades.

Remove dust from lampshades by vacuuming with the dust brush and low suction. Hold the shade steady with your hand, but be careful not to leave fingerprints. You can also use a clothes brush or a dry sponge effectively. Some people use a feather duster, but I think this leaves too much dust within the fabric and seams that other means would remove. Dust gently, because lampshades are breakable and can easily be bent permanently out of shape under pressure.

Long ago, to get the dust out from between the threads of fabric lampshades, the housekeeper would "snap" the shade with a piece of cheesecloth or linen towel, rather as boys snap each other with towels in the locker room. (She duly removed the shades from the lamps before doing this, and stabilized them, or she might have sent the lamp bases flying.) When I was told of snapping, I decided that it would actually be a useful adjunct to vacuuming because it would loosen dust so that it could be sucked up, but I can't say that I noticed any increased cleaning effect when I tried it.

Choosing a Cleaning Method. After years of being dusted and vacuumed, a lampshade may finally reach a point where it needs a more ambitious kind of cleaning. Then you must decide whether you can wash it or whether you must replace it. Not long ago you would also have had the option of sending it to a laundry or dry cleaner, but today it is all but impossible to find a business willing to take on this chore, so home washing is the only option.

Some shades cannot be washed. These include hand-painted lampshades, fabric lampshades with paper interiors, and lampshades whose fabric is glued rather than sewn to the frame. The paint and paper will be ruined and glued places will come unglued if you wet such lampshades. (Some people recommend washing otherwise washable glued shades with detergent-suds foam, then rinsing with a well-wrung, clean cloth. This is worth a try when you have nothing to lose. If trim comes unglued, you can sometimes glue it back on.) I have never had a colored-fabric lampshade, but I have heard that bleeding or running dyes can be a problem. If you have a colored one you had better test the effect of your washing solution first in an inconspicuous area.

Washable-fabric lampshades sewn to the frame can be washed by *immersion* in a washing solution. Parchment, plastic, and laminated or plastic-coated lampshades should not be washed by immersion, but can be washed without being immersed; the parchment and plastic are not harmed by water but, because they do not hold dust the way fabrics do, they can be thoroughly cleaned by dusting and washed by wiping. This is also the safest thing to do, as they may be constructed with glues or other materials that might not survive immersion in water. Instructions for both immersion and nonimmersion cleaning are set forth below.

Note that it would be inadvisable to immerse *any* antique or old fabric shade in water. These are usually exceedingly fragile after long exposure to light and other harmful elements of the environment. I would gently brush such a shade with a soft brush or gently vacuum it with reduced suction power. For any other cleaning, if the shade were valuable or valued, I would consult a professional.

Glass, wood, and bamboo shades should be washed pursuant to the special instructions given elsewhere in this book for those materials. Shades that might shrink a great deal and those made of noncolorfast materials should not be washed. You can regard silk, rayon, synthetic fibers, and preshrunk, colorfast cotton and linen shades—those sewn to the frame—as washable unless the manufacturers' labels state otherwise. If a label states that you cannot wash or dry-clean a shade, I would believe it. Some experts recommend that you not try to wash even "washable" shades because you are so likely to get poor results. I do not think such pessimism is called for, but because I have gotten poor results in at least one attempt at washing a cloth lampshade, I will second the opinion that it is a tricky business. Consider the following suggestions with this caveat in mind. Even faint streaks and spots are terribly noticeable in a lampshade with a light shining behind it.

Fabric Shades: Immersion Method. The hazards to be avoided in home washing are rusting frames (towel dry and then quickly finish air-drying) and streaking or uneven color tone in the end product. The immersion method is best for washable, all-fabric, nonplastic shades because it is the most likely to produce a uniform result. Be as quick as you can through the entire procedure. First remove the shade from the lamp and dust or vacuum the shade thoroughly. Then fill a bathtub with enough lukewarm water to cover the lampshade when it is immersed. Mix in a small amount of a gentle detergent that is safe for the fabric. Immerse the shade. Using a soft brush, cloth, or sponge, start washing at a side seam, working gently in an up-and-down, overlapping motion. Go over the top material first, then the lining. Rinse twice by immersion in clear, lukewarm water. Use white or colorfast terry-cloth towels to dry the shade thoroughly, outside and inside. Blot all excess water with the towels. Then set the shade to dry outdoors on a clean towel or other cloth. Because it is important that the shade dry as quickly as possible, do this only on a sunny, breezy day. If you are an apartment dweller, choose a day when you have a warm, dry room to set the shades in and turn a fan on them while they dry.

Plastic, Plastic-Coated, Laminated Paper, Parchment, and Vellum Shades: No Immersion. Again, begin by removing the shade from the lamp and dusting or vacuuming it thoroughly. Then, to use the nonimmersion method, fill two pails or basins with lukewarm water and add a small amount of mild detergent to one of them. Working quickly on a small area at a time, wash the shade using a well-wrung cloth dampened in the detergent solution, being careful not to soak the shade. Thoroughly rinse each small area with a cloth dampened with clear water and wrung before going on to the next. Wash and rinse both outside and inside and blot with towels as in the immersion method, and finish drying as for the immersion method.

Stains. Stain-removal efforts will be more successful if the shade is first rendered as clean and dust-free as possible. Otherwise, your efforts may simply make a smeary, dark place on the shade.

Try *gently* erasing marks from the shade with a clean eraser. Be sure to supply some backing as you work: hold a clean towel behind the shade as you gently erase the marks. If this does not work, try some solvent-based stain remover or dry-cleaning fluid safe for the fabric. Try to test it first on an inconspicuous area, for discoloration is a big danger, and discoloration on a shade always shows clearly when the lamp is turned on.

Glossary of Rugs and Carpets

American or "sheen-type" Oriental rugs. Reproductions of Oriental rug patterns in Wilton, Axminster, or velvet weave. (The sheen is produced by a chlorine wash or the use of synthetic fibers and is intended to imitate the luster of Oriental rugs.) They may be of good quality and may be woven through to the back, as real Oriental rugs are.

Axminster. A type of cut-pile woven carpet, known for the great variety of colors and designs it can accommodate. It often looks like a hand-knotted carpet.

Backing. The base material into which the pile yarn of tufted carpets is inserted. It may be made of a woven material such as jute or polypropylene or a nonwoven material such as plastic, urethane, vinyl, or latex.

Berber. See "Level-loop pile."

Braided rugs. Rugs made of rags, often of a variety of fibers, braided into long chains, then sewn together, usually in a circle, to form a mat. See "Hooked and rag rugs."

Broadloom. A one-piece carpet in various weaves about twelve to fifteen feet wide. It must be made on a loom broad enough to accommodate this width. Also, a name used for wall-to-wall carpeting.

Brussels. A Jacquard-woven carpet with hard-twisted loops (instead of cut pile like Axminster and Wilton carpets). It is quite durable and of slightly lower quality than Wilton carpets.

Chenille. A type of Axminster rug with a high, dense pile made by weaving together narrow cut strips of woven material with a high pile. It is soft, resilient, luxurious, durable, and expensive. It can be made in a great variety of colors and designs.

Grass rugs. Rugs made of prairie grass harvested in the United States or Canada. The grass is tied into ropes, which are woven into rugs. Sometimes, grass rugs are stenciled or printed with designs, or designs may be woven in. They are usually varnished.

Hooked and rag rugs. Rugs usually used as throw rugs and usually handmade, although some are produced commercially. Loops of fabric or heavy yarn form a pile by being drawn with a hook through some coarse backing—for example, canvas or burlap—that has been stretched on a frame. Hooked rugs can be of wool, cotton, or man-made fibers. Rag rugs are made of pieces of cloth—rags—that are braided, sewn, or crocheted together. Like hooked rugs, rag rugs are available in both machine- and handmade versions. Handmade rag rugs typically are made from rag strips that are braided together into a long rope, which is then coiled and sewn together into an oval or circular shape. Usually the rags are of many different colors and patterns, giving the rugs an irregular design.

Both hooked and rag rugs come in small and large sizes, but are most often used as small scatter rugs. Antiques are likely to be made of fabrics with bleeding dyes, and should not be shampooed.

Oriental rugs. Handmade woven rugs that come from the East, usually Asia, especially Iran, Turkey, the Bukhara region of Uzbekistan, Afghanistan, India, and China. They are woven in a knotted-pile weave using one of two kinds of knots: the *Ghiordes* or *Turkish knot* and the *Senna* or *Persian knot*. The knot secures the pile yarn to the warp yarn, and the ends of its strands stand up as tufts. The Ghiordes knot is actually a twist of the pile yarn. The Senna knot is a real knot. The quality of the rug is in great part determined by the number of knots it has per square inch—the more, the better. Other factors affecting quality are coloring, design, the depth of the pile, the quality of the yarn, and the age and condition of the rug. Oriental rugs are almost always made of wool. A few very fine rugs have a silk pile.

A real Oriental rug can sometimes be identified by two or three characteristics. You should be able to see the entire pattern of the rug in detail on the reverse side. The fringe is produced as an extension of the warp threads; it is never sewn on. The natural dyes used in Oriental rugs fade differently from the aniline dyes used in domestic carpets. The latter fade to different shades; natural dyes fade to paler shades of the original color. To examine the dye, look at the pile closest to the knot. Domestic carpets are lighter in weight in proportion to their size than Orientals. These methods are far from foolproof, however. When in doubt you must ask a reliable expert, who will examine many additional factors such as the knots, the design, and the colors.

Pile. The raised loops, tufts, or yarns on the surface of a rug. A pile is not the same as a nap. Naps are formed by shredding the surface of woven material. Napped materials do not have stand-up loops and tufts. Pile carpets may be produced by many techniques, including weaving, tufting, and gluing.

Rugs and carpets. Sometimes interchangeable terms. Some use the term "carpeting" to refer only to floor covering that is sold by the yard. "Rugs" usually refers to smaller, less substantial floor coverings than carpets. Rugs are usually woven.

Rya rugs. Scandinavian wool rugs with a long pile of one to three inches, often in one-of-a-

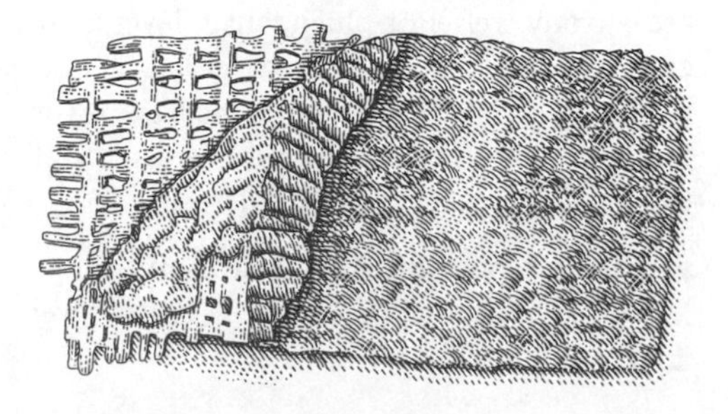

Tufted carpet

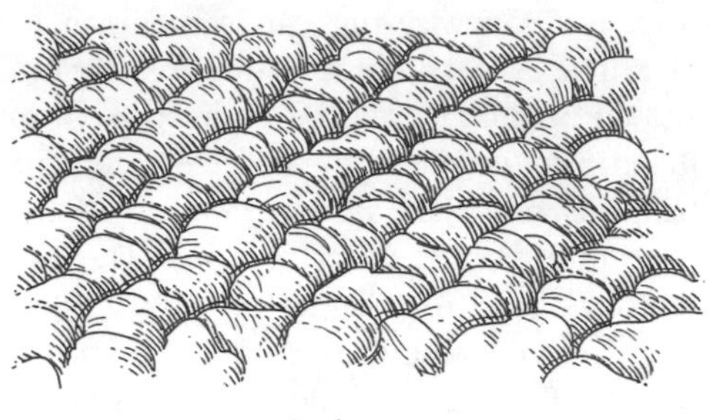
Berber rug

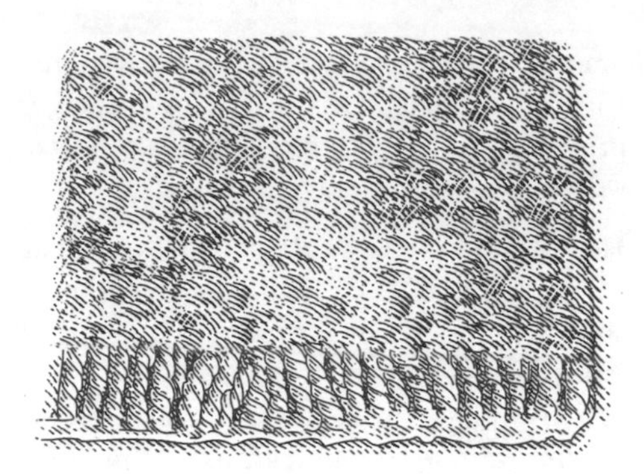
Cut pile

kind abstract patterns of colors in one family. May be hand-knotted with Ghiordes knots (see "Oriental rugs") or machine-made.

Saxony Wiltons. See "Wiltons."

Sisal rugs. Rugs made from the leaf of the sisal plant, grown in Indonesia and Africa. Sisal, a strong and durable fiber, is twisted into strands and woven into rugs.

Shag rugs. Rugs with extra-long pile yarns of an inch or two or even more. The pile yarns flop over in all different directions, because they are so long, and this makes the rug look more densely woven than it is. Shag rugs are hard to clean.

Tufted carpets. Carpets made by inserting pile yarn into a base fabric or backing, which is usually a woven fabric such as jute or polypropylene. Tufted carpets usually use a secondary backing for added strength and stability. Unlike woven carpets, tufted carpets can develop runs: a row of tufts gets pulled out. The chief types of tufted carpets are Saxony, velvet or plush, shag, level-loop, cut-and-loop, and sculptured. Variations on tufting, which glue the tufts to the backing or increase the color and pattern versatility of this type of carpeting, are numerous.

Cut-and-loop pile. A pile with some loops and some cut yarns. It can be either level or multilevel.

Level-loop pile. A pile formed of loops of all the same length. (Multilevel-loop pile has loops of different heights.) What is now called a Berber rug is a level-loop carpet with low, fat loops and a pebbly texture.

Multilevel-loop pile. A pile that has two to three different loop heights, creating patterns.

Saxony tufted carpet. A carpet that uses twisted, plied yarns (but not yarns with a hard twist). It has more twist than velvet rugs, but not much. It has a level-cut pile.

Sculptured carpet. A carpet with a pile surface cut in different lengths to form patterns.

Shag. See "Shag rugs."

Velvet or plush tufted carpet. A carpet with little twist in the surface yarns, in which the cut ends meet closely, giving a smooth, velvety effect. (Plush looks like velvet, but with a longer pile.)

Velvet. A woven rug that, unlike Wiltons and Brussels, is woven on ordinary, not Jacquard, looms, so its color design is limited. The pile is woven over wires that are pulled out, cutting the loops and leaving standing tufts. Because the pile yarn is all brought to the surface, it is quite a durable carpet. It is the least expensive and most common type of woven rug sold in this country.

Wiltons. Cut-pile rugs considered to be among the best of all machine-made woven rugs. Wiltons are expensive. They used to be made only of wool (with pile of either worsted or woolen yarns), but now are made in a number of synthetic fibers as well. Unlike Axminsters, they use only three to six colors and are woven on a Jacquard loom using a method that produces a thick cushion of fibers. Worsted Wiltons, considered the best wool carpets made, are extremely durable and tightly woven, with a fine texture, delicate design, and short pile. A woolen Wilton, which has yarns that are less tightly twisted, is both soft and durable but less resilient than a worsted Wilton. A Saxony is a Wilton made of heavily twisted woolen (rather than worsted) yarns, with a medium-high pile; despite its softness it is quite durable.

Woven carpets. Carpets whose pile yarn is woven in, perpendicular to the warp and backing yarn. They were once the dominant type of carpet but now form a small percentage of all carpets made. The chief types of woven carpets are Axminster, chenille, Wilton, Saxony (a type of Wilton), Brussels, velvet, tapestry rugs, and American Orientals.

Guide to Carpet and Upholstery Stain Removal*

Basic Directions for Carpet Stain Removal†

Use these steps for all the stains listed

For Synthetic Fibers Only

When anything is spilled on carpet surface, removal results are best when stain is treated immediately, before it dries. Water sponging over area will dilute stain, but be careful not to spread stain farther.

For All Carpets

1. Remove excess soil promptly by blotting or scraping with a dull edge first.
2. Apply cleaning materials directly to stain in order listed under numbered steps. Test for 10 seconds and blot in an inconspicuous spot before using a solvent or cleaning materials.
3. Do not rub stain, always blot with clean absorbent white cloth.
4. Avoid getting carpet too wet.
5. When dry, gently brush to restore pile.
6. Some stains are very hard to remove. May need to repeat process two or more times. Some stains are permanent and cannot be removed.

*All material in this guide was written by Anne Field, Michigan State University Extension Specialist, Emeritus, with reference to the Georgia Extension bulletins, "How to Care for Carpets and Rugs" and "How to Care for Your Furnishings," the Hoover Company, Nebraska Extension bulletin "Carpet Care—Cleaning and Stain Removal," the Carpet and Rug Institute, Allied Fibers and Plastics Inc. and DuPont "Clean Up Carpeting" bulletin. All this material is available on the Web site of the Michigan State University Extension (www.msue.msu.edu) under "Home Maintenance and Repair"; a vast amount of further excellent advice on carpets, upholstery, and cleaning throughout the home may also be found on this site.

†See also "Guide to Stain Removal from Clothes, Linens, and Other Household Fabrics," pages 387–90, for further stain-removal suggestions.

to prevent any possible damage to sizings, backings, or stuffing materials. Do not use gasoline, lighter fluid, or carbon tetrachloride.)

2. Mix one teaspoon of a neutral detergent (a mild detergent containing no alkalies or bleaches) with a cup of lukewarm water. Blot.
3. Sponge with clean water. Blot.

Ice Cream

1. Mix one teaspoon of a neutral detergent (a mild detergent containing no alkalies or bleaches) with a cup of lukewarm water. Blot.
2. Mix one tablespoon of household ammonia with a half-cup of water. Blot.
3. Repeat step one.
4. Sponge with clean water. Blot.

Ink (Ballpoint)

1. Sponge with a small amount of dry-cleaning solvent. Blot. (Use small amounts to prevent any possible damage to sizings, backing, or stuffing materials. Do not use gasoline, lighter fluid, or tetrachloride.)
2. Mix one teaspoon of a neutral detergent (a mild detergent containing no alkalies or bleaches) with a cup of lukewarm water. Blot.
3. Sponge with clean water. Blot.

Iodine, Merthiolate

1. Mix one teaspoon of a neutral detergent (a mild detergent containing no alkalies or bleaches) with a cup of lukewarm water. Blot.
2. Mix one tablespoon of household ammonia with a half-cup of water. Blot.
3. Mix one-third cup of white household vinegar with two-thirds cup of water. Blot.
4. Repeat step one. Blot.
5. Sponge with clean water. Blot.

Marking Ink Pen

1. Sponge with a small amount of dry-cleaning solvent. Blot. (Use small amounts to prevent any possible damage to sizings, backings, or stuffing materials. Do not use gasoline, lighter fluid, or carbon tetrachloride.)
2. Mix one teaspoon of a neutral detergent (a mild detergent containing no alkalies or bleaches) with a cup of lukewarm water. Blot.
3. Sponge with clean water. Blot.

Milk

1. Mix one teaspoon of a neutral detergent (a mild detergent containing no alkalies or bleaches) with a cup of lukewarm water. Blot.
2. Mix one tablespoon of household ammonia with a half-cup of water. Blot.
3. Repeat step one. Blot.
4. Sponge with clean water. Blot.

Nail Polish

1. Apply nail polish remover (acetone). Blot.
2. Mix one teaspoon of a neutral detergent (a mild detergent containing no alkalies or bleaches) with a cup of lukewarm water. Blot.
3. Sponge with clean water. Blot.

Paint (Latex)

1. Mix one teaspoon of a neutral detergent (a mild detergent containing no alkalies or bleaches) with a cup of lukewarm water. Blot.
2. Sponge with clean water. Blot.

Paint (Oil-Base)

1. Sponge with a small amount of dry-cleaning solvent. Blot. (Use small amounts to prevent any possible damage to sizings, backings, or stuffing materials. Do not use gasoline, lighter fluid, or carbon tetrachloride.)
2. Mix one teaspoon of a neutral detergent (a mild detergent containing no alkalies or bleaches) with a cup of lukewarm water. Blot.
3. Sponge with clean water. Blot.

Rubber Cement

1. Sponge with a small amount of dry-cleaning solvent. Blot. (Use small amounts to prevent any possible damage to sizings, backings, or stuffing materials. Do not use gasoline, lighter fluid, or carbon tetrachloride.)
2. Mix one teaspoon of a neutral detergent (a mild detergent containing no alkalies or bleaches) with a cup of lukewarm water. Blot.
3. Sponge with clean water. Blot.

Rust

1. Use Whink or Zud or other rust remover. Follow directions on package.

Shoe Polish

1. Sponge with a small amount of dry-cleaning solvent. Blot. (Use small amounts to prevent any possible damage to sizings, backings, or stuffing materials. Do not use gasoline, lighter fluid, or carbon tetrachloride.)
2. Mix one teaspoon of a neutral detergent (a mild detergent containing no alkalies or bleaches) with a cup of lukewarm water. Blot.
3. Sponge with clean water. Blot.
4. Or seek the help of a professional carpet cleaner.

Soft Drinks

1. Mix one teaspoon of a neutral detergent (a mild detergent containing no alkalies or bleaches) with a cup of lukewarm water. Blot.
2. Mix one-third cup of white household vinegar with two-thirds cup of water. Blot.
3. Repeat step one.
4. Sponge with clear water. Blot.

Soy Sauce

1. Mix one teaspoon of a neutral detergent (a mild detergent containing no alkalies or bleaches) with a cup of lukewarm water. Blot.
2. Mix one tablespoon of household ammonia with a half-cup of water. Blot.
3. Repeat step one.
4. Sponge with clean water. Blot.

Tea

1. Mix one teaspoon of a neutral detergent (a mild detergent containing no alkalies or bleaches) with a cup of lukewarm water. Blot.
2. Mix one-third cup of white household vinegar with two-thirds cup of water. Blot.
3. Repeat step one.
4. Sponge with clean water. Blot.

Urine (Dry)

1. Mix one teaspoon of a neutral detergent (a mild detergent containing no alkalies or bleaches) with a cup of lukewarm water. Blot.
2. Mix one-third cup of white household vinegar with two-thirds cup of water. Blot.
3. Mix one tablespoon of household ammonia with a half-cup of water. Blot.
4. Mix one teaspoon of a neutral detergent (a mild detergent containing no alkalies or bleaches) with a cup of lukewarm water. Blot.
5. Sponge with clean water. Blot again.

Urine (Fresh)

1. Blot.
2. Sponge with clean water. Blot again.
3. Mix one tablespoon of household ammonia with a half-cup of water. Blot.
4. Mix one teaspoon of a neutral detergent (a mild detergent containing no alkalies or bleaches) with a cup of lukewarm water. Blot.
5. Sponge with clean water. Blot again.

Vaseline

1. Sponge with a small amount of dry-cleaning solvent. Blot. (Use small amounts to prevent any possible damage to sizings, backings, or stuffing materials. Do not use gasoline, lighter fluid, or carbon tetrachloride.)

2. Mix one teaspoon of a neutral detergent (a mild detergent containing no alkalies or bleaches) with a cup of lukewarm water. Blot.
3. Sponge with clean water. Blot.

Wax (Paste)*

1. Sponge a small amount of dry-cleaning solvent. Blot. (Use small amounts to prevent any possible damage to sizings, backings, or stuffing materials. Do not use gasoline, lighter fluid, or carbon tetrachloride.)
2. Mix one teaspoon of a neutral detergent (a mild detergent containing no alkalies or bleaches) with a cup of lukewarm water. Blot.
3. Sponge with clean water. Blot.

Wine

1. Mix one teaspoon of a neutral detergent (a mild detergent containing no alkalies or bleaches) with a cup of lukewarm water. Blot.
2. Mix one-third cup of white household vinegar with two-thirds cup of water. Blot.
3. Repeat step one.
4. Sponge with clean water. Blot.

*On removing candle wax, see also pages 387–88. On most carpets, especially carpets with high pile, you need not place paper towels under the carpet; and it may not be practical to place the stain facedown, e.g., on wall-to-wall carpeting.

36

Floors and Furniture of Wood and Woodlike Materials

Summary of wood-care basics . . . Protecting wood, substances harmful to wood and wood finishes, water and wood, plasticizer migration, scratches and wear, heat and humidity, light, handling . . . Care of furniture, wood-care products, waxes vs. oils . . . Nourishing wood . . . Waxy buildup . . . Products that interfere with refinishing; silicone oil . . . High vs. low sheen . . . Switching from oil to wax . . . Paste wax . . . Furniture polish . . . Cleaning wood furniture . . . Scratches, marks, and stains on furniture . . . Caring for butcher block in the kitchen . . . Powderpost beetles . . . Protecting wood floors . . . Caring for urethane finishes . . . Special cleaning liquids for sealed-wood floors . . . How to wash urethane or similar hard-finished wood floors, washing on hands and knees, removing scuffs, heel marks, and stains from urethane-finished floors . . . Varnished (nonurethane), shellacked, and lacquered floors, penetrating sealers and natural-wood floors, how to wax, cautions in caring for waxed floors, removing scuffs, heel marks, and stains from waxed floors—Polymer- or acrylic-impregnated wood floors . . . Laminated and prefinished floors . . . Wicker, rattan, cane, and bamboo

No material used in the construction of hard surfaces and furnishings in the home is more important or beautiful than wood. Caring for wood is simple, but, not surprisingly, there is endless controversy about the best ways to do it. Different groups with valid claims to expertise on the subject have different goals and so make contradictory recommendations. Curators and conservators, wax and polish manufacturers, furniture manufacturers, carpenters, furniture makers and finishers, floor manufacturers and installers, and one's relatives all have their own agendas.

No one, however, disputes a few basic ideas about caring for wood. First, everyone agrees on the value of frequent dusting or vacuuming for both wood floors and furniture. Because dust is abrasive, infrequent or improper dusting over the years will create a worn, dull surface. Dust will also accumulate in cracks, grooves, and carvings, where it looks dark and unattractive, and eventually becomes all but impossible to remove. On floors, dust and dirt that are ground into the finish by walkers are the chief cause of deterioration of the finish. Second, skin oils and similar substances that get on wood surfaces over time cause damage to wood and wood finishes. By keeping wood clean you improve its appearance and extend its life. But, third, you should use water in cleaning wood with the greatest possible caution. Last, furniture surfaces should be slippery so that objects and dust glide over them and do not scratch, but floors should not be slippery. Almost anything else anyone can say about caring for wood will be contradicted by some authority somewhere.

Effective care of several delicate and delightful woodlike materials, such as wicker, rattan, cane, and bamboo—used for furniture, shutters, shades, baskets, hampers, and many other home furnishings—follows the same basic principles as care for wood. With these, too, dusting or vacuuming and the occasional damp cleaning will keep them attractive and strong for many years.

Protecting Wood from Physical Mishaps and Environmental Hazards

No wax or polish will protect wood from heat, humidity, light, or rough use. All wood needs protection from these dangers.

Substances Harmful to Wood or Wood Finishes. Alcohol, acetone, and acids and alkalies will harm many finishes—varnishes, shellac, lacquer, and water-based finishes. Alcohol is contained in perfumes, colognes, and many medicines as well as in all wine, beer, and liquor. Acetone is contained in nail polish removers and paint thinners. Various cleaning substances may contain solvents, acids, or alkalies that might harm wood furniture. Fingerprints contain skin oils and perspiration that will over the long haul adversely affect wood

SUMMARY OF WOOD-CARE BASICS

Dust or vacuum furniture and floors frequently.
Never let wood get wet or soaked.
Most wood can occasionally be damp-mopped or damp-wiped without harm so long as the cloth or mop is carefully wrung out and the wood is not permitted to become more than barely damp.
Wax, polish, or clean floors and furniture regularly.
Do not wax or oil urethane-type wood floor finishes.
Natural or nonurethane-finished wood floors should be waxed.
Do not damp-mop waxed floors.

and finishes, especially those that have not been coated with a protective wax or polish. Foods can stain wood and cause the same problems that water does.

Repeated, frequent exposure to even mild alkaline cleaning solutions may soften hardwood finishes over time. (This is why restaurant tables sometimes become gummy or tacky to the touch, even though they are clean. They are cleaned with alkaline cleaning solutions dozens of times each day, and are constantly damp. Chair backs exposed to skin oils over the years also can become tacky.) Only mild or neutral soaps or detergents, therefore, should be used to clean wood, and this should not be done overfrequently. Varnishes, including polyurethane varnish, have better resistance to solvents, acids, and alkalies than do other types of finishes; they also have more resistance to heat. Resistance, however, is not invulnerability; protection and caution are your best bet for all finishes. Against all these dangers, the most vulnerable wood is wood that has no hard finish and that has been given only an oil or wax finish.

Water Is Bad for Wood. When water penetrates a finish, it can cause swelling, warping, and staining. Hard finishes such as shellac, lacquer, varnish, water-based finishes, and polyurethane do not prevent moisture from entering wood, but they slow, or moderate, the rate at which atmospheric moisture enters or leaves the wood, and this is one of the most significant protections they offer. None of these finishes will prevent standing water from eventually soaking through to the wood beneath. Polyurethane varnishes are the most resistant to water; the thicker the finish, the better the resistance. A more resistant finish offers you more time to act in case of spills. When using water to clean wood, carefully avoid getting the wood damp. Follow the instructions on pages 495 and 498–500, below. Use coasters, table pads and cloths, runners, and other protections against water rings and spills.

Plasticizer Migration. Plasticizer migration can occur if you leave plastic objects lying on wood surfaces; color from plastic placemats, tablecloths, notebooks, wrappers, toys,

REMOVING WATER RINGS AND WATER SPOTS FROM FURNITURE

Water rings do not form in wax or polish. If water is left to stand for a few moments on a waxed surface, you may get water marks, but these will come out instantly if you rub them for a moment with a cloth to which a drop of mineral spirits has been applied.

Real water rings—the cloudy or white circles that form when a wet glass or vase is left standing on a finished wood surface and do not go away—are a bigger problem. They form in the finish itself and can be very stubborn. You may have seen suggestions for using mayonnaise mixed with ashes, or toothpaste, to remove such rings. I have tried such methods a dozen times in my life and never succeeded in removing a single water ring—because, I now believe, the real secret is to keep *gently* rubbing for a long time. One friend recently spent forty-five minutes rubbing before she had success. Be careful and observant if you try this! The ashes and toothpaste are abrasive; you are essentially removing the damaged part of the finish with a very mild abrasive. Removing water rings this way may leave an uneven area in your finish; often this will not show if you wax the whole surface when you are through.

Another remedy I have tried is to swipe gently at the spot with a cloth barely dampened with rubbing alcohol. This approach is quite risky, as the alcohol can mar or remove the finish. I have successfully removed one water ring with rubbing alcohol but marred the finish doing so. It looked fine after waxing, however.

and appliance cases can eventually leach into the wood. (This is rather similar to what happens when a magazine is left on a counter or table if it or the surface is damp or if the humidity is high.) Or the plastic may stick to the finish and damage it when the plastic is pulled up. I have observed this dreary phenomenon a couple of times, once when I put a plastic cover under a Christmas tree on a wood floor.

Scratches and Wear. Shellac and lacquer are more vulnerable than polyurethane and other varnishes, and oil and wax finishes have the least resistance to scratching.

To guard against scratches, do not slide objects on wood. Lift them to move them or dust under them. Do not set objects directly on wood, but use coasters, trivets, tablecloths, doilies, and other covers to guard against scratches as well as water, heat, spills, and stains. Use felt bottoms on lamps and decorative objects, but be careful about using colored felt because the color may migrate into the wood. Many experts say to use brown felt, but green is what is often provided.

To conceal minor scratches, use a product such as Old English Scratch Guard in the proper color for your furniture. Follow the directions on the label, putting the product on your wiping cloth, not directly on the furniture.

Heat and Humidity. Wood does best in moderate temperatures and humidity. Temperatures around 70°F and a relative humidity of about 50 percent are ideal for wood. Attics, basements, and warehouses can run to extremes of heat, cold, and humidity. Storage in these places will cause more-rapid aging of wood furniture. (Atmospheric oxygen causes wood to deteriorate over time, just as it makes metals tarnish and rust. There is little you can do to retard this process except keep furniture away from heat.) Wood suffers not only from excess humidity but from too little humidity. High humidity can cause swelling and warping as well as mold and rot; low humidity can cause cracking. Frequent and sudden changes in heat and humidity are a danger in themselves. Repeated exposure to high humidity can cause splitting of the wood and can cause glued furniture to come apart. Wood is more likely to crack when the atmosphere goes suddenly from hot and humid to cool and dry, veneers being particularly vulnerable. This might happen if you shut up your Florida home for a couple of months one summer and set the air conditioner on high immediately upon your return, or if you return to your Maine home in February and set the furnace on high.

Light. Light will bleach any wood surface, no matter what finish, wax, or polish is applied to it. It will also penetrate doilies and tablecloths, although more slowly. Your care strategy should simply be to reduce overall exposure and to expose surfaces uniformly to light. You can do this in several ways: avoid setting furniture where the sun will strike it directly—especially where the sun hits only part of the surface; move objects such as lamps, doilies, artwork, knickknacks, decorations, and other objects that stand on wood surfaces from time to time so that the wood bleaches uniformly. If you close up your home for part of the year or for long vacations, cover the furniture with sheets or blankets while you are gone.

Handling. Try to avoid stacking heavy objects on delicate furniture or overstuffing and overloading drawers. If drawers have two handles, use both to open them. If they stick, apply paste wax to the runners. Heavy or unwieldy pieces of furniture should be lifted by two or more persons; do not slide them along the floor. This will not only harm wood floors, but may bend or harm the furniture legs by subjecting them to too much sideways pressure.

Wood Furniture, Cabinetry, and Woodwork

What Wood-Care Products to Use

Wax vs. Oils. Whether to use oils, waxes, or liquid sprays and polishes on wood furniture is a major ground of disagreement. My father's and grandfather's opinion on the subject provides a useful perspective on this debate, for they believed that you should put nothing at all on such hard finishes as lacquer, shellac, and varnish.

My father made and finished furniture as a hobby that he learned from my grandfather. Both of them were annoyed by the idea of putting wax or polish over a brilliant finish of lacquer, shellac, or varnish painstakingly applied to achieve just the right color, gloss, and satiny texture. Waxes and oils, to a greater or lesser degree depending on the type used and the care employed in application, change the color, shine, and feel of the wood. To the argument that waxes or polishes are necessary to protect the wood, they replied that the finish itself—varnish, lacquer, shellac—is there to protect the wood, and that it is silly to protect the finish with an oily or waxy coating. The finish, they insisted, is tough and long-lasting, given proper care, and when it wears out you are supposed to refinish it—an opinion natural enough in a pair of skilled furniture refinishers with pride of craft.

Many of those interested in the subject dispute only the last point. They believe that it does make sense to try to prolong the life of a finish with protective products. The right product can create a thin protective coating or help preserve the surface simply by making it so slippery that objects sliding along it—lamps or vases or even dust particles—do not scratch. The finish lasts years longer if regularly protected in this way. But authorities disagree on which products provide the best protection.

Once you have made up your mind to polish your finished wood, you must decide what you are going to polish it with. Some people believe that wood needs to be oiled and oppose the use of wax. Others favor wax and oppose the use of oils. Still others think that it does not matter which you use.

Those who favor paste wax contend, first, that furniture paste wax is the hardest, thickest, most long-lasting type of surface protection. This is a claim that I believe, based on my experience and that of my forefathers, who loved the mellow sheen of paste wax on unfinished wood and woodwork. Furniture paste wax is also good on finished wood because it forms a thin, hard coating that prevents dust from penetrating through to the permanent finish and acting as an abrasive on it, and it creates a slippery surface that also reduces abrasion on the finish. Liquid waxes will do the same thing, if to a lesser degree because they go on thinner and sometimes contain less-hard wax. Because waxes dry hard, they do not smear, or attract and hold dust and dirt. Paste wax will last from six months to two or three years, depending on how many coats are applied and how much use the furniture gets. Paste wax, while it certainly does not prevent water rings in the wood's finish, delays their formation and thus can help to reduce their seriousness when they do occur. It gives you a little time to detect the problem and fix it before damage is done. (Use coasters anyway. How quickly water rings form and how serious they are depend on other factors as well, most importantly the type of finish. Shellac is the most vulnerable, and no amount of waxing will prevent water rings in shellac unless you wipe the water up right away. The degree of protection wax offers should not be overestimated.)

Oily polishes, cleaners, and furniture oils will not make a hard, long-lasting coating on the wood, as wax does. The main protection they offer is to increase slipperiness. The shine and more-limited protection last only until they evaporate, which can occur in a few days or, in some cases, a few hours. Those that contain silicone oil last longest, have the highest shine, and create the most slippery surface. (But see cautions about silicone oil below.) Oily products necessarily leave an oily film on wood surfaces that, until it evaporates, smears when you touch it. With oily polishes, as wood-finishing expert Bob Flexner points out, the longer the shine lasts, the longer the smearing lasts, because both indicate that the oil has not yet evaporated.* In my own unscientific home experiments, water rings formed as quickly on finished woods treated with spray and oil polishes as on those to which nothing had been applied.

Does Wood Require Nourishment with Oils or Air to Breathe? The proponents of oily polishes insist that oils provide the only proper way to "feed" or "nourish" the wood, which otherwise will dry out and crack. They argue that wax, unlike oil, stops up the wood's pores, preventing it from breathing, and that wax builds up on furniture, creating a smeary surface and complicating the refinishing process.

Conservators and some refinishers who have looked for a practical or scientific basis for these ideas have found none whatsoever. Wood does not need to be "fed" or "nourished." Furniture wood does not usually contain natural oils, and when it does, the oils never need to be replaced; oil cannot actually penetrate wood cells. Oil does nothing to forestall cracking, and cracking is not caused by failing to oil, polish, or wax the furniture. (The causes of cracking are discussed below.) Nor does wood breathe, and so wax cannot interfere with breathing that does not occur. Humidity definitely affects wood, but wax does practically nothing to keep atmospheric moisture in or out of wood. (The same is true of oils and oily polishes.) The finish, however, if well chosen, actually does moderate the effects of humidity well, beneficially reducing the rate at which it goes in and out.

Should You Worry About Waxy Buildup? Paste and liquid waxes do not cause a waxy buildup. Solvents in the wax dissolve wax left on the surface from prior waxings with each new application. Although an excess of wax might be left on from improper polishing, this is easily avoided and, if it should happen, easily remedied.

Which Products Interfere with Refinishing? The paste wax that you use on your furniture will not get in the way of refinishing in the future. (But do not use it on urethane-type *floor* finishes.) The wax is simply removed first.

Silicone oil is present in 90% of all commercial furniture sprays and polishes. It is inert, does not harm wood, and makes a good shine. But it can cause problems when you wish to refinish furniture. Silicone oil can get through cracks in the finish into the wood, either when polish is applied or during the refinishing process. As Mr. Flexner explains, silicone oil has a low surface tension. When a new finish is applied, silicone oil in the wood makes it go on with an uneven "fish-eye" effect. Unless a skilled refinisher recognizes and deals with this problem (regarded by refinishers as a frustrating one), it can ruin a new finish. If you want to avoid the refinishing problems that silicone oil poses, use products whose labels say that they do not contain silicone oil (such as Guardsman Polish). Caution is necessary because many products that contain silicone oil do not say so on their labels, so you cannot take silence as a guarantee. Look for a product that says it contains none, or call the manufacturer to inquire.

*I am indebted to Mr. Flexner for several enlightening conversations about this and other points in this chapter. For a wealth of further advice on wood furniture care and refinishing, see his outstanding book, *Understanding Wood Finishing* (Rodale Press, 1994).

Other Considerations—Convenience; Appearance. Liquids and sprays of all sorts are most convenient to use for cleaning and dusting wood surfaces. Some of them give a shine more brilliant than wax does, too, if that suits your taste. But a lower sheen more closely resembles fine finishes. Connoisseurs often object to polishes, such as silicone oil, that produce a brilliant shine, because they prefer a softer, more authentic sheen, especially for antiques. When you make your choice, you might also weigh in the balance the desirability of reducing your use of aerosols in the home.

Antiques and heirlooms. Conservators and curators usually oppose the use of anything but paste wax on valuable antiques and heirlooms. Be particularly vigilant against any products that contain silicone oil. Do nothing that will harm or alter the original finish on a very valuable antique or historical piece; it would be wise to consult a conservator about the proper care of such furniture.

Switching from Wax to Oil and Vice Versa. If you have waxed your furniture and wish to switch to a polish containing oil, or the reverse, clean the furniture first with a solvent-based wax remover or use mineral spirits. Do this with plenty of ventilation and far from any sources of sparks, heat, or flame. (Test whatever you use in a safe area before proceeding.) Then wax or polish as you wish. If you should happen to mix wax and oil, you will make the finish look cloudy because the oil will soften the wax. This is an inconvenience, not a permanent problem. Just wipe the mixture off thoroughly, then clean the furniture with a cloth slightly dampened with a solvent-based wax remover or mineral spirits, following the same cautions as above. Let it dry. Then wax or polish as usual.

How to Use Paste Wax on Furniture

Preparing to Wax; Removing Old and Applying New Wax. If a piece of furniture is not heavily used, it can go for as long as a year or two between waxings. Furniture that is constantly used may need paste waxing as often as twice a year. You must go by the look of it. Rewax when you can no longer restore a sheen by gentle rubbing when you dust.

Some wax removers and paste waxes have strong fumes or odors. It is always best to do this work with the windows and doors open, so do this job when the weather is not cold or rainy. First, remove any old wax with mineral spirits or a wax remover. (The reason for removing the old wax is not to prevent a buildup but to get the surface of the furniture cleaner. If you skip removal of the old wax, no harm results other than the loss of a cleaning opportunity.) Apply the removing agent and the wax with a clean cloth, one with no hanging threads, seams, buttons, or anything else that might catch or scratch, and rub the wood with the grain. If the wood has loose slivers, flaking finishes, or damaged or rough areas be careful or you will pull up a sliver or a loose piece of finish or trim and detach it.

Then apply the furniture paste wax to wood that is clean, perfectly dry, and dust-free. With a clean cotton cloth (not the one with which you removed the old wax), dig out a gob of wax about the size of a walnut; if it is too hard to spread, work it in the cloth with your hands until it warms and softens. This will be enough for a whole dresser or wooden chair, depending on how thickly you apply it. Apply the wax *thinly*. If you do not have enough, get another gob and continue in the same fashion until all surfaces of the piece are covered with as thin a coating as possible—carvings, sides, legs, arms, and so forth. Then wait for the time period prescribed on the can (typically about five minutes), or until the wax dries—that is, until the solvent evaporates. If it is a humid day the wax will take longer to dry, and the thicker the coat, the longer the drying period. To remove any excess wax that has dried, apply a little more paste wax to soften a particularly hard spot or, if necessary, use a drop or two of mineral

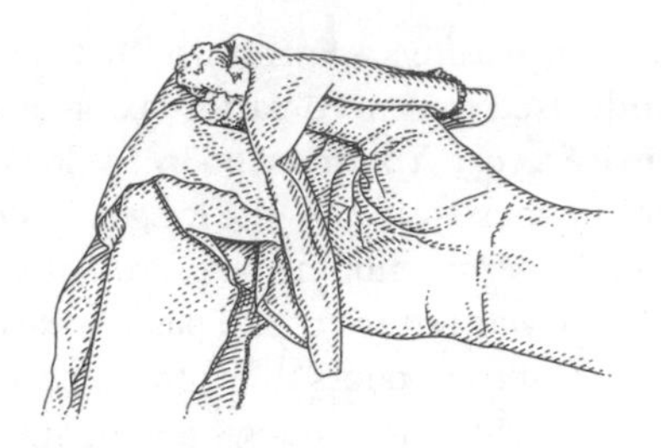

Wax gob in clean cloth

spirits—applied to your cloth, not to the furniture.

Finally, buff the wax with another clean cloth or chamois leather. You can use a power buffer, but I have always done it by hand. When your polishing cloth gets waxy, exchange it for a fresh one. Be careful to avoid getting the wax on upholstery. (You can wash the cloths later in sudsy hot water; add a little ammonia if necessary. *But never mix ammonia with bleach or with wash water to which you have added bleach.* This causes formation of hazardous gases.)

Repeat the entire process for added protection. Two or even three coats last longer and are tougher.

Which Wax? Use a wax whose label says that it is formulated especially for wood furniture. Waxes intended for cars, shoes, or other surfaces may contain substances or abrasives unsuitable for furniture. Use the hardest wax you can find, such as carnauba. (Read labels.) Harder wax lasts longer, protects better, and shines brighter; and dust is less adherent to it. Carnauba wax is so hard that it will always be mixed with other substances to make it workable. Beeswax is rather soft. Liquid waxes are good too. They are liquid simply because they contain solvents, which evaporate in the air when you apply them to furniture. Liquid waxes that contain hard waxes dry just as hard as paste wax, and some people find them easier to apply.

Either natural or colored paste waxes may be used on finished wood. Use only natural wax on unfinished wood. On finished wood, if you use natural wax, you must be more careful to avoid leaving excess deposits of the wax in crevices and cracks, for when it dries there it may leave a whitish residue. Colored waxes will not, and they also do a bit more to minimize the appearance of fine scratches or blemishes—sometimes quite remarkably. However, you must try to get a close color match; an overly dark color will alter the look of your furniture. But do not be dismayed if this should happen, for the effect is temporary, lasting only until the wax wears off or until you remove it (with a commercial solvent-based wax remover or a drop or two of mineral spirits on a clean white cloth). If the polish actually seeps into the wood, that is a sign that your finish is gone. It is time to refinish.

When you buy paste wax, read labels to see what solvent the manufacturer uses. I prefer paste waxes that use mineral spirits or turpentine as a solvent. Those that use toluene seem to me to produce more obnoxious fumes (an unscientific opinion). One authority states that paste waxes that contain toluene (which will be listed in the ingredients on the label) can damage finishes that have not thoroughly cured and can damage water-based finishes even when these are thoroughly cured. Water-based finishes are actually solvent-based acrylic or polyurethane finishes that have been dispersed in water, unlike lacquer, shellac, and varnish, which do not contain water.[1]

How to Use Furniture Polish

When and How to Apply Furniture Polish. Apply furniture polish as often as the furniture appears to need it. Some people like to use spray or liquid polishes designed to aid cleaning and dusting. Not all furniture polishes produce strong fumes or odors, but some do. If yours has a prominent odor, open the windows while you use it.

Follow the instructions on the product. If it is not a cleaning or dusting product, you will be advised to apply it to a clean, perfectly dry, dust-free surface. Use a soft cotton cloth with no hanging threads, seams, buttons, or anything else that might catch or scratch. Apply the polish to the cloth. Typically, the manufacturer instructs you first to wipe the wood with your cloth, spreading the polish lightly and evenly, and then to wipe it off with a second clean cloth.

Which Polish? There are two types of liquid furniture polish. Both are excellent dusting aids, but they contain different cleaners. According to Mr. Flexner, the clear types clean only soil that dissolves in solvents. The milky types clean dirt that dissolves in water as well as dirt that dissolves in solvents. When you have sticky fingerprints, or the remnants of food spills to deal with, you want the milky type.

Cleaning Wood Furniture. Clean wood with water or water-based products only when necessary: if it is covered with fingerprints, stickiness, or food spills, or if it is otherwise dirty in a way that dusting or rubbing cannot remove. You can use a mild or neutral cleaning product designed for wood, following the product directions. If you do not have one of these, you are likely to have several substances in your home that will be fine for this purpose—even a few drops of plain, neutral dishwashing liquid. (See pages 440–41 in chapter 31 and "Detergents and soaps, mild," pages 322–24, and the suggestions for washing wood floors, below. Use a small amount of any such plain, mild, or neutral cleaner in a basin of warm water, or follow the directions on whatever product you are using. *Slightly* dampen a clean cloth (with no hanging strings, buttons, seams, or anything else that might scratch or catch) with the washing solution. Be extremely careful if the furniture has any loose slivers, rough areas, loose trim, or loose, peeling, or cracking finish. (Consider whether you should even subject such pieces to damp cleaning of this sort.) Avoid getting the wood more than barely damp on its surface and avoid letting any water drip or stand on the surface; immediately wipe up any drips. Wipe carefully in the direction of the grain, rinsing your cloth as it becomes soiled, and wringing it hard. Continue until no soil appears on your cloth. Rinse with plain water in the same manner, using a cloth that has been slightly dampened. Then *immediately* rub with a clean, soft, dry cloth in the direction of the grain. Let the wood dry thoroughly before waxing or polishing. This should not take long if the wood is not damp.

You can also clean your furniture with commercial wood cleaners, cleaning polishes, or mineral spirits. Apply the polish, cleaner, or solvent to the cloth, not the furniture surface (unless the product instructions say otherwise), and wipe in the direction of the grain. Rewax or repolish only when the furniture is completely dry. Water-soluble soil, however, such as sticky fingerprints and many food soils, will not be removed by these solvents. If you do not want to use a well-wrung cloth dipped in a little mild detergent and water, try a milky cleaning polish such as Guardsman Polish.

Scratches, Marks, and Stains on Furniture. Camouflage is the best solution for minor damage to wood furniture. Scratch-cover liquids are widely available in various color tones; choose the color that most closely matches the wood. Hardware and paint stores also carry wax sticks and felt-tip touch-up pens designed to conceal scratches and marks. For high-luster finishes only, furniture manufacturers also recommend shoe polish; apply it with a toothpick or cotton swab, and if the resulting color is too dark, partly remove the shoe polish with mineral spirits until you get the color you want. Artist's oil paints (not watercolors) may also be used; apply with a cotton swab or toothpick and wipe dry with a soft cloth. Major damage and all damage to valuable and antique pieces require the services of a professional.

Caring for Butcher Block in the Kitchen. Butcher block used in the kitchen as a food-preparation surface needs only washing (and occasionally, in the proper circumstances, sanitizing—see chapter 13, "Food Safety.") Always rinse it with plain water, then wipe it dry after washing. Even tough butcher block can be damaged by standing water (especially standing sudsy water). Do not use wax or polishes. These contain solvents and other substances that should not come into contact with food. Oils are not necessary, but if you prefer to use one, it should be nontoxic and safe for food-contact surfaces. Mineral oil is usually recommended for this purpose, and, although it offers minimal, if any, protection to the wood, some people like the look of it. Linseed oil, because it is organic, will become rancid over time.

If butcher block becomes pitted or scratched, you can sand it down. Get expert advice on how to do this, or hire help. Replace a cracked chopping board. If a butcher-block table or countertop cracks, consult an expert for a food-safe remedy. The ordinary remedy for this—to fill the crack with a wood filler or wood putty—is not suitable for many surfaces in the kitchen because wood fillers and putty contain solvents and other substances that should not come into contact with food.

Powderpost Beetles. If you find holes in your wood that are round and approximately 1/32 to 1/16 inch in diameter, and if you notice powdery frass or sawdust below the holes, it is possible that you have powderpost beetles. These are insects whose larvae tunnel into wood and emerge as adults one to five years later, through holes to the surface made by the larvae. Infestations may occur in flooring, furniture, antiques, moldings, picture frames, rafters, firewood, and just about anything else made of wood. If you have them in your home, you must do something about them. They can spread from one area or piece of furniture to another and cause a great deal of damage.

If you notice little holes in your furniture, before you panic look for fresh dust or frass, as this indicates that the infestation is active. Holes alone may simply reflect an old, inactive infestation. Powderpost beetles do their damage slowly, so you need not fly immediately into action. You have time to watch the holes, look for frass, and figure out if the infestation is active. This is not always easy to do. I once bought antique chests that were pockmarked with tiny holes, but that luckily proved, after weeks of observation, to be free of insects. Carefully examine any antiques or other wooden items before you bring them into your home.

If you have powderpost beetles, there are several effective EPA-registered insecticides that will work. Look for those that are said to be for use against wood-boring insects. Follow all manufacturers' instructions and observe all cautions on the labels. Or call an exterminator. As a last resort, you may need to fumigate to cure a widespread infestation of powderpost beetles. Only professional, licensed pest-control operators can fumigate your home.

Floors

Protecting Your Floors. Keeping the floors as free of dust as you can is the most important protection you can give them. Weekly, thorough vacuuming or dusting, supplemented by as many daily and partial vacuumings as your schedule permits, is advisable. (See chapter 34.) Dust and dirt ground into the floors when you walk on them will quickly ruin a finish. Doormats at all entrances to your home, preferably one inside and one outside, can remarkably reduce the amount of dust and dirt on your floors and carpets and extend the life of a finish substantially. Dusting by hand is effective. Do not sweep your wood floor with a stiff broom. The bristles may scratch the finish.

Mop up spills quickly, and never let them stand. Place throw rugs (with nonslip backings) in areas where spills are most likely, for example, in kitchens at the sink or refrigerator. Watch out for handmade or other rugs whose color might transfer to the floor, and avoid plastic-backed rugs that might stick to or mar the finish. It is best to rotate rugs now and then so that the floor is uniformly aged by light.

Try to avoid putting furniture directly on the bare floor, for it will easily cause scratches. Place rugs under chairs or tables, or put felt glides, rubber or plastic covers, or other protectors under the furniture legs. Even this will fail to help if you permit grit to collect under the glides. Try to minimize walking on the floor in high heels. Lift and carry, do not slide, furniture across the floor.

In kitchens with wood floors, special caution is necessary to ensure that water and food drips and spills are not left to stand but are immediately wiped up and, particularly where food spills are concerned, that no residues are left behind when you wipe. Some people like to have an area rug (with a nonslip backing) in front of the sink.

In the dry season, cracks will sometimes appear between the boards of wood floors. Indeed, they can become astonishingly wide. These generally go away by themselves when the dry season ends. Keeping your home properly humidified will minimize this problem or prevent it entirely, and is good for all the other wood in your home too, from the piano to the dressers.

Caring for Urethane Finishes. The discussion here applies to all urethane, polyurethane, polyacrylic, and water-based finishes. (Floors treated with penetrating sealers and various prefinished and acrylic-impregnated floors are discussed separately, below.)

Do Not Wax. Although wax will not harm urethane finishes, you should not wax or polish urethane-finished floors. The reasons not to wax urethane-type floors are numerous. To begin with, they do not need to be waxed; they are supposed to be low maintenance. Waxing floors is a time-consuming and laborious task. Waxing can make the floors more slippery, and you will have to exercise appropriate caution. Wax will have to be thoroughly removed before you can refinish the floor because it will prevent any new coat of finish from bonding properly, or will soften the new coat. But wax is extremely tenacious; once it is on a floor it is hard to remove entirely. It seeps into the wood through cracks in the finish. So, to be sure you are rid of it when you refinish, you have to sand waxed floors more deeply; you will not be able to get by with applying a new coat over a shallow sanding of the old. And even if you sand the floor far down, you may not succeed in getting rid of all the wax. Using wax on even small areas to remove marks and scuffs might cause such problems. (None of this is true about furniture with a polyurethane finish because furniture, unlike floors, typically is made of premium wood that is cut and developed differently from floor wood and because floors usually must be refinished more frequently.) Although a few dissenters insist that wax is not a big problem when refinishing, the National Wood Flooring Association (NWFA) comes to the rescue with some common sense. You take a risk in waxing a previously unwaxed floor that will be refin-

WAX THE FURNITURE BUT NOT THE FLOORS

You can use furniture waxes and polishes on wood furniture with any type of finish. You can use floor waxes and polishes on wood floors with old-fashioned hard finishes such as shellac, lacquer, or nonurethane-type varnish and on wood floors without hard finishes of any type (those with oil finishes or wax finishes, for example). Almost all wood floors today, however, are finished with polyurethane or other urethane-type varnishes. Do not wax floors that have urethane-type finishes.

ished, they say, and there is little to be gained by doing so. So why not take it easy instead, and enjoy the natural, long-lasting shine of your floor?

Other Substances to Avoid on Urethane-Finished Floors. You will always be safe if you follow your finish manufacturer's instructions on how to clean and care for your wood floors. If you do not know who your finish manufacturer is, most authorities agree that you will be taking good care of your urethane-finished floors if you use a mild soap or detergent, one with a neutral or near-neutral pH, that leaves no residue, oil, or film behind on the floor. Never allow the floor to be more than barely damp. See "How to Wash Urethane- or Similar Hard-Finished Wood Floors," below. Avoid ammonia, cleaners that contain ammonia, and other strongly alkaline cleaners. Such strong cleaners will dull or damage the finish. Never use any abrasive cleaners, which will scratch the finish and destroy the shine.

Use no sprays designed for dusting and cleaning wood furniture, or any cleaning aids that contain silicone oil or other oils, on such floors. Furniture products will produce a dangerous slipperiness, and silicone oil interferes with refinishing. (Avoid getting silicone oil on your floor by accident too—for example, when you spray an aerosol furniture polish.) Products that contain other oils, as well, may leave a sticky or gummy residue that will dull the finish and impede refinishing. Soaps that contain oil should be avoided, but you cannot necessarily go by the name. Murphy Oil Soap, for example, is simply a soap and contains no oil. It is so named because it is made from oil rather than from fat, as most soaps are. Some experts advise against the use of any soaps, however, on the ground that they leave a soap film that over time will make the floor look dingy or even impede refinishing of the floor. For years I have occasionally washed my polyurethane-finished wood floors with Murphy Oil Soap and have experienced no soap film. But I prefer to buff the floor after washing, both to ensure that the floor is perfectly dry and to heighten the shine.

Cleaning the Floor with Mild Soaps or Detergents; Special Sealed-Wood Floor-Cleaning Liquids. I part company with those experts who say you should never use anything but plain water on your urethane-finished floors. It is simply false that this can keep them clean, and dirty floors are unattractive and unhealthy. Even outside the kitchen, a small admixture of grease is contained in the dirt that collects on floors. You need to put something in the water that will dissolve dirt and grease, and this should be a pH-neutral or mild soap or detergent that will not leave a film or residue. Any mild soap, detergent, or household cleaner is fine—dishwashing liquid (a capful or two in a bucket of warm water), a small amount of Fabuloso, a little Murphy Oil Soap, or even a small amount of neutral, light-duty laundry or mild liquid detergent for washing dishes by hand (the no-bleach, no-brighteners, no-enzymes, and no-additives type). See "Detergents and soaps, mild," pages 322–24, and pages 440–41 in chapter 31. I tend to use Murphy Oil Soap for wood-floor cleaning once every year or two and a little of some neutral cleaner such as Fabuloso or a neutral, plain dishwashing liquid for in-between cleanings. You may prefer to choose any reputable product that advertises that it is designed for wood and is "neutral" or "mild," and use it according to product instructions. Never use ammonia or products that contain ammonia.

To be honest, defying the experts, I do not limit myself to cleaners that really are neutral in pH. My own experience with polyurethane leads me to believe that the occasional cautious use of products that are slightly alkaline, when carried out with normal restraint according to the general instructions given here (especially wringing cloths and mops well and never leaving water or drips standing on the finish), is not going to do your urethane-finished wood floors any harm—at least so long as you do this infrequently. Considering the short period of time your wood finish is in contact with the cleaning solution, your finish is likely to succumb to other causes many years before occasional brief exposures to mildly alkaline cleaning solutions produce any negative results—if they ever do. After many years of washing my own water-based urethane-finished wood floors with a little mild cleaner in water, I find that the finish is still bright and shiny. When a mishap required us to refinish a portion of the floor, there were no refinishing problems.

Following the instructions for care given by the manufacturer of your finish is always the safest bet, and many manufacturers of finishes also produce finish cleaners (to be used according to the instructions on their labels). These are liquid cleaners, not waxes, which are fine except that sometimes they are expensive and sometimes they are hard to find. It is not easy to figure out just what special qualities they may have that are particularly appropriate for a given finish, and I would feel insecure having to depend on any particular product line for something as basic as keeping my floors clean. (In fact, some such products say on their labels that they are designed to work on all sealed-wood floors.)

Several cleaners and care-product lines for sealed wood that are now on the market have been developed especially for polyurethane and its cousins. These cleaners are said to preserve the shine and to cause no refinishing problems. Some are to be rinsed; some are not; some you dilute with water; some you do not. (These cleaners should never be used on oiled, waxed, or unsealed floors. They will turn the wax white and they can roughen or raise the grain on an unsealed floor.) All experts I have spoken to, including those at the NWFA, agree that these cleaning products generally comply with manufacturers' recommendations for good care for urethane-type finishes. I have tried some, which were effective but much more expensive than my mild-detergent-and-water scheme, which seems to get the floor just as clean or perhaps cleaner. I do not know whether these products help the finish last longer. Before using any such specialty product on your urethane-finished floors, test it in an out-of-the-way area to be sure it does not produce excessive slipperiness. Flooring stores, paint and finish stores, and some hardware stores tend to stock them. Many are not available in supermarkets.

White Vinegar? For urethane-type finishes, the NWFA does not condemn one inexpensive cleaning solution that many people like—plain white vinegar in water (a quarter of a cup to a gallon). The Oak Flooring Institute also thinks it all right to use a solution of white vinegar and water. You will nonetheless find some experts who say that over time this mildly acidic solution will cause dulling of the shine on your finish. The commonsense point of view favored by the NWFA is this: the floor is going to grow dull over the years from a number of causes—including those as irremediable as air and light—and it will succumb to those other causes long before the occasional wipe-down with some white vinegar in water produces any harm.

Potential harm aside, however, the problem with vinegar is that it does not do any good. Vinegar, an acid, is not effective as a general cleaner and can do nothing to remove grease; you may as well use plain water and avoid the vinegary smell. Over time, your floors are going to get quite dirty if you never use anything but a little white vinegar and water on them.

Just Plain Water? You can sometimes use plain water on a barely damp mop to clean your urethane-finish floors. But if you stick to plain water alone, soon your floors will become emphatically dirty no matter how often you vacuum or dust. When this happens, not only can you not get all the dirt off, but when you try, you will leave a residue that makes the floor look less shiny and even dirtier than it was. You can restore the shine somewhat by rubbing the floor with a towel, but squeaky-cleanness you cannot have. Still, cleaning with plain water is a good thing to do as an interim cleaning measure now and then. Simply go over the floor with a well-wrung damp mop or cloth occasionally. When you are finished, rub the floor with a towel or buffing pad on a stick, if necessary, to bring up the shine or remove streaks.

How to Wash Urethane- or Similar Hard-Finished Wood Floors. Outside hard-use areas, you will need to do a thorough washing of urethane-finished hardwood floors only infrequently—perhaps once or twice a year. Entryways, halls, and other high-traffic areas may need washing more often, depending on the traffic level; you may wish to wash them seasonally, monthly, or weekly. Kitchens will need washing at least once a week, and probably twice.

First vacuum or dust the floor thoroughly. Then add a little neutral or mild soap or detergent to a bucket of warm water—enough to produce a few bubbles and a slightly slippery feel to the water. Depending on how dirty the floors are, use a little more or a little less of a little stronger or a little gentler cleaner. But never use a strong or strongly alkaline one. Never use anything that contains ammonia. Avoid big suds, which would make the floor too hard to rinse, would dull it, and, in the long run, could even damage the finish. (If you choose to use a specialty product for cleaning urethane-finished floors, follow the product instructions; some are not supposed to be diluted or rinsed.)

Apply the washing-water solution to your mop or cloth, not directly to the floor, and carefully wring out your mop or cloth so that it is only *slightly* damp. (You can use a sponge mop with a wringer attachment.) Pressing down firmly, make several elongated oval strokes in the direction of the grain of the wood. Rinse your mop in the wash water when it becomes soiled and wring it well. Repeat until the entire floor has been washed. *Be sure to wipe up water drops or spills immediately.* If your detergent-and-water solution becomes soiled as you proceed, change it for fresh. Some people use a second bucket of plain water for rinsing out their mop or sponge before reinserting it in the wash-water solution. This keeps the wash water clean longer.

Rinse the floor thoroughly. You can rinse small areas as you go along, using a separate bucket of plain lukewarm water and a separate mop (or sponge or cloth) for rinsing. (This additional bucket is not the one referred to above for rinsing off your washing utensil.) Or first wash the entire floor, then rinse the entire floor. The technique for rinsing is the same as for washing. Use a barely damp, well-wrung mop (or sponge or cloth); make elongated ovals in the direction of the grain of the wood; rinse the mop off as it gets soiled and wring it; and change the water as it soils.

You may or may not think that the floor needs buffing when you are finished. Buff, when necessary, with an electric buffer or with a buffing pad on a stick to bring up a shine. This further cleans and dries the floor.

Scuffs and Heel Marks on Urethane Finishes. On wood floors with urethane-type finishes, you can use one of the new products designed for spot cleaning of scuffs and black marks on sealed-wood floors. Make sure it does not leave the floor slippery. Or use a small amount of mineral spirits on a cloth and rub gently in the direction of the grain to remove such marks. You will sometimes be advised to rub the scuff marks with superfine steel wool, but do this only when matters are serious; it works by taking a bit of the finish off, and in the end you may think the scuff looked better.

Removing Stains from Urethane Finishes. Urethane-type finishes are relatively stain-resistant. Wiping up spills quickly is usually all you need do. For tougher problems see the suggestions in the guide at the end of this chapter. It is a good idea to keep a touch-up kit for surface finishes in your home. These are available from wood-flooring retailers.

Varnished (Nonurethane), Shellacked, and Lacquered Floors, and Floors Without Hard Finishes. If you are among the few who still have floors finished with non-polyurethane varnish, shellac, or lacquer, a good solvent-based floor wax is an advisable protection for your floors. These finishes are not nearly so tough as polyurethane and similar finishes. Wax will help extend their lives; two coats are better than one. Follow the instructions on waxing below. Waxing is particularly important for shellacked floors, which are especially vulnerable to moisture. Never damp-mop shellacked floors (and never let vinegar or ammonia touch them), but you may occasionally clean lacquer and varnish with a neutral cleaning solution in the same manner as you would urethane-finished floors *if the floors have never been waxed*. Wax-finished floors should *not* be damp-mopped. Once they have been waxed, clean them by removing the wax with a manufacturer-recommended or commercial remover or with mineral spirits; then rewax. This cleans the floors quite effectively.

Penetrating-sealer or oil finishes are sometimes used on natural woods. These soak into the pores of the wood and harden there. Some are stained and some are not. These finishes provide much less protection to wood than hard-surface finishes and require more attention. Some natural floors are given no finish at all except wax. All these can be maintained with floor paste wax

WASHING URETHANE-FINISHED WOOD FLOORS ON HANDS AND KNEES

The most effective type of floor washing is done on hands and knees, using a well-wrung, slightly damp cloth, not a sponge. You can feel the floor through the cloth but not through a sponge; you can detect bumpy dirt and the resistance that a sticky area produces. The amount of moisture that comes out of a sponge is less controllable than the amount that comes out of a cloth, and the cloth glides better along the floor. You must make the sponge wetter to get the same smoothness. If you are down on the floor, you can see the dirt better and you can avoid getting the floor more than barely wet. You know exactly how wet the floor is getting because your hands are touching it.

To wash a floor by hand, first vacuum or dust it thoroughly. Then kneel on something soft—an old towel or a flat pillow. Dampen your cloth in the solution of warm water and mild detergent and wring it thoroughly. Then wipe the floor in an oval motion in the direction of the grain of the wood, rinsing your cloth in the bucket of wash water as it becomes soiled and wringing it well. Change the wash water when it becomes soiled. Rinse with plain, lukewarm water in the same manner, using a separate well-wrung cloth, either as you go along or in a separate operation; change the rinse water, too, as it becomes soiled. Buffing by machine is most effective, but you can do this by hand, if you wish, using a clean old towel.

There is no need to go to these lengths if you don't want to or if your knees or other joints won't take it. You can also resort to hand-washing at times—during spring cleaning, for example—and use the mop at others. Or you might want to wash the kitchen by hand once a week or month, and use the mop at other times. Never ask hired housecleaners to clean your floors on their hands and knees; the request is likely to be regarded as degrading. Going on your own knees for your own floors is a different matter.

in the manner described below. You can also use liquid floor wax, but it is not likely to offer so much protection as paste wax, which I much prefer.

How to Wax Nonurethane Finishes, Penetrating-Sealer and Oil Finishes, and Wax-Finished or "Natural" Floors. *Caution: Waxed Floors Can Be Slippery!*

Wax floors about once or twice a year with a high-quality floor paste wax or a liquid floor wax that contains nothing but wax and solvent. If high-traffic areas need attention more frequently, wax those areas alone; you need not always do the whole floor.

Never use water-based or acrylic waxes on wood floors. Try to avoid "one-step" waxes that promise to clean, remove old wax, and lay new wax all at once. They can trap grit on your floor. Paste waxes are excellent; liquid solvent-based floor waxes tend to be easier to apply but tend to go on thinner and may contain less-hard waxes. *Be sure to use a wax formulated for wood floors.* Furniture polishes and waxes will be far too slippery and may contain silicone oil or other substances inadvisable for use on floors.

Before waxing, thoroughly vacuum or dust the floors. Then remove the old coat of wax using a product recommended by the wax manufacturer, following the instructions on the product. Or rub on mineral spirits and then wipe it off with a clean, soft cloth. (Do this only with plenty of ventilation, and away from any source of sparks, flames, or heat.) Let the floor dry thoroughly. Then apply the wax.

Use a wax applicator for liquid wax. If you are using paste wax, apply it directly and spread it with a clean, soft cloth, or work with a gob of wax wrapped in a clean, soft, smooth cloth. Apply wax as thinly as possible; let it dry for the prescribed time period. A longer time may be necessary on humid days. Then buff; a buffing machine is desirable if you are doing entire floors rather than high-traffic spots. (You can rent one.) A second coat, followed by a second buffing, produces extra protection for your floors, and a beautiful sheen. When you buff by hand, rub in the direction of the grain of the wood. Move a buffing machine along the grain too.

As beautiful as is the bright shine on urethane-type finishes, nothing matches the depth and subtlety of the quiet sheen on paste-waxed floors. Buffing occasionally will bring back this look when the floor grows dull; when buffing does not bring it back, it is time to wax again.

Cautions in Caring for Waxed Floors: No Oils. Solvents in oil render wax soft and smeary, so do not use oily products on waxed floors. What was said earlier in this chapter about oiling furniture also applies to oiling floors. The floor needs no oil, and oil alone offers the floor inferior scratch and water protection. If you have oiled your unfinished floors and wish to switch to wax, simply wash them thoroughly first in the manner described above for wood floors with a urethane-type finish. *Be very careful not to let the floor become wet,* and use a very well-wrung mop or cloth. You have no tough finish, such as polyurethane, to protect the wood from the water. If you wet or soak the wood, it will grow rough or harsh or develop a rumpled surface.

Cautions in Caring for Waxed, Oiled, Unsealed, and Other Natural-Finished Woods. On all waxed, oiled, polished, and unsealed floors, avoid the new cleaners for sealed and urethane-finished wood floors. They can turn a waxed finish white. They can also raise the grain on an unfinished wood floor. You can cause the same problems if you try to damp-mop these floors.

Scuff and Heel Marks on Waxed Hard-Finished Floors. Rub the mark with a little paste floor wax and fine steel wool; let dry; then buff. To spot clean waxed floors, rub them with mineral spirits or some other cleaner/remover and a clean cloth, then buff lightly with another soft cloth. Always rub in the direction of the grain of the wood. Put a bit more wax on the spot if it is dull after the spot cleaning.

Removing Stains from Floors Without Hard Finishes (Waxed, Stained, Oiled, Etc.) Suggestions for removing stains from floors without hard finishes, including waxed, oiled, stained, and "natural-finish" floors, may be found in the Guide to Repairing Scratches and Removing Stains on Wood Flooring, pages 504–5.

Polymer- or Acrylic-Impregnated Wood Floors. Suggestions for removing stains from floors without hard finishes, including waxed, oiled, stained, and "natural-finish" floors, may be found in the guide below. Some polymer- or acrylic-impregnated floors also have a urethane-type finish. These floors are to be cared for in the same manner as floors with other urethane finishes. (See "Caring for Urethane Finishes.") For floors that do not have a surface finish, some manufacturers of acrylic-impregnated floors supply a "spray and buff" maintenance and care system relying on products they sell to you. Polymer floors are manufactured with a liquid acrylic forced deep into the wood, and the possibility of water damage is therefore minimal.

Laminated Floors and Other Prefinished Floors. Follow the manufacturers' instructions for care. Before buying such flooring, think about whether these instructions are practical for your intended uses. Some such floors, I have read, cannot be damp-mopped, whereas others are wonderfully washable. Kitchens must have highly washable floors.

Many wood floors are laid with boards that have been finished in the factory. Be sure to find out just how your prefinished floor has been treated and what has been done to it. Some have urethane-type finishes that are to be cared for in the manner described in this chapter for urethane-finish floors. Others have been waxed. It is absolutely necessary for you to know which yours is, for the care and treatment of the two are quite different.

Wicker, Rattan, Cane, and Bamboo

"Wicker" means any pliant twigs or branches, and wicker furniture and furnishings are simply those made of branches flexible enough to be bent and woven into useful and attractive shapes. Rattan, cane, and bamboo, all of which are derived from woody plants, can be cared for in the same way as wicker.

Wicker lasts longer if it is painted with an enamel paint or coated with a clear finish such as polyurethane. These finishes may be touched up, if they grow dull or discolored, with spray lacquer or paint or using a small brush. Do such work outdoors or in well-ventilated areas.

Wicker requires little care. Dusting is most important. This can be done with your vacuum's dusting brush. If and when wicker looks soiled, wash it down with a mild soap or detergent and warm water using a well-wrung cloth or soft brush. Avoid soaking it. Then rinse it in the same way, and immediately wipe it as dry as you can. Let it air-dry someplace where it can dry quickly—in the sun and in a breeze. Make sure that the wicker piece is thoroughly dry before using it again, for it is weaker when wet and may be damaged if you put weight on it.

Remove splinters with a pair of small clippers. You can also use sandpaper on rough spots to make them smooth; then touch them up as above.

Do not let wicker get too dry—especially if it has no finish. Do not leave it to bake in the sun (but you can dry it in the sun after washing), as long exposure to sun can cause warping, splitting, or deterioration. If it seems very dry, wet it a little by wiping it with a damp cloth. Wipe off excess moisture with a towel.

Guide to Repairing Scratches and Removing Stains on Wood Flooring*

If you wish to repair scratches or stains on wood flooring, first determine whether the scratches or stains are in the wood or in the top coat finish.

Natural-finish Floors, Wax-finish Floors, Floors Finished with Penetrating Stains, and Other Wood Floors Without Hard Finishes

If the scratches or stains are in the wood, the floor probably does not have a hard finish.

Scratches. Repair by waxing the area.

Dried milk or food stains. Gently rub with damp cloth. Rub dry and wax. When removing stains from any wood floor always begin at the outer edge of the stain and work toward the middle.

Water stains or white spots. Rub spot with #000 steel wool and wax. If this fails, lightly sand with fine sandpaper and clean the area using #00 steel wool and mineral spirits or a wood floor cleaner. Allow the floor to dry. Stain, wax, and hand-buff.

Heel marks. Rub in small amount of wax with fine steel wool and hand-buff to a shine.

Mold. Rub with a wood cleaner.

Chewing gum, crayon, candle wax. Apply a plastic bag filled with ice until the deposit is brittle enough to crumble off. Crayon or candle wax can be removed by placing an ink blotter on the wax and applying a hot pressing iron to the top of the blotter. Solvent-based wax can also be applied around the area to loosen the deposit.

Oil and grease stains. First rub area with kitchen soap having a high lye content or saturate cotton with hydrogen peroxide and place over the stain. Then saturate a second layer of cotton with ammonia and place over the first. Repeat until stain is removed. Let the area dry and then hand-buff.

Dark spots (dog spots) and ink stains. Try the water spots treatment. If the spot remains, apply a household bleach or vinegar and allow it to soak for an hour. Rinse with a damp cloth, wipe dry, and smooth with fine sandpaper. Stain, wax, and hand-buff.

Cigarette burns. If the burn is not very deep, rub the area with fine sandpaper or steel wool. Moisten the steel wool with wax for better results. If the burn is deep, scrape the area with a pen knife to remove charred fibers. Rub the area with fine sandpaper. Stain, wax, and hand-buff.

Wax buildup. Strip the old wax away with odorless mineral spirits or a wood floor product made for stripping wax. Use cloths and fine steel wool to remove all residue. After the floor is dry, wax and buff.

Wood Floors with Hard Finishes (such as Polyurethane or Other Types of Varnish)

If the scratches or stains are in the finish (superficial), the floor probably has a hard finish.

Scratches. Repair with a touch-up kit made for urethane finishes which are available from any wood flooring retailer.

*The advice given here is adapted from material published on the Internet by the Natural Wood Flooring Association (NWFA) and is reprinted here courtesy of the NWFA.

Food, water, or dark (dog) spots. Use a cleaner developed specifically for urethane finishes to remove the spot or stain. More stubborn spots may require additional scrubbing with the cleaner and a wood flooring scrub pad made for urethane floors.

Greasy spots. Rub the grease, lipstick, crayon, or oil with a cleaner developed for urethane.

Cigarette burns. Most common burns can be treated with a touch-up kit made for urethane finishes (rub with sandpaper, stain, and refinish). For burns that reach deep into the wood, individual plank or parquet boards may need to be replaced.

Chewing gum, crayon, wax. Apply a plastic bag filled with ice on top of the deposit until it is brittle enough to crumble off. Clean area with a product made for urethane finishes. Always use the wood flooring manufacturer's cleaning, repair, and finish products when known.

37

Resilient Floors

Regular care and maintenance . . . Polishing and sealing, using water-based products . . . No-wax floors . . . Spills and stains . . . Cork floors

Resilient floors include those made of vinyl—wax and no-wax—rubber, asphalt, linoleum, and cork. Tiles or sheets of these materials produce floor surfaces that have some "give" as you walk on them. This makes them excellent choices for kitchens and other work areas because they are easy on your feet and legs. Harder surfaces may be more durable, but not nearly so comfortable to walk and stand on for hours at a stretch. Besides being comfortable, most types of resilient floors are easy to keep clean and bright. You can care for them all, except cork, in basically the same manner, using the same kinds of products. Cork is treated separately at the end of this chapter.

Regular Care and Maintenance

Because resilient floors are less hard than stone, wood, and ceramic tile, they are more delicate, and it is even more important to keep them clean. Dust, sand, and dirt will quickly abrade and dull resilient surfaces. Floors that are not regularly cleaned of dirt will also require washing and polishing far more frequently. Use glides or other protective devices under furniture legs to prevent their scratching or gouging the floor. When you are moving furniture, do not drag or slide it across the floor. Always lift it. Area rugs with nonslip backings in places that sustain heavy traffic, such as in front of the kitchen sink, in entryways, and in hallways, also help prevent these areas from looking prematurely worn.

The kitchen can be swept with a broom after each use; this is easier than pulling out the vacuum and it is an effective way to clean grit out of embossed patterns and between floor tiles. (Use a broom properly so as not to raise dust. See chapter 34, "Vacuuming, Sweeping, and Dusting.") In less frequently used areas, sweep, dust, or vacuum thoroughly on cleaning day and less thoroughly—concentrating on heavily used areas—once or twice a week. Resilient-flooring manufacturers will advise you to do this every day, and that would be best for the floor, but few people have time to be so thorough.

Washing resilient flooring once a week is adequate for less frequently used areas. In kitchens or other high-traffic areas, twice-a-week washing is usually required. Some people give the kitchen a quick daily mopping, or might simply damp-mop only the high-use areas and corridors of the kitchen daily.

Before washing the floors, first sweep or vacuum them thoroughly. Wash resilient floors with a solution of all-purpose cleaner or detergent and warm water. If your floors are polished, use a mild cleaner; unless you mean to remove the polish, avoid cleaners that contain ammonia. For particularly stubborn cleaning jobs, go ahead and remove the polish (and repolish when you are finished): use a solution of 1/4 cup of heavy-duty liquid detergent, 1/4 cup of ammonia, and 1/2 gallon of lukewarm water. Wring the mop until it is just damp and not dripping. (Otherwise puddles of water might seep into tile joints and other seams and do damage.) Work on especially stubborn dirt with a medium-stiff brush. Change the cleaning solution as soon as it gets dirty. When you have finished washing, rinse out your mop in fresh, warm water. Then with clean water and a clean, well-wrung damp mop, rinse the entire floor. (Some people use a second mop and bucket of water for the rinsing, and rinse as they go along instead of doing it in a separate operation.) When washing or rinsing, frequently dip the mop to rinse it of all cleaning solution and the soil it has lifted; then rewring it. Change the water for washing or for rinsing when it becomes soiled.

Some people will be unhappy to hear that I prefer to wash kitchen and bathroom floors on my hands and knees, using a piece of thin, old terry cloth to scrub with, and washing the baseboards as I go. Unless you have extremely large floor areas to cope with, however, hand-washing the floors is just as easy as mopping—easier, in my opinion. It unquestionably gets the floors far cleaner. Those with knee or other joint troubles should not try this. Those who would like to try it should wear plastic gloves and kneel on something soft to save their knees. Change the wash and rinse water when it is soiled just as you do when using a mop. You may find that this is actually fast and that you like both the results and the exercise.

Some manufacturers market cleaning and stain-removing products to be used with their floors, and these are always appropriate to the surface. Follow the instructions on the product. If you do not know who manufactured your flooring, you will find similar products available at supermarkets, hardware stores, and home stores. Read the labels and choose one appropriate to your floor type and problem. If you have no-wax floors, be especially careful to choose products that state that they are safe for such surfaces.

I dislike one-step clean-and-polish, no-rinse products. No matter how chemically advanced such products may be, this technique leaves more dirt on the floor than wash-rinse-polish techniques, as you will be able to confirm for yourself; and when the shine-producing chemicals harden (a glossy surface is produced when the water in the solution evaporates), dirt is trapped and begins to build up. People are nonetheless told that they can use several coats—in some cases as many as eight—before removing the old ones. I think it better to use such products only now and then when you are in a special hurry.

Never use undiluted bleach on resilient floors; it may cause yellowing. Abrasives will scratch or dull resilient floors. All strong chemicals are both potentially harmful and unnecessary.

Polishing and Sealing

All resilient floors other than cork may be polished with water-based floor polishes. (On cork floors, use only solvent-based waxes and cleaners. See below.) Water-based polishes for resilient floors are sometimes referred to as "waxes" or "finishes." Such polishes are really clear, water-based acrylic (or other synthetic polymer) finishes that contain no wax, which is solvent-based. Solvent-based polishes or waxes can be used on some resilient floors, but not on asphalt or rubber, in which they will cause severe softening or running of colors. If you do not know what your resilient floors are made of, take no chances and use only water-based polishes, finishes, or sealants. Test any solvent-based product in an inconspicuous area before using it on your floors. When you can, find out the floor manufacturers' instructions about waxes or polishes and follow them.

Before polishing or sealing, thoroughly clean the floor. First sweep or vacuum it, and then wash it. You need not remove the old wax or polish every time you put down new. Removing old polish after three or four coats will be sufficient to prevent a difficult-to-remove buildup or the dulling that comes when dirt is embedded in the old coats. To remove old polish, you may use a solution of 1/4 cup of detergent plus 1/4 cup of ammonia to every 1/2 gallon of water. But you must rinse thoroughly after doing so, or ammonia will remain on the floor and cause the new coat to go on unevenly. Or you may use a commercial product designed to remove this type of polish, following the instructions on the product. Do not use removers for solvent-based waxes unless you have determined that solvents are safe on your flooring and have used a solvent-based wax.

Apply polish or sealant with a sponge mop or a liquid-floor-wax applicator. Follow the product instructions. Often it will be convenient to pour the polish or sealant into a shallow pan, such as a fresh paint tray or an aluminum baking pan, not directly onto the floor. Dip the mop or applicator into the finish and apply a *thin,* even coat to your floor. An excess will not only look bad; it will also attract and hold dirt that is ground into it, and it will be harder to remove. Two coats give greater shine and protection than one.

Water-based polishes for resilient floors are all "self-polishing" these days—that is, you need not buff them. But if you like a higher shine, you can do this with a lamb's-wool pad on a stick, any other soft, clean material, or a buffing machine. Rub quickly and lightly until the surface glows. Turn your cloth or pad as soon as the side you are working on becomes soiled.

Polishing No-Wax Floors

Some readers will be relieved to find out that the name "no-wax" is not an imperative, only a misleading description. Not only can you polish no-wax floors, you probably should. No-wax flooring was first marketed in the 1970s and has since become the most popular type of kitchen flooring. It has many fine qualities, but in most cases shininess without polishes or "finishes" is only a temporary one.

Some manufacturers recommend that you use "restorers" when no-wax floors begin to dull. These, too, wear away, and you must reapply them.

Spills and Stains

Wipe up all spills promptly. Most resilient floors, especially the no-wax types, will not stain if you take care of a spill in a timely manner. If spots remain after the spill is wiped up, quickly rub them with a cleaner suitable for vinyl or no-wax floors. This will almost always be adequate to avoid stains.

Scuff marks can be removed by rubbing them with a nylon abrasive pad, sponge, or soft brush using equal amounts of liquid dishwashing detergent and water. Be sure to rinse thoroughly. Other marks will often come up with a pencil eraser.

Common stains are removed in the following ways. For rust stains, use the old-fashioned lemon-and-salt trick: cut a lemon in half, sprinkle half liberally with salt, and rub it into the stain. Rinse with a sponge and water. Judging by the frequency of claims by floor makers that their no-wax floors resist stains from driveway tar, I assume that this is a common problem. The usually recommended treatment for tar is to rub the spot with mineral spirits. *Warning: mineral spirits may damage the shine of your floor.* Try it on an inconspicuous spot first, and let it dry thoroughly. If it dulls the floor, try to remove the tar by other means. First try chilling it with an ice cube until it is brittle. Then pry it up with a plastic spatula. (If you use a metal one you may scratch the floor.) The tar often will come off in one piece. If a tar-stained mark remains, Consumer Reports' *How to Clean Practically Anything* suggests that you "apply a damp cloth wrapped around a paste made of powdered detergent, chalk, and water. Leave the paste on the stain for several hours."[1] As a last resort, use mineral spirits and then treat the area with an acrylic sealer to make it shine again.

Test all stain-removing solutions in an inconspicuous area before using them where they will show. For stains from alcoholic beverages, juices, coffee, ketchup, mustard, ink, or iodine, use a wet cloth soaked in a solution of 2 to $2\frac{1}{2}$ cups of water and $\frac{1}{4}$ cup of chlorine bleach. For organic stains—blood, grass stains, pet mishaps—and mildew, use either the foregoing bleach solution, straight lemon juice, the lemon-and-salt trick, or hydrogen peroxide.

Cork Floors

Cork, too, is a kind of resilient flooring, but because it is made of an organic material—from the cork oak—its treatment is different from that of the others. It should be swept or vacuumed frequently, as the other resilient floors are. But never clean cork floors with water. Use solvent-type cleaners on them and wax them only with solvent-based waxes. Buff them with a power buffer.

38

Ceramic Tile

Everyday care and cleaning of ceramic tile—excess caution . . . Do vinegar, chlorine bleach, scouring powders harm glazed tiles? . . . Stains and remedies . . . Soap scum and hard-to-remove soil on tiles . . . Sealing unglazed tile and grout

When archaeologists excavate ancient villas in Mediterranean civilizations, they are likely to find the ceramic tiles intact when textiles, leather, and wood have vanished. Ceramic tiles, which vividly evoke the elegance and warmth of these ancient dwellings, provide the same benefits of hardiness, beauty, and grace in our homes today.

"Ceramic tile" is a broad term denoting any tile made from nonmetallic ingredients, such as silica and various types of clay, that is fired to render it hard. Terra-cotta, porcelain, quarry and paver tiles, and ordinary bathroom tiles all are ceramic. Some ceramic tiles have a glaze, a coating that forms a glasslike, lustrous surface on the tile when it is fired. A glaze is not removable or renewable, and, although it is usually extremely durable, after many years it may wear to dullness through scratches and abrasion. Practically all glazes are fairly tough, but delicate glazes are sometimes used on decorative tiles for walls and other places that are not subject to hard wear.

Glazed and unglazed tiles behave differently and require slightly different treatment. Both can endure high temperatures without breaking or scorching. Glazed tiles, however, are more shiny and less porous (more impervious to moisture and spills) than unglazed tiles. The less porous the tile, the more resistant it is to stains. Thus, although hot cookware can be set directly on both glazed and unglazed tile without damaging it, glazed tiles are more popular for kitchen countertops than unglazed because they are highly resistant to food stains. Unglazed ceramic tiles are not strikingly prone to staining, but, being relatively more porous, will sometimes absorb stains, especially if spills are left to stand and especially if the tiles are light in color. Glazed tiles can be quite slippery. Therefore, for floors, matte or semigloss glazes and textured glazes designed to be slip-resistant are preferred. Glazed tiles, being smoother, however, are easier than unglazed tiles to keep clean, because dirt adheres to them less readily.

Porcelain, the most durable ceramic tile, is also almost entirely impervious to liquids. Thus it is the most highly stain-resistant of all tiles. Because its color permeates the body of the tile, scratches and wear show minimally. Porcelain is nearly indestructible with normal use, and therefore is used to make toilets and many sinks and tubs.

Traditional tile grouting, the material used to seal the narrow space between the tiles, is neither so long-lasting nor so dirt-resistant as tile. Sealants will help keep it clean. (See "Sealing Unglazed Tile and Grout," below.) Epoxy grout is considerably more dirt- and stain-resistant than the older cement types of grout.

Everyday Care and Cleaning of Ceramic Tile

All tile floors that are used frequently should be swept or vacuumed daily to remove dirt particles that can accelerate wear. Sand is particularly bad for tile because it is harder than most glazes. Daily sweeping is less urgent for unglazed tiles that benefit from a "worn-in" appearance, but for them, too, frequent sweeping is advisable. All tile floors should also be given a weekly washing to remove dirt. High-traffic areas may need washing two or three times per week. Counters and walls in shower stalls and baths and near sinks need a thorough cleaning once a week to prevent a buildup of scum. Surfaces that are not exposed to water or soap or that are infrequently used should be dusted weekly, and washed as necessary.

Use any neutral, or near-neutral, nonacidic, nonabrasive or low-abrasive detergent or cleanser to wash tile floors or clean tile counters or walls—or use a special tile-cleaning product. Some liquid tile-cleaning products contain gentle abrasives, but these should not worry you unless you have delicate glazes on your tiles. (See "Excess Caution?") Follow all product instructions. If the surface appears dull after cleaning, polish it lightly with a towel. The grout is harder to clean and, being recessed, is passed over when you swipe with a mop, cloth, or sponge. Occasionally you may need to scrub the grout with a brush; a toothbrush can be used on hard-to-reach places. If you have unglazed or matte-finish tiles on your floors, you may find that you must often use an abrasive powdered scouring cleanser to remove marks and scuffs. Such scouring powders are fine for unglazed tiles.

Do not use soap to clean ceramic tile. It leaves a dulling film and eventually may contribute to the formation of hard-to-remove scum.

A prompt cleanup of spills on floors and countertops and splatters on walls prevents soil from hardening and becoming difficult to remove, and prevents staining of the grout and, occasionally, the tile itself. Inks and dyes of any sort, even the dyes in colored grout, are particularly likely to cause a problem. (See "Common Tile Stains and Their Remedies," below.)

To remove mold and mildew from tiles, use a solution of chlorine bleach and water ($^{3}/_{4}$ cup of bleach per gallon of water) and scrub with a brush (or toothbrush, if necessary, to get at the grout). (Test the bleach on inconspicuous areas of tile and grout, especially colored grout, before using.) Mildew will also respond to any commercial mildew-stain remover. Lime and rust deposits will generally give way to scrubbing with a little white vinegar and water followed by thorough rinsing. If that doesn't work, buy a product designed to remove mineral deposits safely. Prevention is easier than cure, however; simply use a squeegee or wipe the tile dry after showering and you will keep mold, mildew, soap scum, and mineral deposits at bay.

Waxing is unnecessary for any glazed ceramic tiles. They generally do not need its protection or its shine, and wax can make tile floors far too slippery. There are tile waxes and finishes designed specially for unglazed, sealed tiles. Such waxes offer no extra protection against stains, but they protect the sealant and increase its life. The only ones I know of, however, render floors more slippery when wet and therefore are not suitable for use in bathrooms, kitchens, or other areas where water gets on the floor. Surfaces on which such waxes have been used can be cleaned with any nonammonia, neutral cleaner.

Using a supermarket kitchen-floor polish, I have successfully polished unglazed, unsealed Saltillo tile. Slipperiness increased modestly but bearably.

Supermarkets, home centers, and tile stores sell many tile-cleaning specialty products, some designed to deal with specific types of stains and soil. Be wary of any that are highly abrasive or highly acidic, but in general they are effective and reliable. If you have hard water, you will probably find it best to make use of a tile-cleaning product to remove scum and mineral deposits now and then. See "Soap Scum and Hard-to-Remove Soil on Tiles," below.

Excess Caution?

You will encounter conflicting advice about the safety for glazed tiles and for grout of white vinegar, bleaches, and powdered scouring cleansers—your grandmother's entire tile-cleaning armamentarium. There is no doubt that certain unusual decorative glazes are delicate and should be cleaned only with nonabrasive, pH-neutral cleaners, or as you have been instructed by your retailer or contractor.

If you have any doubt about whether your tiles have such a soft or vulnerable glaze, ask your contractor or retailer, or test them yourself using either an extra tile or a tile in an inconspicuous area. Test colored grout too. To test a bleach or white-vinegar solution, apply it to a limited area with an eyedropper and let the tile dry overnight. Or scrub it with an abrasive cleanser and observe the results under a magnifying glass. This test will not detect the effects of repeated or long-term use of these substances, but it can reassure you about the effects of a onetime or occasional use.

Leaving the special case of such delicate glazes aside, will any of these substances harm ordinary floor and wall tiles? White vinegar is useful for cutting soap scum, restoring a shine, and removing lime deposits and rust stains, but some experts report that it can etch or damage tile and grout. (This claim is made about all acids, by the way. Other foods besides vinegar are acidic—for example, lemon or other citrus juices and tomatoes; bathroom cleaners are sometimes acidic as well. Read ingredient labels to see if acids are listed.) The experts I vote with, however, insist that a half-and-half solution of white vinegar and water is far too mild to damage today's hardy tiling and that you should feel free to use it when necessary—advice borne out by my own experience. Just limit its use to occasional circumstances and do not use vinegar (or other acids) for your regular cleaning.

A solution of chlorine bleach and water is effective at removing mold, mildew, and many stains. (Try two parts water to one part bleach or a half-and-half solution. Rinse thoroughly.) It is very unlikely to harm ordinary glazed ceramic tile, but test it in an inconspicuous area if you have a doubt. Porcelain tile is always colorfast, and other tiles almost always are. There are some unusual tiles that are not; if you have any type of unusual tiles, it is best to test bleach or any other strong chemical on an out-of-the-way place or on an extra tile that you save for testing purposes, to make sure there will be no untoward reactions. Grout is a different matter. Because some colored grouts are not colorfast to bleach, you must always test yours before using bleach.

Powdered scouring cleansers work magic on soap scum, scuffs, hard-to-remove dirt, and many stains, but the experts are all but unanimous in disapproving of their use on glazed tiles. These cleansers will sooner or later dull and wear out glazes. I have often seen such dulling. On dark-colored tiles, in fact, I have seen the repeated use of abrasives result in "frosting" or lightened places where the glaze has been abraded. Yet I store and use such cleansers. Scouring powders are not needed except in special circumstances—an attack of mold one summer or a scummy film that one day appears on the shower walls. I have not found that the occasional use of these for a special problem has any noticeable negative effect.

For everyday or weekly cleanings, however, use nonabrasive or low-abrasive liquid cleaners, such as Soft Scrub, or mild scouring powders, such as Bon Ami. I can vouch that eight years of regular use of such low-abrasive scouring cleaners has produced no dulling that the eye can detect on new, ordinary, glazed ceramic bathroom tile in my home. And the use of such low-abrasive substances was supplemented by the occasional use of a moderately abrasive scouring powder to deal with special cleaning problems.

Soap Scum and Hard-to-Remove Soil on Tiles

Shower stalls, bathtubs, and bathroom walls near sinks often present special cleaning problems. Soaps, shampoos, and other personal-care products can get on tiles and create a film that is hard to remove. Shower curtains and doors also can develop a soap scum or film. Over time this film builds up, attracts more dirt and scum, and supports the growth of mildew and mold. This is why you are often told that as a preventive measure, you should wipe the walls of the shower or bath to remove body oils and soap and shampoo residues. Ordinarily, a weekly cleaning with your regular cleaner, perhaps supplemented by an extrathorough cleaning every few months, will prevent this problem from developing. (Prevention is always easier than cure.) Vinegar and water will also usually keep scum at bay. If in your case these techniques do not work, you might keep a squeegee or sponge in the shower and clean the walls and doors after each shower, or wipe walls down with a towel destined for the laundry. Wiping the bathroom walls this way also helps preserve your tile by keeping water from standing on it, for minute amounts of chemicals in ordinary tap water may also contribute to gradual wear over the years.

If you develop a serious scum problem—you have been ill or your housecleaner has abused your confidence or your sublessee did not get around to it for three months—you may need to take special steps. First you can try a product formulated for this purpose. Alternatively, if the situation is not too serious, simply wet the surface and sprinkle it with scouring cleanser; let it stand until dry, then scrub it with a brush and rinse thoroughly. If this should fail, or if you can tell from looking at the problem that stronger measures are needed, use this highly effective procedure recommended by the Ceramic Tile Institute: (1) Using a soft cloth or brush, coat the entire surface with *undiluted* liquid detergent. Allow it to dry for several hours. Let badly neglected surfaces stand overnight. (2) Then wet the surface with a solution of liquid detergent and water (in the same proportions as are recommended for ordinary cleaning). (3) While the surface is still wet, sprinkle it with scouring powder; then scrub it with a stiff brush. (4) Rinse it thoroughly,

COMMON TILE STAINS AND THEIR REMEDIES

If you know what caused the stain, seek an appropriate stain-removal agent from the list below (reprinted courtesy of American Olean).

Before trying any remedy described here, first test its safety by trying it on an inconspicuous area of your tiles. If the remedy involves drying, let your test dry. Be sure to test both tile and grout and to observe the results of your test carefully in good light.

Type of Stain	Stain-Removal Agent or Technique
Blood	Hydrogen peroxide or household bleach
Coffee, tea, food, fruit juice, and lipstick	Detergent in hot water followed by hydrogen peroxide or household bleach. Rinse and dry
Nail polish	Dissolve with polish remover. If stains remain, apply liquid bleach. Rinse and dry
Grease and fats	Club soda and water or Spic-and-Span and warm water
Inks and colored dyes	Apply household bleach, let stand until stain disappears, keeping surface wet continuously. Rinse and dry
Iodine (Betadine)	Scrub with ammonia. Rinse and dry
Mercurochrome	Liquid household bleach
Chewing gum, wax, and tar	Use a wood blade (tongue depressor or similar implement) to scrape away the bulk of the material. Chill the material first with an ice cube to reduce smears and spreading. Remove remaining light residue with nonflammable paint stripper (not thinner), *following precautions on label*

Caution! Ammonia and acid, or products containing them, should not be mixed with household chlorine bleach.

and polish it up with a bath towel. This procedure is also what you should do when you move into a home where the bathroom has been neglected and the walls appear dingy or scummy. The results will amaze you.

Sealing Unglazed Tile and Grout

Sealants for unglazed tile and cement grout will prevent many stain and soil problems. (Glazed tiles and epoxy grout need no sealants.) Sealants are clear protective coatings applied to tiles, grout, or both. They are available in different formulations for more- and less-porous tile and greater and lesser shine. Sealants are of two types: surface-applied sealants (usually acrylic or water-based) and "impregnators," or penetrating sealants. Of the two types, the latter is usually preferable, though more difficult to apply. A penetrating sealant enters the pores of tile and grout and renders the surface stain- and dirt-resistant for as long as the sealant lasts—at least one year for surfaces subject to frequent contact and heavy use. If well applied, it will usually last three to five years.

Surface-applied sealants are more widely used because they are the most widely available—you can even find them in some supermarkets—and because they give a glossy finish. However, they will also make a floor more slippery; they may last for as little as six months; and they are not appropriate for countertops. Unlike penetrating sealants, they will scratch and may be susceptible to discoloration from heat. For the intrepid few who have chosen unglazed ceramic tile for their countertops, penetrating sealants will help prevent stains from spills. Any sealant that you plan to use on food-contact surfaces should be nontoxic and otherwise safe and suitable for the kitchen.

Grout benefits from sealing because it soils and stains so much more readily than tile. But even sealants do not completely do away with grout-cleaning problems. It is helpful, therefore, to choose a dark grout to begin with, if possible, or, on floors, to choose to let grout darken naturally.

You may be told that you need use nothing but plain warm water to clean unglazed tile floors that have been sealed, and that all cleaning products will damage or remove the sealant. This is bad advice. It is true that the sealant will last less long if you use cleaning products on it, but it is far from permanent in any event. Even more important, it is impossible to keep tile floors adequately clean, especially in kitchens, using water alone, and you need not choose between a sealant and cleanliness. Continue to use any neutral or near-neutral cleaning product (nonacidic, nonalkaline, nonammoniac), and avoid abrasives on sealed tile floors and counters.

39

Stone

Physical and chemical characteristics of different types of stone . . . Granite, limestone, marble-penetrating sealants, finishes, or dressings for stone, polished stone vs. honed stone, flamed finish . . . Cleaning stone, vacuuming, washing, waxing, specialty products, soap scum on marble . . . Scratches and stains

Stone has always had its niche in the home, but its popularity has grown enormously in the last quarter century. More types of stone—including marble, granite, limestone, slate, and travertine, and other stones—are more frequently used for flooring, furniture, countertops, vanity tops, and walls than ever before. These different types of stone call for different kinds of care and maintenance. But, in important respects, what constitutes the proper use and treatment of stone is a function of which of two main types of stone it is.

Calcareous stone, which includes marble (and marble insets in terrazzo), limestone, and travertine, is composed primarily of calcium carbonate. (Travertine is a limestone, usually buff-colored. It is often sold as marble, but it is not marble. Raw and unpolished, it has a textured appearance because it has hundreds of tiny holes in it. If it is polished, the holes are filled with mastic.) *Siliceous* stone, which includes granite, slate, quartz, sandstone, brownstone (a type of sandstone), and bluestone (another type of sandstone), is composed primarily of silica or a silica-containing compound—the main ingredient in sand. Physically, calcareous stone tends to be more porous and less hard; chemically, it is vulnerable to acids and can be etched or damaged even by weak acids such as vinegar and lemon juice. Siliceous stones are, physically, less porous and harder than calcareous; chemically, they are vulnerable to strong alkalies but can also be damaged by strong acids. The Marble Institute of America counsels that, if you do not know what your stone is, you can test it yourself to find out, in an inconspicuous area, using vinegar dropped from an eyedropper. If the stone is calcareous, the vinegar will etch the surface.

Physical and Chemical Characteristics of Different Types of Stone

The less porous the stone, the less likely it is to stain; the harder it is, the less likely to scratch and crack. Although marble continues to be regarded as the most beautiful and elegant of all stones, granite—a far harder and less porous stone—is superior to marble when durability and ease of care are the criteria. A dark-colored granite is highly stain-resistant, and is more and more commonly being seen on kitchen counters and floors.

Although intrepid designers occasionally use porous stones such as marble and limestone for kitchen countertops, these will stain easily and they are particularly vulnerable to etching by spills of acidic foods and drinks. Acids can also seep into the fissures of the stone and cause damage. Wipe acidic spills—vinegar, citrus fruit juices, wine—off marble and other calcareous stone immediately.

Penetrating sealants are often recommended to render stone more stain-resistant. However, the Marble Institute of America does not recommend the use of penetrating sealants on stone. Although manufacturers of these sealants maintain that they work by penetrating the stone, the Institute is unconvinced by any evidence it has so far examined that this is really true. According to the Institute, the sealants remain on the surface of the stone and easily come off. They fail to prevent stains, and using them gives people a false sense of security. If you nevertheless wish to use a sealant in the kitchen, make sure that on any food-contact surface you use a nontoxic sealant that is safe and suitable for use in the kitchen.

Proper care for stone also depends on whether it is *polished* or *honed*. Polished stone is glossy, sometimes to the point of being reflective. Honed stone has a satin finish; it is smooth but not reflective. The more polished stone is, the more special care it needs, for the polishing on any stone dulls in time. The polish on a hard stone such as granite will last longer than that on marble and other, softer stones. When repolishing is necessary, have it done professionally. To preserve the polished surface for as long as possible, keep it waxed or protect it with a surface sealant.

Less polished, honed finishes are preferred on floors, stairs, entryways, and other places that would be dangerous if slippery and that are going to take hard wear. These honed finishes, too, benefit from a little protection. You can use carpets, area rugs, or throw rugs in high-traffic areas such as entryways. Be sure to use either nonslip backings or nonslip mats under rugs, for a slippery rug on a smooth stone floor is a dangerous state of affairs. Doormats immediately inside and outside entry doors are extremely helpful; tracked in dirt and grit are the main cause of scratched and dull stone surfaces. The Marble Institute of America estimates that it takes at least eight steps before the dirt on your shoes is removed in ordinary walking. (The International Wool Secretariat in England estimates, similarly, that people's shoes are cleaned of dirt only after walking over three meters of absorbent matting.) Regular cleaning using proper methods and materials is also important for protecting stone. Waxing is protective too.

On counters and furniture surfaces of calcareous stone, use coasters, trivets, mats, cloths, and the like under glasses and dishes to protect the surfaces from acidic and staining foods and drinks, such as citrus, fruit, and berry juices, vinegar, and wine. All types of stone should probably be protected from hot objects with trivets or insulating mats, just to be on the safe side. Put cloths, place mats, or runners under dishes and silver.

They can scratch stone's finish. Use protectors of some sort under lamps and decorative objects, too, for these may scratch.

A third type of finish, the flamed finish, is often used on granite floor tiles. Passing the stone under a flame causes it to flake, creating a rather rough surface. This finish is chosen both because it is attractive and because it is less slippery than smoother surfaces.

Cleaning Stone

Vacuuming, Washing, Waxing. Vacuum or dust stone surfaces, including floors, once or twice a week to keep them looking and feeling good. (Use the same methods applicable to any hard, smooth surfaces, as described in chapter 34, "Vacuuming, Sweeping, and Dusting.") This will also help to keep them in good condition because abrasion by dirt dulls them quickly. Do not use dusting sprays or chemically treated mops or cloths on stone.

Wash stone surfaces when they become soiled, using a mop or cloth or soft- or medium-bristled scrub brush, as you prefer, with a small amount of some neutral, mild detergent. Thoroughly rinse (twice if necessary) and dry with a soft cloth. Use no soap, as it may leave a film. Alkaline cleaners—for example, ammonia or strong soaps and detergents—are particularly bad for siliceous stone such as granite and sandstone, but they are not recommended for *any* stone, including marble and other calcareous stone. Although a weakly acidic cleaner is not so potentially damaging to siliceous stone as it is, say, to marble, the experts insist that *all* stone is best maintained with a neutral cleaner. Polished finishes are more vulnerable to all strong cleaners and abrasives. On polished stone, use no scouring powders or liquids that contain abrasives. On duller finishes, mild abrasives, if necessary, can be tried.

Waxing is not needed, but you can improve the appearance of some scratched stone and give a little protection to polished finishes, if you wish, with paste wax. Keep in mind, however, that polished stone will not dull unless it is subjected to abrasion; you should not feel obliged to keep it waxed. Do not use paste wax on travertine or other nonsmooth stone surfaces or on white or white-background marble, however. It will accumulate in the indentations of stone that is not smooth, and will get into the pores of white marble and turn it yellow. You can use a clear, nonyellowing stone-care product for stone that shows any white on the surface. When the surface is clean and dry, apply a thin coat of paste wax, let it dry for a few minutes, then buff. (See chapter 36, pages 494 and 502, for more about paste wax.) Or follow the directions on whatever stone-care product you have chosen.

Some people like to use car wax on marble. The advantage of this, I have been told, is that it resists certain kinds of chemical spills, such as alcohol, well. I do not know whether there are types of car wax that contain ingredients harmful to any type of stone, but a knowledgeable and conservative person in the marble industry confided to me that he has used Simonize car wax on his marble, without incident, for years.

Specialty Products. You need no special or unusual products to take good care of stone. There are many different kinds of specialty cleaners, sealants, waxes, finishes, and "dressings" for stone on the market. These usually are perfectly safe for your stone (assuming you read the labels to determine what uses they are intended for), but some experts feel that such products are unnecessary, and these experts encourage us to feel free to choose the simpler regime, outlined in this chapter, of regular dusting or vacuuming and washing as necessary with a neutral detergent. If you wish, you may also apply a wax or similar finish (after washing, rinsing, and drying). If you prefer the specialty products, you will find different sorts designed for different types of stone, for polished and unpolished stone, for floors, for high sheen or low sheen, and so forth. The manufacturers of these products recommend various care and maintenance schedules for their use. Such schedules may call for frequent buffing or repeated applications of sealants or dressings. Usually you can carry out the regimen yourself without professional help, but you may find yourself committed to more- or less-complicated care routines depending on the products you choose.

Soap Scum on Marble or Other Calcareous Stone. If you have marble in your bathroom, it may collect soap scum. This is a problem because the normal remedies for soap scum—acids and abrasives—are harmful to marble. Do not use vinegar (or any other acid or acidic cleanser) or scouring powders to remove soap scum from marble. The Marble Institute of America recommends that you use ammonia—1/2 cup of ammonia to a gallon of water. But it also notes that with frequent use ammonia will dull the surface, so save this treatment for times of real necessity. Better yet, avoid the problem altogether by wiping down walls and other surfaces where soap scum tends to appear with a towel after baths or showers.

Scratches and Stains

There are stone and marble polishes, also called "rock polishes," that are designed to be used to remove water rings, minor scratches, or dull spots. These are generally mildly abrasive powders that you use to buff the surface. Use them according to the directions on the product, or get expert instruction. You may need very little (one type requires only 1/16 of a teaspoon with a drop of water to make enough to polish ten square feet), and you must proceed cautiously. You can find these at home centers, hardware stores, and retailers of stone-care products.

When you have a potentially staining spill, acting quickly is the best defense. Clean up spills right away, and do not give them a chance to soak deep into the stone. *Blot* the area with a white paper towel or clean white cloth. If you wipe the spill around, you may spread it. Then flush the area with water and a mild detergent solution. Rinse several times. Repeat, if necessary. If a stain remains, refer to the stain removal guide, below.

Guide to Removing Spills and Stains from Natural Stone Surfaces*

Spills and Stains

Blot the spill with a paper towel immediately. Don't wipe the area, it will spread the spill. Flush the area with plain water and mild soap and rinse several times. Dry the area thoroughly with a soft cloth. Repeat as necessary. If the stain remains, refer to the section on stain removal.

Stain Removal. Identifying the type of stain on the stone surface is the key to removing it.

*The material in this guide is excerpted from "Care and Cleaning for Natural Stone Surfaces," Marble Institute of America (1995), and is reprinted here courtesy of the Marble Institute of America.

If you don't know what caused the stain, play detective. Where is the stain located? Is it near a plant, a food service area, an area where cosmetics are used? What color is it? What is the shape or pattern? What goes on in the area around the stain?

Surface stains can often be removed by cleaning with an appropriate cleaning product or household chemical. Deep-seated or stubborn stains may require using a poultice or calling in a professional. The following sections describe the types of stains that you may have to deal with and appropriate household chemicals to use and how to prepare and apply a poultice to remove the stain.

Types of Stains & First Step Cleaning Actions

Oil-based (grease, tar, cooking oil, milk, cosmetics). An oil-based stain will darken the stone and normally must be chemically dissolved so the source of the stain can be flushed or rinsed away. Clean gently with a soft, liquid cleanser with bleach OR household detergent OR ammonia OR mineral spirits OR acetone. DO NOT MIX BLEACH-CONTAINING SUBSTANCES AND AMMONIA!

Organic (coffee, tea, fruit, tobacco, paper, food, urine, leaves, bark, bird droppings). May cause a pinkish-brown stain and may disappear after the source of the stain has been removed. Outdoors, with the sources removed, normal sun and rain action will generally bleach out the stains. Indoors, clean with 12% hydrogen peroxide (hair bleaching strength) and a few drops of ammonia.

Metal (iron, rust, copper, bronze). Iron or rust stains are orange to brown in color and follow the shape of the staining object such as nails, bolts, screws, cans, flower pots, metal furniture. Copper and bronze stains appear as green or muddy-brown and result from the action of moisture on nearby or embedded bronze, copper, or brass items. Metal stains must be removed with a poultice. (See section on "Making and Using a Poultice.") Deep-seated, rusty stains are extremely difficult to remove and the stone may be permanently stained.

Biological (algae, mildew, lichens, moss, fungi). Clean with dilute ($^1/_2$ cup in a gallon of water) ammonia OR bleach OR hydrogen peroxide. DO NOT MIX BLEACH AND AMMONIA! THIS COMBINATION CREATES A TOXIC AND LETHAL GAS!

Ink (Magic Marker, pen, ink). Clean with bleach or hydrogen peroxide (light-colored stone only!) or lacquer thinner or acetone (dark stones only!).

Paint. Small amounts can be removed with lacquer thinner or scraped off carefully with a razor blade. Heavy paint coverage should be removed with a commercial "heavy liquid" stripper available from hardware stores or paint centers. Do not use acids or flame tools to strip paint from stone. Paint strippers can etch the surface of the stone; repolishing may be necessary. Follow the manufacturer's directions for use of these products, taking care to flush the area thoroughly with clean water. Protect yourself with rubber gloves and eye protection, and work in a well-ventilated area. Use only wood or plastic scrapers for removing sludge and curdled paint. Normally, latex and acrylic paints will not cause staining. Oil-based paints, linseed oil, putty, caulks and sealants may cause oily stains. Refer to the section on oil-based stains.

Water spots and rings (surface accumulation of hard water). Buff with dry 0000 steel wool.

Fire and smoke damage. Older stones and smoke or firestained fireplaces may require a thorough cleaning to restore their original appearance. Commercially available "smoke removers" may save time and effort.

Etch marks. Caused by acids left on the surface of the stone. Some materials will etch the finish but not leave a stain. Others will both etch and stain. Once the stain has been removed, wet the surface with clear water and sprinkle on marble polishing powder, available from a hardware or lapidary store, or your local stone dealer. Rub the powder onto the stone with a damp cloth or by using a buffing pad with a low-speed power drill. Continue buffing until the etch mark disappears and the marble surface shines.

Contact your stone dealer or call a professional stone restorer for refinishing or repolishing etched areas that you cannot remove.

Efflorescence. A white powder that may appear on the surface of the stone. It is caused by water carrying mineral salts from below the surface of the stone rising through the stone and evaporating. When the water evaporates, it leaves the powdery substance. If the installation is new, dust mop or vacuum the powder. You may have to do this several times as the stone dries out. Do not use water to remove the powder; it will only temporarily disappear. If the problem persists, contact your installer to help identify and remove the cause of the moisture.

Scratches and nicks. Slight surface scratches may be buffed with dry 0000 steel wool. Or, refer to the section on etch marks and follow the polishing procedure. Deeper scratches and nicks in the surface of the stone should be repaired and repolished by a professional.

Making and Using a Poultice

A poultice is a liquid cleaner or chemical mixed with a white absorbent material to form a paste about the consistency of peanut butter. The poultice is spread over the stained area to a thickness of about 1/4 to 1/2 inch with a wood or plastic spatula, covered with plastic and left to work for 24 to 48 hours. The liquid cleaner or chemical will draw out the stain into the absorbent material. Poultice procedures may have to be repeated to thoroughly remove a stain, but some stains may never be completely removed.

Poultice Materials. Poultice materials include kaolin, fuller's earth, whiting, diatomaceous earth, powdered chalk, white molding plaster or talc. Approximately one pound of prepared poultice material will cover one square foot. Do not use whiting or iron-type clays such as fuller's earth with acid chemicals. The reaction will cancel the effect of the poultice. A poultice can also be prepared using white cotton balls, white paper towels or gauze pads.

Cleaning Agents or Chemicals

Oil-based stains. Poultice with baking soda and water OR one of the powdered poultice materials and mineral spirits.

Organic stains. Poultice with one of the powder poultice materials and 12% hydrogen peroxide solution (hair bleaching strength) OR use acetone instead of the hydrogen peroxide.

Iron stains. Poultice with diatomaceous earth and a commercially available rust remover. Rust stains are particularly difficult to remove. You may need to call a professional.

Copper stains. Poultice with one of the powdered poultice materials and ammonia. These stains are difficult to remove. You may need to call a professional.

Biological stains. Poultice with one of the poultice materials and dilute ammonia OR bleach OR hydrogen peroxide. DO NOT MIX AMMONIA AND BLEACH! THIS COMBINATION CREATES A TOXIC AND LETHAL GAS!

Applying the Poultice

1. Prepare the poultice. If using powder, mix the cleaning agent or chemical to a thick paste the consistency of peanut butter. If using paper, soak in the chemical and let drain. Don't let the liquid drip.
2. Wet the stained area with distilled water.
3. Apply the poultice to the stained area about 1/4 to 1/2 inch thick and extend the poultice beyond the stained area by about

one inch. Use a wood or plastic scraper to spread the poultice evenly.

4. Cover the poultice with plastic and tape the edges to seal it.
5. Allow the poultice to dry thoroughly, usually about 24 to 48 hours. The drying process is what pulls the stain out of the stone and into the poultice material. After about 24 hours, remove the plastic and allow the poultice to dry.
6. Remove the poultice from the stain. Rinse with distilled water and buff dry with a soft cloth. Use the wood or plastic scraper if necessary.
7. Repeat the poultice application if the stain is not removed. It may take up to five applications for difficult stains.
8. If the surface is etched by the chemical, apply polishing powder and buff with burlap or felt buffing pad to restore the surface.

40

Man-Made Solid Surfaces and Other Plastics

Characteristics of man-made solid surfaces . . . Routine care for sinks and counters . . . Regular maintenance . . . Stains . . . Disinfecting sinks and countertops . . . Scratches and cuts . . . Laminates . . . Careful treatment of laminates . . . Cleaning laminates . . . Polishing laminates . . . Other plastics: care and cautions

Plastic is one of the most widely used materials in the home, and many surfaces that are not immediately thought of as plastic are, including stereo equipment and speaker cases, telephones, some bathtubs, paints and varnishes, many parts of computers, vacuum cleaners and other appliances, skylights and storm windows, and a thousand more. In kitchens, bathrooms, and elsewhere in the home, several types of strong, stonelike plastics and a variety of plastic laminates are commonly used for countertops and vanity tops, sinks, shower walls, and similar fixtures. Most of us can afford to learn more about the physical strengths and weaknesses, the chemical vulnerabilities, and the best ways to clean and care for the plastic materials used in the home.

Solid Surfaces

Characteristics of Solid Surfaces. Man-made solid surfaces have grown deservedly popular. They are attractive and functionally superior to every other material for kitchen and bath use. They can be expensive, however.

There is no useful generic name for these solid surfaces, but there is some tendency to call them all "Corian" after the first of them, which was produced by DuPont in the 1970s. The number of brand names is increasing. All types are solid, hard, tough, nonporous synthetics. They have a look and cool feel akin to stone but are lighter than stone. They are quite stain-resistant.

Solid surfaces are given a matte (also called satin) finish when used for sinks and, usually, for kitchen counters. Glossier finishes need more protection and are less well suited to the hard wear that kitchen countertops ordinarily receive. Semigloss, satin, or high-gloss finishes are typically used for vanities and low-wear areas. The color or pattern on solid surfaces goes all the way through the material; thus it does not wear and cannot be rubbed or abraded off, and scratches are hard to see. Surfaces with matte finishes are easily cleanable, which is one of the most important virtues of these materials. You can use abrasives, bleaches, and vigorous cleaning methods to remove stains, scratches, soil, and marks and restore man-made solid surfaces to their original appearance.

Solid synthetic surfaces can withstand fairly strong impacts without cracking or breaking. They are not indestructible, however, so you should never stand on them and you should try to avoid dropping heavy objects on them. But if the worst happens, they are remarkably reparable. If the material should crack, a contractor or other professional can usually insert a new piece with such a fine seam that the eye cannot detect it.

Extreme heat will damage solid synthetics, causing yellowing or scorching. (Such marks are removable, however.) But these surfaces can withstand moderate heat. You might cause cracking if you poured boiling water directly into a solid-surface sink. Manufacturers therefore advise that if you pour boiling water into the sink, you run ample cold water at the same time. Use trivets or heat pads under pots and appliances that get hot.

Strong chemicals can be damaging too; strong acids, oven, drain, toilet cleaners, and paint removers and thinners, nail polish, and anything else that contains acetone are among those that may cause problems. If one of these should be spilled onto the solid surface, immediately clean it off and flush the surface with water.

Do not cut directly on the solid surface; use a cutting board. Knives can scratch the surface, and the surface can dull the knives too. Although knife scratches can be removed fairly readily, it is worth avoiding the trouble of doing so. Abrasives can be used to remove almost all marks and stains.

Routine Care for Sinks and Counters. Follow the manufacturer's care and maintenance instructions. If you do not know the manufacturer, the instructions below are similar to those supplied by several manufacturers. Use any ordinary soap, detergent, or cleaner, including window cleaners and cleaners containing ammonia. Rinse the surface thoroughly and wipe it dry with a tea towel or paper towel to ensure that it does not look dull or streaky.

If you like, you can apply a countertop polish, but this is not necessary. In kitchens, you wash the counter so frequently that soon you will simply wash the polish off. On special occasions, however, you might wish to do this. It gives counters an attractive low luster. The manufacturer of Corian recommends Hopes Countertop Polish for matte (satin) and semigloss finishes; for high-gloss finishes, it recommends a white polishing compound of the same sort that you buy from automotive supply stores for a car—Turtle Wax, for example.

Regular Maintenance. If a surface with a matte finish appears to have grown too shiny during use, wet it and rub it with a green Scotch-Brite pad. To do this properly, flood the surface with water and use even, circular, smooth motions. Do not press too hard. "No white knuckles," said one manufacturer.

To deep-clean a sink, fill the sink with a half-and-half solution of chlorine bleach and water; let it soak for fifteen minutes. Then wash the sides and bottom as the sink drains, rinse, and dry as usual.

Stains (Including Stains and Scorches from Cigarettes). For matte (satin) finishes, the manufacturer of Corian appears to have changed its thinking about stain removal. It used to recommend that you scour with a scouring powder—Ajax, Comet, or a similar abrasive cleanser—using a green Scotch-Brite pad, then rinse and dry as usual. Now it advises that on matte finishes you use the same procedure recommended for semigloss finishes. (I, however, have continued to use the stronger measures on white matte Corian with excellent results and no problems that I can detect.) On both semigloss and matte finishes, it now advises, use an extramild abrasive such as Soft Scrub or Bon Ami on a white (less abrasive than green) Scotch-Brite pad. Scour, then rinse and dry as usual. To even up the gloss after using these procedures on matte and semigloss finishes, you can use Hopes Countertop Polish.

On high-gloss finishes, use an extramild abrasive such as Soft Scrub or Bon Ami, but apply it with a sponge. Rub, then rinse and dry as usual. To restore the shine, the manufacturer of Corian recommends you use a white polishing compound. (See "Routine Care for Sinks and Counters," above.)

Nail polish comes off any finish with *non-acetone-based* nail polish remover. *Acetone can harm solid-surface materials.* Or try the scouring procedures above.

You can use bleach on any finish to deal with stains from wine, tea, and food coloring. But these stains will probably also respond to the treatments described above.

If cigarette burns, scorch marks, or other marks do not come off with this treatment, proceed as for "Scratches and Cuts," below.

Disinfecting Sinks and Countertops. The chlorine bleach solution described for sinks in chapter 13, page 175, is safe to use for sinks of man-made solid surfaces. Man-made solid surfaces, by the way, are also said to be inhospitable locales for bacteria because of their low porosity.

Scratches and Cuts. It is best not to use solid-surface counters as cutting boards, for they will take tiny cuts and scratches from sharp knives or other sharp edges. (Such surfaces will also dull your knives.) However, if scratches occur, it is not a disaster; the scratches can be removed. Scorch marks and other marks that do not respond to the methods prescribed under "Stains," above, can be removed in the same manner as scratches.

On matte finishes, if the scratch is shallow, it may be eliminated when rubbed, wet, with a green Scotch-Brite pad. If it remains, you can sand it off with ultrafine sandpaper. To do this, check your manufacturer's instructions as to how fine the sandpaper should be, and learn how to use it properly. Or call the manufacturer for advice. Although you can probably do the job yourself on matte finishes, on semigloss finishes think about calling a professional. On high-gloss finishes, call a professional unless you are very handy. If you decide to do it yourself, it is important to follow your manufacturer's instructions. Not all solid surfaces are alike.

Laminates

Careful Treatment of Laminates. Laminates are hard materials consisting of two or more layers bonded together: a hard, thick base made of chipboard or similar material, and a thin covering material on the surface made of a plastic derivative. Formica is the most familiar example of a laminate. Until recently, most laminates have been inexpensive and only modestly durable. The plastic coating often separated from the base material. It scratched rather readily. It scorched and stained easily, too.

Newer, often more costly, laminates on the market are sometimes superior to the older ones. They scratch and stain much less easily and therefore are much more durable. However, they will still stain and scratch, and you must be careful when trying to remove spots. Use a cutting board; sharp knives can permanently damage the laminated surface. In "color-through" laminates, the color permeates the entire surface layer, rendering knicks and scratches less visible than on other laminates.

To be sure of the proper care and cleaning of your laminated surface, refer to the manufacturer's care pamphlet. The advice on care and cleaning set forth here is general and may not apply to every type of laminated surface. High-gloss and decorative laminates are quite likely to be more delicate than others, and different manufacturers' laminates may have different vulnerabilities.

Generally speaking, laminated surfaces may be damaged by alkalies, acids, rust removers, abrasives (including metal pot-scratchers, steel wool and soaped steel-wool pads, and powdered cleansers—even mild cleansers and scrubs are not recommended), coffee-pot cleaners, ceramic cooktop cleaners, some countertop cleaners, metal cleaners, oven cleaners, drain cleaners, toilet cleaners, and dyes of any sort, including hair dyes, textile dyes, and food coloring. Watch out for bottles and other containers of these potentially damaging substances too. Don't set one on a laminated surface in case some of its contents have spilled down the side of the bottle. Do not set rags or sponges saturated with these substances on laminated surfaces. If any of these substances should touch your laminated surface, immediately blot it up (don't spread it), wash the counter, rinse it thoroughly, and then dry it.

Heat, too, can scorch, crack, or blister laminates. Never place pots hot from the stove or hot irons on a laminated counter. Use trivets, heat pads, or other appropriate protection. Use such protection, in addition, under all heating appliances such as waffle irons, toasters, electric skillets, and coffee pots.

If you place flowerpots or decorative objects on a laminated surface, put protective pads or cloths under them to prevent scratching when they slide, or other damage to the surface.

Never flood or soak laminated surfaces. The water can enter at the seams and cause the base material to swell, cracking or deforming the smooth laminated surface or causing it to separate.

Avoid heavy blows to laminates, which can gouge or crack them.

Don't set newspapers on a laminated surface, particularly if it is or may become damp. Newsprint can stain.

Cleaning. All laminates may be washed with mild liquid or powdered detergents in water. Rinse and dry with a soft cloth. Rinsing is important. Cleaning solutions left on laminated surfaces for long periods of time can sometimes permanently etch them.

To remove stuck-on soil, first soften it by dampening. To avoid flooding or soaking the laminate, lay a moderately damp (not sopping wet) cloth on the soil for a time. Then brush the soil off with a medium-stiff nylon-bristled brush dipped in a solution of detergent and water. Don't use a very stiff brush, as it might scratch. *Caution: Do not use a brush on high-gloss or metal laminates;* you may damage the finish. These delicate finishes are not recommended for kitchen counters or other places where they will be subject to hard wear.

Stains. When it comes to stains on laminated surfaces, sometimes a wait-and-see policy is best. Food, coffee, tea, and food-coloring stains sometimes just wear away with normal use and washing. If washing and waiting are unsuccessful or if you are dealing with nastier stains, try the stain-removal techniques below. All of them are to one degree or another risky, and may damage your laminated surface. To test whether you will harm the surface, first test in an inconspicuous area. In all cases, when you have a bad stain, first check your manufacturer's care pamphlet or call your contractor or manufacturer.

Intransigent marks may respond to an all-purpose household cleaner. Apply it full strength and leave it for a few minutes. Then blot the surface with a clean, soft cloth and rinse thoroughly.

Some stains can be lightened with a baking-soda poultice. These include stains caused by hair dyes, mercurochrome, iodine, bluing, and silver nitrate. Add enough water to baking soda to form a spreadable paste and gently apply it to the stain. Let the paste stand for a few minutes, then gently wipe it up, rinse thoroughly, and dry. If you see you are making progress, repeat.

Ink stains, among others, will probably not respond to the foregoing methods and may be permanent. Although the major laminated-surface manufacturer in the United States does not recommend this, as a last resort use diluted household chlorine bleach on laminated surfaces to remove ink stains or other bleachable stains, even though *this risks harm*. Try one part bleach to two parts water, or a half-and-half solution; but *test it first* in an inconspicuous area to see just what it does. (I have heard reports of bleach-damage to laminated surfaces.) Leave the solution on the stain for a couple of minutes, then *rinse thoroughly*. If the bleach seems to be helping and not hurting, repeat the process until the spot is gone. Some, who offer personal testimony that this works, say to use the bleach undiluted, letting it stand for one or two minutes *at most* and then rinsing extremely thoroughly and quickly. Certainly you should *test* this in an inconspicuous area before proceeding. *Remember: Never mix any solution containing chlorine bleach with any acid, alkali, or ammonia, or any substance containing any of these. Toxic or deadly gases or other dangerous reactions will result.*

You can try denatured alcohol or other solvents on solvent-soluble stains. Test first, and be sure to follow all safety precautions that apply to the use of solvents. Remember that solvents are flammable and give off flammable fumes. See chapter 60, "Fire."

If the spot remains, call the manufacturer or a professional for help.

Polishing. If you have laminates in places other than a bath or kitchen, ordinary dusting may be sufficient to clean them most of the time. You can also use a non-oily furniture spray, counter polish, or plastic polish a few times a year. This will help conceal fine scratches and add luster.

Other Plastics

The plastics used in such diverse products as telephone receivers, computer mice, toys, radio cases, shelves, kitchen appliances, and storm windows are adapted to their functions, and they can be extraordinarily unlike one another. Despite this diversity, a few generalizations about maintaining and caring for plastics are helpful. Polishes for plastic advertise that they clean, repel dust, eliminate static, and create a shine on all types of plastic. They are all nonabrasive. When you are uncertain what cleaning substance would be safe on plastic, you might turn to one of these.

If it were not for the fact that every rule has its exceptions, I would say that every plastic is washable with a mild or neutral all-purpose detergent. You can use baking soda and water inside the refrigerator. Chlorine bleach solutions are safe for most plastics, but you will have to test them in an inconspicuous area to be sure that you are not dealing with one of the exceptions. Follow manufacturers' instructions exactly when cleaning any electric appliance. You can use all ordinary measures to get rid of soap scum on plastics, including bathroom cleaners designed to do so and mildly acidic solutions, such as vinegar and water. Subject to the caveat concerning ammonia and alkalies under "Cautions to Observe with Plastics," below, window cleaners are effective on many plastics.

Cautions to Observe with Plastics

On most plastics, you should avoid using all harsh cleaners: oven cleaners, drain cleaners, toilet bowl cleaners, or any cleaner containing lye or other strong alkalies, or strong acids. Mild cleaners are safest and best.

When you are in doubt, test any household cleaning substance on an inconspicuous area before using it on something made of plastic.

Some types of plastic used for clock faces, skylights, and windows, and storm doors will turn streaky and cloudy if they are cleaned with alkaline cleaners, including laundry detergents, all-purpose cleaners, and ammonia.

Acetone harms some plastics. The plastic control panels on appliances can be damaged by the solvents in some stain removers. Rarely, alcohol will damage something made of plastic, but usually alcohol is safe. Test first if you have any doubt.

A few plastics, such as Corian and other man-made solid-surface materials, can safely be cleaned with abrasive cleansers (as described above); most would be readily scratched. Acrylic and fiberglass baths or showers would be scratched by powdered cleansers or other abrasives.

Avoid excessive heat on plastics. Many will melt or scar. Hot irons, cooking pans, cigarette ashes, and boiling water can do great damage to some plastics.

Many plastics are breakable. They crack if banged or if a weight falls on them. Some will be marred by knives, scissors, or other sharp objects.

41

Bathrooms

Cleaning and disinfecting bathroom fixtures . . . Porcelain enamel tubs and sinks . . . Nonslip treads in tubs . . . Fiberglass . . . Acrylic . . . Whirlpool baths . . . Reenameled tubs . . . Stainless-steel sinks and basins . . . Bidets . . . Commodes or toilets . . . Faucets, showerheads, metal shower frames

By the early twentieth century, sinks, tubs, and chamber pots had gotten themselves attached to drains and pipes, and the modern kitchen and bathroom had been born. Every bathroom had its toilet of vitreous china and its cast-iron sink and tub coated with "porcelain enamel," which was (and is) actually a remarkably tough vitreous china. The laundry or basement might have housed large cement basins.

Vitreous china and porcelain enamel are still commonly found in kitchens and bathrooms; some new hard plastics have been developed, but these have by no means elbowed the older materials aside. In laundries and basements you'll find a few cement sinks, but plastic ones are more common. If you know who manufactured your sinks, tubs, toilets, whirlpool baths, and basins, follow the manufacturer's care instructions. If not, you may wish to try the procedures given below. All fixtures in the kitchen and bathroom benefit from regular cleaning, using safe products and techniques, and from plumbing that is kept in good repair. Improper cleaning and leaks are the chief causes of damage.

Cleaning and Disinfecting in the Bathroom

The use of disinfectant cleaners is desirable in the bathroom, especially in and around the toilet. (See chapter 30, "Peaceful Coexistence with Microbes.") Follow the product directions, being especially careful to allow the recommended contact time. In addition, if you rinse after using a disinfectant cleaner,

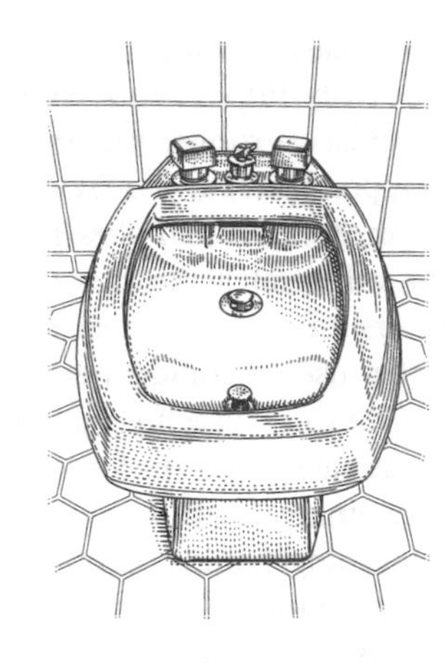

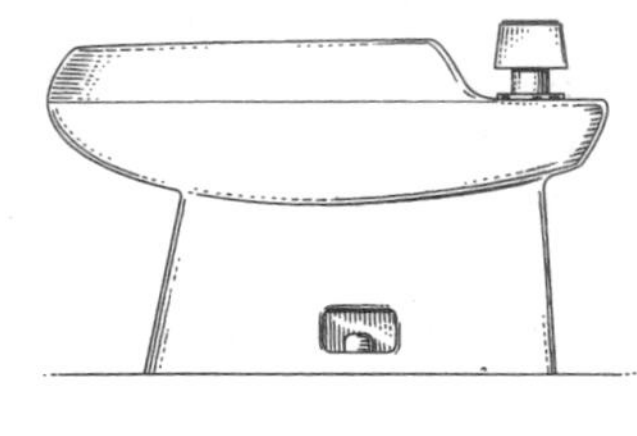

Bidet

people wash their feet in it, as it is considerably lower than a sink basin. Rinse the bidet after using it.

Like the toilet bowl, it is made of vitreous china. You can clean it in the same way as a tub or sink, using any of the same cleaning substances. Any ordinary bathroom cleaners will do. If you have hard water, you must use the same caution as with a toilet to be sure that spray holes are not plugged by lime deposits; you might try Lime-A-Way or a similar product to get rid of them. Use of a disinfectant bathroom cleaner is a good idea.

Care and Cleaning of Commodes (Toilets)

Commodes or toilets by law must be made of nonporous materials. Vitreous china is both tough and nonporous, and is therefore all but universally chosen for this purpose. The exterior of vitreous china toilet bowls can be cleaned in the same way as tubs and sinks. Use of a disinfectant cleaner is desirable. Toilet-bowl cleaners of all sorts are safe for vitreous china toilet bowls. If you have brass fittings inside the tank, however, be cautious about using in-the-tank cleaners. Check labels to make sure the contents will not corrode brass.

When using toilet-bowl cleaners, be careful to avoid splashing them. They often contain harsh chemicals that can be dangerous to your skin or eyes. Read the product instructions thoroughly before beginning to use toilet-bowl cleaners, and follow the instructions carefully. Such products can also be harmful to countertops and other materials.

If the toilet-bowl cleaner is dry—grains or powder—you will usually be instructed to wet the sides of the toilet bowl using a long-handled brush and then to sprinkle the product on the sides and in the water. Let the cleaner stand for at least ten minutes, or longer if you have tough stains. Then scrub with a long-handled brush, being sure to scrub thoroughly under and around the upper rim and as deep into the trap as you can reach. Gel cleaners are touted as having the advantage of adhering to the sides of the bowl better than liquids or dry cleaners, so they work harder during the waiting period. With gels and with liquids you simply squirt the product under the rim, on the sides, and in the water. Some people like to empty the bowl of most of its water before cleaning so that a thick coating of cleaner can work on the portion of the bowl that is normally immersed. To do this, use a plunger or pour half a bucket of water into the bowl. (Some toilet bowls will empty if you simply flush, then flush again before the tank has a chance to refill.) When the bowl is clean, rinse thoroughly by flushing.

If you find that you need to scrub matter off the sides of the toilet bowl by hand, use disposable plastic gloves. Make a paste of powdered cleanser and water or use an all-purpose cleaner, and rub with some cleaning tool that you can throw away or disinfect, such as a paper towel, brush, or rag. Throw away the disposable plastic gloves, too, when you are finished.

If you live in a hard-water area, you can periodically use a product such as Lime-A-Way around the rim to ensure that the holes do not become plugged with lime deposits.

The plastic and enameled-wood lids and seats that are used on many toilets require much gentler treatment. They readily wash up with nonabrasive mild cleaners. Use disinfectant cleaners according to instructions on their labels. Abrasives will leave unattractive dull spots or, on enameled wood, take the enamel off and expose the wood. Ammonia and strong chemicals of any sort are not recommended.

On clearing a stopped-up toilet, see chapter 42, "Pipes and Drains."

Faucets, Showerheads, and Metal Shower Frames

Faucets and showerheads are generally, but not always, made of chrome. Use any nonabrasive bathroom cleaner to wash them. Rinse them and rub them dry to bring up the shine. If yours are not chrome, follow the manufacturers' instructions for cleaning them.

To remove rust or hard-water deposits, try any mildly acidic solution such as a half-and-half solution of white vinegar or lemon juice and water, or use a commercial preparation for this purpose such as Lime-A-Way.

42

Pipes and Drains

Pipe and drain maintenance . . . Clearing drain clogs . . . Stopped-up toilets

Pipes and drains require a little attention to ensure that they remain free flowing and sweet smelling. You also need to know how to remove minor clogs in sink and tub drains and how to unstop the toilet. For more-elaborate repairs and stubborn clogs, call your plumber—and take steps right now to make sure you know a plumber to call when a plumbing emergency arises. Ask a reliable friend or neighbor or check the yellow pages. When you have a name, ask the plumber if he or she is licensed; get the license number and verify it with whoever issues such licenses in your community. Ask the plumber for references from people for whom he or she has recently done work and call those people to see if they were satisfied with the job and the charges for it.

There are many who become fascinated with the pipes and drains and faucets in their homes. They often buy self-help books and appropriate tools and become capable of handling minor plumbing jobs and emergencies themselves. If you are of a mechanical turn and you own a house, check into the books on the subject in your local bookstore. Two of the better ones are *The Stanley Complete Step-by-Step Book of Home Repair and Improvement* (Simon & Schuster, 1993) and *Reader's Digest New Complete Do-It-Yourself Manual* (Reader's Digest, 1991).

Maintenance

To keep your drains free flowing and clean, periodically take steps to prevent clogs from developing. Pour boiling water down drains now and then, especially in the kitchen, to melt grease; do this every time you have any boiling water left over, for example, after making tea or coffee. Now and then use one of the recipes for drain maintenance given in chapter 31 or use an enzyme drain cleaner. Enzyme drain cleaners work gently and will not harm your pipes. But they are slow working and limited in effectiveness. Periodically, disinfect your kitchen drains. See chapter 13, page 175.

Clearing Drain Clogs

If a sink or tub is clogged, first pull out the drain stopper to see if food or a wad of hair or soap is blocking the drain; if so, pull out

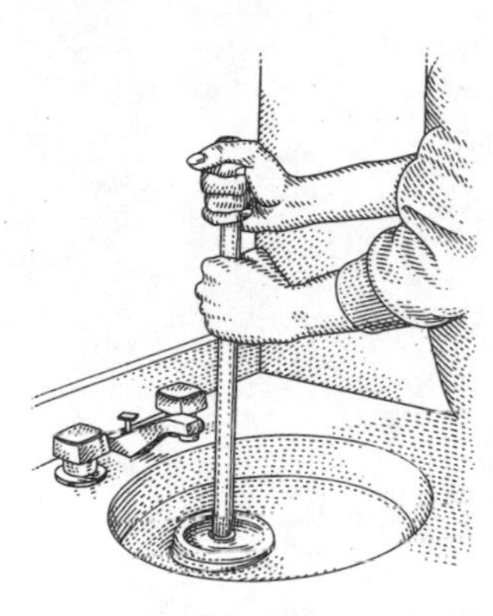

Plunger

the blocking material. Use your fingers (wear plastic gloves if you wish) or a big pair of tweezers that you keep for such purposes. If this does not work, use either of the home remedies for stopped-up drains given in chapter 31. Then use your plunger (sometimes called a "plumber's helper"). Place it tightly over the drain opening and press and pull rapidly and forcefully without lifting the plunger off the drain. It will not work unless you get a seal tight enough to force air or liquid back and forth in the drainpipe. (In a double sink, you must make sure that the other sink is stopped up, airtight.) If the sink or basin is filled with water, do the same thing, trying not to splash. If this doesn't work, you might try letting an enzyme drain cleaner stand in the drain overnight—follow the manufacturers' instructions—and repeating your efforts with the plunger in the morning. If this does not work, call the plumber.

Strong chemical drain cleaners such as Drano are not recommended by many experts because they can harm your pipes. If you decide you want to risk this, use them very cautiously, following the manufacturers' instructions to the letter. They usually contain lye and are dangerous.

Stopped-Up Toilets

If the toilet is stopped up and overflowing, do not flush it. Turn off the water. You'll find the knob behind the toilet, low on the wall. If the bowl is filled to the brim, wait for a while to see if the water subsides to any degree so you need not cause a spill. Another reason to wait is that sometimes a stopped-up toilet will correct itself if you just give it time. If it doesn't, when the water has gone down a little (or when you can see that it isn't going to) place your plunger tightly over the drain hole and press rapidly and forcefully without lifting the plunger off the drain hole. The clog almost always gives way after a few thrusts. If the toilet bowl has drained completely, it often helps to pour enough water in so that the plunger is covered when you press it to the drain hole. Do not flush the toilet to do this or you may cause an overflow.

When you have succeeded in clearing the stoppage, flush a couple of times with the plumber's helper in the toilet bowl to rinse it clean. Then wash the plunger in a solution of water, detergent, and a little chlorine bleach. You can do this right in the toilet bowl, too. Then lift it up, shake off excess moisture into the toilet, and replace it in its ordinary storage place.

If the plunger does not work, the Plumbing-Heating-Cooling Information Bureau recommends that you try a "closet augur" or a "snake," available at a hardware store. This is not necessarily easy to do. The Bureau says to push the hook end in first, gently, and gently twist and work it until it makes a zigzag or "S" shape; then pull it out. Repeat as necessary. Be careful not to let it get stuck in the toilet, because there may be no getting it out without destroying the toilet. I do not know just how you might avoid this, which is why I would call the plumber before matters come to this pass.

43

Walls, Ceilings, Woodwork, and Windows

Walls, ceilings, and woodwork . . . Vacuuming and dusting . . . Washing painted walls, ceilings, and woodwork . . . Cleaning moldy ceilings . . . Cleaning acoustical-tile ceilings and walls . . . Cleaning wallpaper: washable, scrubbable, nonwashable . . . Removing spots and stains . . . Cleaning windows and window coverings . . . Window frames . . . Window screens . . . Storm windows, storm doors, and skylights . . . Window glass . . . Blinds, shades, and shutters

Walls, windows, and ceilings shelter our lives at home, but go unnoticed until walls and woodwork become streaked, fingerprinted, spotted, and dusty, or windows admit little light. Then rooms feel increasingly dark and unkempt until you take action. Vacuuming and dusting will keep walls, ceilings, and windows clean and attractive for long periods. Washing, repainting, or repapering walls becomes necessary only infrequently. This is often one of the chores that is tackled during spring cleaning. Windows, however, need washing more often.

Walls, Ceilings, and Woodwork

Vacuuming and Dusting. Ceilings and walls of all types need an occasional vacuuming to clear away the dust. Use the long brush attachment on your vacuum; start at the ceiling and work your way down the walls to the baseboards. You can use a dust cloth instead if you choose, but it is more likely to knock dust off the ceiling onto the floor. Dry sponges will also work for dusting walls and ceilings, but you would tire yourself trying to cover large areas.

This chore should be carried out at least seasonally, and more often if you can manage it. The 1950s housewife might actually have done it weekly, although often enough she would simply vacuum obvious dust traps and spiderwebs while she did her weekly vacuuming—as you can also do.

Washing Painted Walls, Ceilings, and Woodwork. Older enamel paints were washable, and washing down the ceilings and walls was an onerous spring chore that was highly necessary for those who had heating systems that spewed dust or soot (which was most people). Few of us have this problem anymore, now that we have furnaces with more-effective filters and cleaner fuels, so washing walls is rarely necessary—except, possibly, in the kitchen; vacuuming is sufficient.

Walls, ceilings, and woodwork can be washed if they were painted with enamel, semigloss, or glossy paint. (Paint has a tendency to become less washable as it ages, however, so be sure to test first in an inconspicuous area.) Most latex flat finishes are difficult to wash, although some manufacturers are coming out with new types said to be washable. Most people therefore simply repaint flat-painted walls. Washing them can leave streaks and spots, and all too often fails to remove marks and stains. Test wash an inconspicuous area of a latex flat finish first (according to the instructions given below), let it dry thoroughly, and observe carefully to be sure you are satisfied with the result. Because it is often so difficult to wash latex flat paints, it is best to use semigloss paint in the kitchen because kitchen walls can develop a fine greasy film or become splattered with food or oil, and you will want to be able to wash the film and spots off.

Before washing, lay drop cloths to protect your floors, carpets, and furniture, and provide yourself with a safe ladder. (Cheap plastic drop cloths are available at any hardware store or home center.) Thoroughly vacuum the walls and ceilings before washing; this will make your job infinitely easier. You will need a sturdy, stable ladder or step stool to reach the ceiling.

Use a fairly mild all-purpose detergent or household cleaner diluted in water in a pail according to the instructions on the product; if this does not seem to get the walls clean, try something stronger—Spic and Span, Mr. Clean, or any all-purpose detergent. (Remember to test first; some cleaners will wash paint off, and some paints come off far more easily than others.) Use a second pail of clear water for rinsing. Wipe the surfaces with a clean sponge or cloth dipped in the cleaning solution, then wrung well to remove excess moisture and prevent drips and streaks. Wash a couple of square yards at a time. Then rinse using a new cloth or sponge dipped in the clear water and wrung well. Wipe dry with yet a third cloth. A working partner who follows after you doing the rinsing and drying makes the job faster and less lonely.

The major area of debate concerning wall washing is whether you should start at the bottom and go up, ending at the ceiling, or whether you should start at the top and go down, ending at the baseboards. Most expert cleaners say that you should start at the bottom (contrary to the usual housecleaning rule) because if dirty water runs down the dirty walls as you go, it may streak the unwashed portions and the streaks may remain visible even after you wash that area. The philosophers among us will point out that if you begin at the bottom, the dirty water will run over the part you just washed—a discouraging prospect. The response is that you'll just swipe this with a damp cloth to clean it, whereas the excessive amounts of dirt in the runoff from the top may prove difficult or impossible to remove. Defying the experts and following family custom, I start at the top and never have problems with streaks, but perhaps it all depends on what dirt is on your walls. You will have to observe the effects in your own home.

Cleaning Moldy Ceilings. In the bathroom, you may find mold growing on ceilings and walls. If they are tiled, follow the instructions in chapter 38, "Ceramic Tiles," for cleaning mold off tiles. If they are painted, scrub them with a brush and a solution of $^3/_4$ of a cup of chlorine bleach in a gallon of water. Or try a commercial cleaner effective against mold and safe for painted surfaces. Bathrooms and other areas subject to high humidity benefit from being painted with enamels containing antimildew agents.

Cleaning Acoustical-Tile Ceilings and Walls. Vacuuming and dry sponges work well on acoustical tile, but there may come a time when they too need a good washing. Treat them precisely as you do painted walls, except that you must be even more careful to wipe and rinse with a very well-wrung sponge or cloth and to use a mild cleaner. Specialty cleaners for acoustical tiles are also available. Using such a product normally involves spraying it on, leaving it for a few hours, and then rinsing it off. The solution will probably contain bleach and will drip, so you must be careful to use adequate drop cloths if you use such a product.

You can often remove pencil and other marks from acoustical tile by using an ordinary gum eraser.

Cleaning Wallpaper. Unless it is delicate, peeling, or trimmed with an easily detachable material, wallpaper can be vacuumed or dusted in the same manner as painted walls, but this should be done a bit more frequently. Frequent vacuuming or dusting of nonwashable wallpaper is especially important. Lift your brush or cloth upward when you remove cobwebs or you might cause streaks. If you are dusting with a cloth, turn or change it often, or the dust it collects may streak the paper. On flocked wallpaper, use the softer dusting-brush attachment of your vacuum. When the wallpaper is dirty and vacuuming or dusting does not help, you must either clean the wallpaper or repaper the wall.

Wallpaper today is classified, and usually labeled, as "washable" or "scrubbable" or "nonwashable." "Washable" means you can damp-clean it, using water sparingly. "Scrubbable" means you can wash it as you would painted walls, with mild detergent and water. Vinyl and plastic wallpapers are either washable or scrubbable. "Nonwashable" wallpapers can be cleaned, if at all, using only dry methods. In particular, never try to wash hand-painted, flocked, or textured wallpaper, or silk, linen, or other fabric wall coverings—unless they are vinyl coated. For such materials, call in professionals. Likewise, do not try to clean any old or antique wallpaper by damp methods. As some antique wallpaper is valuable, you might consult a conservator about how to care for it. If you are in doubt about whether your wallpaper is washable and you have a little piece of it, take it to a wallpaper store and ask for an opinion.

Cautions for cleaning all wallpaper: No matter what wallpaper you are trying to clean, never use abrasives (not even Soft Scrub or similar mild ones), scouring powders, or strong cleaners or chemicals of any sort. No matter what method, wet or dry, you use, test it first in an inconspicuous area to see whether you like the results. Test both for deterioration of the paper or its design and bleeding of colors.

When washing wallpaper, your goal is always to avoid soaking the paper and to avoid letting water seep under the paper, where it can cause puckering, bubbling, and peeling. This is less difficult with scrubbable paper.

Washable Wallpaper. Add a small amount of mild detergent to a bucket of lukewarm water. Fill another bucket with plain lukewarm water for rinsing. Dip in the sudsy water, then wring well, a sponge or cloth, and gently wipe the ceiling, using circular motions, first. Then rinse the ceiling with a different, clean sponge or cloth dipped in the plain water, also well wrung. Next, in the same manner, wash the walls, rinsing periodically after you complete a substantial area. Here you run into the same philosophical question about whether to go top to bottom or vice versa that we encountered when discussing painted walls. Wallpaper experts all say bottom to top. Immediately, gently, pat the wall dry with a clean towel so that no water remains on the surface. If any area needs a second wash, wait until it has completely dried, then wash it again following the same procedure.

Scrubbable Wallpaper. Wash these using any all-purpose detergent, in the same manner and order as for washable wallpaper except that a little more vigor and a little less caution are tolerable.

Nonwashable Wallpaper. Try to clean spots and soil on nonwashable wallpaper, after dusting or vacuuming, by rubbing them gently with commercial wallpaper-cleaning putty (Absorene seems to be the only one left) or an art-gum eraser, or—the old home remedy—a wadded-up piece of fresh, soft, moist bread. Brush off any cleaner that adheres to the paper after you have finished. Some in the business recommend that you try washing the occasional spot or stain with a sponge or soft brush dipped in a solution of mild detergent and water. If this does not work, add a tablespoon of bleach to your basin of water and detergent. This is a risky undertaking. Test your washing solution first in an inconspicuous spot, and proceed with caution.

Removing Spots and Stains from Walls and Woodwork. Attempts to wash spots, scuffs, and scars off painted walls often produce a discolored area that looks worse than the spot did. Moreover, any cleaner strong enough to remove the mark also tends to remove some paint, especially when you rub. To minimize these problems, before attempting any spot work, get the wall as dust-free as possible. Then test your proposed remedy in an inconspicuous area.

A thick paste of baking soda and water removes crayon, pencil marks, ink, marker, furniture scuffs, and a variety of other marks from painted walls. First scrape off any excess crayon or other material with a wood or plastic spatula; avoid scratching the wall. Then put some of the paste on a cloth or sponge and gently rub the mark. In my experience, this is less likely than other remedies to leave a discolored area, and it works even on latex flat paints.

Solvent-type cleaners are safe on many types of walls and wallpapers; carefully read instruction labels and, if you have questions about whether the cleaner is safe for your wall, call the manufacturer and ask. On painted and papered walls, you can also try any of the dozens of commercial spot-removing substances sold in supermarkets, hardware stores, and home centers. Just pick one appropriate to the kind of stain and the kind of paper or painted surface on which you will use it, and follow directions. On textured scrubbable vinyl wallpaper, stains—especially crayon—can be stubborn, as they get deep into the crevices of the texture where you cannot reach them. Liquid solvent cleaners, such as WD-40, dry-cleaning fluids, and specialty solvent spot cleaners will work. You may have to brush the cleaner in, gently, to reach the stain. You can also try a solution of chlorine bleach and water to remove ink from scrubbable and washable wallpapers, but pessimism is called for; beware of making things worse by turning a stray line into a discolored smudge. Grease spots on scrubbable and washable papers can usually be gently washed off with water and detergent.

On nonwashable wallpaper, first try to press out as much grease as you can with a paper towel, being careful not to spread the stain. The standard advice is to place absorbent paper over the stain and press it with an iron set at low for several seconds. Change the paper when it has absorbed grease. This technique always leaves me with a stubborn, somewhat fainter grease spot. Perhaps I simply do not try long and hard enough. But if you, too, cannot get all the grease out by this method, look for a commercial product that works on grease and is safe for your paper. You can also try to remove pencil marks and a variety of other spots on nonwashable paper with a commercial putty cleaner. Whatever you try, test first.

Cleaning Windows and Window Coverings

Windows are the home's most important means of controlling air and natural light. Dirty windows darken rooms considerably; bright windows make them light and open. Dusty blinds, screens, and shades also look and feel unattractive and provide a reservoir of dust to pollute the air in your home.

Window Frames. During your weekly housecleaning, vacuum or hand-dust window frames and moldings—the woodwork around the windows. Open the windows so you can reach the corners and edges properly, and clean the entire perimeter of each window.

Dust the windowsills as part of your weekly or semiweekly dusting. In areas where the outdoor air is polluted, dust on your sills can be such a problem that you will find yourself swiping at it every time you pass. When I was a child visiting relatives in New York City, I was astonished to see how a sill that was clean in the morning would be covered with a fine black dust by evening. This happens less often now in New York and many other big cities both because of the decreasing amount of heavy industry in urban areas and because of pollution-control laws that make for cleaner air.

If you wax windowsills, you offer them some protection from rain and rain spotting.

When dusting is not sufficient to get the window frames clean, and always before washing windows, you should wash the frames. First vacuum or dust them, then wash as you would other painted woodwork. Change the cleaning solution as necessary; window frames can become black with dust. Wipe them dry when you are finished.

Window Screens. The dirt that collects on screens can get washed onto the window glass in rainstorms, and dirty screens block much more light than clean ones do.

Vacuum window screens from inside when they look dusty. You can also gently brush them with a medium-stiff brush to loosen the dirt, but beware of creating a dust storm in your home. Do not do this when a breeze is blowing in, and place newspapers down to catch what falls. Once a year, take screens into the yard, squirt them down with a hose, and let them dry in the sun. You might try this in the bathtub if you have no yard, but it is an ordeal. Window-washing services will also clean your screens for you.

Storm Windows, Storm Doors, and Skylights. Storm windows (for the information of those in warm climates) are used in cold climates to provide extra insulation during cold months. They are put up sometime in the fall and taken down in the spring.

Wash glass storm windows as you would other glass windows. Plastic windows and plastic storm windows must be treated differently. Never use ammonia or cleaners containing ammonia on these, for it can cloud the surface permanently. Other alkaline household cleaners may do harm too. Use whatever type of cleaner the manufacturer recommends pursuant to product instructions.

If you do not know the manufacturer, use any mild neutral detergent, rinse, and wipe dry.

Window Glass. Good housewives used to wash their windows, or have them washed, seasonally. Well-to-do households with hired help washed windows more often, and still do. But this is one more good housekeeping habit that has become a luxury. Twice-yearly window washings are as much as many working people can manage now, and some are hard-pressed to get that many.

Remember to wash window frames and screens before washing windows. This will help the glass stay clean longer.

If you wash the windows yourself, do so on a cloudy day. Sunlight will dry them too quickly and cause streaking. You can use a commercial window cleaner such as Windex or use the recipe for a good homemade window cleaner on page 442 in chapter 31. Plain household ammonia in water (1/2 cup per gallon of warm water) also works well. (Ammonia is sometimes not used on mirrors in bathrooms because they may have aluminum frames that the ammonia would damage; a solution of ammonia and water is perfectly all right for cleaning glass or mirrors themselves.)

Wash the window with a nonlinting cloth or a sponge dipped in the cleaning solution; if you are using a commercial cleaner, follow the product instructions. I prefer cloth because your fingertips give you information that you cannot get through a thick sponge about how the surface is reacting to the rubbing. After washing, either squeegee the window, as professionals do, or dry it with another clean, dry, absorbent, lint-free cloth or with paper towels. Old linen or cotton towels are excellent for this purpose. Many veteran window washers, however, think it silly to use anything but squeegees.

Wash the windows inside and out. If your outside windows are high, you should consider hiring an expert rather than risk a tumble.

Blinds, Shades, and Shutters. Regular care of all blinds, shades, and shutters is the same: dust them with a soft, clean cloth or vacuum them each week, using the dusting attachment. Some people prefer brushes with "fingers" for cleaning venetian blinds. Some blinds and shades can and should be washed periodically, for a heavy film that is slightly greasy may eventually form on them from air pollution in the home. You cannot wash shades made of paper, rice paper, or parchment. You can gently dust them, or experiment with vacuuming on a low setting. Be cautious. Remove spots as you would with nonwashable wallpaper; after a thorough dusting or vacuuming, try rubbing them gently with a commercial cleaning putty or artist's gum eraser, or use a commercial spot-removing substance advertised as safe for the

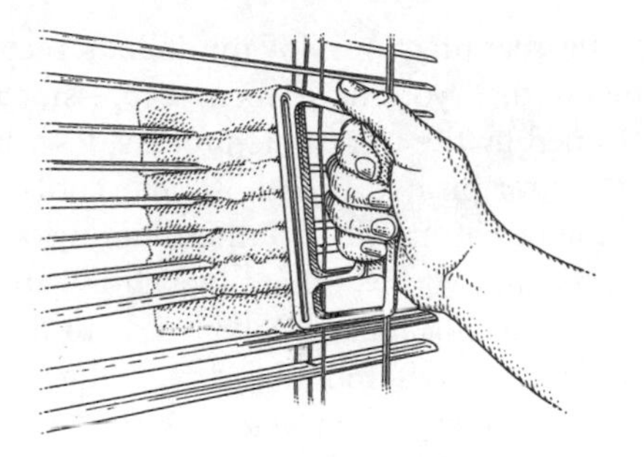

Miniblind cleaning tool

material your shade is made of. Test first in an area that will be hidden when the shade is hung up.

Most roll-up shades today, however, are vinyl or have vinyl coatings, and are washable. To clean one, roll it out to its full length on a clean, flat surface and weigh down the end so that it does not retract accidentally. Wash both sides with a solution of water and detergent; then rinse it and wipe it dry. Make sure the shade is thoroughly dry on both sides before rerolling and rehanging.

Some window-covering experts also advise you never to wash wood or bamboo shades, but I think you must eventually wash them because they become terribly soiled. However, you must clean them with great caution. *Never immerse them,* never permit their surfaces to become soaked or even more than barely damp, and use a small amount of a mild detergent. Wipe them dry with a clean cloth immediately. For both wood and bamboo shades, follow the other instructions for washing wood surfaces in chapter 36, page 503.

Miniblinds, venetian blinds, similar blinds made of aluminum, and vinyl roller shades are all washable. Take them into the yard or put them in the bathtub and wash them with a soft cloth and a mild all-purpose cleaner and water. Rinse them thoroughly, then wipe them dry. Use no harsh cleaners; they are unnecessary, and they might ruin the finish on the aluminum. Ammonia should never be used on aluminum. For the same reason, use no abrasives. Note that some manufacturers of miniblinds recommend that you have them professionally cleaned by the ultrasonic process described below for pleated shades. If your cords are made of natural fibers rather than nylon or plastic and you wet them (which is hard to avoid), do not rehang your blinds until the cords have thoroughly dried; they will stretch and sag when wet.

Pleated shades of plastic or plasticized material are washable, but at least one major manufacturer of such shades recommends that you have them professionally cleaned instead. Professional cleaners of blinds, this manufacturer says, use an ultrasonic generator in a cleaning solution that releases dirt effectively. If you do not wish to hire professionals, it is recommended that you put the shades in the bathtub and proceed as for aluminum shades, using one further caution: be sure not to tear them. Lift them carefully, holding the bottom.

44

China and Crystal

Caring for fine china, washing, automatic dishwashing, safeguards, handwashing, storage and display of fine and antique china . . . Repairing china . . . China in microwaves, ovens, and freezers . . . Caring for glass and crystal, washing and cleaning glass and crystal . . . Curing stains and water lines on crystal and glass . . . Avoiding accidents . . . Storage and display of glass and crystal . . . Lead problems with crystal, china, and other ceramics . . . Packing china and crystal . . . Glossary of china and crystal terms

Traditionally, fine china consisted of all true porcelain and bone china, including tableware, vases, basins, figurines, and decorative objects. The term "porcelain" is commonly used to mean any china at all, but strictly speaking it refers to ceramic containing an admixture of kaolin, fired at high temperatures of 1350° to 1450°C. It is also called "hard-paste" porcelain or "hard" or "true" porcelain. This type of ceramic was produced by the Chinese and Japanese and admired by Europeans for hundreds of years before they discovered in the eighteenth century how, and of what, it was made. It is strong, glasslike—or vitreous—and translucent. True porcelain in white tones often tends to have a slight grayish or bluish cast. Sevres, Meissen, Rosenthal, and Limoges are all examples of true porcelain. Most producers of true porcelain, however, now also make bone china and other types of china.

Bone china is also called English china after the country in which it was invented in the eighteenth century, and which continues to produce the finest types. It is fine china made by the addition of bone ash to the clay mixture that forms its body, which creates a bright white color. Because the clay mixture that forms its body is quite similar to that from which true porcelain is made, bone china is sometimes called "modified porcelain." Bone china, like porcelain, is strong, glasslike, and translucent. Most Staffordshire makers of fine china, such as Wedgwood and Royal Doulton, as well as American makers, such as Lenox, make bone china.

Vitreous china is fired twice to render it glassy and nonporous. The shine on the surface of vitreous china is not a glaze. A crack, therefore, indicates a problem with the body. If you hold a piece up to the light, you can see the shadow of your hand through it, and, characteristically, it gives a clear ring when tapped on the edge. The ring, however, is unreliable as an indicator of fine china. Fine china is so strong that it will not easily shatter even when rendered into fine and delicate shapes and fabriclike folds.

The distinction between fine china and imitation or everyday china has been in the process of collapsing since the 1980s. (It applies, however, to china manufactured before then.) Although it used to be that only fine china was vitreous and strong, today much "everyday" china is also vitreous and is equally strong. The terms *imitation porcelain* and *everyday china* traditionally referred to all porcelainlike imitators of true porcelain, including various types of ironstone and earthenware. (See the Glossary of China and Crystal Terms, pages 550–52.) These imitators were fired at lower temperatures, were not translucent, and were less strong than porcelain. (Even bone china was first referred to as imitation porcelain.) But all vitreous china is about as tough as any other, including fine china. The strength of china is determined more by the shape of a piece than by its inherent qualities. A thin, straight edge will always break more easily than a thick, curved one. Of course, much everyday china on the market is not very strong; still, strength is no longer the reliable mark of distinction between fine and everyday china that it used to be. The price differential between today's fine and everyday china is a function of design and decoration. But even these differences between everyday and fine china are becoming more and more muted. In recent years, many makers of fine china have begun offering attractively designed everyday dishes made of less-expensive imitation porcelains.

Caring for Fine China

Washing Fine China. Always rinse china dishes soon after use, especially if acidic foods such as fruit or vinegar have been served on them. This makes washing much easier, because foods do not have a chance to harden. Abrasive powders and scouring of all sorts are bad for china. Remove flatware from plates before stacking them, and set dishes securely on countertops in preparation for washing. Do not use flatware for scraping china. A rubber spatula or dishcloth is best.

If washing produces hard-water deposits, they will easily come off with a little vinegar. The marks that flatware leaves on dishes during use or sometimes in the dishwasher, if loading is not done carefully, can be removed with a bit of dentifrice powder and gentle rubbing, or a little silver polish. Some manufacturers of fine china recommend Bon Ami to remove these marks. Rinse the china immediately and dry it.

Automatic Dishwashing. Dishwashers clean thoroughly and hygienically. However, they are hard on all china. Even if you set your machine on its most gentle cycle, you put your china in danger each time you use the dishwasher. First, there is the danger of dishes or flatware knocking and rubbing against each other. Chipping, cracking, and scratching are far too likely. This risk can be minimized by proper loading. Consult your manufacturer's instructions, and be sure both that dishes are not touching one another and that they cannot move so as to touch one another. Second, the continuous heat, force of the water, and abrasion of the dirt extracted from the dishes, all endured for the typical long cycles of ordinary dishwashers, are nothing but bad for the dishes. Hand-washing, by comparison, subjects one dish at a time to considerably cooler water temperatures, for shorter periods of time, with a milder detergent, and there is much less danger of abrasion, banging, and the like. Dishes can be washed for years in the machine and not break. However, their surfaces will dull, and they will become constitutionally weaker.

What China Goes in the Dishwasher? When the manufacturers of everyday china insist that it is dishwasher-safe, that does not mean automatic dishwashing does not wear it out. It means that when you are dealing with inexpensive or hardy china, the benefits outweigh the costs. That is a judgment with which I fully concur.

But some fine china, too, nowadays is marketed as being dishwasher-safe—especially bone china. This advice counts on you to load and operate the machine properly and cautiously, for breakage, scratching, and cracking in dishwashers is a constant danger. And, whether or not the manufacturers will admit it, it further presupposes that you are willing to subject the china to some wear and tear and dulling over the years—in other words, that you do not plan to hand it on to your grandchildren in the condition in which you received it. I am not sure that this valuation is one you should necessarily go along with. Fine china is worth preserving. Of course, a rare visit to the dishwasher is not going to cause any detectable dulling in china marketed as dishwasher-safe. Regular automatic dishwashing, however, will cause your fine china to begin to show age at about the same rate you do.

What should never go in the dishwasher, unless the manufacturer explicitly tells you to the contrary, is any fine china that is hand-painted or decorated with gold or silver. The hand-painting and metallic decorations are likely to be harmed in the dishwasher. Porcelain chips a bit more readily than bone china, so you need to be particularly careful with it. In addition, you should put *no* antiques, heirlooms, works of art, or decorative pieces in the dishwasher, and no unglazed or partly glazed wares. Tin glazes on stoneware are too prone to chipping to risk in the dishwasher. (Other types of stoneware are fine in the dishwasher, unless the maker tells you otherwise.) No ceramicware that has known any type of repair should be placed in the dishwasher. Thin, delicate pieces should stay out, as should any pieces with long handles, stems, or other protrusions, because these are especially vulnerable.

Dishwasher Safeguards for Fine China. Be sure that your fine china is described as dishwasher-safe by the manufacturer and be sure to read the preceding section. If you decide to put it in the machine, you should use a water temperature that does not exceed 140°F, use a gentle or fine-china cycle (the short wash or glass-and-china cycle is usually sufficient), and use less detergent than the detergent or machine manufacturer recommends. Rinse off as much food and debris as possible before loading the dishes. This will mean less abrasion caused by food during the wash. Load so that pieces do not touch one another, and avoid overloading. Because porcelain chips a bit more easily than bone china, be particularly careful to set the pieces so that they cannot touch.

Hand-washing Fine China. Rinsing china soon after use is desirable, particularly if it has held acidic foods such as fruit or vinegar. When you are ready to wash the dishes, line the bottom of the sink or basin with a towel. For hand-washing, use a mild soap or detergent and warm water. Wipe the dishes with a sponge or dishcloth. Do not use abrasive sponges or pads. Use a nonabrasive scrubber such as a nylon mesh pad when you have to. Do not soak china for any great length of time, as this may result in water seeping under the glaze, through the kiln marks or cracks, which will weaken the dish. Wash only one piece at a time to avoid knocking one dish against another, and try to keep one

Never store wine or liquor of any sort in a leaded crystal decanter, bottle, or pitcher.

Never store or cook any food or drink—especially acidic ones—in crystal, china, or other ceramicware that contains leachable lead.

Be most careful about any crystal, china, or other ceramicware in which you store or cook any food or drink that will be served to infants or children. (These are among the good candidates for testing with a home lead-testing kit.)

Be especially alert with respect to any pieces you use daily or routinely, especially if children will be using them or be served from them.

Stop using pieces that have a dusty or chalky gray residue on the glaze after they are washed.

Limit the use of older sets of china to special occasions. Avoid serving hot and acidic foods on them. If you serve a vinegary or citrus salad or a tomato sauce, for example, use a nonleaded serving bowl. When you use them, be sure to move food on and off them without delay. Move leftovers into plastic or other proper refrigeration-storage containers. Plain (nonleaded) glass is excellent for refrigerator storage.

Buy crystal from a reputable manufacturer. If you do not know which are reputable, ask any well-established retailer of fine crystalware in your area.

When you buy, look for labels that say "Not for Food Use—Plate May Poison Food. For Decorative Purposes Only." Always obey such labels.

Packing China and Crystal

Newspaper and other materials that absorb moisture can be used when china will be packed for relatively short periods, and indefinitely for glassware. Otherwise, use soft cloth or bubble wrap. Wrap each piece individually, including lids and stoppers. Beware of losing small pieces in the wrappings when you unpack. Gently pack wrapping inside hollowware, bowls, cups, and glasses. Put no weight on glass or crystal, especially on stems. For china, follow the same guidelines that apply to cabinet storage.

Glossary of China and Crystal Terms

Basalt. Black stoneware.

Biscuit or bisque. Unglazed ceramicware that has been fired only once.

Coupe. A term for rimless cups or bowls.

Crackle glass. Glass that is heated, cooled, and then refired so that many small lines appear in it. It dates back to the sixteenth century, but it is still made. It enjoyed a vogue in the 1920s and 1930s.

Crazing. The appearance on ceramicware of a network of fine lines. This is produced when the glaze is compromised and water seeps beneath it, causing expansion of the body, which in turn produces little cracks.

Creamware. A cream-colored earthenware with a porcelainlike appearance, first developed during the eighteenth century, Josiah Wedgwood's being particularly admired. Creamware, queensware, and pearlware were used for table service. Mochaware has a slip decoration in swirling patterns.

Crystal. Superior glassware, usually with a minimum amount of lead added. "Full lead" crystal has 24 percent, but sometimes as much as 30 percent is added. The addition of lead produces a heavy glass that is prized because of its clarity and sparkle and because the lead renders the glass soft enough to be cut and decorated beautifully. Everyone has heard that true crystal rings when tapped and the better the crystal, the longer and clearer the ring. This is by and large true, but the test is not infallible. Some good crystal does not ring; some ordinary glass does. Crystal is either "clear" (blown into shapes), cut, or etched. The lead content of crystal requires that you give some thought to its safe use. Never store wine or juice in lead-crystal decanters. (See pages 548–50.) Makers of fine crystal include Baccarat, Steuben, Lalique, and Waterford.

Delft. Earthenware decorated with a tin-enamel glaze, usually in blue and white or green and white. It is named after the Dutch city that made it popular in the seventeenth century, but the name is also used for the many imitations that were popular in England and other countries. Delft is still produced in the Netherlands.

Earthenware. A low-fired (1000° to 1200°C), opaque, slightly porous—unless glazed—ceramic of which most ancient and antique pottery was made, including much Staffordshire pottery and Dutch and English Delft. Most everyday china is earthenware. Any crack in its glaze will admit moisture that can be absorbed by the body, resulting in cracks to the body. Earthenware is less hard and lighter than stoneware.

Faience. A tin-glazed earthenware with an opaque colored glaze, originating in Faenza in 1714. The word was used to refer to eighteenth-century French, once-fired, tin-glazed wares that were often decorated with hand painting. Quimper faience is produced in Quimper, a town in Brittany.

Glaze. Any liquid coating applied to ceramicware.

Hollowware. Servingware that is hollow inside, including teapots and coffee pots, bowls, platters, and pitchers in china or metal.

Ironstone. A hard, heavy, durable earthenware with a white porcelainlike appearance. Also called Masonware.

Jasperware. A colored stoneware with a raised white decoration.

Lusterware. Ceramicware coated with a thin film of metal, such as copper, gold, silver, or platinum. It has an iridescent sheen.

Majolica. A tin-glazed earthenware similar to faience, characteristically decorated with bright colors on the glaze before firing.

Ormolu. Golden or gilded bronze or brass decorations. Ceramic objects sometimes have ormolu mounts. Do not wash ormolu; dust it.

Overglaze. Colors or decorations applied over rather than under the glaze.

Paste. The material of which the body of ceramicware is made. A glaze is often applied to the body, either before or after a first firing. "Hard paste" refers to the clay mixture, containing a large portion of kaolin, of which true porcelain or hard porcelain is made. "Soft paste" refers to the material of which the body of imitation porcelains, such as earthenware, are made. Soft-paste wares are usually fired at around 1100°, a somewhat lower temperature than that used for hard-paste wares. Because bone china is now made with kaolin, it is often considered a "modified porcelain" or even, in some lexicons, true porcelain. Others consider it a third type of china, neither soft nor hard paste.

Redware. Earthenware made of red clay.

Slip, slip decoration, or slip glaze. An opaque glaze made by thinning clay with water to a smooth, creamy consistency. Slipware has a layer of slip between its glaze and its earthenware body.

Spongeware or spatterware. Ceramicware decorated by applying color with a sponge, scrunched-up rag, or brush tip.

Staffordshire. A county in central England that has been a significant source of ceramics for hundreds of years. Major producers in the area include Royal Doulton (which manufactures Minton, Royal Crown Derby, and Royal Albert), Royal Worcester, Spode,

Wedgwood, Royal Grafton, Coalport (a division of Wedgwood), Birchcroft, Amber China, John Beswick, Blue Denmark, Aynsley, Royal Grafton, Moorcroft Potters (still a family-owned business that produces handmade pottery), and Portmeirion.

Stemware. Glasses with a stem, in plain glass or crystal.

Stoneware. A high-fired (1200° to 1400°C), opaque, vitrified, nonporous, strong, heavy, hard ceramic. Its hardness is the result of the addition of a substance to its body that permits firing at higher temperatures. It is given either a salt glaze, which creates an orange-peel surface, or a lead glaze. Stoneware has a glassy surface but may feel rough. It is durable. It is often used for crocks and jugs, but tableware of stoneware is made too. The body is generally chip-resistant, but may have a glaze that tends to chip.

Transferware. China decorated by prints transferred to its surface from paper that has been pressed on engraved copper plates. Josiah Spode made this process famous in the late eighteenth century, producing highly decorated china that was also inexpensive. Before its invention, decorated china had to be hand-painted and was affordable only by the rich. Transfer printing was used on stoneware, soft-paste porcelain, and bone china.

Yellowstone. Earthenware made from a buff-yellow clay.

45

Metals

What tarnish is . . . "Miracle" cleaners? . . . Silver, how to store, clean, polish . . . Chemical dips and electrolytic cleaning methods . . . Substances that harm silver . . . Pewter . . . Copper, brass, and bronze, waxing, removing corrosion, fireplace accessories, cookware . . . Iron, wrought iron and cast iron, cast-iron pots and pans, "seasoning," enameled cast iron . . . Aluminum, pots and pans, anodized aluminum, substances harmful to aluminum . . . Steel and stainless steel, substances harmful to steel, care of pots and pans . . . Chrome

Every home makes use of a variety of metals in furnishings, tools, furniture, utensils, pots and pans, fireplaces, and dozens of other important objects. Knowing the individual names, characters, strengths and weaknesses, and proper care of these metals is an important part of housekeeping.

When metal objects in the home become dirty and dusty, you can clean them—except for certain antiques—by ordinary dusting with a cloth slightly dampened with water or, when necessary, by washing with a solution of mild, all-purpose detergent and water and rinsing with plain water. If the metal is prone to rust or tarnish, rub it dry immediately afterward with a soft, dry cloth. On valuable and delicate objects, use no harsh chemicals or abrasives, such as steel wool or powdered cleansers.

Tarnish results when metal reacts with some substance in its environment to form a discoloring compound on its surface. When iron oxidizes, for example, rust forms. Tarnishing is hastened by humidity and warmth. Keeping the humidity and temperature in your home at moderate levels, therefore, will help retard tarnishing. Daily use and cleaning may slow it down too, but sooner or later not only iron but silver, copper, and brass are going to tarnish or rust.

Gold, platinum, pewter, bronze, aluminum, stainless steel, and chrome will not rust or tarnish.

Tarnish does not come off with soap and water. When removing tarnish on valuable metals, use only a polish specially designed for the specific metal, not "all-metal" cleaners. Do not use copper cleaner (for example) on silver. Metal polishes all contain abrasives or chemical solvents; those for harder metals have harsher abrasives or stronger solvents. Polishes meant for harder metals are inappropriate on softer metals, and polishes for softer metals are ineffective on harder ones. All-metal polishes are compromises. Use them only on harder, less valuable, more utilitarian metals such as stainless steel, aluminum, chrome, and brass. If you clean all your metal on the same day, be careful not to mix cleaning cloths. Use a fresh cloth for each kind of cleaner and metal.

Generally speaking, but especially when you are cleaning valuable metals, be skeptical of "miracle" cleaners and avoid the "dip-it" or electrolytic cleaners promising magic action that are advertised on television. They will do what they say, but that may be more than you want. Some miracle cleaners do indeed leave a brilliant-looking surface behind, but that brilliant shine appears only because the patina, or surface layer, of the metal has been removed. Over time, raised designs and etchings will be prematurely worn away by such treatments. A gentler cleaning will preserve more of the patina and protect the metal, leaving a quieter luster that does not shout down the true age and subtleties of design of the metal.

No matter what the metal, if it is a historic piece or a valuable antique, seek expert advice before attempting to clean it. In most cases, periodic dusting and gentle washing in a neutral all-purpose cleaner will be fine, but professional guidance should be sought before undertaking more vigorous measures. Polishing metals, it should be stressed, is always a vigorous measure.

Silver

Pure silver is an element; that is, it contains only silver atoms. Because pure silver is so soft, it is usually mixed with other metals to make it harder and more durable. Sterling silver is made of 925 parts of pure silver and 75 parts of copper—92.5% pure silver, in other words. Sterling is imprinted with "Ster" or "925" or even "sterling silver." Silver plate is made of a base metal, such as copper or brass, electroplated with a thin silver coating. This type of silver may have the imprint "EP brass" or "EP copper." Everyday care of sterling silver and silver plate is similar.

The tarnish that eventually forms on all household silver is silver sulfide. It is caused by a reaction between silver and sulfur-containing gases and compounds in the air, such as hydrogen sulfide (H_2S) or sulfur dioxide (SO_2) and other substances with which silver comes in contact: wool, felt, rubber, latex gloves, some paints, eggs, onions, spinach, and many more. Humidity and heat hasten tarnishing. Substances other than sulfur that will harm silver include chlorine bleach, acids, and acidic foods. Salt and sea air will also cause pitting. If you have a silver salt cellar, be sure to empty it immediately following use unless it is lined with glass or some other material that will not react with the salt.

To keep silver bright, use it. Too much polishing will wear silver out prematurely, and frequent use will help retard tarnishing. Rotate pieces in use so that it ages uniformly. Wash it quickly after use so that foods do not have an opportunity to cause tarnish.

Chemically treated products that work well to fight tarnish are available. Soft flannel cloths, bags, or drawer liners that have been treated with silver nitrate or other chemicals should be used for storing silver. Place silver in a chest lined with such cloth, in bags of it, or in drawers lined with it. (Hagerty and Pacific Silvercloth manufacture such cloths and bags.) You do not have to remove the tarnish before storing it. You may as well wait until you are ready to use it again, rather than cleaning it up and exposing new surface areas to tarnish.

Putting silver in plastic wraps or bags is a good antitarnish aid as well—but only if you do it properly. When plastic wraps and bags first came into common household use in the 1960s, people immediately concluded that these would be good for storing silver, as they would keep humidity and air away from it. However, eventually they noticed that plastic can trap moisture next to the silver and hasten its tarnishing. To avoid this effect, according to the Society of American Silversmiths, first wrap the silver in the antitarnish cloths or bags described above, or in nonbuffered tissue paper (archival quality, sulfur-free), and then place it in plastic bags. It is also a good idea to place silica gel packets inside the wrapping with the silver to absorb moisture. I would add that you should make certain that the silver is quite dry before wrapping it, and store the silver out of direct sunlight. (In sunlight, plastic wraps may break down and produce moisture condensation that will attack the silver.) Do not fasten the wrap with rubber bands, which contain sulfur.

Do not wrap silver in chamois leather or felt, which also contain sulfur. If your water has a high sulfur content, you will probably notice that your silver tarnishes rapidly. If you put it in boxes or wrap it in paper, be sure to use archival-quality tissue paper and acid-free boxes. Do not use crumpled newspaper; printer's ink is acidic.

The Society of American Silversmiths advises against lacquering and waxing silver, with one exception. For open displays of silver, it suggests you coat the silver with "a micro-crystalline wax such as Renaissance Wax," even though this may cause a slight dulling.

Wash all silver with a mild soap or detergent and hot water. Rinse it with very hot water, and dry it thoroughly with a soft cloth. Never let it air-dry. Water left standing on silver can corrode it. Using very hot water not only helps clean it, but makes it dry faster.

It is still true that silver does not belong in the dishwasher. I have encountered a few vendors who say that you can put their sterling and silver-plated flatware in the dishwasher, although most stop short of recommending this. (All agree that gold plate should never go in the dishwasher.) This is probably how a few businesses try to counter the tendency of harried buyers to choose only easy-care objects, but it is bad advice. Both sterling and silver plate are so soft that the abrasion and harsh detergents in automatic dishwashers will dull the surfaces of bright pieces and remove the oxidized patina on older pieces. Silver will suffer far more scratching and jostling in the dishwasher than it would if you washed it by hand. Antiques are especially vulnerable; they may have cemented-on parts that will come apart (knife blades, pot legs, and so forth). If water gets into hollow parts of any silver, it can stay there and cause deterioration. And you will most likely need to have your silver-plated ware replated far more quickly if you put it in the dishwasher—an expensive proposition. If you nonetheless choose to wash your silver in the dishwasher, be sure to place silver away from other metals such as copper or steel. If they touch during the washing process, they may mark each other. To help prevent scratching, align forks, spoons, and knives. (But this makes it harder for the machine to get them clean, so check them carefully when you remove them.)

You can use polishing gloves and cloths or a jeweler's rouge cloth (flannel treated with a red polishing powder) to buff your silver between polishings in an effort to retard tarnish or remove light tarnish. You must rub fairly vigorously to have an effect because rouge cloths contain only a mild polishing agent. Silver-polishing cloths and gloves are usually available at department stores and silver retailers.

You should not need to polish silver often—once or twice a year perhaps, but the period varies greatly depending on use and conditions of storage. When the time comes, polish the silver using only the most gentle polishes. A list of polishes suggested by the Society of American Silversmiths includes 3M Tarni-Shield Silver Polish, Goddard's Long Shine Silver Polish, Wright's Silver Polish, Twinkle Silver Polish, and Hagerty Silversmiths' Polish, all of which are gentle. On pieces that should not get wet (because of vulnerable parts or structure), the Society recommends Goddard's Long Shine Silver Polish because it can be left to dry, then buffed off without using water.

Low abrasion is more important in a polish than tarnish inhibition (but many good polishes also help prevent tarnish). The experts remind you that sometimes patience is necessary in polishing. Some conservators advise that for polishing valuable antiques, even gentle commercial products should be avoided, recommending that on such pieces you use only a paste of artists' whiting (available at art-supply stores) in distilled water. Using such mild abrasion always means longer, slower polishing.

Make sure that the silver is completely clean before you begin to polish it. If there is wax on it, remove it. Do not scrape it off, as this may scratch the silver. Soften the wax slightly in a warm oven or with a low-heat hair dryer, if necessary; then peel it off. Or remove it with denatured alcohol, turpentine, or mineral spirits.

When the silver is clean, polish it according to the instructions on the polish. Generally this means that you should apply the cleaning product with a soft, clean cloth, gently, in a circular motion. When polishing a large object, do only a small area at a time. You must be more gentle in polishing silver plate than sterling because overly vigorous polishing can remove the thin silver coating and reveal the base metal underneath. Test the effect of any polish or treatment on silver plate in an inconspicuous area. Use no more polish and no more elbow grease than necessary. As the cloth gets dirty, turn it to a clean area or replace it, because the dirt may be abrasive. Use cotton swabs to clean grooves and crevices if you must, but do not get these areas too clean. Darkening in cracks and crevices of the design makes the design show better and is generally considered attractive. A soft brush can also be used to get at difficult areas on chased silver (ornamented with hammered indentations) or embossed silver (with raised ornamentation).

Thoroughly rinse the polish off with very hot water. Sometimes polish can corrode the silver if it is left on. Then buff the silver to a luster with a clean, soft cloth. Clean flannel, cheesecloth, and well-worn diapers work well. If necessary, use a low-heat hair dryer to blow cracks and crevices dry. Never leave silver to air-dry.

Acid Dips. The use of acid and chemical dips is not a good idea, and the most reliable authorities tell us not to use them. If you have a piece of silver that is terribly blackened with tarnish, you may dread the thought of the labor you face. You may have read that museums and conservators use acid or chemical dips that instantly restore a gleam to silver. They may at times, but I believe they more commonly use even milder, slower methods than we do at home; if they ever resort to acids, they know what they are doing, while most of us at home do not.

Dips can do complicated things to your silver. I have been told that dips can ruin antiques or satin-finished silver. (Satin and dull finishes can be restored only by a professional.) Dips can also remove too much of the surface of your silver. Especially if the piece of silver that you wish to clean is valuable or is an antique, find a reliable professional to clean it for you instead of going this route.

The Society of American Silversmiths, like many other experts, does not recommend chemical dips because of the potential damage they can cause, especially to pieces in which the chemical solution may lodge in areas from which it cannot be removed. At a minimum, it advises, limit their use to heavy, black tarnish that resists all other polishes, and, if you use a dip, do not submerge the piece. Wipe it down with a sponge dipped in the solution. Never use dips on anything that is hollow or has joints or seals; the acid may get inside or in cracks and eat the metal away. If your silver has parts made of ivory, wood, or other vulnerable materials, be careful indeed to protect them from the solution. Wash the silver immediately afterward thoroughly, in a manner safe for the piece, to remove the acid, or it may damage the silver.

Electrolytic Cleaners. Many experts, among them the American Society of Silversmiths, do not recommend electrochemical cleaning either. In this method, you place silver in an aluminum pan and cover it with a sodium carbonate solution. Objects cleaned with this method later retarnish more rapidly because they more readily absorb tarnish-causing substances. Furthermore, it requires immersion to work, and therefore should never be used on pieces with hollow parts, sealed parts, joints, or other cracks and crevices. If the chemical solution gets inside, it will stay and cause deterioration. Electrolytic cleaning also removes the attractive and protective oxidized patina, and harms certain finishes. If you try it, be sure to wash the silver thoroughly immediately afterward.

Never polish gold-plated silver (called "gilded silver," "silver gilt," or "vermeil"). Polishing is not only unnecessary, but it would remove the gold. Keep it out of the dishwasher; wash flatware by hand gently in mild detergent, and wipe it thoroughly dry with a soft cloth, gently buffing. Simply dust decorative pieces.

Pewter

Modern pewter is made primarily of tin, with a small amount of antimony. It is a soft, silverish metal with less luster than silver has. Many people are fond of its low glow. Although tin readily rusts, pewter does not; in fact, pewter will not need polishing if it is used. Antique pewter, however, contains lead—do not put food or drink in old pewter pieces—and will darken with age. (Modern pewter contains no lead and is safe for food.) To keep pewter bright, wash in hot, sudsy water. Some recommend adding two tablespoons of ammonia per quart of sudsy water. Rinse it thoroughly with hot water. Then dry it with a soft cloth, buffing up its shine. Use a soft brush to help get at crevices. Pewter, especially if it is antique, should not go in the dishwasher. Polish it with silver polish in the same way you do silver.

If a valuable, highly prized, or antique piece of pewter has become damaged or appears to be hopelessly darkened, take it to a professional for cleaning.

Pewter is vulnerable to acids; be careful with acidic foods. Note that oak and unseasoned wood contain acids that can cause pewter to deteriorate, if it comes in contact with them.

Copper, Brass, and Bronze

Copper, unlike brass and bronze, is an element. It tarnishes readily and polishes equally readily to a shiny burnt-orange tone. It is considerably harder than silver, but it is still soft. Brass is an alloy of copper and zinc that has a gold color. Bronze is a reddish-gold alloy of copper and tin. Both are harder than copper, and bronze is much harder than brass.

Bronze does not tarnish. Copper and brass readily tarnish and, unless lacquered, will usually need polishing every few months if you intend them to stay bright. If they are lacquered, they will stay tarnish-free until one or more cracks appear in the lacquer. Then you will get problem areas that are difficult to treat because copper or brass cleaners, whether commercial or homemade, cannot penetrate the coating. Therefore the coating will have to be removed with acetone or a lacquer thinner; after this you must clean the metal, and then you can reapply the lacquer. Retouching is not advised. You should remove all of the old coat before applying a new one.

Many experts advise against lacquering. You might instead try waxing the metal with paste wax or oiling it with mineral oil to inhibit tarnish.

Brass pulls and handles on antique furniture should not be polished. Simply dust and wax them as you do the wood. Overly bright brass trim would look out of place on old furniture. If you have modern furniture with unlacquered brass trim that has tarnished, you must ask yourself whether you wish to let it tarnish or whether you wish to keep it bright. If the latter, you must first remove the brass fixtures from the furniture before applying brass polish or cleaner, to avoid damage to the wood. This is a great deal of trouble, and it is easy to learn to like the look of tarnished brass on most furniture.

On unlacquered brass, use a commercial brass cleaner according to its instructions. If the metal is plated brass or copper, rather than solid, be gentle in polishing. First test your polish or procedure in an inconspicuous area. Always rinse the metal thoroughly when you have finished.

If you have highly corroded brass or copper, remove the corrosion before polishing. To do this, try rubbing it with a solution of lemon juice and baking soda (for a little gentle abrasion) or a lemon dipped in salt; then rinse well. Or mix equal parts salt and white flour with white vinegar to form a paste. Rub it on; wait an hour, and rinse it off carefully. Dry it thoroughly with a soft cloth, and then buff. Another home remedy is to boil the item in a solution of vinegar, water, and salt, assuming that it has no trim or decorations that could not withstand the boiling; then rinse and dry well. When it is cleaned, polish as usual.

Brass fireplace screens, andirons, and tools with blackened, sooty soil should first be dusted as free of soot as possible. Then scrub them with a stiff brush and a solution of household detergent and warm water. Rinse them with plain water and dry them with a soft cloth. After they are clean, try polishing them to a shine with commercial brass cleaners or the homemade rubs prescribed above. If the job proves beyond the reach of such remedies, you might try rubbing with very fine steel wool. But this and stronger abrasives (I have heard emery cloth recommended) are likely to mark or scratch your brass.

Copper cookware tarnishes readily and requires plenty of polishing to stay bright. Clean it according to the manufacturer's instructions. When necessary, use a copper-cleaning powder according to instructions. Copper pots that are used regularly will probably have to be retinned every five years or so. (See chapter 8, "The Center of a Dwelling," page 101.) This procedure is performed on the inside of the pot by a professional. House and kitchenware stores will do it or refer you to someone who will.

Chlorine bleach will discolor copper if left to stand on it for more than a few hours. Oven cleaners, chlorine bleach, and Windex will scar, discolor, or corrode brass. Always rinse off acids or polishes left on any of these metals or they will cause rapid retarnishing.

Iron

Iron, an element, readily rusts. *Wrought iron* is a form of iron that is malleable, so that it can be worked into elaborate shapes. Wrought iron is often used inside the home for fireplace grates, pokers, andirons, and other utensils, plant stands, and other pieces of furniture. Simply dust it. If need be, using a stiff brush, cloth, or sponge (whatever best suits the shape and size of the piece), wash it with all-purpose detergent and hot water, rinse it, and dry it thoroughly. Then rub any remaining spots with steel wool. It will gain some luster and rust resistance if you apply a little paste wax with a cloth, let the wax dry, and then buff it with another clean, dry cloth. Be sure that the iron is thoroughly clean and dry before putting on wax. Wipe off rust with a solution of white vinegar and water, or a commercial preparation.

Cast iron is an alloy of iron, carbon, and silicon that is cast in a mold. It is hard, brittle, and nonmalleable. Cast-iron fireplace accessories may be cared for in the same manner as those of wrought iron. To give them a little glow, try some paste stove polish or apply paste wax just as you would for wrought iron. (Of course, waxing is not for cooking pots and pans.)

Iron hinges, locks, and hardware should be oiled with machine oil to prevent rust. Use stove polish to prevent rust on iron stove parts.

Manufacturers and lovers of cast-iron skillets and pans commonly advise you to "season" them. This means first washing them in warm water and detergent, then coating them with cooking oil and heating them in the oven at about 300°F for an hour. If you leave the seasoning on the surface, people say, it will have rust resistance and stick resistance that will improve each time you use the skillet. To preserve the seasoning on seasoned cast-iron pots and pans, you are sometimes told to avoid washing them with detergents. Some say to wash them in plain hot water. Others say that washing cast-iron pans with true soap, rather than detergent, will leave the seasoning on.

There are a few misconceptions here. To begin with, using soap rather than detergent would not do more to preserve the seasoning of the pot. Soaps are not inherently milder than detergents. (See "Detergents and soaps, mild," pages 322–24.) In any event, you really should use soap or detergent to wash all pots, including seasoned cast-iron ones, because plain hot water is much less effective at killing and removing dirt, flavors, odors, and germs from surfaces than sudsy hot water. (Rancid cooking oil is bad for you.) Moreover, washing does not remove the natural "seasoning" that any well-used cast-iron pan develops. Mine (and I use several often) are enthusiastically scrubbed with detergent at each use and over time have become quite as "seasoned" as anyone else's pans. Cast-iron cookware will inevitably turn dark with the passage of years; this is a beneficial and natural part of its aging that you should not try to prevent.

The seasoning of a cast-iron pot is not delicate and, in my experience, you can use any cleaning method on it you wish: scouring pads, pot scratchers, or powdered cleansers. Just try to scour in the direction of the grain of the metal. There are really only two cautions. The first is to dry cast iron thoroughly immediately after washing, for otherwise it will rust. (Even "seasoned" cast iron can rust if left damp.) The second is, for the same reason, to wash it by hand rather than in the dishwasher. But if it should rust, just scour off the rust and dry it. Setting it to heat on the stove for a few seconds will ensure that any moisture has evaporated. The rust, by the way, is a digestible form of iron, and cooking with cast iron generally tends to put a bit of usable iron into your food.

Enameled cast-iron cookware must be treated more cautiously, as the enamel can chip or wear. Remove burnt-on food with plastic scouring pads, not metal or wire ones. Stains respond to rubbing with a powdered cleanser. But do this only as a last resort, and use a low-abrasive cleanser or the enamel will scour right off. It is best to tolerate harmless stains rather than risk this.

Stains on enamelware will often respond to a solution of 1 tablespoon bleach in a quart of warm water. Fill the pan and let it soak for an hour or two; then wash it with hot, sudsy water and rinse thoroughly. This method, too, however, must be used with great restraint, as the bleach will remove the protective glaze on the enamel and cause it to wear.

Aluminum

Aluminum is an element. Mild, ammonia-free detergent and water are all you need for cleaning most aluminum, such as pots and pans and the trim on stoves and mirrors.

You can brighten a dull aluminum cooking pot by boiling a quart of water with 4 tablespoons of white vinegar or cream of tartar in it. Clean off hard-to-remove or burned-on material in a pot or skillet with a metal scouring pad, a soaped steel-wool scouring pad, or a paste of powdered cleanser and water. Always rub with the grain. Copper bottoms on aluminum pans may be scoured with copper cleaner.

Anodized aluminum is made by an electrochemical process that creates a nonlustrous, hard surface that is more stain-resistant, abrasion-resistant, and inert than regular aluminum. Therefore it also resists flavoring foods and absorbing flavors from foods. (Even anodized aluminum, however, will react with foods if they are stored in it overnight or longer.) It is used for cooking pans and pots. In theory at least, you need use no special cooking utensils to protect anodized aluminum, as you would for stick-resistant surfaces that are produced by coatings applied over a metal base. Metal cooking utensils will not harm anodized aluminum. In practice, metal utensils leave marks—not, I am told, because they scratch the surface but because they leave metal streaks on the surface of the pan. You can remove such marks as well as stains or stuck-on dirt with a green Scotch-Brite pad or a powdered scouring cleanser that contains no bleach. Manufacturers of anodized aluminum also recommend the use of cleaning products (Dormónd, for example) specially designed for removing difficult stains and abrasions as well as marks caused by metal utensils on anodized aluminum.

There are nonstick versions of anodized aluminum that have a nonstick coating and must be treated in the same way you care for all other nonstick ware—use no metal utensils, metal scrubbing pads, or scouring powders.

Plain aluminum will darken in the dishwasher, and anodized aluminum will discolor. Some types of nonstick anodized aluminum cookware will gradually lose their nonstick qualities if you wash them in the dishwasher. See pages 102–3 and 113.

Substances harmful to plain and anodized aluminum include chlorine bleach, strong, hot baking-soda solutions and other alkaline cleaners, including oven cleaners, ammonia, and all cleaners containing ammonia. If you are not sure whether a metal is made of aluminum, test an all-purpose cleaner that contains ammonia in an inconspicuous area before using it on the metal. (Ammonia will mottle or otherwise mar the surface.) Stove or mirror trim, for example, that you might take to be chrome may in fact be aluminum.

Steel

Stainless steel is an alloy of steel, chromium, and nickel. It does not rust, corrode, or tarnish.

Good stainless steel is made of 18 percent chromium, 8 or 10 percent nickel, and 74 or 72 percent steel. This combination (sometimes called "18/8" or "18/10") provides the greatest resistance to corrosion. Stainless steel that contains less than 8 percent or 10 percent nickel will be of lower quality. More nickel, generally speaking, guarantees a brighter, more durable, rust-resistant luster. However, practically speaking, the differences between 8 percent and 10 percent are nil; 8 percent sometimes has more luster than 10 percent, and 18/10 may or may not be higher quality than 18/8. If it attracts a magnet, it is not 18/8 (or 18/10).

Good stainless steel is tough, but not indestructible. It may be marked if you leave food on it, particularly acidic or salty foods. Mild acids—vinegar, citrus juices, or pickle juice, for example—should not be left to stand on a stainless-steel sink, flatware, or pots and pans. Some denture cleaners contain acids that may leave permanent stains on stainless steel. Strong acids, such as silver dips and photographers' chemicals, can damage stainless steel. Prolonged exposure to chlorine bleach might pit or stain it. Ammonia or other strong alkalies, such as oven cleaners, can darken stainless steel. In my experience, this can happen if you habitually put stainless steel in the dishwasher; dishwashing detergents are alkaline and may contain chlorine bleach as well. Avoid letting granules of dishwasher detergent rest on stainless steel. (This could happen if you do not run the dishwasher immediately after closing the door. Loose detergent powder might fly onto the pots and remain there.) Makers of stainless-steel flatware recommend that to keep automatic dishwashers from damaging the appearance of your stainless steel you use only powdered cleaners, no liquid or gel detergents, and no detergents with lemon additives. They also advise that you skip the drying cycle and dry your flatware by hand, or open the door and let it air-dry in a cooler environment. If your stainless steel has begun to look dark or dull, a stainless-steel polish can often (but not always) do wonders. The use of harsh abrasives is not recommended.

Brown or blue streaks will appear on the outside or inside of stainless-steel pots and pans if they are overheated, but stainless-steel cleaners will take these marks off. Salted liquids can produce small white dots or pits on the sides of stainless-steel cookware. The pits are permanent, but the white dots will come off with a scouring pad, soaped steel-wool pad, or Scotch-Brite Rescue pad (which is also soaped). They can be avoided by bringing water or other liquids to a boil before adding salt, or adding salt only after food has started to cook, and then stirring well. Remove calcium (hard-water) deposits from stainless-steel pots and pans by boiling a solution of a quart of water and 4 tablespoons of white vinegar in them.

The manufacturers of stainless-steel cookware often say that it can be put in the dishwasher. (If it cannot, that may be because the handle or some other part cannot withstand the dishwasher or because the attractive appearance of the metal will be diminished.) Although some manufacturers advise against it, the interior of most stainless-steel pots can be scrubbed with soaped steel-wool scouring pads or Scotch-Brite Rescue pads, always scrubbing with the grain of the finish. Bon Ami can be used. Use a commercial cleaner for stainless steel to remove stubborn stains. Nylon scrubbing pads are usually all you need for the exterior of just about all types of stainless-steel pots; leading manufacturers say you should use no stronger abrasives on their exteriors.

Following manufacturers' instructions, if possible, is always safest—especially because you never know whether metals have received any special treatments that call for gentler care. Yet I have observed the manufacturers' instructions becoming stricter and more cautious over the years, and I must express doubts about the need to be so terribly careful with such a hearty metal as stainless steel. I believe that often the caution some manufacturers call for is intended only to preserve the brand-new, shiny or satiny finish of much new cookware. I am willing for the pot to show age and the patina of wear, and much prefer the look and shine of an aged, well-scoured, well-used pot to that of a new one. It is an-

and that stones are not loose in their settings. If you have valuable jewelry, let a jeweler do the checking.

Cleaning Jewelry: In General

Ammonia, alcohol, and chlorine or other bleaches should not be used for jewelry cleaning. Alcohol and ammonia will damage some gemstones and the plating on some precious metals. Chlorine can also damage some stones, and may pit or discolor gold or tarnish silver. Ammonia is often recommended because it is an alkaline grease cutter. Thus it removes dulling skin soils and oils from gemstones and restores their sparkle. But neutral, mild detergents do this just as well, without posing any risks. Although it is true that diamonds and certain other stones will not be harmed by an ammonia or alcohol solution, their settings or other stones set with them might be. Use no ammonia, alcohol, salt water, or detergent on any piece that has emeralds, for these substances might remove the oils in the cracks of this stone or erode its finish or polish.

If jewelry is washable (see below), use a mild solution of detergent and water to wash it. Commercial jewelry-cleaning liquids are also fine. Wash jewelry in a plastic basin, rather than the sink, to avoid any danger that something will fall into the drain. If you must wash it in the sink, close the drain tightly first, and remove all the jewelry before opening the drain when you are finished. There are many tragic stories of gems disappearing this way.

Ultrasonic cleaners should be avoided on all jewelry set with gemstones. Even though you may have successfully used ultrasonic cleaning on your diamonds or rubies, crystalline structures magnify vibrations; the vibrations from these machines can therefore cause cracking or shattering if they should happen to strike in just the wrong way. Every ultrasonic cleaning machine and every stone is different from every other, and you never know what will happen. The less hard the gemstone, moreover, the more likely it is that shattering or cracking will occur. Ultrasonic cleaning is fine for metals not set with gemstones.

Whenever you are in doubt about how to clean a piece of jewelry or gemstone, especially a valuable piece, take it to a reliable jeweler for cleaning or advice. This is not expensive (the advice is free), and it is a safer course of action.

Metals. Silver jewelry should be stored and cleaned like all other silver. Use treated polishing cloths between polishings. (See chapter 45, "Metals," pages 554–57.) Delicate silver articles need extra caution. You must make an aesthetic judgment, based on the age and style of the piece, about how much you wish to brighten up indentations and crevices.

Gold and platinum will not tarnish, but gold is often alloyed with other metals. (Twenty-four karat gold is 100% gold; 22 karat is 91.7% gold; 18 karat is 75% gold; 14 karat is 58.3% gold. The lowest legal percentage is 10 karat, at 41.6%. To get the percentage, divide the number of karats by 24.) Alloys will react with skin oils and acids and leave dark smudges on your skin. In this case, or if any gold or platinum should become dirty or dull from skin oils, food spills, or other causes, simply wash it gently in a mild detergent and water and dry it with a soft, dry cloth. Silver-plated and gilded articles need particularly gentle care because the thin layer of gold or silver will easily rub off, and replacing it is quite expensive.

If the metal is set with stones or jewels, however, you must follow the proper cleaning procedures for those stones. For example, in cleaning silver that is set with turquoises or gold that is set with pearls, you must carefully polish or clean around the stones and avoid immersing the piece in water or cleaning solution.

Transparent Gems. Diamonds, sapphires, rubies, garnets, amethysts, topaz, and all transparent gemstones *other than emeralds* that are not glued into their settings can be washed with a mild detergent and warm water. Just be sure that nothing else on the piece of jewelry might be vulnerable to the washing solution. To get behind the stone (on a ring, for example), use a soft brush. Toothbrushes are not recommended; they are too hard and stiff. Dry and buff the gemstones with a soft, clean cloth, if necessary, to bring up the shine after washing.

Opaque Gems, Glued-In Gems. Opaque gemstones need more care, as they are not crystalline in structure. Like ordinary rocks, they absorb water and become wet throughout. (Diamonds, sapphires, and rubies do not.) Thus they can absorb chemicals, soaps, and other substances, which can build up inside them and discolor them. Opals, amber, coral, lapis lazuli, pearls, mother-of-pearl, ivory, malachite, turquoise, and other opaque materials such as bone, ivory, and shells should not be immersed in water or other liquids. Wipe them gently with a slightly damp cloth and pat them dry. Ultrasonic cleaners, which require immersion, are not recommended for this group of materials. Never use ammonia or any other chemical on them. Any gems that are cemented or glued in place also should not be immersed.

Pearls and Mother-of-Pearl. Pearls, cultured pearls, and mother-of-pearl are delicate. They should be stored separately from other jewelry to avoid scratching or breaking them, or tangling or breaking the strings. Hang new pearls until they stretch and loosen. Take pearls and other valuable or valued necklaces to be restrung when the string between the pearls or stones becomes discolored or begins to stretch too much so that they are unevenly spaced. Do not wait for the string to break, for then you may lose some of them. There should be knots in the string between pearls to prevent more than one from falling if the string breaks.

Pearls and mother-of-pearl are vulnerable to extremes in humidity. Overly low humidity, in particular, is bad because it can make them peel. Because pearl and mother-of-pearl come from oysters and mollusks, respectively, they are made primarily of calcium carbonate and hence are also vulnerable to acids and air pollutants of various sorts. (The same is true of coral.) Wipe them after wearing so that acids from your skin do not remain on them. Mothers used to give their daughters this advice, which is still good: do not put on your pearls until you have finished spraying your hair and putting on your perfume and cosmetics, or these materials may get on the pearls and dull their luster or harm them. Dab your perfume on a spot that the pearls will not touch.

Never immerse pearls or mother-of-pearl in water, cleaning solutions, ammonia, or other liquids. To clean them, gently wipe them with a slightly dampened cloth, then pat them dry. If this does not work, take them to a jeweler.

Simulated pearls, by the way, are usually made of plastic, not a calcium compound. Synthetic or cultured pearls, however, do contain calcium carbonate, and they require the same treatment as natural pearls.

Opals. Opals need special care. Do not immerse them or expose them to soaps or other cleaning substances. Simply wipe them with a damp cloth. Opals need humidity, and may crack if left dry. They may also crack if exposed to sudden or extreme changes of temperature, especially excessive heat.

Ivory, Horn, and Tortoiseshell. Ivory, horn, and tortoiseshell are all made of bonelike material that does best in conditions of moderate temperature and humidity (around 50 percent relative humidity and around 68°F). Horn and tortoiseshell should not be exposed to direct sunlight or too much sunlight. Ivory needs a little exposure to sunlight to prevent it from yellowing, but too much is not desirable. Clean all these materials with a cloth slightly dampened with a mild, neutral cleaner in water, well wrung, and rinse with a clean cloth dipped in clear, warm water and well wrung. Do not immerse. Wipe dry with a clean, soft cloth. If your pieces are antique, it would be best to have a professional clean them.

Valuable, Delicate, and Antique Jewelry. If there is the slightest doubt about the safety of any cleaning procedure for valuable, delicate, or antique jewelry, take it to your jeweler or other appropriate professional for cleaning. He or she will not charge you much for this service, and it saves you the considerable risk of damage to something you care about.

Miscellaneous Suggestions for Jewelry Care. Never put jewelry in your checked luggage for an airplane trip. Not only is there a risk of theft, but the extreme temperatures in the hold can crack some gemstones (especially opals).

Remove diamonds and other jewelry when doing chores and washing dishes. Cleaning products can harm jewelry. Oils in dishwater can cloud gems. Some gems might be permanently discolored; others may crack.

If your skin turns green when you wear metal jewelry, you probably have acidic perspiration. (Not everyone does.) Try wearing your jewelry, especially pearls, outside your clothing.

Swimming-pool water contains chlorine and other chemicals. Remove your jewelry before swimming.

DAILY LIFE

47

Kindly Light

Sunlight, ultraviolet A, B, and C radiation, protecting furnishings . . . Artificial light . . . Color temperature on Kelvin scale, color temperatures of familiar light sources . . . Color rendition, Color Rendering Index, CRIs of familiar light sources . . . Quantity of light, lumens per watt, typical LPWs of familiar bulbs . . . Incandescent bulbs . . . Halogen bulbs . . . Fluorescent bulbs . . . Compact fluorescent bulbs . . . Comparison of bulbs . . . Electric lights and ultraviolet radiation . . . Full-spectrum bulbs . . . Making light work, luminaires, light quality, enough light, brightness, contrast and continuity, task lighting, too much light, glare, flickering and other distractions . . . Miscellaneous good lighting practices . . . Energy Star Program

> "Truly the light is sweet, and a pleasant thing it is for the eyes to behold the sun."
>
> —Ecclesiastes 11:7

When I was a child, I noticed that my paternal grandmother's house was dark and my maternal grandmother's light. My paternal grandmother, in small-American-town style, kept her home dim with awnings, venetian blinds, and drapes. In her book, only a careless housekeeper permitted the sun to fade furnishings. The huge flowers on her living room carpets stayed summertime red forever, and her home was deliciously cool no matter what the weather. My maternal grandmother, Italian style, did not erect so strict a division between inside and outside. She kept her home bright and airy; the important thing was to be able to see everything and smell nothing but fresh scents. Despite the fact that electric lighting had been available for more than a generation, in both homes people let their rooms darken as the sun went down. In the evenings, they would sit and talk in near darkness—lit, if at all, only by reading lamps—go to bed early, and rise with the sun. The rhythms of natural light still dominated their habits.

Today, we have seized control of light and dark and make use of a huge and ever-increasing variety of electric lights. But the more we use them, it seems, the less we know about them. This chapter covers basic information on the uses and effects of natural and artificial light sources in our homes.

Sunlight

Modern thinking supports my Italian grandmother's style. Sunlight pouring into your home is in most ways a good thing. Natural light is the most beautiful; the variations in its quality morning to night are primevally meaningful. Sunlight uses up no fuels and creates no pollution. But because it is so powerful, it can do harm as well as good.

The sun emits both visible light and invisible infrared and ultraviolet rays. The infrared radiation creates heat. Although visible light causes damage too, it is the sun's ultraviolet rays that do the most harm. The ultraviolet rays are divided into three classes, called UVA, UVB, and UVC. UVA rays are the longest (315–400 nm, or nanometers; a nanometer equals one-billionth of a meter). These tan skin and fade furnishings. Overexposure to UVA is said to contribute to skin aging and wrinkling. UVB rays, the next longest (280–315 nm), are more dangerous to us and to our furnishings. They cause sunburn and are considered to promote skin cancer, skin aging, and cataracts, although UVA may also contribute to the risk, or promote the growth, of certain types of skin cancer. UVC rays, the shortest (less than 280 nm), are the most dangerous of them all, but they are filtered out by the ozone in the atmosphere and do not reach us. They can be produced artificially, however, and are used for germicidal purposes in hospitals and other places.

The ultraviolet rays of the sun that do reach us are germicidal too. This is why spring cleaning used to mean dragging carpets, mattresses, pillows, upholstery, linens, and laundry into the sun, as well as letting the sun into the home by taking down heavy, light-blocking winter draperies and opening windows to sun and air. Being sun-drenched is one of the things that make air "fresh." A prominent allergist who told me that sunlight will kill dust mites in carpets also commented that if Americans knew what was good for them, they would revert to the ways of their ancestors and sun their things, as many people in the rest of the world still do.

The UV rays that kill germs are also what cause most sun fading; deterioration of fabrics in carpets, upholstery, and draperies; aging and bleaching of wood, plastics, photographs, and paintings; and other damage. The destructive effects of light on both organic and inorganic materials can be amplified by other circumstances: the presence of humidity, oxygen, heat, and various chemicals. Wet fabric fades much more quickly than dry—a principle taken advantage of in grass-bleaching linen. Cellulosic fibers are much more vulnerable to light-bleaching than wool, but wool will fade more readily when it is wet. Silk is most vulnerable to light of all organic fibers. Fabrics will not simply fade and yellow but will also weaken or decompose. If you have ever picked up an old piece of formerly tough cloth left lying in the sun and find that you can rend it effortlessly, you have observed this process at work.

UV light triggers the oxidation of alcohols contained in paper and causes it to turn yellow. Light exposure can also increase acidity in the paper, which in turn causes the paper to decompose. Light can cause dark wood to lighten, light wood to darken, and varnishes to turn yellow.

The trick is to find the happy medium between exposure and protection. Very valuable or historic objects are worth special care to preserve them against the natural processes of aging through exposure to light and heat from the sun. As for more ordinary furnishings, choose those that are as resistant to photodegradation as possible and avoid exposing them to sunlight or other light unnecessarily. Most objects will expire of unrelated causes long before the sun ruins them.

When it comes to minimizing the negative effects of light, you can take a cue from my paternal grandmother and attempt to block light. Ordinary window glass provides some protection against the depredations of sunlight. It blocks half of the UVB and a quarter of the UVA. You can also buy windows, shades, and screens that are specially treated to block all ultraviolet radiation, as well as windows, screens, shades, and coatings that reduce the amount of visible light that enters your home. (Except in special circumstances, it is probably best to avoid permanent visible light–reducing window coatings and tints.) There are also UV-blocking picture and photograph glass and plastics and fibers and dyes that are more light resistant than others. (See chapter 18, "Fabrics that Work," page 268.) Even if you have such UV-blocking windows and picture-frame glass, you cannot assume that other protections for heirlooms and valuables are unnecessary, for visible light is responsible for much fading and other forms of photodegradation.[1]

When you wash carpets or fabrics that you wish to preserve from fading, dry them out of direct sunlight. If you wish to sun bedding, carpets, and upholstery for hygienic reasons, you will have less fading if you do so while they are dry. Carpets, upholstery, fabrics of all sorts, wood, and many other objects will benefit from being rotated or moved from time to time so that all areas receive equal sun exposure. Often enough it is not sun fading per se that bothers us, but unequal sun fading—for example, when one arm of the chair is light blue and the other dark blue. Wood can be protected with fabric covers. Store valuable fabrics, wood, paper, and other organic materials in no light or little light. Close blinds and shades when you are not home. Since electric lights contribute to the negative processes, do not leave lights burning when you are out of the room, and use low UV–emitting types when preservation is very important. See "Electric Lights and Ultraviolet Radiation," below. Museums use low UV–emitting bulbs (or "lamps," as lighting professionals say), UV blockers, and light as low as feasible, and they ordinarily hold temperatures at between 68° and 72°F (18° to 20°C) and humidity at around 50 percent. To the extent that you can preserve such moderate temperatures and humidity in your home, you, too, will help to minimize the damage caused by light. Do not overlook incandescent light bulbs as a source of heat in the home.

Artificial Light

Color Temperature. The sun gives you few choices: it shines or not, and you can block it or not. When you pick artificial light for your home, however, you have options as to color and quality. Acquaintance with two fundamental lighting concepts, "color temperature" and "color rendition," will help you exercise those options.

Color temperature, which actually describes the appearance of light, is measured on a "Kelvin" scale. (The color of the light is indicated on the scale in accordance with a reference source heated to a particular number of degrees Kelvin.) Red-orange light is on the low or "warm" end of the scale. Blue light is on the high or "cool" end of the scale. Light sources that have a color temperature equal to or greater than 4100K appear "cool," and those with a color temperature equal to or less than 3100K appear "warm." What we call warm white light, for example, from an ordinary incandescent bulb, is actually a yellow or gold white. As color temperatures get lower and lower (warmer and warmer), they tilt more and more toward the red end of the spectrum, going from golden to orange to reddish. Light with a color temperature of 3400K is a brilliant, crisp, or neutral white. Cool whites have an icy, bluish tint. As color temperatures exceeding 4000K get higher and higher (cooler and cooler), they tilt more and more toward the blue end of the spectrum. The difference between two color temperatures in the range from, say, 2700K to 4000K is subtle. Unless lamps are set side by side you might not be able to discern it. Yet most people develop a pronounced preference for how things look in warmer light.

Although the brightness of a light source affects its color temperature, color temperature is not a measure of brightness. The chart below lists the color temperature of some familiar types of light, ranging from low/warm to high/cool.

Lighting experts typically recommend that for the home you choose bulbs with color temperatures between 2700K and 3500K. Most people find that such warm color temperatures are more flattering to the skin and have a warmer emotional resonance, perhaps because they are more similar to candlelight and firelight. This recommendation, lighting experts tell me, is primarily based not on science but on familiarity with what people in our corner of the world ordinarily find appealing. Some people—a minority—prefer cooler color temperatures in their home light. What color temperature to choose is a matter of taste. If you have an area in your home in which blues, greens, or purples are prominent, you might find that you like the way a cool light brings these colors out even though in general you prefer warm light.

Light Type	*Color Temperature*
Candlelight	1900K
Sunrise or sunset sunlight	2000K–3000K
Incandescent	2500K–2900K
Halogen	2850K–3300K
Warm white fluorescent	3000K
Rare-earth (triphosphor) fluorescent	3000K–4100K
Cool white fluorescent	4100K
Compact fluorescent	2700K–5000K
Average noon sun	5000K–6000K
"Daylight" fluorescent	6000K–7500K
Uniform overcast sky	7000K
Blue sky	8500K

Color Rendition. You have grappled with the importance of color rendition if you have ever taken a garment you are considering purchasing to a window or out into the street so that you can see what color it "really" is. I have seen people who are getting their hair colored insist on going outdoors to look at it too. Color rendition refers to how accurately or naturally a light shining on objects represents their appearance, or how well it "renders" their colors. This characteristic, too, is measured on a scale, called the Color Rendering Index (CRI). A CRI of 100 indicates that the light in question causes no shift of colors as compared with how things look in a reference light. The lower the number on the scale, the less accurately or naturally the light source renders the colors of objects. All incandescent bulbs have an excellent CRI of 95 to 100. The CRI of fluorescent lights varies widely, from poor to excellent.

The CRI of a given light source is determined by averaging what it does to various colors on the spectrum. This means that two different light sources may have identical CRIs yet show colors quite differently—for example, if they cause different colors to shift but in a way that averages out. You can compare the CRIs only of lights of the same color temperature. Both warm and cool light may have a high CRI, but objects appearing in them may have different color tones.

CRI OF VARIOUS SOURCES OF LIGHT	
Cool white fluorescent	62
Warm white fluorescent	52
Compact fluorescent	82
Rare earth or triphosphor fluorescent	75–89
Incandescent	95–100
Halogen	95–100
Daylight	100

When colors are well rendered, not only are things more attractive but you actually need less light to see well. Bulbs that put out good color light are therefore perceived as brighter, even when they are not. You might need a stronger fluorescent bulb with a lower CRI than an incandescent with a higher CRI.

The Environmental Protection Agency describes the desirability of various CRIs as follows: "CRIs in the range of 75–100 are considered excellent, while 65–75 are good. The range of 55–65 is fair, and 0–55 is poor."[2] These valuations may not be of much help in choosing light for your home, however. Lighting professionals recommend that you choose lights with a CRI of over 70 for the home. But in areas in which color or color discrimination is very important, I am told, you may want CRIs of 80 or higher. A high CRI might not matter much for reading, so long as the black/white contrast is adequate. It might matter a great deal for displaying decorative colors properly, or for certain kinds of activities such as sewing, painting, and various crafts. It certainly matters for kitchens, where judging freshness and doneness of foods is highly dependent upon excellent color rendition. But if in these instances we would do better with CRIs at least in the 80s, the designation of everything over 75 as "excellent" is not terribly meaningful for home choices.

Whatever you choose, evaluate new furnishings in all the kinds of artificial and natural light, at different times of day, in which they really will be used and displayed. This will often require you to bring home samples of fabrics, upholstery, carpeting, and other furnishings and to live with them for a while. Things can look terribly different in a store, on the street, and in your home. They will even look different at different times of day.

Quantity of Light: Lumen Ratings. For generations, people picked lightbulbs based on their wattage. Now, the thing to pay attention to is the lumen; the lumen rating of a bulb is the measure of its total light output. If you thought of one lumen as the amount of light put out by one candle, you wouldn't be terribly far off base, but the lumen is really technically defined and measured with great precision.

The brightest bulb—the one that produces the most lumens—may or may not be the one that uses the most watts. A 60-watt soft white standard incandescent bulb produces, on average, 855 lumens. But there are 20-watt compact fluorescents that produce 810 lumens, which is about the same brightness using only one-third the electricity. Linear fluorescents (see pages 577–78, below) often use even less electricity to produce that many lumens.

To determine how efficient a bulb is, you have to calculate how many lumens per watt (LPW) it gives you by dividing the number of lumens by the number of watts. For example, this is how you would determine the LPW of a 60-watt soft white incandescent bulb:

$$\frac{855 \text{ lumens}}{60 \text{ watts}} = 14.25 \text{ LPW}$$

And this is the calculation of a 20-watt compact fluorescent's LPW:

$$\frac{810 \text{ lumens}}{20 \text{ watts}} = 40.5 \text{ LPW}$$

The compact fluorescent, this shows, is much more efficient (or, as lighting professionals say, "efficacious"). To ensure that you are always able to make this calculation (and to figure out the comparative brightness of bulbs), a law passed in 1992 known as the Energy Policy Act (EPACT) established certain labeling requirements for manufacturers of lightbulbs.* Lightbulb packaging now has to state the number of lumens the bulb produces as well as its wattage rating and the average life expectancy of the bulb. (For fluorescents, whose lives are shortened when they are turned off and on frequently, the average life is calculated assuming that the light is left on for three hours for each start.)

Which Lightbulbs? The four main types of lightbulbs that are used in the home are incandescent, halogen, fluorescent, and compact fluorescent. Incandescents are the old-fashioned or regular type of bulb. Tungsten halogen bulbs are actually another type of incandescent bulb; they are often simply called halogen bulbs. Each type offers a different package of advantages and disadvantages.

Incandescent Lights. "Incandescent" means glowing or luminous with heat, and incandescent bulbs operate by using electricity to heat a filament in a bulb until it glows. Incandescent bulbs are highly flexible in use, since to get different degrees of brightness you need only use a different bulb in the socket, with less or more wattage. (But do not exceed the wattage rating for the light fixture! See chapter 61, "Electrical Safety.") All incandescent bulbs can be used with ordinary dimmers, too, permitting both enormous flexibility in light levels and in efforts to economize. They are easy to remove and replace. Incandescent bulbs provide a steady, pleasant white light with a warm golden tone. They have excellent color rendition of 95 to 100. Their color temperatures range from 2500 to 2900, with 2800 being typical. Some common incandescent bulbs used in the home have these color temperatures: 25 watt—2500K; 40 watt—2650K; 60 watt—2790K; 75 watt—2840; 100 watt—2900K. The color temperature of still bigger bulbs would be higher.

*This was an energy conservation measure that addressed lighting technology used in homes as well as in offices and industry. Among other things, it banned the manufacture of various inefficient bulbs, including the standard 40-watt fluorescent bulb and some incandescents as well, and established minimum lumens per watt (LPW) and CRIs for bulbs to be manufactured in the future.

TYPICAL LPWS FOR COMMON TYPES OF BULB[3]			
Type of Bulb	*Wattage*	*Lumens*	*LPW*
Incandescent A19, Inside Frost	75	1220	16.267
Halogen PAR38 Flood	90	1270	14.1
Fluorescent, 24" T8RE730	17	1325	77.94
Compact Fluorescent CFQ13W	13	900	69.23

Incandescent lights are very good for reading, close work, crafts, and similar activities in the home as well as for background lighting in areas in which you will dine, entertain, and the like. Their warm light is flattering to skin tones.

Incandescent lightbulbs produce heat as well as light—sometimes enough to be a problem in warm weather or to pose a fire hazard if flammable materials accidentally come in contact with a bulb. Because they lose so much energy through the heat they produce, they are less energy efficient and more expensive to use (even though considerably less expensive to buy) than fluorescent bulbs. More energy-efficient types of incandescent bulbs—reduced wattage bulbs with slightly higher LPWs—are appearing on the market. These have a slightly lower light output. Also, with incandescents, bigger means more efficient: a 150-watt bulb has an LPW of 19; a 100-watt bulb, 17.5; a 60-watt bulb, about 12.

Standard incandescent bulbs are much less long-lasting than fluorescents. You can extend their lives by dimming. Otherwise, unless they claim on the package to be long-life, you can expect them to burn for about 750–1,000 hours, which amounts to two or three hours per day, more or less, for about a year. So-called long-life bulbs will last up to 3,000 hours, but they may not put out as much light as others. Bulbs that are both reduced wattage and long-life will have a significantly reduced light output (about one-third less). The latter are not recommended, therefore, except for places where bulbs are hard to replace. Incandescent bulbs grow dim as they age.

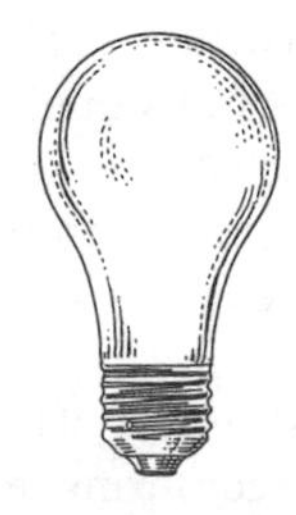

Incandescent lightbulb

"Soft" white, or frosted, bulbs provide a more diffuse light, not a different shade of white. There are also various specialty bulbs on the market. Bulbs that emit strongly colored light are sometimes used for decorative effects in the home, but they are not for reading or other tasks for which you need to see well. Colored lights illuminate like colors but obliterate or distort different colors, so that red lights, for instance, illuminate red things brightly but turn blue things dark. White light is best for your eyes and best for any ordinary activities you might want to engage in in your home. But a tinted filter or bulb does not necessarily produce strongly colored light.

Halogen Bulbs. In halogen bulbs, as with incandescent bulbs, electricity is passed through a tungsten filament, but the filament is enclosed in a glass tube that is filled with pressurized halogen gas. The filament emits a brilliant, bright white light when heated by an electric current. It produces a cooler light

Halogen Flood

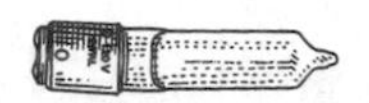

Halogen bulb

than incandescents, with color temperatures ranging from 2850K to 3300K. Typically halogen bulbs have a color temperature of about 3000K and give a crisp or neutral but not "cool" white. Halogens last much longer than incandescents, 2,000 to 4,000 hours, which would give you two hours per day for $2^3/_4$ to $5^1/_2$ years, or three hours per day for almost two to almost four years. This type of bulb also dims very little with age. You can use dimmers with halogen bulbs, but this will not lengthen their lives.

Because halogen bulbs have such a crisp white light, they are favorite choices for task lighting—reading, writing, sewing, crafts, and similar activities.

Halogen bulbs must be used with a glass filter. (Plastic filters cannot be used—they are too susceptible to the heat produced by halogen bulbs.) This glass enclosure both reduces shattering risks and filters out the ultraviolet radiation that halogen lamps otherwise emit, which is suspected of increasing skin cancer risk. (See "Electric Lights and Ultraviolet Radiation," below.) Nowadays in this country you are quite unlikely to be able to buy one that lacks a glass filter. But several years ago when you could, I did. If you, too, own any of these older halogen lamps, it is easy to have them retrofitted with glass filters. Call the manufacturer or contact a local lighting store for advice.

Certain cautions must be observed in handling and using halogen bulbs. Do not touch them with your bare fingers or hands when you take them out of their boxes and install them. Put on a cotton glove or handle them with tissues. They are highly sensitive to skin oils left by your fingers; such oils cause them to deteriorate much faster than they otherwise would.

Before using a halogen bulb, examine it carefully. Never use one if its glass is broken or cracked. A cracked glass could rupture or shatter during use, causing injury or property damage.

You must also be careful to use halogen bulbs only in places in which they cannot be touched by hands or flammable objects such as curtains, bedclothes, or paper, as they become extremely hot, much hotter than incandescents. They have caused many home and dormitory fires as well as accidental skin burns. Make sure lamps are placed where they will not be bumped into and will not be near anything flammable. Do not put torchiere lamps in children's rooms or other rooms where there may be a higher risk of tipping.

Halogen floor lamps, especially the torchiere-style ones, have been particularly hazardous, proving unstable and easily tipped over. In the early days they sometimes specified high-wattage bulbs, as high as 500 watts. In the wake of fires involving these, safety experts advised using no bulb with a wattage exceeding 300 even in a lamp rated for up to 500 watts. But even 300-watt bulbs get exceedingly hot—up to 650°F, according to the March 1997 issue of *Consumer Reports.* More stringent safety standards have been established by Underwriters Laboratories in conjunction with the Consumer Products Safety Commission, the latest of which impose the following requirements on manufactures of halogen torchiere lamps as of June 1, 1999:

> A guard must be affixed to the lamp at the factory that conforms to construction requirements, including the requirement

that it be positioned no more than 3 inches off the bulb.

The lamp must pass a revised "cheesecloth drape test." A 20-layer pad of cheesecloth is draped over the center of the lamp guard while the lamp is turned on. The cloth must not ignite or develop holes in any layer of the cheesecloth.

Halogen torchiere lamps must be equipped with a tip-over switch that will turn the lamp off if it is tipped in any direction, or must pass additional stability test requirements and a vertical wall test. During the vertical wall test, the lamp is laid on its side next to the "wall" (which is plywood covered with cotton terry cloth); it must not flame or char during the test. If you want to continue using older models, Underwriters Laboratories and the CPSC recommend you get wire guards for older halogen lamps that lack them. These are available from Kmart, Home Depot, Montgomery Ward, and many other stores. Additional sources are listed at UL's and CPSC's Web sites.

In addition, if you continue to use older models that do not conform to these requirements, scrupulously observe the cautions described above, especially as to using no bulbs with wattage higher than 300 and placing torchiere-style lamps away from tipping dangers and from potential contact with flammable cloth or other materials. They *never* belong in children's rooms or play areas.

Halogen bulbs are sometimes harder to remove and replace than screw-in bulbs.

Fluorescent Bulbs. Although they cost more at the store, fluorescent tubes are the least expensive to use of all bulbs that you can buy for the home. The superior efficiency of fluorescents is due to the fact that they waste less energy giving off heat. This also makes them the coolest bulbs to use. A fluorescent tube is filled with argon gas and mercury. When a current is passed through this medium, invisible ultraviolet radiation is produced, which excites a phosphor coating on the inside of the tube and causes it to emit light.

Because the light is produced over the large surface area of the tube, fluorescent lighting does not produce unpleasant bright spots and harsh shadows; it is diffuse and bright at the same time.

Fluorescent tubes last anywhere from 10,000 to 20,000 hours, much longer than either incandescents or halogens, and there are types that last much longer. At the end of their lives they tend to flicker and to grow black at the ends, producing less light. Their estimated lives are based on the assumption that each time they are turned on, they are left on for three hours. In fact, they may last longer if left on for more than three hours per start, and they may last less long if operated for less than three hours per start. Generally speaking, all fluorescent bulbs last longer if they are not switched on and off frequently.

Fluorescent lights are sensitive to cold and work better indoors, but newer types are less sensitive than the old models. Fluorescent fixtures for linear fluorescent tubes can accommodate only a single size bulb. At present, most fluorescent bulbs cannot be used with the ordinary dimmers that work with incandescent lights. Some fluorescents cannot be dimmed at all, and for others you have to invest in special dimmers and ballasts. In the past the process has been expensive and difficult. New technology to solve the problems is beginning to look promising, including some aimed at permitting the use of ordinary dimmers with fluorescent lights.

Newer linear fluorescent tubes are often a big improvement over the old "cool white" fluorescents. The problem has been that fluorescent tubes tend to emit lights in "spikes"—that is, various colors in the visible light spectrum are disproportionately strong

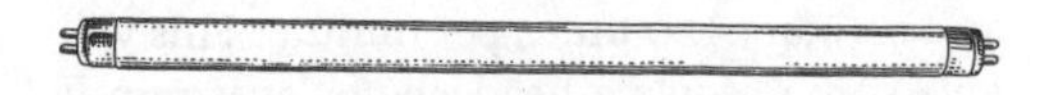

Linear fluorescent tube

in fluorescent light while others are weak, and parts of the spectrums of some colors are omitted. The old cool white fluorescent emits strong light in a narrow portion of the bluish end of the range (along with other color spikes) and is weak in the red range. Its color temperature, therefore, is cool and its CRI a low 62: red tones are distorted, and complexions bathed in the light of the cool white fluorescent acquire a ghostly, yellow-greenish, washed-out look.

Newer types of fluorescents using rare-earth phosphors or triphosphors—T8s and compact fluorescents, for example—significantly diminish the color-distortion problem. A thin coat of rare-earth phosphors produces CRIs ranging from 70 to 79. A thick coat of rare-earth phosphors produces CRIs ranging from 80 to 89. At the same time, fluorescents using rare-earth phosphors have improved efficiencies. Some types achieve even higher CRIs into the 90s, but at a cost of loss of efficiency. Fluorescents with rare-earth phosphors also can provide both a warmer color temperature of around 3000K and cooler color temperatures. (But, generally speaking, the cooler color temperatures have higher CRIs.) For a living area of your home in which it is desirable to have good color rendition, warm light, and compatibility with incandescent bulbs, choose fluorescents with rare-earth phosphors, a color temperature close to 3000K, and a CRI over 80. Currently, these superior fluorescents tend to be more expensive; and the higher the CRI, the higher the cost.

Fluorescent lights need mechanisms known as "ballasts" to provide the correct amount of voltage to start the lamp, and to regulate the current to ensure a steady light output. There are currently two main kinds of ballast: magnetic and electronic. Fluorescent lights operated on magnetic ballasts produce a subtle flicker or pulse—turning off and on some 120 times per minute. This will give some people a headache or eyestrain if they try to read or do close work. Fluorescent bulbs operated on magnetic ballasts may also make a humming noise, which can be terribly annoying. Both problems can be solved by using electronic ballasts. Electronic ballasts are expensive to buy but more energy efficient in use.

Compact Fluorescents. Compact fluorescent bulbs are small. Unlike other fluorescent bulbs, some compact fluorescents have a screw base and can usually screw into regular incandescent light sockets, sometimes with the help of an adapter. This does not necessarily mean that they also fit into the "luminaire" (as lighting professionals call light fixtures and lamps). But they are getting smaller and more versatile over time. They are highly energy efficient—although less efficient than ordinary fluorescents—and offer very good light, much closer to the quality of incandescents. Their typical CRI is 82. At present, they are available in a variety of color

READING THE LABEL

The letters and numbers that identify fluorescent tubes are full of information. On a fluorescent tube labeled RE730, "RE" means "rare earth." The "7" means that it has a CRI in the 70s—from 70 to 79. The "30" means that it has a color temperature of 3000K. A label that says "RE827" indicates a tube coated with rare-earth phosphors with a CRI in the 80s—between 80 and 89—and a low color temperature of 2700. "CF" means "compact fluorescent."

The diameter of fluorescent tubes is measured in eighths of an inch. "T12" refers to a fluorescent tube whose diameter is 12 eighths of an inch (an inch and a half). A "T8" is 8 eighths of an inch in diameter (or an inch). On a fluorescent labeled "F13T5," the "13" means "13 watts," and "T5" means a tube with a ⅝-inch diameter.

Compact fluorescent bulb

temperatures ranging from as low as 2700K and up to 5000K.

I have seen complaints that compact fluorescents are too dim, but I have found my own light of this type, a desk lamp, to provide ample reading light for working long hours at a stretch. The dissatisfaction may arise simply because people do not buy a strong enough compact fluorescent, perhaps assuming optimal conditions that frequently are not present. If you are not sure what to buy, a rule of thumb that one reliable source gave me is this: figure out the wattage of an incandescent bulb that would provide the brightness you desire and divide that by three. Your answer will be the approximate wattage of the appropriate compact fluorescent. So, for example, if you'd like something comparable to a 75-watt incandescent, a 26-watt compact fluorescent would be about right.

Like other fluorescents, most compact fluorescents cannot be used with regular dimmers for incandescent lights; this will damage them and shorten their life. Special

COMPARING BULBS[4]

	Incandescent	Halogen	Linear fluorescent	Compact fluorescent
CRI	95–100	95–100	52–90+	82
Color temperature (typical)	2800K	3000K	3000K–4200K	2700K
Lumens per watt (LPW)	10–20	11–19	65 typical, 50–100 range	65 typical, 40–75 range
Average life span in hours	750–1,000	2,000	10,000–20,000	10,000
Prices	75-watt bulb: $.75 150-watt bulb: $1.75	75-watt halogen A: $4.00 150-watt R40: $5.50	T8RE830 (24" or 36"): $7.00 T5 Cool White 21": $6.00	5-watt: $6.00 26-watt: $14.00
Lumens	75-watt: 1,190–1,220 150-watt: 2,850	75-watt halogen A: 1,090–1,300 150-watt R40: 1,900	T8RE830 24": 1,400 36": 2,250 T5 21": 390–400	5-watt: 250 26-watt: 1800

able: tube lamps, desk lamps, film lamps, nightlights. You can use dimmers. You can get any combination of diffused and focused light that you would like. For help in choosing and placing luminaires, you can turn to a variety of professionals—lighting experts, contractors, architects, decorators—or to any number of excellent books and articles on the subject.* Luminaire placement determines whether your thoughtful choices of bulbs and fixtures are going to make you happy or miserable. The subject is far too large to be covered here, but consider these examples of the importance of placement:

- Place ceiling fixtures so that they are aligned with the front edge of your appliances, counter, or table. Otherwise you will cast a shadow on your work surface.
- Avoid placing wall-mounted lamps at a height at which they will glare into people's eyes. At tables, pendant lamps should be at a height more than two feet above the tabletop.
- Avoid placing light fixtures in stair areas in such a way that someone going up or down looks directly down on or into a light, as it might be blinding and cause a dangerous fall.
- Avoid placing lamps and fixtures so far from the area to be illuminated that they give insufficient light where it is needed (often easier said than done).

Light Quality. In the home, you will want lights with CRIs over 80 or 90 in areas in which color discrimination or color matching is very important—for example, on kitchen countertops and stovetops, on sewing tables, on works of art, on a painting easel, and at desks, chairs, or tables where you read—and in the living room or dining room or any other place where the colors of the furnishings are very subtle or very important. Most people will prefer overall lighting that has a color temperature of between 2700K and 3500K. Your own tastes and habits are the best guide.

Enough Light: Brightness. When light is too dim, eyestrain, fatigue, and headaches can result. You make mistakes and work more slowly. What is too dim, however, is relative to what you are doing and who you are. You do not want bright light for a quiet face-to-face talk, watching videos, listening to music, dancing, walking through your hallway, or hanging up your jacket. But because it takes more light to see small things, you need *very* bright light if you do needlework with tiny stitches or crafts that call for fine discrimination. It also takes more light to do tasks in which there is little contrast between the task and the background, as when you thread a needle with red thread against the background of red cloth. The longer you engage in such demanding activities, the brighter the light you will need to avoid fatigue, eyestrain, error, and just slowing down.

Older people need more light than younger ones to see—*much more.* The older you are, the more light you need. The eyes of someone in his fifties may take in only about half the light of a person of twenty. People in their sixties may show a loss of 60 percent. That is why grandparents so often accuse their grandchildren of sitting and reading in the dark. Guests in your home often need more light than you do because your home is unfa-

*Three that that are particularly valuable are Russell P. Leslie and Kathryn M. Conway (both at the Lighting Research Center in Rensselaer, New York), *The Lighting Pattern Book for Homes* (2d ed., McGraw-Hill, 1996); Randall Whitehead, *Residential Lighting: Creating Dynamic Living Spaces* (Rockport Publishers, 1993); and *Lighten Up! A Practical Guide to Residential Lighting Design* (Light Source Publishing, 1996). You can also write to the American Lighting Association for low-cost brochures on home lighting and helpful references to experts (PO Box 420288, Dallas, TX 75342-0288).

miliar to them, whereas you know its tricks and oddities by heart.

The color of background surfaces affects how much light your bulbs provide. Where there are white or light walls, the reflected light adds brightness to the area and you may need less bright bulbs; where you are working against dark backgrounds or with low contrasts, you will need brighter ones.

Contrasts and Continuities, Task Lighting. "Task lighting" is what we call the increased light we use for specific activities—reading the label on a prescription medicine, sewing, chopping onions, playing Scrabble, working at a workbench. The increased level of illumination is provided only for the small area, the task area, on which our eyes are focused.

The contrast between the brightness of a task area and that of ambient lighting must occupy a happy middle ground, or eyestrain and fatigue will result. If you have a very bright reading lamp in an otherwise pitch-dark room, you are likely to begin to feel eyestrain if you read for long. This is because each time your eyes lift from the page and look at something in the room, they are forced to make a big adjustment to the different light level. You need some light, but less of it, in the area surrounding the task area, say about a third as much light, and it is easier on the eyes if the light gradually declines with distance from the brightly lit task area.

Comfort is not the only benefit of a good ratio between task and ambient lighting. It costs less to use intense light only where that level is needed, with a lower level used for surrounding areas. And focused light on an activity or area of attention surrounded by softer light is generally more attractive. Your dinner table, for example, needs more light than the rest of the room. Take care, though, not to provide light *only* at the table or the overall effect will be stark and glaring.

It is also important to think about the consistency, or continuity, of lighting in different rooms and different areas of the same room. If color temperatures are not in the same range, if you have cool white fluorescent here and warm incandescent there, the changeover can be jarring. But you can easily mix incandescent lights and rare-earth fluorescents, which are available in low color temperatures, of about 3000K.

Too Much Light: Glare. Glare is too much light relative to the eye's adaptation to light at any particular moment. Even if the level of light on a book is proper, an unshielded lightbulb shining into your eyes each time they lift from the page is uncomfortable. This is why you put on a shade of some sort that directs the light at the surfaces you want lit instead of into your eyes. When you are reading or sewing, this is very important. You can also get a glare off a work surface—for instance, from coated, shiny paper or a computer screen—if you have too much or badly directed light. (On glare in computer monitors, see chapter 54, "Home Offices and Computers.")

Flickering and Other Distractions. A flickering light can make reading or close work very fatiguing. When reading and sewing were done by flickering candlelight, complaints of headaches and eyestrain were endless. You will admire Abe Lincoln even more if *you* try reading by firelight for longer than two minutes. Fluorescent lights that use magnetic ballasts may flicker, too, but they do it so quickly that you are not consciously aware of it. Some people may feel eyestrain or get headaches from it nonetheless, as your eyes are still forced to react. Changing to electronic ballasts will solve the problem. Electronic ballasts also eliminate the humming noise of fluorescent lights that so annoys some people.

Miscellaneous Good Lighting Practices.

- Use dimmers in entryways so that you can gradually increase the level of lighting for the hours of darkness.

- Do not leave hallways too dark compared with adjacent areas. This can cause trips and falls.
- Lighting on stairways and steps is *exceedingly* important. Make sure all the steps are uniformly lighted, and that the edge of each step is clearly visible, to prevent trips and missteps. Be especially sure that the top and bottom steps are clearly illuminated, as these are places where trips frequently happen. A further important safety measure on stairs is to make sure that someone going up or down is not going to look directly down on or into a light, as the glare might half blind someone.
- If you have a chandelier or other pendant lamp at your dining table, make sure that it hangs more than two feet above the tabletop or it will glare into people's eyes and obstruct their view.
- In the kitchen you need to accommodate a variety of tasks: reading recipes and newspapers, chopping, stirring, examining raw and cooked foods, washing dishes. You will need excellent task lighting at your sink, stovetop, and countertop for the more visually demanding of these. Dimmers are very useful to enable you to alter the lighting levels. Good color discrimination is indispensable in cooking, so you will want lights with a high CRI.
- To use mirrors effectively, use extra light shining not on the mirror but on you, when you stand two to three feet away. Watch out for the placement of the light. Put it above eye level or shade it so that it does not glare in your eyes. Watch out for harsh shadows from down-directed lights. For makeup or grooming, you want very bright light with a very high CRI.
- For painting and other arts and crafts in which color is key, you want to use as much natural light as possible, so choose a room with several windows, and do not have the light at your back or your shadow will fall on your work. Painters prefer a "daylight" bulb with a CRI over 90, preferably almost 100. This would be as close to real daylight as artificial light could provide. Note that what are called "daylight" bulbs come in a broad range of color temperatures of anywhere from 5000K to 7500K.
- For sewing you will want brighter light when you are working with dark fabrics than when you are working with whites or light colors. In general, however, strong, direct or focused light is needed, with a properly lit background to avoid eyestrain, especially when you are working on a time-consuming project. Anyone who sews needs a neutral white light with an excellent CRI for proper matching of threads and fabrics.
- For task lighting of all sorts, a task lamp with an adjustable focus and multilevel intensities is often useful, say a gooseneck lamp that holds a three-way bulb. You can move its focus or turn it up or down as the task demands. For jobs where very white, very bright light is useful, such as sewing or workbench projects, many people like a maneuverable halogen lamp.
- When setting up desks, work tables, or task areas of all sorts, use desk and task lamps and window light effectively. Place desks and tables at right angles to the window so that the window is at your side when you sit down to work; if the window is in front of you, there will be a glare in your eyes. Right-handed people should have the lamp or window at their left side, left-handed at the right. That way, your main working arm or hand does not cast a shadow on your paper, book, sewing, or other task materials. A lamp might also be placed directly on the wall in front of you so long as it is above eye level and shines directly on your work surface.
- The longer you read and the smaller and fainter the type, the brighter should be

your reading lights. Casual short-term reading usually needs less light. But *never treat reading medicine labels or prescription instructions as a casual matter.* You should always use strong light to decide if you have got the right medicine and have correctly read the dosage and other instructions.

- If, when reading in bed, you want to keep the rest of the room dark, for your mate's sake, get a small, narrowly focused reading lamp that can be aimed right at your book or use a similarly narrow-focused light attached to the wall. This will cause more eyestrain, on account of the high contrast between task light and background light, but less domestic strain.
- If you are sitting in a chair to read and using a reading lamp with a shade or shield, the bottom edge of the shade or shield should be at or slightly above eye level. This will keep light from glaring in your eyes. If the shade were lower than eye level, you might not get enough reading light.
- Most computer monitors sold now are designed to reduce glare and reflections, and they pose few difficulties to the user. Older models and some of the cheaper new ones, however, can have hard-to-solve glare and reflection problems. According to the Lighting Research Center at Rensselaer Polytechnic Institute, you can try moving the light or the computer, and if you cannot do this in such a way as to stop the glare, get a non-glare screen to use with the monitor or get one of the new monitors. Some experts report diminished glare as a result of placing shields or filters over room lights, but this probably also diminishes light output. Some of these filters may warm up the light of fluorescent bulbs at the same time. Place your desk lamp at the left of your monitor (at the right for left-handers). The computer should be at right angles to the window.
- You need bright light in the laundry or it is hard to judge how well you have cleaned your clothes and linens. Although fluores-

cent lighting is usually preferred in such utility areas because it is inexpensive, I find that cool white fluorescent light, which you often encounter in clothing stores, sometimes leaves me yearning for better color rendition; I often carry things out to a window so that I can better judge whether two items look good together. In your laundry you have to judge the color of fabrics accurately, examine soil, match socks, judge the brightness of whites and lights, and find stains. In dim light, stains will be invisible that in daylight are visible, and differing shades of color may be indistinguishable. Optical brighteners in many detergents and laundry products make fabrics look bright white under fluorescent lights but not under incandescent light or daylight. Good window light is therefore useful in a laundry. Position a ceiling light in your laundry so that it is aligned with the edge of the appliances to prevent shadows from your body being cast over them.

- You need fairly bright light to iron; the darker the cloth, the brighter the light you need. Focusing a direct light on your ironing board, with a diffuse overhead light, works well.

THE ENERGY STAR PROGRAM

The Energy Star Program is a joint program of the U.S. Environmental Protection Agency and the Department of Energy aimed at reducing pollution by reducing energy consumption in homes as well as offices. It awards the "Energy Star Label" to a broad range of products and structures that are energy efficient in use while maintaining quality standards in performance. The following may be eligible for the Energy Star Label:

Heating and cooling equipment for the home

Computers, printers, monitors, scanners

Fax machines

Office equipment

Furnaces and other heating and cooling equipment

Home appliances, including dishwashers, refrigerators, room air conditioners

Residential lighting fixtures

For information on these and other products eligible for the Energy Star Label, see the Energy Star site on the Internet http://www.epa.gov/energystar.html; fax a request for information about Energy Star to (202) 233-9659; or call the Energy Star Hotline toll-free at (888) STAR-YES [(888) 782-7937]. For more information about the Energy Star Label Residential Light Fixture Program, write to:

Manager
Energy Star Residential Light Fixture Program
U.S. EPA (6202J)
401 M Street, S.W.
Washington, D.C. 20460

48

Fireplaces

Cleaning the fireplace . . . The exterior, hearth, and bordering walls . . . The interior, the firebox . . . Fireplace accessories . . . Chimneys, inspections and cleaning, creosote and its dangers . . . How to build a fire, dry wood, type of wood, preliminaries, building a fire in standard vs. Rumford fireplaces . . . Additional safety practices . . . Efficiencies

A fireplace is such a potent symbol of home and comfort that "hearth" is still synonymous with "home" even though most people have no fireplace and even though fireplaces are, and always were, a poor means of heating a home. Affection for fireplaces is not simply twentieth-century nostalgia. In the nineteenth century, the open fire was so beloved that many people rejected clean and efficient stoves in favor of fireplaces that baked their fronts, froze their backs, filled the air with smoke, and required constant tending.

Some Victorians insisted that fireplaces were superior to stoves because the chimney provided built-in ventilation and made for fresher air in the home. It does not. The fireplace works by drawing air from the room to feed the fire. As the hot air from the fire rises, it draws the smoke out the flue in the chimney. The problem is that in drawing air from the room to feed combustion, the fireplace actually takes warm air from your house and sends it outside. Nor do fireplaces replace the heat they remove. They produce radiant heat, which warms objects and persons nearby but does not warm the air to any significant degree. (Baseboard heaters, forced hot air, solar heat, and radiators all produce convective heat: that is, they heat the air.) The only practical alternative for someone wishing to use wood for heat is the wood stove.

However inefficient and impractical a fireplace is as a heating device, it remains a source of deep pleasure and beauty. And its efficiency can be improved through the use of the right firewood, skilled firebuilding techniques, and well-designed accessories.

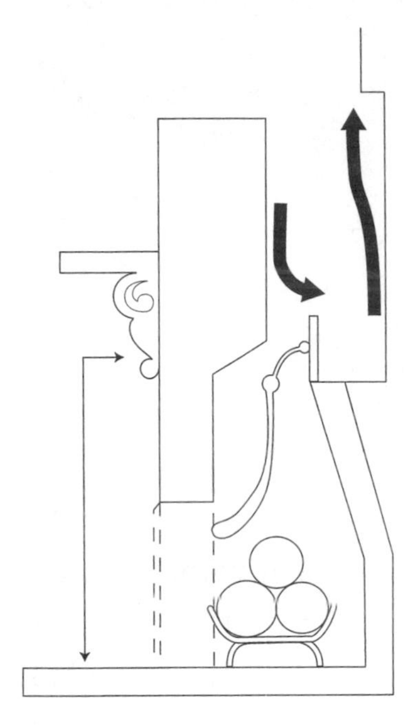

Fireplace structure

STRUCTURE OF THE FIREPLACE

You build the fire in the recessed area called the "firebox," which opens onto the room. The back wall of the firebox is the fireback, and its floor is the inner hearth. The outer hearth is the floor area just in front of the firebox. The hearth is usually made of tile, brick, cement, marble, slate, or some other stone, masonry, or hard material. The chimney is a long, thin, vertical rectangle, directly above the firebox, containing one or more flues, or channels, through which smoke and sparks are carried off to the outside. As smoke and gases first leave the fire, they pass through the "throat" of the fireplace, then through the smoke chamber into the flue. The chimney has a damper, a valve or little door that you open to permit smoke to exit and air to enter when the fireplace is in use. (You close the damper when there is no fire.) The damper can be one of two kinds, a throat damper (just above the firebox) or a top-sealing damper (at the top of the chimney). In some fireplaces, a door in the floor of the firebox leads to an ash pit for dumping ashes.

Cleaning the Fireplace

The Exterior: Hearth and Bordering Walls. The floor and walls near the fireplace often become stained with soot and smoke. These may escape the firebox in small amounts that build up over time. Or the sooty stains may result from smoke pouring suddenly into the room when someone tries to light a fire with the damper closed.

To clean smoke and soot from the hearth and exterior walls of the fireplace, first vacuum off all loose soot and ash. (See the discussion of vacuums below.) Then rub off as much soot as you can with a *dry* brush, sponge, or cloth. When the exterior is as free of soot as you can make it by these methods, wash it in the way recommended for any surface made of the material—stone, marble, cement, slate, tile. Either a solution of the strongest all-purpose cleaner suitable for the surface and water or a specialty cleaner designed for cleaning soot and smoke will work well. TSP, ammonia, or other alkaline cleaner mixed with water and applied with an abrasive, like a good stiff brush, will also work.

If your fireplace has glass doors, wash them in accordance with the manufacturer's instructions or, if you do not know the manufacturer, with ordinary glass cleaner.

The Interior: The Firebox. Ash accumulates in the bottom of the fireplace as logs are burned. During the cold seasons when the fireplace is in use, not all of it should be removed. Remove only enough to allow air to circulate under your andirons or grate and to leave room to place newspaper and kindling for starting new fires. Maintaining a bed of ash in your fireplace is an integral part of good fire making. (See "How to Build a Fire," below.)

Always wait one to two days after using the fireplace before removing any ashes to be sure that they are entirely extinguished. Close the windows, doors, and damper when you remove ashes so that breezes do not blow the ashes about as you work. Wear a dust mask and work gloves, cover your hair, and protect your eyes with goggles from floating dust and debris. If it is a big job, cover the hearth and any nearby furnishings with papers or drop cloths. Brush the ashes into a shovel carefully, so as not to raise dust, and gently empty the shovel into a metal container with a handle, such as a bucket or metal trash can, which will not burn if the ashes are still smoldering. Continue until you have removed enough ashes to leave a proper ash bed. Store the ashes in a metal trash can with a close-fitting lid outdoors. (If your fireplace has an ash pit, you open the trap door in the floor of the firebox and shove the ashes into the pit—when they are completely cold. Empty the ash pit regularly. There will be an access door for doing this either in your basement or outdoors.)

Off-season you can remove all the ashes and, if you wish, clean the firebox and inner hearth more thoroughly. My own feeling is that once any loose material that breezes might blow out into the room are gone, there is no reason to wash down a firebox. But if you are more fastidious, continue with your dust mask, gloves, hair covering, and goggles. After brushing out all the ashes you can, use only vacuums specially designed for ashes to vacuum the last dust out of the firebox. Others will spew fine dust into the air of your home. HEPA filters will catch ash, but call your manufacturer to be sure that yours may be used for fireplaces, because soot can clog the motor of some vacuums.

Fireplace and accessories

Fireplace Accessories. Most people use a grate or andirons to hold the logs, a hearth brush or broom, a fire screen, and a poker, tongs, and a shovel for building and tending their fires. These tools are usually made of cast iron, wrought iron, or brass. To wash them, remove all loose matter with a dry brush, sponge, or cloth, then wash with an all-purpose household cleaner. Use a little paste wax on such accessories for a pleasant shine and rust resistance. (Remember that waxes contain flammable solvents. *Do not* sit by a fire to wax your tools.) See "Metals," under the type of metal yours are made of, for more detailed advice.

Chimneys

The National Chimney Sweeps Guild and the Chimney Safety Institute of America (CSIA) both recommend that chimney inspections be performed by a CSIA-certified chimney sweep. (CSIA is a nonprofit educational association funded in part by the National Chimney Sweep Guild.) Or you might call a building inspector. The National Fire Protection Association (NFPA) says all chimneys should be inspected once a year. There should be an additional inspection after a chimney or furnace fire, when the chimney is physically altered in any way, if there is any suspicion of storm damage, and before closing the purchase of a new home. Get the chimney inspector to provide the results in writing.

The NFPA also recommends annual cleaning by a certified chimney sweep. Otherwise you risk chimney fires or the accumulation of dangerous gases inside your home. If the chimney is blocked, carbon monoxide, for example, might be trapped indoors. A chimney sweep will clean the chimney of soot and creosote, remove birds' nests or other blockages, and alert you to any needed repairs or alternatives. It is *extremely important* to have this done. Chimney fires are common, and sometimes are dramatic and dangerous. Some people think that a fire in the chimney can do no harm. They are terribly mistaken; a chimney fire can and often does burn down the house.

The creosote that collects in chimneys, a flammable by-product of combustion, is the usual cause of chimney fires. It is black or brown and sticky, like tar. Sometimes it hardens and appears shiny. Cleaning the chimney of creosote and other debris is a job for an expert, and you should not try to do it yourself. To reduce the amount of creosote that accumulates in your chimney:

- Burn only "seasoned" or dry wood in your fireplace. Green wood causes the formation of great amounts of creosote.
- Burn hard woods (oak, hickory, madrona, ash) rather than soft ones (fir, pine).
- Do not burn pine boughs or Christmas trees or other sappy woods in your fireplace.
- Do not restrict the air supply to your fire. Make sure that the damper is open wide and that glass doors are not shut while the fire is burning (see page 593, below).
- Do not build fires that are too small. The smoke is cooler and rises more slowly, causing more creosote buildup.

Creosote deposits in your chimney can cause odors in your home, especially when they get wet. This problem is usually worse in the summer, when it is humid and the air conditioner is on. If it is not solved by having the chimney cleaned, consider installing a chimney (or rain) cap. The creosote smells much worse when it gets damp from rain, and a cap helps keep out both rain and wind. You can also buy a commercial chimney deodorant or set a pan of baking soda or cat litter in the fireplace. According to the CSIA, "The real problem is the air being drawn down the chimney, a symptom of overall pressure problems in the house. Some makeup air should be introduced somewhere else in the house. A tight sealing, top mounted damper will also reduce this air flow coming down the chimney." A chimney cap will also help with downdraft problems, but get it inspected regularly because it can become plugged with debris.

How often you should have your chimney inspected and cleaned—in addition to the standard annual inspection and cleaning—depends on many factors, including how often you use it and how much wood you burn. One rule of thumb is to have the chimney checked after you have burned two cords of wood. If you use a wood stove as the primary source of heat, you may need to clean the chimney as often as once a month. Because wood stoves, unlike fireplaces, keep heat in the house, they cause more creosote accumulation. If in doubt, err on the side of safety.

For more information on chimney sweeps and chimney safety, contact the National Chimney Sweep Guild or the Chimney Safety Institute of America or check their sites on the Internet.

How to Build a Fire

Dry Wood. Use wood that is dry or "seasoned." It is easier to light, and, once lit, it produces much greater heat. Green (non-dry) wood, which contains a surprising amount of moisture, will also smoke a great deal and lead to the accumulation of creosote in your flue at a much greater rate, for there will be much less heat to carry the smoke outside the chimney. Never keep a wood pile indoors; this can cause problems with mold and excessive dampness in your home.

Full logs that are dry will have ends that are "checked"—that is, they will have cracks radiating from the center. If the wood is split, bang two pieces of wood together: green wood will make a dull thudding sound, while dry wood will make a sharp crack.

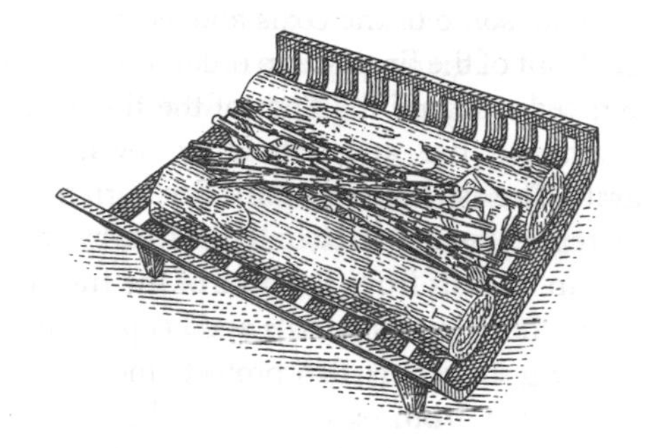
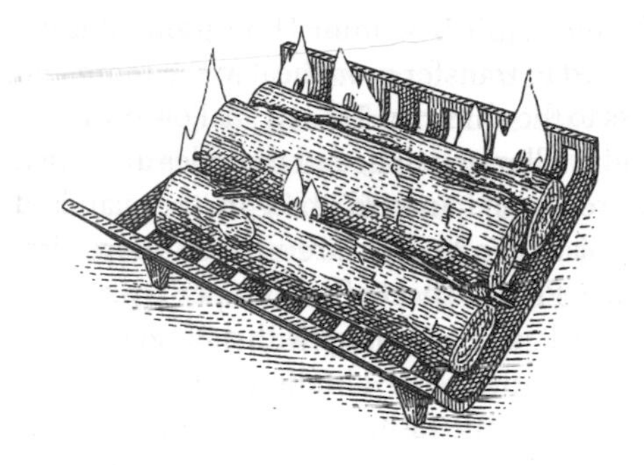

How to build a fire in a standard fireplace

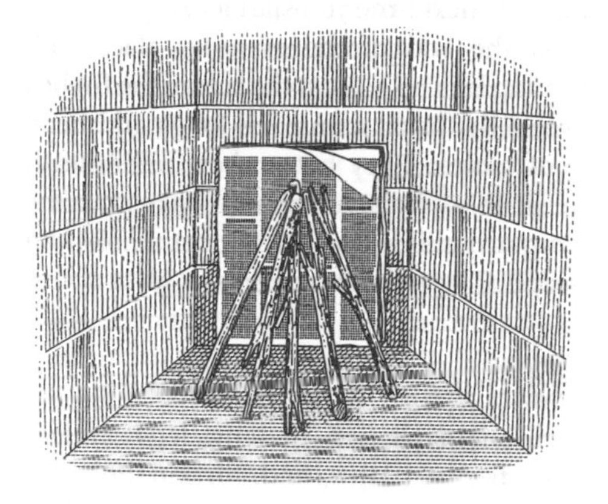

How to build a fire in a Rumford fireplace

Type of Wood. The kind of wood you choose matters greatly too. Different types of wood make fires that are more and less hot, more and less long-lasting, and more and less beautiful. The harder the wood, the longer and hotter the fire will burn.

Preliminaries. Build the fire toward the rear of the firebox, or the smoke may come into the room. Ventilate the room well. Open a window a crack if there is no other source of fresh air. Prime the flue immediately before you light the fire. To do this, make a torch of a twisted-up newspaper and hold the burning torch close to the damper for a minute or two. This will create an upward draft of warm air, pulling air and oxygen over your logs.

Building the Fire. The standard fireplace measures about 36 inches wide, 28 inches high, and 16–20 inches deep. Its inner walls angle inward toward each other somewhat, and often the back wall is sloped forward. To build a fire in a standard fireplace: Open the damper. Place two logs a few inches apart on the fireplace grate. Put crumpled pieces of newspaper between them. Cover the newspaper with kindling. When laying the kindling sticks down, crisscross them to leave plenty of air spaces. Prime the flue to get air flowing up the chimney. Light the paper. When the kindling is burning, add a third log across the top and more logs as necessary.

The Rumford fireplace is less common. Invented in the eighteenth century by Count

49

Some Quiet Occupations

A good place to read . . . A good home library . . . Reference works . . . How to pick cookbooks . . . Books and children . . . Table times, the role of games and cards . . . Television; its addictive potential; using television wisely . . . VCRs and DVDs; watching movies at home . . . Computer games

Your home should offer you a variety of possibilities for quiet occupation. Reading, playing games, watching movies, and other home entertainments promote your sense of well-being, knowledge, mental acuity, and, when we share them with family or friends, social engagement. They are a part of the inner life of the home that reinforces and refreshes the inner life of those who live there.

Reading

A Good Place to Read. A good spot for reading has a bright enough reading light located at your side. If it comes from behind, your head will leave a shadow on the book; if it comes from in front of you, the light will shine in your eyes. The back of the chair or sofa should support your neck and head when you lean back. There should be armrests so that you can hold the book at a comfortable height without getting tired. Unless you are farsighted or nearsighted, the book is most comfortably held 14 to 16 inches from your eyes when you read.

Your reading chair or sofa should have soft cushioning so that you can sit for a good period of time without feeling uncomfortable. It should have enough room for you to move around and change positions. If you like to curl up with your feet tucked under you, you will need either a sofa or a roomy easy chair.

You need a table or chest of some sort next to your reading chair to hold a reading lamp, your book, your glasses, a pencil and notebook, a glass, or whatever you like to keep near you as you read. Many of us like a dictionary at hand to look up an occasional unfamiliar word.

The surrounding area should be quiet with moderate lighting.

A Good Home Library. Most of the books in a home reflect the particular tastes and circumstances of the members of that household. But there are some kinds of books that almost every home has use for. If you are setting up house or being asked about wedding presents, keep the need for certain books in mind. (They can be costly.)

Buy the permanent core of your library in hardback whenever you can afford to. Hardback books usually last much longer. When you can't afford a hardback, buy good-quality paperbacks for now and replace them as you can. If the book is rare or antique, do *not* write in your name, as this will decrease its value.

Reference Works. Every home needs a dictionary. A good one-volume dictionary for each language spoken in your home is all you need for starters. But you might want two, a smaller handy one at your reading chair and a bigger, more inclusive one on your shelf. Real word fanciers will enjoy having a multivolume set. The mother of all dictionaries of the English language is the *Oxford English Dictionary,* which currently has twenty volumes, but you can have the whole thing in a photographically reduced one-volume Compact Edition, affectionately called "the eyestrain edition."

Besides a basic dictionary or two, there are a variety of specialized dictionaries and reference works that many people find useful:

Dictionaries of quotations
A thesaurus
A biographical dictionary
A dictionary of slang
A children's dictionary
On-disk dictionaries
An encyclopedia
A world atlas
An almanac
A gazetteer
A film guide
Home medical guides for adults and children
Guides to child rearing
Religious texts
Housekeeping books
Books about house maintenance
Cookbooks and other books on food

Books and Children. Reading homes raise reading children, and reading children grow up into adults with a capacity for the infinite pleasures of reading. The practical benefits of reading, in fact, are so overstressed in today's schools (better test scores, better colleges, better jobs) that it is important to remind ourselves that an even better reason to hope that children grow into reading adults is that this helps them be happy, enlarges and deepens their private lives, and gives them knowledge and a love of knowledge.

Table Times

Just about every home can make good use of a big table that is not reserved for meals, one that can be used for games, cards, writing, sewing, crafts, planning sessions, meetings, and other activities. If you have no convenient place for such activities, you are far less likely to find time to enjoy them. You need to keep stored at home whatever you use to engage in these activities: decks of cards, checkers, a Scrabble game, and so on.

The psychologist Bruno Bettelheim illuminated the value of games for both children and adults:

> Today, there are relatively few games which are enjoyed as much by adults as they are by children. More often than not, children are experienced as intruders when grown-ups reluctantly feel obliged to make allowances for the child's pres-

HOW TO PICK A COOKBOOK

Those who are setting up house will need at least one basic, comprehensive cookbook such as *Joy of Cooking,* or *The Good Housekeeping Cookbook.* This sort of cookbook includes all basic techniques and dishes and a variety of ethnic dishes that are widely enjoyed. Most people also want a set of narrower cookbooks that address their particular tastes in ethnic cookery, vegetarian cookery, low-fat cooking, and so forth. Books on nutrition and diet are particularly important in homes where someone has health or weight problems.

Read newspaper and magazine reviews. They are not always right, but they often give good tips on useful new cookbooks.

When in doubt, go for authors or books that have enjoyed long popularity or have become classics—Marcella Hazan on Italian cooking, Julia Child on French, Rick Bayless on Mexican, and so on. If a book has gone through two or more editions, that proves at least that it is a survivor.

Read a few recipes. Do they sound appealing? Do they require exotic ingredients you are going to have a hard time finding? Are the instructions clear? Are you looking for something more sophisticated? Easier? Quicker?

Has the book won any awards? Books that have won prizes are often good bets.

Watch out for glossy, expensive cookbooks with lots of colored photographs and few recipes. They take up room on the shelf, and you will not use them very often.

Watch out for gimmicks, theme books about one ingredient, dish, or food; celebrities' cookbooks; and jokey cookbooks. They are mainly money-making ideas by people without deep interest in or knowledge of their subject. But there are exceptions, of course.

If you are trying to learn about some kind of ethnic cookery, look to see whether the author provides suggested accompaniments and menus. If you are not used to Italian or Indian or Japanese cooking, you might need help planning a meal as well as cooking individual dishes. Look also for tips about how a dish is perceived and used in its native land: Is it for holidays? Casual occasions? Is it a seasonal dish? A breakfast dish?

ence and perhaps let him participate. When I was a child in Vienna, things were often different. One of the most common and popular leisure activities of adults was cardplaying. . . . My father spent many of his relatively few leisure hours playing cards with relatives and friends. As they played for hours, I watched them, which they took for granted, since I did not interfere with the game—it was too important to them and to me. . . . That these adults were so serious about a game I also played with my friends was important to me, and so was the fact that they enjoyed it as much as I did. . . . It was from my experience of playing the same card game that I spontaneously understood its importance for my father; and it was from his experience that he had full understanding of and empathy with what playing this game with my friends meant to me. . . . When my father played with us, his role and attitude was that of a parent who enjoys what he is doing because it is enjoyable to his children. This made it very different from the experience when I watched him play with his friends—then he was every bit as serious about it as I was when I played with my friends.

It is from experiences like this that I know the difference between a parent playing with his child—important and enjoyable as this is for both when all goes well—and a parent and his child, each entirely on his own, playing the same game with contemporaries. When parent and child, each for his very own reasons, are engrossed in the same play, this can form a bond between them which is truly *sui generis.*[1]

Television

Television is the bane of the modern home, but only because it is so often abused. People who cannot find time to cook, see their children, entertain, read, visit, listen to music, exercise, talk, clean, or do their laundry nonetheless spend many hours—around twenty hours on average—watching television every week. I agree with those who think that television operates, literally, like a drug, and that many entire families are addicted. In most homes that overdo it with television, the set is on constantly and viewing is largely indiscriminate. Although one station might be preferred over another, any nonsense that happens to be showing is preferred to turning the set off and doing something else. There are people who will go to bed rather than try to cope with a couple of hours without television. Because of this addictive potential, in any household with children in which the parents hope to control the viewing there is likely to be a constant struggle on the part of the children to increase their viewing time. The parents are going to need to exercise constant vigilance.

On the other hand, I also agree with those who think that television is a potentially beneficial force in society and in the home, if only we would use it discerningly. It can breed a sense of commonality in times of crisis, and has an unparalleled potential to bring truths home to the people. It can also be a delightful source of cheap entertainment. But just as you would be unwise to choose to have hot fudge sundaes or a bottle of scotch every night of the week, no one can afford a daily habit of television either.

Television simply needs to assume its rightful, humble place in the scheme of things, through exercise of ordinary rules of moderation. Engage only in discerning viewing, and limit the number of hours anyone spends watching. When deciding how much to watch each week, think of it as a rich dessert with little nutrition—at best it provides an evanescent pleasure while imposing costs in proportion to how much you take in. A little never hurts, and it's not good to forgo all treats. Some desserts are even good for you.

For best television watching, low, diffuse light is best. A bright screen in a perfectly dark room strains the eyes, while overbright light diminishes the picture. Task and reading lamps often cause reflections. For lengthy watching, pick a chair with good back and neck support and soft cushioning.

VCRs and DVDs

The advent of video cassette recorders and DVD players (the initials DVD generally mean digital video disks, although some manufacturers prefer different terms) helps both adults and children to avoid the ever-increasing amount of ever-more-smarmy advertising that afflicts television.

Although you can watch too many movies just as you can watch too much television, watching a rented movie at home, alone, with the family, or with friends, is a wonderful form of home entertainment. This is a particularly good option for invalids or shut-ins, who might search for a video-rental store that delivers and picks up. I hope that the rest of us do our best to support movie theaters as well, as the fun and sociability of sharing the movie with others in a public place is an experience we would all be sorry to lose. Happily, I observe, enthusiastic movie-rental fans also tend to be enthusiastic movie-theater goers.

Home is the place where children today get acquainted with the great movie classics, and every family enjoys this part of their education. Parents have not been slow to realize that videos also offer the opportunity to preview what their children will see, as well as offering a far greater choice of high-quality material than television. Videos are a pleasant and effective way to supplement children's education if the family watches them together and if parents follow up afterward with books, talks, museum trips, and the like.

Computer Games

As with videos and books, there are good and bad computer games. Adults will suit themselves, but children require protection and supervision. The rating systems are some help, but by no means replace your own judgment. And as with television or videos, some people—adults included—become obsessed and addicted to various games. Those with balanced lives find a balanced way to fit computer games into them, if that is their taste.

There are other computer activities besides games—everything from music-writing to programming to conversations with new and old friends around the world. *Consumer Reports* and computer magazines can help you evaluate new software before you buy it and learn about interesting new types.

On a comfortable and effective computer set-up, see chapter 54, "Home Offices and Computers."

50

Sewing

Basic home sewing equipment and skills . . . Sewing basket contents . . . Threading your needle . . . Basic hand stitches: running stitch, basting stitch, back stitch, hem stitch, slip stitch, overhand or whipping stitch, overcast stitch, blanket stitch . . . Four basic machine stitches: regular, basting, backward, zigzag . . . Basic sewing techniques . . . Hemming skirts and uncuffed pants . . . Patching . . . Repairing ripped or torn seams and reinforcing seams . . . Sewing on buttons, two- and four-hole, shank, widening and narrowing buttonholes . . . Snaps and hooks and eyes . . . Broken zippers

Home sewing is enjoying a renaissance. There is no economic justification for this. In many cases, the sewers spend so much money on high-tech sewing machines and aids, including computer helpers, not to mention hours of their time buying materials, cutting, stitching, and fitting, that their sewing is not cost-effective compared with store-bought items. On the other hand, if what you want is not out there to be bought, and you want it badly enough, it makes sense to make it; and only by sewing at home or hiring a tailor can you get clothes made to fit, in precisely the styles, colors, and fabrics you choose, with high-quality workmanship and attention to detail. Now there is even computer software that prints out patterns according to measurements you type in, which makes personalized fit even easier to attain. Most people have never worn well-made, well-fitting clothes, made to taste, in their lives. It is a heady experience. You can also easily make a variety of home furnishings to your exact taste—napkins, curtains, comforter covers, and many other articles.

Sewing itself is more fun, more satisfying, and more challenging than many people would believe without trying it. If you do not know how, there are classes everywhere, and friends are almost always willing to help. Sewing is something that you can do alone or with someone else, a friend or family member.

You need not invest in a lot of expensive equipment if you wish to sew at home. Even advanced sewers can stitch pretty much anything they want on a sturdy portable that does nothing more than go forward and backward. A few "zigzag" stitch patterns and a buttonhole capacity are quite useful but will not get a great deal of use by the the casual or beginning sewer. If you hope to go at sewing seriously, however, you want both a good machine with the latest bells and whistles and, probably, a serger, a machine that is credited with having revolutionized home sewing in the past decade. Without exaggeration, you can say that sergers have certainly contributed enormously to its revitalization. Sergers simultaneously trim, stitch, and finish seams with an overcast stitch. They save great amounts of labor and give articles made at home a professional, finished look that until recently very few could achieve. Some sergers are much more versatile and easier to use than others, and the fanciest ones can be very costly. Check consumer information sources before making a choice.

Basic Home Sewing: Equipment and Skills

Some basic skills in sewing are perennially useful; if you have them, you will use them many times in the course of a year. Not being able to sew on a button, hem a skirt or pants, patch a hole or tear, or repair a seam can be terribly inconvenient, as it is far more trouble to track down a seamstress or tailor to do these little jobs than to take a couple of minutes to do them yourself. With limited skill, you can do these jobs or even make a curtain, napkins, comforter covers, and so forth.

Sewing Baskets. A sewing basket or box in every home is indispensable. Either is preferable to a sewing drawer because you want something that you can carry around with you. If you plan on sewing nothing more than a ripped hem or a loose button, your sewing box need not be elaborate. A sewing basket that includes the following items will see you through all the ordinary sewing chores:

Sewing shears and scissors. You may find it useful to have both a pair of larger shears (six to eight inches) and a pair of smaller scissors (three to six inches). The handles of sewing shears angle upward so that you can cut fabric easily holding the bottom blade against your cutting surface. They have a small hole for your thumb and a large one for a couple of fingers. Scissors have equal-sized handle holes and are straight. (Reserve your sewing scissors for sewing; other jobs, such as cutting paper, will blunt them.)

Pinking shears. These cut zigzag edges on cloth. Pinked edges are sufficient finishing for the edges of cloth that does not unravel badly. (Seam edges should always be finished somehow, with pinking, stitching or serging, or seam binding.)

Seam ripper. The seam ripper is a small cutter with a tiny curved cutting blade used for ripping out seams.

Sewing needles ("sharps"). Buy a package of assorted sizes and lengths. The sizes range from 1 (the thickest) to 12 (the finest), but you will rarely use the very low or high numbers for ordinary household chores. Embroidery needles have long eyes to accommodate several threads. Darning needles have even bigger holes. A variety of lengths is useful.

Straight pins. Medium gauge is the most useful, but use only fine gauge for silks and sheer fabrics. Heavy gauge are necessary for coating, carpeting, and upholstery; lighter ones will break off in the cloth. Those with colored heads are easier

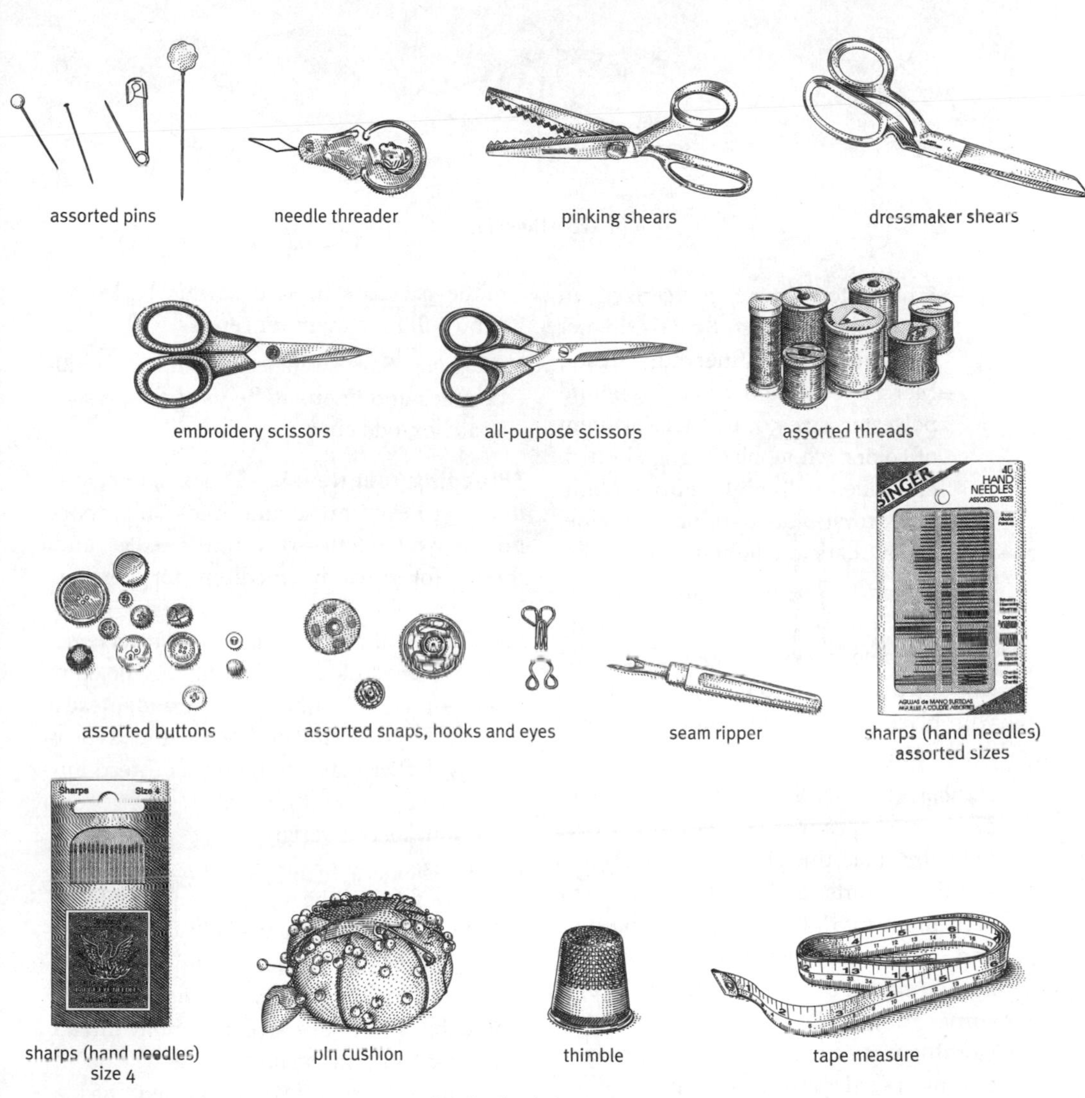

Sewing basket contents

to see. You might like Japanese-made straight pins that have larger, colored heads and longer, finer shafts. (I have heard them called "flowerhead pins.")

Pin cushion

Snaps or hooks and eyes

Tape measure

Dressmaker's chalk

Thimble. Wear the thimble on the middle finger of the hand with which you hold the needle. When it is hard to push the needle through the cloth, do so with the thimble to avoid hurting your finger.

Needle Threader. For those who are far-sighted or have shaky hands, there are completely automatic ones or simple guides—whatever you need.

Thread

—Heavy-duty cotton or cotton-bound polyester in white and black.

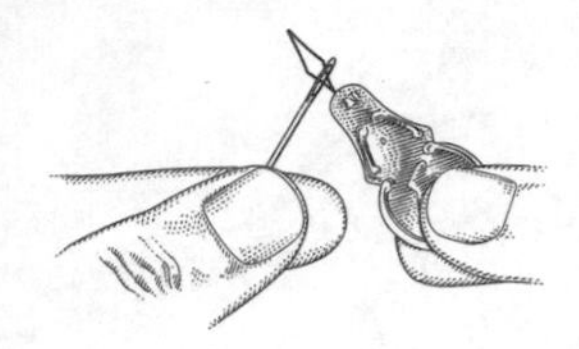
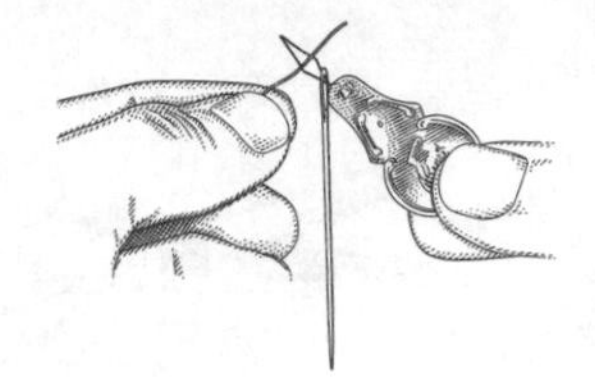
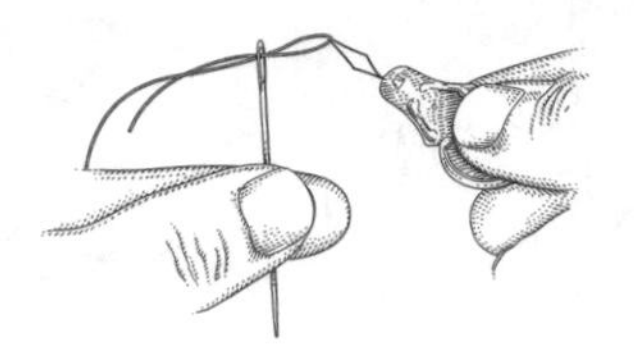

Needle threader

- —Fine cotton thread, mercerized, in white and black, size 80. (The higher the number, the finer the thread.)
- —Mercerized cotton or cotton-bound polyester, size 50, in an assortment of colors: white, black, gray, brown, off-white, red, pink, purple, light blue, royal blue, dark or navy blue, yellow, dark and light green, orange.

Wool threads or fine yarns. Get an assortment in various colors for mending sweaters and socks. Choose either the same colors as you select in threads, or start with black and white and add colors as is convenient.

Buttons. It is useful to have an assortment of sizes, shapes, colors, and styles: two-hole, four-hole, and shank buttons. When you throw shirts, coats, or dresses away or turn them into rags, cut off the buttons and save them, either in a pocket in your sewing basket or in a button box. They'll come in handy. Likewise, when new clothing comes with small packages containing thread, yarn, or buttons, save the little packages in your sewing basket so you will have them for repairs.

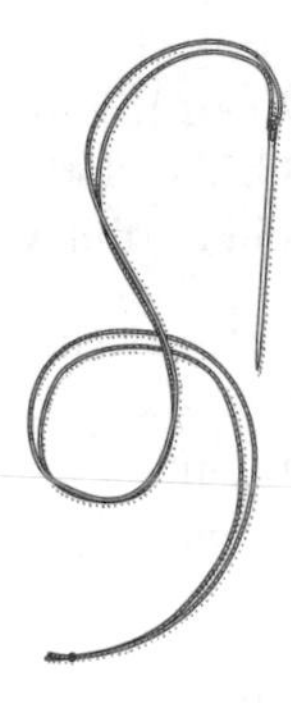

Knotted thread ready for sewing

Rag bag. Save swatches of cloth from old clothes and linens to be used for rags or patches, odd chores, crafts, and so on.

Threading Your Needle. Choose a fine, medium, or heavy thread and needle in proportion to your cloth—very fine needles and thread for organdy, medium for percale, heavy-duty for thick denims. The size numbers for needles and threads are in inverse relation to the thickness of the needle and thread—that is, the finest needles and threads have the highest number. Choose thread color slightly darker than the fabric, as thread appears a bit lighter off the spool.

If you keep a variety of size 50 threads (mercerized if they are cotton), plus a few spools of fine and heavy-duty, you should be able to handle most household chores with what you have on hand. Medium thread will do when medium-heavy or medium-light would be better. But size 50 cotton thread will look bad and create holes and tears in very sheer fabric. If your garment has a satiny or shiny appearance, you will be dissatisfied with the look of mending done in cotton. You can use silk thread on silk, wool, and synthetics with a sheen. Use wool thread to darn wool. There are a variety of threads designed to suit special purposes, too, which you might have occasion to acquire—quilting thread, buttonhole twist, and so forth.

Use a needle threader if you have shaky hands or are farsighted. It makes things easy.

Basic Hand Stitches. Thread your needle and then secure the thread to the fabric so

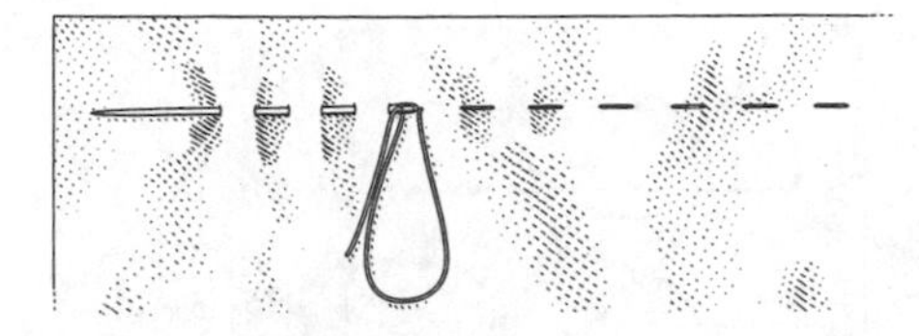
Running stitch

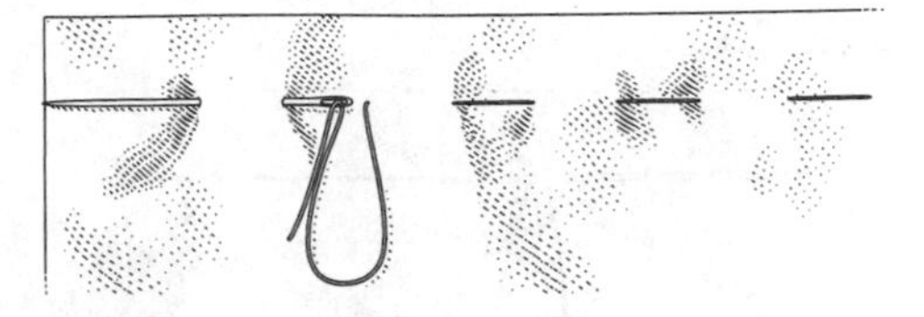
Basting stitch

that it does not pull out. The easiest way to secure the thread is to make a tiny knot at its end. A more attractive way is to take two or three tiny stitches at the beginning of your sewing (you will do so again at the end), as experienced sewers do.

For greater strength, double your sewing thread. When you use a double thread, knot the loose ends together or secure both loose ends by stitching. However, for less visible stitching, desirable in hemming, for example, sew with a single strand of thread. To do this, you knot or secure only one of the loose ends of thread, and leave the other hanging two or three inches down from the eye of the needle. When you are sewing with a single thread, watch out that you do not accidentally catch the loose end in your stitching and begin sewing with a double thread. Do not use a longer thread than you need—the length of your arm extended is the maximum you can comfortably sew with; you sew faster with a shorter thread, and shorter thread is not so prone to tangle and knot. On the other hand, when you are sewing long seams or a hem with a wide circumference, it is annoying to have to keep rethreading your needle, so most of us choose to use a longer thread. Just before you run out of thread, secure it again with tiny stitches or a tiny knot, then snip the thread. (If you let the thread get too short, you will not have enough left to make a knot or a couple of stitches.)

The most common and useful hand stitches are described below.

Running stitch. Used for most basic sewing, mending, seams, and quilting. You use a long, thin needle. Push the needle in and out of one or more layers of cloth every $^1/_{16}$ to $^1/_4$ inch in a straight line, keeping all the stitches even (the same size) and small. The smaller the stitch, the stronger the seam.

Basting stitch. This is just a longer running stitch, from $^1/_4$ to $^1/_2$ inch, used to hold things together temporarily until you do a more permanent stitch. Remove basting when the permanent stitches are in.

Back stitch. This is a strong stitch, a variation on the running stitch, used for repairing ripped seams and reinforcing vulnerable ones. It looks like machine stitching on the right side, but you see overlapping on the wrong side. You use a shorter needle than for the running stitch. After securing the thread, take a small (say $^1/_8$ inch) running stitch, pushing the needle from the right side of the cloth through to the underside and then bringing it back up to the right side. Now reinsert your needle in the first hole of this first stitch and take a running stitch twice as long, say $^1/_4$ inch—and from now on, all the stitches will be the longer length. (Your needle will emerge $^1/_4$ inch ahead of the beginning of the first stitch.) Go back and reinsert the needle at the middle hole—halfway through the second stitch—and take another stitch. Repeat until the seam is completed. Basically, you simply repeatedly reinsert your needle in the hole from which it last emerged.

Hem stitch. This is not a strong stitch, so it is not used where it would be subjected to strain. Begin with your needle coming through the edge of the fold of the hem. (See "Hemming

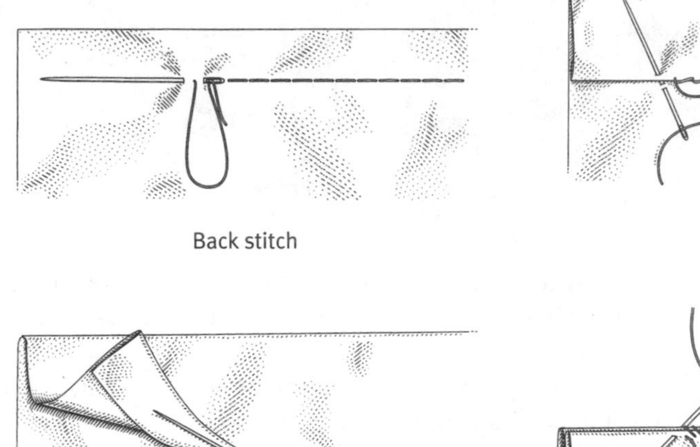

Back stitch

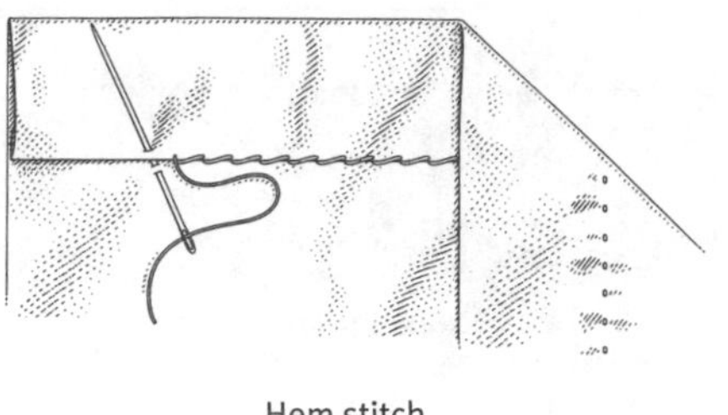

Hem stitch

Slip stitch

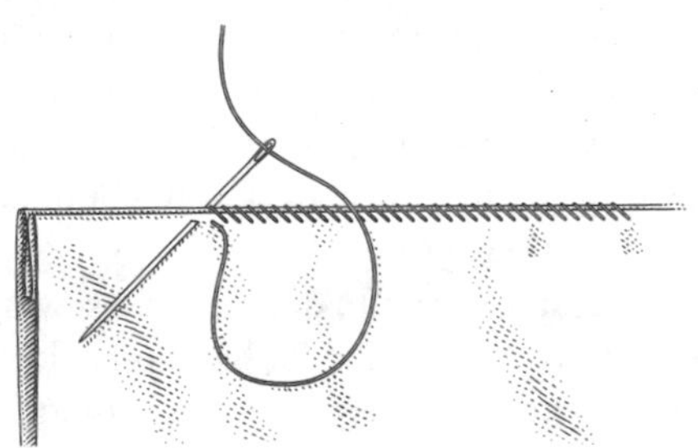

Whipping stitch

Skirts and Uncuffed Casual Pants," below.) Pick up one or two threads of the fabric, then one of the fold of the hem, then one of the fabric, and so forth, creating small slanted stitches. (My grandmother would let me take only one thread of the fabric, but I will approve if you take two.) Do not pull too tight or the hem will pucker. If your stitches are too loose or too far apart, the hem will sag or catch on things and pull out.

Slip stitch. This invisible stitch, similar to hem stitch and likewise not strong, is used to secure hems, facings, and so on. Turn back the edge of the hem or fold about 1/4 of an inch. Secure the thread. Then proceed by taking a small stitch in the fold, then picking up a thread of the fabric, then taking a small stitch in the fold, then picking up a thread of the fabric, and so forth, until it is all hemmed. For heavy fabrics or skirt hems, stitches should be close together, but in other places you can space them widely—up to 1/2 inch apart.

Overhand or whipping stitch. These are basically the same stitch, called overhand if it is perpendicular and whipping if it is slanted. It is used for less visible, strong seams. With whipping stitch, you usually stitch from the right side of the cloth. Hold the folded edges of the seam allowances together. Secure the thread. Then pick up one or two threads from each fold in turn, always beginning with the edge of the cloth in the back and proceeding to the front. Keep the stitches close together.

Overcast stitch. Overcast stitching is used to finish the raw edges of hems and seams. It is similar to the whipping stitch, except that it is done on raw edges of cloth and is about 1/4 inch deep, so it is more visible. Secure the thread. Holding together the two raw edges of the cloth, take slanting stitches over the two together. Proceed from the back of the cloth to the front.

Blanket stitch. This is another stitch for finishing raw edges. Turn under the edge of whatever you are sewing. Secure the thread on the wrong side and push the needle through to the right side. Working from left to right and facing the right side of the article, insert the needle on the right side—at about 1/4 inch from the edge of the fold, at

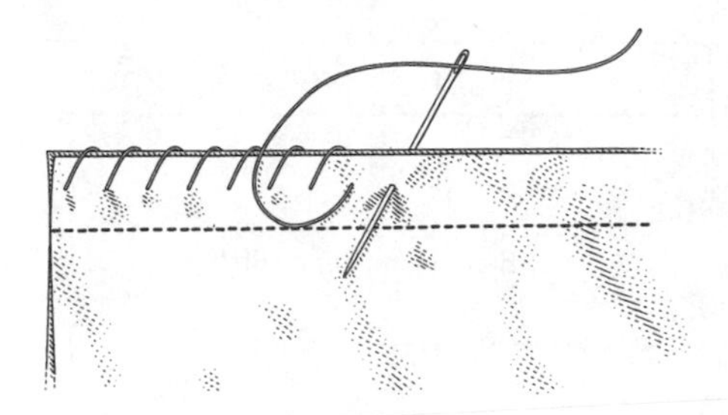
Overcast stitch

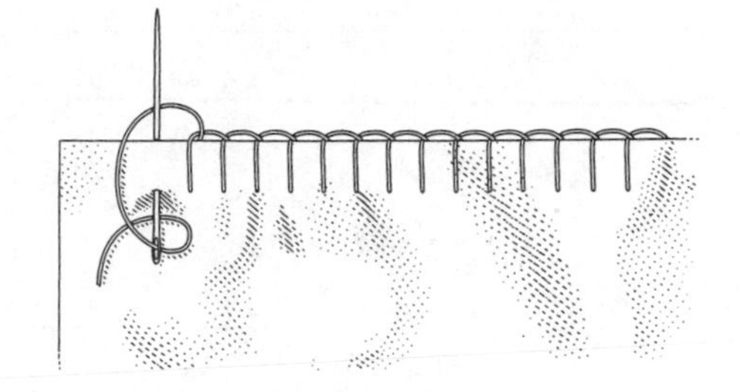
Blanket stitch

the right of the thread—and push it through to the wrong side, holding the thread to the needle's left. You will catch the thread right at the edge of the fold. As you repeat the stitch, a row of stitches forms along the edge of the fold of the cloth.

Four Basic Machine Stitches. Follow your machine's instructions on threading the needle, filling the bobbin, setting the tension, and adjusting the stitch size.

Regular. This is a running stitch. Standard or "regulation" stitching gets 12 stitches per inch. Use 16 per inch on fine and sheer cloth, and 8 to 10 for heavy cloth. Remember to use fine, medium, and heavy-duty needles for cloth of different weights.

Basting. This is a long running stitch. Use 6 to 8 stitches per inch.

Backward. This is a running stitch in reverse.

Zigzag. You set the machine to sew in a pattern instead of in a straight line. You can make the stitches narrower or wider, longer or shorter. See your instruction manual for using the zigzag feature on your machine. Zigzag patterns are used for decoration and reinforcing and finishing seams.

Basic Sewing Techniques

Hemming Skirts and Uncuffed Casual Pants. Besides looking good and preventing unraveling, hemming gives weight and shape at the bottom of a garment to make it hang properly. To lengthen or shorten a hemmed garment, remove the stitching in its hem, iron out the old hem fold-line, and refold the hem to the desired length. When lengthening, especially when the garment is not new, keep in mind that sometimes the original hem fold-line shows as an unattractive line which laundering and ironing fail to remove.

There is no law stating how wide a hem should be. Generally, dresses hang better with a generous hem, say two inches, and the stitch that almost always looks best on dresses is hem stitch. But on blouses, the legs of casual pants without cuffs, and some other articles, narrow machine-stitched hems are often preferable. If the hem is to be on a skirt or dress or uncuffed pants, you must try the garment on and measure how much hem should be turned up to create a good length. With some garments, this can lead to intricacies that are beyond the scope of this book. For example, if the finished hem would be too wide, you will have to cut off some cloth; getting the hem to hang an even distance from the ground can present difficulties; garments that widen toward the bottom, like flared skirts and bellbottoms, must be tucked, gathered, or otherwise narrowed when you turn them up. When such difficulties are all settled to your satisfaction, there are several ways to go ahead and put in the hem.

One standard way of hemming a garment that would be the desired length with, say, a 1½-inch finished hem is this. (Note that making this 1½-inch finished hem will shorten the garment by 1¾ inches.) First, to finish the raw edge of the cloth, turn under

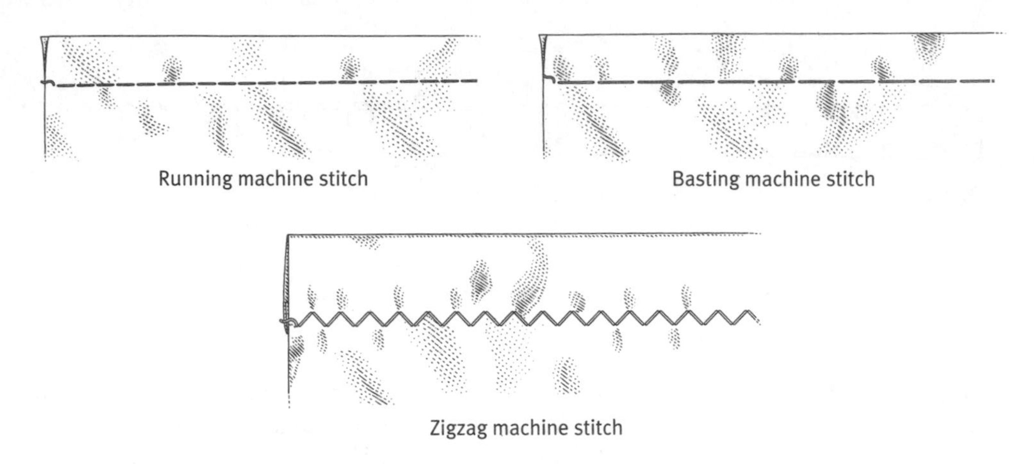

Running machine stitch

Basting machine stitch

Zigzag machine stitch

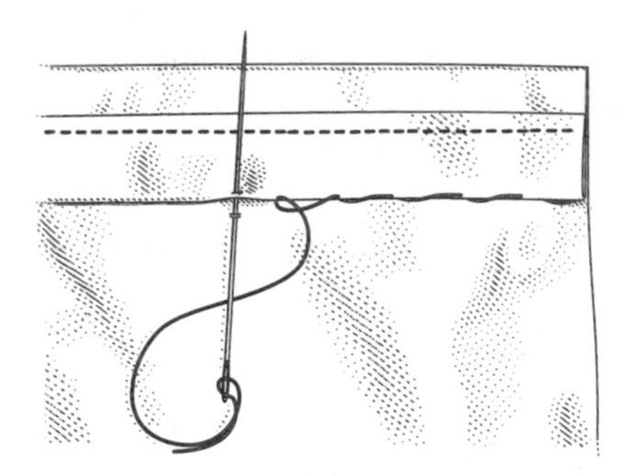

Hem using seam binding

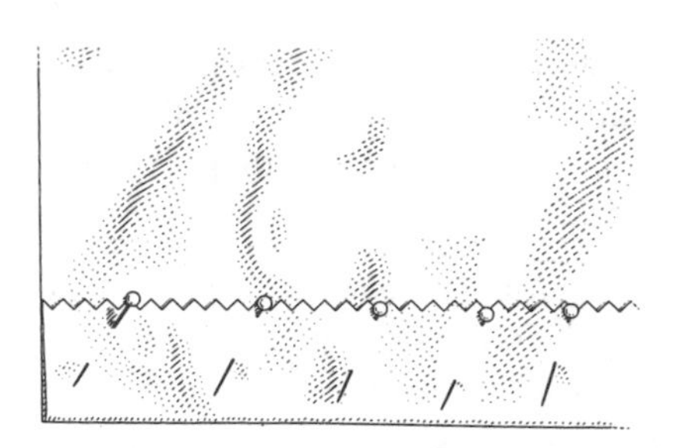

Hem using pinked edge

(to the wrong side) $^{1}/_{4}$ inch of the raw edge and baste it down using either a machine or hand-basting stitch. Then turn the ironed or basted edge under (to the wrong side), making a fold about 1$^{1}/_{2}$ inches wide and, to hold the fold in place while you hem-stitch it to the fabric, pin it or baste it near the fold line so that it stays in place. (You can sometimes avoid basting or pinning these folds and simply iron them in.) Then stitch the hem by hand, using the hem stitch. Some machines will do a hem stitch. Remove the basting stitches. Press or iron.

There are other ways of hemming than simply turning under the raw edge and stitching it down. You might sew seam binding to the raw edge, using a machine (or by hand, if you have no machine). (Seam binding is a narrow, ribbonlike strip of cloth.) Then hem by hand, stitching the outside edge of the seam binding to the cloth, again using the hem stitch. Or you could, for very casual purposes, simply pink the raw edge, assuming that the cloth does not unravel, turn it under, and hem as before. This would be good for a child's Halloween costume, for example.

Patching. You can patch almost any kind of tear, but patches do not look good on everything. There are many ways of patching. You can put patches on the right or wrong side of the garment, and you can make them of the same fabric as the garment or of a different fabric. If you want to make them of the same fabric as a purchased garment, you have to find a place on the garment where you can

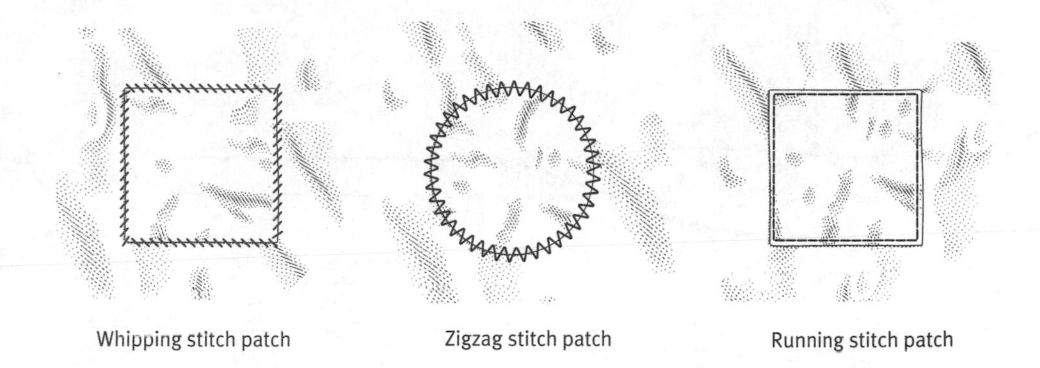

Whipping stitch patch

Zigzag stitch patch

Running stitch patch

snip enough off to make a patch without its being noticeable. Usually this is impossible, but sometimes you can find enough in a hem or facing where the cut-out will be invisible to mend a small tear or hole. (But you may need to know how to repair the place from which you took your patch as well.) Make the patch extend at least an inch beyond the hole or tear in all directions.

First, to make sure that the raw edge of the patch will not unravel, pink it, overcast it, do a running stitch around the border, zigzag it on your machine, or hem it. If you are putting the patch on the wrong side of the garment, you should make sure that the edges of the hole or tear do not fray: turn under the raw edges of the hole or do a zigzag stitch around them with your machine. If you are making a patch of the same fabric, be sure to align it with any pattern, weave, or grain in the fabric. Pin the patch to the garment. If there is to be no strain on the place where the patch is, sew the fabric to the patch with a tiny slip stitch (invisible but weak), with a running stitch (hand or machine), or any other stitch you like. Where strength is not an issue, it is only a question of whether you like the look of the stitch. But if you need a tough patch, as for the knees on children's pants, you should use a generous-sized patch and secure it with an overhand or whipping stitch, a back stitch, or a zigzag machine stitch.

There are also iron-on patches, but they often come off and you have few choices of color and fabric when you use these. Follow the instructions for their use on their labels.

Repairing Ripped or Torn Seams; Reinforcing Seams. Garments are most likely to tear at their seams. Shirts and blouses tear at the point where the sleeve is sewn to the body; trousers tear at the seat of the pants or the crotch; skirts split at the side seam; gloves split along the finger seams. You can re-sew the seam by machine unless the article is too tiny or the tear is in too awkward a spot. Gloves will often have to be sewn by hand; turn them inside out to work.

To repair by hand the portion of a seam that has come undone, use a small running stitch. If the seam must be very strong, use a back stitch. Work on the wrong side of the garment. Begin an inch or so before the rip, stitching right over the old stitches, and continue an inch or so beyond the rip, securing the thread carefully at both ends by making a few tiny stitches. On a machine, you do this with a regular stitch, securing at both ends by stitching backward for a few stitches. Be sure to use the sturdiest thread consistent with the weight of the fabric. Press the seam open after you have finished so that the fabric does not pucker where you have mended.

If you know that you tend to tear your shirts or blouses under the arm or at the shoulder back, or that you often split the seams of your trousers, you can reinforce the seam and prevent the damage from happening. This is a

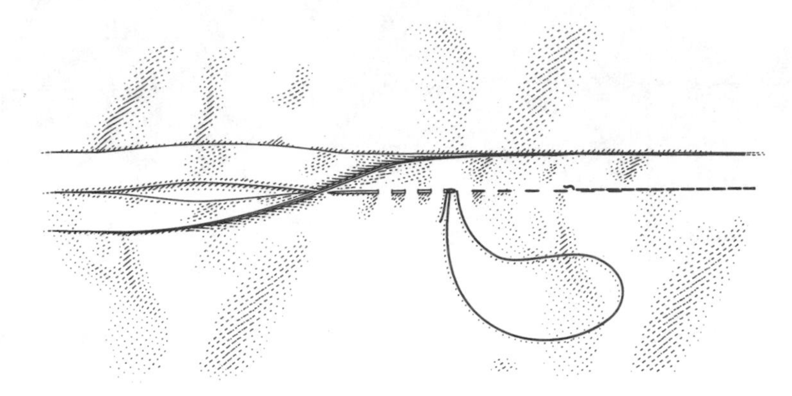

Seam repair

particularly good idea when the garment is made of something sheer that might tear along the seam, or whenever you notice that a garment's stitching does not appear strong. Simply sew along the vulnerable seam, using a small running stitch (or a back stitch when you need a particularly strong seam) in the same way that you would repair a seam.

Sewing on Buttons. I learned about sewing on buttons in 4-H. We were given small, square, pale blue swatches along with what seemed an infinite variety of buttons and arbitrary rules about fastening them to the little blue swatches. The rules were not so arbitrary in retrospect, but we were not told much about what they were for.

Be sure to use strong thread—heavy-duty if the fabric is not delicate. On very delicate fabrics, it is often necessary to put some kind of fabric reinforcement under the button or else the fabric will tear when the button gets pulled.

If you are missing a button on a shirt or a dress in a place where it shows and cannot find a button that matches, remove one from the bottom edge or tail (or some other place where it doesn't show) and put it in the place that does show. Then sew an unmatched button of the right size in the less conspicuous place where you removed the button. Try to make the unmatched button as similar to the others as you can manage.

When you notice that a button is coming loose, reinforce its stitching before it actually falls off and you lose a pretty or unusual button or have to pass half your day half-buttoned. Observe new garments carefully. Often even expensive clothes that should have been made with every attention to detail will have buttons secured by only a couple of threads.

Two- and Four-Hole Buttons. To be sure that you get the button in the right place, close up the garment, buttoning it above and below the missing button so that its buttonhole is at the proper place for buttoning. Mark this place with dressmaker's chalk. Then secure the thread to the right side of the material at that spot by taking several tiny stitches, until the thread feels tight and does not pull out. Place the button so that it is centered at the spot and so that its holes or pattern are parallel to those of all the other buttons. Now insert the needle into one hole of the button from its wrong side. Then insert the needle into the other (or another) hole on the button's right side, passing it through to the wrong side of the cloth. To ensure that the button is not so tight that it cannot be buttoned, you can insert a pin or a matchstick under the thread, between the button and the fabric, as you work.

Repeat the in-and-out stitching five or six times, following the same pattern each time. Try to make the stitches very close together

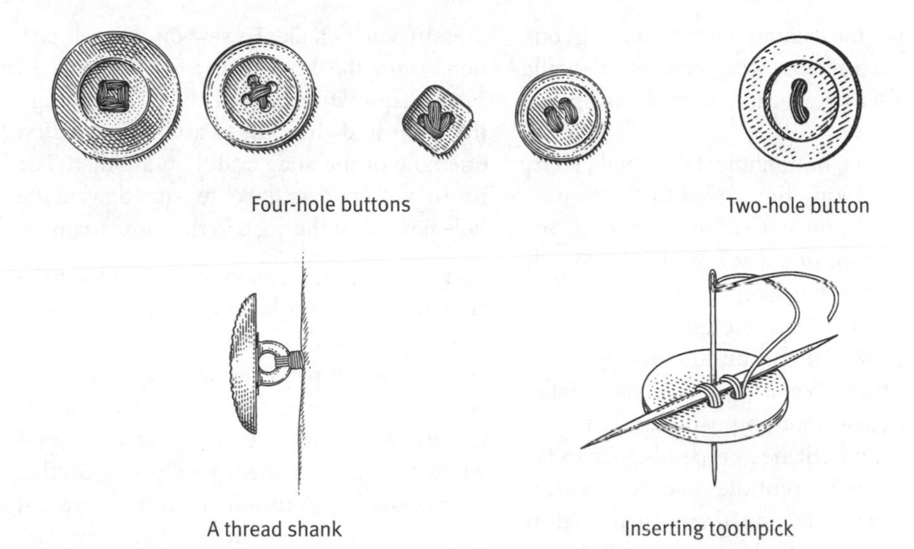
Four-hole buttons

Two-hole button

A thread shank

Inserting toothpick

so that the stitching looks neat on the right and wrong sides of the cloth. Never sew a stitch over the edge of the button.

When the button has been well secured, remove the pin or matchstick and check to see that the button is just loose enough to button easily. (For a heavy item such as a coat, you would need a longer set of threads connecting the button to the fabric, and a good sewer would make a thread shank of the slack. See "Shank Buttons," below.) Then draw the needle through to the wrong side of the cloth and again secure the thread with several tiny stitches. Cut the thread.

Shank Buttons. A shank button has a shank, or a projection on its back that has a hole in it, through which the attaching threads are drawn. Mark the spot where the shank button is to go in the same way as for two- and four-hole buttons. Secure the thread to the right side of the fabric at that spot by taking several tiny stitches. Then pass the needle and thread five or six times from the wrong side of the cloth through the shank hole and back to the wrong side of the cloth again. Try to make the stitches very close to one another. When the button is firmly sewed on, secure the thread on the wrong side of the cloth with a few tiny stitches.

Sometimes with a stiff or thick shank, or when the button and shank form one piece, the button will not lie easily and attractively in the buttonhole unless you make an additional thread shank. (You will not need to do this for the thin metal or plastic shanks that are so often used.) To do this, insert a matchstick between the button and the cloth as before, if this is feasible; if the shank is not properly shaped to allow this, hold the button taut at a slight distance from the cloth, or put the tip of your finger between the button and the cloth, as you stitch in and out of the shank. Then, after the button is sewn on, do not yet cut the thread. Holding the button away from the cloth so that the slack is pulled taut, wrap the sewing thread around it several times, forming the thread shank. Then secure the thread on the underside, as before, with a few tiny stitches.

Widening and Narrowing Buttonholes. Without learning to make buttonholes or to do the buttonhole stitch, on *casual and informal* clothes you can often satisfactorily widen a tight buttonhole or tighten one that is so loose that the button keeps slipping out. Those with limited sewing experience should not try this on elegant, formal, or "good" clothes.

To widen a buttonhole, take small, sharp scissors and snip the corner of the buttonhole a *tiny* bit, no more than 1/16 inch. (If you oversnip, stop; find a sewing friend to help you repair the damage.) Try to fit in the button now. If it is still too tight, take another *tiny* snip. When the button fits perfectly, choose a thread color that will look satisfactory and close your snipped edge with several overhand stitches perpendicular to the buttonhole to prevent the hole from tearing further. Secure the thread very firmly before clipping, as buttonholes take a great deal of strain.

To narrow a buttonhole, sew together one corner of it with several overhand stitches perpendicular to the buttonhole. Before clipping your thread, try the button to see if the hole fits with proper snugness. If it is still loose, take a few more stitches. Secure the thread very firmly before clipping.

Snaps. Choose smaller ones for sheer fabrics, larger ones for heavy. The part with the ball goes on the top of the closure, on the hidden side, and the part with the hole goes on the other side of the closure (the one that gets covered over), on the right side of the cloth. Mark the places where each should go with dressmaker's chalk. To sew on the ball portion, secure the thread with a few tiny stitches. Then, using an overhand stitch, go through the cloth and then up to and through first one hole of the snap and then another. The thread will lap over the outer rim. Sew on the hole portion of the snap in the same manner.

Hooks and Eyes. Hooks and eyes have to be very precisely placed and aligned to work properly. This takes patience, but the actual stitching is simple. Choose smaller ones for sheers and larger ones for heavy fabrics. You use the kind with a straight catch (or eye) when the sides of the opening will overlap when closed. You use the kind with a round eye when the edges meet without overlapping. A hook is often used with just a loop made out of thread.

With dressmaker's chalk, mark the positions the hook and eye will take. Say you are putting the hook and eye on a neck closure that will overlap. Put the hook on the side of the closure that will cover the other, on the underside of the garment and with the hook facing down, placed so that the end of the hook is recessed 1/8 inch in from the edge. Put the eye—the straight type—on the right side of the covered closure, set back to the seam, or about 3/8 inch in from the edge. For a closure that will not overlap, place the round eye so that it extends about 1/8 inch past the edge of the cloth. Using the over-

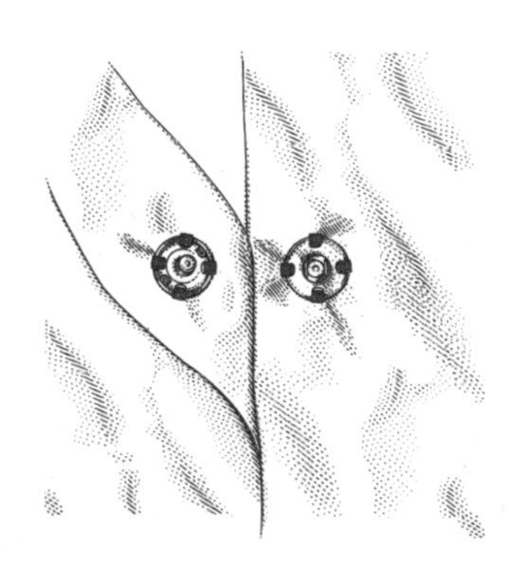

Snaps sewn on

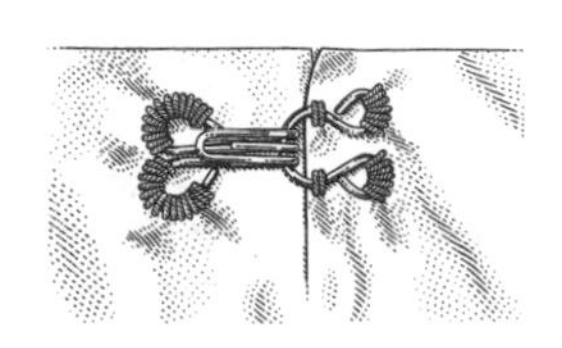

Hook and eye—open

Hook and eye—closed

hand stitch, attach the hook and eye to the spots you have marked.

If you are making a thread loop, just secure the thread at one end of where the loop should be and then insert the needle at the place where the other end should be, leaving the stitch loose. Bring the needle up through the first end and then again down through the second, again leaving the stitch loose. Secure and cut off the thread. You now have a two-stranded loop. To complete the loop, work the entire edge of the loop with blanket stitch (described above).

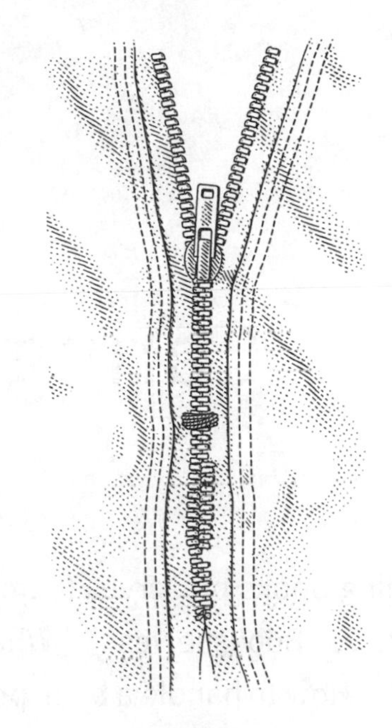

Mended zipper

Broken Zippers. It is rarely possible to repair a zipper, and it takes some practice to learn to remove an old zipper and sew in a new one neatly. But with metal zippers you can sometimes make a rough repair that at least lets you continue to use the garment. One common problem on metal zippers is that the metal teeth at the bottom of the zipper become bent or pulled and the lead cannot be pulled past them. You can repair this sometimes by getting a pair of pliers and straightening the teeth. If the zipper is closed at the bottom (that is, if it is not the kind used on a coat with two unattached sides), you can sometimes fix it in a way that involves limiting how far down you can pull the zipper. What you do, when there is a bump or broken tooth past which the zipper lead will not proceed, is cut the zipper there and reinsert the lead just past the cut. Then sew up the cut with a whipping or overhand stitch, intentionally making a thick block past which the zipper will not go. From now on you'll just zip down to this point. This works on many skirt and trouser zippers, and these often do break at the bottom. You will not, however, be able to use this technique with tight garments, as you probably could not pull them on with the zipper only partially opened.

51

Caring for Books

Reading books preserves them . . . Dust, sunlight, and insect damage to books . . . Bookshelves . . . Whether to preserve or discard book jackets . . . How to handle a book properly when removing it from shelves and when reading it . . . Skin acids are destructive to books . . . Post-its can cause harm . . . Leather bindings . . . Repairing damaged books

The best way to preserve a book is to read it. A book that you take from the shelf and read is a book that has the dust shaken off it, and when you turn the pages one by one, you help keep the spine of the book flexible and lessen the possibility that you will break the spine by opening it abruptly.

Rare and valuable books should be handled with special care, but most books can be preserved by following a few simple procedures and precautions. Dust, sunlight, and insects are the great enemies of books. The top edge of all books on your shelves should be dusted every few weeks and vacuum-cleaned once a year. Very rare and fragile books may be stored in bookcases with glass doors to protect them from dust. But for most books open shelves and occasional dusting will suffice, and glass doors tend to discourage you from reaching for a book when you want it. Sunlight bleaches and weakens cloth bindings, and any books that you especially want to preserve should never be left in direct sunlight. Ordinary books can survive a few hours a day of sunlight but will become bleached after a period of months or years. Silverfish and other insects eat the glue used in book bindings, and if you discover any in your home, you should take steps to exterminate them.

Arrange your shelves so that all the books are tight enough to remain upright but not so tight that you have to work to pull any of them out. If a book is too tall to stand upright on the shelf, lay it flat. If you don't have room to lay it flat and must shelve it on its side, place it with the spine down. If you place it with the spine up, the weight of the pages will eventually make the pages loose in the binding.

As to the shelves themselves, long shelves of softer woods will inevitably sag, which is unpleasant to look at. Choose shorter shelves—$2\frac{1}{2}$ to 3 feet long—set side by side, made of hard wood about $\frac{3}{4}$ inch thick. Or put up metal shelves. A shelf depth of $11\frac{1}{4}$ inches is good, and reasonable heights for bookcases are a matter of your ceiling heights and whether you can easily stand on a stable stool to reach the top shelves. If you have freestanding book cases rather than built-in shelves, however, the higher the case the more important it is that you anchor it to the wall with some sort of brace to make it stable. An adjustable shelf height is desirable to accommodate books of different sizes, but on average allowing one foot works well.

Dust jackets are often worth keeping because they add to the value of the book and help preserve the binding from fading and stains. (In a more pedestrian vein, note too that the flaps make a convenient bookmark.) Some readers routinely discard dust jackets for the sake of the more dignified appearance of cloth bindings, but most readers—and virtually all book collectors—preserve them. You should certainly preserve the dust jacket if the book is valuable enough to be of interest to collectors or libraries or if the jacket contains information not found elsewhere. But dust jackets can become frayed and unappealing when a book gets heavy use, and some dust jackets printed in the first half of the twentieth century leave acid stains on the endpapers. If you want to preserve dust jackets in pristine condition, you can place them in transparent folding plastic that you cut from long rolls. This is available from library suppliers like Brodart Inc., (800) 233-8959. Don't buy the kind that is designed to be affixed to the endpapers of the book; this is used in lending libraries to make sure the jacket stays with the book, but they damage the book itself and are not intended for use in the home.

The way in which you handle a book can help preserve it or help destroy it. The top of the cloth spine is one of the most delicate parts of a book. Never pull on it when you remove a book from the shelf. Instead, grasp the book from both sides if possible. If not, place one or two fingers on the top of the pages and nudge the book out from the shelf until you can grasp it from the sides and pull it the rest of the way. When you open a book for the first time, never start by opening it in the middle because you are likely to crack or weaken the spine. Instead, lay down the front and back covers while holding the pages upright. Then open a few pages at the front, then a few pages at the back, then a few more at the front, and a few more at the back until you gradually reach the middle. This rule applies most of all to books in which the pages are sewn in their binding, but should be applied to any glued books and paperbacks that you want to preserve in the best possible condition.

When holding or reading a book, put your thumbs anywhere except the edge of the pages. You'll leave black marks on the edges and will damage the pages themselves. When you have to hold a book in your hand instead of placing it on a desk or table, cradle it in your left hand (or your right hand if you are left-handed) and, if necessary, gently hold it

Taking a book from a tightly packed shelf

open with the fingertips of your other hand. Do not hold the book open with both thumbs.

These precautions are more than merely aesthetic. They will help your books survive. Virtually all books produced from around 1850 to around 1970 were printed on wood-pulp paper and will eventually disintegrate from the effects of the acid used in breaking the wood into pulp. Every time you leave a thumbprint on the book you add to the chemical processes that are gradually destroying it. Books printed on cheap, newsprint-like paper are probably crumbling already, and nothing can be done to save them except expensive deacidification methods used mostly by professional conservators working in large libraries and museums. But most books from the past 150 years can have their lives extended by careful handling and by being stored in moderate temperature and humidity. Books printed before around 1850 were printed on rag paper, which can last for thousands of years. During the past few decades many serious publishers have begun printing their cloth-covered editions on acid-free pulp-based paper that will last for hundreds of years; these books are usually identified on the copyright page.

Post-its make it easy to take notes and leave bookmarks without writing in the margin or folding down the corner of the page, but they can cause damage to many kinds of paper. Your books will last longer if you don't use Post-its at all; if you have to use them, remove them quickly. Never let yourself be tempted to use Post-its or similar notepapers on illustrated books because the dyes in the inks leach into the adhesive and leave a discolored patch on the page when you remove the note. The worst damage occurs with colored plates, but black-and-white photographic images are also affected, and ordinary text and blank pages will be affected before long.

Leather bindings should be maintained in the same way you preserve any fine leathers. Handling a leather-bound book—with clean hands—will help keep the leather supple. Any discoloration that may result from the oils on your skin is preferable to the irreversible damage that results when leather is left to dry out. An annual application of a mild leather preserver is always advisable.

Repairing damaged books. Major repairs should be performed only by professionals. For highly valuable books, consult the preservation department of a local university library or museum for advice. Damaged bindings can be repaired or replaced by professional binders, but choose specialist craft binders who will let you see samples of their work and will describe the exact details of the work they will do on your book. If the book you want to repair doesn't call for expensive specialist work, you can get excellent results by calling the preservation department of a local library and asking if one of the apprentices can do the job on his or her own time.

Never put clear plastic adhesive coating over a torn binding. Send the book to be repaired. If you have a very careful hand and are willing to practice on a book you don't want to preserve, you can repair a cracked inner hinge of a book by folding back the torn edges of the endpaper, applying a water-soluble adhesive like Sobo Glue, and then folding the torn edges back to their original position. Wipe off any excess before closing the book, and then leave the book closed under a heavy weight for a few hours. Where the inner hinge is not merely cracked but broken, you can repair it with special nontearing tapes that are available from Brodart. For best results, send the book to a professional binder, who can replace the endpapers entirely.

A water-damaged book can be repaired by a conservator, but you can help diminish the effects of warping, after the book has dried, by flattening the book under a heavy weight for a few days. A sheet of glass can be placed between the book and the weight to ensure that the weight rests evenly on the damaged book.

Repairing the inner hinge of a book

Torn pages tend to become more torn and should be repaired. For heavily used books, Scotch Magic Tape is adequate, but I dislike using it on anything but books that young children will outgrow in a few years. For anything better, you should use either Filmoplast P, a clear, ultra-thin, acid-free paper-repair tape, or Archival Aids Document Repair Tape, which can easily be removed without damage; they are both available from Brodart. Both can be used to repair maps and other folded paper as well as books.

Almost all clothbound books are now published in bindings that are glued instead of sewn; good modern glues are so effective and flexible that they are used even on books of high quality. Although the best glued bindings are long-lasting, older and inferior ones may start shedding pages after a brief period of use. If only a few pages fall out of a glued binding, you can "tip" them back in by applying an extremely thin line of Sobo or similar adhesive to the edge of the pages and carefully pushing them back into their proper

BOOKS AND FRIENDS

You must preserve books from your friends' handlings and mishandlings of them as well as your own. I began learning about this as a graduate student at a party, when I took an interesting-looking book from a shelf and opened it widely to peruse it. You could hear the little crack of the binding even in the party din. The host glared at me and asked bitterly, "Why are you breaking the back of my book?" After this I made it my business to learn about being good to books. To preserve the lives of his new books with glued bindings, a friend of mine goes through the book, alternating between front and back, gently turning each page and ending in the middle. If you start in the middle, you risk cracking the binding—as I did at that party.

Friends also pose a danger to books in that they borrow them and never return them. Indeed, people who would be mortified to borrow a cup of sugar without returning it will borrow your favorite novels with nary a thought of return. This is a phenomenon long noticed among moral philosophers, who, as one of my professors pointed out to me in graduate school, build entire moral philosophies on the example of "the friend who breaks his promise to return a book." Having frequently been disappointed in his own friends, one of my acquaintances now refuses to lend anyone any book. My husband will lend a book only when he has privately steeled himself to the certainty of never seeing it again, and even keeps a shadow library of cheap paperback editions that he loans out instead of his good hardback copies.

Pianos

Before recorded music, and even for another two or three decades or so afterward, the piano was the most important means of supplying music in the home. Practically every middle-class home either owned one or aspired to own one. The piano occupied its special position in the home because of its musical versatility. It was both a brilliant solo instrument and the best one for accompanying singing and other instruments. Popular songs and tunes were accessible only to those who had a piano and someone to play it. In addition, unlike most other instruments, the piano permitted you to create complex harmonies and a variety of simultaneous musical voices and rhythms. This meant that people could reproduce in their homes some version of practically any music that existed. Hearing piano renditions of Beethoven's symphonies or Mozart's operas was as close as many people ever got to knowing what these sounded like, for outside urban centers concerts were rare treats and only a few wealthy people could hire musicians.

The piano is still the chief instrument for the home. Not only pianists but singers, violinists, and many others need a piano to make the best home use of their own instruments. The repertoire of piano music, in all styles from all ages, is a vast store of treasures. Sometimes people will still gather around the piano and sing, although in many circles (some of which I belong to), suggesting this activity could get you left off the guest list for the next party. No matter what people say, I think it is fun.

Cleaning and Care of the Case. If you have a grand piano, keep the lid closed when you are not playing or dust and debris will collect inside the piano. On all pianos, it is best to keep the key cover closed when you are not playing to keep the keys and the spaces between them dust-free.

Do your best to expose the piano to as little light as possible, especially sunlight or unshielded fluorescent light. Light will age the finish and alter its color.

Older pianos had lacquered finishes, but new ones—especially those imported from Asian countries—often have polyester or polyurethane. The latter finishes are far tougher and more water resistant but also less reparable. Pianos with the newer finishes, however, should be cared for in the same way as the older ones. Do not use wax or polish or dusting sprays on your piano. (Silicone-containing products make refinishing difficult, and waxes and polishes can gum the works.)

To preserve the finish, dust it as you would any wood furniture. When it is very dusty, you may use a clean, *very slightly* dampened soft cloth. Then immediately wipe with a dry cloth. (Steinway recommends using cheesecloth.) Always wipe in the direction of the grain of the wood. If there are sticky fingerprints or other dirt that rubbing cannot remove, call in a professional technician.

Those experienced with wood and pianos might try cleaning the piano themselves, but I do not recommend this for the inexperienced who might not be as alert to potential accidents or signs of problems. But if you count yourself among the experienced, wipe clean a piano as you would any delicate finished wood, first wiping it with a cloth dipped in water to which you have added a *very* small amount of a neutral detergent and wrung very dry, then rinsing it with a separate cloth wetted with plain water and also wrung very dry, and finally rubbing it down carefully with a third cloth, this one dry. *Do not get the wood wet and do not let water drips go on or in the piano; if this should happen, immediately wipe dry. Do not use sudsy water—use only a tiny bit of detergent in the water. This sort of cleaning should be undertaken only rarely and when absolutely necessary*—to remove jelly fingerprints and similarly extreme soil. Such cleaning is less risky for urethane-type finishes than others.

If a nonurethane-type finish gets a minor scratch, use a little Old English Scratch Cover or a similar remedy in a color that matches your piano's finish. Put it on a soft, clean cloth—*not directly on the piano*—and rub the scratch with it.

A piano is built largely of wood and felt, which is made of wool. For this reason, it is highly sensitive to temperature and humidity. Keep the piano in a place where it will not be exposed to extremes of temperature or humidity. It will do best at around 72°F and 45 to 50 percent relative humidity. Arid air will cause it to go flat. Humid air will make it sharp and possibly cause the strings to rust. Extreme fluctuations in humidity or temperature can cause the soundboard to crack—a major disaster that can be extremely costly to repair. Therefore, place the piano away from direct sunlight, open windows and doors, air conditioners, fireplaces, heating registers, space heaters, radiators, hot pipes, or any other sources of heat. You can use humidifiers and dehumidifiers in the area or room where you keep the piano very beneficially *if you observe two cautions.* First, change the humidity level of the room gradually. Second, do not place any moisture-creating device *next to, near,* or *under* the piano or you may damage the finish or create too much humidity.

Keep drinks away from the piano; liquids will stain the finish, and if they get inside they can do enormous and permanent damage. If liquid gets inside your piano, contact a technician immediately. Parties pose real dangers to pianos, for inevitably someone sets a drink or plate on the lid of the baby grand or the top of the upright. You might resort to placing an elegant cover on the piano when you are entertaining—or even opening the lid (but then you face an increased risk of something spilling inside it).

Although in most homes the top of the upright is adorned with framed photographs, clocks, and china figurines, this is not as good an idea for a grand piano; it prevents opening the lid without a big fuss. Also, such objects are likely to scratch the lid's surface, and repairs to the piano's finish are far more complicated and expensive than they are for furniture. Besides, aesthetically speaking, music lovers often feel that the presence of decorative objects on the lid of a grand piano shows that the piano is considered more as furniture than as instrument. On an upright, this is not an issue. Just be sure to put something under decorative objects or frames so that they do not cause scratches. In the old days, that something would have been a doily, but today people would rather have a scratched piano than a doily—even a lace doily. (People want to show off the wood and no longer have the cautious attitudes about preserving and caring for things that they did in a less wealthy age. They also no longer know how to make doilies.)

You should attempt no repairs or adjustments to the inside of the piano whatsoever. Nor should you attempt to clean inside the case or to remove objects that may have fallen into the case such as pencils or pennies. Let a piano technician deal with all such problems. If a penny or something similar drops between the keys, you can attempt to remove it by carefully sliding a table knife between the keys. But do not attempt much more than this on your own.

If you move, have professional piano movers handle the piano or pick a moving company that has personnel with training adequate for pianos.

Cleaning and Caring for the Keyboard. Keep the dust cover to the keyboard closed when you are not playing; otherwise dust collects on and between the keys. Do not let children pound on the keys; tell them instead to press with their fingers. The pounding may break a key. (Powerful adult players sometimes snap a string or a hammer.)

Many older pianos have ivory keys. Ivory needs some exposure to light or it yellows, but it eventually yellows with age even if it receives light. Any ivory piano keys you see today are old—ivory is no longer used for piano keys—and therefore a bit yellowed. You may wish to lift the cover to expose ivory keys to some sunlight at times, but the yellowing of ivory keys is pleasant-looking and natural. Do not try to cure such yellowing with home remedies! To my knowledge, there are no safe home remedies for the yellowing of old ivory piano keys. Modern pianos have plastic keys that stay white.

Dust the keyboard frequently, and periodically wipe the keys with a clean, white, very slightly damp cloth. Then *dry immediately* with a soft, dry cloth. If there are stains or smudges that are not removed by this method, dip a clean cloth in a small amount of mild detergent and water or a solution of denatured alcohol and water and wring thoroughly so that *it is not dripping*. Then gently rub the spot. Rinse with pure water in the same manner with a well-wrung, nondripping cloth; *dry immediately* with a soft, dry cloth. It is a good idea to use separate solutions and cloths for the black keys. You must be extremely careful, for if water gets on the sides of the keys it may cause the wood under the ivory to swell and the ivory might crack. If a stain persists, you should have a piano repair technician take care of it.

Technicians and Tuners. Choose a competent tuner/technician. The manufacturer of your piano or the store that sold it to you is likely to be able to recommend someone. (In New York and other cities where manufacturers are headquartered, the manufacturer sometimes has a staff of trained technicians you can call upon.) Or ask a good piano teacher, a friend who is knowledgeable, or any institution near your home that keeps good instruments, perhaps a music school or a church. The Piano Technicians Guild, which has a Web site (www.ptg.org), offers certification tests and can provide names of registered piano technicians in your area.

Tuning. Tuning is adjusting the strings of the piano so that they sound at the proper pitch. A piano should be tuned at least twice a year. More frequent tuning is better, but rarely does anyone but a professional musician bother to have it done more than twice. Your piano may need extra attention its first year because of the elasticity of newer wires and because it will have been moved from one environment to another. Piano manufacturers generally recommend three or four tunings in the first year and anywhere from two to four (and more if needed) thereafter. Steinway once put the matter of frequency of tuning in perspective with this reminder: "Remember that a concert piano is tuned before every performance, and a piano in a professional recording studio, where it is in constant use, is tuned three or four times each week as a matter of course." It is not true, as you may have heard, that you have to play the piano to keep it in tune; in fact the more it is played the more frequently it needs tuning.

Voicing. Voicing adjusts the quality of the piano's tones. This is largely a function of the felt that covers the hammers that strike the strings when you press a key. After much use, the felts grow harder and less spongy, and the strings begin to cut into the hammer when it strikes. When this happens, the piano must be revoiced. The technician will reshape and soften the felt. He can also harden it, if the tone is overly mellow. Voicing will be needed every two or three years in a household in which the piano is played regularly. It will need voicing more or less frequently depending upon the habits of your own household.

Regulating the Action. When the technician regulates the action of the piano, he or she adjusts the mechanisms that connect the key that you press with your finger to those that cause the hammer to strike the string. These mechanisms determine how the keys feel when you press them. The action should be even or uniform—the same for each key—and comfortable. (Voicing will also affect these things.) There should be no slack when you depress the key, not even a little. How frequently the action will need regulating will depend upon how much the piano is used.

Storing the Piano. If you are going to turn off the heat in your home and head for the Caribbean or Florida, try to lower the temperature gradually. Sudden cooling is not good for your piano. Gradually warm it when you return too. The same advice is applicable when you place the piano in storage. Damp basements or baking attics can be the end of a good piano. To protect the case, wrap the piano in blankets, top side and underside, and tie the blankets on with twine or string.

Moths. Felt is made of wool, so your piano is vulnerable to moths unless they are mothproofed. All the piano manufacturers that I checked with informed me that they moth-treat their piano felts and have done so for many years. But, it seems, none of the moth treatments last more than a few years. According to manufacturers of fine pianos, a piano that is played regularly will not get moths. If yours is not played regularly or if you want extra protection, one manufacturer's representative suggested, you can put moth repellent inside the piano. In grand pianos, place the repellent on pieces of cardboard on the bronzed plate so that the finish is not damaged. In uprights, place the repellent in cloth bags and hang them on the clamps directly under the top at either side of the piano. My own view is that I do not wish to breathe moth repellents in my living room, but I would certainly take this extra cautionary measure if I were going to store my piano. If you see moths in or near your piano, you had better have a technician in.

Audio Recordings

Storage of Recordings. All audio recordings—LPs, CDs, and audiocassette tapes—should be stored vertically. Keep tapes wound to the head of one side. LPs warp in heat. CDs are much more heat tolerant, but even these may succumb to high temperatures. If you have a warped LP, sometimes you can flatten it by putting it between two thick pieces of plate glass and laying weighty books or similar broad, heavy objects on top. (Remove the cardboard cover but leave on the protective inner sleeve.)

Handling. Do not touch the playing surface of any tape or recording. Hold audiocassette tapes by the outer shell. Hold LPs by the sides or the center label. Handle CDs by the side or center hole only.

Cleaning LPs and CDs. LPs, which are vinyl, can be cleaned with a water-based record-cleaning fluid. A stronger solution of 20% isopropyl alcohol (which *cannot* be used on 78s, which are made of shellac) can also be used on LPs. To clean CDs, moisten a soft, clean cloth with distilled water and wipe, or use a commercial CD cleaning preparation if you have a badly soiled CD. Dust LPs and 78s with a special record-dusting brush, which you can buy in stores that sell records. To dust CDs, wipe with a clean, soft cloth.

Magnetic Tapes. To clean and care for magnetic tapes, see the following chapter.

53

Images and Recordings

Photographs, negatives, and slides . . . Handling photographs . . . Quality of photographic processing . . . Environmental hazards to photographs: light, humidity, temperature, air pollution . . . Where to store photographs . . . Photographic storage and display materials, archival quality, acid- and lignin-free, safe plastics . . . Photographic storage techniques . . . Antiques, daguerreotypes, tintypes . . . Safe photograph display areas . . . Making duplicates of photographs, scanning . . . Repairs on photographs . . . Caring for paintings . . . Caring for videotapes and other magnetic tapes

Every home has its photograph collection, and I have never known a family whose photographs were not charged, cherished symbols of family unity, history, affection, and loyalty. The older the images, the more prized they are, and the harder to share among ever more numerous descendants. As we move into the third century of the photographic arts, thousands of households hold nineteenth-century photographic images of their ancestors; tens of thousands of households hold aging black-and-whites. Hundreds of thousands have all-color photographic records created during the last half of the twentieth century. Now there are families who have turned almost exclusively to videotapes for visual records of family and friends.

If we think about preserving these precious records for posterity, many of us might choose to do things differently. Black-and-white photographs are hardy; they age much better than color ones. Ordinary color photographs deteriorate so rapidly (in as few as ten to twenty years) that some experts say you should regard them as a temporary medium; and although dark storage, when other conditions are optimal, can preserve black-and-white photographs for centuries, most color photographs quickly deteriorate even in the dark. Color slides may last a bit longer than color photographs, but they too show relatively quick deterioration. Videotapes are not even as long-lasting as color photos. The tapes deteriorate each time they are played, and even when not played they will begin to deteriorate within ten years. These are fairly astonishing and unhappy facts when you consider that some people have *only* color photos and videos, or even only videos, to serve as their family records. (Proper storage of all these media is discussed below.)

Perhaps, given current technologies, continuing to take some black-and-white photographs is a good idea. Many people do this simply because they like the way black-and-whites look. Having images in all of these media, in fact, is probably best both practically and aesthetically.

Although a videocamera is a far more complex and remarkable machine than a camera, videotapes are not necessarily superior to photographs. Photos not only last longer than videos, in many ways they constitute a better kind of memento. Videotapes contain very little footage that you are really interested in. It is hard to find the good parts. I do not know anyone who takes the trouble to splice out high moments and create something like a photo album, with images selected on principles of quality, theme or subject matter, or time period. Watching videotapes is more fuss (you have to put something in a machine, rewind, and so forth), so you do not do it so casually. You cannot leave videos in books here and there that people can pick up at will or carry them around in your wallet or put one in the card that you are sending to your grandmother.

Photographs have a conceptual advantage over videotapes too. They stop time, letting you hold on to a single moment. Videotapes, like life, keep right on rolling. It is thrilling to be able to replay an hour of life, but being able to stop change and motion is even more thrilling.

Photographs, Negatives, and Slides

Handling. The care you take in handling your photographs should be in proportion to their importance and your wish for them to last. This section explains how to exercise a high degree of caution. You decide what degree of caution is appropriate to any particular photographs of your own.

Before opening a box or album containing photographs, carefully remove all the dust on the container. Otherwise dust will fall on the photos. Dust acts abrasively on the images.

Never touch photographic images. With less important photographs, wash your hands and touch them only at the very edges. Valuable, antique, and important photographs should never be touched with bare hands at all; wear thin cotton gloves to protect them from your skin oils and acids. These will cause deterioration in and of themselves, and will also furnish molds with nourishment. Very old and fragile photographs should be handled as little as possible. When you have to handle them, hold them on both their right and left sides to avoid stressing them and accidentally causing cracking.

Never fold, crack, or bend photographs. If you hold them up close to your face, your moist, hot breath will get on them.

Quality of Photographic Processing. Whether you are making black-and-white or color photographs, when you want the photographs to last, choose high-quality processing. Better processing tends to be more expensive. Not every family snapshot is worth the expense, but some are.

High-quality processing leaves minimal chemical residues in the paper that might react with the other materials in the photograph and with environmental factors to hasten deterioration. The emulsion (the chemicals out of which the picture is formed) and the quality of the paper on which it is printed are factors in a photograph's longevity. With color photographs, the freshness of the solutions used—how many rolls were processed since the solutions used in processing were changed—is also a factor. To get the best processing, send your film to a reputable professional lab rather than relying on the fast-development shops or drugstore services. (But many fast-development services do decent work for ordinary purposes.) If you do not know of a good lab, ask a photographer friend or try to evaluate a business yourself by asking questions; if the employees have never before encountered someone who is trying to increase the longevity of his or her photographs, it is likely you need another lab. If the store also sells photographic storage and display materials, look around and see if any are archival in quality or acid- and lignin-free. (For the unusually valuable or important photograph, there are also custom labs that can process black-and-whites with archival quality so that they will last centuries if properly handled.)

Different types of negatives also have different life spans, depending on their type and storage conditions. However, negatives are much less delicate than prints mostly because paper is more retentive of chemicals, as well as environmental moisture, than the acetate used for negatives. As for color film, some types are much better than others. To determine the relative longevity of films, check consumer information sources. New types are always being developed.

Environmental Hazards to Photographs. Once the print has been made, you can contribute to its long life by controlling environmental factors that can damage photographs.

Light. Both the paper on which photographs are printed and their emulsions are sensitive to light, especially ultraviolet light. Exposure to light can produce fading, yellowing, and, in color photographs, color shifts, and can cause photos to grow brittle. The ill effects of light are exacerbated by heat and humidity.

If you keep photographs out of direct sunlight and protect them by framing in glass (which filters out much ultraviolet radiation), they will last much longer. There are special UV-filtering types of glass (called "conservation glass") and transparent plastic available from photo supply stores; these filter out even more ultraviolet radiation than ordinary glass. Most colored photos fade much more readily than black-and-white when exposed to light, especially UV light. Although black-and-white photographs that are not displayed but are stored in boxes or albums will last longer than those that are displayed, most color photographs quickly—in a decade or two—fade and show color shifts even in dark storage.

Slides last longer than photographs partly because they rarely see the light. They will eventually fade too, however.

Fluorescent lights and halogen lights, unless filtered, produce significant amounts of ultraviolet radiation. You can get plastic filters to place over fluorescent bulbs to reduce their ultraviolet radiation. Halogen lamps are probably shielded already, but if they are not, get shields. (See chapter 47.)

Humidity and Temperature. All photographs do best in low humidity and cool temperatures. High humidity—anything over 50 percent relative humidity—is bad for photographs. The best humidity level for photographs, negatives, and slides ranges between 15 and 50 percent relative humidity, depending upon what type they are. Some experts advise aiming at 30 percent relative humidity as the safest compromise when you are storing a variety of materials.

Black-and-white photographs are less sensitive to temperature than to humidity, but a combination of high humidity and high temperature is particularly damaging. Avoid temperatures warmer than 77°F; temperatures between 65° and 70°F are reasonable; colder is even better. Most color photographs are more sensitive to temperature than to humidity, and cold storage is one of the few means available to extend their lives. Although some museums routinely use low-humidity cold storage to preserve photographs you should not try this yourself unless you get professional advice. It is a tricky undertaking because of the danger of moisture condensation on cold objects and because fluctuations in temperature and humidity pose extra risks. (You would probably need a separate refrigerator or freezer, along with moisture-proof, archival-quality storage containers.)

Humidity that is too low can cause curling and cracking. High humidity can soften the emulsion, ruining pictures and slides or causing them to become "glazed." Moisture can make the effects of residual chemicals worse, producing brownish or yellowish spots; and it will contribute to mold or fungus growing on the pictures. Molds are also encouraged by matter left on photographs by skin—oils, acids, dirt. The gelatins used in photographic emulsions contain animal matter upon which molds can feed when the gelatins are softened by humidity. Molds can soften the emulsion so that it actually rubs off; they can drastically affect the dyes of color photographs. They can also render the paper brittle or produce brown splotches.

Rapid, drastic fluctuations in humidity and temperature, especially over long periods of time, will cause cracking and crazing; rapid changes are more damaging than gradual ones. If high humidity is your problem, you might put your photographs into archival boxes (see below) with a desiccant (an absorbent material used to take up moisture—a drying agent). You can buy desiccant devices containing silica gel or other substances from photographic supply stores.

Air Quality. In some areas—for instance, those with heavy traffic, heavy industry, or salty sea air—air pollutants can affect the integrity of photographs. Also, insects will munch on photographs. Tight storage boxes, in metal or a neutral plastic, provide adequate protection.

WHERE DO YOU STORE THE PHOTOGRAPHS?

Store photographs in a cool, dark, dry place. One expert told me that he thought people would find it best to keep photographs under the beds (in appropriate storage containers—described below). Most people's bedrooms are fairly cool and dry. The photographs will not get kicked or stepped on or spilled on under the bed either. If you can't do this, a cool closet is another good choice. Just make sure that it is a cool one—that there is no hot pipe going through it and that it has no wall that gets warm. Do not store photographs in kitchens, bathrooms, basements, attics, or garages, as these areas can grow too hot or too humid and may experience damaging abrupt shifts of temperature and humidity. Outside a closet, almost anything stored is better off on a shelf than on the floor; on a shelf there is less danger of photographs being stepped on, eaten by pests, flooded, or lost. Interior rooms tend to have more constant and moderate conditions than exterior ones.

Photographic Storage and Display Materials. When you store photographs, negatives, and slides, you want to keep them free of dirt and dust and safe from insects. You also want to protect them from spills, tears, fingerprints, scratches, and similar accidents. This generally means storage in boxes or albums that provide protection from these dangers and, as well, can provide some protection against changes in humidity. Unfortunately, over time, boxes, albums, and any storage or display materials that are near or touching your photographs, slides, and negatives can sometimes harm them. The very best storage materials can be expensive, and some photographs are not worth so much protection. The point is to be aware of the options and know how to display and store in the safest ways any that are especially important to you.

To ensure very safe display and storage, buy from a reputable retailer, preferably one specializing in archival materials and photographic storage supplies, choosing materials labeled as acid- and lignin-free or archival. When you are having photographs that you wish to preserve framed or mounted by a frame shop or other professional, specify acid-free and lignin-free or archival materials. The need for such materials applies to *everything* you use to store and display your photographs, slides, and negatives: storage boxes, albums, mounting boards, mattes, interleaving (those sheets of paper or plastic that are used to separate photos in boxes), envelopes, sleeves, and so on. If the store personnel seem to brush this idea off or look either puzzled or annoyed, go elsewhere.

Acids and various atmospheric gases (oxidizing gases, ozone, peroxides, ammonia, acidic fumes) all contribute to the deterioration of both negatives and photographs. Acids attack both the photograph's paper and its emulsion (the chemicals out of which the picture is formed)—very slowly but surely. If you have seen newsprint clippings grow yellow and fragile over the years, you have seen this happen; the wood pulp that newspaper is made of contains acid. Materials must also be lignin-free because lignin, a substance present in all plant fibers, reacts with light and heat to produce phenols (or alcohols) and acids, both of which will harm photographic paper and emulsions. If a material contains lignin, it may well be acid-free when you buy it but become acidic years down the road.

Avoid storing photographs, negatives, or slides (or any valuable papers, for that matter) in wooden or cardboard boxes, drawers, cedar chests, and cabinets, as wood and cardboard contain lignin and other potentially damaging substances. There are archival-quality storage boxes that are nearly airtight and quite strong. These tend to be expensive. Less expensive archival boxes tend to be less strong and less airtight. Thus you cannot use them with desiccants so effectively, and they provide less control over atmospheric pollution and fluctuations in humidity. But they may be perfectly adequate for your needs. There is no point in paying for quality you do not need. Metal boxes and files, of steel or coated with baked enamel, are also good storage choices.

When you are storing photographs, always separate them by interleaves. Otherwise, you run the risk that something in or on one photograph will contaminate others. The interleaves also help with the problems of scratching, sticking together, and dust and dirt. Paper interleaves are more absorbent of moisture than the photographs; thus they protectively draw humidity away from the pictures. Never use "magnetic" plastic leaves. Glassine is not recommended for photographic storage. Negatives, too, should not be stored in glassine or Kraft or manila envelopes.

When your photographs are mounted, every part of the mounting materials should be archival. Masking tape, cellophane tape, or household glues should not be used. It is advisable to have a trained professional do the mounting. Dry mounting is preferable to gluing. The glues are likely to be damaging to the photos, and eventually the glues dry and the photograph comes loose.

When you want to display great numbers of photos, photograph albums are the practical choice. Choosing archival, acid-free and lignin-free materials for your albums is very important, but there are many types of safe albums and you can make your own or buy them. Some have photo corners; some have slots; some have plastic pockets. Some have blank pages on which you put your own photo corners. Plastic covers over the pictures are a good idea; they let you see the photograph without your touching it or taking it in and out of something, which over time can cause damage to the photo. But you have to choose the plastic carefully.

The safe plastics (whether for photos, slides, or negatives) are polypropylene, polyethylene, and Mylar or polyester. Never use the magnetic or adhesive plastic overlays; they'll damage your pictures. *Do not use polyvinyl chlorides or PVCs.* These break down to form hydrochloric acid and emit harmful fumes.

Being sure that you have picked a safe plastic can be tricky, as materials often do not state what kind of plastic they are. One expert gave me this tip: when you open the book or package, lean down and sniff. If you smell that familiar plastic smell, it is probably polyvinyl chloride. If a photo album that you are considering buying does not state whether it contains acid- and lignin-free, archival paper, covers, and plastics, do not buy it. Assume that it does *not.* Albums sold in drugstores and gift shops, even expensive ones, that do not specialize in photographic materials typically are not acid-free or archival.

Slides, too, should be stored only in safe plastics: polyethylene, polypropylene, and Mylar (polyester). You can put them in slide pages or sleeves made of these plastics. Or you can store them in metal or safe plastic boxes designed for the purpose and sold at photographic supply stores. There are cabinets, too, if you have great quantities of slides, with removable drawers, and there are modular stackable units.

Photographic Storage Techniques. You can store photographs and negatives vertically or horizontally. The main thing is to store things of like size and like material together. Mixing sizes is more likely to cause accidents or abrasion. Different types of negatives and photos may contain different chemicals and injure one another if stored together. Never bend photographs to fit into a container, and do not jam them in tightly. Give them room. Do not fasten photos, slides, or negatives with rubber bands or paper clips. These will mar them. Check the stores and catalogues for the latest and best archival-quality boxes, negative sleeves, and other storage options. You can buy archival sleeves to put your negatives in, and moisture-proof archival envelopes to put the sleeves in.

When you have great numbers of photographs, an ordering system becomes indispensable. What good are photographs and negatives that can't be found? A good system for ordering negatives for photographs is especially important for color photographs, given the short life span of color photographs. Photographic supply stores and catalogues offer storage "systems," using archival-quality materials, that supply you with a method for orderly storage of negatives cross-referenced to the photographs. Or you can devise one of your own.

There are dozens of potential principles of arrangement for photographs and photo albums: black-and-whites versus color photographs, time, location, subject matter. In our family, we are great believers in chronology. The vast majority of our photographs are stored only in the order in which they were taken. Out of these we sometimes take single photographs for framing or small thematic groups for making mini-albums.

Antiques: Daguerreotypes, Tintypes, and Others. A friend of mine recalls, a few years ago, attending a photographic exhibit in Paris of a collection of Henry Fox Talbot prints from the 1830s. The presentation room was as dark as though it were candlelit. The exhibitors knew that if the prints were to survive for future generations they must receive minimal exposure to light. Antique photographs need special treatment. If you have any daguerreotypes, tintypes, albumin prints, or other antique prints, be exceedingly careful to keep them out of the light in cool, dry conditions. Double-packing these is recommended; use a buffered archival-quality envelope encased in some type of archival plastic. You may then place this in an archival storage box. This does a good job of keeping pollutants in the air away from the photographs.

Antique negatives—nitrate and old acetate—should not be stored in airtight containers. A little air needs to get in. For these some experts recommend the same type of double pack as for antique photos: buffered archival-quality envelope inside, archival plastic on the outside. For further advice consult a conservator, and see the list of sources at the end of this book.

Safe Display Areas for Photographs. Do not hang or display photographs near fireplaces, radiators, air vents, doors, or windows, or in places where sunlight strikes them directly. Bathrooms and kitchens tend to become too humid and too hot, and tend to have fluctuating temperatures and humidities.

Making Duplicates of Photographs. An excellent way to assure that a photograph or slide survives for posterity is to make a duplicate. Display one and put the other in storage.

If you decide to make duplicates, you should be aware that there are three different procedures that can be used. The first is simply photographic duplication of the original photograph or slide: you take a picture or slide of it. Quick-service laboratories will do this for you fairly inexpensively, but the results are often less than good.

The second way is called a "separation." This process produces three black-and-white "separations" in negatives; these are later joined with three different colors and recombined to produce the new color print. The process is guided by careful records of the original colors and tones. Not only is the new print of high quality, but the black-and-white negatives from which it was derived are long-lived and can be reused in the future. Good photographic laboratories do this, but it is an expensive process requiring skill, and inexpensive scanning technology has largely replaced it.

Scanning is the third way of preserving your most valuable photographs. You have them scanned into a computer by a professional photographic lab; you can also use your own scanner or a scanner at a copy shop, but you will not get the same high quality as at a professional lab. The scanned images can be printed on photographic paper by a professional photographic lab whenever you want a fresh copy. Professionally scanned photographs can be almost indistinguishable in detail from the originals, and the colors recorded in the digital files won't fade or change over time. The scanned images, however, require large amounts of storage space on your computer, and you will still have to worry about preserving the digital files themselves (see chapter 54, "Home Offices and Computers," pages 634–35). If your hard disk crashes and you have no backup, your photo is gone. A photo CD, like any other digital storage medium, eventually becomes unreadable or obsolete as the equipment it was designed for is replaced by newer technologies. To preserve it, you have to copy it every few years to an up-to-date storage medium. And even if you are diligent about this, your great-grandchildren are unlikely to have machinery capable of reading it.

Repairs on Photographs. Professionals can sometimes remove stains, repair cracks (at least partially), flatten curling, and perform other minor miracles of restoration. Because such services are costly, they make sense only for highly cherished photographs and antiques. The best professional laboratories can also retouch and "repair" scanned images of damaged photographs on a computer screen and print them out as new photographs; this process is costly, but it lessens the risk that the restoration may inadvertently cause further damage to the original.

When you are willing to take chances with a photo, you can sometimes clean it yourself at home. But this is *risky;* it is terribly easy to ruin a photograph this way. You can buy film cleaner at a photography store. Apply it sparingly to a soft, clean piece of chamois or white, nonlinting cotton. Never use water-based cleaners; these can rub the soil in and damage the emulsion.

Paintings

Paintings like benign neglect. Just make sure that they are displayed in a safe environment and that no cleaning zealot showers them with care.

Keep paintings out of direct sunlight, in fairly cool and dry rooms, say 65° to 70°F and relative humidity below 50 percent. Do not hang paintings in bathrooms or kitchens or other areas with high or fluctuating humidity or temperatures. Do not store (or hang) paintings in basements or attics, which can become too damp or hot. Be careful not to put them near windows where rain might occasionally blow in and the sun might shine on them. Also avoid areas where anyone smokes or candles are burned. All light, natural and artificial, will cause paintings to age, fade, or darken.

Dust the glass over paintings during your normal dusting. Once a year or so, you might wash the glass. *Never spray the glass with window cleaner or water,* for the liquid might get under the glass and ruin the painting. Instead, put a little cleaner on a cloth until it is barely damp and then wipe the glass clean, avoiding the frame. Polish dry with a separate cloth.

Never touch paintings that are not behind glass. Skin oils left on the surface will do harm over time. Once a year or so, or as needed, undertake to dust them. Use a fine, soft brush. Begin at the top of the painting and work your way down, ever so gently brushing the dust off. Naturally, the paintings will do best when the general dust level in the room is kept down with your ordinary cleaning. *Do not* use a feather duster or attempt any cleaning other than gentle brushing away of dust. *Do not* vacuum your paintings. Periodically check for cracks, tears, punctures, and loss of paint or color; if you see a problem, contact a professional for help. An expert would have to undertake any cleaning more ambitious than that described here. Fluctuation in temperature and humidity, over time, can loosen a painting's canvas on the stretcher. A framer or restorer can tighten it again. This should not be done when the humidity is very low, say in winter, or the painting might tear when the humidity rises again.

Carry paintings with two hands, one on each side of the frame. Two people should carry very large frames. If paint is flaking, carry the painting flat, painted side up.

Videotapes and Other Magnetic Tapes

Videotapes are magnetic tapes, like the sound cassette tapes you play on a tape deck. Magnetic tapes are exceedingly delicate and under the best of conditions are not long-lasting. It is a minor tragedy that countless families are relying heavily, and sometimes entirely, on magnetic tape records of important family events. These records will not be around for the children—let alone the grandchildren—unless expensive and troublesome duplications are invested in, and perhaps not even then.

Cool, dry storage is best for magnetic tapes. Magnetic tapes are destroyed by temperatures over 125°F and the combination of heat and humidity is especially destructive. Abrupt changes in temperature and humidity are also damaging. Try storing tapes under a bed or in a cool closet.

Play tapes only on clean equipment. Dirt, even dust particles too small to see, in strategic places in the transport mechanism or on the VCR head will scratch your VCR tape with every touch. Each playing scratches off a little more of the image from the tape.

Not all VCR tapes are equal; some are far more long-lasting than others. (Unlike photographs, black-and-white videotapes do not last longer than color ones.) Check consumer information sources for what brands seem best, and be wary of bargains.

Make duplicates of tapes you cherish, or have a shop make duplicates for you. Keep one as a record and show only the other. The more frequently tapes are played, the faster they wear out. When the user tape begins to fail, use the record copy to make another user copy. Some experts advise copying as frequently as every seven years; others say you might wait as long as ten years. Everyone agrees that you must copy them; they won't last.

Play and rewind all magnetic tapes, including your record tapes, at least once a year. Doing this enables you to spot developing problems before it is too late; it also helps the tape last longer by redistributing tension more evenly along the tape, ensuring that some parts are not unequally stressed. But just before you engage in this annual playing of videotapes, clean your VCR in accordance with the manufacturer's instructions; or, as some experts recommend, have it professionally cleaned. You do not want to ruin all your record copies on a dirty VCR.

Keep all magnetic tapes away from magnets. Loudspeakers and appliances with electric motors, such as vacuum motors, contain magnets.

54

Home Offices and Computers

Advantages of a home office . . . Location and lighting of equipment for maximum comfort, position and type of monitor and keyboard, discomfort caused by the mouse, chair height . . . Wires and cables . . . Backups, keeping disks organized, printing out . . . Cleaning the computer

The great advantage of a home office is that it can be more like a home than an office. A home office imposes no dress code, no hall-prowling supervisors, no piped-in air, and no time-wasting conferences. It usually offers tastier coffee and either friendly company or soothing solitude. The challenge in organizing a home office is the challenge of giving it all the comfort of home without sacrificing the efficiency needed for an effective workplace.

If you work at home, you can usually set your own schedule, unless you work for a corporation or in an industry that requires you to be available at certain fixed hours. Your home office will be a more agreeable place to work if you integrate it into your home and give yourself reasons to move between work life and home life. A quick home-cooked lunch is a calming break in a workday routine, and far more pleasant than a meal delivered from outside and eaten at the desk. Many people who work at home are surprised to find that the sound of children in the house is usually cheering, not an annoyance that makes you want to close the door. But if you do work at home while others are there, you probably should try to find a room with a door that you can close when you need to. I know one family where the children were required to stay in their own room with their baby-sitter while one of their parents was working in a home office—with the result that the parents wasted more time dealing with the misery caused by their rigid rule than they would ever have lost to occasional intrusions by their children.

Home offices used to comprise little more than a typewriter, a writing desk—sometimes merely a kitchen table—and a chair.

Today's home office can include a computer, a printer, a fax machine, an answering machine, and perhaps also a copier and scanner, in addition to file cabinets, disk storage, and bookshelves. It takes some effort to save a home office from resembling a nest built by untidy birds who prefer to use wires and cables instead of twigs and straw, but it can be done. If you can give your home office a room of its own, you will find it easier to concentrate on your work, and you will be able to close the door on it when you want to forget about it. If you must put your home office in your living room or bedroom, try to contain it in a well-defined part of the room so that your paperwork won't spill out into the areas where you want to live.

Good computer setup

Layout, Lighting, and Comfort

When arranging a home office, start by thinking about its layout and lighting. You will need enough desk space to lay out all the papers you need for your work in addition to your computer, printer, and other equipment. Narrow computer stands are generally less efficient and more flimsy than ordinary wide tables that can hold one or more filing cabinets underneath them.

When you look above or to the side of your computer monitor, you should see furniture or a wall, not a window, because your eyes will soon suffer strain from trying to adjust repeatedly to the bright light of the window and then the darker image on the screen. Ideally, the window should be to your left (to your right if you are left-handed) so that daylight will shine on the paperwork on your desk without a shadow from your arm or hand. A window behind you may cause glare on the screen. Position a good desk lamp so that it shines on the desk, not on the screen, and use track lights or other lamps to create a moderately bright ambient light in the room. When planning lighting, keep in mind that soft, indirect light is generally best for viewing surfaces that are essentially two-dimensional objects, like paper or a computer screen.

The vertical position of the monitor is important for comfort. Usually the desktop is the best place for the monitor, not on top of the computer case. If the monitor is too high, you will strain your muscles holding up your head to see it. The top of the screen—not the top of the monitor case—should be just below eye level, and the front of the screen should be about twenty inches from your eyes.

The standard television-style monitor (a cathode-ray tube, or CRT, monitor) causes eyestrain because the image, renewed many times each second, flickers constantly. When setting up a computer attached to a CRT monitor, find the menu that lets you set the "refresh rate" that determines how rapidly the image is renewed, and choose the highest possible rate. (If you don't know how to adjust these settings, any ten-year-old will be happy to do it for you.)

Flat-panel monitors, originally available only on laptop computers and later introduced as separate monitors for use with ordinary desktop machines, are in many ways preferable to CRT monitors. At the time this book was written, their high prices were beginning to decline. Flat-panel monitors are restful to the eye because they have no flicker—since the screen is not continually refreshed, you don't need to set a "refresh rate"—and they save space because they are only a few inches thick. If you value your comfort and your eyesight and you can afford a flat-panel monitor, you may want to replace your CRT as soon as you can.

CRT monitors produced before the late 1980s tended to produce strong electromagnetic emissions and other kinds of radiation suspected of having bad effects on health. Most monitors produced since the early 1990s voluntarily conform to the strict radiation standards imposed by the Swedish government for equipment sold in Sweden. But flat-panel monitors produce far less radiation than even the best CRT types. The radiation generated by CRT monitors is often stronger behind the monitor than in front, so caution would advise placing your monitor so that the back of it faces a wall rather than the middle of a room where another person is likely to sit or stand.

Your keyboard is as important to your health and comfort as your monitor. Keyboards vary enormously in quality and in the way they respond to your typing, and you should consider replacing the cheaply made keyboard that probably came with your computer and buying a better one from the variety available at large computer stores. Some people prefer keyboards with a slightly spongy feel, while others prefer a more snappy and positive response during typing; choose the one that feels most comfortable to you. A variety of "ergonomic" keyboards are available; most of them feature a keyboard layout that looks as if a standard keyboard were pulled into a V shape, with the left-hand keys on one prong of the V and the right-hand keys on the other. Some people prefer these to ordinary keyboards, but they take some getting used to, and if you often have to work on other people's computers, you may find it awkward to switch back and forth between an ergonomic keyboard and a standard one. Avoid novelty keyboards with nonstandard arrangements of the arrow keys or other variations that will make it hard to adjust to a normal keyboard when you need to use one.

To avoid muscle strain, the keyboard should be placed low enough—or your chair adjusted to be high enough—to let your elbows make a right angle (or very slightly larger than a right angle) when your fingertips are on the keyboard. Let your hands float gently over the keys instead of holding them stiffly in one position; use the gentlest possible touch to avoid injuring your fingertips. If you have a wrist rest—a pad that sits in front of the keyboard—rest your wrists on it only when you are not actually typing.

The ubiquitous computer mouse is, for many people, a medical disaster in the making—or a disaster that has already occurred. A few months of constant use of the mouse can leave you with strains in your shoulder and discomfort in your hands. At the first sign of mouse-induced discomfort, try an alternative device like a trackball, which is a stationary device that you manipulate by rotating a ball instead of moving a mouse across the desk. Other comparable devices that you can try include the touchpad, which lets you move the cursor or mouse pointer by moving your fingertip along a small pad; the digitizing tablet, which is a flat plastic surface over which you move a penlike object in order to move the pointer on the screen; or the pointing stick, a small, pencil-eraser-shaped object in the middle of the keyboard, which you manipulate by pressing with your fingertip. Use the one that causes you the least strain.

Your chair should be adjusted so that your thighs are horizontal and your feet are flat on the floor while you work. If you can't lower your chair enough to place your feet flat on the floor, use a footrest.

Computers cause far more medical problems than typewriters did because typewriters forced their users to perform a variety of tasks rather than a single repetitive task. With a typewriter, you periodically had to stop typing to replace the sheet of paper, and this variation in the routine was enough to prevent much physical stress and strain. When working at a computer, take frequent periodic breaks from typing: stretch your arms, perform hand exercises, stand and look away from the screen.

Older models of laser printers, copiers, and similar devices tend to release small amounts of ozone, with bad effects on health and environment, and should be turned off when not in use. Newer models release no appreciable ozone.

Wires and Cables

Everything you add to a home office seems to add two or three wires and cables to an already tangled bird's nest. Take some time to force your cables into some kind of order by labeling them and then hiding them. To do the labeling, buy some vinyl or other permanent stick-on labels at a computer store or well-equipped hardware store; you need enough to attach a label to each end of every cable and wire. Write a brief descriptive term like "printer" or "monitor" on every cable; if you have more than one phone line, attach a label with the appropriate telephone number to each wire, and label each telephone outlet.

Once your cables are labeled, you can begin reducing the clutter. Hardware and computer stores sell plastic ties that you can wrap around a group of cables to hold them together; you can also get flexible tubes and other covers that hold cables together and keep them reasonably well hidden. To avoid electrical interference between cables, don't tie electrical power cords together with telephone wires or with cables that carry data to your monitor, printer, or scanner.

Backups

If you use a computer, backups are the most important element of your home office housekeeping. Every computer eventually breaks down, and the first part to fail is usually the hard disk, a delicate mechanical device that spins at a rate of thousands of rotations per minute. You should get into the habit of saving a backup copy of all your essential files on a set of floppy disks, a tape cartridge, a removable hard disk, or a cartridge disk—anything that you can store away from your computer, and preferably away from your home so that you can recover your files in case of fire, theft, or some other disaster.

Technology changes too rapidly for me to make specific recommendations for backups, but a few general guidelines may be useful. You need two kinds of backups, which you make at different intervals. One kind is an occasional large-scale backup that lets you restore everything on your computer in case the entire system fails or is lost or destroyed; you probably need to make this kind of backup once every few months. The other kind is the more frequent small-scale backup of the files you have created or changed recently. Depending on the kind of computer you own, you may be able to make both kinds of backup using backup programs that came with your computer, but you may have to buy special backup software and install it separately. When buying a new computer, make sure it comes with either a tape or a removable disk drive that lets you make large-scale backups with very little effort; most such drives come with backup software.

You can make your small-scale frequent backups to ordinary floppy disks, but you can also use any large-scale storage medium like digital tapes or removable disks. Alternatively, if you have a fast connection to the Internet, you can consider using a service that lets you transmit your files through the Internet to a remote storage area that acts like a digital safe-deposit box. But think twice before entrusting your files to a service that may or may not close down abruptly; also think twice before entrusting your files to other people who might decide to read them.

After backing up to a floppy disk, removable disk, or tape, always test the backup by restoring one or more files to your hard disk. More than one large corporation has found out too late that the backup disks that they were relying on did not in fact have any data on them. A simple test would have alerted them to the problem.

Use the labels provided when you buy a box of floppy disks to organize and keep track of your files. *Never use pencil* on disk labels: pencil "lead" is carbon, which may interfere with the magnetic particles on the disk and make your data inaccessible. If you prefer not to bother with labels, you can write directly on the disk casing with many kinds of marking pen.

The disks and tapes that you use for most backups are magnetic media, and, like all magnetic storage, they won't last forever. Floppy disks sometimes become unusable after as little as three to five years; digital tapes may not last much longer; even recordable CD-ROM disks of the kind that you can make with specialized computer hardware have a life expectancy of perhaps thirty years. If your only copies of crucial files are on backup disks and not on your computer's hard disk, you should copy them back to your hard disk at least once a year and then back them up again to fresh backup disks.

For the best possible security, you may wish to print out any new or revised files at the end of the day. While I was working on this book, a five-year-old hard disk failed catastrophically, and my most recent tape backup was more than a week old. But I had printed out all the drafts of my chapters as I wrote them, and so, although I had to retype some of the most recent work I had done, nothing was lost.

Although you may want to perform a periodic spring cleaning on your computer's files, it probably makes sense to store all your old correspondence on your computer indefinitely. Up-to-date word processing programs include an address-book feature that lets you enter an address once and reuse it in the future, but even if you don't use or have this feature, you can save much time and effort by copying addresses from old letters into new ones. If you ever wrote a letter of recommendation for a friend or employee, you can reuse the old letter with a new address if needed. When you buy a new computer, make sure you know how to transfer all your old letters and other work from the old machine to the new one; it is worth hiring a ten-year-old expert if you can't do it yourself. You may want to move older correspondence files into directories or folders named with the year the letters were written. (See also chapter 72, "Fond Records.")

Cleaning

Computer screens attract dust and fingerprints. Dust may be wiped off with a clean cloth or a tissue; fingerprints may be cleaned with a very slightly damp cloth, but only after you turn the screen *off*. Special-purpose towelettes sold in office supply stores for cleaning computer screens often leave a soapy film and should be used with caution.

Computer keyboards accumulate highly visible grime and—invisibly hidden beneath the keys—startling accumulations of dust, hair, crumbs, and unidentified miniature objects. Turn off the computer, then clean the grime with rubbing alcohol or, preferably, a spray can of cleaner-degreaser available in electronics stores. Use a spray can of compressed air—available in any hardware store—to blast hair, dust, and crumbs from between the keys. The keyboard is a miniature computer with fragile electronic components inside, and can be damaged by liquids. If you tend to spill coffee over the keys, consider buying a clear, flexible plastic skin that fits over standard keyboards and can be left on while you type. You can find them at large office supply stores.

Computer cases can be cleaned—after turning off and unplugging the computer—with a damp cloth or a spray can of cleaner-degreaser. Be careful when doing this because some electrical current remains in the computer even when it is switched off and unplugged.

55

Pets

Pleasures and benefits of pets . . . Pets and allergies . . . How pets cause allergies . . . Keeping the pet clean to reduce allergens . . . Housekeeping to reduce pet allergens and their effects . . . Pets, muck, and germs . . . Should you keep your pet indoors? . . . Microorganisms, house manners aimed at reducing infection risks . . . Miscellaneous housekeeping problems posed by pets . . . Cats that claw furniture . . . Dogs that chew furniture . . . Cleaning litter boxes and cages . . . Ticks and fleas . . . Pet odors . . . If your dog encounters a skunk or carrion . . . The cat-urine problem . . . Removing hair

A well-chosen pet can transform a home, bringing into it some of the same beneficial changes that a new human member of the household would bring. Among the emotional dividends pets provide are opportunities to give and receive affection, to be a caretaker, and, if you get a protective dog, to feel taken care of. Pets reinforce the spirit of play and whimsy. They introduce an element of the unplanned, unexpected, and unforeseen into home life, which is a large part of why pet owners so often say that their pet is good company. Part of the pleasure of any company is simply the welcome variety given by having to consider another being's point of view on life. To an observant, affectionate owner, an intelligent pet becomes a source of such amusement and interest that only with difficulty do most pet owners refrain from regaling their friends with pet stories.

The value of a pet's company is not only emotional. Some people's pets are good helpers as herders, watchdogs, observers, announcers, messengers, and hunters. Pets can bring health benefits as well. Medical studies indicate that having a pet can actually diminish depression and reduce heart rates and blood pressure. People with a pet, one study shows, had higher survival rates after heart surgery.

Pets require a good deal of care, time, and attention, and their presence occasionally increases housekeeping burdens past what some households can easily cope with. Those living in time-pressed households might consider waiting until the pressure lets up before taking on an intelligent, furry pet. Those with allergies, as well, might read the materials below before making a decision on acquiring a pet. In addition, despite the desirability of a pet as a companion, those who live alone and both work and lead an active social life might also be better off to delay having a pet. The freedom to go out with friends after work, to go away for weekends on the spur of the moment, and simply to be impulsive—whether for the short term or the long term—may be too important to give up.

Pets and Allergies

Households in which allergies are a problem might consider forswearing the pleasure of a furry or feathered pet. Allergens derived from pets, especially cats, are a common cause of allergic conditions. Moreover, in families in which there is a genetic predisposition to allergies, some evidence suggests that infants and young children who are exposed to allergens early in life are more likely later on to develop allergic sensitivities, including asthma, than those who were protected from exposure during the first years of life. Allergists report, however, that when they tell people that they are allergic to their pets and should get rid of them, only one in five does so and the vast majority of those later acquire another pet!

Allergic people who simply love their pets too much to give them up can often get a significant improvement in their symptoms by careful and informed housekeeping, in accordance with their doctor's suggestions. Even when no member of the household is actually or potentially allergic to pets, it is thoughtful to exercise a degree of care to reduce allergens in our homes for the sake of our guests and neighbors, given the astonishing (and growing) number of them who suffer from allergies. The incidence of cat allergies alone is estimated, variously, at between 2 and 15 percent of the population.

How Pets Cause Allergies. Living indoors in intimate contact with a member of another species is not something Mother Nature had in mind when she designed us. This is particularly true when the indoors in question has poor ventilation or is in a very tight, weatherized house. When people are exposed constantly to the bodies or excretions of furry or feathered creatures, they tend to develop allergic conditions such as allergic rhinitis, dermatitis, or asthma. The more they are exposed, the more allergic they tend to become. It is estimated that the average American spends twenty-three of the twenty-four hours in a day indoors, and the average pet probably does too. Whereas our grandmothers' cats prowled the barn, the fields, or the yards looking for mice, ours (like our children) stay inside and play with toys and cause more allergens to be deposited in our airtight, reduced-ventilation homes. Inevitably, therefore, we breathe in many more allergens than people used to; this is thought to be part of the explanation for the ominously increasing rates of asthma and other allergic conditions.

Cats and dogs, like people, constantly give off dander, tiny flakes of skin to which many are allergic. The more of this we are exposed to, the stronger the allergic response tends to become. Dander floats in the air and, sooner or later, settles on surfaces in the house. Pet saliva also contains allergens. When pets lick their fur, the allergens are deposited on their skin and fur. The pets lounge on your carpets or furniture, leaving allergens wherever their bodies touch. Pet allergens are also present in their urine. When, for example, mouse or cat urine dries, its allergens can become airborne and can be inhaled. If you create a dust storm when you change the cat litter or clean the hamster cage, you are spreading allergens into the air.

The major source of pet allergens is dander, not fur. Indeed, the fur itself is not allergenic; it is dander and saliva on the fur that cause the problems. For this reason, by and large it is a myth that short-haired pets cause fewer allergy problems than long-haired; the problems originate with the skin of the animal. Some allergists may admit, grudgingly, that long-haired pets that shed a great deal may simply be more efficient allergen spreaders; the fur falls out and spreads allergens from saliva and skin around your home and on your furnishings. But they insist that the differences in the allergy-provoking qualities of a long-haired and a short-haired pet are minor. That is not to say that a pet is a pet and if you're allergic you're allergic. I should think that a very tiny dog, having much less skin, spreads less dander than a very large one, and four cats produce far more allergens than one. Also, the more time your pet spends outdoors, the more of its dander and hair is left there rather than in your home.

In the case of cats, the allergenic particles are so tiny that they stay airborne for long periods. Dogs' allergens are a bit bigger and tend to settle more readily. (Dust mite allergens are even bigger and tend to go into the air only when disturbed by wind or sweeping or the like.) Thus someone who is allergic to cats may respond almost immediately to the presence of a cat at the other end of a house because the allergens float in the air and circulate (even though the heaviest concentration of them is in the immediate vicinity of the cat). But those who are allergic to dogs may react only if they go near the dog or actually pet the dog. All pet allergens are persistent, but cat allergens are especially so. Even if you gave up your cat and thoroughly cleaned your house, you would continue to have cat allergens for many months. Those who are allergic may experience tearing and sniffling or asthmatic symptoms long after the cat has departed.

Pet allergens tend to stick to surfaces, especially those of fabrics such as upholstery, rugs and carpets, clothes, and draperies, but even to walls and bare floors. After you romp with your pet, your clothes, too, will carry allergens.

Keeping the Pet Clean Helps to Reduce Allergens. When someone in the home is allergic to a pet and you do not want to give the pet up, allergists recommend frequent bathing and grooming of pets as a means of reducing the amount of allergens spread in your home. Although keeping your pet this clean requires considerable effort (especially when water-despising cats are involved), it is likely to make your home appreciably more comfortable for the allergic. There are services you can hire to groom and bathe your pet, if this is hard for you. A frequent recommendation of allergists for households dealing with pet allergies is that you thoroughly brush the pet daily and bathe it, rinsing thoroughly, *once a week*. (Quite apart from the issues of allergies, daily brushing of a cat is also good for the cat: it helps prevent hairballs.) Start bathing kittens and puppies when they are very small so they get used to it. To help prevent a dog's skin from drying out from frequent bathing, you can add a tiny amount of vegetable oil to its diet, a few drops for a small dog and up to a teaspoon for a large one. Do the brushing outdoors; if you are the allergic party in your household, have someone else do this task. There are also "wipes," or anti-allergenic liquids, intended for use on pets' skin and fur to remove dander and saliva and thus reduce the amount that gets spread in your home. A recent study shows that bathing the pet was significantly more effective than using wipes, and the more rigorous the bathing and rinsing, the better. But wipes also removed a substantial amount. (In households where there are no allergy problems, veterinarians may say that dogs need bathing only every three to six months if you brush them frequently.)

Housekeeping to Reduce Pet Allergens and Their Effects.[1] If you or someone else in the home is allergic to a pet and you are unwilling to give the pet up, specific measures can help reduce the level of allergens in the house. Such reductions can translate into greater comfort and fewer symptoms for the allergic. The major remedy, strongly recommended by all allergists, is that you *keep the pet out of the bedroom at all times,* which means, most important of all, *off the bed.* Use as little furniture in the bedroom as possible, and get rid of upholstered furniture. Wall-to-wall carpeting in the bedroom is particularly problematic. Bare floors are best, with perhaps a small bedside rug. Not only in your bedroom but throughout your home, use as little upholstered furniture and carpeting as you can. If possible, keep pets off the furniture. Get rid of stuffed toys and dust-collecting items of all sorts, especially in the bedroom, as these will also collect allergens. Keep the bedroom door closed so that pet allergens cannot waft in and pets cannot stroll in. Close off any air ducts in the bedroom so that pet allergens cannot enter through these. You might even try keeping the pet in only one or two rooms of the house. This is easy enough to accomplish with mice, guinea pigs, and hamsters but seems unkind with dogs and cats (and rather defeats the purpose of having one). Moreover, there are studies showing that although keeping pets in limited areas may reduce allergens in the closed-off rooms, it will not keep allergens out altogether. In one study, although a cat was confined to one room and the door to the room was opened only once a day, cat allergens were nonetheless found throughout the house. Still, reducing the level of allergens in the pet-free rooms can be a major help to the allergic.

If you have a pet, you need to vacuum and dust more often and more thoroughly than other people to keep hair, dander, and airborne allergen concentrations at minimal levels. Vacuuming with a low-emissions vacuum fitted with a HEPA (High Efficiency Particulate Air) filter and dusting with a slightly dampened cloth (to prevent allergen-impregnated dust from flying into the air) are extremely important. If you are the allergic one, try to have someone else do any chores that are dusty and wear an allergen-proof dust mask if you must do them yourself. "Thorough" vacuuming means vacuuming carpets, upholstery, and draperies, as all are major reservoirs of cat allergens. The levels of pet allergens in carpets may be up to one hundred times higher than for bare floors.[2] Vacuum under the furniture and in any place in which either you or the pet tends to spend a lot of time—your bedroom, your favorite reading chair, the cat's favorite cushion. One of our cats used to nest in the laser printer, leaving it coated with hair. We were constantly vacuuming the printer and the whole office. The best vacuum attachments for removing hair, by the way, are simply the proper ones for the surface: use your upholstery attachment for the furniture, the power nozzle on rugs, and so on. (See chapter 34, "Vacuuming, Sweeping, and Dusting.")

For those who have pets but no allergies, two thorough vacuumings and dustings each week are best. In households in which anyone has a serious allergic response, such as asthma, to a pet, daily vacuuming with a low-emissions vacuum cleaner and daily dusting are desirable. (Although vacuuming is known to reduce the amount of allergens significantly, it is difficult to establish that vacuuming also reduces allergic symptoms. But allergists still recommend this as a helpful step.) But since most people cannot manage daily dusting and vacuuming, the recommendation has to be to do these *frequently*—as often as you possibly can. *However often you can manage it, put the bedroom and any other room in which you spend a great deal of time at the top of your list for vacuuming and dusting.*

Air-cleaning machines with HEPA filters can trap cat and other allergens that float in the air, but if the cat is present and sending new allergens to waft around, using such a machine is, obviously, not going to solve the problem completely. Good ventilation, even just opening the windows, can help significantly. Letting the animals go outside for a part of the day—on a covered porch or in a fenced yard if the law forbids your letting them roam—means at least that the concentrations of allergens in the air of your home should be diminished. And, as one prominent allergist commented to me, we should take ourselves outside too. We should especially ensure that our children go outside for a good portion of each day.

Keep the pet's bed, box, crate, den, or cage *clean*. Launder any blankets or pillows and pillowcases that you may use for your pet with very hot, sudsy water, and rinse well with clean water. With sudsy water as hot as the skin can bear, wipe down all hard surfaces or baskets, toys, and any other objects that come in contact with your pet, and rinse thoroughly with clean water. Wash your own clothes, too, after you have played with your pet or after the pet has rubbed against you; and if your pet gets on your bed, wash the bedding—sheets, blankets, comforters and all.

If you have litter boxes, crates, or cages to clean, you know that such operations can be dusty and odorous. If it is possible, go outdoors or to a porch or garage or other well-ventilated area outside your living spaces for these chores. This is immensely helpful for keeping odors down in the home, and for keeping airborne allergens down as well. Allergic people should have someone else do such jobs, or, if there is no one to help, try wearing a dust mask (HEPA filter dust masks are sold for industrial use) or ask your allergist for advice. If you can, arrange to keep cages and cats' litter boxes in a well-ventilated room. Cats' litter boxes are best kept out of living areas, including the bathroom when this is possible (and, for other reasons, away from areas where food is prepared or eaten).

Tannic acid applied to carpets and upholstery can denature cat allergens—make them nonallergenic—but many experts feel it is not very helpful. Test first to see if it stains. Some products are said to be quite unlikely to stain if properly used.

Pets, Muck, and Germs

Pets, like people, can carry diseases and germs. Every home that houses pets needs to have housekeeping routines and manners that recognize and accommodate this fact.

If your dog or cat roams outside or goes for walks, it will sometimes, inevitably, come home with muddy feet, soaked with rain water, or otherwise damp and dirty. Keep old towels in a handy place near the door and wipe your pet down, or its feet, before letting it enter. Then keep it off upholstery and rugs until it is thoroughly dry.

People who let their pets have the run of the house and share dishes, food, and kisses with them may be subjecting themselves—and visitors to their home—to unnecessary risks. These risks may be magnified when the pet is one that goes outdoors, even if it does so on a leash.

Dogs and cats that go outdoors may come into contact with infected animals, wild or tame, with their excrement, and with dead animals. Rodents, bats, raccoons, skunks, other wild animals, and other people's pets carry diseases; sometimes, although rarely, these are dangerous diseases such as rabies or—especially in the southwestern United States—the plague. Rabies can be acquired and transmitted through pets that have not had rabies shots and have had contact with an infected wild animal. Fleas that bite an infected animal may then bite your pet and infect it with some pathogen it acquired from a rodent or skunk. Animal feces left lying on the ground may be infested with worms and pathogenic bacteria or viruses. By investigat-

SHOULD YOU KEEP PETS INDOORS?

Some cat lovers object to the use of cats as mousers, arguing that cats should be kept indoors, protected and petted, because they are pets. It is true that cats, and indeed all pets, are probably safer and live longer if they live entirely indoors. Outdoors, they have more chances of being run over, acquiring a dangerous infection, being attacked by another animal, or suffering some other deadly accident. Safer pets are not necessarily happier ones, however. Other things being equal, cats and dogs who are free to hunt and amuse themselves at will are often saner, brighter, calmer, and more content than pets that spend one hundred percent of their time inside. Even outdoor pets need human company and attention, however. City dogs that live cooped up in apartments but have lots of human company may be happier than country dogs that no one spends time with.

ing animals' holes or nests or areas in which animals have left excrement, or by actual contact with infected animals or in something they find to eat outside, pets can pick up parasites and germs. Don't forget, pets do not wear shoes and they lick their feet and their entire bodies.

Cats' indefatigable grooming has given them the reputation of being clean animals. In many respects that matter in the home, this is not really true. Their constant licking of their fur means that their saliva, which may contain germs (and certainly contains allergens), is more likely to be spread around your home. And cats, even more than dogs, tend to walk on countertops and tabletops. But you need never live with this cat habit; all cats can and should be trained to stay off surfaces used for food preparation and serving. This is especially important for a cat that goes outside. Start the training when it is a kitten. To learn how to do this training, ask your veterinarian to teach you or to recommend a good book on the subject.

Among the diseases that people can acquire from furry pets are ringworm (a fungus you can catch by touching an infected pet), intestinal and other types of worms (eggs are left on the ground in the feces of infected animals), *Campylobacter, Cryptosporidium, Toxoplasmosis* (caused by a parasite whose eggs are found in the feces of infected cats), the plague (from infected rodents, their feces or urine, or fleas that bit them), cat scratch fever, and mange (also called scabies, caused by mites that burrow under the skin). Furry pets are not usually the cause of human infection with tick-borne diseases, such as Lyme disease or Rocky Mountain spotted fever. If you are infected by a tick, that is probably because you went outside and acquired a tick yourself. Ticks on dogs and cats much prefer them as a host and are unlikely to move from a nice furry pet to you, although such a thing is possible. Tick-borne diseases include, in addition to Lyme disease and Rocky Mountain spotted fever, Colorado tick fever, Ehrlichiosis, and tularemia.

Although among pets it is the furry ones that most frequently cause problems, birds and reptiles are not problem-free. You can acquire salmonella by touching infected baby chicks, lizards, turtles, snakes, iguanas, alligators, and similar pets or by direct or indirect contact with their feces. (When the popularity of reptilian pets climbed after the movie *Jurassic Park* became a hit, so did the number of childhood cases of salmonellosis.) If you have broken skin, you might get a bacterial infection if the wound comes into contact with the water in a fish tank. Birds, especially parrots, can give people a disease called psittacosis, sometimes also referred to as parrot fever, which is caused by bacteria in the droppings, on the feathers, and in the nasal secretions of infected birds.

Such facts lie behind the house manners that people have traditionally used to govern their relation with pets:

- Wash your hands after petting, handling, and grooming the pet and before eating.
- Keep cats and other pets off counters and tables.
- Do not let pets eat off the same plates as the family, and wash pet dishes separately from the family's. Keep special water and food dishes for pets, and keep them scrupulously clean. Do not simply refill them with food day after day, but wash them in hot, sudsy water after each use.
- Do not permit pets to beg at the table or to take food from anyone's hand during a meal. Be careful that pets do not eat your baby's or toddler's food. Little ones sometimes enjoy this, but it is a bad habit for the pets and the children to get into.
- Do not feed pets raw or undercooked food. You can give them—or, indirectly, a member of the family—a food-borne illness.
- Do not let pets sleep on the beds. Be particularly careful as to children's beds and furniture.
- Do not let dogs sit on your furniture. Dogs can be trained to stay on the floor and should be provided with a soft, comfortable bed of their own.

The suggestion that one should keep Fido off the furniture (and some of my other suggestions as well) will, I fear, annoy some people. People want to be modern and relaxed, which means not paranoid about germs; they want to make their pet a member of the family. Yet treating the pet as a member of the family does not make sense when the pet cannot act like a member of the family. It is better to treat the pet as a beloved pet. If you use housekeeping methods suitable to the kind of pet you have and teach it good pet manners, you are more likely to want to have the pet live with you for its whole life, and not give it up in a panic when something goes wrong. This is in the pet's best interest, and yours too.

Miscellaneous Housekeeping Problems Posed by Pets

Cats That Claw Furniture. The most important thing you can do to prevent clawing damage to your furnishings is to keep the cat's claws trimmed. Short claws cannot do much damage. There are also training techniques that are highly successful; read a training book recommended by your veterinarian, ask your vet to teach you how to do it, or consult an animal training school. In addition, you must never let your cat be without something that it is permitted to scratch. A vet I know strongly favors a device called a "scratching pad" that is made of corrugated cardboard impregnated with catnip. Scratching posts are traditional favorites, and I have seen many a cat (alas, none of them mine) who will claw nothing else. You might also avoid buying upholstery that is particularly likely to snag a cat's claws. If you are at your wits' end and none of the foregoing measures succeeds, you can have your vet glue on "soft paws." These are little plastic covers that go over the claws and prevent the cat from doing damage. This remedy should, perhaps, be at the very bottom of your list, but it is far better than the dire alternative of declawing. You really need never feel forced to this.

Dogs That Chew Furniture. Get advice from your veterinarian or from a good trainer if your dog chews the furniture. This problem almost always has a solution in good training. Give puppies and dogs things they are permitted to chew on that they enjoy chewing on. There are dog-repelling commercial sprays that are designed to be used on the furniture where the dog chews. These are supposed to be rather ineffective; how-

favorite haunts, *every day* until the problem is cured. (Remember to throw out the vacuum bag after each vacuuming!)

Keeping your lawn well mowed, cutting back underbrush and weeds, and preventing your pets from roaming during the tick season will help keep them tick-free.

If you find yourself with fleas or ticks in the home and you do not use one of the veterinarian-prescribed anti-flea products, the standard advice is that you must treat your home, your yard, and your pet to be sure you are rid of them permanently. Washing the pet with a good pet tick-and-flea shampoo will kill fleas and ticks very effectively but will not prevent them from returning. Flea collars and other over-the-counter measures will do that. See what is available in your local pet supply store, but *be sure to read labels carefully, and choose a product that is appropriate for the type, size, and age of your pet.* For treating your house and yard, pet supply stores also sell anti-flea and anti-tick sprays and bombs. Remember, however, that measures that get rid of adult pests may not kill eggs or larvae; you might find yourself growing ever new generations of fleas unless you make repeat applications in accordance with product instructions. If you buy such pesticides and intend to apply them yourself, *carefully follow every precaution and every instruction on the label* so as to ensure both safety and effectiveness.[3] If you have a bad infestation in your home, you might try calling an environmentally responsible, health-aware pest control service, if there is one in your area.

Pet Odors. Pets have body odor and relieve themselves in cages and litter boxes, and their fur can hold odors. As a result, sometimes homes with pets—and furnishings in the home, particularly those made of textiles—smell like the pet. In the city, one common cause of pet odor in the home is *too many pets living in a small apartment.* Not only do too many animals in a small apartment unavoidably create pet odors that are unpleasant to humans, it is unfair to pets to ask them to live on top of one another. Pets, like people, need social and physical space to be healthy and happy.

In addition to not overcrowding your home with pets, you might try the following highly effective methods to keep pet odors down:

- Frequent bathing and grooming of your pet
- Frequent washing and laundering of your pet's things, especially its bedding or whatever it sleeps on
- Frequent vacuuming
- Frequent cleaning (outdoors, if possible) of cages, crates, and boxes
- Frequent changing (outdoors, if possible) of the litter box
- Keeping litter boxes, cages, crates, and boxes out of living areas and in well-ventilated areas
- Excellent ventilation
- Letting your pet spend time outdoors—on the porch, in the yard
- Preventing pets from roaming where they may encounter skunks, decaying matter, and so on
- More frequent shampooing of carpets than might otherwise be necessary and, if your pets sit on the furniture, more frequent shampooing of upholstery

Commercial products are available for reducing pet odors, including one—Febreze—that works for all types of fabrics. Febreze (available in supermarkets) works well but would be rather expensive to use on large areas of carpet or upholstery. Other commercial deodorizers have enthusiastic proponents too; just visit your local pet supply store and ask patrons and clerks for suggestions. If you find that pet odors cling to your carpets or upholstery between shampoos, you might sprinkle baking soda *amply* over the carpet or furniture, wait 15 minutes, and then vacuum it up. (Baking soda is nontoxic, but shut your pets out of the room anyway when you do this.) I have had great success with baking soda, but you have to use enough, and leave it on long enough, to make a difference. In addition, try keeping the humidity in your home lower with air conditioning or a dehumidifier, since odors are sometimes exaggerated when the air is moister. In my opinion, ordinary air fresheners are no help whatever with the problem of pet odors.

The Cat-Urine Problem. One very common and very difficult odor problem, with which I have all too much personal experience, is caused by cat urine. Once my cat wet the seat of the car when I was taking her to the vet (I do not remember how or why she got out of her pet carrier), and the acrid odor remained as long as we had the car, no matter what remedies we tried. Inside the home, the problem can be equally stubborn and very serious. You think you have gotten rid of it, only to find that it reappears every time it rains. Not only might you find yourself living for years with one of the world's most intransigent bad smells, but the consequences can be financially dire. If your cat has a few off days—say because of feeling unwell or having to get used to a new situation—and sprays your furniture or floors, you may end up having to throw some furniture out and wishing you could throw out the floors. There have been people who were unable to sell or get a decent price for a home that smelled of cat urine, and those who bought a house and discovered an expensive cat-urine problem too late.

If cat urine penetrates wood floors, you may be able to get rid of the odor by resanding and refinishing. But this is not certain, as the urine may have soaked deeply into the wood or even into the underflooring; people sometimes find out to their dismay that every time the weather turns humid or rainy, or if the area becomes wet for any reason, the smell reemerges, right through the fresh finish. When this is the case, you may have to put in new flooring and/or subflooring. If cat urine penetrates porous concrete, sometimes the only way to get rid of the smell is to take out the old concrete and put in new.

IF YOUR DOG ENCOUNTERS A SKUNK OR CARRION

Before attempting to wash your dog clear of the odor of skunk musk or of carrion, don old clothes that may be thrown away when you are finished. Use a metal tub for the bath; plastic ones may take on the unpleasant odor. Wear disposable plastic gloves, and tie something over your hair.

The time-honored method for removing skunk smell from a dog is to give it a tomato-juice bath. Professional groomers tend to scoff at this technique and recommend that you buy some commercial odor eliminator from a pet supply store or from your veterinarian. I have gone through the tomato-juice ritual myself three times, and I must admit that the end result tended to be that my dog and I both smelled like a skunk, even if my dog's smell was somewhat reduced. But for tradition's sake I include the tomato-juice recipe below, in the most effective form I am aware of. I, however, would go for one of the commercial products (used according to package instructions) recommended by my vet or pet supply store. These are supposed to be effective on any strong odor, including skunk, carrion, and excrement.

The tomato-juice remedy for skunk smell requires several large cans of undiluted tomato juice. Pour it on your dog one can at a time, and work it thoroughly into the dog's coat, concentrating on the spots that smell worst. After every square inch of the dog has been saturated with tomato juice and you have rubbed the juice in until your hands are sore, rinse thoroughly all over with tepid water. Then shampoo the dog *three times,* doing a thorough rinse with plenty of tepid water after *each* of the three shampoos.

I tell these stories to convince novices that they should *never* simply get a cat or kitten and turn it loose in their homes. The first thing to do is to read up about cats, their habits, and how to help them adapt safely to your home. Unneutered male cats will spray urine on furniture, walls, and draperies. Spraying urine is, among other things, a way for them to mark territory. Even some neutered males will try to do this, and to some extent may succeed. Products are available that imitate cat pheromones. When used in the home, they may help some cats stop or reduce spraying. If your cat sprays, you might ask your vet what he or she thinks about trying one of these. Any cat may sometimes wet outside the litter box. The reasons that a cat might do this may be medical, behavioral, or a combination of these. For example, cats in new homes (and in a variety of other situations you should know about) may wet, either in many places around the home or in one or two favorite places that the cat returns to repeatedly. If you have been unable to stop your cat's wetting outside the litter box, ask your vet for help *immediately*. The problem almost always has a good solution, whether through medical treatment or training.

Once your cat sprays or wets outside the litter box, it is very important to get rid of the odor at that place entirely. Otherwise, your pet will think of the place that retains the odor as a good place to wet again. Your best bet for success in beating the odor of cat urine is one of the commercial enzyme-cleaner, odor-fighting products carried at pet supply stores or, for fabrics, Febreze. (Note that Febreze, a product that chemically neutralizes odors, is not a cleaner, as some of the other anti-odor products are. You first clean whatever has the odor, and then apply Febreze according to the product label instructions.) Not all such enzyme cleaners are safe for all fabrics or surfaces. Read labels carefully; pick one or two that will be safe for your clothes, carpets, and furnishings, and store them at home for emergencies.

All such commercial products work only if they actually penetrate to all places that the cat urine reached. Thus when the wetting or spraying happens, *act fast* to clean it up. You may be able to prevent it from soaking deeply into the floor or the sofa. If the urine is on a carpet or sofa, do everything you can to limit its penetration and soak it all up, pressing the spot repeatedly with old towels. Put plastic immediately under the carpet so that the urine does not go through to the pad or the floor. If the accident involved only one sofa cushion, remove it immediately from the sofa so none goes on other parts. Sop up every bit with paper towels. After sopping up the urine and preventing its spread, treat the affected area thoroughly with a commercial enzyme cleaner designed for this problem. Follow the product instructions precisely! If you do not have one of these specialized products at hand, use an all-purpose cleaner for the time being. Some say that adding borax to the water may help. Or you might try washing with a solution of enzyme-containing detergent and water—but I would not be surprised if this failed to prevent lingering odors. Reclean with an enzyme cleaner as soon as you can. Do *not* clean up cat urine with ammonia or ammonia-containing products. This smells too much like cat urine to the cat, and encourages it to repeat its crime. Vinegar is another often recommended home remedy that does *not* work on cat urine.

You might also try having sofa cushions, mattresses, carpets, and similar items cleaned professionally by a company that says it can handle cat-urine problems. You may have to have the whole rug or sofa cleaned, even if there is just a small stain, to ensure uniform appearance afterward.

If your cat wets on draperies or clothes or other fabrics, press out as much as you can with paper towels. Then use a commercial enzyme cleaner safe for the fabric according to the directions on the product. Finally, launder with water as hot as is safe for the fabric (which may be only lukewarm or cool, particularly in the case of draperies, which are often prone to shrinking) and an enzyme detergent. If the fabric is chlorine bleachable, you might try chlorine bleach in the amount the manufacturer recommends, but do not add this until the enzyme product has had a chance to work, as it may inactivate the enzymes. If the fabrics are not launderable, take them to a dry cleaner that says it can handle the problem of cat urine.

After laundering fabrics, if an odor still remains, try Febreze or another commercial product for removing odors from fabrics.

Removing Hair. Vacuuming is the best way to get rid of pet hair on floors, carpets, and upholstery. Use whatever attachment is best for the type of surface—wood, carpeting, draperies, upholstery—that you are vacuuming. There are also widgets that can be useful in removing pet hair, however, especially in awkward places and small places that do not seem worth pulling out the vacuum for. These include special pet-hair squeegees, tape rollers, and dry sponges. The tape rollers are especially good for hair on clothes. I find that ordinary clothes brushes and upholstery brushes work less well than any of the foregoing devices.

SLEEP

56

The Cave of Nakedness

The culture of the bedroom . . . Function and decor . . . Furnishings for the bedroom . . . The bed-sitting-room . . . The one-room or small apartment . . . Bedroom privacy, family beds, children . . . Taking care of the bedroom . . . Light and noise . . . Humidity and temperature . . . Clean air . . . Cleaning and laundering routines for the bedroom . . . Daily, weekly, and less frequent types of care for the bedroom . . . Why you wash your underbedding and pillows . . . How often to change the sheets . . . Pests . . . Miscellaneous bed manners . . . Dressing and making the bed . . . Bedclothes . . . How to make the bed . . . Variations . . . Dust ruffles . . . Turning down the bed at night . . . Housecraftly helps for insomnia

. . . Bed-sitting-rooms
soon drive us crazy, a dormitory even sooner
turns us to brutes: bona fide architects know
that doors are not emphatic enough, and interpose,
as a march between two realms, so alien, so disjunct,
the no-man's-land of a stair. The switch from personage,
with a state number, a first and family name
to the naked Adam or Eve, and vice versa,
should not be off-hand or abrupt: a stair retards it
to a solemn procession.

—W. H. Auden, "The Cave of Nakedness"

The bedroom is for sleeping, lovemaking, dressing, and undressing. Not so long ago, it also held the chamber pot. Thus it is a room reserved for all acts that are, or may be, done naked. Because it is made for nakedness, often the bedroom is also the most surprising room in a home. When you visit a hard-bitten lawyer and find a cool, sparsely furnished modern living room and an icy steel and granite kitchen, this is as expected. But it is startling, when you open the door to his bedroom, to find yourself in colonial New England or a sultan's harem or a boudoir on a 1930s movie set. There is a similar lack of congruity between people's public dress and their underwear. It is only natural that the parts of the home (and dress) that have only private and no public or social functions are those that are least censored and most fanciful.

The bedroom is the site of what psychoanalysts call "regression," a normal falling away of the more rational and controlled parts of our personalities, which is necessary to permit both falling asleep and the eruption of sexual feelings. You can call this relaxing if you like, but that is a term I would reserve for playing gin rummy or watching television until stuporous. In your bedroom, not only do you cast off your social security number and your tie or your panty hose, you go to sleep and cast off the part of your mind that grasps the difference between past and present, here and there, real and fanciful. You lose your reasonable, reality-based self in sexual passion too. This makes you feel vulnerable. The bedroom must feel securely private and diminish anxiety; otherwise you will never let yourself be so unguarded as to enjoy being undressed, being sensual, and falling into deep, free dreams.

The Culture of the Bedroom

Function and Decor. Paradoxically, the fact that the bedroom is the place we usually go to express sexual passion does not necessarily mean that the most explicitly sybaritic or sexual style of bedroom decor is the most "functional." Although some people may want to be surrounded by erotic art, the majority tend to find that everything that is supposed to happen in a bedroom happens best if the bedroom simply feels very comfortable and homey. A comfy, homey sort of atmosphere inspires a deeper kind of letting go. It is safe and familiar, so you can permit yourself to fall into sleep, love, or whatever.

The kinds of letting go that you seek in your bedroom are likely to come most easily in a room that feels to *you* homey and comfortable, however it looks or feels to anyone else. The bedroom has to provide encouragement to remove not just your clothes (that's easy) but your social and emotional masks as well. It is one place where you must express your authentic feelings—instead of making a fashion statement—for it to work properly.

The bedroom is where people tend to keep their memorabilia, diaries, precious photographs, and treasures and tokens of loyalty and affection, from love letters to school banners and trophies, displayed or tucked away in drawers and trunks. Bedrooms, or dressing rooms attached to bedrooms, are also where we doff, don, and store our clothes—our second skins—and our jewelry, cufflinks, tie pins, and other adornments. The storage function of the bedroom—the clothes, the cache of photographs, ticket stubs, and old letters—serves the adult in much the same way as an old teddy does the child. These things are wanted in the privacy and denudement of the bedroom because they symbolize the real, historical, and social part of life that one is temporarily giving up; they reassure us that the outside world is still there and that we will resume our place in it tomorrow.

Furnishings for the Bedroom. There is periodically a wave of enthusiasm for putting a great number of pillows and throws on the bed, a decorating trend beloved of merchandisers who wish you to buy much more bedding than you could possibly need. Even if you use lots of throws and pillows just for looks and remove them for sleeping, they are traps for dust and soil and take quite a bit of care—laundering, vacuuming, or dry cleaning. If you leave them on the bed while you sleep, in fact, it's best to launder all of them on the same schedule as your regular bedding. This is make-work that the time-pressed household does not need.

Having all these things on the bed, in any case, does not promote comfort or health. Doctors and grandmothers recommend, for almost everyone, one well-chosen pillow for sleeping. Sleeping with many small or silky throws or wraps can drive you crazy. They slip off your body repeatedly, leave your feet bare, wad up into hard balls, and cannot be anchored. Even if you like them and are skilled in keeping yourself comfortable with them, it is possible that your guests will feel different.

A simple set of furnishings is all that it takes to make a good bedroom. The essential items in a bedroom are the bed, a dresser, a mirror, and a chair. A night stand is convenient for holding a reading lamp, a glass of water, eyeglasses, a book or magazine, or whatever else you may need before sleeping or during the night or when illness forces you to stay in bed. A bit of rug or carpet to rest your feet on when getting in and out of bed is desirable. (More carpeting than this, especially wall-to-wall carpeting, is really not the best choice for health, as it vastly increases the level of dust and allergens in the air you breathe while sleeping—an effect that is even worse if you have pets. The same holds for upholstered furniture and voluminous draperies. See pages 658–60, below, on the importance of good air in the bedroom.) A little sink and a vanity that you can sit at, with drawers and a little mirror, are often welcome and fit for the bedroom or dressing room.

The Bed-Sitting-Room. Despite the poet's insistence that bed-sitting-rooms will soon drive us crazy, there is at present a growing, long-term trend toward more elaborate multifunctional bedrooms. There are those who wish to eat breakfast or other meals in their bedrooms, who therefore add a table and chairs. Some people have large television sets and stereos. Most have radios and telephones. Everyone has an alarm clock. Many have not just a small chair for sitting on while tying shoes but an upholstered, overstuffed reading chair. There are many bedrooms with sofas, bookshelves, desks, and computers. Many people work on their laptop computers in bed. Some people have told me that their entire life at home is spent, essentially, in bed, where they talk on the telephone, read, watch television, eat, and generally recuperate from their stressful working lives.

The impulse to turn a bedroom, or even a bed, into a home in itself bears some examining. Doctors who treat sleep problems tell insomniacs that this is the wrong way to go. (See "Housecraftly Helps for Insomnia" below.) The further you go in the direction of dedifferentiating the bedroom's functions—the more you make the bedroom part of your public life and add to its simple basic functions—the more you take away its ability to encourage the things that are supposed to go on there. I suspect that people are so anxious to experience the feelings that they associate with being in their bedrooms that they try to move more and more of their home lives into the bedroom even though, ironically, this tends to destroy the bedroomlike feeling they are striving for. Often they are so rattled and stress-ridden when they get home from work that they beat an instant retreat to the closest thing to a womb they can find. (I know because I have done it myself so many times.) Others have made homes in which only the bedroom is set up to feel comfortable and warm.

In my experience, a clock radio and a small television that is used occasionally for the late news (or, rarely, for a late movie) do not much get in the way of a bedroom's feeling like a bedroom. I wish I had room for a small table for sitting at to write a note, examine photographs, take stock of my hosiery, sew on a button, examine the catches on bracelets, paint my nails, or have a cup of coffee. But I myself would draw the line at including a sofa, easy chair, stereo system, or computer in the room. Breakfast in bed or at your little tea table is a civilized and enjoyable way to come to on a weekend morning, but lunch and dinner belong to the wide-awake, sociable world. Nor is the bedroom a place for business calls, working, listening to music, and the other chores and pleasures of the waking day. This is a personal line, of course, and everyone must draw his or her own.

The One-Room or Small Apartment. As to the poem's idea that the separation of the bedrooms from the other rooms is so important that it is best to emphasize it with stairs, some people have argued with me about this on the grounds that it is all culturally relative. "The Japanese," they point out, "sleep on futons in the living room with their children, and manage quite well. People who live in studio apartments with only one room do too." But it is also true that the Japanese, when offered room enough to have private bedrooms, gladly do so. And other Japanese go to "love hotels" for marital sex, or sneak out to the car to have a private talk for a couple of minutes. I know few people who prefer studio apartments to those with a bedroom and other rooms too. I speak from experience, having lived in one for several years.

If you, like me, have no stairs or perhaps not even a walled-off space for a bedroom, you can still create the ambience of a bedroom as long as you are clear that this is what you are trying to do. You have to strive to get the eye to separate the bedroom part of the space from the rest; and you have to be careful to set up the studio apartment so that the bedroom corner, alcove, or section is not walked through as you are cooking or going about your household tasks. You can do this by using a separate rug for that area, arranging furniture to create a visual break, using different colors or light levels, and so forth. Or you might put a Japanese screen or curtain in front of the bed or bedroom area, or stand bookshelves at the foot of the bed or wherever they can best serve as a kind of wall.

If you wish, you can have a daybed or convertible that doubles as a sofa in waking hours, or a Murphy bed that folds up into the wall, or a futon that gets put away in the daytime. I tried the sofa-bed option for a while but finally gave up on it because it kept me from arranging my beloved objects, clothes, jewelry, and mirror in a single area, and it did not give a sense of privacy and separation from waking life.

If your apartment or house is small and you must use each room for several functions, you can still make distinctions. If you work at home, for example, you might set up your desk or work space in a corner of the dining room or living room, even if this diminishes the looks of your public rooms. A desk in the bedroom might remind you too much of work, or tempt you to get up and finish one last little chore when you should be unwinding and falling asleep. It is safest to combine only quiet, relaxing uses, such as reading and listening to music, with the central bedroom uses.

Bedroom Privacy; Family Beds; Children. The contemporary bedroom is a very private place, and most of us—not all—like it this way. We keep out not only guests but our own children too, whereas in other parts of the world, people still often sleep in the same room or even the same bed with their children. Indeed, Western parents have been criticized for insisting that tiny babies learn to sleep all by themselves, alone, in the dark.

This is viewed as unnatural, even cruel; and once you have witnessed firsthand an average infant's desperate protests over this treatment, you cannot avoid finding a great deal of wisdom in this attitude. Such ideas have inspired a new, and increasingly popular, family custom of all sleeping together in a "family bed"—defying still another idea in the poem quoted at the outset of this chapter: that a dormitory makes a bad bedroom.

Despite my strong sympathy with the underlying motives, I doubt that many of us Westerners can make a success of a family bed. Not only does it promote a loss of sleep, but it seriously interferes with your sex life. (Many a patient has told many a psychiatrist what they observed when they were supposedly sleeping or were "too young to understand.") Children are hard to sleep with. They snore, toss and turn violently, and mumble. The more people in a bed, the less well anyone sleeps, as the presence of more people multiplies the possibilities of bad feelings toward at least one of them, incidents of others' bad dreams, trips to the bathroom, flailing, crawling over each other to get out, coming and going to bed at different hours, and so forth. If you have a family bed, therefore, I hope you own a very big one, have a thick skin, and are a sound sleeper.

Family beds, as those experienced with them have told me, also eventually pose complicated negotiating problems. What do you do when the children can't sleep without you and you don't want to go to sleep at eight or nine o'clock? Some will remonstrate, saying that human beings have slept grouped together in most of the world from the dawn of history. To them I reply that people from the dawn of history probably experienced much broken sleep. And at the dawn of history and for thousands of years thereafter, there were no alarm clocks, no jobs or rigid working hours, and no school bells; and naps (or perhaps two or three of them) were probably a regular thing. Unless you feel able to guarantee your child a relaxed adult life in a preliterate society on an island where fruit falls to the hand, the fish jump into the nets, and people sleep when the impulse hits them, it is probably best to give children their own rooms when they are quite young and to insist on your right to the privacy of your room. If you do not share a bed with the children, you can give them a great deal of comfort and security with the familiar childhood bedtime rituals: rocking, stories, singing, night-lights, repeated reassurances and explanations, and patience and sympathy with a child's fears.

Just as we adults want the privacy of our own bedroom, so we should respect our children's right to bedroom privacy—a right they begin to assert vigorously as soon as they experience the first, heady taste of school-age independence. We, too, should knock before entering when the door is shut, just as we expect them to knock before entering ours.

Taking Care of the Bedroom

Light and Noise. Children like night-lights in their rooms, but most adults sleep better in darkness, and should pick blackout blinds and curtains for the bedroom. But some people, like an uncle of mine who went to bed and got up early, need to see the sky. My uncle always left the windows uncovered and arranged the bedroom so that he could observe the moon or find constellations and watch the sun rise. He planted highly fragrant flowers under the window—tuberoses, honeysuckle, and Asiatic lilies—so that he could breathe sweet-scented night air.

Most people sleep best in silence, and should keep their door hinges oiled and their faucets dripless. If you live on a noisy street or highway, choose noise-insulating windows and do not overlook the noise-insulating effects of your various window coverings. Thick drapes, curtains, and shades absorb more sound. (Books are superb sound absorbers, but most people do not care for bookshelves in the bedroom.) Some people swear by white-noise generators that mask intrusive sounds, but they keep my husband and me awake. Others like the steady whir of a fan or air conditioner to mask noises. I have friends who have rearranged their homes to place their bedrooms away from the noisy side of the house. Then there are those like my son, born and raised in the city, who find street noises comforting and fear the dark, silent nights in the country.

If the bedroom in your new home has street noise even after all your efforts at muting it, do not despair; most people simply cease to hear familiar, regular noises after a while. My husband describes how, when he was a boy, his family moved into an urban apartment they had always wanted, on a high floor with a lovely view of the river, only to discover what they had never noticed when considering taking the place: there was a constant roar of traffic in the bedrooms. This seemed to them a catastrophe on the first night, and no one slept. But after three days, they no longer heard the noise. Many urban dwellers make such adjustments, causing their country cousins when they visit to wonder how they live with the racket. I suspect that noise you do not "hear" nonetheless takes its toll on nerves and health, at some level. Still, I know from experience that you will find peace and be able to sleep soundly again.

Snoring can be an immense noise problem for the mate of the snorer, and it is often a health problem for the snorers themselves, being associated with inadequate rest, sleep apnea, and other conditions. Snoring often yields to medical intervention. Habitual snorers, therefore, should consult their doctors or a sleep specialist. In the meantime, the mates of snorers can try earplugs; comfortable, effective ones are available in drugstores. You can also gently turn the face of the snorer until the snoring stops. It will soon start up again, but the temporary cessation gives you a window of opportunity for falling asleep. For particularly bad nights, keep another bed made up and ready to receive you so that you do not have to face doing this at 3:00 A.M.

In some cases there are legal remedies for outside noise that invades the peace and quiet of your home. (See chapter 66, "Privacy.")

Humidity and Temperature. Ordinarily, the best relative humidity level for comfort and health is between 40 and 50 percent. Dehumidifiers, humidifiers, or hygrometers may help. (See chapter 29, "The Air in Your Castle.")

The best temperatures for sleeping deeply and soundly are cool: between 55°F and 68°F. The occasional insomniac tends to find that cooling the bedroom works like a magic sleeping pill. Bedrooms for the very young, very old, and ill should generally be kept at the top of this range or, in some cases, even warmer; always get a doctor's advice as to such specially vulnerable people. Choose bedclothes to fit your circumstances, warm or cool, light or heavy. If your home is cooler than 60°F at night, you will toss and turn and sleep poorly unless you choose effective covering of a comfortable weight.

Clean Air. Here is a high priority: the bedroom should have good, clean air. You probably spend more time in your bedroom than in any other room of your home. At least a third of your life is spent in your bed. For this reason, you need to be more careful about all the basics of housekeeping here, especially in children's bedrooms. Children, who may spend up to nine-tenths of their time indoors, spend the bulk of that time in their bedrooms, playing and sleeping the long hours of childhood sleep. Most asthma attacks occur in the night. (It is hypothesized that this is because of allergens in the bedding and bedroom.) Dust, poor ventilation, airborne microbial contamination, mold—all of these cause more injury to health in the bedroom than in the living room because you are exposed to them for so long during your sleeping hours. A failure to clean, vacuum, dust, or wash bedding frequently and properly will result in increased bedroom air pollution.

Dust-mite allergens are found in many places in the bedroom: on carpets, draperies, upholstered furniture, and floors as well as on bedding—pillows, mattresses, sheets, blankets, and comforters. See chapter 33, "Dust and Dust Mites." To reduce dust and dust-mite allergens, consider reducing dust-holding furnishings such as carpets and upholstered chairs in the bedroom. It is the bedding that is most likely to throw up allergens that you will breathe in heavily during the night. For effective laundering methods for killing mites and removing allergens, refer to chapter 27. Use only highly launderable bedclothes, and encase mattresses and pillows in allergen-proof covers. See page 664.

To maintain good air, the job that is the simplest—ventilating—is also one of the most effective things you can do. Open the bedroom windows wide as often as you can to reduce the concentration of dust and all other air pollutants in your bedroom, animate and inanimate. When you are making the bed, try not to fling the bedclothes around more than necessary, as doing so will create a dust storm. If you can stand outside (upwind) and shake the pillow or blanket, you may wish to do so. This was a standard part of the weekly housekeeping ritual in my childhood home. My mother and grandmothers would also lay the blankets on the upstairs porch railing to air when the weather was good, and as you walked down the streets in town in the morning you would see women in their backyards hanging their blankets for airing on the clothesline. This was beneficial. Sunlight, a prominent allergist tells me, kills dust mites, and airing and sunning furnishings and all bedding is a good idea. It also kills microorganisms and keeps things smelling fresh. Three to four hours sunning and airing is effective; or just leave things all day, as people used to do. Remember, however, that this will not by itself remove allergens left by mites, including bits of deceased mites. Laundering is the answer to this.

You should also air the bed and the bedroom simply to freshen them after your long use. On this subject, my Italian and Anglo-American grandmothers exhibited different attitudes. The Italian relatives were outspoken in defense of long airing, insisting on hours of this and putting little stock in making the bed. The Anglo-Saxon attitude combined a suspicion of drafts and a horror of unmade, rumpled beds and beds without taut hospital corners. To the Northern European relatives, such a bed was a symbol of degeneracy and immorality; it suggested not only that you were too lazy to make the bed properly, but that you intended to get back in and be slothful—or worse. Actually, both sides of the family were right; the bed should be aired, along with the room, but then it should be made up. Each morning, pull the bedcovers down and leave them down for an hour or more to freshen and dry the bed, then make the bed neatly.

All the ordinary air pollutants of the home should be banished from the bedroom. Do not smoke in the bedroom or the bed. Hairspray, perfumes, and all strongly odorous substances should be used and stored outside the bedrooms of the allergy-prone and the cautious. Watch out for the off-gassing of new synthetic carpeting, drapes, and certain furniture, and for fumes in rooms that have been recently painted or polyurethaned. (Perhaps you could sleep in another room until your bedroom has thoroughly aired.) Do not hang dry cleaning in the bedroom closet until it is free of all dry-cleaning fluid odors. This sometimes mean you must hang it elsewhere for airing for a couple of days, although a good dry cleaner will send it home to you odor-free. If you have

WHY YOU SHOULD AIR THE BED AND BEDROOM

While you are sleeping, you breathe about two pounds of moisture, along with breath odors and flocks of microorganisms, into the air, your pillow, and your bedding. You also perspire, perhaps a cup's worth, and exude skin oils and body smells. And you use up the room's oxygen and replace it with exhaled carbon dioxide. When there are two or more people in the bed or the room, these effects are multiplied. All this explains why, if you sleep with closed windows, the room has a characteristic stale morning smell (although you might not perceive it until you leave for a few minutes and then return). Unless you leave the bedcovers pulled down and the windows open for an hour or two, the moisture you have left in the bed either does not evaporate or evaporates very slowly, which makes for an environment in pillows and mattress in which dust mites, molds, and other microbial life have more of an opportunity to multiply. Opening the windows lets in new air to dilute the pollutants (microbial and particulate), carry them off, and bring in fresh supplies of oxygen.

pets, keep them out and keep the door to the bedroom closed.

Cleaning and Laundering Routines for the Bedroom. You will often read and hear half-jesting advice to the effect that you should spend your housecleaning time on only those areas of your home that people are going to see when they come to visit. This is bad advice and a bad joke. Keeping dust down in the bedroom does more to promote health and comfort than any other cleaning in your home (with the exception of the kitchen). Your health and comfort, and that of your children, counts far more than what anyone is going to see.

Daily Care of the Bedroom

Each day when you arise, air the bed. Open the windows, if possible; throw the bedcovers back over the foot of the bed. (If the bedding will otherwise drag on the floor, stand a chair at the foot of the bed to support it.) Let the bed stand this way, unmade, while you shower and eat breakfast. The bed should air for at least an hour if you are going to work, or even longer if you are staying home. This helps immensely toward keeping the bed feeling and smelling fresh until you next change the sheets.

Make the bed every day after airing is finished. Plump up down- or feather-filled pillows by punching them back to front and end to end. Smooth sheets and blankets and put them back in their made-up positions, as described below.

Then make sure no clothes are strewn about the room. Hang your nightgown or pajamas and robe for airing, preferably near an open window. Hang up and place in the closet any clothes that belong there. Be sure any dirty laundry has been placed in a laundry hamper. Tidy up as necessary: pick up newspapers, close bottles, carry out cups, and so forth. With a tissue, wipe away any obvious dust or crumbs.

Open blinds and drapery so that the sun will shine in all day. If it is possible, leave the window open all day too.

Weekly Care of the Bedroom

Each week, try to have one major cleaning and one minor cleaning of every bedroom in your home. A twice-weekly dusting and vacuuming is more important for the bedrooms than for any other rooms in your home, and it should ordinarily be a more thorough dusting than in your other rooms, taking in, for example, draperies, shades, and blinds. Vacuum mattresses and pillows too.

Weekly, or more often, change and launder sheets and pillowcases. Change pillowcases twice a week if you wish, as pillowcases grow soiled faster than sheets. Change crib sheets daily or more often if they become wet or soiled.

If you use no top sheet, it is probably best to wash whatever bedding is next to your skin on the same schedule that you follow for sheets.

Less Frequent Types of Care for the Bedroom

Launder pillow covers (the zip-up ones under the pillow cases), mattress covers and pads, blankets, and comforter covers once a month or more often (once a week, or as frequently as the doctor orders, for asthmatics or other allergy sufferers).

Once or twice a year or more often if they become soiled, launder and change the allergen-proof undercovers, if any, on the mattress and on the pillows. (See "Bedclothes: Making the Bed," below.)

Assuming that allergens are not a problem (you have no allergies or you use allergen-proof undercovers), you need to wash pillows and comforters when they smell stale or unpleasant, when they look dirty, or when you have reason to know that they are not clean—typically about once a year or even less often. If you use allergen-proof undercovers and are careful about laundering all their covers and cases, laundering so as to remove dust mite allergens is never necessary.[1]

Turn the mattress and flip it over from time to time. (See page 685.) Traditionally, mattresses were aired and sunned twice a year, in spring and fall. Since this kills mites and discourages molds and funguses, it was and is good housekeeping. Pillows need to be aired and sunned more often. Urban dwellers can try to make up for the impossibility of sunning and airing bedding by careful use and laundering of mattress and pillow undercovers and by diligent vacuuming of pillows, mattress pads, and mattresses.

If you dress the bed properly, you should never need to wash the ticking on your mattress. But if it is soiled by a spill or accident, you would clean it as you would any upholstery. The main thing is not to soak it and to be *extremely careful not to get the interior wet;* otherwise you might get molding or rotting inside.

If you have throw rugs or small carpets in your bedroom, take them out for sunning and airing now and then if that is possible.

Pets. We are better off keeping pets out of bedrooms, especially children's rooms. (See chapter 55, "Pets.")

Pests. Because you spend so many hours in bed, you deposit perspiration, skin, oil, and other bodily products that can attract

WHY YOU WASH YOUR UNDERBEDDING AND PILLOWS

Sheets help keep mattress pads and covers and blankets clean, but the protection is not absolute. The oils and perspiration to some extent get through the sheets; the mattress cover or pad and blanket eventually get soiled, and over the years so does the mattress. The more frequently you wash the sheets, the better your chance of keeping the next layer clean, and the more often you wash that layer, the longer the mattress remains clean.

Pillows get even dirtier than other parts of the bed and bedding. Your eyes tear on the case; your mouth drools on it; your face, which is sweatier and oilier than the rest of you, rubs against it; your hair, which is often dirtier than your face, also rubs against it. And since your nose is pushed into the pillow all night long, you have to make sure you wash your pillow when it is soiled and wash its cases and covers frequently.

HOW OFTEN TO CHANGE THE SHEETS

Long tradition dictates changing sheets and laundering them once a week. This should be considered a minimum. If you or your mate perspires heavily or if ill health causes you to spend extra time in bed, twice a week or more often makes better sense. When you are spending all day in bed recuperating, you will be more comfortable if you change the sheets daily. Likewise, if you make extra use of your bed for any reason—you like to work there on your laptop, you read or watch television there, or you snack there—you may need to change the sheets more often than once a week.

and support pests there. Your own inert presence in the dark, moreover, can be the feast. Nothing chases sleep away like one pesky mosquito buzzing at your ear. Window screens are essential. Each spring check them over for holes. If you find a hole in a screen in use, cover the hole with tape until you repair it or replace the screen. For a quick repair with thread and needle, use heavy-duty polyester thread; it will not rot and it will last a long time.

Cockroaches in the bedroom, especially in an infant's or child's bedroom, should be dealt with *immediately*. Although their presence certainly does not mean that you committed any housekeeping sin, cockroaches spew allergens about just as dust mites do, and they carry disease. (See chapter 33.) Cockroaches are less commonly a problem in bedrooms because conditions there are not so favorable to them as to mites, but bedroom infestations can develop. To help avoid this, keep food out of the bedroom and keep the bedroom dry. Once roaches are established, however, these measures will not cause them to go away, and I would then call a *health- and environment-conscious* exterminator. Such exterminators, unfortunately, do not exist in many communities. Ask your neighbors, check your yellow pages for advertisements that stress these themes, contact your state pest-control association for recommendations (make your wishes clear), or check the blue pages of your telephone book for the number of the state agency that licenses pest-control operators in your state. This agency should be able to help you find such a pest-control operator if one exists in your state. If there is none in yours, boric acid powder in an adult's room is quite effective, but you should keep it out of children's rooms and away from children or pets even though it is less toxic than regular commercial pesticides. *Follow all cautions on the label.* If this does not work, call in a regular exterminator and sleep out of the bedroom for several days after the treatment, while leaving the windows wide open.

Cleaning is extra-important if you have or have had roaches because, as with mites, dead roaches and droppings continue to contaminate your rooms with allergens. Vacuuming, damp-dusting, ventilating, and all the rest of the cleaning routine must be vigorous to get rid of their traces.

You no longer hear much about bedbugs in this country, but they were once a ghastly, intractable problem that might arise in any household, no matter how fastidious. Mamie Eisenhower, when a young bride, fought bedbugs by setting the legs of the bed in pans of kerosene. In the old days people would paint the bedstead white and use all-white bedding so that these bugs (or lice or other undesirable bed companions) could be seen more easily and destroyed more effectively. Extermination involved using chemicals in the bedroom and on furniture and vigorous laundering of bedding—which would have included actual boiling of the sheets, along with all "body linen."

No one can live with bedbugs, which are not only extremely unpleasant but can pass on diseases. The victim may feel the bites and find tiny spots of blood on the sheets before seeing a bug. The bedbug is one-quarter to three-eighths of an inch long, very thin or flat, oval shaped, and dark brown, unless it is engorged, in which case it becomes thickened and elongated and turns dull red. It bites, leaving an extremely irritating fluid on the skin that causes swelling and itching. There is a characteristic bad smell in a room infested with bedbugs. There are various kinds, with slight variations in their appearance. One fairly common type is brought into the home on bats that get into attics or come down chimneys. Bedbugs are often spread on used furniture or mattresses.

Bedbugs occasionally still crop up even in clean homes. I have heard of one case that spread from room to room in a college dormitory, and I can imagine a student innocently transporting them home from there. Be cautious about used furniture, especially used mattresses. If you suspect you have bedbugs, call that environmentally alert exterminator again and check your attic for bats. The bugs can get into cracks and crevices in walls and floors, the frame of your bed, your mattress or box spring, and even such unlikely places as picture frames and stuffed animals. The exterminators generally treat all hard surfaces. You may be advised to treat the mattress yourself with recommended substances, but I think a new mattress would be the way to go. If you are in doubt or need help, call your local cooperative extension service. Washing all bedding in the hottest water, with strong detergent, should be effective to kill any bugs or eggs left on them.

Miscellaneous Bed Manners. For both physical and psychological reasons, a bed treated with respect will be fresher and will more readily induce sleep. Old-fashioned bed manners forbade sitting on a bed in street clothes, especially someone else's bed and most especially a sick person's bed. If you lie down on a made-up bed for your afternoon nap, cover the bedspread with something you can readily launder. Otherwise, wash your face, undress, and crawl between the sheets. Don't put bags, purses, briefcases, shoes, and similar things on the bed; they have been on too many floors, sidewalks, and other questionable places.

Dressing and Making the Bed

A friend of mine remembers being counseled by her elderly aunt long ago that even if she found herself in poverty or sickness she should always make a good bed for herself. Not only is this advice as good today as it was then, the bed that was good then is still good today, too, since people discovered the secrets of good bed-making many centuries ago.

The minimum well-dressed contemporary bed has a mattress for softness (and box springs or some other undermattress to make the bed less hard), which is encased in a cover for cleanliness and comfort. The sleeper lies on a sheet, which serves the dual function of protecting the skin from the scratchiness of the mattress or mattress cover and preventing the deposit of skin oils and perspiration on the mattress. There is also a sheet above the sleeper, and this, too, serves a double function, protecting the skin from the scratchy blanket and protecting the blanket from the skin oils and perspiration of the skin. The sleeper's head rests on a pillow covered in a case, which does the same two jobs as the sheets. On top of the sheets there is a blanket or two—or a quilt or comforter—to keep the sleeper warm. During the day, when no one is sleeping, a decorative cloth covers the whole arrangement, keeping it clean and making it look beautiful while not in use. All this was also true of the bed of any person of means in twelfth-century France. Museums have Renaissance paintings of beds made up just like yours.

Bedclothes; Making the Bed. To dress a modern bed, you need the following items:

- Undercovers for mattresses and pillows
  - Allergen-impermeable undercovers for mattresses, pillows, and duvets or comforters (optional)
  - Mattress pad
  - Pillow cover (zip-up type that goes under the pillowcase)
- Skin-contact linens
  - Bottom sheet
  - Top sheet
  - Pillowcase
- Warmth-providing covers
  - Blankets, quilts, or comforter or duvet
- Day cover for dust
  - Blanket cover, coverlet, or bedspread (counterpane)

You may wish to enclose your pillows, comforters, and mattresses in allergen-impermeable undercovers. These are made of fabrics coated with a polymer membrane that is permeable only to water vapor and heat and prevents dust mites, allergens, and other fine particles from passing through. Such undercovers are indispensable for the bed of anyone who suffers from asthma or other allergies and on the beds of all children as a preventive measure.

Next, on the beds of children still of an age to wet the bed and those of the incontinent or ill, place a rubberized cotton waterproof sheet or some other type of waterproof shield. This prevents the mattress from getting soaked. (If the mattress does become soaked, you can never really get it clean again. You can try the upholstery shampooing machine that injects and then extracts moisture, but this may not be entirely successful.) The all-plastic waterproof shields are less comfortable than the rubberized cotton.

Over the waterproof sheet, or, if there is none, directly on top of the allergenic undercover, or, if there is none, directly on the mattress, you place a mattress cover, a mattress pad plus a cover, or a padded mattress cover. This is to keep the mattress clean and places an additional layer of absorbent, skin-friendly material between you and the mattress, which is likely to be made of a less comfortable synthetic fiber. All-cotton mattress pads with cotton stuffing are sometimes hard to find, but they are preferable. You may think that only the princess in the fairy tale could detect through her sheet whether the mattress pad, or its stuffing, was made of polyester. It is true that many people cannot, or don't mind even if they can. But do not conclude that you cannot unless you give it an all-night test. What feels comfortable for a minute or two might not after a few hours.

On each pillow, place a zippered muslin cover directly next to the ticking if you are not using an allergenic undercover, or over the allergenic undercover if you are using one. (Yes, this means two undercovers and you haven't even gotten to the pillowcase yet.) Place the zipper of the muslin cover at the opposite end from the zipper of the allergenic undercover. Then pull on the pillowcase over the muslin cover, placing the open or buttoning end of the case opposite the zippered end of the muslin cover. This helps keep the pillow and its contents clean longer.

Then, in the manner described below, put on the bottom sheet, the top sheet, a blanket or comforter or other warm cover, and finally the bedspread (also called a counterpane), quilt, or other day cover. Tuck in all sheets and blankets snugly and smoothly. Wrinkles and folds are uncomfortable to sleep on and look unsightly. Use sheets with a generous allowance for tucking to anchor them securely so they do not pull out when you are sleeping; this helps you sleep better and saves you labor making up the bed when you get up. (For recommended tucking allowances and information on sheet sizes, see chapter 57, "Beds and Bedding.")

How to Make the Bed

Fitted bottom sheet. Lay the sheet right side up. For a fitted sheet the only trick is to use enough muscle power. Walk from one corner of the bed to the next, pulling the elasticized corner of the sheet over the corner of the mattress. If the sheet has shrunk, try doing diagonally opposite corners first, as this will hold the sheet in place better while you struggle with the other two. Let the weight of the mattress work for you to stretch the sheet by lifting the mattress corner enough to get the sheet corner on, then letting go. Be sure to purchase preshrunk fitted sheets; if you have deep mattresses, buy sheets that have "deep pockets" or "universal" or "high-contour" corners.

Flat bottom sheet. A flat bottom sheet is tucked under with mitered or "hospital" corners on all four corners. (See instructions for mitered corners below.) The selvages on the long sides of the sheet go along the sides of the bed, the wider hem goes at the head of the bed, and the narrower hem goes at the bottom. (Because sheets wear more at the top of the bed, my Italian grandmother sometimes put the sheets on with the foot at the head and vice versa, for more even wear.)

Top sheet. Assuming that you have folded the top sheet according to the directions in chapter 24, "Folding Clothes and Linens," you now unfold the folds parallel to the selvage ends and lay the sheet, with the crosswise folds still folded, across the width of the bed, in its center. Then grasp the two loose corners of the hem nearest you and give the sheet a flick; it will unfurl, with the wide hem at the top and the narrow hem at the bottom. If the sheet is a print, it should be placed wrong side up so that when the top hem is folded down over the blanket, the print shows its right side. Fold under and miter the two corners at the foot of the bed.

Mitered or "hospital" corners. A properly mitered sheet corner will both look neater and stay securely tucked while you sleep, keeping you comfortable and making the job of making the bed the next day much easier. First, tuck in the bottom edge of the sheet. Then pick up the corner of the sheet (the place on the side edge of the sheet directly opposite the top corner of the mattress) between the thumb and forefinger of one hand, and bring the corner around to the side of the bed. Put the side of the sheet up on the bed, out of your way, for a moment. Tuck in the part of the sheet that is left hanging down while you hold the corner taut at the side of the bed. Let the corner fall and tuck under the side of the sheet near the foot of the bed. The corner is now mitered. (Some people prefer to leave the side of a top sheet untucked.) See next page.

Blankets, quilts, and comforters or duvets. If you intend to use one or more blankets, you put them on now. Put on the blanket, right side up, over the top sheet so that the top of the blanket comes to a point about six to ten inches from the head of the bed. Tuck the blanket in at the foot and make corners at the bottom, as for sheets. Then fold down the top sheet over the blanket. You should have a generous portion of the sheet turned down so as to protect the blanket from body soils and odors. If you like, you can tuck the blanket and top sheet under at the sides of the mattress, but this is a matter of taste. You may, if you wish, add a second top sheet or some other thin, light spread on top of the blanket. This adds a modest degree of weight and warmth and helps keep the blanket clean. Or, in summer, you can use a second sheet in place of a blanket.

Comforters (duvets) are usually left untucked because they are too thick (and sometimes too narrow or too short) for tucking. Some people use no cover over the comforter. Quilts, too, may be used like blankets, under a spread or coverlet, or may be used decoratively as the final cover on the bed.

Day cover. Finally, put on the bed's outermost layer: place the day cover—a blanket

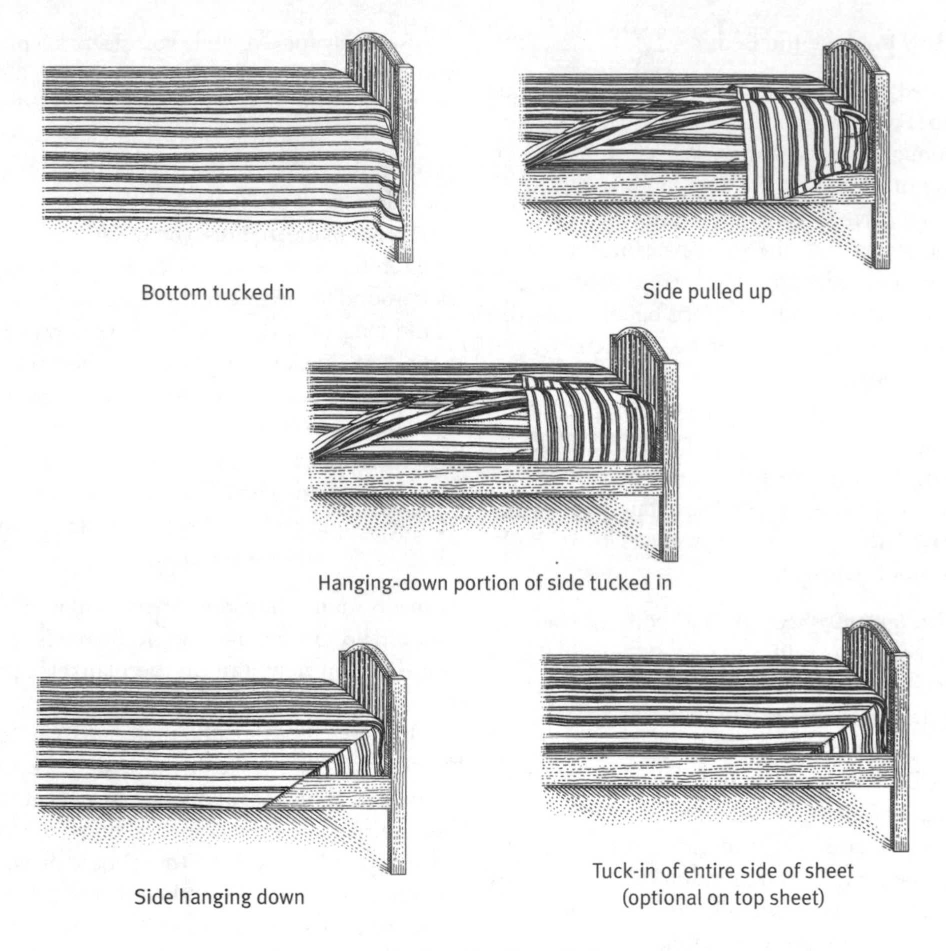

How to make "mitered" or "hospital" corners

cover, coverlet, or bedspread—on the bed to protect the bedclothes from dust and soil and to look good. A bedspread, which used to be used in most homes but is now much less common, may or may not come all the way to the floor. (If it does, it is not used with a dust ruffle.) Although some people sleep under a bedspread for warmth, you may wish to remove it when you sleep, folding it over a rack or placing it over a chair or chest; some people simply fold it neatly at the foot of the bed. If you use a dust ruffle on your bed frame, you usually use a blanket cover or a coverlet over the blanket (or over the comforter or quilt) instead of a bedspread. A blanket cover or coverlet comes down only to the edge of the bed frame, leaving the dust ruffle showing.

Finishing the Bed. Once the day cover is spread evenly and smoothly over the bed, you put the pillows in their cases and finish the bed in any style you like. A very common contemporary style is to fold the top sheet over the comforter or blanket cover, leaving two, four, or more pillows showing at the top of the bed. Any pillows that are not for sleeping are often covered with decorative cases.

Some old-fashioned ways of finishing the bed, which give more daytime protection to the pillows, are these:

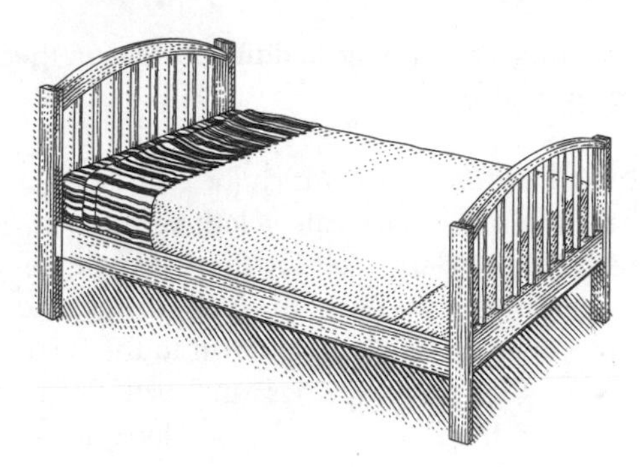

Blanket on bed with sheet folded over top edge of blanket

Bed with bedspread

Blanket cover with pillows exposed and sheet turned down over blanket cover

- Fold the spread over the top sheet fold line, allowing about three feet of it to be turned down. Put the pillows in place, then fold the cover back over the pillows.
- Fold the pillows in half, then push the open-edge sides against the headboard snugly so that they do not unroll. Then cover the pillows with the spread, tucking them in behind.

Variations. In temperate weather, sometimes you are most comfortable using two top sheets and no blanket. In cooler weather, when you are using a blanket it may still be useful to use two top sheets, as described above. The extra sheet adds less warmth and weight than a second blanket but may keep you just warm enough. If you use the second sheet, you may put it on top of the blanket to keep the blanket clean longer.

I do not favor the new style of using no top sheet. People who do this simply spread a comforter or duvet, with or without a removable cover, over the bottom sheet. Or even if they make a more traditional bed for themselves, this simpler bed is what they provide for their children. The main attraction of this ascetic habit is that in the morning the bed can be fixed in an instant simply by pulling the comforter up, or even leaving it attractively rumpled—a system quick enough for the busiest parent and easy enough even for very young children.

The habit of voluntarily forgoing a top sheet to avoid the trouble of pulling up a second one in the morning would have been unfathomable to countless poor people who, over long centuries, could only dream of the luxury of two sheets. I admit that it is unfathomable to me too. This is one of those shortcuts that actually cost a lot in time and trouble and gain you very little. There are concrete reasons to use a top sheet: it is more comfortable, cleaner, and more convenient.

Sheets are designed to be comfortable next to your skin, and there are many different types of sheets to suit many different tastes. (See chapter 57, "Beds and Bedding.") Blankets and quilts and comforter covers are not; they are less skin-friendly, not really being intended for this. Not only are sheets—good ones—meant to feel good on your skin, they are meant to save you the trouble of having to launder your blankets or other warm covers every week or more often.

You can wash sheets—good ones—often and vigorously and easily, but many blankets and comforters are hard to launder or must be sent out to be laundered in commercial-sized machines. (See chapter 25, "How to Launder Tricky Items.") Laundering also makes comforters and blankets age quickly—fade, bunch up, grow thin and spindly, pill, or even pull apart; and they are expensive. Cotton and synthetic blankets are fairly easy to wash, but even they do not hold up to laundering nearly as well as sheets do, and they cost more than sheets. You might think that your comforter is protected by its cover and thus will stay cleaner, but the fewer the protective layers between you and your comforter, the more often you are going to have to wash it. Comforter covers, too, often do not launder easily or well, and are nearly always bizarrely costly for what they are. (You can easily make one by stitching together a couple of sheets of the right size, and putting on snaps or ties to close the opening.) If you are going to use a comforter cover and you do not use a top sheet, keep three covers for each comforter, and change and launder the cover once a week or more often. (If you do not use a comforter cover, you'll have to wash the comforter itself every week.)

Although doing without a top sheet may save you a few seconds straightening the bed in the morning, it costs you time washing duvet covers, comforters, blankets, or quilts, for these definitely become soiled and odorous quickly. In my view, the long-term savings in bed-making time is not worth the cost in laundering, bedding replacement costs (when the appearance or function is damaged by frequent laundering), or loss of comfort. It would be far better to have a more traditional bed and simply not worry about getting it perfectly smooth on rushed mornings: pull up the bedding, throw on the cover, and go.

Dust Ruffles. Dust ruffles (or valances) for beds are ruffles or pleated cloth sewn onto a rectangle of cloth. You lay the rectangle between the mattress and the box springs, and the ruffles or pleats hang down to the floor, covering the box springs and bed frame. They are there to make the bed look attractive, and they are entirely optional. If you find them difficult to take off and replace for laundering, just do without. If you need to cover the sides of your bed entirely, get a spread or other cover that reaches nearly to the floor. Vacuuming dust ruffles regularly will make laundering necessary less often.

Turning Down the Bed at Night. When you turn down the bed at night, you first fold down or remove the day cover; fold it over a rack or the footboard of the bed, or lay it neatly somewhere. Then turn back the corner of the top sheet and blanket in a diagonal fold deep enough to permit someone to insert herself or himself, as into a pocket, without untucking the bedding. This makes the bed feel more welcoming. You can turn down the bed for children or yourself, say before your bath, so that it looks inviting when you come back ready to turn in. Or if you are first in bed, you can turn down the other side for your mate.

Housecraftly Helps for Insomnia

The standard advice for insomniacs is that they should condition themselves to associate their beds and bedrooms with sleeping, and only with sleeping. Therefore, they are often told, do not go to bed before it is near time to fall asleep or lie in bed tossing and turning if you cannot sleep; do not read or watch television in bed; do not let any non-bedroom-like activities invade your bedroom. There is no doubting the beneficial force of habit and association when it comes to going easily to sleep. Such suggestions will definitely help some people, but they will also fail for many. In fact, many of us will be helped to fall asleep by reading for a while or watching a little television in bed. (The gripping page-turner or hair-raising story, perhaps, should be avoided when you need your sleep.) A book or video movie can often take your mind off some nagging worry long enough to let sleep take over if you are not a habitual insomniac but simply have an occasional bad night. Persistent insomniacs may need a psychotherapist's or sleep expert's help.

The causes of insomnia can be divided into those inside you, mental and physical (a worry or a headache), those outside you in the environment (an irritating noise), and those that are a combination of internal and external factors. In the last case, for example, you might have a little worry or a bit of a stiff neck, and there may be a little noise or something slightly uncomfortable about your bed. Neither factor alone would have kept you up, but together they do the trick. Sometimes only the environmental causes are within your power to diagnose and address. Here are some suggestions on how to adjust environmental factors that affect sleep and sleep quality.

First, if the room is warm or simply not too cool, cool down the room further by turning down the heat, opening the windows, or putting on a fan or air conditioning. I don't know why, but sometimes getting quite cool will help you sleep. If you are too cold, however, you may toss and turn and sleep fitfully or too lightly, so make sure you are adequately covered. *Caution: The very young, the sick, and the elderly usually need warmer rooms than ordinary healthy adults. Hypothermia among the elderly is a serious danger. Make the rooms of infants and children, invalids, and elderly people no cooler than their doctors advise.*

If you cannot sleep, put a fresh pillowcase on your pillow or get a fresh pillow. Again coolness helps: get a cold pillow and leave a pillowcase (wrapped in airtight plastic) in the refrigerator for these occasions, if it will not come cool from the linen closet. Try using an ironed pillowcase.

Changing the sheets sometimes helps you to sleep too. If sheets are not fresh, they may cause itching or there may be odors, even very faint ones, that disturb you. Itching and skin irritation can also be caused by sensitivity to laundry detergent, by using too much detergent in the laundry, by failing to rinse bedding adequately, or by allowing pets on the bed. Such problems may occur with your pajamas or nightgown too. Crumbs, dust, or grit in your bed will definitely keep you awake. Brush them out or change the sheets.

Study your sheets. Try replacing polyester-blend sheets with all-cotton or linen. Remember that "satin" sheets are usually polyester, not silk. Sometimes polyester annoys people at a level just below consciousness; you will not sleep well, but you will have a hard time putting your finger on what is bothering you. (By the way, this opinion rests on experience, not a general anti-polyester prejudice—polyester fiber is superb in many types of furnishings and attire. See chapter 18.) Consider the texture and type of sheet you are using. If it has pilled (only polyester and polyester-blend sheets will pill), get rid of it. Pilled fabrics are very uncomfortable next to the skin. Are your sheets too warm? Does a soft, a crisp, a sleek, or a flannelly feel suit you best? Are your sheets sufficiently absorbent? If you are not using a top sheet, consider adding one. Ironed sheets make for a specially appealing bed.

Consider also whether the weight of your blankets suits you. I know people who cannot sleep without the sense of some weight in their blankets; the new, much praised, very lightweight but very warm fibers do not work for them. It is also true that you may toss and turn if your bedclothes are too heavy. The elderly and the arthritic, in particular, may—even unconsciously—be negatively affected by over-heavy blankets; those lightweight ones are a good bet for them. (Sometimes an electric blanket is the solution to the weight problem when the bedroom is too cool.) To reduce the weight of blankets and bedding, you can rest the overhang on a chair or chest at the side of the bed. Some people just can't stand a taut sheet over their toes. They might try making a tuck or fold in the sheets across the width of the bed so that there is extra room for the toes (the opposite of the camp trick of short-sheeting the bed). For the arthritic there are also such things as "blanket tents," which hold up the blankets so that their weight does not rest on tender toes and feet.

The strong odors of potpourris and sachets can most definitely keep you up at night. Any scent you use for bedclothing and lingerie should be exceedingly subtle—barely strong enough to detect. If perfume or cologne bottles on a dresser are leaking odors, try tightening the stoppers, putting them in padded boxes, or, if all else fails, storing them elsewhere.

Of course, your mattress should be comfortable, not uneven or creaky, neither too hard nor too soft.

See chapter 57, "Beds and Bedding," and consider whether your pillow is best for you.

Last, make sure the standard healthy bedroom conditions are met: cleanliness, good ventilation, moderate temperature and humidity, darkness, quiet, and absence of stimulating or stale odors.

57

Beds and Bedding

How much linen to stock . . . Standard mattress, sheet, and pillowcase sizes; calculating desirable sizes for sheets . . . Blanket cover, coverlet, and bedspread sizes . . . Blanket, comforter, and comforter cover sizes . . . Durability of sheets; thread counts, weave and weight, fiber, effect of decorative stitching on durability, whites vs. colors and prints . . . Choosing comfortable sheets . . . Hand, absorbency, warmth, decorative stitching . . . Launderability of sheets; no iron sheets; wrinkly sheets . . . Blankets and comforters . . . Beds, box springs, and mattresses . . . Caring for mattresses . . . Pillows

A good bedroom requires adequate stocks of sheets, well-chosen mattresses and pillows, and good quality in all of them. To be satisfied with your bedroom linens and your bed, you need to know more about bedding than merchandisers today give you credit for. Linen stores once expected their patrons to be knowledgeable, penny-wise women who would pore over merchandise with sharp eyes. Today they seem to expect us to make decisions based purely on the looks of the linens and our supposed love of luxury. I have made more than one foolish purchase of sheets and other bedding, acting just like the naive spender whom advertisers target. Sadder but wiser after these experiences, I describe for you in this chapter many things I wish I had kept in mind during a few shopping trips in the past. We should always try to buy linens we think are beautiful. But when you think through the ways in which sheets and other bedding are used and laundered, you may revise your ideas about what a beautiful sheet looks like.

About Bed Linens

How Much Linen to Stock. For each bed in your home, you will probably find it convenient to stock the following:

3 sets of sheets, top and bottom, (including, if you wish, 1 guest set)

3 sets of pillowcases (including, if you wish, 1 guest set)

2 pillow covers

2 pillow undercovers

2 mattress pads

2 mattress covers

This gives, for each bed, one set of sheets on the bed, one set in the wash, and one in reserve for accidents or extra changes of the bed for guests. (People who keep a set of guest sheets for one or more beds usually choose especially fine or attractive sheets for this purpose and may also use them for a variety of special occasions like anniversaries or special holidays.) Because you change covers, undercovers, and mattress pads less frequently, you will need only one extra set of each of these. Crib sheets and blankets must be changed daily or more often if they become wet or soiled, so stock at least a half dozen of each.

It does not pay to overstock bed linens, for they will simply age on the shelf. An overstocked linen closet also makes more work for you. It is prey to odors and dust. Linens that have sat unused for long periods have had more opportunities to become damp and to develop mold, yellowing, weakness along crease lines, and other problems, so you will have to go in and wash and refold them periodically.

Types of Sheets. What to choose, as opposed to how many, is a more complicated question than it used to be. It pays to understand fibers, fabrics, and their characteristics in making these choices; so the reader is referred generally to chapters 14 through 19. The desiderata in sheets are good fit and resistance to shrinking, durability and resistance to pilling, comfort (a complicated thing in itself), launderability, fit, economy, and beauty. Comfort in a sheet depends greatly on a good hand (and no pilling), warmth or coolness, and absorbency.

Getting the Right Size: Standard Measurements of Bed Linens

Standard Mattress, Sheet, and Pillowcase Sizes. Sheet sizes used to be highly standardized and still are fairly uniform, but you now encounter more variations—reflecting, no doubt, more variation in mattress sizes. Be especially alert for different measurements in European-made sheets and pillowcases, and for differences between linen and cotton sheets and pillowcases. The sizes set out in this section, however, are still considered fairly "standard." They fit the following standard mattress widths and lengths (but see the discussion of extra-deep mattresses below):

Mattress sizes
Twin: 39 × 75
Full/double: 54 × 75
Queen: 60 × 80
King: 78 × 80
California king: 72 × 84

The length and width of sheets will be stated on the package when you buy them. Flat sheets of all sizes are given a 2- to 4-inch hem at top and a 1/2- to 1-inch hem at bottom. Although almost all sheets have selvage edges at the sides, very fine sheets may have hems of an inch or so at the sides. The dimensions of a sheet stated on the package nowadays are the finished sizes, not the "torn" sizes. (The torn size is the size before hemming. When hemmed, sheets are up to 5 inches shorter in length and 2 inches shorter in width. Sheet packages gave the torn size, not the hemmed size, until sometime in the 1970s.)

Dimensions of Standard Sheets

Crib flat: 42 × 72

Crib fitted: 28 × 52

Twin flat: 66 × 96

Twin fitted: 39 × 75

Double or full flat: 81 × 96 (or sometimes 100)

Double fitted: 54 × 75

Queen flat: 90 × 102 (or sometimes 106)

Queen fitted: 60 × 80

King flat: 108 × 102 (or sometimes 106)

King fitted: 78 × 80

California king flat: 102 × 110

California king fitted: 72 × 84

A pillowcase should be 4 inches longer than the pillow and 2 inches greater in circumference.

Dimensions of Pillowcases

Standard: 20 × 26

Queen: 20 × 30

King: 20 × 40; 20 × 36

European: 26 × 26

Boudoir (baby): 12 × 16

Neck roll: 6 × 14

All new sheets will shrink a little when laundered, but the shrinkage is almost entirely in the length, with very little change in the width. The long-term shrinkage in the average cotton sheet will be about 5 percent, which works out to about five inches in a 108-inch sheet. Flannel sheets will shrink more but are cut longer to allow for this. Thus, even if you have standard-length mattresses, it can pay to buy extra-long sheets (these are often 108 inches long) to assure plenty of overhang for tucking after the shrinking. Once upon a time, you would have planned on providing flat sheets large enough to give 10 to 12 inches to tuck on each edge and top sheets that extended 6 to 10 inches past the top of the mattress (so that you could have a generous fold over the top of the blanket). To do this even twenty years ago, you had to buy the next size larger sheet (for example, a queen flat for a double bed) because standard sheet sizes on a standard mattress gave you only 6 or 7 inches for tucking. (Many people regard 6 or 7 inches as quite adequate, by the way, and the 10 to 12 inches I like is a rather old-fashioned standard. But it still works best.)

It is crucial to measure the depth of your mattress before purchasing sheets because of all the extra-deep mattresses being sold today. These not uncommonly have a 14-inch depth, and some are even deeper—up to 20 inches. The mattress most commonly sold today is 8 to 10 inches deep. The old "standard" mattress was 6 to 8 inches deep. With a mattress 14 to 20 inches deep, to get the same allowance for tucking as the standard top sheet gives for a standard 8-inch mattress, you need a sheet that is 6 to 12 inches longer, depending on how deep your mattress is, and 12 to 24 inches wider. (A flat bottom sheet would need as much extra length as width.) If you have a deep mattress, therefore, you must buy the next size larger flat sheet, preferably in an extra-long length, to provide a decent allowance for tucking under and turning down. When purchasing fitted sheets, however, you cannot safely get the next larger size, as they probably will not fit. Instead, if you have a deep mattress, make sure you purchase fitted sheets with "universal" or deep corners. Sometimes the package specifies the corner depth, so check labels. Linen stores will often undertake to make custom-sized sheets for you, and these are often necessary for beds with unusual shapes or unusually deep mattresses.

Common Sizes for Blanket Covers or Coverlets and Bedspreads. Keep two covers or spreads for each bed. People today tend to

CALCULATING DESIRABLE SIZES FOR BED LINENS

Example 1: Calculating top sheet length for standard double (full) mattress Suppose you have a double (full) mattress, 54 X 75, that is 8 inches deep. If you wanted to tuck in 12 inches of your top sheet at the bottom of the mattress and have 10 extra inches at the top, you would have to buy a sheet that is no less than 105 inches in length.

Extra at top	+	mattress length	+	mattress depth	+	tuck		
10"	+	75"	+	8"	+	12"	=	105"

Example 2: Calculating sheet size for an extra-deep queen-size mattress Suppose that you have a queen-size pillow-top mattress, 60 X 80, that is 14 inches deep. You find some linen sheets that come only in flat sizes, and you would like to buy some for your bed. Here is how you would calculate the size of the flat sheet you would need as a bottom sheet, if you were to insist on tucking in 10 inches on all sides. As the calculation shows, you will not be able to buy any standard sheet to fit because no sheet is manufactured in so large a size. In length, it would have to be:

Top tuck	+	mattress depth	+	mattress length	+	mattress depth	+	bottom tuck	
10"	+	14"	+	80"	+	14"	+	10"	= 128"

The width would have to be:

Side tuck	+	mattress depth	+	mattress width	+	mattress depth	+	side tuck	
10"	+	14"	+	60"	+	14"	+	10"	= 108"

leave their pillows uncovered, use dust ruffles, and cover the bed with blanket covers or coverlets that expose the dust ruffle, pillowcases, and sheet tops. Unlike sheet sizes, the sizes of blanket covers and coverlets are not highly standardized. If the exact size matters, measure! Remember to make allowances for extra-deep mattresses. Some common sizes of blanket covers or coverlets are as follows:

Blanket Covers
Twin: 69 x 90
Full/double: 84 x 90
Queen: 95 x 95
King: 102 x 95

It has become hard to find old-fashioned bedspreads that cover the pillows and the sides of the bed down to the floor. Here are bedspread sizes that would work for standard mattresses, but, again, you might need to make allowances if you have an extra-deep mattress:

Bedspreads:
Twin: 74 x 108
Full/double: 88 x 108
Queen/king: 99 x 114

Sizes of Blankets and Comforters. Blankets are sized so as to fit under a coverlet. If you want sufficient overhang for a comforter or blanket to serve also as a bed cover, you must be sure to select a size large enough. Blanket sizes are highly variable, as the following list of sizes I have found in stores and catalogues shows. If the exact size matters, measure and calculate, before buying, just how much overhang or tuck you will need.

Blankets
Crib: 36 x 50
Twin: 68 x 86; 68 x 90; 66 x 96
Full: 81 x 83; 80 x 96
Queen: 91 x 91; 90 x 96
King: 108 x 96
California King: 102 x 102

Comforters (duvets) are variable in size. The sizes of comforter covers are the same as the sizes of the comforters themselves, and they also vary considerably. Measuring is needed if you are concerned about exact fit. The following examples of sizes are typical:

Comforters and Comforter Covers
Twin: 68 x 88; 68 x 86; 66 x 88
Full: 81 x 88
Full/queen: 86 x 86; 88 x 88
Queen: 88 x 96
King: 107 x 96; 102 x 86; 102 x 88

Durability in Sheets

Thread Counts. Do not be deceived into thinking that the higher the thread count, the better the sheet. This is an oversimplified and mistaken idea that is frequently purveyed by merchandisers and fashion writers. It may lead you into paying far more money for a sheet that will not last as long, feel as good, or launder as well as one with a lower thread count. (See chapter 14, "The Fabric of Your Home," page 196.)

Until recent decades, most sheets sold were muslin, a cotton plain-weave cloth with a thread count of about 140. Hospitals and other institutions used muslin sheets exclusively because they were inexpensive, comfortable, and very long-lasting. Most people used them at home, too, especially on children's beds. The next grade of sheet was percale, with a thread count of 180. It felt finer and was also quite durable. In all middle-class homes until lately, there were no aspirations to any sheets better than 180 thread count percale. But in the 1980s increasingly higher thread counts in cotton sheets began to appear—200, 220, 250, 300, and upward—and these typically had ever finer, softer, smoother hand and were made of ever better cotton—Egyptian cotton or pima cotton. Some of these, therefore, were and are good buys. Using fine yarns, high thread counts, and high-quality fiber, they achieve a good balance of durability, launderability, and improved hand. My favorite type of sheet for ordinary home use is a resin-free all-combed-cotton percale with a thread count of 200 to 250 and a care label that says merely "Machine wash."

But super-fine, super-soft, high-thread-count cotton sheets that are somewhat delicate are now on the market. For example, sateen sheets (cotton sheets in satin weaves), which have a slippery, sleek feel and a high luster, are popular today. These sometimes have high thread counts of 300 or 400 or more; yet they are less durable than plain or twill weaves because they use looser twists and floats in the weave, and they are very light and thin. They cannot be bleached; they soon acquire the grayish or yellowish tinge of aging cotton. They wear holes faster. They are costly. Of course, if they suit your fancy and your pocketbook, you should have them; and if you are on a budget, you can reserve them for special occasions, guests' beds, and the like. Just be sure you are not under the impression that you are necessarily getting a long-wearing (or highly launderable) sheet fitted for hard, everyday use. This will depend on many more factors.

Weave and Weight. Most sheets are plain-weave; a few are twill, in general the most durable type of weave. Both twill and plain-weave sheets tend to be more durable than satin weaves, because the latter contain threads with floats and low twist, which are vulnerable to abrasion and tearing. Cotton knit sheets tend to be less durable than woven ones. Heavier weight fabrics tend to be more durable than lighter.

Some of the high-thread-count cotton sheets in plain weave are very sheer and light. They are, therefore, quite lovely and cool, but they are not likely to wear as well as heavier sheeting, particularly if subjected to vigorous laundering and heavy use. You may wish to keep them for special occasions.

Fiber. The best cotton fabric used for sheets is of combed pima or Egyptian cotton. Wrinkle-treated cotton sheets generally do not last as long as untreated cotton or cotton/polyester sheets, but the latter may pill and all-cotton will not. High-quality cotton is extremely durable, even when subjected to frequent vigorous laundering. So is unbleached linen; bleached and dyed linen is less durable. You can, unfortunately, all too easily pay premium prices for linen sheets that are not of the highest quality and will wear poorly. (See chapter 16, "The Natural Fibers," pages 233–35, on how to evaluate linen.) Even very high-quality linen, moreover, will not be able to take hard wear if it is very finely woven and is lacy or bears other delicate decorative needlework.

Decorative Stitching, Cutwork, Lace, and the Like. Decorative stitching on any sheets can make them less durable. Cutwork and lace are highly susceptible to tearing. Embroidery can fray or fade. Even simple hem stitching at the pillow and sheet hem will wear through far, far sooner than the rest of the sheet. If you have bought expensive sheets for special occasions only, you will be using them infrequently and you can launder them gently; thus they will last. But when you are buying sheets for hard everyday use and trying to make economical decisions, your best bet is to choose sheets without these features.

Whites vs. Colors and Prints. The colored and print sheets in linen stores are often as hard-wearing as they are beautiful. In fact, they are so widely appreciated and used to advantage that I feel I need to add only a word of praise for the now overlooked plain white ones. White sheets do not fade. If they are made of a fiber that can take hot water and occasional chlorine bleaching, you can also keep them white and spotless for many years. Most colored and print cotton sheets tend to fade; polyester and polyester blends tend to be more resistant to fading. Some prints and colors are bleachable, but the bleaching will hasten the fading; and unless you wash all pieces of a set at the same time *in the same loads,* some will fade at different rates from others and they will no longer look good together. Off-white and unbleached muslin and other cotton and linen sheets present similar problems. They may come to look dingy over time or begin to lighten with continued laundering. Unbleached linen inevitably whitens over time. You can brighten off-whites and unbleached sets with bleaching, but then you must be sure to do all pieces of the set together or they will turn different shades of off-white. Eventually you will end up with either white or dingy sheets.

The colored, satin-stitched scalloped edging on some cotton sheets has never faded perceptibly in my experience, even with chlorine bleaching. (But you should follow care labels or test the fabric for bleach-fastness before resorting to bleach.) I also find that if you pick your prints carefully and take care to launder sets together, fading may not look bad or may not be noticeable. The bright blue stripes on a blue-and-white-striped sheet, for example, may objectively become less bright blue but do not look washed out. The real problem is dealing with stains: strong stain removers and chlorine bleach may create uneven lightened areas in the print.

There is no denying that white cotton, without wrinkle treatments, is easiest to use and wears best. It is also convenient not to have to worry about matching bottom sheets with top sheets and pillowcases, or with spreads, comforters, and other aspects of the bedroom. White is the color of choice for those who have no time. In fact, because of its launderability I prefer it even for children's bedding. The idea that prints "hide" stains and dirty marks has never really been convincing to me; I find that I see them quite well and that the need to protect the color of the print often interferes with removing marks effectively. Thus, although I find prints hard to resist, I have moved gradually during a very busy period of my life to white and bleachable mostly white bedding of all sorts. If you decide to go with white, you can compensate with plenty of colors and prints in area rugs, spreads or quilts, artwork, wallpaper or wall paint, and the like.

Comfortable Sheets

It is more important to choose comfort in your sheets than in any other fabric you buy, except, possibly, your underwear. A number of factors affect the comfort of a sheet, and some of them are highly subjective. Do not be unduly swayed in your choices by the fads of the day.

Hand: Silky Soft or Crisp? My best friend dearly loves sleeping in silky smooth, softly draping, lustrous sheets; sateen sheets answering to this taste are available in ever greater variety and in several types of fiber. I prefer crisp sheets. My friend's luxurious sheets caress the skin, but they also cling closer to the body, which means that they prevent air from circulating in the little tunnels and valleys that form between your skin and a crisper sheet. The silky feeling can transform into a clammy one, especially if you are the sort of person who perspires a great deal. Satiny sheets also tend to slide all over you. Sometimes this produces a hot feeling, perhaps because of the airless friction of skin against moving, clinging cloth. Satin-weave sheets, moreover, do not let air in or out well, which aggravates the problem.

Still, if you are one of those to whom a silky hand and a soft, light drape appeals, you should look into some of the beautiful all-cotton, high-thread-count sateen sheets. Although you can often find some good buys in these, I wore holes in a costly set of them in three years—a short life for a costly sheet—and they grayed early but could not be chlorine-bleached (presumably because the fine exposed threads in the floats would have been damaged, the luster would have been lost, or, perhaps, the holes would have come even sooner).

Real silk satin sheets, which are extremely costly, are highly absorbent and skin-friendly in many ways. However, they are quite warm, and their care labels call for dry cleaning; they cannot be bleached or subjected to the vigorous laundering you may need to give to sheets. If this type of sheet is your ideal, perhaps you could have a set for "good" or for special occasions, just as once upon a time the real linen sheets were kept for important days and people. Avoid "satin" sheets made of polyester. Polyester, which is unabsorbent, is not a desirable fiber for sheeting.

Those who prefer a crisper or cottony smoothness in sheets will always love, as I do, good combed all-cotton percale with a thread count between 180 and 250—the standard luxury sheet of the prior generation. (At higher thread counts, you lose crispness.) It provides superior comfort, durability, and launderability at lower prices. All-cotton sheets with lower thread counts are no longer sold, which is a shame because muslin sheets (thread count 140) also excel in crisp comfort and durability.* Cotton/polyester blends, which have replaced muslin in the low end of the market, are wrinkle resistant but have a slightly scratchy or harsh hand that is less pleasant than that of all-cotton

*When I discovered, to my amazement, that you could no longer buy a plain, all-cotton muslin sheet, I happened to mention this to my aunt, a chronic over-stocker. Stored on her shelf were several muslin sheets that she had bought some thirty years earlier in Macy's and A & S in Brooklyn, and she sent them to me, still in their original packages, unopened. I have been using them for a few years now, laundering them with the strongest methods. They are extremely comfortable, snowy white, and appear to be indestructible. White muslin sheets, if you could get hold of any, would be an excellent bet for children's beds.

sheets. Wrinkle-resistant, all-cotton percale sheets with moderate thread counts have a better hand than cotton/polyester sheets, although there is a faint rubbery quality to them.

Cotton flannel and knit sheets offer you more softness without crispness, which is just what some people want. Consider lightweight cotton knits for summer and flannels for winter. (But cotton knits sometimes have inconvenient laundering instructions. See "Launderability of Sheets," below.) Even if you generally prefer a crisp sheet, you might find you enjoy the warmth of flannel in winter. If aged percale is what you love best, you can even buy prewashed percale, which has lost its initial crispness. I find it annoying, however, to pay more for sheets that are slightly worn and would rather wear them soft myself.

The queen of fibers when it comes to sheets is real linen (flax), the fiber that gave bed "linens" their name. If real linen sheets sound or look dreamy to you but you have not tried them, do not expect satiny smoothness or silky softness. Linen is very crisp and, until much laundered, rather stiff. If cotton sateen appeals to you, linen probably will not. It is highly absorbent, and although good linen fabric is exceedingly smooth and lustrous, its greater body and crispness gives it something of the quality of good muslin. Like muslin, it softens with age, wears like iron (if of good quality), and wrinkles easily. Many people, including me, like it best of all sheeting. Much of the appeal of linen and muslin to their fans is that because they are crisp they let air in and out, do not cling, and do not slide all over you, as satiny sheets do.

Absorbency. Absorbency is one of the chief factors affecting the comfort of sheets. Linen (flax) sheets are most absorbent, but all-cotton that have received no resin treatments are also highly absorbent. Polyester is unabsorbent and thus uncomfortable in sheets, which are going to have your perspiring bare skin and body weight pressed against them for hours and hours. These are rarely marketed for adults, but I have often seen all-polyester crib sheets. All-cotton knit crib sheets, which do not need ironing either, are a much better choice.

Cotton/polyester blend sheets are superior to all-polyester sheets—the hand is better, and they are more absorbent. They come in both expensive and inexpensive styles. I know many people who find them indistinguishable from cotton, but I believe that those who perspire heavily often can tell the difference readily and are likely to find them uncomfortable. Trading wrinkles for comfort is a bad bargain—better just to let the sheets wrinkle and feel comfortable.

Generally speaking, very light, fine, or flimsy sheets are less absorbent than those with more body simply because there is less fiber present to absorb moisture.

Warmth. Cold sheets are less of a problem in today's warmer houses and apartments. You can always add warmth to the bed by means of blankets or comforters or nightclothes and need not rely on your sheets. If your bedroom gets very cold, however, cotton flannel sheets are best. Flannel and knit sheets do not have that initial icy feeling that is so unpleasant in a cold bedroom. Nor do polyester and polyester-blend sheets and silk, which are all generally less cool than cotton. The coolest sheets of all are lightweight linen (flax). All-combed-cotton percale sheets are also very cool. In general, finer, lighter sheets are cooler that those of heavier weights. Cotton sheets that feel icy in winter when you first get in bed will quickly feel warm again, but you can put a hot water bottle in the bed to take off the initial chill, especially at the feet. A heating pad will do the same thing, but you have to remember to turn it off.

Decorative stitching. Decorative stitching can be scratchy or make uncomfortable ridges on your pillowcase or sheet. When buying pillowcases, look to see that embroidery, lace, or cutwork is positioned on the pillowcase in places where your face will not rest upon it. You can also choose to use plain pillowcases on your sleeping pillow and save fancy work for decorative pillows. Simple hem stitching will not affect your comfort, but the stitching will wear out and tear long before the rest of the pillowcase.

Launderability and Ironing

Launderability of Sheets. Irresponsible merchandising seems to have bred a generation of people who expend time and money on sheets that are much more trouble than they need to be. In the time-pressed household, this can matter. Everyone needs everyday sheets that can take vigorous laundering (the particulars of which are described below). No one should buy everyday bedding that must be dry-cleaned. Dry cleaning is expensive, inconvenient, and does not remove mite allergens. Moreover, you press your face into your bedding, and this might expose you to dry-cleaning fluid fumes that are not healthy to breathe.

Sheets must be changed and washed vigorously once a week or more often if they stop smelling or feeling fresh. It is not a bad idea to change pillowcases twice a week or sometimes more often, as they soil faster than the sheets, particularly in hot weather or when you are perspiring from illness or other causes. Crib sheets for infants should be changed daily or more often if they become soiled. Do not forget that sheets lie next to your skin hour after hour, night after night. They receive saliva, perspiration, body oils and more intimate fluids, skin flakes, and any soil on your body. Sometimes you bleed on them. You sometimes get sick in your bed, and sick people and the very young may be incontinent. Children's beds are subject to a miscellany of stains and spills, including cough syrup and colored medicines. Therefore, your everyday sheets, especially those on infants' and children's beds, should be easy to launder vigorously and should *never* require gentle or complicated treatment. Sheets should be colorfast. You should not have to wash sheets separately, for example. Nor should you have to try to clean them with gentle soaps or detergents. For reasons of health (to decrease the risks of allergies and infections), to remove stains, and to keep the sheets really clean and bright or snowy white, you must be able to wash them in *hot* water (140°F or higher) with strong detergent and, in my opinion, use chlorine bleach—even on print or colored sheets—as necessary to sanitize and to remove stains and dirt.

Your sheets should shrink only negligibly with hot-water washing and drying on the regular setting. You should be able to dry them in the dryer or on the line, as you wish. If sheets are not preshrunk, insist on knowing how much they will shrink and buy them big enough to fit after shrinkage.

The care label you want on sheets will either say all this or may say simply "Machine washable," which implies most of it. Whatever the care label says, plain white cotton percale sheets (preshrunk and not subjected to wrinkle-resistance treatments or other resin treatments) can be laundered in the way you need to launder them.[1] Wrinkle-treated sheets, cotton/polyester sheets, and colored and print sheets sometimes have care labels saying "No bleach" or "No chlorine bleach" or "Wash warm." Check care labels, decide if you believe them (see chapter 19), and decide if the sheets are worth it to you, given these limitations. My white cotton knit twin-size sheets, which I am sorry I bought, had a care label that specified cold water, gentle detergent, no bleach of any sort, and tumbling dry on the low setting—everything that a care label on a sheet should not say. (And even with cold-water washing the sheets shrank, so if you are considering buying any, you might try getting them a size too large.) On the other hand, I ignored the care label on white cotton knit crib sheets and laundered them with regular detergent and chlorine bleach, and encountered no mishap other than shrinking. By the time my son had outgrown the crib, the crib mattress had so outgrown the sheets that it took both my husband and me to stretch them on. But I would buy them again anyway; these crib sheets feel so warm and soft that they are perfect for a baby's skin.

Cotton/polyester sheets launder less well than all-cotton. They tend to hold body oils and as a result sometimes yellow or develop a stale odor. (For curing such problems, refer to chapter 17, pages 264–65.) They may pill as well.

My impression is that when you are buying sheets and towels it is often safest to buy them from manufacturers that specialize in making linens and towels rather than from "designer" companies. Designer sheets and towels, more often than those from specialized manufacturers, have poor durability, fade, and have care labels calling for inappropriate laundering procedures.

No-Iron Sheets; Wrinkly Sheets. Cotton/polyester blend sheets have the highest wrinkle resistance. Resin-treated all-cotton sheets have varying degrees of resistance to wrinkling, some a lot and some a little; their wrinkle resistance diminishes as they age. Knit and flannel sheets are naturally wrinkle-resistant.

Untreated all-cotton and linen woven sheets wrinkle considerably. Traditionally, therefore, they were always ironed. Sleeping on fresh, ironed sheets is one of life's treats, but ironed sheets are not necessary to health or comfort. If you are hard-pressed for time or have better things to do, feel free to laugh loudly at the thought. Certainly giving a guest ironed sheets is gracious. Giving them to yourself for special nights, or anytime you particularly need rest or simply feel like making your room look especially good, is pleasant too. But if you do not want to iron sheets—and this does take time unless you have a mangle—don't conclude that you must buy wrinkle-resistant sheets. Wrinkled cotton or linen sheets look fine. Cover them with a day spread if they do not look fine to you. When you are sleeping in the dark, you'll like the way they feel and you won't be able to see them; and wrinkled cotton tends to smooth out as you sleep on it. (To reduce wrinkles without ironing, see chapter 18, "Fabrics that Work," page 275, and chapter 23, "Ironing," page 349.

Blankets and Comforters

In blankets, you look for functional qualities such as warmth, comfortable weight, a pleasant hand, durability, and static and pilling resistance. Assuming you do not use the blanket next to your skin, absorbency is less important in a blanket than a sheet.

Blankets that are used in the traditional way—layered between sheet and cover—need laundering or cleaning less frequently than sheets, but if you sleep with the blanket next to the skin, you will need launderable blankets that can be washed and changed in the same manner and on the same schedule as your sheets. If you want to avoid breathing dry-cleaning fumes, avoid blankets that need dry cleaning. If you are worried about allergies, choose only blankets that can be frequently laundered in hot water. Read care labels carefully. When high launderability, is your main concern, especially if you want to use hot water, cotton blankets in colorfast colors or white are superior to wool, acrylic, nylon, or comforters. Some wool blankets are washable, but do not purchase a wool blanket expecting to wash it frequently. A polyester blanket will probably be fine with frequent laundering, but you may be forced to second-guess the care labels—it may tell you to use warm or cool wash water.

Some people sleep better with a blanket that has some weight, but those who want a lightweight warm blanket should try acrylic, polyester, or nylon. Acrylic and polyester sometimes pill, which looks and feels unpleasant, but they will keep you warm even if they do pill. The synthetics also tend to develop static electricity, which can start you off in the morning with flyaway hair. Wool, properly cared for, will look good and function well, without pilling, for a very long time. It drapes to the body much better than synthetics. When the atmosphere is very dry, it will develop a little static but less than synthetics. Some wool blankets are soft, smooth, or even fairly silky; others are thick and scratchy. Synthetics tend to feel soft and smooth and fluffier, never scratchy.

When you want only a little warmth, a thin cotton blanket or cotton "thermal" blanket is best. The latter are made in a waffle or honeycomb weave or a knit. Such weaves are also available in wool, acrylic, polyester, and blends. All are machine washable (except, perhaps, the wool), but the synthetics may not take hotter water temperatures. Be sure cotton is pre-shrunk.

Conventional blankets of both natural and synthetic fibers are usually, but not always, napped to produce the comfortable, fuzzy, warmth-holding surface. In cold weather, wool blankets are quite warm, as are quilts. Acrylic blankets are warm, sometimes even warmer than wool. Use two or three blankets for greater warmth, or a down-filled comforter. Or use a blanket plus a comforter for frigid quarters. You may read in newspaper articles or advertisements that a comforter will keep you warm in the winter and cool in the summer. Remember, however, that a comforter is a sack filled with down or some other insulating filler and that covering yourself with it will always make you warm. If you do not find a down-filled jacket comfortable in August, a down-filled comforter will not seem so either. I would not recommend creating a bedroom routine and decor overly dependent upon a comforter that will not be comfortable for half the year. If you are using a comforter or duvet, choose its weight carefully. In any city apartment in which I have ever lived, a lightweight down comforter was too warm even in winter, but in a cold Midwestern house the same comforter was delightful.

Electric blankets can be a godsend in very cold bedrooms. They are not for children, however, and even adults must use them with care. (See chapter 61, "Electrical Safety," page 725.)

About Beds and Mattresses

The ordinary American and European bed consists of a frame, a box spring, and a mattress. Many other sorts of beds are available, and some, such as the futon, have become quite popular. Choosing furniture is a subject beyond the scope of this book, but a little knowledge of what a good bed can do for you is part of housekeeping competence. Standard mattress sizes are given on page 672, above.

The bed frame or bedstead is there to raise you off the floor. In an older day, this gave you some protection from being joined in bed by pests that most people are no longer worried about—mice, insects, bedbugs. It also guaranteed some warmth; warm air rises, so it is colder close to the floor. You could get in and out of a modestly raised bed more easily than one on the floor, particularly if you were aged or infirm. (Actually, beds used to be quite a bit higher than they are now, which was not always so convenient; people used steps and stools for getting in and out of them.)

If your bedroom is quite cold in winter, you too may prefer a higher bed. Anyone whose dusting and vacuuming habits are relaxed or irregular should also prefer a higher bed, as this puts you farther from dust on the floor. If you sleep on the floor on a futon or other low mattress, in fact, you may already have noticed that you can smell the dust when you lie down, and tiny air currents, even your very sleeping motions, rouse the dust all night long. (This would not be the bed-style of choice for asthmatics.) An additional advantage of higher beds, one that my great-grandmother never dreamed of in her sparsely furnished rooms, is that you can store things underneath them.

Four-poster beds, common from the Renaissance, largely disappeared in the late nineteenth century only to make a big comeback in the late twentieth. This is purely a decorating phenomenon driven by nostalgia. The posts on the contemporary bed do not even pretend to any function other than psychological. They originally served to hold up bed curtains, which held in warmth and kept out drafts, and were taken down in warm weather and replaced in cool (and the removal and rehanging and cleaning of the bed draperies was massively labor-intensive). Bed curtains also ensured privacy in earlier times, when the bedchamber might hold many beds, including those of servants. Almost all contemporary bed posts, however, hold up nothing at all; bed curtains are unnecessary to ensure warmth or privacy. Those who want the posts frequently say that they enjoy the sense of enclosure the posts give, or that they just like the look. Some people drape the posts dramatically with cloth intended to evoke grandeur and emphasize a sense of enclosure. Keep in mind that a cloth roof or curtains around your bed can be quite a dust trap and will not be easy to vacuum or clean. They are not for the household short on time or help.

Boards at the head and foot of the bed frame can prevent pillows and bedding from falling off during the night. You can buy railings for the beds of children and the infirm, to prevent their falling out of bed.

The bed frame should provide a sturdy base to hold your box spring and mattress. When I was a graduate student, I had a high antique bed with rather short antique bed slats that tended to move around and, periodically, fall right out, making for unlooked-for flights of adventure in the middle of the night. The box spring is what the modern bed uses in place of the old coil springs or flat springs. A box spring is, essentially, coil springs enclosed in ticking. I remember people cleaning the other sort in my childhood. They not only trapped dust, threads, and miscellaneous toys, but they rusted and sometimes squeaked annoyingly. Flat springs did not provide much spring and often sagged. Springs are there to provide extra softness and springiness. They are not absolutely necessary, but they give a very comfortable feeling to a bed.

In a conventional bed, the mattress itself, known as an "innerspring" mattress, contains more springs and padding. Innerspring mattresses are constructed on a variety of principles with a variety of materials, which you will see advertised when you go looking. Less commonly, people use a mattress without inner springs, such as polyurethane or latex foam, which provide some resilience on their own. Still less commonly, they use a mattress without much resilience that is made of some soft or cushioning material encased in ticking, such as a featherbed or a futon. (When my great-grandmother died, her century-old featherbeds were put into us children's entirely unheated bedrooms, over our regular mattresses, to keep us warm. It is a testament, I suppose, to the draftiness of our room that none of us ever wheezed despite years of sleeping in this ancient bedding.)

In deciding what sort of mattress you would like, you will have to weigh two factors. First, the mattress should provide softness at contact points on your body. If the mattress does not provide enough softness, you will begin to ache where your bones rest against the mattress during your sleep, and you will turn to alleviate the discomfort. If the mattress makes you toss and turn too much, you will sleep too lightly and feel unrested. Second, however, the mattress should also provide support—that is, it should be firm enough to keep your body well aligned during sleep. If your mattress is too soft, your spine will not be supported and you will get a stiff neck and a sore back. Moreover, a soft mattress can also disturb your sleep by making the ordinary turning and moving you do during the night a lot of work—if you have ever slept on a featherbed or a very soft sofa you will have experienced this. An overly soft mattress, therefore, is particularly ill advised for the elderly and the infirm, as such mattresses are hard to turn over in and to pull yourself out of.

Although people with ascetic leanings sometimes believe that the harder the mattress the healthier it is, this does not seem to be true. The experts agree that firm is good, but there is little objective, scientific agreement about what that amounts to, and what one manufacturer calls firm another might call extra-firm. Whatever the word means, everyone agrees that it is possible for a mattress to be too firm. Hospitals and nursing homes are very concerned about the balance between softness and support because bedsores result when a sick person must lie for long periods of time on a hard mattress. The firmer the mattress the more commonly bedsores result, and they appear precisely at the points of greatest pressure. The reason is that the firmer the mattress the less the amount of contact space between your body and the mattress. Imagine that you are lying on your back on a hard wooden board. Your body has natural curves and thus touches the board only at certain points—the middle of the back of your head, your shoulders, your buttocks, your heels, and so on. Your entire weight, therefore, rests on these few contact points. The harder the surface, the smaller the area of the contact points, the greater the pressure on those points, and the worse the discomfort and the sooner the desire to move. A softer mattress alleviates the problem by enabling more of your body to rest on the mattress so that your weight is distributed over a much greater area. Thus the pressure of your weight is lessened at each contact point, the discomfort decreased, and the desire to move delayed; you do not toss and turn. So choosing a good mattress comes down to the question of how you maintain the desired degree of support while increasing the body area that directly receives support.

The best current answer seems to be, first, to get a firm mattress that contours well to your body. (It should also permit someone sleeping next to you to roll over without affecting your sleeping position.) Second, be sure the mattress has sufficient padding for softness. Some mattresses provide this with a "pillow top," an extra layer of softness at the top and bottom. (These mattresses are very thick and require fitted sheets with extra-deep "universal" or "high-contour" pockets.) Or you can buy a firm mattress and lay a separate soft pad or "topper" over it. Hospitals take the latter route when they put foam "egg-crate" pads over hard mattresses to decrease the danger of bedsores, and this is thought to be quite successful. I tried the foam egg-crate topper at a hotel that had excruciatingly hard mattresses, and it did the trick for me. I found, however, that it felt hot. Although you may read that the egg pouches allow air circulation and thus that they are cooling, I suspect that the foam pad may simply act as extra insulation, holding in heat beneath you. But this is one woman's unscientific vote. There are other toppers made of feathers, sheepskin, and other materials.

In the end the only way to pick a mattress is to try it out. You must actually lie on it for as long as you can. If you are sleeping away from home and find yourself on a mattress that you think ideal, by all means do all you can to learn what it was; the opportunity to try out a good mattress so thoroughly is hard to come by. With mattresses, money counts; the more you spend, the more likely you are to get a really good mattress. (This is not true for sheets and some furnishings whose costs are subject to the cost inflation that design faddism brings.) Replace innerspring mattresses every ten years or so, or when they sag. Infrequently used mattresses may last longer than this.

The futons that the Japanese sleep on have become popular in this country. They are thin mattresses with a heavyweight cotton shell. They used to be stuffed with either cotton or buckwheat shelling, but foam and polyester fillings, at least in this country, are now more common. I am told that Japanese futons are quite soft, and that futons sold in this country tend to be too hard for Japanese tastes.

In Japan the futons are laid on the floor every night for sleeping and carried outside during the day for sunning and airing, then put away in a closet until it is time for sleeping again. These habits sound like excellent housekeeping to me. Most Americans will find these thin mattresses, spread directly on the floor or a hard wooden frame, difficult to adjust to after a lifetime of innerspring mattresses and box springs. I know of no studies as to the effects of futon-sleeping versus bed-sleeping on health or back problems. The Japanese appear to adjust to sleeping on mattresses, box springs, and bed frames when they come to this country, but I am told that this is not without some difficulty too. One family I know of gave up futons because they felt self-conscious about the daily sunning and airing, and they were not about to use the futons without this. But when they took to beds, they found it disturbing to sleep so high.

Whatever adjustment problems to sleeping on a futon you might face, you might find, if you are in a transitional stage of life where you move frequently and have guests in and out, that having a small, light futon or two is quite useful. You can always take it with you when you move, which will give you some useful continuity, and it is easy to find room to store one in a small apartment because a thin one rolls up nicely. (Thick, heavy futons will *not* roll up, so if you will have to store yours away when it is not in use, be sure to buy one that rolls up.) The futon can provide a place for friends to sleep, although not, perhaps, your grandmother. It would be a good idea to cover the futon with an allergen-impermeable cover and then put a regular cover over that, which you could remove and wash monthly or more often. You can dress a futon like a Western bed with sheets and blanket and wash the linens each week. You can also provide a platform to rest it on. If you could manage to air and sun it often, it would stay fresh far longer. In Japan, futons are passed on from generation to generation, but periodically they are sent out to professional cleaners who clean and restore them. Your futon will require similar attention to remain healthful and comfortable.

Waterbeds conform brilliantly to the shape of your body and won't collect dust mites. Some of the problems they used to have, such as too much wave action, have been solved by using baffles inside. They are still trouble to fill and keep safe, however, and arthritics may find them hard to get in and out of.

A bed board is a board placed between the box spring and the mattress to shore up the mattress, particularly if it is sagging, and give you firmer support. It makes a phenomenal difference—a most unpleasant one, in my experience. Twice in my life, while spending several weeks away from home, I have unknowingly slept—or tried to—on beds that had bedboards. Although they say you will eventually adjust to a harder bed, I never did, discovering quite by accident the presence of the torture instrument. But these boards are said to be a godsend to many who suffer from back problems, and they also can extend the life of the mattress. If you need one, a piece of plywood 1/2 inch thick will do. You can put it under the entire mattress or under just your side.

Pillows. Most pillows are filled with down, feathers, a mixture of down and feathers, polyester foam, or foam or "synthetic down" made of some other substance, including

CARING FOR MATTRESSES

As they age, mattresses settle and acquire shapes in accordance with the weight and shape of your body. If you are large and your mate small or if you always sleep alone on the same side of the mattress, your side of the mattress may grow flatter. To ensure even aging, therefore, you should turn the mattress every few months. If it is constructed the same on both sides, you should also flip it over. Experts say that you should turn it frequently when it is new, perhaps every month, and decrease the frequency as it gets older. The idea is that the mattress is settling and adjusting more when it is new than when it is older. (They also advise rotating the box spring, although this is less important.) Jumping on the bed will age the mattress.

Vacuum the mattress carefully when you change the cover. Vacuum the cover when you change the mattress pad. Vacuum the mattress pad when you change the sheets. Those fighting allergies may benefit greatly from extra vacuuming of the mattress and frequent washing of the bedding. If you have a yard, drag the mattress outside on a warm sunny day for an airing twice a year, spring and fall. Leave it in the sun for at least three to four hours; all day is even better.

rubber. When it comes to comfort, there is no fixed rule about which you should use or how firm your pillow should be. It is a matter of what feels good to you and what gives you a good night's sleep without a stiff neck or an allergy attack.

The allergy-prone used to be advised to avoid feather pillows and use polyester ones. But some research suggests that polyester pillows, too, hold dust-mite allergens just as feather pillows do and may even constitute a greater risk factor for asthma attacks than feather ones. Asthmatics, and the parents of asthmatic children, should always consult their own doctors on choice of bedding. There appear to be people who are allergic to the feathers themselves, quite apart from their attractiveness to mites, although this idea, too, has been challenged. The clearest lesson seems to be that if you are taking precautions against allergies, you should use allergen-impermeable covers on any kind of pillow; and, of course, people who are allergic to feathers or down should avoid them.

Goose down is the softest, lightest, and most resilient filling for pillows; goose-down pillows are considered to be far superior to any other type. Duck down also makes a superior pillow. Down pillows change shape and bunch when you sleep on them. Synthetic-filled pillows, which are generally firm, do not change shape or bunch. Imitation or synthetic down can be quite soft and cost less than real down. It is said to resist packing down and bunching, but I am not sure this is desirable. At any rate, it is a matter of taste. Replace down and feather pillows in five to ten years or when they grow thin, soiled, and odorous (and when they do not improve upon washing), whichever is sooner. Replace synthetic pillows every two years or so, or sooner if they lose resilience or get irremediably soiled. To test for resilience in a pillow, press it in the middle to see if it springs back. When a loose pillow sags limply over your arm, it is at the end of its days.[2]

Although most people think goose-down pillows are best, feather pillows also have their admirers. Feather pillows are firmer than down, but with more give and flexibility and not so firm as synthetic-fiber pillows usually are—just what many of us want. You can also buy pillows with a mixture of down and feathers in whatever proportions you prefer; this type of pillow is delightfully comfortable and less costly than all-down. Goose feathers are considered highest quality, with duck feathers next, and chicken and turkey feathers last. (Better feathers are softer and more resilient.) If you buy a feather pillow, make sure the ticking is well made—strong, closely woven, and tightly seamed so that feathers cannot poke through. Be sure to sniff a feather pillow. Good ones will not have an unpleasant or strong smell.

You can also buy pillows stuffed with kapok, a vegetable fiber. Although it mats and gets lumpy faster than other types, it dries quickly and thus is sometimes favored for damp places such as seashore cottages and boats.

As to the proper degree of firmness, the rule of thumb you hear is to use a firm pillow if you sleep on your side and a soft one if you sleep on your stomach (but you really should not sleep on your stomach if you can help it). When you sleep on your side, you want your head to stay aligned with your spine, so you want a firm pillow to hold it higher. But if you sleep on your stomach, a firm pillow would hold your head and neck up too high and arch your back improperly. Good sleeping generally means using only one pillow under your head. You might want to add one at your knees, too, particularly if you are pregnant: if you are lying on your side, put it between your knees to keep your back from swaying; if you are lying on your back, put it under your knees to tilt your pelvis into a comfortable position (unarching your back).

In addition to standard pillows, there are many pillows shaped for specialized functions: neck pillows, wedge pillows that tilt the upper body up (good for snorers and apnea sufferers), body pillows, and many more. If you have any particular problems with sleep position, it is worth it to explore the possibilities.

58

Closets for Clothes and Linens

Storing clothes and linens . . . Putting away linens . . . Putting away clothes . . . Caring for your clothes . . . Hats . . . Gloves . . . Shoes

Clothes and linens stay fresher, safer, and cleaner in well-managed closets. Here is a summary of what good management of linen and clothes closets consists of.

In General: Storing Clothes and Linens

Closets should be cool, dry, and airy. Mildew grows in warm, humid conditions, and it can infect cottons, linens, and other materials in your closets, including the very wood the closet is made of. Beware of hot pipes running through closets. Heat can age and discolor fabrics.

Closets need to undergo a major cleaning periodically. During spring or fall cleaning or whenever the mood hits you, empty the closets and chests; dust or wash down shelves, floors, walls, and ceilings. Let closets and chests dry and air thoroughly before you replace things; and wash or clean as many of their contents as feasible, even if they have not been used. Things that are stored for a long time tend to develop a musty smell that will, if not removed, infect the other things stored with them.

To keep clothing and linens fresh-smelling, give them air. Do not overcrowd your drawers and closets. Laying things on slatted shelves that permit air circulation is beneficial. For linens particularly, but for all stored fabrics, narrow shelves are preferable to deep ones both because things are easier to find and because air circulates better. You can also leave the door to the closet ajar now and then so that the closet gets frequent changes of air. (Do this, however, only at times when the air likely to circulate is fresh and sweet.) Air all clothes and linens after laundering and ironing and before replacing them in the closet to be sure that any hint of dampness is entirely dissipated. If you put even slightly damp linens or clothes in your closet, you can produce a musty smell that is impossible to obliterate without totally emptying the closet and cleaning or washing all its contents. If odors afflict your closets, you might try a chemical deodorizer. Calcium carbonate and activated charcoal absorb odors; baking soda effectively neutralizes them. You put one of these substances in an open container and set it in the chest or closet. (Potpourris and perfumes cannot remove odors, and the attempt to mask them usually just makes things worse.) But once the contents of the closet have absorbed the odors, in my miserably experienced opinion, none of these remedies is going to remove the odors from fabrics that have absorbed them. Curing closet mustiness takes so much labor, and fresh closets provide such continual benefits, that it is worthwhile being vigilant. (You can also try using silica gel, activated alumina, anhydrous calcium sulfate, and other desiccants to remove moisture from damp closets and cabinets.)

Although potpourris are not much good for removing odors, many of us enjoy their pleasant scents on our clothes or linens. Potpourris are perfumes. Commercial ones are usually too strong. If you have one that is too strong, take just a tiny bit of it, wrap it in cheesecloth, and tie it with a ribbon. Store the rest in an airtight container in a cool, dark place until you want more. My grandmother always used lavender (that she grew and dried herself)—and so sparingly that you could not detect the odor unless your face was pressed against the pillow. She would sometimes put a quince apple into the chest in which she stored linens to make a good scent. (Watch out for rotten quince apple stains.) Overuse of potpourris can contribute to stale closet odors. It is best if, when you open the closet door, you smell nothing at all, or perhaps if you can just catch the faint, reassuring scent of laundered cloth, one of the best smells in the world.

Wash or dry-clean all clothes and linens before seasonal or long-term storage. Insects and pests of all sorts will be attracted to dirt left on clothes and linens, and in the process of eating the dirt will harm the fibers. It is important to store them unstarched, too, since insects like silverfish will eat the starch and the fabric with it. Soil encourages mildew as well.

Store linen (flax fiber) unironed and loosely folded, since it is brittle and may otherwise crack at creases. Or you can roll linen. When it is stored for long periods, refold it with any creases in new places so that weakness does not develop along a crease line that could cause a crack.

Acid causes deterioration of cellulosic fibers. When doing long-term storage, and storage of antique, delicate, or heirloom linens, you should wrap the articles in acid-free paper and store them in acid- and lignin-free boxes. Acid-free storage materials are now widely available at home centers, photographic supply stores, and archival supply companies.

Do not store cotton or linen in plastic bags from the dry cleaner or in garment bags made of synthetic fibers that do not breathe. These can trap moisture inside. Dry-cleaner plastic bags contain plasticizers that can produce yellow streaks on fabrics. Besides causing yellowing and trapping moisture, these prevent the dry-cleaning fluids and fumes from evaporating. Muslin or canvas garment bags are a good choice. You can also wrap things in clean and well-rinsed sheets or similar articles of white or undyed cotton or linen.

Cedar chests are not recommended for long-term storage or for storage of antique, heirloom, or delicate linens and cottons. The cedar gives off fumes and acids that can yellow and damage cellulosic fibers.

To keep moths out, cleaning wool and silk is the most important thing you can do, for moths, like other pests, are attracted to soils. Moth larvae will attack silk, but it is not as vulnerable as wool and other hair fibers. Carpet beetles will damage wool and other hair fibers as well. In rare instances, silverfish will attack cotton or linen; this is more likely with starched cloth. Never put away cellulosic fibers starched unless you plan to use them within a few weeks. No synthetic fibers are vulnerable to pests; however, pests may attack fabrics made of blends containing man-made fibers. (On mothproofing and the vulnerabilities of natural fibers to pests, refer to chapter 17.)

Putting Away Linens

The time-honored method of stacking linens is to place the freshly laundered pieces on the bottom of the stack. The purpose of this is to make sure that one set of sheets or towels is not used over and over and worn to pieces while others are untouched. Stack sets together so that they are used together and age evenly. Fold as described in chapter 24, "Folding Clothes and Linens."

Putting Away Clothes

Airing and brushing clothes is effective. Air thoroughly garments that you have worn and brush them to remove any superficial dirt or dust before returning them to the closet. Airing and brushing is particularly crucial for wool clothes. This removes dust and perspiration and reduces the number of times you will have to clean or launder them, which helps them last longer. Periodically take out and air wool garments that are infrequently worn.

Let wool garments rest for a day or two after wearing. Through the natural elasticity of the wool, they will regain their proper shape.

Review the contents of clothes closets yearly. Garments that have hung a year without use should be washed or cleaned and then removed to long-term storage. They will begin to smell musty if left month after month or, worse, year after year, and their smell will taint the other clothes. After two years without wearing, give them away to someone who can use them.

Hang clothes with the top, middle, and bottom buttons buttoned and zippers closed. Empty garments' pockets before hanging, especially those of wool garments that are easily stretched, to preserve shape and prevent sagging and bulging. Woven wool, suits, dresses, blazers, and the like should be hung on wide, shaped hangers—padded ones are good—to reduce stress on the fabric at the point of hanging and to preserve proper shape.

Do not hang clothes too close together or they will wrinkle and there will be insufficient air in the closet to keep odors at bay. Clothes that shed will leave fibers on other clothes.

Traditionally, one hung only the clothes of the season in the closet, and the others were stored. This left plenty of room. But now people have far more clothes than they used to, and many city apartment dwellers have little closet space and even less storage space. As a result, closet design companies have sprung up that will renovate your closets, making astonishingly efficient use of their space. If you cannot afford this service, you can do much the same thing on your own by taking advantage of all the gadgetry available at the stores specializing in closet and storage widgets.

Even if you create highly efficient closets, however, seasonal storage of clothes is best. It causes a regular turnover of your closet contents that reduces the possibilities of staleness (and chaos) developing. If storage is proper, it results in slower aging of your clothes. The traditional changeover times are Memorial Day and Labor Day, but it depends upon your local climate; March or April and October or November might be more sensible for you. Some people like to do this at spring and fall cleaning.

When putting away clothes in dressers and on shelves, follow the folding instructions in chapter 24.

Caring for Your Clothes

Do not wash or clean clothes more frequently than necessary. These processes visit wear and tear on garments, contributing over time to fading, pilling, fraying, holes, and the like. If you have worn a shirt for an hour and did not soil it or perspire heavily, hang it, button the neck, middle, and bottom buttons, and air it. Then put it back in your closet. If you have been wearing a garment for a short time and spill a drop of coffee or food on it, try to remove the spot without laundering or cleaning the whole garment.

But if clothes have received a real perspiration bath or heavy soil, wash them sooner rather than later, and wash them frequently. Dirt and sweat will cause fabrics to deteriorate.

Use smocks and aprons when cooking, painting, or doing anything else liable to spot or soil your clothes. In the nineteenth century, the world was hard on people but kind to clothes. The poor clerks who drudged away for miserly wages from early morning to nine o'clock in the evening had sleeve guards to keep their shirts and coats free of ink and other soil. Desk workers today have the same problem with sleeves after leaning all day long on penciled paper, papers from a copier, and newsprint. Although they would be laughed out of the office if they took to wearing sleeve guards, at least they get to go home after eight hours to wash their clothes.

Use scarves to protect the necks and collars of coats (especially leather ones) and other outerwear, because hair and skin oils tend to cause oil staining and soiling in these areas. Such soil is hard to remove and especially unsightly.

Hats

Store hats on shelves in a hat box to keep off dust and prevent crushing and denting. Or wrap them in clean muslin cloth. If a hat has a crown, stuff it with tissue.

Gloves

Put away gloves flat, in a drawer or box. Keep coloreds separate by placing a piece of cloth or tissue paper around them, for occasionally they can transfer color to other gloves.

Shoes

Shoes are safer on shelves than on the floor. Place shoe trees inside them to ensure that they stay straight, and keep them in individual shoe sacks or wrap them in tissue paper, especially if you do not wear them often.

SAFE SHELTER

59

Being Prepared

The importance of safety practices . . . Independent rating agencies, the UL Mark . . . How to use the safety guidelines . . . On emergencies . . . Home emergency chest . . . Calling for help . . . Medicine cabinets, list of desirable contents

I know many people who are afraid of flying in airplanes, being poisoned by pesticides in their food, and getting cancer from secondary smoke. None of them are particularly afraid of going home and falling down or taking the wrong medicine or being burned. Yet they are far, far more likely to be injured or killed at home from the latter causes than to crash in a Boeing 747 or to develop a pesticide- or smoke-induced tumor. The subjective sense of safety can be out of kilter with objective realities. Perhaps this partly accounts for the lack of proper caution that causes huge numbers of deaths and injuries in people's homes each year. It is important to feel safe in one's home but also to continue to modernize home safety practices in accordance with the latest thinking.

The safety recommendations of public health experts work. According to figures published by the National Safety Council, in the course of the twentieth century there have been extraordinary decreases in the rates at which people suffer death and injury through accidents from all causes in all places. The overall death rate from unintentional injuries plunged from 87.2 per 100,000 in 1903 to 35.4 in 1994. Home accidents accounted for 28 percent of deaths in 1912 but for only 10 percent of deaths in 1994. During that period, while the population nearly tripled, the total number of accidental home deaths stayed relatively constant at around 26,000.

The encouraging reduction in the number of accidents and deaths can be ascribed to vastly improved safety practices, the enactment of safety-oriented laws, and excellent programs for public education on safety as well as to improved medical treatment. The National Safety Council estimates that nearly four million lives were saved over the course of the century as a result of the decline. Many times that number were saved from terrible injury, suffering, disability, disfigurement, and impoverishment. Safety consciousness is a huge success story, but the story is a continuing one.

The number of people injured and killed in home accidents continues to be far greater than it need be. Familiarity with the latest safety devices and the latest safety practices could save many more tens of thousands of lives and inestimable amounts of pain, despair, time, and money. It is estimated that in 1993 there were close to 19 million home injuries that resulted either in a need for medical attention or in restrictions on activities lasting not less than half a day. A huge number of these could have been prevented with no expense or trivial expense or simply by initiating a minor or easy change in home habits.

The old and the new are mixed together in the summaries of home safety rules that follow, but the precautions described here are by no means exhaustive. Every household should make a point of finding and reading safety literature. Make a special point of finding safety guidelines for any unusual situations that may exist in your home. All of the following organizations are potentially sources of outstanding advice. Countless others provide safety information relevant to a specific type of danger, appliance, or activity. Addresses for the national organizations listed below are listed in the Acknowledgments and Sources at the end of this book; use the government pages of your telephone book to find the numbers for your local fire and police departments. Your utility company bill most likely has a general information number printed on it somewhere. You can also find excellent information published by some of these and other sources on the Internet.

Centers for Disease Control
Consumer Products Safety Commission
National Fire Protection Association
National Safety Council
United States Department of Agriculture (and local cooperative extension services)
National Electrical Safety Foundation
American Gas Association
National Swimming Pool Foundation
Underwriters Laboratories
American Red Cross
Your local utility companies—water, electric, gas
Your local police department
Your local fire department

Independent Rating Agencies; the UL Mark

In choosing any electrical appliances, cords, fire extinguishers, smoke detectors, or carbon monoxide detectors for your home, always look for a symbol or mark from an independent third-party certification agency or testing laboratory. The one you are most likely to encounter on products used in the home is that of Underwriters Laboratories, whose "UL Mark" can be found on many electric and safety appliances and other equipment you buy for domestic use. Others include the Canadian Standards Association (CSA), and the ETL Testing Laboratories (ETL), which is part of Intertek Testing Services (ITS). These organizations, and others like them, run laboratories that develop safety standards for equipment and appliances used in homes or businesses, and test appliances, products, and materials for electric, fire, burglary resistance, or other hazards. UL and CSA, which are not-for-profit organizations, also engage in public safety education and distribute literature on a variety of safety topics. Some certifying and rating organizations, including those just mentioned, are also Nationally Recognized Testing Laboratories (NRTLs). This means that they meet certain legal standards of the Occupational Safety and Health Administration (OSHA) and are legally qualified to certify that various products used in workplaces meet national safety standards.

If you have questions about particular areas of safety or about particular kinds of products, you can write directly to UL or other testing and certification organizations or check their sites on the Internet.

How to Use the Safety Guidelines

The safety guidelines in chapters 60 through 65 are for reading at your leisure, not for emergency use. Most of them consist of suggestions for cost-free new habits that keep you safer; a few involve buying and installing relatively inexpensive equipment. Pick an area that interests or concerns you and read the relevant sections *in their entirety*. For example, when it is time to put up holiday decorations, read the sections on Christmas decorations and trees, on fires, on candles, and on electrical safety. In the fall, review the materials on furnaces, heating, fireplaces, and space heaters, and think through their applicability to your home. You may find that you need more information or have further questions. You can pursue these by calling or writing to helpful experts or by going to the library and doing a little more reading. Once you have digested what you have learned or raised your safety awareness a notch or two, you may find yourself ready to make some valuable changes.

On Emergencies

Some people panic and lose their heads in an emergency. They have never thought through what they would do if faced with the danger before them. They feel, perhaps rightly, that it is too late now to figure it out. The panic that overwhelms them often prevents them from taking some simple step that would prevent tragedy.

Fear alone, no matter how intense, however, will not disorganize and paralyze you. It is feeling helpless to do anything about what you fear that transforms fear into panic. *Nine-tenths of courage is being prepared. Being prepared gives you enough of a sense of control to enable you to do what you must in an emergency.*

Having even the simplest of plans in place for responding to emergencies both calms panic and reduces risks. A plan for a six-year-old might amount simply to knowing how to dial 911 and give her address (instead of hiding under the bed or crying helplessly). A well-practiced fire escape plan, emergency numbers posted by the telephone, a first-aid kit that has in it what the voice on the telephone tells you to administer, just knowing not to flip on a light switch when there's a strong smell of gas—all will markedly increase your chances of surviving danger and of being able to help others survive too. Everyone should know how to find the shut-off switches or valves for their home's water, gas, oil, and electricity. Label the switch or valve, and record the information in your emergency chest.

Home Emergency Chest

Your home should have an emergency chest prepared for use at all times. Keep it in a cool, dry place and make sure that everyone in the family knows where it is kept. Keep a list of its contents, and once or twice a year review it to see that you have everything. Periodically replace contents that are becoming too old to use. A suggested list of contents for an emergency chest is given below; add or delete items to suit your own needs and special situations.

- Flashlights with fresh batteries
- Radio, battery operated
- Plenty of extra batteries for flashlights and radio
- Matches
- Candles (but rely on flashlights as much as possible to reduce fire hazard)
- Canned or nonperishable packaged foods

- Canned or nonperishable baby foods
- Canned or nonperishable baby formula or milk
- Canned or UHT milk
- Can and bottle opener (nonelectric)
- Bottled water
- Chlorine bleach or other water purifier/ disinfectant (replace every six months)
- Extra prescription medicines for anyone in the household who takes them
- Extra eyeglasses for all in the family who wear them
- Information relating to the health needs of family members—the make and serial number of pacemakers, special items needed by infants, and so on
- Fire extinguisher (ABC)
- Blankets, sleeping bag, or other wraps in cold climates
- First-aid kit
- Extra car keys
- Credit cards and cash
- A list of emergency telephone numbers
  - General emergency number (911)
  - Local police department
  - Local fire department
  - Doctors, including specialists, for all family members,
  - Local poison control center
  - Gas, electric, and other utilities
  - Relatives or friends to be contacted in emergencies (with addresses also)
  - Nearby neighbors

Ask your doctor or health-care provider for suggestions about what to keep in your first-aid kit in the way of antiseptics, emetics, bandages, tools (such as tweezers or blunt-tipped scissors), medicines, painkillers, and the like. Other good sources of information are the Red Cross or a reliable home medical encyclopedia or guide.

Calling for Help

Keep a list of emergency numbers at your telephone as well as in your home emergency chest: your doctors, poison control center number, fire department, police department, utility companies, friends' and relatives' numbers, and the numbers of nearby neighbors. Teach children how to summon emergency help: how to dial 911 or other appropriate numbers and how to give their correct address.

The elderly, invalids, and disabled people might consider carrying a cordless phone about with them. This will enable them to call for help if they should be immobilized at a distance from a regular telephone. There are also various devices that are carried or worn on clothing or the body that will summon aid when you simply push a button. You need not be able to talk. Check consumer advice publications before choosing one.

Medicine Cabinets

Here is a list of items that many experienced households find it useful to keep in their medicine chests.* Ask your family doctor for further suggestions suited to your own household's needs.

- Pain relievers and fever reducers—aspirin, acetaminophen (Tylenol and other brands), or ibuprofen; children's acetaminophen for households with children
- Adhesive bandages, sterile gauze, and adhesive tape, all in various sizes and widths, plus blunt-tipped scissors
- Ace bandage

*This list is adapted from the one given by Hamilton Southworth in his essay "The Home Medicine Chest" in the home medical encyclopedia I prefer, *The Columbia University College of Physicians and Surgeons Complete Home Medical Guide* (Crown, 1989), pp. 810–813. Refer to this essay for further excellent advice.

Antibiotic creams—Betadine, Bacitracin, Neosporin, or similar products

Cotton swabs

Sterile cotton balls

Antacids for heartburn and stomach aches

Mild laxative

Antidiarrhea medication

Itch medicine (antipruritic), such as calamine lotion

Hydrocortisone cream (for eczema, insect bites, and so on)

Sodium bicarbonate (baking soda)

Petroleum jelly (Vaseline)

Over-the-counter cold/allergy remedy (check freshness routinely): antihistamine and decongestant; also in children's versions if you have children

Cough syrup, expectorant

Over-the-counter eye wash (collyrium) with eye cup

Splinter removal equipment—tweezers, fine needle

Rubbing alcohol

Teaspoon for measuring out doses or plastic calibrated liquid medicine cup (for children)

Syrup of ipecac to induce vomiting (when recommended in the event of poisoning), especially in homes with small children or where small children visit

Sunscreen cream or lotion, SPF 15 or higher, effective against UVA and UVB

Oral thermometer (and for infants, an underarm or rectal thermometer)

Miscellaneous items that may or may not fit in your medicine chest but should be kept nearby:

- Your home medical encyclopedia and first-aid instruction book*
- Hot water bottle
- Flashlight for reading labels when lights go out
- Heating pad
- Ice pack holder

Your medicine cabinet should be set up in a cool, dry area. Bathrooms are usually not the best place, as they are often steamy and warm.

*Dr. Southworth suggests the American Red Cross's *Standard First Aid and Personal Safety.*

60

Fire

Fire and burn prevention . . . Smoking . . . Kitchen fires . . . How to put out grease and pan fires . . . Clothing and hair fires . . . Where to store flammable or combustible liquids and gases . . . Using flammable or combustible liquids safely . . . Lawn mowers . . . Gas . . . Pilot lights . . . What to do when you smell gas in your home . . . Other cautions for using gas appliances . . . Supplemental heaters . . . Kerosene and other fuel-burning heaters . . . Charcoal grills and other barbecue grills . . . Furnaces . . . Vents, flues, and chimneys . . . Holiday and Christmas decorations . . . Candles . . . Miscellaneous fire prevention habits . . . Fleeing fires; fight or flight? . . . Fire escape plans, safety ladders . . . Smoke detectors . . . Fire preparedness . . . Fire extinguishers and where to place them . . . Maintenance and disposal of fire extinguishers . . . What kind of fire extinguisher you need . . . How to use your extinguisher . . . Sprinkler systems

Fires cause death and injury both directly and indirectly. Their flames kill, but more people die from inhaling smoke and poisonous gases created by fires than die from burns. These substances act on you like a narcotic, driving you more deeply asleep or reducing your ability to think quickly and react rationally when you are awake. Since fires move fast, people caught in fires may find themselves desperately needing to react fast and reliably just when their ability to do so is compromised. This is why we drill ourselves and our children to prepare for fires. We want to be able to do certain things right almost automatically, so that we will be able to do them even when we are hurt, frightened, groggy, and confused.

Most fire safety rules aim first and foremost at fire prevention (see "Fire and Burn Prevention," below). Another important part of fire safety is knowing when not to fight the fire, how to escape it, where to use smoke alarms and how to maintain them, and how to set up your home so as to facilitate safe escape (discussed in "Fleeing Fires; Fire Preparedness," below). Still other fire safety guidelines aim at helping you control a small, contained fire and safely use extinguishers (discussed in "Fire Control: Fire Extinguishers," below). The prevention of electrical fires is taken up separately in chapter 61.

Fire and Burn Prevention

Smoking. Despite the strength of the antismoking campaign, smoking materials continue to be the leading cause of fire deaths in homes in the United States. As late as 1991, three-fourths of residential fires and 63 percent of fire-associated deaths were attributable to smoking materials.

Smoking in bed can be lethal. The smoker falls asleep holding a lit cigarette. An ash falls on clothes, bedclothes, or bedding or mattresses, smolders for hours, and releases smoke and poisonous gases. These cause the smoker to sleep more and more deeply or even render him unconscious. The same thing can happen if you fall asleep with a lit cigarette while watching television or reading. It is safer not to smoke while viewing or reading.

Never leave a cigarette, cigar, or pipe burning unattended.

Use heavy ashtrays that will not tip over. Never empty an ashtray unless you are certain that the ashes are extinguished.

Empty ashtrays into the toilet, or place them in an empty metal container. Or you can place the ashtray in a sink full of water until its contents are soaked.

Be cautious with cigarettes around flammable materials; avoid getting ashes on clothing and draperies. Watch out for fabrics that blow in the wind, such as curtains.

If someone must smoke in the home, the best policy is to have a safe smoking place and to limit smoking to this place; it is much easier to make one spot safe than a whole home. Make your smoking area near an open window that will carry off the smoke. Keep a sturdy, nontipping ashtray available there and use fire-resistant upholstery and carpeting in that area.

Fires sometimes erupt following a party, when the hosts have gone to bed. An ashtray that contains a lit cigarette can easily be spilled and go unnoticed in a crowd of people. After a party attended by smokers, carefully inspect all rooms in which they were present, looking behind sofas and under furniture.

Keep matches, lighters, and all other smoking materials safely out of the reach of children. Never let children handle them.

Kitchen Fires. Kitchens are another frequent site for the start of residential fires. Careless cooking is usually the cause of kitchen fires. They begin with grease fires or pots that burn up on the stove, or when something flammable like a paper towel or tea towel or clothing accidentally touches a flame or hot burner.

Do not leave cooking pots and pans on the stove unattended. Turn the burner off when you leave the room. If you are simmering something on the stove and forget about it, the moisture in the pot will eventually boil away and what is left in the pan can begin to burn. When something is cooking in the oven, check on it every fifteen minutes or so. Carry the spoon or potholder with you if you leave the kitchen as a reminder that you left something in the oven. Keep it in your hand if you answer the phone.

If you are frying, grilling, roasting, or broiling something, so that grease and oil are present in the cooking pan, a grease fire is always a possibility. For those who have not yet experienced one, a grease fire starts when oil or grease in a pan becomes so hot that it bursts into flame. This can happen in a skillet or pot, in the broiler, or in the oven, and it can be scary enough to leave you feeling weak in the knees. Grease fires sometimes are also caused when grease is allowed to accumulate in the broiler pan, the oven, or the hood vent filter after spattering during cooking.

On the stovetop, do not let a pan of oil overheat; do not forget to turn off the burner under the pot when you have finished cooking. (You can easily forget the oil you are warming when you answer the telephone. Never leave the burner on while you do this.) Always empty and clean the broiler pan after every use. Wipe out any spilled grease in the oven. Clean the vent filters when you know they have been splattered; also do it periodically just for good measure.

When cooking on a gas stove, use small pots only on small burners, and never let flames rise up the sides of the pot. This can lead to mishaps—burns and fires.

Keep potholders at hand to use while cooking, and use only flame-resistant ones. Never use towels as potholders; they might dangle onto the burner or the gas flame and catch on fire. *Never, never use your clothing as a potholder.* Burns caused by loose sleeves or scarves or ties dangling onto hot gas flames and electric burners are common. (See "Clothing and Hair Fires" below. Do not hang curtains where they might blow into a burner's flame. Do not hang towels to dry above the stove.

Pots and pans with flat bottoms are less likely to tilt and spill and cause cooking fires that way. Those with handles that do not get hot are less likely to be dropped and spilled.

Set up your kitchen to minimize the danger of a fire near the stove. Do not keep flammable materials and objects—paper, cloth, wood—hanging around the stove, and make sure that no extension cords are close enough to get scorched or burned. Keep the stovetop free of combustible materials such as matches, recipe cards, and potholders.

Do not store in your oven anything flammable like bread or other food. You can all too easily forget that something is inside when you turn on the oven.

Keep appliances clean and free of crumbs and grease. Toasters and toaster ovens can set grease and crumbs on fire.

Unplug countertop appliances when not in use. Make sure the stove is off when not in use. Check these things when you make your final round for closing down the house at night.

Do not use flammable aerosols in the kitchen, and do not store them in the kitchen anywhere near areas that may be heated up by the stove, oven, or other appliances.

Good housekeeping under the sink is important. Keep containers clean and their labels legible. Clean up spills quickly. Keep all

HOW TO PUT OUT GREASE AND PAN FIRES

If the grease or other fire is in a pan on the stovetop, turn off the burner and put a lid over the pan. This will deprive the fire of oxygen and suffocate it. If the fire is in the oven or broiler, turn off the stove and close the door of the oven or broiler. The fire will soon exhaust the oxygen inside and extinguish itself. You can also throw baking soda over the fire or use your fire extinguisher. *If you use a fire extinguisher, it must be one that says "B" on its label*—for example, an ABC or a BC extinguisher. Salt would smother the fire, but it is not recommended; when salt gets very hot it pops out of the pan and can land on your skin and burn you. *Never pour water on a grease fire.* If you do so, the hot grease will splatter and burn you badly. *Never pick up a pan that contains burning grease and walk with it.* You are likely to spill the burning grease on yourself or, worse, a child who gets in your path or grabs your knees in fear. *Leave the pan on the stove.*

containers tightly closed. Flammable materials—and some cleaning materials are flammable—should not be stored under the kitchen sink. (They should also be kept separate from foods and out of children's reach.)

Clothing and Hair Fires. Clothing fires are remarkably common. People's clothes catch on fire from cigarettes, matches, fireplace sparks, and many other causes. Clothing fires are not only more common among elderly people *but are far more dangerous to elderly people.* The older you are, the more difficult it is for your body to recover from a burn—even a burn that does not seem to you to be serious.

To prevent clothing fires, when you are cooking anything at all, lighting your grill or fireplace, or doing anything involving flames: do not wear loose or dangling sleeves such as those that are common on bathrobes, kimonos, and flowing negligees. Never wear bows or ribbons, anything else that dangles, or anything that a breeze could make billow up. My grandmother once set her apron strings on fire at the stove. People commonly set their bathrobe sleeves on fire while they are making a cup of tea for breakfast.

Use fireplace screens; follow all other safety rules for fireplace operation set forth in chapter 48.

If your clothes catch on fire, the old rule is still best: *Stop, drop, and roll.* Do not walk, run, or spread out your arms, as all these things will fan the flames; dropping to the floor prevents flames from getting to your face and smoke from getting into your lungs. Roll with your arms close to your body, your hands covering your face. Keep rolling until the flames are out.

If your child's clothing catches on fire, the same advice holds. Push the child to the ground and roll the child. If you have a blanket or similar object immediately at hand, you can roll the child in the blanket to suffocate the flames. But, obviously, don't leave to go looking for one.

Hair burns very quickly. If you have long hair, tie it back securely when you are cooking, building a fire in the fireplace, lighting your space heater, leaning toward a lit grill, or doing anything else involving flames.

Where to Store Flammable or Combustible Liquids and Gases. Storing flammable liquids? Don't! The best way to store flammable liquids is *not at all.* Do not keep any flammable liquid longer than you have to. When you no longer need the product, get rid of it.

Some flammable liquids simply do not belong anywhere in anyone's home. Among these are fuels such as gasoline or kerosene; they should not be in your basement, your attached garage, your workshop, your attic, or elsewhere in your home. They should be stored only in a detached structure, such as a shed or detached garage, that is drafty or very highly ventilated. Many other liquids that are commonly stored in the home or the home workshop—such as cleaning fluids, solvents, some aerosol sprays—are also highly flammable. If you can, store these, too, outside the home in a well-ventilated area. Always make sure that they are kept in well-labeled metal cans that are UL-rated safe for the purpose, with tightly closed lids.

Fuels like gasoline and kerosene vaporize so readily that if they are stored in a somewhat enclosed area, such as a basement or a workshop, their fumes can build to a dangerous level. These fumes are highly combustible and can be ignited by a tiny spark, perhaps a spark inside your wall when you switch on a light or a spark inside an electric appliance when you turn it on. Pilot lights on a stove or on a hot-water heater or furnace can also ignite the fumes.

A typical accident scenario involves a spill of gasoline in the basement, which then fills with gasoline fumes. The fumes are ignited by the pilot light on the hot-water heater. Gasoline fumes can build up over time even without a spill, escaping, for instance, from a gasoline can or when the lid is left off the lawn mower's tank.

Gas cylinders holding propane or other compressed or liquefied gases and appliances that use them, such as grills, cookers, or heaters and similar appliances, also *have no business in the home at any time for any reason.* These appliances should never be used indoors in any manner or under any circumstances—not in your fireplace, not on your glassed-in porch.

Read labels on all products stored under your sink, in your bathroom, or in your cleaning cabinet or workshop. You might be surprised by which cleaners, toiletries, or household aids are flammable. Follow all manufacturers' instructions carefully! Never place these substances near old stacks of newspapers or magazines or other junk that would easily burn. If you can, store them in a detached structure, perhaps a garage or shed—never in your basement. Be sure that their containers are properly sealed, sound, leakproof, and clearly labeled as to their contents. As soon as you are finished with one, get rid of it. Keep all products in their original containers or in well-labeled, all-metal, tightly lidded containers that are UL-rated safe for the purpose.

Store flammable liquids in safety containers that bear the UL Mark and have tightly fitting lids. Their contents should be clearly labeled. *Never put gasoline in glass or plastic containers or in containers that have any plastic parts. Never put one kind of flammable liquid or fuel into a container that has ever contained any other kind.* For example, never put gasoline in a container that you sometimes use for kerosene or turpentine or vice versa. If you do, you may mix the two fluids, which can be exceedingly dangerous even if only a trace amount of one is present.

Using Flammable or Combustible Liquids Safely. Whenever you use flammable liquids, be sure that they are kept far away from any heat source, lit match or cigarette, pilot light, flame, or spark.

Use flammable liquids only in well-ventilated areas so that any fumes can be dispersed quickly and safely.

Never use gasoline as a cleaning solvent. This is exceedingly dangerous!

Use starter fluid only on cold coals, *never on lit coals or embers.* If you squirt the fluid onto burning coals or embers and it catches, the flames will travel back up the fluid to the container, which will then explode into flames in your hand. This is not a remote possibility but a likelihood. I know a child who was horribly injured in exactly this way.

Gas. Natural gas, widely used as a fuel in the home, is safe when treated with respect by informed people. Natural gas is naturally odorless, but an odor is added to it so that you will be able to detect its fumes and take proper safety measures. You may get a tiny whiff of this odor when you light your cooking stove, as a tiny bit of the gas escapes in the split second before the burner lights or before the oven goes on.

Pilot Lights. Modern appliances usually lack pilot lights, but older cooking stoves, furnaces, gas heaters and fireplaces, and clothes dryers have them. A pilot light is a place on the appliance at which a tiny amount of gas is constantly emitted and burns in a tiny flame; it is this flame that ignites the appliance's burner or heater when it is turned on. If the pilot flame is extinguished, the gas that feeds it continues to be emitted, and you will smell, faintly at first, the rotten-egg odor of the gas.

LAWN MOWERS

Store your mower outside your home and outside any structure attached to your home—not in your basement and not in your attached garage. Fill your mower with gasoline out of doors. After you have filled it, move it at least ten feet away from the place where you filled it to start it.

A STORY ABOUT VENTILATION AND KEROSENE

The rule about using flammable liquids only with plenty of ventilation is one whose importance I can illustrate with a story of a frightening childhood experience. This story also shows the dangers of storing flammable liquids in the home or basement and illustrates one way not to thaw frozen water pipes.

One January, when I was four or five years old, the water pipes to our farmhouse froze up, as they were apt to do in the depths of each winter. It was early evening, already dark outside, and my parents were preparing to try to thaw the pipes by holding a kerosene lamp near them to warm them.

The entire family had congregated in the cellar, where my father was filling the kerosene lamp, and the doors and windows were shut against the bitter cold. When he struck a match to light the lamp, the very air around us ignited in a flash. The fumes from the kerosene had grown so dense that they caught fire. We somehow ran in front of the wall of flames to the stairs, and we all got out without much more than singed eyelashes. By the time we could get the telephone operator to connect us to the fire department, the fire had extinguished itself. It's probably lucky we had no old Christmas tree or oily rags or old newspapers in our cellar. Our experience is often repeated by other families, some of them less fortunate than we were.

When a pilot light goes out, however, there is a risk, especially in a place with little ventilation, that the unburned gas will continue to accumulate for a long period of time (if no one notices that the pilot light has gone out) until the gas reaches dangerous levels. If this happens, it might ignite or explode if there happens to be a spark in the area or if someone lights a match. Even a tiny spark from turning on a light switch, or static electricity from clothing, might ignite the fumes.

If you have appliances with pilot lights, consult their instruction manuals to learn whether you can relight them yourself, following the manufacturer's instructions, or whether you should call a qualified service person or your gas company. Some, but not all, gas companies will do this free of charge. Some apartment buildings advise tenants to call the supervisor or building maintenance people to have a pilot light relit. Whatever course of action you choose, you should investigate *now* and decide what you will do in each case. If need be, you can discuss it with the service person who does the yearly inspection of your gas appliances. Another wise course of action is to find out what your local utility company recommends you do. One company, for example, instructs its customers to relight the pilot on the stove (if, for example, it is extinguished during cooking inadvertently) only if there is no odor. If there is any odor or if you do not know how long a pilot light has been out, this company tells its customers, evacuate everyone from the premises and call the company for help.

When you can, choose new appliances that have no pilot lights; for example, gas stoves with electric spark ignition. Choose only appliances with the seal of the American Gas Association or that show the mark of a nationally recognized third-party certification agency.

What to Do When You Smell Gas in Your Home. Utility companies want their customers to know what to do if they smell gas. Ask your own company for its advice, or check its site on the Internet. The American Gas Association recommends the following actions if you smell gas inside your home (or any other building):

- Alert others and leave the area immediately.
- Leave open any doors you pass through to help ventilate the area, but don't take time to open windows.

- Do not operate any electrical switches or equipment, including telephones and flashlights.
- Call the local gas company from a telephone outside the area. If you don't know the company number, call the local emergency number (911 in many areas) and ask the operator to call the gas company.
- Remain away from the area until the gas company declares the area safe.

If you are outside and smell gas, call the local gas company from somewhere outside the area where you smelled the gas.

Other Cautions for Using Gas Appliances. Check your gas stove to be sure burners and the oven are completely off after each use.

Have all gas appliances inspected and adjusted by qualified service personnel at least once a year.

Gas flames should burn blue, not yellow. If you are getting a yellow flame, that indicates incomplete combustion and a danger of carbon monoxide. (See chapter 29, page 415.) Call a qualified service representative to have your appliance adjusted. (A little hint of orange in the flame is not a trouble sign.)

If you have a gas heater or gas fireplace log, follow all the safety rules that apply to space and room heaters. See "Supplemental Heaters," below. If you must light the gas heater with a match, light the match first and then turn on the gas. Otherwise gas can accumulate while you are fumbling with a match and cause an explosion when you finally get it lit. If your gas log or heater is vented, be sure that the vent or chimney damper is open when it is lit.

Keep the area around hot-water heaters, furnaces, heaters, and other gas-burning appliances clear of dust, debris, and objects of any sort; and keep all vents clean and clear. Otherwise the dust or debris may easily ignite or you may obstruct air flow to the burner.

Do not line your oven with foil; this will interfere with air flow to the gas flame by blocking the air holes, resulting in carbon monoxide buildup.

Nothing combustible or flammable should be placed in the vicinity of gas appliances. Combustible and flammable liquids, and the fumes emitted by combustible and flammable liquids, are readily ignited by the flame or pilot light on gas appliances or by chance sparks.

Supplemental Heaters—Air Heaters, Room Heaters, or Space Heaters. Supplemental heaters are just that. You are not safe if you are trying to use them as your primary heat source. Many, many fires are caused by these machines. Study all manufacturer's instructions carefully and follow them to the letter. Reread them each year when you get the heater out to use again, so that you do not grow careless or forgetful. *Your oven is not a heater and should never be used for heat.*

All Heaters. Make sure that whatever heater you buy bears the UL Mark or that of another nationally recognized third-party certification agency.

If you have children or pets, place your space or room heater in a safety cage to make sure that they do not get burned by touching it. Or buy a model with a safety grille or safety guard.

Never leave a child or pet alone in a room with a heater that is on. Never permit a child to operate a heater.

Never leave any supplemental heater on while you are asleep or while you are out of the room in which the heater is running. Never leave the space heater running while you are away from home.

Operate all heaters at least three feet away from anything flammable—curtains, upholstery, bedding, firewood, and so on.

Set up the heater in a place in which it is out of walking paths and will not be knocked over or bumped. Never attempt to move the heater while it is lit.

Do not operate a space or room heater in a room in which there are flammable liquids or may be flammable fumes. Do not store liquid fuels such as gasoline or kerosene anywhere near a heater. Do not use paint, lacquer, or solvents such as turpentine or paint thinner in a room in which a space heater is being operated. (Ventilate well whenever you use such substances!) Carefully read the labels of any household cleaners or toiletries that you intend to use in a room with a heater to see whether they are flammable. If so, use them elsewhere! Dry-cleaning fluids, nail polish remover, and many other commonplace household substances should be kept far from space heaters.

Many aerosols are flammable, and aerosol cans exposed to too much heat from a space heater can explode.

Keep a fire extinguisher near the exit of the room in which you keep the heater. Always place a smoke alarm in any room in which you have such a heater.

Never use a heater for any purpose other than heating. Don't even think about using one for drying clothes, drying hair, or burning waste.

Vacuum the area around your supplemental heater frequently to keep it clear of dust and debris. Dust is highly combustible. (This, an experienced firefighter informs me, is why children who have gone under the bed to play with matches so often start a fire. When they strike the match, dust under the bed instantly ignites.)

Do not obstruct air flow in or around the heater by storing *anything* in, on, or around it.

Kerosene and Other Fuel-Burning Heaters. Any heaters that burn any type of fuel must either be vented or operated only in a well-ventilated room. To create adequate ventilation for an unvented heater or stove, open a window near the heater an inch or two, and keep open all doors to the room in which the heater is located.

Ventilation is necessary to admit oxygen and let out carbon monoxide. Without adequate ventilation for fuel-burning heaters, carbon monoxide may build up. Scores of deaths are caused this way each year. It is particularly dangerous to sleep in any room in which an unvented kerosene or gas heater is operating. There are always better ways to keep warm. Fuel-burning heaters also produce nitrogen dioxide, carbon dioxide, and sulfur dioxide as combustion by-products. *Adequate ventilation* is essential to remove or dilute these contaminants too, as evidence suggests that they are unhealthy to breathe. See chapter 29, page 414.)

Kerosene heaters are so dangerous that they are illegal in some places. Safety experts dislike them whether or not they are legal. If you have one, it is very important to know exactly how to handle it. Read the manufacturer's instructions not only before using it for the first time but each year when you get it out again. Have your kerosene heater cleaned and inspected by a qualified service person once a year.

Be sure to buy only a model that automatically turns off if tipped over. In any event, place it where it will not be knocked over or tripped over. The models that have an automatic lighting feature, operated by batteries, are preferable to those that you would have to light with a match. Never let a child light or operate such a heater!

Fill kerosene heaters only with 1-K kerosene, and use only clean, fresh fuel. You are encouraging disastrous fires or explosions if you use gasoline or any other type of fuel in your kerosene heater. Disaster can also occur if gasoline, even in trace amounts, is mixed with kerosene. Never mix kerosene with any other liquid or liquid fuel such as gasoline. Never store kerosene in a container that has ever been used to hold anything else, such as gasoline.

Never fill a kerosene heater when it is hot. Never fill a kerosene heater in your home. Wait until it cools. Then take it, or its tank if it has a removable one, outside for filling. Do the filling only in an area with plenty of ventilation. Do not fill it anywhere near a flame, lit cigarette, or any potential source of a spark.

Even flipping a light switch can cause a spark. Never, under any circumstances, let a child fill your kerosene heater.

Follow the manufacturer's instructions about cleaning the wick. Check it every week or two to see if it is dirty.

Carefully follow all the manufacturer's instructions on proper filling and on not overfilling. Kerosene expands as it heats. If you fill it to the top, you may get spilt kerosene in your house when the kerosene warms from operation of the heater, and this is dangerous.

Store the kerosene heater empty. Not only does the kerosene left in the tank pose a fire hazard, but kerosene spoils.

When you take out the kerosene heater in the fall, you need to inspect it, clean it, and get it ready for new use. Reread the manufacturer's instructions. Make sure there is no old kerosene left in it; if there is, get rid of it. (See chapter 64, "Poisons, Hazardous Substances, and Proper Disposal of Hazardous Household Wastes.") Put in fresh batteries.

Never store kerosene in the home. Store it outside in a detached shed or garage in a container designed for that purpose and bearing the UL Mark.

Charcoal Grills and Other Barbecue Grills. No barbecue grill is safe to use indoors. This means charcoal grills, grills fueled by compressed gas cylinders, and all other types.

Never burn charcoal indoors—not on a grill, in your fireplace, in a stove, or anywhere else. It causes great danger of carbon monoxide poisoning. If you use a charcoal grill in your yard, close the doors and windows to your home to prevent the fumes from coming inside.

Follow the manufacturer's instructions on care, use, and lighting of all grills. *Never, ever pour or squirt starter fluid or lighter fluid on flames, embers, or anything burning or smoldering.* The fluid will light and the fire will travel up the stream of fluid to the container and cause it to explode or burst into flame. Horrible injuries have been caused this way. Children especially are likely to ignore or forget this advice, as they may not understand the danger even after it is explained to them. *You must never let children light a barbecue grill or touch starter fluid or lighter fluid. Put all such dangerous substances out of their reach.*

Never store grills or other appliances with propane cylinders (or other compressed gas containers) in your home, in your basement, or in an attached garage or other attached structure.

Furnaces. Once a year, usually in the fall before heating season begins, have a qualified person come to inspect your heating system and perform any needed cleaning: furnace, heat vents, pipes, filters, blowers and blower compartment, ducts, fan belt, oiling or lubrication, thermostat, temperature controls, air vents, and so on. Make sure that pilot lights and burners are properly adjusted at all times. Follow the manufacturer's instructions to the letter as to how to prepare the furnace for use each fall, how often to check and change filters, and how often to clean the burners, controls, piping, and other parts.

Vacuum away dust and debris in the area around the furnace. Make sure that nothing obstructs air flow in or around your furnace.

Do not store flammable liquids in the same room or near or in the vicinity of your furnace. In fact, store *nothing* in the vicinity of your furnace. Do not leave stacks of old newspapers or magazines or other flammable materials in or near the basement or furnace room.

Install a smoke detector in the basement or wherever your furnace is located.

Fireplaces. See chapter 48.

Vents, Flues, and Chimneys. Each year before the heating season begins, have a qualified person check to see that all vents, flues, and chimneys for your stoves, furnaces, fireplaces, heaters, and all fuel-burning appliances are clear and open and

CONSUMER PRODUCTS SAFETY COMMISSION SAFETY GUIDELINES FOR USING GAS GRILLS*

Liquid petroleum (LP) gas or propane, used in gas grills, is highly flammable. Each year about 30 people are injured as a result of gas grill fires and explosions. Many of these fires and explosions occur when someone first uses a grill that has been left idle for a period of time or just after refilling and reattaching the grill's gas container. To reduce the risk of fire or explosion, routinely perform the following safety checks:

Check the tubes that lead into the burner for any blockage from insects, spiders, or food grease. Use a pipe cleaner or wire to clear blockage and push it through to the main part of the burner.

Check grill hoses for cracking, brittleness, holes, and leaks. Make sure there are no sharp bends in the hose or tubing.

Move gas hoses as far away as possible from hot surfaces and dripping hot grease. If you can't move the hoses, install a heat shield to protect them.

Replace scratched or nicked connectors, which can eventually leak gas.

Check for gas leaks, following the manufacturer's instructions, if you smell gas or when you reconnect the grill to the LP gas container. If you detect a leak, immediately turn off the gas and don't attempt to light the grill until the leak is fixed.

Keep lighted cigarettes, matches, or open flames away from a leaking grill.

Never use a grill indoors. Use the grill at least ten feet away from your house or any building.

Do not use the grill in a garage, breezeway, carport, porch, or under a surface that can catch fire.

Do not attempt to repair the tank valve or the appliance yourself. See an LP gas dealer or a qualified appliance repair person.

Always follow the manufacturer's instructions that accompany the grill.

To avoid accidents while transporting LP gas containers, consumers should transport the container in a secure, upright position. Never keep a filled container in a hot car or car trunk. Heat will cause the gas pressure to increase, which may open the relief valve and allow gas to escape.

Use caution when storing LP gas containers. Always keep containers upright. Never store a spare gas container under or near the grill or indoors. Never store or use flammable liquids, like gasoline, near the grill.

Use extreme caution and always follow the manufacturer's instructions when connecting or disconnecting LP gas containers.

Grills manufactured after October 1, 1995, are required to have three additional safety features to eliminate leak hazards: a device to limit the flow of gas in the event of hose rupture; a mechanism to shut off the grill; and a feature to prevent the flow of gas if the connection between the tank and the grill is not leak proof. Consider purchasing grills that have these safety features.

*This material is excerpted from the Consumer Products Safety Commission Guidelines Press Release #97-128.

functioning properly. They should be free of dust and debris, not to mention birds' and squirrels' nests. Furnace vents can become clogged with mud or other debris from outdoors. Keeping vents, flues, and chimneys free and clear of blockage can prevent fires and the danger of carbon monoxide buildup.

Chimneys need cleaning to remove creosote and soot periodically, too, as well as examination for structural soundness. (See chapter 48, pages 589–90.)

Holiday and Christmas Decorations. An artificial Christmas tree is safest—a thousand times safer than a real tree, an experienced firefighter tells me. If you have a real tree, buy a fresh tree from a reliable source, and do not set it up weeks in advance of Christmas. It will never make it through the end of the season if you do. A fresh tree has flexible twigs that bend rather than crack, and its needles are green.

Keep the Christmas tree from drying out. Cut off a couple of inches at the bottom so the trunk can take in water, and keep the tree well watered—there should be water in the stand at all times. Do not place the tree near radiators, heaters, vents, or other heat sources that might dry it or set it afire.

Never place a Christmas tree anywhere near a fireplace or candle or other flame or source of sparks, and do not use lit candles on the tree.

Do not put flammable decorations on a fireplace or the mantel of a fireplace in which a fire is lit.

Never leave young children or pets alone with a Christmas tree, especially if the lights are on.

Never leave the tree lights or other decorative lights burning when you are out of the home or when you are sleeping.

Keep a fire extinguisher (the ABC type) near the exit of the room in which you have your tree, and make sure that there is a smoke detector near by.

Once a tree is dried out, get rid of it—even if it is not Christmas yet. In that case get another tree; this is trouble, but it is sensible. When you have taken off the decorations, do not leave the dried-out tree sitting in the garage or on the porch. Immediately dispose of it, either by leaving it curbside on the proper day (if that is the procedure where you live) or by taking whatever steps are proper in your area. Do not burn a discarded tree—or discarded giftwrap or decorations—in your fireplace.

Electrical safety rules for Christmas trees and other electric decorations are given in chapter 61, "Electrical Safety."

Candles. Never leave a candle unattended. Never put a candle near anything flammable. Curtains, drapes, flowing sleeves, scarves, ties, and skirts, and other fabrics often are flammable and can easily be picked up by a breeze that touches them to a candle flame. Evergreen Christmas trees and wreaths are flammable too; never decorate them with candles.

Make sure that candles are secure in their holders. Place candles where they will not be knocked over. Make sure that even if they are knocked over they will not land on something flammable. Do not, for instance, light up a bouquet of paper poinsettias with candlelight, no matter how securely the candle stands.

Children of all ages are dangerously attracted to fire. Do not leave them alone with lit candles to be tempted to engage in dangerous play, not even for one second. Store matches and candles out of the reach of children.

Miscellaneous Fire Prevention Habits. Do not keep stacks of newspapers, magazines, cardboard boxes, oily rags, old clothing, and junk anywhere in your home. These are so readily combustible that they often cause fires. If a fire gets started in some other way, these provide quick-burning, extra fuel, increasing the size and danger of the fire.

Store oily or greasy rags in labeled, sealed, all-metal containers.

Buy fireproof and fire-resistant materials insofar as you can for your carpeting, upholstery, mattresses, and draperies and curtains.

Sleep with your bedroom door closed. This will slow down the spread of smoke and fire into your room.

Other Causes of Burns. See chapter 65, "Additional Safety Measures for Children."

Turn pot handles inward on the stovetop so that no one bumps them and so that young children cannot grab them and spill hot food on themselves.

Hot radiators burn many people every year. Put protective covers on them.

Electrically Caused Fires. Electrically caused fires are discussed in chapter 61.

Aerosol Cans. No aerosol can should be punctured or burned, regardless of what it has contained. Keep all aerosols away from heat. They contain gases that expand when heated, creating pressure that may make the can explode. Serious injuries can result. In addition, aerosols may contain chemicals that produce harmful fumes when heated.

Fleeing Fires; Fire Preparedness

Fight or Flight? Fire can grow and spread with astonishing speed. Fire safety experts, therefore, say that when there is a fire you should first get everyone out as fast as you can and then call the fire department. Do not try to fight the fire yourself unless it is quite minor and confined to a small area. Do not try to put out even a small fire if there is a great deal of smoke.

If a fire is quite small and contained or minor, you can try to fight it with your extinguisher. But fire safety experts advise that if you do not succeed in extinguishing it in ten seconds, give up. Get everyone out, and then call the fire department. If the fire is not quite small or minor, do not attempt to fight it, even for ten seconds. Just get everyone out, then call the fire department.

Many people do not realize, however, that even when you succeed in putting out a small fire with your fire extinguisher, you should still call the fire department. The fire department should inspect the premises to make sure that the fire is not still smoldering in hidden areas or in areas distant from the one where you put out the fire. Fire can "skip" floors or bypass areas in ways that only the experts understand.

Fire Escape Plans. Your family should have a fire escape plan down pat. Practice regularly. Everyone, children included, should also try practicing it in the dark. Could you find your way to any exit in the house if a fire had put out all the lights or if the smoke was too thick to see through? Could your children? If you live in an apartment building, does your whole family know all its exits?

Make sure that every room has two exits (a window can be a fire exit) and that every member of the family knows at least two ways out of every room. You should be able to exit without using keys or tools: you will not have time to look for these when there is a fire. You might keep a lightweight, portable, folding safety ladder to be used for emergency exits from bedrooms or other places.

Designate a safe, well-lit meeting place outside your home. That way, if family members have left by different exits, no one is tempted go back in looking for someone who is safely out but cannot be located. Do not waste time looking for valuables, shoes, wallets, purses, or any other possessions.

Do not lock yourself or your family in with a fire. Make sure that windows you rely on as emergency exits can be opened—especially any that open onto the fire escape. If you want security bars at a window, install the type that have a single-action quick release. Everyone in the family should know how to release the bars readily. *Never* use a lock on bars or window gates. (Window gates that require a key to gain access to the fire escape are illegal in many places.) Do not use door locks that you need keys to open from the inside—single deadbolt locks with inside thumb turns. If you must have a double key deadbolt (a bolt that can be locked with a key from both inside

SAFETY LADDERS

Safety ladders can be used for exiting second or third floors. They should be made of metal and constructed in such a way that the steps stand out from the wall, enabling you to get a safe foothold. The top should grip the windowsill firmly.

and outside), leave the key in the inside lock whenever anyone is inside.

As you exit, check the doors for heat before going through them. As I was taught by my four-year-old, who was taught it by a firefighter who visited his nursery school, do not test a door for heat by touching it with the palm of the hand. Test it with the back of the hand, which has fewer nerve endings and will be less hurt if the door is very hot. If a door is hot, *do not enter.* Use an alternative exit. If there is smoke when you open the door, close it and go to the alternative exit. *Close all the doors you pass through as you exit.* This will help keep the fire from spreading.

When getting out of a burning house, stay low; crawl along the floor. There will be less smoke and more oxygen, and it will be cooler lower down. If you can't see, follow the walls to doors and windows. Practice doing this at home with your children.

If all exits are blocked, close the door to the area where you are. Cover the base and cracks of the door with towels or clothes to keep smoke from coming in. If you can, call 911 or signal with a light or white cloth or flashlight or call loudly out windows so that rescuers can find you. A firefighter tells me that you should always yell "Fire!" because people do not listen to "Help!"

Once you are out, call the fire department from a neighbor's. Give your name and address and, if there are any special instructions needed to find the way to your home, be prepared with a quick and easy-to-understand formula for explaining the route. Do not hang up while the person on the other end of the line is still trying to ask you questions. If you are panicky, you may omit some essential information without realizing it.

Never reenter a burning building for any reason.

Make sure that children know the escape plan well and understand that they should follow it if they hear the smoke alarm. Sound the alarm for them so that they are familiar with it. Tell them that if they hear the alarm they should not hide under the bed or in the closet but follow the escape plan. Teach them how to follow walls to windows and doors, and to crawl so as to be able to breathe. Teach them how to call and signal for help and how to telephone for help.

SPECIAL RULES FOR FIREPROOF HIGH-RISE MODERN APARTMENT BUILDINGS

New York and other large cities have many "fireproof" high-rise apartment buildings, generally built after 1960. If you live in such an apartment building, different fire safety rules apply depending on the construction of the building and whether a fire starts in your apartment or elsewhere. (Some rules, however, apply everywhere: make yourself thoroughly familiar with all of your building's stairways and escape routes, and never use the elevator to escape a fire, because it may stop and open into an inferno, or the electricity might fail and leave you trapped.)

The New York City fire department offers these rules for modern fireproof high-rise apartment buildings. Consult your local fire department for advice about your own building. If the fire is in your apartment, get everyone out, close but don't lock the apartment door, alert other residents on the same floor, and exit by the nearest stairway. Call the fire department from a floor below the fire or from the street. If the fire is in another apartment, you are almost certainly safer staying in your apartment rather than going into a smoke-filled hallway or staircase. Keep your door closed, and seal the doorway with duct tape or wet sheets and towels. Turn off air conditioners. Fill the bathtub with water; if the front door gets hot, try to keep it wet. Open windows a few inches at the top or bottom—unless smoke or flame is rising from below. Call the fire department, tell them your apartment number and describe your situation. If you feel you are in grave danger, open a window and wave a bed sheet so firefighters can find you quickly.

Smoke Detectors. Firefighters say that installing smoke detectors is the most important thing you can do to protect yourself from fires. It is a simple and inexpensive step that can increase your chances of surviving a fire by 50 percent. In many locales there are laws requiring smoke detectors for certain types of buildings. Know what the regulations are in your area. Call the local fire department for advice.

Always buy smoke detectors that bear the UL Mark (or the mark of another nationally recognized third-party certification organization), and install them in exact accordance with the manufacturer's instructions.

The Consumer Products Safety Commission recommends that you put a smoke detector on every floor of your home, including the basement. Always put one in any room with a heater. Be sure to put them in garages and workshops too. It is not usually recommended that you put one in the kitchen or bathrooms, since smoke alarms can be triggered by steam from the shower or smoke from cooking. There are smoke detectors, however, that permit you to delay or deactivate the alarm for fifteen minutes; these can be used for kitchens.

Putting smoke detectors near where you sleep is most important, for the sleeping hours are the most dangerous. Place the detectors in the hallways near bedrooms. It would be even better to have them both in the hallway and in the bedroom, but having one in the hallway is more important than having one in the bedroom.

If you have stairs, place a smoke detector at the top of each staircase. Smoke detectors should go on the ceiling at least twelve inches from walls or on the wall twelve inches below the ceiling. In general, make sure they are at least twelve inches away from where ceiling and wall meet; corners tend to be dead air spaces to which smoke might not travel. For cathedral ceilings, place detectors about three feet from the highest point, as there is likely to be a dead space at the peak. Avoid placing them near windows or doors, in closets or other closed-off places, or in the path of heater or air-conditioner vents. In any of these placements, the detector might not be triggered when there is smoke, as the smoke may be blocked or blown away or drawn off. To avoid false alarms, do not place smoke detectors near fireplaces or woodstoves. Cigarette smoke, too, can trigger a smoke alarm. Smoke detectors make a piercing, shrieking noise when they detect smoke.[1] Be sure to familiarize yourself with the sound yours makes, and learn to distinguish its sound from that of any other home alarms you have, such as for carbon monoxide or burglary. It is also helpful to be aware of the noise the smoke detector makes when its battery is running low. Years ago, a few months after I had moved into a new apartment, I began to be troubled by an annoying chirping noise that seemed to begin each evening just as I tried to go to sleep. I searched my apartment and the hallway and called the neighbors, but it took me days to discover that the noise meant that a smoke detector needed new batteries.

Smoke detectors may be battery-powered or hooked into your wiring. The wired-in type also has a backup battery. It must be installed by a certified electrician.

Follow the manufacturer's instructions for checking, testing batteries, and maintaining your smoke detectors. In all those I have seen, you check the battery by pressing a button on the detector. Seniors, invalids, and others who may have trouble reaching the detector to test it may find it easiest to push the battery test button with a broom handle. Check battery-operated alarms once a week and electrically powered ones monthly. In addition, replace the batteries every six months even though they still seem to work. You can remember to do this by planning to do it regularly each spring and fall when you set the clocks forward and back for daylight saving. Be sure that the batteries for your smoke alarms stay in the alarms; do not let anyone remove them to use in a toy or Walkman, meaning to replace them "soon."

When you vacuum your rooms, vacuum the smoke detector grille too. If dust collects on it, it may fail to function properly. If you are painting your rooms, be careful not to paint over the smoke detector, and remind painters not to do so either.

Smoke detectors should be replaced every ten years. Most smoke detectors are simple, inexpensive, and effective. But technology is always developing, so before buying consult a reputable consumers' publication or some organization that is a reliable source of information.

Fire Control: Fire Extinguishers

Fire Extinguishers. All the experts agree: you should have fire extinguishers in your home. When you get your extinguishers, sit down and read their labels and the manufacturer's instruction brochures cover to cover. Learn how to use and care for the extinguishers. (You should also know when *not* to try to put a fire out. See "Fleeing Fires; Fire Preparedness," above.) Periodically review the instructions on use and care of the extinguisher.

Fire extinguishers are useful for putting out only small fires. Most of them will empty themselves in ten seconds or less.

Where to Place Fire Extinguishers. One manufacturer advises using one extinguisher for every 600 square feet of living space; other experts advise at least one on every level of your home, including the attic, basement, garage, and workshop (as well as in campers, boats, and similar vehicles). Fire extinguishers are also advisable in all especially fire-vulnerable rooms and areas such as the kitchen, workshop, or garage, and in any room in which there is a fireplace, space heater, or room heater.

In deciding where to mount a fire extinguisher, the basic rule is to put it where you are unlikely to have to pass by the fire to get it. You should never reach in or near a fire or go into a burning area trying to get an extinguisher. Generally speaking, this means putting it near the exit and at a distance from the potential fire hazard, such as the space heater or fireplace. For example, in a kitchen, put it near the door and remote from the stove. For a basement, the top of the stairs is a good spot, or, if there is a basement workshop, adjacent to the workshop.

Read the manufacturer's instructions on how to mount the extinguisher. The general recommendation is to mount it on a wall, high enough to be out of reach of young children and within easy reach of an adult—say at shoulder height. It should be in clear view and easily accessible, not where you would have to reach over a washing machine or behind a piece of furniture to grasp it. Never put it in a closet or cabinet. Mount the extinguishers so that the operating instructions are in view, not concealed.

Maintenance and Disposal of Fire Extinguishers. Carefully follow the manufacturer's instructions on care and maintenance of your extinguishers. Experts recommend that each month you check the pressure gauge on your fire extinguishers and make sure they are still full and operable. Also make sure that the safety seals and tamper indicators are intact and that there is no obvious physical damage, such as corrosion, leakage, or a clogged nozzle. Buy new extinguishers every ten years. Follow the manufacturer's instructions for disposal of the old ones.

What Kind of Fire Extinguisher You Need. A type of extinguisher well suited to the home is the five-pound multipurpose extinguisher, whose UL rating is "ABC." The letters, which refer to the types of fire the extinguisher may be used on, usually appear prominently on the fire extinguisher's label in an icon: A in a green triangle, B in a red square, C in a blue circle. Some types of fire extinguishers, however, instead use little pictures of the kinds of fires the extinguisher can put out safely.

Type A fires are fires that involve combustible materials such as wood, cloth, and paper. It is safe to extinguish this type of fire with water.

Type B fires involve flammable liquids such as kerosene or gasoline, paint, and oil or grease. Grease or oil fires in your kitchen are type B fires. Never use water on fires of this nature!

Type C fires involve energized electrical equipment or hot wires. In this type of fire, therefore, the extinguishing agent should be nonconducting. Water, a conducting agent, should not be used to put out a C fire!

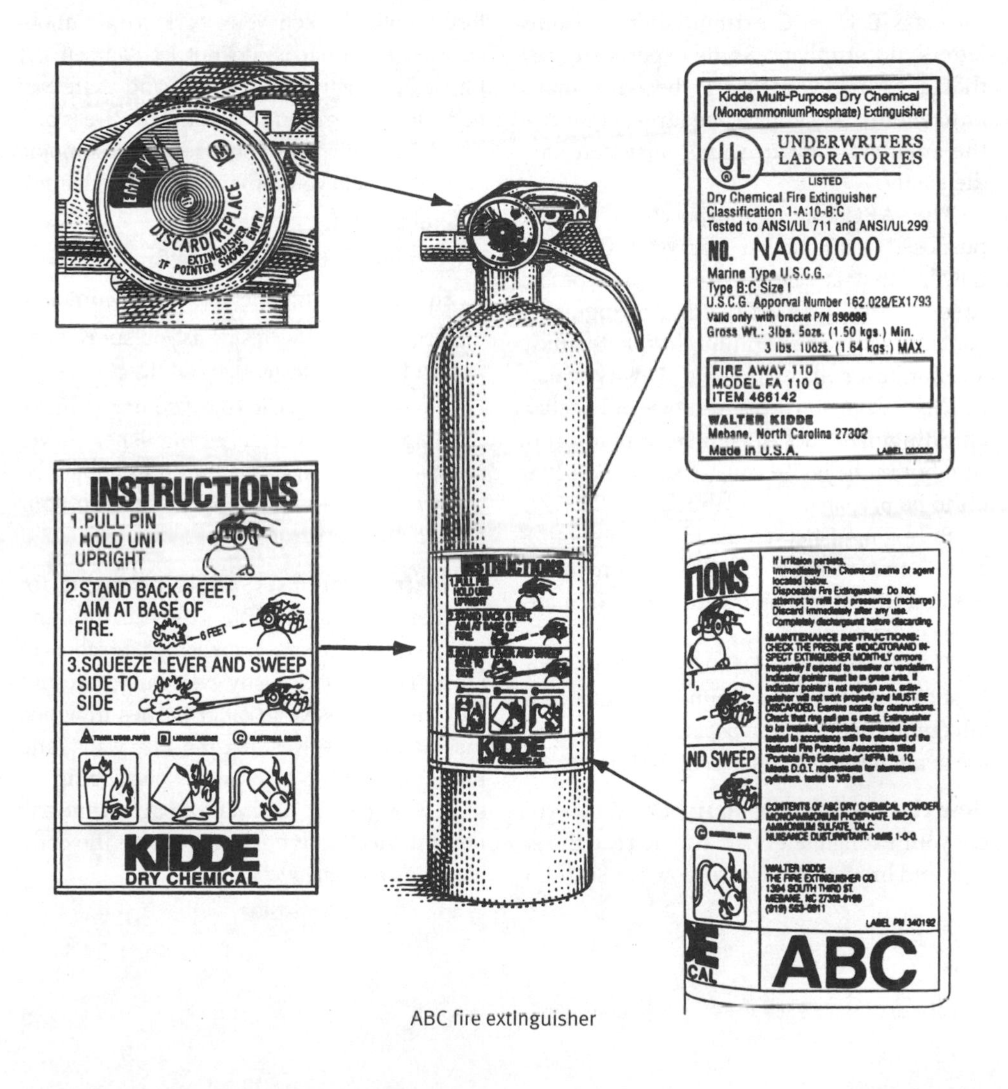

ABC fire extinguisher

The UL classification may have numbers as well as letters. The number would refer to the size of the extinguisher and the size of the fire it can fight. A 4A extinguisher, for example, will put out twice as big a fire as a 2A. The number tells the area (the number of square feet) of fire that the extinguisher can put out. For example, a 60A would put out a 60-square-foot type A fire. If the extinguisher was a 4A:10B:C, that would mean that it could quell a larger B fire (10 square feet) than a class A fire (only 4 square feet). Numbers range from 1 to 40 for class A fires, and from 1 to 640 for class B fires. C extinguishers get only letters, no numbers. Some experts suggest that a 2A:10B:C rating is best for many households. Try to pick the largest one that the smallest adult in your house can handle easily.

The ABC, or "all-purpose" or "multipurpose," extinguisher sprays a fine, dry powder that is safe to use on all types of fires—A, B, and C. My ABC extinguisher contains monoammonium phosphate, mica, ammonium sulfate, and talc. This type may be less efficient on any given type of fire than an extinguisher designed just for that sort of fire, but in the home you are safer and better off to be prepared for anything.

BC extinguishers, rated for use on both B and C fires, usually contain sodium bicarbonate. BC extinguishers are useful in many types of kitchen fires.

There are also type D fires—involving combustible metals such as magnesium, titanium, zirconium, sodium, and potassium—but these are generally not of concern in the home.

How to Use Your Extinguisher. When you get your extinguishers, be sure to read the labels and brochures to learn how to use them. When there is a fire, you will have no time to start studying instructions.

A portable home fire extinguisher is intended to be used only on small, contained fires. If the area is very smoky or the fire is not small, do not try to use the extinguisher. Instead, get out and get help.

To operate an extinguisher, read and follow the manufacturer's instructions precisely. Generally speaking, however, home extinguishers all work the same way. You stand six to eight feet away. You pull the pin and squeeze the handle, pointing the nozzle at the base of the fire. Make a sweeping back-and-forth motion. Keep your back to an unobstructed exit (that is, do not let yourself get trapped with a fire between you and a safe way out). Do not turn your back until the fire is out. The NFPA suggests you use the mnemonic "PASS" to help you remember the guidelines:

Pull the pin.

Aim low, at the base of the fire.

Squeeze the handle to release contents.

Sweep from side to side as you spray, back and forth, until the fire is out.

Do not forget the basic rules: do not go into a burning area to get an extinguisher, never reach into or near a fire trying to get an extinguisher, and when using one keep your back to an unobstructed exit.

Sprinkler Systems. Sprinkler systems for the home are a valuable safety feature and are required in an increasing number of areas. They can be costly even in new homes and very expensive in older homes in which installation involves tearing up walls and pipes. Contact a company specializing in such work (check your yellow pages), and ask for and check references for whom the company has recently worked.

61

Electrical Safety

Preventing electrical fires . . . Causes of electrical fires . . . Safe wiring, electrical and extension cords, switches, and outlets . . . Electrical inspections . . . The National Electrical Safety Foundation . . . When was your home last inspected? . . . Fuses and circuit breakers . . . Overfusing, avoiding overloaded circuits . . . Other rules for avoiding electrical fires . . . Instructions and brochures . . . Overheating . . . Bare wires . . . Outlet plates . . . Using electrical cords safely . . . Additional safety guidelines for extension cords . . . Volts, amps, and watts; wire gauge . . . Electrical shock and electrocution . . . Grounding . . . Polarized plugs . . . Water danger . . . Ground fault circuit interrupters (GFCIs) . . . Testing GFCIs . . . Lightning and power surges . . . Loss of power; low voltage . . . Outlet guards . . . General rules for appliances . . . ALCIs, IDCIs . . . Toasters, electric blankets, electric space heaters . . . Table lamps, floor lamps, and other portable lamps . . . Halogen lamps . . . Metal ladders . . . Electrical safety rules for Christmas trees and other electric decorations

Each year hundreds of people die in electrical fires and electrical accidents in their homes. Each year there are also many thousands of electrical fires in homes that result in shocking injuries and property losses. Most of these tragedies are preventable with a few simple precautions, which, all too often, we do not follow simply because we lack basic information about electrical dangers or because unthinkingly we have developed dangerous habits that go unchallenged.

Preventing Electrical Fires

Causes of Electrical Fires. Electrical fires can occur as a result of overloaded circuits and cords and short circuits. (The dangers of electrical shock and electrocution are discussed separately below.) A circuit consists of wires that carry current to lights and appliances. These wires are designed to carry just so much current safely. If you exceed that amount—in other words, overload the circuit—by plugging too many appliances into an outlet or by plugging in an appliance that uses too much wattage, the fuse in the circuit should open—or "blow," as many of us say—or the circuit breaker should trip. Fuses and circuit breakers are safety devices designed to prevent circuit overload. If they fail, or fail to work quickly enough, more current flows through a wire than the wire can handle. Heat develops, and the result could be a fire.

Electrical wires can also produce heat and fire if they are left bare—without nonconducting insulation—near flammable material, such as wood or sawdust. A short circuit can also cause fires. A short circuit occurs when two bare wires cross that are not supposed to be in contact; this can cause sparks, heat, and fire.

Safe Wiring, Electrical and Extension Cords, Switches, and Outlets

Electrical Inspections. The National Electrical Safety Foundation. The National Electrical Safety Foundation (NESF) is a not-for-profit organization formed in 1994 to promote electrical safety and help prevent electrical accidents. It provides information to the public and sponsors National Electrical Safety Month each year. During this month, May, look for newspaper and magazine articles on the subject of electrical safety, and check your home for compliance with the safety tips.

The NESF strongly recommends that periodically you have your home's wiring checked by a qualified and certified electrician. This is particularly important for people who live in older homes, because most homes have not been inspected for electrical safety since they were built. Not only does wiring, like everything else, grow old and require repair, but today most people have many more electrical appliances than people did forty years ago. If you have an older home or apartment and you are putting in a home office, you should call in a qualified and certified electrician to determine whether your wiring will be adequate for the demands of your office machinery.

When Was Your Home Last Inspected? In areas in which electrical inspections are done by local or state government inspectors, you can determine the date of the last inspection by looking on the door or cover of your electrical panel (the place where your fuses or circuit breakers are located). You'll find there a tag or label with initials or a name, and one or more dates. The most recent date, or the only date, is that of your last inspection. If you find no such tag or label, then you can guess that the last time the electrical system of your house was inspected was probably when it was built—unless you have had it rewired or worked on or know for sure that someone else has.

The NESF offers the following guidelines to help you decide whether you need a new inspection. In applying them, in areas without inspection tags, your best bet is usually to go by the age of your house.

1. If your last inspection was forty or more years ago, an inspection is *overdue*.
2. If your last inspection was ten to forty years ago, inspection is advisable, especially if substantial electrical loads have been added in the interim—high-wattage appliances, lights, wall outlets, extension cords—or if any of the warning signs described below have been observed.
3. If your last inspection was less than ten years ago, inspection may not be needed if you have not noticed any of the warning signs described below.

Potential Electrical Hazards. The NESF urges you to be alert for the following types of electrical hazards and their warning signs:

Power outages: Do your fuses need replacement or circuit breakers need resetting frequently?

Overrated panel: Does your electrical panel contain fuses or circuit breakers rated at higher currents than the current amperage capacity of their branch circuits (that is, is it "overamped" or "overfused")? You will need a qualified, certified electrician to determine whether you have this problem.

Dim or flickering lights: Do your lights dim or does the size of your television picture often shrink?

Arcs or sparks: Are there bright light flashes or showers of sparks anywhere in your electrical system?

Sizzles or buzzes: Do you ever hear unusual sounds coming from your electrical system?

Overheating: Are parts of your electrical system—such as switch plates, wall outlet covers, cords, or plugs—warm or hot, painful to touch, or discolored from heat?

Loose plugs: Do you have any plugs that wobble or pull out of a wall socket easily?

Permanently installed extension cords: Are any extension cords in your home used for long periods, rather than temporarily or short-term, to connect an appliance whose cord is too short to reach the nearest outlet?

Damaged insulation: Do any electrical cords in your home have cut, broken, or cracked insulation?

Fuses and Circuit Breakers; Overloading Circuits; Turning the Lights Back On Safely. Some homes have circuit breakers, and some have fuses and fuse boxes. If you have fuses, keep well stocked with fuses of the sizes you need, not only to avoid inconvenience but also to avoid the dangerous temptation to use the wrong size fuse when you find yourself out of the right size. (See "Do Not Overfuse" below.)

If lights go out in part of your home or if your hair dryer suddenly stops blowing, you may have tripped a circuit breaker or blown a fuse by overloading the circuit. (If the lights go off in your neighbor's house too, this is probably a power outage; let the power company know about it.) If it is very dark, first retrieve your flashlight from your home emergency chest. Then, before touching anything in your fuse or circuit breaker box, *make sure your hands and the floor are dry*. Finally, open the door of your fuse box or circuit breaker box. A "blown" or open fuse shows a dark, burned place in the glass window. A tripped circuit breaker switch will be in the "off" position instead of the "on" position.

Before replacing the fuse or turning the circuit breaker switch on again, reduce the electrical burden on the relevant circuit by turning off, say, the hair dryer or the vacuum cleaner or whatever seems to have been the problem. Then flip the switch back to "on." To change a fuse, first turn off the main power switch. Then remove the old fuse and replace it *with one of the proper amperage.*

If the circuit breaker trips again or the fuse blows again and you cannot determine an obvious source of the problem, do not attempt to turn the switch back on or replace the fuse. Call a qualified, certified electrician.

Do Not Overfuse. If your fuse box has a 15-amp slot for the fuse, use a 15-amp fuse. If you use a 20- or 30-amp fuse instead, which is called "overfusing," the fuse may permit the circuit to overload before it blows. This is very dangerous, as it permits the wires to overheat and could cause a fire. Overfusing is a common cause of fires in older homes. The best way to keep this from happening is to have your fuse panel converted to the type that accepts only a fuse of the proper amperage—S-type sockets.

You should also *never* resort to home remedies such as a copper penny or piece of foil or other piece of metal. This is extremely dangerous, and has caused many a home (and other buildings and structures too) to burn down.

Avoid Overloaded Circuits. Mark each circuit in your circuit breaker box clearly, showing what outlets and lights it includes, for example, "master bathroom plus east master bedroom wall." Each circuit dedicated mostly or wholly to a specific power-hungry appliance should be marked with a descriptive label, for example, "office west wall outlets—laser printer." The whole family should know how to interpret these labels and know when to close a circuit if needed.

Most home outlets are designed to carry 15 amps. A 15-amp circuit can safely carry about 1,500 watts. Thus to ensure that you do not overload your circuits, simply add up the wattage ratings for each of the lights and appliances plugged into that circuit to see if the total exceeds 1,500. (The wattage ratings of the appliances are on their plates or labels.) Remember that each circuit is likely to include several outlets and that you have to add in everything plugged into each outlet, along with any built-in lighting. Avoid using power strips to increase the number of things you can plug into one outlet unless you are quite certain that the total demands of everything drawing from the circuit into which it is plugged will not exceed 1,500 watts. If you attempt to operate an iron, a heavy-duty vacuum cleaner, and an electric space heater simultaneously on the same 1,500 watt circuit, for example, you will trip a circuit breaker.

Ordinary household wiring easily supports personal computers, fax machines, radios, and table lamps. Telephones get the small amount of current they need from the telephone wires, although wall current is needed for an answering machine and the power supply for a portable phone. But machines or appliances that use large amounts of electricity may need their own special wiring or can share a circuit with, at most, a lamp or electric pencil sharpener. These include space heaters, air conditioners, older large laser printers (newer ones are more energy efficient), hair dryers, electric stoves, and clothes dryers, among others. If you notice that the lights flicker or momentarily dim when you turn on some appliance, either find another outlet for it or call a qualified, certified electrician to see about getting some new wiring.

Other Rules for Avoiding Electrical Fires in the Home.

Instructions and Brochures. Always keep instruction booklets, pamphlets, and brochures that come with electrical appliances and tools. Read them cover to cover before using the electrical product, and now and then peruse them to refresh your memory. They generally include safety tips and indispensable advice on safe use. Since most of us have many, many electrical appliances in our homes these days, we have to keep a special file or drawer for these. I keep two thick files, one labeled "Large Appliances" and one labeled "Small Appliances," and I find it necessary to refer to them frequently.

Overheating. If you notice that any of your plugs, switches, or outlets grow warm or hot in use, turn off or unplug the light or appliance, flip the circuit for any such lights, switches, or outlets, and call a qualified, certified electrican to check them.

Appliances can overheat if you block their vents. You must be sure to leave breathing room, in accordance with manufacturer's instructions, around stereos, microwaves, computers, television sets, and other electronic equipment. This type of overheating can not only wreck the equipment but also cause fires.

Lamps and light fixtures can overheat if you use a bulb that is of higher wattage than the manufacturer recommends. When in doubt, check the lighting fixture for maximum bulb wattage ratings and bulb types that can be used safely in the fixture.

Bare Wires. A bare wire visible on an appliance cord requires immediate action; it can cause electric shock or fire. Turn the appliance off, unplug it, and do not use it until the wire is repaired by a qualified repairman. (See "Electrical Shock and Electrocution," below.)

Outlet Plates. Every outlet should be covered with a plate. If children are in the home, use child-proof outlet guards. See page 724.

Using Electrical Cords Safely. Buy only cords that have the UL Mark or the mark of some other nationally recognized third-party certification agency.

Stop using any cord that is beginning to fray or crack, and use cords in a way that protects them from fraying, cracking, or being cut in the first place. If an extension cord shows any such signs of damage or wear, throw it away.

Never remove a cord's warning label or the certification agency's tag that states the appropriate wattage and other details. Leave it on for the sake of the next person who uses the cord, and for your own sake too, because you are unlikely to remember what the label says.

Never lift or carry an electric appliance by its cord. When you unplug an appliance, grasp the plug; do not pull on the cord. If you have any appliances with retractable cords, the same rule applies to them. Unplug them, *then* retract the cord by pushing the retract button or pedal; do not attempt to unplug them by retracting them. Disabled or elderly people, or anyone for whom bending is hard, may be tempted to pull by the cord. Resist the temptation. Instead, ask someone to unplug the appliance for you. Or when you must sit on the floor to pull out the plug, make sure there is something nearby with which you can safely pull yourself up afterward. Or have outlets installed at a more convenient height.

Do not use excessive force to make a plug go into a connection.

Always plug cords fully into outlets.

Never attempt to alter the plug on a cord or to bend or modify any of its metal prongs or pins.

Do not plug a three-pronged plug into a two holed connection or outlet.

Always keep plugs and cords away from heat, flame, and water.

Do not let furniture rest on an electrical cord. Do not run cords under rugs or blankets or cover them with anything.

Do not walk or drive over cords or place them across the floor where they will be walked on. Do not bend them around sharp corners, hang them over sharp edges, or tie them in knots. Beware particularly of bending cords too sharply at the plug. Doing any of these things can cause a crack in the cord's insulation or expose a bare wire. There are cords with flat plugs, by the way, that fit better into many tight spots.

Do not run cords through doorways, holes in ceilings, walls, or floors.

Never nail down or staple a cord (inside or outside your home). Instead, if necessary, secure it with tape; but regard this as a very temporary solution, because duct tape can trap heat. And never remove a staple or nail from a cord unless you first cut off that circuit by flipping the circuit switch.

Put electrical cords and telephone cords behind furniture, along baseboards, and as much as possible where children and pets cannot see, pull, or trip on them.

Never coil a cord in use. But do coil cords neatly in storage.

Never let any cord rest on a wet surface or in water—indoors or outdoors! Water and electricity do not mix!

Never place a cord near anything hot such as a radiator, heater, fireplace, or stove. Certainly *never* drape a cord over anything hot or permit one to rest on a hot surface.

Outdoors, use only cords labeled for outdoor use. Bring them indoors when they are not in use or they will deteriorate from exposure to the sun and may become unsafe.

Never continue to use any cord that becomes warm or hot in use.

Additional Safety Guidelines for Extension Cords. Extension cords very commonly cause fires, typically through overloading and misuse. *All the general rules cited above apply to extension cords as well as appliance cords and all types of electrical cords.* In addition, here are some safety guidelines specially applicable to extension cords.

The first rule is that you should *avoid* using extension cords as permanent wiring. If you must use one, use it for as short a time as possible. Extension cords are a temporary expedient at best. If you find yourself tempted to rely on one permanently, you need to have a qualified, certified electrician in for some work on your wiring. Or get your appliance fitted with a longer cord by a qualified repair person.

Never plug one extension cord into another. Instead, use only one that is long enough.

Always use the shortest extension cord that works. A longer cord poses greater risks of overheating (and destroying the motor on an appliance). If your appliance or tool is only ten feet away from an outlet, don't use a twenty-foot extension cord.

Do not coil up an extension cord in use, as this can result in overheating. But do carefully coil up an extension cord in storage.

Avoiding overloading extension cords. An overloaded extension cord can become so hot that its insulation melts, causing a danger of electrocution and fire. And even if you avoid these terrible hazards, you may end up with stains and marks on whatever the cord was touching. If an extension cord is overloaded, you may notice it beginning to grow warm. If you find an extension cord that is overheating, first flip the circuit breaker that covers the outlet it is plugged into. Then unplug the cord. Throw it away if it is damaged.

To determine what can safely be plugged into an extension cord, you have to look at its label or at the information printed on the plug to determine how many watts or amps it is rated to carry. Then you have to add up how many watts or amps will be used by the appliance or appliances you are plugging into the extension cord. If the total watts or amps used by the appliances is greater than the amount the extension cord is rated to carry, you are overloading the extension cord and creating a grave hazard in your home. Unplug as many appliances as necessary to reduce the total of their wattage ratings to an amount less than or equal to that of the extension cord. (To be on the safe side, make the total less than the extension cord's rating.)

For example, suppose I have an extension cord rated for 1,875 watts, which would be considered heavy-duty. I would dangerously overload it if I plugged into it simultaneously my coffeemaker (which uses 1,500 watts) and my iron (1,200 watts). But either of these appliances alone, plus a 60-watt lamp and a 100-watt pencil sharpener, would not exceed the extension cord's rating.

Do not use extension cords with large appliances; such appliances should always be plugged directly into an outlet. The typical home extension cord is grossly inadequate for an air conditioner, space heater, or any other large or power-hungry appliance.

Whenever possible, avoid using extension cords in the presence of children.

Unplug any extension cord when not in use. Otherwise it continues to create electrical shock and fire hazards.

When using an appliance with an extension cord, turn it off before plugging the cord in.

Do not let an extension cord be wrapped around itself, or anything else, when in use.

With power tools, you should always use heavy-duty cords with a thick protective layer of insulation.

When you use extension cords outdoors, they should be the heavy-duty, rounded-type. They should be marked "Suitable for use with

VOLTS, AMPS, AND WATTS; WIRE GAUGE

Volts are a measure of the force with which electricity passes through wire. An engineer told me to think about volts of electricity as analogous to the pressure of water passing through a hose. Amperes—or "amps"—measure the quantity of electricity (analogous to the volume of water). Watts, which measure the electrical power, are equal to the number of amps multiplied by the number of volts. If you have a tool or appliance cord that states only the wattage it is rated for, you can determine the amperage, if you need to know it, by dividing the wattage by the voltage.

The voltage in most standard outlets in American homes is 120. A cooking range, oven, or electric clothes dryer and certain other appliances will usually have their own circuits, which will have 220 (and sometimes 240) volts. Most circuits in American homes, other than those specially wired for certain large appliances, are wired to carry safely only 1,500 watts of electrical power. When you plug into one circuit appliances that, taken together, use more than this, you trip your circuit breaker or open (blow) a fuse.

A cord's or wire's "gauge" is a number that tells the thickness of the wire. The *lower* the gauge, the thicker the wire and the more electric current (amps or watts) it will be rated for. The wire gauge may be referred to as the "AWG," or American Wire Gauge. A lamp cord ordinarily has a gauge of about 18, which is very thin—adequate only for a lamp bulb.

When current has to travel longer distances through wires, the voltage drops, and the thinner the wire the more the voltage drops. Lowered voltage causes an appliance or tool to draw more amps to compensate for the decrease in voltage. This produces more heat. This is why the motors on the tools and appliances can burn up when you use over-long, over-thin extension cords. This is also why long extension cords with too high a gauge can create an increased risk of fire.

You should be *very careful* about what you plug into any extension cords with a gauge of 18. These can be overloaded far too easily. Many, if not most, household appliances in your home will exceed their wattage ratings. For outdoor uses, gauges of 12 or 14—nothing higher—are recommended. (Look for the heavy-duty, rounded type of extension cord and the statement "Suitable for use with outdoor appliances—store indoors while not in use.")

Electrical cords that have been certified or rated by a nationally recognized third-party certification agency, such as Underwriters Laboratories, come with a tag that states their rated wattage and have the AWG printed on the insulation.

outdoor appliances—store indoors while not in use."

Electrical Shock and Electrocution

Grounding. The wiring in your home should be grounded. Your fuse or circuit breaker box contains wires that run to a metal rod that is driven into the ground. All wiring and everything plugged into the wiring in your home eventually connects with the ground wire. Electricity, as a friend who is an engineer explained to me, is lazy. It always goes down the easiest path, the one with least resistance. Grounding protects you from shock by providing electricity with an easier—more conductive—path to follow than the one provided by your body. A "ground fault" occurs when the electrical current in a product strays outside its intended path. Injury may occur when your body provides a path for the stray current.

When you have three-pronged plugs and three-holed outlets, the third prong and hole attach the appliance to the ground wire inside your outlet. *Never remove the third prong or force a three-pronged plug into a two-holed plug.* Instead, use an adapter. On one side the adapter has a two-pronged plug that you plug into the outlet and a "grounding tab" that you attach to the screw at the center of the outlet cover plate. On the other side the adapter has three holes, into which you plug your three-pronged plug.

Polarized Plugs. Polarized plugs are another antishock safety feature that you should respect. These plugs have two prongs, but one is wider than the other. The wide prong cannot fit into the narrow slot in your outlet, so you can insert the plug only in the intended manner. This aligns the circuit conductors so as to help prevent shock. *Never force a plug into an outlet or attempt to alter a polarized plug so that it will fit.* Have a qualified, certified electrician install a new outlet if the plug does not fit.

Water Danger. Any electrical appliance used anywhere in the vicinity of water is *extremely dangerous,* and fatal accidents from the combination of water and electricity are common and almost too horrible to hear about. *Do not use appliances near any water: pools, spas, Jacuzzis, sinks, tubs, toilets, showers, wet floors, and puddles.* This means lamps, radios, televisions, telephones, hair dryers, blenders, and every other electrically powered product. It means the kitchen sink as well as the bathroom sinks and tubs. If an appliance falls into water, get everyone out of the area (especially children). Then unplug the appliance, if you can. Or, turn off the power at the fuse or circuit breaker box, then unplug and retrieve the appliance. Do not use the appliance again until it has been inspected and repaired by a qualified, certified repairman. Otherwise there is a grave danger of shock, even if the appliance appears to have dried.

The reason for the danger is that tap water is an excellent conductor of electricity. Water will offer an easier path for the current in your wiring than the wiring, so electricity will flow into the water and then into you. Because your body is made mostly of water, you yourself are not a bad conductor. So if you are in or touching water you offer the electricity a path to or from water, and you can be electrocuted.

The bathroom is full of water dangers. Unless you have GFCIs (explained below), if your hair dryer or any other electric appliance falls in a sink or tub of water (or contacts any water that contacts you), anyone in the tub or anyone with hands in the water is in danger of serious injury or death. This is true of electric razors, radios, telephones, televisions: anything electric in a bathroom is dangerous. Remember that sinks, toilets, tubs, showers, and wet floors all pose electrocution and shock dangers.

Drying your hair while you are sitting in the bathtub is unthinkably dangerous. Do not stand on a wet floor drying your hair or warming yourself at an electric space heater. *Never permit any young child to be alone in the bathroom with any electric appliance.* Even older children need careful instruction and supervision. You *must* get GFCIs for your bathrooms. And even if you do have GFCIs, you should observe the foregoing cautions regarding the use of electrical appliances in areas where there is water. If a GFCI should misfunction, your life or that of someone in your household could be at risk.

The kitchen and laundry room pose similar dangers, so they need GFCIs too. Unplug any appliance before washing it or rinsing it or wiping it. Do not turn on the washer or dryer if you are standing on a wet floor. Do not reach over to turn on an appliance with one hand while your other hand is in a basin of water.

Ground Fault Circuit Interrupters. Ground fault circuit interrupters, or GFCIs, are relatively inexpensive safety devices that protect against ground faults and electric shock and electrocution. You should have them installed in every outlet in and around your home where there is water: near kitchen, workshop, and laundry sinks, near bathroom tubs and sinks, and in all outdoor outlets. If everyone did, many lives would be saved every year.

GFCIs work by monitoring the electricity that flows into a circuit and immediately shutting off the current if the amount of current flowing in differs from that flowing out. The amount of current flowing out would be decreased, for example, if some of it was being diverted into you, and you in this case would be about to be shocked or electrocuted. The GFCI would trip and shut off the current so fast that it would save you. (You might still receive a painful shock, however.)

There are several kinds of GFCIs. The wall receptacle type is built right into the wall, in place of a standard electrical outlet. The circuit breaker type, which can be used in homes with a circuit breaker, will shut off the current when there is a ground fault, a short circuit, or an overloaded circuit. Portable ones can be bought and plugged into any standard outlet. You plug one of these into your outlet and then plug your appliances into it.

Testing GFCIs. All GFCIs are supposed to be tested monthly to be sure that they are still working. The National Electrical Safety Foundation suggests that you test by plugging a night-light into the outlet. Then press the "Test" button to make sure the night light goes off. If the night-light does not go off, the GFCI is not working properly. Stop using the outlet and have a qualified, certified electrician come to repair it promptly. If the nightlight goes out, the GFCI is working properly. Press the "Reset" button to get power back in the GFCI outlet.

Lightning and Power Surges. A power surge is a sudden increase of electricity in your circuits. Power surges have many causes, including events at your power plant, lightning, or even conditions in your own home. You may or may not be aware of it when one happens. They can be damaging and dangerous. You should not use telephones, electrical appliances, or computers during a lightning storm. Do not shower or take a bath when there is lightning, and stay out of the pool and the Jacuzzi. Lightning can travel through pipes and water and reach you.

Because lightning and power surges can destroy home electronic devices, unplug computers, answering machines, microwaves, VCRs, stereo systems, and televisions. Some appliances, such as air conditioners, may be damaged or destroyed or have their lives shortened; they too should be unplugged.

You can also use surge protectors, which are available in several types. Some are devices that you install in your fuse or circuit breaker box to give your whole house protection, including telephones and cable lines that are installed on your panelboard. Some are built into power outlet strips; others are small units that fit over your regular outlets. All your computer equipment should be equipped with a surge protector; you may need more than one if you have a heavy-duty laser printer, scanner, or other power-hungry equipment attached to the computer. You can also get devices that provide surge protection for telephone lines used by phones, fax machines, and modems; these can be bought either as stand-alone units or as an additional feature built into standard power strips or surge protectors. Surge protectors reduce the risk of damage, but they are not a guarantee. So even if you have them, you should still unplug your appliances and stay off the telephone during an electrical storm. Surge protectors do not last forever. Replace them in accordance with the manufacturer's recommendations.

If the Power Goes Off; Low Voltage. If your power goes off, unplug appliances. Otherwise, your circuits might be overloaded by a brief surge when the power comes back on. Or the appliances might come on while you are asleep, which can be dangerous. If you leave a lamp or two on, that will tell you when the power is back on.

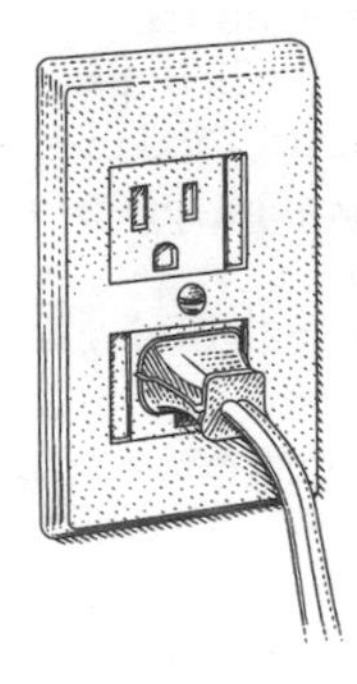

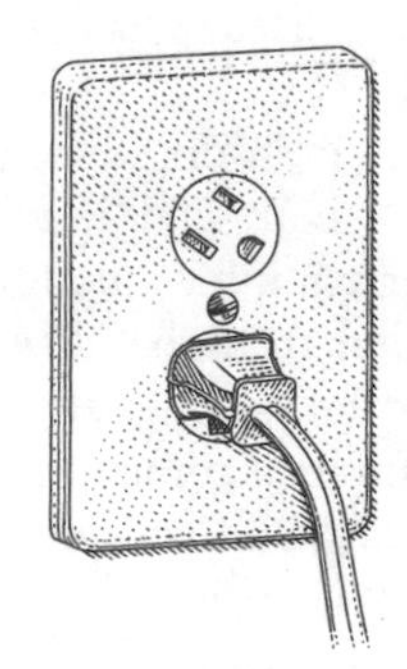

Spring-action outlet guards

If the power is unreliable in your neighborhood, you may want to consider buying an Uninterruptible Power Supply for computer and other sensitive electronic equipment. These units, which typically cost around $100 or more, contain batteries that continue to supply power to your computer when the electric company's power stops or becomes dangerously low. A loud siren alerts you to the problem and gives you time to close down your programs without losing data.

You may sometimes notice that while the power is on, the lights are dim. This is a "low-voltage" situation. You should either turn off or unplug all motor-driven appliances, such as refrigerators, freezers, washers, dryers, and dishwashers, in order to avoid the possibility of damage to them. Notify your utility company of the problem.

See chapter 11, "Cold Comfort," on what to do to keep refrigerated and frozen foods cool for as long as possible during power outages or low-voltage situations.

Outlet Guards. Use outlet guards when you have small children in the house; they might otherwise insert their fingers or objects into unguarded outlets. I know someone who stuck a hairpin into an outlet as a young child and was badly hurt. Check the consumer and safety magazines for what is latest and best. The National Electrical Safety Foundation advises that you not use ornamental safety guards because they may be attractive to children and tempt them to play at the outlets. In my home, we used inexpensive plastic outlet inserts, which babies' fingers are not strong enough to pull out. The problem with these inserts is that they do not provide protection for an outlet in use; when something is plugged in, children can pull out the plug and gain access to the outlet. Or little fingers can pry between the plug and the outlet and receive dangerous shocks. Older children, moreover, can pull them out. Better are the outlet safety covers with inner spring mechanisms that open to permit you to plug something in but spring back to cover the outlet when you take the plug out. When appliances are in use, unless you have safety covers nothing takes the place of eternal vigilance.

General Rules for Appliances. If you ever plug in an appliance and get a tingle, stop using it immediately. You must either have it repaired or discard it. Leaking current is extremely dangerous.

Make sure that plugs are fully inserted.

Bare wires, frayed cords, loose connections, and bent and pulled plugs are all potential causes of dangerous electrical shocks (as well as fire hazards). If you see a worn cord or a plug that is partially pulled off the wire of an appliance or extension cord, immediately cease using it. Either have a qualified person repair or replace it or discard the appliance.

Plug no more than one heat-making appliance, such as an iron, toaster, waffle iron, or hair dryer, into any single wall outlet. (Remember to add up the wattage to be sure you are not overloading the circuit.)

Leave appliances unplugged when they are not in use, especially in the kitchen and bathroom. Otherwise voltage may be present in the appliance, creating a shock danger, even though the appliance is turned off. Make sure not to store appliances—such as a toaster, coffeemaker, or hair dryer—where they could be knocked over into the sink or tub.

Put electrical cords out of the reach of babies and toddlers. They can pull lamps and appliances down on themselves and chew on cords.

Never use any electric appliance for any purpose other than the one it was designed for. Use your oven only to cook, not to heat your room. Use your heater only to heat, not to dry your hair. Many, many accidents and deaths are caused by people using appliances for the wrong purposes. Always read and follow the manufacturer's instructions for use and care, and keep the pamphlets, booklets, and brochures in a handy, safe place.

If you have an appliance that repeatedly opens (blows) a fuse or trips a circuit breaker, unplug it and promptly take it to a qualified repair shop.

Many electric appliances and equipment, such as televisions, stereos, and computers, need ventilation or they will overheat. Carefully follow all manufacturer's instructions, and do not obstruct air vents and fans in any appliance. If you put your television or stereo inside a cabinet, make sure it has enough ventilation, and make sure that it does not overheat, especially with the doors closed.

ALCIs; IDCIs. Some electrical appliances, including UL-listed hair dryers manufactured since 1991, are equipped with built-in personnel protection devices called "appliance leakage current interrupters," or ALCIs, or "immersion detection circuit interrupters," or IDCIs. Like GFCIs, ALCIs protect you against contact with electrified objects or wires and ground faults. ICDIs safeguard against electric shock resulting from the accidental immersion of electrical products. Even if your appliance has such protections, or even if it is plugged into a GFCI, you must *still keep it away from water.* These protections are not guarantees; they are intended to back up, not replace, ordinary safety practices.

Toasters. Unplug the toaster *first. Then* attempt to dig out toast that is stuck in it. It is madness to go poking in a plugged-in toaster. Even when it is not being used to heat anything, voltage is still present.

Electric Blankets and Heating Pads. Electric blankets and heating pads, if improperly used, pose dangers of shock, burns, and fire. Each year when the weather turns cold, check the condition of your electric blanket before using it. Examine it all over on both sides for breaks and cracks, charred spots, or other damage or wear in the wiring, plugs, or connections. If you see any, don't use it.

Do not tuck electric blankets in, and do not put anything, such as other blankets or comforters, over them while they are in use. Do not let your pet sleep on it. Doing any of these things could cause it to overheat, and that is dangerous. *Children should not use electric blankets.*

Turn your heating pad off before you go to sleep. Overheating leading to fires and burns can result if you leave one on too long.

Electric Space Heaters. Use only electric space or air heaters that show the UL Mark. The safety rules governing all supplemental heaters, described in chapter 60, pages 704–5, also apply to electric heaters, including those that tell you to store no flammable liquids in areas where the heater is being used. Such heaters have hot and sparking parts inside, which could light the flammable liquids or the fumes that they might create in the area.

Use electric heaters only for heating.

If you are buying an electric heater, make sure that it is the kind that automatically turns off when it is tipped over.

Follow all safety rules applicable to all other electric products and electric cords. Do nothing to defeat the grounding feature on the plug! Be especially sure not to curl or knot up the cord to an electric heater. Examine the cord for splits, fraying, cracks or other damage. If you find any, have repairs made by a qualified repairman before using the heater.

Avoid using extension cords with electric heaters: plug an electric heater directly into a wall outlet and unplug it when not in use. According to Underwriters Laboratories, if you feel you must use an extension cord, it should have a rating of 1.25 times the wattage rating of the heater. With, say, a 1,500-watt heater, use a cord rated 1,875 watts. Never use an extension cord that is worn, frayed, cracked, or in less than perfect condition. Put the cord where no one will walk over it or trip on it.

Keep any electric heater *far away* from water—sinks, tubs, toilets, showers, and wet floors. Never use an electric heater outdoors or in a bathroom or laundry or other area with water present.

Do not keep plug-in radios or televisions in the bathroom. A battery-powered radio is safe, but store it where it will not fall into the sink, tub, or toilet.

Table Lamps, Floor Lamps, and Other Portable Lamps. You might think you know all you need to know about lamps (switch on for light, switch off for dark), but you should read the manufacturer's labels, pamphlet, or instructions anyway. And you should buy lamps that show the mark of a nationally recognized third-party certification agency. Improperly used lamps can cause fires. (By a "lamp" I mean what lighting and electrical professionals call a "luminaire"; they use the word "lamp" to refer only to a bulb or fluorescent tube. But everyone else uses "lamp" to refer to the appliance or fixture that contains the bulb.)

Unplug or turn off a lamp to replace the bulb, and do not remove the old bulb until it has cooled off or you may get a bad burn. Be sure to keep a bulb in the lamp, too. *A lamp that is plugged in but has no bulb poses a shock risk.*

Never put anything on top of a lamp or on a bulb. This can cause fires. (I once knew some children who started a fire when they made a spotlight out of a lamp by removing the shade and wrapping a little nightgown around the bare incandescent bulb.)

Keep lamps and fixtures in good repair, and when they or their cords and plugs need to be repaired, take them to a qualified technician. Never use a lamp if it shows any bare wires, if the cord is worn or frayed or cracked, or if the switch does not work properly.

Put lamps where they will not be knocked over and where their cords will not be tripped on by people (or pets on a rampage) and where children cannot reach them and pull on them.

Torchiere lamps (the ones with the open tops that shine upward toward the ceiling) should not be placed in children's or dormitory rooms, because children might throw or place objects in it, creating serious fire hazards. Torchiere lamps should also be kept clear of loft beds and bunk beds, as they can catch the bedding on fire; bedclothes might get flung on them accidentally. Retrofit kits are available that can protect the bulb in a torchiere lamp from flying objects. You can buy these at home centers and department stores that specialize in household wares, such as Kmart, Target, Home Depot, and others. Some hardware stores also carry them. Or you can order them directly from the manufacturer. (See chapter 47, "Kindly Light," for other cautions relating to home lighting.)

Read lightbulb package labels and obey all manufacturer's instructions and cautions.

Make sure the lamp or fixture is off, or unplugged, when you change a bulb.

Use only a bulb with the correct wattage in any lamp—the wattage recommended by the manufacturer or lower. Using a higher wattage than the manufacturer specifies can cause overheating and create a danger of fire. Use only the type of bulb specified by the manufacturer.

Halogen Lamps. Safety experts caution against using any bulb with a wattage higher than 300 in any halogen lamp or fixture, even if the lamp specifies one as high as 500. This is simply too hot to take a chance with. Check the lamp or fixture for the recommended wattage and bulb type.

Halogen lamps require a few other cautions as well. See the discussion of torchiere lamps, above, and chapter 47, pages 576–77.

Metal Ladders. Remember that metal ladders conduct electricity. Exercise caution around electrical equipment and appliances.

Electrical Safety Rules for Christmas Trees and Other Electric Decorations. Holiday decorations usually involve electric lights and displays. All the rules for electrical safety set forth in this chapter apply when you use electric lights or other decorations on Christmas trees or elsewhere, indoors or out. (See also the Christmas fire safety rules in chapter 60.)

First read the manufacturer's instructions for each type of electrical decorations that you will be using, both indoor and outdoors.

When you get out your decorations each year, inspect them carefully for cracked or frayed sockets, loose or bare wires, and loose connections. Any items showing such damage must be replaced.

Do not connect more strings of lights or other decorations than the manufacturer recommends. Check the package or string itself for instructions.

Never repair your light strings (or any cords or extension cords) with electrical tape. Some people try to splice strings of lights together, and this has led to predictable disasters. Don't do it! Instead, throw the strings away and get new ones.

Always unplug your lights and cords before replacing bulbs or fuses, and be sure to use only the types of bulbs and fuses prescribed by the manufacturer. Otherwise decorations may overheat, or safety features may not function properly.

Do not staple or nail down any cords, whether for inside or outside lights; rather, tape them in place. If that does not work, try plastic gutter hooks or other hangers, available at retail stores.

Do not use an extension cord for your tree lights, but if you feel you must, use the shortest one possible *and make sure you use one with a proper wattage rating* for the total wattage of *all* the products that will be plugged into it.

Do not put two extension cords together; buy a longer cord if you must, or move the tree.

Watch out for overloaded circuits when you light up your tree. Check the cords and connections for overheating frequently. The combined wattage ratings of all electrical products operating off one circuit should be no more than 1,500 watts.

Children have no business handling or operating lights and electrical decorations. Be careful that pets do not chew on wires, pull at tree branches, or knock the tree over.

If you use an artificial tree, look for the mark of a nationally recognized third-party certification agency to ensure that it meets flammability standards; unfortunately, most artificial trees apparently are not submitted to these agencies by their manufacturers, so you may have to search for one that is certified. Do not use lights on a metal tree; there is a serious danger of shock.

Make sure that all light strings and electrical decorations that you intend to use outdoors have been certified *for outdoor use* by a nationally recognized third-party certification agency.

falls. Their bones are more brittle, and their bodies are more fragile and heal less well. Very often, moreover, injuries suffered by an elderly person in a fall come on top of other serious health problems that can impede or slow recovery. A fall is tragically often the precipitating cause of an older person's loss of independent living.

Stairs and Steps

The most dangerous falls happen on stairs, because they cause people to fall farther and harder. Here are the basics for making stairs safe:

1. Light all the steps well, including the first and last steps, where many falls happen. This goes for inside and outside stairs as well as basement and attic stairs. Falls tend to happen when people think they are at the end of the steps and really they are not. Stairs should be evenly illuminated along their full length, with switches at the top and bottom. When you have guests, you should be particularly careful about lighting the stairs overnight, or at least showing them where the light switches are, for it has happened that guests get up at night and, forgetting just where the stairs are, fall down them. When you have guests coming in the evening, make sure your porch or entryway steps are well lit.
2. Make sure that you have hand rails strong enough to support people's weight, in good repair, running the entire length of any stairs, *including cellar or basement or attic stairs,* on both sides of the stairs. The rails should protrude from the wall at enough of a distance to let you get a good grip.
3. Loose carpeting, loose matting, or loose rubber treading on steps is extremely dangerous. On *each step,* tack or staple down any covering firmly, with heavy-duty carpet staples or tacks. Or pull it up and get rid of it. Periodically check for loose or pulled-out tacks or staples. Not only can this cause carpeting to be loose, which can cause someone to slip and fall, but stepping on one of these can hurt or can make you lose your balance and fall. Never put throw rugs on steps or at the head or foot of steps.
4. If there is no carpeting or other covering on the stairs, make sure that the surface is nonskid. If the steps are wood, the last thing in the world you want to do is wax them to a slippery finish. If the steps are naturally somewhat slippery, you can buy nonskid patches to put on them. Just make sure they are carefully applied.
5. Keep the stairs clean. Dusty wood can get slippery.
6. Keep obstacles *off the stairs.* A major cause of stairway falls is tripping over a box or toy. Of course, you will fall farther if the obstacle is at the top of the stairs, but each step, including the bottom one, should be clear.
7. Use proper footwear with nonskid soles. Clogs, flip-flops, and slippery, backless, or over-loose slippers can easily slip or trip you on the stairs. Plain socks are ex-

THE OLDER YOU ARE, THE HARDER YOU FALL

At around age fifty-five, a person's risk of accidentally dying as a result of a fall begins to increase sharply. In 1992, for example, 522 people in their thirties and 565 people in their forties died as a result of falls. But in that year 655 people in their fifties, 1,326 people in their sixties, 2,366 people in their seventies, and 4,442 in their eighties died as a result of falls. Among all people aged fifty-five and over, deaths from falls (10,731) in 1992 exceeded those related to motor vehicle crashes (9,961), whereas among all people aged twenty-five and over, deaths from motor vehicle crashes (27,753) were more than double the number resulting from falls (12,264).

tremely slippery on bare wood and even on some kinds of carpeting.

8. Teach children to hold the railing, not to play on the stairs, and not to leave toys on the stairs.
9. When there are babies and toddlers living or visiting in the home, place safety gates at the top and bottom of the stairs. These should have latches that the child cannot open, and should be able to withstand the child leaning on them or running into them without giving way.
10. Make sure that the steps are even. A common cause of stairway falls is that one step is shorter or longer than the others. Guests are especially likely to take a tumble because of this, even though you may be used to it.

Sensible Shoes

High heels, slippery soles, floppy footwear of any sort that is prone to flying off your foot—all these can cause injuries. (High heels also cause dents in your wood floors.) They are not especially comfortable either. The safest shoes in the home are low-heeled and rubber-soled with good nonskid treads that offer your foot plenty of coverage and support. Elderly people especially should always use such shoes in the home, and, really, so should everybody else. Sensible shoes are available now in a variety of attractive styles, and are not so grandmotherly and hygienic-looking as they used to be.

Dizziness; Poor Balance

If you get dizzy in high places or if you are suffering dizzy spells or poor balance from any medical condition, you must be sure to alter your habits accordingly. Do not use ladders or climb to high places. Get in and out of bed, chairs, or sofas slowly. Use walking supports, such as canes or walkers, as advised by your doctor or other medical professional.

If you are prone to dizziness, you should also avoid carrying around trays of wine glasses and other breakables, hot foods and liquids that might burn, and especially any sharp objects. Let someone else do these things.

Check with your doctor or other medical adviser for more suggestions tailored to your condition and circumstances.

Ladders, Step Stools

Make sure your ladders and step stools are sound and strong. All their parts should be intact, and all their rungs should be clean, tight, and sturdy.

Do not stand on chairs, boxes, or other makeshifts to reach things in high places. Get a proper stepladder or step stool for this. Preferably, get one that has a railing to hold on to. Make sure your stepladder or step stool is in good repair, with no loose or weak rungs. A one-step step stool is best.

Place the stepladder or stool on a level surface, free of clutter. Open it all the way into its braced-open position. Stand, and step, in the middle of the rungs as you go, or you may cause the contraption to tilt to one side. Do not stand on a higher rung than the manufacturer recommends as safe. Once you are up your ladder, do not lean out or away from the ladder trying to reach something at a distance. This is too likely to tilt the ladder and send you tumbling down. Instead, climb down and move the ladder.

If you have dizzy episodes, *do not go up on any ladder or step stool.* Get someone to help. Store your household goods so that you need not reach anything high except perhaps on unusual occasions, and for those occasions rely on someone's assistance.

Rugs and Carpets

A major cause of household falls is poorly placed, loose, or improperly backed rugs and carpets. Throw rugs, particularly at entrances, that lack nonskid backs are close to assaultive. If there are babies in the home or invalids or elderly people who tend to shuffle, you cannot have any loose rugs that their toes might get under. Put such rugs away until the baby is older or the invalid heals, or tack them down for the older folks.

Never place rugs in such a way that they conceal a bump in the floor. Do not put throw rugs on stairs or at the head or foot of stairs.

Floor Wax

Watch out for wax and cleaning products that make a skating rink out of your home. Test new products for slipperiness in an out-of-the-way area before trying them on your whole floor.

Never use furniture waxes and furniture sprays on floors, as the furniture products are specially designed to produce as much slipperiness as possible. Floor waxes, good ones at any rate, are typically designed to be less slippery, but they will still be somewhat slippery.

Obstacles; Clutter

Keep the floor clear of obstacles. Toys, books, papers, skateboards, vacuum cleaner, boxes—all these, and anything else out of place, constitute something that might trip an unwary walker. They do not belong on the floor, and most especially they do not belong on stairs, in hallways, or pathways of any sort. Clutter causes many falls.

Electrical Cords

These should never, under any circumstances, cross walkways. They have to travel along walls, door jambs, and ceilings to get to the other side. And never tack, nail, or staple them down either. Have an electrician do it, or use tape.

Spills

Anything spilled on any floor in the home may cause a fall. Oily and greasy spills are especially dangerous. Clean them up promptly and be sure that no slick residue is left behind. Detergent cleaners will usually do the trick, but you may need to do several washes and rinses for a big spill.

Bathrooms, Wet Floors

In areas of your home in which the floor is likely to get wet—the bathrooms, kitchen, laundry—try to install a type of flooring that is not slippery or less slippery when wet. For example, in bathrooms, choose matte-finish floor tiles rather than glossy finish; even matte are a bit slippery when wet but not nearly so much as the shinier type. If your kitchen or laundry floor is slippery when wet, you can put down throw rugs with nonskid backs in the areas that tend to get wet. Wipe up spills immediately. When the floor is wet all over from washing, close the door or stand a chair in the doorway so that people stay out until it has dried.

The shower stall and bathtub are notorious fall-inducing areas. Get nonslip bathtubs or shower floors, or put nonslip mats or stickers on the tub and floors you already have. Grab-bars, very securely anchored to the wall, are essential in the tub and shower. Where there are elderly residents, put one next to the toilet too. Outside the tub and shower, put absorbent little rugs or mats with nonskid backs in places where the floor might get wet, such as right outside the bath or shower stall or in front of the sink.

All of us should have learned from cartoons that it is important not to leave wet bars of soap on the floor or in the tub, since stepping on one can really send you flying.

Elderly people may benefit from a shower stool in the shower or tub, plus a spray hose so that they can have a comfortable sit-down shower, with vastly reduced chances of falling.

A night-light in the bathroom, and on the route to the bathroom, can help prevent nighttime falls.

Windows

Install child window guards in all windows, and obey whatever laws exist in your area regarding child safety with respect to windows. In New York City, the law specifies that there can be no more than 4.5 inches of unguarded window in households with children. You can also put in stops to prevent the windows from opening past a certain distance.

Even if you do not have children, most people have friends with children who visit, a niece or nephew, or grandchildren who need this protection. Do not leave young children alone where there are open windows; they are notoriously able to climb up and out. Cribs, children's beds, and high chairs should be placed away from windows. When you have young children in the home, be careful about the placement of other furniture as well. For instance, is your sofa right under a window, giving children a way to crawl up and out? Children learn very young, besides, to push a chair to the spot when they want to climb up somewhere.

Locking any dangerously high windows without guards or locks is some help, but little fingers can be shockingly clever, and besides, sooner or later you will want the window open. Locks, in any event, do not obviate the need for constant, vigilant supervision. So plan on getting window guards as soon as possible.

Level Floors

Steps down to sunken living rooms, door sills, and similar rises and dips in the floor level seem like nothing to the ordinary healthy adult, but to the very young, the very old, and the infirm, they are gulfs, chasms, and mountains. If you cannot avoid having such places in your home, light them well and get used to telling everyone to be careful.

Furniture

Leave wide enough pathways between pieces of furniture to permit adults to pass through without contortions. Make sure nothing protrudes into a walkway. Protruding pieces of furniture will not only bruise a shin or abdomen but might cause someone to trip and fall. Watch out for very low coffee tables; they can be tripped over.

Young children and the elderly are often injured by sharp edges and corners on furniture. Place furniture in such a way as to reduce the likelihood of bumps and collisions.

Low chairs, sofas, and beds can be hard for pregnant women and elderly people to get in and out of. Be sure to lend a hand. Or, if you are elderly or pregnant, master a technique of coping for times when you are alone.

Very low and very high beds can also present problems. If children or others are tending to fall out of bed, get side railings. They are inexpensive, can be put in and taken out easily, and work very well. You can make up the bed with the rails in place, and the child (or other person) can still climb safely out of bed at the openings. Some rails can be lowered and raised to suit your convenience.

Furniture used for support by invalids, the disabled or injured, or the elderly should be strong, stable, and able to withstand the weight put on it. It should not move or slide.

People who experience dizziness should get up from a sitting or lying position slowly.

The Importance of Good Lighting Everywhere

Poor lighting is a frequent cause of falls. It conceals obstacles and tricks the eye as to depths and distances. Your entire home should be set up with adequate lighting.

As eyes grow older, they grow dimmer; the elderly need more light to see well. But they are also more susceptible to glare and adjust less well to strong contrasts. So in your efforts to create adequate brightness for yourself or your parent or other elderly person, avoid falling into the trap of causing glares and strong contrasts. Keep background lighting and task lighting in balance.

Good light on stairs and in halls is especially important. Outdoor walkways and steps, too, should always be lit at night, particularly when you expect guests.

The route from bedroom to bathroom at night, especially when you have overnight guests, should be lit with night-lights. It is a good idea to equip bedrooms with a lamp or light, a telephone, and a flashlight that can all be reached at bedside without getting out of bed or creating any danger of knocking anything over—especially the lamp. Show your guests where the flashlight is and where the lamp switches are.

Keep flashlights or other emergency lights for use in case of power outages. Have a designated place for them, and keep them there at all times. Make it a place in which you will be able to find them.

For additional suggestions on avoiding falls, see chapter 63, "Further Miscellaneous Safety Rules."

63

Further Miscellaneous Safety Rules

The kitchen . . . Avoiding burns . . . Avoiding cuts . . . Avoiding kitchen slips . . . Garbage disposals . . . Bathroom safety . . . Water safety . . . Home swimming pools . . . Inflatable wading pools . . . Buckets and toilets . . . Bathtubs and hot tubs . . . Window glass accidents . . . Garage doors . . . Guns

In addition to the general guidelines on preparedness, fires, electrical safety, and slips and falls that apply throughout the home, there are also specific safety practices required for particular areas and objects in the home. This chapter is a collection of some of the most important of these.

The Kitchen

Avoiding Burns. Never leave handles of cooking pots on the stove protruding outward into the room. Turn them back in such a way that they do not stick out into an area where people walk. You might bump into one and spill the pot's contents, or a child might grab one and suffer a fearful accident. To protect children, use the back burners on your stove.

Keep all hot food and beverages away from young children and pushed back from the edges of counters and tables so that children cannot pull them off.

Keep cords, tablecloths, and placemats where children cannot pull them down.

Keep children away from stoves and ovens at all times, but especially when they are in use.

Make sure that burners are turned off when you are finished using them. Never test an electric burner with your hand to see if it has cooled; never rest your hand on the stovetop.

If you have children, you can get covers for stove knobs to make sure that a young child does not turn them.

Avoid walking around with pots of hot liquids or food. A trip or a spill can be catastrophic, and if there are small children in the room who might get underfoot or grasp you around your knees, a trip or spill is all too possible. If you have a large pot of boiling soup stock that you wish to freeze, put it into several smaller lidded freezing containers at the stove.

When you lift a lid, watch out for steam that might escape and burn your face or hand. Wearing a mitt, let the steam escape out of the side or back of the pan, in a direction away from your face or hand.

Do not use wet towels or wet potholders to lift hot pots. The moisture in them will quickly heat up, and you could be burned.

Wear shoes that offer some coverage. This not only protects you from spilling hot things on your feet—which can lead to a chain reaction of kitchen catastrophes—but also protects your feet from dropped knives, cast-iron skillets, and other objects.

Sometimes dishes get extremely hot in the microwave. Always use a hot potholder when removing them, whether or not you expect them to be hot.

When you wish to add chopped vegetables or other foods to a hot liquid—such as oil, water, or soup—wear a protective mitt and slide the chopped food gently off a plate to the pan. Don't drop the food directly into the hot liquid or it may splash up and burn you.

Any moisture dropped into hot fat will make it sizzle up and send burning droplets flying. Beware of putting damp potato slices or juicy tomatoes or anything else wet or moist in a pan that contains hot oil or grease. Use a long-handled implement, and hold it wearing a mitt. A mesh splatter guard can also help.

The oven causes many burns. Arrange your shelves where you want them before you preheat, so that you need not handle them hot. When you reach in to turn a potato, test a cake, or baste a turkey, or when you lean in to read the thermometer, you can easily burn your hand or face. Be cautious pulling out the oven shelf to do these things, too, as the shelves so often tilt downward, spilling hot grease or food. If the operation is not too delicate (that is, if the dish will not be ruined by slight cooling or gentle bumping), pull the pan out and set it on top of the stove to do it. If your oven shelves tilt, you must *always* do this, no matter how inconvenient it seems.

Put guard latches on any cabinets whose contents—including glass bottles, china, knives, and cleaning substances—are not safe for infants and young children.

Keep electrical appliances and electrical cords far from the sink and any other area in which they might accidentally come into contact with water. Unplug appliances when not in use.

Avoiding Cuts. If you hand scissors or shears to anyone, close them, hold the blades and give them over handle first.

Avoid walking around with knives. When you must walk holding a knife, hold it with your arm at your side, slightly raised, with the knife sloping toward the floor, the blade turned downward, and slightly away from you. That way, if you fall, you don't fall on the point or the blade of the knife.

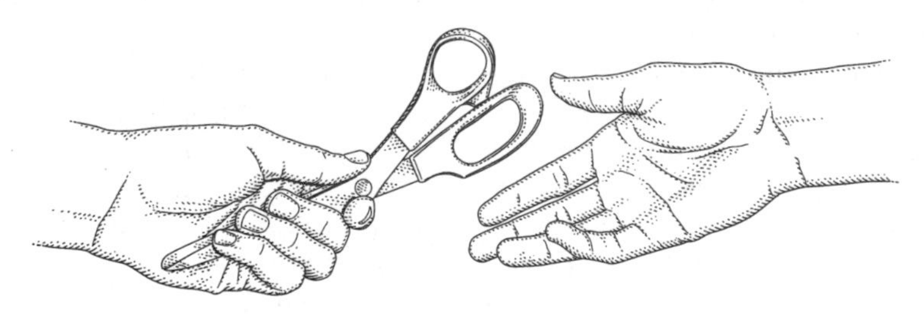

Handing over scissors

Safety experts now advise people not to hand knives to one another. Instead, lay the knife down and let the other person pick it up. (My father taught me that you hand over a knife handle first, holding on to the handle just before it meets the blade, with the point aiming to the floor at a slight angle, blade down. But this is no longer considered acceptable.)

Professionals also advise us not to slice or cut things while holding them in our hands but to put them on chopping boards for chopping. You are more likely to cut yourself this way if your blade is either extremely keen or extremely dull. In the former case, a mere touch will rend the skin; in the latter you may press so hard that the blade slides into your hand with great force.

Treat the blades of food processors with great respect. Never touch them unless the processor is unplugged. Wash them with the same care that you use when you wash knives.

Never lay knives or other sharp implements in a basin or sink full of soapy water. They will be hard to see, and you or the next unwary person may be cut. When washing the knife blade, put the dull edge of the blade against your rag or sponge—never the sharp edge.

Do not put your hands into a glass to wash it; you can break the glass and cut your hand. (This results in a painful characteristic arc-shaped cut.) Instead, insert a bottle brush or other washing tool with a diameter less than the glass's.

Avoiding Kitchen Slips. Wipe up spills and dry any wet spots immediately when you are working in the kitchen. Banana peels really are very slippery. Even worse is mashed banana or pureed anything. The area around the baby's chair, therefore, will be a major slip zone. After the meal is over, check around to see if there are any gobs of food on the floor.

Try to wear nonslip shoes with treads. Bare feet and smooth soles are both much more likely to result in a fall.

Use only rubber-backed or nonskid rugs in the kitchen. But you may find that rugs in the kitchen hurt more than they help, being just one more thing to tangle your feet in.

When the floor is wet after mopping or scrubbing, it may be very slippery. Close the door or set a chair in front of the entrance so that no one comes in and takes a fall (or tracks up the floor).

Garbage Disposals. *Never put your hand in a garbage disposal under any circumstances or for any reason.* If it gets clogged, call a repair person. Follow the manufacturer's instructions about safe operation and what you can and cannot put in it. Among the generally forbidden items are metal, stoneware, glass, and bones. Do not overload the disposal, and use copious amounts of water. If something falls in, turn off the disposal and the water and try to retrieve it with tongs. If the disposal jams, try to clear it only in the manner the manufacturer advises. Some manufacturers provide you with a tool to use to clear a jam. (See chapter 9, "Kitchen Culture," page 118.)

Bathroom Safety

Bathroom electrical appliances should be used in accordance with the cautions discussed in chapter 61.

On avoiding slips and falls, see chapter 62.

Medicine cabinet safety—the safe storage of medicines and pills—is discussed in chapter 64.

Avoid keeping anything made of glass in the bathroom, tub, or shower stall. When your hands are wet, it is easier to let things slip and fall out of your grasp. This can result in bad cuts if the glass shatters on the hard tile. If your shampoo came in a glass bottle, transfer it to one of those plastic ones that you can pick up in the drugstore.

If the bathroom door has a lock, keep a key or other means of entering from outside when the door is locked. That way, if someone inside has an accident and is helpless, you can get in quickly to give aid.

People with children often find it best to disable bathroom and bedroom door locks to avoid the danger of children locking themselves in. Sometimes children can lock doors, but cannot unlock them; and sometimes they will not unlock them even if they can.

If you have young children, lock sharp utensils such as razors or scissors out of their reach. Store electrical appliances, including hair dryers, outside the bathroom.

Water Safety

Children are the typical victims of drowning in the home, with preschoolers and teenagers being the most frequent child victims. Of 900 people who drowned in their homes in 1994, 350 were children under four. The typical home drowning occurs in a pool, but tubs, sinks, toilets, and buckets also occasion drownings. Young children are fatally attracted to the water and do not realize that they can drown. Teenagers exercise poor judgment, take risks, and, sometimes, drink alcohol or take drugs. For every child or adult who drowns, moreover, many others survive near-drowning incidents with profound brain damage, paralysis, and other tragic injuries. Most of the drownings and injuries are caused by negligence. Safe pool construction and pool use rules are ignored, or supervision is inadequate.

Swimming pool safety is outside the scope of this book, but home pools are so common and so dangerous that I feel I must say a little about its importance. To get a real education in water and pool safety, however, you must turn to the reliable authorities on the subject. Learn the safety laws in your area, follow the pool manufacturer's cautions to the letter, take a course in CPR, and get all the information put out by whatever public health authority has jurisdiction in your area.

Unfortunately, it is hard to convince people of how rigorously attentive to water safety they must be without telling them some of the horror stories and without attempting to impress upon them that the stories describe events that are not rare but occur each year hundreds of times.[1] The most common is that a child wanders out of the house or yard and goes into the pool, either just for fun or to retrieve a toy. In most drownings of preschoolers, the child has been missing for less than five minutes when he or she is found; and medical personnel report that the shattered parent typically (and truthfully) says, "I only took my eyes off him for a minute."

A number of states and localities have enacted laws requiring pools to be enclosed in what is called "isolation pool fencing"—that is, a fence that separates the pool from the home, is built to be unclimbable, and has self-closing and self-latching gates. These are known to be highly effective in bringing about a large reduction in the number of preschooler drownings. Some states also require "exit alarms" on doors providing access to the pool and a variety of other safety features. Even if the laws in your area are lax, invest in the best safety features.

Home Swimming Pools. Statistics show that safe home pools—for all age groups—depend upon isolation fencing, pool covers, and other pool safety features (nonslip walking surfaces, nonslip pool bottoms); adequate lifesaving equipment properly placed and knowledge of how to use it; knowledge of lifeguarding and lifesaving techniques and CPR; obedience to safe swimming and diving rules; safe diving boards and pool depths; and *constant adult supervision of all children*. Keep electrical equipment entirely out of the pool area. When the pool is not in use, make sure that all fence gates are closed, and lock all doors and windows that lead to the pool area. Keep a cordless phone near the pool, along with a list of emergency numbers. Besides the foregoing measures, it is important not to tempt unsupervised children into the pool area. Keep toys and other child attractants out of the pool area. There are pool alarms that are supposed to sound if there is motion in the water, but these are not substitutes for supervision; you would be much less safe, not more, if you were ever to rely on an alarm instead of watching the children.

It is not enough that you learn CPR and pool safety, by the way. Your baby-sitters and any other adults who supervise your children should have the same high safety standards that you do. If your baby-sitter is not up on CPR or if your brother is not used to children, then forbid use of the pool in your absence or do not leave your children in their care. If your neighbors have an unfenced pool or lax attitudes, do your best to convince them to reform, but in the meantime you must be unceasingly vigilant.

The Consumer Products Safety Commission provides up-to-date advice on pool safety and pool safety features and products. Check its Web site, or write to the address provided in the Acknowledgments and Sources at the end of this book.

Inflatable Wading Pools. Empty even small inflatable wading pools when playtime is over. Small children can drown in these. (Large inflatable pools should be treated like swimming pools, which are discussed above.) Besides, even though you are watching your own children, can you be sure the neighbor's child will not toddle over, enticed by the water while you are indoors at naptime? Never leave children playing in a wading pool without supervision *for even one second.* If you are worried about the telephone, invest in a cordless one to carry out to the yard with you.

Buckets and Toilets. Never, under any circumstances, leave a baby or young child alone in a room with a bucket full of water. According to the Consumer Products Safety Commission, between January 1984 and June 1993 there were 212 drowning incidents involving five-gallon buckets. It is estimated that there are 50 drowning deaths and 130 emergency-room visits every year attributable to buckets of water.

When you have babies and young children in the home, use child safety locks to keep toilet lids locked at all times.

Bathtubs and Hot Tubs. Never leave an infant or young child alone in the bathtub *for even one second.* If the telephone rings, let it ring. If you feel you must answer it, calmly take your child up out of the tub, wrap him or her up in a towel, and walk sedately to the telephone.

Older children and adults are in danger of drowning in the tub if they fall and become unconscious. Follow all the suggestions on reducing slips and falls in the bathroom listed in chapter 62.

Empty the bathtub as soon as the bath is over, so that it will not remain a dangerously attractive place for young children.

More than 700 deaths have occurred in whirlpool baths, hot tubs, and spas since 1980, and about one-third of these deaths were children under age five. No children should ever be left unattended in whirlpools, hot tubs, or spas. These pose not only all the hazards of ordinary bathtubs, but some others as well. One problem is that long hair can be terribly dangerous in them unless it is securely tied back and up. Otherwise, it can be caught in a suction-fitting drain cover, holding the victim's head underwater until he or she drowns. A safety type of drain cover is available that reduces the risk that hair will become entangled. Another problem is that suction at the drain can become so strong as to be very dangerous, even deadly, especially to children. Current safety guidelines call for at least two drain outlets for each pump; this lessens the suction at any single outlet. The Consumer Products Safety Commission offers these safety guidelines for using hot tubs, spas, or whirlpools:

> Always use a locked safety cover when the spa is not in use and keep young children

away from spas, whirlpools, or hot tubs unless there is constant adult supervision.

Make sure the spa, whirlpool, or hot tub has the dual drains and drain covers required by current safety standards.

Regularly have a professional check your spa, whirlpool, or hot tub and make sure it is in good, safe working condition, and that drain covers are in place and not cracked or missing. Check drain covers yourself throughout the year.

Know where the cut-off switch for your pump is so you can turn it off in an emergency.

Be aware that consuming alcohol while using a spa, whirlpool, or hot tub could lead to drowning.

Window-Glass Accidents

One common type of home accident occurs when people fail to see large picture windows and attempt to walk through them, or when they trip and fall against a glass door or window. Injuries received in these incidents can be serious or fatal, as the jagged glass causes deep cuts and lacerations. To prevent such accidents, station furniture or tall potted plants in front of the large panes, or place decals on them.

Safety glass is a good idea. Tempered safety glass is most common. Wired and laminated types of safety glass also exist. Not only is tempered safety glass five times stronger than normal annealed glass, but it breaks into small cubical pieces that cannot cause deep or serious cuts. New homes will already have safety glass, but those built before 1963 in all likelihood will not.

Garage Doors

Garage-door accidents have decreased significantly since standards have gone into effect requiring them to have a quick-release feature. Even now, however, children are still sometimes crushed by automatic garage doors. Any safety mechanism can sometimes malfunction, so it is important to supervise young children vigilantly around garage doors. Teach children never to stand in the area under the door, and how dangerous it is to activate the door and try to run or ride a bike underneath before it closes. Children have died playing this way with garage doors. Test your own garage door by the method and with the frequency recommended by the Consumer Products Safety Commission or Underwriters Laboratories. Since standards and recommended testing procedures change over time, call or write to such organizations or check the Internet. Recent advice from Underwriters Laboratories was as follows:

> Every month, test the [garage door] operator's anti-entrapment feature by placing a 1½-inch object, such as a piece of two-by-four lumber, flat on the floor in the path of the open door. Activate the door to close. If the door doesn't stop and reverse after contact with the object, disconnect the operator and use the door manually until the operator is replaced or repaired by a qualified technician.
>
> You should also visually inspect the door's springs, rollers and other hardware for breakage or wear. If you see signs of wear or deterioration, contact a qualified technician for repair.[2]

Guns

If you acquire a gun, acquire an education in gun safety at the same time. The likelihood of death to a member of the household from an accidental gunshot wound in the home far exceeds the likelihood of suffering injury inflicted by an intruder.

Some states or locales have laws affecting how you store guns in your home. Learn and obey all regulations in your own area, including those governing licensing and purchasing.

Some places require a trigger lock (or other gun-disabling device) on all stored guns. This is a device that goes over the trigger and prevents firing; typically it is removed with a key. Store all guns *unloaded and uncocked, with the trigger lock secured or the magazine removed.* Store guns in a gun safe—a lockable box or cabinet specially designed to hold guns—and keep it locked! Store ammunition separately in a locked box or cabinet, in a cool, dry place, and keep it locked! Keep all the keys for your trigger locks and gun cabinets on you. Your ordinary keychain with your house and car keys that you keep on your person would be a good place. Do not leave the keys in a drawer somewhere or children may get them and open the cabinet.

64

Poisons, Hazardous Substances, and Proper Disposal of Hazardous Household Wastes

Accidental poisonings . . . Storing toxic substances; childproof locks and latches . . . Original containers; what's on the label . . . Keep different kinds of hazardous products separate . . . Medicines, reading labels in good light . . . Disposing of hazardous household wastes . . . Which wastes are hazardous? . . . Follow manufacturer's instructions . . . Buy less; use it up . . . Down the drain? . . . Not outside in the yard, not on the ground or in a landfill . . . Do not burn . . . Recycle and reuse . . . State and local laws and regulations . . . Hazardous wastes that must or may be taken to collection centers . . . Some acceptable means of disposal in certain circumstances . . . Get advice . . . General safety practices for hazardous wastes . . . Guide to reading container labels

In every home, the potential exists for someone to suffer serious injury or death as a result of swallowing or touching a poisonous or hazardous substance. Accidental poisonings and injuries and illnesses resulting from ingesting or contacting hazardous substances in the home, however, are highly preventable. Guidelines to help reduce the risks and explanations of the best ways to dispose of hazardous household waste are set out in the materials that follow.

Accidental Poisonings

About 90 percent of accidental poisonings occur in the home, and the typical victim is a child under the age of six. More children die of poisoning each year than of all infectious diseases combined. There is an old saw that says "Dose makes the poison." It means that just about anything can poison you if you ingest too much of it, including plain water and ordinary table salt. Being so much smaller and more delicate than we are, children can be poisoned by smaller amounts of substances and even by some substances that would not kill adults. Ordinary vitamin pills, aspirin, cleaning liquids, cold medications, and dozens of other household products are hazardous to little ones. Adults' medicines, including antidepressants and sedatives, are often the cause of death or grave illness in small children

The safety guidelines below will help protect all members of the household from accidental poisoning. If an accidental poisoning should occur in your home, be prepared to react quickly. Post the number of your local poison control center along with your medical emergency numbers and other emergency numbers near your telephone. Call immediately if anyone in your household ingests a hazardous substance. When you call, have with you the container of the substance accidentally ingested so that you can help emergency personnel give you proper guidance. In some cases but not in others, people are advised to administer an emetic (a substance that induces vomiting). Whether you will be advised to use an emetic depends on the nature of the substance ingested and how long ago it was ingested. Keep syrup of ipecac, an emetic, in your first-aid kit or medicine cabinet just in case. Administer or take ipecac only when instructed to by your doctor, your local poison control center, or other competent medical or emergency personnel.

Take a first-aid course, or ask your doctor what is important to know and how you can best acquire the knowledge so that you can handle home emergencies wisely.

Storing Toxic Substances; Childproof Safety Locks and Latches. Households with young children should place a child safety latch on any cabinet in which any substance is stored that might be toxic, harmful, or unhealthy for children. Such substances include pesticides, bug bombs, weed killers, soaps, detergents, cleaning materials, solvents, bleaches, drain cleaners, oven cleaners, aerosols, solvents, paints, paint thinners or removers, spot-removal fluids, liquid fuels, cosmetics, perfumes, nail polish, nail polish remover, rubbing alcohol, pills and medicines of all sorts, including aspirin, Tylenol, and other ordinary household painkillers, cough and cold medicines and other over-the-counter preparations, deodorant, and hydrogen peroxide. Lawn and garden pesticides should be locked up securely in a storage area *outside* the home.

Bathroom and medicine cabinets are prime spots for childproofing as they contain medicines, toiletries, and other dangerous substances, and children can climb up on sinks and gain access to them. Cabinets containing cleaning, hobby, or workshop materials are also important danger spots to render secure and childproof. Children may also go exploring in attics, basements, garages, tool sheds, and other outbuildings too. Wherever you have dangerous substances, it is dangerous not to lock them up, out of sight and out of children's reach.

Whenever you can, buy hazardous substances in childproof packages and bottles.

Original Containers; What's on the Label. *Carefully read labels on every product you bring into your home.* The manufacturer's label tells you how hazardous a substance is, how to be careful around it, what to do in case of accidental ingestion or skin contact, and much else of importance. Keep products in their original containers, make sure their labels are retained, and make sure they remain legible; in an emergency, you will desperately need all the information written there. (See the Guide to Reading Container Labels, page 750.)

Never put dangerous substances in unlabeled bottles or containers. A particularly dangerous practice is using old food containers, as this increases the likelihood that someone will make a fatal or highly injurious error and ingest some. Bleach in a soda bottle looks like something to drink; it belongs *only* in its original container. If a child were to drink out of the soda bottle, it might even be difficult to figure out just what substance it was.

Never use a product for any purpose but the one it is intended for. Never reuse pesticide containers or the containers of any other toxic substances for any purpose.

The Federal Hazardous Substances Act (FHSA) provides that all products that contain "hazardous substances" must post caveats—signal words—on their labels, along with the name and place of business of the manufacturer, the common or chemical name of the hazardous substance, a statement describing what the principal hazards are (such as "Flammable," "Combustible," "Vapor Harmful," "Causes Burns," or "Absorbed Through Skin") and precautionary actions to be followed or avoided. Under the FHSA, the label must use the signal word "DANGER" on substances that are extremely flammable, corrosive, or highly toxic, such as some oven or drain cleaners. (Another statute requires certain very toxic substances, such as pesticides, to display the word "POISON" prominently in red on a contrasting color background, along with first-aid advice.) The label must use the signal word "WARNING" or "CAUTION" on all other hazardous substances, indicating a milder hazard. The latter terms are appropriate when the product is not likely to cause permanent damage so long as first aid is given appropriately. Ordinary all-purpose cleaners, detergents, household chlorine bleach, and disinfectants usually say "WARNING" or "CAUTION."

Any substance bearing any of the statutory signal words—POISON, DANGER, WARNING, or CAUTION—belongs in a childproof cabinet. Pesticides should be locked up someplace *outside* the home.

Keep Different Kinds of Hazardous Products Separate. Do not store pesticides, cleaning fluids, or other toxic substances in the food cabinet. Do not put your dog food next to the kerosene. Do not store medicines near cleaning fluids or foods. Keep things of like kind and purpose and safety level together to reduce the risk of mistaking one for the other. You will not accidentally pick up a bottle of weed killer instead of spray cleaner if you keep your gardening materials in a separate room (and in a separate locked cabinet) from your cleaning materials, and if you

DON'T MIX

Do not mix household chemicals together; you might unwittingly cause a dangerous chemical reaction. In particular, do not mix chlorine bleach with acids or products containing acids or with alkalies or ammonia or substances containing alkalies or ammonia. Hazardous gases will form or other dangerous reactions may occur.

keep your very hazardous substances apart from your relatively safer ones.

Medicines. Lock the medicine cabinet if there are young children in the home; always put medicines on the top shelf, out of children's reach, even if the cabinet is latched or locked. Child safety lids on medicines help lessen the risk, but they are not fail-safe.

Throw away old prescription medicines when you have finished taking them. (See page 751 on throwing away medicines safely.) Never take pills or medicines out of their original container, and never remove labels from medicine containers or bottles. If any container or bottle lacks a label, throw it away. Never store medicines in the same cabinets with foods, cleaning materials, or other household chemicals or substances.

If two different medicines are similar in size, or have similar packages, bottles, or labels, do not store them side by side. You might mistake one for the other.

Read labels in a good light, and use your reading glasses. Otherwise, you may take the wrong thing or misread the instructions or the dosage. Be very careful about taking medicines in the middle of the night, when you are drowsy or bleary-eyed. *Never take, mix, or give medicine in the dark.* Never mix medications (take different ones at the same time) unless your doctor tells you it is safe to do so. If you have taken any medications or other substances or if for any other reason you are drowsy or confused, have someone help you make sure you are taking the right medicine and the right dose.

Do not take medicine in front of children; they may try to imitate you or think you are having something good that they want.

Never tell children that medicine—even their own medicine—is candy. This is giving the opposite message from the one you want. Instead, explain what medicine is and what this medicine will do (stop the hurt, take away the fever, help you get better). I have seen a child insist that his own medicine was candy because it was sweet and fruit-flavored. It is important to insist to the child that, although the nice flavors are there to make it easy for children to swallow, it is still medicine: we take exactly the amount the doctor ordered, not more and not less.

Disposing of Hazardous Household Wastes

Which Wastes Are Hazardous? Some household trash is too hazardous to be thrown in your regular trash or recycling receptacle. It poses risks to people, animals, or the environment. It is important to understand how to dispose of hazardous household wastes safely.

In fact, one way in which housekeeping today is remarkably different from housekeeping fifty years ago is the amount of time you must spend dealing with trash. Most municipalities now have recycling laws, hazardous waste laws, yard waste laws, and others, and learning how to separate and prepare your trash for disposal is not necessarily so simple. Once you get into new habits, however, obeying these important laws ceases to feel like trouble. Typically you can get a brochure from the sanitation or environmental departments in your area that explains everything; or call and ask them your questions. Sanitation workers can often provide invaluable practical advice. If such laws have not yet come to your area, do not be surprised to see them soon. Please note that the discussion here concerns only regulations and recommendations for *private households.* Laws and good practice for businesses may be quite different.

Household hazardous wastes include anything that might harm human beings or animals coming into accidental contact with them, such as sanitation workers, children, or foraging animals. They also include things that might harm the environment unless disposed of properly. Automotive fluids or pesticides, for example, if poured down the storm sewer, contaminate the earth and water. Thus in many municipalities you are required to bring these and other hazardous household wastes to service stations or other drop-off centers or to hazardous waste collection centers.

Federal and state authorities and recycling programs generally break down hazardous household wastes into four categories according to the type of hazard associated with the waste. Some products belong to multiple categories; chlorine bleach, for example, is both "explosive/reactive" and "toxic."

Flammable/Ignitable: This includes products that catch on fire easily and burn intensely. Cans of spray paint, house paint, motor oil, gasoline, kerosene, nail polish, hairspray, furniture cleaners, and butane gas are all examples of flammable/ignitable items.

Corrosive: Products that eat away or dissolve other materials, damaging the body and/or the environment, are corrosive. Some examples of corrosives are bleaches, drain cleaners, lye, oven cleaners, solvents, and batteries.

Explosive/Reactive: These materials will explode or create hazardous by-products such as toxic fumes if exposed to heat, light, or other chemicals. Some examples of explosive/reactive products are drain cleaners, ammonia (when mixed with bleach), bleach (when mixed with acids or alkalies), chemical fertilizers, some pool chemicals, aerosol sprays, and petroleum-based solvents or degreasers.

Toxic: The number of toxic substances is legion, but some examples are bleach, hair dye, some air fresheners, moth killers, rubbing alcohol, nail polish, paint thinner, solvents, weed killers, fertilizers, pesticides, fuels, and antifreeze. Lead or nickel-cadmium batteries are also toxic, as is anything that contains mercury, such as thermostats, thermometers, or some fluorescent lightbulbs.

Disposing of Hazardous Household Wastes

Follow Manufacturer's Instructions. Product labels contain important information about the safe use, storage, and disposal of hazardous products and the containers that hold them. Read and follow all such instructions carefully. Never remove labels or store such substances in unlabeled containers. If the label leaves you with questions as to the nature of the contents or hazards of a product, under right-to-know laws, you can call the manufacturer and request a "Material Safety Data Sheet" or MSDS. This will not give away trade secrets, but it will tell you the chemical nature of the substance and give more information on hazards, safe handling, and disposal. Some MSDSs are posted on the Internet.

Buy Less; Use It Up. To the extent possible, avoid using hazardous household substances. Read labels before you buy, and ask yourself if you really need a product if it is toxic, corrosive, flammable, explosive, or reactive. If you do, and if there is no safer alternative, buy a small amount and use it all up. That way you will not be left with the problem of how to dispose of the leftovers. It is much less difficult to dispose of an empty can that once held paint than to dispose of half a can of paint. If you cannot use all of the substance, try to give it away to someone who can—a neighbor, a church or synagogue or other religious organization, or a civic group. If you give away a hazardous substance, however, be sure that you give it in its original container, with the label and its cautions and instructions intact.

Down the Drain? There are three main types of sewers. Sanitary sewers are pipes leading from residences and other buildings to a wastewater treatment plant. Unless you have a septic tank, your household drains are probably connected to sanitary sewers. Although treatment of wastewater from sanitary sewers can remove most waste products, some may not be removed or may not be entirely removed. Therefore, never pour down your drain any motor oil, transmission fluid, antifreeze, other automotive fluids, gasoline or other fuels, paints, solvents, thinners, strippers, pesticides, or substances containing heavy metals. If you do, these dangerous substances may end up in the water supply.

Products that normally go down the drain when you use them for their intended purpose—laundry detergents, all-purpose cleaners, soaps and shampoos, sink, tile, and tub cleaners, and the like—can usually be disposed of in the drain or toilet. Pour them down with plenty of water, a small amount at a time. Do not dispose of two such products together, as it is dangerous to mix household chemicals—even in the drain. If you have a septic tank, you should not dispose of large quantities of bleach or disinfectant at one time; pour down small quantities, diluted with plenty of water.

Septic tanks are an individual sewer system into which the waste liquids from a single household flow. There are small communities that have constructed septic systems that serve a group of homes, but this is not typical. The solid waste in a septic system settles to the bottom of the tank and is broken down by bacteria. Liquid sewage goes into a "drainfield" to be broken down by other bacteria. If the liquid sewage contains hazardous chemicals, these may pass through the septic system into the ground water. For this reason, those with septic systems must be extremely careful not to dispose of hazardous wastes in their systems; this waste will not pass through a treatment plant.

Storm drains, the third type of sewer, are ditches or pipes that collect water after a storm and channel it into rivers, lakes, and other waterways. (There are some instances of combination storm/sanitary sewers, but this is not typical.) Hazardous waste dumped into storm sewers is transported directly into these waterways. *It is never safe or appropriate to use a storm sewer or gutter for the disposal of any type of hazardous waste.* Yet many people routinely dispose of automotive fluids in this manner. Many people also fail to clean up spills of motor oil and other automotive fluids on streets or in driveways properly, instead just hosing the spill down, which causes the dangerous wastes to be washed into storm sewers and gutters.

Not Outside in the Yard, on the Ground, or in a Landfill. Many materials can eventually contaminate the water supply and the earth if they are poured on or buried in the ground, whether in your own yard, in a deserted country area, or in a landfill. Motor oils, transmission fluid, gasoline, paints, kerosene or turpentine, paint strippers and thinners or similar liquids, and pesticides should *never* be poured on the ground or buried—anywhere. Likewise, never dispose of any hazardous substance in the street or in a dumpster. Empty containers that have held hazardous wastes should not be thrown into a dumpster or buried either.

Do Not Burn. Never burn hazardous waste or empty containers that have held hazardous waste. In particular, never burn any flammable liquids such as gasoline or kerosene or other petroleum-based products, their empty containers, or an aerosol container. Your fireplace or barbecue, by the way, is never a proper place to burn *any* waste. It is dangerous to you and to the environment to use these as incinerators.

Recycle and Reuse. In many communities, recycling is required by law for certain materials and is available for others. Most communities require you to recycle glass, some paper, and some plastic and metal containers, including aerosols in some places; but check the regulations in your particular area. In some communities, you can recycle leftover motor oil, transmission fluid, brake fluid, antifreeze, and other automotive fluids by taking them to an automotive service center, oil recycling station, or authorized collection site in your area. Car batteries, household batteries, and tires can also be turned in for recycling or reusing in some areas. Find out what possibilities exist in your area, and take advantage of them.

Local laws on recycling invariably require that you dispose of recyclable materials in separate containers from regular trash. In other respects, local recycling laws differ. Usually recyclables must be sorted and prepared in one way or another. For example, bottles and cans should be rinsed out and caps and spray pumps removed, corrugated cardboard flattened and tied up with sturdy twine, and newspaper bundles tied up with string. In some areas you are required to separate shiny magazines and catalogues, newspapers, and mail. Check the regulations in your own community.

State and Local Laws and Regulations. State and local laws concerning household hazardous waste and facilities for household hazardous waste also differ greatly from place to place. What you should pour down the drain in your area may depend in part upon the particular capacities of the water treatment facilities in your area. In addition, some areas have recycling and disposal facilities that others lack, and some areas just have more effective environmental laws; all these factors, too, affect what you can throw in the trash or pour down the drain. In my area, but not in others, it is legal to put fluorescent bulbs and ordinary flashlight and household batteries in the regular trash. In some locations it is and in others it is not legal to pour antifreeze down your drain. Whatever the local variations, in most areas today there are some types of hazardous wastes that by law must *never* be disposed of in your regular trash but must instead be delivered to a drop-off center or collection center for hazardous wastes. It is your obligation to find out what these types of waste are in your community. The restrictions discussed below are typical of many municipalities today.

The items listed in the first group below are some that *laws in many areas* require disposing of only at an appropriate drop-off site, service station, retailer, or hazardous waste collection center. The items in the second group may also be disposed of at drop-offs or collection centers in many areas, but laws requiring this may or may not exist. Whether it is required or merely recommended, environmental authorities generally agree that it is good citizenship not to put any of the following items into your regular trash or in dumpsters, not to bury them in the yard or burn them or throw them into landfills, and to avoid pouring them down drains, storm sewers, and gutters.

Where Facilities Exist, Dispose of at Drop-Off Sites and Hazardous Waste Collection Centers

1. *Laws in many areas require drop-off or collection center disposal:*
   - Motor oil
   - Motor oil filters
   - Brake fluid
   - Transmission fluid
   - Antifreeze
   - Tires
   - Car batteries
   - Appliances
   - Any products containing mercury (some fluorescent bulbs, mercury thermometers, mercury thermostats)
2. *Local, state, and federal authorities, recommend drop-off or collection center disposal where possible:*
   - Pesticides, insecticides
   - Flea collars and powders
   - Fungicides
   - Photographic chemicals
   - Wood preservatives
   - Nickel-cadmium rechargeable batteries
   - Lithium batteries
   - Button batteries
   - Weed killers
   - Solvents (mineral spirits, turpentine, naphtha, paint thinner)

Nail polish remover
Empty gas cylinders
Furniture strippers
Pool chemicals
Lighter fluid
Diesel fuel, other fuels
Driveway sealer
Drain cleaners
Oven cleaners
Strong acids, alkalies (lye)
Waxes and polishes for floors, metals, cars
Products containing acetone, xylene, and methylene chloride Products containing heavy metals, including mercury, lead, cadmium, lithium, nickel, chromium, silver, zinc
Cleaners and polishes that contain solvents
Mothballs, moth flakes
Pet sprays and dips
Rat and mouse poisons
Poisons
Lead-acid batteries
Lawn chemicals
Silver polish
Shoe dye
Varnishes, stains
Paint strippers
Paints
Caulk, construction adhesives
Kerosene
Degreasers
Gasoline
Automobile batteries

In most areas, collection centers accept waste only on designated collection days or by appointment. Moreover, different collection centers are not equipped to handle any and all wastes, and some are quite restricted in what they are capable of handling. Call before you go, or read brochures or other literature to learn what sorts of hazardous wastes your center collects. Most will not accept explosives, radioactive material, medical waste, or ammunition. In addition, you may be limited in the amount of materials you will be permitted to bring in, and you may have to offer it packed or sealed in a special manner.

Some Acceptable Means of Disposal in Certain Circumstances. Where local regulations do not forbid it and when you cannot use up, reuse, or recycle hazardous substances or their containers or deliver them for safe disposal to a collection center, authorities in some areas recommend that you dispose of the following materials in the manner described.

Furniture, floor, and metal polishes: Wrap the tightly closed container in newspaper and put it in the trash.

Indoor pesticides (any product formulated to eliminate pests, including weeds, insects, and vermin) and insect repellants: Follow the disposal instructions on the product label. Recycle the empty container if possible. In general, wrap the container well and put it in the trash.

Fertilizers, dry: Wrap the container in newspaper and put it in the trash.

Fertilizers, liquid: Pour quantities of less than one gallon down the drain with plenty of water.

Latex paint: If there is a small amount of paint left in the can, open it and let it air—in a well-ventilated area out of the reach of children and pets—until the paint dries hard. Then put the can in the regular trash with the lid off. You can hasten the drying process by mixing cat litter or sawdust or an oil-absorbent material with the paint. Leave the can open until the paint mixture hardens; then dispose of the can in the regular trash, leaving the lid off. In some areas, facilities exist to recycle empty paint cans.

Oil-based paint: Deliver to a hazardous waste disposal center.

Reading Container Labels

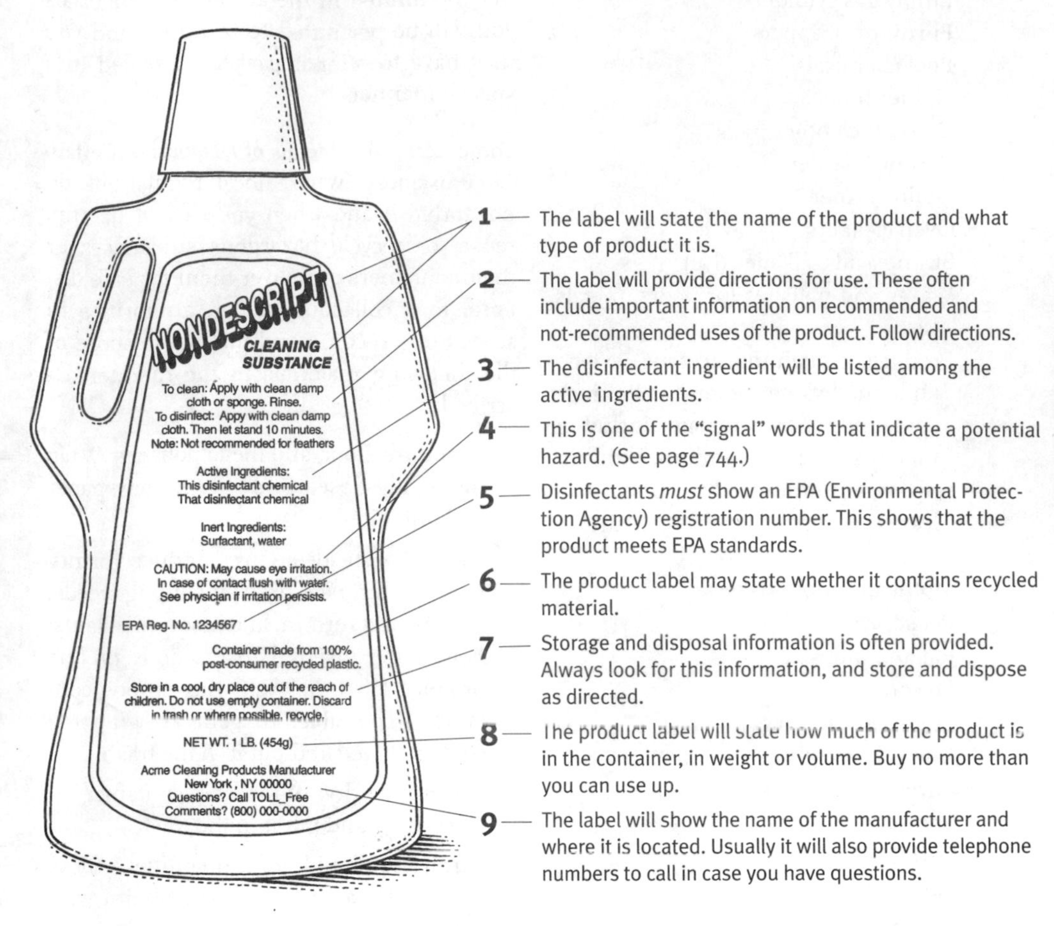

Outdoor pesticides and wood preservatives, or substances such as paints containing them: When these grow old, they probably should not be used but taken to a household waste collection center. Contact your local extension service or other reliable authority for advice (see suggestions below) if there is no such center in your area.

Antifreeze and other automotive fluids: Where permitted by law, pour the remaining product down the drain with plenty of water. Place the empty container in the trash or recycling receptacle. Do not put large quantities of antifreeze into septic a tank at one time.

Brake fluids and car waxes and polishes: Tightly close containers, wrap them well, and place them in the trash.

Makeup: Close the container tightly and place them in the trash.

Nail polish and nail polish removers: Mix with cat litter, sawdust, or sand until solid, then let dry. Close the container tightly and double-wrap in plastic. Place it in the trash. A small amount of remover can be put down the drain with water.

Rubbing alcohol and astringents: Pour down the drain with plenty of water. Rinse the empty container and place it in the trash or recycling receptacle.

Medicines: Pour liquids down the drain or into the toilet and throw solids in the trash, tied up securely. Trash containing pills and other solid medicines, however, should immediately be removed from your home and disposed of in such a way that neither children nor animals can find and ingest them.

Bleach bottles: Rinse when empty and wrap in newspaper.

Leftover bleach: Pour down the drain small quantities at a time, with plenty of water. *Never pour bleach down with any other substances.*

Aerosol cans: Be sure to empty cans completely before placing them in the trash or recycling receptacle. (Turn the can upside down and press the nozzle until all propellant is removed.) *Never put aerosol cans, even if empty, in a trash compactor or incinerator. Do not burn aerosol cans.* Recycle aerosol cans wherever possible.

Get Advice. When you have questions about disposing of hazardous household waste or doubts about whether any substance constitutes a form of hazardous waste, advice is available from your local municipal disposal system or sanitation department, public health agency, the regional office of the EPA in your area or a local environmental agency, or your local cooperative extension service. Private environmentalist groups in your community can often make helpful suggestions or direct you to the relevant authorities.

General Safety Practices for Hazardous Household Wastes. In general, maintain the following practices when dealing with hazardous wastes:

- Recognize a hazardous product for what it is. If the label contains any of the signal words—POISON, DANGER, WARNING, or CAUTION—you are dealing with something that must be used and disposed of with care.
- Keep emergency and poison control telephone numbers handy.
- Understand the hazards of the chemical products you use, and read the labels for instructions on how to treat them.
- Wear protective gloves, goggles, masks, or other protective gear and clothing when using chemicals.
- Use chemicals only in well-ventilated areas.
- Do not mix chemicals.

65

Additional Safety Measures for Children

Teaching children to be safe . . . Tap-water temperature . . . Strangulation and asphyxiation . . . Small objects . . . Plastic bags . . . Cords . . . Balloons . . . Crib bars, rails . . . Mattresses, bedding . . . Miscellaneous risks . . . Tools, knives, and dangerous machines and appliances . . . Keeping your eyes open

In addition to the many child-related safety measures that have already been presented in the "Safe Shelter" section of this book, there are others that fall under no special category relating to housekeeping but pertain solely to the unpredictable nature and unique vulnerabilities of small children. We must remember that their bodies are frail, their store of information small, their judgment weak and their impulses strong, and their foresight all but nonexistent. Adults are there to exercise judgment and control for the young, and in the process, eventually, to teach the children to take care of themselves.

Some children are more impulsive and risk-taking by nature. You can never turn one of these into the cautious, thoughtful type. But since children learn good safety habits by imitation as much as by explicit teaching, even daredevils will usually grow to adopt more moderate behavior if they have a reasonably cautious and caring adult to try to be like. Thankfully, one good way to help your child be one of those children who simply are not particularly "accident-prone" is just to be protective when they are very small. As babies grow into children, they gradually adopt toward themselves whatever attitude of care and concern has been shown toward them. The parents then gradually decrease their protective behavior as the child gradually assumes it and learns how to protect himself or herself. Every child inevitably gets bumps and bruises, and every parent gets shocks and frights. But the child who has been shown concern and whose parents have abhorred his hurts in all likelihood will not be one of those who, by constantly putting himself in danger, keeps his parents in a constant state of terror.

Young children respond better to safety teaching that is firm and protective rather than punitive. You are more likely to get cooperation, for example, if you express concern for the child and say, seriously and firmly, "You must *never* touch electric plugs and cords. They can hurt kids badly." A punitive approach—"You bad boy! Leave that plug alone!"—may be ignored or rebelled against, since it doesn't enlist his support or his understanding. But do not get too wordy. Something brief and clear is what reaches little ones—gently enforced as necessary. Crawling infants must simply be bodily removed from dangers and distracted. You can look serious and concerned and say, "Hot!" or "Ouch!" or similar words.

Of course, teaching safety to young children does not take the place of *vigilant supervision.*

Tap-Water Temperature

Child safety experts urge us to set hot-water heaters in the home at temperatures between 120° and 130°F. The reason is that dangerous scald burns in the young (and the very old) can result from even brief exposure to hot tap water. Such burns can happen nearly instantaneously. Many houses have tap water as high as 140° to 160°F or even higher—140°F being fairly standard. But at 140° to 150°F, adult skin will receive a second-degree burn in *only two seconds.* The skin of infants and young children burns even faster. Such burns are particularly likely to happen to those who cannot immediately remove themselves from the hot water—infants and small children, the handicapped, the elderly, the sick.

Many states have enacted laws requiring newly installed hot-water heaters to be preset at 120°F (49°C) to 130°F (54°C). You can set yours lower; just read the manufacturer's instructions. To check your water temperature if your heater has no degree setting, run the water to its hottest at a tap and hold the stem of a kitchen quick-read or a candy thermometer in the stream.

Such lower temperatures may cause inconvenience. You cannot wash the clothes at hot enough temperatures for certain purposes; unless you have a newer dishwasher that heats its own water, the dishes will not be sanitized as well. There may not be enough hot water for a quick succession of baths and showers. The peace of mind, however, is definitely worth these costs.

You can buy antiscald devices to install in showers and tubs that will automatically block the stream of water if the temperature rises to an unsafe level. This can happen unexpectedly if someone suddenly uses a lot of cold water—for instance, by flushing the toilet. But even if you have your hot-water heater set at a safe temperature or you have installed antiscald devices, you must still be careful. You still need to test the bath temperature and never leave a child (or other vulnerable person) alone in the tub for even one second. There can be scaldings even after the water temperature is safely lowered, since a child will be injured even at 120° or 130°F if the exposure is long enough. But these temperatures at least give you a good opportunity to get the child out of danger.

Strangulation and Asphyxiation

Small Objects. Infants and small children learn about the world by eating and tasting it. When they find small objects on the floor or in other accessible places, their first impulse is to put them in their mouths. When swallowed, such small objects can become lodged in the throat and cause suffocation. Public education and new safety regulations governing toys have reduced the frequency of such tragedies, but they are still all too common.

Leave no small objects lying about the house if there are small children or infants present. Coins, marbles, pins, and buttons are particularly hazardous. Small hard candies, fruit pits and seeds, and grapes can be dangerous to these little ones. Children have also been known to pull knobs off stereos or radios and pop them into their mouths. Children used to chew the eyes off their stuffed toys and mouth small bits of toys of all sorts. Now, on all toys that contain small parts, manufacturers are required to place warning labels to the effect that they are not for children under three. But it is still the parents' job to read and enforce the warnings, by keeping such toys away from their younger ones—not easy to do when you have a six-year-old and a one- or two-year-old.

Plastic Bags. When plastic bags first started to be used in the home, they killed many children before people learned that they had to be careful. Unfortunately, it still sometimes happens. Children put their heads inside, or crawl in, and use up all the oxygen. They die when they cannot extricate themselves, either because they are too weak or uncoordinated or because they panic or lose consciousness. When the dry cleaning comes home wrapped in a thin plastic bag, remove it and either cut it up or tie it into strong knots and dispose of it. Other plastic bags should either be locked out of children's reach or be similarly cut, knotted, and disposed of.

Cords and the Like. Cords, ropes, strings, ribbons, curtains, and similar items can all strangle young children. One study estimates that between 1981 and 1995, 359 children were strangled by window cords. Telephone cords and venetian blind or miniblind cords *must* be placed high, far out of infants' and children's reach. (Don't wind up telephone cords or any other electrical cords in use, but you can wind the others.) Do not give children cords, ropes, ribbons, or similar objects to play with. Put their cribs and beds far away from windows and walls where there are cords or curtains. Keep mobiles out of reach, and do not use any that have strings or cords. Do not put a child's pacifier or mittens on a string or cord around its neck. Mittens can be fastened to coat sleeves. Don't put them on those long strings that go through both sleeves. A child has been killed by the drawstring on her coat.

Children might grab electrical cords left lying on tables, counters, or shelves and pull lamps (or other appliances) down upon themselves.

Balloons. Children can be asphyxiated by inhaling balloons or pieces of broken balloons.

Crib Bars; Rails. Use only standard, regulation cribs with bars a maximum of 2³/₈ inches apart. Children can get their heads between wider bars and strangle. All modern cribs are very likely to meet this standard, but older ones and antiques will quite likely not. I had a vivid illustration of the danger when we received the gift of a charming Victorian child's bed, with white-painted wrought-iron bars, prettily shaped and widely spaced. On the first occasion that my son sat in this bed he immediately put his head between the bars, and the bed had to go.

The same spacing of bars—no wider than 2³/₈ inches—should be observed on stair railings, porch or balcony railings, and bed railings.

Mattresses; Bedding. A mattress poses two sets of problems: first, that the child will somehow get stuck under it and suffocate; second, that it will tear, the stuffing will come out, and the child will suffocate on it. The solutions are snug-fitting, high-quality mattresses in cribs. Make sure there are no rips or tears.

Never put children under six in bunk beds. These beds have too many potential hazards, among them the obvious one of the child falling from a high place and the less obvious dangers of a child's head getting trapped between the rails or of arms or legs getting stuck between the rail and the mattress.

Infants should not sleep with pillows. The danger of suffocation is profound, since they are not strong enough to push a pillow off their faces.

Infants must sleep on firm mattresses (on their backs). Do not let them sleep on any mattress, quilt, comforter, or mattress cover that their face might sink into. You want a smooth surface and freely circulating air.

Infants' mattresses should fit snugly in the crib, with room at most for a finger or two to slide between mattress and crib. The baby's head might get stuck between mattress and crib if there were a larger gap.

Keep pets out of infants' and young children's bedrooms.

Miscellaneous Risks

A surprising number of children are injured when bookshelves, dressers, china cabinets, or other tall pieces of heavy furniture fall on them. They climb up them or stand in the drawers, not realizing the danger. You can bolt such pieces of furniture to the wall with anchors or angle braces. Put television sets on low shelves pushed far back against the wall.

See chapter 63, page 733 for guidelines on preventing children from falling out of windows.

If you are disposing of an old refrigerator or freezer or have one anywhere in your home, garage, basement, or elsewhere on your premises, remove the doors and cut off any electric wires. Children have gotten into old refrigerators, shut the doors, and been suffocated. This can happen in a matter of minutes.

Use safety gates to keep infants and toddlers safe from staircase falls (see page 731) and to keep them from wandering into rooms or areas that might be unsafe for them.

Tools, Knives, and Dangerous Machines and Appliances

Anything that has a blade, a point, or moving parts is probably dangerous to children. Lock children out of your workshop and away from your workbench. Lock up any such dangerous tools, objects, or equipment. Keep your tool chest out of reach or padlocked. Screwdrivers, hammers, nails, wrenches, and other ordinary tools can be lethal weapons in the hands of two- and three-years-olds. Power tools are terribly dangerous for children of all ages. Even older children are far from having enough judgment to be permitted access to tools of any sort without constant adult supervision. Children must be kept away from lawn mowers, saws, weeders, and garden tools, which should be locked away carefully. On keeping children safe from guns, see pages 740–41 in chapter 63.

Keeping Your Eyes Open

Against all dangers to children, the best preventive is *conscientious adult supervision*. No matter what precautions you take and what rules you successfully teach, children will manage to think of something you never dreamed of.

FORMALITIES

66

Understanding Your Castle

Consult your own lawyer . . . Fourth-Amendment protections against governmental intrusions on privacy . . . Laws you can't break in the privacy of your home . . . Privacy, sex, and the Constitution . . . Zoning laws and building codes . . . Co-ops and condominiums . . . Intrusions by private persons: trespass, burglary . . . Self-help against intruders, self-defense . . . Defense of property other than dwelling . . . Defending your home . . . Nuisance . . . Nosiness and prying: the tort of intrusion . . . Modern threats to privacy . . . Door-to-door solicitation . . . Unsolicited mail, unwanted sexually oriented mail . . . Removing your name from marketing lists . . . Unwanted telephone calls, telemarketing . . . Federal regulations . . . State regulations . . . Telephone harassment . . . Caller ID . . . Cellular and cordless telephones . . . Radio, television, and cable television . . . Computers and privacy

> The house of everyone is to him as his castle and fortress, as well for his defence against injury and violence, as for his repose.
>
> —*Semayne's Case,* 5 Co. Rep. 91a, 91b, 77 Eng. Rep. 194, 195 (1604)

A home is a set of rights. A large part of the comfortable feeling of home is nothing more than the familiar sense of enjoying these rights. Chief among them is the right to *privacy,* which is a complex condition based on many related rights, among them the right to be free in our homes from the oppression of scrutiny, from interference by others, and from intrusion, whether by persons, animals, objects, sounds, sights, or even odors. These and other rights also ensure the *security* of home. At home we feel, and are, safe because we have the right to exclude people and things that are dangerous, noxious, or simply unwelcome for any arbitrary or personal reason; this right is protected by the power of government and its enforcement agencies and courts. All the comforts of home—even the familiar freedoms to say what we think, to drop pretense, to relax, to dress and posture our bodies as we wish, to adopt whatever manners appeal to us—are based ultimately on the law. For how could these comforts exist if we lacked the power to control who is admitted to the home, or if we lacked the confidence that what we do in the privacy of the home will not be observed or have dangerous consequences?

An understanding of why and how a home is a castle brings psychological and practical benefits. Such knowledge not only helps you enjoy your home, it helps you protect your rights, recognize your obligations, avoid costly liabilities, increase your security, and promote your interests in a variety of other ways.

But you must consult your own lawyer. The law discussed in this and subsequent chapters is partly the law of individual states, partly the law of the federal government. In the United States, the laws of the various states have a strong family resemblance insofar as they deal with rights related to the home, so it is possible to give a general idea of their nature. But none of the material here is designed to take the place of a lawyer's advice when you have any specific legal problem or question. It is impossible to list all the differences among state laws in a book of this kind. Moreover, the law changes over time, and the laws discussed in books may subsequently be repealed, amended, or reinterpreted. In any event, no explanation of general points of law can provide the level of detail needed to address all the complexities of real-life legal issues. Without hearing all the details of a case, no one can tell you whether general legal principles are likely to dictate the specific ways a court or agency may rule on it, whether it falls under some arcane exception that only your state or city recognizes or that only a lawyer would know about, or whether statutes and legal precedents fail to provide any clear answer. You should get legal advice only from your lawyer; this book provides some useful general information about some laws relevant to home life, but offers no legal advice.

Legal Protections Against Governmental Intrusions on Your Privacy

Constitutional Protections. The government is both the ultimate guarantor of the privacy of the home and potentially the most dangerous intruder upon it. The Fourth Amendment to the Constitution of the United States provides the most important legal protection we have against invasions of the privacy of the home. It is based on the centuries-old legal tradition that your home, however poor, is your castle. Eighteenth-century English law prohibited the king's agents from crossing a subject's threshold, even to search for evidence of a crime, without consent or a proper warrant. Unauthorized entry into someone's home, even by royalty, was trespass, a legal wrong with a legal remedy. The same restriction applies to the officers of our government, from the police to the president.

The Fourth Amendment protects the inviolability of the home by providing that "the right of the people to be secure in their persons, houses, papers, and effects, against unreasonable searches and seizures, shall not be violated, and no warrants shall issue but upon probable cause, supported by oath or affirmation, and particularly describing the place to be searched, and the persons or things to be seized." This means that unless, based on good reasons, you are suspected of a crime, the authorities may not enter your home at all; even if there is good cause to believe you have committed a crime, the authorities may enter and search your home for evidence of that crime only with a warrant, issued by a court, that specifies the limits of the search. Except in unusual circumstances, they must knock first even when they have a warrant. The limits on searches prevent the police from entering your home on a fishing expedition to look for anything and everything that could be used against you, as might be done in a totalitarian state. Fourth Amendment restraints on searches and seizures of property in the home protect you not only against physical entry by police or military personnel but also against government wiretaps, microphones, and other electronic eavesdropping devices. The Fourth Amendment protects only what is really private, however. If you are in the habit of engaging in illegal acts at home with the shades up so that neighbors or passersby can observe, you cannot cry foul if the police should make an arrest based on what you yourself have exposed to view.*

Other parts of the Constitution also protect the home. The Third Amendment, alluding to an eighteenth-century practice, provides that soldiers may not be quartered in people's homes during peacetime or, except "in a manner to be prescribed by law," during wartime. It has been held that the First Amendment guarantees us the right to read anything we want to within the privacy of our homes, including obscene material that might be prohibited elsewhere. But the First Amendment gives no one a right to possess child pornography even in the privacy of the home, nor a right to transmit or receive it on a computer in the home. Nor does it give anyone a right to invade your home with spoken messages you do not want to listen to, or to picket or demonstrate at your home in a manner that disturbs your right to peace, quiet, and privacy.

Laws You Can't Break in the Privacy of Your Home. Although what we do inside our homes is largely our own business, laws restrict our freedom even there. Some of these restrictions are familiar, some less so. As everyone knows, some acts—such as murder, assault, and robbery—are as illegal inside the home as they are everywhere else. Gambling that is illegal outside the home, such as making book or running a numbers game, is also illegal inside the home, but mere "social gambling," a private game played among friends for small amounts of money, is widely held by the courts to be lawful. At home adults may drink as much alcohol as they want, but illegal drugs are still illegal if taken in your own kitchen. (The Supreme Court of Alaska ruled

*Many recent court decisions interpreting the Fourth Amendment were made in drug-related cases, in which the issue was whether the police acted rightly or wrongly in obtaining evidence of illegal drugs or drug dealing in private homes, for example, whether it violates the Fourth Amendment to engage without a warrant in aerial surveillance of a yard (often held that it does not); to do thermal imaging of the heat emanating from a home to detect marijuana growing inside (often held that it does not); to go through garbage someone puts out on the sidewalk to be collected (probably permissible unless the trash was behind a closed fence), to monitor a beeper in a private home (probably illegal without a warrant), and so forth. Some scholars worry that the courts and law-enforcement officials together, in their zeal to suppress drug traffic, will reduce the constitutional protections of privacy in the home.

in 1975 that small amounts of marijuana could legally be held for private use in a private home, but in 1990 a voter initiative required the state legislature to overturn this decision.) Some states' gun-control laws require you to license firearms you keep in your home, although not all do. In some cases, people who have shot burglars who broke into their homes at night have subsequently been charged with possessing an unlicensed gun.

Statutes that prohibit the carrying of concealed weapons often make exceptions for times when you are on your own premises; however, in many jurisdictions you may not carry concealed weapons when you are in common areas in your apartment building, such as hallways, basements, parking lots, and lobbies. Some concealed-weapons laws apply when you are in your own yard and some do not. People who want to pack a six-shooter when mowing the lawn should find out what the local law is. Laws that prohibit taking a weapon to a public gathering might apply to parties you give in your own home. (Even if you are permitted to conceal a weapon, you must still conform to the licensing laws, and even if a gun is licensed, it may still be illegal to conceal it. Licensing and concealment statutes are separate legal requirements.)

Privacy, Sex, and the Constitution. Sexual conduct at home receives rather lackluster constitutional protection. Sodomy laws, although extremely rarely used to prosecute conduct in the home, still exist in many states. They generally forbid specific types of sexual acts that are considered "unnatural," from those with beasts to those involving nonreproductive body parts, even if they harm no one and are engaged in by consenting adults in the privacy of the home. Some of these laws apply only to homosexual acts; some apply to both homosexual and heterosexual acts. Some of these laws also have the entirely valid purpose of prohibiting the sexual abuse of children.

Given the existence of such laws, only married people engaged in sexual relations in their homes can feel confident that their actions are beyond the reach of the sodomy laws. The constitutional protections for married sexual relations are generally traced to a 1965 United States Supreme Court decision in the case of *Griswold v. Connecticut*. Under this decision, no state may make a law forbidding you to use contraceptives in your home, as Connecticut and other states once did. Part of the rationale for the Court's decision was that there would be no way to enforce such a law, even if it were otherwise unobjectionable, without a shocking invasion of the privacy of the home and the marital relation. Courts and commentators who have considered the issue have concluded that the same rationale would protect married sexual relations from prosecution under sodomy laws even though such a case has never actually come before the Supreme Court.

More recently, however, in a case called *Bowers v. Hardwick* (1986), the Supreme Court held that the U.S. Constitution permits states to enact laws that make it a crime to engage in homosexual relations between consenting adults within the privacy of the home. Although some state courts (sometimes relying on their own states' constitutions rather than the U.S. Constitution) have held that their state's sodomy laws are invalid as applied to unmarried heterosexuals, or, rarely, even as applied to homosexuals, others have held to the contrary. The majority position is that sodomy laws may validly be applied to all unmarried people, heterosexual and homosexual. (In 1998, the Georgia state law that was upheld by the Supreme Court in *Bowers v. Hardwick* was overturned by Georgia's state supreme court based on Georgia's state constitution. Kentucky, Pennsylvania, and Tennessee have also recently overturned sodomy laws. The interpretation of the United States

Constitution in *Bowers v. Hardwick*, however, is still binding.)

The possibility of prosecution for engaging in sodomy in the home is remote, but sometimes sodomy laws are enforced against people engaging in sexual conduct in public or quasi-public places such as cars parked at highway rest stops.

Zoning Laws and Building Codes. The Constitution affords your local government considerable control over the physical nature of the home and its functions. There are no constitutional impediments to the enactment of state or local building and health regulations that control who may build your home or sewage system, how, and with what materials. Zoning laws may forbid painting your house purple, building an addition for your mother-in-law or a paying tenant or boarder, building a house under or over a certain size, building on a lot that is too small, carrying on a business or operating a professional office in your home, or many other actions in and affecting your house or apartment.

Those thousands of people now contemplating opening home offices must be sure to check the local regulations. Most local governments forbid operating a business in an area zoned residential, and some home offices will be considered businesses. Home businesses or offices that do not have frequent visits or customers, clients, or employees, and do not cause excessive noise or traffic, or make other unusual demands on the streets, sewers, or trash-disposal systems of a residential area are frequently permitted so long as they do not post signs, display goods in windows, or take other actions that make the home look or operate less like a home. Unobtrusive home offices—for example, an office with one resident worker whose equipment consists of a computer, telephone, fax, and copier—often will be granted a zoning variance (permission not to follow the otherwise applicable zoning regulations). Artists, writers, piano tuners, and musicians typically use home offices and, if a zoning permit is required, generally have no difficulty obtaining one. Even when offices are permitted, however, there may be limits on their size. Be alert to other issues besides zoning laws, such as insurance, real-estate tax, and income tax consequences, that may affect home offices or businesses. Legal issues also may arise out of the substance of the work you choose to do at home. Child care, for example, is usually heavily regulated and requires a license even in a private home. Operating out of your home does not exempt you from complying with the same regulations that apply in formal places of business.

Zoning laws may even affect your choice of whom you live with. They may regulate how many people may live together or whether or to what extent a household may be composed of unrelated people. A zoning regulation in Belle Terre, New York, that forbade more than two unrelated persons from living together, as a means of preserving the character of the neighborhood against an influx of students and transients, was upheld by the U.S. Supreme Court. The Court reached a different conclusion, however, when asked to consider an East Cleveland, Ohio, zoning ordinance that, because of the way it defined "family," did not permit a grandmother, her son, and two grandsons who were merely first cousins (not brothers) to live together. It struck down the ordinance as an impermissible intrusion upon the family.

Rules of the House: Co-ops and Condominiums. Some of your rights to do as you like in and with your home depend on the nature of your ownership. You have the greatest freedom when you own your own home. Landlords of rental properties are in a position to impose special restrictions on you, but these usually must be spelled out in your lease agreement. Cooperative and condominium owners agree to abide by rules that may be highly restrictive. Condominiums and cooperatives, for example, are permitted in some jurisdictions to forbid you to have long-term guests or roommates, or to operate a bed-and-breakfast in your home. They can restrict residency to those over a certain age, prohibit pets, and restrict your right to make improvements such as putting in a balcony or fence or a window different from the windows in the rest of the building. Housing for the elderly can under certain circumstances exclude resident children even if they are your own grandchildren. These restrictions may appear in your lease, ownership agreement, bylaws, or other rules and regulations the board of directors or owners' association may have adopted. You will also have to abide by any new restrictions imposed by the board of directors after your purchase is complete.

Intrusions by Private Persons: Trespass, Burglary, Nuisance

Trespass. Someone trespasses on your property, whether it is your field, lawn, woods, or house, if he or she intentionally enters it without permission or authorization, or intentionally causes someone or something to do so. Trespass is recognized as a wrong both in civil law (in which private citizens go to court and sue for redress of wrongs, most often in the form of money damages or a court order against the defendant) and in criminal law (in which the government prosecutes wrongdoers and imposes fines, forfeitures, or imprisonment as punishment). Trespassing can be a serious problem. People often fear that trespassers will cause damage, whether carelessly, accidentally, or purposely; your flowers or grass will be trampled, fences will be knocked down. In other instances, trespassers annoy you and invade your privacy. Sometimes people also worry about their liability in case an accident befalls the trespasser on their property. In the worst case, people fear that the trespasser is contemplating some harm against them or their property.

Examples of trespass in civil law are common. It would be a trespass (among other things) if the police came into your apartment without a warrant in a case of mistaken identity, if the landlord let himself in simply to check on your housekeeping, if someone decided to take a nap on the swing on your front porch without your permission, if a passing thirsty stranger sneaked into your kitchen for a quick drink of water, or if your neighbor stood on her own land and threw garbage or tennis balls onto yours. Unauthorized entry constitutes trespass even if it is the result of a mistake—for example, a man comes on your land or into your apartment innocently, believing that it is his own or that of his friend.

If warnings or posted notices prove ineffectual to dissuade trespassers, you can go to court and, depending on where you live, either sue for damages or seek an injunction against repeated or continuing trespass. Generally, you can also call on the police for assistance. Criminal trespass or "defiant trespass" statutes usually make it a misdemeanor to trespass, after notice or a warning by posted sign or verbally, not to enter. But they apply without notice or warning in places that people know or should know are private, such as other people's houses.

The extent to which you have a right to use force against trespassers is discussed below.

Burglary. In the old common law—the body of traditional and judge-made law that the colonists brought with them from England—burglary was the crime of breaking and entering the dwelling of another at night with intent to commit a felony. Today, different states define the crime differently, but it generally involves entering any building, not just someone's home, with the intent to commit some sort of crime, such as rape, theft, battery, or murder. State laws hark back to the common-law crime when they impose higher penalties if the building burglarized is someone's house, or if the burglary involves breaking as well as entering, or if it occurs at nighttime, or if it involves the intent to commit a felony. If your home is burglarized, you should call the police as soon as possible even if you are skeptical about the ability of the police to find the offender. The police cannot detect patterns of burglary, nor can local governments justify maintaining a police force of adequate size, if crimes are not reported.

Self-Help Against Intruders: Defense of Self, Property, and Home. To greater or lesser degrees, many states give you a stronger right to resort to force to protect life or property when you are in your home than when you are not. But to understand any special rights you may have at home, it is useful to remind yourself of the law governing your right to defend yourself wherever you may be.

General Principles of Self Defense On the question of permissible acts of self-defense, various jurisdictions differ in detail, but the basic principles are similar everywhere. The essential idea is that under certain conditions you are allowed to use force, up to and including deadly force, in defense of yourself or your family, and often others as well. The law defines deadly force as force sufficient to cause death or serious bodily injury. Deadly force can be applied with weapons, stones, heavy objects, or your bare hands; it only matters whether what you did could reasonably be expected to cause death or serious injury.

The conditions that limit your right to use force in your defense are based firmly on common sense. First, there must be a threat of *unlawful* force against you. If you have just robbed a bank and killed the guard and the police are bearing down on you waving their pistols and shouting deadly threats, you may not shoot at them in self-defense, because they are threatening you with *lawful* force. Assuming that the force threatened against you is unlawful, the threat must also be *imminent*—about to happen soon, not tomorrow—to justify using force in response. If the malefactor gives up and runs away, you lose your right to use force because the threat is gone.

Assuming, however, the threat is imminent, you may not use *excessive* force in response to it; you may use only the degree of force necessary to defend against the threatened harm. In particular, you are justified in using *deadly* force only in response to a threat of deadly force. If someone threatens to slap your hand, it would be excessive to pull out your six-shooter and send him to his maker. It would also be excessive if you shot someone who threatened to punch you on the nose, although I can dream up circumstances that might exonerate you—for example, a world-champion boxer is going to punch you on the nose with all his might despite your heart condition. If you are the aggressor, the law is quite a bit more complicated. The law, obviously, does not like letting you plead self-defense if you kill someone in a fight that you started. Even so, if you originally used nondeadly force and someone responds with deadly force, or if you had subsequently stopped fighting and tried to walk away, you would probably be entitled to defend yourself with deadly force. Cases like this involve great difficulties of proof when they come to trial, as you have seen in many a movie.

The law of self-defense is also complicated by a duty to *retreat* prior to using force if you can do so safely. Society does not want to encourage brawls or private executions, so if you can get away without endangering yourself, society's opportunity to render reasoned judgment against a malefactor is preserved. Nonetheless, under a legal principle called the "castle doctrine," in a majority of states you do not need to retreat when you are in your home, even if you can safely do so. This doctrine is subject to an exception in some jurisdictions: if your assailant is your legal coresident, some courts have held, you still must retreat if you can do so in complete safety. In such jurisdictions, a wife whose coresident husband is attacking her with deadly force must not shoot him if she can run out of the house safely. If she instead stays home and shoots him, she might be convicted of murder. In jurisdictions that do not recognize this exception to the castle doctrine, she would probably have a good plea of self-defense.

All these conditions are further restricted by the requirement that your perception of the situation be reasonable—that is, you must have a reasonable belief that you are imminently threatened with deadly force and that you cannot safely retreat. Thus, although you generally have the right to act on "appearances," you need to have a reasonable take on what the appearances are. Your fear that an intruder's stick, barely visible in the dark, may be a gun is a fear that might be held reasonable; but probably not your fear that the sentimental drunk reclining on your porch swing crooning "Sweet Adeline" is going to murder you and your family.

Defense of Property Other Than Dwelling. The law forbids the use of deadly force to defend property, whether to prevent someone from taking it away from you (theft) or to prevent someone from wrongfully entering your property (trespass). (Most jurisdictions recognize a right to use deadly force to protect your home, but this right is usually *limited* in important ways; see the discussion below.) Instead, you usually must first try a simple request that the malefactor stop or go away or, if this does not work, call the police for help. Assuming that words fail and that you cannot get help in time, you can use *nondeadly* force to prevent the wrong. But even the use of nondeadly force must be limited to the degree of force that reasonably seems necessary to prevent the wrong. If nondeadly force will not prevent the wrong, you must simply suffer the wrong and seek whatever remedy is available to you from the police and courts later. This means, at a minimum, that you cannot shoot and kill a "mere trespasser"—someone who does nothing more than wrongfully enter your yard or grounds or fields or woods, whom you do not have good reason to think will cause death or serious injury to you or others.

In most places you may use nondeadly devices such as spiked fences or barbed wire to keep intruders off your property. But you may *never* use spring guns or set other deadly mantraps to protect your home (or anything else). If your spring gun kills a neighbor who opens your door to call to see if you are home, or even an unarmed cat burglar, you are probably both civilly and criminally liable for the death. Common sense is on the side of the law in condemning the use of any devices that pose deadly risks to innocent people.

Defending Your Home. In most jurisdictions, there are laws known as "defense of dwelling," "defense of habitation," or "home protection" laws. These vary significantly from jurisdiction to jurisdiction, and some states give far greater rights to "defend the home" than others. All of us should know what the laws are in our own home state, but especially those who keep guns for the protection of their homes and members of their households. Such laws do not give anybody a right to shoot a "mere" trespasser. Some such laws require you to give warning before using force against an intruder, and, assuming that doing so will not place you in greater danger, this is probably the wisest course. It is also important to remember that whatever your rights to stand your ground and resist an unlawful intruder, doing so is probably dangerous. The safety of any given course of action is something you would have to judge from the circumstances. Usually, the safest choice is to run away, if possible, or, if not, simply to do what the intruder tells you to do.

In most jurisdictions your right to defend your home is strictly circumscribed in a number of ways, as it should be. Under the most common type of defense-of-dwelling law, you have a right to use a reasonable degree of force, up to and including deadly force, to defend your dwelling or habitation—your home, not other places and not other types of property—when there has been an unlawful entry that is *forcible* and takes place in circumstances that make you *reasonably* fear that the intruder is going to commit a *felony* or that the intruder poses *an imminent threat of serious bodily injury or death* to you or other members of your household. Although some courts interpret this formula to mean that you have a right to shoot an unarmed cat burglar—burglary, after all, is a felony—others have said that "felony" in this context means "violent felony." Assuming the use of force is permissible, in most jurisdictions you may use force in defense of your dwelling or habitation without retreating, even if you could retreat in perfect safety. This is unlike your right to self-defense outside the home, which requires you to retreat if you can do so safely. But otherwise the right to defend your home is typically subject to the same kinds of limits that apply to the right of self-defense: the apprehension of danger must be reasonable; the degree of force used must be proportional to the threat; you cannot use force in response to past acts alone but must have a reasonable fear of imminent danger, and so forth. Further restrictions on the right to defend your dwelling may be specified in the wording of the statute. Often, for example, state laws require that the unlawful entry be made "forcibly," "violently," "riotously," or "tumultuously" before there is a right to defend your dwelling with deadly force.

Some states recognize a considerably broader justification for the use of force in defense of your dwelling. For example, a few (such as Indiana, Louisiana, and Kansas) have laws that make it justifiable to use deadly force to prevent an unlawful entry into or attack on the home, or to compel someone who has unlawfully entered to leave. In these jurisdictions, your action may be regarded as justifiable homicide even in the absence of a fear that the intruder would cause bodily harm or commit a felony in or against the home, or even against an unarmed intruder who refuses to leave. Other states have laws that fall somewhere between this broad justification of the use of deadly force to defend the home and the more circumscribed rights available under the most common type of law.

A number of states that had more restrictive laws amended them during the great crime waves of the 1980s to create statutes more favorable to the occupant of the dwelling who shoots at an intruder. For example, in 1985, Colorado passed a "home protection law," sometimes called the "make my day" statute. The old Colorado law permitted the use of deadly force by the occupant of a dwelling against an intruder who used, or reasonably appeared to be going to use, physical force against the occupant while committing or attempting to commit a burglary. The new law provides, in recognition of citizens' "rights to expect absolute safety within their homes," that occupants of dwellings may use deadly force against anyone who makes an unlawful entry into the dwelling when the occupant reasonably believes that the intruder has committed, or will commit, a crime and might use force, "no matter how slight," against the occupant.

Another group of states retained the basic provisions of the older, more restrictive laws. But they added that, in the event anyone in his or her own home uses force against an intruder who has unlawfully and forcibly entered the home, the occupant will be *presumed* to have held a reasonable fear of imminent peril of death or serious bodily injury. This presumption could be rebutted to show that the fear was not at all reasonable (for example, suppose the intruder, intoxicated, was fast asleep on your sofa) or that you were not at all afraid (the intruder was your former roommate, a peaceable but odious person who had come to retrieve belongings he felt you were wrongfully withholding). Still, this presumption would make conviction of the occupants more difficult, with the probable result that prosecutors would be less likely to indict them in the first place.

The defense of dwelling laws usually shield the occupants of homes only from criminal prosecution or conviction. Someone who is not criminally charged or is acquitted of criminal charges, having claimed justifiable homicide in defense of dwelling, may still be sued in most jurisdictions for damages in a civil suit by the intruder or his or her family or estate.

Nuisance

The intrusions of noise, lights, smells, water, smoke, or dirt can be as unwelcome and as destructive of domestic peace as the intrusion of trespassers. The trespasser interferes with the possession of property; nuisances interfere with the use and enjoyment of property. The legal maxim applied in nuisance cases is that you must use your own property in such a manner as to protect the property of another.

The nuisance most frequently complained of in this age of apartment dwellers and electronic sound equipment is noise. If your neighbor's stereo or television blasts through her supersized speakers day and night, that probably constitutes a nuisance if it prevents you from using your own property for sleeping, working, or entertaining, or enjoying being there. The odor of sewage; frequent noisy parties; a dog that barks loudly all night and every night; floodlights that glare into your bedroom; smoke; dust; a swimming-pool drainage system that floods your cellar several times a year—all might constitute nuisances if they interfered substantially and unreasonably with your use and enjoyment of your property. One case ruled that an artificial pond that was home to malaria-carrying mosquitoes was a nuisance.

Nuisance need not involve physical invasion of one's property by sounds or substances. Any activity that poses an unreasonable risk to the surroundings may constitute a nuisance. Blasting on nearby property may be a nuisance because it poses an unreasonable risk of danger to your property from flying rocks, vibrations, or shifting ground, even though such damage has not yet occurred. The threat of injury may interfere with enjoyment in the present: you probably would not sleep easily if explosives were stored in the house next door or your neighbor had a collection of exotic poisonous spiders or—the more common problem—a vicious dog that every so often escaped its pen. If a swimming pool in a populated area is left unguarded, uncovered, and unfenced, a court could find it legally a nuisance because of the danger it poses to neighborhood children.

A nuisance might be found even if the interference with your use and enjoyment were purely psychological. There have been many successful nuisance suits against funeral homes in residential neighborhoods. The attitude of the courts has been that the funeral homes' constant reminders of death produce a "depression of mind, [and] deprive the home of that comfort and repose to which its owner is entitled" (*Street v. Marshall*, 316 Mo. 698 [1927]).

Nuisance laws can be used against you as well as in your favor. Conflicts arise when something that appears to one person to be a reasonable use of property appears to another to be an unreasonable interference with the latter's use and enjoyment of his or her own property. The law attempts to be fair in nuisance cases by weighing a number of factors. How great would the interference with the rights of each party be if the court were to intervene on behalf of one party or the other? How important is the interest interfered with? How large or small is the annoyance to which the plaintiff is subjected? Is the harm physical, aesthetic, or emotional? Does the defendant's activity have social value? Could the defendant or the plaintiff fix the problem with minimal sacrifice, trouble, or expense?

As a student, I once lived in a little apartment down the street from a factory that manufactured baby food and produced overwhelming and annoying food odors indoors and outdoors several times a week. I would not have stood a chance in a nuisance suit. Not only was the factory there before I was, but its activity was socially valuable and the annoyance to me was not grave. Stewed peaches don't really smell terrible. Suits have been filed in which the defendant has put up a large, lit display each Christmas next door to a plaintiff who is annoyed by it. If the plaintiff simply cannot stand its vulgarity, he or she is probably out of luck. This aesthetic pain is minor and temporary, and the defendant's right to celebrate Christmas at home in his or her own fashion is important. But if the defendant's display is so huge that it shines into the plaintiff's bedroom at night and attracts gawking strangers to the neighborhood who take all the parking places and trample the plaintiff's lawn, the plaintiff would probably have a successful case. In one Christmas display nuisance case, the plaintiff finally got a court to order the defendant to reduce the volume of the sound track that formed part of the gigantic display to a level that the plaintiff could not hear on his own premises.

In evaluating the seriousness of allegations of nuisance, the courts will consider whether complainants' responses are reasonable or whether they are being hypersensitive or cantankerous. Ultrasensitive people generally lose in court. The law, in other words, guarantees each of us the right to use our own property in ways that do not interfere with *reasonable* people's rights to use and enjoy their own property.

If you should successfully sue over a nuisance, it is possible that you would win either monetary damages or an injunction against continuation of the nuisance.

Nosiness and Prying: The Tort of Intrusion

Although many intrusions into the home can be characterized as invasions of privacy, the legal term "invasion of privacy" actually refers to a number of separate but related torts of which only one concerns us here: an "intrusion" into one's solitude or seclusion—in other words, an infringement of your right to be let alone. This offense against privacy, or your right not to have your seclusion broken in upon, can occur only in private places such as your home, or in other places or situations where there is a similar expectation of privacy. As with nuisances, courts will usually say that an intrusion must be unreasonable—that is, offensive to a person of "ordinary sensibilities" before it constitutes a tort. Some jurisdictions construe the tort of intrusion quite narrowly.

A Peeping Tom commits the tort of intrusion, as might someone who goes through your pockets or your mail, or repeatedly spies through your windows with binoculars, or photographs you with telescopic lenses in the privacy of your home without your consent. If someone without your knowledge or consent eavesdropped on you in your home, wiretapped your telephone, or installed any other kinds of listening, recording, or photographic devices in your home, you would have a basis for a lawsuit based on intrusion. (Wiretapping and other kinds of electronic eavesdropping may violate criminal statutes too.) Intrusion may also be found in cases of harassing, repeated, and unwanted telephone calls, unsolicited mail, or house calls. (These types of intrusion are discussed below.) Some authorities speculate that the courts might offer legal recourse for invasion of privacy or intrusion in cases of improper use of confidential information, for example, medical records kept on electronic databases, but so far as I am aware no court has yet done this.

Modern Threats to Privacy

Modern life poses unique threats to the privacy of the home. Burglars and marauders may menace us less than they did a lonely householder in the English countryside of 1600. But today many more of us live packed together in denser urban style, in smaller houses, with increasingly porous barriers against the rest of the world. The vastly extended commercialism of our society creates a constant pressure on the integrity of the home. The king may still be stalled at your castle door, but numerous other unwelcome guests of considerably less dignity have crept in; we live daily with their electronically transmitted voices, images, thoughts, and importunities.

In the continuing struggle for a proper balance between home life and commercial pressures, courts and legislators have done fairly well in formulating law that protects the privacy of the home against the encroachments of new technologies and the media. Their record seems particularly good if you consider how recently they have had to face such innovations as radios, telephones, televisions, computers, the Internet, and newspaper articles that are instantly transmitted by computer throughout the world—at least compared to the centuries-old legal and social values that the lawmakers must protect and accommodate. As to those instances to which the law has not yet made an adequate response, nothing will do more to ensure that it does so than citizens who are aware of what is at stake.

Door-to-Door Solicitation. The door-to-door salesman—as he used to be portrayed in comic strips and movies—stuck his foot in doors that were being slammed in his face; if that didn't work, he gained entry by a dozen other devious stratagems, from crude disguises to barefaced lies. His vacuum cleaner spewed dirt all over the living room rug. He had a dozen foolish contraptions to sell, for each of which he promised, with his fingers crossed behind his back, full satisfaction or your money back.

You may have noticed that he has stopped visiting Dagwood lately and that nowadays you, too, are getting few or no visits from door-to-door salespeople. But you may still receive plenty of visits by people soliciting for political and charitable causes. One reason for the decline in door-to-door sales is the prevalence of local laws prohibiting or regulating them. Another is the fear that makes many people today hesitant about opening their doors to strangers. Even where door-to-door sales are permitted, local laws may require registration or licensing of door-to-door salespeople, fees, background checks, or even fingerprints, and may limit solicitation to certain hours.

Back in the 1950s, the large numbers of door-to-door salespeople led to complaints that they interfered with people's peace, quiet, and privacy at home. Fraud and sharp practice, too, became a problem. The courts upheld properly worded prohibitions of commercial solicitation door-to-door, but they struck down prohibitions of various kinds of noncommercial solicitation. The rights of the Girl Scouts, political parties, the Jehovah's Witnesses and other churches, the United Way, and all other legitimate charitable, religious, and political causes to solicit door-to-door are protected by the First Amendment. The public has been complacent about this turn of events, for it has easy access to well-priced goods in stores, and it has complaints about solicitors.

The federal government, too, has gotten into the act. To help protect consumers against the high pressure and deceptive sales tactics that many home solicitors use, the Federal Trade Commission enacted a "cooling-off" rule. It requires, among other things, that when you make any purchase at home from a door-to-door salesperson of goods worth twenty-five dollars or more, you must be given a written contract or receipt showing the name and address of the seller and the date of the transaction. You must also be given a notice of cancellation that states in boldface type that you have a right to cancel during the three days following the date of the transaction. To register a complaint, get in touch with the FTC; the FTC maintains a Web site, and its telephone number is listed in the United States government listings in the blue pages of your telephone directory. Making a complaint to the FTC is no guarantee of a solution, but it often helps; moreover, it is good citizenship, as the FTC cannot act to correct problems that no one tells it about. Many states have enacted cooling-off laws too, and some of them have good remedies and strong enforcement provisions. For information on how to proceed under state law in your locale, call the office of the state attorney general. The local Better Business Bureau or department of consumer affairs can sometimes help as well.

If you do not wish to be visited by door-to-door solicitors, even those who are lawful in your area, you can simply forbid it. Your right to privacy trumps anyone's right to visit you if you do not want such visits. If you post a "No Solicitation" or "Keep Out" sign, all would-be visitors are obliged to obey and, if they do not, they are trespassers. In some places you can register on a "no solicitations" list kept by the police or the local government. To find out what the options are in your area, call any of the local agencies listed above or try your local police station.

Unsolicited Mail

SOA Forms. Under federal law, if you receive unsolicited obscene or sexually oriented mail from advertisers, you may ask the United States Post Office to tell the senders to stop sending it, to take your name off their mailing lists, and not to trade in lists from which your name has not been deleted. Go to your local post office and request an "SOA" or sexually oriented advertising kit, fill out and return Form PS2201 (if you want to stop SOA from all senders) or PS2150 (if you want to stop mail from a particular sender), and the post office will do the rest. The law that gives you these powers was enacted in 1970 after the post office fielded hundreds of thousands of complaints from people who received unwanted obscene advertising materials from mail-order businesses. A 1970 Supreme Court decision (*Rowan v. Post Office*, 397 U.S. 728 [1970]) upheld the constitutionality of this law against a challenge that alleged that the law violated the First Amendment's guarantee of freedom of speech; the Court spoke particularly of the need to protect children.

If your name has found its way onto nonsexual junk-mail lists and you are inundated every morning, you cannot stop the inundation through the post office, but you can take other effective steps.

Removing Your Name from Marketing Lists. To remove your name from mailing lists, try writing to the Direct Mail Association (DMA). It is a nonprofit marketing trade association that sponsors a free Mail Preference Service, which will get your name off the mailing lists of subscription companies. Write to: Mail Preference Service, Direct Mail Association, P.O. Box 9008, Farmingdale, NY 11735. Or call (212) 768-7277. The DMA will also remove your name from many national telephone solicitation lists. Write to: DMA Telephone Preference Service, P.O. Box 9014, Farmingdale, NY 11735-9014. It will take a few months for the services to start working, but once they take effect they will last for five years—or until you do something to get yourself back on someone's list. DMA will also send you pamphlets containing excellent advice about removing your name from marketing lists, buying by telephone and catalogue, and resolving telephone or mail purchase problems.

Keeping your name off these lists to begin with is not so easy. The basic rule is that whenever you supply your name and address to any organizations—profit or nonprofit—you must instruct them that they are not to give it to anyone else for any reason.

Here are some routes by which your name could wander onto marketing mail lists, and some ways of preventing this from happening:

Warranty Cards. Warranty cards are used to generate marketing information, including lists of names and consumer profiles. The warranty is almost always valid whether or not you send in the card so long as you retain proof of purchase and date of purchase, so do not send in the warranty card (and save your proof of purchase). However, the warranty card is also used to register your purchase with the manufacturer, and you may wish to register so that you will be notified of any future recall of the product. If this possibility seems to matter in a given case and you wish to register, you can try including instructions that your name and address are not to be circulated or sold to anyone else; some manufacturers' cards include a check box you can use to specify this.

Credit Card Companies. Credit card companies often forward your address to other companies who want to send you promotional materials. Write and tell them not to do so.

Telephone Purchases. Instruct the seller not to pass on your name and address.

Magazine Subscriptions. Include a note with your subscription request telling the magazine that it is not to put your name on any mailing lists or pass your name on to any other business. If you are not a new subscriber, write to or call the subscription department now.

Catalogue Orders. Never order anything from a catalogue—and never order a catalogue—without also giving instructions that your name is not to be put on any mailing lists or passed on to any other business.

Credit Bureaus. These organizations cooperate with banks to determine whether you should be offered credit through a credit card. (That is how banks can offer you preapproved credit cards.) You can write to any of the major credit bureaus to ask them not to use your name for prescreening or other marketing purposes. Their names and addresses are available from the DMA.

On-line Shopping. Businesses to which you give your name and address that sell on the Internet may also sell customer lists with your name on them. Some offer a check box you can use to request them not to do so. Check the box; if there is no box, buy elsewhere.

Unwanted Telephone Calls. A hundred years ago, the well-to-do home was protected against unwanted callers by servants and publicly announced visiting hours, during which one undertook to be at home for visitors. It was understood that visitors would not come at other times without an invitation. To make an uninvited and unannounced visit to someone's home remains a fundamental breach of good manners. No similar rule has ever evolved to control the social telephone call.

We all respect some informal rules about time of calling. We try to avoid making calls when we think the person we are calling may be sleeping or eating. But because meals and sleep do not always happen on schedule, all of us sometimes interrupt even when we do not wish to. It is true that one can often simply ignore the ringing telephone, but most of us feel obliged to answer if there is any logical chance that it could be our mate, our elderly parent, the school, our child, or any of a dozen other important possibilities. Telephone answering machines are an unsatisfactory answer to the problem because some people feel uncomfortable screening calls, some people will not leave messages, some messages are inappropriate to leave on an answering machine, such machines still occasionally malfunction, and in any event, the caller can never know whether or when his or her message has been received or listened to or understood.

Telephone calls from beloved parents and friends are often problematic, but there are hardly words to describe what most of us feel about an unsolicited telephone sales pitch for a new credit card, especially when the strange caller insists on going through a spiel even though you say you are not interested and eventually you are forced to hang up on a live voice, with a queasy feeling. At present you are likely to receive a wide variety of unsolicited nonpersonal telephone calls. Some of these we may not mind so long as they are well timed, particularly when they come from organizations or businesses or people with whom we have a legitimate connection: an alumni organization, a familiar department store sales clerk calling to announce a sale, or the garden club or school inviting us to a function. Most people I know object fiercely, however, to unsolicited calls that try to sell them something, such as credit cards or time-share condominiums, or that ask for their opinions for a commercial survey. Calls that solicit or perform surveys for charitable, political, or religious causes seem to be less offensive to some people, but even these are generally annoying. In my home, such calls became so numerous that finally we were forced to begin telling such callers that we make no donations to charities that solicit over the telephone but that we will carefully read and consider a mailed request. The only such call that I am always glad to receive is the one on election day that reminds me to go to the polls and vote.

The telephone is crucial for home safety, quite apart from its urgent social and economic importance. We should not need to unlist our telephone numbers to enjoy peace and privacy and to be protected from those who want us to buy products that are advertised as available in far too many other places as it is. Besides, even unlisting your number does not guarantee immunity. Telemarketers get hold of it one way or another, and once it is on someone's computer database, it tends to circulate. Moreover, fraud and high-pressure tactics in telemarketing have become scandalous, resulting in a number of high-profile prosecutions. Yet, for reasons that are hard to comprehend, the laws protecting us from harassment and invasion of privacy through our own telephones are not so effective as they should be, and there is reason to fear that improvement will be slow in coming.

In the meantime, some telephone companies are working on a technological solution to the problem of telemarketing calls, at least for those who have Caller ID. (See page 775.) For example, some companies have created a service that screens calls that block Caller ID information and calls that show up on Caller ID as "unknown." (In order to have their calls get through, callers must reveal their number.) Please note that "Anonymous Call Rejection," a service that comes free with Caller ID in some areas, screens only calls that have their Caller ID information blocked, and thus will not help (at least not at present) with telemarketers, who do not block their numbers but use equipment that causes them to show up as "unknown" on Caller ID.

Federal Regulations. State and federal laws regulate telemarketing. The federal Telephone Consumer Protection Act of 1991 addressed some of the worst abuses in the field. The act lets anyone who receives more than one call in a twelve-month period in violation of Federal Communications Commission rules promulgated pursuant to the act to sue the caller in state court (where permissible under state laws), and will result in an injunction ordering the calling to stop or a fine of up to five hundred dollars per violation or both. One valuable provision in this act forbids any prerecorded calls to a residence without the party's consent, saving us from the abominations of automatic dialing machine calls. It also prohibits automatic dialing machine calls to emergency service providers, cellular and paging numbers, and hospital rooms, as well as unsolicited advertising to fax numbers. These restrictions leave many permitted uses of automatic dialing machines, but none that poses a threat to the peace and privacy of the home.

The FCC's rules on telemarketing are otherwise rather soft. When you are solicited, if you tell the telemarketer that you want to get off its list, it is required to put you on a "do-not-call" list, which is good for ten years, and to stop calling you. But this doesn't stop a dozen other telemarketers from calling you; each one has to be informed individually. You will not even be put on the do-not-call lists of a telemarketer's affiliates unless you specifically request this. Moreover, the rule regarding the "do-not-call" list does not apply to nonprofit organizations or calls that are not made for a "commercial" purpose.

The FCC regulations also prohibit telemarketing before 8:00 A.M. and after 9:00 P.M., but this does not help people who work at night and sleep during the day, napping babies, sick people, and people who are just busy or troubled or whose dinner has been interrupted too many times. The regulations do usefully oblige the person making the call to provide his or her name, the name of the person or organization on whose behalf the call is made, and a telephone number or address at which that person or organization can be reached.

A second federal act, the Telemarketing and Consumer Fraud and Abuse Prevention Act of 1994 (sometimes called the "Telemarketing Act"), aims primarily at preventing fraud, but its provisions bear upon privacy issues as well. The FTC has prescribed rules enforcing this act that, among other things, forbid telemarketers to call someone repeatedly or continuously with the intent to annoy, abuse, or harass him or her; to call someone who has previously stated that he or she does not wish to receive calls from the telemarketer; to call before 8:00 A.M. or after 9:00 P.M.; or to fail promptly to disclose the identity of the seller, that the purpose of the call is to sell something, and the nature of what is being sold. (By the way, unless you tell the telemarketers never to call again, they can call you as often as they like so long as they do not intend to annoy, abuse, or harass you.) The FTC rules apply only to calls designed to get you to buy goods or services; they do not apply to political, charitable, religious, environmental, or similar solicitations. And they do not apply when a sale that is initiated by a telephone call is not completed, or payment is not required, until after a face-to-face presentation by the seller. The FTC is responsible for enforcing these regulations. If you are aware of violations, you may do yourself and others a good turn if you let the FTC know about them. (Check the FTC Web site or call the Federal Trade Commission at the number in the United States Government listings in the blue pages of your telephone directory.)

State Regulations. Both the Consumer Telephone Protection Act and the Telemarketing Act specifically provide that they do not preempt state laws. This means that states can enact more stringent laws than the federal laws that regulate telemarketers, and states can add local remedies to any existing federal ones, which gives you two possible routes for your complaints. Although federal regulation would seem most effective, because telemarketing is a big interstate business that relies on national databases, several states have gone further and faster than the federal government in protecting the home against telephone intrusions. Current state regulations regarding unsolicited calls vary widely. Sometimes the state regulations are described in the front pages of the telephone directory. (Call the office of your state attorney general for guidance on how to proceed with a complaint under state law.) Hours of permitted telephone solicitation are narrower in some state laws than in federal law. Where the FTC requires "prompt" disclosure of who is calling and what for, some states actually specify the number of seconds the telemarketer has in which to comply—periods from ten to sixty seconds have been specified. Some state laws ban automated dialing and prerecorded messages entirely. State "cooling-off" rules often cover telephone solicitation too, because of the frequency of consumer complaints about high-pressure tactics. (The FTC "cooling-off" rule does not cover telephone solicitations, only door-to-door solicitations.)

Some states, such as Florida, Alaska, Oregon, and Georgia, maintain "do-not-call" lists; if you put your name on the list, telemarketers are obliged not to call you. Similar proposals are being debated elsewhere.

Telephone Harassment. Worse than any telephone solicitations are telephone calls made for the purpose of harassment. These include obscene and threatening calls, some calls from bill collection agencies, hate calls, and the like. Most states have some sort of statute prohibiting harassment by telephone. Telephone directories sometimes describe these laws in the front pages. You can call the office of the state attorney general or check with your local police department if you need more information or guidance on how to deal with a problem. If you are being harassed by a debt-collection agency, call the FTC or the office of your local attorney general.

Caller ID. Caller ID is a telephone service feature that lets you see the telephone number of the person calling before you answer the telephone. Many people have vehemently objected to this on the grounds that it invades the privacy of callers, who can no longer avoid disclosing their telephone numbers to anyone they call. Caller ID means that if you call a business to inquire about the cost of its service it can get your telephone number, even if you decline the service, and call you repeatedly in the hope of persuading you to sign up—or even sell your number to telemarketers. Any business you call for the purpose of making inquiries or complaints can find out how to reach you in the privacy of your home. No one would be able to trust that a call to social-service agencies or anyone else could be made anonymously, and there are legitimate reasons to wish to make anonymous calls. Unlisting your telephone would become much less effective as a means of keeping your number secret.

Most of these objections are obviated by blocking services that let you block your name and number when you call so that it does not show up on the Caller ID of the recipient—either all the time or on a per-call basis. Such services are free, but you must request them. Where offered, they are available whether or not you have Caller ID.

Caller ID seems not to invade any constitutional right of privacy, at least so long as it is offered with adequate blocking services. Because Caller ID is now widespread, if you object to having your name and number disclosed, whether always or sometimes, call immediately to subscribe to the free blocking service.

Cellular and Cordless Telephones. Eavesdropping has always been prohibited by the law. When, centuries ago, it was done by the naked ear at eaves, windows, and doors, eavesdropping was considered a nuisance and it was actionable. In the nineteenth and twentieth centuries, telegraphs and telephones offered amazing new opportunities for eavesdropping. When I was a child living in a backward rural area, telephone party lines were still the rule long after private lines and dial telephones were universal elsewhere. In areas like mine, neighbors sometimes knew each other better than they had any right to. The operator where I lived was my great-aunt Maude, a very knowledgeable lady indeed. If a party line was tied up too long, aunt Maude would listen in for a minute to see why and, if necessary, give a gentle hint or even break in to deliver messages if they were important enough.

Aunt Maude, despite her good intentions, was violating the law. Eavesdropping on conventional telephone conversations has long been prohibited except by law-enforcement officials pursuant to a warrant. (In some places it is also illegal to record a telephone conversation unless you inform the other party or parties, but in the majority of states recording telephone conversations is legal so long as one of the parties to the conversation knows about it.) A California statute prohibited intercepting telegraphs as early as 1862, and wiretapping telephones was first prohibited by statute in Illinois in 1895. The federal Electronic Communications Privacy Act of 1986 protects conversations on cellular telephones from eavesdropping in the same manner conversations on conventional telephones are protected. Conversations on cordless telephones had only partial protection, however, until 1994, when the Communications Assistance for Law Enforcement Act (CALEA) was enacted.

Before CALEA, cordless-telephone conversations were considered "oral communications" insofar as they were broadcast by radio from the handset to the base unit and, as such, were protected from eavesdropping only when they were engaged in with a reasonable expectation of privacy. But because radio broadcasts of cordless telephones could be picked up by ordinary FM radio receivers, baby monitors, and other cordless telephones, as well as scanners legal for any citizen to own, the courts tended to find that there was no expectation of privacy in a cordless-telephone conversation. (In our son's infancy we were often the unwilling auditors, over his baby monitor, of the intimate marital quarrels that our downstairs neighbors conducted on their cordless phone.)

CALEA now makes it illegal to eavesdrop intentionally on cordless-telephone conversations and bans scanners capable of monitoring frequencies that they use. (Conventional wiretapping of cordless-telephone communications transmitted by wire from the base unit has always been illegal except with a warrant.) Moreover, eavesdropping on cordless telephones is harder practically speaking as well as legally. Most cordless telephones are no longer preset to one frequency. Generally they can monitor all available frequencies and operate on one that is unused, making it much less likely that other cordless telephones will pick up the conversation. That cordless-telephone conversations are still relatively less private, however, is evidenced by the continuing requirement of the Federal Communications Commission that cordless telephones be stamped with this warning on the bottom of the base unit: "This cordless telephone operates under part 15 of the FCC Rules. Privacy of communications may not be ensured when using this telephone."

State law is sometimes more protective of cordless-telephone conversations than federal law, so if you are concerned, investigate what state laws apply where you live.

Radio, Television, Cable Television. You have a legal right to exclude unwanted sexually oriented mail, door-to-door solicitation, and noise from sound trucks or loudspeakers on the street whose volume penetrates your home. In the privacy of our homes, we may not be forced to be unwilling listeners to spoken words or viewers of written materials we object to. Some have tried to argue, analogously, that broadcasts of various offensive advertisements and obscenity, pornography, profanity, indecency, and extremely violent programming should be censored on the same grounds—that they, too, intrude on the privacy of the home and that viewers in their homes should not have to view or listen to material that they find offensive, obscene, or immoral. A "householder's right to be left alone" is a powerful constitutional value, but those who oppose restrictions on broadcasts have a compelling argument when they point out that no one makes anyone buy or turn on televisions or radios.

Few of us doubt, however, that some restrictions on broadcast and cable media are required in order to protect children. The law that sets the standard actually forbids the broadcast of "any obscene, indecent, or profane language." But the Federal Communications Commission, which has the responsibility to enforce the statutory standards, bans obscene material from the broadcast media (cable television is not considered a broadcast medium) at all times, but permits "adult" programming during times of the day when children are less likely to be viewing. The rationale for permitting some "indecent" programming, despite the law banning indecent broadcasts, is that what constitutes "indecency" is different for children and adults. A congressional attempt to ban indecent programming twenty-four hours a day was struck down on First Amendment grounds by the District of Columbia Circuit Court of Appeals, and the Supreme Court declined to hear the case. "Indecent" programming is currently permitted from 10:00 P.M. to 6:00 A.M.

The law treats cable TV differently from the broadcast media; the courts have struck down laws that sought to restrict cable companies' freedom to show indecent programming, citing the First Amendment's guarantees of freedom of speech. In 1996, the Supreme Court declared unconstitutional a provision of the Cable Television Consumer Protection and Competition Act of 1992 that required cable operators to put all "indecent" programs on a single channel that would be blocked unless a subscriber specifically requested access to that channel in writing. But other parts of this and other laws make it a bit easier for parents to make sure children are not exposed to indecent or sexually explicit programming.

The 1996 Telecommunications Act requires cable operators, at your request, to scramble or block both audio and video programming of any channels carrying indecent or sexually explicit material on channels to which you do not subscribe. (This is intended to address signal bleed—that is, the partial reception of images from blocked channels.)[1] The 1996 act also requires the FCC to prescribe regulations for circuitry to be built into future televisions that would allow parents to block programming rated as having sexual or violent content; this "V-chip" circuitry allows parents to block all programming rated at a specific level by entering a single command, so it is no longer necessary to block or unblock individual channels. (The rating system, under the act, could either be prescribed by the FCC or the FCC could approve a voluntary system developed by the industry. The FCC has accepted the industry's system of voluntary ratings, which has been adopted almost unanimously by broadcasters.) The FCC has ruled that V-chip circuitry must be built into all new television sets with screens larger than thirteen inches by the start of the year 2000; it will be available to older sets through set-top boxes.

These controls provided in the 1996 Telecommunications Act are in addition to those with which parents have long been familiar. Since 1984, cable operators have been required by the Cable Communications Policy Act to make available on request a "lockbox" that allows parents to block access to individual channels at home. This technology is now built into virtually all televisions and set-top cable boxes, so you can exercise parental control without asking for additional equipment, although the programming procedure may daunt some nontechnical parents. The "addressable converter," which now is universally available, permits the cable operator to block channels that are not on your basic service from appearing on your television at your request. These methods, combined, can go far to protect your home from undesirable programming, and without excessive in-home surveillance and censorhip. They do not protect your child from televisions in other places, however.

Computers and Privacy. Electronic data banks raise serious issues of privacy. Plans to create ever-greater accumulations of data, with links between a person's home and businesses, government agencies, and libraries, promise to raise issues that are even more urgent. Experts agree that these systems pose a dangerous potential for abuse, for they may permit outsiders to gain access to confidential material, such as medical and financial information, about individuals. The legal framework that might adequately protect individuals' privacy against such abuses has yet to be created. There is speculation that the tort of intrusion could serve as the basis for legal action in those jurisdictions that recognize this tort. But even were laws to be drafted that adequately valued privacy, there are serious questions about how effective they might be.

When it comes to computer-transmitted messages, some useful laws have been passed. The Electronic Communications Privacy Act of 1986 protects the privacy of e-mail by making it a felony for someone to intercept your electronic mail without your consent. It applies to e-mail the same principles that make it illegal for someone to tap your telephone. If you connect to the Internet by dialing in from your home computer to an Internet Service Provider (ISP) such as America Online or AT&T WorldNet, your e-mail is extremely secure, both legally and in fact. No one has the time or inclination to intercept e-mail love letters sent over the Internet from one home computer to another, and it is virtually impossible for criminals or mischief-makers to intercept your e-mail or anything else you transmit over the Internet.

But you should be aware of the legal limits on your privacy. The law allows your ISP access to your mail for the purpose of routine maintenance of its computer systems, just as the telephone company is allowed to monitor calls for similar purposes, and your ISP can be obliged to hand over your e-mail to law-enforcement agencies. Any e-mail message you send from your home computer to a friend's computer at work may legally be read by your friend's employer. Although many companies voluntarily refrain from reading employees' e-mail, some keep careful watch.

If you find yourself wanting more privacy than this, you can use encryption software that renders your messages unreadable even by law-enforcement agencies, but all such software is cumbersome to use, and both you and your correspondents must be prepared to put up with its inconveniences.

Many Internet Web sites require that you enter your name, address, and other personal information before you can use their services; some Web sites include a voluntary "privacy policy" statement that tells you whether the information you supply will be made available to other companies, but unless you know and trust the company behind the Web site, you should hesitate before entering information that you want to keep private. Be especially wary of entering your e-mail address, because you may find yourself inundated with unwanted e-mail sales pitches (commonly known as "spam"). If you want to use a site that absolutely requires you to register an e-mail address, you don't have to reveal the address you use for corresponding with friends and coworkers: instead, open an e-mail account on one of the many Web-based services that offer free e-mail that you can access through a browser (two examples are mailcity.com and hotmail.com), and use that address only for registering with Web sites.

The Children's Online Privacy Protection Act of 1998 is the first and, so far, the only law that attempts to protect children who use the Internet. It establishes strict controls on the use of personal information that children supply to Web sites "directed to children." These sites must display the use they intend to make of any information supplied by the children, and must obtain "verifiable parental consent for the collection, use, or disclosure of personal information from children." If you are the parent of a child who has entered information on a Web site covered by the act, the operator of the site must, upon your request, disclose to you the information provided by your child and remove that information from its records.

If you dial into the Internet from your home, your privacy is relatively but not absolutely safe. Any Web site can detect the numerical code that identifies the central computer that you happened to connect to—not your own computer—when you dialed into the office of your Internet Service Provider, but this code does not let the Web site identify you. If you use a dial-in ISP, your home computer does not have a unique numerical code because you are not connected *directly* to the Internet; you are connected only through the ISP's computers. Theoretically, your ISP could be legally forced to identify you as the person who called into one of its computers at the time that this computer was connected to the Web site, but in reality this seems never to have happened.

Computers connected directly to the Internet can be identified, at least to some extent, by their unique identification numbers. If you browse the World Wide Web from a computer at work directly connected to the Internet (not through a dial-in connection), your company's identity can easily be determined by a Web site that you visit. Home computers connected to the Internet through one of the new cable modem systems such as the AtHome network have unique identification numbers, but they can be identified by remote Web sites only as being an element of the cable network; your personal identity and street address will be known only to the cable company.

Some Web sites use programming tricks to obtain your e-mail address from your Web browser without your knowledge, and sell your address to marketers. These tricks won't work with versions of popular Web browsers released after 1998; but if you have an older browser, that may explain how you got on the marketers' mailing lists.

67

Too Late to Say You're Sorry

Negligence and the duty of care . . . The majority view on home accidents . . . Liability to trespassers . . . Liability to licensees (social guests) . . . Liability to invitees (business visitors and domestic employees) . . . The modern (minority) approach . . . Some common types of accidents that result in lawsuits . . . Animals, pets, dangerous animals, watchdogs, nondangerous animals, statutes, and ordinances . . . Snow and ice, public sidewalks, private sidewalks, steps, porches . . . Swimming pools . . . Liability of social hosts for serving alcohol

Most people wonder whether they could successfully be sued for damages if someone were to break a leg on their slippery floor or icy sidewalk. Many people worry about this more than they need to. The laws that govern this kind of liability are intended, at least in theory, to ensure that reasonable people exercising a reasonable degree of caution will usually not be liable for accidents that others may suffer in and around their homes. What the law considers reasonable, moreover, is usually what people with common sense would think reasonable as well. The discussion that follows of some of the legal principles governing liability for accidents at home will give you a number of examples illustrating how the law dovetails with ordinary clear thinking.

Tort law, the law governing private lawsuits over accidents and other noncriminal wrongs, nonetheless is far more complicated than any brief summary such as this one could encompass. It changes over time, and there are many important variations in the fine points of the law from jurisdiction to jurisdiction, although the resemblances among the state laws are generally strong. These are among the many reasons why you must consult a lawyer if you have legal questions about specific circumstances or events.

Wherever conditions in and around your home expose people to a risk of having an accident, you expose yourself to a risk of liability. In tort there are few, if any, absolutes, and the result in a lawsuit would reflect many factors, legal and factual. You cannot say that any one condition—slippery steps or icy walks or rotten stair railings—absolutely will or will not expose you to liability. Nonetheless, you can protect yourself against the risk of lawsuits in two main ways. First, periodically go over your home and grounds looking for situations that might cause accidents; then fix them when possible, and always warn people of any risks. For helpful hints in doing this, refer both to the rest of this chapter and all the chapters in the part of this book called "Safe Shelter." Second, buy good liability insurance in adequate amounts; in some cases, also buy workers' compensation insurance. Refer to chapter 71, "Insurance."

Knock, Knock. Who's There? The Majority View on Home Accidents

If someone breaks a leg in your home and sues you, you are liable to pay damages to that person only if, under the circumstances, you had a legal responsibility to exercise care for that person—called a "duty of care"—and you failed to do so. In that case, you were legally *negligent*. Even though you did not intentionally injure the person, you imposed an unreasonable risk of injury. In deciding just how much care you must exercise toward others so as to avoid being found negligent, the courts usually apply the yardstick of the "reasonable person." When we say things such as, "No reasonable person would act the way he did," the reasonable person we are referring to is probably the same person the law has in mind. Although we rely on our own experience to determine what reasonable behavior is, the courts are constrained by precedent.

Whether you owe a duty of care to a visitor on your premises, and, if so, how much care, depends in most jurisdictions on what kind of visitor he or she is. The majority of the fifty states continue to follow the traditional common-law approach to what lawyers sometimes call "premises liability"—liability for accidents that might befall people on your premises. (The more modern law in the remaining states is briefly described below.) In this traditional approach, your liability to a visitor on your premises depends on whether he or she is a trespasser, licensee, or invitee. Trespassers are those present without permission; licensees have permission to be present; and invitees are present by invitation *for business or similar nonsocial purposes.* The term "invitee" is a legalism that can be confusing, because in most but not all jurisdictions following the traditional approach, social guests count as licensees, not invitees, even though you invited them to come.

You have no duty of care toward a trespasser, and your liability in case of injury to a trespasser is quite restricted (with exceptions, some of which are outlined below). You have a duty of care toward a licensee, but a somewhat limited one, and a correspondingly limited scope of liability. To invitees you owe the highest duty of care, and you have the widest exposure to liability.

Liability to Trespassers. In the majority of jurisdictions the rule is that you owe no duty of care toward trespassers on your property. This means that except in special circumstances you have no liability to trespassers if you fail to make your house and property safe, fail to warn of dangerous conditions there, or fail to inspect your house and property to find out whether there are any unsafe conditions you do not know about.

This rule seems fair to most of us. The law would be "a ass," as Dickens's Mr. Bumble put it, if it imposed on us a legal obligation to provide people with a safe place to trespass. A trespasser, who has no right to be on the property, is presumed to take the premises as he or she finds them and to assume the risk of injury. Suppose that Jones, your neighbor, trespasses on your property to collect leaves for his dried-leaf collection. Several months ago you dug holes for fence posts in your yard but you have not yet put up the fence, and one hole becomes concealed by leaves and other vegetation. While trespassing, Jones steps into it and breaks his leg. If he were to sue you for damages for his injuries (and if he had a good lawyer he would not), as a trespasser he would probably lose the case. Or suppose that a thirsty trespasser sneaks into your house while you are absent, hoping to drink a glass of water and then leave undetected. She has no way of knowing that you are not drinking your own tap water because you have just learned that your well is polluted with dangerous microorganisms. In fact, you are out because you rushed off to buy bottled water. As a result of drinking your water the trespasser develops a serious illness. Again, in jurisdictions that followed the majority approach, you would not be liable.

The basic rule of nonliability to trespassers, however, is riddled with exceptions, most of them congenial to common sense. For example, once you find out the trespasser is present, or if you anticipated, or should have, that the trespasser would be on your property, you must warn him or her of dangers you know about or make that part of your property safe. Or if you know, or should know, that a limited part of your land is habitually used by trespassers—perhaps passers-by often take a short cut across one end of your yard—you might have to make the area safe or warn the trespassers about any dangers. If the trespasser is a child, you face a greater risk of liability, especially if the child was drawn to your property by an "attractive nuisance," such as a pond or high tower or some fascinating machine. If you had reason to know that children were likely to trespass and also knew, or should have known, that on your property or in your home there was a dangerous condition such as a swimming pool or swimming hole or a piece of dangerous machinery that is accessible and fascinating to children, and you failed to take reasonable steps to protect the children, you would face a likelihood of being found liable if some unhappy accident befell a child.

You may be more likely to be held liable to trespassers (and probably licensees or invitees as well) for conditions you created (waxed floors that are slippery or a walkway that your children intentionally hosed down to make a skating area) than natural ones (icy or snowy steps), but, as always, this rule is not absolute. The outcome would turn on many factors.

Liability to Licensees. The term "licensee" may not mean what you expect. A licensee has your permission to be on your premises, but is not invited for a business or professional purpose or for reasons that benefit you economically. The most common licensee is the social guest. (Some jurisdictions, however, treat social guests as invitees.) Your dinner or party guests, your children's playmates, your Thursday night bridge game players are all licensees, not invitees. Others often considered licensees are door-to-door salespeople (so long as you do not ask them in to demonstrate the vacuum cleaner), solicitors for political and charitable causes, a neighbor who wants to borrow a cup of sugar, and usually, but not always, firefighters and police. Letter carriers are invitees.

You have a duty to *warn* licensees of known dangers that are not open and obvious and, in most jurisdictions, to exercise reasonable care in your activities to avoid injuring them. But you need not inspect your premises to find out if there are any dangerous conditions, nor, so long as you give the proper warnings, fix dangerous conditions you do know about. The idea (in jurisdictions that treat social guests as licensees) is that social guests expect and are expected to be treated like members of the family. You do not have to make them safer than you make yourself and your family, but you have to make them at least as safe. That is why you must let them know about unsafe conditions that are not obvious even though you do not have to fix them—so long as a warning will enable your guests to avoid the danger. You would have to warn your guests, for example, about that hidden fence-post hole; if you did, they could avoid stepping in it and be safe. Likewise, if the railing on the upstairs porch will not hold anyone's weight, you are obligated to warn your social guests not to lean on it, but you are not obligated to fix it. If, despite your warning, a guest leans on it, falls, and is injured, in jurisdictions that treat social guests as licensees you are probably not liable for the injuries. If you did not know that the railing would not hold and a licensee—say a local politician going house-to-house asking for votes—leans on it, falls, and is injured, you also will probably not be liable, because you had no duty to a licensee to inspect your property to learn about unknown dangers. To some, this will seem unfair to the poor visitor, which partly explains the trend toward increasing the liability of hosts to guests by treating them as invitees, or through other changes in the law.

Even in jurisdictions that treat social guests as licensees, however, if your social guest is a child, the courts may well hold you to a higher standard of conduct. In several states, the courts have held that the host owes children who are social guests the duty of reasonable care to prevent injury to them. This duty has been held inapplicable if the child's parent or guardian is present. The bottom line is that usually you are responsible for the safety of children visiting in your home without their parents or guardians. If your supervision is negligent, you might be liable for damages if the child is injured as a result of your negligence.

Liability to Invitees. The typical invitee, as the law defines this term, is the invited visitor with a business purpose. The majority of people visiting in the average home are not invitees. People shopping in stores are invitees there. If you invite your insurance agent to the house to discuss your insurance policies, he or she is an invitee in your home. In general, you are obliged to exercise reasonable care to ensure the safety of invitees in your home. With invitees, unlike trespassers and licensees, you have a duty to inspect your premises with reasonable care to find hidden dangers, at least in those areas in which you can expect the invitees to be present, to warn of them, and sometimes to fix them. This means that invitees are entitled to expect that the premises have been made safe for them in light of the invitees' purpose in being there.

Door-to-door salespersons who knock on your door are considered licensees because, not having been invited, they cannot reasonably assume that the premises have been made safe for them. So if there is a termite-infested board in your porch floor that gives way as a salesperson stands there asking you if you need a vacuum cleaner, you probably are not liable for his or her injuries—provided you were unaware of the termites. But if you ask the salesperson to come in and demonstrate the products, he or she becomes an invitee. Now if, while demonstrating the vacuum cleaner in the living room, the salesperson is injured by an electric shock from faulty wiring, you probably are liable, assuming that in the exercise of reasonable care you should have known about and fixed this dangerous condition. But if the salesperson goes poking around your kitchen when you are out of the room and slips and falls, you may not be liable. The kitchen was not an area the salesperson was invited into, nor was it relevant to the purpose for which you invited him or her in.

Sometimes, reasonable care will not require fixing the dangerous condition, and a warning will suffice. You should, for example, tell washing-machine repair people on their way to your laundry room, "Watch out that you don't step on my son's skateboard" or "There is a step down right inside the doorway." It makes both good moral and good legal sense to remind all visitors of unfamiliar hazards. But sometimes a warning will not suffice, particularly when giving the warning cannot ensure the safety of the invitee. You might well be liable, even if you did give a warning, if an invitee slips and falls on your icy porch steps, because in this case giving the warning does not enable him or her to avoid the hazard.

In the majority of jurisdictions, firefighters and police officers are considered licensees, even though they generally enter your home for what seems more like a business purpose than a social one. They cannot reasonably expect that the premises have been rendered safe for them because they often have to enter unexpectedly or in odd ways at odd times. (A few courts have held to the contrary and regard firefighters and police officers as invitees.) But letter carriers are invitees because you know that they are coming and just where they will go on your premises. You must inspect with reasonable care to make sure that there are no dangerous conditions in places where the letter carrier is likely to be, and exercise reasonable care in general to ensure the letter carrier's safety in delivering your mail. When a warning will not suffice, the danger must be removed; just warning about the ice will not help if someone must cross it anyway, so you would have to remove the ice or throw gravel on it or take some other step to make it safe to cross. The same rules apply to other public employees whose entry can be expected at some time or another: the meter reader, the sanitation worker, package and newspaper deliverers, delivery persons, and repair persons are all invitees.

Domestic employees, too, are considered invitees—housecleaners, babysitters, nannies, gardeners, launderers, and others. As a general rule, the employers of domestic employees are liable if a domestic employee is injured as a result of the employer's failure to exercise reasonable care for the employee's safety when the employee is engaged in doing his or her job or doing something that is within the scope of his or her employment. You, as employer, are required to provide a reasonably safe place to work, and safe tools and appliances to work with. You have a duty to inspect your premises to learn about any hidden dangers and defects that might pose dangers, to warn your employee of them, and to correct them if a warning may not suffice to obviate the danger. If your housecleaner suffers injuries in a fall because of your defective stairs or your chauffeur is injured because you failed to have your car brakes inspected or repaired, you may well be found liable for damages.

An exception to these general principles applicable to domestic employees—one that is increasingly disfavored by the courts—is the doctrine of "assumption of risk." If your employee is regarded as having assumed a risk incidental to his or her employment, you may not be liable. For example, if you hire a nurse to take care of you while you recuperate from tuberculosis in your home, he or she might be regarded as having assumed the risk of contracting tuberculosis while caring for you. But this exception to the general rule is usually quite limited and does not spare you from the consequences of your own negligence, especially if the employee's action was taken at your direction—for example, if you were to ask your employee to get the mail when you had failed to clear the walkway or steps leading to the mailbox of slippery snow or ice.

The Modern (Minority) Approach

One version of the modern approach abolishes the distinction between invitees and licensees and imposes a duty of care toward all persons who enter your property with your permission. In jurisdictions that work this way—Florida, for example—your liability to social guests is the same as it is toward business visitors. The law as to trespassers, however, is the same in these places as in the traditional jurisdictions.

In a second modern approach, the hoary legal distinctions among trespassers, licensees, and invitees are abolished for purposes of determining your liability to people who come onto your property, and you are held to have a duty of care to *everyone* who comes on your premises. (California, Colorado, Massachusetts, Minnesota, Rhode Island, Hawaii, and New York are among the states that take this approach.) In practical terms, however, this doctrine is often not so different as it sounds from the majority view, for whether the injured party was a trespasser, a social guest, or a business visitor is considered a fact relevant to determining whether or not you exercised sufficient care. Generally, you are still least responsible if the injured person was trespassing, more responsible if the person was present with your consent, and most responsible if the person came (at your invitation) to fulfill duties or carry on business. Reasonable care with respect to trespassers amounts to something less than it does with respect to your dinner guests or to a doctor making a house call. The main reform that this approach effects has also been instituted in several jurisdictions that retain the traditional categories: social guests are considered to be among those to whom you owe the greatest duty of care.

Some Common Types of Accidents that Result in Lawsuits

The general rules about trespassers, licensees, and invitees apply in all kinds of accidents. Common causes of home accidents that end in litigation are slips and falls caused by slippery waxed floors; throw rugs with slippery backs; invisible glass panels and doors that people walk into; uneven steps; rotten floorboards; overly hot tap water; poor or dim lighting that causes falls, especially near steps and in stairways; obstacles left in passageways and walks that are tripped over; pets; damage caused by trees; snow and ice conditions; and swimming pools. Indeed, about the last three items—injuries caused by pets, icy and snowy walks and steps, and swimming pools—anxiety is so pervasive that I will say a few special words about each of them. On home accident prevention, see the chapters in the part of this book called "Safe Shelter."

Animals

Pets. In certain circumstances, you will be liable both for injuries and for property damage caused by your pet. (Damage caused by livestock or farm animals is not discussed here.) If you live in an area where there are no leash laws or other ordinances governing pets, your liability is determined by common-law principles. Most cities and suburban areas and some rural areas, however, have enacted statutes or ordinances that alter or override common-law principles, either wholly or partly. Both types of law are summarized briefly below.

Dangerous Animals. In most jurisdictions that follow the common-law rules, as well as some statutory jurisdictions, your liability for injuries or damage caused by your pet depends on whether the pet is considered a dangerous animal—that is, whether it is likely to inflict serious damage or injury. The general rule is that a pet owner is "strictly" or "absolutely" liable for injuries or damages caused by a dangerous animal, so long as the owner knew or had reason to know that the animal was dangerous. "Strict liability" means that you are liable regardless of whether you were careless or negligent or somehow at fault. Even if you were careful to restrain and control a dog with a tendency to bite, you would be liable if it escaped through no fault of yours (for example, its pen was destroyed in a tornado, a third party set it loose, or you sprained your ankle while out walking it and could no longer control it) and caused an injury. The law says that the person who insists on keeping a dangerous animal, and not his or her neighbors, should bear the burden of the inevitable risks. This rule usually applies even if the injured person was a trespasser on your property.

It is not necessary for your dog actually to bite someone before you are put on notice that it is dangerous. If you have seen it straining at the leash or otherwise trying unsuccessfully to attack people or other animals, that might be sufficient for a court to deem that you should have known it was dangerous. In some states—Arizona, California, and Florida, for example—the owner need not have had warning of a dog's vicious tendencies to be liable. You are especially likely to be found liable if the animal is considered inherently dangerous—a wolf or shark for example.

In some jurisdictions animals can be legally considered dangerous as a result of doing things other than biting or attacking. A dog that jumps up on people could be considered dangerous because it might knock them down and injure them. A dog with a tendency to destroy crops or gardens might also be considered dangerous. Or it might be deemed dangerous if it chased cars or bicycle riders, barking furiously, potentially causing accidents for those who swerve to avoid hitting it or those who are distracted by it.

Watchdogs. Some people keep ferocious watchdogs; in doing so, they are taking a legal risk. A rule that is commonly followed with respect to watchdogs is that you are liable for any injury caused by your watchdog that you would not have been allowed to inflict in person or to cause the dog to inflict at your command. This means you would be liable if your watchdog attacked a mere trespasser (one who threatens no harm beyond his or her unlawful entry), because you yourself would not have been permitted to inflict injuries on the trespasser. In general, however, liability on your part is less likely to be found by the court when factors justifying the use of more force are present: the trespass occurs at night, evidence exists that the trespasser intended to commit a crime or posed a danger to you or your family, and so forth. Liability is also less likely to be imposed if a clear warning, such as "Beware of the Dog," is posted in an obvious place or if the dog is chained or otherwise effectively restrained. "Less likely," however, does not mean "impossible."

Nondangerous Animals. The general common-law rule regarding a nondangerous pet is that you are liable for damage or injury it causes if the damage or injury occurred through your negligence in controlling the animal. (Most well-populated areas, however, have statutes or ordinances that override the common-law rule and impose strict liability on owners for their pets' misdeeds; see below.) If the injury or damage was not foreseeable, you will not be liable; what is foreseeable is partly determined by your pet's character and your knowledge of it. Thus, if you live near a busy highway, you might be liable if you let your dog run loose, if you knew or should have known that the dog would try to cross it; it would be foreseeable that the dog could cause a serious accident. Similarly, if you know that your dog loves to dig up people's gardens, you could be liable for damages if it does so. You might be liable, too, for failing to restrain your vivacious pet around those who are frail or elderly—it is foreseeable that it might knock them off balance and leave them injured by a fall.

You will be held responsible for knowing the harm that perfectly well-behaved pets can do under special circumstances. For example, you should know that bitches with puppies and cats with kittens may bite those who touch their litter even though they are otherwise entirely gentle.

Statutes and Ordinances. The common law has been altered by statutes or ordinances in most areas. Frequently, a mix of common-law and ordinances or statutes operates simultaneously. In urban and suburban areas, leash laws are all but universal, but they vary widely in content. Some rural and suburban ordinances require restraint only of vicious dogs. But most cities require restraint of all dogs, and under some statutes the owner of an unrestrained dog may be prosecuted for maintaining a nuisance. Some leash laws create civil liability for injuries or damages arising out of violations; some do not. Penalties vary widely, fines being typical. In many cities, ordinances require cleaning up one's pet's droppings in public places.

If you have a pet, you should be sure to learn whether you live in one of the many jurisdictions with laws that create *strict liability* for injuries or damage caused by various domestic animals, dangerous or not. In these places you are potentially liable when your pet hurts someone no matter what you knew or should have known, and no matter how gentle your pet has always been. There are sometimes defenses against liability under these statutes, the most important being that the injured party somehow teased or provoked the animal.

Snow and Ice: Sidewalks, Steps, Porches. Regarding snow and ice, check your local regulations. What follows is a discussion of regulations that are commonly in effect, but there are jurisdictions that do not follow the common rules.

Public Sidewalks. In many areas, local ordinances require you to keep the public sidewalk abutting your property clear and passable. In cold climates, this will mean at least clearing snow and ice. In warmer weather, this may require removing mud or obstacles and repairing holes and cracks. Such ordinances usually require you to clear accumulations of snow and ice within some period of hours. In one state, for example, you have four hours, not including nighttime hours, to clear the accumulations after precipitation has ceased. If you fail to do so, usually you must pay a fine. Apart from such statutes, there is usually no legal duty to keep the sidewalks clear.

A common question is whether you are liable to someone who is injured by a slip on snow or ice when you failed to clear such an abutting public sidewalk. The answer is complex. The fundamental principle in the majority of jurisdictions, surprisingly, is that you are not liable to the public for failing to keep the public walk in a safe condition even though under some local ordinance you are required to clear it. This means that you cannot be sued in tort by someone who slips and falls because you did not obey the ordinance. Nor can the city claim from you the money it has had to pay someone who sued the city after falling on the icy walk. Exceptions to this rule include Pennsylvania, whose common law makes abutting owners liable for such damages (when dangerous elevations and ridges of snow and ice form), West Virginia, and Iowa.

The reasoning behind the principle that makes the local government, and not you, liable, is that the local government should ultimately be responsible for keeping the public walks safe and clear and that, while it should be able to conscript your aid in doing so, it should not be able to evade its responsibility by passing on to you the costs of its failure to do so. This principle of nonliability, therefore, does not apply when the dangerous condition is one you have created or caused through your own negligence. Keep in mind that snow and ice that have naturally accumulated on the public sidewalk are not considered the result of your negligence. Failing to shovel is not the same as actually causing the sidewalk to be covered with snow or ice.

In all jurisdictions, you are potentially liable if you—not Mother Nature—created the condition that caused the injury. Suppose that in shoveling your private sidewalk, you tossed the snow onto the public sidewalk, creating a slippery mess. Or suppose that you hosed down the public sidewalk immediately before a big freeze and created a veritable skating aisle. Or suppose that water from snow melting from your roof was improperly channeled so as to form a river that flowed onto the public sidewalk and froze there overnight, when there was no ice on adjacent sidewalks. In such circumstances, you might well be found liable for negligence in a suit for personal injuries.

Private Sidewalks, Steps, and Porches. The law is different when we move from the public sidewalk onto your private sidewalks, steps, paths, and porches. Here the ordinary rules of premises liability apply. In most jurisdictions, a *trespasser* who is injured by a fall on your slippery private sidewalk, assuming that the slippery condition arose naturally, would not have a case against you except under limited circumstances—for example, the dangerous slipperiness was not open and obvious and you knew that the trespasser was present and failed to warn him or her. If the condition arose not naturally, but through some action of yours, this action would have to amount to wanton misconduct or recklessness: you told your children to water down your sidewalks (so that they could have fun sliding) in freezing weather, creating a treacherous surface for walking, even though you knew that trespassers often used the walks. In jurisdictions that recognize a duty of care toward trespassers, you might be liable in less extreme circumstances.

Even *licensees,* in the majority of jurisdictions, could not easily establish liability on your part if they were injured on your premises by slipping on a natural accumulation of snow or ice. As with public sidewalks, if the condition or accumulation was created wholly or partly by you instead of Mother Nature, however, then you might be liable. Social guests who are licensees take the premises as they find them, although if you know about a concealed hazard, such as ice that is invisible under a dusting of snow, you must warn them. If you do not, you might be liable for any injuries they suffered if they should fall. But in ordinary circumstances you would not be liable for failing to shovel or spread salt or ashes, and, if the iciness were an open and obvious condition, even for failing to warn them. If there were a concealed icy patch of which you were unaware, you would probably still not be liable because you had no duty to inspect to find dangerous conditions. Recall, however, that in some jurisdictions, social guests are treated as invitees and in others the distinction between invitees and licensees is abolished.

If *invitees* are on your premises, you have a duty to inspect your premises to learn of any dangerous conditions, including those attributable to snow and ice, and to fix or, sometimes, warn of them. (A warning may not be sufficient to avoid liability, for example, if the dangerous condition might not be avoided or avoidable despite the warning.) Some jurisdictions hold that there is no liability even to an invitee for injury suffered on a natural accumulation of snow or ice (assuming that there is no failure to warn or that the icy condition is or should be obvious to the invitee). Some jurisdictions, however, say that you must remove the accumulation within a reasonable period of time after the precipitation has stopped, and that you are liable to an invitee if you fail to do so. Considering that invitees are likely to be on your premises every day—letter carriers, meter readers, domestic employees, and others—it is most important that in areas in which they will be present you remove unavoidable risks and adequately warn (repeatedly, if necessary) of others.

Regardless of your legal duties, it is certainly better to be reasonably sure that your dinner guests as well as business visitors have safe means of ingress to and egress from your home. In bad weather, you should inspect the steps, walks, porches, and driveways and warn people of hazards—keeping in mind that what is not hazardous for you might well be hazardous for someone who doesn't see well or is older, younger, more frail, or less familiar with your premises than you are.

Swimming Pools. Swimming pool accidents are tragically frequent; hundreds of drownings occur in private pools each year, many involving children. See chapter 63, pages 738–39.) Although pools are dangerous, ordinary rules of negligence apply and your liability in swimming pool accidents is determined in the majority jurisdictions by whether the injured party was a trespasser, licensee, or invitee.

You have a duty to warn licensees and discovered or anticipated trespassers of defective or dangerous conditions of which you are aware (if these are not open and obvious), but you have no duty to inspect to find defective conditions. But if, for example, one end of the pool is considerably deeper than the other, if there is a slippery pool bottom, or a deep end too shallow for diving, or a steep drop-off from the shallow to the deep end, or another potentially dangerous condition that is not open and obvious, you should warn all persons using the pool. To invitees you have a duty to maintain the pool in a reasonably safe condition and to inspect it to detect any unsafe conditions. Most commonly, swimming pool accidents involve licensees—social guests. But recall that the standards of care applicable to invitees also apply to social guests in some jurisdictions.

If children are swimming in your pool with your permission and their parents are absent, there is an increased likelihood that you will be held liable if any injury befalls them. If there are children in the neighborhood and the pool is unfenced or inadequately fenced, the gate is not self-locking and self-closing or is carelessly left open, or the ladder is left where children can reach it, you are likely to be held liable in the event that a trespassing child is injured or drowns in your pool.

Your risk of liability to any injured party increases to the extent that you violate any ordinary safety standards or construction or design standards, whether these are prescribed by statute or ordinance, or recommended by safety authorities, manufacturers, or installers. These might include cloudy water; a steep drop-off; a slimy pool bottom; an unlocked gate or door; failure to install self-locking and closing gates; lack of a fence or a fence that is too low or otherwise inadequate; lack of a pool cover; failure to post depth markings; a defective diving board; placement of a slide in a dangerous position; failure to have safety and life-preserving equipment handy; failure to warn of insufficient depth to support diving; or an improper pool deck (causing a visitor to fall or fall in easily). In addition, a court will judge harshly the hosts of pool parties at which large numbers of children or teenagers are present with inadequate supervision, where alcohol is served to minors, or where minors have partaken of alcohol whether or not they were served it by their hosts.

It's All Your Fault: Liability of Social Hosts for Serving Alcohol. The widespread revulsion against drunk driving has given rise to a new kind of lawsuit. Suppose you give a party at your home and one of your guests becomes drunk on alcoholic beverages you provide, drives away, and causes an accident in which a third party is seriously injured or killed. Several lawsuits have now been filed by such third parties against such social hosts, complaining that the harm was ultimately caused by the hosts' negligence. The traditional common-law rule was that only the drunken person was responsible for the harm. Although most courts that have considered the question refuse to impose a duty on the social host to protect third parties from the risk of injury by a drunken guest, courts in New Jersey and Massachusetts have imposed such a duty.

The rules applicable to social hosts are somewhat different when minors are concerned. By and large you are not liable to your adult guests if they become drunk on liquor you serve at your party and as a result injure themselves. But if the drinker is a minor, you may be liable for damages if the minor suffers injury or death. Some states have statutes like Georgia's, which provides that

> a person who willfully, knowingly, and unlawfully sells, furnishes, or serves alcoholic beverages to a person who is not of lawful drinking age, knowing that such person will soon be driving a motor vehicle, . . . may become liable for injury or damage caused by or resulting from the intoxication of such minor . . . when the sale, furnishing, or serving is the proximate cause of such injury or damage.

If your underage child should serve his or her underage guests alcohol, you might be in trouble as well, for there have been suits against parents for negligent supervision when a drunken minor guest leaves their home and causes or suffers harm.

68

Promises, Promises

Oral versus written agreements . . . Repairs and other service contracts . . . Sales contracts, made-to-order goods or furnishings . . . Standardized and form contracts . . . Warranties

When you manage a home, you are often responsible for making, reading, or signing agreements, or for entering into a binding handshake with people who supply goods and services, including plumbers, carpenters, repair people, and gardeners. It helps to be aware of when you should, or must, have a written agreement and when a handshake is good enough. You should feel comfortable writing up simple receipts and agreements. You should have some skill in reading contracts that others ask you to sign and determining whether or not they contain worrisome or overreaching provisions and whether you should consult a lawyer.

Oral Versus Written Agreements

A contract is a promise or an agreement, written or oral, to do something in exchange for some benefit or "consideration," as it is called in the law.

Many oral contracts—even brief spoken agreements without so much as the seal of a handshake—are legally valid and binding; many elaborately detailed written contracts are not. For example, a written contract to gamble only in the back room at Joe's Pizza Parlor in exchange for a discount on anchovy pizzas is void wherever gambling is illegal. But an oral contract to supply certain lawn services for a period of three months is valid and enforceable in court—so long as the terms are made definite enough for a court to enforce them. It might be difficult to prove that the terms were what you say they were, or even that the contract existed. Moreover, people commonly forget the details of oral contracts even when there is mutual goodwill. For these and other reasons, written contracts usually are preferable.

In some instances, written contracts are legally required. In such cases, no matter how clear, definite, or provable an oral agreement might be, it will not be enforced by a court. Contracts that *must* be in writing include, most importantly, any contract that state or federal law requires to be in writing, any contract dealing with the sale of some interest in land (including mortgages and purchase contracts), and any contract that would be impossible to perform completely within one year from the date of making. If your neighbor solemnly promises, orally, in front of a half dozen witnesses to sell you an acre of his property (to repay a kindness you showed him years ago) but later reneges, you are out of luck; a promise to sell land is enforceable only if in writing. This sort of case illustrates how a promise that is *morally* binding may not be *legally* binding—your neighbor has behaved badly but the law provides no remedy. Or suppose that you make an oral agreement with a gardener to pay him for taking care of your lawn for a two-year period while you will be out of the country, and he reneges after six months. You have no enforceable agreement with the gardener. A contract for work to be completed more than a year after the date on which you made the contract is enforceable only if it is in writing. Here again, conduct that is *wrong* is unassailable in court.

A written contract is desirable in the following circumstances, even if an oral contract would be enforceable in theory:

1. To record the terms of a complex or unusual agreement.
2. To record the terms of any agreement whose existence and terms would be difficult to prove in the event of subsequent disagreements or to remember after the passage of time.
3. To record the terms of any agreement in which substantial sums of money, labor, or goods are involved, or in which for other reasons the stakes, if not high, are at least significant to your convenience, your pocketbook, or your life.
4. To record the terms of any agreement in which you pay cash up front in exchange for the subsequent performance of services or delivery of goods or products.

These guidelines imply that getting something in writing is often a good thing to do in those informal transactions in which we are frequently engaged in domestic life. For example, suppose you wish to loan baby furniture to a friend. You call a local "man with van" and negotiate terms. The following morning, he is to pick up a crib and an antique chest of drawers at your house and deliver it to your friend, Mary Smith, in exchange for twenty dollars, to be paid by her. When he arrives, you could have him sign this:

> January 22, 2000
>
> I acknowledge receipt of one crib and one chest of drawers from George Black, of 12 Maple Street, Home Town, Home State, to be delivered by me in my van, immediately, to the home of Mary Smith, 34 Oak Street, Home Town, State. I understand that upon delivery Mary Smith will give me $20.00 as payment in full for delivering the crib and chest.
>
> ______________________________
>
> [Signature, Telephone Number, and Address of Man with Van]

This puts in writing what the man took, what he was supposed to do with it, who was supposed to pay him, and where he can be reached. Such a document would be most useful in the event that he later turned out to be unscrupulous (for example, he tried to get you to pay him again, insisting that Mary had not paid him) or careless (he left the furniture on the porch at 43 Oak Street).

It is always safest to pay upon receipt of goods or services, and after making sure that they are acceptable. It is good practice to get and save a receipt for any cash payment. (Mary should get one from the man with the van.) The receipt should state the amount paid, what it was paid for, to whom, and the date. The person whom you pay should sign the receipt. Here is a simple example that could be altered to suit many ordinary household purposes.

> Received as payment in full for delivery of the Local Morning Paper from June through August 1999, from Mr. Neighbor, 12 Elm Street, Home Town, Home State: *$60.00.*
>
> ____________________
>
> [Signature of Newspaper Deliverer and Date]

Repairs and Other Service Contracts

Plumbers, housepainters, appliance repair people, electricians, roofers, carpenters, plasterers, and anyone else who works on floors, walls, ceilings, countertops, and appliances are just some of the people with whom we contract for repairs and other casual work in the home. Ordinarily they accomplish their work in one or two visits. They are rarely paid in advance. They are paid in full upon satisfactory completion of their work, and you should get a receipt or legible copy of an invoice that states that you paid in full (and how much), the worker's address and telephone number, and a clear description of the nature of the work done, broken out into materials and labor. If you have provided the materials—paint, plaster, lumber, and so forth—the receipt should say so. If you mail payment, make a note on the check and in your checkbook explaining briefly what it was for and whether it constituted payment in full—the canceled check will be your proof of payment. Keep copies of all canceled checks, bills, invoices, and receipts. They can help you resolve any disputes over the work or payment for it, locate businesses and people you want to deal with again in the future, and plan your budget.

The description of the work done should be adequate to protect you in case you subsequently discover problems. If the washing machine repair person does some work and leaves with your check, but tomorrow the machine again doesn't work, you want to be able to show that it is the same problem and not a new one for which you must pay anew. My last washing machine repair person wrote on the invoice, fully and accurately, that he had "leveled all four legs and cleaned up the valve inlet hose and screen and checked to see that washer OK."

Sales Contracts

You buy a tremendous number of articles to be used and stored in your home: appliances, furniture, rugs and carpets, furnishings of all sorts, linens, clothes, pots, pans, dishes, tools and utensils, CDs, paintings, and hundreds of others. In most of these transactions, there is no contract. You hand over the money, and immediately get the goods plus a receipt. (It should state what you bought, from whom, what you paid, and the date.) You see what you're getting, and it is your job to determine that the goods are worth what you're paying for them. If the goods are substandard or defective in some way, you often have some protection under a warranty. (Warranties are discussed below.)

When you buy a made-to-order or custom-made article, when you enter into an arrangement for the sale and purchase of goods in the future, or when you take possession now but pay for an article over time in one or more payments, you are entering into a contract. The seller promises to make something for you according to your specifications; you are either going to pay in advance or promise to pay the seller when you get the goods. Or perhaps you promise to make forty-eight equal monthly payments of fifty dollars. In cases such as these, you face the possibility that one or both parties will fail to live up to their side of the bargain. Disputes may arise over whether sellers have delivered what they said they would, and in timely fashion, or whether buyers have paid the amounts they promised to pay at the times when they promised they would. A written contract will help prevent disputes from arising and will make the resolution of disputes easier when they do.

If you have a computer built to specifications from a mail-order house, buy mail-order fruit or other goods out of a catalogue, or buy other goods by mail, you will ordinarily give a credit-card number when you order. The best businesses will not charge your credit-card account until they ship, but some will charge you upon ordering. Inquire before you order which method a company uses and give your business to those who charge upon shipping. You, and not they, should have the free use of your money until they send you what you have ordered.

If you are having furniture made, you will usually pay a hefty deposit (up to half the total amount due), with the rest due on delivery. You should allow yourself the opportunity to inspect the product before paying for it in full. The maker or supplier should agree to correct any problems quickly and free of charge. Storefront businesses will use forms that state the terms of your agreement and provide blank spaces to record your choice of materials, styles, and the rest. Read such forms thoroughly, including the fine print, to make sure that they accurately record what you want to order. If you deal with an individual—a skilled carpenter or furniture maker—rather than a storefront business, you may find that he or she wishes to do business on a handshake basis. Try at least to write out a memorandum of what it is you want made and the price you have agreed upon. In my home, we did this when we had desks made by a carpenter, who worked solo and informally, and it helped all of us considerably. Our memorandum was handwritten on a torn and grubby sheet of lined paper by our carpenter, but it accurately recorded our choice of materials, proposed delivery date, design details, price, and much more. Photocopy it, give one copy to the maker, and keep one. If you make changes in plans as you go along, note the change on your copy or another paper, date it, and send a photocopy of it to the worker so that he or she knows what your understanding of the change is. Carpenters or furniture makers will provide drawings and notes, too, and you should try to get copies of these to attach to your memorandum.

Standardized and Form Contracts

Consumers often must sign form contracts if they are going to get the goods they want. Before paying by credit card became all but universal, many more people bought goods on the installment plan than do now, and they usually signed standardized contracts (also called contracts of adhesion) that contained long passages in fine print, disclaimers, and stringent penalties for failure to make timely payments. Nowadays, people often pay their entire bill to the seller on a credit card, and their installment payments are made on a monthly basis to the credit-card company.

If you should find yourself signing one of these standardized contracts for the sale of goods, be alert. Read the fine print and the warranties. In an installment contract, add up the total payments due under the contract to be sure you are not paying an exorbitant price. The federal Truth-in-Lending Act of 1968 requires all creditors to disclose finance charges as an annual percentage rate, along with other essential terms. If any seller fails to volunteer this information, buy elsewhere and report the seller to the Federal Trade Commission (see the FTC's Web site or find a telephone number in the United States Government listings in the blue pages of your telephone directory), or call your attorney general's office, the Better Business Bureau, or your department of consumer affairs. Read carefully to determine what penalties will be imposed should you miss a payment; contracts of adhesion typically permit the seller to repossess the goods if you miss a payment. This might mean that you could forfeit the goods when you have paid most of the purchase price.

The Truth-in-Lending Act also applies to credit-card agreements. The credit-card company must disclose the effective finance charges on your card along with other information. Typical credit-card agreements provide that the creditor can change the terms of the agreement, including the finance charges, at any time so long as it sends you notice of the changes. It can also assign the agreement—that is, it can let another company take over your account. Your only recourse in these events is to cut your card in half, pay what is due on your account, and notify the company that you are canceling your account. If your card is stolen or lost, notify the company immediately. Typically, you will be liable for no amounts charged once the company receives your notice and, if charges have been made improperly prior to your notice, you will be liable for a maximum of fifty dollars.

When reading form contracts and other contracts that others have written, never let yourself be pressured, and never sign hastily. Take as much time as you need to read every word; do not be embarrassed to ask what various provisions mean; and do not sign *anything* you do not *fully* understand. When a significant amount of money is at stake, have a lawyer read the contract. If you cannot do this, ask an honest and reliable business professional familiar with the kind of transaction at issue, or ask an experienced friend or family member. Make sure you pay careful attention to:

What total amounts are due under a contract, including interest or penalties

When money is due

Who pays if things go wrong

Provisions in which the other party says he or she is not liable

Provisions describing what the other party will do to remedy the situation if the goods or services are not satisfactory

Warranties

Any provision in which you are said to waive any rights

Any provisions describing what and how goods or services are to be supplied, the times they will be supplied, and the nature of the goods or services

If there are blanks in the contract, scribble a line through them before signing. (Otherwise someone could later fill them in and claim you had agreed to the additions.) Sign using blue ink so it is easy to tell the original from copies.

Warranties

Warranties for durable consumer goods are also federally regulated, but the regulations are rather toothless. The Magnuson-Moss Act of 1975 governs written warranties on products costing more than five dollars. This law requires that written warranties be designated either "full" or "limited." If the warranty is designated "full" and the product fails to conform to the warranty, the supplier must promise to repair or replace the product without charge or to refund your money. If there is a written warranty, the supplier cannot disclaim any applicable implied warranties. Implied warranties include the warranty of merchantability (a warranty that the goods are fit for the ordinary purposes for which such goods are sold), the warranty of fitness for a particular purpose (a warranty that the goods are fit for some particular purpose of the buyer's that the seller has reason to know about), and the warranty of title and against infringement (a warranty that the seller has full title, subject to no security interests, to the goods and that the goods do not infringe any patent or trademark).

One trouble with the Magnuson-Moss Act is that it does not require that a written warranty actually be given. Thus the seller can avoid most of its requirements simply by not giving a written warranty of any sort, full or limited. Then the seller need not offer any implied warranties either. The seller need not even warrant by implication that the goods (for example, a vacuum cleaner) are fit for the ordinary purposes to which vacuum cleaners are put (sweeping up household dust). In case the seller gives a limited warranty, study the language carefully to see what you are and are not promised. Look carefully for language such as "as is" or "with all faults" that implies that there are no implied warranties of any sort.

You may at times wish to give some thought to who is and who is not covered by the warranty, especially in light of what you plan to do with the article you are purchasing. Warranty coverage depends on state law. In some states, warranties may extend to all persons who may reasonably be expected to use, consume, or be affected by the goods. In others, the warranty may cover only the relatives or houseguests of a buyer—which would exclude friends and neighbors, for example, under a variety of circumstances.

69

Domestic Employment Laws

Federal labor laws . . . State labor laws . . . When you or your relations do domestic work . . . Federal taxes (the nanny tax laws) . . . Which taxes you must pay . . . Some exemptions to the tax requirements . . . Which forms and numbers you will need . . . Records you must retain . . . State taxes and other regulations . . . Foreign workers and immigration laws . . . Form I-9 . . . Visas, H-2B visa, permanent residence (green card), au pair program, social security numbers . . . Dangers of hiring illegal foreign workers as household employees

Few laws protect domestic employees on the job, but those few deserve our scrupulous observance. Domestic employees—cooks, maids, cleaners, babysitters, nannies, housekeepers, gardeners, and drivers—are those who do work in the home that would otherwise be done by members of the household. In people's private houses, such employees typically experience low pay with no health benefits, no pension plans, no vacation pay, no job security, no hope of advancement, and no redress for grievances and injustices except to leave a job they may desperately need. These problems are all exaggerated for illegal domestic workers, who are sometimes prey to outright mistreatment by unscrupulous employers who take advantage of their reluctance to seek legal protection. On the subject of establishing good relations with household employees, see chapter 70, "Working with Household Help."

Federal Labor Laws

The United States Fair Labor Standards Act (FLSA) entitles employees in domestic service in a private household, with certain exceptions, to receive the minimum wage. (If you live in a state that has a higher minimum-wage requirement than the federal government, you should find out whether it applies to full-time and part-time domestic employees.) The FLSA also requires employers to pay domestic workers at one and one-half times an employee's regular hourly rate for each hour over forty hours worked (for you) per week. Household employees are entitled to the federal minimum wage so long as their cash wages from one employer are at least a thousand dollars in a calendar year (subject to adjustments pursuant to certain statutory requirements) or so long as they work more than eight hours a week for one or more employers. This means you must pay the minimum wage even if your part-time housecleaner works for you only four hours per week so long as he or she works more than eight hours as a domestic employee when you add in hours worked in others' homes. Those who are not covered by the federal minimum-wage requirements include domestic workers who provide casual baby-sitting and those employed as companions for elderly and sick people who are unable to care for themselves. Live-in domestic employees are not subject to the overtime-pay requirements of the FLSA.

The FLSA requires that employers of employees subject to minimum-wage and overtime pay provisions, as household employees are, keep certain records. No special format or type of recordkeeping is required. You should maintain a record of the following:

Personal information—employee's name, home address, occupation, sex, and date of birth, if under nineteen

Hour and day workweek begins

Total hours worked each workday and each workweek

Total daily or weekly straight-time earnings

Regular hourly pay rate for any week when overtime is worked

Total overtime pay for the workweek

Deductions from or additions to wages

Total wages paid each pay period

Date of payment and pay period covered

State Labor Laws

There are no federal laws governing conditions of domestic work, safety regulations, maximum hours, or firing. State common law is usually limited to the "at-will employment doctrine." This is the set of legal precepts that covers relations between employers and employees in the absence of express agreements (explicit ones, whether oral or written) that entitle the employee to a fixed term of employment, limit the employer's right to fire, or in some other way alter the right of either party to end the relationship. Because such express agreements are all but unheard of between employers and household workers, a domestic worker's employment is almost always "at will," which means that it lasts as long as both parties want it to and ends as soon as either party wants to end it. The limits on this freedom are few. If a firing violates public policy, a court might try to find a remedy for an employee (and here we are in the realm of fantasy, because housecleaners rarely have the resources or the will to sue their employers). For example, if you fired your housecleaner for arriving half an hour late because she had stopped to vote on the way in, when she would otherwise have been unable to vote, you could in theory be required to offer her reinstatement or back pay. Or if a firing breached an implied covenant of good faith and fair dealing, a court might be persuaded by the employee to order a remedy.

Note that a promise of lifetime or indefinite employment is usually interpreted by the courts to mean simply that the employee may be fired only *for cause*. It does not mean that the employee cannot be fired at all. You may fire for cause if you fire because of poor performance, absenteeism, dishonesty, drug or alcohol use, or even a change in your financial situation that makes it impossible for you to pay wages. An employer would breach a promise to fire only for cause, by the way, if he or she created such intolerable working conditions that the employee was forced to quit; this comes under the doctrine of "constructive discharge."

When You or Your Relations Do Domestic Work

In general, the law usually presumes that relatives donate domestic services—in other words, the work you do for your mother or sibling is not done for pay. (It makes the opposite assumption about nonrelatives.) Thus a wife generally cannot sue her husband for payment for domestic services. Moreover, some courts have found that certain living arrangements are equivalent to establishing a family relationship and, accordingly, have applied the presumption that domestic services are offered gratuitously to biologically unrelated people who are living together. It tends not to be applied, however, if there is no relationship of support or sexual relationship between the parties, if the relation is not one of mutual affection and devotion, if the claimant is not accorded the rights and privileges of a family member, or if various other indicators of family-type relationships are absent.

Theoretically, someone could overcome the presumption that domestic services were freely donated by proving that there was an express oral agreement to the contrary. But this is often hard to prove. When related, married, or quasi-married people have domestic arrangements that include a mutual expectation that one will compensate the other for domestic services, they would be wise to consult a lawyer and put this in writing. Do not think of compensation solely in terms of a wage or cash. The expected or desired trade-off might be joint ownership of personal or real property, or an inheritance of some sort. Many a disappointed grandchild, niece, or daughter, after having kept someone's house or nursed an invalid for years, has walked empty-handed—and homeless—from a courtroom. Often in such cases, someone has solemnly, even sincerely, promised to "leave you the house in my will" as payment and simply never does so.

On the other hand, people who want to avoid paying compensation for domestic services rendered might sometimes equally well consider entering into a written contract to that effect. Otherwise in a few jurisdictions—ask your lawyer whether you live in one—there is a danger under certain circumstances a court will find that there is an "implied" contract to pay for such services even though no express agreement ever existed. Moreover, there is always the possibility that a claimant could succeed in persuading a court that an express oral agreement to pay exists. (That is what happened in the famous case of *Marvin v. Marvin*, in which the actor Lee Marvin was sued by his former housemate for half of all property acquired during the seven years they lived together.)

Federal Taxes

All employers of domestic workers are subject to federal employment tax laws, including employers of noncitizens working in this country, whether legally or illegally. These laws change often, sometimes in major and sometimes in minor respects, so you must make a point of staying up-to-date. The material presented here does not give the kind of complete account of these laws that would enable you to fulfill your filing requirements and other obligations. Rather, it gives an outline of what is involved, to help people become aware of steps they may need to take. For anything more, you will need to get the proper IRS forms, with their instructions. You may wish to acquire an IRS explanatory booklet; a few of these are recommended below. You may also wish to consult your accountant or your lawyer.

Which Taxes You Must Pay. You are required to withhold and pay social security and Medicare taxes, or FICA taxes, pursuant to the Federal Insurance Contribution Act (FICA), for each of your household employees. You are also required to pay federal unemployment taxes pursuant to the Federal Unemployment Tax Act (FUTA) for all of your household employees who are not covered by the exemptions discussed below. FICA taxes are withheld from your employees' wages. FUTA taxes are paid out of your own pocket. You may, in addition, if you and your employee agree, withhold federal income taxes from your employee's wages, but this is not required. (See IRS Publication 926, "Household Employer's Tax Guide," for the current year, or other guides that the IRS may publish on the subject.)

In the wake of the scandals of 1994, when even the president's nominee for attorney general was found to have failed to comply with the federal employment tax laws applicable to domestic employees, Congress passed the Social Security Domestic Employment Reform Act, which amended both the Social Security Act and the Internal Revenue Code. The Reform Act cut out some of the red tape that had discouraged compliance with the earlier law and raised the threshold amount that triggered the requirement to withhold FICA taxes for social security and Medicare. (The threshold for FUTA was unchanged by the reform act.) Most of us, however, would still regard these laws as being complicated and onerous despite the improvements.

You are now required to pay FICA taxes for each domestic employee to whom you pay at least eleven hundred dollars (as of 1998, but this figure may increase in subsequent tax years) or more in the aggregate in any calendar year. FUTA taxes are due if you paid more than a thousand dollars (subject to certain adjustments) to household employees in any calendar quarter in any tax year or the preceding tax year. The first seven thousand dollars of wages paid to each employee are FUTA wages subject to FUTA taxes, and any of the employee's wages that exceed that amount are not subject to FUTA. For more information on FUTA in any given tax year, refer to the most recent version of the IRS's Publication 926, "Household Employer's Tax Guide," or any similar guide that may be available from the IRS.

If your employee gives you a properly filled out Form W-5, Earned Income Credit Advance Payment Certificate, you are also required to make advance Earned Income Credit payments to him or her. Doing so permits you to reduce the amount of your FICA taxes and federal withholding tax by the amount you pay your employee; but you should not pay more than the combined amounts of FICA and federal withholding tax you would otherwise owe. To learn how much to pay your employee, see Publication 15, Circular E, "Employer's Tax Guide."

Some Exemptions to the Tax Requirements. The exemptions to employee tax obligations are as follows:

Under 18. Since 1995, no FICA taxes have been required to be withheld for employees younger than age eighteen on wages paid during a given year unless their principal occupation in that year was in household employment. This rule exempts wages paid to the typical teenage high-school student who baby-sits for the neighbors on a casual basis. The exemption applies if the baby-sitter was younger than age eighteen at any time during the year, even if he or she turned eighteen on January 2.

Independent Contractors. You need not pay employment taxes for any "independent contractors" who worked for you. An independent contractor is not your employee. Rather, he or she is someone who runs his or her own business or who follows an independent trade, business, or profession, offering services to the general public. (Independent contractors file schedule C, for the self-employed, and they pay their own taxes.) When you control or direct only the result of the work and not the means and methods of accomplishing the result, that is a good indication that the worker is an independent contractor, not your employee. See IRS Publication 926, "Household Employer's Tax Guide." There are many other factors that might be considered in making this determination. If your housecleaner cleans for many other households besides yours, supplies the cleaning tools and materials, and determines what to do and how, these are all indications that he or she is not your employee but is running his or her own business.

If you are in doubt about whether any worker is an independent contractor or an employee, ask your lawyer or accountant for advice, or call the IRS information number in your area and request help. You may want to acquire the following IRS publications (or whatever similar publications are available in future years): Publication 926, "Household Employer's Tax Guide," Publication 937, "Employer Taxes," and Publication 15-A, "Employer's Supplemental Tax Guide."

Employees of Others. You need not withhold or pay employment taxes on wages of anyone who does domestic work in your home as someone else's employee. For example, if a cleaning company sends a cleaner to your house once a week, the cleaner is the company's employee and it pays his or her employment taxes. You pay the cleaning company.

Near Relatives. You need not pay employment taxes on the wages you pay for household services performed by your spouse, your child under age twenty-one, or your parent (except under special circumstances—see Publication 926).

Which Forms and Numbers You Will Need. You pay both FICA and FUTA on your own annual income tax return using Schedule H, Household Employment Taxes. Those who choose to pay household-employee taxes with their business or farm employment taxes, however, should use Forms 941 or 943 (whichever they are using for their non-domestic employees) for their domestic employees' FICA and federal withholding taxes, and Form 940 or 940-EZ for their domestic employees' FUTA taxes.

You must supply a Form W-2, Wage and Tax Statement, to each of your domestic employees by February 1 and to the Social Security Administration by March 1 of each year. File copy A of all Forms W-2 (with Form W-3, Transmittal of Wage and Tax Statements, if there is more than one) with the Social Security Administration at the address provided on the form. If you withhold federal income tax on your employee's wages, you will also need Form W-4, Employee's Withholding Allowance Certificate, for each domestic employee. If your employee is eligible and wants advance payment of the Earned Income Credit for the following year, he or she must fill out Form W-5, Earned Income Credit Advance Payment Certificate.

You will need an Employer Identification Number (EIN) to fill in on the forms you file for your domestic employees. If you do not have one already, apply for one on Form SS-4. You are also required by the Immigration and Naturalization Service to complete Form I-9 for all domestic workers. See pages 802–3, below.

You will need the social security number of each employee for whom you pay employment taxes. If your employee is working for you illegally, he or she will not have a social security number, but you are still legally obligated to pay the taxes. In this case, in the space for the social security number on Form W-2, according to the IRS, you may write "SSA205(c)"—the provision of the Social Security Act that says illegal aliens are not to be issued a social security number. If the employee has applied for a social security number but has not yet received it, write "Applied for."

Records You Must Retain. You must retain records of the employee taxes you pay for a period of at least four years after the due date of the return on which you report the taxes or the date they were paid, whichever is later. The records you must keep, as described in Publication 926, include:

Wage and tax records. On each payday you should record the date and amounts of:

1. Your employee's cash and noncash wages,
2. Any employee social security tax you withhold or agree to pay for your employee,
3. Any employee Medicare tax you withhold or agree to pay for your employee,
4. Any federal income tax you withhold,
5. Any advance EIC [Earned Income Credit] payments you make, and
6. Any state employment taxes you withhold.

Employee's social security number. You must keep a record of your employee's name and social security number exactly as they appear on his or her social security card if you pay the employee:

1. Social security and Medicare wages, or
2. Wages from which you withhold federal income tax.

You must ask for your employee's social security number no later than the first day on which you pay the wages. You may wish to ask for it when you hire your employee.

State Taxes and Other Regulations

State and local tax laws may apply to your household employees; call your state tax department for information. If you are required to withhold state unemployment taxes, the IRS is authorized under the Reform Act to enter into an agreement with a state to collect that state's unemployment tax due for domestic employees. If your state has no such agreement with the IRS, you will have to pay whatever is required directly to the state.

If you and your employee have agreed to withhold federal income taxes from his or her wages, you may agree to withhold state or local income taxes too. You may also agree to withhold state and local income taxes but not withhold federal income taxes.

Some states will require you to register with the state's department of labor as an employer and to comply with its regulations. You may also be required to purchase workers' compensation, disability insurance, or other insurance on behalf of your employees. (Workers' compensation is inexpensive, and it is in your interest to provide it. An employee who is covered by workers' compensation can make no direct claim against you for damages on account of an accidental injury suffered on the job.)

Foreign Workers and Immigration Laws

No reforms have simplified the onerous burdens placed on those employers who wish to employ noncitizens as domestic employees. Nor do any laws offer significant protection to foreign employees against the abuses inherent in the system of reliance on foreign nationals to care for the homes and children of American professionals. The laws applicable in this area do not apply to casual domestic workers—those working in private homes on a sporadic, irregular, or intermittent basis. They apply to both full-time and part-time workers, however: cooks, cleaners, launderers, nannies, gardeners, and so forth.

Form I-9. Every employer, including any employer of domestic workers on a regular basis, is required to complete a Form I-9, Employment Eligibility Verification, for each employee, foreign or not. The only exception is for workers employed on a sporadic, irregular, or intermittent basis. Form I-9 must be completed for part-time domestic employees as well as full-time ones, even if the employee works only a few hours for you each week. You do not need to complete Form I-9 for independent contractors.

The purpose of this form is to require employers to make at least a superficial determination that their employees are working in the United States legally. The form requires you to obtain at least minimal information about your employees and to look at some minimal documentation. You do not have to do any detective work or determine whether the documentation is valid or forged. But you do have to attest to having seen documents that seem to be valid and that would authorize your employee to work. If you properly complete Form I-9, you have a prima facie defense to any charge of hiring illegal aliens to work for you. (Penalties for hiring illegal aliens, by the way, range from fines of a hundred dollars to ten thousand dollars, and even imprisonment for repeated and intentional violators.)

Acquire Form I-9 from the U.S. Immigration and Naturalization Service. Your telephone directory governmental listings will show the INS office nearest you. You should also request the INS's "Handbook for Employers," which provides invaluable advice about how to fill in the form.

After you have completed Form I-9, do *not* send this form in to any governmental agency. Retain it until three years after the date on which employment began or one year after employment is terminated, whichever is *later*. (If employment was terminated in one month, three years after employment began is later. If employment terminated this morning and began ten years ago, one year after termination is later.) Do not discard Form I-9 so long as the employee still works for you.

Visas. There are three basic routes by which domestic workers may acquire visas that permit them to work legally in this country.

H-2B Visas. Domestic workers may try to acquire H-2B "nonimmigrant" visas for unskilled workers, but visas for unskilled workers are limited in number. Domestic workers share those available with all the other unskilled workers. The H-2B visa is not only hard to get, but it permits the employee to stay and work for you for only one year, with extensions up to three years at most, working only at what the application said he or she would be doing. Moreover, if you and the employee have a falling out, the employee will have to leave the country unless he or she can find another employer who wants the same work done. Then a transfer application must be filed before the expiration of the employee's visa.

An H-2B visa will be issued only after the following hurdles have been overcome:

1. You, the employer, must apply to the U.S. Department of Labor for a determination that the service or labor to be performed is truly temporary. This application should include an Application for Alien Employment Certification on Form ETA 750, including a detailed description of the offered employment and describing the terms and conditions of the job offer.
2. The secretary of labor (actually the secretary's staff) must then issue a temporary labor certification. Certification will be granted only when the secretary of labor determines that (i) there are not enough able, willing, and qualified U.S. workers available at the time of the application and (ii) the employment of the foreign worker will not adversely affect wages and working conditions of workers in the United States similarly employed. Certification is by no means automatic. It is often denied.
3. The employer, in this country, files an employment petition (Form I-129) with the Immigration and Naturalization Service requesting work authorization. Notice of approval of this petition is then taken by the would-be employee, in his or

her country, to the United States consulate to apply for an H-2B visa.
4. The Department of State, on the basis of the approved petition, issues one of the visas that Congress permits to be issued annually.

If your employee is already in this country, the employee will need a visa in order to gain legal reentry to this country if he or she should for any reason leave.

Permanent Residence. A "green card" (Alien Registration Receipt Card I-551 or I-151) permits aliens to reside permanently in the United States and work at whatever and for whomever they wish. These visas are also exceedingly difficult for household employees to get. The procedures for applying for a green card are roughly as follows:

1. You, the employer, file an application with the U.S. Department of Labor.
2. The secretary of labor must issue a labor certification. This requires a determination that U.S. workers are not available for the job and that you are offering the prevailing wage for such work.
3. The employer files a petition (Form I-140) with the Immigration Service, which results in getting your employee a place on the waiting list for a visa as of the date the certification application is accepted for filing. (You lose your place if the certification and petition are not approved.)

Then you wait. (As of April 1999, the INS was processing visas for I-140 petitions that were filed in August 1992.) Most of the delay arises because applicants are divided into various categories called "preferences" to which a set number of visas are allocated. Those in the first preference, the supertalented and other outstanding individuals, get visas immediately. But in the third preference, which unskilled workers share with professionals and other workers, there is a long waiting list.

The difficulty, however, is worse than long waits. For some years, domestic employees could live illegally in this country while waiting for their petition for a green card to be approved. In 1997, Congress let lapse the provision of the law that permitted this, with the result that those present in the United States unlawfully are now disqualified for a green card (unless their application for labor certification was filed by January 14, 1998). With very few exceptions, aliens seeking a green card must now do so while living abroad. In addition, in 1996, Congress enacted a law that bars aliens from the United States for a period of ten years if they remain in this country unlawfully for more than one year. (They are barred for only three years if they are present unlawfully for more than 180 days and less than one year and voluntarily leave.)

It used to be that foreign workers could not change employers without losing their places on the waiting list. This rule has changed. Now if an employee gets approval of a new application for certification and a new petition to the Immigration Service for a different job, the employee retains the same place on the waiting list.

The Au Pair Program. Foreign citizens who live in Japan or in the Western European countries that have a reciprocal arrangement with the United States and are between the ages of eighteen and twenty-five may try to become au pairs. Au pairs receive a J-1, an "Exchange Visitor" visa, and most of the red tape for both employer and employee is done by the sponsoring agencies in both countries, to which both would-be sponsoring families and would-be au pairs apply. But here too the number of slots is limited.

The au pair program was founded in 1986 by the U.S. Information Agency pursuant to the Mutual Educational and Cultural Exchange Act of 1961. In this program you provide room, board, pocket money of $125 to

$140 per week, plus other costs (totaling, typically, thirteen or fourteen thousand dollars) to receive in return a maximum of forty-five hours per week in child care. (The au pair's pocket money is not subject to FICA or FUTA taxes, which is one important reason why many people prefer to hire au pairs rather than nannies or babysitters to care for their children.) The arrangement lasts for a maximum of one year. Au pairs are supposed to be treated as members of the family. You are supposed to ensure that they have opportunities to improve their English and to be exposed to sports, cultural, and social events that will enhance their understanding of American mores, customs, and traditions. The USIA complained that in practice the program had come to function as a full-time home child-care work program and not "a valid educational and cultural exchange" and sought to eliminate it, but it is so popular that it has been continued and expanded. Yet the USIA's view certainly fits my observations of many hardworking, lonely au pairs whose employers give them few of the opportunities they are supposed to receive and treat them quite unlike members of the family. Moreover, as a system of full-time care for young children and infants, it has obvious deficiencies in that au pairs lack sufficient training and cannot offer long-term commitment.

Social Security Numbers. All domestic employees, U.S. citizens and noncitizens alike, must have a social security number. (Instructions for acquiring one are given in Chapter 72, "Fond Records," page 835.) Under SSA205(c), however, illegal aliens are not to be issued social security numbers.

Dangers of Hiring Illegal Foreign Workers as Household Employees. Although there is no current policy of prosecuting people who hire illegal aliens to do domestic work in their private households, you are still breaking the law if you do it; and policies can change. (Penalties are described under "Form I-9," above.) If you were to go so far as to help a foreign worker get a tourist visa so that you could hire him or her as your nanny or cook, you would be committing the felony of "harboring" an alien who enters or remains in the United States in violation of the law. The dangers from the employee's point of view are also considerable.

70

Working with Household Help

Social and legal relations . . . How to give orders comfortably and respectfully . . . How to hire, references, character, competence . . . How to give notice . . . Providing references . . . Being considerate . . . Allowing enough time . . . The combination cleaner/baby-sitter . . . Employee information sheets

The best kinds of domesticity are self-sustaining. Households of a size and nature that can be kept up by those who live in them are the most homelike, and housework in itself is physically and emotionally pleasant and restorative. Housekeeping with heavy reliance on domestic employees is not—and never has been—a system that works well. Your own housework can be a joy to you because of the way it is integrated into your life and because of your intense identification with your home and its contents. It does not feel the same to the hired worker. This is similar to the way the feelings of parents about their own children make their experience in taking care of them profoundly different from that of their friends, relatives, and hired caretakers. Among my friends, I know of no one who would argue against these ideas, yet many, myself included, have domestic employees. People who work long hours, especially if they have children, often cannot see any other way to manage.

A hundred years ago, when housework was hard and heavy, just about every urban and suburban household that could afford to hire help did so. It is no surprise to hear that the maids, nurses, and cooks who went into "domestic service" did not like these jobs, and left them for factory and office jobs and upward mobility as soon as they could. It may be something of a surprise, however, to learn how intensely housewives of that era hated having and supervising servants. Complaints of loss of privacy, insubordination, work poorly done, unforeseen absences and abrupt quittings, dishonesty, laziness, dirtiness, and arrogance were unceasing and bitter on the part of employers. When new technology reduced household labor substantially, housewives were glad for a variety of reasons, but prominent among them was that this freed them from having to hire domestic employees. By the 1920s and 1930s, the average middle-class household and even many upper-middle-class ones had given up their cooks and maids, and did not much regret it. (Wealthy households never gave up domestic employees.) Things continued this way without great change until the 1970s and 1980s, when the trend began to reverse itself with the massive movement of women of all classes into the labor force while the growing gap in wages between poorer and richer made household help "affordable."

The enterprise of domestic employment is as fraught with mistrust, tension, and anxiety now as it ever was. But, because so many people must hire domestic employees whether they want to or not, I offer some suggestions on how to be a domestic employer in a way that is more likely to help your household run smoothly and reduce the unpleasantness that so often mars the relationship between domestic employees and their employers.

Social and Legal Relations

If you want smooth relations and employees who want to please you, you would be wise to follow the same rules that all good employers follow even when you are not legally obligated to. Pay a good wage. Give vacations and vacation pay, holiday bonuses, regular raises, and cost-of-living increases. Obey the laws regarding social security, withholding tax, minimum wage, and overtime. A summary of the laws governing domestic employees is set forth in chapter 69. For your own sake as well as that of your employees, take these seriously.

Many people are not accustomed to supervising employees and either fail to assert themselves properly or, going to the other extreme, fail to show the proper respect for the employee. If you are having trouble finding the right tone, try aiming for friendly self-assurance and confidence. You are doing the employee a big favor to be clear and firm about what you want done and how you want it done, and never have I seen this resented. In your own job experience, you surely preferred the employer who did not make you flounder about trying to figure out what in the world your job was supposed to be. What

A HISTORICAL MODEL OF GOOD THINKING ABOUT DOMESTIC HELP

In seventeenth-century Holland, the middle class, domesticity, and republican ideals evolved in tandem. Visitors remarked that the Dutch prized their children first, their houses second, and their gardens third. Small, bright, clean, private homes housing nuclear families were the rule. Holland did not have many servants of any kind, unlike the rest of Europe at that time; society discouraged this and taxed people who hired domestic employees. Dutch society also supported higher status and greater rights for servants. Nannies and nurses were practically unknown. People cared for their own children, houses, and gardens, and this was true no matter how rich or grand they were. If a wealthy household had a maid, the woman of the house was likely to do housework alongside her, and they were likely to eat at the same table. Witold Rybczynski describes how "when the wife of Admiral de Ruyter was visited on the day after her husband's death by an envoy of the Prince of Orange, she could not receive him, since she had recently sprained her ankle—while hanging out the laundry!"*

*Witold Rybczynski, *Home* (Penguin, 1986), pp. 59, 60, 72.

can raise hackles, however, is the employer whose job-description spiel is given with a condescending or punitive undertone, with an apparent assumption that the employee would otherwise do everything wrong, or with an unspoken "or else" at the end of every sentence. It does not hurt to soften instructions by saying, "You probably know this already, but I'll say it anyway. . . ."

Remember the difference between authority and rank. You are the boss but you are not a feudal lord. You need not feel guilty about asking someone to remember to work on the mold on the bathroom tile. However, although some wealthy households still require domestic employees to enter through the back door or a special service entrance, or to wear uniforms, this all seems a bit un-American. Uniforms are sensible for employees who have to deal with many members of the public, as this prevents confusion about who they are and what they are doing without constantly explaining, but otherwise uniforms do not serve much purpose. By and large it is best to let your employees wear whatever they feel comfortable in when doing your work. They need not "sir" or "ma'am" you unless you are going to "sir" or "ma'am" them, and if you call them by their first names you must be sure to let them use yours too. Caregivers for invalids or children, however, should dress "respectably," however old-fashioned that might seem, as this helps them get better treatment from people outside the home and to receive help if they need it. It may not be fair, but caregivers attractively dressed by middle-class standards are more likely to be better treated by the bus driver, the neighbors, the salesclerk, the shoe fitter, the nurse or doctor, and all others they have to deal with in the course of caring for your children or other relatives. And when caregivers are well treated and helped, that benefits your children or other relatives.

If someone works for you all day, make sure he or she takes breaks morning and afternoon, along with a lunch break or other appropriate meal break. Ensure that the working environment is as comfortable, safe, healthy, and pleasant as possible. Establish at the outset whether you are going to provide any meals, transportation costs or transportation, or any other extras.

It is easiest to have a mutually respectful employer-employee relation with professional cleaners who work for agencies. Their taxes are paid by their companies, not you, and they receive health benefits and other ordinary working benefits from the companies they work for, which are also responsible for giving basic training. Often they come with their own cleaning materials, but you may ask them to use yours if you prefer. Calling a company that sends bonded employees helps ensure that you will be compensated in case of theft or damage. You can often set up a regular appointment with an employee who knows you and your home so that you need not worry about showing a new person the ropes every week, which can be onerous.

How to Hire

References. Your employees should ordinarily be able to supply references. Often it is best to begin by asking friends if they can recommend candidates, so that you have a reliable person's judgment to start with. Check your applicants' references, even if friends gave you the names, inquiring about both character and competence. If you are hiring child-care workers, you must be doubly vigilant about checking references. Call the past employers with a list of specific questions. Find out whether the applicants are honest, reliable, courteous, and considerate. Can they do well the work you want done in your home? Are they people you would feel good about having in your home often? If they have never done housecleaning or child care for pay before, you may still want to give them a chance, as many people are good at these tasks who have never done them as jobs. But you should still obtain character references or references from those who have employed your applicants in other capacities—not only past employers but people responsible at the applicants' church, other religious institution, or school, or neighbors. Find out how long the referees have known the applicants and in what capacity. Politely question the referees in ways that indirectly enable you to judge their characters too. If applicants cannot give you references from people who have known them longer than six months, do not hire them. If you should run into a nice young person who has just moved to your area looking for a first job, ask for references from her or his former community.

Character. In all employees, honesty, consideration, pride in work well done, intelligence, motivation, reliability, neatness, and promptness are characteristics to look for. In addition, child-care workers should be kind, warm, gentle, experienced with children, and patient. Do not pick emotionally needy people or people in perilous or deeply unhappy or troubled life circumstances to care for your infant or child. It is hard for those who are needy to be giving without feeling resentful; it is hard for troubled people to focus on a child. Do not pick a disciplinarian so that you take the role of the nice guy. Discipline works only when it comes wrapped with parental love. Remember that children, *including infants,* are persons, and that they like some people and dislike others. Choose someone likable to them as their steady caretaker. You would be bitterly unhappy if forced to spend your days in the company of someone you found petty, selfish, boring, crude, dense, unreasonable, aggressive, irritable, stupid, teasing, judgmental, or cruel; so will your infant or young child. Perhaps most important is the ability of the applicant to understand your child, what he or she wants, likes, and means. It is no fun being entirely dependent for the meeting of every need and wish on someone who never understands what you want—especially when you are tiny, helpless, and incapable of explaining what you want, or how your days are sad or even filled with misery. This is the real situation of many tiny children whom I have observed with full-time caregivers who, without meaning to be unkind, are simply not particularly sensitive to young children or infants.

Even caregivers with the kindest of intentions may, if they are not educated, deal with your child in an improper way. They may think babies should be left to cry if they are neither hungry nor sleepy; they may tease them by taking away their toys; they may refuse to play drop and pick-up with them; they may tease older children in ways that frighten or confuse them (saying that they will take the child's hat or leave the child in the park); and so forth. They may feel contemptuous of age-appropriate fears. They may offer inadequate protection, even for infants and toddlers, against aggressive children at the playground, thinking it best for children to learn to "take care of themselves." Or they may not encourage your child to progress, or they may discourage independence.

Because you cannot know anything of habits, traits, or ideas such as these unless you spend a great deal of time with a caretaker, it is best to have the caretaker come and spend time—preferably a couple of months—with the child while you are present, even though this test is not perfect. Some caretakers derive emotional support from your presence, or control themselves more when you are there. Still, having a caretaker begin work while you are still present, available, and observing is the easiest way for a child to get used to the caretaker so that it is less upsetting when you leave. And it is the best possible way for you to teach a new caregiver the ways and habits of the household, which is one of the most important things you can do to ensure your child's happiness. Most good caregivers will attempt to conform to your ways, knowing instinctively that this is most comfortable for the child.

Competence. A caregiver who is going to spend a significant amount of time with your child should understand child development and the latest and best safety and health rules. This is particularly urgent for infants and preschoolers who cannot tell you about their lives, but it is true even for children who can.

Cleaners should understand cleanliness and follow sanitary methods. If they do not, you will have to teach this or hire someone else. Check to see if they dust under lamps and curios, vacuum under beds and sofas, and vacuum the upholstered furniture and the mattress or mattress pad. Look in corners. Observe their order of work: for example, they should understand that in the kitchen the dishes should be washed before the floor is cleaned. Make sure they do not use dirty cleaning rags and sponges, and that they use different ones for different areas—for floors in different rooms, for table and countertops, especially for dishes—and that they begin with clean ones. Ask them what cleaning products and utensils they prefer, to see how well they know their business. When you find something you want done differently, do not scold or criticize. Say, in a respectful and cheerful voice, "Next time would you please be sure to get under all the furniture with the vacuum?" If this does not help, give the same message in a sober and unsmiling but respectful voice. After that, you can give "final warning" any time you feel fed up. This means that you may tell the employee that you must have things done this way, and that the employee will have to get another job if he or she cannot do so.

How to Give Notice

Tell employees in a serious but respectful voice that you do not feel they have met your standards, and that you have to let them go. Give severance pay in accordance with how long they have been working for you. If only for two or three weeks with no period of satisfactory work, give half the week's pay (for example, if an employee works only one morning per week for you, half of what the employee earns in that morning, plus, of course, the earnings for the day in question, even if the work was not satisfactory). If the employee has been working for you for several months, give a week's pay; if for a year or more, give two weeks' pay. If you are forced to let go someone whose performance has been satisfactory or better or has been with you for years, you should be more generous with severance pay—as generous as you can be.

Providing References

If you have fired an employee for poor performance and the employee asks you for a reference, say gently that he or she should get one from someone who was more pleased with the work done than you were. Cases of stealing or lying that is more than a white lie present serious and painful situations—especially when you feel sorry for the employee you have fired and want to help him or her find a second chance (in some place other than your home). My own feeling is that it is wrong to conceal this kind of misconduct from someone who wants your opinion of an employee, but everyone will have to judge each case on its own merits. If an employee fired for serious misconduct asks you for a recommendation, you might say seriously but pointedly, "I am sorry, but I do not feel able to give you a reference," and explain that you would be obliged to divulge the reason for the firing.

There may be occasions when you have fired someone to whom you can give a reference. For example, I once fired a cleaner who spoke no English because I simply could not communicate to her what I wanted done, which resulted in repeated domestic disasters and frustrations. However, I was able to write a glowing reference for her, as she did many things well and was pleasant, courteous, reliable, and honest. Sometimes you fire someone because you want to do the work yourself or for other reasons that do not reflect badly on the employee, or you must terminate someone's employment because you are moving. In those cases, you will want to do everything you can to help that person get another good job.

There are cases that fall into a gray area, in which you fire someone whose performance was only tolerable, but not really because of poor performance. In such cases, it is best to give a reference. Remember that it is cruel and unfair to hurt someone's chances of finding a new job without strong reasons. But you need not say anything dishonest. Describe the employee's strengths in a matter-of-fact way, and refer only briefly or gently to any weaknesses.

You do not need a salutation in a letter of reference unless your employee asks you to address the letter specifically to a particular person. Keep the letter on your computer and run it off as necessary, adding addresses, to send to prospective employers.

Here is how you might write a letter of reference for an excellent all-round house worker:

> Susan Jones has worked for me as a cleaner one day per week for three years, and she has done a superb job. She is leaving my employment only because I am moving out of town in four weeks. I give her my strongest recommendation.
>
> Ms. Jones is a highly competent cleaner who takes pride in her work and is so skillful that she seems to get everything done in no time. She does an excellent job in all areas of cleaning: dusting, vacuuming, floor washing, etc. She is particularly knowledgeable about laundering. On several occasions she has been willing to stay extra hours to do some ironing, and her ironing is of professional quality.
>
> Ms. Jones is also someone I enjoyed having in my home. She is honest, reliable, cheerful, and well-spoken.
>
> Please call me (222) 222-2222 if you have any questions about Ms. Jones or her period of employment with me.
>
> Sincerely yours,

Here is a letter for a "gray-area" situation, in which you have some reservations about this or that aspect of an employee's work, but no serious ones. For example, perhaps she often wanted to change her hours and this inconvenienced you. Perhaps she did a good job many days, but she too often let your child watch hours of television while she chatted on the telephone or dragged him along to the mall while she shopped instead of taking him to the playground.

> Jenny Gray worked for me as a part-time baby-sitter, for fifteen hours per week, from January through August 1999. Ms. Gray is experienced with young children and always deals with them patiently and kindly. She was conscientious about preparing healthy meals and snacks that Timmy enjoyed and never neglected any safety rules. She is an honest, pleasant person who enjoys and appreciates children. I found that I needed to give her guidance in choosing suitable play activities and, at times, had to be flexible about her hours.

Being Considerate

Do not expect your employee to stay extra hours or to come on different days, especially on little notice, unless you have clearly required a readiness to do so as part of the job. On such occasions, you should pay as generously as you can for the sacrifice of the employee's private life or adjustments in his or her work life that you are requesting.

Provide coffee, tea, or whatever beverages your employee prefers. It is thoughtful to provide fruit or breads or other foods for midmorning or afternoon snacks, if your employee likes them. If your arrangement requires you to provide lunch, make it a pleasant one.

Allowing Enough Time

Do not underestimate how hard the job is or how long it will take to complete. Unfortunately, I know from experience that it is all too easy to decide a job will be quick and simple when you are not the one who does it.

In New York City, the rule of thumb is that a cleaner can usually do the major cleaning of a one-bedroom apartment and some laundry in three to four hours. I would expect an average-sized house with two or three bedrooms and a bath and a half to take five or six hours, and that should allow a good deal of laundry to be done too. To do major cleaning and laundry for big houses and big apartments will take all day, and if you want any special chores done seasonally, monthly, weekly, or otherwise, you should plan to hire someone for an additional day or half day.

It takes half an hour to forty-five minutes to wash an average load of laundry, and anywhere from twenty minutes to an hour to dry it in an automatic dryer. Thus you should allow a minimum of four hours to do four loads using your washer and dryer. This can go faster if you live in an apartment building where more than one machine can be used at a time. Remember that your cleaner can keep the wash going while cleaning.

To save time for your cleaner, separate the wash before the cleaner arrives and get the first load going. Do all the neatening and putting away yourself, too, as most cleaners have a hard time knowing just where you want things to go, and it is difficult and slow work to clean around clothes, books, papers, toys, and other clutter. Keep a list of cleaning materials and tools that the cleaner always uses, and before he or she arrives make sure everything needed is in the house. If you are not going to be at home, leave a note describing any special chores or problems you would like the cleaner to attend to. Or, if you have nothing else to say in a note, just say hello, wish the cleaner a good day, and add your thanks. It can be a lonely business, going to people's empty houses to clean, and the cleaner needs to be appreciated just as the rest of us do.

The Combination Cleaner/Baby-sitter

The complaint that I hear most frequently comes from people who leave their children with a housekeeper/nanny while they work full-time. They often expect to come home to a clean house, washed dishes, and a bathed infant. Having kept a house and cared for an infant full-time, I can vouch that I often was not able to have the house neat, the dishes washed, and the baby bathed by 6:00 or 7:00 P.M., even with a husband who shared the work. The difficulty in accomplishing this was material for many jokes among members of my parents' generation.

Given how hard it is to care for an infant alone and clean house at the same time, it is potentially dangerous to insist on this. You may unwittingly pressure your employee into ignoring your child and doing housework instead. The clean house will speak for itself, but your infant will not be able to tell you for two or three years that he or she is being neglected, and by that time the child may think it is normal. The most important thing this employee does is attend to your infant, getting down on the floor to play, answering the child's cries promptly and lovingly, and doing all the rest that goes into the slow and patient care of the young.

With older children, particularly if they attend school, however, the expectation of a clean house—when it is part of your agreement as to your employee's duties—is not at all unreasonable, so long as you can be sure that your employee permits the children ample free use of the home. You can expect the dishes to be washed, the counters cleared, the beds made, and other light daily chores completed.

You can safely expect major cleaning from your caregiver only when your children are of an age to be quite self-sufficient—say eight and over. By and large, however, with the exception of the light daily routines just described, it is probably best to hire different people to care for your children and to do your housecleaning. And when the child is under three years old, you should often expect to find that the daily routine has been breached; the younger the child, the greater and more frequent the breaches. This may simply mean that you have a good caregiver who has his or her priorities straight.

Employee Information Sheets

It is helpful to make lists of information that cleaners, baby-sitters, and other domestic employees may need to know. I have a list that I give to a substitute cleaner when my regular one is on vacation or ill that includes such items as this on it:

> On the bathroom mirrors and cabinets, please do not use any cleaner that contains ammonia.
>
> On the piano and on the living-room and dining-room furniture, please use no wax or furniture sprays or polishes of any kind. Simply dust with a clean cloth.

The baby-sitter's guide should have blank spaces in which you can write out the name, address, and telephone number of the place you are going, the name and number of your pediatrician, and the names and numbers of a couple of close neighbors who could be called on for help in minor domestic emergencies such as a plumbing problem or a lack of milk. For infants and younger children, also list any allergies and explain where bottles, diapers, favorite toys, and similar necessities are kept.

Show the baby-sitter where your general list of emergency numbers—police, fire department, relatives, and so forth—is posted.

71

Insurance

Homeowners' insurance . . . Liability coverage . . . Property insurance . . . Real property . . . Personal property . . . Insurance for condominiums and co-ops . . . Mobile-home insurance . . . Renters' insurance . . . Special homeowners' coverage issues . . . Earthquake insurance . . . Flood and water damage insurance . . . Hurricanes and tornadoes . . . Computers . . . Other special cases . . . Home-based business insurance . . . Insurance coverage for domestic employees and workers in your home, liability, car, workers' compensation, and medical insurance for domestic employees . . . Administering your insurance policies . . . Paying premiums on time . . . Updating insurance . . . Real estate appraisals . . . Written inventories . . . Safe-deposit boxes . . . Making a claim . . . Insurance glossary

In your home, you ordinarily need several forms of insurance. Most importantly, whether you own or rent your home or live in a co-op, condominium, or some other type of housing, you need a homeowners' insurance policy. If you have a home office or operate a business in your home, you will usually need some form of separate or additional insurance. Households with domestic employees face several insurance issues, among them the desirability—or, sometimes, the necessity—of providing workers' compensation insurance. And insurance policies have to be managed; you cannot simply buy them and tuck them into a drawer. A summary of the relevant types of insurance and the principles of good management of your home insurance is set out below. Medical insurance, which is usually supplied through your job, and automobile insurance are not covered here.

Homeowners' Insurance

All insurance policies for the home may be called "homeowners' insurance policies," even those that are specifically for renters, but home insurance for renters is also called "renters'" or "tenants'" insurance. Homeowners' policies generally provide two basic kinds of insurance: property insurance and liability insurance. Property insurance covers loss of and damage to property from theft, fire, and various other causes or "perils." Liability insurance pays for injuries and damage, whether occurring in or out of your home, to other people or other people's property for which you are legally liable.

Your homeowners' insurance policy will include different types of insurance and different amounts of coverage depending on a variety of factors, such as the value and kinds of property to be insured, the type of home you have, and how much coverage you want or can afford or are required to carry by your mortgage company. The more coverage you buy, the more you will pay for your insurance. Various endorsements and separate policies may be necessary to supplement your basic policy's coverage. Even when you acquire a homeowners' insurance policy, you need separate medical insurance, car insurance, and other kinds of insurance; these areas are not covered by any standard policies for the home.

Liability Coverage Under Ordinary Homeowners' Insurance Policies. All basic types of homeowners' insurance policies, whether your home is rented or owned, include similar provisions for liability insurance. These protect you against liability for unintentional injury or damage you cause to someone else or to someone else's property. (See chapter 67, "Too Late to Say You're Sorry.") You are not insured against things you do intentionally; nor are criminal acts covered. Usually, the policy will make medical payments for injuries suffered by a third party, either at your home or away from it, as a result of something an insured member of your household does, or something a "residence employee" (a household or domestic employee) does in the course of his or her employment, regardless of fault. Read your own policy or call your agent to find out what it provides.

Liability insurance covers you whether or not the accident happens in or about your own home. If your dog bites the neighbor's child in the child's yard or digs up all the landscaping in a yard on the next block, if your child throws a baseball and breaks the neighbor's window, or if an elderly person falls on your steps, breaks a hip, and spends weeks in the hospital, your insurance will pay on your behalf amounts for which you might legally be liable. Generally in such cases, there is no lawsuit, and the parties settle on an amount out of court. The insurance company usually negotiates the amount to be paid.

A typical homeowners' policy offers a hundred thousand dollars' worth of liability insurance, which is not a great deal in the event that you or someone in your family causes serious injury or damage. For modestly increased premiums, you can triple or quadruple that amount, or go even higher, and it is worth doing. Otherwise, a lawsuit might entirely wipe out your savings and leave you financially devastated. You can also buy a "personal umbrella" policy, which is not expensive and offers you liability coverage for greater than that of your homeowners' policy.

Homeowners' (including renters') liability insurance covers injuries and damage caused by you, your spouse, your children or certain other relatives who live with you, your residence employees, and your pets. Unmarried cohabitants may buy insurance policies together just as married people do, but some insurance companies will impose limits on how many roommates or cohabitants can be covered by one policy. One company, for example, limits coverage to two. Homeowners' insurance policies typically exclude liability coverage for lawsuits by one member of the family against other members; for passing on infectious diseases; for injuries or damage arising out of the operation of home businesses, for car and other vehicular accidents; and for accidents that occur on your job. Always read your policy carefully.

A typical policy provides coverage for domestic employees such as baby-sitters, nannies, cleaners, and other regular employees in your home—unless you have workers' compensation insurance for them or are legally required to (even if you do not). It may be wise to buy workers' compensation insurance for your employees, if they are eligible, even when the law does not require you to, and to insist that other people's employees working in or about your home be covered by workers' compensation. (See pages 822–23, below.)

Property Insurance Under Standard Homeowners' Insurance Policies. Homeowners' policies contain fairly standard lists of "perils" or dangers that they insure property against. There are a variety of standard policy forms, which are numbered. HO-1, or basic coverage, which insures against eleven perils (see the list below), is no longer commonly used. HO-2, broad coverage, typically covers seventeen named perils, but it, too, is not used much. The standard form for homeowners today is HO-3, called special or "all-peril" coverage. It covers real property against all perils except for a number of exclusions specifically listed in the policy. The exclusions typically include earthquakes, floods, wars, and nuclear accidents, among others. (You can often buy additional coverage for excluded perils. See pages 819–20.) Under a typical HO-3 policy, personal property does not receive all-peril coverage but is insured against only the same seventeen named perils covered by HO-2. For an increased premium, HO-5 provides all-peril coverage, subject to specified exclusions, for both personal and real property. Or you can add endorsements to HO-3 to extend all-peril coverage to personal property. The HO-4 policy is for renters. It also covers seventeen perils but pays only for damage to personal property, not the structure; the contents of a house, in other words, but not the house itself are covered. HO-6 is the policy appropriate for residents of condominiums and co-ops; it also typically covers seventeen named perils and insures the contents and the interior of the home, but not the exterior structure. HO-8 is an economical policy offered for older homes with valuable but irreplaceable features, which pays only for repairs or actual value; it typically covers eleven perils. (Choose this only on the advice of a trustworthy professional.) The list below sets forth perils typically covered. The first eleven perils (fire through volcanic eruption) are those typically covered in HO-1 and HO-8. Different deductibles may apply to different perils; check your policy.

Fire or lightning

Windstorm or hail

Explosion

Riot or civil commotion

Aircraft

Vehicles

Smoke

Vandalism and malicious mischief

Theft

Breakage of glass that is part of a building

Volcanic eruption (sometimes)

Collapse of buildings (sometimes)

Falling objects

Weight of ice, snow, or sleet

Accidental discharge or overflow of water or steam from plumbing, heating, air conditioning, fire sprinkler, or appliance

Sudden and accidental tearing apart, cracking, burning, or bulging of steam or hot-water heating system, air conditioner, fire sprinkler, or appliance for heating water

Freezing of plumbing, heating, air conditioning, fire sprinkler, or household appliance

Sudden and accidental damage from artificially generated electric current

Insurance for a House You Own. Homeowners' insurance for a house you own usually covers the house plus outbuildings such as garages or toolsheds. Farmers and ranchers, however, would not be adequately insured with standard homeowners' insurance; there are special types of insurance for them. If you own a house, your bank or mortgage lender will insist on real property insurance as a condition of closing on the mortgage. Do not, however, assume that if you get what the bank or lender tells you to buy, you have adequate insurance. The bank may insist only that you acquire insurance in the amount of the mortgage. If your house then burns down, the bank will be fully paid off, but you may be left with too little to rebuild.

Ordinarily, you will want to insure your house for 100 percent of its replacement cost, not what you paid for it or what you might be able to sell it for today. If you do not insure your home for 100 percent of its replacement cost, in the event that it burns down, you will have to dig into your pocket for amounts your insurance does not pay in order to rebuild. Replacement-cost insurance costs more and is generally subject to various limits with which it is important that you familiarize yourself. For example, insurance companies usually impose a hidden penalty if you do not buy a minimum of 80 percent of the replacement cost. Suppose that the replacement cost of your home is $100,000 and you insure it for $80,000, or 80 percent of its replacement cost. Then suppose a fire causes $50,000 in damage. The typical policy will pay you $50,000. But if you had insured the same home only for $75,000, or 75 percent of its replacement cost, and experienced the same amount of damage, the insurance might pay you only 75 percent of $50,000, or $37,500—which leaves $12,500 for you to pay out of pocket.

Replacement-cost insurance also may not guarantee payment of the full replacement cost. In the wake of widespread natural disasters in the 1990s, many insurance companies stopped issuing policies that guarantee the full replacement cost of your home and instead cap payments at various levels, typically 120 to 150 percent of the insured value of your home. This can leave you in grave financial difficulty. If you have insured your house for $100,000, subject to a 120-percent cap, your maximum coverage is $120,000—even if it would cost $150,000 to rebuild.

Check for these and other limits on your potential recovery under your own policy.

Personal Property. No matter whether you own, rent, or live in a condominium or cooperative apartment, you need insurance for your personal belongings. You have clothes, dishes or fine china, furniture, appliances, jewelry, perhaps silver or furs or art work, and many other goods, furnishings, and types of equipment that can be stolen, burned up, or ruined by smoke or water from a burst pipe. Subject to deductibles and recovery limits, these losses will be covered by almost any homeowners' insurance. If you own a house, your homeowners' policy typically will offer coverage for your personal property in an amount up to half the insured value of your home; you can increase this amount by paying higher premiums. If you rent or own a condominium or co-op, coverage is selected for your personal property and other coverages are made a percentage of this amount.

Coverage for your personal property will be limited to the actual cash value of your goods when they were stolen or destroyed, unless you buy replacement-cost insurance. As with real-property insurance, replacement-cost insurance for personal property makes more sense, although it costs more. The upholstered chair for which you paid two thousand dollars five years ago will probably be valued at a fraction of that now. Buying replacement-cost insurance for your house also means that the ceiling on the coverage of your personal belongings—usually 50 percent of the amount for which your house is insured—is raised, typically to 70 or 75 percent.

Watch out for low coverage for items that are particularly vulnerable to loss by theft or fire, such as computers, expensive jewelry, furs, cash, silver, valuable papers, stamp or coin collections, manuscripts, and deeds. You can increase your coverage for such items by means of endorsements to your policy.

The portion of your homeowners' insurance policy that covers personal property loss or damage usually applies when the property is removed from your home—for example, when you are traveling. If your suitcases are stolen on vacation, they are covered, but check your policy for limits on the amount of coverage.

Typical policies may also cover a portion of your expenses when you are forced to live elsewhere as a result of damage to your home by fire or another cause. They generally pay you the difference between how much it ordinarily costs you to live and how much it costs you to live elsewhere (for example, in a hotel) until you can resume living in your permanent residence. There are many restrictions on these payments, and you will probably not get them if you move in with a friend or relative rather than into a hotel. Check your policy for limits on this coverage in dollar amounts and time periods. Some policies require that the insurance company, not the insured, choose the interim accommodations. (Save all your receipts for expenses to prove what you have spent.)

Those who operate home businesses, by the way, should buy extra insurance to cover the businesses. Typical homeowners' insurance policies have "business pursuits" limits or exclusions. See "Home-Based Business Insurance," below.

Insurance for Condominiums and Co-ops. Insurance on condominiums and co-ops covers the interior of the home and personal property against the same perils covered by ordinary homeowners' insurance. Like other homeowners' policies, the HO-6 also includes liability insurance and certain living expenses in case you need temporary accommodations after damage to your home.

Condominium owners sometimes underinsure because they wrongly believe they have adequate coverage through their condominium association. The condominium association will indeed have a master policy that insures the common areas of the building and the building itself, including the physical shell of your home. But this master policy covers nothing inside your unit—none of your furnishings, appliances, finished floors and walls, carpets, lighting fixtures, built-in shelving, wallpaper, or other additions. If you put in expensive flooring or remodel your kitchen or bathroom or build a deck or patio, you must buy your own insurance to cover these. The master policy will not cover them. You should also consider buying "loss assessment" insurance to cover assessments by your building's governing board to pay for uninsured losses or to pay for deductibles on insured losses. Such assessments can be large, and if you do not pay, foreclosure on your home could ultimately result. Before you buy your own insurance, read the master policy to see what it covers.

Mobile-Home Insurance. Mobile-home owners typically use a variation of HO-2. They have to pay more for insurance than those who live in houses and apartments because mobile homes are less sturdy and more vulnerable to wind and storm damage. Basic coverage is of the same types as homeowners' insurance: property insurance for the home itself and for its contents against theft, fire, and other perils, together with liability insurance. Just as with conventional homeowners' insurance, you must choose dollar amounts carefully, decide on cash-value or replacement-cost insurance, and so forth.

Mobile-home insurance has certain features that are different from conventional homeowners' insurance. Among these are the "Consent to Move" endorsement, which, among other things, waives a prohibition against moving the mobile home. Transportation coverage pays for collision damage to the mobile home and its contents while it is being moved to a new location. The lender who lent you money to buy the mobile home may also buy special insurance to protect its interest in your home. You may be subject to "tie-down" requirements if your mobile home is not anchored to a foundation. There may be a wind deductible, which you would have to pay before the insurance company's coverage takes over. Talk to your agent about these and other special issues raised by mobile-home insurance.

Renters' Insurance. If you rent your home, you still need insurance. Your furniture and other property is not covered by your landlord's insurance for his or her real estate. If you are a student and live in an apartment, your parents' homeowners' insurance will not cover you. If you live with roommates, you may or may not be able to share a policy. Check with an insurance agent; the rules are different in different states. Be sure to find out if you will need to update your policy in case one roommate moves out and another moves in. If your former roommate took away property that was specifically insured under the policy you shared, updating your policy will reduce your premiums. Some policies require that each roommate actually be named in the policy or may limit the number of unrelated people in one household that it will insure; others do not. Some companies allow unmarried couples to get insurance together; some automatically extend coverage to a "domestic partner." Be sure to confer with your insurance agent about your situation.

Renters' insurance does not cover your house or apartment itself (real property), only your belongings. Like homeowners' insurance policies, it also provides liability insurance and certain living expenses in case of need for temporary accommodations after damage to your home.

If you rent a house on property that includes other buildings that you want to insure, speak to your agent about additional coverage. The buildings are probably not covered under your basic policy.

Special Homeowners' Coverage Issues

Earthquake Insurance. Ordinary homeowners' insurance does not cover earthquakes; but it can be added to your homeowners' policy as an endorsement. According to the Insurance Information Institute, earthquakes have occurred in thirty-nine states in this century, with California and Washington most at risk. Yet few people have earthquake insurance. Even in California, the country's earthquake capital, most people are without it. Insurance against earthquakes is expensive in the quake-prone areas of the country, with high premiums and high deductibles.[1] In other areas, it is not.

Flood and Water Damage Insurance. Ordinary homeowners' insurance does not cover flood damage and many other forms of water damage. Find out whether you are located in an area that could be flooded. If so, ask your agent or the Federal Insurance Administration about the National Flood Insurance Program. In the event you experience flood damage, you should also check with your tax advisor or the IRS information service about the possibility of deducting flood damage as a casualty loss on your income tax.

Although standard policies cover water damage caused by burst pipes, they exclude any water damage caused by water that "touched the ground" before it did the damage, such as water seepage into your foundations or basement, sewer or drain backups, and any damage from water in or below the ground. They also exclude water damage from slow-leaking or dripping pipes.

Hurricanes and Tornadoes. Most homeowners' policies protect your home from damage from windstorms, snow, or hail. But be sure to read your policy to confirm that windstorms and other potentially dangerous weather conditions are covered. In areas prone to tornadoes and hurricanes, such as Florida and Texas, insurance against damage caused by tornadoes and hurricanes usually must be bought separately; but in areas where these dangers are remote, tornadoes and hurricanes are sometimes covered under ordinary homeowners' policies. Different deductibles may apply to losses from these causes; check your policy.

Computers. If your computer is used entirely for domestic purposes, it is probably insured under your homeowners' policy in the same manner as any of your other personal belongings. Computers nonetheless pose some special problems. Software is sometimes excluded from coverage altogether. Computers depreciate rapidly. Therefore you should check whether you have replacement-cost insurance for your personal property. Otherwise, your insurance may pay you only a fraction of what it would cost to replace the computer in today's market. If your computer is used for business purposes, it will fall under the business-pursuits limits (often around twenty-five hundred dollars for all your business equipment) and exclusions in your policy. Read the list of perils and determine whether damage that might happen to your computer is covered there. A power surge caused by lightning that damages your computer would probably be covered, but a power surge caused by your building management or your electric company would probably not be.

Laptops are usually insured in the same way as other computers while they are in your home, subject to the same limits and exclusions for business uses. (Your insurance will not cover one owned by your employer, even if the loss or damage occurs in your home.) Laptops may be subject to additional limits too. In your car or away from home, they may receive less coverage for theft than other belongings; under some policies, they may have no coverage at all away from home.

To avoid these problems, talk to your insurance agent about whether a business-use endorsement for your policy would be appropriate. Special computer insurance exists that will cover hardware, software, and related equipment; it insures against not only the standard perils but also losses caused by power surges, computer viruses, accidental breakage, and other causes. Special laptop computer insurance also exists that covers laptops used in business travel.

Other Special Cases. You can ask your agent about coverage for many types of loss, in addition to those mentioned above, that particularly concern you and that may not be adequately covered by a standard policy. Below are listed some issues that concern many people. There may be others that are relevant in your circumstances.

Country homes, summer homes, or cottages

Coverage for a garage apartment or separate living unit in your home or on your premises

Boats, planes, and other vehicles

Expensive outbuildings; expensive property stored in outbuildings

Pets

Food spoilage during power outages (for those with large freezers)

Fallen trees

Unauthorized use of your credit cards

Satellite dishes or antennae for television

Septic tanks

Basement flooding

Sewers

Termites or other insect or pest damage

Home-Based Business Insurance

If you operate a business from your home, you definitely need special insurance, and you may be running big risks without it. A homeowners' policy provides only limited and incidental coverage for your home office. Your homeowners' policy probably covers only two to three thousand dollars' worth of business equipment in your home, and only a few hundred dollars' worth toward damage or loss of equipment when it is away from home. For many people with home offices, this amount is grossly insufficient. Your homeowners' insurance probably provides no liability insurance at all for clients or business guests or their property that you keep in your home. It certainly will not insure you for lost income if you have to close up shop for a while because of damage to your home. Business supplies and inventory, records, data stored on computers, client lists, mailing lists, manuscripts, backup tapes, fax machines, copiers, computers, telephone systems—all these and much more may go uninsured if you have nothing more than your homeowners' policy. If you are running your business from an outbuilding of some sort, it may be entirely uncovered by your homeowners' insurance.

If your insurance company considers your home business "incidental," you may be able to add endorsements to your homeowners' policy to extend coverage to your business property and get business-liability insurance. Check with your agent about your insurance company's rules. Some define an incidental business as one that grosses less than five thousand dollars annually.

If your business is not incidental, you have several other options. First, you might buy a business owners' package policy, known as a "BOP." This covers business equipment and property, loss of business income, extra expenses resulting from fire or other insured perils, and business-liability insurance that covers both personal injury and property damage. Second, you might buy a "mini-BOP." This is a policy designed explicitly for a home business. It extends your homeowners' policy so that its personal-property insurance and liability insurance also cover your business. A mini-BOP will also cover loss of income from damage or loss from insured perils. Unfortunately, not all states have these policies, but one can expect such options to become more common as the popularity of running home businesses continues to increase.

Whatever type of policy you choose, it is also important to talk with your agent about all types of insurance that might be required or that it might be wise for you to consider given the nature of your business: umbrella liability policies, health insurance, and so forth. You are required to purchase workers' compensation insurance for business employees of your home-based business unless your business falls under an exemption.

Insurance Coverage for Domestic Employees and Workers in Your Home

Domestic employees, or "residence employees," as insurance policies call them, present many important insurance questions. There is no substitute for talking the issues through with a good insurance agent, and no substitute for reading the exact language of your own policy. The typical policies described below may not be like yours. Residence employees generally include people who help you with your domestic life: cleaners, nannies, maids, cooks, and personal attendants or companions (other than those who perform medical procedures) who care for an invalid or aging person in your home.

Liability Coverage for Domestic Employees. Your homeowners' liability insurance should cover any unintentional injuries or property damage caused by your residence employees during the course of their employment. It will not cover damage or injuries they may cause when they are not working for you.

Injuries suffered by your domestic employees will be covered to the same extent as injuries suffered by others unless the employees are covered by workers' compensation insurance or other legally required benefits, or unless you are required by law to buy workers' compensation insurance even though you have not done so. In the latter case, you are liable to pay for the costs of these injuries out of your own pocket, and you can be sued. See "Workers' Compensation Insurance."

Typical homeowners' policies include a business exclusion that would preclude coverage of business employees. Workers' compensation for such employees is probably required. (See below.)

Car Insurance. Ordinary automobile insurance covers family members who cause injuries or damage property while driving your car. Your domestic employees are probably covered by your insurance while driving your car, but just to be sure, you should add their names as insureds to your policy. (This may increase your premium, especially if your employees' driving record is not outstanding. But it is worth the additional expense.) Your car insurance, however, will not necessarily protect you when they are driving their own cars. As their employer, you will be held liable for damages that exceed the amount of their own coverage if they have an accident in their own car while working for you. For this reason, they should use only your car when on the job, or you should make sure they have high coverage limits on their own car insurance. You might also consider getting yourself listed as an additional insured on their policy.

Another problem to consider is that your employees' car insurance might not cover accidents that occur in a car used for business purposes. If their insurance company takes the view that ferrying around members of your family constitutes a business, your employees might need auto insurance that covers some business uses. These are matters to be discussed with your agent and your employees.

Workers' Compensation Insurance. Workers' compensation insurance is paid for by employers on behalf of employees. It covers injuries suffered on the job and occupational diseases. Workers' compensation does not ordinarily cover injuries suffered while coming from or going to work—only injuries suffered on the job. It covers some injuries suffered by employees while traveling on behalf of their employers. For example, if you send your cleaner out to the market, and he or she is injured in a car accident while doing your shopping, workers' compensation will probably pay. Workers' compensation benefits include the costs of medical treatment as well as disability pay, calculated as a given percentage of wages. The extent of medical coverage and disability pay varies from state to state. Workers' compensation also pays death benefits to the employees' families in case the employee suffers a fatal injury on the job.

Benefits are payable under workers' compensation no matter who (if anyone) is at fault—so long as the injury is not the result of willful misconduct on the employee's part. When a worker is covered by workers' compensation, he or she gives up the right to sue the employer because of on-the-job injuries and occupational diseases, even if the employer is at fault—unless the injury is a result of the employer's willful or intentional misconduct. The worker also gives up the right, which she or he would otherwise have, to sue for compensation for pain and suffering. The employee is limited to workers' compensation. (Exceptions to these rules are quite limited.) Whether or not you are required to obtain workers' compensation for your domestic employees, it is in your interest to do so when they are eligible for it. It is not costly, and it protects you from liability.

If workers' compensation is compulsory for domestic employees in your state and you fail to get it, your liability insurance under your homeowners' policy will not insure you for medical payments for injuries suffered by your domestic employees in the course of their employment. Likewise, if you obtain worker's compensation insurance for your employees, whether or not you are required to do so, your liability insurance under your homeowners' policy will not cover your employees' injuries.

In many states there is no requirement that you purchase workers' compensation for domestic employees such as maids, cleaners, nannies, and gardeners. In other states, you have no choice so long as the employees worked the minimum number of hours or earned more than a certain amount in wages. You may be required to purchase workers' compensation insurance even for part-time workers who work more than a given number of hours per week. The number of hours varies from state to state. In some states, workers' compensation is not required, but employers may choose to buy it anyway. (In New York, for example, it is required for domestic employees who work more than forty hours per week, but those who work fewer hours are also eligible for it.) The law as to which workers are eligible for workers' compensation varies from state to state. If your employees are not domestic employees, but business employees working for you in your home-based business, you are probably required by law to provide workers' compensation insurance for them.

When you obtain workers' compensation insurance, be sure to be thoroughly informed about compliance requirements in your state. Remember that workers' compensation is separate from social security and income tax. You need not pay the latter in order to get the former; neither do you fulfill your requirements for workers' compensation by paying social security or income taxes. In many states, there are regulations that allow you to opt out of workers' compensation under certain circumstances, but opting out may not be desirable. For example, it may entail your agreeing to pay medical expenses and lost wages out of your own pocket. Even if you wish to opt out, it is important to become familiar with the rules governing how you do so, to avoid violating state law. In addition, you should not attempt to provide workers' compensation for a nanny or cook through your business. Because they are actually domestic employees, and do not work for your business, that would be fraud. There are civil and criminal penalties for failure to comply with the workers' compensation laws.

When other people's employees work in or about your home, it is also in your interest to ensure that their own employers provide them with workers' compensation. Never do business with anyone who is not bonded or insured. If you hire a maid service, ask for proof that the service bonds and insures its workers. Ask a contractor for a "certificate of insurance." This means that if the contractor's employees cause injury or damage to you or someone else, their own employer has insurance that will cover it. You can be more confident that losses to you caused by the employees will be made good. If the contractor's employees themselves are injured, they are less likely to think about suing you, and the contractor is less likely to think about looking to you for indemnification.

Your insurance agent will be able to arrange for you to purchase workers' compensation insurance, or will refer you to someone who can provide it.

Employee Medical Insurance. No law requires you to provide medical insurance for your domestic employees. It may still be in your interest to do so, however, as most domestic employees cannot afford to provide it for themselves. Not only will your job look more desirable to the best candidates if you offer medical insurance, but an uninsured worker who is emotionally part of your household may well look to you for help in paying medical bills anyway; and you may feel obligated to provide it or suffer great guilt about refusing to. It is illegal, by the way, to put a domestic employee on your business's payroll for insurance purposes (or any purposes). This amounts to tax fraud.

Administering Your Insurance Policies

Keeping Your Insurance in Order. *Pay your premiums on time!* Write down the dates on which premiums are due in your diary. Your policy is in effect only for the policy period stated on your premium notice. The insurance company will cancel your insurance if your premium is late, but will give you a certain number of days' notice before canceling. Once it has given notice of cancellation, you should consider yourself uninsured as of the cancellation date until you receive written notice from the company that your policy has been reinstated or that the cancellation has been withdrawn. Do not assume that you are still covered if you make a payment after the cancellation date. Insurance companies have the right to take payment but refund it if they decide not to continue the policy. If you are unsure of your status, call the company.

Ask your insurance company what security measures you can take to reduce your premiums. Some companies will give you a discount for using certain types of locks, alarm systems, or other means of increasing the security of your home.

Update your insurance so that you do not become underinsured. When you buy your insurance, inventory the contents of your home so that you can be sure you have adequate coverage. Have a professional determine the accurate replacement cost of your belongings. Have works of art, jewelry, valuable collections, and similar items appraised. In many instances, this will mean getting a formal appraisal from a certified expert. You will receive documentation from the appraiser, which you should store with your insurance policies and inventory list.

Once a year, review your insurance policies. Read them and, if you have questions, call your agent. Learn what is and is not covered and what the coverage limits are. Check your inventory list and update it.

Have your real estate appraised every few years. Every few years get an appraisal of how much it would cost to rebuild your home and make sure you have insurance that would cover the replacement cost. If you go for five years without an appraisal, you may let yourself become seriously underinsured. You can either hire an appraiser or have your agent or insurance company do this. But remember that the insurance company has an interest in coming up with a low appraisal, and you want a high one. If you choose to hire your own appraiser, your bank, a reliable local real-estate agent, or your state's appraisal licensing board will be able to recommend one to you. Make sure that changes in building codes are taken into account. You may need a special endorsement to your policy to cover any extra costs estimated to arise from new code provisions. Save all documents your appraiser gives you. Immediately call your insurance agent if the appraisal shows you have become underinsured.

If you make any additions or improvements to your home, such as a new deck or bathroom or remodeled kitchen or a room addition, do not wait: have an appraisal done immediately and increase your insurance coverage as necessary.

You might consider adding an inflation-protection clause to your policy if you don't have one already. Inflation-protection or inflation-guard clauses are supposed to protect you by automatically increasing the amount of your insurance to keep pace with inflation, but some people making claims have been disappointed with these provisions, which, they say, fail to keep pace with the increase in prices. Do not conclude that because you have such a clause you needn't periodically review your insurance to see whether inflation of one sort or another or other causes have rendered your coverage inadequate. Pay attention to rebuilding costs in particular. Do not forget to consider the impact of changed building codes on building costs; make sure your policy will cover additional costs resulting from building code changes.

Keep a written inventory of your belongings. Make a list of all your personal possessions that shows as much about their value as possible. Remember to include everything you own: each piece of furniture and its cost; draperies, shutters, blinds, and other window coverings; lawn or deck furniture and its replacement cost; appliances; pets; lamps; dishes; stereo systems; televisions; computers; musical instruments; linens; silverware; kitchen equipment; tennis rackets and other items used in games and hobbies; and so forth. You need not count each sock; simply write down "clothing." But you can assign a figure estimating how much it could cost you to replace everything you list under "clothing." Anything you own that is costly (including furs or expensive designer clothes) should be individually listed, and its replacement cost, appraised value, or market value should be written down. Keep all purchase and credit-card receipts showing how much you paid for insured items. Keep all documents showing the appraised values of insured items. Write down the brand names, model numbers, serial numbers, and dates of purchase for all appliances, equipment, and machines. Take photographs or videos of everything in your home. (Two photos and videos of everything are a good idea—one for you and one to give to the insurance company in case you make a claim.) Open every closet door and take pictures of the contents. Take pictures of kitchen drawers and appliances. All this documentation will help you enormously in case you must make a claim on your insurance policy. Some insurance professionals say that the photos are actually easier to deal with than the videos, which take much longer to review and make it much harder to locate any particular item you may be trying to find. Videos also make updating an inventory a bit more complicated.

Keep your inventory list, pictures or videos, and policies in a safe place. A safe-deposit box, a relative's home, or your business office are good choices. If you keep it at home, you must be sure that it is safe from fire, water, and other damage. A home safe that is bolted down and is fireproof may be your best bet. (Wrap the list in plastic, put it in a tightly closed Tupperware container, and place it in the safe.)

Update your inventory list as necessary. When you make a new major purchase, add it to your inventory, along with all the necessary documentation. If it is expensive, call your insurance agent and make whatever changes are necessary in your policy to have it properly insured. A fancy new stereo, carpet, computer, or similar big-ticket item should be protected by insurance without delay. Some of the things that you own may require periodic appraisals: jewelry, watches, furs, works of art such as paintings and sculpture, collections of stamps, antique guns, antiques, silver, china, and valuable musical instruments. Each such item must be written down, along with its appraised value. When an appraisal shows that its value has increased, call your agent and increase your insurance coverage accordingly. Less commonly, you may learn that you are overinsured—if an antique depreciates in value (and replacement cost), or if you sell or give something away.

Finally, keep a running total of the value of your personal belongings as listed. After you update your list, and annually during your insurance review, make sure your insurance coverage is adequate for the total and for each individual item.

Insure all valuables stored in bank safe-deposit boxes. Bank safe-deposit boxes are by and large a secure place to store valuables and important records and papers. They are not fail-safe, however. When your town is flooded, so is your bank, and so is your safe-deposit box in your bank. Banks can suffer fires too. Your diamonds will survive floods and fires both, but your antique watches, deeds, and stock certificates may not. In such a case, the bank will probably not be liable to you for the damage. You must insure the goods in your safe-deposit box yourself. Flood insurance ordinarily will not cover anything stored in a safe-deposit box, so you may need to obtain an endorsement that will. Remember to list the items in the safe-deposit box on your inventory and to check whether you need any special endorsements or additional coverage to insure them adequately.

Making a Claim. First, call the police to report thefts or burglaries. Call credit-card companies, banks, and other card issuers to report theft or loss of credit cards or bank cards. Then call your insurance agent immediately. Take whatever steps you must to prevent continuing damage, but otherwise do not engage in cleanup or repairs until you speak to your agent. Obviously you must call the plumber right away to get the burst pipe fixed or the water turned off. When you must have emergency work done, take before-and-after pictures, if you can, and keep careful records of costs. Get receipts for all work done and materials purchased.

When you speak to your agent, explain what happened: when, how, and what, initially, you think has been lost. Ask about your coverage and whether there is a deductible. Ask how long you will have to wait for your insurance payments. Ask whether to proceed with repairs and whether you need to get estimates. If you are going to have to seek temporary housing, discuss this with the agent. Ask how you go about getting reimbursed under the policy, and about the limits of coverage for living expenses under your policy. (If you accept temporary living accommodations, save receipts proving exactly what you have to spend—for rooms, rent, meals, and so forth.)

After you have called your agent, follow up with a letter repeating what you told the agent on the telephone. He or she will send you a claims form, or a representative will visit you with one. Prepare a comprehensive list of lost or damaged articles. Assemble documentation, including your proof of what you owned and its value (photos, receipts, appraisals) and your proof of its loss or damage. If you have made a report to the police, get a copy of the report from the police station. This will be usually be demanded as part of your proof of theft or burglary. Make photocopies of everything, and keep the originals (or one of your duplicate photographs). When you fill out your forms for the insurance company, provide the photocopies, not the originals, for documentation, unless your insurance company is one of the few that demand the originals. In that case, keep clear copies for your records. Cooperate with the insurance company's representative and fill out any necessary forms promptly. Try not to leave anything out. If you remember something later that should have gone on the list, you may have a hard time getting reimbursed for it. At a minimum, you may slow down the whole process.

The insurance company will probably send an adjuster to estimate the cost of making major structural repairs; the adjuster, who is an employee of the insurance company, will often produce a low estimate. Before you sign off on whatever settlement amount the adjuster comes up with, get a bid from a reputable contractor, in writing, to make sure that the adjuster's estimate will really cover the bill. Usually this will suffice, and the insurance company will accept the realistic bid. But in case you end up in a dispute, involve your agent and a person higher up in the insurance company's claims department. In the worst case, refuse to sign the settlement and call a lawyer. This is uncommon, but if it should happen, you will want all the evidence you can provide that you have met your own obligations under the policy and that the insurance company's offers are too low, so save every scrap of paper and every picture that can support your claim.

Glossary of Insurance Terms

Actual Cash Value. What property is worth for insurance-recovery purposes, calculated as the replacement cost less depreciation.

Deductible. The portion of a loss or claim that you agree to pay. For example, if your home suffers a thousand dollars' worth of damage from a broken water pipe and your deductible is a thousand dollars, your insurance company will pay you nothing. But if your home suffers five thousand dollars' worth of damage from a broken water pipe and your deductible is a thousand dollars, your insurance company should pay you four thousand dollars. By choosing a higher deductible, you can usually lower your premiums considerably.

Domestic Partners. Two people who are unmarried and living together.

Endorsement. An extra provision attached to the end of a homeowners' policy that changes or adds to the policy's original terms.

Fire-Protection Class. A classification assigned to every neighborhood in the country by the Insurance Services Office, according to how good the fire protection is. This assignment reflects such considerations as how far your home is from a water source and how good the firefighting is in your neck of the woods. Your fire-protection class affects how much you pay for insurance. If you have good fire protection, you should get a lower premium.

Floater Policy. An insurance policy whose protection follows movable property around, giving coverage wherever the property is taken.

Personal Property. Furniture, clothes, books, curtains, equipment, and any other material objects that are not real property.

Premium. The amount of money that you pay periodically for insurance.

Real Property. Land, houses, and buildings.

Replacement Cost. What it would cost to replace property in the current market.

72

Fond Records

Safe storage for paper . . . Scrapbooks . . . Important documents and records . . . How long to retain business records . . . Keepsakes . . . Computer records . . . Instruction manuals . . . Safes for valuables and important papers, media safes for videotapes, cassettes, photographic negatives . . . How to replace or acquire important documents: passports, social security cards or numbers, driver's license, divorce decree and other court documents, wills, birth certificates, marriage certificates, stocks and bonds, insurance policies and pension plans, bank documents

Your history is in your home, and record-keeping is therefore an important part of housekeeping. Business records are essential for your financial welfare and security. Personal records—pictures, letters, documents, programs, videos, and objects—remind you of people and events in your past. They help you remember and understand the last generation, and help the next generation remember and understand you. In most homes, mementos are carefully kept, and periodically there are times of reminiscence. Looking at photographs and reading letters is part of the process of integrating a life, and often precedes or follows changes—new ventures or ambitions, moving, graduations, births, and deaths.

Safe Storage for Paper

Most records are on paper. You need not worry too much about business records such as tax forms that are going to be thrown away after a number of years; just keep these dry and out of the heat. But paper records that you want to last your lifetime or your grandchildren's—birth certificates, marriage certificates, deeds, bonds, stock certificates, correspondence, collections of paper objects such as postcards or baseball cards—need a little more care:

- Keep all stored paper in a cool, dry place.
- Paper that is folded will grow weak and tear along the fold line.
- Store paper in acid-free, lignin-free boxes, or safe metal or plastic.
- Do not laminate papers! This may seem to be a way to keep papers from damage, but in fact the materials in the laminate, over time, will accelerate the deterioration of paper.
- Keep papers out of the light, especially direct sunlight and fluorescent light. Very important or cherished papers should be stored in the dark.
- Do not store in adhesive or "magnetic" plastic covers or polyvinyl chloride. Use only safe plastics such as polypropylene, polyethylene, or Mylar for interleaving or plastic covers. (See chapter 53, "Images and Recordings.")

There are ways to de-acidify paper by treating it with alkaline substances. De-acidified paper can then be "encapsulated," placed and sealed within sheets of safe plastic. But it takes training to carry out this operation. Do not attempt it on your own; seek expert help. Among the potential disasters: ink can be dissolved by the de-acidifying solutions.

Scrapbooks

Scrapbooks are a conservator's headache because they usually consist of a variety of media that require different kinds of protection and can potentially damage one another in storage. If you have a prized scrapbook or are thinking of making one, use archival materials whenever you can and similar media to the extent that you can. You might even seek expert advice if you plan on putting cherished pictures or objects into it. Photographic experts or conservators of various sorts can help. Or check the Internet, which lately posts great quantities of material on the subject. But if you decide to follow advice you find on the Internet, be sure that it comes from someone who really knows what he or she is talking about, for example, a librarian, museum curator, conservator, or reputable authority on antiques.

Important Documents and Records

There are many good systems for maintaining important home records and documents. Here is one that is simple and adequate for all but the most complicated households. It calls for you to maintain just two basic business file boxes, one related to long-term and the other to short-term matters. (Keepsakes are best stored separately.)

For the first, maintain a file box called "Long-Term Business Records." Its size will depend upon the quantity of business records you have to store. (You may wish to keep two or three boxes and label their contents. It is better to have two or more small ones that you can lift on and off the shelf than one that is too heavy for you.) A metal or acid- and lignin-free cardboard file box of any sort will be fine, but it should be lidded so that dust does not get into your papers. Include in it, tucked into labeled file folders properly dated, all important family and household documents that you keep in your home. Put the file box in a safe place. *Include in the box a list of all the important papers and documents that you are keeping in a safe-deposit box away from your home.* Be sure to state on the list which banks hold your safe-deposit boxes and what is in each of them.

Here is a list of important papers and documents that most of us must keep safe. I have placed an asterisk after each that you might consider placing in a safe-deposit box. If, when you are at home, you might wish to refer to any of the documents that you are placing in a safe-deposit box, keep a copy of them in your long-term business file at home. Also keep in this file all of the following original documents that you are not putting into your safe-deposit box.

Keep the following records and documents permanently or as long as they are in effect. Keep documents relating to assets, investments, pensions, and property of all sorts for at least seven years after the date on which you dispose of the property. Keep insurance policies, contracts, and similar documents for at least seven years after they have expired.

Documents concerning property ownership
- Leases*
- Deeds and titles*
- Stock certificates*
- Bonds*
- Automobile purchase papers and title*
- Promissory notes*
- Mortgages and loan papers*
- Cancelled checks and documents relating to home purchase, major improvements, and maintenance*

Brokers' statements of assets and holdings

Other investment records and statements, related documents

Pension records and statements, related documents

Insurance policies

Household inventory—list of insured assets; appraisals; photos or videotapes of listed items*

Medical insurance policies, HMO documents and policies

Legal documents
- Copies of wills* (copy at home and/or safe-deposit box, stating name and address of attorney; keep original in attorney's office)
- Marriage certificates*
- Birth certificates*
- Death certificates*
- Prenuptial agreements*
- Court orders and decrees (custody, divorce, alimony, marital separation, adoption)*
- Passports*
- Social security card*
- Naturalization, citizenship, and immigration papers*
- Military draft and discharge papers*
- Trust agreements*

Baptismal certificates and other religious records

Graduation certificates and diplomas

Lists of banks and accounts

List of safe-deposit boxes and their contents

List of contents of home safe

Attorneys' names and addresses

Names and addresses of all family doctors, dentists, and other medical care providers

Contracts (except that you may wish to store appliance service contracts with appliance manuals)

Retain the following records for seven years:

Tax forms and filings plus all supporting documentation for preceding years (current tax documents go in your short-term business file)*

Canceled checks and bank statements*

Receipts, bills, and invoices of purchases and sales and other business transactions (for the preceding three years)

Medical records, medical bills, documents relating to transactions with HMOs and medical insurance companies

Credit card statements and paid bills from previous years (not current ones)

At the beginning of the new calendar year or when you do your taxes, go through your home long-term business file box and remove any documents that no longer need to be kept, such as tax records more than seven years old, or insurance policies that expired more than seven years ago. Periodically do a similar housecleaning of your safe-deposit box. Update inventories, lists, and names and addresses of your lawyer, doctor, dentist, etc.

As for the second type of business records, the short-term ones, in each calendar year label a file box "Monthly Business Records—200X [current year]." In it, place thirteen roomy envelope folders, twelve of them labeled with the names of the months and one labeled "Taxes—200X [current year]." As you proceed through a month, place all business documents that you receive that month into the appropriate envelope. Thus in the folder marked "February" you will tuck the credit card receipts and doctors' bills that you get in February, your February bank statements and bills, premium notices, and other business mail you get in February (other than those that belong in your long-term file box). However, in any month in which you receive a tax document—a form, a statement of wages or interest earned—place those in the folder labeled "Taxes." Thus when in January or February 2001 you receive statements of interest or wages earned in 2000, put them in "Taxes—2000."

At the end of the month, or at whatever time (or times) of the month you pay your bills or submit insurance claims, you will have everything you need in one place. Write out your checks or fill out your forms, and mark the bill in your folder "paid" and initial the date. Retain bill stubs in the folder; do not throw them out. The next month's bank statement, which will contain copies of the canceled checks, will be stored in next month's folder.

When you do your annual taxes or submit them to your accountant or tax preparer for preparation, you will have an easy time finding all relevant documents if you use this system. If you are itemizing your deductions, you simply go through each month's envelope and record the deductible items, both their nature and their amount. If you wish, you can clip all of them together with a label, "Deductibles—February." These documents must be *kept*, as they are your proof that you are entitled to the deduction.

Once you have signed your tax forms for a year—say the year 2000—and you are prepared to submit them, first copy them, including all documents you are submitting with them, such as schedules and W-2's. Place the copies in the tax folder labeled "Taxes—2000" together with all supporting documentation, such as receipts, bills, and canceled checks (or copies of checks, as you will keep your bank records as long as your tax records), and put them in the long-term business file box. Now you have in one box your tax records and the documentation you would need in case of an audit or an error.

If you make estimated tax payments during the course of the year, you can easily put all the relevant material in the tax folder. It makes your life easy when the annual tax time comes around.

When your annual tax forms are filed and any refunds due have been received, go through your short-term business records for that tax year and put anything you need to save in your long-term file.

Keepsakes; Personal Records

Correspondence, programs, children's school records, diaries, and similar records are keepsakes that it makes sense to gather in one central location. You might store them where you keep your business records, in the home office, desk, or file cabinet. Or keep a trunk or storage box for them. Some families like to keep a separate box or chest for each child.

Computer Records

Some household records are conveniently kept on the computer, but whenever possible print out a copy of the material you have stored. Two records are always better than one.

Back up your computer *every time you put anything new on your hard disk that you will need again.* Put your backup tapes in a safe, designated place. Do not shift the storage place from day to day.

Important documents should always be printed out, even if you have a backup. These include children's reports and term papers on which they have labored for long periods, or a memorandum or minutes that you prepared for the PTA, especially when they are based on notes you have not retained.

It is useful to retain all your letters on the computer. This saves you from having to re-input addresses and salutations, and often you can recycle an old letter by simply changing names, addresses, dates, and a few words. For example, if you are writing letters of recommendation for an employee, you can use the first one as a template for all the others. Just copy it into a new file and change as you wish.

Some people input their recipes, or at least those that are not contained in one of their cookbooks. This is useful when you want to be able to search for particular ingredients, since not all ingredients are obvious from the titles of recipes or the categories under which they may be filed. However, you will usually need to print out a recipe to use it in cooking. If you would be devastated to lose your collection of computer recipes, be sure to make backups and print out copies.

Instruction Manuals

Whenever you buy any machine, appliance, or household article that comes with an instruction manual or care instructions, immediately (but after reading it!) slip it into one of three pouch files labeled "Major Appliances" (in which you keep the booklets for your stove, refrigerator, microwave, washer and dryer, air conditioners, lawn mower, vacuum cleaner, and so on), "Small Appliances" (for blenders, food processors, can openers, handheld vacuum cleaner, calculators, telephones, answering machines), and "Miscellaneous Booklets and Instruction Sheets" (on caring for pots and pans, furniture, bicycles, special articles of clothing).

Safes for Valuables and Important Papers

Valuable papers; jewels and jewelry; cherished diaries, photographs, or other items of great sentimental value; hard-to-replace items such as birth certificates, passports, and marriage certificates; and many other important possessions are susceptible to damage or loss from fire, water, smoke, theft, and misplacement or accidents. The two best options for guarding against such dangers are to place them in a safe-deposit box at your bank or to invest in a safe for your home. Many people do both, since each course of action has certain advantages over the other.

The bank gives your valuables great security against theft. Even banks get robbed, but loss of valuables from safe-deposit boxes is extremely rare. Banks are less likely to be burned down or experience smoke damage than a home; and water damage to items stored in a bank is a likelihood only if the whole town is flooded. (But this can happen; it did happen, for example, during the terrible floods in the Midwest in 1993. To guard against losses from a disaster of this kind, you should insure items stored in safe-deposit boxes, in case the bank is not liable for losses stemming from causes other than its own negligence.) The problem with bank safe-deposit boxes, in my experience, is that while they keep cherished items safe, they also keep them where you cannot look at them or enjoy them or show them to your children or relatives or friends. We keep some old family jewelry, which has more sentimental than monetary value, in our safe-deposit box. This keeps it safe, but we might as well not own it, since I have not laid eyes on it for six or seven years now. Although I always plan to go get it and wear it sometimes, I just never remember in time. Perhaps more sensibly, we keep copies of manuscripts in progress in the safe-deposit box when we go out of town, in case our offices and our latest backup tapes burn up with our computers. (Sometimes, though, we just put backup tapes in an outside office.)

A home safe has the advantage of keeping your documents and valuables where you have immediate access to them. The problem is that they are more vulnerable to both theft and damage at home, even in a safe. But there are many different kinds of safes, and if you choose wisely, you can minimize some of the dangers.

Some safes are fire resistant; some safes are burglar resistant; some safes are both; some safes are neither. Some safes will offer good protection from tornado or earthquake damage—they will not break if dropped from heights. Moreover, there are varying degrees of fire and burglar resistance. Roughly speaking, the safer the safe, the more it costs; and the safer the safe (from both fire and theft), the bigger and heavier it is. To spend your money wisely and get the most security, consider just what you want your safe to do. If you have put items of great monetary value in your bank safe-deposit box, what you may really want from a home safe is good fire protection and, maybe, a little security. You can buy just this. But if you are very concerned about theft—if, say, you do not use a bank for some valuables—a safe of this kind will not be enough. And no safe will protect your goods from water damage. Some experts suggest that if you have anything that you want to protect from water, you wrap it in plastic wrap, put it in a closed Tupperware container, and place it in your safe. (But if it is paper or an antique, do not forget that you must be alert to the usual dangers: you need archival storage materials, control over humidity and temperature, and so on.) In general, according to the National Crime Prevention Institute, you are best off with a heavy safe bolted to the basement floor for protection against burglary, fire, or a tornado. But if you are worried about flooding, you want to place the safe upstairs.

When buying a safe, always buy one that has been UL-rated. UL burglary ratings indicate how long the safe will resist the efforts of thieves to get in. Expensive burglary safes can resist a blowtorch for an hour; less expensive safes might withstand burglar tools for fifteen minutes. "X6" on the label would mean that the rating applies to all six sides of the safe. To prevent theft, your safe should either be bolted down securely or be too heavy for anyone to cart off. Otherwise, by getting a safe you are making things easy for the thieves, obligingly placing everything you own that is worth money in one convenient package that they can carry away and open at their leisure someplace else. Note that in some homes you will not be able to bolt down a safe or the floors will not be strong enough to support a very heavy one, so this is something to talk about before you buy a safe. Talk over with the salesperson the issue of where you will put the safe, too. There are wall safes and floor safes and other kinds. Location can greatly add or detract from security.

Fire ratings indicate how long the interior of the safe will remain at a relatively low temperature; for example, a 350°F, one-hour rating means that the interior will not get hotter than 350°F for one hour in an ordinary fire of 1700° to 1800°F. Most fires will not last longer than an hour, and paper will usually not begin to scorch unless it is heated over 350°F; so this rating would vastly increase your fire security.

This sort of safe would be inadequate, however, if you were using it to store computer tapes, tape cassettes, videotapes, or photograph negatives. To protect these, you would need a safe that would keep its contents below 125°F, as magnetic tapes are damaged at temperatures above that. For less money than you would spend on a burglar-resistant safe, you can buy a media "chest" or media safe for these items that will keep them below 125°F for, typically, half an hour. Such safes also offer some degree of protection against magnetic fields (mild ones), humidity, dust, and invasion of privacy.

I Lost It: How to Replace or Acquire Important Documents

It is a good housekeeping practice to conduct a periodic inventory, annual or biannual, of important legal documents and papers to determine that all are present and accounted for and that none have expired. What follows is general advice on how to acquire or replace some important types of documents if you have lost them. An inexpensive booklet titled "Where to Write for Vital Records" (S/N 017-022-01196-4) put out by the U.S. Department of Health and Human Services tells you where to get birth, death, and marriage certificates and divorce decrees in each state. To order this booklet, contact the Superintendent of Documents, U.S. Government Printing Office, Washington, D.C. 20402.

In the material that follows, you will find frequent references to your "county clerk." The county clerk is the clerk of the court for the county in which you reside. The county clerk's telephone number and address are usually to be found in the court listings of the state government section of your telephone directory. (In New York City, because the city and county are coextensive, look under the city government listings.)

Procedures for acquiring the documents listed below may change, and some procedures are quite different in different states and cities. There is no avoiding the need to confirm proper procedure for your area and your situation.

Passports. The forms you will need to fill out in order to replace, renew, or acquire a passport for the first time are available at many U.S. post offices, federal courthouses, county clerk's offices, federal buildings, or other government centers. Check your telephone directory governmental listings under "United States Government, Passport" for the office nearest you. (If you cannot find the information in the directory and a telephone operator does not know the answer, call the Federal Information Center at 800-688-9889.)

First-Time Application. Fill out Form DSP-11. If you are eighteen or older, bring this form and (i) a certified birth certificate, (ii) a valid driver's license with your picture, (iii) two identical passport photographs (taken within six months of the date of your application, 2" X 2," in color or black-and-white), and (iv) $65 ($40 for children under eighteen), to the post office or the office where you got the forms (or to the place to which that office directed you). They will accept your application and mail your passport to you.

For children under eighteen, you need, in addition to Form DSP-11, (i) a certified birth certificate, (ii) two passport photographs (which are subject to the same requirements as adults'), and (iii) $40.

Replacing a Lost or Stolen Passport. If you do not report your passport lost or stolen, the government's records will indicate that you have a passport and you will not be issued a new one until you do so. If it is lost or stolen, report this without delay. Fill out Form DSP-11 and Form DSP-64 (which asks for a description of the circumstances under which the passport was lost or stolen). Then follow the same procedure as for applying for a first-time passport.

Renewing a Passport. You can renew your passport by mail. If you are eighteen or older, fill out Form DSP-82 and mail it together with (i) your old passport, (ii) two passport photographs, and (iii) $55 to the address indicated on the form. To renew a child's passport, follow the same procedure as for a child's first-time passport. This procedure applies even if your passport has expired, so long as it expired not more than two years ago. If it expired more than two years ago, you must follow the same procedure as you would in applying for a first-time passport. Rush procedures are available but cost more. The time that both rush and normal procedures take varies from city to city. In New York, I have renewed by mail in two weeks; I have friends who have succeeded in renewing overnight using a third-party private service specializing in quick passport renewals. (They do the waiting in line for you and often have contacts in the back office.)

Social Security Card/Number. To apply for a first-time social security number, you must fill out Form SS-5. To obtain this form, you can either visit the nearest Social Security Administration office (check your telephone directory's U.S. government listings for an address and telephone number) or call the Social Security General Information number, (800) 772-1213, and request that the form be mailed to you. If you apply for a card for your child, you will need the child's birth certificate (an original, not a copy) and one more document showing identity, such as a doctor or hospital bill or school record. You will also need to identify yourself with two forms of identification: a birth certificate and one more, such as a driver's license, passport, marriage certificate, or doctor's records. You can deliver the form together with the required documentation to your local social security office personally, or you can mail them in. In the latter case, however, you will receive no guarantee as to the return of your documents, so it is best to go personally if you can possibly manage it. Non-U.S. citizens must show their birth certificates or passports plus Immigration and Naturalization Service documents—green card (I-151 or I-551) or Form I-94. (Only originals will be accepted.)

Driver's License. The requirements vary enormously from state to state. Call or visit the relevant state office. It is called the Department of Motor Vehicles in many states; call your state government information number if you cannot determine the name of the appropriate agency from your telephone directory.

In order to get a license, in most states you must be sixteen years of age or older and you will have to pass a written test as well as a driving test. The motor vehicles department will supply you with preparation materials. You will be required to supply proof of identity, for example, one or more of a certified birth certificate, passport, major credit card, or social security card. Call or write or drop by in advance to find out just what your state accepts.

A permit is issued to allow you to practice driving in preparation for your driving test; it will expire after some period of time. Driver's licenses must also be renewed at regular intervals (in my own state, every four years). Some states require some type of examination upon renewal, often an eye examination.

When you move from one state to another, you are invariably required to get a driver's license from that state and to give up your old one. Sometimes getting the new license requires various examinations and proof of identity; sometimes it does not.

Deeds. If you have lost the deed to your house, you can get another from the county in which the property is located. Very often these records are obtainable in the county courthouse; you must simply find the right room. For information you can call the county clerk. The proper office may be known as the Registry of Deeds, the Register and Recorder's Office, or the Hall of Records. In New York City, you go to the City Register. You will usually be charged $.25 to $1 per page for an uncertified copy and between $.50 and $2 per page for a certified copy ($4 in New York, plus a three- or four-day wait), together with a separate certification fee of $1 or more. A deed tells exactly who owns the property (one or more people), what property is owned, and exactly where it is. You need the deed to prove your title to the property—not only that you have title but what kind of title (fee simple absolute or "for ten years" or a life estate)—and to pass title to anyone else.

Divorce Decree. You may usually obtain a copy of your divorce decree from the county clerk's office in the county or court in which the divorce was granted or from your state health department. The office of the state health department that you contact is usually located in your state capitol and is usually called something like Office of Vital Statistics, Vital Records, Health Statistics, or Vital Registration. But sometimes you look for a very different-sounding office. For example, if you got divorced in Cambridge, Mass., you would go to the Copy Department of the Middlesex County Probate Court, located in the Middlesex Probate Court Building. Charges are similar to those for copies of deeds, including separate certification charges.

Other Court Documents. Copies of court-issued documents, certified and not, such as judge's opinions and orders, rulings, motions, transcripts, probate documents, and so on, are generally available from the clerk of the issuing court. If you are uncertain which court issued a document, you might try talking your problem over with the county clerk. Your lawyer, of course, will have copies of all documents issued in matters in which he or she was involved, and he or she will also be able to help you track down other documents.

Wills. The original of the will is customarily stored in your lawyer's office, and you keep a copy (with the lawyer's name and address stated on the copy). But if you were keeping the original of your will in your home and you have lost it, the lawyer who drafted it will have a copy. You would have to reexecute the will (sign it, date it currently, and have it properly witnessed again), however, because the law makes a presumption that if the original is not available, it was revoked. For this reason, too, you should act promptly, for in the meantime you are without a will. If you cannot find your original lawyer or if he or she for some reason does not have a copy of your will, of course you must make another one.

If you lost only a copy, and the original is in a safe-deposit box or in your lawyer's office or somewhere else, then simply have another copy made and put the copy with your other important documents at home, returning the original to its safekeeping place. If you are in the process of making a new will and the original of your previous will cannot be found anywhere, your lawyer will know how to phrase the new will so that it is clear that the old one is revoked.

Birth Certificates. Call the state department of health, or the equivalent, or a general state government information number, to find out where to get a certified copy of a birth certificate in your state. The office in the state health department that you must contact is usually located in your state capitol and is called something like Office of Vital Statistics, Vital Records, Health Statistics, or Vital Registration. There are restrictions on who can obtain a certified copy of a birth certificate. For example, in New York State, you can get only your own or your child's birth certificate. You apply by mail, sending in a check or money order ($15 per copy requested), the full name of the person whose birth certificate is sought and—if that person is not you—your relation to that person, the full name and maiden name of the person's mother, and the full name of the person's father. Vital Statistics will send back the birth certificate. In some places this can take weeks or even months. Call the office to learn about expedited procedures.

Anyone born in New York City (a notorious special case) gets his or her birth certificate in the Bureau of Vital Records, Department of Health, City of New York. All other persons born in New York State apply to the Albany office.

Marriage Certificates. The county clerk in the county where you were married probably has a record of your marriage and for a fee of a few dollars can give you a certified copy of your marriage certificate.

Various rules govern the issuance of marriage certificates. Usually you may ask for the certificate by mail or in person. In most places, only the bride and groom themselves, or someone with written authorization from one of them, may obtain the certificate; proof of identity will be required. There is generally a fee, and checks may not be accepted.

Stocks and Bonds. If stock certificates stored at home have been lost or destroyed and you receive dividends on these stocks, on the dividend check you will find printed the name of the "transfer agent," usually a bank. Call that bank and ask for the loss department. They will take information, reissue your stock, and stop payment on the old certificates.

If you are not receiving dividends, contact the brokerage house to get the name of the transfer agent. In this situation you may find valuable any records of ownership you have: the stubs of the certificates you lost (which have the stock certificate numbers on them) or your broker's statements of account.

Nowadays your broker will usually keep your stock certificates, which makes this kind of loss less common. Treasury bills and bonds, too, are typically mere book entries now, rather than elegant pieces of paper yellowing in your safe. U.S. Savings Bonds, however, are bearer bonds that you have possession of. If you should lose them, the Treasury will replace them if you fill out and mail in Form PD F 1048, "Application for Relief on Account of Loss, Theft, or Destruction of US Savings and Retirement Securities" (retaining a copy for your files). Call the number of the Federal Reserve in your area and request the form.

Insurance Policies, Pension Plans. Your insurance agent will get replacement policies for you. If you have no agent, call the nearest office of your insurance company. Likewise, simply contact the organization through whom you acquired your pension plan (your employer, union, or other group). Or contact directly whatever organization administers your pension plan; they will either provide a copy of the plan or direct you to someone who will.

Bank Documents. Report lost checks and ATM cards to your bank immediately. The bank will issue you new checks and cards or stop payment on lost ones, as the situation calls for. You can also get copies of canceled checks, statements of account, and most other bank documents simply by requesting them at the bank.

Notes

Chapter 3. Neatening

page 30. 1. Some of the currently popular choices are Candace Ord Manroe, *Storage Made Easy: Great Ideas for Organizing Every Room in Your Home* (Reader's Digest, 1995); Stephanie Culp, *How to Conquer Clutter* (Writer's Digest Books, 1989); Don Aslett, *Clutter's Last Stand* (Writer's Digest Books, 1984); Jeff Campbell, *Clutter Control* (Dell Books, 1992); and Deniece Schofield, *Confessions of an Organized Homemaker* (Betterway, 1994).

Chapter 5. Breakfast, Lunch, and Dinner

page 50. 1. If you are beginning to cook at home and wish to bone up on good nutrition, one of the most readable, reliable, intelligent, and down-to-earth introductory books I am aware of is *Jane Brody's Nutrition Book* (Bantam, 1989). *The Tufts University Guide to Total Nutrition,* by Stanley Gershoff, with Catherine Whitney (Harper & Row, 1990) is also excellent. You will also find basic nutritional concepts presented in a clear and useful manner in all-purpose cookbooks such as *Joy of Cooking* (Scribner, 1997) and *The New Good Housekeeping Cookbook,* edited by Mildred Ying (Hearst, 1986), as well as in your home medical guide or encyclopedia.

page 51. 2. Grains and vegetables usually contain a couple of grams of protein per serving too, and some, such as quinoa or corn or peas, contain a bit more than others. Meat- or poultry-based broths often contain a fair amount of high-quality animal protein. Note that many types of beans—for example, kidney beans and black beans—contain high carbohydrate levels as well as substantial amounts of protein. The distinction between fruits and vegetables is not hard and fast. Fruits are the typically sweet, pulpy parts of the plant that contain the seeds or pit. But tomatoes, which are technically considered fruits, are not sweet and are treated as vegetables for menu-planning purposes, as are squashes and pumpkins—except when the latter are made into pies and custards. And citrus fruits, which are often sour, are fruits for menu purposes. Vegetables can include the leaves, stalks, seeds, seedpods, or roots of plants.

Chapter 7. Stimulating Beverages

page 71. 1. Pregnant women and women striving to become pregnant are usually advised by their doctors to cut out or cut back on coffee and tea. Heavy coffee drinkers (or those consuming more than 300 mg of caffeine daily) tend to take longer to become pregnant and show a higher rate of miscarriage. Some people find that drinking caffeinated beverages gives them heartburn or aggravates a stomach ulcer. Caffeine may cause excess calcium loss in those not getting enough in their diets, thus increasing the risk of osteoporosis. Caffeine is associated with anxiety attacks or heart palpitations in some sensitive people. Sometimes people on certain medications will be advised to avoid caffeine.

page 71. 2. Some evidence indicates that substances in tea have an antioxidant effect that protects against some cancers, help the heart by reducing total blood cholesterol and affecting "bad" LDL blood cholesterol in a beneficial way, and by inhibiting the formation of blood clots (which can cause heart attacks or strokes).

page 79. 3. If you repeatedly set glass pots on the electric drip coffeemaker's heated burner or on a diffuser over a stove-top burner, they eventually weaken and crack.

page 82. 4. For example, among those herbal teas that may pose health hazards are sassafras (one that we always made at home when I was a child) and comfrey, both potentially harmful to the liver and carcinogenic as well. Senna and comfrey have a laxative effect, and fennel and nettle are diuretics. Their overuse could result in dangerous dehydration. *Ma huang* can cause increased blood pressure and heart rate. Valerian can create a variety of side effects. Many, many other plants contain ingredients that should be used with caution. Herbal teas are pleasant and helpful, but those who go in for them should be sure to ask their doctors about them and to read up on them so as to learn of any potential health hazards.

page 86. 5. *Jancis Robinson's Wine Course,* p. 43.

Chapter 9. Kitchen Culture

page 113. 1. Automatic Dishwashing Procedures, in "Dishwashing Facts from the Soap and Detergent Association."

Chapter 10. To Market, to Market

page 127. 1. A bill to impose country-of-origin labeling on imported fresh produce (and some meats) has been introduced in Congress but so far has not been enacted. This would require the country of origin of fresh produce to be identified by signs near retailers' bulk displays.

page 131. 2. The Food Keeper was developed by Food Marketing Institute, 800 Connecticut Avenue, NW, Washington, D.C. 20006, (202) 452-8444 with Cornell University, Institute of Food Science, Cornell Cooperative Extension, (607) 255-3262.

Call USDA's Meat and Poultry Hotline toll-free at 1-800-535-4555 10:00 A.M. to 4:00 P.M. Eastern time, Monday through Friday, for more information about the safe handling and storage of food.

Call FDA's Center for Food Safety and Applied Nutrition toll-free at 1-800-FDA-4010.

Information is also posted at the USDA's Web site at www.fsis.usda.gov and the FDA's Web site at www.fda.gov.

Chapter 11. Cold Comfort

page 143. 1. 1999 *Food Code,* United States Public Health Service, Food and Drug Administration, pp. 401–402.

page 145. 2. Note that The Food Keeper recommends cold storage only for genuine maple syrup (see page 133). The reason for refrigerating maple syrup is that it may grow moldy if stored outside the refrigerator. Some food-storage experts, however, recommend that you refrigerate *all* syrups for the same reason. See, e.g., *Handbook of Food Preparation,* Food and Nutrition Section, American Home Economics Association (Kendall/Hunt, 1993), p. 158.

page 147. 3. According to the Kansas State University Cooperative Extension Service, however, this advice applies to foods that were purchased from self-service markets, such as the average supermarket. It does not apply to foods that are wrapped for you by your butcher or at the fish market. The reason for the difference is that meat packages in self-service counters have been handled by many shoppers. Opening these before storage provides the opportunity for far more contamination. But things you bought from the butcher or fishmonger that were specially wrapped for you should be removed from the package or paper and wrapped loosely in waxed paper to refrigerate. This allows the surface to dry, and the dryness retards bacterial growth. To freeze such items, rewrap them securely with safe freezer wrap.

Chapter 12. Bread and Honey

page 155. 1. Canning involves sterilizing foods in sealed containers, such as cans or jars, by heating them to high enough temperatures to kill practically all microorganisms and their spores. As long as the containers remain sealed, no new microorganisms can enter. Thus the food is preserved until you open the bottle or can, at which point refrigeration is usually necessary. The canning process itself causes some loss of nutrients in the foods. The extent of the loss depends on several factors, especially how quickly the canning process is carried out.

Chapter 13. Safe Food

page 163. 1. Robert B. Gravani, "The pH of Foods," *Food Science Fact Sheets,* No. 124, Aug. 1983, p. 2, explains: "Most microorganisms grow best at pH values around 7.0 while only a few grow below pH 4.0. Yeasts and molds are generally more acid tolerant than bacteria and can grow at lower pH values." Low-acid foods are considered those with pH between 4.6 and 7.0. Acid foods are those with pH of 4.5 or below.

page 165. 2. USDA Food Safety and Inspection Service, "Use a Meat Thermometer and Take the Guesswork Out of Cooking," U.S. Department of Agriculture, Food Safety and Inspection Service, Cooperative State Research, Education and Extension Service, 14th Street and Independence Ave., S.W., Washington, D.C. 20250, in cooperation with National Grocers Association and Food Marketing Institute.

page 167. 3. Source: "Egg and Egg Product Safety," Consumer Information from USDA, Food Safety and Inspection Service, *Food Safety & Consumer Education Office,* October 1996.

page 172. 4. Waxy coatings are applied to some fruits and vegetables to help maintain freshness by holding in moisture. Washing and scrubbing with a brush will remove much of them. I have read nothing about them that especially troubles me, but there are those who believe that they contain harmful substances. Since 1994, FDA regulations have required packing cartons to state whether wax has been applied and to tell whether it is an animal-based or vegetable-based type of wax (a fact in which vegetarians are often interested). A vegetable-based wax, however, under the regulations, includes vegetable, petroleum, beeswax, or shellac-based waxes and resins. *FDA Consumer,* March 1997.

page 174. 5. The *Food Code* is published by the FDA and endorsed and recommended by the Centers for Disease Control and Prevention and the Food Safety Inspection Service, U.S. Department of Agriculture. It is revised periodically. While it is a highly influential model for the states' regulatory policies, it has been substantially adopted only in one or two states and a few localities. Other jurisdictions are currently considering taking this step.

page 174. 6. See Sections 4-703.11 and 4-501.111 of the the 1999 *Food Code.*

page 175. 7. After studies a few years ago suggested that wood chopping boards were more sanitary than plastic ones, government oversight agencies undertook research to find out whether this was true. The answer was no. The USDA's report said:

"Recent studies by the Food and Drug Administration's Center for Food Safety and Applied Nutrition found that microorganisms became trapped in wood surfaces and were difficult to dislodge by rinsing. Once trapped, bacteria survive in a dormant stage for long periods of time. The next time the cutting board is used, these bacteria could contaminate other foods, potentially causing foodborne illness.

"On the other hand, the study found that the microorganisms were easily washed off plastic surfaces." (Excerpted from "Focus On: Cutting Board Safety," U.S. Department of Agriculture, Food Safety and Inspection Service, Washington, DC 20250, Consumer Publications, Dec. 1994, slightly revised Sept. 1997.)

page 176. 8. The 1999 *Food Code* states that sponges "may not be used in contact with cleaned and *sanitized* or in-use *food contact surfaces.*"

page 176. 9. There are "antibacterial" sponges on the market that do not develop odors. These are said to contain substances that discourage the growth of bacteria in the sponge. However, they are not intended for killing bacteria on the surfaces they are used to clean and cannot be used for sanitizing.

page 185. 10. Julie Miller Jones, *Food Safety* (Eagan Press, 1992), p. 161.

Chapter 14. The Fabric of Your Home

page 196. 1. Kathryn L. Hatch, *Textile Science* (West, 1993), p. 320; Bernard P. Corbman, *Textiles: Fiber to Fabric* (McGraw-Hill, 1983), p. 78.

Chapter 15. Transformations

page 222. 1. Germany and the Netherlands have recently banned the import of certain dyed goods whose colors might, if subjected to reduction treatments, produce carcinogenic dye degradation products.

page 222. 2. Frosting tends to plague some permanent-press clothes made of cotton/polyester blends. In such clothes, the cotton fibers tend to be a bit darker than the polyester ones, and, weakened by the resin treatment that creates the resistance to wrinkling, the cotton fibers also tend to wear away faster than the polyester. In areas subject to abrasion, such as the knees, a lighter area may appear.

page 230. 3. Kathryn L. Hatch, *Textile Science* (West, 1993), p. 422.

Chapter 16. The Natural Fibers

page 239. 1. Fergusons Irish Linens, manufacturer of linens and damasks, recommends hot water, a "color care" detergent free from optical brightening agents, and no bleach on sturdy washable linens. The following *maximum* wash-water temperatures are suggested (I have converted from centigrade to Fahrenheit): (1) White linen without special finishes, 200°F. (2) Linen without special finishes, where colors are fast, 140°F. (For 1 and 2, a temperature of 122°F is generally sufficient.) (3) Linens that are colorfast at 104°F but not at 140°F should be washed at 104°F. (Test first for fastness at different temperatures.) (4) Fine hand-embroidered linen should be hand-washed at 104°F.

page 245. 2. Kathryn L. Hatch, *Textile Science* (West, 1993), p. 147.

page 248. 3. Kathryn L. Hatch, *Textile Science,* p. 417.

Chapter 17. The Man-Made Fibers and Blends

page 257. 1. Bernard P. Corbman, *Textiles: Fiber to Fabric* (McGraw-Hill, 1983), p. 347.

page 263. 2. The natural fibers other than silk (which is the only natural fiber that is a filament fiber) are measured by their diameters, stated in micrometers. Sheep's wool ranges from 17 to 40 micrometers (17 being fine and 40 coarse), cotton from 16 to 21 micrometers. Flax is slightly finer than cotton, from about 15 to 20 micrometers. Only filament fibers are measured in deniers, and what counts as a filament fiber is determined by its length, which is indefinitely long. See Kathryn L. Hatch, *Textile Science,* pp. 90–91.

page 263. 3. Joyce A. Smith, Ohio State University Extension Factsheet, available on the Internet: (ohioline.ag.ohio-state.edu/hyg-fact/5000/5546.html).

Chapter 19. Carefully Disregarding Care Labels

page 284. 1. I once spilled a glass of milk on a crêpe dress of a viscose rayon acetate blend that had a "Dry-clean only" label. After the dry cleaner failed to remove the milk stain, I convinced myself that the dress could safely be washed by hand in lukewarm water with gentle, neutral detergent. In fact, the shrinkage was astonishing. It had been a loose-fitting dress, but after this gentle washing and hanging dry I could not even pull it over my shoulders.

Chapter 27. Sanitizing the Laundry

page 378. 1. See R. Sporik et al., *New England Journal of Medicine,* August 23, 1990, pp. 502–507, quoted in "House-dust mites may cause childhood asthma," Child Health Alert, October 1990.

Chapter 29. The Air in Your Castle

page 395. 1. The Environmental Protection Agency defines a volatile organic compound as "any compound of carbon, excluding carbon monoxide, carbon dioxide, carbonic acid, metallic carbides or carbonates, and ammonium carbonate, which participates in atmospheric photochemical reactions." *Federal Register,* vol. 62, no. 164, 40 CFR, part 51, sec. 100. This means they are organic (carbon-containing) compounds that evaporate and react with light or other radiant energy.

page 395. 2. A. Custovic and A. Woodcock, "Avoiding Exposure to Indoor Allergens: ABC of Allergies," *British Medical Journal,* 316, no. 7137 (1998): 1075.

page 396. 3. K. J. Collins, "Low Indoor Temperatures and Morbidity in the Elderly," *Age and Ageing,* 15, no. 4 (1986): 212–20.

page 397. 4. "Cooling Your Home Naturally," U.S. Department of Energy, October 1994, DOE/CH10093–221.

page 398. 5. "Cooling Your Home Naturally," p. 6.

page 400. 6. A. K. Munir et al., "Cat, Dog, and Cockroach Allergens in Homes of Asthmatic Children from Three Climatic Zones in Sweden," *Allergy*, 49, no. 7 (1994): 508–16.

page 401. 7. V. A. Arundel et al., "Indirect Health Effects of Relative Humidity in Indoor Environments," *Environmental Health Perspectives,* 65 (1986): 351–61. See also F. L. Schaffer et al., "Survival of Airborne Influenza Virus: Effects of Propagating Host, Relative Humidity, and Composition of Spray Fluids," *Archives of Virology,* 51 (1976): 263–73; and M. K. Ijaz et al., "Effect of Relative Humidity, Atmospheric Temperature, and Suspending Medium on the Airborne Survival of Human Rotavirus," *Canadian Journal of Microbiology,* 31 (1985): 681–5.

page 402. 8. Arundel et al., "Health Effects," p. 359.

page 404. 9. "Household Care Products and Indoor Air Quality," Chemical Specialties Manufacturers Association, Inc., 1913 I Street N.W., Washington, DC 20006, (202) 872-8110.

page 412. 10. "Questions and Answers about Carbon Monoxide and CO Detectors," Underwriters Laboratories.

page 414. 11. "Questions and Answers about Carbon Monoxide and CO Detectors," Underwriters Laboratories.

Chapter 30. Peaceful Coexistence with Microbes

page 420. 1. APIC is a not-for-profit organization dedicated to "advancing healthcare epidemiology through collaboration, research, practice, and credentialing," 1016 Sixteenth Street NW, Washington, DC 20036; (202) 296-2742; fax: (202) 296-5645; E-mail: APICinfo@apic.org.

page 420. 2. Stuart B. Levy is professor of molecular biology and microbiology, professor of medicine, director of the Center for Adaptation Genetics and Drug Resistance at the Tufts University School of Medicine, president of the Alliance for the Prudent Use of Antibiotics, and president-elect of the American Society for Microbiology. The quotation is from "The Challenge of Antibiotic Resistance," *Scientific American,* March 1998, 46–53.

page 424. 3. Paul D. Ellner and Harold C. Neu, *Understanding Infectious Disease* (Mosby Year Book, 1992), p. 175.

page 424. 4. J. Tilden et al., "A New Route of Transmission for Escherichia Coli: Infection from Dry Fermented Salami," *American Journal of Public Health,* 86 (1996): 1142–45.

Chapter 31. The Chemistry of Household Cleaning

page 442. 1. Frank L. Wiseman, *Chemistry in the Modern World* (McGraw-Hill, 1985), p. 472.

Chapter 33. Dust and Dust Mites

page 450. 1. Alfred, Lord Tennyson, "The Vision of Sin."

page 451. 2. P. Cullinan et al., "Asthma in Children: Environmental Factors," *British Medical Journal,* 308 (1994): 1585.

page 453. 3. D. P. Strachan and I. M. Carey, "Home Environment and Severe Asthma in Adolescence: A Population Based Case-Control Study," *British Medical Journal,* 311 (1995): 1053–56.

page 453. 4. Kathryn V. Blake, "Asthma Management," *American Druggist,* July 1998, p. 57.

Chapter 36. Floors and Furniture of Wood and Woodlike Materials

page 494. 1. Flexner, *Understanding Wood Finishing,* p. 230.

Chapter 37. Resilient Floors

page 509. 1. Edward Kipel, ed., *How to Clean Practically Anything* (Consumer Reports Books, 1996), p. 31.

Chapter 47. Kindly Light

page 571. 1. See Mark S. Rea, ed., *Lighting Handbook: Reference and Application* (Illuminating Engineering Society of North America, 1993), p. 609.

page 573. 2. "Lighting Fundamentals," Lighting Upgrade Manual, EPA's Green Lights Program, January 1995.

page 575. 3. See Russell P. Leslie and Kathryn M. Conway, *The Lighting Pattern Book for Homes* (2d ed., McGraw-Hill, 1996), pp. 100ff.

page 579. 4. The information in this table is drawn in part from Leslie and Conway, *The Lighting Pattern Book for Homes.*

page 581. 5. C. D. Lytle et al., "An Estimation of Squamous Cell Carcinoma Risk from Ultraviolet Radiation Emitted by Fluorescent Lamps," *Photodermatology, Photoimmunology & Photomedicine,* 9(6) (Dec. 1992), 268–74; A. J. Swerdlow et al., "Fluorescent Lights, Ultraviolet Lamps, and Risk of Cutaneous Melanoma," *British Medical Journal,* 297: (1988): 647–50.

Chapter 49. Some Quiet Occupations

page 597. 1. Bruno Bettelheim, *A Good Enough Parent* (Knopf, 1987), pp. 186–87.

Chapter 55. Pets

page 640. 1. On issues relevant to this section, see generally Andrew W. Murphy and Thomas A. E. Platts-Mills, "Asthma: Realistic Ways to Help Your Patient Control Indoor Allergens," *Consultant,* 36 (1996): 1022–27.

page 640. 2. Ashley Woodcock and Adnan Custovic, "Avoiding Exposure to Indoor Allergens," *British Medical Journal,* 316 (1998): 1075.

page 646. 3. If insecticides, sprays, or fogs for fleas and ticks are used in your home, you might let the children sleep at their grandparents for a few days. (I would get pets out of the home too.) According to a recent study, pregnant women who used flea and tick foggers and sprays gave birth to children who suffered increased rates of brain tumors. There has long been a suspicion that certain chemicals used in some such products are associated with increased tumor rates in children. These investigators gathered statistics on the use of several different kinds of pesticides. *Only* the tick and flea foggers and sprays were associated with increased risk. No increased risks for tumors were observed with lice, yard or garden insecticides, herbicides, snail killer, or termite treatments. The association with flea and tick foggers was higher in cases when the child got the tumor before age five. There was increased risk with an increase in the number of pets treated. There was significant increased risk if the ordinary safety precautions were ignored, such as evacuating the house after spraying or dusting, delaying the harvesting of food after pesticide use, or following instructions on pesticide labels. "These findings indicate that chemicals used in flea/tick products may increase risk of pediatric brain tumors and suggest that further research be done to pinpoint specific chemicals involved," wrote the investigators. Janice M. Pogoda and Susan Preston-Martin, *Environmental Health Perspectives,* November 1997.

Chapter 56. The Cave of Nakedness

page 661. 1. Without allergen-proof undercovers, allergists recommend laundering the pillows and comforters of those with allergies anywhere from once every three months to once every other week. This is a troublesome, time-consuming job, and it is of course infinitely easier to use the allergen-proof undercovers. A representative of one company that manufactures allergen-proof undercovers told me that they block dander and mite allergens but not necessarily molds. If you should get moldiness in a pillow or comforter, stop using it. If you cannot get a new one, air and sun the moldy one vigorously and wash it thoroughly, then repeat.

Chapter 57. Beds and Bedding

page 679. 1. If the sheets have been treated with optical brighteners, it is conceivable that chlorine bleach could cause yellowing. But I have never encountered this problem in any brand of cotton sheet. See "Optical brighteners" in the appendix to chapter 21 and "Yellowing" in chapter 26.

page 685. 2. Isabel B. Wingate, *Textile Fabrics and Their Selection* (Prentice-Hall, 1976), p. 500.

Chapter 60. Fire

page 711. 1. There are also fancier smoke detectors. Some will light up to guide you out of the house in case of fire; these are particularly good to use along your likely exit route in case of fire down stairways or along hallways. There are also detectors that strobe light, rather than sound, to alert the hearing-impaired. You can pay even more money and get them wired into your home's security system and programmed so as to call the fire department or you at the office in case smoke is detected. This system might be good for seniors or the disabled. Make sure you understand how to maintain and operate it correctly, however, so as to avoid the problem of false alarms. Whatever smoke detectors you buy, be sure to look for the UL Mark.

Chapter 63. Further Miscellaneous Safety Rules

page 738. 1. In California alone, 71 children aged one to four drowned in 1993, and another 250 were hospitalized as a result of near drowning. Drowning was the leading cause of death by injury among California children this age, exceeding the number who were killed in car crashes—a staggering fact when you consider how much more time all children spend riding in cars than swimming. Although I was not able to learn exactly how many of these drownings occurred in home pools, *Public Health Reports* (January 11, 1997) asserts, "A private pool at a single family home is the site for most swimming pool drownings and near-drownings . . . [T]he literature is clear that approximately one-half to two-thirds of all immersion incidents occur in the child's own home pool, with the remainder occurring at the residence of a friend, relative, or neighbor." The danger of a child's dying in this fashion thus rises with income level. Only four percent of black preschooler deaths derived from drowning; fifty-five percent of white preschooler deaths were drownings.

page 740. 2. Underwriters Laboratories, "Home Safety and Inspection Checklist" (1996).

Chapter 66. Understanding Your Castle

page 777. 1. One provision of the federal Telecommunications Act of 1996 was declared unconstitutional in 1996 by the Court of Appeals for the Third Circuit, in a decision affirmed by the Supreme Court in 1997. The provision that was struck was also intended to deal with signal bleed. It would have required cable operators to scramble or block any indecent or sexually oriented programming on any channel devoted primarily to sexually oriented programming, so that it could not be received by anyone who did not subscribe to it. Until this could be done, the cable operator would have been required to broadcast sexually explicit programming only during hours when children were unlikely to be viewing.

Chapter 71. Insurance

page 819. 1. Earthquake insurance, historically, has been hard to find in states such as California that are prone to quakes. But California now has the California Earthquake Authority (CEA), which makes quake insurance available to all residential-property owners, mobile-home owners, and renters in California. Any insurance company selling homeowners' insurance in California is required by law to offer earthquake coverage, either by participating in the CEA plan or writing its own. The CEA insurance will cover structural damage to dwellings but not damage to pools, patios, fences, driveways, or detached garages. The deductible is high: 15 percent of the total coverage on the home. The CEA also has limits on how much insurance Californians will be able to get for personal belongings and living expenses. Wraparound or supplemental policies from other insurers may be available to insure part or all of the deductible or to increase the various limits.

Acknowledgments and Sources

I owe a great debt to the many people who helped me to write this book—my family, friends, colleagues, and all the delightful people whom I met during the course of my research. Every page of the book benefited from the attention of Edward Mendelson, my most astute reader, who early on adopted this unruly child of a book and in countless ways helped me to civilize it. James Mendelson's contributions on safety, his insistence that the book address children's issues, and his editorial acumen have helped immensely to improve it. Blanche Neel, who taught me more about housekeeping than anyone else, read the entire manuscript, contributed research, shared innumerable thoughtful suggestions, corrections, and recollections, and endured endless telephoned questions without once objecting. Lucy Neroni, another major housekeeping talent who also read the entire manuscript and let herself be conscripted into my telephone research campaign, was a storehouse of good information, memories, corrections, wit, and good humor.

Never was an author more fortunate in her editor than I have been. Without Maria Guarnaschelli's generous support, this book would never have been completed. She edited with genius and sensitivity, and always had a clear view of the forest when I got lost in the trees. The illustrations by Harry Bates clarify much that I was unable to say in words. Katya Rice, M. C. Hald, and Jane Lincoln Taylor, each with her own special genius, improved the manuscript and proofs in thousands of large and small details. Marjorie Miller lavished invaluable care on the final draft. Doe Coover, the ideal agent, believed in the book when it was an inchoate stack of paper, and warmly supported it and me through the long years of its making.

Patricia Bauer repeatedly came to my aid with knowledge and friendship. Professor Marcia Folsom of Wheelock College read early drafts of several chapters and made invaluable suggestions. I am indebted for research, experimentation, and much else to Senta German, Sonia Walsh, Elise MacAdam, Ella Larkin, Marie Maloney, Robert Fendell of Columbia Hardware, Noelle Clancy, Suzanne Lamb, Cheryl Lewis, Menachem Martin Maimon, Jason Mandela, Dan Ronnen, Derek Dalmer, and many others. Over and over, Matt Thornton's intelligent calm and quiet good judgment helped me stay on course, and Laura Wise came to my rescue more than once. I also want to offer thanks to everyone who helped with the book whose names are omitted here, either because they modestly insisted on anonymity or because of my oversight.

Many individuals and organizations read or helped confirm information contained in one or more chapters of this book. Among those who gave generous help with large portions of the book were Professor J. Richard Aspland of Clemson University, Professor Kathryn Hatch of the University of Arizona; Bessie Berrie, U. S. Department of Agriculture Meat and Poultry Hotline; Dora Carter and the National Electrical Safety Foundation; Kevin Hesslin of the Lighting Research Center, Rensselaer Polytechnic Institute; the American Lung Association; and Dennis Inch. Acknowledgments for the separate sections of the book are listed below. A list of addresses, telephone numbers, and Web sites of helpful agencies and organizations appears at the end.

I am especially indebted to the Cooperative Extension Services of many states; these services, established by federal law, disseminate information derived from agricultural experimentation stations and other departments of land-grant colleges and universities. Answers to many questions on housekeeping, farming, gardening, and related matters may be found at extension service Web sites; many local extension services may be found in the county government listings in telephone directory blue pages.

Any errors that may remain in the book are my sole responsibility, and I will be grateful to readers who inform me of possible corrections and additions, which may be sent in care of the publisher.

Beginnings

Printed sources that I found useful in preparing this section include, among many others, Witold Rybczynski, *Home: A Short History of an Idea* (Viking, 1986); Margaret Horsfield, *Biting the Dust* (St. Martin's, 1998); Laurie Abraham et al., *Reinventing Home* (Plume, 1991); Caroline Davidson, *A Woman's Work Is Never Done: A History of Housework in the British Isles 1650–1950* (Chatto & Windus, 1982); Jane and Leslie Davison, *To Make a House a Home* (Random House, 1994); Dorothy Hayden, *The Grand Domestic Revolution: A History of Feminist Designs for American Homes, Neighborhoods, and Cities* (MIT Press, 1981); Elizabeth Wayland Barber, *Women's Work: The First Twenty Thousand Years* (Norton, 1994); Glenna Matthews, *"Just a Housewife"* (Oxford, 1987); Laura Shapiro, *Perfection Salad: Women and Cooking at the Turn of the Century* (Farrar, Straus & Giroux, 1986); Ruth Schwartz Cowan, *More Work for Mother: The Ironies of Household Technology from the Open Hearth to the Microwave* (Basic Books, 1983); Susan Strasser, *Never Done: A History of American Housework* (Pantheon, 1982); Katherine Kish Sklar, *Catharine Beecher: A Study in American Domesticity* (Norton, 1973).

Older books that remained fascinating or useful include Mary Randolph, *The Virginia Housewife* (1824), ed. Karen Hess (University of South Carolina Press, 1984); Catherine Sidgwick, *Home* (James Munroe, 1835); Catharine E. Beecher, *A Treatise on Domestic Economy for the Use of Young Ladies at Home and at School* (T. H. Webb, 1841); Harriet Beecher Stowe, *House and Home Papers* (Ticknor and Fields, 1865), and *Motherly Talks with Young Housekeepers* (J. B. Ford, 1875); Catharine Beecher and Harriet Beecher Stowe, *American Woman's Home* (J. B. Ford, 1872); *Cassell's Book of the Household* (4 vols., Cassell, 1875); Eunice Beecher, *All Around the House; or How to Make Homes Happy* (Appleton, 1879); Annie Fields, *Life and Letters of Harriet Beecher Stowe* (Houghton Mifflin, 1897); Julia McNair Wright, *The Complete Home* (J. C. McCurdy, 1879); Marion Harland, *House and Home* (Clawson Brothers, 1889), and *The Housekeeper's Week* (Bobbs-Merrill, 1908); Mrs. C. E. Humphrey, ed., *The Book of the Home* (6 vols., Gresham, 1912); Marion Talbot and Sophonisba Preston Breckinridge, *The Modern Household* (Whitcomb & Barrows, 1912); L. Ray Balderston, *Housewifery* (Lippincott, 1928); Henry Humphrey, *Woman's Home Companion Household Book* (P. F. Collier, 1950).

Food

I am especially grateful for information and other guidance provided by Bessie Berry (U. S. Department of Agriculture Meat and Poultry Hotline); Linda Madsen (U. S. Department of Agriculture); Joseph Madden, Dr. Diane Robertson, and Kevin Budich (Food and Drug Administration); Professor Robert Gravani and Donna L. Scott (Cornell Cooperative Extension); Joe Corby (New York State Department of Agriculture and Markets); Anne Austin Sydnor, Manager, Consumer Affairs, Food Marketing Institute.

Published sources include a variety of pamphlets, datasheets, and Web pages from government agencies, extension services, and industry groups. Among the most valuable sources were the following:

U. S. Department of Agriculture, Food Safety and Inspection Service ("Preventing Foodborne Illness: A Guide to Safe Food Handling," Home and Garden Bulletin 247, Sept. 1990; "Kitchen Thermometers," Oct. 1997; "A Quick Consumer Guide to Safe Food Handling," Home and Garden Bulletin 248, Aug. 1995; "Use a Meat Thermometer and Take the Guesswork Out of Cooking"; "Take the Guesswork Out of Roasting a Turkey"; "E. coli O157:H7: What You Need to Know if There Is an Outbreak in Your Community," July 1995; "Focus On: Cutting Board Safety"; "Basics for Handling Food Safely," Sept. 1997; "Food Storage Chart," Sept. 1997; "Egg and Egg Product Safety").

U. S. Department of Agriculture, Agricultural Marketing Service ("How to Buy Fresh Vegetables," Home and Garden Bulletin 258, Jan. 1994; "How to Buy Canned and Frozen Vegetables," Home and Garden Bulletin 259, Jan. 1994; "How to Buy Fresh Fruits," Home and Garden Bulletin 260, Jan. 1994; "How to Buy Canned and Frozen Fruits," Home and Garden Bulletin 261, Jan. 1994).

U. S. Department of Agriculture, Human Nutrition Information Service ("Preparing Foods and Planning Menus Using the Dietary Guidelines," Home and Garden Bulletin 232-8; "Shopping for Food & Making Meals in Minutes Using the Dietary Guidelines," Home and Garden Bulletin 232-10).

U. S. Department of Health and Human Services, Public Health Service, Food and Drug Administration (*Food Code,* 1997; "If You Eat Raw Oysters, You Need to Know . . . ," DHHS Publication FDA 95-2293; "Eating Defensively: Food Safety Advice for Persons with AIDS," DHHS Publication FDA 92-2232; and several articles in the excellent periodical *FDA Consumer,* especially Paula Kurtzweil, "Can Your Kitchen Pass the Food Safety Test," Oct. 1995, and "On the Road to Safer Food, *FDA Consumer,* Sept.–Oct. 1998).

Centers for Disease Control, National Center for Infectious Diseases, Division of Bacterial and Mycotic Diseases ("Preventing Foodborne Illness: Escherichia coli O157:H7).

Northeast Regional Agricultural Engineering Service (Susan Mackay, "Home Storage of Fruits and Vegetables," August 1992).

Cornell Cooperative Extension, Department of Food Science (Safe Food Handling Tips Brochures: "Keep It Clean," "Cook It Safe," "When Eating Out," "Use Appropriate Thermometers"; Robert B. Gravani, *Food Science Fact Sheets,* Sept. 1981–May 1984).

Food Marketing Institute ("Dinnertime USA," and "The Food Keeper," developed in cooperation with the Cornell University Institute of Food Science, Cornell Cooperative Extension).

National Cattlemen's Beef Association (Louise A. Berner, "Heterocyclic Amines in Foods and Their Implications to Health: A Special Report of Current Status").

Soap and Detergent Association ("Understanding Automatic Dishwashing" and "Automatic Dishwashing Procedures").

American Spice Trade Association ("Spice Questions Consumers Often Ask").

Tea Council of the U.S.A.

I have also relied on many exceptionally well-informed books, notably: M. R. Adams and M. O. Moss, *Food Microbiology* (Royal Society of Chemistry, 1995; Ronald M. Atlas, *Microorganisms in Our World* (Mosby, 1994); Janet Baily, *Keeping Food Fresh* (Doubleday, 1985); Paul D. Ellner and Harold C. Neu, *Understanding Infectious Disease* (Mosby, 1992); Stanley Gershoff, with Catherine Whitney and the editorial advisory board of the *Tufts University Diet and Nutrition Letter, The Tufts University Guide to Total Nutrition* (HarperCollins, 1996); Julie Miller Jones, *Food Safety* (Eagan Press, 1992); Corby Kummer, *The Joy of Coffee* (Houghton Mifflin, 1995); Harold McGee, *On Food and Cooking* (Macmillan, 1984) and *The Curious Cook* (Macmillan, 1990); Jack Murdich, *Buying Produce: A Greengrocer's Guide to Selecting and Storing Fresh Fruits and Vegetables* (Hearst, 1986); James Peterson, *Fish and Shellfish: The Cook's Indispensable Companion* (Morrow, 1996); Jancis Robinson, *Jancis Robinson's Wine Course* (Abbeville Press, 1996); Joel, David, and Karl Schapira, *The Book of Coffee and Tea,* (St. Martin's, 1996); American Home Economics Association, Food and Nutrition Section, *Handbook of Food Preparation,* (Kendall/Hunt, 1993).

These articles were among many that proved useful: Alfred A. Bartlett et al., "Diarrheal Illness Among Infants and Toddlers in Day Care Centers," *Journal of Pediatrics,* Oct. 1985; W. O. Ellis et al., "Aflatoxins in Food: Occurrence, Biosynthesis, Effects on Organisms, Detection, and Methods of Control," *Critical Reviews in Food Science and Nutrition,* 30:4, 1991; Richard L. Guerrant and David A Bobak, "Bacterial and Protozoal Gastroenteritis," *New England Journal of Medicine,* Aug. 1, 1991; Craig W. Hedberg and Michael T. Osterholm, "Outbreaks of Food-Borne and Waterborne Viral Gastroenteritis, *Clinical Microbiology Reviews,* July 1993; Gregory R. Istre et al., "Campylobacter Enteritis Associated with Undercooked Barbecued Chicken," *American Journal of Public Health,* November 1984, Melvin A. Kohn et al., "An Outbreak of Norwalk Virus Gastroenteritis Associated with Eating Raw Oysters," *Journal of the American Medical Association,* Feb. 8, 1995; Arnold N. Kornblatt et al., "Epidemiologic and Laboratory Investigation of an Outbreak of Campylobacter Enteritis Associated with Raw Milk," *American Journal of Epidemiology,* November 1985; Melvin I. Marks, "Infectious Diarrhea: Introduction and Commentary," *Pediatric Annals,* Oct. 1994; David O. Matson, "Viral Gastroenteritis in Day-Care Settings: Epidemiology and New Developments," *Pediatrics,* Dec. 94; Michael C. Peterson, "Clinical Aspects of *Campylobacter jejuni* Infections in Adults," *Western Journal of Medicine,* Aug. 1994; Janet Raloff, "Sponges and Sinks and Rags, Oh My! Where Microbes Lurk and How to Rout Them," *Science News,* Sept. 14, 1996; J. F. Robens and J. L. Richards, "Aflatoxins in Animal and Human Health," *Reviews of Environmental Contamination and Toxicology,* 1992; P.C.B. Turnbull and Phyllis Rose, "*Campylobacter jejuni* and *Salmonella* in Raw Red Meats: A Public Health Laboratory Service Survey," *Journal of Hygiene,* 1982; "Foodborne Outbreak of Gastroenteritis Caused by *Escherichia coli* O157:H7, North Dakota, 1990," *MMWR: Morbidity and Mortality Weekly Review,* Apr. 26, 1991; "Microbial Attachment Similar for Wooden, Plastic Cutting Boards," *Food Chemical News,* Sept. 30, 1996.

Cloth

I owe special thanks to Professor J. R. Aspland of Clemson University and Professor Kathryn Hatch of the University of Arizona. Invaluable advice was also provided by Jane Borthwick, Ingrid Johnson, Sandy Sullivan of the Clorox Company, Damon Jones of Procter & Gamble, as well as by employees and officials of many other companies, including the American Society for Testing and Materials, Fergusons

Irish Linens, Inchcape Testing Services, Schweitzer Linens, Bergdorf Goodman, Bloomingdale's, Procter & Gamble, and Jana Starr of Jana Starr Antiques, New York.

Books used as sources for this section include *1997 Annual Book of ASTM Standards* (American Society for Testing and Materials, 1996; the figure on page 287 has been reproduced by the Simon & Schuster Consumer Group under license from ASTM. This figure is reprinted from ASTM Standard D 5489-96c, Standard Guide for Care Symbols for Care Instructions on Textile Products, copyright 1996 American Society for Testing and Materials, 100 Barr Harbor Drive, West Conshohocken, PA 19428, USA [phone: 610-832-9585, fax 610-832-9555]. Copies of the official standard should be obtained directly from ASTM.); J. R. Aspland, *Textile Dyeing and Coloration* (American Association of Textile Chemists and Colorists 1997); Bernard P. Corbman, *Textiles: Fiber to Fabric* (McGraw-Hill, 1983); Françoise de Bonneville, *The Book of Fine Linen* (Flammarion, 1994); Kathryn Hatch, *Textile Science* (West, 1993); Judith Jerde, *Encyclopedia of Textiles* (Facts on File, 1992); Marjorie L. Joseph, *Essentials of Textiles* (Holt, Rinehart and Winston, 1988); J. J. Pizzuto, *Fabric Science Swatch Kit* (Fairchild, 1990); Arthur Price and Allen C. Cohen, *J. J. Pizzuto's Fabric Science* (Fairchild, 1994); Phyllis G. Tortora, ed., *Fairchild's Dictionary of Textiles* (Fairchild, 1996); Isabel B. Wingate, *Textile Fabrics and Their Selection,* (Prentice-Hall, 1976); Frank L. Wiseman, *Chemistry in the Modern World* (McGraw-Hill, 1985).

Among many valuable articles, I relied especially on Lindy G. McDonald and Euan Tovey, "The Role of Water Temperature and Laundry Procedures in Reducing House Dust Mite Populations and Allergen Content of Bedding," *Journal of Allergy and Clinical Immunology,* Oct. 1992; R. Sporik et al., "Exposure to House-Dust Mite Allergen (Der p I) and the Development of Asthma in Childhood: A Prospective Study," *New England Journal of Medicine,* Aug. 23, 1990 (cited in *Child Health Alert,* Oct. 1990); T. Vandenhove et al., "Effect of Dry Cleaning on Mite Allergen Levels in Blankets," *Allergy,* May 1993; Donna L. Wong et al., "Diapering Choices: A Critical Review of the Issues," *Pediatric Nursing,* Jan.–Feb. 1992.

I found detailed, reliable information in pamphlets and Web pages provided by corporations and organizations, especially:

Centers for Disease Control, National Center for Infectious Diseases, Hospital Infection Program ("Laundry"), and Office of Safety Information ("Guidelines for Laundry in Health Care Facilities").

Michigan State University Extension ("Kinds of Soil and Appropriate Cleaners").

Mississippi State University, Cooperative Extension Service ("Stain Removal Guide," revised by Dr. Everlyn S. Johnson).

University of Missouri–Columbia, University Extension ("Stain Removal from Washable Fabrics," by Sharon Stevens).

Ohio State University Extension ("Quick 'n Easy Stain Removal," by Janis Stone; "Microfibers: Functional Beauty," by Joyce A. Smith).

Arm & Hammer ("Super Solutions for Tough Day-to-Day Chores: Super Washing Soda," "Arm & Hammer Baking Soda: The Little Yellow Box with a House-full of Uses").

Dial Corp. Consumer Information Center ("20 Mule Team Borax Laundry Booster: A Guide to Laundry and Household Uses").

DowBrands ("Your Guide to Tough Laundry Problems from the Stain Removal Experts at DowBrands").

Economist Intelligence Unit ("Textiles and the Environment," by Jack Watson).

Fergusons Irish Linen ("Fergusons Care Guide for their Genuine Irish Linen").

International Fabricare Institute ("Clothing Stains," and the "Professional Cleaners Care" series of pamphlets on a variety of subjects).

Lever Brothers ("Optical Brighteners," "Dirty Secrets and Clean Facts: The Wisk Laundry Guide," "Home Laundering Guide: Deterioration of Laundry Items," "Get It *All* Clean")

Maytag Company ("Special Baby, Special Cleanup: How to Care for Baby Laundry," "Automatic Washer Model A9800 User's Guide," "Automatic Dryer Model D9700 User's Guide").

Procter & Gamble ("Stain Removal Guide for Water Washable Items," "Laundry Tips," "Home Fabric Care Made Easy," "What Causes Color Loss in Fabrics?").

Soap and Detergent Association ("Removing Stains from Washable Items," "Laundering Facts from the Soap and Detergent Association, " "Laundry Detergent Package Directions, " "Sorting It Out," "Soaps and Detergents," "Laundry Detergent Package Directions" "A Handbook of Industry Terms," "Laundry Products and High-Efficiency Washers").

Seymour Housewares ("Handbook on Laundry Care and Ironing").

Woolite ("Caring for the Clothes You Care About").

This section includes logos and other symbols reprinted by permission of la Confédération Européene du Lin et du Chanvre and Masters of Linen (PO Box 1630, New York NY 10028, 212-734-3640); Cotton Incorporated; the Woolmark Company; the American Wool Council; and the Harris Tweed Authority.

Cleanliness

Among the many experts who helped with this section, I want to offer special thanks to Dr. Israel Lowy; the late Jess McIlvain; Professor William Rutala, University of North Carolina; Professor Thomas A. E. Platts-Mills, University of Virginia; Dr. Elaine Larsen, Columbia University; Cheryl Wrightmeyer, Iowa State University; Bonnie Holmes (National Wood Flooring Association); Susan Eddy (Butcher Paste Wax); Sandy Sullivan (Clorox); Julia Hewgley (Center for Food Safety and Applied Nutrition, Food and Drug Administration); Bill Sothern (Micro Ecologies); Dale Remmien (Home Ventilating Institute); Jennifer Jeffries (Market Support Inc.); Vincent Migliore and the Marble Institute of America); also staff members at the American Lung Association; International Gemmological Institute; Plumbing-Heating-Cooling Information Bureau; Environmental Protection Agency; Kathleen Young of the Alliance for the Prudent Use of Antibiotics; the Association for Practitioners in Infection Control and Epidemiology; and Miele Appliances, Inc.

Books that were especially useful include: American Chemical Society, *ChemCom: Chemistry in the Community* (Kendall/Hunt, 1988); David Battie, ed., *Sotheby's Concise Encyclopedia of Porcelain,* (Conran Octopus, 1990); Seymour S. Block, *Disinfection, Sterilization, and Preservation* (Lea & Febiger, 1991); Robert J. Charleston, ed., *World Ceramics: An Illustrated History from Earliest Times* (Crescent, 1990); Thomas R. Donovan et al., *Chemicals in Action* (Holt, Rinehart and Winston, 1987); Paul D. Ellner and Harold C. Neu, *Understanding Infectious Disease* (Mosby Year Book, 1992); Bob Flexner, *Understanding Wood Finishing* (Rodale, 1994); Robert Fournier, *Illustrated Dictionary of Practical Pottery* (Chilton, 1992); Glenn Haege, *Glenn Haege's Complete Hardwood Floor Care Guide* (Master Handyman, 1995); John R. Holum, *Elements of General and Biological Chemistry* (Wiley, 1975); Brad Hughes, *The Complete Guide to Restoring & Maintaining Wood Furniture and Cabinets* (Betterway, 1993); Bruce Johnson, *The Wood Finisher* (Ballantine, 1993); Frank A. Oski, *Pediatrics* (Lippincott, 1990); Hermione Sandwith and Sheila Stainton, *The National Trust Manual of Housekeeping* (Viking, 1991); Mette Tang Simpson and Michael Huntley, *Sotheby's Caring for Antiques* (Simon and Schuster, 1992); Isaac Turiel, *Indoor Air Quality and Human Health* (Stanford University Press, 1985); Frank L. Wiseman, *Chemistry in the Modern World* (McGraw-Hill, 1985); *Good Housekeeping's Guide to Successful Homemaking, Revised Edition* (Harper & Row, 1961).

Articles I consulted for this section include: Shamim A. Ansari et al., "Potential Role of Hands in the Spread of Respiratory Viral Infections," *Journal of Clinical Microbiology,* Oct. 1991; Anthony Arundel et al.,"Indirect Health Effects of Relative Humidity in Indoor Environments," *Environmental Health Perspectives,* Mar. 1986; David Bardell, "Survival of Herpes Simplex Virus Type 1 on Some Frequently Touched Objects in the Home and Public Buildings, *Microbios,* no. 256–57, 1990; B. Bean et al., "Survival of Influenza Viruses on Environmental Surfaces," *Journal of Infectious Diseases,* July 1982; Kathryn V. Blake, "Asthma Management: What You Need to Know," *American Druggist,* July 1998; Edward J. Bottone et al., "Loofah Sponges as Reservoirs and Vehicles in the Transmission of Potentially Pathogenic Bacterial Species to Human Skin," *Journal of Clinical Microbiology,* Feb. 1994; Clive M. Brown et al., "Asthma: The States' Challenge," *Public Health Reports,* May–June 1997; K. J. Collins, "Low Indoor Temperatures and Morbidity in the Elderly," *Age and Ageing,* July 1986; Jacquelynne P. Corey, "Environmental Control of Allergens," *Otolaryngology: Head and Neck Surgery,* Sept. 1994; P. Cullinan et al., "Asthma in Children: Environmental Factors," *British Medical Journal,* June 18, 1994; Robert E. Dales, "Respiratory Health Effects of Home Dampness and Molds Among Canadian Children," *American Journal of Epidemiology,* July 15, 1991; G. D'Amato et al., "Environment and Development of Respiratory Allergy: II. Indoors," *Monaldi Archives for Chest Disease,* Dec. 1994; Rupali Das and Paul D. Blanc, "Chlorine Gas Exposure and the Lung: A Review," *Toxicology and Industrial Health,* May–June 1993.

Also: J. S. Garner et al., "CDC Guideline for Handwashing and Hospital Environmental Control," *Infection Control,* Apr. 1986; Dinah Gould, "Nurses' Hands As Vectors of Hospital-Acquired Infection: A Review," *Journal of Advanced Nursing,* Oct. 1991; Dinah Gould, "Infection Control: Making Sense of Hand Hygiene," *Nursing Times,* July 27, 1994; M. K. Ijaz et al., "Effect of Relative Humidity, Atmospheric Temperature, and Suspending Medium on the Airborne Survival of Human Rotavirus," *Canadian Journal of Microbiology,* Aug. 1985; W. R. Jarvis, "Handwashing—the Semmelweis Lesson Forgotten?" *Lancet,* Nov. 12, 1994; E. C. Kaltenthaler and J. V. Pinfold, "Microbiological Methods for Assessing Handwashing Practice in Hygiene Behaviour Studies," *Journal of Tropical Medicine and Hygiene,* Apr. 1995; Arthur M. Kodama and Robert I. McGee, "Airborne Microbial Contaminants in Indoor Environments: Naturally Ventilated and Air-Conditioned Homes," *Archives of Environmental Health,* Sept.–Oct. 1986; Leonard R. Krilov and S. Hella Harkness, "Inactivation of Respiratory Syncytial Virus by Detergents and Disinfectants," *Pediatric Infectious Disease Journal,* July 1993; Patricia A. Kuster, "Reducing Risk of House Dust Mite and Cockroach Allergen Exposure in Inner-City Children with Asthma," *Pediatric Nursing,* July–Aug. 1996; Elaine L. Larson, "APIC Guideline for Handwashing and Hand Antisepsis in Health Care Settings," *American Journal of Infection Control,* Aug. 1995; Stuart B. Levy, "The Challenge of Antibiotic Resistance," *Scientific American,* March 1998; John N. Mbithi et al., "Survival of Hepatitis A Virus on Human Hands and Its Transfer on Contact with Animate and Inanimate Surfaces," *Journal of Clinical Microbiology,* Apr. 1992; William D. Morain, "Out, Damned Spot," *Annals of Plastic Surgery,* May 1994; A. K. Munir et al., "Cat, Dog, and Cockroach Allergens in Homes of Asthmatic Children from Three Climatic Zones in Sweden," *Allergy,* Aug. 1994.

Also: Thomas A. E. Platts-Mills, "There's Something in the Air: Common Household Airborne Allergens," *Discover,* March 1998; Alan M. Rauch et al., "Outbreak of Kawasaki Syndrome in Denver, Colorado: Association with Rug and Carpet Cleaning," *Pediatrics,* May 1991; L. Christine Oliver and Bruce W. Shackleton, "The Indoor Air We Breathe: A Public Health Problem of the '90s," *Public Health Report,* Sept.–Oct. 1998; William A. Rutala, "APIC Guideline for Selection and Use of Disinfectants," *American Journal of Infection Control,* Aug. 1996; William A. Rutala and D. J. Weber, "Uses of Inorganic Hypochlorite (Bleach) in Health-Care Facilities," *Clinical Microbiology Review,* Oct. 1997; Syed A. Sattar et al., "Chemical Disinfection to Interrupt Transfer of Rhinovirus Type 14 from Environmental Surfaces to Hands," *Applied and Environmental Microbiology,* May 1993; Syed A. Sattar et al., "Interruption of Rotavirus Spread Through Chemical Disinfection," *Infection Control and Hospital Epidemiology,* Dec. 1994; F. L. Schaffer et al., "Survival of Airborne Influenza Virus: Effects of Propagating Host, Relative Humidity, and Composition of Spray Fluids," *Archives of Virology,* vol. 51 (1976); Elizabeth Scott et al., "An Investigation of Microbial Contamination in the Home," *Journal of Hygiene,* Oct. 1982; Elizabeth Scott et al., "Evaluation of Disinfectants in the Domestic Environment under 'In Use' Conditions," *Journal of Hygiene,* Apr. 1984; Elizabeth Scott and Sally F. Bloomfield, "The Survival of Microbial Contamination via Cloths, Hands, Utensils," *Journal of Applied Bacteriology,* Mar. 1990; Joanne E. Sheldon, "Twenty-five Tips on Hand Washing," *Nursing,* Jan. 1994; D. P. Strachan and I. M. Carey, "Home Environment and Severe Asthma in Adolescence: A Population-Based Case-Control Study," *British Medical Journal,* Oct. 21, 1995.

Also: J. Tilden et al., "A New Route of Transmission for Escherichia Coli: Infection from Dry Fermented Salami," *American Journal of Public Health,* Aug. 1996; Brett T. Volpe et al., "Hypersensitivity Pneumonitis Associated with a Portable Home Humidifier," *Connecticut Medicine,* Oct. 1991; R.P. Wenzel and M.A. Pfaller, "Handwashing: Efficacy versus Acceptance, a Brief Essay," *Journal of Hospital Infection,* June 1991; Robert A. Wood, "Environmental Control in the Prevention and Treatment of Pediatric Allergic Disease," *Current Opinion in Pediatrics,* Dec. 1993; Ashley Woodcock and Adnan Custovic, "Avoiding Exposure to Indoor Allergens: ABC of Allergies," *British Medical Journal,* Apr. 4, 1998; Kazuko Yoshida et al., "Prevention of Summer-type Hypersensitivity Pneumonitis: Effect of Elimination of *Trichosporon cutaneum* from the Patients' Homes," *Archives of Environmental Health,* Sept.–Oct. 1989.

Pamphlets and Web pages by government agencies and other organizations have also been invaluable. Among them are:

U. S. Department of Energy ("Cooling Your Home Naturally"; the illustration on page 396 is based on a drawing from this pamphlet.).

U. S. Environmental Protection Agency ("Consumer's Guide to Radon Reduction: How to Reduce Radon Levels in Your Home," "Home Buyer's and Seller's Guide to Radon," "Protect Your Family from Lead in Your Home," "Lead in Your Home: A Parent's Reference Guide," "Fact Sheet: EPA and HUD Move to Protect Children from Lead-Based Paint Poisoning; Disclosure of Lead-Based Paint Hazards in Housing"), and the U. S. Consumer Product Safety Commission ("The Inside Story: A Guide to Indoor Air Quality").

National Safety Council, Environmental Health Center ("Lead in Dishes and Crystal").

Michigan State University Extension Service ("Home Maintenance and Repair" Web pages prepared by Anne Field).

American Lung Association ("Asbestos in Your Home," prepared in association with the Environmental Protection Agency and Centers for Disease Control, and "Air Pollution in Your Home?").

Arm & Hammer ("Super Solutions for Tough Day-to-Day Chores from Arm & Hammer Super Washing Soda," "Baking Soda Basics").

Ceramic Tile Institute of America ("Care of Ceramic Tile," "Acids and Acid Cleaning—Friend or Foe").

Chemical Specialties Manufacturers Association ("No Wax Floors: A Mirage or a Miracle?" "Floor Maintenance Manual," "Consumer Products in the Home and Community," "Waste Not: Disposal Options for Consumer Products," "Household Care Products and Indoor Air Quality").

Clorox ("The Clorox Bleach Simple Solutions Guide").

Consumer Federation of America ("How Healthy Is the Air in Your Home?").

DowBrands ("Sparkle and Shine: A Little Chart for Big Cleaning Jobs Inside and Out").

Environmental Defense Fund ("What You Should Know About Lead in China Dishes," "Shopper's Guide: List of Low-Lead China Patterns," "A Dish Buyer's Guide").

Household and Institutional Products Information Council ("Household Products: Smart Choices for Cleaner Living").

Marble Institute of America ("Care and Cleaning for Natural Stone Surfaces").

National Asthma Education and Prevention Program ("Expert Report II: Guidelines for the Diagnosis and Management of Asthma").

National Institute of Allergy and Infectious Diseases ("Something in the Air: Airborne Allergens").

Natural Wood Flooring Association.

Soap and Detergent Association ("Household Cleaning Facts," "A Handbook of Industry Terms," "All the Dirt on Cleaning House," "Soaps and Detergents").

Westchester County, New York, Environmental Management Council ("Non-Toxic Alternatives and Disposal Recommendations for Unsafe Household Products," "Hazardous Household Products," "Proper Disposal and Recycling").

Valuable information is also available from the EPA Safe Drinking Water Hotline (1-800-426-4791), Indoor Air Quality Hotline (1-800-438-4318), Asbestos Ombudsman (1-800-368-5888), and from the EPA's extensive Web site (www.epa.gov).

Daily Life

Among many experts who were generous with their advice, I want especially to thank Professor Stephen D. Walter, McMaster University; Kevin Hesslin and Russell P. Leslie (Lighting Research Center, Rensselaer Polytechnic Institute); W. Howard Cyr (Center for Devices and Radiological Health, Food and Drug Administration); Dr. Andrea Kaufman (Westside Animal Hospital, New York); Martin Rankle (Ins-U-Clear Ltd.); Richard Krasilovsky (Safe-at-Home); Greg Flanders and Dennis Inch (Light Impressions); and the staff of the Acme Safe Co., New York City.

Published sources for this section include these books: Roger A. Caras and Robert William Kirk, *Dogs: Harper's Illustrated Handbook of Dogs* (Harper, 1992); Fayal Green, *The Anatomy of a House* (Doubleday, 1991); Laurence E. Keefe and Dennis Inch, *The Life of a Photograph* (Focal, 1990); Russell P. Leslie and Kathryn M. Conway, *The Lighting Pattern Book for Homes* (McGraw-Hill, 1996); J. Murdoch et al., eds., *IESNA Lighting Ready Reference* (Illuminating Engineering Society of North America, 1996); Mark S. Rea, ed., *Lighting Handbook: Reference and Application* (Illuminating Engineering Society of North America, 1993); Craig A. Tuttle, *An Ounce of Prevention: A Guide to the Care of Papers and Photographs* (Rainbow, 1995); Randall Whitehead, *Residential Lighting: Creating Dynamic Living Spaces* (Rockport, 1993), and *Lighten Up! A Practical Guide to Residential Lighting Design* (Light Source Publishing, 1996).

Among articles consulted, these were among the most useful: C. D. Lytle et al., "An Estimation of Squamous Cell Carcinoma Risk from Ultraviolet Radiation Emitted by Fluorescent Lamps," *Photodermatology, Photoimmunology and Photomedicine,* December 1992; Andrew W. Murphy and Thomas A.E. Platts-Mills, "Asthma: Realistic Ways to Help Your Patient Control Indoor Allergens," *Consultant,* May 1996; A. J. Swerdlow et al., "Fluorescent Lights, Ultraviolet Lamps, and Risk of Cutaneous Melanoma," *British Medical Journal,* Sep. 10, 1988; Stephen D. Walter et al., "The Association of Cutaneous Malignant Melanoma and Fluorescent Light Exposure," *American Journal of Epidemiology,* Apr. 1992.

I also used pamphlets and other material prepared by the Environmental Protection Agency's Green Lights Program ("Lighting Fundamentals," "Lighting Upgrade Technologies," "Compact Fluorescents: In Demand for All the Right Reasons," "Quality & Efficient Fluorescent Lamps").

Safe Shelter

I received extensive and generous help on this section from many public-spirited experts in their fields, and am especially grateful to Lieutenant Joseph Di Pietro of the City of New York Fire Department. I and my readers have also benefitted from help given by, among many others, Christine Branche and Judy A. Stevens (National Center for Injury Prevention and Control, Centers for Disease Control), and Dora Carter (and others at National Electrical Safety Foundation); Tracey Maloney (Underwriters Laboratories); Susanne Ogaitis (School of Hygiene and Public Health, The Johns Hopkins University); Nelda Werkmeister, City of Apple Valley, Minnesota.

The following books and articles were among those I found especially informative: *The Columbia University College of Physicians and Surgeons Complete Home Medical Guide* (Crown, 1989); Robert A. Dershewitz and Edward R. Christophersen, "Childhood Household Safety," *American Journal of Diseases of Children*, Jan. 1984; P. C. Holinger, "The Causes, Impact, and Preventability of Childhood Injuries in the United States," *American Journal of Diseases of Children*, June 1990; Leonard Krassner, "TIPP Usage," *Pediatrics*, Nov. 1984; Patrick W. O'Carroll et al., "Drowning Mortality in Los Angeles County, 1976–1984," *Journal of the American Medical Association*, July 15, 1984; J. Pearn et al., "Accidental Poisoning in Childhood: Five Year Urban Population Study with 15 Year Analysis of Fatality," *British Medical Journal*, Jan. 7, 1984; Frederick P. Rivara, "Injury Control: Issues and Methods for the 1990s," *Pediatric Annals*, July 1992; Juan G. Rodriguez et al., "Incidence of Hip Fractures, United States, 1970–83, *American Journal of Preventive Medicine*, May–June 1989; Carol Runyan et al., "Risk Factors for Fatal Residential Fires," *New England Journal of Medicine*, Sept. 17, 1982; "Safe at Home: What to Do about Lead Radon, Asbestos, and Other Worries," *Consumer Reports*, July 1995; and the articles gathered in *Home and Leisure Injuries in the United States: A Compendium of Articles from the Morbidity and Mortality Weekly Report 1985–1995* (National Center for Injury Prevention and Control, 1996).

National and local government agencies provided invaluable booklets and other printed material, notably the U.S. Consumer Product Safety Commission ("Your Home Fire Safety Checklist," "Home Safety Electrical Safety Audit—Room by Room Checklist") and the Fire Department of the City of New York ("Window Gates That Require a Key to Be Opened Are Against the Law [in New York City] and Endanger Your Life," "Safe at Home: Fire Dos and Don'ts," "Home Fire Extinguishers," "Fire Safety Tips for Senior Citizens," "Fire Safety and You! Know What to Do! Stop...Drop...Roll").

I also received valuable information in printed and Internet form from industry and other groups, especially:

National Safety Council ("Your Home Safety Checklist," "Accident Facts," "The E's of Electrical Safety," and the periodical *Family Safety and Health*).

American Lung Association ("Fact Sheet—Carbon Monoxide").

National Electrical Safety Foundation ("Plug into Electrical Safety: A Home Electrical Safety Check," "Plug into Electrical Safety: Extending Electrical Safety," "Plug into Electrical Safety: An Electrical Lifesaver," "Plug into Electrical Safety: News About Appliances," "Plug into Electrical Safety: Post-Holiday Safety," "Electrical Safety Questions and Answers").

American Red Cross and the Federal Emergency Management Agency ("Emergency Preparedness Checklist").

The New York Hospital/Cornell Medical Center Burn Center ("Burn Wise! Burn Prevention Information of Special Interest to Observant Jews").

Chemical Specialties Manufacturers Association (Jay M. Arena, "Your Child and Household Safety").

Soap and Detergent Association ("Clean and Safe: The Facts About Using Household Cleaning Products Effectively *and* Safely").

National Safe Kids Campaign ("Is Your Home Childproof," "Fact Sheet: Home Injury").

American Gas Association ("Home Energy Safety Issue: Accidental Ignition," "Using Home Appliances Properly," "Home Energy Safety Issue: Carbon Monoxide").

Insurance Information Institute ("Kerosene Heater Safety").

National Fire Protection Association.

National Swimming Pool Foundation.

Children's Safety Network.

A uniquely valuable source of information is Underwriters Laboratories ("Decorating for a Safe and Happy Holiday Season," "Questions and Answers about Carbon Monoxide and CO Detectors," "Appliance Safety Quiz," "Questions and Answers about the UL Mark," "Smoke Detectors," "Home Safety Inspection Checklist," "Consumer Safety Guide," "Playing It Safe: Toy and Recreational Safety for Kids of

All Ages," and Norm Bezane, "This Inventive Century: The Incredible Journey of Underwriters Laboratories 1894–1994"); these and other brochures may be ordered from Underwriters Laboratories, Literature Stock, 333 Pfingsten Road, Northbrook, IL 60062-2096; (847)272-8800, ext. 43731.

Formalities

This section, or parts of it, benefited from careful reading by Lawrence G. Spivak, Thomas Hauser, Derek Dalmer, Dan Ronnen, Kate McHale, Cheryl Lewis; the section on insurance was reviewed by, among others, Jean Salvatore of the Insurance Information Institute.

Helpful Agencies and Organizations

American Gas Association
400 N. Capitol St., NW
Washington, DC 20001
(202) 824-7000
Fax (202) 824-7115
www.aga.org

American Lung Association
1740 Broadway
New York, NY 10019
(800) 586-4872
www.lungusa.org
The number listed above calls the local office in your area; check the Web site or your telephone directory for the local office's address.

American Red Cross
Public Inquiry Office
11th Floor
1621 N. Kent Street
Arlington, VA 22209
(703) 248-4222
www.redcross.org
Check the Web site or your telephone directory for the address of the local chapter.

Centers for Disease Control and Prevention (CDC)
1600 Clifton Rd., NE
Atlanta, GA 30333
(404) 639-3311
(800) 311-3435
www.cdc.gov

CDC, Division of Unintentional Injury Prevention
Mail Stop K-63
National Center for Injury Prevention and Control
4770 Buford Highway, NE
Atlanta, GA 30341-3724
(770) 488-4652
www.cdc.gov/ncipc/duip/duip.htm

U. S. Consumer Products Safety Commission (CPSC)
Washington, DC 20207
(301) 504-0990
Hotline (800) 638-2772
www.cpsc.gov

USDA Food Safety and Inspection Service
U. S. Department of Agriculture (USDA)
Food Safety Education and Communications Staff
Room 2932–South Building
1400 Independence Ave. SW
Washington, D.C. 20250
(202)720-7943
Fax (202)720-1843
www.fsis.usda.gov

USDA Meat and Poultry Hotline
(800) 535-4555 or (202) 720-3333

Environmental Protection Agency (EPA)
401 M Street, SW
Washington, DC 20460-0003
(202) 260-2090
www.epa.gov

EPA Asbestos Ombudsman
(800) 368-5888

EPA Indoor Air Quality Information Clearinghouse
Hotline (800) 438-4318
www.epa.gov/iaq

U. S. Food and Drug Administration (FDA)
HFE-88
5600 Fishers Lane
Rockville, MD 20857
(888) 463-6332
www.fda.gov

Home Ventilating Institute
30 W. University Drive
Arlington Heights, IL 60004
(847) 394-0150
www.hvi.org (Web site in preparation)

National Electrical Safety Foundation
1300 North 17th Street, Suite 1847
Rosslyn, VA 22209
(703) 841-3211
www.electricnet.com/orgs/nesf.htm

National Fire Protection Association (NFPA)
1 Batterymarch Park
P.O. Box 9101
Quincy, MA 02269-9101
(617) 770-3000
www.nfpa.org

National Lead Information Center
(NLIC)
(800) 424-5323
www.epa.gov/lead/nlic.htm

National Safety Council
1121 Spring Lake Drive
Itasca IL 60143-3201
(630) 285-1121
Fax (630) 285-1315
www.nsc.org

National Swimming Pool Foundation
P.O. Box 495
Merrick, NY 11566
(516) 623-3447
Fax (516) 867-2139
www.nspf.com

National Radon Information Hotline
Consumer Research Council
(800) 767-7236

Underwriters Laboratories
333 Pfingsten Road
Northbrook, IL 60062-2096
(847) 272-8800 (for literature, ext. 43731)
www.ul.com

For United States government publications, books, pamphlets, posters, periodicals, or subscription services on a variety of subjects of importance to the home, contact the Superintendent of Documents at the address and telephone number given below. If you do not know which publications or other material you are looking for, a useful booklet to ask for is *A Guide to U.S. Government Information,* also referred to as "The Subject Bibliography Index"; the order form in this booklet lets you request specialized lists of publications in various areas of interest. You might also ask for the *U.S. Government Information Catalog,* a helpful selective listing issued periodically.

Superintendent of Documents
P.O. Box 371954
Pittsburgh, PA 15250-7954
(202) 512-1800
Fax (202) 512-2250
www.gpo.gov

Index

B

D

E

M